Hit Songs,
1900–1955

Hit Songs, 1900–1955

American Popular Music of the Pre-Rock Era

DON TYLER

McFarland & Company, Inc., Publishers
Jefferson, North Carolina, and London

Table of Contents

Preface

Legendary songwriter E. Y. "Yip" Harburg said, "Songs are the pulse of a nation's heart. The fever chart of its health. Are we at peace? Are we in trouble? Are we floundering? Do we feel beautiful? Do we feel ugly? Listen to our songs." One of America's most famous and prolific songwriters, Irving Berlin, once told Abel Green, the editor of *Variety*, that the history of the United States could be traced through its music. Berlin also said, "Songs make history and history makes songs. It needed a French Revolution to make a 'Marseillaise' and the bombardment of Fort McHenry to give voice to 'The Star Spangled Banner.'" In addition, our songs also evince our moods, manners and mores. The songs a nation sings or listens to are evidence of that nation's outlook, its passions, its social conscience or lack of it, its patriotism, its morals and the need of its citizens to love and be loved.

This book affords the reader the chance to read about the most popular songs in America during the pre-rock era. It is my hope that most of my readers will be able to reminisce about where they were and whom they were with when they heard these songs. Even those readers unborn in the pre-rock era will still recognize a remarkable number of songs in this book. There aren't many Americans alive today who haven't heard "Take Me Out to the Ball Game," "Over There," "God Bless America," "White Christmas," and numerous others.

Portions of this book were published in my earlier one, *Hit Parade: An Encyclopedia of the Jazz, Depression, Swing and Sing Eras* (1985). After twenty additional years of research into the popular music of the United States, I decided to re-edit that book and expand it with newfound information.

The previous book was a chronology of the most popular songs in the United States from 1920 through 1955, when rock began its rise. All the authorities argue about the date rock 'n' roll began,

but I chose to end my book in 1955 since Elvis Presley definitely made rock 'n' roll a national phenomenon in 1956. *The Billboard Book of No. 1 Hits* starts on July 9, 1955, when Bill Haley and His Comets hit No. 1 with "Rock Around the Clock." I preferred to finish 1955, rather than stop in the middle of the year.

The present book follows the same basic format as the previous one, but it begins twenty years earlier. I chose to begin the previous book with 1920 because that date represented the birth of radio and its dissemination of music to a larger public. With this new book I wanted to include the pre-radio era — but how far back to go? I explored sources like the Songwriters' Hall of Fame, which includes the years 1880–1953 as "the Tin Pan Alley years." I used those dates as a beginning reference point. As I explored the songs back to the 1860s, however, I found relatively few in each year that are still well known today, except for the songs of Stephen Foster. I found a few historically important songs from the Civil War period, and a lot of hymns and gospel songs that are still in use today in many denominations. I considered trying to make the book cover the one hundred years from 1856 to 1955, but decided against that because of a lack of information about the songs from that far back in history; few of them are still known and performed. Even in the 1880 decade, I could find fewer than a dozen songs that might fit the criteria for inclusion. The 1890 decade was a little more profitable with approximately thirty songs that might be remembered by some of us today; however, many of them were popularized in sheet music sale and the infant recording industry in the early 1900s. Therefore, I selected 1900 as an appropriate starting date.

For each year, the book describes the top hits and how they were created and popularized. If chart information is available, it is presented. During the early years, sheet music sales were far more important than record sales, but I have listed the recording artists who helped popularize the songs.

The years are divided into eras corresponding to shifts in musical tastes and often to historical developments as well. "The Good Old Days" covers the first 15 years of the 20th century. "The Ragtime Years" covers the second half of the second decade of the new century (although the second half of the 1910s could also be called "The War Years" because of the tremendous influence exerted by the First World War). "The Jazz Age" covers the Roaring Twenties of the flapper and her beau (during the twenties all popular music was called jazz). "The Depression Years" includes the songs of 1930 to 1934, the primary years of the Great Depression. "The Swing Era" refers to the time of the big bands; it covers 1935 to 1944, and includes most of World War II. The period from the end of the war to the advent of rock 'n' roll is "The Sing Era" (1945–1955) in which singers became more important than bands.

Sometimes it was difficult to verify which songs actually were the top hits of each year. The information available often seemed contradictory. The Recording Industry Association of America began certifying million-selling recordings only in 1958. Before that, often the company or recording artist estimated the sales figures. Beginning in 1935, *Your Hit Parade* radio program compiled and featured a list of top songs for every week. After 1940 there were weekly charts published in *Variety* and *Billboard* of the biggest popular songs.

Lists compiled by *Variety* magazine also suggested which songs should be included. On its fiftieth anniversary in 1956, *Variety* published a *Hit Parade of a Half-Century* covering 1905 to 1955. Although it lists the songs alphabetically rather than by popularity, it indicated some of the most famous songs of these years. In January 1981, *Variety* published "The Top Ten, 1941 to 1980," which ranks each year's top ten by popularity. *Variety* also published its list of *Golden 100 Tin Pan Alley Songs, 1915–1935*, which helps greatly in a period where factual information is difficult to obtain. *Variety*, however, did not disclose how it determined which songs to include in their lists. I also used *Cash Box* popular music singles charts from 1950 through 1981 to document the most popular hits. Often *Variety*, *Billboard*, *Cash Box*, and especially *Your Hit Parade* disagree, but their rankings make interesting comparisons and were worthy of inclusion. The books from Record Research were a valuable source, especially in the years before the advent of *Your Hit Parade* and the other charting services.

Another source of outstanding hits was the *ASCAP* (American Society of Composers, Authors and Publishers) *All-Time Hit Parade*, sixteen songs chosen by this performing-rights organization on its fiftieth anniversary in 1964 as the greatest hits during those fifty years.

The further back in history we go the less information is available. One of the most pertinent criteria for inclusion in the book is a song's longevity. When I examined the early years prior to the days of charts, I tried to determine a song's popularity by counting how many versions were available on early disks and wax cylinders and how many times it was revived over the years. The versions available helped determine the popularity at that particular time, within a year or two at least, and the revivals suggested longevity.

It was often a difficult task to decide which songs to write about, but I tried very diligently to write about songs that were either No. 1 hits on any or all of the charts, songs that were *Variety Hit Parade of a Half-Century* and/or *Golden 100 Tin Pan Alley* songs, *ASCAP All-Time Hit Parade* selections, songs that were award winners or had something so outstanding about them that they just could not be ignored.

As far as I could control my emotions, the selections have not been influenced by my personal preferences or opinions.

I have included lyrics when they could be found and were no longer under copyright. The quoted lyrics or lyric excerpts are meant to help the reader to remember a song, to help set the era in the reader's mind and to remind the reader why a particular song became popular with the public.

Unfortunately I cannot provide these songs for listening, but numerous websites today offer a lot of these songs either as listening files, downloads or purchases in tape or CD format. I have included as many web addresses as I could find where the reader can go to hear the song free in a vintage recording or in a midi musical version. I've also included websites that have the sheet music cover and sometimes the entire musical score for viewing and/or printing and have also provided sites where the reader can read the lyrics of most of the songs.

The final section of the book contains biographical sketches of the composers and lyricists whose songs are listed in this book, and of every performer who introduced a listed song or whose version of the song was the highest ranked of all recorded versions within the period covered. The biographical information is in the form of sketches, not definitive accounts of their lives. In many instances entire books have been written about these people. I present brief information about their lives and then list the most famous songs they wrote, introduced, or popularized. In most cases, many other songs could have been included, but I chose to include only the best known, the most famous, and the most popular.

I want to especially thank my wife, Doris, for helping in the research process. She's definitely my soulmate. She loves all these songs as much as I do. Her willingness to help made it more fun and a lot less time consuming.

I

The Good Old Days: 1900–1914

The story of American popular music of the pre-rock era is the story of Americans' lives, because music is a reflection of history. There have been songs about wars, political campaigns, heroes, villains, highs and lows, national successes and calamities, loves and losses. Some of the songs are trivial, some were here and gone almost immediately, but some are still being whistled and hummed into the 21st century.

Popular music is the people's music — what the people sing, hum, whistle, play or listen to in live performances or in mechanical reproductions. This has always been true of every era. But it is obvious that the beginning of the 20th century brought about a marked change in quality and style of the words and music being written by American songwriters.

When one looks back to the Civil War era, Stephen Foster seems like a beautiful, lush island in a gigantic ocean of nothingness. His songs have proved amazingly durable. His songs seem far ahead of their time and compare very favorably to later songs. But little else remains except a few Civil War songs that are historically significant.

The sentimental ballads of the 1890s seem extremely old-fashioned. A few songs from the period are still remembered, however, including "American Patrol," "Ta-ra-ra-boom-de-ay," "After the Ball," "The Bowery," "Daisy Bell (A Bicycle Built for Two)," "Good Morning to All (Happy Birthday to You)," "The Sidewalks of New York," "The Band Played On," "The Streets of Cairo" (the hootchy-kootchy tune), Sousa's marches including "King Cotton," "El Capitan" and "Hands Across the Sea," plus "A Hot Time in the Old Town," "Sweet Rosie O'Grady" and "On the Banks of the Wabash, Far Away." There are a few others, but they were also popular during the early years of the 1900s.

The First Decade of the 20th Century

The people alive today were not around at the dawn of the 20th century. But, believe it or not, there are at least a few songs from the era that people remember.

The first several years of the new century were peaceful. A few incredibly rich men owned private railroad cars and gave outlandish parties for their friends and business acquaintances. By today's standards, goods and services were incredibly cheap: a shirt cost 23 cents, a parlor table was $3.95, a couch was $9.98, a brass bed would set you back $3.00, corned beef cost 3 cents per pound, a felt hat was 89 cents and an entire suit was only $10.65.

The new century brought the automobile, which spawned such songs as "In My Merry Oldsmobile" and "He'd Have to Get Under, Get Out and Get Under to Fix Up His Automobile." As Americans began to reach for the sky and the first flight experiments brought flying machines, they celebrated that success with "Come, Josephine, in My Flying Machine." Baseball became the "national pastime," and the country was singing "Take Me Out to the Ball Game."

This is the decade in which the Associated Press was founded, a tornado and tidal wave killed 6,000 in Galveston, Texas, Teddy Roosevelt became president, wireless telegraphy became a reality, Henry Ford organized the Ford Motor Company and mass production of automobiles began, the Wright Brothers launched the first successful mechanical airplane and air travel became a reality, the Olympic games were held for the first time in the U.S., a catastrophic earthquake devastated San Francisco, movements against drinking of liquor and smoking became more earnest and Admiral Peary made it to the North Pole.

In the entertainment world, John Philip Sousa's band made its first European concert tour, phonograph recordings began to become more popular, Enrico Caruso made his American debut, George M. Cohan made his musical comedy debut, silent motion pictures were a new phenomenon, the first animated cartoon was filmed, the vaudeville circuit was established and Florenz Ziegfeld inaugurated his *Follies*.

Recordings: Disks or Cylinders

Phonographs and gramophones were making their way into the nation's homes. At first, sound recordings were made by the acoustic process, that is, without amplification or electricity. The musician had to play or sing directly into the recording horn. It wasn't until the mid–1920s that electronic recordings with microphones and amplifiers replaced the acoustic process.

Almost all popular recordings were on wax cylinders until Emile Berliner's Gramophone was produced in the mid–1890s and flat disks began to be marketed.

Only the more prosperous citizens could afford the one-sided disks featuring popular songs. For example, "Meet Me in St. Louis, Louis" as sung by Billy Murray on a Columbia disk, could be purchased in 1904 for a dollar, but members of the working class earned below $500 a year and they could not afford to spend much, if anything, on entertainment. Even the more affluent people who had a little disposable income had to be extremely selective when buying disk recordings priced at a dollar each. Cylinders, priced at fifty cents a few years earlier, had come down in price, so a person could buy a wax cylinder version for twenty-five cents. The wax cylinders were more fragile than disks, so for multiple reasons, including a superior sound, more famous artists, longer playing time and more effective marketing, music lovers began to favor the relatively new disk format. Before '05, records were too primitive and expensive to be the barometer for making hits of songs.

By the end of the decade it was clear that the cylinder was on the way out and the disk was the future. Of the almost thirty million recordings that were sold in '09, the huge majority were disks.

Columbia stopped producing the cylinders in 1912. Edison continued to produce cylinders, now unbreakable, for another couple of decades, primarily for the rural market. But disk sales were definitely predominant.

Sheet Music and Tin Pan Alley

At the turn of the century, the average worker earned less than twenty-five cents an hour. However, sheet music and player pianos were selling in substantial quantities. In the previous decade, sheet music had been expensive; it was not uncommon to find a copy of a popular song selling for as much as two dollars. The new century brought cheaper ways to print music and increased sales. Gradually the price fell to twenty-five cents.

By the 1900s a song's availability in sheet music was crucial. The number of copies of sheet music a song sold was the chief element in determining a song's popularity. Most new songs were published in sheet music form, with the music transcribed for voice and piano. The publishers needed the song to be performed by famous entertainers in front of large audiences. They hired song pluggers who performed the songs for entertainers trying to convince them to perform their company's songs. But the song was available to the public in sheet music.

Publishing songs became lucrative after Charles K. Harris published his "After the Ball" in 1892. Harris' success convinced businessmen that sizeable profits could be made from publishing popular songs. The sheet music industry soon was the prominent medium of disseminating popular music to the public.

So what or where was Tin Pan Alley? It is simply a nickname for the New York City neighborhood that once was the home of several music publishers. By the late 1890s, New York City had become the center of the songwriting and music publishing business. Many songwriters gravitated to a block of West 28th Street between Broadway and Sixth Avenue and their competing pianos in all the neighboring buildings created a sound that journalist Monroe Rosenfeld said sounded like tin pans clanging together. Some of the pianos had been muted with paper and the "rinky-tink" sound of the competing pianos coming from open windows created a cacophony of sound. In one of his newspaper articles in the early 1900s, Rosenfeld gave the area the title "Tin Pan Alley." By the '20s most music publishers had moved uptown, to 42nd Street and elsewhere, but the term stuck as a nickname for the popular music industry.

Tin Pan Alley has come to refer to New York City's music publishing business in general. At least during this era, most of the major publishing firms, such as Witmark, Harms, Feist, and Von Tilzer, were based in Manhattan. Other cities like Philadelphia, Boston, Detroit, St. Louis, and Chicago had music publishers also, but even most of those had major New York City offices.

Tin Pan Alley grew in importance as vaudeville was becoming popular. More Americans heard new songs in vaudeville, in New York City or on the vaudeville circuit, than in any other form of live entertainment. The publishers turned to the vaudeville stars to introduce their songs, which usually encouraged the public to buy the sheet music. The vaudeville entertainers were always looking for good new material.

Tin Pan Alley writers turned out almost 100 songs that sold more than a million copies of sheet music during this decade. Almost all the department stores, the music shops and many of the five-and-ten-cent stores hired demonstrators who played the songs for patrons. The result was a thriving sheet music business. Most middle class homes had a piano in the parlor and usually the mother, or at least one of the children in the family, played the piano for family sing-alongs. With no radio, television, and in most cities and towns, no live entertainment, the family music time after dinner was a major form of entertainment. Sheet music was necessary for these sing-along sessions.

What Is a Popular Song?

Popular music is the people's music. It is, generally speaking, simple enough for anyone to grasp without having any special training. The famous early songwriter Charles K. Harris laid out six rules for writing a successful popular song. He recommended the writer keep his audience in mind — "the masses, the untrained musical public" — and reminded them that the subject matter and melody must appeal to their ears. Second, he advised them to keep an eye on their competitors. Third, "Take note of the public demand." Fourth, he felt slang and vulgarisms never succeeded. Fifth, he recom-

mended avoiding "many-syllabled words and those containing hard consonants." Finally, the writer should endeavor to be concise: "Get to your point quickly, and then make the point as strong as possible." Many years late, Irving Berlin offered his nine rules for writing popular songs in an interview printed in *The American Magazine*. Summarized, the rules were as follows: the melody should be within the singer's range, the title should be attention-getting and should be repeated in the body of the song, the song should be "sexless" (could be sung by male or female), the song requires "heart interest" (as opposed to head interest, appeal to the heart more than the intellect) and it should be an original idea, words, and music. Further, Berlin advised sticking to nature, meaning homely, concrete, everyday things, and he advocated sprinkling the lyrics with open vowels so they would sound euphonious. To conclude, he encouraged making the song as simple as possible and advised potential songwriters to look upon their writing as a business.

Generally, popular songs, at least during the eras covered by this book, began with a verse, which is similar to the recitative section of operatic songs. Recitative is a sort of declamation with musical tones or operatic dialogue in the rhythm of speech. Popular songs adapted the recitative into the verse, which establishes the song's premise. If the song had a dramatic context, the performer could "get into" the character during the verse. The most memorable section of popular songs, the part the audience would whistle or hum, is the chorus or refrain. That section is equivalent to the aria in operatic terms. It is the more lyrical, melodic section and is often more emotional than the verse. By the 19th century, the chorus usually was eight or sixteen bars (measures) long, while the verses were often much longer, as long as sixty-four bars. Stephen Foster popularized the symmetrical eight-bar verse and eight-bar chorus form. However, for his more classical compositions like "Beautiful Dreamer," Foster used the sixteen-bar chorus. By the time Irving Berlin wrote "Alexander's Ragtime Band" in 1911, the thirty-two-bar chorus had gained acceptance. It was built of four equal length sections: the first eight bars stated the song's principal melodic idea. The second eight bars repeated that melody, but the lyrics changed. The third eight bars, often called the bridge, most often introduced a new musical idea. The final eight bars inevitably repeated the original melody with a repeat of former lyrics or with new ones.

The form AABA served as the basic structure of most popular songs for many years. Three-fourths of the song is the same musical idea. After the first sixteen bars, the bridge offers eight measures of a refreshing new idea so the melody doesn't become monotonous. The other form used in some popular songs is the verse-chorus (AB or AABB) type. Early gospel songs often used this form and a few popular songs gravitated to this type of structure. There actually seem to be more of the two-part, verse-chorus, songs during the rock era than during pre-rock.

Irving Berlin noted his vocabulary was somewhat limited through lack of education, so it follows that his lyrics are simple. Similarly, his lack of musical education enabled him to write his songs without worrying about the laws of musical form or harmony. In his opinion, his lack of musical training was an asset.

What Type of Songs Were Popular?

Male quartet arrangements were popular, with tunes sung by a first tenor, second tenor (who usually sang the melody), baritone, and bass. They harmonized on the songs, but these were not "barbershop quartets." That phrase caught on in the '20s and became widely used in the '40s. In other words, no singers were identified by that term during this period.

Victor had the Haydn Quartet, while Columbia boasted the Peerless Quartet and the Columbia Male Quartet. Harry MacDonough was the lead singer for the Haydn Quartet, while Frank Stanley, and later Henry Burr, was the chief singer for the Columbia quartets.

Songs that could be sung around the family piano dominated sheet music sales, and most of those fall into the sentimental ballad category. Through the 1880s and into the early 1900s, the European operettas were a heavy influence on American songs. This period is referred to as the golden age of the ballad. In the early years of the twentieth century, some of the most popular songs were tearjerkers. Sentimental ballads were designed to stir the emotions. Songs in this genre include "When You Were Sweet Sixteen," "In the Sweet Bye and Bye," "Absence Makes the Heart Grow Fonder," "Shine on Harvest Moon," "In the Shade of the Old Apple Tree," "Put on Your Old Grey Bonnet," "My Old New Hampshire Home," "I Wonder Who's Kissing Her Now" and "A Bird in a Gilded Cage."

The minstrel tradition dates back to slavery when white entertainers imitated the slaves. Touring minstrel groups, both African Americans and whites that blacked their faces with burnt cork, were still popular in the early 20th century. A few minstrel-type songs that were popular during this era were "Arkansas Traveler" in '02, "The Preacher and the Bear" in '05, and the songs of black performer and recording artist Bert Williams, particularly "Nobody" in '06.

Ragtime began as a folk music developed by African Americans. Exactly where or how it developed is unknown. The term "ragtime" first appeared on sheet music in 1897. The music's heyday followed Scott Joplin's career as a composer, from the end of the 1890s until his death in '17. Between '00 and '10, more than 1800 rags were published.

The "coon song" was an important genre, and no discussion of popular music of the era can be complete without acknowledging it. Sheet music of such songs, generally with cover illustrations that seem demeaning to African Americans today, sold well. Popular "coon songs" with ragtime-influenced melodies include Hughie Cannon's "Bill Bailey, Won't You Please Come Home?" Bob Cole's "Under the Bamboo Tree," and Joe Howard's "Good-Bye, My Lady Love." Even though the infectious syncopation of ragtime inspired many songs of the early 1900s, it was the following decade that was even more important for ragtime.

The first decade of the new century was rich with topical songs about the events of the day. Examples of topical songs include "Meet Me in St. Louis, Louis," which was inspired by the Louisiana Purchase Exposition of '04 which was held in St. Louis. The Wright brothers' flights were the inspiration for "Come Take a Trip in My Air Ship." The first cross-continental trip by automobile inspired "In My Merry Oldsmobile" in '05.

Brass bands were very popular during this era. Every city of any size had a band that played in the city park on Sunday afternoons. But by far the most important band was John Philip Sousa's. Beginning with the United States Marine Band in the 1890s and continuing with his own band of 100 players, Sousa and his band toured America as well as Europe and recorded often. Important march-type songs include "The Stars and Stripes Forever" and "Semper Fidelis," but even George M. Cohan's "The Grand Old Rag (Flag)" has a march quality to it.

By the beginning of the 20th century, live

entertainment, particularly in the form of the theater, was well established and had proven to be the great medium for introducing the American public to a wide variety of entertainment.

European operettas were a popular favorite of theater audiences. Productions of Victor Herbert's operettas were very well received, as were those of Franz Lehar and Oscar Straus. Examples would include *Mlle. Modiste, The Red Mill, The Chocolate Soldier* and *The Merry Widow.* The musical theater also offered other divertissements like *Floradora, The Wizard of Oz* (not the same as the famous '39 film; for instance, Dorothy didn't have a dog named Toto, she had a pet cow named Imogene), *Babes in Toyland* (by Victor Herbert, but not quite as operatic as his other works), George M. Cohan's *Little Johnny Jones* and *Forty-Five Minutes from Broadway,* plus the *Ziegfeld Follies.* For the first half of the second decade, the following musicals were particularly popular on Broadway: *Madame Sherry, Naughty Marietta, The Firefly, Sweethearts, The Girl from Utah* and *Watch Your Step.*

A few classical numbers were popular with the public, chiefly due to the popularity of Enrico Caruso. Some the classical pieces that were popular during this decade include "Vesti la Giubba" from *I Pagliacci,* "Celeste Aida" from *Aida* and "Solenne in quest' ora" from *La forza del destino.*

What Is ASCAP?

In '14, five composers, one librettist and three publishers' representatives formed the American Society of Composers, Authors and Publishers (ASCAP) to protect and license public performance of musical compositions. Restaurants and other establishments were playing the popular songs of the day to lure customers. They were advertising, "Come in and hear our orchestra play [insert a famous writer's name]'s latest hit song from [insert the name of a Broadway show] and enjoy our delicious food." However, the songwriters and publishers were not receiving any royalties for the use of the songs. Many people even today don't understand the problem, but if you can, try to imagine that you have just written a song that will become enormously popular. How do you make money from that song? When it is published, you will receive royalties from sheet music sales. When it is recorded, you will receive royalties from sales. But unless an organization like ASCAP had come along, you would not receive anything for the millions of times your song was played on radio, on TV, in public performances, or in eating establishments, bars, casinos, etc. Those people would be making money off of your song, but they wouldn't have to compensate you one penny. Unfair, isn't it? That's why ASCAP and other performing rights organizations came along: to protect songwriters and publishers' rights.

1900

Because

Words: Charles Horwitz; Music: Frederick V. Bowers

The most famous "Because" song today is the '02 song of wedding fame (see '02), but this 1898 song by Horwitz and Bowers was perhaps even more popular during the first half of the first decade of the new century.

Sheet music sales were the primary indication of popularity with the general public, but on some occasions, music was mechanically produced by a music box, a player piano, or by rather primitive phonographs, however, only the more prosperous could afford wax cylinders and one-sided disks featuring popular songs. Albert Campbell's 1899 recording, plus the Haydn Quartet's '00 disk were both very popular.

Horwitz's first verse follows: *At night I sit alone and dream, of days when you were always near. / And mem'ry then recalls the time, when both our lives were happy dear. / I would I knew where you can be, I trust your heart is still the same, / When nature sleeps and all is still, I whisper fondly one sweet name.*

The lyrics never reveal the "one sweet name" that the singer whispers. The chorus lyrics follow: *Because I love You! Because I love you! / My only one regret, since then, we've never met, / Because I love you! Because I love you! / Yes, my heart is yours, Because I love you!*

Evidently, this is an example of unrequited love. The singer is still very much in love and regrets he hasn't met his love since they parted.

The non-descript sheet music cover and musical score of this song are available at http://levysheetmusic.mse.jhu.edu/browse.html.

A Bird in a Gilded Cage

Words: Arthur J. Lamb; Music: Harry Von Tilzer

"A Bird in a Gilded Cage" became an enormously successful sentimental ballad during the early years of the 20th century. A sentimental ballad is an effusive, perhaps even mushy, song often playing upon the listener's emotions.

The "bird in the gilded cage" is a young woman who is bound by the wealth of an older man. Von Tilzer was hesitant to write the music unless the song's lyrics made it clear that the woman in the "cage" was the man's wife, not his mistress.

The first verse tells us that a very beautiful woman passes by a man and his girl friend at a dance. The girl tells her beau that the beautiful woman has "riches at her command." He replies that she may live in a mansion, but she "married for wealth, not for love."

The famous chorus sings about this beautiful woman who is not happy, "though she seems to be." One of the song's key lines is "youth cannot mate with age." This girl's "beauty was sold, for an old man's gold, she's a bird in a gilded cage."

The seldom-sung second verse is about the death of the beautiful woman. The lyrics speculate that "she is happier here at rest, than to have people say when seen" after which the chorus comes in again with "She's only a bird in a gilded cage."

Even though sheet music sales were the primary barometer of a song's popularity at his point, both Jere Mahoney and Steve Porter helped the song's popularity with almost equally successful recordings. Porter's Columbia recording may have been slightly more popular than Mahoney's Edison recording. Harry MacDonough also helped popularize the song with numerous performances and a successful recording on Edison.

"A Bird in a Gilded Cage" was used in the '41 motion picture *Ringside Maisie*.

See the sheet music cover and listen to a midi musical version (if you download the free SCORCH software, you can follow the musical score while you listen; the download is free. This software is wonderful; it follows the music for you; a line in the music shows exactly where you are, so even if you don't read music, it is well worth the effort) at http://parlorsongs.com/issues/2001-10/this month/featurea.asp. The sheet music cover and musical score are available at http://levysheetmusic.mse.jhu.edu/browse.html (use the search function).

Hello, Ma Baby

Words & Music: Joe E. Howard & Ida Emerson

"Hello, Ma Baby" was Joe E. Howard's first successful song and it became one of the most successful early ragtime songs. It is also one of the earliest successful songs about the telephone.

The lyrics of the first verse tell us this singer talks to a girl on the telephone that he has never seen. Nevertheless, he considers her his girl and advises other men to "take my tip an' leave this gal alone." Every morning he picks up the telephone and says, "Hey, Central, fix me up along the line!" The chorus is what he says to "baby mine."

Some modern editions of the song have removed some of the racial language, but the original chorus lyrics follow: *Hello, ma baby! Hello, ma honey! / Hello, ma ragtime gal! / Send me a kiss by wire, Baby, my heart's on fire! / If you refuse me, honey, you'll lose me / Then you'll be left alone; / Oh, baby, telephone, and tell me I'se your own.*

A twenty-nine-year-old inventor, Alexander Graham Bell, had patented the telephone in 1876. The first commercial use of the invention came within a couple of years and it quickly became a public necessity. AT&T was organized in 1886 and by 1892 Bell controlled 240,000 telephones. By '03 there were two million telephones, 1,278,000 managed by Bell. So the telephone quickly went from phenomenon to necessity, at least in the big cities.

"Hello, Ma Baby" was used in Joe E. Howard's screen biography *I Wonder Who's Kissing Her Now* ('47). For an entire generation of cartoon watchers in film and on TV, the most famous performance of the song is probably the one where a man discovers a singing and dancing frog in the cornerstone of a demolished building. He envisions all the money he's going to make with this song-and-dance frog, but of course, the frog refuses to perform on demand. That cartoon became so famous that the WB television network uses that frog as its mascot. The cartoon was *One Froggy Evening* ('55). Originally, the frog didn't have a name, but later was called Michigan J. Frog.

Arthur Collins and Len Spencer competed with each other to see whose recording of the song would be most successful. It was a virtual dead-heat.

The sheet music cover and the musical score are available at http://scriptorium.lib.duke.edu/dynaweb/sheet music/1900-1909/@Generic_BookTextView/9963;nh=1? DwebQuery=Hello#X. Another sheet music cover and the musical score of this song are available at http://levysheet music.mse.jhu.edu/browse.html (use the search function). See two different sheet music covers and hear a midi musical version at http://www.perfessorbill.com/index2.htm.

The Little Brown Jug

Words & Music: R. A. Eastburn

"The Little Brown Jug" was written by J.E. Winner, using the pseudonym R.A. Eastburn in 1868. The sheet music copyrighted in 1868, claims the song was written by George Cooper and W.F. Wellman, Jr. Another sheet music publication in 1869 titled "The Original Little Brown Jug" named the writer as Betta. Most authorities accept Winner as the writer.

The song was popularized by Steve Porter in '00 Columbia recording. Glenn Miller and his orchestra revived it in '39 in a popular recording.

The chorus lyrics are rather folk-like and simplistic: *Ha! Ha! Ha! 'tis you and me, / Little Brown Jug Don't I love thee.*

Perhaps the tune's popularity as an instrumental indicates the melody is more interesting than the words.

The song was used in the '30 film *Dodge City*, in the '39 movie musical *The Story of Vernon and Irene Castle*, which starred Fred Astaire and Ginger Rogers, in the '44 movie musical *Twilight on the Prairie*, and in the '54 film biography *The Glenn Miller Story*.

The sheet music cover and musical score of this song are available at http://levysheetmusic.mse.jhu.edu/browse. html (use search; the 1868 Copper and Wellman version and 1869 Betta version are there).

Ma Tiger Lily

Words: Clay M. Greene; Music: A. B. Sloane

"Ma Tiger Lily" is a very popular '00 coon song (see "When Chloe Sings a Song: for more about so-called coon songs). Unfortunately, the lyrics are grossly racial, but the coon song with its racial language was very much the fad. According to the sheet music cover, "Ma Tiger Lily" premiered in the musical comedy *Aunt Hannah*, which was produced at the Bijou Theatre in New York City.

The first verse begins with the singer singing "I'd frow down any coon fur her, she frowed down piles for me." His "Tiger Lily" is "wicked as kin be." The chorus lyrics follow: *Fur she's ma Lily, ma Tiger Lily, / She draws de niggers like a crowd of flies. / A queen in shape and size, got diamonds in her eyes, / She is ma sweetest one, ma baby Tiger Lily.*

Both Arthur Collins and Len Spencer had extremely

popular recordings of "Ma Tiger Lily" in '00 helping make it one of the year's biggest hit songs.

The music score is available at http://levysheetmusic. mse.jhu.edu/browse.html. The sheet music cover and musical score are available at http://digital.library.ucla.edu/ apam/librarian?ITEMID=SY103024.

Mandy Lee

Words & Music: Thurland Chattaway

Thurland Chattaway wrote "Mandy Lee" in 1899. It became a barbershop quartet, or perhaps more aptly stated, a male quartet, favorite. Since the phrase "barbershop quartet" was not used in music trade journals or on sheet music at this time, it is the male quartet that was important.

Male quartet arrangements of popular songs were popular, with tunes most often sung by a group consisting of a first and second tenor (second tenor usually carried the melody), baritone, and bass. Some of the leading singers of the time, like Arthur Collins, were the lead singers of these male quartets.

Although recordings were not the most reliable method to determine popularity during this time, Arthur Collins, Albert Campbell and Harry MacDonough helped popularized "Mandy Lee" with important recordings.

The lyrics of the chorus follow: *Mandy Lee, I love you, 'deed I do, my Mandy Lee. / Your eyes they shine like diamonds, love, to me. / Seems as though my heart would break without you, Mandy Lee. / 'Cause I love you, Mandy, 'deed I do, my Mandy Lee.*

The sheet music cover and musical score of this song are available at http://levysheetmusic.mse.jhu.edu/browse. html (use search).

My Wild Irish Rose

Words & Music: Chauncey Olcott

"My Wild Irish Rose," "Mother Machree" and "When Irish Eyes Are Smiling" are considered the most popular Irish ballads of all time.

"My Wild Irish Rose" was interpolated into the 1899 show *A Romance of Athlone*, where Chauncey Olcott, the writer, performed it. He recorded it for Columbia in '13. In '06 it was used in the musical *The Little Cherub*.

Chauncey Olcott was one of the most popular performers of his day. He was also a well-known composer. His performances of "My Wild Irish Rose" were so impassioned and expressive that he became known as the "Irish Thrush."

The lyrics to the famous chorus follow: *My wild Irish Rose, / The sweetest flow'r that grows, / You may search ev'rywhere but none can compare / With my wild Irish Rose. / My wild Irish Rose, / The dearest flow'r that grows, / And some day for my sake, she may let me take / The bloom from my wild Irish Rose.*

For the era, the last two lines of the chorus are shocking. This is an extremely chaste, prim and proper period, so to sing "And some day for my sake, she may let me take the bloom from my wild Irish Rose" seems rather daring. Was this really sexually suggestive? It certainly sounds suggestive, but considering the prudish morals of the era, it is difficult to imagine a song becoming a national hit that includes a sexually suggestive thought.

There have been three significant ethnic influences in American popular music: the Jews, the African Americans and the Irish. These nationalities were transplanted into American society and for many years they were severely oppressed. One of the avenues available to them to rise above their oppressed station in life was music and many of them took advantage of their opportunities.

The Irish were an important influence in American popular songs especially during the first couple of decades of the 20th century. The Irish have always been proud of their heritage and they loved to sing about it. In addition to "My Wild Irish Rose," "Mother Machree" (see '11) and "When Irish Eyes Are Smiling" (see '13), a couple of the most prominent Irish songs were "A Little Bit of Heaven, Shure They Call It Ireland" (see '15) and "Too-ra-loo-ra-loo-ral" (see '14). George M. Cohan was also proud to show his Irish heritage in his songs, notably "Harrigan" (see '07). And that only mentions some of the most obviously Irish songs, but the Irish influence continued in American popular songs for many years.

When music was played in the home during these opening years of the 20th century, it was most often performed with someone at the piano accompanying family members who sang. With the price of pianos gradually decreasing in the late 19th century, Americans purchased pianos for their parlors, and that fueled the public's desire for more published songs. "My Wild Irish Rose" was one of the most popular songs to sing during these family or community songfests, especially if several mixed voice singers were present so they could harmonize. The sheet music industry was a booming business supplying the sheet music for the pianist and singers.

Sometimes music was produced mechanically, that is, by a music box, a player piano, or by phonograph, which was often called a talking machine, however, only members of more prosperous classes could afford wax cylinders and one-sided disks featuring popular songs. The most popular recordings of "My Wild Irish Rose" were by Albert Campbell and by George Gaskin in 1899 and by Harry MacDonough in '00. The Haydn Quartet revived it in '05, while the writer, Chauncey Olcott, scored with it in a '13 recording. John McCormack revived it once again in '15. Then, during the big band era, Jan Garber and his orchestra had a popular recording of the song in '37.

The song was featured in several Hollywood films, including *Doughboys in Ireland* ('43) and *My Wild Irish Rose* ('47).

The rather bland sheet music cover and musical score are available at http://digital.nypl.org/lpa/lpa_search.cfm. See a slighly different, and even blander, sheet music cover and hear a midi musical version at http://www.perfessor bill.com/index2.htm or see a different, but equally bland, cover at http://parlorsongs.com/issues/2002-3/thismonth/ featurea.asp.

Old Folks at Home

Words & Music: Stephen C. Foster

Stephen Foster's "Old Folks at Home," or as it may be more famous "Swanee River," written in 1851, was introduced by the Christy Minstrels.

Foster wanted to find a river to write a song about. His brother suggested several, including the Yazoo and the Pedee, but Foster rejected them. Then his brother took down an atlas and inspected the state of Florida. He came upon the Suwanee River and Stephen immediately liked the name, except he contracted the name to "Swanee."

The Christy Minstrels, headed by Ed Christy, were looking for a new Foster song to perform and agreed to introduce it. Christy also wanted song writing credit. Foster finally sold the song to Christy for $500, but it is doubtful that Foster was paid that amount. The first sheet music described the song as an "Ethiopian melody" probably to avoid using the term "Negro." It also credited E.P. Christy as the writer and Christy continued to appear as the writer on published sheet music until 1879, when the first copyright expired.

By the mid–1850s the song had sold a reported 150,000 copies of sheet music.

Popular recordings of the song were issued by Len Spencer (1892), Vess Ossman ('00), the Haydn Quartet ('04), Louise Homer ('05), Alma Gluck ('15), the Taylor Trio ('16), and Oscar Seagle and the Columbia Stellar Quartet ('19). Then during the big band era, the song was revived by Jimmie Lunceford and his orchestra and by Bunny Berigan and his orchestra (1936–37). If the number of revivals is an indication of longevity, "Old Folks at Home" certainly qualifies. "Old Folks at Home" became one of the most recorded songs of the pre-rock era.

In most modern printings of "Old Folks at Home," the racially sensitive language has been modified, but, for authenticity, the original lyrics to the first verse and chorus follow: *'Way down upon de Swanee ribber, Far, far away, / Dere's wha my heart is turning ebber, Dere's wha de old folks stay. / All up and down de whole creation, Sadly I roam, / Still longing for de old plantation, and for de old folks at home. / All de world am sad and dreary, Ebry where I roam, / Oh! darkeys how my heart grows weary, / Far from de old folks at home.*

"Old Folks at Home" or "Swanee River" has appeared in several Hollywood films, including *Mississippi* ('35), where it was sung by Bing Crosby and a black chorus, *Harmony Lane*, a biopic about Stephen Foster, *Swanee River* ('39), another fictious account of the life and music of Stephen Foster, *Babes on Broadway* ('42), with Judy Garland and Mickey Rooney and *I Dream of Jeanie* ('52), yet another film about the life of Stephen Foster.

Several sheet music covers and the musical score of this song are available at http://levysheetmusic.mse.jhu.edu/browse.html (use search). See the sheet music cover, the lyrics and the musical score at http://www.pbs.org/wgbh/amex/foster/gallery/pop_ie_oldfolks_listen.html (a musical sample is also available in QuickTime or RealAudio).

When Chloe Sings a Song

Words: Edgar Smith; Music: John Stromberg

"When Chloe Sings a Song" is described as a "coon song." The sheet music proclaimed it as "a southern plantation number." The New Grove Dictionary of American Music defined the coon song as "a genre of comic song, popular from around 1800 to the end of World War I, with words in a dialect purporting to be typical of black American speech."

Coon was a slang word for African Americans. Even though many of the coon songs evidence a sort of racism through music and are offensive to African Americans today, the songs are important historic documents and no discussion of popular music of this era can be complete without acknowledging the genre.

One of the first coon songs to become a hit was "(Jump) Jim Crow" performed by Thomas Dartmouth Rice in

1828. Most states in the South had passed anti–African American legislation, known as the Jim Crow laws. Of course, it wasn't until 1964's Civil Rights Act that discrimination became illegal.

As bad as the coon songs were in stereotyping African Americans, they were not the only ethnic group to be affected. There were comic songs about virtually every ethnic group. For example, the Irish were also berated in songs like "The Mick Who Threw the Brick."

Reportedly approximately one fifteenth of new songs each month were coon songs. Characterizing any comic number as a coon song helped sales. When Thomas A. Edison's National Phonograph Company issued "Bedelia" in '03 sung by Billy Murray, promotional literature characterized the song as an "Irish coon serenade" and the sheet music states almost the same thing: "Irish Coon Song Serenade."

The catchy tunes of the coon songs, which were usually heavily syncopated, made them instant favorites, but the words, in dialect slang, may have helped reinforce prejudices.

Lillian Russell introduced "When Chloe Sings a Song" at Weber and Fields' Music Hall in an extravaganza titled *Whirl-I-Gig* in 1899. An extravaganza was a lavishly staged, spectacular form of entertainment. It often contained elaborate scenic effects, colorful costumes and rather scantily clad dancing girls.

George J. Gaskin further popularized the song in an early Columbia recording.

The lyrics are filled with dialect. The song's title might have been "Dar is music" because the phrase is used often in the verse. In the first verse, the singer tells us there are many different kinds of music, but "de sweetes' music ever dat I hear" is when his sweet Chloe sings. The chorus lyrics follow: *Do yo' hear dem tones a-comin' wid de ole banjo a-strummin' / Why de bees dey stop dere hummin' when dey hears 'em come along, / O'er de whole o' dis plantation, it's de cause ob a sensation, / Sweetes' music in creation is when Chloe sings a song.*

The sheet music cover and musical score of this song are available at http://levysheetmusic.mse.jhu.edu/browse.html (use search).

When You Were Sweet Sixteen

Words & Music: James Thornton

On a particular occasion James Thornton's wife asked him if he still loved her; his reply turned into a tremendously successful song. Thornton told his wife he loved her just as much as he did when she was sixteen. His wife, Bonnie, encouraged James to turn the thought into a love song in 1898. Then Bonnie Thornton had the honor of introducing the song in vaudeville. The song quickly caught on and became a particular favorite of male quartets.

Thornton sold publication rights to the song to Joseph W. Stern & Co. for $25, but when the company failed to publish the song right away, Thornton sold it to Witmark for $15. Witmark published it right away and sold millions of copies of sheet music. As the song became a hit, Stern sued Witmark. The suit was settled out of court when Witmark agreed to pay Stern $5000 for the rights.

The lyrics of the verse and chorus of this famous song follow: *When first I saw the love light in your eyes, / I thought the world held naught but joy for me. / And even though we drifted far apart, / I never dream but what I dream of thee. / I love you as I've never loved before, / Since first I saw you on the village green. / Come to me or my dream of love is o'er, / I love you as I loved you / When you were sweet sixteen.*

George J. Gaskin and Jere Mahoney both released very popular recordings of the song in '00. Gaskin's version on Columbia most likely made "When You Were Sweet Sixteen" the biggest hit of the year. With both Gaskin's Columbia recording and Mahoney's Edison recording selling very well, the song was certainly one of the, if not the, biggest hit of the year. Then in '01, Harry MacDonough and J.W. Myers added to the song's popularity when they both released popular recorded versions. All these popular recordings meant that "When You Were Sweet Sixteen" became one of the biggest hits of the first decade of the 20th century.

The song was featured in the Shirley Temple film *Little Miss Broadway* ('38) and in *The Jolson Story* ('46). It was used as a leitmotif in the '41 film *The Strawberry Blonde* and it was sung by Bing Crosby on the soundtrack of *The Great John L.* in '45.

Then in '47, Perry Como had a million selling recording of the song. The Mills Brothers and Dick Jurgens both also released popular recordings of the song in '47.

The sheet music cover and musical score of this song are available at http://levysheetmusic.mse.jhu.edu/browse. html (use search).

1901

Absence Makes the Heart Grow Fonder

Words: Arthur Gillespie; Music: Herbert Dillea

This expression, or similar ones, existed long before this song came out in '01. One such quote, "Absence makes the heart grow fonder," was by Thomas Haynes Bayly who lived from 1797 to 1839.

We've all heard this famous quote, which implies the time we spend away from the one we love makes us love that person even more. When we're away from someone we care for very much, we miss that person and think about them often, and that feeling makes us want to be with them even more. In meaningful relationships, we at least hope this expression is true. Of course, one might think of it as the need of a specific person to leave so we might grow fonder of them.

Harry MacDonough had the most popular recording of "Absence Makes the Heart Grow Fonder" in '01, but recordings by George J. Gaskin and by Jules Levy were also popular in '01 and '02.

In the sheet music, there are the original lyrics and a school version. In the first verse, the singer is telling his sweetheart he has grown lonely living away from her. Before they parted, harsh words were spoken, but he is hoping she still cares for him. The chorus lyrics follow: *Absence makes the heart grow fonder, that is why I long for you; / Lonely thro' the nights I ponder, wond'ring, darling, if you're true. / Distance only lends enchantment, tho' the ocean wave divide, / Absence makes the heart grow fonder, longing to be near your side.*

Edwin S. Timmons wrote another song with the same title in 1896. Lyricists Sam M. Lewis and Joe Young and composer Harry Warren wrote another song titled "Absence Makes the Heart Grow Fonder (For Somebody Else)" in '30.

View a couple of sheet music covers and the musical score at http://digital.library.ucla.edu/.

American Patrol

Music: F. W. Meacham

Meacham's march creates the illusion of a passing band. It begins softly, as if the patrol is in the distance, and grows louder; the sound becomes distant at the end, as if the band had passed by. Sousa's Band popularized it in a very popular Gram-o-phone recording in '01. Meacham had written the march in 1885.

Prince's Orchestra revived the march in a popular '17 recording. Then in '42, Glenn Miller and his Orchestra revived it again. Miller's recording can be heard on various compilations, including *The Essential Glenn Miller*. A recording by Six Brown Brothers is available at http://www.redhotjazz.com/6brownbrothers.html.

Meacham, by the way, was a one hit wonder; he composed no other famous marches or songs.

"American Patrol" appeared on the soundtracks of *Thousands Cheer* ('43) and *Patch Adams* ('98).

The sheet music cover and musical score of this song are available at http://levysheetmusic.mse.jhu.edu/browse. html. See the sheet music cover and hear a midi musical version at http://www.perfessorbill.com/index2.htm or http://parlorsongs.com/issues/2002-7/thismonth/feature b.asp.

Any Old Place I Can Hang My Hat Is "Home Sweet Home" to Me

Words: William Jerome; Music: Jean Schwartz

Will Denny had a particularly popular recording of "Any Old Place I Can Hang My Hat Is 'Home Sweet Home' to Me" in '01. The song's title is sometimes listed as "Any Old Place I Hang My Hat Is 'Home Sweet Home' to Me."

In *The Longing for Home*, Frederick Buechner says: "Home sweet home. There's no place like home. Home is where you hang your hat, or as a waggish friend of mine once said, 'Home is where you hang yourself.'" All of Buechner's quotes, except for perhaps the last, are famous expressions of love for home, wherever that may be. To most of us, home is where we "hang our hat," whether that's a palatial mansion or a run-down shack. And we tend to be nostalgic about that home, the place we grew up, the place of our memories.

In the case of the singer in this song, he has wonderlust. He wants to be free and easy so home must be any place he can hang his hat. Whenever the spirit whispers "roam," he looks for another welcome mat.

A famous bluegrass song by Bill Monroe, "The Brakeman's Blues," quotes the line "Any old place I hang my hat is home."

Good-bye, Dolly Gray

Words: Will D. Cobb; Music: Paul Barnes

"Good-bye, Dolly Gray" is basically a march written, according to David Ewan in *American Popular Songs*, in

1898, but it was not copyrighted until '00. Ewan also said the song was sung by our soldiers during the Spanish-American War, which was in 1898. However, the most popular recordings of the song were by J.W. Myers in '00 on Columbia and by the Big Four Quartet in '01 for Edison.

Although this song was written almost two decades before World War I, it was a favorite during that war. Many "goodbye" songs were popular during that time. The lyrics of the first verse and chorus follow: *I have come to say goodbye, Dolly Gray. / It's no use to ask me why, Dolly Gray. / There's a murmur in the air / You can hear it ev'rywhere / It is time to do and dare, Dolly Gray. / Don't you hear the tramp of feet, Dolly Gray. / Sounding thro' the village street, Dolly Gray. / 'Tis the tramp of soldiers true / In their uniforms of blue, / I must say good-bye to you, Dolly Gray! / Good-bye Dolly, I must leave you, / Tho' it breaks my heart to go, / Something tells me I am needed / at the front to fight the foe. / I see the boys in blue are marching, / And I can no longer stay. / Hark! I hear the bugle calling, / Good-bye Dolly Gray!*

Hear Harry MacDonough's '01 recording of "Good-bye, Dolly Gray" at www.firstworldwar.com/audio/pre 1914 or hear Hugh Donovan and the Broadway Quartet's recording of the song at http://www.authentichistory. com/audio/civilwar/Victrola-Goodbye_Dolly_Gray.html. The sheet music cover and musical score of this song are available at http://levysheetmusic.mse.jhu.edu/browse.html.

Hello, Central, Give Me Heaven

Words & Music: Charles K. Harris

"Hello, Central, Give Me Heaven" is a song by Charles K. Harris about a child who uses a telephone to try to contact her deceased mother. "Hello, Central..." indicates the needs to go through an operator who then connected the caller to the party they were trying to reach.

The lyrics of the first verse are the child speaking to her father. She tearfully tells him she's lonely "since dear Mamma's gone to Heaven." The child decides she'll call her on the telephone to tell her to come home. The chorus lyrics, which follow, are what the child speaks to the operator: *Hello central, give me Heaven, / I've a Mamma there. / You will find 'er with the angels / On the golden stairs. / She'll be glad it's me whose speaking, / Tell her won't you please, / For I want a surely tell her, / We're so lonely here.*

Another "telephone" song was the World War I classic "Hello, Central, Give Me No Man's Land."

"Hello, Central, Give Me Heaven" was popularized in '01 in an Edison recording by Byron Harlan.

See the sheet music cover and musical score at http:// lcweb2.loc.gov/cocoon/ihas/loc.natlib.ihas.100006409/ or http://levysheetmusic.mse.jhu.edu/browse.html. See the sheet music cover and listen to a midi musical version of this song at http://parlorsongs.com/issues/2001-11/this month/featurea.asp.

My Blushin' Rosie (My Posie Sweet)

Words: Edgar Smith; Music: John Stromberg

Fay Templeton and a chorus of girls introduced "My Blushin' Rosie (My Posie Sweet)" in Weber and Fields' new burlesque production *Fiddle-Dee-Dee*, which opened in '00 (the sheet music cover also indicates that Ms. Templeton sang the song in the Weber and Fields' production *Quo Vass Iss*). The song's title is sometimes listed as "Ma Blushin' Rosie (Ma Posie Sweet)."

Stromberg had written the melody earlier as a dance tune for Bessie Clayton, but she never used it, so when he needed a replacement number in *Fiddle Dee Dee*, he reworked the original as a song for Fay Templeton. It became the hit of the show and one of the most successful numbers to originate in a Weber and Fields presentation.

Al Jolson also became interested in the song and sang it in his Sunday evening Winter Garden concerts in the '20s. As a result, the song was featured in the movies *The Jolson Story* ('46) and *Jolson Sings Again* ('49).

"Ma Blushin' Rosie" was also used in the movie musicals *Broadway to Hollywood* ('33), *Lillian Russell* ('40), *The Naughty Nineties* ('45) and *The Daughter of Rosie O'Grady* ('50).

The lyrics of the verse tell us that the singer has "a little bunch of sweetness" that he hopes will be his bride. This girl's "baptismal name was Rosie, but she put's the rose to shame." The lead-in to the chorus is, "And almost every night, you'll hear me call her name." The chorus (using "my" instead of "ma") follows: *Rosie, you are my posie, / you are my hearts bouquet. / Come out here in the moonlight, / There's something sweet love, / I wanna say. / Your honey boy I'm waiting, / Those ruby lips to greet. / Don't be so captivating, / My blushing rosie, / My Posie sweet.*

The sheet music cover and music score are available at http://levysheetmusic.mse.jhu.edu/browse.html.

The Stars and Stripes Forever

Music: John Philip Sousa

"The Stars and Stripes Forever" is a patriotic march by John Philip Sousa. By an act of the U.S. Congress, it was declared the "National March of the United States of America."

In his autobiography, Sousa said he composed this march on Christmas Day 1896. He had just learned that David Blakely, the manager of his band, had died. Sousa was on a ferry in Europe at the time. Sousa composed the march in his head and later committed it to paper.

The manuscript of his full score is dated April 26, 1897; the march's official premiere was in Philadelphia on May 14, 1897. "Stars and Stripes Forever" became one of the most recorded songs of the pre-rock era. Over a hundred interpretations are available on compact disks.

In turn-of-the-century America, dancers favored the march over the waltz as a musical form since the regular rhythm in 2/4, 4/4, or 6/8 meter was perfect for the new and wildly popular two-step dance. Eventually, the term "fox-trot" replaced "march" as a term in printed music. During the late 1800s and early 1900s marches were often used to accompany dances like the cakewalk or two-step.

Bands were once so pervasive in America that almost every town of any size sponsored a community band. They were heard almost everywhere, from parading on Main Street to playing in the park on Sunday afternoon, to providing background music for skating or providing dance music for wedding receptions. In an article for Harper's Weekly in 1889, Leon Mead wrote, "At present there are over ten thousand military bands in the United States. In the smaller cities they average twenty-five men each. In small county towns they number twelve to eighteen members."

Several famous bands toured widely and always drew large crowds. They were professional concert bands not affiliated with any military institution, not marching or parade bands, they most often performed under a band shell in a park or seated in the open air or in a concert hall.

Sousa had left the U.S. Marine Band in 1892 to form Sousa's New Marine Band, soon renamed Sousa's Grand Concert Band. This band was always identified on recordings as Sousa's Band. It was the nation's most popular concert ensemble. Even though Sousa was worried that mechanical music, records and player pianos, threatened the livelihood of musicians, over a thousand recordings are credited to Sousa's Band.

"Stars and Stripes Forever" (it is most often referred to today without the "The" at the beginning) is in standard march form: Introduction, the March (AABB) Trio (CDCDC). The Trio section is most often a more mellow tune than the March section. Sousa set lyrics to this Trio melody, but it may be more well known today in other lyric versions like "Three cheers for the red, white and blue..." or even "Be kind to your web-footed friends..."

One of the most significant parts of "Stars and Stripes Forever" is the piccolo obbligato that is played on the first repeat of the Trio melody. Later the low brass join the piccolos with a powerful counter-melody that brings a majestic mood towards the end of the piece.

Of course, it was Sousa's band that popularized the song, but many other bands, national and local, played it often. Sousa wasn't fond of recordings. He called it "canned music," but he was rather pleased with the profits he received from them.

Sousa's band was one of the first to make commercial records, but he would not conduct the band while recording. Arthur Pryor usually did the conducting. It wasn't until the mid–'20s that Sousa would direct his band in a recording. Hear Sousa's Band's '06 recording of this march at http://www.edisonnj.org/menlopark/vintage/victor.asp or hear the Sousa band's 1890-something recording of this march at http://lcweb2.loc.gov/cocoon/ihas/loc.natlib. ihas.200001552/. The sheet music cover and musical score of this song are available at http://levysheetmusic.mse.jhu. edu/browse.html.

The march's title served as the title for a '52 Sousa biographical motion picture starring Clifton Webb. A medley of Sousa marches including "Washington Post March," "Semper Fidelis," "El Capitan" and "Stars and Stripes Forever" was danced by Dick Powell in *Rosalie* ('37) and "Stars and Stripes Forever" was also performed in *Babes in Arms* ('39).

The Tale of a Bumble Bee

Words: Frank Pixley; Music: Gustav Luders

Gertrude Quinland and William Norris introduced "The Tale of a Bumble Bee," sometimes listed as "The Tale of the Bumble Bee," in *King Dodo*. The sheet music cover uses "a" instead of "the."

The song has three verses and three choruses. The lyrics use the Bumble Bee as a metaphor for men who go from blossom to blossom collecting honey from each. Even though they promise to be true, they flit from girl to girl or in the case of the song's lyrics, from blossom to blossom and even though they promise to return, they seldom actually do.

Harry MacDonough had a very popular recording of "The Tale of a Bumble Bee" in '01.

The sheet music cover and musical score are available at http://levysheetmusic.mse.jhu.edu/browse.html.

Tell Me, Pretty Maiden *and* The Shade of the Palm

Words: Owen Hall; Music: Leslie Stuart

At the turn of the century, American musical theater was still heavily influenced by European shows. For instance, Gilbert and Sullivan's British comic operas were very popular. Another import from England was *Florodora*, which opened in late '00. It became the second show in Broadway history to have a run of over 500 performances.

The plot of *Florodora* was a story of a young woman seeking romance and the restoration of a stolen inheritance. The protagonist in the tale is the elderly manufacturer of Florodora perfume who wants to marry the young heroine, Dolores, whose father has been cheated into losing his fortune. At first, New York City producers thought the show was "too British" for American audiences, but that did not prove to be the case. Read the show's complete plot synopsis at http://www.geocities.com/Vienna/1052/ floro/floroplot.html.

TELL ME, PRETTY MAIDEN

The most memorable part of the show was the production number "Tell Me, Pretty Maiden." Six five-foot fourinch; 130-pound women with twirling parasols joined by six well-dressed men sang the song. Audiences were enthralled as they sang: MEN: *"Oh tell me, pretty maiden, are there any more at home like you?"* / GIRLS: *"There are a few, kind sir, But simple girls, and proper too."* / MEN: *"Then tell me pretty maiden What these very simple girlies do."* / GIRLS: *"Kind sir, their manners are perfection and the opposite of mine."*

The original *Florodora* sextet of chorines — Daisy Green, Marjorie Relyea, Vaughn Texsmith, Margaret Walker, Agnes Wayburn, and Marie Wilson — received an inordinate amount of adulation and publicity. A claim has been perpetuated for many years that all six married millionaires, but this is unsubstantiated. It is true, however, that these young ladies fascinated the public.

The song was popularized in recordings by Harry MacDonough and Grace Spencer and by Byron G. Harlan, Joe Belmont and the Florodora Girls. Hear Harry MacDonough and Grace Spencer's '02 Edison recording of this song at http://www.archive.org/audio/audio-details-db. php?collectionid=tellmaiden&collection=opensource_ audio. The sheet music cover and musical score are available at http://levysheetmusic.mse.jhu.edu/browse.html.

The song's popularity spawned some parodies, including "Tell Us Pretty Ladies" and Tell Me, Dusky Maiden" by Bob Cole and the Johnson Brothers.

The original London cast recording is available on CD (see www.musicalheaven.com/f/florodora.shtml)

A '30 movie musical titled *The Florodora Girl* included a Technicolor sequence of "Tell Me Pretty Maiden."

THE SHADE OF THE PALM

Leslie Stuart's "The Shade of the Palm" was introduced in *Florodora*. The song was introduced by the character Frank Abercoed, the manager of the Island of Florodora. According to the sheet music cover the song was sung by Sydney Barraclough.

In the musical's plot, after Frank Abercoed refuses to marry Lady Holyrood, his boss, Gilfain, decrees he will marry her or be discharged. Once discharged, he will return to England. In the song "The Shade of the Palm," he tells Dolores he must go but will return for her if she waits patiently.

The lyrics sing about a garden on a island in an Eastern sea where a maid is waiting for the singer "in the shade of the palm." In the chorus, we find out that the maiden's name is Dolores. The singer calls her the "Queen of the Eastern Sea" and asks her to be waiting "in the shade of the shelt'ring palm."

J.W. Myers had the most popular recording of "The Shade of the Palm" in '01, but Harry MacDonough and Emilio DeGogorza also had popular versions of the market.

The musical score is available at http://lcweb2.loc.gov/cocoon/ihas/loc.natlib.ihas.100009238/. The nondescript sheet music cover and music score are available at http://digital.library.ucla.edu/apam/librarian?SEARCH. Hear Harry MacDonough's Gram-o-phone recording of this song at http://www.archive.org/audio/audio-details-db.php?collectionid=2552&collection=opensource_audio.

When Reuben Comes to Town

Words: J. Cheever Goodwin; Music: Maurice Levi

A rube, or in this case a reuben, is a country bumpkin. The dictionary defines it as slang for "an unsophisticated rustic." In '06, George M. Cohan made the people of New Rochelle, New York mad because he accused them of being rubes who had "whiskers like hay" in his song "Forty-five Minutes from Broadway."

J. Cheever Goodwin's lyrics are not unlike Cohan's except he doesn't accuse any specific locale as been filled with reubens. The song could very well have been titled "Just Like That Before," since the phrase is used so often in the four verses of the song. It seems a Reuben, not a person named Reuben, but a rube, came to town from the country. "His clothes were rahter seedy and his whiskers long and gray." He chooses a cab driver, a cabby, who charges him "five dollars for a ride of seven blocks." The chorus lyrics follow: *When Reuben comes to town, he is sure to be done brown, / It's really very shocking, and the fact we should deplore, / But it can't be helped alas! / When a chump's as green as grass; / He'll meet the fate of hundreds who have gone before.*

The sheet music cover tells us the song was premiered with "cyclonic success in the Rogers Bros. latest farce *In Central Park.*

S.H. Dudley helped popularize "When Reuben Comes to Town" in '01 with a very popular recording. Dan Quinn had issued his popular version in '00.

The sheet music cover and musical score are available at http://levysheetmusic.mse.jhu.edu/browse.html.

1902

Arkansas Traveler

Music: Mose Case

Julius Mattfeld in *Variety Music Cavalcade*, lists the origin of "Arkansas Traveler" as 1851. Some sources list Joseph Tosso, a violinist, as the song's writer, but Mattfeld discredits that claim. According to http://memory.loc.gov/learn/educators/workshop/discover/arkansas.html, the history of "Arkansas Traveler" is as follows: it was published in 1847 with a melody by W. C. Peters under the titles "Arkansas Traveler" and "Rackinsac Waltz." In 1851, the tune was called "A Western Refrain." The most famous version, a combination of music and dialogue story, by Mose Case appeared first in 1858. In 1863, Oliver Ditson & Co., Boston published a version crediting Case as the writer. Another version appeared in 1858 by Col. Faulkner that contained the melody, but no dialogue. In 1870, Currier and Ives published two prints entitled "The Arkansas Traveler" and "The Turn of the Tune." In 1876, Col. S.C. Faulkner or B.S. Alford printed a large cardboard printing of the song. Faulkner claims to have been the original Arkansas Traveler in 1840.

The prologue to the song in the Mose Case sheet music says, "This piece is intended to represent an Eastern man's experience among the inhabitants of Arkansas, showing their hospitality and the mode of obtaining it." Later, it says, "In the door sat a man playing a violin; the tune was the then most popular tune in that region, namely: the 'Arkansas Traveler.'" It seems the man repeated the first part of the tune over and over because he couldn't play the second part. The stranger approached the man who was playing the song and said "How do you do?" The man only glanced at him, continued playing, and said: "I do as I please." That's an example of the humorous exchanges that take place in between each of the musical sections. One of the cleverest examples was: "Stranger: Why don't you cover your house? It leaks. Old Man: Cause it's raining. Stranger: Then why don't you cover it when it's not raining? Old Man: Cause it don't leak."

Len Spencer popularized "Arkansas Traveler" with a very popular recording in '02; his recording had also been successful in '00, but not quite as popular as in '02.

Fiddlin' John Carson revived the song again in '24 with a reasonably popular recording.

The sheet music cover and musical score of this song as credited to Mose Case are available at http://levysheetmusic.mse.jhu.edu/browse.html (use search).

Because

Words: Edward Teschemacher; Music: Guy d'Hardelot

"Because" became an institution when it was sung in an enormous number of weddings in the first half of the 20th century. Thankfully, since it needed a rest, the song has not remained quite so popular in late 20th and early 21st century weddings.

The song was published in England in '02 and arrived in this country very quickly. "Because" sold over a million copies of sheet music rather easily.

Along with "Oh, Promise Me" (1889), "Because" became *the* featured vocal solo at weddings.

Some of the lyrics sound rather antiquated: *Because you come to me with naught save love, / And hold my hand and lift mine eyes above, / A wider world of hope and joy I see, / Because you come to me. / Because you speak to me in accents sweet, / I find the roses waking 'round my feet, / And I am led through tears and joy to thee, / Because you speak to me. / Because God made thee mine I'll cherish thee / Thru light and darkness thru all time to be, / And pray His love may make our love divine, / Because God made thee mine.*

Even allowing for poetic license, people did not then nor

do not now talk like that. Popular song lyrics are supposed to be in the vernacular. The words are also chauvinistic. It sounds like the woman in the song is the man's property: "God made thee mine."

The song was popularized in recordings by Evan Williams in '10, by Enrico Caruso in '13, by Perry Como in '48 and by Mario Lanza in '51. Fifty years of longevity is quite remarkable.

Deanna Durbin sang "Because" in the '38 movie musical *Three Smart Girls Grow Up*, it also appeared in *Thrill of Romance* ('45), *The Great Caruso* ('51), which starred Mario Lanza and in *The Stars Are Singing* ('53), where it was sung by Lauritz Melchior.

Bill Bailey, Won't You Please Come Home?

Words & Music: Hughie Cannon

"Bill Bailey, Won't You Please Come Home" became very popular soon after it was published. Hughie Cannon, a famous song-and-dance man, wrote the words and music to this song.

It seems that the real-life Bill Bailey's wife was in the habit of kicking him out of the house whenever she gets disgusted with him and his late night carousing. However, Bill keeps going back for more punishment over and over again. Cannon, a friend of the real Bill Bailey, gave his friend a few dollars and suggested he stay away for a while. Later Cannon began to wonder what would happen if Bill suddenly became rich. He could just imagine Bill's wife begging him to come back. He quickly wrote the lyrics and set them to a rag-style melody.

The song's lyrics follow the story pretty closely: *Won't you come home, Bill Bailey, / Won't you come home? / She moans the whole day long; / I'll do de cooking, darling, / I'll pay de rent, / I knows I done you wrong. / 'Member dat rainy eve dat I drove you out, / Wid nothin' but a fine tooth comb? / I knows I'se to blame, well, ain't dat a shame? / Bill Bailey, won't you please come home?*

One of Cannon's friends, a black-faced minstrel performer, John Queen, introduced the song at the Newburgh Theater in New York City.

In more modern times, Eddie Jackson, who frequently appeared on TV with Jimmy Durante, revived the song.

Although recordings were not the chief method of popularizing songs at this point, "Bill Bailey..." was recorded by Arthur Collins for Columbia, by Dan Quinn for Victor and by Silas Leachman, also for Victor. Their recordings certainly helped disseminate the song to a nationwide audience among those who could afford the "talking machines." Arthur Collins' recording of "Bill Bailey..." is available at www.archive.org/audio.

The song inspired a few once-popular but now-forgotten sequels, including "I Wonder Why Bill Bailey Won't Come Home," "He Done Me Wrong, or, The Death of Bill Bailey," and "When Old Bill Bailey Plays the Ukalele (sic)."

"Bill Bailey..." was used in the following movie musicals: *Meet Me at the Fair* ('52) and *Paradise Hawaiian Style* ('66), an Elvis Presley film.

The sheet music cover and musical score are available at http://levysheetmusic.mse.jhu.edu/browse.html and at http://scriptorium.lib.duke.edu/dynaweb/sheetmusic/. See the sheet music cover and hear a midi musical version at

http://www.perfessorbill.com/index2.htm or http://parlorsongs.com/issues/2002-1/thismonth/featureb.asp.

Good Morning, Carrie!

Words: Cecil Mack; Music: Chris Smith & Elmer Bowman

Bert Williams and his partner George Walker had a very popular recording of "Good Morning, Carrie" in '02.

Cecil Mack's lyrics tell about a girl who lives in "Car'lina," the daughter of Aunt Dinah, named Caroline. However, people call her "Carrie." "In the light of early dawn" the singer, with his banjo, wakes Carrie with his song, which is the chorus, that follows (in the sheet music there wasn't any punctuation, only dots between phrases of the lyric): *Good morning, Carrie.... how you do this morning..... / Was you dreaming 'bout me..... my pretty maid..... / Say look here Carrie..... when we gwine to marry..... / Long springtime honey.... good morning babe.*

The sheet music cover and musical score are available at http://levysheetmusic.mse.jhu.edu/browse.html.

In the Good Old Summer Time

Words: Ren Shields; Music: George Evans

"In the Good Old Summer Time" is one of the first successful songs about a season of the year. Publishers were very skeptical about seasonal songs, but this one proved to them that such a song could be extremely popular.

Renowned minstrel George "Honey Boy" Evans, comedian Ren Shields and singer Blanche Ring were dining together at the Brighton Beach Hotel in Brooklyn one summer evening in '02. Evans mentioned that while some people preferred the winter, he liked the good old summertime. Shields and Ring immediately saw the statement as a potential song. Evans and Shields collaborated on the writing, while Blanche Ring got to introduce the song in *The Defender*. Audiences loved the song and often joined Ms. Ring in singing the chorus.

The lyrics enumerate some of the things people enjoyed doing in the summer at the beginning of the 20th century, like holding hands while strolling through shady lanes. The second verse, which is seldom heard, mentions playing hooky from school to go swimming, playing "ring-a-rosie," and stealing cherries. The lyrics to the classic chorus follow: *In the good old summer time, / In the good old summer time, / Strolling thro' the shady lanes / With your baby mine; / You hold her hand and she holds yours, / And that's a very good sign / That she's your tootsey wootsey / In the good old summer time.*

Notice the use of the endearment, "tootsey wootsey," which was a particularly popular expression during this era.

"In the Good Old Summertime" was popularized in a Columbia recording by J.W. Myers and in an Edison recording by William Redman in '02. It was further popularized by the Haydn Quartet's Victor recording, another Victor recording by Sousa's Band with vocals by Harry MacDonough and S.H. Dudley and another Victor recording by Harry MacDonough in '03. It was revived again in a recording by Les Paul and Mary Ford in '52.

The song provided the title for and was used as background music in a '49 film starring Judy Garland. The film was one of several versions of Miklos Laszlo's play *The Shop Around the Corner*.

Hear Paul Whiteman's '28 recording of this classic

popular song at http://www.redhotjazz.com/pwo.html or hear William Redmond's '02 Edison recording of this classic at http://nfo.net/ogg3.htm.

The sheet music cover and musical score are available at http://levysheetmusic.mse.jhu.edu/browse.html or at http://digital.library.ucla.edu/apam/. See the sheet music cover and hear a midi musical version at http://www.perfessorbill.com/index2.htm. See the original sheet music cover and musical score, and hear a midi musical version at http://www.geocities.com/dferg5493/songfiles.htm.

The Mansion of Aching Hearts

Words: Arthur J. Lamb; Music: Harry Von Tilzer

"The Mansion of Aching Hearts" is a sequel to Lamb and Von Tilzer's extremely successful sentimental ballad "A Bird in a Gilded Cage" (see '00). Once again they stressed that gold and diamonds, weath in general, do not buy happiness. One might easily assume that the mansion of aching hearts was a bordello.

The lyrics of the first verse set the stage. It is the end of an evening of dancing and "a few men were saying their last goodbyes, to the beautiful belle of the ball." A young man, who has had his heart stolen away by the woman, is "startled to hear someone say:" *She lives in a mansion of aching hearts, / She's one of a restless throng, / The diamonds that glitter around her throat, / They speak both of sorrow and song; / The smile on her face is only a mask, / And many the tear that starts, / For sadder it seems, when of mother she dreams, / In the mansion of aching hearts.*

The song was popularized in recordings by Harry Mac-Donough for Victor, by Byron Harlan for Edison, and by J.W. Myers for Columbia in '02.

The sheet music cover and musical score are available at http://levysheetmusic.mse.jhu.edu/browse.html. See the sheet music cover and listen to a midi musical version at http://parlorsongs.com/issues/2001-10/thismonth/featurea.asp.

On a Sunday Afternoon

Words: Andrew B. Sterling; Music: Harry Von Tilzer

Harry Von Tilzer was an extremely successful songwriter during these first few years of the new century. He had tremendous success with "A Bird in a Gilded Cage," "The Mansion of Aching Hearts," and "On a Sunday Afternoon" within the first few years of the decade.

"On a Sunday Afternoon" reportedly had sold a million copies of sheet music within a year of its publication. Von Tilzer got the idea for the lyric at the beach one day. He thought about most people having to return to work on Monday after a fun day at the beach on Sunday. He presented the thought to lyricist Andrew Sterling, who adapted the idea into the following lyrics of the chorus: *On a Sunday afternoon / In the merry month of June / Take a trip on the Hudson or down the bay, / Take a trolley to Coney or Rockaway, / On a Sunday afternoon, / You can see the lovers spoon. / They work hard on Monday, / But one day that's fun day / Is Sunday afternoon.*

The song was used in the '44 film *Atlantic City* and in the '45 Abbott and Costello film *Naughty Nineties.*

The song was popularized in recordings by J.W. Myers for Columbia, by Edward M. Favor for Victor and by J. Aldrich Libbey for Edison in '02.

The sheet music cover and musical score are available at

http://levysheetmusic.mse.jhu.edu/browse.html. See the sheet music cover and musical score, and hear a midi musical version at http://www.geocities.com/dferg5493/songfiles.htm.

Semper Fidelis

Music: John Philip Sousa

"Semper Fidelis" is the title of the official march of the United States Marine Corps. It was composed by John Philip Sousa in 1888. Sousa was director of the United States Marine Corps Band when a replacement for "Hail to the Chief" was requested, but later rejected. Sousa considered it to be his "most musical" march.

Sousa's U.S. Marine Corps Band helped popularize the march with a 1890 recording and Sousa's Band (the non-military unit) recorded it successfully in '02. Hear the U.S. Marine Band's '09 recording of this march at http://www.archive.org/audio/audio-details-db.php?collectionid=EDIS-SRP-019413&collection=opensource_audio.

The sheet music cover and musical score of this song are available at http://levysheetmusic.mse.jhu.edu/browse.html.

Under the Bamboo Tree

Words & Music: Bob Cole & the Johnson Brothers

Exactly who deserves songwriting credit for this song is difficult to ascertain. The cover of sheet music gives credit to Bob Cole and the Johnson brothers; the first page of music only credits Bob Cole; some music reference books credit Cole and J. Rosamond Johnson, suggesting that Rosamond's brother James Weldon Johnson did not contribute.

David Ewan says the song was originally titled "If You Lak-a Me" and was written by Cole and J. Rosamond Johnson during the time they were a vaudeville team. Cole had suggested they perform the spiritual "Nobody Knows the Trouble I See" in their act, but Johnson objected. They compromised by inverting the melody of the spiritual and writing new lyrics.

The seldom-heard verse tells us a royal dusky maid lived in the jungle. She had made quite an impression on "a Zulu from Matabooloo." He would be waiting for her every morning beneath a bamboo tree. When she arrived, he sang: *If you lak-a-me, lak I lak-a-you; / And we lak-a-both the same, / I lak-a say, this very day, / I lak-a-change your name; / 'Cause I love-a-you and love-a-you true / And if you-a love-a-me, / One live as two, two live as one / Under the bamboo tree.*

Marie Cahill interpolated this African marriage proposal into *Sally in Our Alley* ('02). Later it was also interpolated into *Nancy Brown* ('03).

The song was popularized in an Edison recordings by Arthur Collins in '02 and in a duet recording by Arthur Collins and Byron Harlan in '03.

A particularly delightful performance of the song was by Judy Garland in *Meet Me in St. Louis* ('44). She was joined by her screen sister, Margaret O'Brien, as they sang the song and danced the cakewalk. It was also used in the '44 film *Bowery to Broadway.*

The sheet music cover and musical score are available at http://levysheetmusic.mse.jhu.edu/browse.html. See the sheet music cover and hear a midi musical version at http://www.perfessorbill.com/index2.htm or http://www.

geocities.com/dferg5493/songfiles.htm. See the '44 sheet music cover from *Meet Me in St. Louis* at www.hulapages.com/covers_5.htm.

Way Down in Old Indiana
Words & Music: Paul Dresser

Paul Dresser was very nostalgic about his home state. His most famous song was "On the Banks of the Wabash, Far Away," which became the Indiana state song. Another of his popular songs that celebrated his home state was 1902's "Way Down in Old Indiana," not to be confused with 1917's "Indiana," sometimes called "Back Home Again in Indiana."

Other songs celebrating Indiana in the popular repertoire include "Indiana Moon," "You're My Little Indiana Rose," "Wabash Moon," "Dreaming of My Indiana Sweetheart," and "Hoosier Sweetheart."

J.W. Myers had a particularly popular recording of "Way Down in Old Indiana" in '02.

1903

Any Rags?
Words & Music: Thomas S. Allen

The lyrics of "Any Rags?" tell the story of "ragged, jagged Jack," a ragpicker. He comes down the street waking up all the neighbors with his yell for "Any rags? ... Any bones? Any bottles today?"

The song is definitely a racial stereotype, but it is unfortunately probably true.

"Any Rags?" was popularized in a successful recording by Arthur Collins, who sang many of the coon songs of the era. A recording of this song by Arthur Collins is available at www.archive.org/audio.

View the sheet music, including a colorful cover, at http://lcweb2.loc.gov/cocoon/ihas/loc.natlib.ihas.10000 4483/. The sheet music cover and musical score are also available at http://levysheetmusic.mse.jhu.edu/browse.html. Hear a midi musical version of the song at http://www.primeshop.com/midlist3.htm.

Come Down Ma' Evenin' Star
Words: Edgar Smith & Robert B. Smith; Music: John Stromberg & W.T. Francis

Lillian Russell introduced "Come Down, Ma Evenin' Star" in the Weber and Fields extravaganza *Twirly-Whirly* ('02). Lillian Russell was thereafter closely associated with the song.

The song's manuscript was found in the composer's pocket when he was found dead of an apparent suicide.

Most of the lyric is unfortunately in dialect. The chorus lyrics follow: *Ma evenin' star I wonder where you are, / Set up so high like a diamond in de sky; / No matter what I do I can't go up to you, / So come down from dar, ma evenin' star. / Come down! Come down! Come down from dar, ma evenin' star.*

The song was popularized in recordings by Mina Hickman and by Henry Burr.

The song was used in the film *Broadway to Hollywood* ('33), in the film biography *Lillian Russell* ('40) and in

Chauncey Olcott's film biography *My Wild Irish Rose* ('47).

The sheet music cover and musical score are available at http://levysheetmusic.mse.jhu.edu/browse.html.

Lillian Russell didn't record the song until '12 when she was well past her prime and the record company never released the recording. Her recording of the song can be downloaded at http://www.archive.org/details/LillianRussell.

Down Where the Wurzburger Flows
Words: Vincent P. Bryan; Music: Harry Von Tilzer

"Down Where the Wurzburger Flows" was introduced by Nora Bayes at the Orpheum Theater in Brooklyn. At the first performance, Ms. Bayes was overcome by emotions, but Harry Von Tilzer, seated in the audience, immediately began singing and continued until Ms. Bayes regained her composure to resume her performance. The audience was so impressed by the exchange that the theater management insisted that Von Tilzer and Bayes continue the same collaboration for the rest of opening week. The song became such a success for Miss Bayes that she was often identified as "The Wurzburger Girl."

The song's lyrics are nostalgic for Bohemia. The singer is toasting her native land with beer. Vincent Bryan's chorus lyrics follow: *Take me down, down, down where the Wurzburger flows, flows, flows / It goes down, down, down but nobody knows where it goes / Just order two seidels of lager, or three / If I don't want to drink it, please force it on me, / The Rhine may be fine but a cold stein for mine, / Down where the Wurzburger flows.*

In '03, Von Tilzer wrote a sequel to "Down Where the Wurzberger Flows" entitled "Under the Anhauser Bush," with lyrics by Andrew B. Sterling.

"Down Where the Wurzburger Flows" was popularized in recordings in a duet by Arthur Collins and Byron Harlan and by Arthur Collins as a soloist.

The sheet music cover and musical score are available at http://levysheetmusic.mse.jhu.edu/browse.html and at http://scriptorium.lib.duke.edu/dynaweb/sheetmusic/. See the sheet music cover, read the lyrics and hear a midi musical version at http://www.halcyondaysmusic.com/january/january2005.htm.

Goodbye, Eliza Jane
Words: Andrew B. Sterling; Music: Harry Von Tilzer

Arthur Collins helped popularize "Goodbye, Eliza Jane" with a very successful recording in '03.

Andrew Sterling's coon song lyrics tell us that Liza hasn't been the gal she promised. She "went a driving with Mister Brown," so the singer has become "the laughing stock of the town" and he's leaving. However, before he goes, he tells Eliza Jane goodbye with the chorus lyrics, which follow: *Goodbye, Eliza Jane, I'm gwine a' for to leave you! / Well, you'll know when I go that I was the fellow with the 'dough, dough, dough;' / So I'm gwine for to sing a little song, and travel along, just travel along; / Wish you goodbye, Babe; I'm on my way; Goodby, Eliza Jane. (The last time "Goodbye" was spelled "Goodby" in the sheet music).*

The sheet music cover makes it appear that the song title should be spelled "Good Bye, Eliza Jane."

The sheet music cover and musical score are available at http://levysheetmusic.mse.jhu.edu/browse.html and at http://scriptorium.lib.duke.edu/dynaweb/sheetmusic/.

Hurrah for Baffin's Bay

Words: Vincent Bryan; Music: Theodore F. Morse

The '03 musical version of *The Wizard of Oz* was mostly a showpiece for comedians Dave Montgomery and Fred Stone. In the story, Dorothy doesn't have a dog named Toto, but a pet cow named Imogene. They are blown by a tornado to Munchkinland. They meet the Tin Woodman, the Scarecrow, and the Cowardly Lion and go through a number of adventures together before they finally get to meet the Wizard.

The musical score was a mismash of songs written by various composers and lyricists. The comedy song "Hurrah for Baffin's Bay" was one of the several interpolations. Fred Stone and Dave Montgomery who played the Scarecrow and Tin Woodman respectively sang this song of nautical nonsense. The song is a near riot of puns and it can take several hearings to understand them all.

It's easy to see from the words to the chorus of the song that it has little to do with the plot and it aptly illustrates some of the nonsense in the musical: *Avast, belay — Hurrah for Baffin's Bay! / We couldn't find the pole, / Because the barber moved away. / The boat was cold, / We thought we'd get the grip, / So the painter put three coats / Upon the ship! / Hip, hip! Hip, hip! / Hurrah for Baffin's Bay!*

The '39 film version of *The Wizard of Oz* starring Judy Garland had a new musical score by Harold Arlen and E.Y. Harburg. *The Wiz*, an African American cast variation on the original L. Frank Baum story, opened on Broadway in '75. It also had a new musical score by Charlie Smalls.

"Hurrah for Baffin's Bay" was popularized in a recording by Bob Roberts in '03.

You can hear two different recordings of this song at http://www.hungrytigerpress.com/tigertunes/baffinsbay.shtml.

Hiawatha

Words: James O'Dea; Music: Neil Moret

"Hiawatha" caught on primarily because John Philip Sousa included it in his band's repertoire. The composer recalled late in life that he learned about the song's success from this telegram sent by Sousa: "Congratulations, dear boy. Hiawatha the biggest hit I've ever played."

The Hiawatha in the song was not the one from Longfellow's famous poem, but was a small Kansas town. The composer, Neil Moret, had lived in Kansas City and had dated a girl from Hiawatha. One day enroute to visit the girl the melody came to him and he jotted it down. It was first published as an instrumental in '01 and was introduced by Sousa and his band.

James O'Dea added the lyrics in '03 and the song became even more popular. The lyric version of "Hiawatha" sparked an Indian song fad, including Kerry Mills' "Red Wing," Percy Wenrich's "Silver Bell," Egbert Van Alstyne's "Navajo" and "Seminole" and Fred Hager's "Laughing Water." The song even spawned a parody, "Parody on Hiawatha," that was recorded by Arthur Collins and Byron Harlan. Sousa's Band also recorded a "Hiawatha Two-Step."

The verses are much longer than the chorus, which is a bit unusual. Below are the first verse and chorus: *Oh the moon is all agleam on the stream / Where I dream here of you my pretty Indian maid. / While the rustling leaves are singing high above us overhead / In the glory of the bright summernight / In the light and the shadows of the forest glade / I am waiting here to kiss your lips so red. / There's a flood of melodies on the breeze / From the trees and of you they breathe so tenderly / While the woodlands all around are resounding your name. / Oh, my all in life is you only you / Fond and true and your own forevermore I'll be. / Hear then the song I sing with lips aflame.*

Chorus (a little faster tempo): *I am your own your Hiawatha brave; / my heart is yours you know / Dear one I love you so. / Oh Minnehaha gentle maid decide, / decide and say you'll be, My Indian bride.*

"Hiawatha" was popularized in recordings by Harry MacDonough, by Dan Quinn, and by the Columbia Orchestra. Hear the '03 recording of this song by the London Regimental Band at http://www.archive.org/audio/audio-details-db.php?collectionid=hiawatha1903&collection=opensource_audio.

The sheet music cover and musical score are available at http://levysheetmusic.mse.jhu.edu/browse.html and at http://scriptorium.lib.duke.edu/dynaweb/sheetmusic/. See the sheet music cover and hear a midi musical version at http://www.perfessorbill.com/index2.htm.

In the Sweet Bye and Bye

Words: Vincent P. Bryan; Music: Harry Von Tilzer

This "In the Sweet Bye and Bye" is not the famous gospel song by Sanford Bennett and Joseph Webster, but it was a very big hit in '03 for its writers, Vincent Bryan and Harry Von Tilzer.

John Bieling and Harry MacDonough both had very successful recordings of the song.

The lyrics tell us that "two lovers wait, by the old garden gate, telling tales of love." The male tells the female to "cease repining" because he promises they'll be happy together "in the sweet bye and bye." The chorus continues: *In the sweet bye and bye; In the sweet bye and bye; / We'll have a cottage that's built for two, / Then lovey'll love dovey and dovey'll love oo; / In the sweet bye and bye, in the sweet bye and bye, / Love's dream will seem sweet as peaches and cream / In the sweet bye and bye.*

The sheet music cover and musical score to this song are available at http://levysheetmusic.mse.jhu.edu and at http://scriptorium.lib.duke.edu/dynaweb/sheetmusic/.

Mighty Lak' a Rose

Words: Frank L. Stanton; Music: Ethelbert Nevin

Frank Stanton was a writer for the *Atlanta Constitution*. He wrote the original lyrics of "Mighty Lak' a Rose" in African American dialect.

The song was a favorite for family sings around the parlor piano.

It's a tender song sung by a Mammy to her son, or perhaps one of her Master's sons under her care, in the style of a lullaby. She sings: *Sweetest little fellow, everybody knows; / Don't know what to call him but he's mighty like a rose! / Lookin' at his mammy with eyes so shiny blue, / Makes you think that heaven is comin' close to you. / When he's there a-sleepin' in his little place, / Think I see the angels looking thro' the lace. / When the dark is falling, when the shadows creep, / Then they come on tiptoe to kiss him in his sleep. / Sweetest little fellow, everybody knows, / Don't know what to call him but he's mighty like a rose! / Lookin' at his mammy with eyes so shiny blue, / Makes you think that heaven is comin' close to you.*

"Mighty Lak' a Rose" was popularized by George Alexander in a recording in '03. The song was revived in a recording by Marguerite Dunlap in '11 and by Geraldine Farrar in '16. At http://www.songwritershalloffame.org/exhibit_audio_video.asp?exhibitId=304 you can hear an audio clip of "Mighty Lak' a Rose" performed by Paul Robeson.

The non-descript sheet music cover and musical score are available at http://levysheetmusic.mse.jhu.edu/browse.html.

My Old Kentucky Home, Good Night

Words: Stephen C. Foster

"My Old Kentucky Home, Good Night," most often known today as "My Old Kentucky Home," was introduced in 1853 by Ed Christy and his minstrel troop. Within a year of its publication, it had sold approximately 100,000 copies of sheet music, a remarkable sales figure for the 1850s.

Foster supposedly wrote the song one morning when he was visiting his Rowan cousins at Federal Hill in Bardstown, Kentucky. That morning he heard the mockingbirds singing and was watching the little slave children playing. He wrote, "The sun shines bright on the old Kentucky home, 'Tis summer, the darkies are gay. Later in the lyrics he mentions the birds making music all day long. Later, the word "the" in the first phrase was changed to "my" and "darkies" was changed to "people."

In '22 a fund was raised to purchase that Bardstown home and it is now a part of My Old Kentucky Home State Park.

The song has been the official state song of Kentucky since '28 and it is the official song of the Kentucky Derby at Churchill Downs.

"My Old Kentucky Home" became one of the most recorded songs of the pre-rock era.

The song appeared in the following movie musicals: *Harmony Lane* ('35), *Swanee River* ('39) and *I Dream of Jeanie* ('52), the last two screen biographies of Stephen Foster.

In this song, the verse and chorus seem almost inseperable. Only the first verse and chorus are well known, however. *The sun shines bright on my old Kentucky home / Tis summer, the darkies are gay / The corn top's ripe and the meadow's in bloom / While the birds make music all the day / The young folks roll on the little cabin floor / All merry, all happy and bright / By 'n by hard times come a-knocking at the door / Then my old Kentucky home good night / Weep no more, my lady / Oh, weep no more, today / We will sing one song for the old Kentucky home / For the old Kentucky home far away.*

The Edison Male Quartet had the first successful recording of "My Old Kentucky Home" in 1898. The Haydn Quartet had great success with their version in '03. It was revived again at least four more times: Harry MacDonough in '06, Geraldine Farrar in '10, Alma Gluck in '16, and the Columbia Stellar Quartet and Lucy Gates both revived it in '18.

The sheet music cover and musical score of this song are available at http://levysheetmusic.mse.jhu.edu/browse.html and at http://lcweb2.loc.gov/cocoon/ihas/loc.natlib.ihas.200000743/. See the sheet music cover and hear a midi musical version of "My Old Kentucky Home" at http://parlorsongs.com/issues/2003-5/thismonth/feature.asp.

The Rosary

Words: Robert Cameron Rogers; Music: Georgia B. Welles

There were at least three popular settings of Robert Cameron Rogers' "The Rosary." Composer Ethelbert Nevin wrote his version in 1898. Robert A. King composed his version in '05. Georgia B. Welles was the composer of the '03 version. There is no information that specifies which version was popular in '03, however, since Welles' version was copyrighted in that year, it seems logical to assume her version was the popular one at this juncture. However, since Nevin is the most well known composer of the group, his version may actually be the one that was most popular. Most of the settings were written for the concert stage, but this sentimental ballad became a favorite of regular folks in parlors throughout America.

This song would have been especially popular among those of the Catholic faith who use the Rosary in their prayers. The lyrics follow: *The hours I spent with Thee, Dear Heart! / Are as a string of pearls to me, / I count them over, every one apart, / My rosary, my rosary... / Each hour a pearl, each pearl a prayer, / To still a heart in absence wrung, / I tell each bead unto the end, / And there a cross is hung... / O' memories that bless and burn, / O' barren gain and bitter loss, / I kiss each bead and strive at last to learn, / To kiss the cross, Sweet Heart, / To kiss the cross... / I kiss each bead and strive at last to learn, / To kiss the cross, Sweet Heart, / To kiss the cross... (to kiss the cross).*

The song even inspired the comic "When Ragtime Rosie Ragged the Rosary" ('11) though the song did not become a big hit.

"The Rosary" was popularized in recordings by William H. Thompson and by Henry Burr in '03. Alan Turner revived it with success in '06, as did Ernestine Schumann-Heink in '08. John McCormack revived it in '12 and the Taylor Trio did the same in '16.

"The Rosary" became one of the most recorded songs of the pre-rock era.

Both Welles' and Nevin's sheet music cover and musical score are available at http://scriptorium.lib.duke.edu/sheetmusic/.

1904

Alexander (Don't You Love Your Baby No More?)

Words: Andrew B. Sterling; Music: Harry Von Tilzer

This Von Tilzer coon song came to the composer while he was watching the blackface vaudeville team of McIntyre and Heath and by overhearing a remark by a theater patron. At a particular point in the vaudeville team's act, McIntyre called Heath "Alexander." It got a big laugh from the audience. Later as the audience was leaving the theater, Von Tilzer heard an African American lady ask her boy friend, "Don't you love your baby no more?"

Von Tilzer quickly relayed the name "Alexander" and the quote to one of his favorite lyricists Andrew B. Sterling. The song was soon finished and became very popular in vaudeville and in minstrel shows.

Sterling's lyrics begin with the girl, the singer of the song, apologizing to Alexander for saying "another coon" was ruling her heart. She begs him not to leave, to take her back and she promises to remain true to him. She promises that he can be Boss and ends the verse by asking to stay with him.

The lyrics to the chorus follow: *Can't you see the rain and hail am fastly falling, Alexander, / Don't you hear your lady love a-softly calling, Alexander, / Take me to your heart again and call me honey, / All I want is lovin,' I don't want your money, / Alexander, don't you love your baby no more?*

Montgomery and Stone, a popular turn-of-the-century minstrel act, were white entertainers who performed in blackface. They were certain to get a laugh whenever they would call each other "Alexander," because audiences considered the name too sophisticated for a black man (an African American).

This song may very well have been one of Irving Berlin's inspirations for using the name "Alexander" again when he wrote "Alexander and His Clarinet" in '10 and revised the song in '11 into "Alexander's Ragtime Band."

The most popular recording of "Alexander (Don't You Love Your Baby No More?)" was by Billy Murray.

See the sheet music cover and the musical score at http://ucblibraries.colorado.edu/cgi-bin/sheetmusic.pl?RagAlexander&Rag&main.

All Aboard for Dreamland

Words: Andrew B. Sterling; Music: Harry Von Tilzer

Dreamland, a Coney Island amusement park, opened in '04. It was a very popular destination until it burned in '11. "All Aboard for Dreamland" was written to celebrate the park's opening.

Andrew Sterling's lyrics tell us that sweethearts love to call this amusement park "the land of dreams." The singer is encouraging all the sweethearts to take a ride at the close of day to the park that is "just outside of the town not so far away." He continues his plea in the chorus lyrics, which follow: *All aboard for Dreamland, Jump on a trolley with Maudie or Mollie,/ And all aboard for Dreamland, it's out of sight; / That's the place for sweethearts, ice cream and kisses, / Oh, there's where the bliss is, / So all aboard for Dreamland, on a summer's night.*

Byron Harlan had a very popular recording of the song in '04.

The sheet music cover and musical score are available at http://levysheetmusic.mse.jhu.edu/browse.html.

Bedelia

Words: William Jerome; Music: Jean Schwartz

Building songs around girls' names has always been popular, and this one may have been the most popular of this era. Others from the era include "My Gal Sal," "Elsie from Chelsea," and "Mariah," to name a few. "Bedelia" is notable for its use of Irish folk material.

The most popular recordings of the song were issued by the Haydn Quartet, by Billy Murray, by George J. Gaskin and by Arthur Pryor's Band in '04. Jan Garber and his orchestra revived the song in '48.

The sheet music cover proclaims that the song is "The Novelty Song of the Century," and calls the song "An Irish Coon Song Serenade." One might assume that the publishers were making a racial comment here, equating the

Irish immigrants with the coons (African Americans). On the other hand, perhaps the publisher was just trying to capitalize on the coon song craze by claiming this song was that type even though it had more Irish influence than African American.

William Jerome's first verse and chorus lyrics follow: *There's a charming Irish lady with a roguish winning way, / Who has kept my heart a bumpin' and a jumpin' night and day; / She's a flower from Killarney with a Tipperary smile, / She's the best that ever came from Erin's Isle / And I find myself a singing all the while / Bedelia, I want to steal ye, Bedelia, I love you so, / I'll be your Chauncey Olcott If you'll be my Molly O.' / Say something sweet Bedelia, Your voice I like to hear, Oh Bedelia, elia, elia, / I've made up my mind to steal ye, steal ye, steal ye, Bedelia dear.*

"Bedelia" was used in the '33 movie musical *Broadway to Hollywood* and in *Hello, Frisco, Hello* ('43).

See the sheet music cover and musical score at http://lcweb2.loc.gov/cocoon/ihas/loc.natlib.ihas.100007925/ or at http://levysheetmusic.mse.jhu.edu/browse.html or see the sheet music cover and listen to a midi musical version at http://parlorsongs.com/issues/1999-8/aug99feature.asp.

Blue Bell

Words: Edward Madden & Dolly Morse; Music: Theodore F. Morse

Byron Harland and Frank Stanley, the Haydn Quartet and Henry Burr all helped popularize "Blue Bell" with very successful recordings in '04.

The sheet music says the song is a "march song and chorus." The sheet music cover shows a solider saying goodbye to a woman in a beautiful white dress, Blue Bell. The idea of the song's lyrics is a man is leaving his sweetheart to enter the military service. He's come to say goodbye because he hears the bugle calling all brave hearts, so, even though his heart is breaking, he must go.

The chorus lyrics follow: *Goodbye my Blue Bell, Farewell to you. / One last fond look into your eyes so blue, / 'Mid camp fires gleaming, 'mid shot and shell / I will be dreaming of my own Blue Bell.*

The song was also used in the '46 film biography of Al Jolson.

See the sheet music cover and musical score at http://lcweb2.loc.gov/cocoon/ihas/loc.natlib.ihas.100007847/ or at http://levysheetmusic.mse.jhu.edu/browse.html or at http://scriptorium.lib.duke.edu/dynaweb/sheetmusic/.

Dear Old Girl

Words: Richard Henry Buck; Music: Theodore F. Morse

In the first half of the first decade of the new century, working hours were long and transportation was still extremely crude by today's standards. What entertainment there was for the huge majority of Americans centered around the home, very often singing after the evening meal around the parlor piano. Americans of the time appear to have been very sentimental and the songs of the era were often expressions of sentiment in the form of sentimental ballads. "Dear Old Girl" is one of those sentimental ballads that was a favorite of harmonizers around the family piano.

British minstrel-show tenor, Richard "Dick" Jose, loved

the song and performed it from coast to coast. Audiences loved Jose's performance and bought copies of the sheet music so they could sing it at home.

The lyrics begin with a summer wedding, but soon we discover that the "Dear Old Girl" has died and the husband is mourning brokenheartedly for his lost love.

In recordings, the song was popularized by J.W. Myers in '03 and by the Haydn Quartet in '04.

The sheet music cover and musical score are available at http://levysheetmusic.mse.jhu.edu/browse.html and at http://digital.library.ucla.edu/apam/. A PDF is available of this song at http://odin.indstate.edu/about/units/rbsc/kirk/sh-group.html.

Listen to the Mocking Bird

Words & Music: Alice Hawthorne

Septimus Winner wrote this famous song in 1855 using the pseudonym Alice Hawthorne. The sheet music cover of "Listen to the Mocking Bird" describes the song as "a sentimental Ethiopian ballad."

The lyrics to the first verse say the singer is dreaming of "sweet Hally." Even though she is dead, "the tho't of her is one that never dies." She is buried (sleeping) in the valley where the Mocking Bird is singing. The chorus continues: *Listen to the Mocking Bird, Listen to the Mocking Bird, / The Mocking Bird still singing o'er her grave; / Listen to the Mocking Bird, Listen to the Mocking Bird, / Still singing where the weeping willows wave.*

By '50, this song had sold approximately 20,000,000 copies of sheet music, but the writer, Septimus Winner, never really profited from the song's huge success, since he had sold the rights to the song for $50.

John Yorke Atlee had a very important recording of "Listen to the Mocking Bird" in 1891. Whistler Joe Belmont revived it in 1899. A duet version by Frank Stanley & Corrine Morgan was popular in '04. Alma Gluck revived it again in '15.

A song sheet of "Listen to the Mocking Bird" is available at http://levysheetmusic.mse.jhu.edu/browse.html and the 1884 sheet music cover and musical score are available at http://lcweb2.loc.gov/cocoon/ihas/loc.natlib.ihas.200002397/.

Meet Me in St. Louis, Louis

Words: Andrew B. Sterling; Music: Kerry Mills

"Meet Me in St. Louis, Louis" became a promotional song for the '04 Louisiana Exposition or World's Fair in St. Louis. The exposition also included the first Olympic games held in the United States.

The writers, Mills and Sterling, were ordering drinks in a bar when Mills asked for a popular drink of the time known as a "Louis" (pronounced Louie). The bartender's name also happened to be Louis, so when Mills ordered another round, he called out, "Another Louie, Louie." The two writers were amused by the repetition of names, but also quickly associated it with the approaching World's Fair that would be held in St. Louis. Sterling wrote the lyrics, which Mills bought for $200. The song became a major hit, perhaps, along with "Sweet Adeline," the biggest hit of the year.

The lyrics to the first verse inform us that when Louie comes home he finds a note from his wife, Flossie. It says, "Louis, dear, it's too slow for me here, so I think I will go

for a ride!" The note continued as the chorus: *Meet me in St. Louis, Louis, Meet me at the fair, / Don't tell me the lights are shining any place but there, / We will dance the hoochee kooche, I will be your tootsie wootsie, / If you will meet me in St. Louis, Louis, Meet me at the fair!*

Notice the reference to the "hoochee kooche" (sometimes spelled "hoochie koochie"), a Middle Eastern dance similar to belly dancing and to the term of endearment "tootsie wootsie," which we had heard earlier, slightly differently, in "In the Good Old Summer Time."

Four singers who popularized the song on disks and cylinders in '04 were Billy Murray, S.H. Dudley, J. W. Myers and Will F. Denny. Those fortunate enough to have the machines to play recordings could also buy a "Meet Me in St. Louis Medley" performed by Arthur Pryor's Band. Billy Murray's Columbia version of the song was selling for a dollar in the summer of '04. That doesn't sound like a lot today, but in '04 most families had very little extra income to spend on such extravagance. Of course, for only twenty-five cents, one could buy a wax cylinder version of the song. Wax cylinders were much more fragile, however.

The song was sung under the titles and was used as background music for the closing scene in the '44 movie musical *Meet Me in St. Louis*, which starred Judy Garland. The movie soundtrack was inducted into the Grammy Hall of Fame in 2005.

The sheet music cover and musical score are available at http://levysheetmusic.mse.jhu.edu/browse.html.

Navajo

Words: Harry H. Williams; Music: Egbert Van Alstyne

"Navajo" was one of the first successful popular songs about an American Indian, but the song is as much, or more, coon song than Indian. The song's success, along with the lyric version of "Hiawatha," helped start a vogue for songs on Indian subjects, including Kerry Mills' "Red Wing," Percy Wenrich's "Silver Bell" and Fred Hager's "Laughing Water."

Marie Cahill interpolated the song into the musical *Nancy Brown* after it had opened in New York City.

The first of two verses introduce us to a Navajo Indian maid in New Mexico and an African American who has come to reveal his love. When they were alone, he softly sings the chorus: *Nava, Nava, my Navajo, / I have a love for you that will grow, / If you'll have a coon for a beau, / I'll have a Navajo.*

Billy Murray, Harry MacDonough and J.W. Myers all helped popularize the song with successful recordings in '04.

The song was published as an instrumental and in a different edition with lyrics.

The sheet music cover and musical score are available at http://levysheetmusic.mse.jhu.edu/browse.html and at http://scriptorium.lib.duke.edu/dynaweb/sheetmusic/. See the sheet music cover and hear a midi musical version at http://www.parlorsongs.com/issues/2003-8/thismonth/feature.asp.

Silver Threads Among the Gold

Words: Eben E. Rexford; Music: Hart Pease Danks

Sentimental songs may have sold better than any other type of popular music. Such music had long been popular and remained popular decades afterwards.

The composer, Danks, paid the lyricist, Rexford, three dollars for the rights to set one of his poems to music. The poem had first been published in a Wisconsin farm magazine. When Rexford accepted, he forwarded several poems to Danks for consideration. Among that batch of poems was "Silver Threads Among the Gold," which Rexford had written for his wife. Ironically, Danks would divorce his wife a year after this sentimental ballad was published in 1873. Unfortunately for Danks, he sold the song to the publishers and failed to capitalize on his great success.

The song was very popular in the second half of the 1870s and into the 1880s, but it found new life in '03.

"Silver Threads Among the Gold" may have been the most recorded song from '03 until the Great Depression, with record companies issuing over a hundred different versions, vocal and instrumental. When one version became dated and removed from a company's catalog, another was recorded to take its place. "Silver Threads Among the Gold" became one of the most recorded songs of the pre-rock era.

Richard Jose popularized it with a very successful recording in '04, Will Oakland's version was popular in '09, while John McCormack's '12 version and Charles Adams' '15 version also continued the popularity of the song well into the second half of the decade.

Rexford's first verse and chorus lyrics follow: *Darling, I am growing old, / Silver threads among the gold / Shine upon my brow today, / Life is fading fast away. / But, my darling, you will be, will be, / Always young and fair to me, / Yes, my darling, you will be, / Always young and fair to me. / Darling, I am growing old, / Silver threads among the gold, / Shine upon my brow today, / Life is fading fast away.*

The song was used in the '33 Mae West movie musical *She Done Him Wrong.*

The rather bland sheet music cover and musical score are available at http://levysheetmusic.mse.jhu.edu/browse.html.

Sweet Adeline

Words: Richard H. Gerard; Music: Henry W. Armstrong

"Sweet Adeline" became one of the most successful sentimental ballads of the era. For some reason, it has come to be associated with being inebriated. It certainly became a favorite of barbershop quartets, as a matter of fact, the women's barbershop-style singing organization is called "The Sweet Adelines."

The composer, Henry Armstrong, had written the melody in 1896 as an instrumental titled "Down Home in New England." He finally asked Richard Gerard to set words to his melody. Gerard used the title "You're the Flower of My Heart, Sweet Rosalie." Publishers at first were not enthusiastic, so Gerard felt the problem was the non-commercial appeal of the name "Rosalie." (That didn't appear to be the case in the long run, at least. Cole Porter wrote the music for the '37 movie musical titled *Rosalie* and the title song was very popular.) Gerard saw the name Adelina Patti, a celebrated opera star, on a poster advertising her tour and decided to change the name in the ballad to "Adeline." Witmark then bought and published the song.

Gerard later admitted in an interview that the song was inspired by a girl who worked at the music counter of a New York department store.

The song is best known today as "Sweet Adeline," but it was originally published as "You're the Flower of My Heart, Sweet Adeline."

The Quaker City Four introduced the song at Hammerstein's Victoria Theater in New York City in '03. The song began to catch on with the public and its popularity soon soared.

The song has two verses. The first verse says that the singer often sits alone dreaming of bygone days when his love was near. He wonders where she is and "if your heart to me is still the same." He says "the sighing wind and nightingale ... are breathing only your own sweet name." It's almost impossible to think of the chorus lyrics without imagining it being sung by a barbershop quartet: *Sweet Adeline, My Adeline, / At night, dear heart, for you I pine; / In all my dreams Your fair face beams, / You're the flower of my heart Sweet Adeline.*

"Sweet Adeline" became closely identified with John F. "Honey" Fitzgerald, the Mayor of Boston.

In '29, Oscar Hammerstein II and Jerome Kern used the song's title for a Broadway musical.

The Haydn Quartet, the Columbia Male Quartet, plus Albert Campbell and James F. Harrison popularized the song in '04 with successful recordings. The Mills Brothers revived it successfully in '39.

The song was used in the Marx Brothers film *Monkey Business* ('31).

The sheet music cover and musical score are available at both http://levysheetmusic.mse.jhu.edu/browse.html and http://scriptorium.lib.duke.edu/.

Toyland

Words: Glen MacDonough; Music: Victor Herbert

Producers Fred Hamlin and Julian Mitchell wanted a successor to the popular children's fantasy, *The Wizard of Oz.* They found what they were looking for in *Babes in Toyland.*

The plot of the musical was fairly flimsy, but wove together various characters from nursery rhymes. Children Jane and Allen must survive a storm at sea and a frightening journey through the woods before they arrive at a fantastic land of the toys.

Songs from the score include "I Can't Do the Sum," "March of the Toys," and "Toyland." "Toyland," was introduced by Bessie Wynn, as Tom Tom, and the chorus. It was the most popular song from the musical, but "I Can't Do the Sum" was also very popular. "March of the Toys" became more popular in '11.

Glen MacDonough's famous chorus lyrics follow: *Toyland, toyland little girl and boy land, / when you dwell within it, you are ever happy there! / Childhood toyland, mystical merry toyland, / once you pass its borders you can never return again!*

Most people today know the musical from movie versions: either the '34 Laurel and Hardy film or the '61 color version by Disney. There was also an '86 television version that featured Drew Barrymore and Keanu Reeves.

The song "Toyland" is often heard during the Christmas season. It was popularized in a duet recording by Corrine Morgan and the Haydn Quartet in '04. Billy Murray had a popular recording of "I Can't Do the Sum."

The sheet music cover and musical score are available at http://levysheetmusic.mse.jhu.edu/browse.html and at http://digital.library.ucla.edu/apam/. See the sheet music

cover and listen to a midi musical version at http://parlor
songs.com/issues/2002-1/thismonth/featureb.asp.

1905

Claire de Lune

Music: Claude Debussy

The famous French Impressionist composer, Claude Debussy began his *Suite bergamasque* in 1890. He had completed most of it by the turn of the century, but it was not
completely finished until '05. The third movement of this
piano suite is his famous "Clair de lune," one of the most
beautiful evocations of moonlight in classical piano literature.

As strange as it may seem, this classical piano piece was
a hit in the popular music arena in '05 enough to be included in *Variety's Hit Parade of a Half-Century.*

"Clair de lune" was revived in recordings by Jose Iturbi
in '46, and by Paul Weston and his orchestra in '48. Their
recordings were popular enough to chart.

Come Take a Trip in My Air Ship

Words: Ren Shields; Music: George Evans

In '03, American aviation history witnessed an epoch-
making event. Man had been attempting to fly for many
years. A German engineer had been experimenting since
1891 in flights with a glider. In the United States in 1896,
Octave Chanute had flown in a glider over the sand dunes
of northern Indiana. Man's attempts to fly were being
slowly realized scientifically. Wilbur and Orville Wright,
who had been experimenting with gliders, installed a light
motor in their equipment and launched from Kill Devil
Hill, near Kittyhawk, North Carolina, the first successful
mechanical airplane. In that first flight, Orville travelled
120 feet in twelve seconds. On the fourth attempt the same
day, December 17, '03, Wilbur flew 852 feet in fifty-nine
seconds. In September '05, Orville accomplished the first
officially recorded airplane flight at Dayton, Ohio. He
flew 11.12 miles in eighteen minutes, nine seconds. In October '05, Orville and Wilbur again demonstrated their
airplane by flying 25 miles in thirty-eight minutes. What
once seemed only a dream was becoming a reality.

Ren Shields and George Evans, the same writers who
penned "In the Good Old Summer Time," were inspired
by the Wright Brothers' first successful flights to write
"Come Take a Trip in My Airship," one of the earliest
songs about aviation. However, according to the sheet
music cover illustration, the airship is more like a blimp or
a dirigible. Topical songs like this one were a very important type of song during this first decade of the 20th century. Ethel Robinson introduced the song in vaudeville.

The song's verse is a girl singing about her sailor who has
an airship and he's coming to take her for a ride. The chorus is what the boy says to her: *Come, take a trip in my
airship, / Come, take a sail 'mong the stars, / Come, have a
ride around Venus, / Come, have a spin around Mars. / No
one to watch while we're kissing, / No one to see while we
spoon. / Come, take a trip in my airship, / And we'll visit the
man in the moon.*

Billy Murray and J.W. Myers both helped popularize
the song with successful recordings.

Hear J.W. Myers' '04 recording of this song at http://
www.archive.org/audio/audio-details-db.php?collectionid=
airship1904&collection=opensource_audio. See the sheet
music cover and the sheet music score at http://lcweb2.loc.
gov/cocoon/ihas/loc.natlib.ihas.100005954/.

Dearie

Words & Music: Clare Kummer

Sallie Fisher introduced "Dearie" in the musical *Sergeant
Brue* in '05.

Corrine Morgan and the Haydn Quartet had the most
popular recording of the song in '05, but Harry MacDonough's recording was also popular. George Alexander's
version was reasonably popular in '06.

The lyrics talk a lot about dreams. In the first verse, the
singer tells us the world is getting older and colder and it
"has no place for a dreamer of dreams." Therefore, there's
no place for him because he dreams of his "Dearie" all day
long. In the chorus he says, "Nothing's worth while, but
dreams of you."

The sheet music cover and musical score are available at
http://levysheetmusic.mse.jhu.edu/browse.html.

Give My Regards to Broadway *and* The Yankee Doodle Boy

Words & Music: George M. Cohan

"Give My Regards to Broadway" and "The Yankee
Doodle Boy" were introduced in George M. Cohan's third
Broadway musical, but his first real hit, *Little Johnny Jones.*
The plot revolved around Johnny Jones who had traveled
to Britain to ride his horse named Yankee Doodle in the
English Derby. Johnny is accused of throwing the race.
He hires a private detective who discovers that Johnny was
framed by an American gambler, which, of course, clears
his name. In the third act, with the locale suddenly in San
Francisco's Chinatown, Johnny's girlfriend, Goldie Gates,
is kidnapped. When Johnny and his private detective ap-
prehend the abductor, he turns out to be the same villain
who framed him in the derby.

Cohan was literally born into show business; his entire
family was in the theater as members of the famous vaudeville team The Four Cohan's, with his sister, Josephine, and
their parents. George became one of the most multi-
talented men of the musical theater. In almost all of his
productions, he was composer, lyricist, librettist, playwright, actor, director and producer. He wrote twenty-
one musicals and twenty plays. Not only did Cohan fill almost every conceivable position in his musicals, he also
hired his family members to appear in them as well. For
instance, his father, Jerry, played the American gambler
who framed him in the race and his then-wife, Ethel
Levey, was his love interest, Goldie.

GIVE MY REGARDS TO BROADWAY

In the musical, Johnny must remain in England until his
name is cleared while the others return home. He is standing on the Southhampton pier watching the ship depart,
waiting for a signal, a flare from the ship that will indicate
he has been exonerated. At first he sings "Give My Regards to Broadway" plaintively because he can't return to
the United States with the others, but once he sees the
flare and realizes he has been cleared of any wrongdoing,
he performs the song in an exuberant song-and-dance
style. In the '68 Broadway musical, *George M,* Joel Grey

performed the song basically the same as the original scene from the musical.

Along with Cole Porter's "There's No Business Like Show Business," Cohan's song has become one of the unofficial anthems of the American theatrical industry.

The lyrics of the verse are not very familiar, especially in comparison to the chorus. They don't completely agree with the story from the musical. Johnny is in England, not France and he is waiting for his name to be cleared, so as he watches others sail away, he tells them to give his regards to Broadway. These, however, are the lyrics for the first verse: *At a port in France one morning, / Waiting for my ship to sail, / Yankee soldiers on a furlough / Came to get the latest mail; / I told them I was on my way / To old Manhattan Isle; / They all gathered about, / As the vessel pulled out, / And said, with a smile:*

The lyrics of the famous chorus follow: *Give my regards to Broadway, / Remember me to Herald Square; / Tell all the gang at Forty-Second Street / that I will soon be there. / Whisper of how I'm yearning / to mingle with the old time throng; / Give my regards to old Broadway / And say that I'll be there, ere long.*

It was first heard in the movies in *The Broadway Melody* ('29) and again in the film version of *Little Johnny Jones* ('29) starring Eddie Buzzell (actually Warner Bros. had filmed a silent version in '23; why film a silent version of musical?). Then several years later, it was used in *The Great American Broadcast* ('41). James Cagney's performance of it in Cohan's screen biography, *Yankee Doodle Dandy*, is a film classic. The song was also the title for a '48 movie musical, where Charles Winninger and Dan Dailey sang it. It then appeared in *Jolson Sings Again* ('49) and in Jane Froman's film biography *With a Song in My Heart* ('52). "Give My Regards to Broadway" was nominated for the American Film Institute's list of greatest songs from movies for its appearance in *Little Johnny Jones* ('29), but it did not make the final list.

Billy Murray and S.H. Dudley helped popularize the song with successful recordings in '05. Hear Billy Murray's '05 recording of this song at http://www.edisonnj.org/menlopark/vintage/columbia.asp. See the sheet music cover and listen to a midi musical version at http://parlorsongs.com/issues/2002-1/thismonth/featureb.asp. See the sheet music cover and the musical score at http://levysheetmusic.mse.jhu.edu/browse.html or a PDF is available at http://library.indstate.edu/.

THE YANKEE DOODLE BOY

This jaunty patriotic song was Cohan's entrance song in *Little Johnny Jones*. It introduces the character and the lyrics are also reasonably autobiographical. Cohan thought of himself as "a real-live nephew" of his Uncle Sam. And he claimed to have been "born on the fourth of July," even though his birth certificate says July 3, 1878. The lyrics also say this Yankee Doodle boy had come "to London just to ride the ponies."

Sometimes the song is listed as "Yankee Doodle Boy" minus the "The," and sometimes as "Yankee Doodle Dandy."

As usual, the verse is not nearly as well known as the chorus. However, the lyrics of the verse set up the chorus very well: *I'm the kid that's all the candy, / I'm a Yankee Doodle dandy, / I'm glad I am, So's Uncle Sam. / I'm a real*

live Yankee Doodle, / Made my name and fame and boodle / Just like Mister Doodle did, by riding on a pony. / I love to listen to the Doodle strain, / I long to see the girl I left behind me; / And that ain't a josh, She's a Yankee, by gosh, / Oh, say can you see / Anything about a Yankee that's phony?

Cohan was always patriotic, so the quote lyrically and melodically of the phrase "Oh, say can you see" from "The Star Spangled Banner" is not surprising.

The very patriotic lyrics of the famous chorus follow: *I'm a Yankee Doodle dandy, / A Yankee Doodle, do or die; / A real live nephew of my Uncle Sam's, / Born on the Fourth of July. / I've got a Yankee Doodle sweetheart, / She's my Yankee Doodle joy. / Yankee Doodle came to London, / Just to ride the ponies, / I am a Yankee Doodle boy.*

The sheet music cover and musical score are available at both http://levysheetmusic.mse.jhu.edu/browse.html and http://lcweb2.loc.gov/cocoon/ihas/loc.natlib.ihas.100005162/. Go to the following website, http://www.geocities.com/dferg5493/yankeedoodleboy.htm, click on a song title to hear hit the song and see the lyrics.

Like "Give My Regards to Broadway," "Yankee Doodle Boy" was in the '29 film version of *Little Johnny Jones*. It was also used in the Judy Garland and Mickey Rooney movie musical *Babes on Broadway* ('42). Jimmy Cagney's exuberant singing and dancing of the song in *Yankee Doodle Dandy* ('42) was one of the film's highlights. Bob Hope and Cagney's dance of the song in *The Seven Little Foys* ('55) is another classic. AFI's (American Film Institute) *100 Years ... 100 Songs* (2004) named "The Yankee Doodle Boy" the No. 71 greatest song ever from an American film for its performance by James Cagney in *Yankee Doodle Dandy*.

Billy Murray's recording of the song was very popular in '05. By mid-'05 Victor advertised that Murray's recording of the song was the top-selling record in its history. Fred Waring and his Pennsylvanians revived it in a reasonably successful recording in '43.

A Good Cigar Is a Smoke

Words: Harry B. Smith; Music: Victor Herbert

Harry B. Smith's lyrics for this song were inspired by a Rudyard Kipling quote from *The Betrothed*: "A woman is only a woman, but a good cigar is a smoke." This quote became a catch phrase of the early 1900s.

Melville Stewart introduced this comedy number in *Miss Dolly Dollars* in '05.

The verses of this song are in 6/8 time, while the more famous chorus is in waltz time (triple meter). The first verse lyrics sing to men who feel they have been wronged by some woman. The singer tells his fellowman, "If a pair of blue eyes have deceived you, and a pair of red lips said you nay," they should not drink champagne to ease their sorrows. Instead, they should go to the club and "light up a long dark cigar." The chorus lyrics begin with the song's subtitle: *Puff, puff, puff, puff, watching the smoke arising; / Puff, puff, puff, puff, soon you'll be realizing / That which the poet has written is true, / All love is a practical joke, / For a woman is only a woman, my boy, / But a good cigar is a smoke.*

This song was selected by *Variety* for its *Hit Parade of a Half-Century* for '05, listed as "Woman Is Only a Woman, but a Good Cigar Is a Smoke."

The musical score is available at http://levysheetmusic.mse.jhu.edu/browse.html.

I Don't Care

Words: Jean Lenox; Music: Harry O. Sutton

Eva Tanguay popularized this *Variety Hit Parade of a Half-Century* song in vaudeville. Her Ethel-Merman-like delivery of this song was so successful that she became known as "The I Don't Care Girl."

Judy Garland performed this rowdy number in the '49 movie musical *In the Good Old Summertime* and Mitzi Gaynor performed it in Eva Tanguay's screen biography *The I-Don't-Care Girl* ('53).

The multiple verses are in common time (4/4) and are marked "Moderato," while the chorus is in cut time (2/4) time and is marked "Faster." Following is the first verse and chorus: *They say I'm crazy, got no sense But I don't care. / They may or may not mean offence, But I don't care; / You see I'm sort of independent, of a clever race descendent, / My star is on the ascendant, That's why I don't care. / I don't care, I don't care, What they may think of me. / I'm happy go lucky, Men say I am plucky, / So jolly and care free. I don't care, I don't care, / If I do get the mean and stony stare. If I'm never successful, / It won't be distressful, 'Cos I don't care.*

At http://www.perfessorbill.com/index2.htm you can also hear a midi musical version and see the sheet music cover.

In My Merry Oldsmobile

Words: Vincent P. Bryan; Music: Gus Edwards

The first commercial automobile appeared in Detroit in 1896. By 1899, the automobile had become such a nuisance that it was barred from Central Park in New York City. In '03, Henry Ford left the Detroit Automobile Company and organized the Ford Motor Company. Although the automobile was not the most reliable form of transportation during these early years of the new century, Americans were fascinated by the contraptions. In '03 Dr. H. Nelson Jackson and Sewell K. Crocker made the first trans-continental automobile trip from San Francisco to New York City in seventy days.

"In My Merry Oldsmobile" is a topical song inspired by the first trans-continental automobile race. In '05, two tiny, primitive 7-horsepower Olds Runabouts followed the historic ruts of the Oregon Trail across the West in the first transcontinental automobile race from New York City to Portland, Oregon (some reports say Detroit to Portland, but that's not technically trans-continental). Basically buckboards with motors, these were the first motorized vehicles to travel the Oregon Trail, the first to cross the United States from east to west (the trip in '03 was not a race, and traveled west to east) and the first to cross the Cascade Mountain range. Although parts of the United States were reasonably civilized by '05, the 20th century had not made much of an impact on the western part of the country. The little cars and their drivers faced a rough trip of bad weather, sickness, wild animals, thirst, accidents and unforeseen breakdowns.

The Oldsmobile brand is one of the oldest. In 1895, Ransom Eli Olds teamed with Frank Clark to successfully produce a self contained, gasoline-powered carriage. Olds and a group of Lansing businessmen created the Olds Motor Vehicle Company in 1897. Sadly, in the early 21st century, General Motors announced that the brand would be discontinued so it appears the song will outlive the car.

The lyrics sound very much like a commercial jingle for Oldsmobile: *Come away with me, Lucile / In my merry Oldsmobile, / Down the road of life we'll fly / Automobubbling you and I. / To the church we'll swiftly steal, / Then our weddin' bells will peal, / You can go as far as you like with me, / In my merry Oldsmobile.*

Was there any double entendre meaning in the line "you can go as far as you like with me"? That's difficult to judge, but considering the prudishness of the era, it seems doubtful.

Billy Murray's solo recordings and Arthur Collins and Byron Harlan's duet version helped popularize the song in '05.

Donald O'Connor, Jack Oakie and Peggy Ryan performed the song in the film *The Merry Monahans* in '44. It was also used in the '48 movie musical *One Sunday Afternoon*.

The sheet music cover and musical score are available at http://levysheetmusic.mse.jhu.edu/browse.html, at http://scriptorium.lib.duke.edu/dynaweb/sheetmusic/ and at http://digital.library.ucla.edu/apam/.See the sheet music cover and listen to a midi musical version at http://parlorsongs.com/issues/2001-2/thismonth/featureb.asp. A foxtrot and a waltz version by Jean Goldkette and his orchestra in '27 are available at http://www.redhotjazz.com/goldo.html. Go to the following website: http://www.geocities.com/dferg5493/inmymerryoldsmobile.html, to hear the song and see the lyrics.

This song was selected by *Variety* for its *Hit Parade of a Half-Century* for '05.

In the Shade of the Old Apple Tree

Words: Harry H. Williams; Music: Egbert Van Alstyne

Though "Wait 'Till the Sun Shines, Nellie" and perhaps a few others came close, no songs of '05 matched the popularity of this sentimental one about the apple tree.

At the time Williams and Van Alstyne wrote "In the Shade of the Old Apple Tree," they were working as song pluggers for Remick, the famous music-publishing house. This song became their first major success as songwriters. They were reportedly inspired by a visit to Central Park in New York City, which, incidentally, didn't have any apple trees.

The lyrics of this famous song follow: *In the shade of the old apple tree / Where the love in your eyes I could see / When the voice that I heard like the song of a bird / Seemed to whisper sweet music to me / I could hear the dull buzz of the bee / In the blossoms as you said to me / 'With a heart that is true, I'll be waiting for you / In the shade of the old apple tree.'*

Irving Gillette, Albert Campbell, the Haydn Quartet and Arthur Pryor's Band all helped popularize "In the Shade of the Old Apple Tree" with very successful recordings in '05. Duke Ellington and his orchestra had a reasonably popular recording of the song in '33.

The sheet music cover and musical score are available at http://levysheetmusic.mse.jhu.edu/browse.html and at http://scriptorium.lib.duke.edu/dynaweb/sheetmusic/ or a PDF of this song is available at http://library.indstate.edu/. You can see the sheet music cover, read the lyrics and hear a midi musical version to this song at the following website: http://www.halcyondaysmusic.com/october/october2002.htm. Go to the following website, click on a song title to hear the song and see the lyrics: www.geocities.com/dferg5493/songfiles.htm.

This song was selected by *Variety* for its *Hit Parade of a Half-Century* for '05.

Kiss Me Again *and* I Want What I Want When I Want It

Words: Henry Blossom; Music: Victor Herbert

Victor Herbert's *Mlle. Modiste* was set in Paris. Fritzi Scheff starred as the stage-struck girl, Fifi, who works in a hat shop. With some help from a rich American, she becomes the toast of Paris.

Kiss Me Again

The operetta's most enduring song was "Kiss Me Again," which was introduced by Ms. Scheff. Actually the song was part of a trilogy routine called "If I Were on the Stage." Fifi sings that if she were on the stage as a country girl she would sing a gavotte, if she were a historical lady she would perform a polonaise and if she were a romantic heroine, she would sing a waltz. The waltz was "Kiss Me Again." Some parts of the three songs were particularly low for Miss Scheff and she expressed her feelings to Herbert, but the composer refused to change the music. Even so, it became one of her greatest musical triumphs.

The lyrics of the most famous part of the trilogy, the waltz, follow: *Sweet summer breeze, whispering treesStars shining softly above. / Roses in bloom, wafted perfume / Sleepy birds dreaming of love. / Safe in your arms, far from alarms, / Daylight shall come but in vain. / Tenderly press close to my breast, / Kiss me, kiss me again.*

Variety selected "Kiss Me Again" for its *Golden 100 Tin Pan Alley Songs* and *Hit Parade of a Half-Century*.

The motion picture version of the operetta was filmed in '31, but the plot was changed considerably. The "If I Were on the Stage" segment was used in the film. In '39 Paramount filmed *The Great Victor Herbert*, the rather fictionalized screen biography of the composer. Susanna Foster performed "Kiss Me Again" in the film.

Olive Kline helped popularize the song with a '16 recording. Victor Herbert himself issued an instrumental recording of the song in '19.

The non-descript sheet music cover and musical score are available at http://levysheetmusic.mse.jhu.edu/browse.html. See the sheet music cover and hear a midi musical version at http://parlorsongs.com/issues/2003-9/thismonth/featureb.asp.

I Want What I Want When I Want It

William Pruette, as Henri de Bouvray, introduced this comic song in *Mlle. Modiste*. Frank Stanley recorded a popular version of the song in '06. The verse is in 6/8 time, while the chorus in the common meter (4/4).

Blossom's lyrics are the epitome of male chauvenism. The singer is extremely happy as a bachelor: "I'm happier far than men are, who are cursed with a shrew of a wife." He drinks all he wants, hangs out with his old friends and stays out all night if he so chooses. He doesn't have anyone "to nag me or scold." The chorus lyrics follow: *For I want what I want when I want it! / That's all that makes life worth the while. / For the wine that tonight fills my soul with delight, / On the morrow may seem to me vile. / There's no worldly pleasure myself I deny, / There's no one to ask me the wherefore or why, / I eat when I'm hungry, and drink when*

I'm dry. / For I want what I want when I want it! / I want what I want when I want it!

This song was selected by *Variety* for its *Hit Parade of a Half-Century* for '05.

The Preacher and the Bear

Words & Music: George Fairman

At the beginning of the 20th century, the best-known coon song was Ernest Hogan's "All Coons Look Alike to Me," but by the middle of the first decade "The Preacher and the Bear" became the most popular coon song of the era.

Joe Arzonia is most often credited as the song's writer, but it was actually written by George Fairman. He sold all rights to the song to Arzonia, the owner of a café where Fairman played piano, for $250. At this time, if a writer sold a song, it was perfectly legal for the buyer to publish the song as if he were the writer.

Arthur Collins, one of the most famous coon song and rag or ragtime singers, first recorded "The Preacher and the Bear" in early '05, and was then forever closely associated with the song. Collins was the first recording artist to obtain a hit based on sales figures (cylinders and disks). He reportedly sold between one and two million copies of "The Preacher and the Bear." It was not at all unusual for recording artists to record the same song for virtually every record company in the country. By '20, Collins had done just that with "The Preacher and the Bear."

In '47 Phil Harris' recording of the song was reasonably popular, but some of the racially sensitive lyrics had been changed. Country singer Jerry Reed's '70 version of the song charted on *Billboard*.

"The Preacher and the Bear" is a comical song. In his recordings of the song, Collins imitated black vocal style and speech. It is interesting to note that the word "coon" was used in reference to the preacher in the original version. In later versions "preacher" replaced "coon."

The lyrics tell about a preacher who went hunting on a Sunday even though he knew he shouldn't. After he had bagged a quail and a hare, he was returning home when he came face to face with a "great big grizzly bear." The preacher "climbed a persimmon tree" while the bear sat down to wait. The preacher began to pray: *Oh Lord, didn't you deliver Daniel from the lion's den? / Also delivered Jonah from the belly of the whale and then / Three Hebrew chillun from the fiery furnace? / So the Good Book do declare / Now Lord, if you can't help me / For goodness sakes, don't you help that bear!*

The sheet music cover and musical score are available at http://levysheetmusic.mse.jhu.edu/browse.html and at http://scriptorium.lib.duke.edu/dynaweb/sheetmusic/. To hear Arthur Collins sing "The Preacher and the Bear," go to http://www.nb.no/html/the_world_s_first_big_hit.html

What You Goin' to Do When de Rent Comes 'Round? (Rufus Rastus Johnson Brown)

Words: Andrew B. Sterling; Music: Harry Von Tilzer

Like several other songs by Sterling and Von Tilzer, the idea for this one was an overheard remark. Von Tilzer was in a Miami train station when he heard two African American women lamenting the shiftless nature of a man. One of the women said she asked the man "What you goin' to do when de rent comes 'round?"

The name in the title, Rufus Rastus Johnson Brown, is, of course, the man to whom the question is being asked. The lyrics to the comic chorus follow: *Rufus Rastus Johnson Brown, / Whatcha gonna do when the rent comes 'round. / Whatcha gonna do and whatcha gonna say. / If you can't pay rent at the break of day. / Oh you know, I know, anybody knows / That you can't pay rent if you ain't got the dough. / Rufus Rastus Johnson Brown, / Whatcha gonna do when the rent comes 'round.*

Once again, "The King of Coon Songs," Arthur Collins helped popularize the song with a successful recording in '05.

"What You Goin' to Do When de Rent Comes 'Round? (Rufus Rastus Johnson Brown)" was selected by *Variety* for its *Hit Parade of a Half-Century* for '05.

The sheet music cover and musical score are available at http://levysheetmusic.mse.jhu.edu/browse.html and at http://scriptorium.lib.duke.edu/dynaweb/sheetmusic/. Hear a midi musical version at http://www.primeshop.com/midlist3.htm.

Where the Morning Glories Twine Around the Door

Words: Andrew B. Sterling; Music: Harry Von Tilzer

Byron G. Harlan helped popularize "Where the Morning Glories Twine Around the Door" with a very popular recording in '05.

This song is another example of a sentimental ballad. Sterling's lyrics are reminiscing about a homestead "in New England, far, far away." The singer is dreaming of his loved ones "down where the morning glories twine." The chorus lyrics follow: *Now, the same old moon is shining, and the roses bloom as fair, / And the same dear hearts are pining, they are waiting for me there. / Mother dear will come to meet me, and a sweetheart's kiss will greet me, / Where the morning glories twine around the same old door.*

A PDF of this song's musical score is available at http://library.indstate.edu/level1.dir/cml/rbsc/kirk/sheet_titles.html.

Where the River Shannon Flows (see 1910)

This song was selected by *Variety* for its *Hit Parade of a Half-Century* for '05.

The Whistler and His Dog

Music: Arthur Pryor

Arthur Pryor wrote "The Whistler and his Dog" in '05. Pryor was a trombonist and arranger for John Philip Sousa's band.

The earliest recorded version of the tune was probably the Edison Military Band on an Edison Cylinder. Many people have recorded the song, most notably the composer himself, Arthur Pryor's Band on Victor.

The melody of this piece is probably familiar to most of you, but you may not recognize it by its title. It was used as background music for many early films to suggest a relaxed background or a lackadaisical attitude. The whimsical song is in AABACCA form with a 4-bar introduction and a 4-bar interlude between the CA strains.

The sheet music cover shows a small boy sitting on a barrel as he whistles. Also on the cover is a small dog sitting in front of its doghouse that seems to be listening to and enjoying the boy's whistling. Several mischievous boys are looking over a fence that has a poster on it advertising an upcoming performance of Arthur Pryor's Band.

Variety included "The Whistler and his Dog" on its *Hit Parade of a Half-Century* for '05.

Listen to the song at the following website: http://www.whistlingrecords.com/78s/78s.htm where you can hear Sybil Sanderson Fagan's Federal 78rpm recording (does not give the date, but it is an early recording).

See the sheet music cover and the musical score at http://scriptorium.lib.duke.edu/dynaweb/sheetmusic/.

1906

Anchors Aweigh

Words: A.H. Miles; Music: Charles A. Zimmerman

The U.S. Navy song, "Anchors Aweigh," was selected by *Variety* for its *Hit Parade of a Half-Century* for '06.

The lyricist, A.H. Miles graduated from the Naval Academy in '07 and later served as the chapel choir director. The composer, Charles Zimmerman, was the Academy's band director. They wrote the song for the '06 Army/Navy football game. The corps sang the song as they marched onto the football field before the game.

For the next two decades, the song was used primarily in connection with that football game. The lyrics printed below are the original football chorus: *Stand Navy down the field, Sail set to the sky! / We'll never change our course so, Army you steer shy-y-y-y. / Roll up the score Navy Anchors Aweigh / Sail Navy down the field and sink the Army, sink the Army gray.*

In '26, Royal Lovell, a Midshipman, added more verses. D. Savino is credited with revising the melody in a later edition. George D. Lottman was also credited in some additions as a co-writer. Lottman's lyric revision of the chorus follows: *Stand Navy out to sea, Fight our battle cry; / We'll never change our course, So vicious foe steer shy-y-y-y. / Roll out the T.N.T. Anchors Aweigh / Sail on to victory and sink their bones to Davy Jones hooray! / Anchors Aweigh, my boys, Anchors Aweigh, / Farewell to college joys, we sail at break of day-day-day-day! / Through our last night on shore, Drink to the foam. / Until we meet once more here's wishing you a happy voyage home.*

The most popular recordings of the song were issued by the U.S. Naval Academy Band in '21 and by Paul Tremaine in '30.

The song was included in a medley in the '37 movie musical *Rosalie* and in the '45 movie musical *Anchors Aweigh*, where it was played by an orchestra conducted by Jose Iturbi. The song has probably been used in many other films, but was uncredited. According to http://www.imdb.com/, it appeared, credited, in *Down Periscope* ('96).

The sheet music cover and musical score are available at http://levysheetmusic.mse.jhu.edu/browse.html (2 editions avialable). Hear the U.S. Marine Band recording of this song at http://lcweb2.loc.gov/cocoon/ihas100010481/.

Chinatown, My Chinatown (see 1915)

Variety Hit Parade of a Half-Century for '06.

Everybody Works but Father

Words & Music: Jean Havez

"Everybody Works but Father" was first popularized by the Lew Dockstader's Minstrels.

The song was inspired by so many women and children entering the work force in the early 1900s. The song is comical, but, as comedy often does, it raised a serious social issue.

Child labor had been an issue in this country, especially in the huge Northeastern cities like New York City, since the 1850s. The problem had grown even worse as immigration increased around the beginning of the new century. Children from poor families as young as six or seven years of age were expected to earn their keep and contribute to the family's economy. There were reportedly about three quarters of a million child laborers under age fifteen at this time in history. The movement for child labor laws began to gain support.

At the beginning of the 20th century, approximately 20 percent of white women and 40 percent of black women were in the paid workforce in the United States.

So where was Father? Why wasn't he working? In many cases, he had been laid off because industry could get cheaper labor by using the women and children.

The lyrics of the first verse must be sung by one of the man's children. They are griping about having to get up every morning at six o'clock and about the winter weather they have to fight as they go to work. What they would prefer is to stay at home like father. The chorus follows: *Everybody works but father and he sits around all day, / Feet in front of the fire — Smoking his pipe of clay, / Mother takes in washing So does sister Ann, / Everybody works at our house but my old man.*

Billy Murray's '06 recording of the song was very popular, but recordings by Lew Dockstader's Minstrels and by Bob Roberts had helped it get started in '05.

The sheet music cover and musical score are available at http://levysheetmusic.mse.jhu.edu/browse.html and at http://scriptorium.lib.duke.edu/dynaweb/sheetmusic/.

The Good Old U.S.A.

Words: Jack Drislane; Music: Theodore F. Morse

There seems to have been a lot of patriotic fervor in the country in '06, with this song, "Anchors Aweigh" and "You're a Grand Old Flag" being very popular, but there doesn't appear to be any significant war that involves the U.S., except perhaps the Russo-Japanese War, during this time.

This patriotic march tune is a conversation between a son and his father. In the verse, the little boy asks his father why a big crowd reacts so proudly when the brass band plays "My country 'tis of thee." The father tells his son he'll understand "one of these days." Then he explains further with the chorus, which follows: *Makes no diff'rence where you wander, / Makes no diff'rence where you roam, / You don't have to stop and ponder, / For a place to call your home. / When they ask where were you born, lad, / Speak right up, be proud to say / That your home's the land of Uncle Sam, / The good old U.S.A.*

Byron G. Harlan's recording was very popular in '06, plus J.W. Myers' version was also pretty well received.

The sheet music cover and musical score are available at http://levysheetmusic.mse.jhu.edu/browse.html.

How'd You Like to Spoon with Me?

Words: Edward Laska; Music: Jerome Kern

"How'd You Like to Spoon with Me?" became Jerome Kern's first hit song in America (he had one earlier in England). Georgia Caine and Victor Morley introduced this invitation to romance in *The Earl and the Girl* in '05. The scene featured six girls in beautiful dresses swinging in flower decorated swings.

The female sings the first verse: *I don't know why I am so very shy, / I always was demure, / I never knew what silly lovers do, / No flirting I'd endure; / In all my life I've never kissed a man, / I've never winked my eye. / But now at last I'm going to break the ice / So how'd you like to try?*

The refrain of the song begins with the girl asking, "How'd you like to spoon with me?" To which the man replies, "I'd like to." The girl continues to ask several questions including things like "How'd you like to hug and squeeze? Dangle me upon your knees? How'd you like to be my lovey dovey? How'd you like to spoon with me?" In between each question the man's responses in the affirmative, but each reply is slightly different. Of course, we seldom, if ever, hear the word "spoon" today used in this context, but it basically meant to engage in amorous behavior, such as kissing or caressing. Another expression we have heard frequently is the endearment "tootsie wootsie," and it appears again in this song's chorus, spelled differently, in the phrase "call me little tootsy wootsy baby."

Corrine Morgan and the Haydn Quartet's recording of the song was very popular in '06.

"How'd You Like to Spoon with Me?" was performed by Angela Lansbury in Kern's screen biography *Till the Clouds Roll By* in '46.

View several sheet music covers and the musical score at http://digital.library.ucla.edu/apam/.

Let It Alone

Words: Alex Rogers; Music: Bert A. Williams

This Bert Williams song has a potential eight verses and choruses; six are printed on the last page of the sheet music. In the lyrics, Williams is giving advice about giving advice. His advice? "Let it alone!" *Let it alone, let it alone, if it don't concern you, / Let it alone, don't go four-flushin' an' puttin' on airs, / And dippin' into other folks affairs, / If you don't know, say so! / Mind your own bus'ness and let it alone.*

Bert Williams' recording of his song was very popular in '06 and the sheet music sold very well as well.

The sheet music cover and musical score are available at http://levysheetmusic.mse.jhu.edu/browse.html and at http://scriptorium.lib.duke.edu/dynaweb/sheetmusic/. Notice that Williams is pictured on the cover in black face, which illustrates that sometimes African Americans blacked their faces in the minstrel tradition.

Love Me, and the World Is Mine

Words: Dave Reed, Jr.; Music: Ernest R. Ball

This ballad was introduced at Proctor's 5th Avenue Theater in New York City in '06. Vaudevillian Maude Lambert, composer Ernest Ball's second wife, was one of the performers who helped make the song a success. It was such a huge success, as a matter of fact, that Witmark, the famous music publishing house, rewarded Ball with a twenty-year contract as staff composer. Such a long term contract was unheard of at the time.

Henry Burr, Albert Campbell and Harry Anthony released popular recordings of the song in '06. It was revived by the Haydn Quartet in '08.

The verses of this song are in common or 4/4 time, while the chorus, which is unusually short, is in 12/8 time (which is like 4/4 time in triplets). The lyrics of the verses are rather antiquated with words like "'twould," and phrases like "yet lo, dear heart, 'tis only thee" and "be mine for aye."

The lyrics of the four line chorus follow: *I care not for the stars that shine, / I dare not hope to e'er be thine, / I only know I love you, / Love me, and the world is mine.*

The song became a favorite of barbershop quartets, not just male quartets, the barbershop quartets of SPEBSQSA (Society for the Preservation and Encouragement of Barber Shop Quartet Singing in America).

"Love Me, and the World Is Mine" was heard in several movie musicals, including *San Francisco* ('36), where it was sung by Jeanette MacDonald, *The Strawberry Blond* ('41), the Ernest R. Ball screen biography *Irish Eyes Are Smiling* ('44) and *The Eddie Cantor Story* ('54).

Variety selected this song for its *Hit Parade of a Half-Century* for '06.

The non-descript sheet music cover and musical score are available at http://levysheetmusic.mse.jhu.edu/browse.html.

Mary's a Grand Old Name, So Long, Mary *and* Forty-Five Minutes from Broadway

Words & Music: George M. Cohan

Forty-Five Minutes from Broadway was more of a comedy with music than what we've come to expect from a Broadway musical. There were only five songs, but three of them are still remembered by many people.

The show is set 45 minutes from Broadway in New Rochelle. The plot revolves around a missing will left by a deceased millionaire. Kid Burns, a chronic horse track gambler, discovers that the will leaves everything to the man's housekeeper, Mary Jane Jenkins. Even though Burns loves Mary, he will not marry her, because she has too much money (such a thing would hurt his manly pride). So Mary, in a magnanomous jester, tears up the will so Burns and she can be married. In the '06 production, Victor Moore played Kid Burns, while Fay Templeton was Mary. In a '12 production, Cohan himself played the Kid, opposite Mary played by Sallie Fisher.

Cohan's musicals were American; people in this country could readily identify with the characters and with the plots in comparision to the strong European influence of the operettas that were also popular with theater-goers.

MARY'S A GRAND OLD NAME

Fay Templeton introduced "Mary's a Grand Old Name." The song became one of the show's hit songs and sold many thousands of copies of sheet music.

Many of the new immigrants to America changed their names when they arrived. In many cases, the change was to hide ethnic origins of some of the groups who found discrimination in this country. Jewish, Irish and some eastern European songwriters and/or entertainers changed

their names seemingly to avoid any potential problem. In some cases, the name change was simply to Americanize the name, to fit in better in their new country. In that context, "Mary's a Grand Old Name" is a topical song affirming that the name, a name popular in the past, but not in current fashion, is indeed a wonderful name.

The lyrics of the first verse tell us that Mary was the name of the singer's mother. She explains that since her mother's "name was Mary, she called me Mary too." She says her mother was not a gay person, but rather plain. Then the last phrase of the verse is difficult to understand: "I hate to meet a fairy who calls herself Marie." The second verse clears up the previous phrase by explaining that there's no falseness in the name Mary, but if a girl is named Marie, "she'll vary, she'll surely bleach her hair." We are warned to "beware of sweet Marie." The famous chorus follows each verse: *For it is Mary, Mary, plain as any name can be. / But with propriety, society will say Marie. / But it was Mary, Mary, long before the fashions came, / And there is something there that sounds so square, it's a grand old name.*

The schottische tempo of the song made it an ideal soft-shoe dance number.

The song was also performed in the Broadway musical about Cohan, his life and music, *George M* ('68). James Cagney sang the song in Cohan's motion picture biography *Yankee Doodle Dandy* ('42). Cagney and Bob Hope danced to the song in the movie musical *The Seven Little Foys* ('55). The song was also used in the Judy Garland–Mickey Rooney movie musical *Babes on Broadway* ('42).

Bing Crosby's recording of the song was popular in '43.

"Mary's a Grand Ole Name" was selected by *Variety* for its *Hit Parade of a Half-Century* for '05.

Hear Billy Murray's '06 recording of this song at http://www.authentichistory.com/audio/1900s/1906_45_Minutes_From_Broadway.html. The musical score is available at http://levysheetmusic.mse.jhu.edu/browse.html, at http://lcweb2.loc.gov/cocoon/ihas/loc.natlib.ihas.100005146/ and at http://digital.library.ucla.edu/.

SO LONG, MARY

Fay Templeton and the chorus introduced this farewell song at the New Rochelle railroad station in the musical. "So Long, Mary" may have been the most popular song to come out of the musical in the mid- to late 1900s, but it has not stood the test of time as well as "Mary's a Grand Old Name."

Corrine Morgan had a particularly popular recording of the song, and Ada Jones' version was not far behind in popularity.

The chorus lyrics alone don't seem to fit the character Mary who seems to be singing goodbye to herself. The first verse explains that she is leaving on the train and several girls have accompanied her to the station. She's surprised the girls cared enough to make the effort. She tells them it reminds her of her family as they said goodbye to her when she left Schenectady. In that instance, the chorus is what her family had sung to her. In the second verse it is a group of males who are seeing her off. She's surprised that anyone in New Rochelle would come to the depot and say: *So long, Mary! Mary, we will miss you so. / So long, Mary! How we hate to see you go; / And we'll all be longing for you, Mary, / While you roam, So long, Mary, / Don't forget to come back home!*

In the Broadway musical *George M* ('68) the song was

performed by Joel Grey, who played Cohan, Harvey Evans, Loni Ackerman and Angela Martin. Like all the other Cohan song classics, "So Long, Mary" was performed in *Yankee Doodle Dandy* ('42). Irene Manning, playing the legendary Fay Templeton, performed both "Mary's a Grand Old Name" and "So Long, Mary" in the film.

The musical score is available at http://levysheetmu sic.mse.jhu.edu/browse.html and the sheet music cover and musical score at http://lcweb2.loc.gov/cocoon/ihas/ loc.natlib.ihas.100005157/ and at http://digital.library. ucla.edu/. A recording of this song by Ada Jones is available for downloading at www.archive.org/audio-details-db. php?collection=78rpm&collectionid=AdaJones_part1& from=BA.

This song was selected by *Variety* for its *Hit Parade of a Half-Century* for '05.

FORTY-FIVE MINUTES FROM BROADWAY

Victor Moore and the chorus introduced the title song from the musical. The song sings about New Rochelle, but Cohan got in trouble with the town's Chamber of Commerce and its citizens who didn't like being referred to as "rubes" and to the suggestion that they had "whiskers like hay." The first verse lyrics follow: *The West, so they say, Is home of the jay, / And Missouri's the state That can grind them. / This may all be, But just take it from me, / You don't have to go Out West to find them. / If you want to see The real jay delegation, / The place where the Real rubens dwell. / Just hop on a train At the Grand Central Station. / Get off when they shout 'New Rochelle.'*

The famous chorus continues its dubious praise of New Rochelle: *Only forty-five minutes from Broadway, / Think of the changes it brings; / For the short time it takes, / What a diff'rence it makes / In the ways of the people and things. / Oh! What a fine bunch of rubens, / Oh! what a jay atmosphere; / They have whiskers like hay, / And imagine Broadway / Only forty-five minutes from here.*

Joel Grey and Loni Ackerman performed the song in the Broadway musical *George M* ('68). It was also performed in Cohan's screen biography *Yankee Doodle Dandy*.

Billy Murray had a popular recording of the song in '06. Hear Billy Murray's '06 recording at http://www.ar chive.org/audio/audio-details-db.php?collectionid=broad way1906&collection=opensource_audio or http://www. edisonnj.org/menlopark/vintage/blackwax.asp. The sheet music cover and musical score are available at http:// levysheetmusic.mse.jhu.edu/browse.html and at http:// digital.library.ucla.edu/.

"Forty-Five Minutes from Broadway" was selected for *Variety's Hit Parade of a Half-Century* for '05.

Nobody
Words: *Alex Rogers; Music: Bert A. Williams*

"Nobody" became Bert Williams' signature song. He introduced it in vaudeville as the member of a team with George Walker. He performed the song is a slow mournful style that made people laugh. The song and Bert Williams became even more famous when he performed it in the *Ziegfeld Follies of 1910*. His appearance in the *Follies* was the first for an African American with whites in a major Broadway musical production.

The song is about a person who doesn't do anything for anybody ("nothing for nobody") because nobody does anything ("nobody does nothing") for him.

The verses are more spoken than sung: *When life seems full of clouds and rain / And my body is racked with pain, / Who soothes my achin' brain? Nobody! / When winder comes with snow and sleet / I'm so tired with cold feet / Who says, "Here's two bits, Bert, / Go and eat"? Nobody!*

Williams performs the chorus wonderfully. His stage personality, as Mr. Nobody, fits the lyrics perfectly: *I ain't don't nothin' to nobody. / I ain't never got nothin' from nobody no time / And 'til I get me somethin' from somebody sometime, / Well, I don't intend to do nothin' for nobody no time.*

Williams recorded "Nobody" for Columbia in mid-'06 and his recording became very popular. Williams' recording of the song was revived in '13. Arthur Collins' '05 version was also quite successful.

In a '18 article in *American Magazine* Williams said, "Before I got through with 'Nobody,' I could have wished that both the author of the words and the assembler of the tune had been strangled or drowned or talked to death. For seven whole years I had to sing it. Month after month I tried to drop it and sing something new, but I could get nothing to replace it, and the audiences seemed to want nothing else. Every comedian at some time in his life learns to curse the particular stunt of his that was most popular."

To hear Bert Williams sing "Nobody," go to this website: http://www.pbs.org/wnet/broadway/stars/williams_ b.html. The sheet music cover and musical score are available at http://levysheetmusic.mse.jhu.edu/browse.html (Williams is pictured again in black face).

The song was performed by Bob Hope in the movie musical *The Seven Little Foys* ('55).

This song was selected by *Variety* for its *Hit Parade of a Half-Century* for '05.

The Streets of New York, Every Day Is Ladies' Day with Me *and* Because You're You
Words: *Henry Blossom; Music: Victor Herbert*

Victor Herbert usually wrote operettas, but *The Red Mill* in '06 was more of a farce with music; it only had six songs and they weren't very operatic.

The plot of the show concerned the adventures of Kid Conner and Con Kidder, played by Dave Montgomery and Fred Stone, the same two clowns who had starred in *The Wizard of Oz* in '03. They portrayed two innocents abroad who were stranded in Katwyk-aan-Zee, Holland. As they tried to raise enough money to return home, they were involved in several misadventures.

THE STREETS OF NEW YORK
(OR IN OLD NEW YORK)

The waltz "The Streets of New York," also known as "In Old New York," was introduced by Montgomery and Stone as they reminisce about home.

The lyrics of the song praise the women of New York and claim "you cannot see in gay Paree, in London, or in Cork! The queens you'll meet on any street in old New York." *In dear old New York it's remarkable very! / The name on the lamp-post is unnecessary! / You merely have to see the girls / To know what street you're on! / Fifth Avenue beauties and dear old Broadway girls! / The tailor made shoppers the Avenue A girls, / They're strictly all right but they're different quite / In the diff'rent parts of town. / In Old New*

York! In old New York! | The peach crop's always fine! | They're sweet and fair and on the square! | The maids of Manhattan for mine! | You cannot see in gay Paree, | In London or in Cork! | The queens you'll meet on any street | In old New York!

Billy Murray helped popularize this song with a popular recording in '07.

The musical score is available at http://levysheetmusic. mse.jhu.edu/browse.html and the sheet music cover and musical score are available at http://scriptorium.lib. duke.edu/dynaweb/sheetmusic/1900-1909/@Generic __BookTextView/31151. See the sheet music cover and hear a midi musical version at http://www.perfessorbill. com/index2.htm.

EVERY DAY IS LADIES' DAY WITH ME

"Every Day Is Ladies' Day with Me" was introduced by Neal McCay who played the rather baudy governor of Zeeland. The governor explains that he is in great debt because he "afforded anything that I could get." He also says he's never been married, even though he admits "it's the proper thing to do you'll all agree." Neither did he really care about the affairs of state or business. As for women, he readily confesses his roving eye could never "find any fun in wasting all my time on one, so ev'ry day is ladies' day with me."

Variety selected this song for its *Hit Parade of a Half-Century* for '06.

The sheet music cover and musical score are available at http://levysheetmusic.mse.jhu.edu/browse.html.

BECAUSE YOU'RE YOU

Neal McCay and Allene Crater introduced "Because You're You" in *The Red Mill*. A very successful duet recording by Harry MacDonough and Elise Stevenson helped popularize the song beyond the theater in '07.

The song has rather confusing lyrics. The words of the song are: *Not that I am fair, dear, | Not that I am true. | Not my golden hair, dear, | Not my eyes of blue. | When we ask the reason | Words are all too few! | So I know I love you, dear. | Because you're you.*

The confusion is concerned with who is unfair, untrue, has golden hair and eyes of blue? The singer? The lover? Regardless, we understand that the loved one is loved just because they are themselves.

The sheet music cover and musical score are available at http://levysheetmusic.mse.jhu.edu/browse.html.

Wait 'Till the Sun Shines, Nellie

Words: Andrew B. Sterling; Music: Harry Von Tilzer

"Wait 'Till the Sun Shines, Nellie" is yet another example of the genesis of a song being an over heard remark. Von Tilzer seems to make a habit of eavesdropping on other people's conversations to get song ideas.

One version of the story of the song's birth is that Von Tilzer was standing outside a theater waiting for a sudden rain shower to subside, when he overheard someone near him say "wait till the sun shines." Another version says that Von Tilzer and Sterling were sitting in a hotel lobby when they overheard a young groom consoling his new bride, "wait till the sun shines, Nellie." And yet another claims that a newspaper report of a close friend comforting a down-and-out family with the remark, "the sun will shine after the storm."

Perhaps the verse of the song can shed some light on its origin: *On a Sunday morn sat a maid forlorn | with her sweetheart by her side | Thro' the window pane she looked at the rain | 'We must stay home, Joe,' she cried | 'There's a picnic too at the old Point View. | It's a shame it rained today.' | Then the boy drew near, kissed away each tear, | And she heard him softly say...*

Then follows the famous chorus: *Wait 'till the sun shines, Nellie, | And the gray skies turn to blue. | You know I love you Nellie, | 'Deed I do. | We'll face the years together, | Sweethearts you and I. | So won't you wait till the sun shines Nellie, | Bye and bye.*

Byron Harlan and Harry Tally helped popularize the song in '06 with very successful recordings. Prince's Orchestra also had a popular version on the market.

Variety named "Wait 'Till the Sun Shines, Nellie" as a *Golden 100 Tin Pan Alley Song* and for its *Hit Parade of a Half-Century* for '05.

Mary Martin performed "Wait 'Till the Sun Shines, Nellie" in the '41 movie musical *Birth of the Blues*. The song was also used in *Rhythm Parade* ('42), in *Bowery to Broadway* ('44) and in *In the Good Old Summertime* ('49).

The sheet music cover and musical score are available at http://levysheetmusic.mse.jhu.edu/browse.html. See the sheet music cover and listen to a midi musical version at http://parlorsongs.com/issues/2002-1/thismonth/featureb. asp. Read the lyrics and hear a midi musical version at http://www.geocities.com/dferg5493/nellie.htm.

Waltz Me Around Again, Willie

Words: Will D. Cobb; Music: Ren Shields

Blanche Ring introduced this song in the musical *Miss Dolly Dollars*. It was popularized in vaudeville by Della Fox.

Billy Murray and the Haydn Quartet helped popularized it with a successful recording in '06.

The first verse of the song introduces us to Willie Fitzgibbons, who stood on his feet all day selling ribbons. Willie "grew very spoony on Madelaine Mooney, who'd rather be dancing than eat." Every evening Madelaine would drag Willie to the dance hall, and even though he was tired, she'd say: *Waltz me around again, Willie, | Around, around, around! | The music is dreamy, | It's peaches and creamy, | O don't let my feet touch the ground! | I feel like a ship on an ocean of joy, | I just want to holler out loud, 'Ship Ahoy!' | Waltz me around again, Willie, | Around, around, around!*

Variety selected this song for its *Hit Parade of a Half-Century* for '06.

The sheet music cover and musical score are available at both http://levysheetmusic.mse.jhu.edu/browse.html and at http://lcweb2.loc.gov/cocoon/ihas/loc.natlib.ihas. 100008866/ or see the sheet music cover and read the complete lyrics at http://holyjoe.org/poetry/cobb.htm.

Will You Love Me in December (as You Do in May)?

Words: James J. Walker; Music: Ernest R. Ball

Composer Ernest R. Ball had a great year in '06. His "Love Me and the World Is Mine" and "Will You Love Me in December as You Do in May?" were both extremely popular songs of the year. This was just the beginning for Ball, who had a very successful songwriting career.

Janet Allen, a member of the vaudeville team of Allen and McShane, introduced "Will You Love Me in December as You Do in May?" The song was quickly recorded by the Haydn Quartet and by Albert Campbell and the song's fame began to spread. It reportedly sold several hundred thousand copies of sheet music and earned each of the writers more than $10,000 in royalties, quite a large sum for the time.

"Will You Love Me in December as You Do in May?" was played at the wedding of lyricist James J. Walker and Janet Allen, the girl who introduced the song, in '12. This same James Walker became Mayor of New York City in '26 and the song was continually associated with him and played to honor him everywhere he went.

The first verse lyrics contend that "in the summer of life ... you say you love but me." However, the singer can't help but wonder if the sweetheart will love them when they are old and gray as much as when they were young.

The chorus lyrics ask the title question and continue with other queries: *Will you love me in December as you do in May? / Will you love me in the good old-fashioned way? / When my hair has all turned gray, / Will you kiss me then and say, / That you love me in December as you do in May?*

The sheet music cover and musical score are available at http://levysheetmusic.mse.jhu.edu/browse.html and at http://digital.library.ucla.edu/. See the sheet music cover and read the entire lyrics and hear a midi musical version at http://www.halcyondaysmusic.com/february/february 2004.htm.

This sentimental ballad was heard in the '54 screen biography of Eddie Cantor (*The Eddie Cantor Story*). It also appeared in the '57 Bob Hope film *Beau James*, in which Hope portrayed New York City's colorful mayor, the lyricist Jimmy Walker.

This song was selected by *Variety* for its *Hit Parade of a Half-Century* for '05.

You're a Grand Old Flag

Words & Music: George M. Cohan

"You're a Grand Old Flag" was introduced by George Cohan in his musical *George Washington, Jr.* in '06. Cohan had met with a Civil War veteran who told Cohan that he had fought to save this tattered flag, which he called "a grand old rag." George then wrote this salute to the stars and stripes and it was introduced as "The Grand Old Rag." Billy Murray had recorded the song for Victor six days before the show opened on Broadway and cut it for other record companies shortly afterwards. Nearly all of his versions have the original words: "You're a grand old rag, you're a high-flying flag..." Soon after the show opened, Cohan was besieged with criticism from several patriotic societies and the press that referring to the American flag as a "rag" was not suitable. Actually, Cohan was one of the most patriotic of American citizens and he was stung by the criticism. He agreed to revise the chorus, with some printed versions of the song merely changing "rag" to "flag." Some other versions have the words, "You're a grand old flag tho' you're torn to a rag..." (see chorus lyrics below).

The lyrics of the rapid-fire first verse follow, using the word "flag" instead of "rag": *There's a feeling comes a stealing and it sets my brain a reeling / When I'm listening to the music of a military band. / Any tune like 'Yankee Doodle' simply sets me off my noodle, / It's that patriotic something that*

no one can understand. / 'Way down South in the land of cotton,' melody untiring, ain't that inspiring! / Hurrah! Hurrah! We'll join the jubilee, and that's going some for the Yankees, by gum! / Red, white and blue, I am for you. Honest, you're a grand old flag.

As usual the chorus lyrics are most famous, but the more common first line today is "You're a grand old flag, you're a high flying flag": *You're a grand old flag, though you're torn to a rag, / And forever in peace may you wave. / You're the emblem of the land I love, / The home of the free and the brave. / Every heart beats true under red, white and blue. / Where there's never a boast or brag; / 'But should auld acquaintance be forgot,' / Keep your eye on the grand old flag.*

Notice the quote of the phrase and melody from "Auld Lang Syne" in the next to last line.

Not only was Billy Murray's recording of the song very popular, but also Arthur Pryor's Band's version. Their versions used the "You're a Grand Old Flag" title. Prince's Orchestra revived the song successfully in '17.

Cohan sang "You're a Grand Old Flag" in his first talking picture, *The Phantom President* ('32). James Cagney performed it in Cohan's screen biography *Yankee Doodle Dandy* ('42).

See this Library of Congress website to see the sheet music cover and the sheet music score: http://lcweb2.loc. gov/cocoon/ihas/loc.natlib.ihas.100010512/ or at http:// digital.library.ucla.edu/apam/. Or at this Library of Congress site, listen to Billy Murray's '06 recording of this song: http://lcweb2.loc.gov/cocoon/ihas/loc.natlib.ihas. 100010366/. The song is titled "You're a Grand Old Flag" in this publication. The following one is titled "You're a Grand Old Rag:" http://lcweb2.loc.gov/cocoon/ihas/loc. natlib.ihas.100010513/.

Variety chose "You're a Grand Old Flag" for its *Hit Parade of a Half-Century* for '06.

Another song from the score of *George Washington, Jr.*, "You Can Have Broadway," was popularized by Billy Murray in a successful '07 recordings.

1907

Auld Lang Syne

Words: adapted by Robert Burns; Music: Traditional Scottish

Along with "Happy Birthday" and "For He's a Jolly Good Fellow," "Auld Lang Syne" may be one of the most well known and most often sung or performed songs in American history.

The traditional Scottish melody is built on a pentatonic scale (a five note scale; like the five black keys of the piano). The melody's origin goes far back into Scottish history.

During the reign of King Charles I from 1625 until 1649, "auld lang syne" was a commonly used expression. After the mid–1600s, several poems used the expression, sometimes coupled with the phrase "should auld acquaintance be forgot." Some of these poems were set to folk melodies and at least one of them was published during the latter part of the 17th century. One surviving version began, "Should old acquaintance be forgot and never thocht upon" and concluded "on old long syne." This appears to be what eventually developed into the first verse of the song we know today.

In the late 1790s, the Scotch poet Robert Burns wrote two additional verses and George Thomson set the verses to an old Scottish tune that had been used as the melody for several texts, including "I Fee'd a Lad at Michaelmas," "The Miller's Wedding" and "The Miller's Daughter." This coupling of verses and tune is the "Auld Lang Syne" as we know it today.

During the immigrations from the British Isles of the late 1790s, "Auld Lang Syne" came to the U.S. and quickly became a part of America's music. The lyrics are familiar to most people: *Should auld acquaintance be forgot, and never brought to mind? / Should auld acquaintance be forgot and days of Auld Lang Syne? / For Auld Lang Syne, my dear, for Auld Lang Syne, / We'll tak' a cup o' kindness yet, for Auld Lang Syne.*

It has been the song of New Year's Eve for so long, no one can remember when it wasn't associated with the event. Guy Lombardo and his Royal Canadians adopted it as their theme song and played it for New Year's Eve celebrations on radio and television for thirty years or more beginning in the late '20s or early '30s.

In '07, Frank Stanley recorded and popularized the song. The Peerless Quartet revived it with a '21 recording. The song became one of the most recorded of the pre-rock era. Don Redman and his orchestra's recording of "Auld Lang Syne" is available at http://www.redhotjazz.com/redmano.html.

Campmeetin' Time

Words: Harry Williams; Music: Egbert Van Alstyne

Arthur Collins and Byron Harlan helped popularize this coon song with a very popular recording in '07. The sheet music cover spells the title "Campmeetin' Time, but the first inside sheet spells it "Camp Meetin' Time." The chorus lyrics appear to go with the cover spelling.

It seems there is great excitement in the African American community because flags and banners are "wavin' in the breeze, tents a-rockin,' coons a-flockin' ... fightin' to get in." It isn't a circus that causing all the excitement, it's a "campmeetin' down in southern Alabam." The chorus lyrics follow: *Campmeetin' Time, Campmeetin' Time, / Hear the parson say, wash dem sins away, / One only time in any southern clime, / That a chicken or a goose / Can run around loose, is Campmeetin' Time.*

The sheet music cover and musical score are available at http://levysheetmusic.mse.jhu.edu/browse.html.

For hundreds of years, campmeetings have been held where Christians come together to worship and socialize. The groups began meeting under brush arbors, then often in open-sided tabernacles, or churches. They came many times from miles away, so they usually camped out, first in tents or lean-tos, and later in rather primitive cabins. These campmeetings usually lasted a week or more. Campmeetings are still held today, especially in the south.

Harrigan *and* When We Are M-a-double-r-i-e-d

Words & Music: George M. Cohan

Edward "Ned" Harrigan was a famous performer in the Harrigan and (Tony) Hart partnership. Harrigan and Hart presented a series of farces with music back in the early 1890s. Many of these shows were about the Mulligan Guards, which dealt with Irish, German, Italian and Jewish immigrants. Their humor and their songs were topical, but would probably be considered too caustically racial today.

Harrigan

"Harrigan," the song, was George M. Cohan's tribute to Ed Harrigan. James C. Marlowe introduced the song in *Fifty Miles from Boston.* The song opens by spelling the name: "H-A-double R-I-G-A-N spells Harrigan." This Irishman is extremely proud of all his Irish blood. He dares anybody to "say a word agin' me" and claims proudly that no shame has ever been connected with his name.

The song was recorded by Billy Murray and Edward Meeker in '07, but was premiered in the musical in '08.

The sheet music cover and musical score are available at both http://levysheetmusic.mse.jhu.edu/browse.html and at http://lcweb2.loc.gov/cocoon/ihas/loc.natlib.ihas.100005148/ or see the sheet music cover and hear a midi musical version at http://www.perfessorbill.com/index2.htm.

Joel Grey performed the song in the '68 Broadway musical *George M.* James Cagney sang it in the Cohan's screen biography *Yankee Doodle Dandy* ('42).

When We Are M-a-double-r-i-e-d

Ada Jones and Billy Murray recorded a very popular duet version of "When We Are M-a-double-r-i-e-d," another example of a spelling song, by Cohan from *Fifty-Miles from Boston.*

The musical score indicates the song is "Tempo di Polka." Most of the song is exchanges between the males and females with the girls beginning "What would you say if I asked you to wait another year?" The guys beg "Oh! Don't dear." Later in the verse to lead into the chorus the girls sing, "Love's but a spell so poets tell." To which the boys reply, "Spell a little love for me," which leads directly into the chorus, which follows (it begins with both girls and boys singing together): *When we are M-A-double-R-I-E-D / H-A-double-P-Y we'll be; / (boys) I'm going to B-U-Y you'll see, a nice little H-O-U-S-E. / (girls) / We'll have a B-A-B-Y boy (boys) and a G-I-R-L too. / When I'm M-a-double-R-I-E-D to Y-O-U.*

A recording of this song by Ada Jones and Billy Murray is available for downloading at www.archive.org/audio. The musical score is available at http://levysheetmusic.mse.jhu.edu/browse.html.

He's a Cousin of Mine

Words: Cecil Mack; Music: Chris Smith & Silvio Hein

Bert Williams was primarily responsible for popularizing "He's a Cousin of Mine" with a very popular recording of the song in '07, but Bob Roberts also had a popular recording as well.

Marie Cahill had introduced the song in the musical *Marrying Mary.*

We find out in the song's verse that a scandal has hit the neighborhood because Julie Brown's "long lost cousin, Jeremiah" had come to town. Julie's "feller" caught them spooning, but Julie claimed it was perfectly appropriate to hug and kiss her cousin. Julie tries to explain further in the chorus lyrics which follow: *Why he's a cousin of mine, just a cousin of mine, / You're li'ble for to see him here any old time,*

I Jes' like a bee all the time a buzzin' | 'Tain't no harm for to hug and kiss your cousin. | I haven't see Jerry in the last ten years, | You know that's a mighty long time. | His mother's sister's angel child, | He's a cousin of mine.

The sheet music cover and musical score are available at http://levysheetmusic.mse.jhu.edu/browse.html.

I Just Can't Make My Eyes Behave *and* It's Delightful to Be Married
Words & Music: Various

I Just Can't Make My Eyes Behave

Anna Held interpolated "I Just Can't Make My Eyes Behave" in the musical *A Parisian Model* in '06. This coquettish song became one of her greatest successes and she and the song became inextricably associated. The sheet music cover proclaims this number as "Anna Held's Sensational Eye Song." Will D. Cobb wrote the words, while Gus Edwards furnished the music.

Anna Held had been born in Warsaw, Poland, but grew up in France. She became famous as a French entertainer in London music halls, then performed in French and German cabarets. Famous producer Florenz Ziegfeld brought her to New York City, married her, starred her in several Broadway productions and then divorced her. She was famous for her eyes. This song was an excellent one to capitalize on Miss Held's charms, and particularly her eyes.

The provocative chorus lyrics follow: *For I just can't make my eyes behave | Two bad brown eyes I am their slave, | My lips may say run away from me | But my eyes say come and play with me, | And you won't blame poor little me, | I'm sure, 'Cuz I just can't make my eyes behave.*

Ada Jones had a particularly popular recording of "I Just Can't Make My Eyes Behave" in '07. A recording of this song by Ada Jones is available for downloading at www.archive.org/audio-details-db.php?collection=78rpm&collectionid=AdaJones_part1&from=BA

The song was used in the Judy Garland and Mickey Rooney movie musical *Strike Up the Band* in '40.

The sheet music cover and musical score are available at http://levysheetmusic.mse.jhu.edu/browse.html. See the sheet music cover and hear a midi musical version at http://parlorsongs.com/issues/2004-1/thismonth/feature.asp.

It's Delightful to Be Married

Anna Held, who wrote new English lyrics, introduced this French song, originally "La petite Tonkinoise," in *The Parisian Model*. Vincent Scotto had written the music. She performed the song while holding a hand mirror in the faces of the men in the audience.

The coquettish Miss Held had been brought to the U.S. from Europe by producer extraordinaire Florenz Ziegfeld, they lived together and eventually married. He starred her in many of his Broadway productions. She had been born in Poland, was raised in France, began her performing career in London music halls, and became a big star in Paris and Berlin prior to coming to America.

The Parisian Model was one of Miss Held's biggest stage triumphs. It ran for a full season on Broadway and toured for several years. While this musical would seem harmless by modern standards, it was condemned as scandalous and obscene when it premiered. Of course, the condemnations only perked the public's interest, so it played to full houses.

This song became one of Miss Held's best-remembered numbers. It's interesting to note that the lyrics sing about a subject that was not, by all reports, important to Anna Held. Married life and children were not a priority for her. One of the noteworthy things in the lyrics is the stammered "to be" just prior to the word "married" in the second phrase. *It's delightful to be married. | To be, to be, to be, to be, to be married. | There is nothing half so jolly as | A jolly married life. | And I love to play with baby, | With my pretty little, darling little baby. | You are papa, I am mama, | What a jolly family!*

Variety selected this song for its *Hit Parade of a Half-Century* for '07.

The song was used in the movie musical *The Great Ziegfeld* ('36).

The sheet music cover credits the music to Scotto and Christine, however inside the musical score only credits Vincent Scotto. The sheet music cover and musical score are available at http://lcweb2.loc.gov/cocoon/ihas/loc.natlib.ihas.100007975/.

I Love a Lassie (My Scots Bluebell)
Words: Harry Lauder & George Grafton; Music: Harry Lauder

Harry Lauder was a famous Scottish entertainer. He was tremendously popular as a music hall and vaudeville performer. Over his forty years of touring the world, he made over twenty U.S. appearances. Harry also entertained the troops in France during World War I. After the war, King George V knighted him.

This Harry Lauder song was reportedly inspired by his love for his wife Nancy, but he changed the name in the song to Mary.

The wonderful Scottish-flavored lyrics to the verse and chorus follow: *I love a lassie, a bonnie Hielan' lassie, | If you saw her you would fancy her as well: | I met her in September, popped the question in November, | So I'll soon be havin' her a' to masel.' | Her faither has consented, so I'm feelin' quite contented, | 'Cause I've been and sealed the bargain wi' a kiss. | I sit and weary weary, when I think aboot ma deary, | An' you'll always hear me singing this... | I love a lassie, a bonnie bonnie lassie, | She's as pure as a lily in the dell, | She's sweet as the heather, | the bonnie bloomin' heather, | Mary, my Scots bluebell.*

Sir Harry Lauder's recording of "I Love a Lassie (My Scots Bluebell)" was very popular in '07. It was his first recording released in the U.S. There was also a short film of Lauder singing his song released in '07.

Variety selected this song for its *Hit Parade of a Half-Century* for '06.

Read more about Sir Harry Lauder, The World's Most Beloved Musical Humorist at http://www.parlorsongs.com/issues/2004-12/thismonth/feature.asp.

Let's Take an Old-Fashioned Walk

There have been several songs with this title. Irving Berlin wrote a song for *Miss Liberty* in '49, plus Fred Wise, Buddy Kaye and Sidney Lippman had written one in '48, but, of course, neither is this '07 song. The writers of this song cannot be found.

Ada Jones and Billy Murray recorded a very successful version of "Let's Take an Old-Fashioned Walk" in '07. The song was, according to Joel Whitburn's *A Century of Pop Music*, one of the top hits of the year.

Maple Leaf Rag

Music: Scott Joplin

Exactly where or how rag or ragtime developed is unknown. All we know for sure is that it developed among the African Americans. The music had been around for years before rags surfaced into public awareness. One of the first hints of the music in public was piano players pounding out rags at the Chicago World's Fair of 1893.

Scholars aren't even sure why this type of music is called "ragtime" (by the way, the term was two words until around the late 1890s). Scott Joplin speculated that the name came from the music's "ragged movement," but he was only trying to explain a style that had been around quite a few years before any of his rags were published.

We know that ragtime is a heavily syncopated music and started, at least, as piano music. The pianist's left hand kept the steady, march-like rhythm with an "oom-pah" effect, while the right hand played the melody in a much more syncopated rhythm. Ragtime was usually written for the piano but was later transcribed for ensembles, especially military bands and sometimes for banjo players.

The music's heyday spanned Scott Joplin's composing career from the late 1890s until his death in '17.

After his death, Joplin's rags were virtually forgotten until a renewed interest in ragtime during the '40s. Then they lay almost dormant again until ragtime was used on the soundtrack of the '73 movie The Sting. Then the listening public rediscovered his music and other rags.

Joplin's "Maple Leaf Rag" is the best known of his compositions. No piano version of the song was recorded during Joplin's lifetime primarily because the piano didn't record well on the primitive equipment of the era. When recording companies wanted to record ragtime they recorded bands, such as Sousa's and banjoists such as Vess Ossman. As one indication of the song's popularity, "Maple Leaf Rag" was recorded eight times between 1899 and '17. Vess Ossman and the U.S. Marine Corps Band recorded the two most popular versions of the song in '07. "Maple Leaf Rag" became one of the most recorded songs of the pre-rock era.

Joplin is generally considered the greatest, or at least as one of the greatest, composers of ragtime music, but he could be viewed as a one-hit wonder. None of his other compositions approached the popularity of "Maple Leaf Rag."

The sheet music cover and musical score of this song are available at http://levysheetmusic.mse.jhu.edu/browse.html. See the sheet music cover and hear a midi musical version at http://www.perfessorbill.com/index2.htm.

The Merry Widow Waltz (I Love You So)

Words: Adrian Ross; Music: Franz Lehar

The Merry Widow and other Viennese operettas had a great influence on Broadway productions in the early 20th century. The Viennese influence declined only as anti–German sentiments were stirred during the World War I years.

One of the most celebrated and successful shows of its kind ever written, The Merry Widow opened on Broadway in '07. The success of The Merry Widow revived an interest in European operetta in general, but also had a major influence on fashion, with the introduction of Merry Widow hats, gowns, corsets and cigarettes.

The story was set in Paris and concerned the efforts of the ambassador of the imaginary kingdom of Marsovia to convince Prince Danilo to marry the wealthy widow Sonya so that she would contribute money to the country's depleted treasury. Danilo tries to resist her charms because he doesn't want to be accused of being a fortune hunter. At a party at the widow's Paris home, she arouses Danilo's jealousy, convinces him that she will be penniless if she remarries and gets him to propose. Under the terms of the will, her inheritance from her late husband goes to her new husband.

The extremely popular "Merry Widow Waltz" was recorded and primarily popularized in '07 by the Victor Orchestra, the record label's house orchestra.

The waltz became so popular that it was heard everywhere, so it spawned the '08 song "I'm Looking for the Man That Wrote 'The Merry Widow Waltz.'" The author wants to do away with the person responsible for inflicting "The Merry Widow Waltz" on the public.

Although this famous waltz was sung with lyrics, it is by far more well known today as an instrumental.

Variety selected "The Merry Widow Waltz" for its Hit Parade of a Half-Century for '07.

See the sheet music cover and music score at http://lcweb2.loc.gov/cocoon/ihas/loc.natlib.ihas.100002082/. The sheet music cover and musical score are available at http://levysheetmusic.mse.jhu.edu/browse.html (listed as both "For I Love You So" and "I Love You So."). Paul Whiteman and his orchestra's recording of "The Merry Widow Waltz" is available at http://www.redhotjazz.com/pwo.html.

Other familiar songs from The Merry Widow include "Maxim's" and "Vilia." Paul Whiteman and his orchestra's recording of "Vilia" is available at http://www.redhotjazz.com/pwo.html. The sheet music cover and musical score are available at http://levysheetmusic.mse.jhu.edu/browse.html (listed as "Vilja-Lied").

A silent version of the operetta had been filmed in '25, but why film a silent movie of a musical production? In '34, Hollywood filmed a version of the operetta with Maurice Chevalier and Jeanette MacDonald. Lorenz Hart supplied new lyrics for "The Merry Widow Waltz" and several others songs from the operetta. A Technicolor version was filmed in '52 starring Lana Turner and Fernando Lamas.

My Gal Sal

Words & Music: Paul Dresser

Since the spelling of their last name is different, not very many people realize that Paul Dresser, the writer of many popular songs of the era, is the brother of the famous novelist Theodore Dreiser. Paul substituted an "s" for the "i" to become Dresser.

Paul, at only forty-eight years old, was at the end of his illustrous career when he wrote "My Gal Sal," which is also sometimes known as "They Call Her Frivolous Sal." Paul died in '06 and did not get to enjoy the satisfaction of one final hit after several years of hard times. Paul's wife, Louise, introduced this sentimental ballad in vaudeville. "My Gal Sal" sold millions of copies of sheet music and Byron Harlan's recording of the song was very successful, one of the top ten hits of the decade.

The song's lyrics indicate that the singer is losing his girl friend to death. She was his best pal, "an all 'round good fellow." He concludes that she may not have been the most beautiful girl, in fact she was frivolous, peculiar and "a wild sort of devil," but she shared his "troubles, sorrows and cares." He confesses his love for her and she promises she will meet him "on the other side."

The Columbia Steller Quartet revived the song successfully with a '21 recording. The Charleston Chasers' recording of "My Gal Sal" is available at http://www.red hotjazz.com/charleston.html.

The song was included in the first talking picture, *The Jazz Singer*, in '27. Paul Dresser's '42 screen biography was titled *My Gal Sal*.

This song was selected by *Variety* for its *Hit Parade of a Half-Century* for '05.

Read the lyrics and hear a midi musical version at http://www.geocities.com/dferg5493/mygalsal.htm.

Nobody's Little Girl

Words: Jack Drislane; Music: Theodore F. Morse

Byron G. Harlan helped popularize "Nobody's Little Girl" in '07 with a very popular recording.

According to the lyrics of this sentimental ballad, a little girl is standing on the corner "with a letter in her hands." She asks a passing postman to take the letter to her Mother. The postman asks her name. Her tearful reply is the chorus, which follows: *They say I'm nobody's baby, You'll find my Mama, sir, maybe, / If someone cared for me only, I wouldn't be sad and lonely, / Papa and Mamma have parted, I'm all alone, broken hearted / I guess that's why they all call me, Nobody's little girl.*

The sheet music cover and musical score are available at http://levysheetmusic.mse.jhu.edu/browse.html.

Oh, Promise Me

Words: Clement Scott; Music: Reginald DeKoven

"Oh, Promise Me" was written in 1889 and introduced by Jessie Bartlett Davis in the musical *Robin Hood* in 1890. The song was added after the show's first performance in Chicago in 1890. The temperamental Ms. Davis, who played Alan-a-Dale, demanded another song that would compliment her beautiful alto voice (it was not unusual for women to play men's parts, especially if they were young men; the practice goes back to Mozart's day and beyond). Reginald DeKoven had written "Oh Promise Me" earlier and it had been published, but needing a song quickly and not wanting to write a new one immediately, he offered the ballad to Ms. Davis. It was performed as a marriage proposal in the second performance.

"Oh, Promise Me" became the hit song of the show and sold over a million copies of sheet music. For many years, "Oh, Promise Me" and Edward Teschemacher and Guy d'Hardelot's "Because" (see '02) were the most common vocal solos performed at weddings in America.

The song was recorded by many singers. The most popular recorded versions include George J. Gaskin's 1893 recording, Henry Burr's '05 recording, Corrine Morgan's '07 recording and Alan Turner's '13 recording. Hear Harry MacDonough's recording of this song at http://www.archive.org/audio/audio-details-b.php?collectionid=oh prom1900&collection=opensource_audio.

The non-descript sheet music cover and musical score of "Oh, Promise Me!" are available at http://levysheetmu sic.mse.jhu.edu/browse.html.

Red Wing (An Indian Fable)

Words: Thurland Chattaway; Music: Kerry Mills

The sheet music covers of "Red Wing" are beautiful covers, but they depict a Native American woman in full makeup, eye shadow, rouge, and lipstick. That is not a very realistic rendering. That may have been how most Americans of the early 20th century thought of Indian maidens.

The music of the song is popular music not Native American, but, after all, this is a popular song written to make money. A truly Native American melody might not have been as successful.

The song is subtitled "An Indian Fable" and the lyrics of the verse relate a tale about a shy little Indian maid who lived on the prairie. She sang a love song to a bold warrior as he rode off to battle. The chorus continues: *Now, the moon shines tonight on pretty Red Wing, / The breeze is sighing, the night bird's crying, / For afar 'neath his star her brave is sleeping / While Red Wing's weeping, her heart away.*

Frank Stanley and Henry Burr had a popular duet recording of the song in '07. The song was revived by Sam Donohue with a popular recording in '47.

The sheet music cover and musical score are available at http://levysheetmusic.mse.jhu.edu/browse.html and at http://scriptorium.lib.duke.edu/dynaweb/sheetmusic/. See the absolutely gorgeous sheet music cover, the lyrics and a midi musical version at http://parlorsongs.com/issues/2000-4/2000-4.asp.

Variety selected "Red Wing" for its *Hit Parade of a Half-Century* for '07.

School Days (When We Were a Couple of Kids)

Words: Will D. Cobb; Music: Gus Edwards

Gus Edwards is famous for his company of child stars that toured the vaudeville circuit for many years. Among the stage and screen stars who started in Edwards' company of children were George Jessel, Eddie Cantor, Groucho Marx, Lila Lee and Georgie Price.

"School Days" was introduced by Gus Edwards and his company, as it was called. The song sold in excess of three million copies of sheet music.

We can learn some things about the schools of the era by looking at the lyrics. The primary subjects that were taught were "readin' and 'ritin' and 'rithmetic." Those subjects were "taught to the tune of a hick'ry stick," which meant the teacher carried a stick around and would whack the knuckles of students who were not doing their school work in a good and timely manner. The school work was written on a slate with chalk. The teacher periodically checked each student's work; they erased their slate and began a new lesson. A popular fabric for girls' dresses was calico and the boys usually went barefooted.

Byron Harlan and Albert Campbell both had popular recordings of the song in '07 and '08 respectively.

The sheet music cover and musical score are available at http://levysheetmusic.mse.jhu.edu/browse.html and at http://lcweb2.loc.gov/cocoon/ihas/loc.natlib.ihas.10000 5129/. See the sheet music cover and listen to a midi musical version at http://parlorsongs.com/issues/2002-1/this month/featureb.asp.

"School Days" was used in the '39 movie musical *The Star Maker*, which was based on Gus Edwards' career as a maker of stars. Then it was performed by Gale Storm and Phil Regan in the '45 movie musical *Sunbonnet Sue*.

Variety chose "School Days" for its *Hit Parade of a Half-Century* for '07.

Vesti la giubba

Words & Music: Ruggero Leoncavallo

In Leoncavallo's opera *Pagliacci*, a troupe of players is touring the small villages in Calabria. Canio, the principal actor and clown of the troupe, is unaware that his wife, Nedda, has a secret lover in the village. After Canio catches the lovers together and they escape unharmed, he must dress in his harlequin costume and put on his clown makeup for the evening's performance. As he prepares to perform in the comedy that evening he sings of his great heartbreak. The scene is one of the most poignant in all of opera and the tenor aria he sings has become world famous.

One of the world's most famous tenors, Enrico Caruso, had come to America from his native Italy in '03 and had won immediate fame. Even though he had a powerful operatic voice, he was a popular recording star. He popularized "Vesti la giubba" in '04 and again, with even greater popularity, in '07. Hear Caruso sing "Vesti la giubba" in his '07 recording at http://www.geopaix.com/caruso/.

Also see "Laugh, Clown, Laugh" in 1928. A film and the song are loosely based on *Pagliacci*.

Won't You Come Over to My House?

Words: Harry H. Williams; Music: Egbert Van Alstyne

This *Variety Hit Parade of a Half-Century* song was popularized in '07 recordings by both Byron Harlan and Henry Burr.

There are a couple of verses to this sentimental ballad, but the first verse sets the scene. It is June, the bees are humming, and the perfume of roses fills the air. The singer sees "a baby" seated all alone and crying. She pleads with a passer by to come to her house to play with her. *Won't you come over to my house, / Won't you come over and play, / I've lots of playthings, a dolly or two / We live in the house 'cross the way, / I'll give you candy and sweet things, / I'll put your hair in a curl, / Won't you come over to my house, / And play that you're my little girl.*

The sheet music cover and musical score are available at http://levysheetmusic.mse.jhu.edu/browse.html and at http://scriptorium.lib.duke.edu/dynaweb/sheetmusic/.

1908

Any Old Port in a Storm

Words: Arthur J. Lamb; Music: Kerry Mills

Frank Stanley popularized "Any Old Port in a Storm" with a successful recording in '08.

The verses of the song are in 6/8 meter, while the chorus changes to 12/8. This song of the sea is obviously meant for a bass to sing; the last ending of the chorus concludes on a low D.

Any old port in a storm lads! Whatever that port may be, / And thanks be given our Father in Heav'n / Who watches o'er you and me, / Tho we're far, far away from the land we seek / Where the heart of true love beats warm; / For the shelter there, is a haven fair; / Any old port in a storm, Any old port in a storm.

Variety selected this song for its *Hit Parade of a Half-Century* for '08.

"Any Old Port in a Storm" can be heard in the '43 movie musical *Tahiti Honey*.

The musical score is available at http://levysheetmusic.mse.jhu.edu/browse.html.

Are You Sincere?

Words: Alfred Bryan; Music: Albert Gumble

Alfred Bryan's lyrics tell about a young man and maiden walking together. He tells her that he likes her better every day, in every way, and asks if he could call her "dear."

She questions him: *Are you sincere? If you're sincere, / I'll let you call me your Dearie, / Say what you mean, mean what you say, / And you can always be near me, / If I give my heart to you, / I'll have none and you'll have two, / If you're sincere, call me your Dear, / Answer me: Are you sincere?*

In the next verse, we learn that the girl is ready to marry. She says it's leap year so "what's the use, to tarry, marry, Harry." She tells him that if he's "too bashful" just say "yes" and she'll "do the rest," but only once you answer her question: "Are you sincere?"

Elise Stevenson's recording of this waltz was very popular in '08. Byron Harlan also had a popular recording of the song on the market.

The sheet music cover and musical score are available at http://levysheetmusic.mse.jhu.edu/browse.html. See the sheet music cover, read the complete lyrics and hear a midi musical version at http://www.halcyondaysmusic.com/march/march2004.htm or see the sheet music and hear a midi musical version at http://parlorsongs.com/issues/2005-3/thismonth/feature.asp.

A '58 hit song had the same title, but the songs are not at all the same, of course.

As Long as the World Rolls On

Words: George Graff, Jr.; Music: Ernest R. Ball

According to Julius Mattfeld in *Variety Music Cavalcade*, Ernest R. Ball and George Graff, Jr. wrote "As Long as the World Rolls On" in '07. And according to Joel Whitburn's *A Century of Pop Music*, Alan Turner's recording of the song was very popular in '08. Reinald Werrenrath, Henry Burr and the Peerless Quartet each also released versions of the song that were popular in '08. The song even challenged "Take Me Out to the Ball Game" as the year's biggest hit song.

The song hasn't remained as well known as many of the other hit songs of the era, however.

Cuddle Up a Little Closer, Lovey Mine

Words: Otto Harbach; Music: Karl Hoschna

"Cuddle Up a Little Closer, Lovey Mine" had been created for a vaudeville sketch, but the writers were never paid for the material, so they decided to use it instead in the '08 operetta *The Three Twins*. Alice Yorke introduced this cuddly come-on in that production.

As usual, the verses are not nearly as well known as the

chorus. According to the first verse, it is summer at the beach. The lovers talked for a while, "then she grew more cold, and he grew more bold." The girl thought they should leave, but the guy murmured the chorus: *Cuddle up a little closer, Lovey mine, / Cuddle up and be my little clinging vine, / Like to feel your cheek so rosey, / Like to make you comfy, cozy, / 'Cause I love from head to tosey, Lovey, mine.*

The song has been included in several films, including *The Story of Vernon and Irene Castle* ('39), *The Birth of the Blues* ('41), *Is Everybody Happy?* ('43), *Coney Island* ('43), *Four Jills in a Jeep* ('44), *Shady Lady* ('45) and *On Moonlight Bay* ('51).

Ada Jones and Billy Murray's duet recording of the song was very popular in '08. The song was revived successfully in '42 by Dick Jurgens and in '43 by Kay Armen. Ted Lewis and his Band's recording of "Cuddle Up a Little Closer, Lovey Mine" is available at http://www.redhotjazz.com/tlband.html.

Variety selected "Cuddle Up a Little Closer" for its *Hit Parade of a Half-Century* for '08.

Read the lyrics and hear a midi musical version at http://www.geocities.com/dferg5493/cuddleupalittlecloser.htm. Or see the sheet music cover and the musical score at http://levysheetmusic.mse.jhu.edu/browse.html.

The Glow Worm (Gleuhwuermchen)

Words: Lilla Cayley Robinson; Music: Paul Lincke

"The Glow Worm" was written by Paul Lincke for the operetta *Lysistrata* in '02. The original German lyrics were by Heinz Bolten-Backers.

It was heard for the first time in the U.S. in the '07 musical *The Girl Behind the Counter*, where it was sung by May Naudain. The song sold well in Europe and the U.S., selling more than 4 million sheet music copies.

The original Lilla Cayley Robinson words are: *Shine, little glow worm, glimmer, (glimmer) / Shine, little glow worm, glimmer! (glimmer!), / Lead us, lest too far we wander, / Love's sweet voice is calling yonder! / Shine, little glow worm glimmer, (glimmer), / Shine, little glow worm, glimmer! (glimmer!) / Light the path, below, above, / And lead us on to love!*

Lucy Isabelle Marsh and the Victor Orchestra both had extremely popular recordings of the song in '08. Almost fifty years later if was revived by the Mills Brothers into a No. 1 hit (see '52 for more). Johnny Mercer wrote new lyrics in '52. His recorded version was reasonably popular in '52. The Mills Brothers' version uses both the original and the new lyrics.

Variety selected "The Glow Worm" for its *Hit Parade of a Half-Century* for '07.

See several sheet music covers of "The Glow Worm" at http://digital.library.ucla.edu/apam/librarian?SEARCH.

My Dear

Words: Dave Reed, Jr.; Music: Ernest R. Ball

Harry MacDonough had a very popular recording of "My Dear" in '08, but Reinald Werrenrath also contributed to the song's success with a successful recording of the song in late '07.

According to Dave Reed's lyrics, everything, or almost everything, in the world is for you, "My Dear." The "world is bright and fair," the skies are clear, and the flowers bloom their finest all for you, "My Dear."

The non-descript sheet music cover and musical score are available at http://levysheetmusic.mse.jhu.edu/cgi-bin/display.pl?record=148.112.000&pages=5.

Sunbonnet Sue (When I Was a Kid So High)

Words: Will D. Cobb; Music: Gus Edwards

"Sunbonnet Sue" was the first song published by Gus Edwards when he established his new publishing house in '06. It proved to be profitable, since it sold more than a million copies.

Will Cobb's lyrics tell about a boy's infatuation with a girl called "Sunbonnet Sue." He was so fascinated with this Sue that "sunshine and roses ran second" to her. He gave her a couple of "kid" kisses that "tasted lots nicer than pie," and soon found he was "dead stuck" on her. All this happened "when I was a kid so high."

The Haydn Quartet had a very popular recording of the song in '08 and Byron Harlan's recorded version was also popular.

The song provided the title for a '46 movie musical starring Gale Storm and Phil Regan. It also appeared in Gus Edwards' screen biography *The Star Maker* in '39.

Variety selected "Sunbonnet Sue" for its *Hit Parade of a Half-Century* for '06.

The sheet music cover and musical score are available at both http://levysheetmusic.mse.jhu.edu/browse.html and http://lcweb2.loc.gov/cocoon/ihas/loc.natlib.ihas.10000 5886/.

Take Me Out to the Ball Game

Words: Jack Norworth; Music: Albert Von Tilzer

Lyricist Jack Norworth wrote the words to "Take Me Out to the Ball Game" while riding the New York City subway. Norworth noticed a sign that advertised a baseball game at the Polo Grounds that day and his mind began to conjure up baseball-related lyrics. He took the lyrics to composer Albert Von Tilzer who set them to music. The resulting song has become the most famous baseball song and perhaps one of the most famous sports-related songs of all time. The song's verses are not familiar to most people, but the chorus has become one of the most played or sung songs in the U.S., after only "The Star-Spangled Banner" and "Happy Birthday."

It's difficult to believe that Norworth nor Von Tilzer had never been to a baseball game, but that's the legend. It's quite understandable that the composer of the melody would not need to understand the game, but one would think that the lyricist would need at least a fundamental understanding of the sport. Perhaps Norworth had not been to an organized or professional baseball game, but had enough acquaintance with the game to write the lyrics. One odd thing about the words is that they are written from the viewpoint of someone not currently watching a game.

Nora Bayes, Norworth's wife, introduced the song in vaudeville.

Baseball, or something like the game that became baseball, began in this country in the early 19th century when several sources mention the growing popularity of a game called "townball," "base" or "baseball." During the early 1800s, many small towns fielded teams and baseball clubs formed in some cities. Around the mid–1800s, Alexander

Cartwright, who should probably be honored as the game's founder, not Abner Doubleday, formalized the rules. Historically, things progressed nicely until the Civil War, which curtailed a lot of such activities. One result of the war was that Union soldiers spread the game to other parts of the nation.

By the turn of the century, professional baseball clubs were playing in major northeastern cities. Singing the song during the seventh-inning stretch of those baseball games quickly became a tradition (the seventh-innning stretch is the time between the halves of the inning; after six and a half innings people needed to stand up and stretch).

There are two versions of the verses, the original '08 version and a '27 one. Here are the original words to the first verse: *Katie Casey was baseball mad, | Had the fever and had it bad. | Just to root for the home town crew, | Ev'ry sou | Katie blew. | On a Saturday her young beau | Called to see if she'd like to go | To see a show | But Miss Kate said "No, | I'll tell you what you can do:*

The chorus is what most people remember: *Take me out to the ball game, | Take me out with the crowd | Buy me some peanuts and Cracker Jack, | I don't care if I never get back. | Let me root, root, root for the home team, | If they don't win, it's a shame. | For it's one, two, three strikes, you're out, | At the old ball game.*

Billy Murray and Haydn Quartet had a particularly popular recording of "Take Me Out to the Ballgame" in '08. Harvey Hindemyer and Edward Meeker also released popular recordings of the song in '08. Hear Edward Meeker's '08 wax cylinder recording at http://www.tinfoil.com/cm-9808.htm#e09926. View the sheet music cover and musical score at http://library.indstate.edu/levell.dir/cml/rbsc/kirk/PDFs/sm1908_take.pdf.

The '44 movie musical *Shine on Harvest Moon* was the screen biography of songwriter Jack Norworth and his wife, the famous vaudeville star Nora Bayes. "Take Me Out to the Ballgame" was among the songs in the film. In '49, MGM filmed *Take Me Out to the Ball Game*, a movie musical starring Gene Kelly and Frank Sinatra as baseball players and occasional vaudevillians on a team managed by Esther Williams. Gene Kelly and Frank Sinatra performed the title song. The song also appeared on the soundtrack of *The Princess Bride* ('87), *Hook* ('91), *A League of Their Own* ('92), *Sleepless in Seattle* ('93), *Angels in the Outfield* ('94) and *Mr. 3000* (2004), plus in most films about baseball even though it was often uncredited (like *The Pride of the Yankees* in '42).

"Take Me Out to the Ballgame" is a *Variety Golden 100 Tin Pan Alley Songs* honoree and a *Hit Parade of a Half-Century* selection for '08.

There Never Was a Girl Like You

Words: Harry H. Williams; Music: Egbert Van Alstyne

Byron Harlan popularized "There Never Was a Girl Like You" with a successful '08 recording. James McCool had first released a popular recording of the song in '06. Harry MacDonough released his version, that did well, in '09.

Variety selected this song for its *Hit Parade of a Half-Century* for '07.

In the first verse, we find that the girl, Lou, and the singer had gotten married. As they ride along "folks along the way stopped a-makin' hay just to come and wish us joy for life."

The chorus lyrics follow (notice the title line uses "gal" not "girl"): *My darling Lou, Lou, how the birds are callin' | And the morning glories miss you too, my honey. | Lou, Lou, how ma' tears are fallin' | For there never was a gal like you.*

There was also a song with the same title in '06 by Charles Baer.

The sheet music cover and musical score are available at http://scriptorium.lib.duke.edu/dynaweb/sheetmusic/. Page five of the sheet music is a male quartet arrangement of the song.

Under Any Old Flag at All

Words & Music: George M. Cohan

Victor Moore starred in George M. Cohan's *The Talk of New York*, a sequel to *45 Minutes from Broadway*.

Cohan's lyrics tell us he has a friend who is "a patriotic crank" who plays patriotic pranks. This person had plenty of money in the bank until he traveled around the would and spent all his money. When he came back to the U.S., he supposedly wrote the chorus to this song (which follows): *Makes no diff'rence if you're Yankee, English, Irish, Scotch or Dutch, | If your bank checks there and its on the square, | You needn't care if you're here or there. | When you're rich, you're the smoke, | When you're broke, it's a joke. | It's the man behind the dough that gets the call. | With a good supply of money ev'rything is milk and honey, | Under any old flag at all.*

Cohan himself was so patriotic some people thought he was "a patriotic crank." So in some ways, this lyric may have been autobiographical.

Billy Murray helped popularize "Under Any Old Flag at All" with a very popular recording in '08.

The musical score is available at http://levysheetmusic.mse.jhu.edu/browse.html (no sheet music cover available).

Wouldn't You Like to Have Me for a Sweetheart?

Words: Wallace Irwin; Music: Alfred G. Robyn

"Wouldn't You Like to Have Me for a Sweetheart?" was introduced in the musical *A Yankee Tourist*. According to the sheet music cover, the song was introduced by Raymond Hitchcock.

Ada Jones and Billy Murray's duet recording of "Wouldn't You Like to Have Me for a Sweetheart?" was particularly popular in '08, while Ada Jones' solo recording was also well received.

A Victor recording of this song by Ada Jones and Billy Murray is available for downloading at http://ia200106.eu.archive.org/l/audio/AdaJonesBillyMurray_part2/AdaJonesBillyMurray-WouldntYouLiketoHaveMeForaSweetheart.mp3.

1909

El Capitan

Words: John Philip Sousa and Tom Frost; Music: John Philip Sousa

Not only was John Philip Sousa a composer of marches, but he also composed the music for an 1896 operetta, *El Capitan*.

El Capitan was a very popular attraction on Broadway in 1896. Sousa not only composed the music, but he collaborated with Tom Frost on the lyrics.

The producer of the operetta was also its star, De Wolf Hopper, who introduced the title song, "El Capitan." The song combines two musical ideas from the operetta.

Sousa's Band popularized the march with successful recordings in 1895 and in '09.

The sheet music cover and musical score of this song are available at http://levysheetmusic.mse.jhu.edu/browse. html and at http://digital.library.ucla.edu/apam/.

Good Evening, Caroline

Words: Jack Norworth; Music: Albert Von Tilzer

Frank Stanley and Elise Stevenson helped popularize Jack Norworth and Albert Von Tilzer's "Good Evening, Caroline" in '09 with a very popular recording, but Billy Murray's version was not very far behind in popularity.

The singer was out strolling one evening. He began wondering if his girl, Carolina, was as lonesome as he was. When he saw her, she turned away as if she didn't see him. Even so, he got up the nerve to approach her and the chorus, which follows, is what he said to her: *Good evening, Carolina, Never saw you looking finer, / How's your Ma? How's your Pa? But tell me first just now you are, / For you, dear, my heart is pining, Say that you'll be mine; / Just take your time, make up your mind, Good evening, Caroline.*

The sheet music cover and musical score are available at http://lcweb2.loc.gov/cocoon/ihas/loc.natlib.ihas.10000 9588/default.html.

I Love, I Love, I Love My Wife but Oh! You Kid!

Words: Jimmy Lucas; Music: Harry Von Tilzer

Variety included "I Love My Wife; But, Oh, You Kid!" in its *Hit Parade of a Half-Century* for '09, however, they probably meant "I Love, I Love, I Love My Wife, but Oh You Kid" instead. Harry Armstrong and Billy Clark wrote "I Love My Wife; but Oh, You Kid!," while Jimmy Lucas and Harry Von Tilzer wrote "I Love, I Love, I Love My Wife but Oh! You Kid!" both with '09 copyright dates. It's difficult to ascertain which song was published first or which *Variety* actually meant to include in their *Hit Parade of a Half-Century*, however, from all accounts the more popular one was Lucas and Von Tilzer's.

We do know that "I Love My Wife; But, Oh, You Kid!" became a catch phrase of the early 1910s.

Arthur Collins had the most popular recording of "I Love, I Love, I Love My Wife but Oh! You Kid!" on the market, but Bob Roberts and Edward M. Favor also recorded versions that were popular. Arthur Collins' recording of the song is available at www.archive.org/ audio.

The lyrics of "I Love, I Love, I Love My Wife, but Oh! You Kid!" tell about a married man named Jonesy who stopped to speak to a sweet single girl. He told her he was married, however, there was a large "BUT" to his statement. The chorus lyrics follow: *I love, I love, I love my wife, but oh you kid, / For my dear wife I'd give my life, but oh you kid, / Now wifey dear is good to me, a wrong she never did, / I love, I love, I love my wife, but oh you kid.*

The sheet music cover and musical score of "I Love, I

Love, I Love My Wife, but Oh You Kid" are available at http://levysheetmusic.mse.jhu. edu/browse.html.

The lyrics of Armstrong and Clark's rival song, "I Love My Wife; But, Oh, You Kid!," tell about a married man named Henry Green who had family troubles. His wife fussed at him every night. One night Henry and a friend went out to dine and a lady at the next table caught Henry's eye. "She looked at Hen and sigh'd, Hen looked at her and cried:" *Well I love my wife but oh you kid, oh you kid, oh you kid, / You've got me clean off my lid and I'm dead gone on you, / I could love you in the summer time, winter time, rain or shine, / I love my wife with all my life, but oh you kid.*

A PDF of "I Love My Wife; But, Oh, You Kid!" is available at http://odin.indstate.edu/about/units/rbsc/ kirk/sh-group.html.

I Wonder Who's Kissing Her Now

Words: Will M. Hough and Frank R. Adams; Music: Joe E. Howard and Harold Orlob

"I Wonder Who's Kissing Her Now" was introduced in the '09 musical *The Prince of Tonight* and sold more than three million copies of sheet music. Henry Burr had a particularly popular recording of the song in '09. Billy Murray's recording of it was more popular in '10, as was one released by Manuel Romain.

Then, in '47, Joe E. Howard's film biography, *I Wonder Who's Kissing Her Now*, was filmed. The movie musical helped the song to become popular again, and it climbed to No. 1 on *Your Hit Parade*. It was No. 1 for only the September 6th broadcast. Perry Como's recording with Ted Weems' Orchestra, the most popular version on the market, reached No. 2 on *Billboard's* chart. Other popular '47 recordings of the song were those by Ray Noble and his orchestra and by the Dinning Sisters.

The song's renewed popularity resulted in Harold Orlob's attempting to prove that he, not Joe E. Howard, had composed the song. He said he did not want financial reward, he only wanted due credit for composing this famous song. As it turned out, he had written the music as an employee of Joe E. Howard and was paid for the job. Since Howard paid Orlob for the song, it was perfectly legal (but perhaps a little unethical) for him to publish the song as if he were the composer of the music. Eventually, the case was settled out of court when Howard agreed to share credit with Orlob.

The verses of this famous song are not performed nearly as often as the chorus, but the first verse is well worth reading to set the stage for the chorus: *You have loved lots of girls in the sweet long ago, / And each one has meant heaven to you / You have vowed your affection to each one in turn, / And have sworn to them all you'd be true; / You have kissed 'neath the moon, / While the world seemed in tune / Then you've left her to hunt a new game. / Does it ever occur to you later boy, / That's she's prob'ly doing the same?*

In the chorus of this famous waltz, the singer worries about the things others may be doing with the girl he once loved: *I wonder who's kissing her now; / Wonder who's teaching her how; / Wonder who's looking in to her eyes? / Breathing sighs! Telling lies! I wonder who's buying the wine / For lips that I used to call mine; / Wonder if she ever tells him of me, / I wonder who's kissing her now?*

ASCAP chose "I Wonder Who's Kissing Her Now" as

one of only sixteen numbers to appear in its *All-Time Hit Parade*. It was also in *Variety*'s *Hit Parade of a Half-Century* in '09 and was also included as a *Golden 100 Tin Pan Alley Song*.

The sheet music cover and musical score are available at both http://levysheetmusic.mse.jhu.edu/browse.html and the musical score at http://lcweb2.loc.gov/cocoon/ihas/loc.natlib.ihas.100006515/.

"I Wonder Who's Kissing Her Now" was used in the movie musical *The Time, the Place and the Girl* ('29), in *Moonlight in Havana* ('42), in addition to *I Wonder Who's Kissing Her Now* in '47.

During the late '40s and early '50s several songs from former eras were revived into popularity. It almost seems that, as we approached the birth of rock 'n' roll, writers were running out of something new and original to write about, so performers turned to the past to find musical gems to record. This song is an example. Others include "Peg o' My Heart," "For Me and My Gal," and "Heartaches" which were re-popularized in '47. "I'm Always Chasing Rainbows" and "Prisoner of Love" had been revived in '46. "I'm Looking Over a Four Leaf Clover," "Little White Lies," "My Happiness" and "Twelfth Street Rag" were big hits in '48.

I've Got Rings on My Fingers (or Mumbo Jumbo Jijji Boo J. O'Shea)

Words: R. P. Weston & F. J. Barnes; Music: Maurice Scott

Blanche Ring introduced "I've Got Rings on My Fingers" in the '09 musical *The Midnight Sons*. The song became a hit and was closely identified with Ms. Ring. She also interpolated it into the '10 musical *The Yankee Girl*. Ms. Ring also recorded the song for Victor and her recorded version was very popular with the public. Ada Jones also had a recording of the song on the market and it competed with Blanche Ring's recording extremely well. A recording of this song by Ada Jones is available for downloading at www.archive.org/audio-details-db.php?collection=78rpm&collectionid=AdaJones_part1&from=BA.

The words are so Irish that the song seems to demand an Irish brogue to sing it, with "me fingers" rather than "my fingers" for instance. For us today, the lyrics are rather difficult to understand. First of all, they sound like they should be sung by a man, but the song was primarily popularized by women. Some parts of the text sound like a combination of African American ("Mumbo Jumbo Jijji Boo") and Irish ("Patrick's Day" and "O'Shea"). "Nabob" is a wealthy person or a person of prominence. *Sure, I've got rings on my fingers, bells on my toes, / Elephants to ride upon, my little Irish Rose, / So come to your nabob, and next Patrick's Day, / Be Mistress Mumbo Jumbo Jijji Boo J. O'Shea.*

Blanche Ring performed the song in the '40 movie musical *If I Had My Way* and the song was used in the '42 Judy Garland and Mickey Rooney movie musical *Babes on Broadway*.

The sheet music cover and musical score are available at both http://levysheetmusic.mse.jhu.edu/browse.html, at http://lcweb2.loc.gov/cocoon/ihas/loc.natlib.ihas.100007972/ and at http://scriptorium.lib.duke.edu/dynaweb/sheetmusic/.

My Pony Boy

Words: Bobby Heath; Music: Charles O'Donnell

Lillian Lorraine introduced "My Pony Boy" in the Anna Held musical *Miss Innocence*.

The song is supposedly a rousing "cowboy" number, but it doesn't sound particularly western. In the first verse, we find out that every maid on the prairie is interested in this "Broncho Boy." The lead-in for the refrain is, "So each little peach made a nice little speech of love to him." And the chorus follows: *Pony Boy, Pony Boy, Won't you be my Pony Boy? / Don't say no, Here we go, Off across the plains; / Marry me, Carry me, Right away with you. / Giddy up, giddy up, giddy up, whoa! / My Pony Boy!*

The bouncy "giddy up, giddy up, giddy up, whoa!" line in the chorus of the song is the most intriguing part.

Ada Jones helped popularize the song with a successful recording in '09. A recording of this song by Ada Jones is available for downloading at www.archive.org/audio-details-db.php?collection=78rpm&collectionid=AdaJones_part1&from=BA. The Peerless Quartet's recorded version was also quite popular.

Variety selected "My Pony Boy" for its *Hit Parade of a Half-Century* for '09.

The sheet music cover and musical score are available at http://scriptorium.lib.duke.edu/dynaweb/sheetmusic/. See the beautiful sheet music cover, lyrics for the chorus and a midi listening version at http://parlorsongs.com/issues/2000-4/2000-4.asp.

On Wisconsin!

Words: Carl Beck; Music: W.T. Purdy

"On Wisconsin!" is not only the University of Wisconsin fight song, but it is also the official state song of Wisconsin. It is probably one of the most well-known college fight songs. John Philip Sousa reportedly said that "On Wisconsin!" was "the finest of college marching songs."

W.T. Purdy, a corporation clerk who had never been to the state before, composed the melody in '09. Carl Beck, a former University of Wisconsin student, supplied the lyrics. The pair couldn't afford the $50 to publish their song, but they were able to raise $10 as a down payment at the printers to have 500 copies printed.

The college glee club (or choir) reportedly first performed the song and then W.T. Purdy performed it at a pep rally before the Minnesota football game. It was an immediate hit with students.

In '18, Purdy sold his copyright for less than $100.

The lyrics to the song as University of Wisconsin fight song follow: *On, Wisconsin! On, Wisconsin! / Plunge right through that line! / Run the ball clear down the field, (originally "Run the ball clear 'round Chicago") / A touchdown sure this time. / On, Wisconsin! On, Wisconsin! / Fight on for her fame / Fight! Fellows!—fight, fight, fight! / We'll win this game. / On, Wisconsin! On, Wisconsin! / Stand up, Badgers, sing! / "Forward" is our driving spirit, / Loyal voices ring. / On, Wisconsin! On, Wisconsin! / Raise her glowing flame / Stand, Fellows, let us now / Salute her name!*

In '59, "On Wisconsin!" became the official state song. The lyrics of the song as the official state song were changed to: *On, Wisconsin! On, Wisconsin! / Grand old Badger state! / We, thy loyal sons and daughters / Hail thee good and great. / On, Wisconsin! On, Wisconsin! / Champion of the right. / "Forward," our motto—God / Will give thee might!*

Variety selected "On Wisconsin!" for its *Hit Parade of a Half-Century* for '09.

Prince's Orchestra had a popular recording of the song in '15.

See the sheet music cover and the musical score at http://scriptorium.lib.duke.edu/dynaweb/sheetmusic/, at http://digital.library.ucla.edu/apam/ or hear the University of Wisconsin band play the song at http://www.badger band.com/music/onwis.html.

Put on Your Old Grey Bonnet

Words: Stanley Murphy; Music: Percy Wenrich

Composer Percy Wenrich took the completed song, "Put on Your Old Grey Bonnet," to the Remick Publishing Company. After he performed it, Remick wasn't convinced the song was worth publishing. Remick was going to Atlantic City for a weekend holiday, so he took the song along for further consideration. By the time he returned from his trip, he was convinced it would be a big hit song. He told Wenrich that he couldn't get the song off his mind all weekend. Remick claimed he couldn't carry a tune, so if even he couldn't forget it, then it had to be a hit.

And it was! It sold over a million copies of sheet music and was popularized in recordings by the Haydn Quartet in '09 and by both Arthur Clough and Byron Harlan in '10. Jimmie Lunceford and his orchestra revived the song with a successful recording during the Big Band era in '37.

Murphy's original lyrics were "Put on your old sun bonnet," but the words were changed by the publisher and remained "grey" instead of "sun." Murphy's lyrics have remained well known all these years, partly due to the song's popularity at community sings for many years. *Put on your old grey bonnet, / with the blue ribbon on it, / While I hitch old Dobbin to the shay; / And through the fields of clover, / We'll drive up to Dover / On our golden wedding day.*

Is it "grey" or "gray"? Several sources spell the title differently; however, the sheet music cover spells it "grey."

The song was used in the '43 movie musical *Here Comes Elmer.*

Variety selected this song for its *Hit Parade of a Half-Century* for '09.

The sheet music cover and musical score are available at http://levysheetmusic.mse.jhu.edu/browse.html and at http://scriptorium.lib.duke.edu/dynaweb/sheetmusic/ or hear a midi musical version at http://www.geocities.com/dferg5493/songfiles.htm.

Shine on Harvest Moon

Words: Jack Norworth; Music: Nora Bayes & Jack Norworth

Nora Bayes, the "Queen of the Two-a-Days," co-wrote and introduced "Shine on Harvest Moon" in the *Ziegfeld Follies of 1908.* The song became her musical trademark. Bayes' husband and co-writer, Jack Norworth, often performed the song in his vaudeville act also.

Duet recordings by Harry MacDonough and Elsie Stevenson and Ada Jones and Billy Murray were both extremely popular in '09, as was a duet recording by two males: Frank Stanley and Henry Burr. Bob Roberts had a '09 solo recording that was popular and Arthur Pryor's Band had a popular recording of it in '10. Ethel Waters revived the song with a popular recording in '31 and Kate Smith revived it again in '43.

Norworth's lyrics are about a guy begging the harvest

moon to shine brightly so he and his girl can "stay outdoors and spoon." The harvest moon would have been in the fall and he knew that the approaching winter season would not be a good time to stay outdoors, or as he says it "snow time ain't no time to stay outdoors and spoon." The last phrase of the song, "for me and my gal," was reportedly what gave Edgar Leslie the idea for his famous song "For Me and My Gal."

The harvest moon is the full moon that occurs nearest the date of the autumn equinox in our hemisphere (it comes in the spring in the southern hemisphere). Most harvest moons occur in September, but from time to time, it may occur in October. Some people believe the harvest moon is brighter than normal full moons. Farmers could continue harvesting their crops by this bright moon, so it became known as a "harvest moon."

The song was also interpolated into the '08 musical *Miss Innocence,* which starred Anna Held. Ruth Etting revived the song in the *Ziegfeld Follies of 1931.* A '44 movie musical, *Shine on Harvest Moon,* starred Ann Sheridan and Dennis Morgan as Nora Bayes and Jack Norworth. It also appeared in Marilyn Miller's screen biography *Look for the Silver Lining* in '49. Jane Powell, Ann Sothern and Louis Calhern performed the song in *Nancy Goes to Rio* in '50. For some reason, it was also used in Gus Kahn's '52 screen biography *I'll See You in My Dreams.* Carmen Cavallaro played it for the star Tyrone Power in *The Eddy Duchin Story* ('57). The song was also used in the '37 non-musical film *Ever Since Eve.*

Variety selected "Shine on Harvest Moon" for its list of *Golden 100 Tin Pan Alley Songs* and for its *Hit Parade of a Half-Century* for '08.

See the sheet music cover and hear a midi musical version at www.perfessorbill.com or www.parlorsongs.com. Or see the sheet music cover and musical score, and hear a midi musical version at http://www.geocities.com/dferg 5493/songfiles.htm. The sheet music cover and musical score are available at both http://levysheetmusic.mse.jhu. edu/browse.html or at http://scriptorium.lib.duke.edu/ dynaweb/sheetmusic/1910-1920/@Generic__BookText View/39558.

That's A-Plenty

Words: Henry Creamer; Music: Bert A. Williams

Arthur Collins helped popularize "That's A-Plenty" with a popular recording in '09.

Collins, the King of the Coon Song, was often called upon to record the songs of black artists like Bert Williams. In his '09 recording of "That's A-Plenty" for Columbia, Collins performed the song in Williams' deadpan manner.

Lew Pollack wrote another song titled "That's A-Plenty" in '14.

Variety selected this song for its *Hit Parade of a Half-Century* for '09.

To the End of the World with You

Words: George Graff, Jr.; Music: Ernest R. Ball

Henry Burr had a particularly popular recording of "To the End of the World with You" in '09, but Manuel Romain's version was also popular with the public.

This song is a sentimental ballad. The verses, in common time or 4/4 time, are almost overly romantic. The singer gushes about "a wonderful power" that has entered his life once his love's "eyes reached my heart." All of his "joys are because I love you" and will continue to love you "until Heaven's roll call." The chorus, which follows, switches meter to 12/8 time (feels like 4/4 with triplets): *Tho' stars of hope are burning low, dear, | And all the world is filled with woe, dear, | My heart will bid me go, dear, | To the end of the world with you!*

Notice the internal rhyme scheme. Three lines of the chorus end with the word "dear," but the rhyme words are "low," "woe" and "go."

The non-descript sheet music cover and musical score are available at http://levysheetmusic.mse.jhu.edu/browse.html.

The Whiffenpoof Song
Words: Meade Minnigerode & George S. Pomeroy; Music: Guy Scull

For years, the composer credited for writing this song was Tod B. Galloway, an Amherst graduate, but in more recent years, it appears to have been Guy Scull, a Harvard student.

The song originated in '09 when The Yale University Whiffenpoofs, a senior *a cappella* men's singing group, a branch of the Yale Glee Club, was formed.

The lyricists, Minnigerode and Pomeroy, were members of the '10 Yale senior class. They freely adapted some lines from Rudyard Kipling's poem "Gentleman Rankers" for the lyrics, however, the word "whiffenpoof" comes from an imaginary character in the Victor Herbert operetta *Little Nemo*, which had been produced in '08.

Rudy Vallee had heard the song when he was a Yale student. Vallee revised and adapted the song in '36 and popularized his new version over his radio program and with an RCA Victor recording.

The song did not reach national prominence, however, until '46–'47, when recordings by Tex Beneke, Rudy Vallee, Robert Merrill and Bing Crosby with Fred Waring's Pennsylvanians became popular. Crosby's version was by far the most popular version. Bing and Bob Hope sang an excerpt from the song in their '53 movie musical *The Road to Bali*.

The verse is a little difficult to understand for those of us who did not attend Yale, but the Whiffenpoofs often gathered, as men often did during previous centuries, in a restaurant (Mory's) or pub ("the dear old Temple bar") to drink ale and lustily sing "the songs we love so well," like "Shall I Wasting" and "Mavourneen." The lyrics say they are serenading "our Louie," whoever that is, as long as their voices will last (there was a drink called a "Louis," pronounced "Louie," maybe that's what they were serenading). Then, they say, they'll "pass and be forgotten with the rest" (graduate and move on to other things). The famous chorus follows: *We're poor little lambs who have lost our way Baa, baa, baa | We're little black sheep who have gone astray Baa, baa, baa | Gentleman songsters off on a spree Doomed from here to eternity | Lord have mercy on such as we Baa, baa, baa.*

Variety selected this song for its *Hit Parade of a Half-Century* for '09.

The song can also be heard in the '50 Bing Crosby film *Riding High*.

Read the lyrics and hear Bing Crosby's recording of the song with Fred Waring and his Pennsylvanians at http://www.the-lambs.org/whiff.htm.

To read an extensive history of the Whiffenpoofs of Yale, go to http://www.yale.edu/whiffenpoofs/history/.

The Yama Yama Man
Words: O.A. Hauerbach; Music: Karl Hoschna

Bessie McCoy introduced this spooky comedy song in the musical *The Three Twins* in '08. She wore a clown costume and a witch's hat. Her performance of the song became so famous that she became known as "The Yama Yama Girl."

The song had not been written for the musical. During pre–Broadway tryouts in Chicago, the producer decided he needed a stand-out number for his star, Ms. McCoy. Hoschna and Hauerbach quickly wrote the song and it was immediately put into rehearsal for the show.

Yama is the god of death in the Hindu religion. He is the lord of the infernal regions. The Yama Yama Man, in the song's context, is that creature that all little children are afraid of when the lights go out. Considering the song's subject, it's surprising that it hasn't remained popular for Halloween, if for nothing else.

The two verses are quite short (the sheet music had four extra topical verses by Collin Davis). The first verse is: *Ev'ry little tot at night, | Is afraid of the dark you know | Some big Yama man they see, | When off to bed they go. |* The chorus is the most famous part of the song. | *Yama, Yama, the Yama man, | Terrible eyes and a face of tan. | If you don't watch out | He'll get you without a doubt, If he can. | Maybe he's hiding behind the chair, | Ready to spring out at you unaware. | Run to your mama, for here comes the Yama Yama Man.*

Ada Jones and Victor Light Opera Company released a very popular recording of the song in '09. A recording of this song by Ada Jones is available for downloading at www.archive.org/audio-details-db.php?collection=78rpm&collectionid=AdaJones_part1&from=BA.

The song was used in the '39 movie musical *The Story of Vernon and Irene Castle*. It also appeared in Marilyn Miller's screen biography *Look for the Silver Lining* in '49.

The sheet music cover and musical score are available at http://levysheetmusic.mse.jhu.edu/browse.html.

Yip-I-Addy-I-Ay!
Words: Will D. Cobb; Music: John H. Flynn

Blanche Ring introduced this novelty song in the musical *The Merry Widow and the Devil* in '08. She also popularized it with a popular recording in '09. Arthur Collins and Byron Harlan also had a popular recording of this waltz on the market.

The first verse tells about a young man named Herman Von Bellow, who played the cello every night at a dance garden. One night he became completely entranced by a maid dancing there. This girl waltzed up to him and this is what she sang: *Yip-I-Addy-I-Ay-I-Ay! Yip-I-Addy-I-Ay! | I don't care what becomes of me, | When you play me that sweet melody, | Yip-I-Addy-I-Ay-I-Ay! | My heart wants to holler, "Hooray!" | Sing of joy, sing of bliss, | Home was never like this! Yip-I-Addy-I-Ay!*

Variety selected this song for its *Hit Parade of a Half-Century* for '09.

"Yip-I-Addy-I-Ay!" was used in the '44 movie musical *Bowery to Broadway* and in *Sunbonnet Sue* ('45).

The sheet music cover and musical score are available at both http://levysheetmusic.mse.jhu.edu/browse.html and

You're in the Right Church but the Wrong Pew

Words: Cecil Mack; Music: Chris Smith

R.C. McPherson used the pen name Cecil Mack to write his song lyrics. He and Chris Smith wrote "You're in the Right Church but the Wrong Pew" for the famous vaudeville team of Bert Williams and George Walker. Bert Williams interpolated the song into the '08 musical *My Landlady*. Williams performed the song in his famous half-comic, half-serious performing style.

The song has three verses and a chorus. The first verse tells us that a man, named Jim Johnson, knocks on 'Lizabeth Thompson's door very late one night. She decides to "fool him and pretend I don't live here no more." She explains in the chorus lyrics that follow: *You're in the right church but the wrong pew, / You've got the right neighborhood that's true, / You're in the right street and what's more, / You're in the right house but on the wrong floor, / Now when you're out late, get the name straight before you attempt to call, / You're in the right church, but the wrong pew, dat's all.*

Arthur Collins and Byron Harlan's duet recording of the song was very popular in '09. Eddie Morton's recording, released in '08, was also popular.

Variety selected this song for its *Hit Parade of a Half-Century* for '08.

The sheet music cover and musical score are available at http://digital.nypl.org/lpa/ and at http://digital.library.ucla.edu/apam/. This sheet music cover indicates the song was from *Bandana Land* not *My Landlady* and Bert Williams is pictured on the cover.

1910

Ah! Sweet Mystery of Life, Tramp! Tramp! Tramp!, I'm Falling in Love with Someone *and* Italian Street Song

Words: Rida Johnson Young; Music: Victor Herbert

Originally titled *Little Paris*, Victor Herbert and Rida Young's operetta *Naughty Marietta* is set in New Orleans in the 1870s. Marietta d'Altena has come there to avoid an unhappy marriage in her native Naples. Marietta is first attracted to the lieutenant governor's son, but she eventually falls for Captain Dick Warrington, who, as leader of the Rangers, is trying to round up a pirate gang. This operetta in generally knowledged as Victor Herbert's best.

Ah! Sweet Mystery of Life

Marietta is only able to recall fragments of a melody. She vows to give her heart to the man who can complete the melody. Of course, the man who accomplishes the task is Captain Dick. The completed song was "Ah! Sweet Mystery of Life." Orville Harrold, as Capt. Dick, and Emma Trentini, as Marietta, introduced the song in the operetta.

Although the lyrics seem a bit antiquated, they express a profound thought. The mystery of life has been found. And that mystery is? "'Tis love and love alone, the world is seeking ... 'Tis the answer, 'tis the end and all of living." The weakest part of the lyric is the last phrase: "For it is love alone that rules for aye!" "For aye" in this context means always or forever, but that expression is just not a part of our venacular.

Rather surprisingly, "Ah! Sweet Mystery of Life" was not popularized greatly in recordings until '28. In '28, Fred Waring's Pennsylvanians and Leo Reisman and his orchestra popularized it with recordings. It was revived into popularity in '35 when a film version of the operetta was released starring Jeanette MacDonald and Nelson Eddy. Eddy's recording of the song helped popularize it in '35. Bing Crosby revived it again in '39 in a reasonably popular recording.

The song was given a comical treatment in the film *Young Frankenstein* ('74). In addition to the song's prominence in the '35 film version of *Naughty Marietta*, it was also used in the '39 fictionalized screen biography of Victor Herbert, *The Great Victor Herbert*.

Variety chose "Ah! Sweet Mystery of Life" for its *Golden 100 Tin Pan Alley Songs* and *Hit Parade of a Half-Century*. This song was nominated for the American Film Institute's list of the greatest songs ever from American films, but did not make the final list. It was nominated for the '35 film version of *Naughty Marietta*.

See the sheet music cover and the musical score at http://scriptorium.lib.duke.edu/dynaweb/sheetmusic/1910-1920/@Generic__BookTextView/232 or http://levysheetmusic.mse.jhu.edu/browse.html.

Tramp! Tramp! Tramp!

Orville Harrold, as Capt. Dick, and his Rangers introduced the march "Tramp! Tramp! Tramp!" According to *A Century of Pop Music*, Byron Harlan and Frank Stanley's duet recording of the song was very popular in '10. The song can be heard in the '35 film version of the operetta, but not in *The Great Victor Herbert*.

This is not the famous Civil War song by George Frederick Root. The subtitle of Root's song was "The Prisoner's Hope," while the '10 "Tramp! Tramp! Tramp!" was subtitled "Along the Highway." Both, of course, were marching songs.

I'm Falling in Love with Someone

By the middle of the second act of the operetta, it was obvious that Capt. Dick and Marietta's friendship had developed into more. Orville Harrold sings about the symptoms of falling in love. He sings that he is falling for a one particular girl and his head is awhirl. It's plain to see, he sings, "I'm sure I could love someone madly, if someone would only love me!"

Notice the composer's melodic leap of a ninth (perhaps not unheard of in operetta, but unusual in more popular fare) to accentuate the words "one girl" and "to see."

John McCormack had a particularly popular recording of "I'm Falling in Love with Someone" in '11. Charles Harrison popularized it with a recording in '12. When the film version was released in '35, Nelson Eddy's recording of the song became popular.

In addition to being heard in the film version of the operetta, it was also used in *The Great Victor Herbert*.

Variety chose this song for its *Hit Parade of a Half-Century* representing '10.

The non-descript sheet music cover and musical score are available at http://levysheetmusic.mse.jhu.edu/browse.html.

ITALIAN STREET SONG

Emma Trentini introduced this *Variety Golden 100* song. It is a soprano showpiece in which Marietta recalls her youthful days in her native Naples. She dreams of the "mandolinas playing sweet, the pleasant fall of dancing feet." She would love to return to her native Napoli.

The chorus is just a lot of nonsense words for the singer to show off their vocal skills ("Zing, zing, zizzy, zizzy, zing, zing, Boom, boom, aye"). Normally, the second time through the chorus a virtuoso obbligato is sung.

In addition to being heard in the film version of the operetta, the song was also used in the '39 movie musical *Broadway Serenade*, which starred Jeanette MacDonald and in the '46 movie musical *Holiday in Mexico*, which starred Jane Powell.

Lucy Isabelle Marsh and the Victor Light Opera Company had a popular recording of the song in '11

The rather non-descript sheet music cover and musical score are available at http://levysheetmusic.mse.jhu.edu/browse.html.

Read the plot of the film version at http://www.san.beck.org/MM/1935/NaughtyMarietta.html or http://www.musicalheaven.com/n/naughty_marietta.shtml.

The Victor Light Opera Company had a popular '11 recording called "Gems from Naughty Marietta" that was very popular.

Another song from the operetta's score, "'Neath the Southern Moon" was popularized in '11 in a recording by Merle Tillotson.

Any Little Girl That's a Nice Little Girl Is the Right Little Girl for Me
Words: Thomas J. Gray; Music: Fred Fisher

Variety chose "Any Little Girl That's a Nice Little Girl Is the Right Little Girl for Me" for its *Hit Parade of a Half-Century.*

The American Quartet had a popular recording of this song in '10, while Ada Jones' version was more popular in '11.

In the first verse a guy is upset with his girl because she flirts. She asks "What's a girl to do, please tell me do?" He replies "that's eas'ly told," and the chorus, which follows, is his reply: *Any little girl, that's a nice little girl, is the right little girl for me. / She don't have to look like a girl in a book. / If a good cook she should be. / She don't have to wear rats in her hair, / Or a straight front X. Y. Z. / Any little girl, that's a nice little girl, is the right little girl for me.*

In the second verse, however, we find newly weds "in a pullman parlor car." The wife says she's "going out to look about" and will return shortly. When she doesn't return, the man asks the porter if he has seen her. The porter tells the groom "she left you flat." To which, the newly wed man replies — and the chorus repeats.

The sheet music cover and musical score are available at both http://levysheetmusic.mse.jhu.edu/browse.html and http://lcweb2.loc.gov/cocoon/ihas/loc.natlib.ihas.100006031/.

By the Light of the Silvery Moon
Words: Edward Madden; Music: Gus Edwards

"By the Light of the Silvery Moon" was introduced in vaudeville by child star Georgie Price as a member of Gus Edwards' troup of children. They were appearing in a revue called *School Boys and Girls.* Georgie was a stooge seated in the audience. At some point in the song, Georgie would be invited up from the audience to sing it again or to prove that he could do a better job than the first performer.

Lillian Lorraine interpolated it into the *Ziegfeld Follies of 1909.*

This is a great example of "moon-June-spoon" lyrics. The rhyme words are moon, spoon, tune, June and soon. The lyrics share basically the same sentiment as "Shine on Harvest Moon" from '08. The singer wants the silvery moonlight so he can spoon with his best girl. He'll croon (sing) his girl a love song so she'll agree to marry in June. He trusts the moon's beams will make his love dreams a reality and they'll "be cuddling soon, by the silvery moon."

Billy Murray and the Haydn Quartet had a very popular recording of the song in '10, as did the Columbia Male Quartet and Ada Jones. The Billy Murray and the Haydn Quartet recording was one of the top five hits of the decade. Hear a '12 recording of "By the Light of the Silvery Moon" by Ada Jones and a chorus at http://www.edisonnj.org/menlopark/vintage/blueamberol.asp.

A '53 movie musical was titled *By the Light of the Silvery Moon* and starred Doris Day and Gordon MacRae. The song has been used in several Hollywood films, including *Ruggles of Red Gap* ('35), *The Story of Vernon and Irene Castle* ('39), *The Birth of the Blues* ('41), *Babes on Broadway* ('42), *Hello, Frisco, Hello* ('43), *Sunbonnet Sue* ('45), *The Jolson Story* ('46), *Always Leave Them Laughing* ('49) and *Two Weeks with Love* ('50).

Variety chose "By the Light of the Silvery Moon" for its *Hit Parade of a Half-Century* representing '09.

The sheet music cover and musical score are available at http://levysheetmusic.mse.jhu.edu/browse.html and at http://scriptorium.lib.duke.edu/dynaweb/sheetmusic/. A PDF of this song is available at http://library.indstate.edu/level1.dir/cml/rbsc/kirk/sheet_titles.html.

Call Me Up Some Rainy Afternoon
Words & Music: Irving Berlin

Irving Berlin had previously been collaborating with other songwriters like Ted Snyder to produce his songs. "Call Me Up Some Rainy Afternoon" is one of the first that he wrote both the words and the music. It is also an early example of a song inspired by the telephone.

The lyrics tell us that Nellie Green and Harry Lee met at a masquerade and liked each other right away. He walked Nellie home at the end of the evening and got her telephone number. Just as he was about to leave, she whispered this invitation, "Call me up some rainy afternoon, I'll arrange for a quiet little spoon." She goes on to say that she'll see that her mother takes a walk so they can hug and talk. But she admonishes him to not tell anyone. In the second verse, Harry calls Nellie to tell her he is coming over. However, when he arrives no one answers the doorbell. He can hear Nellie talking to someone else on the telephone saying exactly the same things she had said to him.

Ada Jones and the American Quartet had the most popular recording of the song, but Ada Jones' solo version was also popular in '10. A recording of this song by Ada Jones is available for downloading at www.archive.org/audio-details-db.php?collection=78rpm&collectionid=AdaJones_part1&from=BA.

See the sheet music cover and the musical score at http://lcweb2.loc.gove/cocoon/ihas/loc.natlib.ihas.1000 4626/.

Carrie (Carrie Marry Harry)

Words: Junie McCree; Music: Albert Von Tilzer

Junie McCree's catchy phrase "Carrie Marry Harry" must have been the key to this song's great success. Otherwise, the lyrics are not particularly novel.

The first verse is about Harry apologizing that he offended Carrie and wanting to "make up with a kiss." The chorus tells us that they expect to marry in June (as usual). She had "promised to travel... Away out west on a honeymoon" to Oklahoma. The next phrase is unusual: "with your mama, yama, yama, yama." It seems strange that mama would accompany them on their honeymoon to Oklahoma, plus the repeated "yama," which may have been just a rhyming repeat with no particular meaning. But "The Yama Yama Man" ('08), a song about the devil or those things that freighten children at night, was still very much on the minds of the populous. The chorus ends with the sentiment that "Carrie marry Harry, is a sweet and most beautiful rhyme."

The second verse is Carrie telling Harry he is a naughty tease whose flirting has hurt her deeply. However, she's willing to forgive and forget if he'll be good. She'll then allow him to sing the chorus again.

Albert Von Tilzer's melody is full of rather wide melodic leaps (6ths) and quite a few sixteenth notes, which cover a lot of syllables fairly quickly. In other words, the tune is not especially easy to sing.

If it wasn't the lyrics or the tune that made the song memorable, perhaps it was Billy Murray's popular recording of the song in '10.

"Carrie Marry Harry" was used in the '45 movie musical *Billy Rose's Diamond Horseshoe*, which starred Betty Grable. It also appear in *Flame of Barbary Coast*, a John Wayne film.

The sheet music cover and musical score are available at both http://levysheetmusic.mse.jhu.edu/browse.html and http://lcweb2.loc.gov/cocoon/ihas/loc.natlib.ihas.10000 9583/.

Casey Jones

Words: T. Lawrence Seibert; Music: Eddie Newton

Casey Jones, that famous railroad man, was known as an engineer who always brought his train, the Cannonball, in on time. Casey, whose real name was John Luther Jones, was known among railraod men for his skill with the locomotive's whistle. People learned to recognize Casey's distinctive whistles.

On April 29, '00, Casey had just finished his run, but volunteered to take another shift to replace a fellow worker who had fallen ill. He and his fireman, Sim Webb, pulled out of Memphis headed south late on a Sunday evening, an hour and half or more late. Casey was determined to make up the time. When they reached Vaughn, Mississippi

about 4 a.m., there was a freight train on a sidetrack, but the train was too long to get all of its cars safely on the siding. When Casey realized there was no way of preventing a smashup, he called to his fireman, "Jump, Sim, and save yourself!" Sim jumped, landed in some bushes and lived to tell about the wreck. Casey quickly put the engine in reverse and applied the brakes, but could not avoid a wreck. When they found Casey's body in the wreckage, he had one hand on the whistle cord, the other on the brake lever. Casey had tried to warn the freight train's conductor in the caboose of the impending crash so he could jump.

The lyrics are far too long to include here, but they can be read at http://www.trainweb.org/caseyjones/song.html.

Wallace Saunders, an African American engine wiper, wrote the first poetic verses about Casey Jones. Then Wallace made up a catchy little tune for the verses. The song was picked up by other railroad men and soon spread from station to station.

Legend has it that one of the railroad men shared it with his brothers who were vaudeville performers. They reworked the lyrics and added a chorus. They began performing the song on the vaudeville circuit. The popularity of the song on the vaudeville circuit helped Casey Jones become a folk hero. When the song was published in '02, T. Lawrence Seibert was credited as the composer and Eddie Newton as the lyricist. Ironically, or perhaps typically, Casey's family nor Wallace Saunders ever received any compensation.

The Casey Jones Home and Museum is in Jackson, Tennessee, and the Casey Jones Railroad Museum State Park is in Vaughn, Mississippi.

Billy Murray and the American Quartet had a very popular recording of the song in '10. Billy Murray's solo version and Arthur Collins and Byron Harlan's duet version were also popular. "Casey Jones" became the biggest recorded hit of the decade.

Variety selected "Casey Jones" for its *Hit Parade of a Half-Century* representing '09.

Hear Billy Murray's '12 recording of "Casey Jones" at http://www.edisonnj.org/menlopark/vintage/blueam berol.asp or http://www.authentichistory.com/audio/1900s/1912_Billy_Murray_Chorus-Casey_Jones.html (sheet music cover also at this website).

See the sheet music cover, the musical score and hear a midi musical version at http://parlorsongs.com/insearch/collecting/collecting1.asp. See the sheet music and musical score at http://digital.library.ucla.edu/apam/. A PDF is available of this song at http://library.indstate.edu/level1.dir/cml/rbsc/kirk/sheet_titles.html.

There was a '58 TV series about Casey Jones, starring Alan Hale.

Don't Wake Me Up I Am Dreaming

Words: Beth Slater Whitson; Music: Herbert Ingraham

Variety selected "Don't Wake Me Up I Am Dreaming" for its *Hit Parade of a Half-Century* representing '10 (listed as "Don't Wake Me Up, I'm Dreaming."

Walter Van Brunt helped popularize this waltz with a successful recording in '10.

The melody is rather operatic and has several high notes, especially at the climax ("If I should wake") where it reaches a high G. The chorus lyrics follow: *Don't wake me up I am dreaming, / Dreaming of one I love. / Don't wake me up I am dreaming, / Where skies are blue above. / Dreaming of days spent together, / Days when you loved me too. / If I should wake, my heart would break, / Let me dream, dream, dream.*

The sheet music cover and musical score are available at http://levysheetmusic.mse.jhu.edu/browse.html.

Every Little Movement

Words: Otto Hauerbach; Music: Karl Hoschna

Karl Hoschna and Otto Harbach (still spelling his name Hauerbach) wrote the musical *Madame Sherry*. It was based on a '03 English musical, which in turn had been based on a French musical. The plot centers around a tale of mistaken identity. Ed Sherry gets his wealthly uncle to believe that his Irish landlady is his wife and a dancing teacher's pupils are their children. At first Ed begins to court Lulu, the dancing teacher, but eventually sets his sights on Yvonne, his cousin.

The characters who sing "Every Little Movement (Has a Meaning of Its Own)" are Lulu and Leonard. Lulu first sings that she is bored by the waltz, the two-step, ragtime, the schottische and the polka swing." The dance of the day is "aesthetic dancing." The chorus further explains: *Ev'ry little movement has a meaning all its own, / Ev'ry tho't and feeling by some posture can be shown, / And ev'ry love-thought that comes a-stealing / o'er your being must be revealing / All its sweetness in some appealing / little gesture all, all its own.*

Then Leonard sings that all of us, whether fat or slim, need to express ourselves through the dance. He suggests we let our "arms and legs grow eloquent" so we can express ourselves "with temp'rament while you (we) are keeping time" with the music. And the chorus repeats.

Harry MacDonough and Lucy Isabelle Marsh's duet recording of "Every Little Movement" was very popular in '10.

Variety chose "Every Little Movement" for its *Hit Parade of a Half-Century* representing '10.

The song was used in the '43 movie musical *Presenting Lily Mars*, which starred Judy Garland, in Nora Bayes' screen biography *Shine on Harvest Moon* in '44, in *The Jolson Story* in '46 and in *On Moonlight Bay*, which starred Doris Day, in '51.

The rather non-descript sheet music cover and musical score are available at both http://levysheetmusic.mse.jhu.edu/browse.html and at http://lcweb2.loc.gov/cocoon/ihas/loc.natlib.ihas.100006484/.

Another song from the score, "The Birth of Passion," was popularized in '10 in a recording by Prince's Orchestra. The sheet music cover and musical score are available at http://levysheetmusic.mse.jhu.edu/browse.html.

Has Anybody Here Seen Kelly?

Words & Music: C.W. Murphy, Will Letters, John Charles Moore & William C. McKenna

"Has Anybody Here Seen Kelly?" was an English popular song. The British version was used originally in *The Jolly Bachelors*, but was not well received. The original title was "Kelly from the Isle of Man," and the lyrics dealt mainly with English geography and customs that American audiences knew little about. The show's producer, Lew Fields, decided the lyrics had to be rewritten. He hired William McKenna to adapt the lyrics for the U.S. audience.

These are the lyrics (first verse and chorus) that McKenna wrote: *Michael Kelly with his sweetheart came from County Cork, / And bent upon a holiday, they landed in New York. / They strolled around to see the sights; alas, it's sad to say, / Poor Kelly lost his little girl upon the Great White Way. / She walked uptown from Herald Square to Forty Second Street / The traffic stopped as she cried to the copper on the beat: / Has anybody here seen Kelly? / K.E. double L. Y, / Has anybody here seen Kelly? / Have you seen him smile? / Sure his hair is red, his eyes are blue, / And he's Irish through and through, / Has anybody here seen Kelly? / Kelly from the Emerald Isle.*

Nora Bayes introduced McKenna's version and it became an immediate hit. The song became one of the most frequently demanded songs in her vaudeville repertoire. Miss Bayes' '10 recording of the song was quite popular, as was Ada Jones' recorded version. A recording of this song by Ada Jones is available for downloading at www.archive.org/audio-details-db.php?collection=78rpm&collectionid=AdaJones_part1&from=BA. A PDF of this song is available at http://library.indstate.edu/level1.dir/cml/rbsc/kirk/sheet_titles.html. The sheet music cover and musical score are available at http://levysheetmusic.mse.jhu.edu/browse.html.

Variety selected this song for its *Hit Parade of a Half-Century* representing '09.

"Come Along, My Mandy," written by Tom Mellor, Alfred J. Lawrence and Harry Gifford, was also introduced in *The Jolly Bachelors*. Nora Bayes and Jack Norworth wrote new lyrics for the song. Bayes and Norworth also had a popular recording of the song in '10. The Norworth's version of the sheet music cover and musical score are available at http://levysheetmusic.mse.jhu.edu/browse.html.

If I Was a Millionaire

Words: Will D. Cobb; Music: Gus Edwards

Gus Edwards introduced "If I Was a Millionaire" in a vaudeville revue that he wrote, produced and starred in.

Gus Edwards is most famous for his troup of child stars. This song is directed towards the kids. He tells them if he "was a real live, regular, first class, cross my heart, millionaire," he'd buy all the schools in the country and give the children two six month vacations twice a year. They wouldn't have "school when it was raining, I'd let you stay at home when it was fair." Soda fountains would be free and he'd build them "ice-cream mountains."

Variety selected this song for its *Hit Parade of a Half-Century* representing '10.

"If I Was a Millionaire" was heard in Gus Edwards' screen biography *The Star Maker* ('39) and in *The Eddie Cantor Story* ('53).

The sheet music cover and musical score are available at http://levysheetmusic.mse.jhu.edu/browse.html.

In the Valley of Yesterday

All we know about this song is that Harry MacDonough recorded a popular version of it for Victor in '10. According to Joel Whitburn's *A Century of Pop Music*, it was one of the top hits of '10.

Macushla

Words: Josephine V. Rowe; Music: Dermot MacMurrough

"Mascushla" is one of Ireland's most famous and popular songs, and it is very well known there, but it is much less well known in the U.S. The word, "macushla," is an Irish term expressing affection, like darling.

The song is full of emotion and the love the writer (or singer) has for his darling "macushla." The song is almost religious in its expressive emotion.

The melody ends on a high note that could be a problem for most singers, except an Irish tenor or perhaps a real soprano.

The lyrics begin with repeated pleadings for "Macushla!" Macushla's voice is softly calling, but the singer cannot hear her. Her arms are reaching and he wants his "lost love, Macushla," to find him and bind him again. The song's last strain follows: *Macushla! Macushla! I Your red lips are saying I That death is a dream, I And love is for aye, I Then awaken, Macushla, I Awake from your dreaming, I My blue-eyed Macushla, I Awaken to stay.*

Variety selected this song for its *Hit Parade of a Half-Century* representing '10.

The song can be heard on the soundtrack of the '38 movie musical *Hawaii Calls* (how did a famous Irish song end up in a Hawaiian film?).

The non-descript sheet music cover and musical score are available at http://levysheetmusic.mse.jhu.edu/browse. html. Hear a midi musical version and see the sheet music cover at http://parlorsongs.com/issues/2003-12/thismonth/feature.asp.

Meet Me Tonight in Dreamland

Words: Beth Slater Whitson; Music: Leo Friedman

An internet website claims "Meet Me Tonight in Dreamland" was written for Dreamland Park's opening day in '04. The park was part of Coney Island's amusements, but it burned in '11. The lyrics (see below) appear to be consistent with the park's opening, but the song was not published until '09. It's more likely that "All Aboard for Dreamland" in '04 was written for the park's opening.

The song became very successful, selling over two million copies of sheet music. Unfortunately, the writers, Whitson and Friedman, did not profit from the song's huge success. The publisher, Will Rossiter, bought the song for a trifle and refused to pay royalties. So Rossiter reaped all the rewards.

When Rossiter's brother formed a publishing company the next year and was willing to pay royalties, Whitson and Friedman signed up with the new company. Their next song, "Let Me Call You Sweetheart," was even more successful than "Meet Me Tonight in Dreamland." Both the writers and the publisher shared the profits from that song, a much better arrangement for Beth Whitson and Leo Friedman.

The song's verse tells us that the person is dreaming of his sweetheart night and day. Since they are in love in his dreams, he wants to meet "in the land of dreams." The chorus continues: *Meet me tonight in Dreamland I Under the silv'ry moon I Meet me tonight in Dreamland I Where love's sweet roses bloom I Come with the lovelight gleaming I In your dear eyes of blue I Meet me in Dreamland I Sweet, dreamy Dreamland I There let my dreams come true!*

Henry Burr had the most popular recording of the song in '10, but Elizabeth Wheeler and Harry Anthony's duet version was also popular. Jimmie Davis revived the song successfully in '38. Pat Boone revived it again in '65.

"Meet Me Tonight in Dreamland" was used in the '49 movie musical *In the Good Old Summertime*.

Variety chose this song for its *Hit Parade of a Half-Century* representing '09.

The sheet music cover and musical score are available at both http://levysheetmusic.mse.jhu.edu/browse.html, at http://digital.library.ucla.edu/apam/ and http://lcweb2.loc.gov/cocoon/ihas/loc.natlib.ihas.100006089.

Play That Barbershop Chord

Words: William Tracey; Music: Lewis F. Muir

The first written use of the term "barbershop" when referring to a male harmony-singing group came in '10 with the publication of the song "Play That Barbershop Chord." Evidently the word was in common usage by this time.

Bert Williams introduced the song in '10 at Hammerstein's Victoria Theater in New York City. The song became so successful that Williams interpolated it into his act for the *Ziegfeld Follies of 1910*.

The composer, Lewis Muir, later admitted that he adapted his melody from an earlier one called "Play That Fandango Rag."

Muir had originally asked Ballard MacDonald to write lyrics for his tune, but when Ballard procrastinated about finishing the job, Muir got William Tracey to work on the project. Once the song became successful, MacDonald claimed he had written the lyrics and got his publisher, Edward B. Marks, to sue MacDonald's publisher, J. Fred Helf. The court awarded $37,000 in damages to MacDonald, causing Helf to go out of business.

"Play That Barbershop Chord" was used in the '49 movie musical *In the Good Old Summertime*. The lyrics of the song, as sung in the film, follow: QUARTET: *"Oh, Mr. Lord. I* ALL: *Play the barbershop chord I* GUY FROM QUARTET: *Mr. Jefferson Lord I* VERONICA: *Thomas Jefferson Lord I* GUY FROM QUARTET: *play that barbershop chord I* VERONICA: *play the barbershop chord I* QUARTET: *that soothing harmony I* VERONICA: *sweet harmony I* ALL: *makes a terrible, terrible, terrible I* QUARTET: *terr-boo-hoo-hoo-hoo I* VERONICA: *hit with me. I* QUARTET: *Play that strain I* VERONICA: *Play that strain I* QUARTET: *just to please me again I* VERONICA: *just to please me again. I 'Cause, Mister, when you start that minor part, I I feel your fingers slippin' and a-grippin' my heart. I Mr. Jefferson Lord I* GUY FROM QUARTET: *Mr. Jefferson Lord I* ALL: *Play that barbershop chord!*

Bert Williams' '10 recording of the song was very popular, as was a version by the American Quartet.

Of course, the song became a barbershop quartet favorite. There were several recordings available on the Internet by various barbershop quartets.

Variety chose this song for its *Hit Parade of a Half-Century* representing '10.

See the sheet music cover with Bert Williams on the cover at http://www.archeophone.com/features/recordings/302.php. On the same site, you can hear Arthur Collins' wax cylinder recording of the song. The sheet music cover and musical score are available at both http://levysheetmusic.mse.jhu.edu/browse.html and at http://lcweb2.loc.gov/cocoon/ihas/loc.natlib.ihas.100007896/.

So where did barbershop singing originate? Did guys really sit around the barbershop harmonizing? It may have been like the origin of "doo-wop," where singers got together on street corners to sing. Except in this case, it was the barbershop, where many men went daily to receive a shave.

Male quartets had been the rage during the previous decade and the American Quartet, the Peerless Quartet, the Haydn Quartet and the Columbia Stellar Quartet were still very popular recording groups.

The barbershop style of music may actually have southern African American origins. Famous African American poet and songwriter James Weldon Johnson wrote, "every barbershop seemed to have its own quartet." (Lynn Abbott wrote an article for the Fall '92 issue of *American Music* titled "'Play That Barber Shop Chord': A Case for the African American Origin of Barbershop Harmony.")

Barbershop harmony is a style of unaccompanied singing with three voices harmonizing to the melody. The second tenor or lead usually sings the melody, with the tenor, bass and baritone harmonizing with the lead. A key ingredient that gives barbershop its distinctive sound is its use of dominant seventh or major-minor seventh chords.

For more information on barbershop singing, go to the SPEBSQSA (Society for the Preservation and Encouragement of Barber Shop Quartet Singing in America) website (http://www.barbershop.org/).

That's Why They Call Me "Shine"

Words: Cecil Mack; Music: Ford Dabney

In '10, Ada Walker introduced "That's Why They Call Me 'Shine'" in an African American road show called *His Honor the Barber*. The song was supposedly written about an actual man named Shine.

Often known as "Shine," the song was recorded with success years later by the California Ramblers ('24), Louis Armstrong ('32), Bing Crosby and the Mills Brothers ('32) and Frankie Laine ('48). Crosby and the Mills Brothers version was the most successful of the recordings mentioned above.

"Shine" was used in the '41 movie musical *Birth of the Blues*, in the '43 movie musical *Cabin in the Sky*, played by Harry James in *The Benny Goodman Story* ('56) and in *The Eddy Duchin Story* ('56).

Variety selected this song for its *Hit Parade of a Half-Century* representing '10.

Washington and Lee Swing

Words: C.A. Robbins; Music: Thornton W. Allen & Mark Sheafe

The country was becoming more and more interested in things collegiate. Not academia, but the life of the collegiate: singing groups, fraternity life, and sports. College songs began to become popular. There was "The Whiffenpoof Song" from Yale in '09, the University of Maine's "Stein Song" in '10 (popularized by Rudy Vallee in '30), "The Sweetheart of Sigma Chi" and this Washington and Lee fight song, for example.

Washington and Lee University's fight song, "Washington and Lee Swing," is one of the most famous of the college fight songs. Mark Sheaf taught the tune to members of the guitar club in '06. C.A. Robbins wrote the words and Thornton Allen composed additional music for the verses.

The song caught on and by '24 was popular all over the country. Meyer Davis had a reasonably popular recording of "Washington and Lee Swing" in '25.

The original words of the fight song are: *Come cheer for Washington and Lee, / We're going to win another victory! / The White and Blue we will ever wave in triumph / For the University. RAH! RAH! RAH! / Fight to the finish we are with you, / Break through the line on every play; / Rush the ball on down the field / And we will win this game today. / When Washington and Lee's men fall in line, / We're going to win again another time; / For W&L I yell, I yell, I yell, / And for the University, I yell, like hell! / And we will fight! fight! fight! for every yard; / Circle the ends and hit that line right hard! / And we will roll those Wahoos on the sod! / Yes, by God! RAH! RAH! RAH!*

Variety selected this song for its *Hit Parade of a Half-Century* representing '10.

The sheet music cover and musical score are available at http://digital.library.ucla.edu/apam/.

Where the River Shannon Flows

Words & Music: James J. Russell

By the early 20th century, as the United States became a power internationally, its culture became more diverse. The U.S. was becoming more complex culturally as immigrants poured into the country, settling especially in the metropolitan Northeastern cities. Our social diversity began to find expression in the popular music of the period. Tin Pan Alley was overflowing with immigrant talents who helped define American music. Songwriters of German, Irish, Jewish, and Scandinavian ancestry began to find an audience. Many of these writers focused on nationalistic themes, recalling the homeland or pining for what they remembered fondly about the land of their birth.

Such seems to be the case of "Where the River Shannon Flows," which was written by James J. Russell in '05. He's remembering the land "where the fairies and the blarney will never, never die. It's the land of the shillalah; My heart goes back there daily." And he's thinking about the girl he left behind when he came to this country.

The chorus indicates the guy is planning to return to Ireland to see his little Irish rose: *Where dear old Shannon's flowing / Where the three-leaved shamrock grows / Where my heart is I am going / To my little Irish rose / And the moment that I meet her / With a hug and kiss I'll greet her / For there's not a colleen sweeter / Where the River Shannon flows.*

The second verse confirms that he intends to return to "Erin's shore" to "settle down forever."

Harry MacDonough had a very popular recording of the song in '10 and had popularized it originally in '06 (even more popular in '10 than in '06, however).

Variety selected this song for its *Hit Parade of a Half-Century* representing '05.

The sheet music cover and musical score are available at http://levysheetmusic.mse.jhu.edu/browse.html. See the sheet music cover, read the lyrics and hear a midi musical version at http://parlorsongs.com/issues/2002-3/this month/featurea.asp.

The River Shannon is Ireland's longest river. It divides the west country from the east and south. The river has served as an important waterway since antiquity. The river is a national treasure for the Irish. The city of Limerick is the nearest town where the river meets the sea.

1911

Alexander's Ragtime Band

Words & Music: Irving Berlin

Irving Berlin often wrote a song, decided it wasn't quite right, put it aside, later pulled it out, revised it and it became a monster hit song. Such was the case for "Alexander's Ragtime Band." Berlin had written a ragtime song in '10 called "Alexander and His Clarinet," but decided it wasn't quite right, so he stuck it in his musical idea trunk for future consideration. Then in '11, when he was asked to write a song for the annual Friars' Club *Frolic*, he dug around in his idea collection and resurrected the lyrics from "Alexander and His Clarinet" and a ragtime tune he had written earlier. The result was *the* most famous ragtime song, "Alexander's Ragtime Band." The song made the entire country "ragtime" conscious.

The song never got performed at the Friars' Club *Frolic*, but was popularized by Emma Carus, Sophie Tucker and other performers in vaudeville. By midsummer, the song had sold a respectable half-a-million sheet music copies, and had sold a million by the end of the year. The next year, it sold another million copies in the U.S. and England. By '13, it had sold over a half-a-million copies of sheet music in England alone. The song eventually earned Berlin, now in his mid-twenties, $30,000 in royalties.

Critics say that "Alexander's Ragtime Band" is not a ragtime tune, but more like a march. Admittedly, there isn't much syncopation, but it was chiefly responsible for the nationwide ragtime craze.

In critiquing his own song, Berlin said, "The melody ... started the heels and shoulders of all America and a good section of Europe to rocking. The lyric, silly though it was, was fundamentally right."

In the song's first verse the singer is trying to get his honey to hurry "to the leader man, ragged meter man." He wants to take her "to Alexander's grand stand, brass band."

The opening words of the chorus are an invitation to "come," to join in, and "hear" the singer and his song: "Come on and hear ... Alexander's Ragtime Band." He tells her it's "the bestest band what am, honey lamb." He also tells her he can get the leader of the band to play "Swanee River" in ragtime for her.

Alexander was often used comically as a name for African American males during this period as a name that was too grand, too exalted for a "coon," as they were regretfully called.

Arthur Collins and Bryon Harlan had a particularly popular recording of "Alexander's Ragtime Band" in '11 (their duet recording was inducted into the Grammy Hall of Fame in 2005), but Billy Murray's version was not far behind in popularity. Prince's Orchestra and the Victor Military Band released popular recordings of the song in '12. The song became one of the top five hits of the decade. Hear Billy Murray's '11 recording of "Alexander's Ragtime Band" at http://www.archive.org/audio/audio-details-db. php?collectionid=EDIS-SRP-0194-15&collection=open source_audio. Then fifteen years later, in '27, famous blues singer, Bessie Smith, revived it. The Boswell Sisters recorded a fairly popular version in '35 and Louis Armstrong did the same in '37. "Alexander's Ragtime Band" was popularized again in '38. (For more about that, see '38.)

Variety selected "Alexander's Ragtime Band" for its *Golden 100 Tin Pan Alley Songs* list and for its *Hit Parade of a Half-Century* representing '11. The song became one of the most recorded songs of the pre-rock era.

Berlin's songs are still under copyright, so the lyrics to any of his songs will not be printed here, but they are available on the internet at one of the following websites: http://www.thepeaches.com/music/composers/berlin/ or http://www.lyricsdepot.com/irving-berlin/. The copyright law indicates that the duration of the copyright is the owner's life plus 50 years. Therefore, Berlin's works should still be under copyright until 2039.

See the sheet music cover and musical score at http:// lcweb2.loc.gov/cocoon/ihas/loc.natlib.ihas.100004621/ or http://scriptorium.lib.duke.edu/dynaweb/sheetmusic/1910-1920/@Generic__BookTextView/547. A PDF of this song is available at http://odin.indstate.edu/about/units/rbsc/kirk/sh-group.html. See the sheet music cover and hear a midi musical version at www.perfessorbill.com.

Irving Berlin tried diligently to capitalize on the success of "Alexander's Ragtime Band" and the ragtime craze with "The Ragtime Jockey Man," "Ragtime Mocking Bird," "Ragtime Soldier Man" and "Ragtime Violin!" These songs were more popular in '12, and although they were successful, they weren't nearly as successful as "Alexander..."

Come, Josephine in My Flying Machine

Words: Alfred Bryan; Music: Fred Fisher

Blanche Ring introduced "Come, Josephine in My Flying Machine" in vaudeville. Her historic recording of it was a big hit in '11, but it wasn't the only one. The breezy, light-hearted singing style of Ada Jones and Billy Murray along with the American Quartet made their recording of the song a big hit recording as well in '11. Harry Tally's recording was popular, but paled in comparision with Blanche Ring's and with the disk by Ada Jones, Billy Murray and the American Quartet.

Of course, the song deals with that new fangled thing people called "aeroplanes." *Come, Josephine in my flying machine, / Going up she goes! Up she goes! / Balance yourself like a bird on a beam, / In the air she goes! There she goes! / Up, up, a little bit higher, / Oh! My! The moon is on fire / Come Josephine in my flying machine, / Going up, all on, "goodbye!"*

The song appeared in the movie musical *The Story of Vernon and Irene Castle* and also in Fred Fisher's screen biography *Oh, You Beautiful Doll* ('49). This song made an appearance in the movie *Titanic* in '97.

Variety chose this song for its *Hit Parade of a Half-Century* representing '10.

See the sheet music cover and musical score at http:// levysheetmusic.mse.jhu.edu/browse.html.

A recording by Ada Jones, Billy Murray and the American Quartet is available at www.archive.org/audio. At the following website, you can hear Harry Talley's recording of "Come Jospehine in My Flying Machine: http://www.edisonnj.org/menlopark/vintage/columbia.asp or http://www.authentichistory.com/audio/1900s/1911_Harry_Tally_Come_Josephine_In_My_Flying_Machine.html.

Down by the Old Mill Stream

Words & Music: Tell Taylor

Tell Taylor wrote "Down by the Old Mill Stream" in '10. The song became one of the biggest hits of the decade, selling more than two million sheet music copies and being popularized in a very successful recording by Arthur Clough and the Brunswick Quartet. Harry MacDonough recorded an even more popular version of the song in '12.

The song became a barbershop quartet favorite, and it remained popular with other a cappella singing groups for many years.

In the first verse of this sentimental ballad we learn that the singer, a male apparently, is "dreaming of days gone by" when he and his sweetheart were younger. Even though her hair has turned to silver, he is remembering fondly when they first met "down by the old mill stream." The chorus continues to tell us that the woman's eyes are blue, she was dressed in gingham, she was sixteen, and his "village queen." The second verse tells us that the old mill wheel and the old oak tree have fallen down, but their love has lasted "forty years or more."

The original sheet music was published with not only the piano version but also with an arrangement for male vocal quartet.

Variety chose this song for its *Hit Parade of a Half-Century* representing '10.

See the sheet music cover and the musical score at http://lcweb2.loc.gov/cocoon/ihas/loc.natlib.ihas.10000 9310/ or http://scriptorium.lib.duke.edu/dynaweb/sheet music/ or http://digital.library.ucla.edu/apam/ or a PDF is available of this song at http://library.indstate.edu/level1.dir/cml/rbsc/kirk/sheet_titles.html.

Gee, but It's Great to Meet a Friend from Your Home Town

Words: William Tracey; Music: James McGavisk

Billy Murray helped popularize this song with a successful recording in '11. *Variety* chose this song for its *Hit Parade of a Half-Century* representing '10. Jack Oakie performed the song in the '43 movie musical *Hello, Frisco, Hello.*

The sheet music cover has a picture of a woman, presumably Sadie Helf, because beside the picture is the following: "Sung with Tremendous Success by Vaudeville's New Star Dainty Sadie Helf." The song was published by the J. Fred Helf Company. Any relation to Sadie? Seems likely.

William Tracey's lyrics, especially the first verse, are very conversationally written; *Have you ever stopped to think when you've been traveling here and there, / What a great big lonesome world this seems to be, / And how hard it is to find a pal who's really on the square, / It's a problem that has often puzzled me. / Though you make friends very easy and they seem good and true / There are few that have that good old fashioned way; / You will find there's something different in the things they say or do, / And when you have met them all you're bound to say:*

Some sources listed the song's title as "Gee, but It's Great to Meet a Friend from Your Old Home Town," but the sheet music cover and the song's lyrics do not use the word "old." The verses are in common time (4/4), while the chorus is in 2/4 time. The lyrics follow: *Gee, but it's great to meet a friend from your home town, / What*

diff'rence does it make if he is up or down, / When he shakes you by the hand, / There's a feeling you can't understand! / Oh, Gee, but it's great to meet a friend from your home town.

The musical score is available at http://levysheetmusic.mse.jhu.edu/browse.html and the sheet music cover and musical score are available at the Library of Congress website: http://lcweb2.loc.gov/cocoon/ihas/loc.natlib.ihas.100007175/.

Good Night, Ladies

Words: Harry Williams; Music: Egbert Van Alstyne

Variety chose "Good Night, Ladies" for its *Hit Parade of a Half-Century* representing '11.

The lyrics and melody to "Good Night, Ladies" are extremely simple. One would assume the song was of folk origin it is so completely uncomplicated. *Good night, ladies (repeat twice), we're going to leave you now. / Merrily we roll along, roll along, roll along, / Merrily we roll along o'er the deep blue sea.*

See the sheet music cover and musical score at http://levysheetmusic.mse.jhu.edu/otcgi/llscgi60 (listed under "College Songs, Song No. 2").

Hear Nick Lucas' '32 recording of "Good Night, Ladies, spelled "Goodnight, athttp://www.redhotjazz.com/lucas.html. The song appeared in the '62 movie musical *The Music Man* sung by the barbershop quartet The Buffalo Bills.

I Love the Name of Mary

Words: George Graff, Jr.; Music: Ernest R. Ball & Chauncey Olcott

According to the sheet music cover Chauncey Olcott introduced "I Love the Name of Mary" in *Barry of Ballymore.*

Will Oakland helped popularize "I Love the Name of Mary" with a very popular recording of the song in '11, while Walter Van Brunt had a popular version on the market in '12. It may well have been one of the top hits of '11 in sales of sheet music, wax cylinders and other recordings, but it has not lasted nearly as well as many other Ernest R. Ball, Chauncey Olcott or George Graff, Jr. songs.

The verses of this song are in 6/8 time, while the more famous chorus changes to waltz time (triple meter). In the first verse, we find that the singer hasn't found the right girl to marry. He finally realizes that the only place he'll find the appropriate girl is in Ireland. The girl of his dreams is named Mary. The chorus lyrics, not the greatest example of the lyricist's art, follow (no punctuation in the chorus): *I love the name of Mary, Gentle and sweet nor airy / Tender as e'er a fairy Just as true / And from my hearts glad singing, / And from the hopes there springing / Future days joys are bringing and you too Mary.*

The sheet music cover and musical score are available at http://digital.library.ucla.edu/.

I Want a Girl (Just Like the Girl That Married Dear Old Dad)

Words: William Dillon; Music: Harry Von Tilzer

The Columbia Male Quartet and Walter Van Brunt and the Peerless Quartet helped popularize "I Want a Girl" with a popular recordings in '11.

The first verse tells us that a boy's mother had told him

to get married and you'll be happy. He's looked all over the place, but can't find a girl like the girl he has in mind. Then he explains what that kind of girl is: *I want a girl Just like the girl That married dear old Dad / She was a pearl and the only girl That Daddy ever had. / A good-old fashioned girl With heart so true, / One who love Nobody else but You / I want a girl, Just like the girl That married dear old Dad.*

Variety chose this song for its *Hit Parade of a Half-Century* representing '11.

The song was performed in the '46 movie musical *The Jolson Story*.

The sheet music cover and musical score are available at http://levysheetmusic.mse.jhu.edu/browse.html and at this Library of Congress website: http://lcweb2.loc.gov/cocoon/ihas/loc.natlib.ihas.100009635/. Hear a midi musical version, see the sheet music cover and the musical score at http://www.geocities.com/dferg5493/iwantagirl.html.

Let Me Call You Sweetheart

Words: Beth Slater Whitson; Music: Leo Friedman

"Let Me Call You Sweetheart" became one of the most successful ballads of the decade, selling approximately five million copies of sheet music. *Variety* chose the song for its list of *Golden 100 Tin Pan Alley Songs* and for its *Hit Parade of a Half-Century* representing '10.

Whitson and Friedman had written "Meet Me Tonight in Dreamland" (see '10). They had sold their rights to the song to the publisher, Will Rossiter, and didn't benefit from its huge sale of sheet music. When Harold Rossiter opened his music publishing company in '10 and was willing to pay royalties, the writers left Harold's brother, Will, and allowed Harold to publish "Let Me Call You Sweetheart." Both publisher and writers profited hugely from the song's popularity.

This waltz became a favorite of sing-a-longs, of barbershop quartets, and of many harmony groups.

The famous and familiar words of the chorus follow: *Let me call you sweetheart, I'm in love with you. / Let me hear you whisper that you love me, too, / Keep the lovelight glowing in your eyes so true. / Let me call you sweetheart, I'm in love with you.*

In addition to sheet music sales, recordings by the Columbia Male Quartet and by Arthur Clough were very popular in '11. As a matter of fact, the Columbia Male Quartet's version was the number two recorded hit of the decade next to Arthur Collins and Byron Harlan's "Alexander's Ragtime Band."

The song was used in several Hollywood movie musicals, including *Coney Island* ('43), starring Betty Grable, *Thousand's Cheer* ('43), *Billy Rose's Diamond Horseshoe* ('45), and *The Rose* ('79).

The sheet music cover and musical score are available at http://levysheetmusic.mse.jhu.edu/browse.html and at this Library of Congress website: http://lcweb2.loc.gov/cocoon/ihas/loc.natlib.ihas.100006088/. Also see www.perfessorbill.com to see the sheet music cover and hear a midi musical version.

Look Out for Jimmy Valentine

Words: Edward Madden; Music: Gus Edwards

The real Jimmy Valentine was a safecracker who got caught and did time in jail. William Sydney Porter, alias O. Henry, also did time on an embezzlement charge. Porter and Valentine met in jail. When Porter got out he moved to New York and began writing short stories under the name O. Henry. One of his tales, "A Retrieved Reformation," related what happened to Jimmy Valentine after he got out of jail. Jimmy intended to go straight, but felt he had to do one more job. He moved to a particular small town, took a job in a shoe store to watch the bank, and met and fell in love with the banker's daughter. The story gets even more complicated, far too much so to tell the entire story here. But he ends up saving a little girl who got locked in the bank's safe with his safe cracking skills.

The story was a natural drama. O. Henry sold the rights to the story to a playwright for $500 and the tale was dramatized as *Alias Jimmy Valentine*. It was a Broadway success and many years later became a '30s movie.

Gus Edwards saw the Broadway play and the story inspired him to write the song "Look Out for Jimmy Valentine (or sometimes called Jimmy Valentine)" with lyricist Edward Madden. It became a hit in '11. The following are the lyrics Edward Madden wrote: *Look out, look out, Look out for Jimmy Valentine / For he's a pal of mine, A sentimental crook / With a touch that lingers in his sandpapered fingers / He can find the combination of your pocketbook. / Look out, look out, for when you see his lantern shine / That's the time to jump right up and shout Help! / He'd steal a horse and cart, / He'd even steal a girlie's heart / When Jimmy Valentine gets out.*

The Peerless Quartet recorded a successful version of "Jimmy Valentine" in '11. Bing Crosby performed "Jimmy Valentine" in the '39 movie musical *The Star Maker*, Gus Edwards' screen biography.

Variety chose "Jimmy Valentine" for its *Hit Parade of a Half-Century* representing '11.

The sheet music cover and musical score are available at http://levysheetmusic.mse.jhu.edu/browse.html.

Mother Machree

Words: Rida Johnson Young; Music: Ernest R. Ball & Chauncey Olcott

Along with "My Wild Irish Rose" and "When Irish Eyes Are Smiling," "Mother Machree" is one of the most famous Irish ballads to come out of Tin Pan Alley. Co-writer Chauncey Olcott introduced the song in the '10 musical *Barry of Ballymore*, then, it was so successful, he repeated it in the '12 musical *Isle of Dreams*.

The lyrics definitely have an Irish flavor. In the first verse we hear that "no coleen" will ever take a certain spot in his heart, "no other can take it, no one ever will." According to the American Heritage Dictionary, coleen simply means an Irish girl. The word came from the Gaelic word "cailin."

Then the famous chorus tells us his special feelings about Mother Machree. *Sure, I love the dear silver that shines in your hair, / And the brow that's all furrowed and wrinkled with care. / I kiss the dear fingers so toilworn for me. / Oh, God bless you and keep you, Mother Machree.*

The second verse tells us that his mother has made all his sorrows and cares brighter by "that smile in your eye." And her love has guided him in the right path.

John McCormack and Will Oakland had equally popular recordings of the song in '11 and both were very successful. Chauncey Olcott's recording of the song was popular in '13. Then the Taylor Trio revived it again in '15.

The song has appeared in several Hollywood movie musicals, including Ernest R. Ball's screen biography *Irish Eyes Are Smiling* ('44) and in Chauncey Olcott's screen biography *My Wild Irish Rose* ('47). It was also used in the '43 movie musical *Doughboys in Ireland*, which starred tenor Kenny Baker.

Variety chose "Mother Machree" for its *Hit Parade of a Half-Century* representing '10.

The non-descript sheet music cover and musical score are available at http://levysheetmusic.mse.jhu.edu/browse. html and at http://scriptorium.lib.duke.edu/dynaweb/ sheetmusic/1910-1920/@Generic__BookTextView/30608 or hear Charles Harrison's recording of "Mother Machree" at http://www.turtleserviceslimited.org/machree.htm.

My Rosary of Dreams

Words & Music: E.F. Dusenberry & C.M. Denison

Variety chose "My Rosary of Dreams" for its *Hit Parade of a Half-Century* representing '11. There are no listings in *A Century of Pop Music* or *Pop Memories* of any recordings of the song.

The verse, in 6/8 meter, tells us the singer has wanted for years and years "to meet a face I've met in dreams." In the chorus, which changes to 12/8 meter, we hear: *You are my Rosary of dream, You're all the joy I know, / Tho' just a dream face you seem real as thro' the world I go, / Those dreams of you from out the past each one a pearl it gleams, / I take them all and weave them in my Rosary of dreams.*

The sheet music cover and musical score are available at http://levysheetmusic.mse.jhu.edu/browse.html.

Put Your Arms Around Me, Honey

Words: Junie McCree; Music: Harry Von Tilzer

"Put Your Arms Around Me, Honey" was interpolated into *Madame Sherry* (see '10), even though all the other songs were written by Otto Harbach and Karl Hoschna. It was then popularized in performances by Elizabeth Murray. Later it became a song speciality for vaudevillian Blossom Seeley.

Junie McCree's lyrics for the verse set the stage. It's evening, everything is still, and "the pale moon is shining from above." Cupid is calling "ev'ry Jack and Jill" to spoon. The chorus lyrics are about a guy wanting to be held tightly by his honey. He wants to "huddle up and cuddle up." Honey's eyes are particularly attractive: *Oh, babe, won't you roll dem eyes, Eyes that I just idolize. / When they look at me, my heart begins to float / Then it starts a-rockin' like a motor boat.*

The chorus concludes with a strong statement of admiration: "I never knew any girl like you," which is also the subtitle.

Arthur Collins and Byron Harlan's duet recording was very popular in '11, as were recordings by Ada Jones and the "That Girl" Quartet. Dick Kuhn revived the song in '42–'43 and Dick Haymes had a popular version of the song on the market in '43.

The song has been used in several Hollywood movie musicals. Betty Grable sang it in *Coney Island* ('43), it also appeared in *Slightly Terrific* ('44), in *Mother Wore Tight* ('47) and in *In the Good Old Summertime* ('49).

Variety chose this song for its *Hit Parade of a Half-Century* representing '10.

See the sheet music cover and musical score at http:// lcweb2.loc.gov/cocoon/ihas/loc.natlib.ihas.100009609/ or http://scriptorium.lib.duke.edu/dynaweb/sheetmusic/ 1910-1920/@Generic__BookTextView/37347. See the sheet music cover, read the lyrics, and listen to a midi musical version at http://parlorsongs.com/issues/2002-2/this month/featurea.asp.

Under the Yum Yum Tree

Words: Andrew B. Sterling; Music: Harry Von Tilzer

"Under the Yum Yum Tree" should not be confused with "Under the Bamboo Tree, which came from '02. The "Bamboo Tree" song is a famous ragtime tune.

The lyrics to "Under the Yum Yum Tree" are a bit silly by Andrew Sterling standards (verse one and chorus): *There's a place to go where the breezes blow / And the hum of the bumble bee / As he busses by 'Neath a tinted sky / In a sweet honeyed melody; / Take your sweetheart true, to this place with you / There's a spot where on one can see. / You can lovey, love, love, / With your dovey, dovey, dove, / Under the Yum Yum tree. / Under the Yum Yum tree, That's the yummiest place to be, / When you take your baby by the hand / There'll be something doing down in Yum Yum land; / That is the place to play, with your honey, and kiss all day, / When you're all by your lonely, You and your only, / Yum! Yum! Yummy, Yummy, Yum / Under the Yum Yum tree.*

Arthur Collins and Byron Harlan's duet recording of "Under the Yum Yum Tree" was very popular in '11.

The song was used in the non-musical film *Wharf Angel* in '34. There was a '63 film comedy starring Jack Lemmon titled *Under the Yum Yum Tree.*

The sheet music cover shows a male and female presumably under a Yum Yum tree. He is leaning back against her for support and comfort, which seems a little odd for the time period.

The sheet music cover and musical score are available at http://levysheetmusic.mse.jhu.edu/browse.html and at this Library of Congress website: http://lcweb2.loc.gov/co coon/ihas/loc.natlib.ihas.100009660/.

1912

Be My Little Baby Bumble Bee

Words: Stanley Murphy; Music: Henry I. Marshall

This cute little song, "Be My Little Baby Bumble Bee," was introduced by the Dolly Sisters in the *Ziegfeld Follies of 1911.*

The lyrics tell the story of Queenie, the honey bee. She would meet Billy Bumble "round the Rosemary" and she would treat him "to some honey sprees." Then she would continue with the chorus: *Be my little baby bumble bee, / (buzz around, buzz around, keep a buzzin' round) / Bring home all the honey, love, to me. / (little bee, little bee, little bee) / Let me spend the happy hours roving with you 'mongst the flow'rs, / And when we get where no one else can see, / (cuddle up, cuddle up, cuddle up) / Be my little baby bumble bee, / (buzz a-round, buzz a-round, keep a buzz-in' round) / We'll be just as happy as can be, / (you and me, you and me, you and me) / Honey keep a buzzin' please, / I've got a dozen cousin bees, / But I want you to be my baby bumble bee.*

Ada Jones and Billy Murray had a very popular duet recording of the song in '12. Ada Jones also recorded a duet version with Walter Van Brunt that was popular in '12.

The song appeared in the '44 movie musical *Irish Eyes Are Smiling*, Ernest R. Ball's biopic, in the '53 Doris Day movie musical *By the Light of the Silvery Moon* and in *The Eddie Cantor Story* ('53).

Variety chose this song for its *Hit Parade of a Half-Century* representing '12.

There is another song with a similar title: "Be My Little Bumble Bee" by Alb. H. Fitz copyrighted in '01.

The sheet music cover and musical score of this song are available at http://levysheetmusic.mse.jhu.edu/browse.html and at this Library of Congress website: http://lcweb2.loc.gov/cocoon/ihas/loc.natlib.ihas.100007539/. Read the lyrics and hear a midi musical version at http://www.geocities.com/dferg5493/bemylittlebabybumblebee.htm.

Down by the Old Mill Stream (see 1911)

Popularized by Harry MacDonough with a very successful recording in '12.

Everybody Two-Step

Words: Earl C. Jones; Music: Wallie Herzer

The American Quartet had a particularly popular recording of "Everybody Two-Step" in '12.

The sheet music cover advertises the song as having been sung by Nellie Beaumont in *A Lucky Hoodoo*.

In addition to ragtime, the two-step dance was in vogue. This song tries to get everybody involved and encourages doing the dance by offering a few instructions.

The first verse asks if we "hear the latest music hit?" Then it tells us it was written by "Mutt and Jeff," not by Rubenstein, referring to cartoon characters as compared to some classical composer. The text refers to the two-step as the "old Havana style." In order to do this dance, you must "act like you were made of rubber, chile." The chorus lyrics follow: *Ev'rybody two-step and grab a girlie girl. / Ev'rybody two-step and do the twirly-whirl. / Shake your feet with all your might, / Ev'rybody two-step and two-step right. / If you want to two-step just like a Polar bear, / Ev'rybody does it, nobody ought to care.*

Then comes the following spoken part to end the song: *Ev'body wiggle waggle. Then you make a bow. Ev'rybody two-step now.*

The sheet music cover and musical score of this song are available at http://levysheetmusic.mse.jhu.edu/browse.html. A PDF is available of this song at http://library.indstate.edu/level1.dir/cml/rbsc/kirk/sheet_titles.html. See the sheet music cover and listen to a midi musical version at http://www.halcyondaysmusic.com/september/september2001.htm.

Everybody's Doin' It Now

Words & Music: Irving Berlin

Quite a few new dances evolved around '11 or so with the nationwide spread of ragtime. The ragged rhythms of rags and similar songs demanded dances with jerky motions. They were a new breed of vigorous, highly sexual, African American–inspired dances, with names that shocked the genteel. Many of the couple dances of the time had names such as bunny hug, monkey, lame duck, ostrich, horse trot, kangaroo dip, grizzly bear, maxixe, half-in-half, gotham gobble, humpback rag, come-to-me-tommy and even the Fox Trot that would become popular about '14. One of the new dances that evolved during this time was a rather ungraceful dance called the Turkey Trot, which included flapping the arms like turkeys.

Vernon and Irene Castle, the most popular "society" dance team of the era, thought the Turkey Trot should be eliminated from polite society. Some communities tried to ban it, but that only added to its popularity.

Irving Berlin's "Everybody's Doin' It Now" attempted to exploit the dance craze and helped popularize the turkey trot. The lyrics were actually shamelessly shocking for the time. To even suggest that everybody was doin' "it" was like suggesting everyone was making love.

In the first verse a guy asks his honey to listen to this infectious music that keeps going to their brains like a bottle of fine wine. He says let's take a chance and get in line so we can enjoy this dance like others are doing. The chorus begins by telling us that "ev'rybody's doin' it, doin' it, doin' it." The guy tells his girl to watch "that ragtime couple over there, Watch them throw their shoulders in the air." Then the "ev'rybody's doin' it" strain is repeated, before he asks, "ain't that music touching your heart?" So, he encourages her to come on and start doing it like everybody else is doing it. The second verse indicates how exhausting this dance is; he needs a chair to rest, but then decides he is as capable as the rest of the dancers who are still going strong. So they dive right back into the chorus again.

The song was used in the '38 movie musical *Alexander's Ragtime Band* and in *Easter Parade* ('48), both films with Irving Berlin songs. It was also used in the '47 film *The Fabulous Dorseys*, the screen biography of Tommy and Jimmy Dorsey.

Arthur Collins and Byron Harlan helped popularize the song with a very popular duet recording in '12. The Peerless Quartet also had a popular recording of the song in '12. Hear Paul Whiteman's '55 recording of this Berlin classic at http://www.redhotjazz.com/pwo.html.

Variety selected "Everybody's Doin' It Now" (listed as Everybody's Doin' It) for its *Hit Parade of a Half-Century* representing '11.

See the sheet music cover and the musical score at http://lcweb2.loc.gov/cocoon/ihas/loc.natlib.ihas.100004629/. Or read the lyrics and hear a midi musical version at http://www.geocities.com/dferg5493/everybodysdoingit.html.

I Love You Truly

Words & Music: Carrie Jacobs-Bond

"I Love You Truly" was written around the turn of the century by Carrie Jacobs-Bond. Ms. Jacobs-Bond had a tough life, but produced several famous songs.

She had been severely burned as a child, her father declared bankruptcy when she was twelve and died shortly afterward, she married and was divorced by her early twenties. She married again at age twenty-five to Dr. Frank Lewis Bond. They lost their life's savings in the depression of 1893. At age thirty-three, she lost her second husband. Now with a young son and no money, Ms. Jacobs-Bond tried making a living painting china and renting rooms.

She finally turned to writing songs and with the help of some friends, opened a music publishing business around the turn-of-the-century.

"I Love You Truly" was included in a collection of songs that was one of the first publications of the new company. In '06, the song was published as a separate song and sold millions of copies of sheet music.

The song became a standard at wedding ceremonies around the country.

Ms. Jacobs-Bond was invited to sing "I Love You Truly" at the White House for Presidents Theodore Roosevelt, Warren G. Harding, and Calvin Coolidge.

Elsie Baker had the most popular recording of the song in '12.

Variety selected "I Love You Truly" for its *Hit Parade of a Half-Century* representing '06.

Read the lyrics and hear a midi musical version at http://www.geocities.com/dferg5493/iloveyoutruly.html. See the sheet music cover and the musical score at http://levysheetmusic.mse.jhu.edu/browse.html or http://digital.library.ucla.edu/apam/ or a PDF of this song is available at http://library.indstate.edu/levell.dir/cml/rbsc/kirk/sheet _titles.html.

I'm the Lonesomest Gal in Town

Words: Lew Brown; Music: Albert Von Tilzer

Lew Brown and Albert Von Tilzer's "I'm the Lonesomest Gal in Town" was a popular ballad in '12.

This woman is really desperate! She wants somebody to find a man for her to save "a poor girl from her grave." The chorus lyrics follow: *I'm the lonesomest gal in town, / Ev'rybody has thrown me down; / I ain't got no angel child to call me dear, / Got no honey man for me to cuddle near. / But I'm learning to roll my eyes, / And someday you may be surprised, / When I steal somebody's lovin' man and kiss him with a smack, / I'll hug him and I'll squeze him but I'll never give him back, / 'Cause I'm lonesome, so very lonesome, / Yes, I'm the lonesomest gal in this here town.*

Variety chose this song for its *Hit Parade of a Half-Century* representing '12.

There are no listings in *A Century of Pop Music* or *Pop Memories* of a recording of this song in '12, but Morton Downey and his orchestra had a popular recording of "Lonesomest Girl in Town" in '26.

The song was used in a couple of films including *Make Believe Ballroom* ('49) and *South Sea Sinner* ('50).

Love Is Mine

Words: Edward Teschemacher; Music: Clarence G. Gartner

Enrico Caruso popularized "Love Is Mine" with a particularly popular recording in '12.

The lyricist Teschemacher was also responsible for the famous wedding song "Because" (see '02).

Caruso was at his prime in '12. He had important recordings of "Dreams of Long Ago," "The Lost Chord," and "Canta Pe' Me (Neapolitan Song)" in '12 in addition to "Love Is Mine."

The Victor Company paid Caruso $1,825,000 in royalties from his recordings during his life, which was more than his earnings at the Metropolitan Opera. Since his death his estate has collected another near $2,000,000 in royalties from his records.

Moonlight Bay

Word: Edward Madden; Music: Percy Wenrich

Even though this decade was very ragtime conscious, not every song was fast and jerky. "Moonlight Bay" calmed things considerably.

"Moonlight Bay" was introduced and popularized in vaudeville. The American Quartet's recording of the song became one of the top ten recordings of the decade. Dolly Connolly also had a popular recording of the song in '12. Father and son, Bing and Gary Crosby, revived the song in the early '50s with their recording.

Harmony groups loved this song. It's been a favorite of barbershop quartets for many years.

The famous and familiar lyrics of the chorus are: *We were sailing along on Moonlight Bay, / We could hear the voices ringing / They seemed to say 'You have stolen her heart, / Now don't go 'way!' / As we sang love's old sweet song, on Moonlight Bay.*

The song was used in several Hollywood movie musicals, including the Judy Garland and Mickey Rooney film version of *Babes in Arms* ('39) and *Tin Pan Alley* ('40) with Alice Faye. Frank Sinatra, the Pied Pipers and Tommy Dorsey's orchestra performed it in *Ship Ahoy* ('42), and of course, it was prominent in *On Moonlight Bay* ('51), which starred Doris Day and Gordon MacRae.

Variety chose this song for its *Hit Parade of a Half-Century* representing '12.

The sheet music cover and musical score of this song are available at http://levysheetmusic.mse.jhu.edu/browse. html. Hear the Premier Quartet's '15 recording of this song at http://www.archive.org/audio/audio-details-db. php?collectionid=EDIS-SRP-0164-01&collection=open source_audio. Read the lyrics at http://lirama.net/song/ 16595.

Oceana Roll

Words: Roger Lewis; Music: Lucien Denni

Lucien Denni, a French composer, wrote "Oceana Roll" with lyricist Roger Lewis. Ragtime was actually quite popular in France.

The U.S. Navy did not seem to object to its cruiser *Alabama* being mentioned prominently in Roger Lewis' lyrics. It is possible that Lewis had served aboard the ship.

There is a good amount of ragtime syncopation throughout the chorus of the song.

The lyrics of the verse tell us about a musical guy named Billy McCoy, who was on the cruiser the U.S.S. *Alabama*. He would play the "piana" in a ragtime syncopation that kept his fellow shipmates up all night listening. The chorus follows: *Each fish and worm Begins to twist and squirm / The ship goes in a dip and does a corkscrew turn, / You see that smoke so black Sneak from that old smokestack? / It's floatin' right to heaven and it won't come back. / Now here and there You'll see a stool and chair / A-slippin' round the cabin Sayin' "I don't care!" / Then the hammock starts a-swingin' and the bell begins a-ringin' / While he's sittin' at that piana There on the Alabama / Playin' the Oceana Roll!*

Variety selected "Oceana Roll" for its *Hit Parade of a Half-Century* representing '11.

Arthur Collins had a popular recording of "Oceana Roll" in '12; Eddie Morton had first introduced it in a '11 recording.

Jane Powell and a chorus of kids performed this song in the movie musical *Two Weeks with Love* ('50).

The sheet music cover and musical score of this song are available at http://levysheetmusic.mse.jhu.edu/browse. html or at this Library of Congress website: http://lcweb2. loc.gov/cocoon/ihas/loc.natlib.ihas.100005572/. See the sheet music cover and hear a midi musical version at http://www.perfessorbill.com/index2.htm or http://parlor songs.com/issues/2001-3/thismonth/feature.asp.

Oh! You Beautiful Doll

Words: A. Seymour Brown; Music: Nat D. Ayer

"Oh! You Beautiful Doll" is another of the songs of the period that got its start in vaudeville. Billy Murray and the American Quartet had a very successful recording of the song in '12.

The definition of beauty or attractiveness has changed over the years. From around the early 15th century until the beginning of the 18th century, western culture's beautiful women were big-breasted, plump, and somewhat maternal-looking. As the new century opened, upper-class women set the standards of fragility with their pale skin. Women would powder their faces and seek shelter from the sun under the shade of an umbrella or a large hat. Then the hourglass figure and the corset became popular. In '00, the Florodora girls were considered the epitome of feminine allure. The six girls were 5 feet 4 inches tall and weighed 130 pounds each. By today's standard, they would be considered plump. But in that era, plump was beautiful. The men of the early 1900s would consider many of the beautiful women of the 21st century under nourished. Whatever the judge of beauty may have been in '12, the woman in the painting on the sheet music cover is a beautiful woman.

The sheet music cover (one of the most beautiful ones; the cover artist was Starmer) and musical score of this song are available at http://levysheetmusic.mse.jhu.edu/browse. html or at this Library of Congress website: http://lcweb 2.loc.gov/cocoon/ihas/loc.natlib.ihas.100004221/ or see the sheet music cover and listen to a midi musical version at http://parlorsongs.com/issues/2002-2/thismonth/fea turea.asp, or see the sheet music cover and hear a midi musical version at http://www.perfessorbill.com/index2. htm.

The lyrics to the verse follow: *Honey dear, Want you near, / Just turn out the light and then come over here, / Nestle close Up to my side, My heart's a fire / With love's desire. In my arms, rest complete, / I never thought that life could ever be so sweet / Till I met you, some time a go, / But now I know I love you so.*

The lyrics of the famous chorus: *Oh! you beautiful doll, you great big beautiful doll! / Let me put my arms about you, / I could never live without you; / Oh! you beautiful doll, you great big beautiful doll! / If you ever leave me how my heart will ache, / I want to hug you but I fear you'd break / Oh, oh, oh, oh, Oh, you beautiful doll!*

"Oh! You Beautiful Doll" has become a staple of Hollywood movie musicals. It was heard in *The Story of Vernon and Irene Castle* ('39), in *For Me and My Gal* ('42) where it was performed by Gene Kelly and Judy Garland, in *Broadway Rhythm* ('44) where it was performed by Charles Winninger, in *The I-Don't-Care Girl* ('53), in *The Eddie Cantor Story* ('53) and of course, in *Oh You Beautiful Doll* ('49).

Variety chose this song for its *Hit Parade of a Half-Century* representing '11.

Hear Billy Murray and the American Quartet's '12 recording of "Oh, You Beautiful Doll" at http://www.first worldwar.com/audio/ohyoubeautifuldoll.htm.

Ragging the Baby to Sleep

Words: L. Wolfe Gilbert; Music: Lewis F. Muir

Al Jolson popularized "Ragging the Baby to Sleep" with a very popular recording in '12.

Ragtime was at its peak. The list of popular '12 songs with rag or ragtime in their title is impressive: "Ragtime Cowboy Joe," "When Uncle Joe Plays a Rag on His Old Banjo," "Ragtime Violin," "Alexander's Ragtime Band" (left over from '11), "Red Pepper, a Spicy Rag," "That Mysterious Rag," "Ragtime Jockey Man," "Ragtime Mockingbird," "Ragtime Soldier Man," "Skeleton Rag," "Another Rag (A Raggy Rag)" and that only includes the ones with rag or ragtime in the title. Others that seem to fit the genre include "Waiting for the Robert E. Lee" and "Everybody's Doing It Now," among others.

However, nothing is available to tell us specifics about "Ragging the Baby to Sleep." From the title, it doesn't sound like something that would really put any baby to sleep. Did they take some lullaby and juice it up in a rag style like Ed Claypoole did with the musical scale in his '15 song "Ragging the Scale"? That's merely conjecture.

Bill Edwards, of http://www.perfessorbill.com/ fame, said in an email correspondence, "It doesn't have one of those clever composition stories that I know of, and was simply another Tin Pan Alley (a second-rate one compared to many "hits") knockoff composed by the duo who had recently produced their first mega-hit, 'Waiting for the Robert E. Lee.'"

Ragtime Cowboy Joe

Words: Grant Clarke; Music: Lewis F. Muir & Maurice Abrahams

This ragtime classic became a favorite with barbershop quartets.

The first verse of the song begins by setting the stage: "Out in Arizona where the bad men are." The roughest, toughest of these men is Ragtime Cowboy Joe, who got his name from singing his cattle to sleep each night. The chorus continues: *How he sings, Raggy music to his cattle / As he swings Back and forward in his saddle / On his horse (A pretty good horse), / Who is syncopated gaited, / And with such a funny meter / To the roar of his repeater. / How they run, When they hear the feller's gun, / Because the western folks all know: / He's a hifalootin,' scootin,' shootin' / Son-of-a-gun from Arizona, Ragtime Cowboy / (Talk about your cowboy), Ragtime Cowboy Joe.*

The song has a loping melody to imitate the horse's syncopated gait.

Bob Roberts helped popularize the song in '12 with a very successful recording. It was revived in '39 by Pinky Tomlin, in '49 by Eddy Howard and in '49 by Jo Stafford. The song was also revived by David Seville and the Chipmunks.

"Ragtime Cowboy Joe" can be heard in the following movie musicals: *Hello, Frisco, Hello* ('43) where it was performed by Alice Faye, Jack Oakie and June Havoc, and *Incendiary Blonde* ('45) where it was performed by Betty Hutton.

Hear Paul Whiteman's '40 recording of this ragtime

classic song at http://www.redhotjazz.com/pwo.html. See the sheet music cover and hear a midi musical version at http://www.perfessorbill.com/index2.htm.

Roamin' in the Gloamin'

Words & Music: Harry Lauder

This is one of Harry Lauder's most famous songs. "Roamin' in the Gloamin'" means "Wandering in the twilight."

In the first verse, he claims that he has seen "lots of bonnie lassies" as he has traveled around the world, but his heart has been given to Kate McBride. The chorus follows: *Roamin' in the gloamin' on the bonnie banks o' Clyde, / Roamin' in the gloamin' wi' ma laddie by ma side, / When the sun has gone to rest, that's the time that we like best, / O, it's lovely roamin' in the gloamin'.*

There are a total of three verses. In the second, he asked her to be his bride one night as they were walking side by side in the twilight. Both of them were shy, but he got braver on the journey home (the chorus repeats). In the third verse, they are sitting around the kitchen fire late one evening when she agreed to marry him. He was so happy, he "got up and danced the Hielan' Fling" (the chorus repeats).

Variety chose this song for its *Hit Parade of a Half-Century* representing '11.

See the sheet music cover and the musical score at http://scriptorium.lib.duke.edu/dynaweb/sheetmusic/1910-1920/@Generic__BookTextView/37989, http://digital.library.ucla.edu/apam/ or see the sheet music and hear a midi musical version of this song at http://www.parlorsongs.com/issues/2004-12/thismonth/feature.asp and there is a link there to hear Harry Lauder sing the song, which also includes him talking and laughing.

The Sweetheart of Sigma Chi

Words: Byron D. Stokes; Music: F. Dudleigh Vernor

"The Sweetheart of Sigma Chi" was written in '11 by two undergraduates at Albion College in Michigan. The song has become one of the most popular, if not *the* most popular, college fraternity songs. Byron Stokes wrote the words one June day while in class at Albion College. He took the words to "Dud" Vernor, who completed the music that same day. According to the Albion College website, Mrs. Darleen Wellington Miller, a local piano and vocal teacher, assisted Vernor, one of her pupils, in composing "The Sweetheart of Sigma Chi."

The most popular recorded versions of "The Sweetheart of Sigma Chi" were in late '27 and early '28. The most popular version was by Fred Waring and His Pennsylvanians, a "collegiate glee club" group that was extremely popular in the '20s and 30s. The song rose to No. 3 in December of '27, and it stayed in the top ten for seven weeks. Gene Austin's recording of the song was almost as popular as Waring's.

There have been two *The Sweetheart of Sigma Chi* movies. The first was made in '32, and starred Buster Crabbe and Burr McIntosh. The song is sung in the movie several times by Ted FioRito, a popular bandleader of the era. In '46, the second movie musical *The Sweetheart of Sigma Chi* was released. It starred Marjorie Ann Hoerner. The song was sung in the film by Phil Brito and played in the background.

The famous chorus lyrics are: *The girl of my dreams is the sweetest girl / Of all the girls I know / Each sweet co-ed like a rainbow trail / Fades in the afterglow / The blue of her eye and the gold of her hair / Are a blend of the western sky / And the moonlight beams on the girl of my dreams / She's the sweetheart of Sigma Chi.*

Variety chose this song for its *Hit Parade of a Half-Century* representing '12.

See the sheet music cover and the musical score at http://scriptorium.lib.duke.edu/dynaweb/sheetmusic/1910-1920/@Generic__BookTextView/42859 or at http://digital.library.ucla.edu/apam/.

That Haunting Melody

Words & Music: George M. Cohan

George Cohan was at his peak during this decade; he produced eleven shows in '11 alone and many of his songs became very popular. "That Haunting Melody" is an example. The song first appeared in the Broadway show *Vera Violetta* starring the great Al Jolson. Most of the show's music was not by Cohan, but he did contribute this song (Jolson becomes famous for interpolating songs into his shows and they often have absolutely nothing to do with the plot).

Jolson not only introduced the song in the show, he recorded it for Victor with "Rum Tum Tiddle," also from *Vera Violetta*, on the reverse side. His recording was very popular in '12.

The song is basically about a ten-note theme that haunts the singer; he can't get it out of his head. We hear enough of the haunting little happy tune that it begins to stick with us also. The first verse opens with a question: "Tell me, have you ever heard this melody?" Then he hums the tune in question. He doesn't remember where he heard it, but he liked it right away. It sticks in his brain so much he has "nearly gone insane." *Oh, how I love that strain of melody! (Hum) / Where have I heard that melody? / It seems so familiar to me; (hum) / It's floating in the air It's ev'rywhere / I hear it here, I here it there, (hum) / I love, I love, I love it so! It follows whereever I go, / What is it from? I can't help but hum (hum) / I couldn't live without, I'm mad about, / That haunting melody.*

The sheet music cover and musical score are available at both http://levysheetmusic.mse.jhu.edu/browse.html and at http://lcweb2.loc.gov/cocoon/ihas/loc.natlib.ihas.100005158/. See the sheet music cover and hear a midi musical version (the SCORCH version is great; it allows you to follow the score as you listen) at http://parlorsongs.com/issues/2004-7/thismonth/feature.asp .

Waiting for the Robert E. Lee

Words: L. Wolfe Gilbert; Music: Lewis F. Muir

"Waiting for the Robert E. Lee" has become a ragtime classic. The lyricist, L. Wolfe Gilbert, was inspired to write this lyric when he was in Baton Rouge, Louisiana and witnessed some African Americans unloading freight from a Mississippi River boat named the *Robert E. Lee.*

The verse lyrics name a "levee in old Alabamy," not in Baton Rouge; perhaps Baton Rouge didn't rhyme very well. Below are L. Wolfe Gilbert's wonderful lyrics for the first verse and chorus: *Way down on the levee in old Alabamy, / There's daddy and mammy, there's Ephriam and Sammy, / On a moon light night you can find them all, /*

While they are waitin' the banjos are syncopatin' / What's that they're sayin'? What's that they're sayin'? / While they keep playin' they're hummin' and swayin'.' / It's the good ship Robert E. Lee that's come to carry the cotton away. / Watch them shufflin' along. See them shufflin' along. / Go take your best gal, real pal, go down to the levee, I said to the levee / And join that shufflin' throng, hear that music and song. / It's simply great, mate, waitin' on the levee, waitin' for the Robert E. Lee.

After it was published by F.A. Mills, a song plugger, convinced Al Jolson to perform the song. He sang it at one of the Sunday evening concerts he gave at the Winter Garden Theater. The theater was usually closed on Sunday evening, but Jolson began giving concerts on those evenings so he could sing whatever he wanted to sing with no restrictions. Sometimes, but not often, he felt restricted by appearing in a musical that had a story and musical score. Ruth Roye helped popularize the song with her performances in vaudeville. Gus Edwards' kid troupe also performed the song often in their vaudeville appearances.

The Billy Murray and the Heidelberg Quintet had the most popular recording of the song in '12, but Arthur Collins and Byron Harlan's duet recording and Dolly Connolly's solo version were also popular.

The song has been unusually popular with Hollywood movie musicals, beginning with the first "talkie" *The Jazz Singer* ('27), *Applause* ('29), *The Story of Vernon and Irene Castle* ('39), *Hellzapoppin'* ('41), *Babes on Broadway* ('42), *Cairo* ('42), *Lake Placid Serenade* ('44) and *The Jolson Story* ('46).

Variety chose this song for its *Golden 100 Tin Pan Alley Songs* and *Hit Parade of a Half-Century* representing '12.

The sheet music cover and musical score of this song are available at http://levysheetmusic.mse.jhu.edu/browse. html and at this Library of Congress website: http://lc web2.loc.gov/cocoon/ihas/loc.natlib.ihas.100007899/ or http://scriptorium.lib.duke.edu/dynaweb/sheetmusic/1910-1920/@Generic__BookTextView/47134. Or see the sheet music cover and hear a midi musical version at http:// www.perfessorbill.com/covers/relee.htm or http://parlor songs.com/issues/2001-3/thismonth/featureb.asp.

Hear the Billy Murray and the Heidelberg Quintet's recording of this song at http://www.turtleserviceslim ited.org/Waiting%20for%20the%20Robert%20E%20Lee .htm.

'Way Down South

Music: George Fairman

Variety selected a song they listed as "Down South" for its *Hit Parade of a Half-Century* representing '12.

The Heidelberg Quintet had a popular recording of a song titled "'Way Down South" in '12. "'Way Down South" was written by George Fairman. The *Variety* list does not give composer credit, but it's very doubtful they intended Sigmund Spaeth and W. H. Myddleton's "Down South," which appeared in the '29 film version of *Show Boat* or Earl Welch and Pat Ballard's song from '22.

W.H. Myddleton was a name that was well known in England early in the 20th century, primarily for his classical arrangements and his collection of Welsh, English and American folk melodies. He is also known for his cakewalk rhythm song "Down South" written in '12.

When I Was Twenty-One and You Were Sweet Sixteen

Words: Harry H. Williams; Music: Egbert Van Alystyne

Harry Williams and Egbert Van Alystyne had a good year with "Goodnight Ladies" and "When I Was Twenty-One and You Were Sweet Sixteen."

This song is about a couple, Hiram and Malinda, who are celebrating their 50th wedding anniversary. In the first verse, Malinda asks Hiram if he remembers the importance of that particular day. He does remember and says he'll "hitch old Yankee Doodle to the wagon right away." Next comes the chorus: *Put on your gingham gown, dear, / Come on to town with me. / Let's make believe we're young again, / Just as we used to be. / I'll be your bashful beau, dear, / You'll be my village queen / As in days when I was twenty one, / and you were sweet sixteen.*

Henry Burr and Albert Campbell had a very successful recording of this song in '12. Harry McDonough and the American Quartet also had a recording of it that was popular in '12.

Variety chose this song for its *Hit Parade of a Half-Century* representing '11.

See the sheet music cover and the musical score at http://scriptorium.lib.duke.edu/dynaweb/sheetmusic/1910-1920/@Generic__BookTextView/49393 or see the sheet music cover and hear a midi musical version at http://par lorsongs.com/issues/2004-12/thismonth/feature.asp.

1913

The Curse of an Aching Heart

Words: Henry Fink; Music: Al Piantadosi

Variety chose "The Curse of an Aching Heart" for its *Hit Parade of a Half-Century* representing '13. The sheet music cover advertises the song as "Emma Carus' wonderful hit" and suggests the song is "the moral song with a blessing."

Will Oakland had the most popular recording of this song in '13. Manuel Romain also released a successful recording of it in '13. It was revived in a '36 recording by Fats Waller and his Rhythm, which is available at http:// www.redhotjazz.com/rhythm.html.

The lyrics are rather bitter. The singer says that the loved one dragged him down until his soul was dead. She shattered all his dreams, but he says, "though you're not true, may God bless you, That's the curse of an aching heart." The song's subtitle is "You Made Me What I Am Today."

See the sheet music cover, the lyrics and hear a midi musical version at http://www.halcyondaysmusic.com/ june/june2004.htm. The sheet music cover and musical score of this song are available at http://levysheetmusic. mse.jhu.edu/browse.html and at the Library of Congress website: http://lcweb2.loc.gov/cocoon/ihas/loc.natlib. ihas.100008453/ or a PDF is available of this song at http://library.indstate.edu/level1.dir/cml/rbsc/kirk/sheet_ titles.html.

Danny Boy

Words: Fred E. Weatherly; Music: Londonderry air

An English lawyer, Frederic Edward Weatherly, who was also a radio entertainer and a songwriter, wrote "Danny Boy." He wrote the words and a tune in '10, but the song did not get much attention. Two years later, Weatherly's sister-in-law sent him a tune called "Londonderry Air." He immediately noticed that the melody was perfect for his text. In '13 Weatherly published a revised version of his lyrics with the Londonderry Air tune.

Variety chose "Danny Boy" for its *Hit Parade of a Half-Century* representing '13. The song became one of the most recorded songs of the pre-rock era.

The beautifully sad lyrics follow: *Oh, Danny boy, the pipes, the pipes are calling / From glen to glen and down the mountain side / The summer's gone, and all the leaves are falling / 'Tis ye, 'tis ye must go, and I must bide. / But come ye back when summer's in the meadow / Or when the valley's hushed and white with snow / 'Til I'll be here in sunshine or in shadow / Danny boy, Oh Danny boy, I love you so. / And when ye come and all the flowers are dying / If I am dead, as dead I well may be / Ye'll come and find the place where I am lying / And kneel and say an "Ave" there for me / And I shall hear, 'though soft ye tread around me / And all my grave shall linger sweeter be / Then ye will bend and tell me that ye love me / And I shall sleep in peace until ye come to me.*

Ernestine Schumann-Heink recorded a popular version of "Danny Boy" in '18. Glenn Miller and his orchestra revived it with a popular recording in '40. Those are the only recordings that were popular enough to chart, but there have been a tremendous number of recordings of the song.

Hear a midi musical version and read the lyrics at http://www.geocities.com/dferg5493/dannyboy.html. Or see the non-descript sheet music cover and the musical score at http://scriptorium.lib.duke.edu/dynaweb/sheetmusic/1910-1920/@Generic__BookTextView/4744.

The Green Grass Grew All Around

Words: William Jerome; Music: Harry Von Tilzer

Variety chose "The Green Grass Grew All Around" for its *Hit Parade of a Half-Century* representing '12. Walter Van Brunt helped popularize this song with a popular recording in '13, so it is listed here for that year. The song is often called "And the Green Grass Grew All Around," undoubtedly because the chorus opens with those words, however, the sheet music does not use the "And" in the title.

There are three verses and three choruses to this song, in other words, it can go on forever. Verse one tells us that Johnnie Green and Sallie Brown are spooning in the park. "Underneath a tree, they were making love" sounds unusually risqué for the period, but so does "if you will share my lot I'll give you all I've got," except that in this case Sally was talking about money. The chorus continues: *And the green grass grew all around, all around, all around, / and each little bird in the tree top high said "Oh you Kid" and winked his eye, / and the green grass grew all around, all around, on the ground, / with all your gold my turtle dove, said he "How can you doubt my love?" / and the green grass grew all around, all around, and the green grass grew all around.*

On the sheet music cover illustration is a small bird that is supposedly saying "Oh, you kid," which must have been a very fashionable aphorism during the era. There were two '12 songs that also used the phrase ("I Love, I Love, I Love My Wife, but Oh, You Kid" and "I Love My Wife, but Oh, You Kid!"

The sheet music cover and musical score of this song are available at http://levysheetmusic.mse.jhu.edu/browse.html. See the sheet music cover, read the complete lyrics and hear a midi musical version at http://www.halcyondaysmusic.com/june/june2001.htm.

Hitchy Koo

Words: L. Wolfe Gilbert; Music: Lewis F. Muir & Maurice Abrahams

"Hitchy Koo" was a ragtime song written by Lewis F. Muir, Maurice Abrahams and L. Wolfe Gilbert in '12.

In '17, Raymond Hitchock mounted a series of Broadway revues titled *Hitchy Koo*.

L. Wolfe Gilbert's lyrics for the first verse and chorus follow: *If you've got an ear for music then just gather near, / Tell me, can't you hear it buzzin' in your ear; / Is it music? Sure it's music, it's the best you'll ever hear, / It's my ever lovin' honey calling baby dear. / Say ain't that music weired, strangest you ever heered? / Say, don't you be a-skeered, listen! / Oh, ev'ry evening hear him sing, it's the cutest little thing, got the cutest little swing, / Hitchy Koo, Hitchy Koo, Hitchy Koo. / Oh, simply meant for Kings and Queens, don't ask me what it means, I just love that / Hitchy Koo, Hitchy Koo, Hitchy Koo. / Say he does it just like no one could, / When he does it, say, he does it good. / Oh, ev'ry evening hear him sing, it's the cutest little thing, got the cutest little swing, / Hitchy Koo, Hitchy Koo, Hitchy Koo.*

The American Quartet had a popular recording of "Hitchy Koo" in '13.

Variety chose this song for its *Hit Parade of a Half-Century* representing '12, it is listed in '13 here because it was more popular with the public that year.

The sheet music cover and musical score of this song are available at http://levysheetmusic.mse.jhu.edu/browse.html and at http://lcweb2.loc.gov/cocoon/ihas/loc.natlib.ihas.100007901/. Joseph C. Smith's Orchestra's recording of "Hitchy Koo" is available at http://www.redhotjazz.com/jcso.html.

Last Night Was the End of the World

Words: Andrew B. Sterling; Music: Harry Von Tilzer

This is a touching sentimental ballad that aptly illustrates the musicianship of Harry Von Tilzer. The 12/8 time signature is a little unusual, especially for a popular song. It is even more unusual that the tune switches from 12/8 to 4/4 and back to 12/8 (12/8 is basically like 4/4 with triplets). The range is pretty high in the original key of G with a high G (and even a higher A on the second ending) at the song's climax.

Andrew B. Sterling's lyrics match the music perfectly, but by our modern standards, the words are overly dramatic or sentimental, however that was the style called the sentimental ballad.

The lyrics for the first verse set the stage for the chorus. The man and his supposed sweetheart were "alone in the moonlight," but she told him she "loved another, Last night when you said goodbye." The chorus lyrics follow: *Last night the stars were all aglow, / Last night I loved, I loved you so; / My heart was glad for you were near. / I held your hand and called you dear, my dear, / And then the stars grew dim and cold, / The moon grew pale, my heart grew old, / My dream is o'er, to live no more, / Last night was the end of the world.*

"Last Night Was the End of the World" was popularized by Henry Burr in a very successful recording in '13. Charles Harrison also had a popular recorded version on the market. Lina Cavalieri, a celebrated opera singer of the time, helped popularize the song by performing it on her concerts during her '12–'13 American tour.

The rather non-descript sheet music cover and musical score of this song are available at http://levysheetmusic. mse.jhu.edu/browse.html and at the Library of Congress website: http://lcweb2.loc.gov/cocoon/ihas/loc.natlib. ihas.100009642/. See the sheet music and hear a midi musical version of this song at http://parlorsongs.com/issues/2000-9/2000-9b.asp.

On the Road to Mandalay

Words: Rudyard Kipling; Music: Oley Speaks

"On the Road to Mandalay" is a '07 art song setting of Rudyard Kipling's famous poem. It isn't often that an art song has become popular, but this song is one example. Several baritones popularized it in vaudeville.

Kipling's poem, the lyrics for Speaks melody, follow: *By the old moulmein pagoda Looking eastward to the sea / There's a burma gal a settin' and I know that she waits for me / And the wind is in those palm trees and the temple bells they say / Come you back you mother soldier Come you back to mandalay, / Come you back to Mandalay Come you back to Mandalay Where the old flotilla lay / I can here those paddles chonkin' From rangoon to mandalay / On the road to Mandalay Where the flying fishes play / And the dawn comes up like thunder Out of china across the bay / Ship me somewhere east of Suez Where the best is like the worst / And there ain't no ten commandments and a cat can raise a thirst / And those crazy bells keep ringing 'cause it's there that I long to be / By the egg foo yong pagoda Looking eastward to the see.*

Frank Croxton helped popularize the song with a successful recording of it in '13. There was a '13 song by Al Bryan and Fred Fisher titled "I'm on My Way to Mandalay"

Variety selected this song for its *Hit Parade of a Half-Century* representing '07.

See the sheet music cover and hear a midi musical version at http://parlorsongs.com/issues/2002-1/thismonth/featureb.asp. The sheet music cover and musical score are available at http://levysheetmusic.mse.jhu.edu/browse. html and at http://scriptorium.lib.duke.edu/dynaweb/sheetmusic/.

Peg o' My Heart

Words: Alfred Bryan; Music: Fred Fisher

Jose Collins introduced "Peg o' My Heart" in the *Ziegfeld Follies of 1913* as an interpolation.

The sheet music cover pictures Laurette Taylor. She is sitting with a valise on her lap and a dog in her arms. The cover also includes the following dedication: "written around J. Hartley Manners wonderful character "Peg" in Oliver Morosco's production of the comedy *Peg o' My Heart* at the Cort Theatre N.Y. Dedicated to the star, Miss Laurette Taylor."

Charles Harrison had the most popular recorded version

of the song in '13, but Henry Burr's version was not far behind. Walter Van Brunt's '14 recording was also popular. The song was revived in '47 into a major hit with three No. 1 recordings: by the Harmonicats, by the Three Suns, and by Buddy Clark. In addition, Art Lund, Ted Weems and Clark Dennis released recordings of the song that were popular enough to chart in '47. (For more see '47)

There are the typical two verses and refrain in this classic. The chorus is by far the most popular and most heard part of the song. In fact, the verses are not well known at all. The lyrics of the first verse follow: *Oh! My heart's in a whirl, Over one little girl, / I love her, I love her, yes, I do, / Altho' her heart is far away, / I hope to make her mine some day. / Ev'ry beautiful rose, ev'ry violet knows, / I love, I love her fond and true, / And her heart fondly sighs, as I sing to her eyes, / Her eyes of blue, Sweet eyes of blue, my darling!*

In most recordings, it is the chorus that is sung. The following are the original lyrics for the chorus, which are different than later editions: *Peg o' my heart, I love you, / We'll never part, I love you, / Dear little girl, sweet little girl, / Sweeter than the Rose of Erin, / Are your winning smiles endearin,' / Peg o' my heart, your glances / With Irish art entrance us, Come be my own, / Come, make your home in my heart.*

Somewhere between '13 and the '40s, the lyrics changed. There doesn't seem to be any explanation for the changes. The most common lyrics of the chorus of the '47 recordings are: *Peg o' my heart, I love you / Don't let us part, I love you / I always knew, it would be you, / Since I heard your lilting laughter, / It's your Irish heart I'm after. / Peg o' my heart, Your glances make my heart say / "How's chances," Come, be my own, / Come make your home in my heart.*

The song was used in the '44 movie musical *Babes on Swing Street*, where it was sung by Ann Blyth, and in *Oh You Beautiful Doll* ('49), the screen biography of composer Fred Fisher.

Variety named "Peg o' My Heart" to its *Golden 100 Tin Pan Alley Songs* list and to its *Hit Parade of a Half-Century* representing '13.

The sheet music cover and musical score of this song are available at http://levysheetmusic.mse.jhu.edu/browse. html and at the Library of Congress website: http://lcweb 2.loc.gov/cocoon/ihas/loc.natlib.ihas.100006039/ or at http://scriptorium.lib.duke.edu/dynaweb/sheetmusic/1910-1920/@Generic__BookTextView/36274. See the sheet music cover and hear a midi musical version at http://www.perfessorbill.com/index2.htm.

Row, Row, Row

Words: William Jerome; Music: Jimmie V. Monaco

Elizabeth Brice introduced this cute song in the *Ziegfeld Follies of 1912*. The song tells us how some young couples of the early 1910s courted. Parents were generally very strict and there were only a few things that boys and girls could do together. They had to work at finding ways to be alone. One was a row in the park on a Sunday afternoon. One of the sheet music covers shows a guy in typical early 1910s attire with oars in hand, while the girl is seated at the opposite end of a canoe-looking boat in what appears to be a seat made from a chair back. She's dressed immaculately and shades her skin from the sun with a large umbrella.

The lyrics of the first verse tell about a young "Wisenheimer" named Johnnie Jones who liked to take all the girls for a ride in his little boat. Every Sunday afternoon he'd take his favorite girl, Flo, for a boat ride so they could spoon.

The chorus explains further: *And then he'd row, row, row, way up the river / He would row, row, row. A hug he'd give her, / Then he'd kiss her now and then, she would tell him when, / He'd fool around and fool around, and then they'd kiss again, / And then he'd row, row, row, a little further He would row, oh, oh, oh, oh. / Then he'd drop both his oars, take a few more encores, / And then he'd row, row, row.*

In the second verse, we find out that this "rowing Romeo" would take Flo to an island where he would tell her "tales of love ... until it was time for them to go." Then the chorus is repeated to complete the song.

Ada Jones had a particularly popular recording of the song in '13. A recording of this song by Ada Jones is available for downloading at www.archive.org/audio-details-db.php?collection=78rpm&collectionid=AdaJones_part1&from=BA. Other popular recordings were by Arthur Collins and Byron Harlan and by the American Quartet. Mitchell Ayres and his orchestra revived the song successfully in '40.

"Row, Row, Row" was used in *The Story of Vernon and Irene Castle* ('39), in *Incendiary Blonde* ('45), where it was performed by Betty Hutton, *Two Weeks with Love* ('50), and *The Seven Little Foys* ('55).

Variety chose this song for its *Hit Parade of a Half-Century* representing '12.

The sheet music cover and musical score of this song are available at http://levysheetmusic.mse.jhu.edu/browse.html and at the following Library of Congress website: http://lcweb2.loc.gov/cocoon/ihas/loc.natlib.ihas.100000 7792/ and at http://digital.library.ucla.edu/apam/.

Somebody's Coming to My House

Words & Music: Irving Berlin

Sophie Tucker helped popularize this Irving Berlin song in vaudeville. She introduced it at Hammerstein's Victoria Theater in New York City.

The first verse lyrics tell us that everybody is excited at the singer's house. She says we can't "guess why so she's going to tell us. In the chorus we hear that somebody's coming to her house and they're coming to stay. Her Father is "so happy he's jumping with joy," and he hopes it's a boy. Her mother thinks "He'll be president soon." By this time, we've all figured out that it is a baby that is coming.

Variety chose this song for its *Hit Parade of a Half-Century* representing '13.

The sheet music cover and musical score of this song are available at http://levysheetmusic.mse.jhu.edu/browse.html and at http://scriptorium.lib.duke.edu/sheetmusic/.

The Spaniard That Blighted My Life

Words & Music: Billy Merson

Al Jolson introduced "The Spaniard That Blighted My Life" at the Winter Garden Theater in *The Honeymoon Express*. He also popularized it with a very successful recording in '13.

The sheet music cover identifies this waltz as "Al Jolson's Great Spanish Song," but the number is not a particularly Spanish number. The song's popularity is probably more due to Jolson's performance of it than the song itself; in other words, it might not have become nearly as popular had not Jolson performed it. That's true of a lot of our most famous performing artists, of course. A lot of songs became hits for Elvis Presley or the Beatles that would have remained virtually unknown had they not performed the song in their unique charismatic performing style.

The composer, Billy Merson, had introduced the song in a London music hall in '11, but the song did not become a major hit until Jolson performed and recorded it.

A '30s recording of the song by Al Jolson and Bing Crosby is now a collector's item. The two stars made some ad lib remarks during the recording session that were left on the record. Their lighthearted banter is really refreshing to hear from two such major stars.

In the first of three verses, the singer is telling the story of how this Spaniard blighted his life. At a bullfight, the singer left his future wife to buy some refreshments. While he was gone, "the dirty dog stole her away." And the singer swears his revenge! In the chorus, we find out that the Spaniard is "Alphonso Spagoni, the Toreador." In a particularly catchy, but silly, part of the chorus, the singer sings: *And when I catch the bounder, the blighter I'll kill, / He shall die! he shall die! / He shall die tid-dly-i-ti-ti-ti-ti-ti ti!... / For I'll raise a bunion on his Spanish onion.*

Jolson performed the song in his second "talkie" film, *The Singing Fool* ('28), and in *The Jolson Story* ('46).

Variety chose this song for its *Hit Parade of a Half-Century* representing '11.

The sheet music cover and musical score of this song are available at http://levysheetmusic.mse.jhu.edu/browse.html. See the sheet music cover and hear a midi musical version at http://www.perfessorbill.com/covers/spaniard.htm or http://parlorsongs.com/issues/2002-12/thismonth/feature.asp.

Sweethearts *and* The Angelus

Words: Robert B. Smith; Music: Victor Herbert

Sweethearts has a typical operetta plot. An infant princess is taken to live with the owner of the Laundry of the Wild Geese to protect her from harm during a war. The laundress raises the princess as her own daughter. A Prince, traveling incognito, of course, meets and falls in love with the girl. Once her true identity is revealed, they wed and are crowned co-rulers of the fictitious country of Zilania.

SWEETHEARTS

Christine MacDonald introduced "Sweethearts" in the operetta *Sweethearts*.

Christie MacDonald helped popularize this romantic waltz with a very successful recording in '13. Grace Kerns and Victor Herbert and his orchestra both had popular versions of the song on recordings.

The verses of this Victor Herbert song are in duple meter, while the chorus or refrain is in triple or waltz time. The principal female character, Sylvia, sings this song about trying to find true love.

"Sweethearts" can be heard in the '38 film version of the operetta sung by Jeanette MacDonald, except it had new lyrics by Bob Wright and Chet Forrest. It can be heard with the original lyrics in the '39 screen biography of Victor Herbert, *The Great Victor Herbert*, and in the '51 screen biography of Caruso, *The Great Caruso*. It was also used in the '48 movie musical *Three Darling Daughters*, with Wright and Forrest's lyrics.

The musical score is available at http://levysheetmu sic.mse.jhu.edu/browse.html and the sheet music cover and musical score are available at http://lcweb2.loc.gov/co coon/ihas/loc.natlib.ihas.100006637/.

THE ANGELUS

Christine MacDonald, as Sylvia, introduced this prayer song in the comic opera *Sweethearts*. After a verse and chorus, the Prince and Sylvia join in a duet.

Musically, the song begins in 12/8 time, but occasionally shifts to 9/8 for a measure or two. When the Prince enters the song, the meter shifts to 4/4.

The chorus or refrain is the actual prayer part of the song: *Oh, give me the guiding hand which I so need! / For that only I plead. / Send knowledge unto my wond'ring heart, / And unto the darkness light impart. / Grant me some token, / Some word that's spoken, / One that will be Help to me.*

Christine MacDonald and Reinald Werrenrath had a popular duet recording of "The Angelus" in '13. Prince's Orchestra also had a popular recording of the song in '13.

"The Angelus" did not appear in the screen version of the operetta.

See the sheet music cover and the musical score at http://lcweb2.loc.gov/cocoon/ihas/loc.natlib.ihas.10000 6621/ or at http://levysheetmusic.mse.jhu.edu/browse. html.

Sympathy *and* Giannina Mia
Words: Otto Hauerbach; Music: Rudolf Friml

The Firefly's plot concerns an Italian street singer in New York City who disguises herself as a cabin boy to be near a wealthy man on his yacht. A music teacher becomes impressed with her voice and she soon becomes a star and marries the wealthy man.

SYMPATHY

Audrey Maple and Melville Stewart introduced this romantic waltz in *The Firefly* in '12, Rudolf Friml's first Broadway score. Notice that lyricist Otto Hauerbach had not yet changed his last name to "Harbach."

The song was sung by Jeanette MacDonald and Allan Jones in the '37 film version of *The Firefly*, however as Hollywood often does, the story was changed.

A duet recording by Walter Van Brunt and Helen Clark was very successful in '13.

The song begins with the character Thurston asking "Has some one been such a naughty boy?" Geraldine answers affirmative. Then he asks another similar question, to which she again answers yes. He tells her to dry "those dew-drops," and tells her at the end of the verse and the beginning of the refrain that she needs some sympathy.

This waltz has two verses and different refrains, plus a third refrain as a duet.

Variety chose "Sympathy" for its *Hit Parade of a Half-Century* representing '12.

The non-descript sheet music cover and musical score of this song are available at http://levysheetmusic.mse. jhu.edu/browse.html.

GIANNINA MIA

Emma Trentini introduced "Giannina Mia" in *The Firefly*. In the '37 film version of the operetta, it was sung by Jeanette MacDonald.

The character Nina sings this song in *The Firefly*. In the verse, she sings about gliding over a blue lagoon in a gondola. "Giannina" is a girl's name, similar to "Jane." "Mia" is "my," so the title means "My Jane." In the chorus, she sings: *For I adore you, Giannina mia! / More, more and more, / I adore you, Giannina mia! / Queens there have been, who in ages of old / Shone more resplendent with jewels and gold, / Precious jewels not half so rare, dear, / As the splendor of your wondrous hair, dear. / For I adore, I adore you, Giannina mia, / More, more and more, / I adore you, Giannina mia! / My heart's your throne, dear, / My heart's your throne, dear, / There you should rule alone, alone!*

Variety chose "Giannina Mia" for its *Hit Parade of a Half-Century* representing '12.

Another song from the musical, "When a Maid Comes Knocking at Your Heart," was popularized in a recording in '13 by Olive Kline. Another famous song from this comic opera is "Love Is Like a Firefly," which was not terribly popular in any recordings, but the melody of the chorus is well known, especially as an instrumental.

The rather non-descript sheet music cover and musical score are available at http://digital.library.ucla.edu/apam/.

Till the Sands of the Desert Grow Cold
Words: George Graff, Jr.; Music: Ernest R. Ball

Ernest Ball wrote this waltz in '11, but it was popularized in a particularly popular recording by Alan Turner in '13. Frank Croxton also had a popular recording of the song in '13, as did Donald Chalmers in '12.

This song is an instrumental that starts in the key of C, modulates to E-flat and then back to C. In the sheet music, there were no lyrics; it was strictly an instrumental. There appears to have been a vocal version with lyrics by George Graff, Jr. published in '12. The song also starts in waltz time, but changes to 12/8 (more like 4/4 in triplets) for the chorus.

In the first verse, the singer wants the hot winds that blow over desert sands to "tell thee that I love thee," and will love "thee, till desert sands grow cold."

The chorus continues: *Love me, I'll love thee, / Till the sands of the desert grow cold, / And their infinite number are told. / God gave thee to me, and mine thou shalt be, / Forever to have and to hold. / Till the story of Judgement is told, / And the myst'ries of Heaven unfold, / I'll turn love, to thee, My shrine thou shalt be, / Till the sands of the desert grow cold.*

The sheet music cover and musical score of this song are available at http://levysheetmusic.mse.jhu.edu/browse. html, at http://scriptorium.lib.duke.edu/dynaweb/sheet music/1910-1920/@Generic__BookTextView/46017 and at http://digital.library.ucla.edu/apam/. The sheet music at Duke doesn't credit Graff as the lyricist because it is the instrumental version.

The Trail of the Lonesome Pine
Words: Ballard MacDonald; Music: Harry Carroll

"The Trail of the Lonesome Pine" appears at first glance to be a "cowboy" song, but it is set in the Blue Ridge Mountains of Virginia. There was a popular novel of the same title by John Fox, Jr. on the market at the time the song was written, but it was set in the Cumberland Mountains of Kentucky. Muriel Window interpolated the song into *The Passing Show of 1914*.

The first verse tells us that the singer's girl, June, lives in a cabin on a Virginia mountain where a lonesome pine stands. He intends to marry this girl very soon, but in the meantime, he's sure she is waiting "'neath that lone pine tree." The most famous part of the song, of course, is the chorus: *In the Blue Ridge Mountains of Virginia, / On the trail of the lonesome pine / In the pale moonshine our hearts entwine, / Where she carved her name and I carved mine; / Oh, June, like the mountains I'm blue / Like the pine I am lonesome for you, / In the Blue Ridge Mountains of Virginia, / On the trail of the lonesome pine.*

Henry Burr and Albert Campbell had a very popular recording of this song in '13. Elsie Baker and James F. Harrison also had a popular recording on the market in '13.

Laurel and Hardy's performance of the song in *Way Out West* ('37) is particularly memorable. Their rendition is both delightful and comic.

Variety chose "Sweethearts" for its *Hit Parade of a Half-Century* representing '13.

See the sheet music cover and hear a midi musical version at http://www.halcyondaysmusic.com/april/april 2002.htm or http://parlorsongs.com/insearch/cowboys/ cowboys.asp. The sheet music cover and musical score of this song are available at http://levysheetmusic.mse.jhu. edu/browse.html and at http://library.indstate.edu/level1. dir/cml/rbsc/kirk/ or http://scriptorium.lib.duke.edu/dyna web/sheetmusic/1910-1920/@Generic__BookTextView/ 46350.

When I Lost You

Words & Music: Irving Berlin

One of the aspiring young singers who came to the publishing office of Waterson, Berlin and Snyder looking for free professional copies of new songs was the twenty-year-old sister of songwriter Ray Goetz, Dorothy. Instead of a new song to perform, Dorothy got a date with Berlin and within a few weeks a proposal of marriage. On their Cuban honeymoon, Dorothy contracted typhoid fever and died shortly after they returned to New York City.

Berlin attempted to write about his wife's death in the tragically autobiographical "When I Lost You." It was unlike any song he had written previously. Melodically, it was a simple waltz with bittersweet harmony that enhanced the melancholy of the lyrics.

Berlin's poignant lyrics list the things he feels he lost when his beloved young wife died: *the sunshine and roses, ... the heavens of blue, ... the beautiful rainbow, the morning dew, ... the angel who gave me summer, the whole winter too, ... the gladness that turned into sadness.*

Henry Burr had a very popular recording of the song in '13. Manuel Romain also had a popular recording of the song on the market.

Berlin never allowed a movie to be made about his life before he died, but the tragic loss of his young wife and his love affair with Ellin MacKay in the early '20s before they married would make an excellent love story film. Add in Berlin's wonderful music, particularly the love songs, and a boxoffice hit would certainly be the result.

Berlin's tragic song appeared in the movie *The Cat's Meow* (2001).

The sheet music cover and musical score of this song are available at http://levysheetmusic.mse.jhu.edu/browse. html and at http://scriptorium.lib.duke.edu/dynaweb/ sheetmusic/1910-1920/@Generic__BookTextView/49327. Read the lyrics at http://www.lyricstime.com/irving-ber lin-when-i-lost-you-lyrics.html.

When Irish Eyes Are Smiling *and* Isle o' Dreams

Words: Chauncey Olcott & George Graff, Jr.; Music: Ernest R. Ball

WHEN IRISH EYES ARE SMILING

Along with "My Wild Irish Rose" and "Mother Machree," "When Irish Eyes Are Smiling" is considered one of the most popular Irish ballads of all time. This lilting Irish waltz was first sung by co-writer Chauncey Olcott in the '12 musical play *The Isle o' Dreams.*

The chorus is very familiar. It is heard yearly during St. Patrick's Day celebrations around the world. *When Irish eyes are smiling, / Sure it's like a morn in Spring. / In the lilt of Irish laughter / You can hear the angels sing. / When Irish eyes are happy, / All the world seems bright and gay, / And when Irish eyes are smiling, / Sure they steal your heart away.*

Chauncey Olcott's recording of the song was the most popular version on the market, but Harry MacDonough's was also well received.

The song can be heard in the movie musical *Let Freedom Ring* ('38), *Doughboys in Ireland* ('43), *Irish Eyes Are Smiling* ('44), Ernest R. Ball's screen biography, *My Wild Irish Rose* ('47), Chauncey Olcott's screen biography, and *Top o' the Morning* ('49).

Variety chose "When Irish Eyes Are Smiling" for its *Hit Parade of a Half-Century* representing '12.

The non-descript sheet music cover and musical score of this song are available at http://levysheetmusic.mse.jhu. edu/browse.html and at http://scriptorium.lib.duke. edu/dynaweb/sheetmusic/1910-1920/@Generic__Book-TextView/49465. Read the lyrics at http://www.images ofireland.net/song15.html.

ISLE O' DREAMS

Another song from the musical *The Isle o' Dreams* was "Isle o' Dreams." Chauncey Olcott also introduced this song, which he and Frederic Knight Logan co-wrote. The song's alternate title is "Goodbye, My Emerald Land."

The singer is sad to be leaving his hometown. He hopes his native land will at least pretend to say: "Lad, if you ne'er return 'twill break my heart, 'twill break my heart!" He promises he'll never find another place half as dear to his heart.

Variety chose "Isle o' Dreams" for its *Hit Parade of a Half-Century* representing '12.

See the sheet music cover and musical score at http:// digital.library.ucla.edu/apam/.

When That Midnight Choo-Choo Leaves for Alabam'

Words & Music: Irving Berlin

After Irving Berlin lost his young wife to typhoid fever, he escaped into his musical world. His next big hit was "When That Midnight Choo-Choo Leaves for Alabam.'" It was more like "Alexander's Ragtime Band." It was a syncopated, upbeat crowd pleaser.

Arthur Collins and Byron Harlan's duet recording of the song was very popular. The Victor Military Band also had a popular recording of the song.

According to the first verse of the song, a person is packing his things, giving the landlord back the key to the dreary flat and getting ready to catch the train back home.

In the chorus he claims he has his fare and will tell "that rusty-haired conductor man" that he's to stop the train in Alabam'. He intends to remain there with his honey-lamb.

In the second verse, the singer says he intends "to over-feed my face 'cause I haven't had a good meal since the day I went away." He is going to kiss his "Pa and Ma a dozen times for ev'ry star shining over Alabama's new mown hay." A repeat of the chorus concludes the song.

Alice Faye performed the song in the movie musical *Alexander's Ragtime Band* ('38), Judy Garland and Fred Astaire sang it in *Easter Parade* ('48), and Ethel Merman, Dan Dailey, Mitzi Gaynor and Donald O'Connor performed it in *There's No Business Like Show Business* ('54).

Variety chose this song for its *Hit Parade of a Half-Century* representing '12.

See the sheet music cover and hear a midi musical version at http://www.perfessorbill.com/covers/midchoo. htm. See the sheet music cover and the musical score at http://library.indstate.edu/level1.dir/cml/rbsc/kirk/ or http://scriptorium.lib.duke.edu/dynaweb/sheetmusic/1910-1920/@Generic__BookTextView/50156 or http://libraries. mit.edu/music/sheetmusic/childpages/whenthatmidnight. html. The lyrics and chord chart are available at http:// www.jbott.com/wmnchoo.html.

Where Did You Get That Girl?

Words: Bert Kalmar; Music: Harry Puck

"Where Did You Get That Girl?" was introduced and popularized in vaudeville.

The first verse of the song tells us that Johnnie Warner is sitting in a corner of a café feeling lonesome because he does not have a girl friend. At another table he sees a guy he knows with a girl named Mable. He asks the guy: *Where did you get that girl? Oh! you lucky devil. / Where did you get that girl? tell me on the level. / Have you ever kissed her, If she has a sister / lead me, lead me, lead me to her mister. / Gee! I wish that I had a girl, I'd love 'er I'd love 'er, / Oh goodness how I'd love 'er. / If you can find another, I'll take her home to mother, / Where! Where! Where did you get that girl?*

The song provided the title for a '41 movie musical. Harriet Parrish sang the song in the film and it was also the theme song for the movie. Fred Astaire and Anita Ellis sang it in *Three Little Words* ('50), the screen biography of Bert Kalmar and Harry Ruby.

Variety chose this song for its *Hit Parade of a Half-Century* representing '13.

Walter Van Brunt helped popularize the song in '13 with a popular recording.

The sheet music cover and musical score of this song are available at http://levysheetmusic.mse.jhu.edu/browse. html and at the following Library of Congress website: http://lcweb2.loc.gov/cocoon/ihas/loc.natlib.ihas.10000 8565/. See the sheet music cover, read the lyrics and hear a midi musical version at http://www.halcyondaysmusic. com/june/june2001.htm.

You Made Me Love You

Words: Joseph McCarthy; Music: James V. Monaco

"You Made Me Love You," a *Variety Golden 100 Tin Pan Alley Song*, originated in '13. Al Jolson introduced it in the Winter Garden extravaganza *The Honeymoon Express*.

One of the song's greatest honors came in '63, when ASCAP selected it as one of sixteen numbers for its *All-Time Hit Parade*.

Jolson reportedly first appeared as the black-faced character Gus in *The Honeymoon Express*. He appeared in black-face in almost all of his later Winter Garden musicals. He also introduced what became one of his trademarks: getting down on one knee, stretching out his arms as if pleading to the audience. Apparently Jolson was suffering from an ingrown toenail and to relieve the pressure, he knelt and flexed the troubled toe. Then to justify kneeling, he stretched out his arms as if to emphasize a poignant part of the lyrics. The audience loved it! And a Jolson trademark was born.

Joseph McCarthy's famous lyrics follow: *You made me love you, / I didn't want to do it, I didn't want to do it, / You made me love you / and all the time you knew it, / I guess you always knew it. / You made me happy sometimes, you made me glad, / But there were times, dear, you made me feel so bad. / You made me sigh for, / I didn't want to tell you, I didn't want to tell you, / I want some love that's true, yes I do, 'deed I do, you know I do. / Gimme, gimme what I cry for, / you know you got the brand of kisses that I'd die for / You know you made me love you.*

Al Jolson helped popularize the song in '13 with a very successful recording. William J. Bailey also had a popular recording of the song in '13. The song's next success came in '38, when the young Judy Garland sang it to a photograph of Clark Gable in the film *Broadway Melody of 1938*. Her recording of "{Dear Mr. Gable} You Made Me Love You" was inducted into the Grammy Hall of Fame in '98. Roger Edens added the following lyrics to the original ones for Judy's scene with Gable's photograph: *Dear Mr. Gable, I am writing this to you / and I hope that you will read it so you'll know, / My heart beats like a hammer and I stutter and I stammer / every time I see you at the picture show. / I guess I'm just another fan of yours, / and I thought I'd write and tell you so.*

Judy Garland's version of the song was nominated for the American Film Institute's list of the greatest songs ever from American films, but did not make the final list.

Bing Crosby revived it with a moderately successful recorded version in '40. Harry James further enhanced his reputation as one of the most popular bandleaders and trumpeters of the Big Band Era with a schmaltzy rendition of "You Made Me Love You" in '41. James featured the song in the motion pictures *Syncopation* and *Private Bucka-roo*, also in '41. James's recording of the song peaked at No. 5 on *Billboard*, but never charted on *Your Hit Parade*. However, the song has developed into a standard over the years, and James's recording of the song is one of his most famous ones.

"You Made Me Love You" was used in several other movie musicals, including *The Jolson Story* ('46), *Three Darling Daughters* ('48), *Jolson Sings Again* ('49), and Ruth Etting's screen biography *Love Me or Leave Me* ('55).

Variety chose this song for its *Hit Parade of a Half-Century* representing '12.

The sheet music cover and musical score of this song are available at http://levysheetmusic.mse.jhu.edu/browse. html and at the following Library of Congress website: http://lcweb2.loc.gov/cocoon/ihas/loc.natlib.ihas.10000 7799/ or http://scriptorium.lib.duke.edu/dynaweb/sheet music/1910-1920/@Generic__BookTextView/53347.

1914

The Aba Daba Honeymoon

Words & Music: Arthur Fields & Walter Donovan

This cute novelty song is about a monkey wedding and honeymoon. Ruth Roye introduced it at the Palace Theater in New York City in '14.

Most of the lyrics a nonsensical. "'Aba, daba, daba, daba, daba, daba, dab,' said the Chimpie to the Monk, 'Baba, daba, daba, daba, daba, daba, dab,' said the Monkey to the Chimp." Later it explains that all that gibberish means "Monk, I love but you" or "Chimp, I love you too." The big baboon married them and they went on their "Aba Daba Honeymoon."

Arthur Collins and Byron Harlan's duet recording helped popularize the song nationwide in '14.

"Aba Daba Honeymoon" was used in the following movie musicals: *King of Jazz* ('30), *Billy Rose's Diamond Horseshoe* ('45), and *Two Weeks with Love* ('50), where it was performed by Debbie Reynolds and Carlton Carpenter. "Aba Daba Honeymoon" was nominated for the American Film Institute's list of the greatest songs ever from American films, but did not make the final list.

Kitty Kalen's '50 recording of the song sold well, but Debbie Reynolds and Carlton Carpenter's rendition from the soundtrack of the film sold even better in '50 and '51; it became a million seller. Several other recorded versions were popular in '51, including those by Richard Hayes, by Freddy Martin, by Cliff Stewart and by Hoagy Carmichael and Cass Daley.

Hear Arthur Collins and Byron Harlan's '14 recording of this song at http://www.firstworldwar.com/audio/1914.htm.

The sheet music cover and musical score are available at http://levysheetmusic.mse.jhu.edu/browse.html and at the following Library of Congress website: http://lcweb2.loc.gov/cocoon/ihas/loc.natlib.ihas.100006022/. Read lyrics at http://lirama.net/song/16576.

Ballin' the Jack

Words: James Henry Burris; Music: Chris Smith

Billy Kent and Jeanette Warner introduced this ragtime dance number in vaudeville in '13. "Ballin' the Jack" began as a piano piece, a very popular style during these ragtime years. The song was billed as a "Fox-Trot" dance.

The original piano version was written in '12; James Burris added in lyrics in '13. *Variety* selected "Ballin' the Jack" as one of its *Golden 100 Tin Pan Alley Songs* and for its *Hit Parade of a Half-Century* representing '13.

The title of this Dixieland toe-tapper comes from railroad slang. "Jack" was an African American term for "locomotive" and "highball," which was the starting signal. So, "ballin' the jack" meant moving fast and having a good time.

In the first verse of this song, we learn that the "folks in Georgia's bout to go insane" because this new dance came to the state. The singer admits he is to blame for introducing it. He says he'll demonstrate the dance and when he does, we'll "say that it's a bear."

The lyrics of the chorus then instruct us how to do this dance: *First you put your two knees close up tight, / Then you sway 'em to the left, / Then you sway 'em to the right. / Step around the floor kind of nice and light, / Then you twis' around and twis' around with all your might. / Stretch your lovin' arms straight out in space, / Then you do the Eagle Rock with style and grace, / Swing your foot way round, then bring it back; / Now that's what I call "Ballin' the Jack."*

Prince's Orchestra had a big hit recording of the song in '14. Although it wasn't terribly popular, Chubby Checker released a twist version of the song during the early '60s.

Judy Garland performed "Ballin' the Jack" with Gene Kelly in the movie musical *For Me and My Gal* in '42, while Danny Kaye performed it the '51 movie musical *On the Riviera*. Dean Martin sang it in the '51 film *That's My Boy*.

The sheet music cover and musical score of this song are available at http://levysheetmusic.mse.jhu.edu/browse.html, at http://digital.library.ucla.edu/ and at http://lcweb2.loc.gov/cocoon/ihas/loc.natlib.ihas.100008982/. Red Nichols' Five Pennies' recording of "Ballin' the Jack" is available at http://www.redhotjazz.com/rn5p.html or Paul Whiteman's at http://www.redhotjazz.com/pwo.html. Hear the National Promenade Orchestra's '14 recording of "Ballin' the Jack" at http://www.archive.org/audio-/audio-details-db.php?collectionid=balljack1914&collection=opensource_audio or at http://www.edisonnj.org/menlopark/vintage/blueamberol.asp. See the sheet music cover and hear a midi musical version at http://parlorsongs.com/issues/2002-2/thismonth/featurea.asp.

By the Beautiful Sea

Words: Harold R. Atteridge; Music: Harry Carroll

"By the Beautiful Sea" was introduced in vaudeville by the Stanford Four. The publisher hired a group of boys in sailor suits to perform the song in the Coney Island amusement park area to help familiarize the public with the song. The marketing effort worked. The song became a huge hit. Muriel Window further popularized the song when she interpolated the song into the revue *The Passing Show of 1914*.

The first verse of the song, which is not nearly as well known as the chorus, tells us that "Joe and Jane were always together." Joe loves summer weather and invites Jane to go to the beach. Jane liked the idea "so he'd get his Ford, Holler 'all board'" and off they'd go. Then comes the familiar chorus: *By the sea, by the sea, by the beautiful sea. / You and I, you and I, oh, how happy we'll be. / When each wave comes a-rollin' in, we duck or swim. / And we'll float and fool around the water. / Over and under and then up for air. / Pa is rich, Ma is rich, so, now what do we care. / I'd like to be beside your side, beside the sea, beside the seaside by the beautiful sea.*

Now, the second verse, which is almost never heard, is really surprising. It starts out telling us that even though Joe is "quite the sport on Sunday," he "eats at Childs on Monday," implying a less-than-fashionable restaurant. Jane was also less than she appeared to be, because she'd "go to work marcelling hair" ("marcelling" meant to style the hair with deep, regular waves, using a curling iron). Now the really surprising part. It seems that Joe had a wife and he'd leave her on Sunday to ostensibly go to work. He'd miss the train into the city and "get his Ford and Jane" and off they'd go to the beach. Extramarital affairs may have been nothing new in the early 1910s, but the surprising thing is that the subject was part of a very popular song.

The Heidelberg Quintet and Ada Jones and Billy Watkins both had very popular recordings of the song in '14. Prince's Orchestra also had a popular recorded version on the market.

The song was used in the movie musical *The Story of Vernon and Irene Castle* ('39), *For Me and My Gal* ('42), where it was performed by Gene Kelly and Judy Garland, and *Atlantic City* ('44), where it was sung by Constance Moore.

Variety chose this song for its *Hit Parade of a Half-Century* representing '14.

The sheet music cover has a photo of the Hippodrome Four, as if they were the ones who popularized the song. The cover also is a painting of a typical beach scene of the era (the artist is uncredited). It's interesting to see the bathing attire that was fashionable. The men in the painting are not dressed in swimsuits; they have on coats, ties, hats, and are carrying canes. One woman is in a dress and shields herself from the sun with an umbrella. A couple of sailboats float placidly in the distance. The sheet music cover and musical score are available at http://lcweb2.loc.gov/cocoon/ihas/loc.natlib.ihas.100005022/, at http://digital.nypl.org/lpa, and at http://levysheetmusic.mse.jhu.edu/browse.html.

Can't Yo' Heah Me Callin' Caroline?

Words: William H. Gardner; Music: Caro Roma

William H. Gardner wrote the dialect lyric for "Can't Yo' Heah Me Callin,' Caroline" to Caro Roma's tune. Roma's given name was Carrie Northey.

The following is the chorus of the song so the reader can get an idea of the dialect lyrics: *Can't yo' heah me callin,' Caroline, / It's mah heart acallin' dine. / Lordy, how I miss yo' gal o' mine. / Wish dat I could kiss yo' Caroline! / Ain't no use now fo' de sun to shine, / Caroline, Caroline, / Can't yo' heah mah lips a-sayin' / Can't yo' heah mah soul a-prayin,' / Can't yo' heah me callin' Caroline.*

Variety chose this song for its *Hit Parade of a Half-Century* representing '14.

George MacFarlane helped popularize this sentimental "coon" song with a successful recording in '14. Red Nichols' Five Pennies' recording of this song is available at http://www.redhotjazz.com/rn5p.html.

The song, as "Can't You Hear Me Callin,' Caroline," was used in the screen biography of Marilyn Miller, *Look for the Silver Lining*, in '49.

The non-descript sheet music cover and musical score of this song are available at http://levysheetmusic.mse.jhu.edu/browse.html. See the sheet music cover and hear a midi musical version at http://parlorsongs.com/issues/1999-8/aug99gallery.asp.

The Good Ship Mary Ann

Words: Gus Kahn; Music: Grace LeBoy

Nora Bayes helped popularize "The Good Ship Mary Ann" with a popular recording in '14.

The words of the first verse tell us that a woman is standing on a pier "strainin' her eyes" as she waits for the boat that is bringing her honey. The verse ends leading into the chorus with "No use to hold her, no use to scold her, She wants the world to hear her singing!"

The chorus is what she sings: *It's the good ship Mary Ann / Bringing back my lovin' man, / Step aside and let me meet him, let me greet him. / Lordy, I could eat him! / Bless the captain, bless that crew, / Bless the dear old Mississippi too! / For bringing back my lovin' man, / On the good ship Mary Ann, / Bless the good ship Mary Ann!*

See the sheet music cover and the music score at http://lcweb2.loc.gov/cocoon/ihas/loc.natlib.ihas.100006829/ or a PDF of this song is available at http://library.indstate.edu/level1.dir/cml/rbsc/kirk/sheet_titles.html.

Variety chose this song for its *Hit Parade of a Half-Century* representing '14.

He's a Devil in His Own Home Town

Words: Grant Clarke & Irving Berlin; Music: Irving Berlin

There are a couple of verses to this song, but in the first verse we learn about an uncle who has a two thousand acre farm. This uncle "has a reputation in the village" as "a gosh darn dude." His behavior might be okay for his hometown, but not in the big city.

The chorus begins by repeating "He's a devil" three times. Then the lyrics tell us some of the devilish things he does: he's a clown, he spends money foolishly (five cents, as if it were nothing), he tells "stories in a groc'ry store," makes everybody laugh and he cheats playing checkers. In summary, "He's a devil in his own home town."

Variety chose this song for its *Hit Parade of a Half-Century* representing '14.

Billy Murray had a very popular recording of "He's a Devil in His Own Home Town" in '14. Eddie Morton also had a popular recording of the song in '14.

The sheet music cover and musical score of this song are available at http://levysheetmusic.mse.jhu.edu/browse.html and at http://scriptorium.lib.duke.edu/dynaweb/sheetmusic/1910-1920/@Generic__BookTextView/12347. See the sheet music cover and to hear a midi musical version at http://parlorsongs.com/issues/1998-5/may98feature.asp (this website says that Berlin not only wrote the music and lyrics, but did the cover art for the sheet music cover).

I Love the Ladies

Words & Music: Grant Clarke

Florenze Tempest introduced "I Love the Ladies" in the musical *Our American Boy* in '14. Arthur Collins and Byron Harlan helped popularize the song with a very successful duet recording in '14. The song became a barbershop quartet favorite.

The sheet music cover has a picture of a person, Florenze Tempest it seems, but it's difficult to tell if it is a young male or a female. We know Florenz Ziegfeld is male, but what about Florenze? If the singer isn't male, it doesn't make a lot of sense for a female to sing "I Love the Ladies."

The lyrics are not the greatest example of the lyricist's art. Perhaps that is why the song has not remained as longlastingly popular as some others from this era. The first verse introduces us to the twenty-one year old Johnny Dunn, who "liked to dance in each café." The reason he danced in each café is because he liked the ladies. He had a soft life because his father was rich. Even so, the father told Johnny to find a job, but Johnny replied "I'm having too much fun."

The chorus begins "I love the ladies, I love the ladies, I love to be among the girls." When he's having tea, he wants to have it with a brunette. The next phrase: "And in the good old Summer time," is a melodic quote from "In the Good Old Summer Time." When he goes swimming, he wants women around. When he's "in London, Paris, and old Vienna, or any other town," he doesn't like it unless the ladies are around. He loves the small ones and tall ones. As a matter of fact, he thinks "The world can't twirl around without a beautiful girl."

The sheet music cover and musical score are available at http://levysheetmusic.mse.jhu.edu/browse.html and at http://lcweb2.loc.gov/cocoon/ihas/loc.natlib.ihas.10000 7939/.

I Want to Go Back to Michigan (Down on the Farm)

Words & Music: Irving Berlin

The ragtime craze was fading slightly by '14 and some songs had a more romantic feel. Many songs speak to home, family and sweethearts; this Irving Berlin song is an example.

In the first verse we learn that the singer was born in Michigan and wants to return to his hometown "to fish again in the river that flows beside the fields of waving corn." To set up the chorus, he tells us what a lonesome soul he is and he'll tell us why.

Not unlike Berlin's "He's a Devil in His Own Hometown," the chorus to this song begins by repeating "I want to go back" three times. Then he enumerates some of the things he misses: away from harm, a milk pail on his arm, and the rooster that woke him at 4 a.m. He confesses that he thinks the "great big city's very pretty," but he wishes "That I was in Michigan down on the farm."

Variety chose "I Want to Go Back to Michigan" for its *Hit Parade of a Half-Century* representing '14.

Elida Morris had a very popular recording of "I Want to Go Back to Michigan" in '14. Morton Harvey had a successful recording of the song in '15.

Judy Garland performed this song in the '48 movie musical *Easter Parade*. It also appeared in the films *Sing Again of Michigan* ('51) and *Bowling for Columbine* (2002).

The sheet music cover and musical score are available at http://levysheetmusic.mse.jhu.edu/browse.html and at http://scriptorium.lib.duke.edu/sheetmusic/b/b05/b0598/. See the sheet music cover and hear a midi musical version at http://parlorsongs.com/issues/1998-11/orignov98feature.asp.

I'm on My Way to Mandalay

Words: Al Bryan; Music: Fred Fisher

Alfred Bryan and Fred Fisher's "I'm on My Way to Mandalay" was popularized by the trio, Henry Burr, Albert Campbell and Will Oakland with a very successful recording in '14.

Mandalay is a popular destination for songs during this era. There's "On the Road to Mandalay" and "I'm on My Way to Mandalay."

The lyrics tell us that the singer's loved one is far away in the "Land of Love," which is Mandalay. He's going there "to find someone who waits for me across the sea." The chorus follows: *I'm on my way to Mandalay, / Beneath the shelt'ring palms I want to stray, / Oh, let me live and love for aye, / On that Island far away; / I'm sentimental for my Oriental love, so sweet and gentle, / That's why I'm on my way to Mandalay, / I've come to say "Good-bye."*

The sheet music cover and musical score are available at http://levysheetmusic.mse.jhu.edu/browse.html and at http://lcweb2.loc.gov/cocoon/ihas/loc.natlib.ihas.10000 6033/ and http://scriptorium.lib.duke.edu/dynaweb/sheet music/1910-1920/@Generic__BookTextView/19599. See the sheet music cover, read the lyrics and hear a midi musical version at http://www.halcyondaysmusic.com/april/april2003.htm.

If I Had My Way

Words: Lou Klein; Music: James Kendis

Variety chose "If I Had My Way" for its *Hit Parade of a Half-Century* representing '13. The Peerless Quartet had a popular recording of "If I Had My Way" in '14, so it is listed here rather than '13. The song was revived by Bunny Berigan and his orchestra in '36 and by Glen Gray and the Casa Loma Orchestra in '39. On the sheet music cover Ethel Green is pictured, with a caption that reads, "introduced in vaudeville with unprecedented success by Ethel Green."

The song provided the title for a movie musical starring Bing Crosby in '40. It can also be heard in the '46 movie musical *Sunbonnet Sue*, where it was sung by Gale Storm and Phil Regan.

The lyrics of the verse say "If I only had my way," your dreams would come true and the world would be a paradise. The chorus continues: *If I had my way, dear, forever, / There'd be a garden of roses for you and for me. / A thousand and one things, dear, I would do, / Just for you, just for you, only you. / If I had my way, we would never grow old, / And sunshine I'd bring ev'ry day. / You would reign all alone, / Like a queen on a throne, If I had my way.*

See the sheet music cover, the lyrics and hear a midi musical version at http://www.halcyondaysmusic.com/may/may2004.htm or see the sheet music and the musical score at http://lcweb2.loc.gov/cocoon/ihas/loc.natlib.ihas.100006805/.

It's a Long, Long Way to Tipperary (see '15)

Little Grey Home in the West

Words: D. Eardley-Wilmot; Music: Hermann Lohr

D. Eardley-Wilmet and Hermann Lohr wrote this sentimental song in '11, but it was popularize in '14.

The lyrics paint a lovely picture of the "Little Grey Home in the West." The golden sunset in the hills at the end of a long day and even though the toil may be tiring, he forgets to be weary, because all the cares of the world are charmed away "In my little grey home in the west." He is always welcomed home, finds "lips I am burning to kiss," and "a thousand things other men miss." It may be "a tumble-down nest," but "no place can compare with my little grey home in the west."

Charles Harrison popularized "Little Grey Home in the West" with a successful recording in '14. Maggie Teyte also had a popular recording of the song in '14.

The song (spelled "Little Gray Home in the West") was used in the '38 film version of *Sweethearts*.

Variety chose this song for its *Hit Parade of a Half-Century* representing '11.

The non-descript sheet music cover and musical score are available at http://levysheetmusic.mse.jhu.edu/browse.

html and at http://scriptorium.lib.duke.edu/dynaweb/sheetmusic/1910-1920/@Generic__BookTextView/26842. Hear Peter Dawson's '12 recording of this song at http://www.firstworldwar.com/audio/littlegreyhomeinthewest.htm.

Love's Own Sweet Song

Words: C.C.S. Cushing & E.P. Heath; Music: Emmerich Kalman

Variety chose "Love's Own Sweet Song" for its *Hit Parade of a Half-Century* representing '14. The song was introduced in the operetta *Sari*.

In the first verse, the singer is completely caught up in the happiness of love. The lovers had never known "there was a joy like this." The refrain lyrics follow: *Oh let us come and dance with joy / Since love and life are ours, / For youth is strong and blood grows warm / Beneath the scent of flow'rs / Music light and laughter bright shall carry us along / Singing with our hearts on fire love's own sweet song.*

Charles Harrison and Grace Kerns had a popular duet recording of this song in '14.

A PDF of "Love's Own Sweet Song" is available at http://library.indstate.edu/level1.dir/cml/rbsc/kirk/sheet_titles.html.

The Memphis Blues

Words: George A. Norton; Music: William Christopher Handy

In '09, W.C. Handy wrote a song for a political candidate for Mayor of Memphis, Tennessee. The song became so popular that the candidate, Edward Crump, was elected.

In '12, Handy revised the piece as a piano blues and published it himself. Renamed "The Memphis Blues," it was the first commercial blues ever published. Later in '12, Handy sold the rights to the song to a New York publishing company for $50. The new owner, Theron A. Bennett Company, hired George Norton to write the lyrics. The song was then reissued in '13.

In '31, Charles Tobias and Peter DeRose wrote a new set of lyrics for the melody. Their version was published by Joe Morris Music Company.

The original version, Handy's melody with Norton's lyrics, was used in the '34 movie musical *Belle of the Nineties*, which starred Mae West, and in the '41 movie musical *The Birth of the Blues*.

Variety chose this song for its *Hit Parade of a Half-Century* representing '12.

Prince's Orchestra and the Victor Military Band had popular recordings of "The Memphis Blues" in '14. Arthur Collins and Byron Harlan had a popular duet recording of the song in '15. It was revived by Ted Lewis in '27 and again by Harry James and his orchestra in '44. Ted Lewis and his Band's '27 recording is available at http://www.redhotjazz.com/tlband.html.

The sheet music cover and musical score are available at http://levysheetmusic.mse.jhu.edu/browse.html and at http://lcweb2.loc.gov/cocoon/ihas/loc.natlib.ihas.100006378/ and at http://scriptorium.lib.duke.edu/dynaweb/sheetmusic/1910-1920/@Generic__BookTextView/29633.

Play a Simple Melody (see '50)

Variety chose this song for its *Hit Parade of a Half-Century* representing '14.

Rebecca of Sunny-Brook Farm

Words: A. Seymour Brown; Music: Albert Gumble

The Kate Douglas Wiggin '10 novel inspired the song "Rebecca of Sunny-Brook Farm." Most people today probably remember the '38 movie of the same name that starred Shirley Temple. That film was loosely based on the Wiggin novel, but has no relation to this song.

Jose Collins helped popularize the song by interpolating it into the *Ziegfeld Follies of 1913*. The American Quartet had a very popular recording of the song in '14. Henry Burr and Helen Clark's duet recording was also popular.

The seldom-heard verse tells us that Rebecca is waiting for the singer on a farm in Maine. The chorus continues: *Where the honey suckle vine twines itself around the door, / A sweetheart mine, Is waiting patiently for me; / I can hear the whippoorwill Tell me softly from the hill, / Her mem'ry haunts you, Rebecca wants you / So come back to Sunny-Brook Farm.*

The chorus of this song is reminisent of the way "By the Light of the Silvery Moon" is often performed. The soloist sings the first phrase, then a second voice or a chorus repeats the phrase. And that pattern continues, except at the phrase "Is waiting patiently for me," the echo is "for me" after "patiently" and after "me."

See the sheet music cover and the musical score at http://lcweb2.loc.gov/cocoon/ihas/loc.natlib.ihas.100005530 or http://scriptorium.lib.duke.edu/sheetmusic/1910-1920/@Generic__BookTextView/37745 or see the sheet music cover and to hear a midi musical version at http://parlorsongs.com/issues/2003-12/thismonth/feature.asp.

The Song That Stole My Heart

Words: Andrew B. Sterling; Music: Harry Von Tilzer

The sheet music cover touts this song as Harry Von Tilzer's most beautiful ballad. It did become one of the most successful songs of '14, but it hasn't remained very well known over the years.

Henry Burr's recording of the song was extremely successful and his was the only really successful recorded version.

The song has two verses and a chorus. The first verse follows: *One night in June 'twas in the long ago / You sang a song so tenderly / An old time tune that set my heart aglow / So soft and sweet You sang to me / The song I heard you play / I long once more to hear / You stole my heart away that night my dear.*

The much more familiar chorus continues: *Play that melody so sweet / I love it so, I love it so, / Soft and low those words repeat, / "Oh don't you remember sweet Alice Ben Bolt," / The song that stole my heart away.*

The quoted line is from a 19th Century song "Ben Bolt" by Nelson Kneass.

The sheet music cover and musical score are available at http://levysheetmusic.mse.jhu.edu/browse.html.

St. Louis Blues (see '20)

Variety chose this song for its *Hit Parade of a Half-Century* representing '14.

The Springtime of Life

Words: Robert B. Smith; Music: Victor Herbert

"The Springtime of Life" from *The Debutante* by Robert

B. Smith and Victor Herbert was chosen by *Variety* for its *Hit Parade of a Half-Century* representing '14.

The Debutante was a musical comedy in two acts, with the book written by Harry B. Smith and Robert B. Smith. The musical only lasted forty-eight performances on Broadway. The sheet music cover indicates the star of the musical was Hazel Dawn.

"The Springtime of Life," sung by a character named Elaine, has verses in duple meter, while the chorus is in triple meter or waltz time. Robert B. Smith's first verse and chorus lyrics follow: *My life is like a boat that's sailing on a sunlit azure sea—away; / Love is the pilot, he is guiding to a land unknown to me—today. / A distant island undiscovered ev'ry happy girl must find at last. / Ah! May the journey be as happy as the dear days past. / The springtime of life is fairest, the future a pearl appears, / And the days that to us are the rarest Are seen thro' the mist of years. / Dream days! Fondly we gaze, Then time gently turns the page, / And the things that we dreamed Are not what they seemed in the beautiful golden age.*

The sheet music cover and musical score are available at http://digital.library.ucla.edu/apam.

Sylvia

Words: Clinton Scollard; Music: Oley Speaks

Oley Speaks was primarily an art song composer. His "On the Road to Mandalay" was popular in '13. And his "Sylvia," also an art song, was popular enough in '14 that *Variety* chose this song for its *Hit Parade of a Half-Century.*

Clinton Scollard's lyrics follow: *Sylvia's hair is like the night, / Touched with glancing starry beams; / Such a face as drifts thro' dreams, / This is Sylvia to the sight. / And the touch of Sylvia's hand / Is as light as milkweed down, / When the meads are golden brown, / And the autumn fills the land. / Sylvia:- just the echoing / Of her voice brings back to me, / From the depths of memory, / All the loveliness of spring: Sylvia! Sylvia! / Such a face as drifts thro' dreams, / This is Sylvia to the sight.*

No popular recordings of "Sylvia" can be found in the literature on sheet music and recording sales of the period.

That International Rag

Words & Music: Irving Berlin

By '13 Berlin's "Alexander's Ragtime Band" had sold 500,000 copies of sheet music in England, so he decided to make a good will gesture to his audience there. He was performing the next evening at the Hippodrome, so he went to work and stayed up all night, which was not particularly novel for him, composing "That International Rag." With Cliff Hess accompanying him, Berlin performed the song and all of his other hits that were well known in England at his Hippodrome performance that evening.

This Berlin rag was found listed by several titles. It was titled variously as "International Rag," "The International Rag" and "That International Rag." One sheet music publication has "The International Rag" as the title, but another, also published by Berlin's company, had "That International Rag" on the cover, but "The International Rag" on the inside sheet music as the title. Therefore, either is probably acceptable.

The primary idea of the first verse is that America is to blame for making the entire world ragtime crazy. The second verse is basically the same idea: that America has every nation dancing to this syncopation.

In the chorus, Berlin lists some of the places that have become addicted to rags, including London, France, Germany, Spain, Russia, and Italy. The whole world "goes 'round to the sound of the International Rag."

Arthur Collins and Byron Harlan helped popularize this song with their duet recording in '14. Their recording was titled "International Rag." The Victor Military Band and Prince's Orchestra also recorded popular versions of the song. Their versions were titled "That International Rag."

Variety chose this song for its *Hit Parade of a Half-Century* representing '13.

The sheet music cover and musical score are available at http://levysheetmusic.mse.jhu.edu/browse.html and at http://scriptorium.lib.duke.edu/dynaweb/sheetmusic/1910-1920/@Generic__BookTextView/44243 or a PDF of this song is available at http://library.indstate.edu/level1.dir/cml/rbsc/kirk/sheet_titles.html.

This Is the Life

Words & Music: Irving Berlin

Irving Berlin's "This Is the Life" was introduced by Al Jolson at the Winter Garden Theater in New York City in '14.

In the first verse, we meet Farmer Brown who came to New York City to take in the sights. He went to "Cabarets, swell cafes" for a week or so. "After seeing ev'ry show, After meeting May and Flo," Farmer Brown admitted that he loved the farm, but "This is the life." He liked the cabareting, the musical comedies, the wine and the cocktail cherries. For him, "this is the life!"

Variety chose this song for its *Hit Parade of a Half-Century* representing '14.

The Peerless Quartet and Billy Murray both had popular recording of "This Is the Life" in '14.

The sheet music cover and musical score are available at http://levysheetmusic.mse.jhu.edu/browse.html.

Too-Ra-Loo-Ra-Loo-Ral (That's an Irish Lullaby)

Words & Music: James R. Shannon

The famous Irish performer, Chauncey Olcott, introduced "Too-Ra-Loo-Ra-Loo-Ral" in the musical extravaganza *Shameen Dhu* in '13. Olcott's '14 recording of the song was very popular. This "Irish Lullaby" has probably become one of the most famous Irish songs of all time.

The verse is distinctively Irish: "Over in Killarney... Me Mither sang a song to me ... a simple little ditty, In her good ould Irish way." The singer wishes he could hear his mother sing the song again. The chorus doesn't make much sense, but it is a beautiful lullaby: *Too-ra-loo-ra-loo-ral, Too-ra-loo-ra-li, / Too-ra-loo-ra-loo-ral, Hush now don't you cry! / Too-ra-loo-ra-loo-ral, Too-ra-loo-ra-li, / Too-ra-loo-ra-loo-ral, That's an Irish lullaby.*

Bing Crosby, as Father O'Malley, singing "Too-Ra-Loo-Ra-Loo-Ral" in *Going My Way* to the elderly Father Fitzgibbon, played by Barry Fitzgerald, was a particularly memorable and sentimental rendition. Crosby's recording of the song charted into the top five on *Billboard*. In addition to *Going My Way*, the song can be heard in the '45 movie musical *Nob Hill*.

Variety chose this song for its *Hit Parade of a Half-Century* representing '14.

The sheet music cover and musical score are available at

http://levysheetmusic.mse.jhu.edu/browse.html and at http://lcweb2.loc.gov/cocoon/ihas/loc.natlib.ihas. 100008000/. See the sheet music cover and hear a midi musical version at http://www.parlorsongs.com/issues/2004-8/thismonth/feature.asp.

Twelfth Street Rag (see '48)

Variety chose this song for its *Hit Parade of a Half-Century* representing '14.

Vienna, City of My Dreams (Wien, du Stadt meiner Traume)

Music: Rudolf Sieczynski

Variety included "Vienna, City of My Dreams" in its *Hit Parade of a Half-Century* representing '14. It was listed by its German title "Wien, du Stadt meiner Traume," but the song is also known as "Wien, Wien nur du allein."

This song is probably the best-known Viennese song of the years just preceding World War I. The writer dedicated the song to a Liesl, but no one seems to know exactly who this person was. The song became a worldwide hit and is still known even today.

As World War I approached, Vienna was the capital of the Austro-Hungarian empire. Unfortunately this "city of my dreams," changed drastically after the war. During the war, this song was spread around the world as the Austrian soldiers dreamed of home, of their Vienna. They sang "Wien, Wien nur du allein" with all their hearts.

Way Out Yonder in the Golden West

Words & Music: Percy Wenrich

Variety chose "Way Out Yonder in the Golden West" for its *Hit Parade of a Half-Century* representing '14.

The only popular recording of the song was by the Avon Comedy Four in '27.

When You're a Long, Long Way from Home

Words: Sam M. Lewis; Music: George W. Meyer

Variety chose this song for its *Hit Parade of a Half-Century* representing '14.

Henry Burr had a very popular recording of "When You're a Long, Long Way from Home" in '14.

The chorus lyrics follow: *When you're a long long way from home / It makes you feel like you're alone / It's hard to find a pal that's true / That you can tell your troubles to / And when you send a letter home / Your mother's voice rings in your ears / And then you cross the T's with kisses / What a strange world this is, / Then you dot the I's with tears / And all the sunshine turns to gloom / When you're a long way from home.*

The sheet music cover and musical score are available at http://levysheetmusic.mse.jhu.edu/browse.html or at http://lcweb2.loc.gov/cocoon/ihas/loc.natlib.ihas.10000 7275/ or the score is available at http://scriptorium.lib. duke.edu/dynaweb/sheetmusic/1910-1920/@Generic__ BookTextView/51523. See the sheet music cover, read the lyrics and hear a midi musical version at http://www.hal cyondaysmusic.com/june/june2001.htm.

II

The Ragtime Years: 1915–1919

The Ragtime Years

During the second decade of the 20th century several things occurred historically that had a huge impact; particularly the events leading up to and including World War I were monumental and were on the minds of millions of people around the globe. The history of the era can be traced in our music, what we whistled, hummed, played and danced to. But our songs not only reflect the historical events, but also the moods, manners and mores of our country at this particular point in its history. This period exhibits skepticism about our involvement in the war with songs like "I Didn't Raise My Boy to Be a Soldier," but then becomes extremely patriotic as world events convince the populous that the war is necessary with songs like "Over There" and "Sister Susie's Sewing Shirts for Soldiers."

The assassination of the Archduke Franz Ferdinand, heir to the Austrian throne, and his wife by Serbian terrorist in Sarajevo, Bosnia in '14 was the trigger that started what became a struggle that engaged more than twenty countries. At first, the United States declared its neutrality and was steadfastly against entering this war of nations for three years. When a German U-boat sank the *Lusitania* in '15 American sentiment began to shift. Then in '17 when Germany announced its U-boats would fire on anything, the U.S. became involved. We quickly mobilized 4,355,000 troops. With our entry into the war, those at home supported their "boys over there" in any way they could. Mothers and sweethearts knitted for the boys. Home windows displayed flags starred with the number of men from the family serving in the war. "Meatless," "wheat-less," "fuel-less" days were observed to conserve food and fuel for the war effort.

The war officially came to an end in late '18. A wild and noisy public demonstration greeted the announcement of the armistice.

So what other historical events shaped the decade? The Panama Canal opened; evangelist Billy Sunday, a former baseball player, toured the country drawing huge crowds; the Boy and Girl Scouts were founded; many women marched in suffrage parades; the U.S. adopted daylight savings time in '18 (it had been used by England and Germany as an economy measure during the war) and Congress ratified liquor prohibition in '19.

In the entertainment field, the motion-picture industry began to flourish. By '15, movie houses were springing up everywhere. D.W. Griffith's silent movie classic *The Birth of a Nation* was released in '15. The Victor phonograph company introduced the Victrola, its new record-playing machine. "Class" dancers like Vernon and Irene Castle became popular. Cowboy philosopher, Will Rogers joined the *Ziegfeld Follies of 1917*. Bert Williams became the first African American to appear with whites on Broadway. Jim Thorpe, American part-Indian athlete, was an Olympic hero and was proclaimed the world's greatest all-around athlete. Jack Johnson, the first African American heavyweight-boxing champ, lost his title to Jess Williard in '15. Baseball was shocked by the "Black Sox" gambling scandal at the 1919 World Series.

A Melting Pot of Cultural Influences

What kind of music did the Americans like in the 1910s? Some people listened to folk music or classical music from Europe. However, popular music became the dominant style at least when it comes to sales figures.

In the United States, musical traditions of many cultures, African American, Eastern European, Irish, Jewish, English and others, were being mixed, resulting in a new and distinctly American form of popular music. Popular music of the second decade of the 20th century was incredibly varied, with many genres being popular.

No one type of music dominated. The period may be called The Ragtime Years, but it does not mean that ragtime is the only music of the era. Even though there had been some rags in the previous decade, about '10 pianos around the nation really began thumping out ragtime. This ragtime fever brought sizeable revenues to the music publishing business, especially after the five-and-ten-cent stores hired piano players to demonstrate popular songs in their stores. In addition, the craze produced a batch of new dance steps, most popular of which was the fox (or turkey) trot. Variations on the turkey trot include the crab step, kangaroo dip, fish walk, the Texas Tommy, the snake and the grizzly bear. The waltz and two-step were not as fashionable.

Actually ragtime was only a small part of the popular music scene of the 1910s. Ragtime's heyday spanned Scott Joplin's career as a composer, from 1899 until his death in '17, though many superb rags were written after '17. The syncopated rhythms of ragtime were very important during this decade. Irving Berlin's "Alexander's Ragtime Band" made the entire country ragtime conscious in '11 and gave America's dancing feet the music it needed to "shake a leg." Hotels and restaurants soon provided after-dinner dancing. Special tea time dances were promoted, as well as after-theater dancing. At least at first, all this dancing was confined to the large cities. The country's rural areas were years behind; news of the newest fads, whatever they were, traveled very slowly. If they reached the rural communities at all, it was months, or more likely years, later.

Sheet Music, Wax Cylinders, Disks?

To understand popular music of the era we need to know a little about the sheet music industry and the still infant recording industry.

As this period began, the demand for popular music was greater than ever. Sheet music sales were climbing to unprecedented heights. Two six million sheet music sellers were "Let Me Call You Sweetheart" and "Down by the Old Mill Stream." From approximately '15, five-and-ten-cent stores sold sheet music. The stores often hired pianists and sometimes vocalists to demonstrate the songs. The added exposure of the songs in many cities and towns across the country definitely helped boost sheet music sales.

A great deal of sheet music was sold in five-and-ten-cent stores like F.W. Woolworth. By the World War I years, Woolworth was selling 20 million copies of sheet music per year.

When our nation is at peace, our economy is reasonably strong, and our citizens are generally happy, they want to dance. And the dances are generally hotter, faster tempo music (conversely, once we entered the war, if the theory is correct, the mood changes and the tempo of songs slows a bit). As the public became more interested in dancing, the record companies scrambled to produce dance-able records.

The most popular recording artists of the decade were Henry Burr, Arthur Collins, the American Quartet, Byron Harlan, the Peerless Quartet, Billy Murray, John McCormack, Albert Campbell, Al Jolson and Ada Jones. Two male quartets, one female, several important recording artist from the previous decade, and a big newcomer in Al Jolson, these were the big names of the recording industry of this era.

Vaudeville

Vaudeville consisted of acrobats, jugglers, animal acts, comedians, dancers, singers and personalities (people who were famous for one reason or another). These acts traveled around the country on the vaudeville circuit often introducing the nation to the newest songs and dances. Vaudeville had been around for a couple of decades or more, but the Keith and Proctor chain of vaudeville theaters across the country were at their heyday during this period. By '14, the company supervised over 400 vaudeville theaters. The Keith and Proctor chain was later incorporated in the Radio-Keith-Orpheum circuit. The leading vaudeville theater was the Palace in New York City. It became the goal of every vaudeville performer. If they played the Palace, they had made it to the big time.

Thousands of songs were introduced or popularized or both in the vaudeville theaters. Many of the headline entertainers became identified with the songs they introduced and popularized in vaudeville.

A few of the songs introduced and/or popularized in vaudeville during this decade include "Alexander's Ragtime Band," "The Aba Daba Honeymoon," "The Darktown Strutters' Ball," "Down by the Old Mill Stream," "Let Me Call You Sweetheart," "My Melancholy Baby," "Waiting for the Robert E. Lee" and "You Made Me Love You."

Broadway

Jerome Kern was probably the most important composer on Broadway during the 1910s. He revolutionized the musical theater with his innovative shows. Victor Herbert and Rudolf Friml were important forces with their European-style operettas.

Some of the decade's most famous Broadway shows were *The Blue Paradise, Very Good Eddie, Oh, Boy!, Maytime, Leave It to Jane, Oh, Lady! Lady!!, Sinbad,* the *Greenwich Village Follies* and the yearly productions of the *Ziegfeld Follies.* One can almost tell from the titles which ones were more operatic and which were less in the operetta style. Starting with Jerome Kern's *The Girl from Utah* in '14, more of the musical productions tended toward musical comedy. *Irene* opened in '19, but its songs were more popular in '20.

Some of the important songs birthed on Broadway during the era include "Till the Clouds Roll By," "Has Anybody Here Seen Kelly?," "When Irish Eyes Are Smiling," "The Girl on the Magazine," "Poor Butterfly," "A Pretty Girl Is Like a Melody" and "Rock-a-bye Your Baby with a Dixie Melody."

The Silent Movie Industry

What could the silent movie industry possibly have to do with the popular music of this era? Well, movie houses employed at least a pianist or organist and sometimes a band or orchestra to accompany the silent films. Often in between reels, the theater would conduct sing-along sessions to keep the audience occupied. The audiences seemed to love the opportunity to sing their favorite songs, often some of the biggest hits of the day.

The Blues

The blues, although virtually unknown outside the African American community, originated from the field hollers and work songs of black slaves. "Blue notes," the flatted third, fifth and seventh notes of the normal scale that were used melodically, not harmonically, are a chief characteristic of the blues. The clash of the flatted tones against the un-flatted ones in the harmony creates a distinctive sound. The slaves were trying to recreate the quartertone system of their native African music, seeking a note that isn't in our normal seven-note diatonic scale.

The traditional blues text is a rhymed couplet in iambic pentameter in which the first line is repeated. Actually only about half of the 12 bars is sung, while the rest of the measures are usually filled in with instrumental improvisation.

The blues began to reach the general public during the second decade of the 20th century, when W.C. Handy's first compositions were published. His first hit was "Memphis Blues," followed a couple of years later by the tremendously famous "St. Louis Blues." Other blues songs of the period include Handy's "The Hesitating Blues," "Joe Turner Blues," and "Beale Street Blues." Blues songs by other writers include "The Honolulu Blues," "Livery Stable Blues," "Regretful Blues," plus a couple of blues lamenting the beginning of prohibition: "Alcoholic Blues" and "Prohibition Blues."

There are several blues songs, notably ""St. Louis Blues," Wabash Blues" and "Wang Wang Blues," that were very popular during the early '20s. By this point, the traditional 12-bar blues format was not usually adhired to, but the character of the blues was definitely present.

Today the blues remain an active and vital source of inspiration to many musicians, especially jazz musicians. Some modern singers, like Janis Joplin, were greatly influenced by the early blues and those who sang them. Many hits like Elvis Presley's "Hound Dog" are based on the 12-bar blues form.

Jazz

The history of jazz is well documented in hundreds of books and articles. However, the exact origins of the genre remain rather obscure. All we really know is that the roots of jazz are African American, but what emerged is a uniquely American style. The former slaves used the rhythmic and harmonic traditions of the whites and mixed in some of the left-over African elements that had survived their assimilation into American culture.

Jazz is a performer's art; it was the music of the moment. It was not written down like most of the other popular music of this country. Therefore, it is mostly speculation to chronicle the early years of jazz.

As far as can be determined, the early development of jazz came from the following sources: minstrel music, the blues, brass bands, ragtime and the introduction of instruments like the banjo and the saxophone.

Jazz made an appearance in New Orleans around the turn of the century, but the first jazz recordings were not made until the Original Dixieland Jass Band recorded and popularized their versions of "Tiger Rag" and "The Darktown Strutters' Ball" in '18. It probably should be pointed out that the Original Dixieland Jazz Band was an all-white instrumental ensemble. If you are a student of American popular music, you probably know that Elvis Presley brought "black rhythm and blues" into respectability and it was accepted because he was white. Basically, the same thing happened with jazz. A black (or African American) band would not have been accepted in the racial climate of the mid–1910s. Jazz would have remained a strictly black music if a white group had not first popularized it. Other all-black bands like King Oliver's Creole Jazz Band may have been more authentic, but they only became well known after the Original Dixieland Jazz Band popularized the music first.

Early in the development of the genre, the word was spelled "jass" and meant to fornicate, and "jassing" meant sexual intercourse. A "jassbo" was a ladies' man. Later the word evolved into "jazz," but nobody really seems to know why, except perhaps to become more accepted by polite society, it had to get away from the sexual connotations.

1915

Auf Wiedersehn

Words: Herbert Reynolds; Music: Sigmund Romberg

Vivienne Segal, in her Broadway debut, introduced "Auf Wiedersehn" in the operetta *Blue Paradise*. This teary goodbye song was Sigmund Romberg's first popular song success. Harry MacDonough and Olive Kline helped popularize "Auf Wiedersehn" with a successful duet recording in '15.

Helen Traubel sang the song in Romberg's screen biography *Deep in My Heart* ('54).

The song begins as a duet between Rudolph and Mizzi. Rather unusually, it modulates from the key of F to A flat and back to F during the verse section. The verse is in common time (quarduple meter), while the chorus is in triple meter (waltz time). Herbert Reynolds' chorus lyrics follow: *Love lives ever, knowning no word like goodbye, / Hearts may sever, True love can never die! / Calm all your fears and dry all your tears, / Love will remain when all else shall wane, / Guiding me on thro' the years: / Auf Wiedersehn! Auf Wiedersehn!*

Variety Hit Parade of a Half-Century chose this song representing '15.

The sheet music cover and musical score are available at http://levysheetmusic.mse.jhu.edu/browse.html and at http://digital.library.ucla.edu/apam/. Hear Harry MacDonough and Olive Klein's '15 recording of this song: at http://www2.collectionscanada.ca/plsql/gramophone/.

There were several other "Auf Wiedersehn" songs, including one written by Lucy H. Hooper and J. Remington Fairlamb in 1869, by Vernon Roy and W.T. Francis in '05 and by George V. Hobart and Silvio Hein in '08.

By Heck

Words: L. Wolfe Gilbert; Music S. R. Henry

"By Heck" is a *Variety Hit Parade of a Half-Century* selection representing '15. Byron Harlan and Will Robbins helped popularize the song with a successful recording.

The Dorsey Brothers Orchestra's recording of "By Heck" is available at http://www.redhotjazz.com/dorseybros.html or hear a midi musical version at http://www.primeshop.com/midlist3.htm.

By the Waters of Minnetonka

Words: J. M. Cavanass; Music: Thurlow Lieurance

"By the Waters of Minnetonka" is subtitled "An Indian Love Song."

According to a typewritten account from Thurlow Lieurance's estate papers "By the Waters of Minnetonka" was inspired by a Sioux love song recorded by Lieurance in '11 on the Crow Reservation in Montana. He copied the tune as sung by Sitting Eagle, a Sioux. The song was based upon the following Sioux legend:

"Moon Deer, daughter of the Moon Clan, loved Sun Deer of the Sun Clan. Tribal law forbade marriage between the two clans. The two lovers ran away far to the east and north. They came to a beautiful lake called Minnetonka (Minne means water; Tonka means large and round). Their traditional enemies, the Chippewa, lived on the north shore of this lake. They could not return home, so finally in desperation they decided to end it all. The legend states that they disappeared beneath the waves and were no more.

Many moons afterwards the Sioux warriors drove the Chippewa north to Lake Superior. One night while they were camped on the shores of Lake Minnetonka, they heard the waters singing a weird melody and, in the moonpath on the waters, two lilies appeared and grew to the skies. The lilies were the spirits of Moon Deer and Sun Deer."

Alice Neilson helped popularize this song with a successful '15 recording. Paul Whiteman's recording of this song is available at http://www.redhotjazz.com/pwo.html.

The song is in triple meter (waltz) and the sheet music has accompaniment for piano and violin or flute. The lyrics are rather disjointed, trying, one would assume, for authenticity: *Moon Deer, How near, Your soul divine; / Sun Deer, No fear in heart of mine. / Skies blue o'er you, Look down in love; / Waves bright, Give light As on they move. / Hear thou my vow to live, to die / Moon Deer, thee near Beneath this sky.*

The sheet music cover and musical score are available at http://levysheetmusic.mse.jhu.edu/browse.html and at http://www.nla.gov.au/apps/cdview?pi=nla.mus-an 20222093-t-cd or at http://scriptorium.lib.duke.edu/ dynaweb/sheetmusic/1910–1920/@Generic__Book TextView/3256.

Variety chose this song for its *Hit Parade of a Half-Century* representing '14.

Carry Me Back to Old Virginny
Words & Music: James A. Bland

The official song of the state of Virginia, "Carry Me back to Old Virginny" was written by an African American minstrel, James Bland, in approximately 1878, and has been Virginia's state song since '40.

George Primrose and his minstrels introduced the song and it became a staple in the repertoire of most of the minstrel groups.

Bland reportedly was inspired by a couple of things when he wrote this song: a peaceful scene on a plantation on the James River near Williamsburg, Virginia and a chance remark made to him by a female student at Howard University in Washington, D.C. The student was explaining to Bland a dream had carried her back home "to old Virginny."

The lyrics contain several pseudo–African American colloquialisms, words that today may be too racially sensitive: *Carry me back to old Virginny, / There's where the cotton and the corn and tatoes grow, / There's where the birds warble sweet in the springtime, / There's where the old darkey's heart am long'd to go, / There's where I labored so hard for old massa, / Day after day in the field of yellow corn, / No place on earth do I love more sincerely / Than old Virginny, the state where I was born. / Carry me back to old Virginny, / There's where the cotton and the corn and tatoes grow, / There's where the birds warble sweet in the springtime, / There's where this old darkey's heart am long'd to go. / Carry me back to old Virginny, / There let me live 'till I wither and decay, / Long by the old Dismal Swamp have I wandered, / There's where this old darkey's life will pass away. / Massa and missis have long gone before me, / Soon we will meet on that bright and golden shore, / There we'll be happy and free from all sorrow, / There's where we'll meet and we'll never part no more.*

Alma Gluck had a particularly popular recording of this old song in '15. Len Spencer had released a popular recording of it in 1893.

"Carry Me Back to Old Virginny" became one of the most recorded songs of the pre-rock era.

The sheet music cover and musical score are available at http://levysheetmusic.mse.jhu.edu/browse.html and at http://digital.library.ucla.edu/apam/.

Chinatown, My Chinatown
Words: William Jerome; Music: Jean Schwartz

African Americans were not the only ones who faced discrimination in the United States. As a matter of fact, most of the immigrants found they were looked upon as less than desirable. Actually, not only immigrants, but our own native Americans were just as discriminated against as any other racial group. Orientals in general were another group that often faced racial stereotyping and were sometimes portrayed in discriminatory ways in songs. Some of the most popular songs of the era were based on racist themes. "Chinatown, My Chinatown" is a good example. The song had been written in '06 and was interpolated into the '10 revue *Up and Down Broadway*.

The exotic was alluring in '15, and Chinatown seemed like a mysterious, exotic location that was fascinating to the average American.

The lyrics of the verse are peppered with stereotypical references, such as "Pigtails flying here and there," and racial slurs such as "That's the time the festive Chink starts to wink his other eye." However, the words to the chorus don't seem especially offensive, except for perhaps the phrase "almond eyes of brown": *Chinatown, my Chinatown, Where the lights are low. / Hearts that know no other land Drifting to and fro. / Dreamy, dreamy Chinatown, Almond eyes of brown, / Hearts seem light and life seems bright in dreamy Chinatown.*

The American Quartet's vocal version was very successful in '15. Grace Kerns and John Barnes Wells duet version also sold very well, and Prince's Orchestra had a popular version on the market also. The song was revived in '32 in recordings by Louis Armstrong and by the Mills Brothers. It was revived again in '35 by Ray Noble and his orchestra. Bobby Maxwell revived it yet again in '52 with a recording that was popular enough to chart. Louis Armstrong and his Orchestra's recording is available at http://www.redhotjazz.com/lao.html.

The song has appeared in several Hollywood movie musicals, including *Bright Lights* ('31), *Nob Hill* ('45), *Jolson Sings Again* ('49), *Young Man with a Horn* ('50), and *The Seven Little Foys* ('55).

See the sheet music cover and the musical score at http://lcweb2.loc.gov/cocoon/ihas/loc.natlib.ihas.100007926/ or at http://levysheetmusic.mse.jhu.edu/browse.html. See the sheet music cover and hear a midi musical version at http://parlorsongs.com/issues/1999–8/aug99feature.asp. Hear a midi musical version and read the lyrics at http://www.geocities.com/dferg5493/chinatown.htm.

The sheet music cover is tasteful, but it may be generic Oriental rather than specifically Chinese. For instance, the instrument depicted appears to be a Japanese long necked lute rather than the Chinese short-necked version. This probably just demonstrates that the publisher thought that anything Oriental was sufficient.

Variety selected this song for its *Hit Parade of a Half-Century* for '06.

Close to My Heart
Words & Music: A.B. Sterling

Henry Burr and Albert Campbell help popularize "Close to My Heart" with a very successful recording in '15. According to Joel Whitburn's *A Century of Pop Music* it was one of the top ten song hits of the year, however, if that is true, it certainly did not sustain its popularity in subsequent years.

Down Among the Sheltering Palms
Words: James Brockman; Music: Abe Olman

The Lyric Quartet helped popularize "Down Among the Sheltering Palms" in '15 with a successful recording.

One of the sheet music covers says that the song is Al Jolson's sensational hit and has his picture on the cover.

The song can be heard in the '49 movie musical *That Midnight Kiss*, where it was performed by Keenan Wynn and a quartet, and in the '53 movie musical *Down Among the Sheltering Palms*. It was performed by a girls' chorus in the '59 film *Some Like It Hot*.

The lyrics tell us that the singer is way down east pining his heart out while his lover is way out west. He's going by train, a six day trip, to see her "down among the sheltering palms." He asks her to meet him "by the old golden gate" (bridge?). And he pleads, "Oh, honey wait for me."

See the sheet music cover, read the lyrics and hear a midi musical version at http://www.halcyondaysmusic.com/february/february2003.htm. The sheet music cover and musical score are available at http://levysheetmusic.mse.jhu.edu/browse.html, at http://scriptorium.lib.duke.edu/dynaweb/sheetmusic/ and at http://lcweb2.loc.gov/cocoon/ihas/loc.natlib.ihas.100008275/ or at http://lcweb2.loc.gov/cocoon/ihas/loc.natlib.ihas.100008276/. Hear a midi musical version, see the lyrics, two sheet music covers and the musical score at www.geocities.com/dferg5493/songfiles. See sheet music covers from '15 and two from '17 at http://www.hulapages.com/covers_2.htm.

Variety selected "Down Among the Sheltering Palms" for its *Hit Parade of a Half-Century* representing '15.

Goodbye, Girls, I'm Through

Words: *John Golden; Music: Ivan Caryll*

"Goodbye Girls, I'm Through" was introduced in the musical *Chin-Chin*, which starred Dave Montgomery and Fred Stone. Lambert Murphy helped popularize it with a successful recording in '15.

This song has two verses and two choruses. In the first verse, the singer is happy because he has finally found the girl he has sought to be his wife. He admits he has dallied with "lotus lips and almond eyes." But he is ready for the straight and narrow and willing to bid his former life, and the women of it, goodbye.

The first chorus lyrics follow (including the spellings and capitalizations from the sheet music): *Good Bye Girls, I'm through / Each Girl that I have met I say Good Bye to you / Without the least regret I've done with all flirtations / You've no more fascination / There's but one to whom I'm true / Good Bye Girls. Good Bye Girls. I'm through.*

In the second verse, we find out that the girl he has found is a "Yankee Princess."

The sheet music cover and musical score are available at http://levysheetmusic.mse.jhu.edu/browse.html, at http://digital.library.ucla.edu/apam/ and at http://lcweb2.loc.gov/cocoon/ihas/loc.natlib.ihas.100005048/.

Variety chose this song for its *Hit Parade of a Half-Century* representing '14.

He's a Rag Picker

Words & Music: *Irving Berlin*

The Peerless Quartet helped popularize Irving Berlin's "He's a Rag Picker" with a '15 recording.

The lyrics to the song are not about a person who collects old rags from other people's trash, but a guy who plays ragtime tunes night and day. He just sits at the piano hour after hour tickling the ivories with syncopated tunes.

The sheet music cover and musical score are available at http://levysheetmusic.mse.jhu.edu/browse.html and at

http://scriptorium.lib.duke.edu/dynaweb/sheetmusic/1910–1920/@Generic__BookTextView/12429. See the sheet music cover and hear a midi musical version at http://www.parlorsongs.com/issues/2001–6/thismonth/feature b.asp. This website also points out the similarities of Berlin's song with Percy Wenrich's "Red Rose Rag" and compares the similarities.

Variety chose this song for its *Hit Parade of a Half-Century* representing '14.

Hello, Frisco!

Words: *Gene Buck; Music: Louis A. Hirsch*

"Hello, Frisco!" was a topical song that saluted the first transcontinental telephone service in the U.S. Ina Claire introduced the song in the *Ziegfeld Follies of 1915*. For "Hello, Frisco," the chorus girls appeared as various cities.

AT&T had been expanding telephone service out of New York City since the late 1880s. By '14, technology had progressed enough that service could be extended to 2,000 miles or more. In '15, the first transcontinental telephone service became a reality.

Alice Green and Edward Hamilton had a very popular duet recording of "Hello, Frisco!" in '15. Elida Morris and Sam Ash's duet recording was also popular.

Most of the listings for this song indicate that the title is "Hello, Frisco, Hello," but the sheet music has the title as "Hello, Frisco!" The subtitle is "I Called You Up to Say 'Hello.'"

In the verse, the man is talking to the operator placing a call to San Francisco to a girl named Frisco, rather than the city, San Francisco. He is impatient: "Please, long distance, do connect me, Get her on the telephone."

There are two refrains, the first, the most familiar is what the man says to Frisco. The second refrain is a duet between Frisco, saying "Hello New York, hello" and the man's patter in between "How do you do, my dear? I only wish that you were here." The lyrics to the more famous first refrain follow: *Hello, Frisco, hello (repeat) / Don't keep me waiting, it's aggravating, / Why can't you hurry Central you're so slow, / Hello, now can you hear You know I love you, dear, / Your voice is like music to my ear, / When I close my eyes you seem so near, / Frisco, I called you up to say "hello."*

The song can be heard in the movie musical *The Story of Vernon and Irene Castle* ('39), where it was sung by a chorus and danced by Ginger Rogers and Fred Astaire, *Hello, Frisco, Hello* ('43), where it was performed by Jack Oakie and John Payne and by Alice Faye and John Payne in the film's closing scene, and *The I-Don't-Care Girl* ('53), the screen biography of Eva Tanguay.

The sheet music cover and musical score are available at http://levysheetmusic.mse.jhu.edu/browse.html, at http://digital.library.ucla.edu/apam/ and at http://lcweb2.loc.gov/cocoon/ihas/loc.natlib.ihas.100006682/.

Variety selected "Hello, Frisco!" for its *Hit Parade of a Half-Century* representing '15.

Home, Sweet Home

Words: *John Howard Payne; Music: Sir Henry Rowley Bishop*

John Howard Payne, a descendant of one of the signers of the Declaration of Independence, went to London to act in, write and produce dramas. In 1823, he teamed with Sir Henry Rowley Bishop to write the operetta *Clari* or *The Maid of Milan*. It premiered at Covent Garden, London, on May 8, 1823.

Maria Tree introduced "Home, Sweet Home" at the end of the first act of the operetta. The song was extremely well received and quickly spread from London to the rest of England and then throughout the rest of Western civilization. It became one of the most famous songs of the 19th century. Jenny Lind, one of the world's most famous singers of the era, performed it in her tours spreading its fame to many countries including the United States.

For many years, the melody was thought to have come from a Sicilian folk song. Bishop had published a couple of volumes of folk material in 1821 and 1822. If he could not find authentic melodies, he created tunes of his own. To represent Sicily, he created a tune he called "A Sicilian air." This was the melody that he used for "Home, Sweet Home."

A statue of John Howard Payne was erected in Prospect Park, Brooklyn and was unveiled in 1873.

There have been many popular recordings of "Home, Sweet Home," but Alice Neilsen had a particularly popular version of the song in '15. Elsie Baker's '15 recording was also popular. John Yorke Atlee issued his popular version in 1891, Harry MacDonough's '02 version was also popular. Richard Jose's '06 recording was well received. Alma Gluck revived it again in '12. "Home, Sweet Home" became one of the most recorded songs of the pre-rock era.

The song appeared in the following movie musicals: *The Prodigal* ('31), *Let Freedom Ring*('38), *First Love*('39) and *Cairo*('42).

Hear Harry MacDonough's '04 recording or Harry MacDonough and the Haydn Quartet's '03 recording at http://www2.collectionscanada.ca/plsql/gramophone/brow se.display_titles?bet=H&lang=e. The sheet music cover and musical score are available at http://levysheetmusic. mse.jhu.edu/browse.html.

I Didn't Raise My Boy to Be a Soldier
Words: Alfred Bryan; Music: Al Piantadosi

The assassination of the Archduke Franz Ferdinand, heir to the Austrian throne, and his wife, Duchess of Hohenberg, by a Serbian terrorist in Sarajevo, Bosnia in '14, started what became World War I. As an ally of Austria, Germany declared war on Russia, ally of Serbia. Great Britain, as an ally of Russia, issued a declaration of war against Germany. President Wilson declared the United States' neutrality. By '15, the Central Powers were comprised of Germany, Austria-Hungary, Turkey and Bulgaria. The Allies were comprised of Russia, Great Britain, France, Belgium, Serbia, Montenegro, Japan and Italy. American sentiment was generally to remain uninvolved until the German armies introduced poison gas, attrocities were reported in Belgium, and U-boats attacked and sank American vessels, especially the steamer *Lusitania*, which sank off Ireland with the loss of 1,198 lives.

Even then, not everyone was pro war. This song illustrates the anti-war sentiment that was prevalent during the years before America's involment in '17.

The Peerless Quartet and Morton Harvey both had very popular recordings of the song that were popular in '15. Hear Morton Harvey's '16 recording of this song at http://www.authentichistory.com/audio/ww1/Morton_ Harvey-I_Didnt_Raise_My_Boy_To_Be_A_Soldier.html. The sheet music cover depicts a gray-haired woman

hugging her son as she invisions the horrors of war. The subtitle is "A Mother's Plea for Peace," and was "respectfully dedicated to every mother — everywhere."

The lyrics to the first verse begin by telling us that millions of soldiers have gone to war and have not returned. For all those who have died in vain, mother's hearts have been broken. Then the chorus is what the mother said: *I didn't raise my boy to be a soldier, / I brought him up to be my pride and joy, / Who dares to place a musket on his shoulder, / To shoot some other mother's darling boy? / Let nations arbitrate their future troubles, / It's time to lay the sword and gun away, / There'd be no war today, If mothers all would say, / "I didn't raise my boy to be a soldier."*

"I Didn't Raise My Boy to Be a Soldier" was involved in a plagiarism suit in '16. A composer named Cohalin claimed that the melody of this song was stolen from his song "How Much I Really Cared." The melodies were similar and since Piantadosi had worked for the publisher of Cohalin's song and may have come in contact with the song at that time, the court ruled in Cohalin's favor.

As American sentiment began to change, numerous songs came out to refute this one, including "I Didn't Raise My Boy to Be a Coward," "I Didn't Raise My Boy to Be a Molly Coddle," "I Didn't Raise My Boy to Be a Slacker" and "I Didn't Raise My Boy to Be a Soldier but He'll Fight for the U.S.A."

"I Didn't Raise My Son to Be a Soldier" *was selected for Variety's Hit Parade of a Half-Century* representing '15.

The sheet music cover and musical score are available at http://levysheetmusic.mse.jhu.edu/browse.html and at http://lcweb2.loc.gov/cocoon/ihas/loc.natlib.ihas.1000084 57/ or at http://scriptorium.lib.duke.edu/dynaweb/sheet-music/1910–1920/@Generic__BookTextView/14371. See the sheet music cover and hear a midi musical version at http://parlorsongs.com/issues/2004–4/thismonth/feature.a sp. A PDF of this song is available at http://library. indstate.edu/level1.dir/cml/rbsc/kirk/sheet_titles.html.

In a Monastery Garden
Music: Albert William Ketelbey

"In a Monastery Garden" was a *Variety Hit Parade of a Half-Century* selection representing '15. According to *A Century of Pop Music* and *Pop Memories*, there aren't any famous recordings of "In a Monastery Garden," therefore, its popularity must have been in sheet music sales. Its fame appears to have been more in the classical or semi-classical vein rather than as a popular song.

The song's composer, Albert Ketelbey, displayed musical talent at a young age; he was composing classical-type compositions by his teens. He attended England's Trinity College of Music in Oxford. His greatest success in composition was his descriptive pieces with exotic subjects. His "In a Persian Market," "In a Chinese Temple Garden" and "In a Monastery Garden" were particularly popular with theater orchestras and in sheet music sales.

The reader can download a '21 recording of this song by the Peerless Quartet: http://memory.loc.gov/cgi-bin/ query/r?ammem/papr:@filreq(@field(NUMBER+@band (edrs+50812r))+@field(COLLID+edison)).

It's a Long, Long Way to Tipperary
Words & Music: Jack Judge & Harry Williams

Jack Judge was a British music-hall entertainer and composer of popular songs. He is famous for writing "It's a Long, Long Way to Tipperary" in '12. A battalion of the Connaught Rangers Regiment of the British Army adopted the song because the Rangers were mostly Irishmen and they had connections with the town of Tipperary. The Connaught Rangers spread the song's fame when they went to France at the beginning of World War I in '14.

After a particular evening's performance at a music hall, Jack went to a pub near the theater. Someone at the pub bet Judge that he could not write a new song the next day and perform it on stage during the next evening's performance. Judge accepted the bet. On the way home, he overheard a fragment of a conversation between two men. In giving directions, one man said to the other "It's a long way to..." He liked the sound of the partial phrase and, even though he had never been to Ireland, added the town "Tipperary" to it. One source claims the original was "It's a long way to Connemara." The next morning, he went to a nearby pub and wrote the song in a very short time. A friend wrote down the musical notation by listening to Jack singing the song.

Another friend was Harry Williams. Williams had often lent Judge money and Jack promised if he ever wrote a best-selling song, he would put Williams' name on it also. He kept his promise. It has been alleged by Williams' relatives that he was the composer. Both men made a good deal of money from the song's royalties.

Judge won his bet by singing "It's a Long, Long Way to Tipperary" at the next evening's performance (New Year's Eve '12). Its catchy tune quickly caught on with the public. Once it was published, it was popularized on the English music-hall circuit by singer Florrie Forde, who was a very popular music-hall performer of the time.

The song sold a million sheet music copies in '14 and it became one of the most popular songs with the British, German and Russian armies during World War I. Even though it is known as a war song, it really has nothing to do with war.

The chorus is the most famous part of the song: *It's a long way to Tipperary, It's a long way to go. / It's a long way to Tipperary to the sweetest girl I know. / Goodbye Piccadilly, Farewell Leicester Square, / It's a long, long way to Tipperary, but my heart lies there.*

The American Quartet had a very successful recording of the song in '14, but John McCormack's '15 recording was just as popular. Prince's Orchestra and Albert Farrington also had popular recordings of the song in '15.

Variety chose this song for its *Hit Parade of a Half-Century* representing '12.

Hear John McCormack's and/or Billy Murray and the American Quartet's '14 recording of this song at http://www.firstworldwar.com/audio/1914.htm.

The sheet music cover and musical score are available at http://levysheetmusic.mse.jhu.edu/browse.html and at http://lcweb2.loc.gov/cocoon/ihas/loc.natlib.ihas.1000071 09 and http://scriptorium.lib.duke.edu/dynaweb/sheet music/1910–1920/@Generic__BookTextView/22436.

It's Tulip Time in Holland (Two Lips Are Calling Me)

Words: Dave Radford; Music: Richard A. Whiting

"It's Tulip Time in Holland (Two Lips Are Calling Me)" was Richard Whiting's first successful popular song. It sold over a million and a half copies of sheet music. Henry Burr helped popularize the song with a successful recording in '15.

Whiting accepted a Steinway grand piano from the music publishing company, Remick, in lieu of royalties on this song. His royalties would have bought him considerably more than a piano, but his previous published songs had not sold well, so he considered the grand piano a good deal.

The first of two verses sets the stage: an old fashioned windmill beckons the singer "to a little maid of Holland."

The chorus lyrics follow: *It's tulip time in Holland, Two lips I know are lonely, / The sweetest lips in Holland, Are blooming for me only. / I'd give the world if I could be, Back there beside her / By the Zuider Zee, It's tulip time in Holland, / Two lips are calling me.*

The song was used in the '43 movie musical *Hello, Frisco, Hello* and in *April Showers* ('48).

The sheet music cover and musical score are available at http://levysheetmusic.mse.jhu.edu/browse.html and at http://lcweb2.loc.gov/cocoon/ihas/loc.natlib.ihas.1000099 16/.

Variety selected "It's Tulip Time in Holland" for its *Hit Parade of a Half-Century*.

A Little Bit of Heaven (Shure, They Call It Ireland)

Words: J. Keirn Brennan; Music: Ernest R. Ball

Chauncey Olcott introduced this Irish song in the '14 musical *The Heart of Paddy Whack*. George McFarlane had a very successful recording of the song in '15, and Charles Harrison's version was almost as popular. John Barnes Wells and John McCormack also had solo recordings that were popular in '15.

The song's lyrics begin with a question: "Have you ever heard the story of how Ireland got its name?" Then the singer proceeds to tell the story as "me dear old mother told the tale to me": *Shure, a little bit of heaven fell from out the sky one day / And nestled on the ocean in a spot so far away. / And when the angels found it, shure it looked so sweet and fair, / They said suppose we leave it, for it looks so peaceful there. / So they sprinkled it with star dust just to make the shamrocks grow, / 'Tis the only place you'll find them no matter where you go. / Then they dotted it with silver, to make it's lakes so grand, / And when they had it finished shure they called it Ireland.*

The seldom heard second verse reminds us that Ireland is the "dear old land of fairies," and that no other place on earth has "such lakes and dells."

The song was used in the Hollywood movie musical *A Little Bit of Heaven* ('40), in Ernest R. Ball's screen biography *When Irish Eyes Are Smiling* ('44), where it was sung by Dick Haymes, and in Chauncey Olcott's screen biography *My Wild Irish Rose* ('47), where it was sung by Dennis Morgan.

Variety chose "A Little Bit of Heaven" for its *Hit Parade of a Half-Century* representing '14.

The sheet music cover and musical score are available at http://levysheetmusic.mse.jhu.edu/browse.html. See the sheet music cover and hear a midi musical version at http://www.perfessorbill.com/covers/ireland.htm.

My Bird of Paradise

Words & Music: Irving Berlin

The Peerless Quartet had a particularly popular recording of Irving Berlin's "My Bird of Paradise" in '15.

The lyrics tell about a girl in Honolulu, his "bird of paradise," who is feeling much better since she received a letter from her Hawaiian lover. The chorus is what he wrote. He asks her to wait for him because he is coming back to her and the Hawaiian Islands. In his dreams he hears a ukulele strumming and her asking him to come back to her.

The sheet music cover and musical score are available at http://levysheetmusic.mse.jhu.edu/browse.html and at http://scriptorium.lib.duke.edu/dynaweb/sheet music/1910–1920/@Generic__BookTextView/31016. See the sheet music cover, the complete lyrics (two verses and the chorus) and hear a midi musical version at http://www.halcyondaysmusic.com/september/september2002.htm.

My Little Dream Girl

Words: L. Wolfe Gilbert; Music: Anatol Friedland

James F. Harrison and James Reed had a very popular duet recording of "My Little Dream Girl" in '15.

In the first verse of Gilbert's lyrics, the singer, a male, is ready to go to sleep so he can dream of his girl. The chorus lyrics follow: *My little dream girl, you pretty dream girl, / Sometimes I seem, girl, to own your heart. / Each night you haunt me, by day you taunt me, / I want you, I want you, I need you so. / Don't let me waken, learn I'm mistaken, / Find my faith shaken, in you sweetheart. / I'd sigh for, I'd cry for, sweetdreams forever, / My little dream girl goodnight.*

The sheet music cover and musical score are available at http://levysheetmusic.mse.jhu.edu/browse.html and at http://scriptorium.lib.duke.edu/dynaweb/sheetmusic/'10-'20/@Generic__BookTextView/31467.

My Melancholy Baby (see '28)

Variety chose this song for its *Golden 100 Tin Pan Alley Songs* and *Hit Parade of a Half-Century* representing '12, but it was most popular in '28. It was popularized in '15 in a recording by Walter Van Brunt.

On the Beach at Waikiki (or the Golden Hula)

Words: G.H. Stover; Music: Henry Kailimai

"On the Beach at Waikiki" was a *Variety Hit Parade of a Half-Century* selection representing '15. According to the www.huapala.org website the song was the most popular Hawaiian song during the '30s, earning the writers and publisher $50,000 in royalties.

There are five short verses to this song, which seems folk-like in character. Each of the verses begins with "Honi kaua wikiwiki." The first verse lyrics follow: *Honi kâua wikiwiki / Sweet brown maiden said to me / As she gave me language lessons / On the beach at Waikîkî.*

The lyrics and a midi musical version can be found at http://www.huapala.org/O/On_The_Beach_At_Waikiki.html. The sheet music cover can be seen at http://www.hulapages.com/00078b.jpg.

Song of Songs (Chanson du Coeur Brise)

Words: Clarence Lucas; Music: Moya

Grace Kerns helped popularize "Song of Songs" with a popular recording in '15. Paul Whiteman and his orchestra revived it successfully in '24.

The French lyrics were by W. Maurice Vaucaire. The lyrics of Clarence Lucas' English version of the first verse asks several questions of the loved one, like "Do you recall that night in June when first we met?" However, it seems that "all our tenderest vows were made but to be broken."

The chorus lyrics follow: *Song of songs, song of memory, / And broken melody of love and life, / Never more to me can that melody / Fill the heart with joy once it knew. / O night of bliss, night of June and love, / Beneath the stars, amid the roses / O dream of delight that faded at dawn / O song of song, O night of bliss / When you were my whole world of love.*

The sheet music cover and musical score are available at http://levysheetmusic.mse.jhu.edu/browse.html and at http://scriptorium.lib.duke.edu/dynaweb/sheetmusic/'10-'20/@Generic__BookTextView/41268.

Variety chose this song for its *Hit Parade of a Half-Century* representing '14.

Song of the Islands

Words & Music: Charles E. King

"Song of the Islands (Na Lei O Hawaii)" was first published in Honolulu, then was popularized on the mainland.

Exotic destinations must have been on the minds of the populous during '15. Several of the popular songs of the year had exotic locales in their subject matter: Chinatown, San Francisco (Frisco), Tipperary and Ireland in general, Holland, plus the Hawaiian Islands. This song and Irving Berlin's "My Bird of Paradise," which were both popular in '15, had Hawaiian subject matter. There does not seem to be any particular thing historically that would have caused the nation to be fascinated by these exotic locales. The trend continues in '16 with several Hawaiian flavored songs.

Wayne King and his orchestra's '30 recording and Bing Crosby's '36 version are the most popular recorded versions of "Song of the Islands."

The song was included in the '29 movie musical *Melody Lane*, in *Ice-Capades Revue* ('42) and in the non-musical film *Cheaper by the Dozen* ('50). A '42 film titled *Song of the Islands* starred Betty Grable, Victor Mature and Jack Oakie.

Variety chose this song for its *Hit Parade of a Half-Century* representing '15.

See the sheet music cover at http://www.hulapages.com/covers_2.htm.

They Didn't Believe Me

Words: Herbert Reynolds; Music: Jerome Kern

Producer Charles Frohman brought the British musical hit *The Girl from Utah* to the United States. The plot involved an American girl who flees to London rather than become a rich Mormon's latest wife. The British score proved to be unsuitable, so Frohman hired composer Jerome Kern and lyricist Herbert Reynolds to write five new songs. One of their additions was the wonderful "They Didn't Believe Me."

Julia Sanderson and Donald Brian introduced "They Didn't Believe Me" in the musical *The Girl from Utah*. The musical had premiered in London, but came to New York City in '14.

The song became a major success, Kern's first, both the song and the musical, success in this country. The song became a million selling sheet music song.

Harry MacDonough and Alice Green helped popularize this song with an usually successful duet recording in '15. Grace Kerns and Reed Miller and Walter Van Brunt and Gladys Rice had popular recordings of the song in '16. Morton Downey and his orchestra revived it with some success in a '34 recording. Red Nichols' Five Pennies' recording of this Kern classic song is available at http://www.redhotjazz.com/rn5p.html.

Reynolds rejected the flowery poetry of most period love songs and produced a lyric with the easy cadence of everyday conversation. The lyrics tell about a guy and girl who are determined to marry even though they cannot convince their friends how wonderful the other one is: *And when I told them how beautiful you are, / They didn't believe me. They didn't believe me. / Your lips, your eyes, your cheeks, your hair / Are in a class beyond compare. / You're the loveliest girl that one could see! / And when I tell them, and I'm certainly gonna tell them, / That I'm the man whose wife one day you'll be, / They'll never believe me. They'll never believe me, / That from this great big world you've chosen me.*

The song was used in Jerome Kern's '46 screen biography *Till the Clouds Roll By*, where it was sung by Dinah Shore, and in the '49 movie musical *That Midnight Kiss*, where it was performed by Kathryn Grayson and Mario Lanza.

Variety chose this song for its *Hit Parade of a Half-Century* representing '14.

See the sheet music cover and the musical score at http://lcweb2.loc.gov/cocoon/ihas/loc.natlib.ihas.100006967/, at http://digital.library.ucla.edu/apam/ or see two different sheet music covers and listen to a midi musical version at http://parlorsongs.com/issues/2002-2/thismonth/featurea.asp.

When I Leave the World Behind

Words & Music: Irving Berlin

The idea for this song came when the playwright Wilson Mizner told Irving Berlin about a Chicago lawyer's unusual will. The lawyer, Charles Lounsbery's will said, "I leave to children exclusively the dandelions of the field and the daisies thereof, with the right to play among them freely, according to the custom of children." Other clauses in the will read similarly. After the song had become a success, it was discovered that the will was a fake concocted by a man named Willston Fish as a joke.

Berlin's sentimental song tells about a man facing of his own mortality and the legacy he would like to leave behind. Berlin's lyrics sing about a millionaire who is concerned about the distribution of his wealth after his death. Then he compares that to a man without wealth who simply wants to leave behind peace and beauty. The simple man enumerates the things he'll leave behind when he dies. They include the sunshine to the flowers, springtime to the trees, the night time to the dreamers, songbirds to the blind, and the moon above to those in love.

Fritzi Scheff, a well-known Viennese operatic singer who had become a vaudeville star, introduced the song at the Palace Theater. Berlin was in the audience for the first performance. After Ms. Scheff finished her performance of the song, Berlin rose from his place in the audience and sang it several more times. After that successful introduction, Berlin took the song to Al Jolson, who milked tears from audiences with his emotional performances of it.

Later, Belle Baker and other vaudeville stars continued the song's success. Recordings by Henry Burr and Sam Ash helped popularize this Irving Berlin song.

Variety Hit Parade of a Half-Century representing '15.

See the sheet music cover and the musical score at http://scriptorium.lib.duke.edu/dynaweb/sheetmusic/'10-'20/@Generic__BookTextView/49236.

When You Wore a Tulip and I Wore a Big Red Rose

Words: Jack Mahoney; Music: Percy Wenrich

The American Quartet helped popularize this song with a popular recording in '15. After Judy Garland and Gene Kelly performed the song in the '42 movie musical *For Me and My Gal*, their recording of the song was popular enough to chart.

"When You Wore a Tulip and I Wore a Big Red Rose" was popular during World War I, so many films about the era have used the song. It was included in *Larceny in Music* ('43), where it was sung by Allan Jones and the King Sisters, in *Hello, Frisco, Hello* ('43), in *Greenwich Village* ('44), in *The Merry Monahans* ('44), where it was sung by Ann Blyth, in *Chicken Every Sunday* ('49), in *Cheaper by the Dozen* ('50), and in *Belles on Their Toes* ('52).

The verse of this song is rather fast, but the chorus slows down considerably. The lyrics to the fast verse follow: *I met you in a garden in an old Kentucky town, / The sun was shining down, You wore a gingham gown; / I kissed you as I placed a yellow tulip in your hair, / Up-on my coat you pinned a rose so rare. / Time has not changed your loveliness, You're just as sweet to me, / I love you yet, I can't forget the days that used to be.*

The lyrics for the much more familiar chorus follow: *When you wore a tulip, A sweet yellow tulip, / And I wore a big red rose, When you caressed me, / 'twas then Heaven blessed me, / What a blessing, no one knows, / You made life cheery, When you called me dearie, / 'Twas down where the blue grass grows, / Your lips were sweeter than julep, / When you wore that tulip, and I wore a big red rose.*

Variety chose "When You Wore a Tulip and I Wore a Big Red Rose" for its *Hit Parade of a Half-Century* representing '14.

The sheet music cover and musical score are available at http://levysheetmusic.mse.jhu.edu/browse.html and at http://lcweb2.loc.gov/cocoon/ihas/loc.natlib.ihas.100009812/. Hear a midi musical version and read the lyrics at http://www.geocities.com/dferg5493/whenyouworeatulip.html or at http://parlorsongs.com/issues/2001-9/thismonth/featureb.asp.

When You're Away

Words: Henry Blossom; Music: Victor Herbert

Wilda Bennett introduced "When You're Away" in the musical *The Only Girl*.

Henry Blossom's lyrics are full of exclamation marks, as if he was trying over emphasize his point. Some of Blossom's lyrics are also rather antiquated. In the verse (not printed here) he uses the term "ashen-cold," for instance. And in the refrain, he uses "'twere" and "naught," which are not, and have not been, a part of our everyday language for many years: *When you're away, dear, / how weary the lonesome hours! / Sunshine seems gray, dear! / The fragrance has left the flow'rs! / If I knew 'twere but dreaming!*

Ne'er to be! | Then when you're near me, | There's naught that I strive to do, | Save to endear me more fondly my love to you! | Never again let us part, dear! | I die without you, mine own! | Hold me again to your heart! | I love you alone! Love you mine own! | I love you alone!

Olive Kline helped popularize the song beyond the Broadway stage with a popular recording in '15. Deanna Durbin performed the song in the '43 movie musical *His Butler's Sister*.

The sheet music cover and musical score are available at http://levysheetmusic.mse.jhu.edu/browse.html.

Variety included this song in its *Hit Parade of a Half-Century* representing '14.

1916

America (My Country 'Tis of Thee)

Words: Samuel Francis Smith; Music: "God Save the King"

The father of public school music in America and the father of the singing school movement, Lowell Mason, wanted Samuel Francis Smith, then a student at Andover Theological Seminary, to write a song for a children's choir. Mason gave Smith several books of songs and hymns to try to find an appropriate melody to use. As Smith leafed through the books, he came upon a German patriotic song that inspired him to write a patriotic verse of his own. Since the words he read were in German, he did not realize that the tune was the British "God Save the King."

A children's choir in Boston first performed the song on July 4, 1832 and the song was published in Lowell Mason's 1832 collection *The Choir, or Union Collection of Church Music*.

In '16, patriotic feelings were aroused in the U.S. because World War I had already begun in Europe. The government was doing its best to remain neutral, but the country was wary and feeling inevitably drawn into the conflict. Patriotic songs were very popular.

The Columbia Mixed Double Quartet recorded and released a very popular version of "America" in '16. Louis Gravieure had another popular recording of the song in '17. Sousa's Band and George Alexander had popular recorded versions of the song in '05.

Hear George Gaskin's 1899 recording of "America" at http://lcweb2.loc.gov/cocoon/ihas.1351/ or Arthur Middleton's '17 recording: http://lcweb2.loc.gov/cocoon/ihas.100010382/.

Baby Shoes

Words: Joe Goodwin & Ed Rose; Music: Al Piantadosi

"Baby Shoes" is a '11 sentimental ballad that was popularized first in vaudeville. Henry Burr had a popular recording of the song in '16. It had been popularized by the American Quartet with a '11 recording.

This waltz sings about a mother's love. In the first verse, the lyricists ask us to "imagine the love of a child for its toys," "a bird for its mate," and "a miser for gold." Then "multipy each love a million times o'er, It won't be half the love that a mother has for": *Baby shoes, Baby shoes, | Mother will never forget them, | You have forgotten when*

your feet were bare, | Mother remembers, she still has a pair of | Baby shoes, Baby shoes, | To keep them the world she'd refuse, | If she had to choose, her life she would lose, | Before she'd part with her baby's shoes.

See the sheet music cover and the musical score at http://lcweb2.loc.gov/cocoon/ihas/loc.natlib.ihas.100008451/.

Variety chose "Baby Shoes" for its *Hit Parade of a Half-Century* representing '16.

Beale Street Blues

Words & Music: W.C. Handy

W.C. Handy, the Father of the Blues, originally published this song in Memphis as "Beale Street."

The lyrics of this W.C. Handy classic tell us that he has seen Broadway, old Market Street in San Francisco, he has "strolled the Prado ... gambled on the Bourse." But he advises us to "see Beale Street first!" He tells us some of the things we'll see on Beale Street: "pretty browns in beautiful gowns ... tailor-mades and hand-me-downs ... honest men, and pick-pockets." The street's businesses never close unless "somebody gets killed." There's no place he'd rather be, but he's "goin' to the river ... because the river's wet, and Beale Street's done gone dry!"

Prince's Orchestra and Earl Fuller both helped popularize it in '17 with popular recordings. Marion Harris revived it in '21 with a popular recording. Alberta Hunter revived it again in '27, Joe Venuti again in '32, and Guy Lombardo and his Royal Canadians once again in '42 with recordings that were popular enough to chart.

Mitzi Gaynor performed the song in the screen biography of Eva Tanguay *The I-Don't-Care Girl* ('53). The song was also included in W.C. Handy screen biography *St. Louis Blues* ('58).

See the sheet music cover and the musical score at http://scriptorium.lib.duke.edu/dynaweb/sheetmusic/1910–1920/@Generic__BookTextView/2228. Or see the sheet music cover and hear a midi musical version at http://www.parlorsongs.com/issues/1999–9/sep99feature.asp. Read the lyrics at http://www.mixed-up.com/lyrics/round/beale-street-blues/.

Variety chose "Beale Street Blues" for its *Hit Parade of a Half-Century*.

Bring Me a Rose

Words & Music: Charles Shisler

Variety included "Bring Me a Rose" in its *Hit Parade of a Half-Century* for '16, even though it reportedly wasn't copyrighted until '18.

The song is a ballad in waltz time. No important recordings of the song can be found, but a man named Sam Ash is on the cover of the sheet music for introducing and helping popularize the song. This particular Sam Ash was a popular vaudeville performer, not the same person who founded the Sam Ash music store chain.

See the sheet music cover and follow a SCORCH version of the musical score as you listen to a midi musical version at http://parlorsongs.com/issues/2001–8/thismonth/featurea.asp.

Forever Is a Long, Long Time

Words: Darl MacBoyle; Music: Albert Von Tilzer

Variety included this song in its *Hit Parade of a Half-Century* representing '16. The most popular recording of the song was Charles Hart's version in '19.

The singer is trying to warn his girl against saying "Goodbye forever": *Forever means when summer brings the roses, / They'll waken mem'ries in your heart; / Forever means the songs we love together / Will lose their sweetness when we part. / Forever dear, means that we near / The twilight of a day sublime, / When you say "Goodbye forever," just remember / That forever is a long, long time.*

The sheet music cover and musical score are available at http://levysheetmusic.mse.jhu.edu/browse.html.

The Girl on the Magazine *and* I Love a Piano

Words & Music: Irving Berlin

The original title of *Stop! Look! Listen!* was *Watch YourStep.* Harry Smith's libretto told the story of a chorus girl who aspired to replace a leading lady who had recently married and retired from the stage. She was coached by a helpful assistant played by Harry Fox. After various vicissitudes, she accomplishes her goal. The show's two most famous songs were "The Girl on the Magazine" and "I Love a Piano."

The Girl on the Magazine

Joseph Santley introduced Irving Berlin's "The Girl on the Magazine" in the musical *Stop! Look! Listen!* The song was staged as a glamorous production number whose sole purpose was to extol feminine beauty. As Santley sang in front of a giant reproduction of *Vogue* magazine, four showgirls came to life and walked off the page.

Harry MacDonough helped popularize the song with a very popular '17 recording.

In the first verse of the song the singer (apparently a male) tells us that his "head is a dizzy whirl" since he "met a certain girl." He is terribly sad because he knows "she never could be mine."

In the chorus, he thinks they painted the girl on the cover just for himself. He would fall in love if he could find a girl as "nice as she." If he met "a girl as sweet" he'd claim her for his own. He swears he would love her the same as he loves her "on the cover of a magazine."

In the movie musical *Easter Parade* the song was titled "The Girl on the Magazine Cover."

The sheet music cover and musical score are available at http://levysheetmusic.mse.jhu.edu/browse.html.

I Love a Piano

Harry Fox introduced Irving Berlin's "I Love a Piano" in the musical *Stop! Look! Listen!* in '15. The set for "I Love a Piano" consisted of an immense keyboard running from one end of the stage to the other. Before this keyboard six pianists played six pianos. They were all playing the melody of this song about the love of music. For many years, Irving Berlin insisted "I Love a Piano" was his best effort.

This song about the possibilities of music tells the story from the performer's point of view. In the verse lyrics, Berlin says he has been fascinated by everything about bands since he was a child. He was wild about the director, "clarinets were my pets, and a slide trombone I thought was simply divine." But now those instruments jar his system, because "there's one musical instrument that I call mine."

The chorus lyrics are simply delightful. He says he loves the piano, he loves to hear somebody play "an upright or a high toned baby grand" (he particularly mentions Steinway pianos). He loves to run his fingers over the ivory keys and "with the pedal I love to meddle." He says to keep the fiddle, give him a "P-I-A-N-O."

Billy Murray further popularized the song with a very popular '16 recording.

Judy Garland and Fred Astaire performed the song in the '48 movie musical *Easter Parade.*

The musical score is available at http://levysheetmusic. mse.jhu.edu/browse.html (no sheet music cover this time). Hear a midi musical version, see the lyrics, and access sheet music files (no cover) at http://www.geocities.com/dferg 5493/iloveapiano.htm.

Goodbye, Good Luck, God Bless You

Words: J. Keirn Brennan; Music: Ernest R. Ball

"Goodbye, Good Luck, God Bless You," written in '14 by J. Keirn Brennan and Ernest R. Ball, was popularized in vaudeville and in a very popular recording by Henry Burr.

The lyrics of Brennan's chorus follow: *Goodbye, good luck, God bless you, / Is all that I can say. / But when you leave, my heart will grieve / Forever and a day. / Though other arms caress you, / I cannot bid you stay. / Goodbye, good luck, God bless you, / Is all that I can say.*

The sheet music cover and musical score are available at http://levysheetmusic.mse.jhu.edu/browse.html. See the sheet music cover and to listen to a midi musical version at http://www.parlorsongs.com/issues/1999-3/mar99 feature.asp.

Hello, Hawaii, How Are You?

Words: Bert Kalmar & Edgar Leslie; Music: Jean Schwartz

In '15, the telephone and wireless telephony were progressing technologically, but for most communities the telephone and radio were still novelties. In '15, the first New York to San Francisco telephone line was opened and the speech was experimentally transmitted from Arlington, Virginia to Honolulu.

This song is about a sailor contacting his honey in Honolulu.

Prince's Orchestra had a particularly popular recording of the song in '16, but Billy Murray's version was almost as popular. Recordings by Nora Bayes and by Anna Chandler were also popular in '16.

The sheet music cover and musical score are available at http://levysheetmusic.mse.jhu.edu/browse.html and at http://lcweb2.loc.gov/cocoon/ihas/loc.natlib.ihas.1000079 36/ or see the sheet music cover at www.hulapages.com/ covers_2.htm.

Variety selected "Hello, Hawaii, How Are You?" for its "Hit Parade of a Half-Century" representing '15.

I Ain't Got Nobody

Words: Roger Graham; Music: Spencer Williams & Dave Peyton

"I Ain't Got Nobody" became a Bert Williams standard. Sophie Tucker also helped popularize this song in her vaudeville act. As a matter of fact, Sophie Tucker's recording of the song was popular in '24. Other popular recordings include Marion Harris' in '21 and blues queen Bessie Smith's in '26. During the rock era, "I Ain't Got Nobody" was used in a medley by David Lee Roth. Roth's medley was popular enough to chart in '85.

Roger Graham's lyrics follow: *There's a saying going 'round and I begin to think it's true, / It's awful hard to love someone, when they don't care 'bout you, / Once I had a lovin' man, as good as many in this town, / But now I'm sad and lonely, for he's gone and turned me down, now / I ain't got nobody and nobody cares for me. / I got the blues, the weary blues, / And I'm sad and lonely, won't somebody come and take a chance with me? / I'll sing sweet love songs honey, all the time / If you'll come and be my sweet baby mine. / 'Cause I ain't got nobody, and nobody cares for me. / Won't somebody go and find my man and bring him back to me? / It's awful hard to be alone and without sympathy. / Once I was a loving gal, as good as any in this town, / but since my daddy left me, I'm a gal with her heart bowed down.*

The song was used in the '38 movie musical *Paris Honeymoon* and in the '44 movie musical *Atlantic City*.

Variety chose "I Ain't Got Nobody" for its *Hit Parade of a Half-Century*.

I Sent My Wife to the Thousand Isles

Words: Andrew B. Sterling & Ed Moran; Music: Harry Von Tilzer

Al Jolson popularized "I Sent My Wife to the Thousand Isles" with a very popular '16 recording.

What a chauvinist song! Of course, chauvinism was the accepted way of life in the mid–1910s. In the first verse lyrics a man is standing on the pier telling his wife goodbye. She sees a tear in his eye and assumes it means he will miss her, but he tells us "those tears were tears of joy." In the second verse, he says he loves his wife "because she's far away." The lyrics of the chorus follow: *I sent my wife to the Thousand Isles today, she's on her way. / She'll spend a week on every Isle, and say, that's why I'm gay. / So everybody come and give three cheers, / She's going to be away for twenty years, / 'Cause I sent my wife to the Thousand Isles today, Hooray!*

The sheet music cover and musical score are available at http://levysheetmusic.mse.jhu.edu/browse.html. See the sheet music cover and listen to a midi musical version at http://www.perfessorbill.com/covers/thsndisl.htm.

If I Knock the "L" Out of Kelly (It Would Still Be Kelly to Me)

Words: Sam M. Lewis & Joe Young; Music: Bert Grant

Marguerite Farrell helped popularize "If I Knock the 'L' Out of Kelly" with a very popular recording in '16. But its sheet music sale was also considerable.

This cute waltz novelty tells us about Timothy Kelly, a store owner, and Pat Clancey, the painter man. Timothy wanted his name painted over the door of his store. When Clancey painted it he misspelled Kelly by leaving out one "L." He decided not to charge Kelly, but "reasoned it out in" his "own little way," which is the chorus of the song: *If I knock the "L" out of Kelly, / It would still be Kelly to me; / Sure a single "L-Y" or a double "L-Y" / Should look just the same to an Irishman's eye. / Knock off an "L" from Killarney, / Still Killarney it always will be, / But If I knock the "L" out of Kelly, / Sure he'd knock the "L" out of me.*

There are several accent marks in the music over certain words followed by rests, as if a blow has been delivered and the singer is absorbing a punch.

The sheet music cover and musical score are available at http://levysheetmusic.mse.jhu.edu/browse.html.

Ireland Must Be Heaven, for My Mother Came from There

Words: Joseph McCarthy & Howard Johnson; Music: Fred Fisher

The Irish have had an important and prominent influence on American popular music. Many Irish songs or songs about Ireland have reached hit status and many have endured over the years. "Ireland Must Be Heaven, for My Mother Came from There" became particularly nostalgic among all Irish Americans and the general population soon loved it as well. The song sold millions of copies of sheet music.

Fred Fisher, the composer, was from Germany and neither of the lyricists, McCarthy nor Johnson, were from Ireland.

The lyrics of this Irish ballad yearn for Ireland primarily because mother, the basis of all good Irish homes, was from there.

There are many "mother" songs during the early years of the 20th century. In '15, the anti-war song "I Didn't Raise My Boy to Be a Soldier," which was the expression of many mothers and in '16 we had the famous "M-O-T-H-E-R" (see below). Then there was "Mother Machree" in '10, just to name a few.

Then there are numerous Irish-themed songs, including "A Little Bit of Heaven (Shure They Call It Ireland) from '14, "Peg o' My Heart" and "When Irish Eyes Are Smiling" from '13, "Has Anybody Here Seen Kelly," "Where the River Shannon Flows" and "Machushla" from '10, again to name only a few.

So a sure success for a popular song would be to combine "mother" and "Irish." The formula worked.

Charles Harrison helped popularize the song with a very successful '16 recording.

The sheet music cover and musical score are available at http://levysheetmusic.mse.jhu.edu/browse.html. See the sheet music cover and hear a midi musical version at http://parlorsongs.com/issues/2002–2/thismonth/featureb.asp.

Variety chose this great Irish song for its *Hit Parade of a Half-Century*.

Keep the Home Fires Burning (Till the Boys Come Home)

Words: Lena Guilbert Ford; Music: Ivor Novello

Several English songs associated with World War I became popular in the U.S., including "It's a Long Way to Tipperary," "Pack Up Your Troubles," "Roses of Picardy" and "Keep the Home Fires Burning."

Frederick J. Wheeler had a particularly popular recording of the song in '16, and James F. Harrison and James Reed's duet recording was also quite popular. John McCormack's '17 recording of the song was also popular, as popular as Reed's had been in '16.

The first verse of the song tells about men being called into military service and "the Country found them ready." The lyrics say we should not cry because that makes their job even more difficult. Even though our hearts are breaking, "make it sing this cheery song." The chorus follows: *Keep the home fires burning, / While your hearts are yearning, /*

Though your lads are far away / They dream of home; / There's a silver lining / Through the dark cloud shining, / Turn the dark cloud inside out, / Till the boys come home.

The non-descript sheet music cover and musical score are available at http://levysheetmusic.mse.jhu.edu/browse. html or at http://lcweb2.loc.gov/cocoon/ihas/loc.natlib. ihas.100008252/ or at http://scriptorium.lib.duke.edu/ dynaweb/sheetmusic/1910–1920/@Generic__Book TextView/25103.

Variety selected this song for its "Hit Parade of a Half-Century" representing '15.

The Lights of My Home Town

Words & Music: Charles K. Harris

Charles K. Harris wrote this sentimental ballad and the Peerless Quartet popularized it with a very successful Victor recording in '16. According to Joel Whitburn's *A Century of Pop Music*, the song was one of the year's No. 1 hits.

The singer is far away from his home. He often feels lonesome, particularly for the "sight of my dear mother and the lights of my home town." The chorus continues: *Just to see the lights of my old home town, / Just to see the gay crowd's move along / Just to sometimes hear the music playing / Just to hear the laughter and the song / Just to see the girl that used to love me, / Rosebuds in her hair and gingham gown / I would gladly give up fame and wealth and glory / Just to see the lights of my home town.*

You can hear a 30 second audio clip of the Peerless Quartet's recording of the song at http://www.archeophone.com/product_info.php?products_id=63. The sheet music cover and musical score are available at http://lcweb2.loc.gov/cocoon/ihas/loc.natlib.ihas.100006416/default.html. The first page of the musical score is a four part arrangement of the chorus for male quartet.

Li'l Liza Jane

Words & Music: Countess Ada DeLachau

Variety selected "Li'l Liza Jane" for its *Hit Parade of a Half-Century.*

The sheet music says the song was "used as incidental music in the three act comedy *Come Out of the Kitchen.* Ruth Chatterton is pictured on the sheet music cover as Jane Ellen from *Come Out of the Kitchen.*

This folk-like song has nine very simple verses and a chorus that follows each verse. As an example, the first verse and chorus follow: *I'se got a gal an' you got none Li'l Liza Jane, (repeat) / Ohe, Liza, Li'l Liza Jane (repeat).*

The sheet music cover and musical score are available at http://levysheetmusic.mse.jhu.edu/browse.html and at http://digital.library.ucla.edu/apam/.

Memories

Words: Gustave Kahn; Music: Egbert Van Alstyne

"Memories" was one of lyricist Gus Kahn's first successes; notice that he still used "Gustave," rather than "Gus."

John Barnes Wells and Henry Burr both had popular recordings of "Memories" in '16.

The lyrics of the first verse follow: *Round me at twilight come stealing, / Shadows of days that are gone; / Dreams of the old days revealing / Mem'ries of Love's golden dawn.*

The lyrics of the famous chorus continue: *Memories, Memories, Dreams of love so true. / O'er the Sea of Memory*

I'm drifting back to you. / Childhood days, Wildwood days, / Among the birds and bees You left me alone, / But still you're my own! In my beautiful Memories.

Danny Thomas sang it in the '52 movie musical *I'll See You in My Dreams*, Gus Kahn's screen biography.

The sheet music cover and musical score are available at http://levysheetmusic.mse.jhu.edu/browse.html. See the sheet music cover and to hear a midi musical version at http://parlorsongs.com/issues/2002–2/thismonth/featurea.asp (the sheet music cover is rather unusual; a tall lamp with a red shade is the only object on the page).

Variety chose "Memories" for its "Hit Parade of a Half-Century" representing '15.

M-O-T-H-E-R (a Word That Means the World to Me)

Words: Howard Johnson; Music: Theodore F. Morse

Mother songs have been popular for years, especially among the sentimental ballads of the 1890s and the early years of the 20th century.

This mother ballad is a spelling song that gives a meaning to each of the letters.

The famous chorus follows (the "'T' is for the tears were shed to save me" phrase seems stilted somehow; like it should be "that were shed," but that doesn't fit rhythmically or musically): *"M" is for the million things she gave me, / "O" means only that she's growing old, / "T" is for the tears were shed to save me, / "H" is for her heart of purest gold; / "E" is for her eyes, with lovelight shining, / "R" means right, and right she'll always be, / Put them all together, they spell "MOTHER," / A word that means the world to me.*

Sophie Tucker helped popularize the song by performing it in her vaudeville act. Henry Burr had a particularly popular recording of it in '16. George Wilson Ballard also had a popular version on the market.

The song was used in the '47 movie musical *Mother Wore Tights.*

There are two verses and two choruses.

There were at least two sheet music covers that were on the market and both identify the song as "Eva Tanguay's Great 'Mother' Song."

See the sheet music cover and the musical score at http://lcweb2.loc.gov/cocoon/ihas/loc.natlib.ihas.100007859/ or see the sheet music cover and hear a midi musical version at http://www.parlorsongs.com/issues/2000–5/2000–5.asp.

Variety named "M-O-T-H-E-R" to its "Hit Parade of a Half-Century" representing '15.

Nola

Music: Felix Arndt

"Nola" is a Felix Arndt piano composition published in '15. Lyrics were added by Sunny Skylar in '59.

The instrumental was an engagement gift for his girl friend, Nola Locke, a singer and pianist, who became his wife.

Variety chose "Nola" for its *Hit Parade of a Half-Century* representing '16.

The most popular recordings of the song did not come until the '20s. Vincent Lopez and Carl Fenton and their orchestras both had popular recordings of the song in '22 (Lopez' version was by far more successful; it became his theme song). Tommy Dorsey and his orchestra revived it successfully in '37. Les Paul revived it in '50; his version made it to No. 4 on the *Billboard* chart. Guy Lombardo and his Royal Canadians also had a popular version on the market in '50.

An instrumental version of "Nola" was used in the '30 Paul Whiteman movie musical *King of Jazz*, Vincent Lopez and his orchestra performed it in the '32 movie musical *The Big Broadcast*, and it also appeared in the '45 movie musical *That's the Spirit*.

The sheet music cover and musical score are available at http://scriptorium.lib.duke.edu/dynaweb/sheet music/1910–1920/@Generic__BookTextView/33004;nh=1? DwebQuery=Nola#X.

Oh! How She Could Yacki Hacki Wicki Wacki Woo

Words: Stanley Murphy & Charles McCarron; Music: Albert Von Tilzer

Hawaii was certainly in style on Tin Pan Alley during the mid–1910s. Not authentic Hawaiian music, of course, but Tin Pan Alley's version of the Islands and their music.

Eddie Cantor performed this number in his Broadway debut in a Ziegfeld production on the Midnight Roof of the New Amsterdam Theater in '16.

Arthur Collins and Byron Harlan had a very successful duet recording of the song in '16.

The song's subtitle is "That's love in Honolu," not Honolulu. The lyrics are rather silly, but that does not mean they are bad. It is extremely difficult to determine what the American public will buy. And in the case of popular music, if they buy the sheet music and the recordings, it is a hit!

The verses are in the key of D, while the chorus modulates to G, which is a little unusual for a popular song.

In the first verse, the singer tells us that he has been a Romeo. He loved a girl in Timbuctoo and other places, but a "little Hula Hula" in Honolulu broke his heart in two.

The lyrics of the chorus follow: *She had a Hula, Hula, Hicki, Boola in her walk, / She had a Ukalele, Wicki, Wicki, Walli in her talk, / And by the big Hawaiian moon, / Beneath a banyan tree we'd spoon, / I've been tryin' to learn Hawaiian, / Since that night in June, / She had a blinky, blinky, little naughty winky in her eye, / She had a "Come and kiss me, don't you dare to miss me" in her sigh, / Beneath the banyan parasol / She couldn't talk my talk at all, / But, Oh, how she could Yacki, Hacki, Wicki, Wacki Woo, That's love in Honolu.*

The sheet music cover and musical score are available at http://levysheetmusic.mse.jhu.edu/browse.html and at http://lcweb2.loc.gov/cocoon/ihas/loc.natlib.ihas. 100009604/ or see the sheet music cover and to hear a midi musical version at http://www.parlorsongs.com/ issues/1999–12/dec99gallery.asp or see the sheet music cover at www.hulapages.com/covers_2.htm.

Variety selected this song for its "Hit Parade of a Half-Century."

Pretty Baby

Words: Gus Kahn; Music: Tony Jackson & Egbert Van Alstyne

One of Egbert Van Alstyne's biggest hit songs is "Pretty Baby," on which he shared composer credit with Tony Jackson.

According to Gus Kahn's son, Donald, his father and Van Alstyne frequented the black nightclubs of Chicago. One evening they apparently heard Tony Jackson and his "Pretty Baby." What they heard was not the song exactly as we know it today, but Kahn and Van Alstyne saw potential in the song and convinced Jackson to sell it to them.

According to http://www.redhotjazz.com, Tony Jackson was gay and wrote his version of "Pretty Baby" for his boyfriend.

There are conflicting accounts as to the complete history of this song, but most likely Kahn rewrote the lyrics, perhaps cleaning them up a bit (many of the early rhythm and blues songs of the '50s also had to have their lyrics cleaned up before they would sell to the general public). Some researchers claim that Van Alstyne stole the tune from Jackson. Others say that Ziegfeld bought it and had Kahn and Van Alstyne rewrite it for Fanny Brice. Some imply that Van Alstyne made no contribution to the song at all. Others claim that the Shubert brothers bought the tune, but couldn't use the original slang lyrics and didn't like the melody for the verse. They supposedly hired Kahn and Van Alstyne to clean up the lyrics and rewrite the verse melody.

Kahn's lyrics for the famous chorus follow: *Ev'rybody loves a baby that's why I'm in love with you, / Pretty Baby, Pretty Baby; / And I'd like to be your sister, brother, dad and mother too, / Pretty Baby, Pretty Baby. / Won't you come and let me rock you in my cradle of love, / And we'll cuddle all the time. / Oh! I want a lovin' baby and it might as well be you, Pretty Baby of mine.*

However it actually evolved, Dolly Hackett introduced this delightful, jaunty little song in *The Passing Show of 1916*. Billy Murray's recorded version was very popular in '16.

"Pretty Baby" has appeared in several movie musicals including *Applause* ('29), Mae West's *She Done Him Wrong* ('33), *Rose of Washington Square* ('39), where it was sung by Al Jolson, *Coney Island* ('43), where it was sung by Betty Grable, Ted Lewis' screen biography *Is Everybody Happy?* ('43), Nora Bayes' screen biography *Shine on Harvest Moon* ('44), Gloria DeHaven and Charles Winninger sang it and danced to it in *Broadway Rhythm* ('44), Danny Thomas sang it in Gus Kahn's screen biography *I'll See You in My Dreams* ('52), and it also appeared in Eva Tanguay's screen biography *The I-Don't-Care Girl* ('53).

See the sheet music cover, the lyrics and hear a midi musical version at http://www.halcyondaysmusic.com/ april/april2004.htm, or http://www.parlorsongs.com/ issues/2004–10/thismonth/feature.asp. The sheet music cover and musical score are available at http://levy sheetmusic.mse.jhu.edu/browse.html and at http:// lcweb2.loc.gov/cocoon/ihas/loc.natlib.ihas.100007059/ or at http://scriptorium.lib.duke.edu/dynaweb/sheetmusic/ 1910–1920/@Generic__BookTextView/37085.

Variety included "Pretty Baby" in its "Hit Parade of a Half-Century."

Somewhere a Voice Is Calling

Words: Eileen Newton; Music: Arthur F. Tate

John McCormack had a particularly popular recording of this '11 song in '16. Henry Burr and Elizabeth Spencer and Vernon Archibald had popular recordings of it in '14.

The rather simplistic lyrics of the chorus follow: *Dusk and the shadows falling o'er land and sea, / Somewhere a voice is calling, calling for me. / Dusk and the shadows falling* o'er land and sea, / Somewhere a voice is calling, calling for me. / Dearest, my heart is dreaming, dreaming of you, / Somewhere a voice is calling, calling for me, calling for me.

It must have been John McCormack's performance that popularized an otherwise rather ordinary song.

The non-descript sheet music cover and musical score are available at http://levysheetmusic.mse.jhu.edu/browse. html. See the sheet music cover and hear a midi musical version at http://www.parlorsongs.com/issues/1999–3/ mar99gallery.asp.

The Star Spangled Banner

Words: Francis Scott Key; Music: tune "To Anacreon in Heaven"

Even though the United States was not directly involved in World War I in '16, patriotic feelings were intense.

Prince's Orchestra recorded a very successful version of "The Star Spangled Banner" in '16. John McCormack released his equally popular version of the song in '17. Margaret Woodrow Wilson, the daughter of President Wilson, had recorded a popular version in '15. Back in 1892, Patrick Gilmore's Band had recorded a popular version.

Most of us probably know the story of the origin of our national anthem, but the basic story is worth repetition. During the last days of the War of 1812, a young Baltimore lawyer, Francis Scott Key, was one of a commission who were sent to negotiate the release of Dr. William Beanes by the British, who were anchored near Fort McHenry in Baltimore harbor. Key and the rest of the party reached the British vessel just prior to their attack on Fort McHenry. During that evening aboard the British vessel, Key witnessed the battle. When dawn broke and he saw the American flag still flying above the fort, he was moved to pen the verses we know and love so well.

Key appropriated the English song "To Anacreon in Heaven" for the melody to his verses.

For many years, the United States did not have an official national anthem. It was not until '31 that both houses of Congress passed the bill and President Hoover signed the legislation that officially made the song our national anthem. It was not the only song considered, "Columbia, the Gem of the Ocean" received a lot of support.

There have been several movements over the years to replace this militaristic song as our national anthem with songs like Irving Berlin's "God Bless America" or "America, the Beautiful," but such efforts have failed to muster enough support.

Hear Anna Case's '17 recording of "The Star Spangled Banner" at http://lcweb2.loc.gov/cocoon/ihas/100010383/. A PDF of this song is available at http://library. indstate.edu/level1.dir/cml/rbsc/kirk/sheet_titles.html.

Our national anthem became one of the most recorded songs of the pre-rock era.

The Sunshine of Your Smile

Words: Leonard Cooke; Music: Lilian Ray

"The Sunshine of Your Smile" was first popularized in vaudeville. John McCormack's '16 recording of the song was very popular.

The lyrics seem a bit antiquated, more like those of the late 1800s than the mid–1910s: *Dear face that holds no sweeter smile for me, / Were you not mine, how dark the world would be. / I know no light above that could replace /*

Love's radiant sunshine in your dear face. / Give me your smile, the love light in your eyes, / I could not hold a fairer paradise. / Give me the right to love you all the while, / My world forever, the sunshine of your smile.

The non-descript sheet music cover and musical score are available at http://levysheetmusic.mse.jhu.edu/browse. html and at http://lcweb2.loc.gov/cocoon/ihas/loc. natlib.ihas.100008592/.

There's a Broken Heart for Every Light on Broadway

Words: Howard Johnson; Music: Fred Fisher

Which came first the song or the expression? There's no definitive answer, but chances are the saying came first.

The statement "There's a broken heart for every light on Broadway," of course, means that many talented actors and actresses had their dreams shattered because they did not find the success they anticipated on Broadway.

There were, even in the mid–1910s, millions of lights on Broadway; in fact, it had become known as "The Great White Way." In 1891, the first electric marquee had been erected at a Broadway theater. By the early years of the 20th century, the street was ablaze with white lights as each theater tried to outdo the others as they announced their shows and stars.

"There's a Broken Heart for Every Light on Broadway" was first popularized in vaudeville, but Elsie Baker helped popularize the song with a successful recording in '16.

The sheet music encourages the singer to perform the verse at an ab lib tempo. The singer is giving advice to any young potential Broadway hopefuls. The verse says the young dreamers would "never leave the village if he knew."

Knew what? The chorus (in a more even tempo) tells us: *There's a broken heart for ev'ry light on Broadway, / A million tears for ev'ry gleam they say, / Those lights above you think nothing of you, / It's those who love you, that have to pay, / There's a sorrow lurking in each gloomy shadow / And sorrow comes to ev'ry one some day, / Twill come to our brothers but think of the mothers with broken hearts for each light on Broadway.*

The song was used in Fred Fisher's screen biography, *Oh, You Beautiful Doll* ('49). Bill Shirley dubbed the song for Mark Stevens in the film.

Variety included this song in its *Hit Parade of a Half-Century.*

There's a Long, Long Trail

Words: Stoddard King; Music: Zo Elliott

This '13 song became a World War I classic. *Variety* included it in its *Hit Parade of a Half-Century* representing '13.

The writers, King and Elliott, were seniors at Yale in '13 when they wrote this song for a banquet being held at their fraternity. At first it made little impression and all the publishers they submitted it to turned it down.

Elliott transferred to Trinity College, Cambridge, England in the fall of '13. There he heard that an London publisher was searching for songs, so Elliott submitted "There's a Long, Long Trail." The publisher agreed to publish it only if Elliott paid for the initial printing; if the song proved to be successful, he would be refunded the printing cost.

When World War I began in Europe, Elliott was traveling in Germany. When he returned to London, he found a nice royalty waiting for him. He then returned to the U.S. and convinced the Witmark publishing company to buy the copyright. Witmark's version didn't start out particularly well, but as America moved closer and closer to involvement in the War, the song began to catch on. It eventually sold over two and a half million copies of sheet music.

James F. Harrison and James Reed released a particularly popular duet recording of the song in '16, but there were several other popular versions on the market: Charles Harrison's '15 recording, John McCormack's '17 version, Oscar Seagle and the Columbia Stellar Quartet's '18 recording and Riccardo Stracciari's '19 version.

The song has been used in several films with a World War I context, most notably *What Price Glory* ('52).

The lyrics don't really have anything to do with War, or directly with soldiers or their loved ones. The verses, which are not nearly as well known as the chorus, indicate that the singer is very lonely night and day. He keeps remembering his loved one. The more famous chorus follows: *There's a long, long trail awinding / Into the land of my dreams, / Where the nightingales are singing / And a white moon beams. / There's a long, long night of waiting / Until my dreams all come true; / Till the day when I'll be going / Down that long, long trail with you.*

The non-descript sheet music cover and musical score are available at http://levysheetmusic.mse.jhu.edu/browse. html. Hear a midi musical version and see the complete lyrics at http://www.geocities.com/dferg5493/theresalong longtrail.htm.

There's a Quaker Down in Quaker Town

Words: David Berg; Music: Alfred Solman

Henry Burr and Albert Campbell had a very successful recording of "There's a Quaker Down in Quaker Town" in '16, but the Peerless Quartet version was also quite popular. Hear Henry Burr and Albert Campbell's '16 recording at http://nfo.net/ogg.htm.

The verses to this song are quite short in comparison to most of the others of the era. The first verse follows: *Two hours ride from old Broadway / There is a sleepy town, they say; / "Old Philadelphia," You opened my eyes / And I apologize.*

The chorus is not as ethnic as one might suspect. The lyrics might not have had the same exotic flavor without the Quaker reference, but the lyrics could easily have been referring to any girl in any town. The lyrics to the chorus follow: *There's a Quaker down in Quaker town, / When I am around she sighs, / But down in her heart, I know, / She's not so slow, for oh, oh, oh, oh! Those eyes! / Like the waters still she's very deep, / She knows a heap, I found, / She has that "Meet me later" look, / And oh, she knows her book, / This little Quaker down in Quaker town.*

The sheet music cover and musical score are available at http://levysheetmusic.mse.jhu.edu/browse.html and at http://lcweb2.loc.gov/cocoon/ihas/loc.natlib.ihas.1000090 55/ or at http://scriptorium.lib.duke.edu/dynaweb/sheet music/1910–1920/@Generic__BookTextView/45505. See the sheet music cover, the lyrics and hear a midi musical version at http://www.halcyondaysmusic.com/may/may 2002.htm.

Turn Back the Universe and Give Me Yesterday

Words: J. Keirn Brennan; Music: Ernest R. Ball

The Orpheus Quartet popularized "Turn Back the Universe and Give Me Yesterday" with a particularly popular recording in '16.

The two verses are in 4/4 (or common) time, which is not usual, of course. The basic idea is that a couple has said some things in anger and they would like to turn back time to repair the hurt feelings. The lyrics to the first verse follow: *It seems so long ago, / Although 'twas only yesterday, / When just a word in anger heard / Our lives should part for aye. / With faith so strong we thought no wrong / Could tear our heart strings then; / What would I give could I but live / The days that might have been!*

A rather unusual thing comes next when the chorus changes the meter to waltz-time (triple meter): *Turn back the universe and give me yesterday; / Unclasp the hands of time that hold life's golden ray. / Take back that bitter hour when our love passed away, / Turn back the universe and give me yesterday!*

The sheet music cover and musical score are available at http://levysheetmusic.mse.jhu.edu/browse.html and at http://lcweb2.loc.gov/cocoon/ihas/loc.natlib.ihas.1000042 82/. See the sheet music cover, the lyrics and hear a midi musical version at http://www.halcyondaysmusic.com/march/march2001.htm.

Where Did Robinson Crusoe Go with Friday on Saturday Night?

Words: Sam M. Lewis & Joe Young; Music: George W. Meyer

Al Jolson premiered this novelty song in the Winter Garden extravaganza *Robinson Crusoe, Jr.* in '16. It was in this show that Jolson was first billed as "The World's Greatest Entertainer."

In most of the productions that Jolson appeared in on Broadway, he was the black-face servant Gus. At some point during the evening, Jolson would step forward, get completely out of character and sing whatever songs he wanted to sing. At least in *Robinson Crusoe, Jr.*, this song and "Yaaka Hula Hickey Dula" seem related to the overall theme. However, Jolson also interpolated "Where the Black-Eyed Susans Grow" and "Down Where the Swanee River Flows" into the show, which doesn't appear to have any relation to the topic.

The extravaganza was loosely based on Daniel DeFoe's *Robinson Crusoe* (1719), but "loosely" is the key word.

The verse to the song sets the stage. Robinson Crusoe has landed on an island with "no rent to pay, no wife to obey." He and Friday, his only companion, built a hut and lived there until they would apparently go somewhere else on Saturday night.

The comedic, slightly suggestive, chorus follows: *Where did Robinson Crusoe go with Friday on Saturday night? / Every Saturday night they would start in to roam / And on Sunday morning they'd come staggering home. / They went hunting for rabbits when the weather grew colder / But Crusoe came home with a hare on his shoulder. / Now, where did Robinson Crusoe go with Friday on Saturday night?*

There are several verses and choruses. Go to one of the websites mentioned below to read more of the lyrics.

The sheet music cover and musical score are available at

http://levysheetmusic.mse.jhu.edu/browse.html and at http://lcweb2.loc.gov/cocoon/ihas/loc.natlib.ihas.1000072 76/ or hear a midi musical version, see the lyrics, and see the sheet music cover at http://parlorsongs.com/issues/ 2002–12/thismonth/feature.asp.

Variety chose this Al Jolson hit song for its *Hit Parade of a Half-Century*.

You Belong to Me

Words: Henry Blossom; Music: Victor Herbert

Victor Herbert and Henry Blossom wrote "You Belong to Me" for a Florenz Ziegfeld produced revue titled *The Century Girl*. It played at the cavernous Century Theater for 200 performances.

Blossom's lyrics are extremely possessive! The verse tells us the singer has searched his whole life for this girl, so he has no intention of letting her go. He certainly doesn't know how to accept "No"; he says "No often means "Yes." The chorus lyrics follow: *So don't forget wherever you are that you belong to me. / Led by fate, soon or late my own you're bound to be. / The flow'rs belong to the Sunlight, the pearls belong to the Sea. / So don't forget that you'll love me yet for you belong to me.*

Variety included "You Belong to Me" in its *Hit Parade of a Half-Century*.

The musical score is available at http://levysheetmusic. mse.jhu.edu/otcgi/llscgi60. Another song titled "You Belong to Me" was written by Pee Wee King, Redd Stewart and Chilton Price and popularized by Jo Stafford and Patti Page in '52.

1917

The Bells of St. Mary's

Words: Douglas Furber; Music: A. Emmett Adams

Bing Crosby and Ingrid Bergman starred in a '45 motion picture titled *The Bells of St Mary's*. Australian composer, A. Emmett Adams and lyricist Douglas Furber, wrote the song that gave the film its title. They were inspired to write the song when they heard some church bells ringing in '14.

The song was introduced into the United States in '17 and became a classic. The tune also became the college song of the New York State Maritime College.

The sheet music cover shows a girl and boy walking together near a church.

The lyrics of the chorus are by far more famous than the verses. The words to the chorus follow: *The Bells of St. Mary's, Ah! Hear they are calling / The young loves, the true loves Who come from the sea, / And so my beloved, When red leaves are falling, / The lovebells shall ring out, ring out for you and me.*

Variety included this song in its *Hit Parade of a Half-Century*.

The rather bland sheet music cover and musical score are available at http://digital.library.ucla.edu/apam/.

For Me and My Gal

Words: Edgar Leslie & E. Ray Goetz; Music: George W. Meyer

Writing of any kind is a discipline. Generally, the more one practices the craft, the easier it becomes. J.S. Bach

wrote volumes of music during his lifetime. Quite a few of his composition are considered among the greatest ever written. Irving Berlin wrote thousands of songs and not all of them became monster hits, but a good percentage are now considered some of the greatest of American popular music. In this instance, George Meyer was simply plying his craft; he was a songwriter. He needed to write a song, a good song, one that would become a hit; he needed the money. He set to work and wrote the music for this ballad. He thought up a title, took the music and title to lyricists Edgar Leslie and E. Ray Goetz, who wrote the words for Meyer's melody. It was as simple as that. A composer and a couple of lyricists practicing their crafts. And a popular song classic was born. Many people have been credited with the quote, "Genius is 90% perspiration and 10% inspiration," but whoever said it, the thought applies here.

By the way, it is amazing that so many of our popular songs were not word born, but the music came first and words were added later. It just seems that the words would suggest a rhythm and melody, but that doesn't seem to be the case in numerous examples.

Such vaudeville headliners as Belle Baker, Sophie Tucker, Eddie Cantor and George Jessel were some of the first performers to popularize "For Me and My Gal." Al Jolson sang it at some of his Winter Garden Sunday evening concerts (the theater was normally closed on Sunday evening, so Jolson began giving concerts that evening; that way he could sing whatever he wanted with out any worrys about a musical plot).

The song eventually sold more than three million copies of sheet music. Van and Schenck had the most popular recording of the song in '17, but Prince's Orchestra, Henry Burr and Albert Campbell, and Billy Murray also had popular recordings of the song in '17. After Judy Garland and Gene Kelly performed the song in the '42 movie musical *For Me and My Gal*, their recording of the song was quite popular. Guy Lombardo and his Royal Canadians had a somewhat popular recording of the song in '43. The song was also used in the '49 movie musical *Jolson Sings Again*.

The famous chorus lyrics follow: *The bells are ringing for me and my gal, / The birds are singing for me and my gal. / Everybody's been knowing / To a wedding they're going / And for weeks they've been sewing, / Ev'ry Susie and Sal. / They're congregating for me and my gal, / The Parsons waiting for me and my gal. / And sometime I'm goin' to build a little home for two, / For three or four or more, / In Loveland for me and my gal.*

The sheet music cover and musical score are available at http://levysheetmusic.mse.jhu.edu/browse.html and at http://lcweb2.loc.gov/cocoon/ihas/loc.natlib.ihas.1000072 56/ or see the sheet music cover and hear a midi musical version at http://parlorsongs.com/issues/2002–2/this month/featureb.asp.

The song was selected by *Variety* for its *Golden 100 Tin Pan Alley Songs* and *Hit Parade of a Half-Century*. "For Me and My Gal" was nominated for the American Film Institute's list of the greatest songs ever from American films for it appearance in *For Me and My Gal* ('42), but did not make the final list.

Good-bye Broadway, Hello France

Words: C. Francis Reisner & Benny Davis; Music: Billy Baskette

"Good-bye Broadway, Hello France" was introduced

as the finale of the Broadway revue *The Passing Show of 1917.* Patriotic feelings were very high in the U.S. When Germany instituted unrestricted submarine warfare in early '17, the United States began to arm all merchant ships. The U.S. declared war on Germany on Good Friday, April 6, 1917. American troops arrived in France in early summer and entered into the conflict in the fall. Before the year was over, we had also declared war on Germany's ally, Austria-Hungary. The United States was at war.

This song became a big hit, selling approximately four million copies of sheet music. The American Quartet's recording of the song was also very successful. The Peerless Quartet's version was also popular.

Hear the American Quartet's recording of this song at http://www.authentichistory.com/audio/ww1/American_ Quartet-Goodbye_Broadway_Hello_France.html or to www.firstworldwar.com/audio/1919.

The song was used in the '40 movie musical *Tin Pan Alley*, and in the '42 movie musical *For Me and My Girl*, where it was sung by a male chorus.

There are a couple of verses and a chorus to this song. The first chorus lyrics follow: *Good-bye Broadway, Hello France, / We're ten million strong, / Goodbye sweethearts, wives and mothers, / It won't take us long, / Don't you worry while we're there, / It's for you we're fighting too, / So good-bye Broadway, hello France, / We're going to square our debt with you.*

You can read the rest of the lyrics to the verses and second chorus at one of the websites mentioned below.

Variety included "Good-bye Broadway, Hello France" in its *Hit Parade of a Half-Century* representing '17.

The sheet music cover and musical score are available at http://levysheetmusic.mse.jhu.edu/browse.html and at http://lcweb2.loc.gov/cocoon/ihas/loc.natlib.ihas.1000045 39/ or at http://scriptorium.lib.duke.edu/dynaweb/sheet music/1910–1920/@Generic__BookTextView/11058.

Indiana

Words: Ballard MacDonald; Music: James F. Hanley

Many people think the name of this song is "Back Home Again in Indiana," because that's how the chorus begins, but the name is simply "Indiana." And many people probably think it is the official state song of Indiana, but it is not. It is, however, the song that starts the Indianapolis 500 race each year (like "My Old Kentucky Home" is played before the Kentucky Derby).

The composer, James Hanley, was born in Indiana and the song was his first major hit.

Recordings of "Indiana" by Conway's Band and the Original Dixieland Jazz Band were popular in '17. Their recording is available at http://www.redhotjazz.com/ odjb.html. Red Nichols and his Five Pennies revived it successfully in '29. Many jazz ensembles have recorded the song over the years.

The lyrics of the famous chorus follow: *Back home again in Indiana, / And it seems that I can see / The gleaming candlelight still shining bright / Thru the sycamores for me, / The new mown hay sends all its fragrance / From the fields I used to roam, / When I dream about the moonlight on the Wabash, / Then I long for my Indiana home.*

The quote from "On the Banks of the Wabash" in the seventh line of the chorus was intentional, was used by permission, and was somewhat of a tribute to Paul

Dresser's 1897 ballad that became the official state song of Indiana in '13.

"Indiana" was interpolated into the film version of Jerome Kern's Broadway musical *Roberta* in '35. It also appeared in the screen biography of Red Nichols, *The Five Pennies* ('59).

See the sheet music cover and the musical score at http://lcweb2.loc.gov/cocoon/ihas/loc.natlib.ihas.1000063 80/ or http://scriptorium.lib.duke.edu/dynaweb/sheet music/1910–1920/@Generic__BookTextView/21845 or see the sheet music cover, read the lyrics and hear a midi musical version at http://www.halcyondaysmusic.com/ december/december2004.htm or see the sheet music and hear a midi musical version at http://parlorsongs.com/ issues/2003–5/thismonth/feature.asp. A PDF of this song is available at http://odin.indstate.edu/about/units/rbsc/ kirk/sh-group.html.

Variety included "Indiana" in its *Hit Parade of a Half-Century.* The song became one of the most recorded songs of the pre-rock era.

It's a Long Lane That Has No Turning

Words & Music: Manuel Klein

Variety included "It's a Long Lane That Has No Turning" in its *Hit Parade of a Half-Century* representing '17, however, it appears to have been more popular in '12. First, the song had been copyrighted in '11 and had appeared in the New York Hippodrome production *Around the World* in its 1911–12 season. Second, the Peerless Quartet had the most popular recording of the song in '12.

The singer has "wanted to meet a little girl like you" for many years and he always thought good luck would come his way. He's "traveled in ev'ry land," but couldn't find a sweetheart. In the chorus, which follows, we find out that he has finally found the girl that he can love: *It's a long lane that has no turning, / And I think I can plainly see / That the girl I love is learning just to care a bit for me. / Oh yes, it's a long lane that has no turning, / And the saying is old but true, / But I wouldn't care how long it was if I could walk through it with you.*

The sheet music cover and musical score are available at http://levysheetmusic.mse.jhu.edu/browse.html and at http://digital.library.ucla.edu/apam/.

Leave It to Jane

Words: P.G. Wodehouse; Music: Jerome Kern

Edith Hallor introduced the title song of the musical *Leave It to Jane* in '17. The musical was based on George Ade's play *The College Widow*. The musical is another example of the public's fascination with things collegiate. It was set at Atwater College and deals primarily with the efforts of the college widow, Jane, to get the star player on a rival college's football team to play for Atwater under an assumed name.

The lyrics begin like a cheer for a football team: "Leave it to Jane, Jane, Jane." The singer thinks Jane is a girl with brains who can tackle any problem, so the answer to their collegiate predicament is "just hand over the whole thing to Jane."

The song was used in Jerome Kern's screen biography *Till the Clouds Roll By* ('46), where it was performed by June Allyson.

The Victor Light Opera Company had a popular recording of the song in '17.

Variety included "Leave It to Jane" in its *Hit Parade of a Half-Century*.

The sheet music cover and musical score are available at http://digital.nypl.org/lpa/.

Lookout Mountain

Henry Burr and Albert Campbell's duet recording of "Lookout Mountain" for Victor was very popular in '17. According to Joel Whitburn's *A Century of Pop Music*, it was one of the year's top hit songs.

M-I-S-S-I-S-S-I-P-P-I

Words: Bert Hanlon & Benny Ryan; Music: Harry Tierney

Frances White introduced this spelling song in the Ziegfeld revue *Midnight Frolics* in '16. Grace LaRue then performed it in the '17 revue *Hitchy Koo*.

Anna Wheaton had a popular recording of the song in '17, as did Ada Jones.

The lyrics tell us about a person who was terrible at spelling in school, especially when they were around seven years old, because they had a lisp that was a particular problem when it came to the letter "s." Therefore, they thought the "word Mississippi was awful hard to spell." The chorus explains how he now finds it easy to spell: *M-I-S-S-I-S-S-I-P-P-I / That used to be so hard to spell It used to make me cry / But since I've studied spelling It's just like pumpkin pie / M-I-S-S-I-S-S-I-P-P-I.*

There was another song with this same title in '50.

Variety included "M-I-S-S-I-S-S-I-P-P-I"on its *Hit Parade of a Half-Century* representing '16, but it was more popular in '17.

The sheet music cover and musical score are available at http://levysheetmusic.mse.jhu.edu/browse.html.

Missouri Waltz (Hush-a-bye Ma' Baby)

Words: J.R. Shannon; Music: John Valentine Eppell & Frederick Knight Logan

"Missouri Waltz" was originally published as a piano instrumental in '14. Frederick Knight Logan was credited as the "arranger" on the original sheet music, which claimed that the song had come from "an original melody procurred by John Valentine Eppell." The Missouri State Archives website (www.sos.state.mo.gov/archives) lists a number of individuals variously credited for the original melody; all are African American. Several websites now credit the music to Eppell, with Logan as the arranger. Two years later, another edition of the song was published with lyrics written by James Royce under the pseudonym J.R. Shannon.

"Missouri Waltz" sold over a million copies of sheet music. It became the official state song of Missouri in '49. The lyrics, like many of the period, are in African American dialect. The most famous part of the song follows: *Hush-a-bye ma baby, slumber time is comin' soon. / Rest yo head upon my breast, while mammy hums a tune. / The sandman is calling, where shadows are falling, / While the soft breezes sigh as in days long gone by. / 'Way down in Missouri where I heard this melody, / When I was a pickaninny on ma mammy's knee. / The darkies were hummin', / Their banjos were strummin', So sweet and low.*

The song had several recorded versions: the Victor

Military Band, Prince's Orchestra and Jaudas' Society Orchestra had popular recordings of the song in '16. Elsie Baker recorded an especially popular version in '17, while Henry Burr and Albert Campbell's duet recording was also popular. Earl Fuller had a moderately successful version of it in '18. Earl Fuller's Rector Novelty Orchestra's recording is available at http://www.redhotjazz.com/fuller-srector.html.

"Missouri Waltz" was used in the '39 movie musical *The Story of Vernon and Irene Castle*.

Variety chose this song for its *Hit Parade of a Half-Century* representing '14.

The sheet music cover and musical score are available at http://levysheetmusic.mse.jhu.edu/browse.html and at http://lcweb2.loc.gov/cocoon/ihas/loc.natlib.ihas.1000059 36/ or at http://scriptorium.lib.duke.edu/dynaweb/sheet music/1910–1920/@Generic__BookTextView/13739.

My Own Iona

Words: L. Wolfe Gilbert; Music: Anatol Friedland & Carey Morgan

"My Own Iona" is subtitled "Moi — One — Ionae." The sheet music cover says this song is Hawaii's favorite love song. It seems rather doubtful that it was originally heard in Hawaii, in fact, it doesn't sound like authentic Hawaiian music.

Of course, our concept of Hawaii and its music is most probably not completely authentic. In the case of this song, it is what our culture expects Hawaiian music must be.

In the first verse, the singer longs to see his Iona "down among the Hula Hula hills." He says he misses "those sighing croons, Hawaiian tunes" and Iona. Gilbert's chorus lyrics follow: *My own Iona, from old Halona, / Your dark and dreamy eyes they speak of paradise. / My Ukulele, played the Mauna Loa gayly (sic), / Halona's calling me, Iona dear, my own.*

Horace Wright popularized "My Own Iona" with a very popular recording in '17. Charles King and Elizabeth Brice had a popular duet recording of the song in '16. Ted Lewis and his Band's recording of this song, listed as "Iyone-My Own Iyone," is available at http://www.redhotjazz.com/tlband.html.

The sheet music cover and musical score are available at http://levysheetmusic.mse.jhu.edu/browse.html. See the sheet music cover and hear a midi musical version at http://parlorsongs.com/issues/1999–12/dec99feature.asp. Or see the sheet music cover at www.hulapages.com/covers_2.htm.

Oh Johnny, Oh Johnny, Oh!

Words: Ed Rose; Music: Abe Olman

Nora Bayes and Henry Lewis introduced "Oh Johnny, Oh Johnny, Oh!" as an interpolation, into the musical *Follow Me* in '16.

The sheet music sold a million or more copies and the song was popularized in recordings by the American Quartet and by Elizabeth Brice in '17. The American Quartet's version was particularly popular.

More than twenty years later, in '40, Orrin Tucker and his orchestra with vocalist "Wee" Bonnie Baker revived the song with a popular recording. Their disk reportedly sold a million copies. The Tucker recording stayed at the top of the jukebox charts for a dozen weeks in '40 and was the second best sheet music seller of the year. The song made eleven appearances on *Your Hit Parade*, peaking at No. 2 in early '40.

The lyrics are cheerful and talk about all of Johnny's (aimed at all the guys headed to both Wars) loving qualities: *Oh Johnny, Oh Johnny, how you can love. / Oh Johnny, Oh Johnny, heavens above, / You make my sad heart jump for joy, / And when you're near I just can't—sit still a minute! / I'm so ... Oh Johnny, Oh Johnny, please tell me do / What makes me love you so, / You're not handsome it's true, but when I look at you, / I just ... Oh Johnny, Oh Johnny, Oh!*

The song was used in several movie musicals, including *Oh Johnny, How You Can Love!* ('40), where it was sung by Betty Jane Rhodes, *You're the One* ('41), which starred "Wee" Bonnie Baker and the Orrin Tucker Orchestra, *For Me and My Gal* ('42), where it was danced by Gene Kelly, and *Spotlight Scandals* ('43).

Hear the American Quartet and Billy Murray's '17 recording of this song at www.firstworldwar.com/audio/ 1917. The sheet music cover and musical score are available at http://levysheetmusic.mse.jhu.edu/browse.html and at http://lcweb2.loc.gov/cocoon/ihas/loc.natlib.ihas.1000082 77/.

Variety included "Oh Johnny, Oh Johnny, Oh!" in its *Hit Parade of a Half-Century* representing '17 and '40.

The Old Grey Mare (The Whiffle Tree)
Words: unknown; Music: Frank Panella

"The Old Grey Mare" (some spell it "Grey," some "Gray") sounds considerably older than its '15 copyright. It sounds like folksong material or at least music from prior to the 1890s. Music historian Sigmund Spaeth, in his '48 *History of Popular Music in America*, thinks the melody came from an 1858 song titled "Down in Alabam.'" An instrumental version of the same melody appeared in 1860 titled "Get Out of the Wilderness."

The automobile had progressed nicely, but even in '15, and especially anywhere outside a metropolitan area, the horse and buggy were still the most reliable form of transportation. Even to those with automobiles, this song would have been nostalgia.

The song's subtitle is "The Whiffle Tree." So what is a whiffle tree? Most of us who aren't farmers or horse people haven't a clue. A whiffle tree is the wooden members and cross members that harness animals to a cart or wagon.

The song was popular during World War I and the verse lyrics mention "The Old Grey Mare was fighting at the front," but since it was written in '15, it must be talking about an earlier war. The lyrics of the song are printed on the inside cover of the sheet music as if the music and the words came from two completely different sources.

The sheet music says the song is a "one-step" and "two-step" march. That isn't particularly unusual, since marches were danced to during Sousa's heyday.

The lyrics to the chorus follow: *Oh, the old gray mare, she ain't what she used to be, / Ain't what she used to be, Ain't what she used to be. / The old gray mare, she ain't what she used to be, / Many long years ago.*

In '17, Prince's Orchestra had a popular recording of "The Old Grey Mare." Arthur Collins and Byron Harlan had a popular duet recording of the song in '18.

See the comical sheet music cover and the musical score at http://lcweb2.loc.gov/cocoon/ihas/loc.natlib.ihas.

100008312/ or see the sheet music cover and hear a midi musical version at http://parlorsongs.com/issues/2001–2/ thismonth/featureb.asp (this site also offers a midi version of "Down in Alabam'" to compare with "The Old Grey Mare").

Variety named "The Old Grey Mare" to its *Hit Parade of a Half-Century* representing '15.

Over There
Words & Music: George M. Cohan

"A nation that sings can never be beaten," declared a *Saturday Evening Post* article during World War I. The article, titled "A Nation's Songs — the Popular Songs of America at War," was quickly appropriated by song publisher Leo Feist and appeared on the back of much of Feist's sheet music in the war years. "Each song," the article continued, "is a mile-stone on the road to victory. Songs are to a nation's spirit what ammunition is to a nation's army ... When the boys march down the Avenue, it's the martial crash of "Over There" that puts the victory swing in their stride."

George Cohan was at his Long Island home when he read in the newspaper that the United States had declared war on Germany. His patriotic mind immediately began to formulate a tune and by the time he got into the city, he had completed the chorus and the verse. The opening phrase, "Johnny, get your gun," had been an 1886 popular song. The song quickly became America's call to arms. It was sung in cities, large and small, and in the tiniest villages all over the country.

Cohan performed it for some troops at Fort Myers, near Washington, D.C. to only a luke warm crowd. Charles King next performed it at the Hippodrome Theater in New York City for a Red Cross benefit concert. Then Nora Bayes adopted it for her vaudeville act and popularized it to hit status.

Publisher Leo Feist paid $25,000 for the publishing rights and quickly made back his investment. The song sold over four million sheet music copies by the end of the war. The song became *THE* song of World War I. And it was popular again with the soldiers of World War II.

The American Quartet's recording of "Over There" was one of the biggest recordings of the decade, and Nora Bayes' and the Peerless Quartet's versions were also very popular. Billy Murray's recording was also popular in '17. Hear Nora Bayes or Billy Murray's '17 recording of this song at www.firstworldwar.com/audio/1917 or hear Billy Murray's version at http://lcweb2.loc.gov/cocoon/ihas/ loc.natlib.ihas.100010567/. Opera star Enrico Caruso's '18 recording of the song was also very popular. Hear Caruso's '18 recording of this song at http://www.edisonnj.org/ menlopark/vintage/victor.asp or www.firstworldwar.com/ audio/1918. Prince's Orchestra also had a popular recording of the song in '18.

President Franklin D. Roosevelt presented Cohan with the Congressional Medal of Honor in recognition of Cohan's writing of "Over There" and "You're a Grand Old Flag."

"Over There" was first used in film in the '29 movie musical *The Cock-Eyed World*. It was, of course, used in Cohan's screen biography, *Yankee Doodle Dandy* ('42), and in the '44 movie musical *Four Jills in a Jeep*.

The lyrics of the famous chorus follow: *Over there, over there, / Send the word, send the word, over there, / That the*

Yanks are coming, the Yanks are coming, / The drums rum-tumming ev'rywhere. / So prepare, say a pray'r, / Send the word, send the word to beware, / We'll be over, we're coming over, / And we won't come back till its over over there.

See three different sheet music covers and the musical score at http://lcweb2.loc.gov/cocoon/ihas/loc.natlib.ihas.100005155/ (original cover) or http://lcweb2.loc.gov/cocoon/ihas/loc.natlib.ihas.100010517/ (London cover) or http://lcweb2.loc.gov/cocoon/ihas/loc.natlib.ihas.100010516/ (Army cover) or also at http://levysheetmusic.mse.jhu.edu/browse.html (five covers: original, London, Army, Navy, and Norman Rockwell). See a sheet music cover, read the lyrics and hear a midi musical version at http://www.halcyondaysmusic.com/july/july2004.htm.

Variety named "Over There" for its *Hit Parade of a Half-Century.*

Pack Up Your Troubles in Your Old Kit Bag and Smile, Smile, Smile!

Words: George Asaff; Music: Felix Powell

"Pack Up Your Troubles in Your Old Kit Bag and Smile, Smile, Smile!" is another of the World War I era's most famous songs. From the way the title is printed, one would assume the song is better known as "Smile, Smile, Smile!," however, that doesn't appear to be the case.

The Knickerbocker Quartet recorded the most popular version of it in '17, but there were several other popular versions on the market, including those by the Victor Military Band, Reinald Werrenrath, and Helen Clark. Oscar Seagle and the Columbia Stellar Quartet had a '18 recording of it that also was popular.

The lyrics are about Private Perks. It seems this guy is "a funny little codger" who loves to tell jokes and make people smile. In one of the several verses to the song we learn that "Private Perks went a-marching into Flanders with a smile ... When a throng of 'Bosches' came along ... Perks yelled out 'This little bunch is mine!'" and encouraged the rest of the guys to sing the famous chorus, which follows: *Pack up your troubles in your old kit bag and smile, smile, smile! / While you've got a lucifer to light your fag, / Smile, boys, that's the style! / What's the use worrying? / It never was worth while. / So, pack up your troubles in your old kit bag and smile, smile, smile!*

Hear Murray Johnson's '16 recording at www.firstworldwar.com/audio/1916 or Reinald Werrenrath's '17 recording at www.firstworldwar.com/audio/1917.

The sheet music cover and musical score are available at http://levysheetmusic.mse.jhu.edu/browse.html. Hear a midi musical version and read the lyrics at http://www.geocities.com/dferg5493/packupyourtroubles.html.

Variety chose this song for its *Hit Parade of a Half-Century* representing '15.

Poor Butterfly

Words: John Golden; Music: Raymond Hubbell

Haru Onuki introduced "Poor Butterfly" in the Hippodrome extravaganza *The Big Show* in '16. The lyricist, John Golden, mistakenly thought he was writing a song for the Japanese opera star Tamaka Mirua, who had starred in Puccini's opera *Madame Butterfly.* Golden decided to write a popular song lyric that basically told the story of the opera. As it turned out, it was Ms. Haru Onuki who introduced this lovely ballad. Golden was quite upset that

his song was not to be introduced by the Japanese opera star, but by then it was too late for him to write a replacement.

The Victor Military Band helped popularize the song with a very successful '17 recording. Prince's Orchestra, Charles Harrison, Grace Kerns and Fritz Kreisler all had popular recorded versions on the market in '17. In '54, the Hilltoppers revived the song with a recording that was popular enough to chart. Red Nichols' Five Pennies' recording of this song is available at http://www.redhotjazz.com/rn5p.html or Joseph C. Smith's Orchestra's recording at http://www.redhotjazz.com/jcso.html.

In the opera *Madame Butterfly*, the heroine falls in love with an American seaman. He leaves without knowing that she is pregnant with his child. All the time he is gone, she yearns for his return and tells her servant, Suzuki, the things she will do when he returns. When he eventually comes back, Butterfly learns that he has married an American girl. In a powerfully dramatic moment, she gives him the baby and kills herself. The same basic story was the plot of the '91 Broadway musical *Miss Siagon*, which was written by Richard Maltby, Jr., Alain Boublil and Claude-Michel Schonberg, but based in Viet Nam.

The lyrics of the first verse begin by telling us that we're going to hear a story "of a little Japanese sitting demurly 'neath the cherry blossom trees." Her name is Miss Butterfly. She was sweet and innocent until a young American seaman came to her garden. They met daily and he "taught her how to love in the 'Merican way, to love with her soul!" When he sailed away, he promised to return. Next comes the chorus, notice how nicely it follows the story of the opera: *Poor butterfly! 'neath the blossoms waiting / Poor butterfly! For she loved him so. / The moments pass into hours The hours pass into years / And as she smiles through her tears, She murmurs low, / The moon and I know that he be faithful, / I'm sure he come to me bye and bye. / But if he don't come back Then I never sigh or cry / I just must die. Poor butterfly.*

The seldom-heard second verse is just as sad. It tells us that "once Butterfly she gives her heart away, she can never love again, she is his" forever. So, even though she smiles, "her heart is growing numb" as she waits for his return.

Julie Andrews sang "Poor Butterfly" in the '67 movie musical *Thoroughly Modern Millie.*

The sheet music cover and musical score are available at http://levysheetmusic.mse.jhu.edu/browse.html and at http://scriptorium.lib.duke.edu/sheetmusic/a/a13/a1306/.

Variety included "Poor Butterfly" in its *Golden 100 Tin Pan Alley Songs* and its *Hit Parade of a Half-Century* representing '16.

They Go Wild, Simply Wild, Over Me

Words: Joseph McCarthy; Music: Fred Fisher

Marion Harris popularized "They Go Wild, Simply Wild, Over Me" with a popular recording in '17. Hear Ms. Harris' recording at http://www.redhotjazz.com/marionharris.html.

What a sport! The guy that this song is about thinks he's God's gift to women. Check out the lyrics to the chorus: *They go wild, simply wild, over me, / They go mad, just as mad as they can be, / No matter where I'm at, / All the ladies, thin or fat, / The tall ones, the small ones, / I grab 'em off like that! / Every night how they fight over me, / I don't know what it is that they can see, / The ladies look at me and sigh / In my arms they want to die, / They go wild, simply wild, over me.*

Gene Kelly danced to this song in the '42 movie musical *For Me and My Gal.*

The sheet music cover and musical score are available at http://levysheetmusic.mse.jhu.edu/browse.html and at http://lcweb2.loc.gov/cocoon/ihas/loc.natlib.ihas.1000060 54/.

Variety included this song in its *Hit Parade of a Half-Century* representing '17.

They're Wearing 'Em Higher in Hawaii

Words: Joe Goodwin; Music: Halsey K. Mohr

During the Hawaiian song craze of the mid–1910s, "They're Wearing 'em Higher in Hawaii" was popularized first in vaudeville. Then Arthur Collins and Byron Harlan's duet recording of the song was popular in '17. Morton Harvey also had a popular recording of the song.

The lyrics tell us about a man named Henry Meyer, who was a buyer of ladies wear. He was sent to Hawaii to study the fashions there. When his work wired him to come back, he replied, "I'm busy, I'm getting dizzy, the styles here turn my head!" He tells them they'd think the same thing if they were there. And the chorus continues: *For they're wearing 'em higher in Hawaii, / Higher, higher, higher, higher in Hawaii, / The beautiful beach at Waikiki / Is not the only pretty sight that you can see. / In Hawaii the maidens there are flyer, / They simply sway your heart away. / Hula maids are always full of pep. / All the old men have to watch their step. / For they're wearing 'em higher in Hawaii, / They're going up every day.*

In the second verse, Meyer's boss goes to Honolulu to check things out. He finds Meyer weaving grass skirts, but soon Meyer's boss catches "the fever" and decides to move his office to Hawaii.

See the sheet music cover and the musical score at http://lcweb2.loc.gov/cocoon/ihas/loc.natlib.ihas.1000077 43/ or see the sheet music cover at www.hulapages.com/covers_2.htm.

Variety included this song in its *Hit Parade of a Half-Century.*

Thine Alone

Words: Henry Blossom; Music: Victor Herbert

The Dublin born Victor Herbert had dreamed of writing an Irish opera, so he was very disappointed when *Eileen*, his Irish operetta produced in '17, had a disappointing run of only two months on Broadway. The operetta's most famous song was "Thine Alone."

The plot of the operetta was set in 1798 and dealt with an Irish revolutionist who is arrested by the British for treason. His wellborn British sweetheart, Eileen, and her aunt help him to escape disguised as a servant, but he is recaptured and is about to be shot when a pardon arrives not only for him, but provided a happy ending for all the revolutionaries.

Walter Scanlon and Grace Breen introduced the zealous duet "Thine Alone" in *Eileen.* Allan Jones and Mary Martin sang it in Victor Herbert's screen biography *The Great Victor Herbert* ('39).

Variety included "Thine Alone" in its *Hit Parade of a Half-Century.*

The sheet music cover and musical score are available at

http://lcweb2.loc.gov/cocoon/ihas/loc.natlib.ihas.1000066 39/.

Till the Clouds Roll By

Words: P.G. Wodehouse & Guy Bolton; Music: Jerome Kern

Jerome Kern, P.G. Wodehouse and Guy Bolton produced several musicals for the relatively small 299-seat New York City Princess Theater. These musicals, which have become known as the Princess Theater musicals, attempted to offer modern, cohesive, funny, intimate stories with songs that fit the characters and situations. The musicals ran between '15 and '19. *Oh, Boy!* ('17) became the most successful of the seven Princess Theater musicals.

The story was a funny but believable tale of modern marital misunderstanding. While a newlywed man's wife leaves to inform her parents she has eloped, he allows a college girl to avoid a lecherous judge by hiding out in his apartment. As one might imagine, all sorts of complications develop, but all the misunderstandings were resolved by the final curtain.

Anna Wheaton and James Harrod helped popularize "Till the Clouds Roll By" beyond the musical with a particularly popular recording, but Prince's Orchestra also had a very popular recording of the song as well. Vernon Dalhart's '17 recording was also popular.

The lyrics of the chorus of the duet follow: *Oh, the rain comes a pitter, patter, / And I'd like to be safe in bed. / Skies are weeping, while the world is sleeping, / Trouble heaping on our head. / It is vain to remain and chatter, / And to wait for a clearer sky, / Helter skelter, I must fly for shelter / Till the clouds roll by.*

June Allyson and Ray McDonald sang the song in Jerome Kern's screen biography *Till the Clouds Roll By* ('46).

See the sheet music cover and the musical score at http://lcweb2.loc.gov/cocoon/ihas/loc.natlib.ihas.1000069 68/.

Variety included this song in its *Hit Parade of a Half-Century.*

You're in Love

Words: Otto Harbach & Edward Clark; Music: Rudolf Friml

Lawrence Wheat, Marie Flynn and the chorus introduced the title song of the musical *You're in Love.* The Lyric Quartet helped popularize the song with a popular recording in '17. Joseph C. Smith's Orchestra's recording of "You're in Love" is available at http://www.redhotjazz.com/jcso.html.

The sheet music cover shows a wistful young lady standing at a ship's guard rail (the ship is named the High Hope) looking out into nothingness. A little naval angel stands on the rail pointing at the girl as if he is giving her advice or is the Navy version of Cupid.

The song's verse lyrics talk about love puzzling fools and saints "from Noah's time to now." It says we've all given advice to our neighbor about the complications of love, but we really don't know anything about it until it has hit us, too.

The song's refrain follows: *And some strange, peculiar feeling / O'er you comes slowly stealing. / It throws your nerves at sixes and sevens, / Makes you feel as tho' you're climbing up to the heavens; / Then dear, divine emotions / Give you such frisky notions! / First, you're glad, and then you're sad, / Lose whatever sense you had, / And you're in love, in love!*

The phrase "sixes and sevens" is an expression that means confused or chaotic. Earlier, it may have been a Hebrew expression. The expression was used in the singular (six and seven) in the Bible, and by Chaucer and by Shakespeare. Several sources suggest that the plural form of the expression came from an Old English dice game.

See the sheet music cover and the musical score at http://lcweb2.loc.gov/cocoon/ihas/loc.natlib.ihas.100006096/ or http://scriptorium.lib.duke.edu/dynaweb/sheetmusic/1910–1920/@Generic__BookTextView/53832.

Variety included "You're in Love" in its *Hit Parade of a Half-Century* representing '16.

1918

The Battle Hymn of the Republic

Words: Mrs. Dr. S.G. (Julia Ward) Howe; Music: William Steffe

Julia Ward Howe wrote the lyrics to "The Battle Hymn of the Republic" in 1861 during the Civil War. Her verses were set to the tune of "John Brown's Body," which had been taken from "Glory, Hallelujah," a tune that has been credited to William Steffe.

Mrs. Howe was visiting Washington, D.C. in 1861, when she was invited to review the Union troops in nearby Virginia. A sudden attack caused the troops to rush back to their camp. As they went, they were singing patriotic songs, including "John Brown's Body." A Reverend James F. Clarke, a member of Mrs. Howe's party, encouraged her, since she was a celebrated poet, to write a new wartime lyric to the tune. That evening at the Willard Hotel in the capital, she wrote the verses. The poem was published in the *Atlantic Monthly* in February, 1862. The magazine's editor suggested the title "The Battle Hymn of the Republic."

In the mid–1850s William Steffe of South Carolina wrote a camp-meeting song with the traditional "Glory Hallelujah" refrain. It started with the words "Say, brothers, will you meet us on Canaan's happy shore?" The tune was catchy and was soon widely known.

Early in the Civil War, a soldier named John Brown was a member of a regiment stationed in Boston. The regiment used Steffe's tune to sing a song about John Brown of Kansas who had recently made a stand against slavery. Their song was directed in jest towards their regiment's John Brown.

This version, using the words "John Brown's body lies a-mouldering in the grave, but his soul goes marching on," soon became popular among the Union troops.

Patriotic fervor was at a peak in '18 because of World War I. The Columbia Stella Quartet's recording of "Battle Hymn of the Republic" was especially popular that year. Thomas Chalmers also had a '18 recorded version that was popular. Reinald Werrenrath's '17 recording was also popular with the public and the Columbia Mixed Double Quartet's '16 version was equally popular. The Columbia Mixed Quartet's recording had been popular in '12. "Battle Hymn of the Republic" became one of the most recorded songs of the pre-rock era.

Hollywood movie musicals used the song in *San Francisco* ('36), in John Philip Sousa's screen biography *Stars and Stripes Forever* ('52), where it was sung by an African American choir, in *The Five Pennies*, the film about cornet player Red Nichols, and rather surprisingly in *Elvis* ('79).

Several sheet music covers and the musical score are available at http://levysheetmusic.mse.jhu.edu/browse.html. Download a midi file and read the complete lyrics at http://www.contemplator.com/america/battle.html or at http://www.authentichistory.com/audio/civilwar/Victrola-The_Battle_Hymn_of_the_Republic.html hear Reinald Werrenrath sing this patriotic song.

The Darktown Strutters' Ball

Words & Music: Shelton Brooks

By '18, songwriters were beginning to realize that American popular music's potential was boundless. "The Darktown Strutters' Ball" is a good example of that potential. Music and lyrics are artfully wedded.

In the first verse, a man tells his girl that he has some good news, they've been invited to the "Darktown Ball," which is "a very swell affair. All the 'high-browns' will be there." He proceeds to describe that he'll wear his silk hat and frock tail coat and she should wear her Paris gown and new silk shawl. He expects them to "be the best dressed in the hall." Next, comes the famous chorus, which follows: *I'll be down to get you in a taxi, Honey, / You better be ready about half past eight. / Now dearie, don't be late, / I want to be there when the band starts playing. / Remember when we get there, Honey, / The two-steps, I'm goin' to have 'em all, / Goin' to dance out both my shoes, / When they play the "Jelly Roll Blues," / Tomorrow night at the Darktown Strutters' Ball.*

Sophie Tucker first popularized "The Darktown Strutters' Ball" in her vaudeville act. Arthur Collins and Byron Harlan recorded a very successful version of the song that was popular in '18. This rowdy syncopated novelty was recorded by the Original Dixieland Jazz Band at their first recording session in '17. This first nominal jazz record sold like hotcakes, and the sheet music sales exceeded three million. This Original Dixieland Jazz Band's recording is available at http://www.redhotjazz.com/odjb.html. Another '17 popular recording was released by Six Brown Brothers. Jaudas' Society Orchestra also had a popular recording on the market in '18. Ted Lewis revived the song successfully in '27 with a popular recording. Lewis' recording is available at http://www.redhotjazz.com/tlband.html. In '48, Alan Dale and Connie Haines' duet version was popular enough to chart. And Lou Monte's '54 revival was pretty popular, rising to No. 4 on the *Billboard* chart.

The rests after "goin' to dance out both my shoes" and "when they play the Jelly Roll Blues" may have been meant for a tap dancer or an instrumental riff.

Variety included the song in its *Golden 100 Tin Pan Alley Songs* and *Hit Parade of a Half-Century* representing '17. "Darktown Strutters' Ball" became one of the most recorded songs of the pre-rock era.

The sheet music has a wonderful cover; unfortunately the caricature of blacks with big lips is too racially provocative. The sheet music cover and musical score are available at http://levysheetmusic.mse.jhu.edu/browse.html

and at http://lcweb2.loc.gov/cocoon/ihas/loc.natlib. ihas.100004308/ or at http://scriptorium.lib.duke.edu/ dynaweb/sheetmusic/1910–1920/@Generic__BookText View/4803. Hear the '17 recording of this song by the Original Dixieland Jazz Band at http://www.redhot jazz.com/odjb.html. Read the lyrics and hear a midi musical version at http://www.geocities.com/dferg5493/ darktownstruttersball.htm.

Give Me the Moonlight, Give Me the Girl

Words: Lew Brown; Music Albert Von Tilzer

Sam Ash had a very popular recording of "Give Me the Moonlight, Give Me the Girl (and Leave the Rest to Me)" in '18.

The verse is a super confident man saying he never worries if a girl is bashful, shy or "if she has that 'don't you dare to kiss me' in her eye." Then this perhaps overly confident man proceeds in the chorus to tell us: *Give me the moonlight, Give me the girl, | And leave the rest to me. Give me a babbling brook, | Give me a shady nook, Where no one can see. | Give me a bench for two, Where we can bill and coo, | And mine she's bound to be, If there's anyone in doubt, | And they'd like to try me out, Give me the moonlight, | Give me the girl, and leave the rest to me.*

The song was used in the '45 movie musical *The Dolly Sisters.*

"Give Me the Moonlight, Give Me the Girl" was revived in the '50s by the popular British singer Frankie Vaughan.

Variety chose this song for its *Hit Parade of a Half-Century* representing '17.

The sheet music cover and musical score are available at http://levysheetmusic.mse.jhu.edu/browse.html.

Hail! Hail! The Gang's All Here

Words: D.A. Esrom; Music: Arthur Sullivan

Theodore A. Morse's wife, using the pen name D.A. Esrom (Morse backwards), took a tune out of Gilbert and Sullivan's comic opera, *The Pirates of Penzance,* "The Pirate's Chorus," or "Come, Friends, Who Plough the Sea," and set new words to it for "Hail! Hail! The Gang's All Here." The song became famous and was a favorite of many American soldiers during World War I.

Irving Kaufman's '18 recording of the song was very popular. The Shannon Four also had a popular recording of the song in '18.

The chorus lyrics sound like a football cheer: *Hail! Hail! The gang's all here, | What the heck do we care? | What the heck do we care? | Hail! Hail! The gang's all here! | What the heck to we care now?*

Variety included the song on its *Hit Parade of a Half-Century* representing '17.

The sheet music cover and musical score are available at http://levysheetmusic.mse.jhu.edu/browse.html. See a '17 Saturday Evening Post ad for "Hail, Hail, the Gang's All Here" at http://www.militarysheetmusic.com/hail-hail-the-gangs-all-here.htm.

Hello, Central, Give Me No Man's Land

Words: Sam M. Lewis & Joe Young; Music: Jean Schwartz

Al Jolson introduced "Hello, Central, Give Me No Man's Land" in the musical extravaganza *Sinbad* in '18.

Then he popularized it further with a very popular recording.

The war had an enormous effect on those left at home. Children and family were sung about in several songs of the war era (see "Just a Baby's Prayer at Twilight" below, for instance). In this tearjerker, the simplicity of a child's understanding of the war makes a powerful impact. "Hello Central Give Me No Man's Land" tells about a child trying to call her Daddy and trying to understand why her mother cries when she prays her bedtime prayer each night.

The first verse tells us that baby climbs down the stairs at night, "toddles up to the telephone" and whispers to the operator: *Hello, Central! Give me No Man's Land, | My daddy's there, my mamma told me; | She tip-toed off to bed | After my prayers were said; | Don't ring when you get the number, | Or you'll disturb mamma's slumber. | I'm afraid to stand here at the 'phone | 'Cause I'm alone. So won't you hurry; | I want to know why mamma starts to weep | When I say, "Now I lay me down to sleep"; | Hello, Central! Give me No Man's Land.*

Hear Al Jolson's '18 recording of this song (includes lyrics & sheet music cover) at http://www.authentichistory.com/audio/ww1/Al_Jolson-Hello_Central_Get_Me_No_Mans_Land.html or hear Henry Burr's '18 recording at www.firstworldwar.com/audio/1918. The sheet music cover and musical score are available at http://levysheetmusic.mse.jhu.edu/browse.html and at http://lcweb2.loc.gov/cocoon/ihas/loc.natlib.ihas.1000079 35/ or at http://scriptorium.lib.duke.edu/dynaweb/sheet music/1910–1920/@Generic__BookTextView/12251. Or see the sheet music cover and hear a midi musical version at http://www.parlorsongs.com/issues/2000-12/2000-12b. asp.

I Don't Know Where I'm Going, but I'm on My Way

Words & Music: George Fairman

George Fairman's World War I song, "I Don't Know Where I'm Going, but I'm on My Way," was popularized by the Peerless Quartet's very well-received recording in '18. (There had been a previous song in '06 with the same title.)

In the first verse, a new soldier is telling everybody goodbye because his "Uncle Sammy" is calling him to fight.

The shorter than normal chorus lyrics follow: *And I don't know where I'm going but I'm on my way. | For I belong to the regulars I'm proud to say | And I'll do my duty-uty night or day | I don't know where I'm going but I'm on my way.*

Hear the Peerless Quartet's '17 recording of this song at www.firstworldwar.com/audio/1917. See the sheet music cover and musical score at http://levysheetmusic.mse.jhu. edu/browse.html and at http://scriptorium.lib.duke.edu/ dynaweb/sheetmusic/1910–1920/@Generic__Book-TextView/14547 or see the sheet music cover, read the lyrics and hear a midi musical version at http://www. halcyondaysmusic.com/october/october2002.htm.

I'm All Bound 'Round with the Mason Dixon Line

Words: Sam M. Lewis & Joe Young; Music: Jean Schwartz

Al Jolson popularized "I'm All Bound 'Round with the

Mason Dixon Line" with a particularly successful recording in '18. The song's title could have been "Away Down South," since the line is used several times.

In the first verse, we're told that the singer's mother and father courted and married "in Alabamy, away down South." He, the singer, was born in Dixie and considers it "the finest place on earth." He grew up "in sunny Caroline," and Dixie is deeply entrenched "in the heart of mine."

The chorus lyrics follow: *I'm all bound 'round with the Mason Dixon Line; | It's pulling me, back where I used to be; | When I was younger I knew ev'ry lane, | Now I hunger to be once again; | Back where the robin keeps throbbin' pretty melodies; | And when I'm all bound 'round with a pair of lovin' arms, | Oh! Mother mine! I'll know I'm in Caroline; | I've read a lot about Heaven, | But give me Dixie all the time; | For I've found that I'm bound, | Bound all around, with the Mason Dixon Line.*

Neither of the verses is as well known as the chorus, but the second verse is even more obsure than the first. However, that verse is interesting because it talks about Abraham Lincoln and the Civil War. The lyrics say that Lincoln "surely loved the stars and stripes, the Southern and the North," and that "no one loved old Dixie more than he."

The sheet music cover and musical score are available at http://levysheetmusic.mse.jhu.edu/browse.html and at http://lcweb2.loc.gov/cocoon/ihas/loc.natlib.ihas.1000079 41/. See the sheet music cover, read the lyrics and hear midi musical version at http://www.halcyondaysmusic.com/december/december2000.htm.

I'm Always Chasing Rainbows

Music: Harry Carroll

Harry Fox introduced "I'm Always Chasing Rainbows" in the musical *Oh, Look!*. The Dolly Sisters starred with Harry Fox in the musical.

The song's chorus melody was taken from Chopin's "Fantaisie Impromptu in C-sharp minor." This was one of the first instances of a popular song being lifted from a famous classical composition. It was so successful that in later years there will be almost an epidemic of borrowing from the classics. "I'm Always Chasing Rainbows" sold over a million copies of sheet music and was popularized in popular recordings by Charles Harrison, Harry Fox, Prince's Orchestra and Sam Ash in '18.

Perry Como revived the song successfully in '45. Helen Forrest and Dick Haymes's duet recording was also popular in '45. Harry James and his orchestra's '46 recording was also popular. Joseph C. Smith's Orchestra's recording of this song is available at http://www.redhotjazz.com/jcso.html.

The song appeared in several Hollywood movie musicals, including *Ziegfeld Girl* ('41), where it was performed by Judy Garland, *Nobody's Darling* ('43), *The Merry Monahans* ('44), and *The Dolly Sisters* ('45), where it was sung by Betty Grable.

The lyrics to the verse tell us that this person (the singer) has tried to find happiness, but "my dreams have all been denied." Then they question, "Why have I always been a failure, what can the reason be? I wonder if the world's to blame, I wonder if it could be me?"

The famous chorus lyrics come next: *I'm always chasing rainbows, | Watching clouds drifting by, | My schemes are just like all of my dreams, | Ending in the sky. | Some fellows look*

and find the sunshine, | I always look and find the rain, | Some fellows make a winning sometime, | I never even make a gain. | Believe me, I'm always chasing rainbows, | waiting to find a little blue bird in vain.

The sheet music cover and musical score are available at http://levysheetmusic.mse.jhu.edu/browse.html.

Variety included "I'm Always Chasing Rainbows" in its *Hit Parade of a Half-Century* representing '18.

I'm Sorry I Made You Cry

Words & Music: N.J. Clesi

Clesi's "I'm Sorry I Made You Cry," written in '16, became one of the most successful ballads of the late 1910s and was especially popular in '18.

Henry Burr had a very popular recording of this waltz in '18. Fats Waller revived it in '37 with a popular recording (hear Waller's recording with his Rhythm at http://www.redhotjazz.com/rhythm.html).

All of the music during this period was not war related. Normal life continued at home. Love and its hurts and pains did not change because of the war. Clesi's lyrics express an apology to a hurt lover: *I'm sorry dear, so sorry dear, I'm sorry I made you cry, | Won't you forget, won't you forgive, don't let us say goodbye. | One little word, one little smile, one little kiss won't you try. | It breaks my heart to hear you sigh, I'm sorry I made you cry. | One little word, one little smile, one little kiss won't you try. | It breaks my heart to hear you sigh, I'm sorry I made you cry.*

The song was used in the '39 movie musical *Rose of Washington Square*, where it was sung by Alice Faye, and in *Somebody Loves Me* ('52).

The sheet music cover and musical score are available at http://levysheetmusic.mse.jhu.edu/browse.html and at http://lcweb2.loc.gov/cocoon/ihas/loc.natlib.ihas.10000511 2/ or see two sheet music covers, the standard edition and the war edition at http://www.lib.duke.edu/music/sheet_music_images.html#clesi_1 or hear a midi musical version and read the lyrics at http://www.geocities.com/dferg 5493/imsorryimadeyoucry.html or http://parlorsongs.com/issues/2001-10/thismonth/featureb.asp.

Variety included "I'm Sorry I Made You Cry" in its *Hit Parade of a Half-Century* representing '18.

Just a Baby's Prayer at Twilight (for Her Daddy Over There)

Words: Sam M. Lewis & Joe Young; Music: M.K. Jerome

Sam M. Lewis and Joe Young's lyrics sing about a child's prayer for their father who is overseas fighting in the war. This sweet ballad touched many hearts during the war. This is another tearjerker, not unlike "Hello, Central, Give Me No Man's Land" (see above).

The first verse lyrics talk about prayer in general. The singer has "heard the prayers of mothers" and others praying for "those who went away." But this child's prayer "made me cry." The chorus lyrics follow: *Just a baby's prayer at twilight When lights are low | Poor baby's years are filled with tears | There's a mother there at twilight | Who's proud to know Her precious little tot | Is Dad's forget-me-not | After saying "Goodnight, Mama" | She climbs up stairs quite unawares | And says her prayers | "Oh! kindly tell my daddy That he must take care" | That's a baby's prayer at twilight | For her daddy, over there.*

Henry Burr's '18 recording became the second biggest recorded hit of the decade, but his was not the only recording of the song that was popular. Other releases include those by Prince's Orchestra, by Edna White's Trumpet Quartet, and by Charles Hart.

Hear Henry Burr's '18 recording of this song at www.firstworldwar.com/audio/1918 (includes the lyrics and sheet music cover). The sheet music cover and musical score are available at http://levysheetmusic.mse.jhu.edu/browse.html and at http://scriptorium.lib.duke.edu/dynaweb/sheetmusic/1910–1920/@Generic__BookTextView/24314. Or see the sheet music cover and hear a midi musical version at http://parlorsongs.com/insearch/worldwar1-2/wwlno2.asp.

K-K-K-Katy

Words & Music: Geoffrey O'Hara

On the sheet music cover of "K-K-K-Katy," above the title was the following statement: "The Sensational Stammering Song Success Sung by the Soldiers and Sailors." The song became extremely popular during the war years as a "goodbye" song.

The Katy in the song was Katherine Richardson of Kingston, Ontario. Geoffrey O'Hara, a Canadian, wrote the song at Richardson's house in '17. The sheet music cover identifies O'Hara as an Army Song Leader.

The song was first played at a garden party fund-raiser for the Red Cross in Collins Bay on Lake Ontario. Billy Murray helped the song become well known with a popular recording of it in '18.

The lyrics to the first verse tell us about Jimmy, "soldier brave and bold," and Katy, "a maid with hair of gold." Katy was standing at her gate watching a parade of soldiers go by when she saw Jimmy. He showed up at her garden gate that evening at eight and stuttered this song to Kate: *K-K-K-Katy, beautiful Katy, / You're the only g-g-g-girl that I adore; / When the m-m-m-moon shines, / Over the c-c-c-cowshed, / I'll be waiting at the k-k-k-kitchen door.*

It's interesting to note that the sheet music was printed in a wartime edition that was smaller than normal to save paper. At the bottom of the cover is the following statement about the War Edition from Leo Feist, the publisher: "To co-operate with the Government and to conserve paper during the War, this song is issued in a smaller size than usual. Save! Save! Save is the watchword to-day. This is the spirit in which we are working and your co-operation will be very much appreciated."

The song was used in the Hollywood movie musical *The Cock-Eyed World* ('29) and in *Tin-Pan-Alley* ('40), where Jack Oakie performed it.

Hear Billy Murray's '18 recording of this song at www.firstworldwar.com/audio/1918. The sheet music cover and musical score are available at http://levysheetmusic.mse.jhu.edu/browse.html and at http://lcweb2.loc.gov/cocoon/ihas/loc.natlib.ihas.100008266/ or at http://scriptorium.lib.duke.edu/dynaweb/sheetmusic/1910–1920/@Generic__BookTextView/24860. Hear a midi musical version and read the lyrics at http://www.geocities.com/dferg5493/kkkkaty.html. Or see the sheet music cover, read the complete lyrics and hear a midi musical version at http://www.halcyondaysmusic.com/february/february2004.htm.

Variety included this stuttering song in its *Hit Parade of a Half-Century.*

Oh! How I Hate to Get Up in the Morning

Words & Music: Irving Berlin

"Oh! How I Hate to Get Up in the Morning" was introduced by Irving Berlin and a chorus of soldiers in *Yip, Yip, Yaphank,* an all-soldier revue.

Arthur Fields helped spread the song's fame with a very popular recording in '18. Irving Kaufman also had a popular recording of the song in '18.

Irving Berlin had been born in Russia and had immigrated to the U.S. with his family. He had never become a U.S. citizen. When the first World War broke out, he, like most people in the entire country, became very patriotic. It was then that he decided to become a citizen. Consequently, Berlin became eligible for the draft and shockingly, at age thirty, found himself drafted into the army and assigned to Camp Upton, primarily a staging area for soldiers bound for the war in France, in Yaphank, Long Island, to become a member of the 20th Infantry, 152nd Depot Brigade.

Berlin said, "I found out quickly ... there were a lot of things about army life I didn't like, and the thing I didn't like most of all was reveille. I hated it. I hated it so much that I used to lie awake nights thinking about how much I hated it." Berlin once remarked about the question in the opening line of "The Star Spangled Banner" that he couldn't see anything "by dawn's early light."

In addition, Berlin was forced to share crowded sleeping quarters with dozens of other men and being rather small and fragile looking, the strenuous physical drills were not to his taste.

Berlin decided to incorporate his hatred of the military life in a song. He discovered that soldiers everywhere felt precisely as he did. Berlin's plaintive "Oh! How I Hate to Get Up in the Morning," with its threat to murder the bugler, definitely struck a chord. The song's comic complaining appealed not only to the soldiers, but also to the country at large. It eventually sold a million and a half copies of sheet music.

The camp's commanding officer wanted to build a community house where friends and relatives could visit the soldiers. He asked Berlin to put on a musical show to raise the $35,000 cost. Berlin agreed to write the show, if the commanding officer would allow him to stay up late writing and avoid getting up at 5 a.m. for reveille.

In keeping with the shows vaudeville format, Berlin even devised a romantic show stopper, "Mandy" (see '19), which would serve as the centerpiece of a minstrel section.

Berlin also wrote one very patriotic song, "God Bless America." He decided to cut it from the score and filed it away for future reference (see '40).

The all-soldier cast bivouacked at the Seventy-first Regiment Armory, at Park Avenue and Thirty-fourth Street, and each day they marched in military formation to the Century Theater, rehearsed under the direction of Sergeant Berlin, and then marched back to the armory, where they remained under military discipline.

The show's playbills proclaimed: "Uncle Sam Presents ... a military mess cooked up by the boys at Camp Upton."

The revue was basically an old-fashioned minstrel complete with an interlocutor, but it was also part vaudeville with acrobats, jugglers, dancers, a boxing demonstration and military drills set to Berlin's music. There also was a great deal of comedy, with the soldiers appearing as hairy-chested chorus girls in Ziegfeld-like numbers.

Berlin finally appeared as one of the final acts of the evening. A Camp Upton-style tent appeared onstage and after several calls for "Sergeant Berlin," when he failed to appear, two soldiers dragged him out of the tent, seemingly arousing him from a sound sleep. Then he sang, in his peculiar little voice: "Oh! how I hate to get up in the morning, Oh! how I'd love to remain in bed."

The show had been expected to earn $35,000, but it eventually collected $80,000.

On closing night, when the soldiers marched down the aisles singing the finale, "We're on Our Way to France," they marched out the doors and into the street. That much was a usual part of the show, but this time they were actually going to France and the war. There was considerable crying, fainting and cheering by the audience as the soldiers proceeded in formation to a troop carrier. They boarded it and sailed within the week to France. Berlin, however, stayed behind.

Hear Arthur Fields recording of this song at http://www.authentichistory.com/audio/wwl/Arthur_Fields-Oh_How_I_Hate_To_Get_Up_In_The_Morning.html or www.firstworldwar.com/audio/1918 (Eddie Cantor's '18 recording of the song is also at this site). Hear a midi musical version and read the lyrics at http://www.geocities.com/dferg5493/ohhowihatetoge-tupinthemorning.htm or the sheet music cover and musical score are available at http://levysheetmusic.mse.jhu.edu/browse.html.

Original Dixieland One Step (Dixie Jass Band One Step)

Music: Original Dixieland Jazz Band

Dixieland jazz developed in New Orleans around the turn of the century. Like other jazz styles, it spread to Chicago and New York City in the 1910s.

Dixieland combos usually had a rhythm section consisting of drums, upright bass, piano and perhaps banjo or guitar. The lead instruments were usually trombone, trumpet and clarinet. The distinctive element of Dixieland jazz is the simultaneous inprovising by the lead instruments.

The Original Dixieland Jazz (earlier spelled "Jass") Band was a white band who capitalized on this African American music, but their music has remained well known for decades. They made the first jazz recording in early '17. The record had "Livery Stable Blues" on one side, with "Original Dixieland One-Step" on the flip side. The recording was very successful and signaled the coming Jazz Age of the '20s.

The band consisted of Nick LaRocca, a left-handed cornet player, who was the leader of the group, clarinetist Larry Shields, Eddie Edwards playing tailgate trombone, Henry Ragas playing piano and Tony Sbarbaro playing drums.

Variety included "Original Dixieland One-Step" on its *Hit Parade of a Half-Century.*

At http://www.redhotjazz.com/odjb.html you can hear the Original Dixieland Jazz Band recordings of "Original Dixieland One Step" recorded in '36 and "Dixie Jass Band One Step" recorded in '17.

Over There (see '17)

Rock-a-Bye Your Baby with a Dixie Melody

Words: Sam M. Lewis & Joe Young; Music: Jean Schwartz

Al Jolson is infamous for interpolating completely unrelated songs into the Broadway musicals in which he was appearing. Each evening, Jolson would stop the show, walk to the edge of the stage and sing whatever song or songs he wanted to sing that evening. Such arrogance was a Jolson trademark, but he got away with it. The audiences loved it!

Jolson interpolated "Rock-a-Bye Your Baby with a Dixie Melody" into the musical extravaganza *Sinbad* in '18. Jolson also popularized it in a recording that was among the top ten recordings of the decade. Jolson also sang it in the '39 movie musical *Rose of Washington Square* and in his screen biography *The Jolson Story* ('46) and in *Jolson Sings Again* ('49). His recording of the song from the soundtrack of the '46 film was popular all over again.

The song also appeared in the movie musicals *The Show of Shows* ('29) and in *The Merry Monahans* ('44).

In *Sinbad*, Jolson appeared in his usual black-face. This time he was a comical character named Inbad in Bagdad who poses as Sinbad. As in most Jolson musical extravaganzas the book or plot was not very important. The audience came to see and hear Jolson.

And the crowds loved to hear him sing: *Rock-a-bye your baby with a Dixie melody; / When you croon, croon a tune from the heart of Dixie. / Just hang my cradle, Mammy mine, / Right on that Mason Dixon Line / And swing it from Virginia to Tennessee with all the love that's in ya. / "Weep No More, My Lady": sing that song again for me, / And "Old Black Joe," just as though you had me on your knee. / A million baby kisses I'll deliver the minute that you sing the "Swanee River"; / Rock-a-bye your rock-a-bye baby with a Dixie melody.*

Quoted songs in the lyrics include Stephen Foster's "Old Black Joe" from 1860 and "Old Folks at Home (Swanee River)" from 1851. "Weep no more, my Lady" is a phrase from Foster's "My Old Kentucky Home" (1853).

The sheet music cover and musical score are available at http://levysheetmusic.mse.jhu.edu/browse.html. See the sheet music cover and hear a midi musical version at http://parlorsongs.com/issues/2002-12/thismonth/feature.asp.

Variety included this song in its *Hit Parade of a Half-Century.*

Another popular song from *Sinbad* was "'N' Everything" by Al Jolson, B.G. DeSylva and Gus Kahn. Jolson also popularized it with a successful recording in '18. Later, Jolson interpolated "Avalon" (see '21) and "Swanee" (see '20) into the show.

Roses of Picardy

Words: Frederick E. Weatherley; Music: Haydn Wood

"Roses of Picardy" is a famous World War I song popularized by Lambert Murphy in a successful '18 recording.

Written in '16 by English composer Haydn Wood in conjunction with the famous British lyricist Fred E Weatherly, "Roses of Picardy" is considered by many to be one of the most beautiful songs of the Great War. It became a favorite of all the troops, but especially by British soldiers who had left behind a sweetheart when they enlisted (or were conscripted) and were sent to the front lines in France.

A film of the same name, and set during World War I, was produced in '27.

Reportedly, Weatherley wrote the words after a French widow offered him protection in her home in France. So Weatherley's lyrics are about "Colinette with the sea-blue eyes" who "is watching and longing and waiting." She hears a song on the wind; she listens to this "first little song of love": *Roses are shining in Picardy / In the hush of the silvery dew, / Roses are flow'ring in Picardy, / But there's never a rose like you. / And the roses will die with the summertime, / But our roads may be far apart; / But there's one rose that dies not in Picardy, / 'Tis the rose I keep in my heart.*

Hear Ernest Pike's '17 recording of this song: at www.firstworldwar.com/audio/1917 or hear John McCormack's '19 recording at www.firstworldwar.com/audio/1919. The sheet music cover and musical score are available at http://levysheetmusic.mse.jhu.edu/browse.html and at http://lcweb2.loc.gov/cocoon/ihas/loc.natlib.ihas.100010042/ or hear a midi musical version and read the lyrics at http://www.geocities.com/dferg5493/rosesofpicardy.htm.

Variety included "Roses of Picardy" in its *Hit Parade of a Half-Century.*

Send Me Away with a Smile

Words & Music: Louis Weslyn & Al Piantadosi

"Send Me Away with a Smile" became one of the World War I Doughboys' favorites. It was a particularly popular goodbye song.

The top of the sheet music cover proclaims "A War Song with Universal Appeal." There's a drawing of a girl at a garden gate waving goodbye (with her handkerchief) to a soldier, pictured in the distance.

In the lyrics of the first verse, the soldier is telling the girl not to cry as they say "Goodbye." He asks if she doesn't hear the bugle call and the fife and drum bidding "the fellows come." Even though he loves her, he knows it is time to go, and she would not have him stay behind. The chorus lyrics follow: *So send me away with a smile, little girl, / Brush the tears from eyes of brown, / It's all for the best, and I'm off with the rest, / Of the boys from my own home town. / It may be forever we part, little girl, / And it may be for only a while. / But if fight, dear we must, in our Maker we trust, / So send me away with a smile.*

The famous Irish tenor, John McCormack, had a very popular recording of the song in '18. M.J. O'Connell also had a popular recording of the song in '18.

Hear John McCormack's '17 recording of this song at www.firstworldwar.com/audio/1917. The sheet music cover and musical score are available at http://levysheetmusic.mse.jhu.edu/browse.html and at http://lcweb2.loc.gov/cocoon/ihas/loc.natlib.ihas.100009815/.

It's interesting to note that the same composer, Al Piantadosi, also wrote the pacifist song "I Didn't Raise My Boy to Be a Soldier" in '15. That simply illustrates how much the country's views of the war had changed in three years.

Smiles

Words: J. Will Callahan; Music: Lee G. Roberts

Nell Carrington and a chorus of girls introduced this wartime morale booster in the revue *The Passing Show of*

1918. It is a "war" song only in the sense that it was popular during the Great War. It was extremely popular, perhaps because it was not directly related to the war. It gave the soldiers and their loved ones back home a break from the war.

The composer, Lee Roberts, heard a lecture on the value of a smile in business at a convention of music dealers in Chicago. He wrote the melody and sent it, along with the suggestion of a lyric about smiles, to J. Will Callahan. Roberts included the phrases "there are smiles that make us happy, and smiles that make us blue" that he had thought of after hearing the lecture. Callahan expanded on the idea and came up with the following classic lyrics for the chorus: *There are smiles that make us happy; / There are smiles that make us blue, / There are smiles that steal away the teardrops. / As the sunbeams steal away the dew, / There are smiles that have a tender meaning, / That the eyes of love alone may see, / And the smiles that fill my life with sunshine, / Are the smiles that you give to me.*

After several music publishers rejected the song, the writers formed a new company to release the song. Within six months, it had sold more than two million sheet music copies and eventually exceeded three million.

Joseph C. Smith's Orchestra recorded a particularly popular version of the song in '18. Hear Smith's recording at http://www.redhotjazz.com/jcso.html. Henry Burr and Albert Campbell's duet recording wasn't too far behind in popularity. Lambert Murphy also released a popular recording of the song in '18.

The song has been used in several Hollywood movie musicals, including *Applause* ('29), *For Me and My Girl* ('42), where it was sung by Judy Garland, *The Dolly Sisters* ('45), where it was sung by a chorus of soldiers, *Somebody Loves Me* ('52), and *The Eddy Duchin Story* ('56).

The sheet music cover is of a lovely smiling girl. The back cover, by the way, has an ad for buying war bonds with the slogan "Buy Bonds for Your Boy and My Boy." Other interesting slogans on the page include "The safest investment in the world — a Liberty Bond!," "If you can't jab a bayonet, grab a bond!," "Between meals buy War Saving Stamps! And at meals save food! Put America first!," and "We'll win the war — with bread and lead."

The sheet music cover and musical score are available at http://levysheetmusic.mse.jhu.edu/browse.html and at http://lcweb2.loc.gov/cocoon/ihas/loc.natlib.ihas.100008689/ or at http://scriptorium.lib.duke.edu/dynaweb/sheetmusic/1910–1920/@Generic__BookTextView/40085. Hear a midi musical version and read the lyrics at http://www.geocities.com/dferg5493/smiles.htm.

Variety listed "Smiles" in its *Hit Parade of a Half-Century* for both '17 and '18.

Sweet Little Buttercup

Words: Alfred Bryan; Music: Herman Paley

A song titled "I'm Called Little Buttercup" and which contains the lyrics "Poor little Buttercup, sweet little Buttercup" comes from Act I of the Gilbert and Sullivan operetta *H.M.S. Pinafore*. The Gilbert and Sullivan song and "Sweet Little Buttercup" from '18 are easily confused.

Elizabeth Spencer and the Shannon Four popularized this '18 song with a popular recording.

This is another World War I era goodbye song. The following are the lyrics for most familiar part of the song, the chorus: *Sweet little Buttercup, Shy little Buttercup, /*

Dry your eyes of blue. I'll come back to you. / When the war is through, Safe in your sylvan dell, / Far from the shot and shell. Let your lovelight shine. / Angels guide you, Watch beside you, / Sweet little Buttercup mine.

The sheet music cover and musical score are available at http://levysheetmusic.mse.jhu.edu/browse.html and at http://lcweb2.loc.gov/cocoon/ihas/loc.natlib.ihas.1000083 06/ or http://scriptorium.lib.duke.edu/dynaweb/sheet music/1910–1920/@Generic__BookTextView/42529 or see the sheet music cover, the lyrics and hear a midi musical version at http://www.halcyondaysmusic.com/may/ may2003.htm or http://parlorsongs.com/issues/1997–11/ nov97feature.asp.

Variety chose "Sweet Little Buttercup" for its *Hit Parade of a Half-Century* representing '17.

Tiger Rag (see '31)

Variety included "Tiger Rag" in its *Golden 100 Tin Pan Alley Songs* and *Hit Parade of a Half-Century*. "Tiger Rag" became one of the most recorded songs of the pre-rock era.

1919

After You've Gone

Words: Henry Creamer; Music: Turner Layton

Al Jolson and Sophie Tucker were among the first entertainers who popularized "After You've Gone," Jolson at his Winter Garden Sunday evening concert and Tucker in her vaudeville act. African American vaudevillians, Creamer and Layton, penned this classic song.

This *Variety Golden 100 Tin Pan Alley Song* and *Hit Parade of a Half-Century* selection representing '18, was further popularized in a particularly popular '19 recording by Marion Harris, but there were several other popular recordings of the song over the years. Hear Ms. Harris' recording of "After You've Gone" at http://www.redhot jazz.com/marionharris.html. Henry Burr and Albert Campbell's duet version was almost as popular in '18 as Harris' was in '19. Billy Murray and Gladys Rice also had a popular version on the market in '19. Famous blues singer Bessie Smith and Sophie Tucker both had '27 recordings of the song that gained popularity. Paul Whiteman and his orchestra, with a Bing Crosby vocal, revived it successfully in '30, as did Louis Armstrong in '32 and Benny Goodman in '35. A '29 recording of this song by Louis Armstrong is available at http://www.redhotjazz.com/ lao.html. Vibraphonist Lionel Hampton and his band recorded a popular version in '37. For some reason France has always loved American jazz. The Quintet of the Hot Club of France's '37 recording also scored well with the public. "After You've Gone" became one of the most recorded songs of the pre-rock era.

There are two verses, but the first one is by far the more familiar: *After you've gone and left me crying; / After you've gone, There's no denying; / You'll feel blue; You'll feel sad; / You'll miss the dearest pal you've ever had. / There'll come a time, Now don't forget it; / There'll come a time When you'll regret it. / Someday, when you grow lonely, / Your heart will break like mine and you'll want me only, / After you've gone, After you've gone away.*

"After You've Gone" has appeared in several Hollywood movie musicals, including *For Me and My Gal* ('42), where it was performed by Judy Garland, the Olsen and Johnson comedy *Ghost Catchers* ('44), *Atlantic City* ('44), where it was sung by Constance Moore, Disney's *Make Mine Music* ('46), where it was played by Benny Goodman's Quartet, in *Jolson Sings Again* ('49), *Some Came Running* ('58), where it was performed by Shirley MacLaine, *The Five Pennies* ('59) and *All That Jazz* ('79). Loudon Wainwright III sang "After You've Gone" on the soundtrack of *The Aviator* (2005).

The sheet music cover and musical score are available at http://levysheetmusic.mse.jhu.edu/browse.html and at http://lcweb2.loc.gov/cocoon/ihas/loc.natlib.ihas.1000052 91/. A PDF of this song is available at http://library.ind state.edu/level1.dir/cml/rbsc/kirk/sheet_titles.html. Hear a midi musical version and read the lyrics at http://www. geocities.com/dferg5493/afteryouvegone.htm or http:// parlorsongs.com/issues/2002–2/thismonth/featureb.asp.

Beautiful Ohio

Words: Ballard MacDonald; Music: Mary Earl

Robert A. King wrote the music for "Beautiful Ohio" using the pseudonym Mary Earl. The song is a waltz and was first released as a piano instrumental. It was first used to accompany acrobatic acts in vaudeville. Later in '18, Ballard MacDonald wrote the lyrics. As a vocal, the song sold over five million copies of sheet music.

King was a writer for the music publishing firm Shapiro and Bernstein. His contract called for him to write four songs per month. The songs he wrote as a salaried employee became the exclusive property of the company. It was under those terms that he wrote "Beautiful Ohio," in other words, his publishers were not legally bound to pay him any royalties. They did, however, pay King $60,000, a magnanimous gesture, for this song.

The lyrics of the chorus follow: *Drifting with the current down a moonlit* stream / While *above the Heavens in their glory gleam / And the stars on high Twinkle in the sky / Seeming in a Paradise of love divine / Dreaming of a pair of eyes that looked in mine / Beautiful Ohio, in dreams again I see / Visions of what used to be.*

Henry Burr released a particularly popular recording of "Beautiful Ohio" in '18; it became the No. 7 recording of decade. The Waldorf-Astoria Dance Orchestra and Prince's Orchestra both had very popular recordings of the song in '19. Olive Kline and Marguerite Dunlap, Fritz Kreisler, and Sam Ash each had popular recordings of the song on the market in '19. Paul Whiteman and his orchestra's recording of "Beautiful Ohio" is available at http://www.redhotjazz.com/pwo.html.

"Beautiful Ohio" became the offical state song of Ohio in '89. The lyrics were changed slightly for the state song version. Even though it was originally a waltz, the song has also been used for many years as a march for the Ohio State University Marching Band.

The song can be heard in the '42 Hollywood movie musical *Cairo*, which starred Jeanette MacDonald.

Variety included "Beautiful Ohio" in its *Hit Parade of a Half-Century* representing '18.

The sheet music cover and musical score are available at http://levysheetmusic.mse.jhu.edu/browse.html and at http://scriptorium.lib.duke.edu/dynaweb/sheet music/1910–1920/@Generic__BookTextView/2359. Hear a midi musical version and read the lyrics at http://www.geocities.com/dferg5493/beautifulohio.htm.

Chinese Lullaby

Words & Music: Robert Hood Bowers

Variety included "Chinese Lullaby" in its *Hit Parade of a Half-Century*. The song originated in the musical production *East Is West*. Fay Bainter performed the song according to the sheet music cover.

During the silent movie days, pianist knew exactly what to play when anything Oriental appeared, "Chinese Lullaby." In that era anything Oriental was compressed into one generic entity.

The song's verse is in duple meter, while the chorus switches to triple. The verse begins plaintively, "Sing song, sing song, so Hop Toy, allee same like China boy." The chorus lyrics follow: *A ripple I seem on life's mystic stream, / Tossed at the waters' will; so I dare dream I'll be, / Like the poor ripple, free; when the troubled waters grow still.*

The only popular recording of the song was by Paul Whiteman and his orchestra in '32 and it was only marginally popular. Hear Whiteman's recording of "Chinese Lullaby" at http://www.redhotjazz.com/pwo.html.

The sheet music cover and musical score are available at http://levysheetmusic.mse.jhu.edu/browse.html.

Chong (He Come from Hong Kong)

Words & Music: Harold Weeks

Variety chose "Chong" for its *Hit Parade of a Half-Century*. The Columbia Saxophone Sextet had the most popular recording of "Chong." Joseph C. Smith's Orchestra's recording of this song is available at http://www.redhotjazz.com/jcso.html.

Unfortunately "Chong" is an example of Oriental racism in music. The lyrics are full of Orientals' poor English skills. "Chong" plays his Tom Tom in a Chinese café. But he "no likee that song, where Chineeman cry 'way up high." Instead, he "loved his rag the same as you." When he returns to Hong Kong, he "teachee peachee Melican song all day long to his China girl in old Hong Kong."

The sheet music cover and musical score are available at http://levysheetmusic.mse.jhu.edu/browse.html.

Dear Old Pal of Mine

Words: Harold Robe; Music: Lt. Gitz Rice

The name Lieutenant Gitz Rice became closely associated with one patriotic song he wrote during the First World War: "Dear Old Pal of Mine" in which a soldier laments his absence from his girlfriend. Rice was on active duty in Ypres, Belgium, when he composed the tune for the song.

Sascha Jacobsen helped popularized "Dear Old Pal of Mine" with a recording in '19. *Variety* chose this song for its *Hit Parade of a Half-Century* representing '18.

The singer's life seems empty since he left his old pal who also happens to be his sweetheart. He wants an angel to "guard you while I stray." The chorus lyrics, basically a prayer, follow: *Oh how I want you, dear old pal of mine, / Each night and day I pray you're always mine. / Sweetheart may God bless you, Angel hands caress you, / While sweet dreams rest you, dear old pal of mine.*

"Dear Old Pal of Mine" got more exposure, along with other Rice patriotic war-time compositions, as part of the army recruitment play, *Getting Together*, which was staged in New York City in '18. One edition of the Edison Amberol Records newsletter said about "Dear Old Pal of Mine": "It is one of those simple melodies that goes straight to the heart, and is unforgettable."

The sheet music cover and musical score are available at http://levysheetmusic.mse.jhu.edu/browse.html. The sheet music cover pictures the composer in his Canadian military uniform. The cover also advertises that the song is often sung by John McCormack in his performances.

Hindustan

Words & Music: Oliver G. Wallace & Harold Weeks

Joseph C. Smith's Orchestra and Henry Burr and Albert Campbell both had popular recordings of "Hindustan" in '19. Ted Weems and his orchestra revived the song with a popular recording in '48.

The song seems to be better known as an instrumental, except for Henry Burr and Albert Campbell's '19 duet recording. The lyrics are not nearly as interesting as the music. The words to the chorus follow: *Hindustan, where we stopped to rest our tired caravan, / Hindustan, where the painted peacock spread his fan, / Hindustan, where the purple sunbird flashed across the sand, / Hindustan, where I met her and the world began.*

Hear a '18 recording by Joseph C. Smith and his orchestra of this song at http://www.redhotjazz.com/jcso.html. The sheet music cover and musical score are available at http://levysheetmusic.mse.jhu.edu/browse.html and at http://scriptorium.lib.duke.edu/dynaweb/sheetmusic/1910–1920/@Generic__BookTextView/12520. Or hear a midi musical version and read the lyrics at http://www.geocities.com/dferg5493/hindustan.html or http://www.halcyondaysmusic.com/april/april2001.htm.

Variety included "Hindustan" in its *Hit Parade of a Half-Century* representing '18.

I'll Say She Does

Words & Music: B.G. DeSylva, Gus Kahn & Al Jolson

Al Jolson introduced "I'll Say She Does" in the Winter Garden extravaganza *Sinbad*. Jolson had already introduced "Rock-a-Bye Your Baby with a Dixie Melody" and "'N' Everything," and will interpolate "Swanee" and "Avalon" into the show in the future. This song is just one of many that Jolson would sing during the Broadway production even though they have nothing to do with the show's plot.

Jolson also popularized the song beyond Broadway with a very successful recording in '19, however, other popular recordings were released by Wilbur Sweatman's Original Jazz Band and by the All-Star Trio.

The lyrics of this song seem to be similar in idea to the Marx Brother's show *I'll Say She Is* and may have served as a source of inspiration for their production: *Does she make everybody stare? I'll say she does. / Was she happy to get the ring? You bet she was. / And can she dance? Can she twist? / Does she do a lot of things I can't resist?*

The sheet music cover and musical score are available at http://levysheetmusic.mse.jhu.edu/browse.html.

I'm Forever Blowing Bubbles

Words: Jean Kenbrovin; Music: John W. Kellette

James Kendis, James Brockman, and Nat Vincent all had separate contracts with publishers that led them to emerge their names into Jean Kenbrovin for lyricist credit on "I'm Forever Blowing Bubbles."

The sheet music cover says Helen Carrington introduced the song in the revue *The Passing Show of 1918* (other sources credit June Caprice with introducing it). It became a big hit selling over two and a half million copies of sheet music.

Ben Selvin and his Novelty Orchestra and Henry Burr and Albert Campbell competed with each other for the most popular recording of the song; both versions were very successful. Hear Ben Selvin's recording of this song at http://www.redhotjazz.com/benselvino.html.

The lyrics are not literal, of course, but speak about our hopes and dreams. The words of the famous chorus follow: *I'm forever blowing bubbles, Pretty bubbles in the air. / They fly so high, nearly reach the sky, / Then like my dreams, they fade and die. / Fortune's always hiding, I've looked ev'ry where / I'm forever blowing bubbles, Pretty bubbles in the air.*

The song was used in the '51 movie musical *On Moonlight Bay*, where it was performed by Jack Smith. It was also used in the non-musical films *Stella Dallas* ('34) and *Men with Wings* ('38).

The sheet music cover and musical score are available at http://levysheetmusic.mse.jhu.edu/browse.html and at http://scriptorium.lib.duke.edu/dynaweb/sheetmusic/1910–1920/@Generic__BookTextView/18380. Hear a midi musical version and read the lyrics at http://www.geocities.com/dferg5493/imforeverblowingbubbles.html or http://parlorsongs.com/issues/1999–10/oct99feature.asp.

Variety included "I've Forever Blowing Bubbles" in its *Hit Parade of a Half-Century.*

It's Nobody's Business but My Own

Words & Music: Will E. Skidmore & Marshall Walker

Bert Williams introduced this ragtime tune in the *Ziegfeld Follies of 1919.* He also helped popularize it beyond Broadway with a very successful recording of the song in '19.

The sheet music says this song is the sixth in a series called the "Deacon Series." There are two verses and three variations of the chorus, therefore, it's possible that the chorus was sung first, then alternating verses and choruses.

The words of the first verse tell about a delegation of church Deacons "from a 'Hardshell' congregation" went to visit Parson Brown. They inform him that some scandalous information is making the rounds about the Preacher. They want to hear his side of the story. His reply is the chorus, which follows: *It's nobody's bus'ness but my own, / What I do when my preachin' thru, / So refrain from messin' 'round my home, / Leave me alone, / What I do in church you all can see, / Don't you worry 'bout me privately, / It's nobody's bus'ness but my own.*

The fifth and sixth lines of the chorus have three versions: the second one probably came after the first verse: "There's a time to preach, a time to shout, Then there's other things to think about."

In the second verse, the Deacons threaten to fire the Preacher if he doesn't stop. Parson Brown's answer to them was, "I ain't no Diplomat, but here's what's on my mind" and the chorus repeats, probably with the third variation of lyrics: "When a flock of sisters seek my door, You Old Jealous Deacons all get sore."

There's a very similar song titled "Ain't Nobody's Business

(But My Own)" that was popularized in '50 by Kay Starr. It was written by Irving Taylor.

See the sheet music cover and the musical score at http://scriptorium.lib.duke.edu/dynaweb/sheetmusic/1910–1920/@Generic__BookTextView/22823.

Ja-Da (Ja-Da Ja-Da Jing Jing Jing)

Words & Music: Bob Carleton

The sheet music cover of "Ja-Da" identifies the writer as "Bob Carleton, U.S.N.R.F," which meant that Carleton was in the U.S. Navy Reserve Force.

Beatrice Lillie introduced "Ja-Da" in the stage musical *Bran Pie.* Arthur Fields helped popularize this famous novelty song with a popular '19 recording. A recording by the Original New Orleans Jazz Band is available at http://www.redhotjazz.com/onojb.html.

This bit of fluff has a sparkling melody and infectious rhythm that lends itself to improvisation. As the lyrics say, "There ain't much to the words, but the music is grand."

The lyrics of the first verse and chorus (the musical instructions at the chorus say "with lots of 'Ja-Da'") follow: *You've heard all about your raggy melodies, / Ev'ry thing from opera down to harmony, / But I've a little song that I will sing to you, / It's going to win you thru and thru. / There ain't much to the words but the music is grand, / And you'll be singing it to beat the band. / Now you've heard of your "Will-o'-the-wisp," / But give a little listen to this; / It goes: Ja Da, Ja Da, Ja Da Ja Da Jing, Jing, Jing, / That's a funny little bit of melody, / It's so soothing and appealing to me, / It goes: Ja Da, Ja Da, Ja Da Ja Da Jing, Jing, Jing.*

The reference to "Will-o'-the Wisp" in the verse is strange. Perhaps people in '19 knew more about this phrase than we do today. It apparently means "an erroneous perception of reality, a delusion."

Most good improvisational songs have few chords so the musicians can improvise more freely, but actually "Ja-Da" has more chord changes and some some rather complicated changes than normal. Chords like F7, G9, Cdim, C7+ and Fdim in the key of F are not simple chords.

The song appeared in the following movie musicals: *Rose of Washington Square* ('39), the screen version of *Babes in Arms,* where it was performed by Charles Winninger, and *That's the Spirit* ('45).

The sheet music cover and musical score are available at http://levysheetmusic.mse.jhu.edu/browse.html. The sheet music cover is a wartime edition, smaller to conserve paper, and says "The sale of this song will be for the benefit of the Navy Relief Society. The Society that guards the home of the men who guard the seas." Pictured on the cover are three guys dressed in Navy apparel, the song's writer, Carlton, along with Sobol and Rosenberg as the Ja-Da Trio. Hear a midi musical version and read the lyrics at http://www.geocities.com/dferg5493/jada.html or http://parlorsongs.com/issues/2002–2/thismonth/featureb.asp.

Variety included "Ja-Da" in it *Hit Parade of a Half-Century* representing '18.

Mandy *and* A Pretty Girl Is Like a Melody

Words & Music: Irving Berlin

MANDY

Irving Berlin wrote "Mandy" for his all-soldier show *Yip, Yip, Yaphank* in '18. He staged this cakewalking marriage proposal as a drag number with a hairy-chested blackface male chorus decked out in ribbons and curls. It may have been tasteless and racist, but it was also funny. One reference indicates that Private Dan Healy portrayed Mandy, while another says an African American woman, not a person in blackface or a drag queen, played her.

Then in '19 Van and Schenck performed the song as part of the first act finale, "The Follies Minstrel," in the *Ziegfeld Follies of 1919*. It was sung by the entire company, including a corps identified in the program as "The Follies Pickaninnies." Then it was performed elegantly by Marilyn Miller and it began to achieve the popularity it had failed to gain in *Yip, Yip, Yaphank*.

Van and Schenck also had a popular recording of the song in '19, as did the Shannon Four. Ben Selvin and his Novelty Orchestra had a popular recording of the song in '20. Fats Waller and his Rhythm's recording of "Mandy" is available at http://www.redhotjazz.com/rhythm.html or Paul Whiteman's at http://www.redhotjazz.com/pwo.html.

A minstrel chorus performed the song in the '42 Broadway musical *This Is the Army*. Eddie Cantor performed an energetic rendition of the song in the '34 movie musical *Kid Millions* (that performance also had a minstrel setting). The song was used as background music in *Blue Skies* ('46), which starred Bing Crosby and Fred Astaire, and in *White Christmas* ('54), where Vera-Ellen, John Brascia and the ensemble sang it.

The sheet music cover and musical score are available at http://levysheetmusic.mse.jhu.edu/browse.html and at http://scriptorium.lib.duke.edu/dynaweb/sheet music/1910–1920/@Generic__BookTextView/29365 or hear a midi musical version and read the lyrics at http://www.geocities.com/dferg5493/mandy.htm.

Variety included "Mandy" in its *Hit Parade of a Half-Century* representing '19.

A Pretty Girl Is Like a Melody

John Steel introduced "A Pretty Girl Is Like a Melody" in the *Ziegfeld Follies of 1919*. The song became the unofficial song of all subsequent *Follies*. It was Ziegfeld's intent "to glorify the American girl," and this song seemed particularly appropriate.

The number was staged around the Ziegfeld girls representing various classical compositions. As the girls emerged, the melody they were associated with was played. Some of the classical pieces that were interpolated into the number include Dvorak's "Humoresque," Mendelssohn's "Spring Song," Massenet's "Elegy," Offenbach's "Barcarolle," Schubert's "Serenade," and Schumann's "Traumerei."

John Steel also helped popularize the song beyond the *Follies* with a very popular '19 recording. Sam Ash also had a popular recording of the song on the market. Red Nichols' Five Pennies' recording of this song is available at http://www.redhotjazz.com/rn5p.html or Paul Whiteman's at http://www.redhotjazz.com/pwo.html.

The song has been used by several Hollywood movie musicals, including a spectacular revolving wedding cake scene in *The Great Ziegfeld* ('36), which won an Academy Award for dance direction for Seymour Felix, in *Alexander's Ragtime Band* ('38), in *The Powers Girl* ('43), where it was sung by Carole Landis and Anne Shirley, in *Blue Skies* ('46), performed by Fred Astaire and a male chorus, and in *There's No Business Like Show Business* ('54), where

it was performed by Ethel Merman and Dan Dailey. The song also appeared in *The Cat's Meow* (2001).

This song was nominated for the American Film Institute's list of the greatest songs ever from an American film, but did not make the final list. It was nominated for its inclusion in *The Great Ziegfeld* ('36).

The sheet music cover and musical score are available at http://levysheetmusic.mse.jhu.edu/browse.html. Hear a midi musical version and read the lyrics at http://www.geocities.com/dferg5493/aprettygirlislikeamelody.htm.

Variety included "A Pretty Girl Is Like a Melody" in its *Golden 100 Tin Pan Alley Songs* and *Hit Parade of a Half-Century* lists.

O Death, Where Is Thy Sting?
Words & Music: Clarence A. Stout

Many famous composers have set the Biblical text from 1 Corinthians 15:55: "O death, where is thy sting? O grave, where is thy victory?" However, the most famous setting is most likely Handel's duet for alto and tenor from *Messiah*.

In the popular music field, Clarence Stout's use of the phrase is definitely not serious. The song's first verse tells about a preacher, Parson Brown, who is giving his congregation advice concerning sin and vice. He tells them "Hell is full of vampire women, whiskey, gin and dice." One of his parishioners, Mose Johnson, thinks Rev. Brown's description of Hell sounds like a place he'd like to be. In the song's chorus Mose says, "If what you say is the positive truth, O Death, where is thy sting?" He swears he'll be plenty happy with the "booze and women down below."

Bert Williams had a particularly popular recording of "O Death Where Is Thy Sting?" in '19.

Oh! What a Pal Was Mary
Words: Edgar Leslie & Bert Kalmar; Music: Pete Wendling

Is it possible that women were taking a different role by '19? Could they really have gained enough equality that a woman could be a man's pal? It was not until '20 that the Nineteenth Amendment to the U.S. Constitution was ratified, which gave women the right to vote and there were many more women's equality issues to be resolved.

We learn in the first verse that Mary, his sweetheart and friend, is gone, dead, we presume. The lyrics to the chorus follow: *Oh! what a gal was Mary, Oh! what a pal was she, / An angel was born on Easter morn, / And God sent her down to me. / Heart of my heart was Mary, Soul of my soul divine, / Though she is gone, Love lingers on, / For Mary old pal of mine.*

The song is a beautiful waltz that conveys heartfelt feelings of deep love.

Henry Burr popularized the song with a very popular recording in '19, while Edward Allen released a popular version of it in '20. The All Star Trio's recording of this song is available at http://www.redhotjazz.com/allstartrio.html or Joseph C. Smith's Orchestra's recording at http://www.redhotjazz.com/jcso.html.

The sheet music cover and musical score are available at http://levysheetmusic.mse.jhu.edu/browse.html and at http://scriptorium.lib.duke.edu/dynaweb/sheetmusic/1910–1920/@Generic__BookTextView/33908 or see the sheet music cover, the lyrics and hear a midi musical version at http://www.halcyondaysmusic.com/october/

october2001.htm or http://www.parlorsongs.com/issues/
1999–11/nov99feature.asp or http://www.geocities.com/
dferg5493/ohwhatapalwasmary.html. There are two
different sheet music covers; one is of a beautiful woman
in a large, fashionable hat, the other is a more virginal
looking woman dressed in what appears to be a wedding
outfit.

Variety included "Oh! What a Pal Was Mary" in its *Hit
Parade of a Half-Century* representing '19.

Till We Meet Again

*Words: Raymond B. Egan; Music: Richard A.
Whiting*

"Till We Meet Again" became one of the most successful ballads of the World War I era. This bittersweet waltz
was the last best-selling sheet music piece, selling five million copies within the first year of publication. According
to Whiting's daughter, songstress Margaret Whiting, her
father wrote this waltz tune in '17, but decided it wasn't
right and tossed it away. Whiting's wife retrieved it from
the garbage and took it to Remick, the publishing company. They accepted it and began the publishing process.
During that period, a Detroit movie theater held a war-
song contest. Someone entered "Till We Meet Again" and
it was voted the winner.

Henry Burr and Albert Campbell had a particularly
popular recording of the song in '19, the sixth biggest
record of decade, but Nicholas Orlando and Charles Hart
and Lewis James both had recordings that rivaled Burr

and Campbell's version for popularity. Vernon Dalhart
and Gladys Price and Prince's Orchestra also had popular
recordings of the song in '19. Hear Vernon Dalhart and
Gladys Price's '18 recording of this song at www.firstworld
war.com/audio/1918.

Marta Eggerth, in her U.S. movie debut, performed the
song in *For Me and My Gal* ('42), Doris Day and Gordan
MacRae sang it in *On Moonlight Bay* ('51), and it was used
in the screen biography of pianist Eddy Duchin, *The Eddie
Duchin Story* ('56).

For many years the song was frequently sung as the U.S.
Congress adjourned.

Raymond Egan's lyrics were particularly moving to all
the soldiers and their loved ones. Actually, the words fit any
farewell between lovers. The lyrics follow: *Smile the while
you kiss me sad adieu, / When the clouds roll by I'll come to
you; / Then the skies will seem more blue / Down in lovers'
lane, my dearie. / Wedding bells will ring so merrily, / Ev'ry
tear will be a memory. / So wait and pray each night for me,
/ Till we meet again.*

The sheet music cover and musical score are available at
http://levysheetmusic.mse.jhu.edu/browse.html and at
http://lcweb2.loc.gov/cocoon/ihas/loc.natlib.ihas.1000099
21/ or at http://scriptorium.lib.duke.edu/dynaweb/sheet
music/1910–1920/@Generic__BookTextView/46119 or
hear a midi musical version and read the lyrics at http://
www.geocities.com/dferg5493/tillwemeetagain.htm or
http://parlorsongs.com/issues/2000–11/2000–11b.asp or
http://www.halcyondaysmusic.com/july/july2003.htm.

The Jazz Age:
1920–1929

The '20s — characterized by flappers and "jazz babies"— were known as the jazz age. Suitable theme songs for the era might include "Ain't We Got Fun?," "Let's Do It" and "Runnin' Wild." The flapper and her beau would do practically anything as long as it was fun: They supposedly kissed indiscriminately, wore provocative clothing, used profanity, drank plenty of liquor, danced whenever they had the chance, sang their favorite songs with gusto, and laughed and giggled with abandon (sounds more like today).

The Lost Generation flapper bobbed her hair and wore skirts that flirted with exposing the knee. She danced the Charleston and the Black Bottom and twirled her ever-present pearl necklace. The "in" sayings of the day included "the cat's pajamas," "the bee's knees," "twenty-three skiddoo," "Oh, you kid" and "stew in your own juice." Millions were entertained by playing Mah-Jongg or the Ouija board.

When the United States is prosperous and politically stable, people are generally happy. When people are happy and successful, they sing and dance to fast, hot music. Although the '20s were not all smooth sailing, the country sang and danced its way through the decade as if it had nothing to worry about but having a good time. A popular expression of the time sums up that outlook: "Goin' to hell in a hand-basket."

The popular music of the decade included silly songs, like "Barney Google," girl songs, like "Sweet Sue," boy songs, like "Sonny Boy," mammy songs, like "My Mammy," baby songs, like "Yes Sir, That's My Baby," blues songs like "Wang, Wang Blues," and of course, there was jazz, like "Jazz Me Blues."

The Emergence of Popular Jazz

Actually jazz had been around for years. In New Orleans, by 1880, the basic format of the jazz ensemble, two cornets, tuba, clarinet, and drums, had developed. Early jazz flourished in the Storyville section, the "sporting district," until it was closed down in 1917. Jazz men sought new territory in cities along the Mississippi River, like Memphis and St. Louis, eventually reaching Chicago.

The prevailing style of jazz in the '20s was Dixieland, usually characterized as hot, loud, and fast. The Original Dixieland Jazz Band was one of the first nationally popular jazz bands. But compared with later years, jazz had a small following.

True jazz, as black musicians played it, was rare on the top-seller lists. There was symphonic jazz, with its leader, the so-called "King of Jazz," Paul Whiteman, and sweet jazz, which retained many of the nuances of jazz but was appropriate for dancing. Many of the most popular tunes of the twenties are "jazzy" only in the sweet sense. Pure primitive jazz was refined into music more palatable to white middle-class and working-class ears.

Legendary names associated with this period in jazz include Sidney Bechet, Johnny Dodds, and Jimmie Noone; cornetists Johnny Dunn, Jabbo Smith, and, of course, Louis Armstrong; trombonists Jimmy Harrison, Bennie Morton, and Claude Jones; pianists Jelly Roll Morton, James P. Johnson, and Fats Waller.

The Dance Band

Paul Whiteman's was by far the most popular dance band of the '20s. It featured a symphonic string section, sweet, lush arrangements and a danceable beat. Whiteman was called the "King of Jazz," but his music sounds rather unjazzy to modern ears. As it turns out, all popular music of the period was called "jazz," so more appropriately, Whiteman was the "King of Popular Music" rather than jazz and that he definitely was!

It was Whiteman who commissioned George Gershwin to write a jazz concerto to prove that jazz was an idiom that commanded respect; the result was "Rhapsody in Blue."

Several of the most important songs of the decade were popularized by Whiteman's orchestra, including "Whispering" backed with "The Japanese Sandman," "Wang Wang Blues" and "Hot Lips," which featured trumpet soloist Henry Busse, "Three O'Clock in the Morning," a classic Whiteman recording and "Valencia," which had been featured in the Broadway musical *Great Temptations*.

Other sweet bands that emerged in the '20s included Ben Selvin and his Novelty Orchestra, the Buddy Rogers Orchestra, Art Landry and his Call of the North Orchestra, Lew Gold and his Club Wigwam Orchestra, Ted FioRito, Isham Jones, Ted Weems, Harry Richman, Ted Lewis and their orchestras, and toward the end of the decade Guy Lombardo and his Royal Canadians and Rudy Vallee and his Connecticut Yankees.

Musical Theater Enthusiasts

The '20s may be known as the Jazz Age, but the decade should really be remembered for producing wonderful music for the theater. Composers like George Gershwin, Irving Berlin, Richard Rodgers, Vincent Youmans, Rudolf Friml, Sigmund Romberg, Ray Henderson, and Walter Donaldson were at their peak, while Victor Herbert was still around for a few more bows and Cole Porter was just beginning his string of successful musicals.

The '20s may have expressed themselves most completely in the musical comedy and revue. Despite an overused formula for success — bring on the chorus at the beginning and the end of each act, empty the stage instantly by asking, "Anyone for tennis?," insert at least one big sidesplitting drunk scene, have the juvenile leads break into a tap dance or soft-shoe shuffle at the end of their duet — the big musicals of the decade yielded some of the great standards of all times.

Sigmund Romberg's *Blossom Time* in '21 inspired a revival of interest in the operetta style. Operettas that premiered over the next few years included Victor Herbert's *Orange Blossoms*, Rudolf Friml's *Rose Marie* and *The Vagabond King*, plus Sigmund Romberg's *The Student Prince in Heidelberg* and *The Desert Song*.

The Broadway musicals introduced a number of giant hits. *Irene*, which opened in 1919, set the style of the musical of the decade and spawned the hit "(In My Sweet Little) Alice Blue Gown." More than 400 shows were produced on Broadway during the decade, introducing such hit songs as "Look for the Silver Lining," "The Love Nest," "My Mammy," "Toot, Toot, Tootsie!," "Indian Love Call," "I Want to Be Happy," "Tea for Two," "The Desert Song," "Can't Help Lovin' Dat Man," "'S Wonderful," "I Wanna Be Loved by You" and "More Than You Know," to name only a few.

The stars of the musicals were the likes of Al Jolson, Marilyn Miller, Eddie Cantor, Fred and Adele Astaire, Dennis King, Helen Morgan, Ed Wynn, Julia Sanderson, Edith Day, Gertrude Lawrence, and Beatrice Lillie.

Of all the significant musicals, a Jerome Kern and Oscar Hammerstein II collaboration had the greatest impact; they remodeled Edna Ferber's novel *Show Boat* into one of the classics of the Broadway stage. The music was stunning; the lyrics were pertinent; the story was touching; the effect of the whole production was stupendous.

The plush Broadway revue was in its full glory in the twenties. Gorgeous, long-limbed chorines in sequins and ostrich-feathered headdresses were a major attraction of such revues as *George White's Scandals*, Irving Berlin's *The Music Box Revues*, and Florenz Ziegfeld's *Follies*. The *Ziegfeld Follies*, the yardstick by which revues were measured, had passed its heyday, but it remained one of the ultimate stage entertainments of the era. The *Follies of 1921* introduced "My Man" and "Second Hand Rose," sung by Fanny Brice, and showcased the interpolation by Van and Schenck of "Wang Wang Blues." Comedians Gallagher and Shean stole the '22 show with a topical song "Mister Gallagher and Mister Shean." Van and Schenck scored again in the '23 *Follies* with "That Old Gang of Mine." Eddie Cantor's big song of '27 was an interpolation of Walter Donaldson's "My Blue Heaven" into the last edition of the *Follies* of the '20s.

In 1919 a rival challenged the supremacy of Ziegfeld in the field of revues. *George White's Scandals* contributed several memorable songs to the decade: I'll Build a "Stairway to Paradise," "Last Night on the Back Porch," "Somebody Loves Me," "Birth of the Blues" and "Black Bottom." Other important revues included *Earl Carroll's Vanities, The Greenwich Village Follies, The Music Box Revue,* and *Charlot's Revue.*

White Broadway audiences first heard jazz in all-black revues like *Shuffle Along, Lew Leslie's Blackbirds* and *Connie's Hot Chocolates.*

The World's Greatest Entertainer

Many of the musicals of the period were tailor-made for certain stars, and no one more than Al Jolson. Jolson seldom, if ever, sang a note from the score of the numerous musicals in which he appeared. Instead, at a particular point in each act, he would step entirely out of character, move to the front of the stage, and perform whatever song he chose to sing at that performance. What gall! But the audiences loved it. Jolson was billed as "The World's Greatest Entertainer," and he lived up to the billing.

Jolson always appeared in blackface, usually as the servant, Gus. He became a star in 1912 and continued his enormous successes into the twenties. Some of Jolson's most famous Broadway show appearances were in *Robinson Crusoe, Jr., Sinbad, Bombo* and *Big Boy.*

The Sound Motion Picture

Because of his extraordinary popularity, Jolson had a hand in the first sound motion picture in '27. In the film *The Jazz Singer,* which actually was only partially sound, Jolson sang six of his favorite songs. The phenomenal success of what was first regarded as a mere novelty launched the sound age in the movies. Next for Jolson was *The Singing Fool.* This '28 film featured Jolson singing "I'm Sitting on Top of the World," "There's a Rainbow 'Round My Shoulder" and "Sonny Boy." The sound process was improved in '28, and as the decade closed, "All-Talking! All-Singing! All-Dancing!" films like *Broadway Melody* and *The Hollywood Revue* arrived.

Theme songs for major nonmusical pictures also became popular. Even a few silent films had theme songs (example: "Charmaine" for *What Price Glory* in '27). But soon virtually every picture had a hackneyed theme song, which caused a public backlash against theme songs and against musical films.

The Early Record Industry

At the beginning of the '20s, sheet music was the main source of profit in music. As early as the late 1870s, recorded music had been possible, but at the turn of the century, a record was still a novelty. By the end of World War I, though, many of America's stage stars were entering homes via records. The recording industry had become a reality by '20, and by the mid-'20s 130 million records were being sold annually.

At first, these records were played on the gramophone. It had to be wound up, and the needle had to be changed for every record. By the end of the decade, electric automatic record changers and long-lasting tungsten needles had been introduced. The disks were weighty ten- or twelve-inch records, which played at seventy-eight or eighty revolutions per minute.

The Birth of Radio

On November 2, 1920, station KDKA, installed at the Westinghouse plant in East Pittsburgh, Pennsylvania, went on the air with the news that Warren Harding had been elected President of the United States. A year later there were 8 more stations. Within two years there were 564 — and a shortage of wavelengths. Millions of Americans made new friends with radio personalities.

In '22, $60 million worth of radio sets were sold in the United States. By '29, $842 million had been sold. Radio quickly traveled from infancy to maturity. Many bands and singers of the decade owe their fame to the radio. Paul Whiteman and his orchestra appeared regularly on radio, as did Rudy Vallee and his Yale Collegians. Vaughn DeLeath was one of the first female singers to gain national recognition over radio. Wendell Hall became the singing star of *The Eveready Hour,* one of radio's earliest variety programs. Others who may have owed their stardom to radio included Little Jack Little, Whispering Jack Smith, Lanny Ross, Jessica Dragonette, and the "Sweethearts of the Air," Peter De Rose and the Ukulele Girl, May Singhi Breen.

The radio microphone and perhaps the intimacy it afforded was uniquely suited for the birth of the crooning style of singing. The singers who adapted their singing style to the gentle, relaxed, soft crooning style became the most successful radio singers.

The torch singer, the thrush of the speakeasy, was also the rage. Perched on a piano, singing in a throaty, heartbreaking, breast-beating fashion, Libby Holman, Ruth Etting, and Helen Morgan were the epitome of the torch singer.

As much as radio helped the music business, there were drawbacks. Irving Berlin lamented, "We have become a world of listeners, rather than singers. Our songs don't live anymore. They fail to become part of us. Radio has mechanized them all. In the old days Al Jolson sang the same song for years until it meant something — when records were played until they cracked. Today, Paul Whiteman plays a song hit once or twice or a Hollywood hero sings them once in the films and the radio runs them ragged for a couple of weeks — then they're dead."

Vocal Quality vs. Showmanship

Which is more important, vocal quality or showmanship? The popular music industry has, in most instances, been more interested in entertainment, showmanship or charisma than in vocal skills or singing ability. That's not to discredit the singers, but to say that a native singing ability has not been necessary to achieve success on Broadway, in movie musicals, or in recordings.

Fred Astaire and Gene Kelly were wonderfully talented dancers with limited vocal skills, but they were both extremely successful, particularly Astaire in the recording field. Nobody would credit Carol Channing with having a good voice, but she was a successful Broadway and film actress/singer and has recorded often. What about Gene Austin, who was an amazingly successful recording artist in the '20s? Austin had such a small voice he had difficulty being heard above his band in live performances. Helen Kane, the "boop-boop-a-doop" girl, was mostly known for her high, squeaky voice. Or, consider Louie Armstrong's constantly hoarse-sounding, raspy voice; entertaining, yes; great God-given vocal instrument, no. But the audiences loved it!

Of course, there are a few quality singers who have had success, many more it would seem in the early days of the recording industry than more recently. Enrico Caruso, Jeanette MacDonald, Nelson Eddy, Grace Moore, Mario Lanza, and Kathryn Grayson particularly come to mind. But the numbers of great vocalists pales in comparison to the Mickey Rooney's, the Carmen Lombardo's, the Louis Armstrong's, Fats Waller's, and the Nat "King" Cole's of the entertainment/recording industry.

People adored Satchmo's and Nat Cole's raspy sound! The audiences of Broadway musicals loved Ethel Merman's blasting, strident, belting singing. Movie audiences haven't been turned away by the singing of stars who weren't singers. And one can never predict what the record buying public will purchase. Vernon Dalhart's "The Prisoner's Song" was one of the biggest hits of the '20s, yet it is exceedingly unpleasant to listen to today. Nick Lucas' voice reminds us of Tiny Tim of the '60s, but he had a great deal of success with "Tip Toe Through the Tulips" and others during the '20s. It would be stretching the point to say Lucas or Tiny Tim had great voices. Eddie Cantor was known more for his bulging eyes and frantic performances than for his singing ability. Ted Lewis half-talked, half-sang most of his hits. "Whispering" Jack Smith used a half-whispering singing style because of an injury from gas in World War I. Even the crooners had voices that suit radio and recording, but without the aid of microphones would have been unheard in live performances.

And it often isn't even vocal quality vs. entertainment that is the deciding factor. Sometimes it is the song itself. Who could have predicted the unusual success of "Yes! We Have No Bananas" by several different singers, "Minnie the Moocher" by Cab Calloway, or "Three Little Fishies" by Kay Kyser and his orchestra.

When it comes to judging the American public's taste, one must be extremely careful. However, it seems the public would prefer showmanship over quality.

Never had popular music been so diverse and so lucrative or had such national impact. An examination of the most popular tunes of each year of the decade will give an even clearer picture of an era that can be only remotely connected with reality at one moment and so enduringly memorable at another.

1920

Alice Blue Gown

Words: Joseph McCarthy; Music: Harry Tierney

The '19 Broadway musical *Irene* set an endurance record of 670 performances that it held for 18 years. What made it such a hit for its day was an intelligent libretto, interesting comedy situations, fast pacing, singable songs that fit rather well into the plot, and talented performers.

Actually, the plot was little more than another version of the Cinderella tale. A chatty upholsterer's assistant, Irene O'Dare, played by Edith Day, is sent to a Long Island mansion to mend some cushions. There she meets Donald Marshall who is instantly attracted to Irene. Donald persuades his friend, a male couturier known as Madame Lucy, to hire Irene to pose as a socialite in order to show off his latest fashion creations. Even though she doesn't get away with the masquerade, Irene makes a hit at an elegant party wearing her "Alice Blue Gown," and ends up in Donald's arms.

"Alice Blue" was the name given a particular shade of blue favored by President Theodore Roosevelt's daughter, Alice.

In the musical, Irene sings about her "sweet little Alice blue gown." When she went to town, she was proud, but shy, because she could sense everyone was looking at her. She'd stop at each shop window to primp. Then as the fashion of the day demanded, she'd frown, as if she didn't appreciate the attention. She loved the dress and wore it "till it wilted," but she will always remember it fondly.

Edith Day's recording of the song was the most popular version. The song was revived again in the early forties in recordings by Frankie Masters, Ozzie Nelson, and Glenn Miller and their orchestras. Isham Jones and his Rainbo Orchestra's recording of "Alice Blue Gown" is available at http://www.redhotjazz.com/jonesrainbo.html.

In '40, Hollywood made a screen version of *Irene* starring Anna Neagle. In '73, *Irene* was revived on Broadway in a production starring Debbie Reynolds.

Variety chose "Alice Blue Gown" for its *Hit Parade of a Half-Century* representing '19.

The sheet music cover and musical score are available at http://levysheetmusic.mse.jhu.edu/browse.html and at http://scriptorium.lib.duke.edu/sheetmusic/a/a55/a5569/. A PDF is available of this song at http://library.indstate.edu/level1.dir/cml/rbsc/kirk/sheet_titles.html.

The title song, "Irene," was also popularized by Edith Day in a successful recording. The sheet music cover and musical score are available at http://levysheetmusic.mse.jhu.edu/browse.html. A PDF is available of this song at http://odin.indstate.edu/about/units/rbsc/kirk/sh-group.html. Joseph C. Smith's Orchestra's recording of "Irene" is available at http://www.redhotjazz.com/jcso.html.

Blues (My Naughty Sweetie Gives to Me)

Words & Music: Charles McCarron, Carey Morgan & Arthur Swanstrom

Variety included "Blues (My Naughty Sweetie Gives to Me)" in its *Hit Parade of a Half-Century* representing '19.

Ted Lewis popularized the song with a successful '20 recording. Hear Lewis' recording of "Blues" At http://www.redhotjazz.com/tlband.html.

The lyrics begin with questions: "What is that song about kissing? What is that song about smiles?" The singer tells us he wouldn't sing about anything but his "weary blues." Next, in the chorus, he describes different types of blues. "There are blues that you get from pain ... when you're lonely for your one and only ... that you get from longing." However, for him, the "bluest blues" are "the blues my naughty sweeties gives to me." Read the complete lyrics at http://www.perfessorbill.com/index2.htm.

See the sheet music cover and musical score at http://digital.library.ucla.edu/apam/.

Dardanella

Words: Fred Fisher; Music: Felix Bernard & Johnny S. Black

This rag-style fox-trot novelty number is the song for which composer Fred Fisher is probably best remembered and that is rather odd, since he didn't really write it. Johnny S. Black wrote a piano rag entitled "Turkish Tom Tom," which Fred Fisher wrote lyrics for, then published it himself as "Dardenella." As lyricist and publisher of "Dardanella," Fisher is believed to have earned more than $1 million. After the song had become successful, Felix Bernard, a vaudevillian, claimed he had written the tune but had renounced his rights for a cash settlement of $100. After a court fight, later sheet music publications carried Fisher's name as lyricist and Black and Bernard as composers.

Published in '19, within its first year "Dardanella" had sold almost 2 million copies of sheet music. It was an important record for Ben Selvin's Orchestra in '20. Selvin recorded "Dardanella" under many different names for several record companies. Within a few years it is said to have sold 6.5 million records on various labels. Hear Ben Selvin's recording at http://www.redhotjazz.com/ben-selvino.html. Other important recordings were by Prince's Orchestra, Harry Raderman's Jazz Orchestra, and a duet recording for Henry Burr and Albert Campbell.

In the song's lyrics, Dardanella is an Oriental beauty the singer wants to see again to capture her heart; however, the song is best remembered as an instrumental, so the lyrics are not well known. Even the sheet music says, right under the title, "published as an instrumental number," like this was the lyric version of an instrumental tune.

"Dardanella" has been featured in a couple of movie musicals including *Two Girls and a Sailor* ('44) and *Oh You Beautiful Doll* ('49).

It was selected for *Variety*'s *Hit Parade of a Half-Century* (listed in '19).

See the sheet music cover and musical score at http://levysheetmusic.mse.jhu.edu/browse.html and at http://digital.library.ucla.edu/apam/. Or a PDF is available of this song at http://odin.indstate.edu/about/units/rbsc/kirk/sh-group.html. Or see the sheet music cover and hear a midi musical version at http://parlorsongs.com/issues/1998-5/may98gallery.asp.

Hold Me

Words: Art Hickman; Music: Ben Black

Florenz Ziegfeld was most famous as the producer of his spectacular *Follies*. He began his show business career managing the strong man Sandow. He later brought European star Anna Held to the United States and managed her career here. They married in 1897 and divorced in '13, so Ziegfeld could marry actress Billie Burke.

The first *Follies* was staged in '07, and the *Follies* appeared yearly through the '20s. The '11 edition was the first to be known as the *Ziegfeld Follies*. They were lavish spectacles that "glorified the American girl." Many of the most popular performers of the day were featured in the casts and many of the best songwriters wrote material for them to present.

"Hold Me" was introduced in the '20 edition of the *Follies*. The composer, Art Hickman, had the most popular recording of the number. Hear Art Hickman's recording of "Hold Me" At http://www.redhotjazz.com/hickman.html. It was revived again in '33 with popular recordings by the Hotel Commodore Orchestra, by pianist Eddy Duchin and his orchestra, and by sometimes composer, Ted FioRito and his orchestra.

The song's first verse is a girl confessing that she'd like "a man to steal a kiss," but she doesn't want to be thought too bold or to be scolded for that thought. The chorus lyrics tell us that the girl simply wants to be held. She craves "your affection." She wants to be teased, squeezed and thrilled. Finally, she begs, "Please don't scold me, just hold me tight in your arms."

See the sheet music cover and the musical score at http://scriptorium.lib.duke.edu/dynaweb/sheetmusic/1910–1920/@Generic__BookTextView/12596 or a PDF of this song is available at http://odin.indstate.edu/about/units/rbsc/kirk/sh-group.html.

I'll Be with You in Apple Blossom Time

Words: Neville Fleeson; Music: Albert Von Tilzer

"I'll Be with You in Apple Blossom Time: was initially popularized by Nora Bayes, "Queen of the Two-a-Days," in vaudeville.

Variety chose this number as one of its *Hit Parade of a Half-Century* selections.

Important recordings were released by tenor Charles Harrison, Henry Burr and Albert Campbell, and operatic tenor Reed Miller in '20. In the early '40s, the Andrews Sisters revived it into popularity when they performed it in the Abbott and Costello film *Buck Privates* and released a popular recording of it.

The lyrics talk about changing "your name to mine" when I see you again "in apple blossom time." The singer expects their wedding day in May to be a wonderful day. The "church bells will chime" when "you will be mine in apple blossom time."

See the sheet music score at http://scriptorium.lib.duke.edu/dynaweb/sheetmusic/1910–1920/@Generic__BookTextView/17885 or see the sheet music cover and hear a midi musical version at http://parlorsongs.com/issues/1999–5/may99feature.asp.

I've Got My Captain Working for Me Now

Words & Music: Irving Berlin

By '20 most of the troops who had fought in World War I had been discharged. A topical song that appealed to many of the former soldiers, "I've Got My Captain Working for Me Now," was interpolated into the *Ziegfeld Follies of 1919* by Eddie Cantor. It was Al Jolson, and to a lesser degree Billy Murray, who popularized it around the nation with popular recordings. The Original Dixieland Jazz Band's recording of this song is available at http://www.redhotjazz.com/odjb.html.

The song is a rather jazzy, mock-military style number by Irving Berlin. The lyrics are very clever and express the ultimate joy the singer feels because he is now the boss of his former commanding officer. Millions of draftees would have sympathized with the song's sentiments.

"I've Got My Captain Working for Me Now" was revived again during World War II in the film *Blue Skies*, where it was performed by Bing Crosby.

The sheet music cover and musical score are available at http://levysheetmusic.mse.jhu.edu/browse.html and at http://scriptorium.lib.duke.edu/dynaweb/sheetmusic/1910–1920/@Generic__BookTextView/23179.

The Love Nest

Words: Otto Harbach; Music: Louis A. Hirsch

The musical comedy *Mary* primarily owed its run on Broadway to its hit song, "The Love Nest." This was the greatest song success of composer Louis Hirsch, who had his first successful song included in a '11 stage production. "The Love Nest" became the theme song for the Burns and Allen radio and television series.

The plot of *Mary* concerns building "portable houses" (mobile homes) to sell for $1,300 each. "The Love Nest" was sung by Jack McGowan (as Jack) to Janet Velie (as Mary), detailing his plans for the love nest that will make him rich. Little did anyone in '20 know to what proportions the mobile home and trailer business would later grow.

Popular recordings by Art Hickman and his orchestra and by Broadway musical veteran John Steel helped popularize "The Love Nest." See the sheet music cover and hear a midi musical version at http://www.redhotjazz.com/hickman.html. The lyrics sing about a "love nest" that is "cozy with charm." It is "better than a palace with a gilded dome," because it "is a love nest you can call home."

"The Love Nest" was featured in Hollywood's tribute to George M. Cohan, *Yankee Doodle Dandy* ('42) and in *The Helen Morgan Story* ('57).

The sheet music cover and musical score are available at http://levysheetmusic.mse.jhu.edu/browse.html.

Variety selected "The Love Nest" for its *Hit Parade of a Half-Century*.

Joseph C. Smith's Orchestra popularized the title song from the musical with a successful '20 recording.

Palesteena

Words & Music: Con Conrad & J. Russel Robinson

Con Conrad came to songwriting from the vaudeville stage, on which he had been appearing since '07, when he was still in his teens.

"Palesteena (or Lena from Palesteena)" was introduced and popularized by the Original Dixieland Jazz Band in '21. Hear the ODJB's recording of "Palesteena" at http://www.redhotjazz.com/odjb.html. Eddie Cantor and Frank Crumit also released popular recordings of the song under the title "Palesteena" in '21.

Although the song may be primarily known as an instrumental, it did have lyrics. It tells us about a "not so pretty" girl, "Lena is her name" from the Bronx in New York City. She played her concertina really well and got a "swell position" to play in Palesteena. Even though she only knew one song, she played so well, she is now called "the Queen o' Palesteena."

Variety chose this song for its *Hit Parade of a Half-Century*.

The sheet music cover and musical score are available at http://levysheetmusic.mse.jhu.edu/browse.html.

Rose of Washington Square

Words: Ballard MacDonald; Music: James F. Hanley

"Rose of Washington Square" was copyrighted in '20, but it was introduced by Fanny Brice in the *Ziegfeld Midnight Frolic* of '19. She repeated the performance in the '20 edition. It provided the title for a '39 screen musical that was loosely based on Brice's career. The song recalls a time when beauty was appreciated from afar; beautiful women were "seen but not heard."

Even though Fanny Brice introduced this song and it became one of her musical trademarks, hers was not the most popular recorded version. The Kentucky Serenaders and Henry Burr released the best selling versions. Benny Goodman revived the song in '39. The All Star Trio's recording of this song is available at http://www.redhotjazz.com/allstartrio.html.

Variety chose "Rose of Washington Square" for its *Hit Parade of a Half-Century*.

The lyrics tell Rose that "nature did not mean that you should blush unseen but be the queen of some fair garden." The singer, a male it seems in the lyrics, says he'll "bring the sunbeams from the heavens to you and give you kisses that sparkle with dew."

See the sheet music cover and musical score at http://lcweb2.loc.gov/cocoon/ihas/loc.natlib.ihas.100006381/ or at http://digital.library.ucla.edu/apam/.

St. Louis Blues

Words & Music: W.C. Handy

St. Louis Blues became the most famous blues song ever written and for a time, was the most recorded song in the world. The song is on of *Variety*'s *Golden 100 Tin Pan Alley Songs* list. *Variety* chose this song for its *Hit Parade of a Half-Century* representing '14.

W.C. Handy had written "The Memphis Blues" in '13, but sold it to a publisher for $50. He wrote "St. Louis Blues" in '14 and formed a partnership with Henry Pace of Memphis to publish it themselves. The song didn't experience much success until Handy took it to New York City where Sophie Tucker became interested in it and used it successfully in her vaudeville act.

Prince's Orchestra had the first popular recording of the song in '16, but Marion Harris, one of the decade's most popular singers, had a more popular version in '20. Ms. Harris' version is available at http://www.redhotjazz.com/marionharris.html. The Original Dixieland Jazz Band issued their very successful version in '21. Original Dixieland Jazz Band's version is available at http://www.redhotjazz.com/odjb.html. One of the most famous versions of the song is the '25 recording by blues legend Bessie Smith with Louis Armstrong accompanying her on trumpet; that record was inducted into the Grammy Hall of Fame in '93. Armstrong's recording is available at http://www.redhotjazz.com/lao.html. Two W.C. Handy versions are available: with his Memphis Blues Band at http://www.redhotjazz.com/handymbb.html and with his orchestra at http://www.redhotjazz.com/handyo2.html.

Handy's "St. Louis Blues" is the second most recorded song of the pre-rock era behind "Silent Night."

"St. Louis Blues" has been used in numerous movie musicals including *Is Everybody Happy?* ('29), *Banjo on My Knee* ('36), *St. Louis Blues* ('38), *Birth of the Blues* ('41), *Is Everybody Happy?* ('43), *Jam Session* ('44) and *The Glenn Miller Story* ('54), where it appeared as "St. Louis Blues March."

See the sheet music cover and the musical score at http://digital.library.ucla.edu/apam/ or at http://scriptorium.lib.duke.edu/dynaweb/sheetmusic/1910–1920/@Generic__BookTextView/41594 or see the sheet music cover at http://parlorsongs.com/issues/1999–9/sep99feature.asp.

Swanee

Words: Irving Caesar; Music: George Gershwin

Irving Caesar and George Gershwin met at Dinty Moore's Restaurant in New York City one day in '19 to discuss new ideas for songs. After lunch they rode a bus to Gershwin's apartment where they finalized the details of "Swanee."

For the opening of a new motion-picture theater in October of '19, a stage show was presented before the film. Gershwin's "Swanee" had its premier in that stage show with sixty chorus girls, with electric lights glowing on their slippers, dancing to its rhythms on an otherwise dark stage. The reception wasn't particularly spectacular.

However, Al Jolson became interested in the song and performed it at one of his Sunday evening concerts at the Winter Garden Theater. That performance by Jolson was a smashing success. The song then caught on throughout the country and became George Gershwin's most commercially successful song ever. Even though this was his first of many famous and beautiful popular songs, he never had a commercial success that topped "Swanee."

Al Jolson's recording of "Swanee" was tremendously successful and helped popularize the song around the nation.

Variety listed "Swanee" as one of its *Golden 100 Tin Pan Alley Songs*.

The lyrics are memorable for their fast patter of "how I love you, how I love you" and "waiting for me, praying for me," and for spelling Dixie so that the last letter ("e") goes right into the words "Even" (what a clever writing devise!).

The Grammy Hall of Fame Award was established by the Recording Academy's National Trustees in '73 to honor recordings of lasting qualitative or historical significance that are at least 25 years old. Winners are selected annually by a special member committee of eminent and knowledgeable professionals from all branches of the recording arts. Jolson's recording of "Swanee" was inducted into the Grammy Hall of Fame in '98.

Other popular versions of "Swanee" were recorded by the All-Star Trio and by the Peerless Quartet.

"Swanee" was, of course, used in Gershwin's film biography *Rhapsody in Blue* ('45), *The Jolson Story* ('46), *Jolson Sings Again* ('49), and *The Jazz Singer* ('54).

Variety chose this song for its *Hit Parade of a Half-Century* representing '19.

The sheet music cover and musical score are available at http://levysheetmusic.mse.jhu.edu/browse.html and at http://digital.library.ucla.edu/apam/. See the sheet music cover, read the lyrics and hear a midi musical version at http://www.parlorsongs.com/issues/2002–12/thismonth/featureb.asp.

When My Baby Smiles at Me

Words: Andrew B. Sterling & Ted Lewis; Music: Bill Munro

Ted Lewis introduced this song, which became his theme song, in '18 before interpolating it into *The Greenwich*

Village Follies of 1919. It was still a top song in '20 when it was finally copyrighted.

Ted Lewis' recording was by far the most popular version, but a duet release by Billy Murray and Gladys Rice and a solo version by Henry Burr also helped popularize the song. Ted Lewis' version was revived into popularity in '38. Hear Lewis' '19, '26, '38 or '57 recordings of his theme song at http://www.redhotjazz.com/tlband. html.

The chorus lyrics begin with "when my baby smiles at me my heart goes roaming to paradise." A familiar part of the lyrics, especially in Ted Lewis' recording, is "I sigh, I cry," where he sounds like he's sighing and perhaps crying a little too. The chorus ends with the singer saying that it is "just a glimpse of heaven when my baby smiles at me."

"When My Baby Smiles at Me" was used in several movie musicals including *Sing, Baby, Sing* ('36), Shirley Temple's first film, *Hold That Ghost* ('41), an Abbott and Costello comedy, *Behind the Eight Ball* ('42) and *When My Baby Smiles at Me* ('48).

"When My Baby Smiles at Me" became a *Variety Hit Parade of a Half-Century* selection.

See the sheet music cover and musical score at http://lcweb2.loc.gov/cocoon/ihas/loc.natlib.ihas.100008021/ or http://scriptorium.lib.duke.edu/dynaweb/sheet music/1910-1920/@Generic__BookTextView/49880.

Whispering *and* The Japanese Sandman

Words & Music: Various

WHISPERING

"Whispering" and "The Japanese Sandman" were two sides of the same disk that established Paul Whiteman and his orchestra as major show business personalities. The phenomenally successful disk had sold nearly 2 million copies by '21. Considering the number of record players in use in '20, an equivalent sale today would be about 20 million. Hear three different Whiteman recordings of this song, the '20 acoustical version, the '28 electrical version and a '54 recording at http://www.redhotjazz.com/pwo. html. Paul Whiteman's recording of "Whispering" was inducted into the Grammy Hall of Fame in '98.

The Whiteman orchestra began playing "Whispering" during an engagement at the Ambassador Hotel in Los Angeles early in '20. Later the same year they recorded their arrangement of the song by Ferde Grofe for Victor.

The song has a basic stepwise melody, simple harmony, and no syncopation, which is common for the major hits of these years. The harmony lends itself to banjo and guitar accompaniment, and the melody encourages group singing, a prevalent form of home entertainment during the era. During pre–Victrola years, families often gathered in parlors around player pianos for singing sessions. Widespread in the first decade of the century, the tradition was still being carried on by many families, especially those who could not afford the Victrolas or the records.

"Whispering," written by the brothers, Malvin and John Schonberger, sold more than a million copies of sheet music soon after its publication.

Even though the new jazz age music had arrived, it did not immediately replace the older style. In this period, the adults, not the young, made the hits, and jazz was the music of the flaming youth of the '20s, particularly in the later half of the decade.

Whiteman's recording was extremely popular, one of the biggest recorded hits of the decade, but there were other recordings available including those by West Coast dance band leader, Art Hickman, and Broadway performer, John Steel. Les Paul, who invented multi-track recording and was an electric guitar pioneer, revived it with good success in '51. Gordon Jenkins and his orchestra also had a recording released in '51 that did pretty well. The brother and sister team of Nino Tempo and April Stevens charted with their version of "Whispering" in '64 and Dr. Buzzard's Original "Savannah" Band revived it again in '77 with moderate success.

The chorus lyrics begin with the title: "Whispering," and continue with a couple of reasons for the whispering — "while you cuddle near me" and "so no one can hear me." Later, the lyrics tell us the singer's lover is "whispering why you'll never leave ... never grieve me." But the principal thing that is whispered is "I love you."

"Whispering" was used in the '41 movie musical *Ziegfeld Girl, Greenwich Village* ('44) and *Give My Regards to Broadway* ('48).

See the sheet music cover and musical score at http://lcweb2.loc.gov/cocoon/ihas/loc.natlib.ihas.100007909/ or at http://digital.library.ucla.edu/apam/.

THE JAPANESE SANDMAN

"The Japanese Sandman" was written by Raymond B. Egan (words) and Richard A. Whiting (music).

During the '20s, transportation was still primitive enough that to most people the Orient was excitingly exotic and distant. Tin Pan Alley adapted authentic Far Eastern music to appeal to Americans, who accepted it as genuine.

Nora Bayes first popularized "The Japanese Sandman" in vaudeville, but it was Paul Whiteman and his orchestra who made a big hit record of it for Victor. On the flipside of "Whispering," the Whiteman disk reportedly sold nearly 2 million copies by '21. Nora Bayes and Ben Selvin and his orchestra also made popular recordings of the song, but not nearly as popular as Whiteman's. Hear several different Paul Whiteman recordings of this song, the '20 acoustical version, the '28 electrical version, the '38 version (Swinging Strings) and a '54 version at http://www.redhotjazz.com/pwo.html. Benny Goodman and his orchestra revived it at the beginning of the Swing Era with some success.

The first verse of the song asks us to stretch our imaginations "for the moment and come with me ... over the western sea." There we will find a Japanese lady singing a lullaby to her baby. The chorus continues by telling us the "Japanese Sandman" is "sneaking on with the dew" and taking "every sorrow of the day that is through." This sandman is "just an old second hand man trading new days for old."

"Japanese Sandman" was featured on the soundtrack of Julie Andrews' movie musical, *Thoroughly Modern Millie* ('67).

The sheet music cover and musical score are available at http://levysheetmusic.mse.jhu.edu/browse.html. See the sheet music cover and hear a midi musical version of

"Japanese Sandman" at http://www.parlorsongs.com/issues/2003–1/thismonth/featureb.asp.

Both "Whispering" and "Japanese Sandman" were selected for *Variety*'s *Hit Parade of a Half-Century*.

The World Is Waiting for the Sunrise

Words: Eugene Lockhart; Music: Ernest Seitz

Listed by *Variety* in its *Hit Parade of a Half-Century* as a top song of '20, this '19 song reflects the hope of a return to better days.

The lyricist, Eugene Lockhart, is better known to movie fans as Gene Lockhart.

"The World Is Waiting for the Sunrise" had the optimism that people needed in the aftermath of World War I, which had ended in '18 — a word of cheer about the loveliness of things like a rose, the song of a thrush, and love.

Isham Jones, John Steel and Theo Karle issued the most popular recorded versions of "The World Is Waiting for the Sunrise" in '22.

Les Paul and Mary Ford revived the song and had a million seller with it in '51; their rhythmic version was much different than the original slow ballad. Comedian Stan Freberg's version charted in '52.

The chorus is rather short. It opens by proclaiming to "Dear one" that "the world is waiting for the sunrise." The singer continues by painting a picture or two of the dawn: roses heavy with dew and a thrush calling his mate. And the chorus ends with the singer saying that just as the thrush is calling his mate, his "heart is calling you."

The non-descript sheet music cover and musical score are available at http://lcweb2.loc.gov/cocoon/ihas/loc.natlib.ihas.100007984/.

You'd Be Surprised

Words & Music: Irving Berlin

This saucy Irving Berlin number was introduced by Eddie Cantor in the *Ziegfeld Follies of 1919*. Cantor also helped popularize the song beyond Broadway with a popular recording. Cantor's Emerson recording became Berlin's first hit record, selling 888,790 copies. In addition, the song sold 783,982 copies of sheet music, and 145,505 piano rolls. The All Star Trio's recording of this song is available at http://www.redhotjazz.com/allstartrio.html.

"You'd Be Surprised" told of an unassuming, perhaps even an unattractive, man who became a surprisingly ardent lover when he was alone with his woman.

The first verse begins by telling us that a boy named Johnny was bashful and shy. A girl named Mary loved him, but everybody asked her why she picked him as her beau. "With a twinkle in her eye she made this reply," and she proceeds in the chorus to tell us that he may not be good in crowds, but when they are alone "you'd be surprised." The rest of the chorus is in a similar vein revealing some of the things Johnny does that would surprise us.

The sheet music cover and musical score are available at http://levysheetmusic.mse.jhu.edu/browse.html and at http://digital.library.ucla.edu/apam/.

Variety chose this song for its *Hit Parade of a Half-Century* representing '19.

1921

Ain't We Got Fun?

Words & Music: Richard A. Whiting

Richard Whiting's song, "Ain't We Got Fun?," would have made a good theme song for the decade's youth who were hell-bent on seeking fun, except the typical flapper and her beau were more a fixture of the last half of the decade rather than the first half.

This *Variety Hit Parade of a Half-Century* song was originally introduced, according to the sheet music cover, by Van and Schenck (Gus Van and Joe Schenck), a popular musical comedy team that was featured in vaudeville and in several Broadway musicals. Another sheet music cover claims the song was introduced by Arthur West in *Fanchon and Marco Satires of 1920*.

Van and Schenck had the most popular recording of the song, but the Benson Orchestra of Chicago and by Billy Jones, one of the famous "Happiness Boys" had popular recordings also. Hear Van and Schenk's '21 recording of this song at http://www.authentichistory.com/audio/1920s/Van_and_Schenck-Aint_We_Got_Fun.html or hear the Benson Orchestra of Chicago's recording at http://www.redhotjazz.com/benson.html.

The song was featured in the '52 movie musical *I'll See You in My Dreams*, in *By the Light of the Silvery Moon* ('53)and in the '74 film *The Great Gatsby*, which starred Robert Redford and Mia Farrow. The song also appeared in *The Cat's Meow* (2001).

The song has three verses and three choruses. Read the complete lyrics and hear a midi musical version at http://www.geocities.com/dferg5493/aintwegotfun.htm. The first verse tells us that bill collectors are haunting the singer. The grocer, butcher and landlord have all sent men to collect. However, this "happy chappy and his bride of only a year" are oblivious and remain cheerful. The chorus is what the young lovers think about the situation. They're having fun "ev'ry morning, ev'ry evening" even though "times are bum and getting bummer." One of the song's most famous lines and an axiom for the ages is "there's nothing surer, the rich get rich and the poor get children."

The sheet music cover and musical score are available at http://digital.nypl.org/ and at http://digital.library.ucla.edu/apam/.

All by Myself

Words & Music: Irving Berlin

"All by Myself" was one of Irving Berlin's most successful ballads up to the early '20s. It sold 1,053,905 copies of sheet music, 1,225,083 records, and 161,650 piano rolls for the player pianos that were tremendously popular.

The most successful recording was made by Ted Lewis, the famous bandleader who was famous for his half-spoken, half-singing vocals. Hear Ted Lewis' recording of this song at http://www.redhotjazz.com/tlband.html. Other popular recordings were made by Frank Crumit, the popular entertainer who appeared in several Broadway musicals of the decade and later hosted a popular radio show, by Aileen Stanley, by Benny Krueger, the former sax player with the Original Dixieland Jazz Band, by

Vaughn DeLeath, one of the most famous of the early radio performers (supposedly the first woman to sing on radio) and by the extremely popular Ben Selvin and his Orchestra.

"All by Myself" is a meditation on solitude and the misery of growing old alone. The lyrics begin by telling us that the singer is so unhappy they don't know what to do. They are tired of living alone and feel unloved. The singer is "all by myself in the morning" and at night. They sit alone playing solitaire and "watching the clock on the shelf." They admit to being afraid of growing old alone. This text may have been autobiographical of Berlin. He had lost his bride who died shortly after their honeymoon in '12 and had not remarried.

Bing Crosby performed the song in the '46 movie musical *Blue Skies*.

The sheet music cover and musical score are available at The sheet music cover and musical score are available at http://levysheetmusic.mse.jhu.edu/browse.html. A PDF is available of this song at http://odin.indstate.edu/about/units/rbsc/kirk/sh-group.html.

Avalon

Words & Music: Vincent Rose and Al Jolson

Borrowing tunes from the classics became very popular and highly profitable if the borrowers were not sued in the '20s. Vincent Rose wrote "Avalon," and Al Jolson helped make it popular. Chances are that Rose shared writing credit with Jolson so he would perform it. Knowing that Jolson's performance would likely make him a lot of money, Rose was willing to share credit.

The melody was borrowed from the aria "E lucevan le stelle" from Puccini's opera *Tosca*, although the key was changed from minor to major. Puccini's publishers brought suit and were awarded damages of $25,000 and all future royalties.

Borrowing from the classics was not novel. Harry Carroll and Joseph McCarthy had adapted the middle section of Chopin's "Fantaisie Impromptu in C-sharp minor" into "I'm Always Chasing Rainbows" in '18.

Jolson interpolated "Avalon" into the musical *Sinbad*, which had opened on Broadway in '18, after it had been running for a couple of years. Jolson's recording of "Avalon" was most popular in '21. After the release of his film biography, *The Jolson Story*, a new recording of "Avalon" by Jolson was released and became reasonably popular again.

"Avalon" has been used in several movie musicals including *Cairo* ('42), which starred Jeanette MacDonald, *The Jolson Story* ('46), *Margie* ('46), *The Benny Goodman Story* ('56) and *The Helen Morgan Story* ('57). The song also appeared in *Sweet and Low Down* ('99) and *The Cat's Meow* (2001).

The song was chosen for *Variety*'s *Hit Parade of a Half-Century*. "Avalon" became one of the most recorded songs of the pre-rock era.

Jolson (or the singer) tells us he found his "love in Avalon beside the bay" and he left his "love in Avalon and sail'd away." Now, he dreams "of her and Avalon" and thinks he'll "travel on to Avalon."

Hear several different Paul Whiteman recordings of this song at http://www.redhotjazz.com/pwo.html. The sheet music cover and musical score are available at http://levy sheetmusic.mse.jhu.edu/browse.html or see the sheet

music cover, read the lyrics and listen to a midi musical version at http://www.parlorsongs.com/issues/2002–12/this month/featureb.asp

Broadway Rose

Words: Eugene West; Music: Martin Fried and Otis Spencer

Variety chose "Broadway Rose" for its *Hit Parade of a Half-Century* representing '20.

The Peerless Quartet had a popular recording of "Broadway Rose" in '21. Hear the Original Dixieland Jazz Band's recording of this song at http://www.redhotjazz.com/odjb.html or Ted Lewis and his Band's at http://www.redhotjazz.com/tlband.html.

The verses of the song are in 4/4 or common time. The lyrics tell us about a "pretty flower" that is growing "along old Broadway." The singer, presumably male, found this "faded little rose" among the "gay life" and "white light's glare" of Broadway and his heart went out to her. Read the complete lyrics and hear a midi musical version at http://www.halcyondaysmusic.com/april/april2001.htm.

The chorus switches to triple meter or waltz time. This girl called "Broadway Rose" wears fancy clothes and smiles to hide the fact that she is really alone. The singer tells us "still at heart you're a gem." And even though the world tends to condemn her, no one really understands her woes.

See the sheet music cover and the musical score at http://scriptorium.lib.duke.edu/sheetmusic/a/a03/a0328/ or at http://digital.library.ucla.edu/apam/.

Cherie

Words: Leo Wood; Music: Irving Bibo

Paul Whiteman and his orchestra released a very successful recording of "Cherie" in '21, but theirs was not the only popular recording by far. Recordings of the song by Carl Fenton and his orchestra, Nora Bayes, Ben Selvin and his orchestra and Harry Raderman's Jazz Orchestra were also popular with the public in '21.

The sheet music says this song is "An American Fox Trot with a Parisian Twist." The song has three verses, but all of them are not very well known. In the first verse we meet this sweet French coquette who loves to dance. As she dances every dance, the fellow she's dancing with whispers the following words (the chorus) in her ear: *Cherie, Cherie, You're sweet, just as sweet as can be; / Cherie, to me, You're fair as the rare "fleur-de-lis"; / Dance on with anyone you see, / But save your kisses all for me, Cherie Baby! / You're part of my heart, Ma Cherie.*

Hear Paul Whiteman's recording of this song at http://www.redhotjazz.com/pwo.html. The sheet music cover and musical score are available at http://levysheetmusic.mse.jhu.edu/browse.html and at http://digital.library.ucla.edu/apam/. Art Phillips' artwork on the cover, a painting of Cherie, is very beautiful.

I Never Knew I Could Love Anybody Like I'm Loving You

Words & Music: Tom Pitts, Ray Egan & Roy Marsh

Jane Green inserted this *Variety Hit Parade of a Half-Century* selection into the revue *The Century Revue* and also into the *Midnight Rounders of 1921*. However, it was primarily popularized by Paul Whiteman and his orchestra in '21. Hear Whiteman's recording at http://www.red

hotjazz.com/pwo.html. It was successfully revived in '41 and was performed in several motion pictures.

The chorus lyrics begin with the title phrase: "I never knew I could love anybody, Honey, like I'm loving you." He didn't realize what her yes and smile could do to him. He's so in love he can't sleep or eat. The chorus closes with a repeat of the title phrase.

See the original sheet music cover and the musical score at http://levysheetmusic.mse.jhu.edu/browse.html or at http://digital.library.ucla.edu/apam/. See the sheet music cover, read the lyrics and hear a midi musical version at http://www.geocities.com/dferg5493/ineverknewicould loveanybody.html.

Jazz Me Blues

Music: Tom Delaney

This tune, a *Variety Hit Parade of a Half-Century* selection, illustrates people's fascination with both jazz and the blues in the '20s.

The blues, although largely unknown to the general public before the decade, can be traced back to the field hollers and call-and-response work songs of the slaves on the southern plantations. The harmony of the blues, consisting of the primary chords of a key (tonic, the I or key chord; subdominant or the IV chord; and dominant or the V chord) is decidedly European.

Authentic blues has a 12-bar form. Its most common characteristic is so-called "blue" notes (the flatted 3rd, 5th, and 7th tones of the scale) that are used only melodically. The unflatted notes remain in the harmony, almost causing the chord to sound out of tune. It's as if the performer was searching for a note that doesn't exist in our semitone system, which is exactly true. The slaves who birthed the blues were accustomed to the quarter tone system in their native country and were searching for a note that isn't possible in a seven note scale.

The traditional blues text is a rhymed couplet in iambic pentameter in which the first line is repeated. Actually only about half of the 12 bars is sung, while the rest of the measures are filled in with instrumental improvisation. Today the blues remain an active and vital source of inspiration to many musicians, especially jazz musicians. Some much later singers, like Janis Joplin, were greatly influenced by the early blues and those who sang them.

Many hits like Elvis Presley's "Hound Dog" are based on the 12-bar blues form. And that's only one example.

"Jazz Me Blues" was introduced on records by Lucille Hegamin, but the Original Dixieland Jazz Band had the most success with the song. Bix Beiderbecke recorded Tom Delaney's tune in his first recording with the Wolverines. Hear the Original Dixieland Jazz Band recording of this song at http://www.redhotjazz.com/odjb.html.

Look for the Silver Lining

Words: B.G. DeSylva & Clifford Grey; Music: Jerome Kern

Jerome Kern's *Sally* got the musical theater of the '20s off to a superb start. Just as *Irene* was a Cinderella tale created to feature the singing talents of Edith Day, so *Sally* was a Cinderella story featuring the dancing talents of Marilyn Miller. It was the year's biggest hit, running 570 performances.

Sally is a dishwasher at the Elm Tree Alley Inn in Greenwich Village. An aristocratic member of society arrives to book a party at the Inn. He is captivated with Sally and urges her never to be dismayed but rather to "Look for the Silver Lining." Before the musical ends Sally is propelled into dancing stardom in the *Ziegfeld Follies*.

One of the decade's most popular singers, Marion Harris, had the most successful recording of the song, but a duet recording by Elsie Baker (recorded as Edna Brown) and Charles Harrison, by Isham Jones and his orchestra, by tenor Lewis James and by Elizabeth Spencer also had popular recordings as well. Hear Marion Harris' recording of this famous Jerome Kern song at http://www.red-hotjazz.com/marionharris.html.

The film version of *Sally* was filmed in '29 starring Marilyn Miller. "Look for the Silver Lining" was also used in Jerome Kern's screen biography *Till the Clouds Roll By* ('46) and *Look for the Silver Lining* ('49), the screen bio of Marilyn Miller.

"Look for the Silver Lining" was a *Variety Hit Parade of a Half-Century* selection.

The first verse, sung by a male (Irving Fisher in the original Broadway cast), tries to lift Sally's (Marilyn Miller in the original cast) spirits. He asks her not to be offended if he sounds like he's preaching to her. He says he has a secret that can make her "very biggest troubles small." The secret is the chorus: "Look for the silver lining when e'er a cloud appears in the blue." He continues by reminding her that the sun is shining somewhere in the world, so she must simply make the sun shine for herself. And how can she accomplish this? With "a heart full of joy and gladness" which "will always banish sadness and strife." She must simply "try to find the sunny side of life."

The sheet music cover and musical score are available at http://levysheetmusic.mse.jhu.edu/browse.html and at http://scriptorium.lib.duke.edu/dynaweb/sheetmusic/1910–1920/@Generic__BookTextView/27630 or see the sheet music cover and hear a midi musical version at http://parlorsongs.com/issues/2002–2/thismonth/featureb.asp.

Joseph C. Smith's Orchestra had a popular recording titled "Medley from *Sally*" in '22. The musical's title song was also popularized by Joseph C. Smith's Orchestra in '21. A PDF of the musical score is available at http://library.indstate.edu/level1.dir/cml/rbsc/kirk/PDFs/sm1921_sally.pdf. The song appeared in the '29 film version of the musical. Another song from *Sally*, "Whip-poor-will," was popularized in a recording by Isham Jones and his orchestra. Read the lyrics at http://www.thepeaches.com/music/composers/kern/WhipPoorWill.htm. "Whip-poor-will" also appeared in Marilyn Miller's screen biography *Look for the Silver Lining*.

Ma! (He's Making Eyes at Me)

Words: Sidney Clare; Music: Con Conrad

This comedy number was written by Conrad and Clare for Eddie Cantor, who introduced it in *The Midnight Rounders of 1921*.

The text exclaims to Ma: "he's making eyes ... he's awful nice ... he wants to marry ... he's kissing me." Those lyrics sound like they are to be sung by a female, but hearing and seeing a male singer (namely Eddie Cantor) clapping his hands as he jumped and skipped around the stage, singing "Ma — He's Making Eyes at Me" was a showstopper.

Variety chose this Cantor classic for its *Hit Parade of a Half-Century*.

Listen to or download the '21 recording of this song by the Benson Orchestra of Chicago at http://www.redhot jazz.com/benson.html. See the sheet music cover and musical score at http://digital.library.ucla.edu/apam/. A PDF of this song is available at http://library.indstate.edu/level1.dir/cml/rbsc/kirk/PDFs/sm1921_ma.pdf.

Make Believe

Words: Benny Davis; Music: Jack Shilkret

Nora Bayes had a particularly popular recording of "Make Believe" in '21. Paul Whiteman and his orchestra, Isham Jones and his orchestra and Ben Selvin and his orchestra also contributed popular '21 recordings.

This "Make Believe" is not the same song that became popular after it premiered in *Show Boat*. That "Make Believe" was most popular in '28.

The song's two verses are trying to recommend making believe and smiling as remedies for feeling sad and blue. The chorus lyrics, which follow, continue the idea: *Make believe you are glad when you're sorry, / Sunshine will follow the rain; / When things go wrong, it won't be long, / Soon they'll be right again. / Tho' your love dreams have gone, Make believe, don't let on, / Smile tho' your heart may be broken; / For when bad luck departs, you will find good luck, / Don't grieve, just make believe.*

The sheet music cover and musical score are available at http://levysheetmusic.mse.jhu.edu/browse.html. Hear Paul Whiteman's recording of this song at http://www.red hotjazz.com/pwo.html. See the sheet music cover, read the lyrics and hear a midi musical version at http://www.halcyondaysmusic.com/september/september2005.htm.

Margie

Words: Benny Davis; Music: Con Conrad & J. Russel Robinson

"Margie" was written about Marjorie, the five-year-old daughter of Eddie Cantor. Cantor introduced and popularized this song, interpolating it into the revue *The Midnight Rounders of 1921*. Cantor's recording of "Margie" was the most popular recorded version.

Even though the song was written about Cantor's daughter, it is mostly a love song, not to a little girl, but about the singer's girl friend named "Margie." He's always thinking about her and wants to tell the world he loves her. He has "bought a home and ring and ev'rything." She's his inspiration. The chorus ends with the singer telling her she is his only one, "Oh! Margie, Margie, it's you!"

Ted Lewis and his band, popular entertainer Frank Crumit and the Original Dixieland Jazz Band had popular recordings of "Margie." Hear Ted Lewis' recording of "Margie" at http://www.redhotjazz.com/tlband.html. Claude Hopkins and his orchestra with vocalist Orlando Robertson revived the song in '34 and Don Redman and his orchestra revived it again in '39.

"Margie" has been used in several movie musicals including both the '40 and '46 film versions of *Margie, Hit Parade of 1941* ('40) and *The Eddie Cantor Story* ('53). The song also appeared in *The Cat's Meow* (2001).

"Margie" became a *Variety Hit Parade of a Half-Century* selection.

The rather innocuous sheet music cover and musical score are available at http://levysheetmusic.mse.jhu.edu/browse.html or see the same sheet music cover at http://

www.parlorsongs.com/issues/2005-1/thismonth/feature.asp.

My Mammy

Words: Joe Young & Sam Lewis; Music: Walter Donaldson

William Frawley introduced "My Mammy" in vaudeville, but it became a hit when Al Jolson interpolated it into *Bombo* in '21.

One of the best-remembered of Jolson's routines was his singing this song and falling on his knees, pleading with his mammy. He says "the sun shines East, the sun shines West, but" he's "learned where the sun shines best." And where is that? His "heart strings are tangled around Alabamy." He tells his Mammy that he's coming, he's sorry he made her wait and hopes he's not too late because he'd "walk a million miles" for one of her smiles.

One questionable aspect of America's popular music culture is its insensitive depiction of blacks in songs. Until the mid–'40s, and sometimes even beyond, the tradition of the coon and minstrel song continued without anyone (including African American performers) making much of an effective protest. The "mammy" and "darky" songs were hardly ever ill-intentioned or deliberately hostile, but they tended to perpetuate the stereotype of a lazy, simpleminded race that were all born with natural rhythm. Songs like "My Mammy," "Swanee," "Mississippi Mud," "Black Bottom," and "That's Why Darkies Were Born" are a few songs that perpetuated the tradition. However, there are several that seem to come from genuine admiration of the race and their contribution to our musical heritage, including "Ol' Man River," "Without a Song" and the American folk-opera *Porgy and Bess*. Most lyricists have allowed direct references to words like "darky" to be changed to less offensive words once society decided they were offensive.

It is rather remarkable that Jolson, Eddie Cantor, and others, appeared in black-face with such success during the late teens and twenties. The heyday of minstrel groups, who tended to be white performers that made up as blacks with burnt cork makeup on their faces, was from approximately 1843 through the turn of the century. Jolson was capitalizing on an old tradition, but by the '20s, it wasn't a major thrust in the show business community. Jolson certainly made the most of it in his career, however.

"The King of Jazz," Paul Whiteman and his orchestra had the most popular recording of "My Mammy" during the early '20s. Hear this Whiteman recording at http://www.redhotjazz.com/pwo.html. Other contemporary popular recordings were released by the all-time great foursome, the Peerless Quartet, by Aileen Stanley, by the Yerkes Jazarimba Orchestra, and by Isham Jones and his orchestra. Jolson had a popular recording of "My Mammy" in '28 after he had performed the song in the first sound motion picture *The Jazz Singer* in '27 and again in '47 after his movie biography *The Jolson Story* was released. Jolson also performed it in the '39 movie musical *Rose of Washington Square*.

Variety listed this song in its *Hit Parade of a Half-Century* for '21. This song was nominated for the American Film Institute's list of the greatest songs ever from an American film, but did not make the final list. It was nominated for its inclusion in *The Jazz Singer* ('27). The song also appeared in the non-musical film *The Pelican Brief* ('93).

A group called the Happenings charted with their version of "My Mammy" in '67.

The sheet music cover and musical score are available at http://levysheetmusic.mse.jhu.edu/browse.html and at http://digital.library.ucla.edu/apam/. See the sheet music cover and hear a midi musical version at http://www.parlorsongs.com/issues/2002-12/thismonth/featureb.asp.

Al Jolson also popularized "Yoo-hoo" from *Bombo* with a '21 recording. "Yoo-hoo" was written by Bud DeSylva and Al Jolson. The sheet music cover and musical score are available at http://levysheetmusic.mse.jhu.edu/browse.html. See the sheet music cover , the lyrics and hear a midi musical version at http://parlorsongs.com/issues/2002-12/thismonth/featureb.asp

My Man *and* Second Hand Rose
Words & Music: Various

MY MAN

Mistinguett had made "Mon Homme" a hit in France and had planned to use it in her American debut in the *Ziegfeld Follies of 1921*. Channing Pollock wrote English lyrics (original French lyrics were by Albert Willemetz and Jacques Charles) to Maurice Yvain's melody for Mistinguett's *Follies* appearance, but Ziegfeld lost interest in her and dropped her from the show before it was opened.

Although Fanny Brice had previously been used as a comedienne in the *Follies*, Ziegfeld selected her to do the song, perhaps because of the strong parallel between the subject of the lyrics and Brice's ill-fated marriage to the gangster Nicky Arnstein. Brice, dressed in tattered clothes, leaning against a lamppost, created a classic with her poignant rendition of the ballad. In a newspaper article a few years later, Arnstein blamed the song for ruining their marriage.

The chorus opens with a lament: "It's cost me a lot, but there's one thing that I've got, it's my man." Even though she's "cold and wet, tired you bet," she'll soon forget it all with her man. Her man is "not much for looks, and no hero out of books," and he has two or three other girls. Even though she doesn't know why she should, she loves him. "He isn't good, he isn't true" and he beats her. However, "when he takes" her "in his arms the world is bright." So even if she says she'll give him up, she'll "come back on" her "knees some day" because "whatever my man is I am his forever more!"

Brice sang "My Man" in her talking film debut, *My Man* ('28), and in *The Great Ziegfeld* ('36). The song was also used in *Rose of Washington Square* ('39). It became a hit for a new generation when Barbra Streisand performed it in *Funny Girl* ('68), the movie version of the Broadway smash of '64, which loosely chronicled Fanny Brice's career. "My Man" was not used in the original Broadway production, but as often happens in Hollywood, several of Brice's famous songs were interpolated into the film. It was also used in *Lady Sings the Blues* ('72), the film biography of blues immortal Billie Holiday.

Fanny Brice was a comedienne, not a particularly accomplished singer, but her recording of the song was the most popular version, followed closely by Paul Whiteman and his orchestra's version. Hear Paul Whiteman's recording of this song at http://www.redhotjazz.com/pwo.html. Another popular recording of "My Man" was by Aileen Stanley. Belle Baker revived it with some success in '28,

while Billie Holliday's vocal with Teddy Wilson's band gained a following in '38. Wayne King and his orchestra further popularized it in '39. Dinah Shore's version in '41 was also well received.

Fanny Brice's '22 recording of "My Man" was inducted into the Grammy Hall of Fame in '99.

This song was nominated for the American Film Institute's list of the greatest songs ever from an American film, but did not make the final list. It was nominated for its inclusion in *Funny Girl* ('68).

The sheet music cover and musical score are available at http://levysheetmusic.mse.jhu.edu/browse.html and at http://digital.library.ucla.edu/apam/.

SECOND HAND ROSE

Fanny Brice also introduced "Second Hand Rose," which became one of her trademark songs, in the *Ziegfeld Follies of 1921*. Barbra Streisand revived the song also in the movie version of the Broadway musical *Funny Girl* in '68. Brice also used this number in her first starring role in talking pictures, *My Man* ('28). "Second Hand Rose" was written by lyricist Grant Clarke and composer James F. Hanley.

In a bittersweet Yiddish accent, Rose sings that everything she has is a hand-me-down. The song opens with the singer (Fanny Brice, in this instance) telling us her father owns a second hand business that sells "everything from toothpicks to a baby-grand" piano. All the stuff in their "apartment came from father's store," including her clothes. She laments that she never gets anything that hasn't been used, she never gets anything that's new. "Even Jake, the plumber," the man she adores, told her he'd "been married before!" Everybody knows her as "Second hand Rose from Second Avenue!" Fanny Brice and Ted Lewis had very successful recordings of "Second Hand Rose" in 1921–22. Hear Ted Lewis' recording of "Second Hand Rose" at http://www.redhotjazz.com/tlband.html.

Variety's Hit Parade of a Half-Century included "Second Hand Rose" as one of the outstanding songs of '21.

The sheet music cover and musical score are available at http://levysheetmusic.mse.jhu.edu/browse.html or see the sheet music cover and hear a midi musical version at http://www.perfessorbill.com/index2.htm.

In the same '21 *Follies*, "(I Hold Her Hand and She Holds Mine) Ain't Nature Grand?" was introduced. Van and Schenck's recording of the song, written by Billy Rose, Ben Ryan and Irving Bibo, was popular in '21. The sheet music cover and musical score are available at http://digital.nypl.org/. The song appeared in the movie musical *Dangerous When Wet* ('53).

Also from the same *Follies*, came "Sally, Won't You Come Back?" written by Rudolf Friml. Ted Lewis and his band popularized the song with a successful recording in '21. Hear Lewis' recording of this song at http://www.redhotjazz.com/tlband.html.

O-HI-O (O, My! O!)
Words: Jack Yellen; Music: Abe Olman

In several instances, this song is listed incorrectly as "Down by the OHIO" or "(Down by the) O-HI-O (I've Got the Sweetest Little O, My! O!)." Even though that line appears in the lyrics, the original sheet music cover indicates the song's title is "O-HI-O (O, MY! O!)."

In the first verse the singer (seemingly a male) tells us

he has had all the girlies: slim, tall, plump and small; wild ones and mild ones. However, he's through with all of them but one. That one is "down by the O-hi-o." He's "going right back there to meet her." Even though "she's just a simple country girl," we'd be surprised to find out "they've got that O, My! O!" He can't wait 'till he gets "back to O-hi-o." A catchy tune and clever lyrics made this song a lasting hit.

Van and Schenck popularized the song initially in vaudeville and it was later recorded by Billy Murray and Victor Roberts with the "(Down by the) O-HI-O (I've Got the Sweetest Little O, My! O!)" title. However, Al Jolson's version, titled "O-HI-O (O-My!-O!) was the most popular one in '21.

"O-HI-O" was revived in '40 by the Andrews sisters and by the Smoothies.

The song appeared in the comedy film 1941 in '79.

See the sheet music cover, the lyrics and hear a midi musical version of this song at http://parlorsongs.com/issues/2003–8/thismonth/featureb.asp.

Peggy O'Neil

Words & Music: Harry Pease, Ed. G. Nelson & Gilbert Dodge

This slow waltz was a hit in vaudeville. Singing a fast patter on the second chorus became very popular at family and community sings. The tune and lyrics are nostalgically reminiscent of 1890s songs like "The Sidewalks of New York."

The verse lyrics tells that "Peggy O'Neil" can "steal any heart, anywhere, any time." Then the chorus tells us how to recognize "this wonderful girl." "If her eyes are blue as skies," if she smiles all the time, if she has a roguish walk, "talks with a cute little brogue," and has a rascality personality, "That's Peggy O'Neil."

The most popular recordings of "Peggy O'Neil" were by Billy Jones and by Charles Harrison. Both Frankie Carle and the Harmonicats revived the song in '47.

Variety selected "Peggy O'Neil" for its *Hit Parade of a Half-Century.*

The sheet music cover and musical score are available at http://levysheetmusic.mse.jhu.edu/browse.html. The sheet music cover appears to have been from the late '40s or early '50s. Nine sheet music covers are available at http://digital.library.ucla.edu/apam/. Hamilton King's beautiful painting, a reproduction from *The Theatre Magazine*, is the most interesting cover by far. See Hamilton King's '19 painting on the sheet music cover, read the lyrics and hear a midi musical version at http://parlorsongs.com/issues/2005–3/thismonth/feature.asp.

Say It with Music

Words & Music: Irving Berlin

Broadway saw a new, exquisitely beautiful theater open in '21, The Music Box, with the first of five revues. The theater and revue were Irving Berlin products. The theater was built specifically to showcase Irving Berlin's music.

In the '21 edition of the *Music Box Revue,* "Say It with Music" was introduced by Wilda Bennett and Joe Santley. Their performance of the song didn't receive a great reception. Part of the reason for its lukewarm reception may have been the song's relatively simple staging. Berlin had wanted the song to receive the attention he felt it deserved, but the audience, apparently, wanted spectacle. The song was on *Variety's Hit Parade of a Half-Century* list.

The *New York Times* critic, Alexander Woollcott," in his review of the production said, Berlin "has written only one real song. It is called 'Say It with Music,' and by February you will have heard it so often that you will gladly shoot at sunrise any one who so much as hums it in your hearing."

The song has two verses: one female, one male. The first (female) verse reminds us that music is the language of lovers and that "melody and romance" go hand in hand. If we have something sweet to say to our lover we should "Say It with Music" (which starts the chorus). Even though the first verse is feminine, the chorus is the same for both sexes. The lyrics claim that "they'd rather be kissed" while listening to the music of "Chopin or Liszt." Further, Cupid is helped along with a mellow melody played by a cello. So, if we have something to say to our lover, we should "say it with a beautiful song."

Paul Whiteman and his orchestra once again had the most popular recording of the song. Hear two recordings by Whiteman of this song: one from '21 and one from '39 at http://www.redhotjazz.com/pwo.html. Other not quite so popular versions were by Ben Selvin and his orchestra, by John Steel, who starred in several Broadway productions, and by the Columbians, another band, not unlike Ben Selvin's group.

"Say It with Music" sold 374,408 copies of sheet music, 102,127 piano rolls, and 1,223,905 recordings.

"Say It with Music was used in the movie musical *Alexander's Ragtime Band* ('38), which was about Irving Berlin. It also appeared in *The Cat's Meow* (2001).

The sheet music cover and musical score are available at http://levysheetmusic.mse.jhu.edu/browse.html. Read the lyrics at http://www.lyricsdownload.com/irving-berlin-say-it-with-music-1921-lyrics.html.

Song of India

Words: Al Wilson & Jim Brennan; Music: Nicolai Rimsky-Korsakoff

Paul Whiteman and his orchestra had a very popular recording of Rimsky-Korsakoff's "Song of India" from the first movement of his *Le Coq D'Or Suite* and from his opera *Sadko* in '21. The original tune was called "Chanson Indoue (Hindu Song)." Hear two recordings by Whiteman of this song: one from '21 and one from '39 at http://redhotjazz.com/pwo.html.

Other bandleaders, like Tommy Dorsey and Glen Gray, revived it into popularity during the late thirties during the heyday of the big bands.

The lyrics are pretty contrived and the melody is far too florid for the words to really flow easily. Thank goodness the song is by far more well known in its instrumental versions.

The sheet music cover and musical score are available at http://levysheetmusic.mse.jhu.edu/browse.html. A PDF of this song is available at http://library.indstate.edu/level1.dir/cml/rbsc/kirk/images/sm1922_song.jpg.

Wabash Blues

Words: Dave Ringle; Music: Fred Meinken

Recorded by Isham Jones and his orchestra, featuring Louis Panico on trumpet, "Wabash Blues" was one of the biggest hits of 1921–22. Hear Jones' recording that supposedly sold nearly 2 million copies at http://www.redhotjazz.com/ishamjones.html. The version by the Benson Orchestra of Chicago sold more than 750,000. The Benson recording is available at http://www.redhotjazz.com/benson.html.

For more on the blues as a form, see "Jazz Me Blues" above.

We tend to think of the blues as being slow and depressing, however, both "Wabash Blues" and "Wang Wang Blues" (see below) are examples of up-tempo, rather cheerful blues.

"Wabash Blues" is a good example of a commercial blues, written in Tin Pan Alley for the general market (it doesn't follow the classic 12-bar blues form). Harmonic changes are few, approximately every two measures, allowing time for instrumental improvisation. The text is not a rhymed couplet in iambic pentameter, and the text sounds contrived, however it is better known as an instrumental so the text isn't a key ingredient.

"Wabash Blues" was used in the movie musical *Joan of Ozark*, starring Judy Canova in '42 and was chosen for inclusion in *Variety*'s *Hit Parade of a Half-Century*.

Hear Isham Jones and his orchestra's '21 recording of this song at http://www.authentichistory.com/audio/1920s/Isham_Jones_and_His_Orchestra-Wabash_Blues.html. See the sheet music cover and musical score at http://digital.library.ucla.edu/apam/ or see the sheet music cover and hear a midi musical version at http://www.parlorsongs.com/issues/1999-9/sep99feature.asp.

Wang Wang Blues

Words: Gus Mueller & Buster Johnson; Music: Henry Busse

Henry Busse — composer, trumpeter, conductor, and radio and recording artist — joined the Paul Whiteman orchestra in '18 and stayed for ten years. "The Wang Wang Blues" was Busse's first important composition, written in collaboration with Gus Mueller and Buster Johnson, clarinetist and trombonist respectively with the orchestra. The most popular recorded version was by Paul Whiteman's orchestra that featured Henry Busse's trumpet. Hear several versions of Whiteman's recording, the '20 acoustical version, the '27 electrical version and two '45 versions at http://www.redhotjazz.com/pwo.html.

Although the song is primarily known as an instrumental, it did have lyrics. The words have the singer telling us that they have "the bluest blues" because his sweetie sweet has left him. He is pleading with this girl to come back and "chase away those Wang, Wang Blues." And the number ends with an emphatic "Wang Wang!"

See the sheet music cover and musical score at http://digital.library.ucla.edu/apam/. A PDF of this song is available at http://library.indstate.edu/level1.dir/cml/rbsc/kirk/images/sm1921_wang_c2.jpg.

"Wang Wang Blues" was used in the movie musical *Somebody Loves Me* ('52) and was selected for *Variety*'s *Hit Parade of a Half-Century*.

1922

April Showers

Words: B.G. DeSylva; Music: Louis Silvers

This *ASCAP All-Time Hit Parade*, *Variety Golden 100 Tin Pan Alley Song* and *Hit Parade of a Half-Century*

selection became a specialty of the decade's most charismatic performer, Al Jolson, who introduced it in the Winter Garden musical extravaganza *Bombo*. There was the merest hint of a plot in this musical extravaganza. Jolson played his blackface servant boy, but this time instead of Gus, Jolson was named Bombo and served none other than Christopher Columbus.

The official score was by Sigmund Romberg, but all of the show's hits were interpolations. Jolson was interjecting new songs for the run of the musical, even after the show had left New York to go on tour. Of course, he was famous for his interpolations, whatever the production. In *Bombo*, Jolson introduced three of his greatest song hits: "April Showers," "Toot, Toot, Tootsie" in '22, and "California, Here I Come" in '24.

"April Showers," which enthralled most of the opening night audience, was, as one critic noted, not even on the program. Another critic reported that Jolson "sang with his old-time, knee-slapping, breast-beating, eye-rolling ardor, sang with a faith that moved mountains and audiences. You should have heard them cheer."

Jolson recorded "April Showers" for Columbia in the fall of '21, and his was the best-known version, but Paul Whiteman and his orchestra's version was a close second. Hear Whiteman's recording of this song at http://www.redhotjazz.com/pwo.html. Other popular renditions on recordings included those by Ernest Hare, by Charles Harrison, and by Arthur Fields.

The lyrics remind us that even "though April showers may come" our way, "they bring the flowers that bloom in May." Of course, the rain is synonymous with bad things or troubled times and the May flowers with good things and a brighter future. We are told to "keep on looking for a blue bird and list'ning for his song," which again is urging us to look for the good and not dwell on the bad things in life.

After a decline in popularity in the late '30s, Jolson won renewed fame when the movie musicals *The Jolson Story* and *Jolson Sings Again* became big box office successes in the late forties. As a result of *The Jolson Story* ('46), "April Showers" became popular again in a new recording by Jolson and also by Guy Lombardo and his Royal Canadians. The song was also used in *Margie* ('46), 1948's *April Showers*, *Jolson Sings Again* ('49) and *The Eddy Duchin Story* ('56). According to http://www.imdb.com/, "April Showers" appeared in the non-musical film *The Cat's Meow* (2001).

The sheet music cover and musical score are available at http://levysheetmusic.mse.jhu.edu/browse.html. See the sheet music cover, read the lyrics and listen to a midi musical version at http://www.parlorsongs.com/issues/2002-12/thismonth/featureb.asp.

Chicago (That Todd'ling Town)

Words & Music: Fred Fisher

Most songs about towns are nostalgic, but this one about Chicago would tend to elicit finger-snapping or dancing the Charleston more than nostalgia as one's hometown. But Chicago wasn't the writer's hometown anyway.

A million seller in sheet music in '22, Fred Fisher's "Chicago" was popularized in '22 by Ben Selvin's orchestra and by the Bar Harbor Society Orchestra in recordings. It found new fame as a popular recording by the Tommy Dorsey orchestra in the late '30s and was popularized again by Frank Sinatra in '57. Hear Ben Selvin and his orchestra's recording of "Chicago" at http://www.redhotjazz.com/benselvino.html. Blossom Seeley first popularized "Chicago" in vaudeville, even though by this time other forms of entertainment were replacing vaudeville in many areas. "Chicago" became a *Variety Hit Parade of a Half-Century* selection and a *Variety Golden 100 Tin Pan Alley Song.*

The "windy city," Chicago, was such a "toddling town," the song's lyrics tell us, that even the famous evangelist Billy Sunday couldn't shut it down. In the context of the song, a "toddling town" probably meant a drinking, carousing town. The lyrics also tell us we'll lose our blues in Chicago. The song proclaims proudly that they do things on State Street, Chicago's main thoroughfare, that aren't done on Broadway in New York City. As an example, "I saw a man, he danced with his wife in Chicago."

"Chicago" was used in several movie musicals including Fred Astaire and Ginger Roger's *The Story of Vernon and Irene Castle* ('39), *In the Good Old Summertime* ('49), *Oh, You Beautiful Doll* ('49) and Frank Sinatra's *The Joker Is Wild* ('57). The song also appeared in *Orphans* ('87) and *Michael* ('96), plus, according to http://www.imdb.com/ films where it was uncredited.

The sheet music cover and musical score are available at http://digital.library.ucla.edu/apam/ and at http://digital.nypl.org/lpa/max_milleimage.cfm?bibid=12267&query=Chicago&qtype=MC.

China Boy

Words & Music: Dick Winfree & Phil Boutelje

The Paul Whiteman orchestra first popularized "China Boy," a *Variety Hit Parade of a Half-Century* song, in a recording. Revived by Benny Goodman in the mid–'30s, it became one of his specialties. The unusual opening chord structure that alternates between major and augmented chords gives "China Boy" a distinctive sound.

The song lyrics are unusually long. They begin: *Hey there, China Boy, would you like to take me home with you? / I'll hold you in my arms and ask you questions. / Hey there, China Boy, would you like to fall in love with me? / Hey don't you know that you're supposed to have the answers.*

Then the lyrics continue with several "Tell me" or "promise me" phrases. There are also several questions, like "If I asked you to go would you stay?"

Isham Jones and his orchestra's recording of "China Boy" can be heard at http://www.redhotjazz.com/ishamjones.html or Paul Whiteman's version at http://www.redhotjazz.com/pwo.html.

Do It Again

Words: B.G. DeSylva; Music: George Gershwin

Irene Bordoni introduced this Gershwin/DeSylva collaboration in the musical *The French Doll.*

The amusing lyrics play on a double entendre, the "it" in the title refers to kissing but is left ambiguous, so listeners can interpret "it" however they prefer. For this reason, the song was banned from most radio stations. The chorus lyrics ask for "it" to be done again even if "I may say, 'No, No, No, No, No.'" Then it explains that the "it" is kissing: "my lips just ache to have you take the kiss that's waiting for you." Even though her "Mama may scold" because she's been told "it is naughty," she begs "Oh, do it again, please, do it again!" Read the complete lyrics at

http://www.carlinamerica.com/titles/titles.cgi?MODULE=LYRICS&ID=315&terms=___terms___.

"The King of Popular Music of the Twenties," Paul Whiteman and his orchestra helped popularize "Do It Again" with a big-selling recording. Hear this recording at http://www.redhotjazz.com/pwo.html. Surprisingly "Do It Again" was not included in *Variety's Hit Parade of a Half-Century.*

"Do It Again" was used in Gershwin's screen biography *Rhapsody in Blue* ('45) and *Thoroughly Modern Millie* ('67), where Carol Channing performed it.

See the sheet music cover and musical score at http://digital.library.ucla.edu/apam/. A PDF is available of this song at http://odin.indstate.edu/about/units/rbsc/kirk/shgroup.html.

(When He Plays Jazz He's Got) Hot Lips

Music: Henry Busse, Henry Lange & Lou Davis

Trumpeter Henry Busse composed this showcase tune for trumpet with a couple of the other members of Paul Whiteman's orchestra as collaborators. The distinctive sound of Busse's vibrato on soft, muted trumpet with Paul Whiteman and later with his own group became his trademark.

Quite naturally, Paul Whiteman's orchestra had an extremely popular recording of "Hot Lips." Hear Whiteman's recording of "Hot Lips" at http://www.redhotjazz.com/pwo.html. Recordings by the Cotton Pickers and Ted Lewis were also popular. Henry Busse and his band revived it with a popular recording in '34 and again in '40. Horace Heidt and his Musical Knights revived it again with good success in '37.

"Hot Lips" was a *Variety Hit Parade of a Half-Century* selection.

See the sheet music cover and musical score at http://digital.library.ucla.edu/apam/.

I'm Just Wild About Harry

Words & Music: Noble Sissle and Eubie Blake

Blake and Sissle, two African American entertainers, had been a vaudeville team since '15 and had appeared as the number two attraction or top headliners for several years (in vaudeville the headline act, the prestige position, was next to closing; the number two spot was the next most preferred spot on the evening's fare, but by the late 1910s billing did not reflect merit).

In '21 Blake and Sissle wrote the songs for the first successful all-black revue produced in New York City, *Shuffle Along.* Although African Americans had performed on Broadway and all-black shows had played in principal houses, in some respects discrimination was more severe after World War I than before, so it was a remarkable accomplishment that *Shuffle Along* was such an outstanding success.

In the script Harry Walton (played by Roger Matthews) announces he is a reform candidate for mayor of Jimtown, and every citizen responds, "I'm Just Wild About Harry." The song was originally written as a waltz, but Lottie Gee, the young singer who was to perform it, complained that she couldn't sing it in waltz time, and the up-tempo "I'm Just Wild About Harry" became a hit. The foot-stomping score for the entire show had audiences shouting for more. Almost single-handedly *Shuffle Along* made all-black shows popular with white audiences.

The lyrics begin with a very short introduction to the chorus. It basically says I'm here to state, relate, explain, and make it plain that: "I'm just wild about Harry and Harry's wild about me." His kisses are ecstasy, he's sweet "like sugar candy" and "honey from a bee." Those lyrics don't sound much like a campaign song, do they? That may have been the original usage in *Shuffle Along*, but the song is known more today as a fun, fast love song.

There were three equally popular recordings of this song in '22, by Marion Harris, Ray Miller and Paul Whiteman. Vaughn DeLeath and Vincent Lopez also had popular recordings of the song in '22. Marion Harris' recording is available at http://www.redhotjazz.com/marionharris. html, Paul Whiteman's is also available at http://www.red hotjazz.com/pwo.html, but Miller's is not available at this website.

For you cartoon-atics, Daffy Duck sang the song in *Yankee Doodle Daffy*. The song also appeared in the non-musical films *Harry and the Hendersons* ('87) and *The Cat's Meow* (2001).

Variety selected "I'm Just Wild About Harry" for its *Hit Parade of a Half-Century*.

The sheet music cover and musical score are available at http://levysheetmusic.mse.jhu.edu/browse.html. Read the lyrics and hear a midi musical version at http://www.geoc-ities.com/dferg5493/imjustwildaboutharry.htm.

Paul Whiteman and his orchestra popularized another song from *Shuffle Along*, "Gypsy Blues," in '22. Hear Whiteman's recording of this song at http://www.redhot jazz.com/pwo.html.

Ben Selvin and his orchestra's recording of "Love Will Find a Way" from *Shuffle Along* was popular in '22. The sheet music cover and musical score are available at http://levysheetmusic.mse.jhu.edu/browse.html. Noble Sissle and his Sizzling Syncopators' recording of this song is available at http://www.redhotjazz.com/sissless.html.

Eubie Blake and his Shuffle Along Orchestra popular-ized "Bandana Days," also from *Shuffle Along*, in '21. See the sheet music cover and musical score at http://digital. nypl.org/lpa/max_milleimage.cfm?bibid=12470&query= Bandana&qtype=MC. Hear Blake's recording of this song at http://www.redhotjazz.com/shufflealong.html.

A Kiss in the Dark

Words: B. G. DeSylva; Music: Victor Herbert

Orange Blossoms was the last show Victor Herbert wrote before his death in '24. Actually Herbert's great musical ca-reer had, for all practical purposes, ended with World War I. His had been the age of the waltz, and his music sounded out of place in the postwar world of ragtime and jazz. He had numerous operetta successes before the first decade of the new century. Then he scored with five suc-cesses between '00 and '19.

Orange Blossoms was not a huge financial or artistic suc-cess, but it did boast the song "A Kiss in the Dark," which was introduced by Edith Day. The heroine sings the song to her godfather as she recalls a kiss in the dark from a stranger when she had been on vacation in Deauville.

The first verse recalls "a lovely dance, and a stroll into a night trembling with romance." The singer says the stranger tells her of her charms and suddenly holds her in his arms and kisses her. She also says that the "kiss in the

dark" may have been nothing to him, but to her it was a supreme thrill.

The most popular recordings of "A Kiss in the Dark" were by Amelita Galli-Curci and by Fritz Kreisler.

Variety chose "A Kiss in the Dark" for inclusion in its *Hit Parade of a Half-Century*.

The musical score is available at http://levysheetmusic. mse.jhu/browse.html and at http://digital.library.ucla. edu/. See the non-descript sheet music cover, read the lyrics, and hear a midi musical version at http://parlor songs.com/issues/2003-9/thismonth/featureb.asp.

L'Amour-Toujours-L'Amour — Love Everlasting

Words: Catherine Chisholm Cushing; Music: Rudolf Friml

This Rudolf Friml song became a favorite of sopranos and tenors in both concert hall performances and in vaudeville. Despite the French title, it was sung with En-glish words.

The 6/4 time signature is rather unusual for a popular song. Also the range of an octave and a sixth usually sug-gests an instrumental performance, but this song is by an operetta composer and was a concert specialty for the op-eratic singer whose range was large.

The chorus lyrics celebrate that love at last has found the singer. He pleads "Hold me and fold me away, thrill me and fill all my day." The chorus concludes with "yearning, burning glory, L'amour toujours l'amour."

Variety selected this number for its *Hit Parade of a Half-Century*.

Read the lyrics that were added later by Paul Francis Webster at http://www.digitaltimes.com/karaoke/singers/ L_Amour.html.

Love in the Sand

This *Variety Hit Parade of a Half-Century* song is a mys-tery. The song was not listed in *Variety Music Cavalcade, Revised Edition* among sixty-one songs published in '22 or the seventy-seven songs listed at http://en.wikipedia. org/wiki/1922_in_music. Neither was it listed in any other year, for that matter. Nor is it listed in Joel Whitburn's *A Century of Pop Music* or his *Pop Memories*.

There was a famous Rudolph Valentino '22 film titled *Blood and Sand*. Could the song and the film be related?

Mister Gallagher and Mister Shean

Words & Music: Ed Gallagher & Al Shean

Gallagher and Shean introduced this comedy routine, in the *Ziegfeld Follies of 1922*. This edition of the *Follies* highlighted the shimmy sensation Gilda Gray and folk humorist Will Rogers. Unfortunately, the musical score was not particularly strong, and the only memorable song was this comedy patter performed by a pair of dialect co-medians who had been recruited from vaudeville. Their act — billed as "By, About and for Themselves" — featured this number, which they wrote. The song was chosen by *Variety* for its *Hit Parade of a Half-Century*. Read a sam-ple lyric of this song at http://www.musicals101.com/ lygallagher.htm.

According to the sheet music cover, the correct title of the song should be "Oh! Mister Gallagher and Mister Shean," but the song is more commonly known minus the "Oh!"

Although it seems strange that anyone other than Gallagher and Shean would record this song, which was not the case. Ernest Hare and Billy Jones, Furman and Nash, plus Irving Kaufman and Jack Kaufman issued popular recordings of the song in '22. Bing Crosby and Johnny Mercer revived it in '38. Hear Paul Whiteman's recording of this comic song at http://www.redhotjazz.com/pwo.html.

The song was performed by Charles Winninger and Al Shean, himself, in the '41 blockbuster movie musical *The Great Ziegfeld* and by Al Shean again with Jack Kenny as Gallagher in *Atlantic City* ('44).

Ed Gallagher and Al Shean starred in vaudeville and the musical stages of the '20s. The team split permanently in '25. Incidentally Shean was the uncle of the Marx Brothers.

The sheet music cover and musical score are available at http://levysheetmusic.mse.jhu.edu/browse/html.

Paul Whiteman and his orchestra popularized another song from *Ziegfeld Follies of 1922*, "My Rambler Rose" by Gene Buck, Louis A. Hirsch and Dave Stamper, with a successful recording. The sheet music cover and musical score are available at http://levysheetmusic.mse.jhu/browse.html. Hear Whiteman's recording of this song at http://www.redhotjazz.com/pwo.html.

Paul Whiteman and his orchestra also popularized "'Neath the South Sea Moon" from *Ziegfeld Follies of 1922*. Buck, Hirsch and Stamper also wrote this song. The sheet music cover and musical score are available at http://levysheetmusic.mse.jhu.edu/browse/html and at http://digital.library.ucla.edu/. Hear Whiteman's recording of this song at http://www.redhotjazz.com/pwo.html.

My Buddy

Words: Gus Kahn; Music: Walter Donaldson

In '22 Walter Donaldson began working with the lyricist Gus Kahn. They initiated the partnership with a big hit: "My Buddy." Al Jolson sang it to national popularity. It was picked up by several ballad singers in vaudeville, who also helped make it popular.

"My Buddy" is quite a tearjerker: "Nights are long since you went away ... my buddy ... your buddy misses you." This tender, sentimental ballad is in triple meter, which generally suggests a waltz, but this song is usually sung with enough rubato to destroy the waltz feel.

The most popular recordings were released by Henry Burr, by Ernest Hare, and by Ben Bernie and his orchestra. Sammy Kaye's band revived it in the early '40s.

"My Buddy" was used in Gus Kahn's screen biography *I'll See You in My Dreams* ('52) and became a *Variety Hit Parade of a Half-Century* selection. The song also appeared in the non-musical film *Buddy* ('97).

See the sheet music cover and musical score at http://levysheetmusic.mse.jhu/browse.html and at http://digital.library.ucla.edu/. See the sheet music cover and hear a midi musical version at http://www.perfessorbill.com/index2.htm.

On the Alamo

Words: Gilbert Keyes & Joe Lyons; Music: Isham Jones

Isham Jones composed the music to "On the Alamo," which Gilbert Keyes and Joe Lyons furnished with lyrics. Jones' orchestra was chiefly responsible for popularizing the song. Hear Jones' recording of this song at http://www.redhotjazz.com/ishamjones.html.

The Norman Petty Trio revived the song with a moderately successful recording in '54.

This song's words aren't the greatest of the lyricist's art. It seems most likely that Isham Jones' music came first and Keyes and Lyons did their best to fit some words around the melody. The singer, a male, is waiting for a girl who had promised to meet him "by the garden gate." In the light of day ("noonlight") he thinks he should give up, but every evening when "the moon swings low on the Alamo" he finds himself wandering to that garden gate "in a garden fair where roses grow."

See the sheet music cover and musical score at http://digital.library.ucla.edu/apam/.

The Sheik of Araby

Words: Harry B. Smith & Francis Wheeler; Music: Ted Snyder

"The Sheik of Araby" was introduced in the '21 musical *Make It Snappy*. Rudolph Valentino's film *The Sheik* had been a sensation, so this song was at least partially inspired by that film or trying to capitalize on the film's success.

The Club Royale Orchestra and Ray Miller had equally popular recordings of "The Sheik of Araby" in '22. Jack Teagarden revived the song successfully in '39, Spike Jones had a popular comedy version of it in '43, and the Super-Sonics revived it again in '53. Hear the California Ramblers' recording of "The Sheik of Araby" at http://www.redhotjazz.com/caramblers.html.

The lyrics are sung by the sheik, introducing himself and proclaiming "your love belongs to me." At night while we're asleep he'll creep into our tent, and he'll steal us away to "rule this world" with him.

The song was used in the '40 movie musical *Tin Pan Alley*, where Billy Gilbert, Alice Faye and Betty Grable performed it comically.

The sheet music cover and musical score are available at http://levysheetmusic.mse.jhu.edu/otcgi/llscgi60.

Variety included this song in its *Hit Parade of a Half-Century*. "The Sheik of Araby" became one of the most recorded songs of the pre-rock era.

Another song from *Make It Snappy*, "I Love Her — She Loves Me (I'm Her He — She's My She)" by Irving Caesar and Eddie Cantor, was popularized by Eddie Cantor with a successful '22 recording. See the sheet music cover and musical score at http://digital.nypl.org/ and at http://digital.library.ucla.edu/. Hear Ray Miller and his orchestra's recording of this song at http://www.redhotjazz.com/miller.html.

Song of Love

Words: Dorothy Donnelly; Music: Sigmund Romberg

The Broadway season of '21 had its biggest hit with the musical *Blossom Time*. This musical biography of Franz Schubert employed the composer's melodies for its songs. The evening's biggest hit was "Song of Love" taken from the *Unfinished Symphony's* first movement. Bertram Peacock, who played Schubert, and Olga Cook, who played Mitzi, introduced the song.

This duet between Schubert and Mitzi tells a story about a sad and lonely young prince and a pure and holy maid whose love broke the enchantment the prince was under. The refrain is the song that "he laid at her feet." Schubert begins the refrain with "You are my song of love, melody immortal." Schubert and Mitzi alternate lines of the song until towards the end they sing the climax of the song together.

It has been estimated that Romberg earned more than $100,000 in royalties from this one song, whereas Schubert's earnings from his output of symphonies, songs, quartets, operas, sonatas, and other musical works amounted to the equivalent of about $500.

Lucy Isabelle Marsh and Royal Dadmun, Edwin Dale, and Prince's Orchestra popularized the song with popular recordings.

Variety selected this song for its *Hit Parade of a Half-Century.*

See the sheet music cover and musical score at http://lcweb2.loc.gov/cocoon/ihas/loc.natlib.ihas.100007913/ or at http://levysheetmusic.mse.jhu/browse.html.

Stumbling
Words & Music: Zez Confrey

This song comments in lyrics and syncopated melody on the intricacy of the social dances that were popular during the first years of the '20s. The tune was used as a leit motiv in the '67 movie musical *Thoroughly Modern Millie.* It was also used in *Mother Wore Tights* ('47).

Recordings by Paul Whiteman and his orchestra, by Billy Murray, by Frank Crumit, by Ray Miller, and by the Broadway Dance Orchestra helped spread the song's fame nationally. Hear Paul Whiteman's recording of "Stumbling" at http://www.redhotjazz.com/pwo.html.This song is far more famous as an instrumental, but it did have lyrics written by Confrey. He takes his girl to a dance and as they begin to dance they stumble all around. Neither of them seems especially adept, so they claim their stumbling is the newest dance step. The lyrics of the chorus follow: *Stumbling all around, stumbling all around, / Stumbling all around so funny, / Stumbling here and there, stumbling everywhere, and I must declare, / I stepped right on her toes, and when she bumped my nose, / I fell and when I rose, I felt ashamed, and told her, / That's the latest step, that's the latest step, / That's the latest step, my honey / Notice all the pep, notice all the pep, notice all the pep; / She said, "Stop mumbling, tho' you are stumbling, / I like it just a little bit, just a little bit, quite a little bit."*

Variety included "Stumbling" in its *Hit Parade of a Half-Century.*

See the sheet music cover and musical score at http://levysheetmusic.mse.jhu/browse.html and at http://digital.library.ucla.edu/.

Ten Little Fingers and Ten Little Toes — Down in Tennessee
Words: Harry Pease & Johnny White; Music: Ira Schuster & Ed. G. Nelson

Variety chose "Ten Little Fingers and Ten Little Toes — Down in Tennessee" for its *Hit Parade of a Half-Century.*

Irving Kaufman helped popularized the song with a popular recording in '22, but Billy Murray and Ed Smalle's duet recording was also popular. Hear Ted Lewis' recording of this song at http://www.redhotjazz.com/tlband.html.

The song tells us that the singer "met a pal from Tennessee" who was very happy because he had gotten good news from home. The good news was "ten little fingers, and

ten little toes, down in Tennessee," which, of course, was a baby. The baby was one day old and weighed ten pounds. He is so proud, he says he'd give up "the world and its gold," because of that baby waiting down in Tennessee.

See the sheet music cover and musical score at http://levysheetmusic.mse.jhu/browse.html. See the sheet music cover, the lyrics and hear a midi musical version at http://www.halcyondaysmusic.com/november/november2000.htm.

Three O'Clock in the Morning
Words: Dorothy Terriss; Music: Julian Robeldo

Another big hit for Paul Whiteman and his orchestra, this waltz by Julian Robeldo was first published in New Orleans in '19. Lyricist Theodora Morse, writing under the pseudonym of Dorothy Terriss, later set it to words that changed it from a ribald drinking song to a ballad. It was introduced in the closing scene of the revue *The Greenwich Village Follies of 1921* by Rosalinde Fuller and Richard Bold.

A distinctive feature of "Three O'Clock in the Morning" is its middle strain, which echoes a chiming clock. Whiteman's recording reportedly sold 3.5 million copies. Hear two Whiteman recordings of this song, the '22 acoustical recording and the '26 electrical recording at http://www.redhotjazz.com/pwo.html. Sheet music sales surpassed a million copies. While the Whiteman recording was extremely popular, there were other successful renditions available for the public to buy on records including those by Carl Fenton, by Frank Crumit, by Joseph C. Smith's Orchestra, and by Ben Selvin and his orchestra during the early twenties. Ted Lewis and his orchestra revived it with considerable success in '30, while Monty Kelly's '53 version was only moderately successful.

The lyrics talk about dancing until three o'clock in the morning. Daylight is coming soon, but the singer requests "one more waltz with you." He wants to dance "forever, dear, with you." Read the lyrics at http://www.geocities.com/Paris/Cafe/8636/three.html.

A '23 silent film was titled *Three O'Clock in the Morning.* "Three O'Clock in the Morning" was used in several movie musicals including *Presenting Lily Mars* ('43), *Margie* ('46), *That Midnight Kiss* ('49) and *The Eddy Duchin Story* ('56).

The sheet music cover and musical score are available at http://levysheetmusic.mse.jhu/browse.html and at http://digital.library.ucla.edu/apam/.

Another song, "Georgette," from *Greenwich Village Follies* by Lew Brown and Ray Henderson was popularized by Ted Lewis with a successful recording. See the sheet music cover and musical score at http://levysheetmusic.mse.jhu/browse.html. Hear Lewis' recording of this song at http://www.redhotjazz.com/tlband.html.

Tuck Me to Sleep (in My Old 'Tucky Home)
Words: Sam Lewis & Joe Young; Music: George W. Meyer

"Tuck Me to Sleep..." is one of composer George Meyer's most important songs after '17. A recording by Vernon Dalhart was particularly popular in '22. Ernest Hare, Al Jolson's former understudy, and Billy Jones, one of the famous "Happiness Boys," also issued recorded versions that sold well.

The chorus lyrics follow: *Tuck me to sleep in my old 'Tucky home, / Cover me with Dixie skies and leave me there alone. / Just let the sun kiss my cheeks ev'ry morn; / Like the kissin' I've been missin' / From my Mammy since I'm gone. / I ain't had a bit of rest, / Since I left my Mammy's nest, / I can always rest the best in her lovin' arms. / Tuck me to sleep in my old 'Tucky home, / Let me lay there, stay there never no more to roam.*

You can listen to this song played by the Oakland Banjo Band, with a vocal by John Green, at http://www.jbott.com/tucky.html.

The song is one of *Variety's Hit Parade of a Half-Century* selections, but has not maintained its popularity in subsequent years.

See the sheet music cover and musical score at http://digital.library.ucla.edu/apam/. A PDF of this song is available at http://library.indstate.edu/level1.dir/cml/rbsc/kirk/images/sm1921_tuck.jpg.

'Way Down Yonder in New Orleans *and* Angel Child

Words & Music: Various

'WAY DOWN YONDER IN NEW ORLEANS

Spice of 1922 ran for only about eight weeks, but it introduced the classic "'Way Down Yonder in New Orleans." The song was inserted into *Spice* after it had been discarded from the score of *Strut Miss Lizzie*, which had lasted for only four weeks. It was popularized by vaudeville star Blossom Seeley and Paul Whiteman and his orchestra in popular recordings of the time. Hear Paul Whiteman's recording of "'Way Down Yonder in New Orleans" at http://www.redhotjazz.com/pwo.html. The Peerless Quartet also had good success with their version. It also reportedly sold a million copies of sheet music. Freddy Cannon revived the song with a popular recording in '59.

"'Way Down Yonder in New Orleans," by Henry Creamer and J. Turner Layton, is a direct descendant of ragtime and exhibits considerable blues influence. A clever textual and melodic correlation occurs on the word "stop," for the song — melody and accompaniment — actually stops: "Stop! — Oh, won't you give your lady fair a little smile, Stop — you bet your life you'll linger there a little while." The lyrics tell us that New Orleans is "a garden of Eden" full of "Creole babies with flashin' eyes." It's a "heaven right here on earth." Read the lyrics at http://www.oldielyrics.com/lyrics/dean_martin/way_down_yonder_in_new_orleans.html.

"'Way Down Yonder in New Orleans" was used on the soundtrack of movie musicals such as *The Story of Vernon and Irene Castle* ('39), which starred Fred Astaire and Ginger Rogers, *Is Everybody Happy?* ('43), *Somebody Loves Me* ('52), which was based on the lives of Blossom Seeley and her husband, Benny Fields, and *The Gene Krupa Story* ('59), the screen biography of the famous drummer. According to http://www.imdb.com/, the song also appeared in the '81 film *Bix*.

This song was chosen by *Variety* for its *Hit Parade of a Half-Century*.

See the sheet music cover and musical score at http://digital.library.ucla.edu/apam/.

ANGEL CHILD

Al Jolson popularized another song from *Spice of 1922*, "Angel Child" by Benny Davis, George Price and Abner Silver, with a very successful recording in '22. The sheet music cover says the song was "sung with great success by Georgie Price in *Spice of 1922*." Price was one of the song's co-writers.

Ben Selvin and his orchestra's recording of the song was also popular. The Benson Orchestra of Chicago's recording of "Angel Child" is available for listening at http://www.redhotjazz.com/benson.html. See the sheet music cover and hear a midi musical version at http://parlorsongs.com/issues/1997–10/oct97feature.asp.

There are two verses and a chorus to this fox trot. The first verse's basic idea is its opening line: "You're just as sweet as an angel." The chorus lyrics are not particularly noteworthy. As a matter of fact, they seem amateurish in comparison to some of the gems from this period. The singer is "just wild about you, Angel child," which he states twice in the chorus with a slight variation.

See the sheet music cover and musical score at http://levysheetmusic.mse.jhu.edu/browse.html and at http://digital.library.ucla.edu/.

1923

Annabelle

Words: Lew Brown; Music: Ray Henderson

Variety chose "Annabelle" for its *Hit Parade of a Half-Century* representing '23.

According to *Pop Memories*, the only popular recordings of "Annabelle" were Lawrence Welk's and the Hoosier Hot Shots' in '39.

The song's basic idea can be summed up with, "Oh! Annabelle, Oh! Annabelle! You've made a wild man out of me."

Several sheet music covers, including this one, are available at http://digital.library.ucla.edu/apam/ (the musical score was not available).

Bambalina

Words: Herbert Stothart, Otto Harbach & Oscar Hammerstein II; Music: Vincent Youmans

Wildflower opened in early '23. This operetta had the longest run of any Vincent Youmans musical — 586 performances. "Bambalina," which was the operetta's biggest hit song, established Youmans as a major figure in the musical theater. "Bambalina," however, has a rather monotonous fiddle tune and does not evidence the genius Youmans exhibits in later endeavors.

The lyric relates how the caller and fiddler, Bambalina, calls a stop in a square dance so that the dancers can embrace.

Edith Day, one of the era's female musical stars, introduced "Bambalina" in the operetta.

"Bambalina" was chosen for *Variety's Hit Parade of a Half-Century*.

It seems like Paul Whiteman and his orchestra popularized everything during the decade and that is practically true. Hear Whiteman's recording of "Bambalina" at http://www.redhotjazz.com/pwo.html. Once again, they had the most popular recording of the song, with Ray Miller and his orchestra's version a distant second.

Ben Bernie and his orchestra popularized the title song from *Wildflower* with a successful recording in '23.

Barney Google

Words: Billy Rose; Music: Con Conrad

This *Variety Hit Parade of a Half-Century* song inspired by a popular cartoon character helped feed the decade's appetite for crazy songs. Some of the many nonsense songs of the era became hits while others were popular, but did not achieve long-lasting hit status. Examples include "Who Ate Napoleons with Josephine When Bonaparte Was Away?," "Does the Spearmint Lose Its Flavor on the Bedpost Overnight? (revived later as "Does the Chewing Gum Lose Its Flavor on the Bedpost Overnight?"), "Diga Diga Doo," "Who Takes Care of the Caretaker's Daughter — While the Caretaker's Busy Taking Care?," "I Faw Down an' Go Boom," "I Got a 'Code' in My 'Doze,'" and "Yes! We Have No Bananas."

The comic strip hero Barney Google debuted June 17, 1919 as *Take Barney Google, F'rinstance*. The creator, Billy DeBeck, soon changed the name to *Barney Google*. The cartoon character was a henpecked gambler. In a particular comic strip, Barney was in the wrong place at the right time, just standing around outside of the Jockey Club. During a rather physical argument, a man was thrown out a window and landed on top of Barney. The man felt Barney had saved his life, so he gave him one of his horses, which became Barney's horse, Spark Plug, in the comic strip (and song). DeBeck approved the lyrics of the song and even contributed the sheet music cover. Many people bought the music even though they couldn't read it or had no instrument, just because of the cover.

Conrad and Rose wrote this comical song for Eddie Cantor (perhaps there is a correlation between Barney's "goo-goo-googly eyes" and Cantor's bug-eyed performing). Cantor introduced "Barney Google" in '23, but it was popularized in recording by Ernest Hare and Billy Jones, radio's most famous comedy singing team, and by former vaudeville child-star, Georgie Price. Hear a recording of this comic classic by the Georgians at http://www.redhotjazz.com/georgians.html.

This comical song has two verses and two choruses, plus seven additional choruses available on the last page of the sheet music. By far the most well known part of the song is the chorus, which begins: "Barney Google, with his Goo Goo Googly eyes." It seems that Barney's wife was three times his size and was suing him for divorce. As a result, he's now sleeping with his horse, Spark Plug.

Access DeBeck's sheet music cover, read the lyrics and hear a midi musical version at http://www.perfessorbill.com/index1.html.

Carolina in the Morning

Words: Gus Kahn; Music: Walter Donaldson

The Passing Show of 1922's gift to posterity was "Carolina in the Morning," a schottische introduced by the Howard Brothers (Willie and Eugene).

The text — "Nothing could be finer than to be in Carolina in the morning" — is world-famous, even though the melody for those words is just two notes, two complete measures that alternate back and forth between just two notes. The next phrase also alternates between two notes for two measures in a sequence one step higher. After a short bridge, the "A" theme is repeated with new text,

which begins, "Strolling with my girlie..." After the "A" theme is completed, the melody and lyrics change. The singer tells us that if he had Aladdin's lamp he'd make a wish, but then the next phrase is a repeat of the opening phrase of the chorus.

The famous comedy-musical team of Van and Schenck had the most popular recording of "Carolina in the Morning," followed by versions by Marion Harris, by Paul Whiteman and his orchestra and by the American Quartet. Danny Winchell, accompanied by Leroy Holmes and his orchestra, revived it again in the mid-'50s with moderate success. Hear Paul Whiteman's recording of this song at http://www.redhotjazz.com/pwo.html or hear Marion Harris' version at http://www.redhotjazz.com/marionharris.html.

"Carolina in the Morning" was used in several movie musicals including *The Dolly Sisters* ('45), *April Showers* ('48), *Look for the Silver Lining* ('49), *Jolson Sings Again* ('49) and Gus Kahn's screen biography *I'll See You in My Dreams* ('52).

This Donaldson/Kahn classic was selected as a *Variety Hit Parade of a Half-Century* number.

The sheet music cover and the musical score are available at http://levysheetmusic.mse.jhu.edu/browse.html. Six sheet music covers and the musical score are available at http://digital.library.ucla.edu/apam/. Access the lyrics and hear a midi musical version at http://www.parlorsongs.com/issues/2003-8/thismonth/featureb.asp or at http://www.perfessorbill.com/index1.html.

Crinoline Days *and* Lady of the Evening

Words & Music: Irving Berlin

CRINOLINE DAYS

Grace LaRue introduced Irving Berlin's "Crinoline Days" in *The Music Box Revue of 1922–23*, the second *Music Box Revue*. As she sang, a stage elevator lifted her higher and higher while her hoop skirt kept growing fuller and wider until the dress engulfed the entire stage.

Berlin's lyrics yearn for the return of the past, back to the days when a girl would not allow her ankles to be displayed. In the refrain, the lyrics continue wishing for the return of the time when a man married the girl he courted and when women's complexions weren't the result of cosmetics.

Paul Whiteman and his orchestra had a very popular recording of the song in '23. Whiteman's recording is available at http://www.redhotjazz.com/pwo.html.

"Crinoline Days" became a *Variety Hit Parade of a Half-Century* selection.

The musical score is available at http://levysheetmusic.mse.jhu.edu/browse.html. Read the lyrics of this song at http://www.oldielyrics.com/lyrics/irving_berlin/crinoline_days.html.

LADY OF THE EVENING

Irving Berlin's "Lady of the Evening" was introduced by one of the greatest revue tenors, Irish-brogued John Steel, in the second edition of *The Music Box Revue*. Steel sang this serenade, one of Berlin's personal favorites, in a simple moonlight rooftop setting. The idea of the lyrics is that the "lady of the evening" is calling us. She can make our cares and troubles disappear.

John Steel had a popular recording of the song in '23, as did Paul Whiteman and his orchestra. Whiteman's recording is available at http://www.redhotjazz.com/pwo.html.

The musical score is available at http://levysheetmusic.mse.jhu.edu/browse.html. Read the lyrics of this song at http://www.oldielyrics.com/lyrics/irving_berlin/lady_of_the_evening.html.

Variety selected "Lady of the Evening" for its *Hit Parade of a Half-Century* representing '22.

Another song from *Music Box Revue of 1922*, "Pack Up Your Sins and Go to the Devil," was popularized by Emil Coleman. The musical score is available at http://levysheetmusic.mse.jhu.edu/browse.html. Hear Paul Whiteman's recording of this Berlin song at http://www.redhotjazz.com/pwo.html. This song also appeared in the '38 movie musical *Alexander's Ragtime Band*.

Down Hearted Blues

Words: Alberta Hunter; Music: Lovie Austin

Famous blues singer Bessie Smith helped popularize "Down Hearted Blues" in '23 with a recording. Hear Bessie Smith's recording of this blues at http://www.redhotjazz.com/bessie.html.

Songwriters and vaudeville performers Noble Sissle and Eubie Blake's recording of the song was also fairly successful in '23.

Bessie Smith was a rough, crude and sometimes violent woman, but she also became one of the greatest of the classic blues singers of the '20s. Bessie started out as a street musician in Chattanooga, Tennessee, but by the early '20s she was one of the most popular blues singers in vaudeville. She made her recording debut on Columbia in '23. Accompanied by pianist Clarence Williams, she recorded "Gulf Coast Blues" and "Down Hearted Blues." The disk sold more than 780,000 copies in six months and eventually became a million seller.

The lyrics are typical of a commercial blues song. The singer, Ms. Smith in this instance, is disgusted and broken hearted because it's difficult to love someone when that someone doesn't love you. The next part of the song is in the traditional 12-bar blues format with the first line repeated: "Trouble, trouble, I've had it all my days." Then comes the "catch" line: "It seems like trouble going to follow me to my grave." The rest of the song continues to follow the same form. Read the complete lyrics at http://blueslyrics.tripod.com/lyrics/bessie_smith/downhearted_blues.htm.

A couple of sheet music covers of this song are available for viewing at http://digital.library.ucla.edu/apam/ (no musical score was available).

Dreamy Melody

Words: Frank Magine & C. Naset; Music: Ted Koehler

Art Landry, bandleader, clarinetist, and violinist, recorded this waltz with his Call of the North Orchestra. It reportedly sold about 1.5 million copies.

The wide range of the melody and, to a degree, its chromatic melody suggests an instrumentally conceived melody that was intended to be played rather than sung.

The first verse and chorus indicate that the singer has found a "dreamy melody" that has captured his heart. It's

haunting him and he keeps asking for it to be played again "sweet and tenderly."

The sheet music cover and musical score are available at http://levysheetmusic.mse.jhu.edu/browse.html. See the sheet music cover, the lyrics and hear a midi musical version at http://parlorsongs.com/issues/2002–4/thismonth/featureb.asp.

I'll Build a Stairway to Paradise

Words: Ira Gershwin & B.G. DeSylva; Music: George Gershwin

Between '20 and '24, George Gershwin wrote the complete scores for five editions of George White's *Scandals*. In the songs for these productions, he began to completely reveal his true musical genius.

By '22, Gershwin's skill as a composer was very evident in "I'll Build a Stairway to Paradise," which he wrote with his brother, Ira, using the pen name Arthur Francis, and B.G. "Buddy" DeSylva. The song was originally called "A New Step Every Day," but DeSylva suggested revisions in the lyrics that gave him equal billing with Ira as lyricist. George's melodic and harmonic genius is evident in the unexpected flatted thirds and sevenths, the subtle enharmonic changes, and jazz accentuations.

Winnie Lightner, Pearl Regay, Colette Ryan, Olive Vaughn, George White, Jack McGowan, Richard Bold, Newton Alexander, and the chorus, accompanied by Paul Whiteman's orchestra, introduced this selection as the Act One finale of the '22 edition of *Scandals*.

The lyrics begin with a warning to ministers who berate dancing teachers. The singer thinks the fastest way to paradise is to dance "the steps of gladness" as we build "a stairway to paradise with a new step every day." Read the lyrics of this song at http://www.soundtracklyrics.net/song-lyrics/an-american-in-paris/stairway-to-paradise.htm.

The ever-present Paul Whiteman and his orchestra had the most popular recorded version. Hear Paul Whiteman's recording of this song at http://www.redhotjazz.com/pwo.html. Other popular releases were by Ben Selvin and his orchestra and by Carl Fenton and his orchestra. The song was one of Gershwin's that was featured in his screen biography, *Rhapsody in Blue* ('45) and in *An American in Paris* ('51). Rufus Wainwright sang "I'll Build a Stairway to Paradise" on the soundtrack of *The Aviator* (2005).

Variety chose this song for its *Hit Parade of a Half-Century* representing '22.

Just a Girl That Men Forget

Words: Al Dubin & Fred Rath; Music: Joe Garron

Variety selected "Just a Girl That Men Forget" for its *Hit Parade of a Half-Century* representing '23.

The song was popularized in '23–'24 in recordings by Henry Burr and by Lewis James.

The girl pictured in the lyrics is the type of girl that men enjoy for a while, but soon forget. It says that men want to settle down with an old-fashioned girl. The girl in the song, however, is a vamp or a flapper with modern ways. She's told she is not the kind of girl that men marry.

The sheet music cover and musical score are available at http://levysheetmusic.mse.jhu.edu/browse.html, however, it was not yet online.

Love Sends a Little Gift of Roses

Words: Leslie Cooke; Music: John Openshaw

John Openshaw and Leslie Cooke wrote "Love Sends a Little Gift of Roses" in '19. Reinald Werrenrath and Charles Hackett popularized it in '21 in recordings but in '23 the Carl Fenton Orchestra's recording was even more popular. Other contemporary recordings were by the famous tenor, John McCormack, the Bar Harbor Society Orchestra, singer Sam Ash, and the Columbia Orchestra.

Cooke's chorus lyrics open with the title phrase, then continue with "breathing a pray'r unto my posies," which sounds rather antiquated, much older than its '19 copyright date. Later in the chorus the singer asks her lover's heart to be more tender, his eyes to glow with the brightness of love, and just a kiss.

This song was chosen by *Variety* for its *Hit Parade of a Half-Century* representing '19.

A court case between "In Sunny Kansas" and "Love Sends a Little Gift of Roses" was tried in '42. Go to http://ccnmtl.columbia.edu/projects/law/library/cases/case_mcmahonharms.html to read about the case results.

The non-descript sheet music cover and musical score are available at http://levysheetmusic.mse.jhu.edu/browse.html. See the sheet music cover and hear a midi musical version at http://www.parlorsongs.com/issues/1999-3/mar99gallery.asp.

Lovin' Sam (the Sheik of Alabam')

Words: Jack Yellen; Music: Milton Ager

Grace Hayes introduced this *Variety Hit Parade of a Half-Century* selection representing '22 in the musical *The Bunch and Judy*, where it was an interpolation.

Nora Bayes had the most popular recording of "Lovin' Sam (the Sheik of Alabam')" in '23.

In '22 Milton Ager helped found the song publishing house of Ager, Yellen & Bornstein, which published "Lovin' Sam." With this hit, Ager began an association with lyricist Jack Yellen, with whom he wrote several outstanding songs during the '20s.

The verse is in the key of D, while the chorus modulates to the key of G; such key changes are not unheard of in popular music, but neither are they extremely common.

The first verse of Yellen's lyrics starts as if a preacher was singing them: "Listen, sister and brothers, I suppose you've heard of the Sheik." He says he knows a man who is a greater lover than the Sheik. All the girls in town would love to be the bride of this Romeo. Some of the lyrics are racial, like "high browns" and "cullud" (meaning black).

The chorus lyrics tell about "Lovin' Sam, the Sheik of Alabam'." Sam is a "mean love makin', a heart-breakin' man!" We're told that if we could love like Sam, we could have our eggs and ham in Alabam's finest kitchens.

The sheet music cover and musical score are available at http://levysheetmusic.mse.jhu.edu/browse.html and at http://lcweb2.loc.gov/cocoon/ihas/loc.natlib.ihas.100004178/ and a PDF of the song is available at http://library.indstate.edu/level1.dir/cml/rbsc/kirk/images/sm1922_lovin.jpg.

My Sweetie Went Away (She Didn't Say Where, When, or Why)

Words: Roy Turk; Music: Lou Handman

Variety selected "My Sweetie Went Away" for its *Hit Parade of a Half-Century* representing '23.

Billy Murray and Ed Smalle had a popular duet recording of the song in '23 and Dolly Kay's version was also popular. Hear Bessie Smith sing this song accompanied by her Down Home Trio at http://www.redhotjazz.com/smithdownhome.html.

The sheet music cover is available for viewing at http://digital.library.ucla.edu/apam/ (no musical score was available).

No! No! Nora!

Words: Gus Kahn; Music: Ted FioRito & Ernie Erdman

"No, No, Nora" was introduced by the co-composer, Ted FioRito and his orchestra. Sheet music covers vary the punctuation; some use commas, others use exclamation points, some use no punctuation.

The song was used in lyricist Gus Kahn's screen biography, *I'll See You in My Dreams* ('51), where it was performed by Doris Day.

Eddie Cantor had a big hit recording of the song in '23.

In the chorus, the singer, Cantor in this instance, assures Nora that she is his only love and promises to stay true to her. He asks, "And would I trade you for Venus?" And answers, "No, no, Nora!"

Variety selected "No, No, Nora" for its *Hit Parade of a Half-Century* representing '23.

At http://www.ruthetting.com/songs/no-no-nora.asp you can see the sheet music cover with Ms. Etting on the cover and read the lyrics of this song. Or you can hear a '23 recording by the Benson Orchestra of Chicago at http://www.redhotjazz.com/benson.html.

Oh! Gee, Oh! Gosh, Oh! Golly, I'm in Love

Words: Ole Olsen & Chic Johnson; Music: Ernest Breuer

The writers of "Oh! Gee, Oh! Gosh, Oh! Golly, I'm in Love," the comedy team of Olsen and Johnson, introduced this comic song, which became a *Variety Hit Parade of a Half-Century* selection. It became identified with Eddie Cantor because of his many famous performances of the song. Cantor interpolated it into the *Ziegfeld Follies of 1923*.

Eddie Cantor's recording and a duet recording by Ernest Hare and Billy Jones were the most popular versions of this song on the market.

Parade of the Wooden Soldiers

Music: Leon Jessel

"Parade of the Wooden Soldiers" was introduced to American audiences in the Russian revue *Chauve Souris* ('22), which had been imported to Broadway from Paris. The song had originated in '11 as a German instrumental number, "Die Parade der Holzsoldaten."

Paul Whiteman and his orchestra's recorded version was the most popular one, but others by Vincent Lopez and Carl Fenton's groups were also very successful. Whiteman's orchestra re-released the song with success in '28. Hear two Whiteman recordings: the '23 acoustical version and the '28 electrical version at http://www.redhotjazz.com/pwo.html.

"Parade of the Wooden Soldiers" was used in the Shirley Temple movie musical *Rebecca of Sunnybrook Farm* ('38).

The song is not necessarily a seasonal song, but it is often heard around the Christmas season.

Variety chose this song for its *Hit Parade of a Half-Century* representing '11.

The sheet music cover and musical score are available at http://levysheetmusic.mse.jhu.edu/browse.html. The sheet music cover only credits Leon Jessel as its writer, but some sources credit Ballard MacDonald as lyricist.

Swingin' Down the Lane

Words: Gus Kahn; Music: Isham Jones

The songs Isham Jones wrote and made popular were closely associated with an orchestra of violins, clarinets, saxophones, and muted brass. Jones wrote more than 200 tunes, and several of them became standards for dance bands. It's interesting that he used the same ending for "Swingin' Down the Lane" as for "I'll See You in My Dreams." Hear Jones' recording of this song at http://www.redhotjazz.com/ishamjones.html.

In addition to Isham Jones and his orchestra's recorded version, which was the most successful one, Ben Bernie and his orchestra's was a close second. Another, slightly less successful version was release by the Columbians.

Gus Kahn's lyrics start with everybody walking hand in hand, as they are "Swingin' Down the Lane," then tells us everybody is feeling grand, followed again by the title phrase. The rest of the lyrics are about a guy who is alone, wishing he were with his girl as other lovers are on this particular night as they stroll, or in this case, swing, down the lane. Access the lyrics at http://www.spiritofsinatra.com/pages/Lyrics/s/Swingin_Down_The_Lane.htm.

"Swinging Down the Lane" was used in the movie musical *Greenwich Village* ('44). It was also a *Variety Hit Parade of a Half-Century* selection.

That Old Gang of Mine

Words: Billy Rose & Mort Dixon; Music: Ray Henderson

The famous team of Van and Schenck introduced "That Old Gang of Mine" in the *Ziegfeld Follies of 1923*; it became *a* gigantic success for the writers.

The text speaks of barbershop quartet camaraderie. He can't forget the old quartet that sang "Sweet Adeline," and the days when sweethearts and pals were a part of "That Old Gang of Mine." Read the lyrics of this song at http://lyrics.duble.com/lyrics/P/perry-como-lyrics/perry-como-that-old-gang-of-mine-lyrics.htm.

This famous song was chosen by *Variety* for its *Hit Parade of a Half-Century*.

The most popular recordings of the song included those by Billy Murray and Ed Smalle, by Benny Krueger and his orchestra, by Ernest Hare and Billy Jones, by the Benson Orchestra of Chicago, and by Irving and Jack Kaufman. Dick Robertson revived it again with some success in '38. Benny Krueger's recording of "That Old Gang of Mine" is available at http://www.redhotjazz.com/krueger.html.

The song was used as the musical theme for the Warner Bros. film *The Country Kid*.

Several different sheet music covers are available for viewing at http://digital.library.ucla.edu/apam/.

There'll Be Some Changes Made (see 1941)

Variety chose this song for its *Hit Parade of a Half-Century* for '23.

Toot, Toot, Tootsie (Goo' Bye)

Words & Music: Gus Kahn, Ernie Erdman, Dan Russo & Ted FioRito

Bombo began its run at the Winter Garden Theater in late '21, and this song was added in '22. This exuberant farewell became one of Jolson's specialties.

Anyone who has heard Jolson sing "Toot, Toot, Tootsie goodbye, Toot, Toot, Tootsie don't cry" will certainly remember it. Jolson was such a distinctive and charismatic performer. The rest of the lyric talks about how sad he is because the train is taking him away from his Tootsie. He asks for a kiss and tells her to watch for a letter from him. He says the only way she wouldn't get a letter from him was if he were in jail.

Even though it was a Jolson specialty, other successful recordings of it were on the market. Ernest Hare and Billy Jones, Vincent Lopez and his orchestra and the Benson Orchestra of Chicago issued other '23 hit recordings of the song. Art Mooney and his orchestra, who revived many songs from the '20s in the late '40s, revived "Toot, Toot Tootsie" in '49, as did Mel Blanc, the famous voice of many cartoon characters.

"Toot, Toot, Tootsie" was used in several movie musicals including the one that started it all, *The Jazz Singer* ('27). Jolson also performed it in *Rose of Washington Square* ('39), *The Jolson Story* ('46) and again in *Jolson Sings Again* ('49). It was also in *I'll See You in My Dreams* ('52), Gus Kahn's screen biography.

This hit was selected by *Variety* for its *Hit Parade of a Half-Century* representing '22. It was also nominated for the American Film Institute's list of the greatest songs ever from an American film, but did not make the final list.

The sheet music cover and musical score are available at http://levysheetmusic.mse.jhu.edu/browse.html. See the sheet music cover and hear a midi musical version at http://www.parlorsongs.com/issues/2002-12/thismonth/featureb.asp.

Al Jolson also popularized "Who Cares" from *Bombo*. Jack Yellen and Milton Ager wrote "Who Cares." The sheet music cover and musical score are available at http://levysheetmusic.mse.jhu.edu/browse.html. Hear Marion Harris' recording of "Who Cares" at http://www.redhotjazz.com/marionharris.html.

Yes! We Have No Bananas

Words: Irving Cohn; Music: Frank Silver

This novelty song, a *Variety Hit Parade of a Half-Century* selection, became a sensation when Eddie Cantor introduced it in the '22 revue *Make It Snappy*. He added it after the New York City opening. The audience demanded that Cantor repeat the song for a quarter of an hour.

Frank Silver consciously or unconsciously borrowed a great deal of the tune from Handel's *Messiah* and Balfe's "I Dreamt That I Dwelt in Marble Halls."

Equally popular recordings by Billy Jones and by Ben Selvin and his orchestra helped spread the song around the nation. Hear Billy Jones' '23 recording of this song at http://www.authentichistory.com/audio/1920s/Billy_Jones-Yes_We_Have_No_Bananas.html. Other successful recordings included those by the Great White Way Orchestra with vocalist Billy Murray, by Benny Krueger, and by Sam Lanin. Hear the Great White Way Orchestra's recording at http://www.bassocantante.com/flapper/music.html.

The lyrics introduce us to a Greek fruit seller who rattles off an inventory of his produce ending with a resounding and paradoxical "Yes! we have no bananas."

The song was so successful that it spawned a spoof version entitled "I've Got the Yes! We've Got No Bananas Blues."

The song has been used in several movie musicals beginning with Maurice Chevalier's French version ("Les Ananas") in *Innocents of Paris* ('29). It next appeared in *Mammy* ('30), where its lyrics were sung to the melody of various well-known opera arias. Next the Pied Pipers performed it in *Luxury Liner* ('48) and finally, it was used in *The Eddie Cantor Story* ('53).

The sheet music cover and musical score are available at http://levysheetmusic.mse.jhu.edu/browse.html (German edition). Read the lyrics at http://lyricsplayground.com/alpha/songs/y/yeswehavenobananas.shtml.

You've Got to See Mamma Ev'ry Night

Words: Billy Rose; Music: Con Conrad

The "Last of the Red Hot Mamas," Sophie Tucker was responsible for popularizing this song, which insists that "you've got to see your mamma ev'ry night or you can't see mamma at all."

The first verse of the lyrics opens with Mamma telling Daddy that she's feeling blue because she doesn't see much of him, and she says that will never do. She tells him she's laying down the law and proceeds with the chorus where she tells him he must see her every night, kiss her and treat her right or she won't be home when he calls.

Variety chose this Tucker specialty for its *Hit Parade of a Half-Century*.

Dolly Kay's recording, accompanied by Frank Westphal and his orchestra, competed with Sophie Tucker's as the most popular one, while those by Billy Murray and Aileen Stanley and by Mamie Smith were also successful. Hear a recording of this song by the Georgians at http://www.redhotjazz.com/georgians.html or hear Marion Harris' version at http://www.redhotjazz.com/marionharris.html.

See the sheet music cover and hear a midi musical version at http://parlorsongs.com/issues/1999-11/nov99feature.asp. Several sheet music covers are available for viewing at http://digital.library.ucla.edu/apam/.

1924

California, Here I Come

Words: Al Jolson & B.G. DeSylva; Music: Joseph Meyer

Even in '24 Al Jolson was still introducing new material into *Bombo*, which had opened in '21, but that's nothing novel for Jolson. "California, Here I Come" was added by Jolson after the show had left New York City and gone on tour.

Jolson is listed as a co-writer, but he most likely took no part in the writing process. He negotiated $5,000 from the publisher to have his name and picture on the sheet music cover. It is difficult to tell in retrospect whether Jolson actually had anything to do with the writing of any of the songs for which he is given credit, but it was a fairly common practice to give entertainers of his caliber composer or lyricist credit to get them to perform them. The performer, in this case Jolson, then received writing royalties from songs. The true writers, in this case lyricist Buddy DeSylva and composer Joseph Meyer, were willing to share the royalties, since getting performers like Jolson to perform the song practically guaranteed its success.

Jolson's was the most popular recording of "California, Here I Come," but Georgie Price and the California Ramblers also charted with their versions. Jolson's recording of the song was inducted into the Grammy Hall of Fame in 2005. Hear Paul Whiteman's recording of this song at http://www.redhotjazz.com/pwo.html.

The first verse lyrics begin by painting a wintry, snowy picture that causes us to think about a warmer climate like Southern California. The singer, Jolson, in this instance, sings that's the place he loves best of all. He's been blue because he's been away from California. He can't wait to go back there and he is beginning to hear it calling him. Next comes the famous chorus: "California here I come, Right back where I started from." Flowers are blooming and the birds sing each morning at dawn. The "sun-kiss'd misses" don't want him to be late; so he tells them to open up the golden gate, he's on his way. Read the lyrics at http://www.lyricsvault.net/songs/19804.html. Many films have used this song in film soundtracks to suggest going to California. The song was used in several movie musicals including *Lucky Boy* ('29), starring George Jessel, *Rose of Washington Square* ('39), where it was performed by Jolson, *The Jolson Story* ('46), and *Jolson Sings Again* ('49), performed by Jolson's voice for Larry Parks who portrayed Jolson in both films. It was also used in Jane Froman's screen biography, *With a Song in My Heart* ('52).

Variety selected this classic song for its *Hit Parade of a Half-Century*.

See the sheet music cover and hear a midi musical version at http://www.perfessorbill.com/index2.htm or see the sheet music cover at http://voxlibris.claremont.edu/sc/exhibits/cacroonin/cacroonin.html.

Al Jolson also popularized "I'm Goin' South," which was written by Abner Silver and Harry Woods, from *Bombo*. Hear Ray Miller and his orchestra's recording of "I'm Goin' South" at http://www.redhotjazz.com/miller.html.

Charleston

Music: James P. Johnson; Words: Cecil Mack

African American musical comedy had its greatest success since 1921's *Shuffle Along* with *Runnin' Wild* in '23. One number from that show, "Charleston," a gawky, zesty, irresistible dance, dominated social dancing for the next several years. Although a number of dances — shimmy, black bottom, varsity drag — were popular in the '20s, the Charleston is most identified with the era.

"Charleston" combined ragtime syncopation with a swinging bass that ushered in the most distinctive sound of the decade. The dance originated on a small island near Charleston, South Carolina among the African Americans. The dance had been around since right after the turn of the century, but didn't become well known among the general public until the '20s.

Learn more about the Charleston as a dance at http://www.mixedpickles.org/jazzdance.html.

Variety chose "Charleston" for its *Hit Parade of a Half-Century.*

In '24, the most popular recordings of "Charleston" were by pianist Arthur Gibbs and His Gang and Paul Whiteman and his orchestra. Hear Gibbs' recording at http://www.redhotjazz.com/gibbsgang.html; three Whiteman recordings of "Charleston" are available at http://www.redhotjazz.com/pwo.html, two recorded in '25 and one in '55. Ben Selvin and Isham Jones and their orchestras released popular recordings in '25 and '26 respectively.

"Charleston" was featured on the soundtrack of *Margie* ('46) and *Tea for Two* ('50), which starred Doris Day. The song also appeared in *The Great Gatsby* ('74) and *The Cat's Meow* (2001).

Charley, My Boy

Words: Gus Kahn; Music: Ted FioRito

Gus Kahn and Ted FioRito dedicated "Charley, My Boy" to Charley Foy, the famous vaudevillian, who became particularly well known for "The Seven Little Foys."

The Russo-FioRito Oriole Orchestra introduced this *Variety Hit Parade of a Half-Century* song at the Edgewater Beach Hotel in Chicago.

The image conjured up by this song is that of the flapper with few brains singing of her love for Charley and dancing giddily to its upbeat tempo. The lyrics tell us that Charley is a pretty ordinary fellow to everyone but Flo, who is convinced he is an extraordinary beau. Charley thrills her and gives her shivers of joy. She thinks Romeo should take love lessons from Charley. Read the lyrics at http://lyricsplayground.com/alpha/songs/c/charleymyboy.s html.

"Mr. Banjo Eyes," Eddie Cantor, had the most popular recording of "Charley, My Boy," but the International Novelty Orchestra also had a popular version on the market. Hear the California Ramblers' recording of this song at http://www.redhotjazz.com/caramblers.html.

Fascinating Rhythm, The Man I Love *and* Oh, Lady Be Good

Music: George Gershwin; Words: Ira Gershwin

Although George and Ira Gershwin's *Lady, Be Good!* was not the biggest smash of the '24 Broadway season, it may well have been its most important musical. It was in this show that jazz was first used for an entire score. Gershwin had experimented with the style earlier with individual pieces in various shows, but the score for *Lady, Be Good!* broke out of the musical and operetta mold.

FASCINATING RHYTHM

"Fascinating Rhythm," or sometimes called "Fascinatin' Rhythm," has an unusual beat that made it one of *Lady Be Good*'s outstanding hits. In the context of Ira's lyrics, fascinate meant "to bewitch; to enchant; to influence in some wicked manner." This rhythm has the singer "all aquiver." At the end of each workday he finds he hasn't accomplished a thing. He longs to be the man he once was before this "fascinating rhythm" grabbed him and wouldn't let go. Read the lyrics at http://www.rosemaryclooney.com/LyricPages/fascinatingrhythm.html.

It has been suggested that George perfected the rhyth-

mic device that was first heard in Zez Confrey's "Stumbling," but it appeared so novel in Gershwin's skillful hands that one questions his need to borrow ideas.

The brother and sister song-and-dance team of Fred and Adele Astaire originally introduced this number in *Lady, Be Good!* Cliff "Ukulele Ike" Edwards and Sam Lanin, one of the most recorded bandleaders of the decade, released the best-known recordings of "Fascinating Rhythm" in '25. Hear Paul Whiteman's recording of this song at http://www.redhotjazz.com/pwo.html.

"Fascinating Rhythm" was, of course, featured in the film version of *Lady Be Good* ('41) and in *Rhapsody in Blue* ('45), Gershwin's screen biography. It was also performed by Tommy Dorsey and his orchestra in 1943's film version of *Girl Crazy.*

Variety selected "Fascinating Rhythm" as a *Hit Parade of a Half-Century* song.

THE MAN I LOVE

Not many songs had as much of a struggle as "The Man I Love" making it as a hit song. Gershwin wrote it in '23 as the verse for a song he was writing for *Lady Be Good*, but he threw away the chorus and kept the verse. The song had been intended for Adele Astaire to sing in the first act of *Lady, Be Good!.* However, the producer removed it from the show during pre–Broadway tryouts because it slowed the action of the opening act and the audience didn't seem to respond to it. It was next tried unsuccessfully in the original version of *Strike Up the Band* ('27) and again in *Rosalie* ('28). By the time the '30 version of *Strike Up the Band* opened, the song, which had become successful in Britain and on the Continent, finally registered as a hit.

It was first identified with Helen Morgan as one of her specialties and has become one of the most treasured of Gershwin's standards. It is particularly interesting for the contrapuntal accompaniment figure against the blues-influenced tune.

"The Man I Love," which was published in '24, sold only 893 copies in the first two years. Eva Gauthier, accompanied by the composer, is credited with the first official performance of the song in '25. The occasion was a repeat of the famous Aeolian Hall recital of November 4, 1923, this time in Derby, Connecticut. After a couple of years the song seemed to die. When it was resurrected in early '28, it sold 60,133 copies of sheet music and 162,518 copies of various recordings. Marion Harris, Sophie Tucker, Paul Whiteman, and Fred Rich each had hit recordings of "The Man I Love" in '28. But that was only the beginning. It was revived again in the mid–'30s and has remained a standard ever since.

The chorus lyrics sing about a man who will come into the singer's life. She says when he comes she'll do her best to keep him. Ira's bridge lyrics are very cleverly written: "Maybe I shall meet him Sunday, maybe Monday, maybe not; still I'm sure to meet him one day, maybe Tuesday will be my good news day." She hopes they will build a little home where they'll stay. Above all else, she's waiting for the man she loves. Read the lyrics at http://www.musicsonglyrics.com/B/billieholidaylyrics/billieholidaythe manilovelyrics.htm.

Variety selected "The Man I Love" for its *Golden 100 Tin Pan Alley Songs* list. The song became one of the most recorded songs of the pre-rock era.

"The Man I Love" was featured in Gershwin's screen

biography *Rhapsody in Blue* ('45), *Young Man with a Horn* ('50), *Sincerely Yours* ('55), *The Eddy Duchin Story* ('56), *Lady Sings the Blues* ('72), and *New York, New York* ('77).

Read the lyrics at http://www.allthelyrics.com/lyrics/george_gershwin/gershwin_jazz_round_midnight/the_man_i_love-156193-lyric/.

OH, LADY BE GOOD

Walter Catlett introduced the musical's title song. The musical was originally titled *Black-Eyed Susan*, but this song became so popular during pre–Broadway tryouts that the title was changed.

In the title song chorus, the singer is pleading with the "sweet and lovely lady" to be good to him. He begs for pity because he feels all alone in such a big city. Read the lyrics at http://www.oldielyrics.com/lyrics/ella_fitzgerald/oh_lady_be_good.html.

Paul Whiteman and his orchestra had the most popular recording of the song, but Carl Fenton and Cliff Edwards also had popular recordings on the market. Whiteman's recording is available at http://www.redhotjazz.com/pwo.html.

I Love You

Words: Harlan Thompson; Music: Harry Archer

The biggest Broadway hit in '23 was *Little Jesse James.* "I Love You" was the most successful song to come out of any musical during the year, and its great popularity probably lengthened the show's run considerably. Harry Archer's score, played by the Paul Whiteman orchestra in the pit, was not otherwise noteworthy. Although Archer wrote the music for four other Broadway musicals during the decade, none achieved distinction. Introduced by Ann Sands and Jay Velie in the show, "I Love You" is a straightforward declaration of affection.

The chorus begins with "I love you" twice and then the singer confesses that is all he can say. Then he says it again, "the same old words ... in the same old way." The chorus ends with the singer waiting to hear his lover tell him she will be his. Read the lyrics at http://www.risa.co.uk/sla/13/13388.html.

Variety selected "I Love You" for its *Hit Parade of a Half-Century.*

As might be expected since his orchestra was playing in the pit for this musical, Paul Whiteman's orchestra had the most popular recording of the song. Paul Whiteman recordings of this song are available at http://www.redhotjazz.com/pwo.html, one in '23, another in '54. Other successful, but less popular versions, included those by tenor Lewis James and Charles Hart, former tenor of the Shannon Four.

I Wonder What's Become of Sally

Music: Milton Ager; Words: Jack Yellen

Van and Schenck introduced this *Variety Hit Parade of a Half-Century* waltz that is reminiscent of the barbershop quartets of the turn of the century.

The singer wonders where Sally is these days. He says there's no sunshine since she went away. He pleads to anyone who knows where she is to send her back home so he can welcome back "my Sally, that old gal of mine." Read the lyrics at http://lyricsplayground.com/alpha/songs/i/iwonderwhatsbecomeofsally.shtml.

Al Jolson popularized "I Wonder What's Become of Sally" with a very popular recording. Van and Schenck and Ted Lewis also helped popularize the number with successful recordings. Hear Ted Lewis' recording of this song at http://www.redhotjazz.com/tlband.html.

"I Wonder What's Become of Sally?" was used in the movie musical *Night and Day* ('46), which was Cole Porter's screen biography (why a non–Porter song was used is puzzling).

It Ain't Gonna Rain No Mo'

Words & Music: Wendell Hall

Wendell Hall, composer, author, poet, singer, guitarist, and radio, film, and television artist, appropriated this tune from a southern folk song of the 1870s. His recording, in which he accompanied himself on the ukulele, reportedly sold more than 2 million copies. It sold more than 5 million combined record and sheet music copies.

This song has five very simple choruses. All the first chorus says is, "It ain't gonna rain, it ain't gonna snow, it ain't gonna rain no mo'. Come on ev'rybody now, it ain't gonna rain no mo'." All the other lyrics are just as simplistic. Read all five choruses: at http://ingeb.org/songs/itaintgo.html.

Hall, known as the "Red-Headed Music Maker," helped make the ukulele a popular instrument. His phenomenal success with "It Ain't Gonna Rain No Mo'" quickly made him a star on the vaudeville circuit and on radio.

Wendell Hall's classic was chosen for *Variety*'s *Hit Parade of a Half-Century.*

See two sheet music covers at http://digital.library.ucla.edu/apam/.

It Had to Be You

Words: Gus Kahn; Music: Isham Jones

This beautiful ballad was introduced by composer Isham Jones's band, and theirs was the most popular recorded version of the song. Hear Isham Jones and his orchestra's recording of "It Had to Be You" at http://www.redhotjazz.com/ishamjones.html. Marion Harris and Cliff ("Ukulele Ike") Edwards also had very popular versions. Marion Harris' version is available at http://www.redhotjazz.com/marionharris.html. Others by Billy Murray with Aileen Stanley, Paul Whiteman and his orchestra, and Sam Lanin were also popular. It has remained popular through the years with revivals in '30, '41, and '44 by Red Nichols and his Five Pennies, by Artie Shaw and his orchestra (in both '41 and '44), by Helen Forrest and Dick Haymes, by Betty Hutton and by Earl Hines.

The chorus lyrics begin with "It Had to Be You" presented twice. Then the singer tells us he has been wandering around trying to find the person to whom he could be true. Even though others aren't mean, cross or bossy, they won't do because they don't thrill him like she does. It just had to be "wonderful you, it had to be you." Read the lyrics at http://www.ruthetting.com/songs/it-had-to-be-you.asp.

Variety selected "It Had to Be You" for its *Hit Parade of a Half-Century.*

"It Had to Be You" has been featured in several movie musicals including *Nobody's Darling* ('43), *Is Everybody Happy?* ('43), *Show Business* ('44), *Incendiary Blonde* ('45), *Living in a Big Way* ('47) and, of course, Gus Kahn's screen biography, *I'll See You in My Dreams* ('52). Most film buffs will also remember that Harry Connick, Jr. performed "It Had to Be You" in the movie *When Harry Met Sally* ('89). AFI's *100 Years ... 100 Songs* (2004) named "It Had to Be You" the No. 60 greatest song from an American film for its appearance in *When Harry Met Sally*. According to Ruth Etting's website, she performed the song in the '36 film *Melody in May*. The song also appeared in *The Great Gatsby* ('74) and *Eyes Wide Shut* ('99).

Jealous

Music: Jack Little; Words: Tommie Malie and Dick Finch

Composer/pianist/singer Little Jack Little introduced this *Variety Hit Parade of a Half-Century* song. He was a particularly popular radio personality during the decade.

The singer is jealous of the moon, pretty flowers, birds in the trees, and the clock on the shelf because they are close to you. He is even sometimes jealous of himself.

The opening melodic phrase is practically a chromatic scale, not typical popular song fare.

Marion Harris and Ben Selvin and his orchestra had the most popular recordings of "Jealous" in '24. The Andrews Sisters revived it in '41 with moderate success. Marion Harris' recording can be heard at http://www.redhot jazz.com/marionharris.html.

"Jealous" was used in the '52 movie musical *Somebody Loves Me*.

June Night

Words: Cliff Friend; Music: Abel Baer

Variety included "June Night" on its *Hit Parade of a Half-Century*.

Ted Lewis and his band had a popular recording of "June Night" in '24. Hear Ted Lewis' recording of "June Night" at http://www.redhotjazz.com/tlband.html. Fred Waring and his Pennsylvanians also had a successful disk of the song in '24. Hear Waring's recording at http://www.redhotjazz.com/waringspa.html.

The singer just wants "a June night, the moonlight and you." Read the lyrics from a much later Jimmy Dorsey recording at http://www.top40db.net/Lyrics/?SongID=57090&By=Year&Match=.

The song appeared in the movie musical *Somebody Loves Me* ('52).

Last Night on the Back Porch

Words: Lew Brown; Music: Carl Schraubstader

Lew Brown, most usually lyricist for Ray Henderson, wrote the words to this comical song. Winnie Lightner sang it in *George White's Scandals of 1923*.

The lyrics of this *Variety Hit Parade of a Half-Century* selection speak of a lover and his date kissing on the back porch: "last night on the back porch I loved her best of all." It is doubtful anything more risqué was implied. Read the lyrics at http://www.lyricsvault.net/songs/19776.html.

The song was popularized in recordings by Paul Whiteman and by the duo Ernest Hare and Billy Jones. Paul Whiteman's recording of "Last Night on the Back Porch" is available at http://www.redhotjazz.com/pwo.html or you can hear the Original Memphis Five's recording with Billy Jones as vocalist at http://www.redhotjazz.com/om5.html.

George White is primarily remembered for the *Scandals*

revues that he presented from '19 through '39, which rivaled the *Ziegfeld Follies* in popularity. In addition, he produced several nightclub revues and some films, plus wrote lyrics for several songs with composer Cliff Friend.

See eleven sheet music covers of this song at http://digital.library.ucla.edu/apam/.

Linger Awhile

Music: Vincent Rose; Words: Harry Owens

"Linger Awhile" was another million-selling record for Paul Whiteman and his orchestra. It is one of the best examples in all of popular music for economical use of a small number of notes (46).

Rather unusually the chorus lyrics do not begin with the title, but instead set the stage: "the stars shine above you ... they whisper 'I love you.'" When they part, he tells her each hour apart will seem like a day. He has something to tell her so he asks her to "Linger Awhile." Read the lyrics at http://www.lyricscafe.com/b/ball_david/dball07.html.

Whiteman's recording featured the banjo playing of Mike Pingatore, who played with Whiteman for twenty-five years. Hear Whiteman's recording at http://www.red hotjazz.com/pwo.html. Prior to Whiteman's success with "Linger Awhile," it had been introduced by Lew Gold and his Club Wigwam Orchestra. A duet recording by Lewis James and Marcia Freer also helped popularize "Linger Awhile" in '24.

The song was featured in the '30 movie musical *The King of Jazz*, which, of course, featured Paul Whiteman and his orchestra. It was also used in *Give My Regards to Broadway* ('48).

Variety chose "Linger Awhile" for its *Hit Parade of a Half-Century*.

Memory Lane

Words: B.G. DeSylva; Music: Larry Spier and Con Conrad

The collegiate group, Fred Waring and his Pennsylvanians, popularized "Memory Lane" with a very successful recording in '24. Hear Waring's recording of "Memory Lane" at http://www.redhotjazz.com/waringspa.html. Paul Specht and his orchestra also had a recording that helped the song to become known nationwide.

DeSylva's lyrics say, "I am with you wandering through Memory Lane." The singer is reminiscing about the years, the laughter and the tears. Even though the loved one is gone, his love will remain as he strolls Memory Lane with you.

"Memory Lane" was revived in '44 in the Abbott and Costello film *In Society*.

Nobody's Sweetheart

Words: Gus Kahn and Ernie Erdman; Music: Billy Meyers and Elmer Schoebel

Ted Lewis introduced this *Variety Hit Parade of a Half-Century* song in the revue *The Passing Show of 1923*.

It was revived in a '31 recording, backed by "Tiger Rag," in the first million-selling record by a vocal quartet, by the Mills Brothers. It was also an important recording for the Benny Goodman Trio in '35. Isham Jones' recording of this song is available at http://www.redhotjazz.com/ishamjones.html.

The song's lyrics tell about a sweet hometown girl who has changed into a woman of the world with "fancy hose, silken gown ... painted lips, painted eyes..." Read the lyrics at http://www.stlyrics.com/lyrics/illseeyouinmydreams/ nobodyssweetheart.htm.

The song was used in the '31 movie musical *The Cuban Love Song*, in *Hit Parade of 1943*, in *Stormy Weather* ('43), in *Atlantic City* ('44), and in Gus Kahn's screen biography *I'll See You in My Dreams* ('52).

Rhapsody in Blue
Music: George Gershwin

George Gershwin's significant serious jazz composition "Rhapsody in Blue" was almost not written. Paul Whiteman had been planning a serious concert hall performance devoted exclusively to American popular music. Whiteman wanted to prove that jazz was as worthy as any other type of music. He asked Gershwin to write a new work for him in a jazz idiom. Gershwin, burdened by other projects, forgot all about his promise to Whiteman until he happened to read a notice in the newspaper concerning the forthcoming concert. With just a few months to go, Gershwin began what became a jazz piano concerto that moved jazz from the speakeasy to the world of concert music. "Rhapsody..." made Gershwin wealthy and gained him the world's admiration. The original Paul Whiteman orchestra recording featuring the composer at the keyboard was a huge success, especially for a serious music composition. The same recording was re-released in '27 and sold well again. "Rhapsody in Blue" became the Whiteman orchestra's theme song.

The rhapsody is scored for solo piano and symphony orchestra. A concerto is for a solo instrument pitted against the symphony orchestra, but a concerto requires a form that would have bound Gershwin too much. A rhapsody is a free-form piece, so it did not have to conform to any particular structure requirements.

The opening clarinet portamento is magnetic and sets the tone. Two principal melodies are developed during the composition.

"Rhapsody in Blue" was selected by *Variety* for its *Hit Parade of a Half-Century*. The '27 recording of "Rhapsody..." by George Gershwin with Paul Whiteman's orchestra was inducted into the Grammy Hall of Fame in '74.

Paul Whiteman and his orchestra, with George Gershwin at the piano, performed "Rhapsody in Blue" in *King of Jazz* ('30). It was also used in *The Great Ziegfeld* ('36), in *Rhapsody in Blue* ('45), Gershwin's film biography, in *Sincerely Yours* ('55) and in Disney's *Fantasia 2000*. According to http://www.imdb.com/, the song also appeared in *Lisa* (2001).

Modern audiences will recognize part of "Rhapsody in Blue" as the commercial theme for United Airlines.

Hear Paul Whiteman and George Gershwin's '24 recording of "Rhapsody in Blue" at http://www.edisonnj. org/menlopark/vintage/victor.asp (it's in two parts, each over four and a half minutes long). Hear Whiteman's recording of this song in six different recordings, one with Gershwin at the piano at http://www.redhotjazz.com/ pwo.html.

Serenade
Words: Dorothy Donnelly; Music: Sigmund Romberg

Sigmund Romberg's score for *The Student Prince in Heidelberg* was his finest achievement. The producers, the Shubert brothers, were skeptical about the operatic score, apprehensive about the show's unhappy ending, and aghast that Romberg demanded a large male chorus rather than a chorus line of feminine lovelies. They almost threw Romberg and his music out of the show. But Romberg prevailed and made the Shuberts a handsome profit through the original 608 performances and nine touring productions. Dorothy Donnelly was lyricist for this masterpiece, which outranks Romberg's adaptation from Franz Schubert that became *Blossom Time* and seriously challenges *The Desert Song*, his '26 hit, for the honor of being his most successful Broadway work.

The Student Prince in Heidelberg opens in the palace of the mythical kingdom of Karlsberg in 1860. The heir to the throne, Prince Karl Franz, is bored with his royal life. He and his tutor, Dr. Engel, plan to visit the German University town of Heidelberg. Prince Karl meets Kathie, the lovely young daughter of an innkeeper. Before long, Kathie and the Prince fall in love. One beautiful evening the Prince is inspired to sing a serenade under her window ("Serenade"). However, their love is doomed when news arrives that the king is dead, Prince Karl must return home to ascend the throne and marry Princess Margaret. Once back in Karlsberg, the new king cannot forget Kathie or Heidelberg. He returns to Heidelberg where he meets Kathie again, but they realize a permanent reunion is impossible. They say goodbye for a last time, with a pledge to keep their memories of each other alive as long as they live. Read the lyrics at http://www.lyricsandsongs.com/ song/572107.html.

Prince Karl's serenade to Kathie begins, "Overhead the moon is beaming." "Serenade" was almost cut from the score by the Shuberts, but through Romberg's persistence it remained and went on to become one of the score's major successes. It is a tenor showpiece, with a range of almost two octaves climaxing on a high A flat as the singer pledges his eternal love.

The film version of *The Student Prince* was released in '54.

"Serenade" was a *Variety Hit Parade of a Half-Century* selection.

Other famous songs from the musical's score include "Golden Days," "Drinking Song," and "Deep in My Heart, Dear."

Franklyn Baur popularized "Deep in My Heart, Dear" in '24 with a successful recording. The song appeared in the '54 film version of *The Student Prince*.

Sleep
Words & Music: Earl Lebieg

Fred Waring's Pennsylvanians' closing theme song, "Sleep," was a very successful recording for the group in '24. Hear Waring's recording of "Sleep" at http://www. redhotjazz.com/waringspa.html. Ben Selvin and his orchestra also helped popularize the song.

Waring and his band and later a chorus of singers, called the Pennsylvanians, became famous on radio on various shows in the '20s. They later had a popular television series. Choral singing had most often been associated with church, but Waring's group had wide appeal singing secular songs.

Waring's closing theme was "Sleep," although they called it "Sleep, Sleep, Sleep."

The song's writer is listed as Earl Lebieg, but the

writers were really Earl Burtnett and Adam Geibel. They used Burtnett's first name with Geibel spelled backwards for their pseudonym.

Benny Carter and Les Paul revived the song again in '40 and in '53 respectively.

The sheet music cover and musical score are available at http://levysheetmusic.mse.jhu.edu/browse.html. Read the lyrics at http://ntl.matrix.com.br/pfilho/html/lyrics/s/sleep.txt.

Somebody Loves Me

Words: B.G. DeSylva & Ballard MacDonald; Music: George Gershwin

Winnie Lightner introduced George Gershwin's third big hit of '24 ("Rhapsody in Blue" and "Fascinating Rhythm" are the others) in *George White's Scandals of 1924*. Rich in jazz age harmonies, this cozy, intimate song became identified with Blossom Seeley because of her frequent outstanding performances of the song.

The slow, legato ballad's chorus begins with the statement "Somebody loves me" but asks, "I wonder who she can be?" It ends by suggesting that the lover may be you. Read the lyrics at http://www.allthelyrics.com/lyrics/george_gershwin/gershwin_songbooks_paradise/somebody_loves_me-156176-lyric/.

Once again, Paul Whiteman's orchestra had the most popular recorded version, with other popular releases by Ray Miller and Marion Harris. Hear Paul Whiteman's recording of "Somebody Loves Me" at http://www.redhotjazz.com/pwo.html or hear Ms. Harris' version at http://www.redhotjazz.com/marionharris.html.

Variety selected this Gershwin classic for its *Hit Parade of a Half-Century* and for its *Golden 100 Tin Pan Alley Songs* list.

"Somebody Loves Me" was used in several movie musicals including *Broadway Rhythm* ('44), *Rhapsody in Blue* ('45), *Lullaby of Broadway* ('51), *Somebody Loves Me* ('52), a film based on the lives of Blossom Seeley and her husband Benny Fields, and *Pete Kelly's Blues* ('55). The song also appeared in the non-musical film *The Cat's Meow* (2001).

Some sources also credit Ira Gershwin, George's brother, as one of the lyricists, but the sheet music only lists B. G. DeSylva and Ballard MacDonald.

Somebody Stole My Gal

Words & Music: Leo Wood

Leo Wood wrote "Somebody Stole My Gal" in '18, but it didn't become popular until Ted Weems and his orchestra's '24 recording became a big hit. Hear Ted Weems' recording at http://www.redhotjazz.com/weems.html. Ted Lewis revived the song successfully in '31 and Johnnie Ray revived it again in '53. You can hear Ted Lewis' version at http://www.redhotjazz.com/tlband.html.

Since the song was copyrighted in '18, the familiar chorus lyrics follow: *Somebody stole my gal, Somebody stole my pal, / Somebody came and took her away / She didn't even say she was leavin', / The kisses I loved so He's getting now I know / And Gee! I know that she would come to me / If she could see Her broken hearted lonesome pal / Somebody stole my gal.*

The Original Memphis Five's version of "Somebody Stole My Gal" was used on the soundtrack of *The Aviator* (2005).

See the sheet music cover and hear a midi musical version at http://www.perfessorbill.com/covers/ssmgal.htm.

Spain

Words: Gus Kahn; Music: Isham Jones

"Spain" was introduced and popularized by composer Isham Jones and his band in '24. However, Paul Whiteman and his orchestra also had a recording of the song that achieved a lot of support from the public.

Gus Kahn's lyrics compare Spain to a fair maiden. The singer and his lover are apart, but she reminds him of a "lover's refrain, soft as the pattering rain, singing of beautiful Spain."

What'll I Do?

Words & Music: Irving Berlin

In late '23, Irving Berlin attended a birthday party for Donald Ogden Stewart. During the evening, he went to the piano and played the first part of a song he was working on called "What'll I Do?" He played what he had written over and over until he had finished it that evening. The song, telling of a profound loneliness because his love is far away, and which no amount of partying and drinking could alleviate. Read the lyrics at http://www.oldielyrics.com/lyrics/irving_berlin/whatll_i_do.html. Subsequently it became an important hit, selling more than a million copies of sheet music and a million records.

Since Berlin wrote the song in '23, it must not be directly related to his falling in love with Ellin MacKay in '24, even though the lyrics seem to perfectly fit. Ellin's father did every thing he could to break up the romance. It was at this time of frustration and hurt that Berlin's beautiful love songs "What'll I Do?" and "All Alone" (see '25) seem particularly appropriate; however, Berlin would never admit they were in the least autobiographical.

Grace Moore and John Steel introduced Irving Berlin's "What'll I Do?" during the run of *The New Music Box Revue*.

This Berlin love song was selected for *Variety's Hit Parade of a Half-Century* representing '24.

As usual, it seems, Paul Whiteman's orchestra had the most popular recorded version, but there were several others competing for that honor, including a duet version by Henry Burr and Marcia Freer, Lewis James, Vincent Lopez and his orchestra, Carl Fenton and his orchestra, and singer Irving Kaufman. Hear Paul Whiteman's recording of "What'll I Do?" at http://www.redhotjazz.com/pwo.html. Nat "King" Cole and Frank Sinatra revived "What'll I Do?" in '48. The song was also used in *Westward Passage* ('32) and *Alexander's Ragtime Band* ('38). Danny Thomas performed it in the '48 movie musical *Big City*. The film *The Great Gatsby* ('74), which starred Robert Redford and Mia Farrow, used several authentic songs from the twenties on its soundtrack. "What'll I Do?" was prominently featured several times during the film. "What'll I Do?" also appeared in *Radioland Murders* ('94) and *The Kid Stays in the Picture* (2002).

Linda Ronstadt has recorded several albums of standards with Nelson Riddle and his orchestra. The first of those LPs was titled "What'll I Do?" and, of course, the song was one of the album's key selections.

1925

Alabamy Bound

Words: B.G. DeSylva & Bud Green; Music: Ray Henderson

Al Jolson introduced "Alabamy Bound," before Eddie Cantor interpolated it into the musical *Kid Boots* after it opened in New York City. Only the interpolation of "Alabamy Bound" and the extraordinary "Dinah" kept *Kid Boots* from closing. "Alabamy Bound" reportedly sold more than a million copies of sheet music.

Jolson seemed to specialize in songs with a southern flavor; this bright march-type ditty is a good example. The singer is going to Alabama on a train, the twenties' ultimate means of fast, safe, and luxurious transportation. Several songs have been inspired by the railroads, and "Alabamy Bound" is an excellent example of people's fascination with traveling by rail.

Vaudeville and Broadway singer/dancer Blossom Seeley had the most popular recording of "Alabamy Bound." Isham Jones and his orchestra also had a popular version. The Mulcays revived it in '54 with a charted recording. Hear Paul Whiteman's recording of this song at http://www.redhotjazz.com/pwo.html.

The lyrics begin with a goodbye to the blues because he is going back home to Alabama (Alabamy). One of the cute phrases is when he says there are "no heebie jeebies hanging round," meaning he doesn't have the jitters; there's no feeling of uneasiness or nervousness. Access the sheet music cover, the lyrics and listen to a midi musical version at http://www.perfessorbill.com/index1.html.

"Alabamy Bound" was a *Variety Hit Parade of a Half-Century* selection.

"Alabamy Bound" has been featured in several movie musicals including *The Great American Broadcast* ('41), *Babes on Broadway* ('42), which starred Judy Garland and Mickey Rooney, *Broadway* ('42), *Show Business* ('44), which starred Eddie Cantor, and *With a Song in My Heart* ('52), which starred Susan Hayward as Jane Froman.

All Alone

Words & Music: Irving Berlin

Once again Irving Berlin composed a song that seems to fit his falling in love with Ellin MacKay, the Comstock Lode heiress. Ellin's father did every thing he could to break up the romance. Once they married, against his will, her father disinherited her for marrying a Jew. It was during his often rocky, frustrating romancing of Ellin that Berlin's "All Alone" seems to fit so precisely, even though it was written earlier.

Grace Moore and Oscar Shaw introduced "All Alone" in the *Music Box Revue of 1924*. Ms. Moore sat at one end of the stage under a spotlight, singing into a telephone, while Mr. Shaw sat at the other end, doing the same.

Radio was now spreading songs to a wider audience than sheet music and live performances could ever hope to reach. A prime example was John McCormack's singing "All Alone" in '24 over a small network of radio stations that reached eight million listeners in one performance while only a thousand or so had heard the song in the *Music Box Revue*. McCormack's radio performance increased the demand for the recording of "All Alone," which sold 250,000 copies in a month. The song eventually sold another million copies in various recordings, a million in sheet music, and 160,000 in player-piano rolls.

The first verse lyrics begin by comparing the loved one to a melody that lingers and haunts us all the time. The more famous chorus is filled with lonesome feelings. The singer is waiting by the telephone for a call that doesn't come. He is alone every evening "wond'ring where you are and how you are and if you are all alone too." Read the lyrics at http://www.oldielyrics.com/lyrics/irving_berlin/all_alone.html.

This Berlin love song was selected for *Variety's Hit Parade of a Half-Century* representing '24.

Three almost equally popular recordings, by Al Jolson, John McCormack and Paul Whiteman and his orchestra helped popularize this Berlin ballad in '25. Hear Paul Whiteman's recording of "All Alone" at http://www.redhotjazz.com/pwo.html. Other recordings that were popular included those by Cliff "Ukulele Ike" Edwards, Abe Lyman, Ben Selvin and his orchestra and Lewis James.

"All Alone" was used in the movie musical *Alexander's Ragtime Band* ('38). The song also appeared in *The Great Gatsby* ('74).

Cecilia

Words: Herman Ruby; Music: Dave Dreyer

"Whispering" Jack Smith, a singer elevated to stardom by his radio appearances, popularized "Cecilia" during '25.

The singer asks Cecilia several questions, like "Does your Mother know you're out?," then asks her for a little kiss and finally asks if she will be his girl. Read the lyrics at http://www.heptune.com/lyrics/cecilia.html.

Variety chose "Cecilia" for its *Hit Parade of a Half-Century*.

"Whispering" Jack Smith's recorded version of "Cecilia" was the most popular one, but Johnny Hamp and his orchestra, with vocals by Charles Buckwalter, Frank Master, and Elwood Groff, also had a successful version. It was Hamp's first really successful recording. Hear Hamp's recording of "Cecilia" at http://www.redhotjazz.com/jhks.html. Dick Jurgens and his orchestra with Ronnie Kemper doing the vocal revived the song in '40.

Collegiate

Words & Music: Moe Jaffe & Nat Bonx

In the '20s, people had an extraordinary curiosity about things collegiate — not the life of the classroom, but the extracurricular activities that took place on the sports fields, in fraternity houses, and at dances. There were college musicals, collegiate dance bands, and songs inspired by college life. This preoccupation with campus life helped "Collegiate" become a hit song.

The stereotypical male college student of the '20s wore a raccoon-skin coat, carried a ukulele under one arm, a college pennant in the other hand, had a hip-flask presumably filled with liquor in his back pocket, drove a Stutz Bearcat and danced the Charleston endlessly. This caricature is actually more accurate for the last half of the decade, but it does seem appropriate for this song.

After graduating from high school, Moe Jaffe, the song's co-writer, worked his way through the University of Pennsylvania's Wharton School and Law School by playing piano and leading a campus dance band called Jaffe's Collegians.

The band's theme song, "Collegiate," turned Jaffe from law student toward Tin Pan Alley. Written by Moe and fellow law student Nat Bonx, "Collegiate" was well known on the Penn campus when Fred Waring, a Penn State grad, brought his Pennsylvanians to play at a Penn campus dance. Waring received so many requests for "Collegiate" that he first assumed it was a published song. When he learned that the writers were on campus, introductions were made and in the early Spring of '25, Waring's Pennsylvanians recorded "Collegiate" at the Victor studios in Camden, New Jersey. If the recording had not become a hit, it would still have historical significance as the first electronic recording of a song; that is, the first to use electronic microphones rather than acoustical recording horns.

Fred Waring and his "collegiate" outfit interpolated the song into the revue *Gay Paree* in '26.

Within the year, Waring's recording helped make "Collegiate" a big hit around the country, selling over one million copies of sheet music. Over the years, the song sold over five million disks and was interpolated into several movies.

"Collegiate" was used in the '29 movie musical *The Time, the Place and the Girl*, the Marx Brothers farce *Animal Crackers* ('30) and *Margie* ('46).

It was selected by *Variety* for its *Hit Parade of a Half-Century*.

Waring's Collegians, later called the Pennsylvanians, with the band members singing, also had the most popular recording of "Collegiate," but Carl Fenton and his orchestra also had a successful version on the market. Hear Waring's recording at http://www.redhotjazz.com/waringspa.html.

The Waring band singing the contraction "C'llegiate, c'llegiate" sounds like a bunch of guys just singing for fun. There are some typical mid-'20s college fashions mentioned in the lyrics, like baggy trousers and raggy looking clothes and they say they never wear garters or red hot flannels. They very seldom get in a hurry and never worry. The song ends with a "Rah! Rah! Rah!" cheer.

Dinah (see 1932)

Everybody Loves My Baby

Words & Music: Jack Palmer & Spencer Williams

The first recording of this '24 *Variety Hit Parade of a Half-Century* song featured Louis Armstrong on trumpet with Clarence Williams' Blue Five band. "Everybody Loves My Baby (But My Baby Don't Love Nobody but Me)" is not much more than a riff repeated three times. A riff is an ostinato phrase usually with instrumental improvisation.

As important as jazz was during the decade, not many authentic jazz recordings are listed among the most popular versions of the song. Remember, the word "jazz" had come to include all of popular music during the era.

The chorus lyrics begin with the title phrase then continues with "But my baby don't love nobody but me." The three "A" phrases in the AABA form are lyrically practically identical with only a word or two different. Read the lyrics at http://www.elyricsworld.com/go/d/Doris-Day-lyrics/Everybody-Loves-My-Baby-lyrics.html.

Aileen Stanley's recording was the most popular one in

'24, but Clarence Williams' version was also well received. Clarence Williams' recording of this song with Eva Taylor's vocals is available at http://www.redhotjazz.com/williamsb5.html.

"Everybody Loves My Baby" was used in Ruth Etting's screen biography, *Love Me or Leave Me* ('55). It also appeared in the Broadway musical *Black and Blue* ('89).

If You Knew Susie

Words & Music: B.G. DeSylva

Al Jolson introduced this classic song in the musical *Big Boy*, then decided it was not his style, so he encouraged Eddie Cantor to use it. Cantor first performed it at a New York City benefit concert, where it was a smash hit, and it became one of his specialty numbers for the rest of his career.

"If You Knew Susie (Like I Know Susie)," along with "Five Foot Two..." is often used thematically in films to suggest a flapper of the '20s.

In the chorus lyrics we are told that if we knew this girl, Susie, like the singer knows her, we would say "Oh! What a girl!" Furthermore, there aren't any other girls "so classy as this fair lassie." Read the lyrics at http://www.ceder.net/recorddb/viewsingle.php4?RecordId=2499.

Cantor's recording of "If You Knew Susie" was the most popular version, but a solo version by Cliff Edwards, a duet version by Ernest Hare and Billy Jones and Jack Shilkret and his orchestra, with Billy Murray doing the vocal, also had good success.

The sheet music only credits DeSylva as the writer, but other sources, like David Ewen in *American Popular Songs* and Stanley Green in *Encyclopedia of the Musical Theater*, also credit Joseph Meyer as either co-writer or composer.

The sheet music cover claims the song was "the Hit of Five Productions," including Jolson performing it in *Big Boy*, Cantor showcasing it in *Kid Boots*, Willie Howard singing it in *Sky High*, Jack Rose interpolating it into *The Passing Show* and Jay C. Flippen using it in *June Days*.

Variety selected "If You Knew Susie" for its *Hit Parade of a Half-Century*.

"If You Knew Susie" was used in the following movie musicals: *The Great Ziegfeld* ('36), where it was performed by Buddy Doyle imitating Eddie Cantor, *Anchors Aweigh* ('45), where it was performed by Gene Kelly and Frank Sinatra, *If You Knew Susie* ('48), where Cantor performed it, and *The Eddie Cantor Story* ('53), where it was performed by Keefe Brasselle as Cantor.

I'll See You in My Dreams

Words: Gus Kahn; Music: Isham Jones

This *Variety Hit Parade of a Half-Century* classic and *Golden 100 Tin Pan Alley Song*, introduced by Isham Jones and his orchestra, furnished the title for a '51 movie musical based on the life and songs of lyricist Gus Kahn. In addition to that movie musical, the song was also used in *Pardon My Rhythm* ('44), *Follow the Boys* ('44) and *Margie* ('46). The song also appeared in *Stardust Memories* ('80), *Sweet and Low Down* ('99) and was used as theme music for a 2003 film titled *I'll See You in My Dreams*.

This standard makes excellent use of a minimum of notes: 50. Most really good melodies can stand alone — that is, they don't rely on harmony or rhythm for their interest. "I'll See You in My Dreams" is such a melody. It is strong enough to sound good *a cappella*.

Isham Jones conducting Ray Miller's Orchestra had the

most successful recording of "I'll See You in My Dreams," but the public had others to choose from including those by Marion Harris, by Paul Whiteman, by Ford and Glenn and by Lewis James. Hear Isham Jones' recording of this song at http://www.redhotjazz.com/ishamjones.html. Frank Bessinger was the vocalist on Jones' recording. Hear Marion Harris' recording at http://www.redhotjazz.com/marionharris.html.

The famous lyrics begin with "I'll see you in my dreams, hold you in my dreams." Even though someone else took her away, the singer can feel her charms. Her lips and eyes will light his way tonight because "I'll see you in my dreams." Read the lyrics at http://www.allthelyrics.com/lyrics/ill_see_you_in_my_dreams_soundtrack/.

Indian Love Call *and* Rose Marie

Words: Otto Harbach and Oscar Hammerstein II; Music: Rudolf Friml

Rudolf Friml's operetta *Rose Marie* had the longest Broadway run of any of Friml's musicals, 557 performances. Set in the Canadian Rockies, the show was a resounding success, undoubtedly because of the tuneful score and perhaps because of its North American, rather than European, setting. It was not only the biggest hit of the season but the biggest grossing musical until *Oklahoma!* broke the record nearly twenty years later.

INDIAN LOVE CALL

The show's most lasting song is unquestionably "Indian Love Call," originally published as "The Call," which was introduced by Mary Ellis and Dennis King. However, it is most closely identified with Jeanette MacDonald and Nelson Eddy, who starred in the second film version of *Rose Marie* in '36. Reportedly, their duet recording was the first musical show tune to top the million mark. Another film version of *Rose Marie* was released in '54; it starred Ann Blyth and Howard Keel.

The distinctive call in the melody has become an operetta cliché. Unfortunately, the song was performed so often through the years, many times by singers who put on operatic airs, that it has become undeservedly comical. In that vein, the song appeared in the '99 film comedy *Dudley Do-Right*.

Variety chose "Indian Love Call" for its *Hit Parade of a Half-Century* representing '24 and '29. This song was nominated for the American Film Institute's list of greatest songs ever from an American film, but was not on the final list. It was nominated for its appearance in the '36 film version of the musical.

Paul Whiteman and Leo Reisman and their orchestras popularized "Indian Love Call" in recordings in '25. Paul Whiteman's recording of "Indian Love Call" is available at http://www.redhotjazz.com/pwo.html. Jeanette MacDonald and Nelson Eddy's version from their movie version did very well when the recording was released in '37. Artie Shaw and his orchestra's first big hit recording was "Indian Love Call" backed by "Begin the Beguine" in '38. "Indian Love Call" may have been intended for the "A" side of the disk, but "Begin the Beguine" proved to deserve the honor. Country singer Slim Whitman had considerable success with his version in '52. Read the lyrics at http://www.lyricsvault.net/songs/15017.html.

See the sheet music cover and musical score at http://lcweb2.loc.gov/cocoon/ihas/loc.natlib.ihas.100006092/.

ROSE MARIE

Like "Indian Love Call," the title song was a hit song from *Rose Marie*. It was introduced by Dennis King and Arthur Deagon in the original show and sung by Nelson Eddy in the '36 film version.

This expressive operetta aria sings of the love the Canadian fur trapper Jim Kenyon and the Mountie Sergeant Malone both have for Rose Marie la Flamme. Particularly potent is the closing: "Of all the queens that ever lived, I'd choose you to rule me, my Rose Marie." Read the lyrics at http://homepage.ntlworld.com/gary.hart/lyricsw/whitman.html.

Paul Whiteman and his orchestra, the famous Irish tenor John McCormack, organ soloist Jesse Crawford, and Lambert Murphy a popular concert tenor released recordings of "Rose Marie" that helped popularize the song. Country singer Slim Whitman had considerable success with his version in the mid–'50s. Hear Paul Whiteman's recording of this song at http://www.redhotjazz.com/pwo.html.

Variety also included "Rose-Marie" in its *Hit Parade of a Half-Century.*

Manhattan

Words: Lorenz Hart; Music: Richard Rodgers

In the spring of '25, the junior members of the Theatre Guild staged a revue at the Garrick Theater entitled *The Garrick Gaieties.* The revue was a skillful production, even though it was small-scaled. The most lasting part of the evening proved to be the songs, seven of which were written by a new songwriting team, Richard Rodgers and Lorenz Hart.

Lyricist Lorenz "Larry" Hart and composer Richard Rodgers first became known to the general public through the hit song "Manhattan" in the first edition of the *Gaieties* and through "Mountain Greenery" in the second edition.

Hart and Rodgers were opposites in personality, temperament, outlook, living and working habits, but their collaboration carried them to the pinnacle of Broadway success.

The song "Manhattan" is a tribute to New York City. The lyrics mention several major landmarks: the zoo, Delancey Street, the subway, Mott Street, Greenwich Village, Coney Island, Central Park, Fifth Avenue, plus several others. Read the lyrics at http://www.lorenzhart.org/manhattansng.htm.

Ben Selvin and his orchestra, with the Knickerbockers, and Paul Whiteman and his orchestra both had popular recorded versions of "Manhattan." Whiteman's recording of his song is available at http://www.redhotjazz.com/pwo.html.

The song has been used in several movie musicals: Mickey Rooney performed it in the rather fictitious movie biography of Rodgers and Hart, *Words and Music,* in '48, Tony Martin crooned it in *Two Tickets to Broadway* in '51, it was featured in *The Eddy Duchin Story* ('56) and in *Beau James* ('57). The song also appeared in the non-musical film *The Rat Race* ('60) and *Mighty Aphrodite* ('95).

The '48 film *Words and Music* was based on Rodgers and Hart's partnership.

Ben Selvin and his orchestra popularized another Rodgers and Hart song from *The Garrick Gaieties,* "Sentimental Me," which was revived again in '50 into a No.

1 hit by the Ames Brothers. Read the lyrics at http://www.lorenzhart.org/sentiment.htm.

Montmartre Rose

Words & Music: Tommy Lyman & C.E. Wheeler

Variety included "Montmartre Rose" in its *Hit Parade of a Half-Century* representing '25.

By the end of the 19th century, the section of Paris known as Montmartre became the center of the artistic bohemian life style in the city. The name comes from "Mont des Martyrs" (a bishop, a priest and an archdeacon were all decapitated there around the year 250). Many artists, from Berlioz to Picasso, lived, worked, and played in Montmartre.

Other than the songwriters, we know no specifics about this song.

The song is not listed in *Pop Memories* or *A Century of Pop Music* as being popular enough in any recordings to be included.

Moonlight and Roses

Words & Music: Ben Black & Neil Moret

Tunesmiths of the '20s now and then borrowed from the classics, as in "Avalon" ('20, borrowed from Puccini's "E lucevan le stelle") and "Song of Love" ('21, borrowed from Schubert's "Unfinished Symphony"). Another prime example of tune lifting was Harry Carroll's "I'm Always Chasing Rainbows" ('18, which used the middle section of Chopin's "Fantaisie Impromptu" for its melody).

"Moonlight and Roses" came from an organ piece by Edwin H. Lemare ("Andantino in D-flat," 1892). Ben Black and Neil Moret, a pseudonym for Charles N. Daniels, were responsible for taking Lemare's music and adapting it into a popular song.

The lyrics to this sentimental ballad claim that "Moonlight and roses bring wonderful memories of you." Read the lyrics at http://www.lyricsdir.com/suzy-bogguss-moonlight-and-roses-lyrics.html.

Variety chose this song for its *Hit Parade of a Half-Century.*

Irish tenor John McCormack and Ray Miller and his orchestra had successful recordings of "Moonlight and Roses" in '25, and the Three Suns revived it with moderate success in '54. Vic Damone revived it again in '65. Hear Ray Miller's Orchestra's recording of this song at http://www.redhotjazz.com/miller.html.

"Moonlight and Roses" was used in the following movie musicals: *Tin-Pan-Alley* ('40), and *Mr. Big* ('43).

O, Katharina!

Words: Fritz Lohner & L. Wolfe Gilbert; Music: Richard Fall

A revue conceived in Russia, revived in Paris, and brought to Broadway in '22 proved to be a sensation. It was *Chauve Souris*. "O, Katharina!" came from the show. L. Wolfe Gilbert wrote English lyrics to replace the original German.

"O, Katharina!," a *Variety Hit Parade of a Half-Century* song, is as timely today as it was in the '20s. It addresses the diet-conscious American woman who is told by her lover if she wants to keep his love, she must lose weight.

Clarinetist/singer/bandleader Ted Lewis had a very popular recorded version in '25. Hear Ted Lewis' recording of this song at http://www.redhotjazz.com/tlband.html.

Other versions on the market included those by Vincent Lopez and his orchestra and by Carl Fenton and his orchestra.

Oh, How I Miss You Tonight

Words: Mark Fisher & Benny Davis; Music: Joe Burke

Joe Burke had been an arranger in Tin Pan Alley before he became a composer. He waited ten years for his break, which came in '25, when he teamed with Mark Fisher and Benny Davis to write the dreamy waltz "Oh, How I Miss You Tonight." Benny Davis introduced the song in vaudeville.

In the chorus lyrics, the singer misses his girlfriend when evening comes and whenever they are apart. He says he'd "rather be lonely, and wait for you only." Read the lyrics at http://lyrics.duble.com/lyrics/P/perry-como-lyrics/perry-como-oh-how-i-miss-you-tonight-lyrics.htm.

This song was selected by *Variety* for its *Hit Parade of a Half-Century.*

Ben Selvin's orchestra had a very popular recorded version, while the Benson Orchestra of Chicago, Lewis James, and Irving Kaufman also had successful recordings of the song. Hear the Benson Orchestra of Chicago's recording of this song at http://www.redhotjazz.com/benson.html.

Another song from *Chauve Souris*, "I Miss My Swiss (My Swiss Miss Misses Me)" by Abel Baer and L. Wolfe Gilbert, was popularized by Ernest Hare and Billy Jones in a '25 recording. Hear Paul Whiteman's recording of this song at http://www.redhotjazz.com/pwo.html.

The Prisoner's Song

Words & Music: Guy Massey

Vernon Dalhart's recording of "The Prisoner's Song" became the largest-selling Victor record of the pre-electric era. Estimates run as high as 7 million disks sold. His recording of "The Prisoner's Song" was inducted into the Grammy Hall of Fame in '98.

After receiving formal music training, Dalhart went to New York City to sing light opera, but after hearing Henry Whittier's recording of "The Wreck of the Old 97" he decided that his best chance of making money was in hillbilly music. He recorded "Wreck of the Old 97" for Edison Records and then for Victor, coupled with "The Prisoner's Song." Dalhart recorded for 30 or more companies and recorded "The Prisoner's Song" for at least 28 labels using 70 names for an estimated total of 25 million records sold.

Hearing the Dalhart recording today makes us wonder how it could possibly have sold such a huge number of records because it sounds corny and shallow. Part of the sound can be attributed to the early recording equipment, but not all of it. Evidently enough early hillbilly music fans and others found it worthy to make it one of the most successful recordings of the early days of the recording industry. It was most popular in the last few months of '25 and into the first part of '26. Hear Dalhart's recording at http://www.lib.unc.edu/mss/sfcl/hillbilly/HTML/Sounds/Dalhart_19427b.htm.

According to Novie Massey, the wife of Robert Massey, Guy's brother, Robert wrote "The Prisoner's Song." She said she was with the brothers when her husband sang it and Guy wrote it down. Guy took it to New York and copyrighted it in his own name. Guy then convinced his cousin, Vernon Dalhart, to record it, and it became a huge hit. In his will, Guy willed the song back to Robert, but he never admitted Robert wrote it.

"The Prisoner's Song" was selected for inclusion in *Variety's* *Hit Parade of a Half-Century*.

There are five verses to this song. They seem similar to the folk song "Lonesome Valley" in several instances. The singer wishes for someone to love him and "someone to live with 'cause I'm tired of livin' alone." In the next verse, the singer asks his girl to meet him tonight so he can tell her a sad story. The next verse reveals that he is going to jail. The fourth verse doesn't seem to fit the others. It talks about him owning a ship that he would gladly sell to ease his darling's suffering. In the last verse, he wishes he "had the wings of an angel" so he could fly over the prison walls to his darling's arms. Read the lyrics at http://www.bobdylanroots.com/prisoner.html.

Remember

Words & Music: Irving Berlin

The love affair of Irving Berlin and Ellin MacKay produced some of the most touchingly sentimental ballads that have ever been written. "Remember" is a prime example. Clarence Mackay was adamant that Irving Berlin, a Jewish songwriter, was an unsuitable match for his daughter, so he bribed her with a European tour in hopes she would forget about this tunesmith. Her absence didn't cause Berlin to forget her, as a matter of fact, he kept thinking about her so much he expressed his anxiety over their separation by writing the self-pitying lament "Remember." It seems, according to the song's lyrics, that Berlin is afraid Ellin has forgotten to remember. Although Berlin denied the song was autobiographical, it certainly seems to fit the circumstances. Read the lyrics at http://www.oldielyrics.com/lyrics/irving_berlin/you_forgot_to_remember.html.

Originally copyrighted under the title "You Forgot to Remember," it was introduced in vaudeville by Gladys Clark and Henry Bergman and became a song that Ruth Etting performed regularly. Isham Jones and his orchestra had the most popular recording of "Remember," but other popular versions by Jean Goldkette and his orchestra and Cliff Edwards internationally known as "Ukulele Ike," were on the market. Hear Isham Jones' recording of "Remember" at http://www.redhotjazz.com/ishamjones.html or hear Cliff Edwards' version at http://www.redhotjazz.com/ike.html.

"Remember" was used in *Alexander's Ragtime Band* ('38), *So This is Love* ('53), and *There's No Business Like Show Business* ('54).

Variety included "Remember" in its *Hit Parade of a Half-Century* representing '26.

Song of the Vagabonds

Words: Brian Hooker; Music: Rudolf Friml

Rudolf Friml brought a new operetta, *The Vagabond King*, to Broadway in '25. It was his greatest box-office success after *Rose Marie*. From the lovely score came the hit "Song of the Vagabonds."

This romantic operetta about Francois Villon, the 15th Century French vagabond poet, was based on J.H. McCarthy's *If I Were King*. Villon was appointed King of France for a day. During his brief reign, he manages to save both his neck and Paris by leading his followers against the Duke of Burgundy. Villon also manages to win the hand of the beautiful Katherine de Vaucelles.

Dennis King, who played Villon in the Broadway pro-duction, popularized "Song of the Vagabonds," a rousing summon to arms, with a successful recording in '26. Vincent Lopez and his orchestra also had a popular recording of the song on the market.

Variety chose "Song of the Vagabonds" for its *Hit Parade of a Half-Century*.

People from the mid-west may recognize this song as the "signature" tune of the University of Nebraska Cornhusker Marching Band. New lyrics were set to the melody and are sung when the band is on parade as an introduction to the school fight song, "Hail Varsity." In '41, the band was to perform in the Rose Bowl parade. ASCAP had banned all of its music from radio. Since the parade would be broadcast, the director, Don Lentz, had to find something the band could play that was not written or published by a member of ASCAP. The ensemble had previously adapted "Song of the Vagabonds" into the "Band Song." Several bandsmen quickly added some words and the band sang as they marched. The parade audience found the singing marching band quite unique.

The song appeared in the movie musical *Song of the Vagabonds* ('30), plus the film version of *The Vagabond King* in '56.

Read the lyrics at http://lyricsplayground.com/alpha/songs/s/songofthevagabonds.shtml.

Sweet Georgia Brown

Words & Music: Ben Bernie, Maceo Pinkard & Kenneth Casey

Ben Bernie and his orchestra introduced this tune, which is today identified with the Harlem Globetrotters and their warm-up routine.

Other popular recordings besides Ben Bernie's orchestra included those by Isham Jones and his orchestra and blues singer Ethel Waters. Bing Crosby had a popular version on record in '32. It was revived again in the late forties by Brother Bones. Isham Jones' '32 recording of this song is available at http://www.redhotjazz.com/ishamjones.html. The uncredited vocalist on the recording sounds very much like young Bing Crosby, complete with some scat singing in the second chorus.

"Sweet Georgia Brown" is one of the most recorded songs of the pre-rock era, and was even recorded by the Beatles during the rock era.

The chorus lyrics assure us there is no gal has ever been made like "Sweet Georgia Brown." She may have two left feet, but she is really neat. The only men she can't attract are those she hasn't met. The chorus ends with "Georgia claimed her, Georgia named her, Sweet Georgia Brown." Read the lyrics at http://www.topthat.net/DWT/Music/lyrics.html.

"Sweet Georgia Brown" was featured in the '42 movie musical *Broadway* and in the all-black Broadway musical *Bubbling Brown Sugar* ('76). The song also appeared in the film *Oscar* ('91) and *Sweet and Low Down* ('99).

Tea for Two *and* I Want to Be Happy

Words: Irving Caesar; Music: Vincent Youmans

No, No Nanette was the most successful musical comedy of the '25 season. The story was a '20s trifle, but it produced two hit songs: "I Want to Be Happy" and "Tea for Two." Vincent Youmans' musical score to Irving Caesar's lyrics was catchy and endearing.

TEA FOR TWO

"Tea for Two" is one of Youmans and Caesar's most memorable songs. It was included as one of sixteen songs in the ASCAP *All-Time Hit Parade*, which was selected to publicize the organization's golden anniversary in '63. It is also a *Variety Hit Parade of a Half-Century* selection. The song became one of the most recorded songs of the pre-rock era.

Louise Groody and John Barker introduced "Tea for Two" in the original Broadway show. Caesar's lyrics, intended to be temporary, were dashed off in five minutes but were never changed. Youmans had been playing around with a new melody all day and when Caesar came by late in the afternoon on his way to a party, Youmans insisted that he write a lyric for the new melody. Caesar didn't want to take the time, but after much coaxing, he complied, mostly to get Youmans off his back. Caesar intended to revise the lyric later, but the impromptu words seemed to fit so well, they were never changed. This could be why even though the title is "Tea for Two," the only reference to tea occurs at the beginning with the rest of the lyric devoted to the happiness of marriage.

The chorus lyrics encourage us to "picture you upon my knee just tea for two and two for tea." These two lovers don't want anyone to see or hear them, they don't even want their friends or relations to visit or know they have a telephone. They plan to raise a family and live happily ever after. Read the lyrics at http://www.stlyrics.com/lyrics/teafortwo/teafortwo.htm.

The most popular recordings of "Tea for Two" in '25 in descending order were by Marion Harris), by the Benson Orchestra of Chicago and by Ben Bernie and his orchestra. The Ipana Troubadors revived it in '30, and Teddy Wilson and his band revived it again in '37. Jazz pianist Art Tatum's '39 recording of "Tea for Two" was inducted into the Grammy Hall of Fame in '86. Warren Covington with the Tommy Dorsey orchestra revived it again in '58 in a cha-cha version that sold very well. Hear Marion Harris' recording at http://www.redhotjazz.com/marionharris.html and the Benson Orchestra's version at http://www.redhotjazz.com/benson.html.

"Tea for Two" was also used in *With a Song in My Heart* ('52) and *Sincerely Yours* ('55). The song also appeared in the non-musical film *Oscar* ('91).

See the sheet music cover and musical score at http://lcweb2.loc.gov/cocoon/ihas/loc.natlib.ihas.100010096/. Hear a midi musical version at http://www.primeshop.com/midlist3.htm.

I WANT TO BE HAPPY

Louise Groody and Charles Winninger introduced "I Want to Be Happy," which was a comedy number in the show. Winninger was Nanette's father's lawyer, but he has a passion for the younger Nanette. He claims he can't be happy until he makes her happy. Read the lyrics at http://www.stlyrics.com/lyrics/teafortwo/iwanttobehappy.htm.

Variety selected this song for its *Hit Parade of a Half-Century.*

Successful recordings by Carl Fenton, Vincent Lopez's orchestra, Jan Garber's orchestra, and the Shannon Four helped popularize "I Want to Be Happy" nationwide. Red Nichols and His Five Pennies revived it in '30 and Benny Goodman and his orchestra revived it again in '37. Hear

this song as recorded by the California Ramblers at http://www.redhotjazz.com/caramblers.html.

Two Hollywood versions of *No, No, Nanette* were filmed: one in '30 and another in '40. Both songs were also used in *Tea for Two* ('50), which was loosely based on *No, No, Nanette.* "I Want to Be Happy" also appeared in *Torch Song Trilogy* ('88).

Ukulele Lady
Words: Gus Kahn; Music: Richard A. Whiting

This *Variety Hit Parade of a Half-Century* song illustrates the popularity of the ukulele during the '20s. Cliff "Ukulele Ike" Edwards, May "The Ukulele Girl" Singhi Breen, and Wendell Hall playing the uke and singing "It Ain't Gonna Rain No Mo'" are further testimony of the popularity of this four-stringed instrument, which originated in Hawaii. A typical caricature of the jazz age male collegiate often consists of a raccoon coat, a flask in the hip pocket, a college pennant in one hand, and a uke in the other. The first verse sets the scene: it's a beautiful moonlight night on Honolulu Bay. The beach is filled with girls ("peaches") who have brought their ukeleles along so they can sing this song (the chorus). The chorus lyrics are reminiscent of "Under the Bamboo Tree," with its "If you lak-a-me lak I lak-a-you." This song says instead, "If you like Ukulele Lady, Ukulele Lady like a' you." If you linger in the shade, Ukulele Lady will linger with you. If you kiss her and promise to be true and then she sees you fooling around some other Ukulele Lady, she'll drop you. Read the lyrics at http://www.arlo.net/lyrics/ukulele-lady.shtml.

This song was popularized by Vaughn DeLeath, one of the first women singers to gain recognition on radio and one of the people who is credited with originating the style of singing called crooning. Hear Paul Whiteman's recording of this song at http://www.redhotjazz.com/pwo.html.

See four different sheet music covers at www.hulapages.com/covers_3.htm.

Yes Sir, That's My Baby
Words: Gus Kahn; Music: Walter Donaldson

The Walter Donaldson-Gus Kahn partnership that produced "My Buddy" and "Carolina in the Morning" among others, continued with "Yes Sir, That's My Baby" in '25.

The song was written for and introduced by Eddie Cantor. Gus Kahn got the idea for the lyrics in Cantor's living room, playing with a toy pig that belonged to Cantor's daughter. As the windup toy toddled around the room, Kahn improvised the lines that became the song's beginning. Cantor insisted Kahn complete the lyrics, as he, of course, did. Donaldson wrote the melody and a popular music classic was born.

The chorus begins: "Yes, Sir, that's my baby, No, Sir, don't mean maybe." The bridge section reveals a wedding is about to take place, then the opening is repeated again. Read the lyrics at http://www.apluslyrics.com/lyrics/35390/Frank_Sinatra/Yes_Sir,_That's_My_Baby/.

Sweet-voiced Gene Austin had the most popular disk version, followed closely by Blossom Seeley's and Ben Bernie and his orchestras. Two other moderately successful recordings were released by Ace Brigode and the Coon-Sanders Orchestra. Hear the Coon-Sanders Orchestra version at http://www.redhotjazz.com/coonsanders.html.

Variety chose "Yes Sir, That's My Baby" for its *Hit Parade of a Half-Century.*

1926

Always

Words & Music: Irving Berlin

This *Variety Golden 100* and *Hit Parade of a Half-Century* Irving Berlin love song is a pledge of everlasting love: "I'll be loving you always." The song came about when Irving Berlin's musical secretary, Arthur Johnson's girlfriend, Mona, asked him to write a song about her sometime. Berlin replied, "Why sometime? Why not right now?" He asked her name and began humming a melody. Meanwhile, Johnson wrote on a napkin, "I'll be loving you, Mona." Nothing came of the song immediately, but in '25, Berlin rediscovered his unfinished song and changed "Mona" to "Always." Voila! A hit song was born.

When Irving and Ellin MacKay were married in early '26, he turned over all the rights to "Always" to her as a wedding gift. Ellin's father, Clarence MacKay, disinherited her when she married Berlin and refused to have anything to do with her. Her father, the Postal Telegraph and Cable Corporation mogul and the head of a family listed on the Social Register, was absolutely against Ellin even considering marriage to the son of Russian Jews, but even worse, a musician. He drew up a new will excluding Ellin; her share of the MacKay estate would have amounted to $10 million. Perhaps the royalties from "Always" took some of the sting out of her disinheritance.

However, their love must truly have been sincere love, because Irving and Ellin lived together as husband and wife for over 60 years until her death.

"Always" is a great wedding song because of its wonderfully loving lyrics. The chorus opens with a promise: "I'll be loving you, always, With a love that's true, always." He promises when her plans don't go right or when her days are cloudy, he'll be there to help. As the chorus ends, he further promises to be there not for an hour, a day, a year, but always. Read the lyrics at http://www.oldielyrics.com/lyrics/irving_berlin/always.html.

Gladys Clark and Henry Bergman introduced this classic in vaudeville. Vincent Lopez and George Olsen's orchestras had the most successful recordings of "Always" in '26. Other successful '26 versions included those by Henry Burr, Nick Lucas and Lewis James. Hear Nick Lucas' recording at http://www.redhotjazz.com/lucas.html. Gordon Jenkins and his orchestra and Paul Lavalle and his orchestra revived it in '44. Sammy Kaye and Guy Lombardo's groups also charted with their recordings of it in '45. "Always" became one of the most recorded songs of the pre-rock era.

"Always" was performed in *Roar of the Dragon* ('32), *Young Bride* ('32), *The Pride of the Yankees* ('42) and by a chorus in the '46 movie musical *Blue Skies*. Deanna Durbin sang the song in the Universal Pictures '44 film *Christmas Holiday*. The song also appeared in *Blithe Spirit* ('45).

Baby Face

Words: Benny Davis; Music: Harry Akst

"Baby Face" reportedly became a million-selling record for Art Mooney and his orchestra in '48, but it was originally introduced and recorded in '26 by Jan Garber and his orchestra with the lyricist, Benny Davis, doing the vocal. Recordings by Ben Selvin and his orchestra, by "Whispering" Jack Smith and by the Ipana Troubadors also helped popularize the song in '26. Other '48 popular recordings included those by Sammy Kaye and his orchestra, Jack Smith and Henry King. Hear Ben Selvin's recording of "Baby Face" at http://www.redhotjazz.com/ben selvino.html.

Along with "Five Foot Two," and "If You Knew Susie," "Baby Face" is one of the songs often chosen by filmmakers to identify the '20s flapper and her scatterbrained mentality. "Baby Face" was one of the musical numbers in Rudy Vallee's '30 movie musical, *Glorifying the American Girl*. It was also used in *Jolson Sings Again* ('49) and in Julie Andrews' movie musical *Thoroughly Modern Millie* ('67).

In the first verse lyrics the singer says he never knew why he loved this girl so much. He then surmises that perhaps it's the way she looks at him when she gets up each morning. Next he confesses that he fell in love with her "little baby face." He's sure there isn't any other person that could replace her, because she makes his heart jump. When he's in her embrace, he's in heaven. Read the lyrics at http://kinks.it.rit.edu/cgi-bin/MusicSearch.cgi?song=regular/showbiz/song-babyface.

The Birth of the Blues *and* Black Bottom

Words: B.G. DeSylva & Lew Brown; Music: Ray Henderson

THE BIRTH OF THE BLUES

Introduced by Harry Richman as the first-act finale of *George White's Scandals of 1926*, "The Birth of the Blues" was the first big hit for the team of Henderson, DeSylva and Brown. The trio came together with considerable prior experience and then for the rest of the decade were without peer in capturing the spirit of the times in song.

The setting for "The Birth of the Blues" was the gates of heaven, where a debate takes place between jazz and classical music. This song was presented to Beethoven and Liszt as evidence that the blues are an important part of music. At the end of the scene the pearly gates open to accept blues and jazz into this musical Valhalla.

"The Birth of the Blues" was one of sixteen songs selected in '63 for the ASCAP *All-Time Hit Parade*. *Variety* selected the song as one of its *Golden 100* and *Hit Parade of a Half-Century*.

Paul Whiteman and his orchestra's recorded version was the most popular one, but Harry Richman's was also very well received. The Revelers also had another successful version on record. Frank Sinatra revived "The Birth of the Blues" with some success in '52. Hear Paul Whiteman's recording of "The Birth of the Blues" at http://www.redhotjazz.com/pwo.html.

The song has been featured in several movie musicals including *Birth of the Blues* ('41), which was a tribute to the Original Dixieland Jazz Band, *When My Baby Smiles at Me* ('48), which starred Betty Grable and Dan Dailey, *Painting the Clouds with Sunshine* ('51), another "gold diggers" tale, 1953's version of *The Jazz Singer*, which starred Danny Thomas, and *The Best Things in Life Are Free* ('56), a tribute to the work of the songwriting team of Henderson, DeSylva and Brown.

Read the lyrics at http://www.lyricsfreak.com/f/frank-sinatra/56003.html.

BLACK BOTTOM

A second hit song, "Black Bottom," from the *Scandals of 1926* became one of the big dance sensations of the late '20s. The muddy flats or bottom land of the Suwannee River inspired the dance rather than the slapping of the rear-end that was one of its movements. It also featured sluggish foot movements that suggested plodding through the mud. Considering the fast tempo of the song, plodding through anything doesn't seem appropriate.

The Black Bottom dance supposedly originated in New Orleans and later migrated to New York City. Blues singer Alberta Hunter is often given credit for introducing the dance, but others say Perry Bradford introduced it in Nashville, Tennessee in '19 when he wrote a song titled "The Black Bottom." The sheet music has the dance instructions printed along with the music. Jelly Roll Morton wrote a song called "Black Bottom Stomp" in '26 about a predominantly African American area of Detroit referred to as the Black Bottom. The dance became much more famous when it was performed at the Apollo Theater in the George White *Scandals*.

The chorus lyrics tell us about a dance called "Black Bottom." It's sure captivated everyone as they clap their hands and dance this "raggedy trot." Even old men with lumbago are giving it a try. The bridge lyrics move to the muddy river bottom that is oozing with mud; they start to squirm "just like a worm!"

"Black Bottom" was selected for *Variety's Hit Parade of a Half-Century*.

Johnny Hamp and his Kentucky Serenaders had the most popular recording of "Black Bottom" during '26. Hear Johnny Hamp's Kentucky Serenaders' '26 recording of "The Black Bottom" at http://www.redhotjazz.com/jhks.html.

The song was used in the '54 version of *A Star Is Born*, which starred Judy Garland, and *The Best Things in Life Are Free* ('56).

George Olsen and his orchestra's recording of "Lucky Day" from *George White's Scandals* was also popular in '26.

The Blue Room *and* The Girl Friend

Words: Lorenz Hart; Music: Richard Rodgers

The Girl Friend, one of Rodgers and Hart's earliest musicals, was a vehicle for the husband and wife dance team Eva Puck and Sammy White. They introduced the Charleston-styled title song and one of the writing team's loveliest ballads, "The Blue Room."

The musical's plot has something to do with a bicycle rider farmhand becoming the toast of the town, thanks to some help from his female admirer. It concerns a Long Island dairyman, Leonard Silver, played by Sammy White, who hopes to become a great six-day bicycle rider. His girl friend, played by Eva Puck, is his trainer, manager and promoter.

THE BLUE ROOM

Sammy White and Eva Puck introduced "The Blue Room," which praises romantic seclusion in *The Girl Friend*, the musical that Sandy Wilson used as the model for his '53 musical *The Boy Friend*.

The singers are dreaming of the "blue room" they will have in their future home. In that room every day will be a holiday because they're married to each other. Read the lyrics at Lorenz Hart's website: http://www.lorenzhart.org/broom.htm.

The Revelers and the Melody Sheiks popularized "The Blue Room" with successful recordings in '26. Perry Como revived it with moderate success in '49. Hear Isham Jones' recording of "Blue Room" at http://www.redhotjazz.com/ishamjones.html.

The song was one of *Variety's Hit Parade of a Half-Century* selections.

The song was used in the biopic of Rodgers and Hart, *Words and Music* ('48), *Young Man with a Horn* ('50), and *The Eddy Duchin Story* ('56).

THE GIRL FRIEND

Sammy White introduced the Charleston-style title song, which describes his girl friend as cute and sweet. Describing her, he says she's gentle, "mentally, nearly complete," and she's so beautiful it shouldn't be legal. Not only does she have a heart and a mind, she's ideal! The chorus ends with: "In my funny fashion I'm cursed with a passion for the girl friend."

George Olsen and his orchestra had the most popular recording of "The Girl Friend" in '26. Hear "The Girl Friend" recorded by the California Ramblers at http://www.redhotjazz.com/caramblers.html (listed under "The").

Variety included "The Girl Friend" in its *Hit Parade of a Half-Century*.

"The Girl Friend" was played as an instrumental in Rodgers and Hart's screen biography *Words and Music* ('43).

Breezin' Along with the Breeze

Words: Seymour Simons & Richard A. Whiting; Music: Haven Gillespie

This collaborative song was a record hit for singer Johnny Marvin, for drummer Abe Lyman and his orchestra, and for the Revelers in '27. It also was Fred Waring's theme music for his radio program in the '30s. The Hoosier Hot Shots revived "Breezin' Along with the Breeze" with some success in '38. Hear a recording of this song by Josephine Baker at http://www.redhotjazz.com/bakerfb.html.

In the first verse lyrics, the singer confesses to being a rover since his childhood, because nobody loved or cared for him. He grew up rather wild. Now, nobody wonders where he is, nor is anyone missing him. He's like a bird that flies wherever he wants. That line leads into the chorus which begins with the title phrase: "I'm just breezin' along with the breeze" by rails or by sea. When he gets tired, he makes his bed in Mother Nature with the sky as his roof. The song ends with the title again: "Breezin' along with the breeze." Read the lyrics at http://www.ruthetting.com/songs/breezin-along.asp.

"Breezin' Along with the Breeze" was used in the following movie musicals: *Shine on Harvest Moon* ('44), *The Jazz Singer* ('53), and *The Helen Morgan Story* ('57). The song also appeared in the Lucille Ball and Desi Arnez film *The Long, Long Trailer* ('54), in *The Violent Road* ('58), and in *Alice* ('90).

Bye Bye Blackbird

Words: Mort Dixon; Music: Ray Henderson

Following "Birth of the Blues" and "Black Bottom," Ray Henderson had a third hit song in '26 with "Bye, Bye Blackbird." This time Henderson worked with lyricist

Mort Dixon, with whom he had collaborated earlier on "That Old Gang of Mine" ('23).

"Bye, Bye Blackbird" was first made popular by Eddie Cantor, then served as the theme song for vaudevillian Georgie Price. Gene Austin had the most successful recording of the song; his recording of the song was inducted into the Grammy Hall of Fame in 2005. Other popular recordings were issued by Nick Lucas, by Benny Krueger and his orchestra, and by Leo Reisman and his orchestra. Russ Morgan and his orchestra revived it with moderate success in '48. Hear Josephine Baker's recording of "Bye Bye Blackbird" at http://www.redhotjazz.com/bakerfb.html.

The lyrics to "Bye, Bye Blackbird" helped the song continue its popularity into the early '30s because of the opening phrase: "Pack up all my cares and woe," which seemed particularly meaningful to the people of our nation during the Great Depression. The melody is narrow in range and moves in scale-wise patterns, with few skips. These characteristics give the melody a folk song character. Read the lyrics at http://www.fortunecity.com/tinpan/new bonham/6/byebyeblackbird.htm.

The song was used in *Rainbow Round My Shoulder* ('52), *The Eddie Cantor Story* ('53), and *Pete Kelly's Blues* ('55).

A Cup of Coffee, a Sandwich and You
Words: Billy Rose & Al Dubin; Music: Joseph Meyer

Gertrude Lawrence and Jack Buchanan introduced this song in *Charlot's Revue of 1926*. Lawrence was never well known as a great singer, but according to contemporary critics, she had a fantastic stage personality that could sell any song. In this song, she sold the idea that she did not need the finer things of life, all she required for happiness was "a cup of coffee, a sandwich and you."

Al Dubin's daughter has said that the inspiration for the title was a line from an Omar Khayyam poem: "A loaf of bread, a jug of wine, and thou beside me in the desert."

Coffee has become an important part of many Americans' lives. The coffee pot begins the day for many and the coffee break is one of the most anticipated times of the work day. Coffee houses, latte stations and other assorted java joints have become a familiar part of the American landscape. Coffee has become a universally accepted stimulant in the U.S. and in many other countries.

In the context of this song, perhaps all the singer needs is " A Cup of Coffee, a Sandwich and You."

The song was chosen for inclusion in *Variety's Hit Parade of a Half-Century* representing '25.

Gertrude Lawrence and Jack Buchanan's duet recording was the best-known version on the market. Hear Nick Lucas' recording of this song at http://www.redhotjazz.com/lucas.html.

This song was used in *Margie* ('46), where Barbara Lawrence and Jeanne Crain performed it. In '42, Bud Abbott and Lou Costello performed a comedy routine based on "A Cup of Coffee, a Sandwich and You" in the film *Keep 'em Flying*.

Five Foot Two, Eyes of Blue
Words: Sam M. Lewis & Joe Young; Music: Ray Henderson

This early Ray Henderson success is closely identified with the '20s because it describes the stereotypical flapper: "turned up nose, turned down hose..." However, the lyrics warn us if we happened to see a girl walking down the street with furs, diamond rings and such things, "that ain't her." Read the lyrics at http://www.digitaltimes.com/karaoke/singers/fivefoottwo.html.

As popular as this song is in identifying the flapper, the only movie musical that it was found in was *Love Me or Leave Me* ('55), the screen biography of nightclub singer and *Follies* star, Ruth Etting. However, it also appeared in the non-musical *The Great Gatsby* ('74).

The most popular solo singer of the decade, Gene Austin, had the most popular recorded version, but Art Landry and his orchestra, with a vocal by Denny Curtis, and Ernie Golden and his orchestra had other successful releases of the song in '26. It was revived with limited success by Tiny Hill in '40 and by Benny Strong in '49. The song was the theme song of Ina Ray Hutton and her All-Girl Orchestra. Hear Art Landry's '25 recording of "Five Foot Two, Eyes of Blue" at http://www.redhotjazz.com/landryo.html.

"Gimme" a Little Kiss, Will "Ya" Huh?
Words: Roy Turk & Jack Smith; Music: Maceo Pinkard

One of the lyricists, "Whispering" Jack Smith, had great success with this song; it became one of his most famous recordings. Smith's recorded version was by far the most popular one, with one by Billy Jones being moderately successful. April Stevens revived the song in '51 to Top Ten status. Hear Jean Goldkette and his orchestra's recording of the song at http://www.redhotjazz.com/goldo.html.

The singer assures the girl that if she'll give him a kiss; he'll give it right back. Read the lyrics at http://www.spiritofsinatra.com/pages/Lyrics/g/Gimme_A_Little_Kiss.ht.

I'm Sitting on Top of the World
Words: Sam M. Lewis & Joe Young; Music: Ray Henderson

I'm Sitting on Top of the World" was popularized by Al Jolson. Its optimistic text proclaims that this is the best of all possible worlds in the best of all possible times.

The Great Depression is a few years away yet, but this song sounds like the type of anti-Depression philosophy used in many of the songs of that era. The chorus lyrics say the singer is "sitting on top of the world, just rolling along." He's leaving the blues of the world behind by singing a song. He just phoned his "parson" to warn him to get ready for a wedding because "just like Humpty Dumpty" he's ready to fall in love. The chorus ends with a repeat of the opening line. Read the lyrics at http://www.oldielyrics.com/lyrics/bobby_darin/im_sitting_on_top_of_the_world.html.

Other recordings were available by alto saxophonist/bandleader Roger Wolfe Kahn and his orchestra and radio/Broadway personality Frank Crumit in '26. Les Paul and Mary Ford revived the song with success in '53. Hear Isham Jones' recording of the song at http://www.redhotjazz.com/ishamjones.html.

Jolson sang it in his '28 part-talkie *The Singing Fool* and again in *The Jolson Story* ('46). It was also used in Ruth Etting's screen biography *Love Me or Leave Me* ('55) and *Thoroughly Modern Millie* ('77).

Moonlight on the Ganges

Words: Chester Wallace; Music: Sherman Meyers

Variety chose "Moonlight on the Ganges" for its *Hit Parade of a Half-Century.*

Paul Whiteman and his orchestra had a popular recording of the song in '26. Hear Whiteman's recording of this song at http://www.redhotjazz.com/pwo.html. Fred Rich and his orchestra had a fairly successful recording of the song on the market in '27.

Whiteman's arrangement has a definite Far Eastern, or perhaps more accurately Indian, flavor.

The singer is crooning to his "little Hindu." He expects all their dreams and schemes to come true. Read the lyrics at http://www.nomorelyrics.net/song/91111.html.

Show Me the Way to Go Home

Words & Music: Irving King

"Show Me the Way to Go Home" has been a favorite of the imbibing set since it was written in '25.

Variety chose this song for its *Hit Parade of a Half-Century.*

Vincent Lopez and his orchestra and Ernest Hare and Billy Jones had popular recordings of this song in '26. Hear this song recorded by the California Ramblers at http://www.redhotjazz.com/caramblers.html.

The singer requests that we show him the "way to go home" because he's exhausted and he wants to go to bed. He confesses that the drink he had about an hour ago went straight to his head. Read the lyrics at http://www.guntheranderson.com/v/data/showmeth.htm.

Sleepy Time Gal

Words: Joseph R. Alden & Raymond B. Egan; Music: Ange Lorenzo & Richard A. Whiting

"Sleepy Time Gal" was a popular recording for Ben Bernie and his orchestra, for Gene Austin, and for Nick Lucas. Other not quite so popular versions were available by Art Landry, Ben Selvin, Lewis James and their orchestras. It was revived in the early forties by Harry James and his orchestra. Hear Art Landry's recording of "Sleepy-Time Gal," with a vocal by Henry Burr, at http://www.redhotjazz.com/landryo.html.

This song is so well known, so much a part of the American popular music tradition that it could probably pass for a folk song. It was and still is a favorite of sing-along groups, such as Mitch Miller's Sing-alongs during the late '50s. But as easily singable as it is, the melody and harmony are the product of craft rather than of the folk tradition.

The sheet music cover says this is a "Wide Awake Fox Trot Song."

The lyrics begin by the singer telling this "Sleepy time gal" that she is turning night into day because they've danced the entire evening away. The singer asks for a little kiss then tells her they should say "Goodnight." He promises when her dancing days are finished, he'll find them a cottage where she can become domestic by learning "to cook and to sew." He assures her that she'll love being "a stay-at-home, play-at-home, eight o'clock sleepy time gal!" Read the lyrics at http://lyricsplayground.com/alpha/songs/s/sleepytimegal.shtml.

Valencia

Words: Clifford Grey; Music: Jose Padilla

The Great Temptations, another of the Shuberts' Winter Garden revues, introduced one interpolation that has remained popular: Jose Padilla's "Valencia (A Song of Spain)."

The original lyrics were written by Lucienne Boyer and Jacques Charles, but Clifford Grey furnished the English version.

"Valencia" had first been sung by Mistinguett in the Moulin Rouge nightclub revue in Paris. Hazel Dawn, Halfred Young, and Charlotte Woodruff introduced it into the United States in *The Great Temptations.* Grace Bowman sang it in the '27 revue *A Night in Spain.*

Variety selected "Valencia" for its *Hit Parade of a Half-Century* representing '25.

Paul Whiteman and his orchestra's recording of "Valencia" was one of the biggest successes of the decade. Hear three Whiteman recordings at http://www.redhotjazz.com/pwo.html (two from '26 and a London recording from '27). Other popular recorded versions included those by Ben Selvin and his orchestra, the famous vocal group, the Revelers, Ross Gorman and his orchestra (Gorman was clarinet soloist for the world premiere of Gershwin's "Rhapsody in Blue"), and organist Jesse Crawford. Singer Tony Martin revived it with some success in '50.

The lyrics sing the praises of the town. The singer says Valencia, with its orange trees and sea breeze, has always seemed to beckon because it was there "long ago we found a paradise of love."

When the Red, Red Robin Comes Bob, Bob, Bobbin' Along

Words & Music: Harry Woods

Harry Woods, a prominent composer of songs of the '20s and '30s, had his first major hit with this song. It was introduced by Sophie Tucker in Chicago, but it was Al Jolson who popularized it nationwide with a very successful recording. Other '26 recorded releases included those by Paul Whiteman and his orchestra, by "Whispering" Jack Smith, by Cliff "Ukulele Ike" Edwards, and by the Ipana Troubadors, with vocalist Franklyn Baur. Doris Day made the *Billboard's* Top 30 with her version in '53. Hear Paul Whiteman's recording at http://www.redhotjazz.com/pwo.html.

The famous chorus lyrics begin with the title phrase, after which we're encouraged to wake up, get out of bed, cheer up and "live, love, laugh and be happy." Even though the singer may have been blue, now he's "walking through fields of flowers." He's feeling just a kid again. Read the lyrics at http://lyricsplayground.com/alpha/songs/w/whentheredrobincomesbobbinalong.shtml.

Jolson's voice performed it in the '49 movie musical *Jolson Sings Again.* The song also appeared in non-musical film *Bullets Over Broadway* ('94).

Who?

Words: Oscar Hammerstein II; Music: Jerome Kern

In the first half of the '20s, Jerome Kern had two extremely successful musicals: *Sally* ('20) and *Sunny* ('25), both starring Marilyn Miller. In *Sally*, Ms. Miller, the most adored musical-comedy actress of the decade, introduced "Look for the Silver Lining," and in *Sunny*, she introduced the breezy love duet, "Who?," with Paul Frawley.

Kern had written a catchy tune that posed a problem for

his lyricist. The first note was held for nine beats. The same thing happened five times during the tune. Hammerstein had to find a word that could be repeated over and over, without becoming monotonous. It also needed to be a word that ended on an open vowel so that the singer could hold it for more than two measures each time it appeared. Hammerstein's answer to the problem was "who." Kern credited Oscar's choice of words with saving his tune and making it the hit song that it became.

Sunny was the first Kern-Hammerstein collaboration, a partnership that eventually produced one of Broadway's all-time great musicals: *Show Boat* ('27). The musical's plot is another rags-to-riches tale. A circus bareback rider in England stows away aboard a New York bound ship to avoid marrying the circus owner. Without the proper papers, she can't enter the U.S. until she marries a rich American named Jim. Sunny thinks she loves Tom, but after getting a divorce from Jim, she realizes its Jim she loves after all.

Variety selected "Who?" for its *Hit Parade of a Half-Century* representing '25 and as one of its *Golden 100 Tin Pan Alley Songs*.

George Olsen and his orchestra had the most success recording of "Who?" in '26. The Brox Sisters had moderate success with their release in late '25. Tommy Dorsey and his orchestra revived it successfully in '37. Hear Red Nichols' Five Pennies' recording of "Who?" at http://www. redhotjazz.com/rn5p.html.

Hollywood filmed *Sunny* in '30 and in '41. "Who?" was also used in Jerome Kern's screen biography *Till the Clouds Roll By* ('46) and in Marilyn Miller's screen biography *Look for the Silver Lining* ('49).

"Who?" was the theme song of the NBC-TV show *It Could Be You* from '56 to '61 in the daytime show and from '58 to '60 in the primetime version.

The chorus is rather short and concise. It asks several "who" questions, like "who stole my heart away" and "who makes me dream all day?" The answer is "no one, but you." Read the lyrics at http://www.cfhf.net/lyrics/it-could.htm.

George Olsen's orchestra popularized the title song of the musical, "Sunny," with a successful recording.

1927

Ain't She Sweet?

Words: Jack Yellen; Music: Milton Ager

Eddie Cantor, Sophie Tucker, and Lillian Roth adopted "Ain't She Sweet?" for their respective vaudeville acts after it was introduced by Paul Ash and his orchestra in Chicago.

This song established its composer, Milton Ager, and its lyricist, Jack Yellen, as hit songwriters.

"Ain't She Sweet" is another song that is closely associated with the flapper. She walks down the street so all the guys can "look her over once or twice." Read the lyrics at http://lirama.net/song/18334.

Ben Bernie and his Hotel Roosevelt Orchestra had a big hit recording of "Ain't She Sweet?" in '27. Vocalists Gene Austin and Johnny Marvin also had successful

recordings of the song at the time. In '49, Mr. Goon Bones and Mr. Ford, whoever they were, revived it with a Top 20 recording. Even the Beatles recorded "Ain't She Sweet," with John Lennon doing the lead vocals. Hear Ben Selvin's recording at http://www.redhotjazz.com/benselvino.html.

"Ain't She Sweet?" was used in movie musicals such as *Margie* ('46), *You Were Meant for Me* ('48), and *The Eddy Duchin Story* ('56).

At Sundown (When Love Is Calling Me Home)

Words & Music: Walter Donaldson

This Walter Donaldson hit song reportedly sold more than 2 million disks in various versions in the late '20s. George Olsen and his orchestra, with vocalists Fran Frey, Bob Borger and Bob Rice, had the most popular recorded version of "At Sundown (When Love Is Calling Me Home)," but the Arden-Ohman Orchestra (piano duo Victor Arden and Phil Ohman) and vocalist Franklyn Baur also helped popularize the song with successful recordings. It was also a favorite of Ruth Etting's, so it was used in her biopic *Love Me or Leave Me* ('55). Hear the Clicquot Club Eskimos' recording of "At Sundown" at http://www. redhotjazz.com/eskimos.html.

Donaldson's lyrics sing of breezes sighing of undying love. The singer hears love calling him home as the sun begins to fall. The opening notes of the phrase "Every little breeze" are enough for most popular music connoisseurs to identify the song. Read the lyrics at http://www.spirit ofsinatra.com/pages/Lyrics/a/At_Sundown.htm.

"At Sundown" has been used in several movie musicals including *Glorifying the American Girl* ('30), *This Is the Life* ('44), *Music for Millions* ('44), *Margie* ('46), *The Fabulous Dorseys* ('47), *Love Me or Leave Me* ('55) and *The Joker Is Wild* ('57), where it was sung by Frank Sinatra.

The Best Things in Life Are Free *and* The Varsity Drag

Words: B.G. DeSylva & Lew Brown; Music: Ray Henderson

The first book musical by Henderson, DeSylva and Brown was a collegiate caper, *Good News*. It explores a "burning issue" often a part of the twenties' collegiana: will the star football player be allowed to play in the big game against the arch-rival school despite his failing grade in astronomy? The answer? Since college spirit is more important than grades, he plays ... and wins.

THE BEST THINGS IN LIFE ARE FREE

In the plot of the musical, the rich football hero leads up to the song "The Best Things in Life Are Free" by trying to convince the poor heroine that money is not the answer to everything. This paean to the priceless things in life was introduced by John Price Jones and Mary Lawlor.

And what are those things about life that are best and free? The stars, the flowers, the robins, and the sunshine. The best thing of all is love and all these things are free. Read the lyrics at http://www.songlyrics.com/song-lyrics/George_Olsen/Miscellaneous/ Best_Things_In_ Life_Are_Free/192785.html.

"The Best Things in Life Are Free" was a *Variety Hit Parade of a Half-Century* selection.

George Olsen and his orchestra, one of the most

popular sweet bands of the decade (with vocalist Bob Borger), recorded the most popular version of the song, but Frank Black and his orchestra's recording also helped popularize it. Superstar vocalists Dinah Shore and Jo Stafford both revived it in '48 with moderate success. Luther Vandross and Janet Jackson's duet recording of a different song with the same title charted in '92. Hear Ted Lewis' recording of this classic song at http://www.redhotjazz.com/tlband.html.

Film versions of *Good News* came out of Hollywood in '30 and '47. A '56 movie musical titled *The Best Things in Life Are Free* was a tribute to these songwriters — Henderson, DeSylva and Brown. The song also appeared in *White Men Can't Jump* ('92).

THE VARSITY DRAG

Another hit song from *Good News* was the Charleston-type number "The Varsity Drag." The song cue in the musical occurs when Zelma O'Neal, playing the co-ed Flo, tells the other students, "Let the professors worry about their dusty old books, we'll make Tait famous for the Varsity Drag!"

Variety listed "The Varsity Drag" in its *Hit Parade of a Half-Century.*

George Olsen and Cass Hagan and their orchestras both had popular recordings of "The Varsity Drag" in '27. Hagan's recording featured vocalists Franklyn Baur, Lewis James, and Elliott Shaw, with future-famous bandleader Red Nichols on trumpet.

Hear George Olsen and his orchestra's '27 recording of this song at http://www.authentichistory.com/audio/1920s/George_Olsen-The_Varsity_Drag.html or hear a '27 recording of this song by Cass Hagan and His Park Central Hotel Orchestra at http://www.edisonnj.org/menlopark/vintage/columbia.asp.

The lyrics of "Varsity Drag" are cleverly written. In typical collegiate fashion, in the verse, the students declare that knowledge is not everything. Instead, they need to learn to dance, specifically the great new dance called the drag. So the dance lesson begins. The chorus teaches the drag dance, and begins with "Down on the heels, up on the toes, That's the way to do the Varsity Drag." This new dance is hot, new, mean, and blue. The students are told they can pass their classes whether they're dumb or smart, but what they really need to do is stay after school to learn the "Varsity Drag." Read the lyrics at http://lyricsplayground.com/alpha/songs/v/varsitydrag.shtml.

Film versions of *Good News* came out of Hollywood in '30 and '47. "The Best Things in Life Are Free" and "The Varsity Drag" were important songs in both film versions. "The Varsity Drag" was also used in the '49 movie musical *You're My Everything.* "Varsity Drag" was nominated for the American Film Institute's list of the greatest songs ever from an American film, but it did not make the final list.

George Olsen and his orchestra also popularized "Lucky in Love" and the title song from *Good News* with successful recordings.

Blue Skies

Words & Music: Irving Berlin

The idea that love can turn gray skies to blue is aptly illustrated in this Irving Berlin song, introduced by Belle Baker in the musical *Betsy.* Richard Rodgers and Lorenz Hart wrote all the other songs for the musical, but Belle Baker called Berlin begging him for a song. She told him there wasn't a Belle Baker–type song in the entire score. All Berlin had to offer was one of his trunk songs that was unfinished. He went to Ms. Baker's apartment with only eight measures of the song complete. By the next morning Ms. Baker called producer Florenz Ziegfeld to tell him Berlin had just finished a great Belle Baker song. Rodgers and Hart had a no interpolation contract, but Ziegfeld finally agreed to allow Ms. Baker to perform it. It came near the end of the show and Ms. Baker and "Blue Skies" electrified the audience, which demanded encore after encore. After the twenty-third time, she forgot the lyric, but Berlin, who was sitting in the front row, came to the rescue by shouting out the words, then he sang a twenty-fourth encore. "Blue Skies," of course, proved to be the biggest hit of the production.

In the musical, Betsy's mother wouldn't allow any of her other children to get married until Betsy, who had no boyfriend, finds a husband.

Variety selected "Blue Skies" for its *Hit Parade of a Half-Century.* The song became one of the most recorded songs of the pre-rock era.

In the first sound film, *The Jazz Singer* ('27), Al Jolson included "Blue Skies" among several of his favorites that he performed in the film. Other movie musicals that used the song included *Glorifying the American Girl* ('30), *Alexander's Ragtime Band* ('38), *Blue Skies* ('46), which starred Bing Crosby and Fred Astaire, and *White Christmas* ('54), where the song was performed by two of the film's stars, Bing Crosby and Danny Kaye. The song also appeared in *Glengarry Glen Ross* ('92), *Star Trek: Nemesis* (2000) and *Romeo Must Die* (2000).

Ben Selvin and his orchestra's recorded version was the most popular one, but several others helped popularize the song nationwide. Others included those by George Olsen and his orchestra, by Vincent Lopez and his orchestra, by vocalists Johnny Marvin and Ed Smalle, plus Harry Richman, and Vaughn DeLeath. Johnny Long and his orchestra revived it with some success in '41; Count Basie and Benny Goodman and their orchestras revived it again with improved success in '46. Ted Lewis' recording of "Blue Skies" is available at http://www.redhotjazz.com/tlband.html.

It is interesting to note that each of the three main sections of the lyric begins with something "blue"— blue skies, bluebirds, and blue days — an excellent example of text writing technique. Berlin's lyrics for the first verse tells us that the singer thought every day was cloudy until good luck came along and the skies weren't gray any more. In the chorus he explains that he sees "nothing but blue skies," and "bluebirds all day long." The sun is shining brightly and everything is going right because he's in love. From now on all of his blue days are gone. Read the lyrics at http://www.oldielyrics.com/lyrics/irving_berlin/blue_skies.html.

Charmaine

Words: Lew Pollack; Music: Erno Rapee

Erno Rapee had the distinction of being the first to write a successful movie theme song. He took a melody that had been written in Hungary in '13 and transformed it into the theme for the silent film *What Price Glory* in '26.

The title of the song could easily have been "I Wonder"

since each phrase of the chorus lyrics begins with those words. The singer wonders if the lover will return to the waiting Charmaine. See the sheet music cover and read the lyrics at http://www.bischel.com/charmaine.html.

The song was chosen for *Variety*'s *Hit Parade of a Half-Century*.

"Charmaine" reportedly became a million sheet music seller and was a very popular recording for Guy Lombardo and his Royal Canadians. Singer Lewis James had a moderately successful '27 record release of it also. Mantovani and his orchestra and Gordon Jenkins and his orchestra revived "Charmaine" in '51, while Paul Weston and his orchestra took the song to Top 10 status in '52. Billy May and Vaughn Monroe and their orchestras issued other '52 recordings.

"Charmaine" was used in the following movie musicals: *Two Girls and a Sailor* ('44), *Margie* ('46) and *Thoroughly Modern Millie* ('67).

The Desert Song, One Alone *and* The Riff Song

Words: Otto Harbach & Oscar Hammerstein II; Music: Sigmund Romberg

Sigmund Romberg's operetta *The Desert Song* has become one of the most durable of all Broadway operettas, with lyrics and book by Otto Harbach and Oscar Hammerstein II. The authors tried to integrate modern news and literary events into the story: an uprising in Morocco, the exploits of Lawrence of Arabia, and the novel *The Sheik*, which had been turned into a film starring Rudolph Valentino.

THE DESERT SONG

At the end of Act One, the Red Shadow comes to take Margot away with him into the desert and sweeps her off her feet with this impassioned song, which is sometimes called "Blue Heaven" because that's how the lyrics begin.

At the end of out of town tryouts for *Lady Fair*, the original title for the musical, Oscar Hammerstein was on a train from Boston to New York City. On that train ride, he wrote the lyrics to an unused Kern melody for the song that would produce the title for the musical: "Blue Heaven and you and I and sand kissing the moonlit sky ... the desert song..."

"The desert song, calling, Its voice enthralling will make you mine" is the basic idea of the chorus lyrics. Read the lyrics at http://www.mixed-up.com/lyrics/round/show.html?name=desert-song.

"The Desert Song" was selected for *Variety*'s *Hit Parade of a Half-Century*.

Nat Shilkret and the Victor Orchestra had the most popular recording of this operetta classic.

ONE ALONE

Another well-known song from the score of *The Desert Song*, "One Alone," was presented in the operetta as the third song in a musical debate concerning love. A desert chieftain advocates brief, uninvolved flings, a lieutenant proposes a harem, but the hero, the Red Shadow, rejects both views in favor of the "one alone" philosophy. Robert Halliday, who originally portrayed the Red Shadow, introduced this gorgeous love song.

Nat Shilkret and the Victor Orchestra had a successful recording of "One Alone," and Don Voorhees and his orchestra also had a worthy recording of the song.

"One Alone" was selected by *Variety* for its *Hit Parade of a Half-Century*.

See the sheet music cover of this song from the '53 film version: http://www.patfullerton.com/gm/ms/desertsong.html.

THE RIFF SONG

"The Riff Song" is a battle call sung by the Red Shadow, Sid El Kar and their band of Riffians (bandits) in the opening scene of the operetta.

This riding song was selected by *Variety* for its *Hit Parade of a Half-Century*.

There have been three screen versions of *The Desert Song*, one in '29 that starred John Boles, one in '43, which starred Dennis Morgan, and one in '53 with Gordon MacRae. "The Desert Song" and "One Alone" were also featured in the screen biography of Sigmund Romberg, *Deep in My Heart* ('54).

Forgive Me

Words: Jack Yellen; Music: Milton Ager

"Forgive Me" was popularized by Gene Austin in a popular recording in '27. Austin's Victor recording was backed by "Someday, Sweetheart." His version of the song was most popular in the summer of '27.

The February 22, 1928 issue of *Variety* reported, "The biggest selling popular vocal artist on all records now is Gene Austin, exclusive Victor artist whose 'Forgive Me' recording went over 500,000 disks."

Eddie Fisher revived it again with some success in '52.

Hallelujah! *and* Sometimes I'm Happy

Words: Clifford Grey & Leo Robin; Music: Vincent Youmans

Hit the Deck was Vincent Youmans's second most memorable musical, after *No, No, Nanette*. Louise Groody played the owner of a coffee shop near a U.S. Navy installation. This nautical production boasts two all-time Youmans hits: "Hallelujah!" and "Sometimes I'm Happy."

HALLELUJAH!

"Hallelujah!" is a revival number featuring a male chorus and Lavinia (Stella Mayhew) in blackface. Lavina tells everyone to sing "Hallelujah!" and they'll chase the blues away. When they're burdened with cares, singing "Hallelujah!" will get them through their darkest days. Satan is just waiting to undo us with gray skies, but if we sing "Hallelujah!" it "helps to shoo the clouds away." Read the lyrics at http://www.stlyrics.com/lyrics/hitthedeck/hallelujah.htm.

The melody had been composed by Youmans during World War I, but was first heard in *Hit the Deck*.

Nat Shilkret and the Victor Orchestra had the most successful '27 recording of "Hallelujah!," but the Revelers and Cass Hagan and his orchestra also helped popularize the song with recordings. The California Ramblers' recording of "Hallelujah!" is available at http://www.redhotjazz.com/caramblers.html.

SOMETIMES I'M HAPPY

Another hit song, "Sometimes I'm Happy," was introduced by Louise Groody and Charles King in *Hit the Deck*. Its melody had been written earlier in a quicker tempo to the title "Come on and Pet Me." The lyricists for the original version were by William Carey Duncan and Oscar

Hammerstein II, but Irving Caesar wrote this lyric for a never-opened musical, *A Night Out*. At a slower tempo "Sometimes I'm Happy" became a hit in *Hit the Deck*.

In the chorus lyrics, the most familiar part of the song, the singer sings that he can sometimes be happy, sometimes blue. His disposition depends on this girl. A particularly comical part of the lyrics is "sometimes I love you, sometimes I hate you, but when I hate you, it's 'cause I love you." Then the singer confesses that's just how he is and there's nothing he can do about it; he's happy when he's with this person. Read the lyrics at http://www.johnnymercer.com/FAQ/Sometimes%20I'm%20Happy.htm.

Louise Groody and Charles King competed with Roger Wolfe Kahn's orchestra for the most popular recorded version of "Sometimes I'm Happy" in '27. Kahn's version featured vocalist Franklyn Baur. Hear Kahn's recording at http://www.redhotjazz.com/rwkahno.html. Benny Goodman and his orchestra revived it in '35, while Sammy Kaye and his orchestra redid it again in '38.

Hollywood filmed versions of *Hit the Deck* in '30 and '55. Both songs were featured in both film versions. Jane Powell and Vic Damone performed "Sometimes I'm Happy" in the '55 version.

Variety selected both songs for its *Hit Parade of a Half-Century* and "Sometimes I'm Happy" for its *Golden 100 Tin Pan Alley Songs* list. "Sometimes I'm Happy" became one of the most recorded songs of the pre-rock era.

I Know That You Know

Words: Anne Caldwell; Music: Vincent Youmans

Top comic talents Beatrice Lillie and Charles Purcell introduced this bouncy romantic duet in Vincent Youmans' *Oh, Please!* It is the one song from the score that has survived. The number uses a readily identifiable Youmans technique of a simple repeated series of notes over numerous harmonic changes.

The lyrics ask, what do "I know that you know?" The answer is I'll go where you go and won't lose you. It will soon be goodbye time, so the singer asks to be held tightly and for one more little goodnight kiss. Read the lyrics at http://libretto.musicals.ru/text.php?textid=343&language=1.

The most popular recording of "I Know That You Know" was by Nat Shilkret. Benny Goodman and his orchestra revived the song with reasonable success in '36. Hear Cliff Edwards' recording of the song at http://www.redhotjazz.com/ike.html.

The song was used in the '30 film version of *Hit the Deck*, in *The Powers Girl* ('43), in the '50 film *Tea for Two*, and in the '55 film version of *Hit the Deck*.

The song was selected by *Variety* for its *Hit Parade of a Half-Century*.

I'm Looking Over a Four-Leaf Clover (see 1948)

Ida! Sweet as Apple Cider

Words & Music: Eddie Leonard

The last of the great minstrels, Eddie Leonard, wrote "Ida! Sweet as Apple Cider" in '03 while appearing with the Primrose and West Minstrels. Leonard later interpolated it into the Broadway musical *Roly Boly Eyes* ('19).

The song became particularly associated with Eddie Cantor, who performed it regularly partially because his wife was named Ida.

Since the copyright is '03, it is possible to print the lyrics. What follows is the verse and chorus: *In the region where the roses always bloom, / Breathing out upon the air their sweet perfume, / Lives a dusky maid I long to call my own, / For, I know my love for her will never die; / When the sun am sinking in dat golden west, / Little robin red breast gone to seek their nests, / And I sneak down to dat place I love the best, / Every evening there along I sigh. / Ida! sweet as apple cider, Sweeter than all I know, / Come out! in the sil-v'ry moonlight, / Of love we'll whisper, so soft and low! / Seems as tho' can't live without you, / Listen, please, honey do! / Ida! I idolize ya. I love you, Ida, 'deed I do.*

In '27, jazz great Red Nichols' Five Pennies had a particularly successful recording of "Ida! Sweet as Apple Cider." Hear Nichols' recording at http://www.redhotjazz.com/rn5p.html. Popular entertainer Frank Crumit had a reasonably successful recording of it in '24, and Glenn Miller and his orchestra took it into the Top 30 in '41.

"Ida..." has remained a standard and was used in the following movie musicals: *Babes in Arms* ('39), *If I Had My Way* ('40), where it was performed by Eddie Leonard, *Broadway Rhythm* ('44), *Incendiary Blonde* ('45) and *The Eddie Cantor Story* ('53).

See the '03 sheet music cover and the musical score at http://scriptorium.lib.duke.edu/sheetmusic/b/b06/b0603/.

In a Little Spanish Town

Words: Sam M. Lewis & Joe Young; Music: Mabel Wayne

The "King of Jazz," Paul Whiteman and his orchestra, Ben Selvin and his orchestra, and Sam Lanin and his orchestra all had successful recordings that helped popularize "In a Little Spanish Town" in '27. David Carroll and his orchestra revived it in '54 with moderate success. Hear Paul Whiteman's recording at http://www.redhotjazz.com/pwo.html.

Virginia O'Brien performed the song in MGM's wartime movie musical *Thousands Cheer* ('43).

The song's success in '27 started a Tin Pan Alley vogue for Spanish-styled songs. At the same time, it launched Mabel Wayne on a career as a successful popular composer.

A subtitle for this hit could easily be "'Twas on a night like this," which appears in the text more often than the title phrase. Read the lyrics at http://www.lyricsvault.net/songs/13874.html.

Just a Memory

Words: Bud G. DeSylva & Lew Brown; Music: Ray Henderson

"Just a Memory" was published as an independent song (not written for a stage or screen production), but it was quickly interpolated into the musical *Manhattan Mary*. Subsequently, it was heard in Marilyn Miller's screen biography *Look for the Silver Lining* ('49), and in Henderson, DeSylva and Brown's screen biography *The Best Things in Life Are Free* ('56).

The chorus lyrics sing about a memory of days the singer had spent with his loved one, but all that's left is the memory. The singer wonders if they will ever share the night, the moon, or the stars again. He also wonders if he dares hope, sing, smile, laugh, or love again. He dreams of her dear face, even "though it's just a memory."

Paul Whiteman and his orchestra had the most popular recording of the song in '27, but there were also successful recordings released by Vincent Lopez and by Franklyn Baur. Hear Paul Whiteman's recording of this song at http://www.redhotjazz.com/pwo.html.

The song was selected by *Variety* for its *Hit Parade of a Half-Century*.

Me and My Shadow

Words: Billy Rose; Music: Al Jolson & Dave Dreyer

This '27 hit was added to the '75 movie *Funny Lady*, the sequel to *Funny Girl*, because Billy Rose, Fanny Brice's second husband was lyricist for the song. In addition to *Funny Lady*, "Me and My Shadow" appeared in Bud Abbott and Lou Costello's *Hold That Ghost* ('41), and *Feudin', Fussin' and A-Fightin'* ('48), a movie musical that starred Donald O'Connor.

"Me and My Shadow" is very closely associated with Ted Lewis. He often performed this number with "shadow" Eddie Chester, who duplicated Lewis's gestures behind a shadowy background while Lewis sang in his half-talking, half-singing style.

As famous as Ted Lewis's performance of "Me and My Shadow" may have been, it was "Whispering" Jack Smith who had the most popular recording of the song in '27, and it was extremely successful. Nat Shilkret and the Victor Orchestra also had a very popular recorded version (Johnny Marvin was the vocalist). Johnny Marvin released his own version on Columbia Records, which had a reasonable amount of success. Although their recordings didn't make the Top 40, Frank Sinatra's solo recording and a duet by Robbie Williams and Jonathan Wilkes of "Me and My Shadow" were also successful.

Frank Fay introduced the song originally in the revue *Harry Delmar's Revels* in '27.

The original chorus lyrics begin with the singer and his shadow walking down the avenue. The singer only has his shadow as a companion. When they return home at twelve o'clock and climb the stairs to their apartment, they don't bother knocking because they know "nobody's there." It's just "me and my shadow, all alone and feeling blue." Some modern recordings, like those by Frank Sinatra and Robbie Williams, use different lyrics.

Miss Annabelle Lee

Words & Music: Sidney Clare, Lew Pollack & Harry Richman

Harry Richman introduced "Miss Annabelle Lee" but it was Ben Selvin and his orchestra that principally popularized the song with a successful recording in '27. Although it wasn't popular enough to chart, Frank Sinatra had a well-known recording of "Miss Annabelle Lee." Ben Selvin's recording of this song is available at http://www.redhotjazz.com/benselvino.html.

The song lyrics ask several questions, like "Who's wonderful, who's marvelous?" The answer is "Miss Annabelle Lee." Miss Annabelle is also kissable, loveable, pretty, and dignified. Read the lyrics at http://www.spiritofsinatra.com/pages/Lyrics/m/Miss_Annabelle_Lee.htm.

The song was used in the '55 movie musical *Gentlemen Marry Brunettes*.

The song was selected by *Variety* for its *Hit Parade of a Half-Century*.

My Blue Heaven

Words: George Whiting; Music: Walter Donaldson

There are a few songs that could be considered *The* Song of a Generation. "My Blue Heaven" could very well be *the* song of the '20s. It became one of the most recorded songs of the pre-rock era.

Lyricist George Whiting introduced this song in vaudeville; Tommy Lyman then popularized it further. Eddie Cantor sang it in the *Ziegfeld Follies of 1927*, where he dominated the show, thanks in part to this outstanding song. But it was singer Gene Austin who made the most lasting impression with "My Blue Heaven." His recording of it is reputed to have sold 5 million copies, and made him rich and famous. His '27 disk remained the top all-time seller until it was replaced by Bing Crosby's "White Christmas" fifteen years later. To have the most successful recording for fifteen years should qualify Gene Austin and his recording of "My Blue Heaven" as *the* song of this generation. Hear Gene Austin's recording of "My Blue Heaven" at http://www.bassocantante.com/flapper/music.html.

The popular refrain begins, "When whip-poor-wills call and ev'ning is nigh, I hurry to my blue heaven." In his little heaven, he finds a smiling face beside a fireplace in a cozy room. Just he, Mollie and their baby are happy in their blue heaven. Read the lyrics at http://lirama.net/song/67218.

Paul Whiteman and his orchestra's recording of the song was practically as popular as Austin's. Hear a '27 recording by Paul Whiteman and his orchestra of this song at http://www.edisonnj.org/menlopark/vintage/victor.asp or http://www.redhotjazz.com/pwo.html. Vocalist Nick Lucas, Don Voorhees and his orchestra, and Seger Ellis also had very successful releases of the song in 1927–28. Sammy Kaye and his orchestra (or "Swing and Sway with Sammy Kaye" as it said on the record) revived it in '39 into a Top 20 hit. Fats Domino revived the song again successfully in '56. The Smashing Pumpkins included the song on their *The Aeroplane Flies High* album in '96.

"My Blue Heaven" was used in the following movie musicals: *Never a Dull Moment* ('43), where it was performed by Frances Langford, *Moon Over Las Vegas* ('44), *My Blue Heaven* ('50) and *Love Me or Leave Me* ('55), the screen biography of Ruth Etting. The song also appeared in *Heaven* ('87) and *The Next Best Thing* (2000).

Variety included "My Blue Heaven" in its *Hit Parade of a Half-Century* and its *Golden 100 Tin Pan Alley Songs* list. Gene Austin's recording of the song was inducted into the Grammy Hall of Fame in '78.

Rio Rita *and* The Rangers' Song

Words: Joseph McCarthy; Music: Harry Tierney

Since *Show Boat* wasn't ready, Florenz Ziegfeld opened his new Ziegfeld Theater in New York City with *Rio Rita*, a flashy spectacle of old Mexico.

The plot of *Rio Rita* concerns the Texas Rangers hunting a notorious bandit known only as the Kinkajou. The Rangers leader, Captain Jim, falls in love with Rio Rita but General Esteban, who also loves her, persuades Rita that Jim courts her because he believes that the man they are looking for is her brother. Only when Jim arrests Esteban as the real villain can he and Rita hope for happiness.

RIO RITA

"Rio Rita" is the principal love song from the musical *Rio Rita*. J. Harold Murray introduced this *Variety Hit Parade of a Half-Century* song. Captain Jim has found love in this tempestuous Rio Rita.

The chorus lyrics begin "Rio Rita, life is sweeter, Rita, when you are near." The singer (Captain Jim) only asks to one day hear her say "I love you." The chorus ends with Captain Jim giving this Senorita his heart.

Recordings by Ben Selvin and his orchestra and by Nat Shilkret and his orchestra helped popularize the song beyond Broadway.

The sheet music cover and musical score are available at http://levysheetmusic.mse.jhu.edu/browse.html.

THE RANGERS' SONG

This robust march in honor of the Texas Rangers was introduced by J. Harold Murray and a chorus of Rangers in *Rio Rita*.

The chorus lyrics are very masculine. They're rootin', tootin' scootin' and shootin' pals. The principal idea of the text is summed up at the end of the chorus: "You're not alone for when you belong to the Lone Star Rangers..."

The U.S. Forest Service has unofficially adopted the song. A Service Bulletin article in '33, "Seeking a Forest Service Song," says, "'The Rangers Song,' to a tune from *Rio Rita*, has now become identified with the Forest Service in the minds of thousands throughout the country through its use for more than a year as the signature song for the radio drama, 'Uncle Sam's Forest Rangers.' It is a lively addition to our repertory. But since it is used with music from a popular musical comedy, we can not claim it exclusively as our own."

"The Rangers' Song" was a *Hit Parade of a Half-Century* selection by *Variety*.

There were two film versions of *Rio Rita*, '29 and '42. "The Ranger's Song" and "Rio Rita" were used in both the films.

Russian Lullaby

Words & Music: Irving Berlin

Irving Berlin's "Russian Lullaby" was inspired by his ancestry. Berlin was born to Russian Jewish parents who named him Israel Baline. He and his family had immigrated to America to escape the Czar's torment. Berlin and his wife, Ellin, had a new daughter, Mary Ellin Berlin. Her birth may have reminded her father of his homeland and his childhood.

The hauntingly beautiful "Russian Lullaby" was written in the key of D minor.

His "Russian Lullaby" hit a responsive chord with the record-buying public in '27. Roger Wolfe Kahn and his orchestra, with vocalist Henry Garden, released the most popular recorded version of "Russian Lullaby," but several others helped popularize the song. Other releases included those by vocalist Franklyn Baur, organist Jesse Crawford, Ernie Golden and his orchestra, with vocalist Vaughn DeLeath, and the Revelers. Bunny Berigan and his orchestra revived "Russian Lullaby" in '38. Hear Ted Lewis' recording of the song at http://www.redhotjazz.com/tlband.html.

The song, along with several other Berlin hits, was used in the score of the movie musical *Blue Skies* ('46).

The verse tells us that a "lonely Russian Rose" lives near the Volga River. She is singing "a Russian lullaby" to a baby on her knees. In the lullaby, the refrain, she dreams of a land that's free for her and her baby. Read the lyrics at http://www.oldielyrics.com/lyrics/irving_berlin/russian_lullaby.html.

Some of These Days

Words & Music: Shelton Brooks

Sophie Tucker introduced Shelton Brooks' "Some of These Days" in Chicago in '10. It became such a successful number for her that it became her theme song. Sophie Tucker's recording with Ted Lewis in '27 was a big hit with the record buying public. She had originally released a recording of it in '11 and it was very popular then also. Hear Sophie Tucker and Ted Lewis' '26 recording of this song at http://www.edisonnj.org/menlopark/vintage/columbia.asp or at http://www.redhotjazz.com/tlband.html.

Shelton Brooks had been wrestling with a minor key melody for several days, but couldn't seem to come up with any appropriate words to go with the tune. One day in a restaurant, he overheard a spat between an African American woman and her boyfriend. Brooks heard her say something like, "some of these days, you're gonna miss me, honey." Brooks immediately thought her phrase matched his tune and, once he had the start, the rest of the song came easily. As soon as it was printed he took it to Sophie Tucker, who had often been helpful to aspiring Afro-American songwriters. Tucker was so enthusiastic about the song she performed it the very next day! "Some of These Days" eventually sold more than two million units on the sheet music market. It was also destined to become a jazz standard. Barry Singer, in his biography of lyricist Andy Razaf, claims that this number was "...perhaps the landmark song of this Tin Pan Alley epoch, whereby Brooks, with sophisticated lyric colloquialism and heartfelt passion, elevated the coon song into the realm of expressive emotion."

The American Quartet in '11, the Original Dixieland Jazz Band in '23, and Bing Crosby in '32 released popular recordings of "Some of These Days."

See the sheet music cover and the musical score at http://lcweb2.loc.gov/cocoon/ihas/loc.natlib.ihas.100004309/, at http://levysheetmusic.mse.jhu.edu/browse.html and at http://digital.library.ucla.edu/apam/ (2 different covers).

Since the song was published in '10, the chorus lyrics follow: *Some of these days You're gonna miss me honey / And I'm talkin' about days When you feel all blue. / You're gonna miss my huggin' You're gonna miss my kissin' / You may even miss me, baby When I'm long gone away. / I hope you feel lonely and want me only / 'Cause you know lover Ya always had your way. / And if you-a leave me You know it's gonna grieve me / You'll miss your brown eyed mamma Some of these days.*

Variety selected "Some of These Days" for its *Golden 100* list. *Variety* chose it to its *Hit Parade of a Half-*Century representing '10. The song became one of the most recorded songs of the pre-rock era.

"The Last of the Red-Hot Mommas," Sophie Tucker performed "Some of These Days" in *Honky Tonk* ('29), *Broadway Melody of 1938*, and *Follow the Boys* ('44). Lillian Roth performed it in the Marx Brothers' *Animal Crackers* ('30). It was also used in *Broadway* ('42) and *All That Jazz* ('79). It was even interpolated into the '36 film version of the operetta *Rose Marie*. The song also appeared in *Forbidden Zone* ('80), *Pi* ('98) and Kevin Spacey performed the song in the movie *Beyond the Sea*, the 2004 screen biopic of singer Bobby Darin.

Tonight You Belong to Me
Words: Billy Rose; Music: Lee David

Billy Rose, Fanny Brice's second husband, wrote the lyrics for "Tonight You Belong to Me" and Lee David contributed the music in '26.

Gene Austin's recording of the song was a major hit in '27. Other popular recordings during the time included those by vocalist Franklyn Baur, by Roger Wolfe Kahn and his orchestra and by singer Irving Kaufman. Frankie Laine revived it with moderate success in '53, but the song was a big hit in '56 for Patience and Prudence.

Patience and Prudence were the daughters of orchestra leader Mack McIntyre. Patience was 11 years old and Prudence was 14 years old when their father brought his daughters into the Liberty Records recording studios in Los Angeles in the summer of '56. One of the songs on their audition tape was a cover version of "Tonight You Belong to Me."

The Lennon Sisters often performed the song on the Lawrence Welk television show.

The chorus lyrics contend the loved one may "belong to somebody else," and realizes at dawn that they will be gone, "but tonight you belong to me." Read the lyrics at http://lirama.net/song/16962.

Steve Martin and Bernadette Peters performed the song in film *The Jerk* ('79). Martin played the ukulele and Ms. Peters played the flugelhorn.

1928

Among My Souvenirs
Words: Edgar Leslie; Music: Horatio Nicholls

"Among My Souvenirs" was originally introduced by Jack Hylton and his orchestra in England. Paul Whiteman and his orchestra introduced it to the United States and their recording of it was among four very popular versions on the market in '28. Hear Whiteman's recording at http://www.redhotjazz.com/pwo.html. Other versions were released by Ben Selvin and his orchestra, by the Revelers, and by Roger Wolfe Kahn and his orchestra. Thirty years later it became a big recording hit for Connie Francis.

The singer is living in memories, reviewing the souvenirs of a broken romance. Read the lyrics at http://lirama.net/song/17310.

Hoagy Carmichael sang "Among My Souvenirs" in the '46 film *The Best Days of Our Lives*.

"Among My Souvenirs" was selected for *Variety's Hit Parade of a Half-Century* representing '27.

Angela Mia (My Angel)
Words: Lew Pollack; Music: Erno Rapee

One of the earliest movie theme songs that swept the hit lists of the late '20s was "Angela Mia (My Angel)," which served as a recurring theme in the synchronized score for the movie *Street Angel*. The film starred Janet Gaynor.

The singer believes that Angela is an angel sent from heaven in answer to his prayers.

Variety selected "Angela Mia" for its *Hit Parade of a Half-Century* representing '28.

Recordings by Paul Whiteman and his orchestra, with vocalists Jack Fulton, Charles Gaylord, and Al Rinker, by Vincent Lopez and his orchestra, with vocalist Lewis James, and by vocalist Scrappy Lambert helped popularize the song nationally. It was revived in '54 by Don, Dick, N' Jimmy and by the Ralph Flanagan Orchestra. Their versions were only moderately successful. Hear Whiteman's recording at http://www.redhotjazz.com/pwo.html (listed as "My Angel").

See the sheet music cover and hear a midi musical version at http://www.parlorsongs.com/issues/1998–2/feb 98feature.asp.

Can't Help Lovin' Dat Man, Make Believe, Ol' Man River *and* Why Do I Love You?
Words: Oscar Hammerstein II; Music: Jerome Kern

Broadway history was made on December 27, 1927, when Florenz Ziegfeld presented Jerome Kern and Oscar Hammerstein II's *Show Boat*, which led the way toward a musical theater of increased scope. The musical became the most lastingly effective and third-longest-running Broadway musical of the decade.

Kern and Hammerstein had been determined to write a musical beyond the conventions of the typical musical comedy of the day. They wanted to write a musical with dramatic continuity and one where each song was an integral element of the plot. They chose Edna Ferber's novel *Show Boat* for the experiment, and the result was a new genre of musical play, integrating all the elements of the plot, music, and characters into one cohesive artistic concept.

The primary plot follows Magnolia Hawks, the daughter of the owner of the show boat, and Gaylord Ravenal, a riverboat gambler, from their first meeting on a levee in Natchez around 1885 to their reunion some thirty-seven years later. In between, they impulsively fall in love at first sight, act together in the showboat productions, marry, move to Chicago during the World's Fair, Gaylord loses what little money they had gambling, and leaves Magnolia before he knows she is pregnant. Magnolia tries to make ends meet as a singer, until her father takes her back to the show boat to make raising her child a little easier. A second romance between the mulatto Julie and the show boat's leading man, Steve, was revolutionary because it dared deal with the subject of miscegenation.

CAN'T HELP LOVIN' DAT MAN

Kern's score has become one of the best known of all Broadway musicals. "Can't Help Lovin' Dat Man" was introduced in the Cotton Blossom's pantry by Julie, while Queenie and Magnolia listen. Magnolia has just told Julie that she is in love and Julie warns her, "Love's a funny thing — there's no sense to it — that's why you got to be so careful..." and begins to sing. The chorus lyrics compare fish swimming and birds flying with the inevitability of Julie loving one man, because she "can't help lovin' dat man of mine." He's lazy and slow, and she may be crazy for loving him, but Julie sings, "Home without him ain't no home to me." The song is supposed to be a traditional song of ardent love that only "colored folks" know. Julie, a mulatto, is passing for white, but is soon removed from the showboat by the sheriff after her background is revealed. Read the libretto and the lyrics at http://www. theatre-musical.com/showboat/lyrics.html (Song No. 7).

Helen Morgan, who played Julie, had the most famous recording of "Can't Help Lovin' Dat Man," but Ben Bernie and his orchestra also had a successful one of the song in '28. More recently, Barbra Streisand included the song on her first Broadway album, with Stevie Wonder featured on harmonica in the accompaniment.

Variety picked this Kern/Hammerstein song for its *Hit Parade of a Half-Century* representing '27.

MAKE BELIEVE

"Make Believe" was sung at the first meeting of Magnolia Hawks, the daughter of the owner of the show boat, and Gaylord Ravenal, a river boat gambler. They had noticed each other and are attracted but express their mutual interest in vague "make believe" terms. Read the libretto and lyrics at http://www.theatre-musical.com/showboat/lyrics.html (Song No. 5).

"Make Believe" was selected by *Variety* for its *Hit Parade of a Half-Century* representing '27. This song was nominated for AFI's list of greatest songs in movies, but was not among the final list.

Hear Paul Whiteman and his orchestra's recording at http://www.redhotjazz.com/pwo.html.

OL' MAN RIVER

In the plot of *Show Boat*, the sheriff warns the gambler, Gaylord Ravenal, that he is not wanted in town and should move on. Magnolia, who has been attracted to Gaylord, quizzes Joe, a black worker on the levee, about Gaylord. Joe refuses to tell her anything. In one of the show's most memorable hits, Joe suggests that if anyone can give her the answer, it must be "ol' man river," who sees all and knows all. Read the libretto and lyrics at http://www.theatre-musical.com/showboat/lyrics.html (Song No. 6).

When Edna Ferber, the author of the novel *Show Boat*, heard "Ol' Man River" for the first time she said: "I give you my word, my hair stood on end, tears came to my eyes. I knew that this wasn't just a musical comedy number. This was a great song. This was a song that would outlast Kern and Hammerstein's day and my day and your day."

Variety selected this *Show Boat* classic for its *Hit Parade of a Half-Century* representing '27 and its *Golden 100 Tin Pan Alley Songs* list. AFI's (American Film Institute) *100 Years ... 100 Songs* (2004) listed "Ol' Man River" as the No. 24 greatest song from an American film even though it was originally introduced in a Broadway musical. AFI named it to their list for the '36 film version where Paul Robeson performed the song. "Ol' Man River" became one of the most recorded songs of the pre-rock era.

Paul Whiteman and his orchestra's recording of "Ol' Man River" was a big hit (actually there were two popular Whiteman recordings in '28: one by the orchestra alone and one with vocalist Paul Robeson; both were very popular, but the orchestra version appears to have been the most successful one). Hear Whiteman's recording with Robeson's vocal and also one with Bing Crosby doing the vocal at http://www.redhotjazz.com/pwo.html. Al Jolson's recording of the song was also well received, as was

one by the Revelers. Jazz pianist Luis Russell and his orchestra, with vocalist Sonny Woods, revived it again in '34 with a moderately successful recording.

WHY DO I LOVE YOU?

"Why Do I Love You?," also from *Show Boat*, was popularized in a '28 recording that was reasonably successful by Nat Shilkret and his orchestra. Hear Paul Whiteman's recording at http://www.redhotjazz.com/pwo.html.

The basic idea of the lyrics can be summed up with three questions from the song: "Why do I love you? Why do you love me? Why should there be two happy as we?" Read the libretto and lyrics (Song No. 18) at http://www. theatre-musical.com/showboat/lyrics2.html.

"Why Do I Love You?" was also included in *Variety*'s *Hit Parade of a Half-Century* representing '27.

Film versions of *Show Boat* were made in '29, a part-talking production; in '36, generally considered the most faithful screen version, and in '51, a Technicolor version. "Can't Help Lovin' Dat Man," "Make Believe," and "Ol' Man River" were used in all three versions, as well as in Jerome Kern's screen biography *Till the Clouds Roll By* ('46). "Can't Help Lovin' Dat Man" was also used in *The Helen Morgan Story* ('57). "Bill" and "Make Believe" were omitted from the '29 version, but were a part of the other two.

A '32 recording of the songs from *Show Boat* by Paul Roberson, Helen Morgan, James Melton, Frank Munn, Countess Albani with Victor Young's orchestra and chorus was inducted into the Grammy Hall of Fame in '91.

Chloe (The Song of the Swamp)

Words: Gus Kahn; Music: Neil Moret

"Chloe" was deemed worthy of inclusion in *Variety*'s *Hit Parade of a Half-Century* representing '27.

When Gus Kahn wrote the lyrics to this novelty song, he turned to his wife and said, "I wrote this song and never once mentioned Chloe in the chorus." He and Neil Moret finally decided to leave it as it was; Chloe is mentioned often in the verse, however.

Paul Whiteman and his orchestra popularized the song with a successful recording in '28. Hear Whiteman's recording at http://www.redhotjazz.com/pwo.html. Whiteman's recording sounds spooky, but is also comical. The singer says he "has to go where you are" even if it's through the swamp.

However, "Chloe" may have been even more popular in the mid-'40s when Spike Jones and his City Slickers' comical version was popular. Louis Armstrong revived the song again in '53 with a somewhat popular version.

The song appeared in the movie musical *Bring on the Girls* ('45).

Diane (I'm in Heaven When I See You Smile)

Words: Lew Pollack; Music: Erno Rapee

An unidentified singer performed the song "Diane" for the '27 film *Seventh Heaven*. The "soundtrack" was recorded separately, that is, this was a silent film, but there was an accompanying soundtrack.

The film's plot concerns Chico, a Parisian sewer worker, rescuing Diane from her cruel sister and gives her shelter in his home.

The lyrics of this *Variety Hit Parade of a Half-Century*

selection for '28 request a smile from Diane. Something so simple puts the singer in heaven.

Nat Shilkret and the Troubadors had the most popular recording of "Diane" in '28.

I Can't Give You Anything but Love (Baby) *and* Diga Diga Doo

Words: Dorothy Fields; Music: Jimmy McHugh

Beginning in '26, white producer/director Lew Leslie staged a popular series of *Blackbirds* revues. Although these productions showcased African American talent, they were almost completely created by Caucasian writers and composers.

Blackbirds of 1928 was the zenith of the series. This production opened at the Liberty Theater in New York City's prime theater district, not in Harlem, with an all-black cast and an all-white creative team.

I CAN'T GIVE YOU ANYTHING BUT LOVE (BABY)

The big hit song from *Blackbirds of 1928* was "I Can't Give You Anything but Love." Patsy Kelly had initially introduced it in the '27 revue *Harry Delmar's Revels.* "I Can't Give You Anything but Love" was then interpolated into *Lew Leslie's Blackbirds of 1928* by Aida Ward in her Broadway debut. She performed it with Willard Mclean and Bill Robinson, who was also known as "Mr. Bo Jangles."

Numerous recordings helped popularize "I Can't Give You Anything but Love," including those by Cliff "Ukulele Ike" Edwards, by Ben Selvin and his orchestra, by Johnny Hamp and his orchestra, by singer Gene Austin, by Nat Shilkret and the Victor Orchestra, and by Seger Ellis and his orchestra. Hear Johnny Hamp's Kentucky Serenaders' recording of this song at http://www.redhotjazz.com/jhks.html. Pianist Teddy Wilson and his orchestra with legendary blues vocalist, Billie Holiday, revived it in '36, as did pianist/singer Rose Murphy in '48.

The success of the song was partially due to jazz recordings that never made the pop charts by Louis Armstrong, Benny Goodman, and Fats Waller. By the mid-'60s there were more than 450 recordings of this tune, and it had reportedly sold a total of more than 2.5 million records. "I Can't Give You Anything but Love" became one of the most recorded songs of the pre-rock era. Hear Louis Armstrong's recording of the song at http://www.redhotjazz.com/lao.html.

This song was included in *Variety's Hit Parade of a Half-Century* representing '28 and its *Golden 100 Tin Pan Alley Songs* list.

Reportedly the idea for this hit song came when the writers overheard a young man outside Tiffany's in New York City tell his girlfriend, "Gee, honey, I can't give you nothin' but love." Dorothy Fields picked up on that quote almost literally: "I can't give you anything but love, Baby, That's the only thing I've plenty of, Baby." He would love to help her look great, but the only jewels he can afford come from a 5-&-10-cent store ("diamond bracelets Woolworth doesn't sell"). Read the lyrics at http://lirama.net/song/15980.

Hollywood used the song in several movie musicals beginning with *I Can't Give You Anything but Love* in '40. Additionally it appeared in *True to the Army* ('42), *Stormy Weather* ('43), Charlie Barnet and his band performed the song in *Jam Session* ('44), Gloria DeHaven performed the song in French in *So This Is Paris* ('55), and *The Helen Morgan Story* ('57). The song also appeared in *Miss Mary* ('96), *The Mambo Kings* ('92), *Nixon* ('95), *The Green Mile* ('99), *Catch Me If You Can* (2002) and jazz violinist Django Reinhardt's recording of the song was used on the soundtrack of *The Aviator* (2004).

DIGA DIGA DOO

Adelaide Hall introduced a second hit, "Diga Diga Doo," in her first starring role on Broadway in the all-black revue *Blackbirds of 1928*. It also was the Broadway debut for the composer and the lyricist, Jimmy McHugh and Dorothy Fields.

In the presentation of the song, Hall was supported by a bevy of girls dressed in two-piece red sequined costumes with red feathers to suggest African Zulus. The "diga diga doo" of the title is supposedly the beat of a Zulu man's heart when he is in love.

"Diga Diga Doo" was performed by Lena Horne in the '43 movie musical *Stormy Weather*. The song was also used in the 2004 film *The Notebook*, where it was performed by Rex Stewart and the Ellingtons.

Variety selected this song for its *Hit Parade of a Half-Century* representing '28.

Jazz legend Duke Ellington and his orchestra had the only popular record of the song. Hear Ellington's recording of the song at http://www.redhotjazz.com/dukecco.html.

Ben Selvin and his orchestra's recording of "I Must Have That Man!," also from *Blackbirds of 1928*, was popular in '28. Hear this song as recorded by Duke Ellington and his Cotton Club Orchestra at http://www.redhotjazz.com/dukecco.html.

Here Comes the Show Boat

Words: Billy Rose; Music: Maceo Pinkard

Variety selected "Here Comes the Show Boat" for its *Hit Parade of a Half-Century* representing '27.

Even though both "Here Comes the Show Boat" and the musical *Show Boat* came out in '27, they are not related. Kern and Hammerstein, of course, wrote *Show Boat*, while Billy Rose and Maceo Pinkard wrote this song. "Here Comes the Show Boat" could have been influenced by the success of *Show Boat*.

Vaughn DeLeath had the most successful recording of the song, but hers was only marginally popular. Hear Jean Goldkette and his orchestra's recording of this song at http://www.redhotjazz.com/goldo.html.

The song is a typical southern-flavored number. The lyrics begin, "Here comes the show boat, puff, puff, puff, puff, puff, puff, puffin' along." "Mammy and Pappy" are so happy they're shufflin' along.

I Wanna Be Loved by You

Words: Bert Kalmar; Music: Herbert Stothart & Harry Ruby

"I Wanna Be Loved by You" is the "boop-boop-a-doop" song. Because Helen Kane introduced it in the musical *Good Boy,* she assumed the title "the Boop-Boop-a-Doop Girl." This song was the only memorable number from the score of *Good Boy*. Delivered in Kane's distinctive delivery, the song became a hit, perhaps one of the biggest novelty hits of the decade. Hear Kane's '28 recording of the song at http://nfo.net/ogg.htm (listed as "I Want to Be Loved by You").

The principal idea of the chorus lyrics can be summed up in the following excerpt: "I wanna be loved by you, just you, and nobody else but you." Those thoughts appear at the beginning and end of the chorus. Read the lyrics at http://kopteri.net/koti/milaja/mm/lyrics/Loved.htm.

The song was performed by Helen Kane's voice in *Three Little Words* ('50), the screen biography of Harry Ruby and Bert Kalmar. Debbie Reynolds mouthed the words to Ms. Kane's voice. It was also used in *Gentlemen Marry Brunettes* ('55), which was set in the '20s.

The song was deemed worthy of inclusion in *Variety*'s *Hit Parade of a Half-Century* representing '28 (listed as "I Want to Be Loved by You).

Jeannine (I Dream of Lilac Time)

Words: L. Wolfe Gilbert; Music: Nat Shilkret

Gene Austin helped popularize "Jeannine (I Dream of Lilac Time)" with a very successful recording. The song's composer Nat Shilkret and the Victor Orchestra also had a popular recorded version. Ben Selvin and his orchestra and famous Irish tenor John McCormack also helped make it a national hit with their recordings of "Jeannine." Hear Paul Whiteman and his orchestra's version at http://www.redhotjazz.com/pwo.html.

The chorus lyrics begin with the title phrase. Next come metaphors about her eyes, her smile, and her cheeks. The singer is evidently going away and will return during lilac time. He sings, "When I return, I'll make you mine ... Jeannine, I dream of lilac time."

The song was written to accompany the silent film *Lilac Time* ('28), which starred Delores del Rio.

The song was deemed worthy of inclusion in *Variety*'s *Hit Parade of a Half-Century* representing '28.

Laugh, Clown, Laugh

Words: Sam M. Lewis & Joe Young; Music: Ted FioRito

Fred Waring and his Pennsylvanians had a very successful recording of "Laugh, Clown, Laugh" that helped make it nationally known. Hear Waring's recording at http://www.redhotjazz.com/waringspa.html. Ted Lewis also had a popular recording of the song.

"Laugh, Clown, Laugh" is a popular song version of the tale of the tragic clown from Leoncavallo's opera *I Pagliacci*. The opera's basic plot tells a story about a traveling troop of actors. We soon learn that Canio is an extremely jealous husband, for good reason it appears. Nedda, his wife, has a lover, Silvio, in this village. One of the traveling players observes the lovers together and rushes to tell Canio. When Canio arrives, Silvio gets away. Canio and Nedda argue about the identity of her lover. Then Canio is reminded of their upcoming performance and that he needs to get ready. As Canio slowly puts on his make-up and clown costume he sings the touching "Vesti la Guibba" (see 1907). During the evening's performance, Colombina (Nedda) brings another man home to eat with her since her husband, Pagliacci (Canio), is away for the evening. Pagliacci returns unexpectedly and interrupts them. Reality and stage become intertwined. Canio kills Nedda and as her lover, Silvio, rushes to the stage, he also stabs him. Then as Canio closes the curtain, he declares, "The comedy is over!"

The 1928 American silent film *Laugh, Clown, Laugh* starring Lon Chaney was a variation on *Pagliacci*, though it did not use the actual plot. The sheet music cover advertises the MGM film with Chaney's picture in his clown outfit on the cover. Even though the film was silent, this song was the film's theme song.

Lyricists Lewis and Young provided a recitation on the back cover of the sheet music (the first 16 lines fit "Vesta la Guibba," the last 7 lines fit the last 16 bars of the chorus of the song; the last line was to be sung). The recitation suggests the whole world is a masquerade party, because we all wear a mask to cover up the real person underneath. We're just actors playing our parts, entering and exiting to play our role, not really having much choice in the matter. The performer played the part of a lover, but the one he wanted is unattainable. Even though the world may think he's merry, playing the part of the clown, his mask now covers tears. Even though it hurts, he must just keep acting the part: "Just like Pagliacci — Laugh, clown, laugh!"

Let's Do It (Let's Fall in Love) *and* Let's Misbehave

Words & Music: Cole Porter

E. Ray Goetz, a Broadway producer, encountered musician-international playboy Cole Porter at the Lido in Venice, Italy. Goetz, who knew of Porter's famous parties, at which he would perform some of his cute, often sexy, songs for his guests, was planning a musical as a vehicle to star his wife, Irene Bordoni. He decided to try to convince the wealthy Porter to write the music and lyrics for an entire Broadway musical. Most people didn't think Porter would do it, after all, if a person doesn't need the money, why would they work? Porter wrote a remarkable musical score for his Broadway debut. From it came "Let's Do It (Let's Fall in Love)." However, "Let's Do It" was not the first song that Porter wrote for that particular place in the show. "Let's Misbehave" was originally intended to be used, but it was dropped in favor of "Let's Do It." Both songs are cute, clever, and slightly risqué.

In the musical's plot, a Massachusetts matron is summoned to Paris for the marriage of her son to Vivienne Rolland, played by Ms. Bordoni, the darling of the Paris stage. The mother schemes to terminate the engagement and her plan succeeds. By the final curtain, Vivienne and her devoted dancing partner, Guy, realize they are in love, and her former suitor, Andrew, turns his attention to an equally dim-witted girl named Brenda.

LET'S DO IT (LET'S FALL IN LOVE)

Irene Bordoni and Arthur Margetson introduced the incredibly clever "Let's Do It" in Cole Porter's first Broadway show, *Paris*. The lyrics enumerate the mating habits of numerous flora and fauna, insinuating that the two lovers should do the same thing. Cole Porter is *the* master of ingenious and imaginative lyrics. Read these delightful lyrics at http://www.thepeaches.com/music/composers/cole/LetsDoItLetsFallInLove.htm.

The most popular recordings of "Let's Do It" were by Irving Aaronson and his orchestra. Hear Aaronson's recording of this song with vocalists Phil Saxe and Jack Armstrong at http://www.redhotjazz.com/aaronson.html. Paul Whiteman and his orchestra, with vocalists Jack Fulton, Charles Gaylord, and Austin Young, and the Dorsey Brothers Orchestra, with vocalist Bing Crosby also had popular recordings of the song.

Cole Porter's screen biography, *Night and Day* ('46), used the song in its score, as did *Can-Can* ('60), where it was performed by Frank Sinatra and Shirley MacLaine. "Let's Do It" was sung by Alanis Morissette on the soundtrack of the 2004 Cole Porter movie musical *De-Lovely*.

LET'S MISBEHAVE

Porter wrote "Let's Misbehave" for Irene Bordoni to perform in *Paris*, but it was deleted from the show in favor of "Let's Do It" during pre–Broadway tryouts. Not unlike "Let's Do It," "Let's Misbehave" enumerates the love life of several members of the animal kingdom. Read the lyrics at http://www.thepeaches.com/music/composers/cole/LetsMisbehave.htm.

"Let's Misbehave" was used in the '75 movie musical *At Long Last Love*, which starred Burt Reynolds, Cybill Shepherd, and Madeline Kahn. Irving Aaronson and his Commanders' recording of "Let's Misbehave" was featured in the '82 movie musical *Pennies from Heaven*. Hear Aaronson's recording of the song at http://www.redhotjazz.com/aaronson.html. "Let's Misbehave" was performed by Elvis Costello in the 2004 Cole Porter movie musical *De-Lovely*.

Ben Bernie and his orchestra had a moderately successful recording of "Let's Misbehave" in '28. It probably was a little too risqué for the sensitive ears of most of the listening public during the late '20s.

Marquita (Marcheta)

Words & Music: Victor Schertzinger

Variety included "Marquita" in its *Hit Parade of a Half-Century* representing '28, however that seems strange. The only popular recordings of "Marcheta" are by Olive Kline and Elsie Baker in '22, by Isham Jones and his orchestra in '23, and by John McCormack in '24. And Victor Schertzinger wrote a song titled "Marquita (Marcheta)" in '13. None of those dates matches '28 by any means.

Gene Autry performed "Marcheta" on his December 24, 1950 telecast in an episode title *The Sheriff of Santa Rosa*. He pronounced "Marcheta" exactly the same as "Marquita."

"Marcheta" was used as background music for the non-musical film *They Were Expendable* in '45.

The lyrics of Victor Schertzinger's "Marcheta" are available at http://kokomo.ca/early_years/marcheta_lyrics.htm.

My Heart Stood Still *and* Thou Swell

Words: Lorenz Hart; Music: Richard Rodgers

A Connecticut Yankee was a musical version of Mark Twain's novel *A Connecticut Yankee in King Arthur's Court*. In the musical's prologue, Martin, the Yankee, is visiting his former fiancée, Alice Carter, on the eve of his marriage to Fay Morgan. Fay discovers them together and knocks Martin out with a champagne bottle. During his unconsciousness, Martin dreams he is back in Camelot in the days of King Arthur. He falls in love with Demoiselle Alisande Le Carteloise, is dubbed "Sir Boss," and is charged with industrializing the country. To the astonishment of the Knights of the Round Table, Sir Boss introduces telephones, advertising and radio. The King's evil sister Morgana Le Fay has Alisande kidnapped, but Sir Boss rescues her just before he awakens. Back in reality, he realizes it is Alice not Fay whom he really loves.

MY HEART STOOD STILL

"My Heart Stood Still" was first introduced in a '27 English revue *One Damn Thing After Another*, then by William Gaxton and Constance Carpenter in the '27 American musical *A Connecticut Yankee*.

Rodgers and Hart got the idea for the song while they were in Paris. They and a French girl were in a near accident in a taxi, when the girl exclaimed "Oh, my heart stood still!" Hart took note of the exclamation, thinking it would make a good title for a song. Upon their return to London to resume work on the revue, Rodgers supplied music and Hart added words to go with the phrase from the near accident.

In the chorus lyrics, the singer takes "one look at you" and his heart stood still. He sings he "never lived at all until the thrill of that moment." Read the lyrics at Lorenz Hart's website: http://www.lorenzhart.org/stoodsng.htm.

George Olsen and his orchestra, with vocalists Fran Frey, Bob Borger and Bob Rice, recorded the most successful version of "My Heart Stood Still." Their disk was most popular during '28. Two other disks were very successful: Ben Selvin and Paul Whiteman and their orchestras. Hear Whiteman's recording of the song at http://www.redhotjazz.com/pwo.html.

"My Heart Stood Still" was listed as a *Variety Golden 100 Tin Pan Alley Song* and *Hit Parade of a Half-Century* selection representing '27.

THOU SWELL

Another hit song from the score was "Thou Swell," which was introduced by William Gaxton and Constance Carpenter.

The combination of King Arthurian English and American slang in the lyrics made this sprightly duet a classic lyric. The chorus lyrics begin: "Thou swell! Thou witty! Thou sweet! Thou grand!" which illustrates the King Arthurian English. American slang is represented by "hear me holler I choose a sweet lollapalooza..." Read the lyrics at Lorenz Hart's website: http://www.lorenzhart.org/swellsng.htm.

Ben Selvin and his orchestra had the most successful recording of "Thou Swell." "My Heart Stood Still" and "Thou Swell" were back to back on the same Selvin record. Bix Beiderbecke and his Gang's recording of "Thou Swell" can be heard at http://www.redhotjazz.com/bixgang.html.

The film version of the musical in '49 starred Bing Crosby, but it omitted "My Heart Stood Still" and "Thou Swell." However, "Thou Swell" was performed in Rodgers and Hart's screen biography, *Words and Music* ('48), by June Allyson and the Blackburn twins.

Variety included "Thou Swell" in its *Hit Parade of a Half-Century* representing '27.

My Melancholy Baby

Words: George A. Norton; Music: Ernie Burnett

"My Melancholy Baby," a *Variety Golden 100 Tin Pan Alley Song* and *Hit Parade of a Half-Century* selection representing '12, was copyrighted in '11. It was first popularized in vaudeville, then in a '15 recording by Walter Van Brunt. In '28 Gene Austin revived it with a very successful recording. That wasn't the end, however; it has been revived further in '35, '36, '39 and '47 by Al Bowlly, Teddy Wilson, Bing Crosby and Sam Donohue respectively. Gene Austin's '28 recording was apparently the most successful. Walter Van Brunt had recorded it in '15. "My Melancholy Baby" became one of the most recorded songs of the pre-rock era. Hear Paul Whiteman's recording of this song at http://www.redhotjazz.com/pwo.html.

The song, Ernie Burnett's only hit song, was involved in a much-publicized legal suit in '40. When the song was originally written lyrics were furnished by Burnett's wife, Maybelle E. Watson. That version, titled "Melancholy," was published in '11. The next year the publisher hired George A. Norton to revise the lyric and it was re-published as "My Melancholy Baby," crediting Norton for the words. In '40 Maybelle Watson, divorced from Burnett by this time, sued to establish her interest in the copyright. She won the case and was awarded back royalties by the court.

The '11 version of the sheet music cover and musical score titled "Melancholy" can be accessed at http://levysheetmusic.mse.jhu.edu/browse.html, however this edition lists George A. Norton as the lyricist. A '12 edition can be accessed at http://scriptorium.lib.duke.edu/dynaweb/sheetmusic/1910–1920/@Generic__BookTextView/31747, also with Norton as lyricist.

In the mid-'60s, the son of composer Ben Light claimed that his father wrote the song but failed to have it copyrighted. He charged that Burnett stole the melody and copyrighted it as his own. That claim was never substantiated.

The chorus lyrics urge the loved one to be his melancholy baby. These lyrics also anticipate the mood of the Great Depression: "Ev'ry cloud must have a silver lining. Wait until the sun shines through." The singer tells his girl to smile or he will be melancholy. Read the lyrics at http://lirama.net/song/17399.

The song has appeared in several Hollywood musicals, including an instrumental version in *East Side of Heaven* ('39), plus *Swing It Soldier* ('41), *Birth of the Blues* ('41), *Follow the Band* ('43), *Minstrel Man* ('44), *Billy Rose's Diamond Horseshoe* ('45), and the '54 version of *A Star Is Born*. The song also appeared in the non-musical film *Scarlet Street* ('45).

Ramona

Words: L. Wolfe Gilbert; Music: Mabel Wayne

"Ramona" was commissioned by the film studio to help promote a movie of the same name. The sheet music cover says the song was dedicated to Dolores Del Rio, the star of the film.

"Ramona" was introduced by Paul Whiteman and his orchestra on a coast-to-coast radio broadcast before the motion picture opened.

The chorus lyrics tell Ramona the singer hears mission bells "ringing out our song of love." He sings that they'll meet that evening beside a water fall. He dreads the dawn when she'll be gone. Read the lyrics at http://lirama.net/song/23199.

Paul Whiteman and Gene Austin's recordings were both extremely successful. Reportedly Gene Austin's version sold 2 million copies, making it one of the first multi-million selling recordings. Torch singer Ruth Etting and vocalist Scrappy Lambert both released successful recordings of "Ramona." The song also sold well on piano rolls and in sheet music. The Gaylords revived the song in '53; their recording topped out at No. 12 on the *Billboard* chart. Hear Paul Whiteman's recording of "Ramona" at

http://www.redhotjazz.com/pwo.html.

"Ramona" was chosen by *Variety* for its *Hit Parade of a Half-Century* representing '27.

'S Wonderful

Words: Ira Gershwin; Music: George Gershwin

The Gershwins created the songs for the musical *Funny Face*, which starred the brother and sister team of Fred and Adele Astaire, Allen Kearns, and Victor Moore.

Funny Face was first dubbed *Smarty* but the name was changed during pre–Broadway tryouts. The plot was shallow, but the show's main attractions were Gershwin's music and the Astaires.

The top tune from the show, made all the more memorable by Ira's clever shorthand lyrics, was "'S Wonderful." Ira's goal was to write rhymed conversation. He had an unusually keen ear for the way people actually speak. When we speak, we elide words, slide into some syllables, drop some parts of the words, and communicate in ways that are almost impossible to put in writing. In "'S Wonderful" we have a contraction with the elimination of *it* from *it's* and the elision of the remaining *s* with *wonderful*. Such usage is common in colloquial conversation. Other elided words include "'s marvelous," "'s awful nice," "'s paradise" "'s what I love." Read the lyrics at http://www.thepeaches.com/music/composers/gershwin/SWonderful.htm.

This love duet was introduced by Adele Astaire and Allen Kearns, the lovers in the story.

Recordings of "'S Wonderful" in 1927–28 were available by popular entertainer Frank Crumit, accompanied by Jack Shilkret on the pipe organ and by Sam Lanin's Ipana Troubadours, featuring vocalist Scrappy Lambert. Hear Frankie Trumbauer and his orchestra's recording of "'S Wonderful" at http://www.redhotjazz.com/fto.html.

"'S Wonderful" was included by *Variety* in its *Hit Parade of a Half-Century* representing '27.

The song was used in Gershwin's biopic *Rhapsody in Blue* ('45), *American in Paris* ('51), where it was performed by Gene Kelly and Georges Guetary, and *Funny Face* ('57), where Fred Astaire and Audrey Hepburn performed it. This song was nominated for the American Film Institute's list of the greatest songs ever from an American film, but did not make the final list. It was nominated for the '57 film version of *Funny Face*. The song also appeared in the movies *Torch Song Trilogy* ('88) and *Grumpier Old Men* ('95).

The Arden-Ohman Orchestra popularized the title song, "Funny Face," with a successful '28 recording.

Jane Green popularized "My One and Only," also from *Funny Face*, with a successful '28 recording.

Sonny Boy *and* There's a Rainbow 'Round My Shoulder

Words & Music: Various

SONNY BOY

While Al Jolson's second talking-picture, *The Singing Fool*, was being rehearsed, "Sonny Boy" became a last-minute replacement for a song that had been judged unsuitable. Jolson telephoned Buddy DeSylva to urge the Henderson, DeSylva, and Brown songwriting team to write a number that would fit into the specific spot in the film. The next morning the song had been written.

It has been suggested that the writing team created "Sonny Boy" tongue in cheek. They did write it originally under the pen name Elmer Colby, as if they didn't want anyone to know that it came from such a famous and prestigious songwriting team. Nevertheless, Jolson took it seriously and sang it into immortality when he "sobbed" it to little Davey Lee in the film.

In addition to *The Singing Fool*, "Sonny Boy" was also used in *Leathernecking* ('30), a reworking of Rodgers and Hart's *Present Arms*, which starred Jolson, in *Jolson Sings Again* ('49), and Henderson, DeSylva, and Brown's biopic *The Best Things in Life Are Free* ('56).

Jolson's recording of "Sonny Boy" was one of the biggest hits of the decade. Hear Al Jolson's '28 recording of this song: at http://www.authentichistory.com/audio/1920s/Al_Jolson-Sonny_Boy.html. Other popular recordings of it were released by Ruth Etting, by Jan Garber and his orchestra, and by Gene Austin. The Andrews Sisters revived it with reasonable success in '41.

Variety placed "Sonny Boy" on its *Hit Parade of a Half-Century* representing '28. Jolson's recording of the song was inducted into the Grammy Hall of Fame in 2002. "Sonny Boy" was nominated for the American Film Institute's list of the greatest songs ever from American films, but it did not make the final list.

Jolson sings: "Climb upon my knee, Sonny Boy." He tells this three year old how much he means to him. This little tike makes the gray skies blue for him. Even if his friends forsake him, "I still have you, Sonny Boy." See the sheet music cover and hear a midi musical version at http://www.perfessorbill.com/covers/sonnyboy.htm or read the lyrics and hear a midi version at http://www.smickandsmodoo.com/lyrics/sonny.htm.

THERE'S A RAINBOW 'ROUND MY SHOULDER

In addition to "Sonny Boy," another Al Jolson specialty was introduced in the movie *The Singing Fool*. Jolson's '28 recording of "There's a Rainbow 'Round My Shoulder," coupled with "Sonny Boy," is estimated to have sold a million copies. Jolson also sang the song for his '46 screen biography *The Jolson Story*, where Larry Parks played the part of Jolson. It was also featured in the '52 movie musical titled *Rainbow 'Round My Shoulder*, which starred Frankie Laine.

"There's a Rainbow 'Round My Shoulder" was written by lyricists Billy Rose and Al Jolson with music composed by Dave Dreyer.

McKinney's Cotton Pickers' recording of this song can be heard at http://www.redhotjazz.com/cotton.html.

The lyrics say that being in love gives one all the right things, including "a rainbow 'round my shoulder," which is symbolic of everything in the world being in tune — all's right with the world. Read the lyrics at http://briansetzer-orchestra.the-lyrics.com/there's-a-rainbow-round-my-shoulder-323795.html.

Al Jolson also popularized "Golden Gate" from *The Singing Fool* with a successful recording. Billy Rose and Dave Dreyer contributed the lyrics, while Al Jolson and Joseph Meyer provided the music.

Sweet Sue — Just You
Words: Will J. Harris; Music: Victor Young

The "Sue" in the title of this song was Sue Carol, later Mrs. Alan Ladd, whose portrait appeared on the cover of the sheet music and to whom the song was dedicated.

The most popular recordings were by Earl Burtnett and his Los Angeles Biltmore Hotel Orchestra, with a vocal performance by the Biltmore Trio, and by Ben Pollack and his Californians, with vocalist Franklyn Baur. Hear Ben Pollack and his Californians' version at http://www.redhotjazz.com/pollackcalif.html. It was revived several times: by the Mills Brothers with good success in '32, by Tommy Dorsey and his orchestra in '39 and by Johnny Long and his orchestra in '49. Several jazz oriented recordings of the song have been made, some of them critically acclaimed, but they never were nationally popular. Hear Paul Whiteman's recording with Bix Beiderbecke on cornet and Jack Fulton on vocals at http://www.redhotjazz.com/pwo.html.

"Sweet Sue" was used in the Fred Astaire movie musical *Second Chorus* ('41), in *Rhythm Parade* ('42), and in *The Eddy Duchin Story* ('56). The song also appeared in the non-musical films *Sweet and Low Down* ('99) and *Red Betsy* (2003).

Variety chose "Sweet Sue" for its *Hit Parade of a Half-Century* representing '28 and its *Golden 100 Tin Pan Alley Songs* list. "Sweet Sue" became one of the most recorded songs of the pre-rock era.

The chorus lyrics open with "Ev'ry star above knows the one I love, Sweet Sue, just you." The singer says she's the only one that ever shared his dreams. He assures her that she lives in his heart all the time. Read the lyrics at http://lirama.net/song/22327.

The Sweetheart of Sigma Chi (see 1912)

Variety named this song to its *Hit Parade of a Half-Century* twice, for 1912 and 1928.

That's My Weakness Now
Words: Bud Green; Music: Sam H. Stept

"That's My Weakness Now" was introduced at the Paramount Theater in New York City by a still unknown Helen Kane. She added a few "boop-boop-a-doops" to the chorus, which started her road to stardom. "The Boop-Boop-a-Doop Girl" had established her trademark.

And what was the weakness? The sheet music's lyrics were written from the male perspective. Presumably, Ms. Kane would have changed the gender. The male singer had a weakness for whatever a particular girl had: "She's got eyes of blue, I never cared for eyes of blue, but she's got eyes of blue, and that's my weakness now."

Helen Kane's recording was the only popular version in '28, but it was revived by Russ Morgan and his orchestra with moderate success in '49. Hear Paul Whiteman's recording of this song featuring the Rhythm Boys at http://www.redhotjazz.com/pwo.html. This song was selected for inclusion in *Variety's Hit Parade of a Half-Century* representing '28.

"That's My Weakness Now" was used in the '29 movie musical *Applause*.

Together
Words: B.G. DeSylva & Lew Brown; Music: Ray Henderson

The collaborations of Henderson, DeSylva, and Brown lasted only from '25 through '30, but those years were extremely productive for the team: six Broadway musicals, songs for five Hollywood films and nearly two dozen major hit songs.

The lovely old-fashioned waltz "Together" was one of their successes. The lyrics seem very nostalgic of days gone by: "We strolled the lane..., laughed in the rain..., Sang love's refrain..." Read the lyrics at http://lirama.net/song/17793.

Paul Whiteman and his orchestra, with vocalist Jack Fulton, had a very successful recorded version of "Together." Hear Paul Whiteman's recording of "Together" at http://www.redhotjazz.com/pwo.html. Cliff Edwards ("Ukulele Ike") and Nick Lucas also each released successful versions of the song in '28. A duet version by Helen Forrest and Dick Haymes was very popular when they revived it in '44. Guy Lombardo and his Royal Canadians and Dinah Shore also released success versions in '44.

Its popularity in '44 was probably due to its interpolation into the Claudette Colbert-Joseph Cotton film *Since You Went Away* or visa versa. Shirley Temple performed the song in the film. Connie Francis revived the song again in '61.

The song was a part of the score of Henderson, De-Sylva, and Brown's biopic *The Best Things in Life Are Free* ('56) and was featured in the film *Since You Went Away*.

When You're Smiling

Words & Music: Mark Fisher, Joe Goodwin & Larry Shay

Seger Ellis had a popular recording of "When You're Smiling" in '28. Louis Armstrong revived it in '29 and Ted Wallace revived it again in '30. Hear Louis Armstrong's recording of this song at http://www.redhotjazz.com/lao.html.

The subtitle of the song is "the whole world smiles with you." Read the lyrics at http://lirama.net/song/13392.

The song was used in the movie musical *You're a Lucky Fellow Mr. Smith* ('43), *When You're Smiling* ('50) and in the Frank Sinatra film *Meet Danny Wilson* ('52).

Contemporary big-band vocalist Michael Buble recorded the song on his first album.

Variety selected this song for its *Hit Parade of a Half-Century* representing '28.

1929

Ain't Misbehavin' *and* Honeysuckle Rose

Words: Andy Razaf; Music: Fats Waller & Harry Brooks (on "Ain't Misbehavin')

AIN'T MISBEHAVIN'

"Ain't Misbehavin'" was co-written by the famous African American pianist/singer/songwriter Fats Waller with Harry Brooks and Andy Razaf. Margaret Simms and Paul Bass introduced it, however, in *Connie's Hot Chocolates*, a nightclub revue. It was later taken over by another famous jazz pioneer, Louis, usually pronounced "Louie." Armstrong when he joined the cast shortly after the show opened. The song subsequently became closely identified with him. Armstrong credited his appearance in this revue with the beginning of his international fame. His '29 recording of "Ain't Misbehavin'" has become a jazz classic.

Hear Armstrong's recording of this song at http://www.redhotjazz.com/lao.html.

Leo Reisman and his orchestra, with vocalist Lew Conrad, appear to have had the most popular recording of "Ain't Misbehavin'," but Louis Armstrong's version wasn't far behind. Other popular releases included Irving Mills' Hotsy-Totsy Gang's recording of the song which has a vocal and tap dancing by Bill "Mr. Bojangles" Robinson. Hear it at http://www.redhotjazz.com/hotsytotsy.html. Other popular recordings were by Gene Austin, Ruth Etting, and, of course, Fats Waller. Hear Waller's recording of the song at http://www.redhotjazz.com/rhythm.html. Teddy Wilson and his band revived it in '37. Country singer Willie Nelson also revived it. The song became one of the most recorded songs of the pre-rock era.

According to the chorus lyrics, the singer "ain't misbehavin'" because he doesn't have anyone to talk to or walk with. However, he's happy to be out of circulation ("on the shelf"). He's saving his love for this specific girl because her kisses are worth the wait. Instead of being out misbehavin', he's home each evening listening to his radio. Read the lyrics at http://www.allthelyrics.com/lyrics/fats_waller/aint_misbehavin_200000/aint_misbehavin-146153-lyric/.

"Ain't Misbehavin'" was performed by Mary Beth Hughes in the '43 movie musical *Follow the Band*, and by Fats Waller in *Stormy Weather* ('43). It was also used in the '44 movie musical *Atlantic City, You Were Meant for Me* ('48), *The Strip* ('51), *Gentlemen Marry Brunettes* ('55), and *Ain't Misbehavin'* ('55).

"Ain't Misbehavin'" was nominated for the American Film Institute's list of the greatest songs ever from American films, but did not make the final list. It was nominated for its inclusion in *Stormy Weather* ('43).

This Fats Waller classic was included in *Variety's Hit Parade of a Half-Century*.

In '79 Broadway honored Waller with a revue, *Ain't Misbehavin'*, which featured many of his best works and other songs that were identified with him. Nell Carter, later a television personality, was one of the stars of that revue.

The sheet music cover and musical score are available at http://levysheetmusic.mse.jhu.edu/browse.html. Hear a midi musical version at http://www.primeshop.com/midlist3.htm.

HONEYSUCKLE ROSE

Waller's two most famous songs — "Ain't Misbehavin'" and "Honeysuckle Rose" — both came out in '29. Both songs have been inducted into the Grammy Hall of Fame: Waller's piano solo recording of "Ain't Misbehavin'" inducted in '84 and his '34 recording of "Honeysuckle Rose" inducted in '99.

Andy Razaf also wrote the lyrics for "Honeysuckle Rose." The song was introduced in a revue at Connie's Inn, a New York City nightclub in '29.

"Honeysuckle Rose," which was most popular in '37, also became one of the most recorded song of the pre-rock era. Fletcher Henderson and his orchestra's recording of it was popular in '33, Red Norvo's, Fats Waller's and the Dorsey Brothers Orchestra's in '35, while sort of an all-star version with Fats Waller, Tommy Dorsey, Bunny Berigan and Dick McDonough was the most popular version in '37.

"Honeysuckle Rose" was also nominated for the American Film Institute's list of the greatest songs ever from

American films, but did not make the final list. It was nominated for its inclusion in *Thousands Cheer* ('43). The song also appeared in the movie musicals *Tin-Pan-Alley* ('40), *Walking My Baby Back Home* ('53), and *New York, New York* ('76). Willie Nelson successfully revived the song in '80. In '81 it was the title of a movie that starred Nelson.

The Dorsey Brothers' Orchestra's recording of "Honeysuckle Rose" can be heard at http://www.redhotjazz.com/dorseybros.html, while Waller's version is available at http://www.redhotjazz.com/rhythm.html

Am I Blue?

Words: Grant Clarke; Music: Harry Akst

One of the world's most famous blues singers, Ethel Waters, sang "Am I Blue?" in the '29 movie musical *On with the Show*.

The chorus lyrics begin by asking "Am I blue?" twice. Then the singer asks if we can't tell she's blue by the tears in her eyes. She sings that we'd be blue also if our plans with our lover had fallen through like hers. Her man is gone and they're through, so she asks again "Am I blue?" Read the lyrics at http://lirama.net/song/10466.

Clarke and Akst had copyrighted "Am I Blue?" in '19. The sheet music cover and musical score are available at http://levysheetmusic.mse.jhu.edu/browse.html.

Ethel Waters' recorded version was the most popular one and was extremely successful. Hear Ms. Water's recording at http://www.redhotjazz.com/waters.html. Other versions available to the record buying public in '29 were by torch singer Libby Holman, by radio star Annette Hanshaw, by Nat Shilkret and the Victor Orchestra, by Ben Selvin and his orchestra, with vocalist Smith Ballew, and by Tom Gerun and his orchestra, with vocalist Jimmy Davis. Years later, famous rhythm and blues performer, Ray Charles, had a particularly soulful recording of "Am I Blue?"

Variety selected "Am I Blue?" for its *Hit Parade of a Half-Century.*

"Am I Blue?" was used in several movie musicals in addition to *On with the Show* including *So Long Letty* ('30), *Is Everybody Happy?* ('43), which starred Ted Lewis and Larry Parks and *Funny Lady* ('75), which starred Barbra Streisand. The song also appeared in *Slaves of New York* ('89) and *U.S. Marshalls* ('98).

"Am I Blue?" was nominated for the American Film Institute's list of the greatest songs ever from American films, but did not make the final list. It was nominated for its inclusion in *On with the Show* ('29).

Ethel Waters also popularized "Birmingham Bertha" from *On with the Show*. Hear Jean Goldkette and his orchestra's recording of "Birmingham Bertha" at http://www.redhotjazz.com/goldo.html.

Button Up Your Overcoat

Words: B.G. DeSylva & Lew Brown; Music: Ray Henderson

Henderson, DeSylva, and Brown's musical *Follow Thru* came to Broadway in '28 and included in the score was "Button Up Your Overcoat." *Follow Thru* was a commentary on country club life and the swanky golf club hoi polloi that starred Jack Haley, Zelma O'Neal, and Eleanor Powell. This was Powell's first Broadway success and headed her career toward the successes she had in the

screen musicals of the '30s. It was also the first starring role on Broadway for Jack Haley, who became almost immortal for his role as the Tin Man in the '39 movie musical *The Wizard of Oz*. Haley was particularly adept at playing the bewildered, inept, reluctant hero.

Variety picked the song for its *Hit Parade of a Half-Century* representing '28.

The lyrics of "Button Up Your Overcoat" are a catalog of health admonitions: wear proper clothing, eat correct foods, be careful crossing streets, don't stay up too late, and stay away from bootleg liquor. Read the complete lyrics at http://www.lyricsdownload.com/helen-kane-button-up-your-overcoat-lyrics.html.

"The Boop-Boop-a-Doop Girl," Helen Kane, had the most popular recording of "Button Up Your Overcoat" in 1928–29. Paul Whiteman and his orchestra, Fred Waring and his Pennsylvanians and Broadway star Ruth Etting also helped popularize it with successful recordings. Hear Fred Waring's recording of the song at http://www.redhotjazz.com/waringspa.html or hear Paul Whiteman's version at http://www.redhotjazz.com/pwo.html.

Hollywood's version of *Follow Thru* was released in '30. "Button Up Your Overcoat" was featured in the score, as it was in *The Best Things in Life Are Free* ('56), a film tribute to Henderson, DeSylva, and Brown. The song also appeared in *The Front Page* ('74) and *The Sure Thing* ('85).

Paul Whiteman and his orchestra popularized "My Lucky Star," also from *Follow Thru*, in a '29 recording. This is not the "(You Are My) Lucky Star" from *The Broadway Melody of 1936*. Arthur Freed and Nacio Herb Brown wrote that song for that '35 film. Hear Paul Whiteman's recording of "My Lucky Star" at http://www.redhotjazz.com/pwo.html.

Helen Kane also popularized the spicy song "I Want to Be Bad" from *Follow Thru*. Hear Annette Hanshaw's recording of this song at http://www.redhotjazz.com/hanshaw.html. "I Want to Be Bad" appeared in the screen version of *Follow Thru* ('30).

Can't We Be Friends?

Words: Paul James; Music: Kay Swift

Libby Holman introduced this torch song in *The Little Show*.

Variety included this song in its *Hit Parade of a Half-Century.*

The song appeared in the movie musical *Young Man with a Horn* ('50) and was used as an orchestral episode in *The Man I Love* ('46).

The lyrics tell us that this singer thought she'd found the man of her dreams. However, now he just wants to be friends. Read the lyrics at http://www.lyricsfreak.com/e/ella-fitzgerald/45697.html.

Carolina Moon

Words: Benny Davis; Music: Joe Burke

"Carolina Moon" was originally popularized by Guy Lombardo and his Royal Canadians. It became identified with popular ballad singer Morton Downey because the song was his radio theme song. The first recording of it was by Gene Austin.

"Carolina Moon" is a dreamy waltz that has remained a pop music staple over the years. The singer pleads with the moon that shines on Carolina to shine on the person who is waiting for him and let her know he's blue and lonely. Read the lyrics and hear a midi musical version at http://www.moonlightsys.com/themoon/lyrics.html.

Gene Austin's recording was a big seller, but Ben Selvin and his orchestra and Nat Shilkret and the Victor Orchestra also helped popularize it with successful recordings. Hear Annette Hanshaw's recording of "Carolina Moon" at http://www.redhotjazz.com/hanshaw.html.

Variety also included this song in its *Hit Parade of a Half-Century* representing '28.

Deep Night

Words: Rudy Vallee; Music: Charlie Henderson

Rudy Vallee was the musical sex symbol of the late '20s for many young girls, the predecessor of such entertainment idols as Frank Sinatra, Elvis Presley, and the Beatles.

"Deep night, stars in the sky above ... deep in the arms of love" was sung in Vallee's thin, crooning voice that captivated his fans. The young girls swooned when he crooned romantic songs like "Deep Night." Read the lyrics at http://www.seeklyrics.com/lyrics/Frank-Sinatra/Deep-Night.html.

In addition to Vallee's popular recording of the song, Ruth Etting had a successful version of it also.

Variety selected this Vallee specialty for its *Hit Parade of a Half-Century.*

See the sheet music cover and hear a midi musical version at http://www.parlorsongs.com/issues/1998-3/mar98gallery.asp.

Great Day!, More Than You Know *and* Without a Song

Words: Billy Rose & Edward Eliscu; Music: Vincent Youmans

The musical *Great Day!* must have had a dreadful plot; Stanley Green's *Encyclopedia of the Musical Theatre* doesn't even mention the musical, nor can a plot summary be found on the internet. However, three well-known songs came from the musical's score.

GREAT DAY!

"Great Day!" is a supercharged revival number that was introduced by Russell Wooding's Jubilee Singers in the musical of the same name. This hymn to the power of positive thinking remained popular through the next several years. The people who lived during the Great Depression needed to hear "When you're down and out, lift up your head and shout 'There's gonna be a great day.'" Read the lyrics at http://www.stlyrics.com/lyrics/funnylady/agreatday.htm.

The ever-present Paul Whiteman and his orchestra had the only recording of "Great Day!" that was popular enough to mention, but it was extremely successful. Hear this Whiteman recording at http://www.redhotjazz.com/pwo.html. In more modern times, Kellogg's has used the song in its commercial for Sugar Frosted Flakes, the Tony the Tiger cereal.

Barbra Streisand performed "Great Day" in an unusually slow tempo rendition in the '75 movie musical *Funny Lady.* Several of Billy Rose's song were featured in that film, since Rose became Fanny Brice's second husband.

Variety listed "Great Day" as one of its *Golden 100 Tin Pan Alley Songs*, but for some reason was not on its list of *Hit Parade of a Half-Century.*

MORE THAN YOU KNOW

"More Than You Know," a song of obsessive love, was a second hit song that was introduced in *Great Day.* It was performed originally by Mayo Methot. The musical was not a financial success, but Youmans and his collaborating lyricists were in top musical form. "More Than You Know" has become a standard and is particularly associated with Jane Froman because of her outstanding performances of the song.

Ruth Etting had the most popular recording of "More Than You Know," which was most successful in the early months of the new decade. Mildred Bailey and Perry Como both revived the song with moderate success in '37 and '46 respectively.

"More Than You Know" was interpolated into the screen version of Youmans' *Hit the Deck* in '30 and in '55. It was, like "Great Day," also featured in *Funny Lady* ('75).

Variety selected the song to be included in its *Hit Parade of a Half-Century.*

The verse of the song tells us it doesn't matter whether the person she is singing to is here or somewhere else, or if he is false or true, she is growing fond of him. The chorus begins by stating the title twice. She finds him on her mind "more than you know." Whether he's right or wrong she'll string along. She says she'd cry if he tired of her and said goodbye. Read the lyrics at http://lirama.net/song/15583.

WITHOUT A SONG

"Without a Song," a powerful and emotional affirmation of the force of music in our lives, was introduced by baritone Lois Deppe and Russell Wooding's Jubilee Singers in *Great Day.*

Paul Whiteman and his orchestra's recording of "Without a Song" was on the flip side of their very successful recording of "Great Day." Hear Paul Whiteman's recording of this song at http://www.redhotjazz.com/pwo.html. The song has been revived numerous times over the years, but none of the recordings were successful enough to chart on *Billboard, Variety,* or the other charting services.

The powerful lyrics sing that our days would seem endless, and we would seem friendless "without a song." The original lyrics were typically racist for the time. The line "A man is born..." was originally "A darkie's born..." The singer is confident that he'll be all right as long as his song is strong in his soul. He confesses there are many things he doesn't know, but he knows "there ain't no love at all without a song." Read the lyrics at http://lirama.net/song/15597.

"Without a Song" was used in the '31 movie musical *The Prodigal,* which starred Lawrence Tibbett.

Variety listed "Without a Song" as a *Golden 100* Tin Pan Alley Song and *Hit Parade of a Half-Century* song.

Honey

Words: Seymour Simons & Haven Gillespie; Music: Richard Whiting

Sensationally popular Rudy Vallee and his Connecticut Yankees introduced and popularized "Honey" on his radio program and with a popular recording of the song. The song had reportedly sold more than a million copies of sheet music by '30.

Besides Vallee's recording, Ben Selvin and his orchestra also had a successful release of it in '29.

The lyrics begin with "I'm in love with you Honey" and asks for a reply in a like manner. The singer insists that, even though it may seem funny, no one else will satisfy them. The chorus concludes with "Ev'ry day would be so sunny, Honey, with you."

"Honey" was performed in the television show *I Love Lucy*, episode #88, "Ricky's Hawaiian Vacation." The song also appeared in the '45 MGM film *Her Highness and the Bellboy* starring Hedy Lamarr, Robert Walker and June Allyson.

Variety selected the song to be included in its *Hit Parade of a Half-Century* representing '28.

I Kiss Your Hand, Madame (Ich kusse ihre Hand, Madame)

Words: Sam M. Lewis & Joe Young; Music: Ralph Erwin

"I Kiss Your Hand, Madame" originated in Europe in '12. The original German lyrics were by Fritz Rotter. With English lyrics, the American version was introduced and popularized by Rudy Vallee in '29. It became Lanny Ross' theme song on his Campbell soup radio show during the '30s. Bing Crosby sang it in the '48 movie musical *The Emperor Waltz*. Hear Paul Whiteman's recording of this song at http://www.redhotjazz.com/pwo.html.

"I Kiss You Hand, Madame" was included in *Variety*'s *Hit Parade of a Half-Century* for '28.

In the lyrics we find out very quickly that the singer is dreaming: "In dreams I kiss your hand, Madame." Continuing in slumberland, he begs for her lips. Each time he holds her tightly, she vanishes into the night. The chorus ends the same phrase as the first phrase and adds: "And pray my dreams come true." See the German sheet music cover and hear a midi musical version at http://www.parlorsongs.com/issues/2000-7/2000-7b.asp.

I'll Get By (see '44)

I'm Just a Vagabond Lover

Words & Words: Leon Zimmerman & Rudy Vallee

Rudy Vallee introduced this song on radio and had a very popular recording of the song. He sang it in the movie musical *Glorifying the American Girl*, which starred Mary Eaton, Eddie Cantor, and Helen Morgan. The success of the song led to the filming of another movie musical titled *The Vagabond Lover*, which starred Vallee. Hear Vallee's recording of this song at http://cfelt.com/0507_1.html.

The song was the object of several plagiarism suits, all of which were discredited.

Variety selected this song for inclusion in its *Hit Parade of a Half-Century*.

I've Got a Feeling I'm Falling

Words: Billy Rose; Music: Harry Link & Thomas Waller

Helen Morgan introduced "I've Got a Feeling I'm Falling" in the '29 movie musical *Applause*.

Gene Austin helped popularize the song with a popular recording of it in '29. Hear Annette Hanshaw's recording of this song at http://www.redhotjazz.com/hanshaw.html.

The song was also used in the Broadway musical about Fats Waller's music titled *Ain't Misbehavin'*.

Variety selected this song for inclusion in its *Hit Parade of a Half-Century*.

The chorus lyrics say that the singer is "flying high," but is feeling like she's falling in love. She's used to being single, but now she's "a tingle over you." See the sheet music cover and hear a midi musical version at http://www.perfessorbill.com/covers/falling.htm.

Ruth Etting popularized "What Wouldn't I Do for That Man?," another song from *Applause*. E.Y. Harburg and Jay Gorney wrote the song. Annette Hanshaw's recording of this song can be heard at http://www.redhotjazz.com/hanshaw.html. The song also appeared in the '30 movie musical *Glorifying the American Girl*.

Little Pal

Words: B.G. DeSylva & Lew Brown; Music: Ray Henderson

Henderson, DeSylva and Brown wrote "Little Pal" for the '29 movie musical *Say It with Music*. They and Jolson had hoped to repeat the success of "Sonny Boy," but, although popular, the song didn't generate the same appeal.

Jolson's recording of "Little Pal" did find a lot of success among the record buying public. Gene Austin and Paul Whiteman and his orchestra also had popular recordings of the song on the market. Hear Paul Whiteman's recording of this song at http://www.redhotjazz.com/pwo.html.

Louise

Words: Leo Robin; Music: Richard A. Whiting

The debonair French entertainer Maurice Chevalier made his American stage debut in the last midnight revue produced by Florenz Ziegfeld on the roof of the New Amsterdam Theater in New York City in '29. His bow on the American screen took place in *Innocents of Paris* ('29), where he introduced "Louise." His jaunty air, charm, and sex appeal immediately made him famous in this country. He is particularly associated with two songs: "Louise" and "Mimi" ('32).

Recordings by Maurice Chevalier and by Paul Whiteman and his orchestra, with vocalist Bing Crosby, helped the song become known throughout the country. Read the lyrics and hear Maurice Chevalier sing "Louise" at http://members.tripod.com/~compmast/chevalie/louise.html or hear Paul Whiteman's recording at http://www.redhotjazz.com/pwo.html.

"Louise" was chosen for *Variety*'s *Hit Parade of a Half-Century*.

Since '29, "Louise" has appeared in the following movie musicals: *You Can't Ration Love* ('44), *The Stooge* ('53), which starred Dean Martin and Jerry Lewis, and the '80 version of *The Jazz Singer*, which starred Neil Diamond.

The song is so thoroughly associated with Chevalier that the lyrics seem to need his French accent. The lyrics of the chorus tell us that every breeze and the birds in the trees are saying "Louise." Every small sigh confirms to him that he adores Louise. But he can't believe his good fortune. Could it be that someone like Louise could love him?

Love Me or Leave Me *and* Makin' Whoopee

Words: Gus Kahn; Music: Walter Donaldson

One of 1928's famous Broadway hit shows was *Whoopee*. Walter Donaldson was an established Tin Pan Alley composer, but this was his first complete Broadway score and Eddie Cantor's most famous Broadway musical.

The musical's setting is a California ranch where a hypochondriac, Eddie Cantor, has been sent for health reasons. Sally Morgan runs off with Cantor's character, Henry Williams, to avoid her fiancé Sheriff Bob, whom she doesn't really love. They end up in an Indian camp where they discover that Sally's true love is not the half-breed everyone supposes him to be. The most intriguing part of the production was Cantor and his humor, the opulence of the production and some "Indian" lovelies on horseback.

LOVE ME OR LEAVE ME

The standout ballad of the show was "Love Me or Leave Me," which was performed by Ruth Etting . The song became so identified with her that her '55 movie biography, which starred Doris Day as Ms. Etting, was titled *Love Me or Leave Me*.

Quite logically, Ruth Etting's recording of "Love Me or Leave Me" was most popular one in '29. Ms. Etting's recording of "Love Me or Leave Me" was inducted into the Grammy Hall of Fame in 2005. Benny Goodman and his orchestra revived the song in '34 and again in '36.

The song was used in *Tell It to a Star* ('45), Gus Kahn's biopic *I'll See You in My Dreams* ('52), and as mentioned above, Ruth Etting's screen biography.

"Love Me or Leave Me" is listed by *Variety* as a *Golden 100 Tin Pan Alley Song*, but, surprisingly, not among its *Hit Parade of a Half-Century*.

The lyrics of the chorus begin with "Love me or leave me and let me be lonely." She says to her lover that he may not believe her, but she loves only him. Even though this love isn't ideal, to say the least, she intends to remain "independently blue." The chorus ends with the confirmation of her love. Read the lyrics at http://lirama.net/song/15064.

MAKIN' WHOOPEE!

A second big hit song from the show was "Makin' Whoopee!" Eddie Cantor introduced the song, which became one of his all-time popular hits.

The lyrics to "Makin' Whoopee!" warn of the dangers of married life. Cantor played a shy hypochondriac who is induced to elope with Sally Morgan, but ends up with the faithful nurse, Mary. Read the lyrics at http://lirama.net/song/10542.

Again quite logically, Eddie Cantor's recording of "Makin' Whoopee!" was the most popular but the ever-present Paul Whiteman and his orchestra weren't too far behind with their version. Whiteman's recording featured vocalists Bing Crosby, Jack Fulton, Charles Gaylord, and Austin Young. Hear Eddie Cantor's '28 recording of this song at http://www.authentichistory.com/audio/1920s/Eddie_Cantor-Making_Whoopee.html or hear Paul Whiteman's recording of this song at http://www.redhotjazz.com/pwo.html. Ben Bernie and his orchestra also had a successful version on the market.

"Makin' Whoopee!" was nominated for the American Film Institute's list of the greatest songs ever from an American film, but did not make the final list. It was nominated for its appearance in *The Fabulous Baker Boys* ('89).

The movie adaptation of *Whoopee* ('30) was Cantor's talking-picture debut. Only three songs were retained from the stage score, and several new ones, including "My Baby Just Cares for Me," were added for the movie. Other

movie musicals that used "Makin' Whoopee!" include *Show Business* ('44), where Cantor performed it again, Gus Kahn's '52 biopic *I'll See You in My Dreams*, and *The Eddie Cantor Story* '53). The song also appeared on the *Sleepless in Seattle* ('93) soundtrack as sung by Dr. John.

Another song from the score that was popular enough to chart was "I'm Bringing a Red, Red Rose," which was popularized in a recording by Ruth Etting.

Lover, Come Back to Me *and* Softly, as in a Morning Sunrise

Words: Oscar Hammerstein II; Music: Sigmund Romberg

Sigmund Romberg's *The New Moon*, the only show of the '28 season to run for more than 500 performances, almost didn't make it to Broadway. During tryouts it was canceled, but after being rewritten and recast, it reopened. All but one of the hits from the show were from the revision.

The New Moon marked the second collaboration between Romberg and Oscar Hammerstein II (the first had been 1926's *The Desert Song*). The play was set in 18th century New Orleans and was loosely based on the life and exploits of a French aristocrat, Robert Mission.

LOVER, COME BACK TO ME

The biggest hit from the show was "Lover, Come Back to Me," one of Romberg's best-known melodies. It was introduced by Marianne, Evelyn Herbert, who pleads with Robert, Robert Halliday, to return her affection. Robert thinks Marianne has betrayed him into enemy hands.

The lyrics have Marianne eagerly asking her lover to return. When he finally returns, the love lasted for a time, but now that time has past. Now her heart is singing: "Lover, come back to me" again. Read the lyrics at http://lirama.net/song/41274.

"Lover, Come Back to Me" has been the most popular of the songs from the score in recordings. Popular versions were issued by Paul Whiteman and his orchestra, with vocalist Jack Fulton, by the Arden-Ohman Orchestra, by Rudy Vallee, and by Perry Askam. Nat "King" Cole revived it in '53 with good success. There also have been a few jazzy recordings of the song, but they did not chart. The song became one of the most recorded songs of the pre-rock era. Hear Paul Whiteman's recording of the song at http://www.redhotjazz.com/pwo.html.

Variety chose "Lover, Come Back to Me" for its *Hit Parade of a Half-Century* representing '28 and its *Golden 100 Tin Pan Alley Songs* list.

SOFTLY, AS IN A MORNING SUNRISE

At a tavern, Robert Mission's friend Philippe cautions Robert that while love steals in "Softly, as in a morning sunrise," its vows are always broken. It is such a beautiful song to carry such a pessimistic message about love. Read the lyrics at http://www.sh-k-boom.com/ghostlight/newMoon_lyrics.htm#08.

Nat Shilkret and the Victor Orchestra, with vocalist Franklyn Baur, had the only popular recording of this number from the score. The Shilkret recording had "Softly, as in a Morning Sunrise" on one side of the disk, with "One Kiss" on the flip side.

Variety selected "Softly, as in a Morning Sunrise" for its *Hit Parade of a Half-Century* representing '28.

There were two motion-picture adaptations of *The New*

Moon. The first starred Grace Moore and Lawrence Tibbett ('30), and the second starred Jeanette MacDonald and Nelson Eddy ('40). "Softly, as in a Morning Sunrise" did not appear in the first screen version.

Nat Shilkret and the Victor Orchestra had a popular recording of "One Kiss," one of the musical's most beautiful songs.

The Arden-Ohman Orchestra popularized another song from the score, "Marianne," in a '29 recording. Hear Paul Whiteman's recording of "Marianne" at http://www.red hotjazz.com/pwo.html. The song also appeared in the '30 and '40 film versions of *The New Moon.*

Another well known song from the score, "Stout-Hearted Men," was more popular in '30 in a recording by Perry Askam.

"Wanting You" is a beautiful duet from the score.

All of the songs mentioned above were featured in Sigmund Romberg's motion-picture biography *Deep in My Heart* ('54).

Marie (see 1937)

Moanin' Low *and* I Guess I'll Have to Change My Plan

Words: Howard Dietz; Music: Ralph Rainger (Moanin' Low) & Arthur Schwartz (I Guess I'll Have to Change My Plan)

Moanin' Low

Torch singer Libby Holman, impersonating a mulatto, premiered "Moanin' Low" in the intimate revue *The Little Show.* The scene was a dingy, shabby tenement apartment. After rousing her lover, played by Clifton Webb, from a drunken stupor, the girl brings him to his feet, and they perform a sultry dance to the song. At the end of the number, he strangles her.

Libby Holman's recording of "Moanin' Low" was the most popular version on the market. The jazz band, the Charleston Chasers, also recorded the song with a vocal performance by Eva Taylor. Jazz trumpeter Red Nichols directed the group while clarinetist and alto saxophonist Jimmy Dorsey was one of the members. Hear the Charleston Chasers' recording at http://www.redhotjazz.com/charleston.html. Pianist Teddy Wilson and his orchestra with vocalist Billie Holiday revived it in '37.

"Moanin' Low" was included in *Variety*'s *Hit Parade of a Half-Century.*

Rainger's lyrics to this torch song aptly illustrate the breast-beating, everything-is-wrong feelings expressed by this genre of song. Even though the man she loves is mean to her, she calls him her sweet man. She also thinks she's the kind of woman for this type of man. She confesses that she doesn't really know why he treats her so badly. Read the lyrics at http://lirama.net/song/13372.

I Guess I'll Have to Change My Plan

A second hit song from the score of *The Little Show,* "I Guess I'll Have to Change My Plan," written by lyricist Howard Dietz, this time with composer Arthur Schwartz, was a casual acceptance of the end of a love affair. The great character actor Clifton Webb introduced the song. The song's subtitle is "The Blue Pajama Song." In the second chorus, the singer regrets he bought a pair of blue pajamas.

Webb's character has discovered that his lover is married.

At first he is determined to call off the affair, change his plan as it were, but later in the song he changes his plan again as he decides it might be fun having an affair with someone who is married. Read the lyrics at http://www.ilyric.net/Lyrics/B/Band-Wagon/I-Guess-I'll-Have-To-Change-My-Plan.html.

Rudy Vallee had a very popular version of the song released on record in '32. Guy Lombardo and his Royal Canadians also had a popular version on the market in '32.

Hear Paul Whiteman's recording of the song at http://www.redhotjazz.com/pwo.html.

"I Guess I'll Have to Change My Plan" was performed by Jack Buchanan and Fred Astaire in the movie musical *The Band Wagon* ('53). The song was performed by Peg La Centra in *Humoresque* ('46).

Pagan Love Song

Words: Arthur Freed; Music: Nacio Herb Brown

Nacio Herb Brown and Arthur Freed's second assignment at Metro-Goldwyn-Mayer was to write music for a dramatic film, *The Pagan,* for Ramon Navarro. One morning, at eleven o'clock, they were asked to write the title song for the film. They delivered "Pagan Love Song" a couple of hours later.

Reportedly the song sold over 1,600,000 copies of sheet music for its publisher, Jack Robbins, but official figures were not kept at this point.

Bob Hope used this piece in his debut act in vaudeville in New York City at Proctor's Eighty-sixth Street Theater in '29. He sang it straight, not comically, and, according to the *Variety* reviewer, performed it well.

The lyrics urge us to come away to Tahiti, where we can sing the "Pagan Love Song" to each other. Read the lyrics at http://www.huapala.org/Poly_Tahiti/Pagan_Love_Song.html.

The Copley Plaza Orchestra directed by Bob Haring had the most popular recording of the song, and his was extremely successful. Nat Shilkret and the Troubadors Orchestra (basically the same as the Victor Orchestra) and the Columbians also had highly successful releases of the song. Hear Paul Whiteman's recording of the song at http://www.redhotjazz.com/pwo.html.

Hollywood movie musicals featured the song twice after '29. It was used in *Night Club Girl* ('44) and again in *Pagan Love Song* ('50), an Esther Williams film with a Tahitian setting.

See two sheet music covers of the song at www.hulapages.com/covers_3.htm.

A Precious Little Thing Called Love

Words: Lou Davis; Music: J. Fred Coots

J. Fred Coots and Lou Davis submitted "A Precious Little Thing Called Love" to Paramount for consideration as a theme song for the Gary Cooper film *A Shopworn Angel* ('29). Out of 150 songs that were submitted, their song was chosen. Nancy Carroll performed it in the film.

It was further popularized by George Olsen and his orchestra with Ethel Shutta, Olsen's wife, doing the vocal. Their recorded version was very popular around the entire nation. Other recordings by the Ipana Troubadours and a duet version by Johnny Marvin and Ed Smalle also helped spread the song's message. Annette Hanshaw's recording of this song can be heard at http://www.redhotjazz.com/hanshaw.html.

The chorus lyrics begin by wondering why the singer's heartbeat rises when she hears this man's footsteps coming down the street? The answer: "It's a precious little thing called love." The singer envisions a June wedding and a honeymoon cruise.

Siboney

Words: Dolly Morse; Music: Ernesto Lecuona

"Siboney (Canto Siboney)" is a Cuban instrumental by Ernesto Lecuona that Dolly Morse added English lyrics to in '29.

Alfredo Brito had a reasonably popular recording of the song in '31, but *Variety* chose "Siboney" for its *Hit Parade of a Half-Century* representing '29.

The song appeared in the '37 movie musical *When You're in Love*, which starred opera singer Grace Moore, Gloria Jean sang "Siboney" in the '42 movie musical *Get Hep to Love* and it also appeared in the '44 movie musical *Babes on Swing Street*.

"Siboney" is a song they sing and a dance they dance at a café in Havana. Read the lyrics at http://www.lyrics 007.com/Nana%20Mouskouri%20Lyrics/Siboney%20Lyr ics.html.

Singin' in the Rain

Words: Arthur Freed; Music: Nacio Herb Brown

Once again the songwriting team of Nacio Herb Brown and Arthur Freed collaborated to produce a standard: "Singin' in the Rain." The song was introduced by Cliff "Ukulele Ike" Edwards in the movie musical *Hollywood Revue of 1929*. It has been revived several times in films since, including Jimmy Durante's performance of it in *Speak Easily* ('32) and Judy Garland's interpolation of it into *Little Nellie Kelly* ('40). By far the most famous rendition came in the '52 movie musical *Singin' in the Rain* in an unforgettable performance by Gene Kelly; Kelly's recording from the soundtrack of the film was inducted into the Grammy Hall of Fame in '99. The film's trio of stars: Gene Kelly, Debbie Reynolds, and Donald O'Connor, also performed the song in the same film. *That's Entertainment* ('74) saluted this song and several of its film performances. The narrator suggested that MGM used it so often that it might be considered their theme song.

Cliff Edwards' recorded version of the song was extremely popular. Earl Burtnett and his Los Angeles Biltmore Hotel Orchestra, with vocalist Paul Gibbons, and Gus Arnheim and his orchestra's disk versions also helped spread its fame. Surprisingly, Gene Kelly's version from the '52 film never charted. Hear the Dorsey Brothers' Orchestra's recording of "Singin' in the Rain" at http://www.redhotjazz.com/dorseybros.html.

The movie *Singin' in the Rain* was recently voted one of the 10 Best American Films Ever Made and, by a vote of international film critics conducted by the prestigious magazine *Sight and Sound*, it was chosen as No. 3 of the 10 Best Films of All Time. AFI's *100 Years ... 100 Songs* (2004) named "Singin' in the Rain" as the No. 3 greatest song from American films ever. However, it was named to that honor for its '52 film appearance not its debut in '29. The song also appeared in *Little Nellie Kelly* ('40), *North by Northwest* ('59), *A Clockwork Orange* ('71), *Die Hard* ('88) and *What About Bob?* ('91).

"Singin' in the Rain" was picked by *Variety* for its *Hit Parade of a Half-Century*.

The singer is ecstatic! He's "singin' in the rain" and thinks it's glorious because he's happy. He laughs at the dark clouds because he has the sun in his heart. He's ready to fall in love. He's smiling as he walks down the lane singing a happy song. Read the lyrics at http://www.lyrics ondemand.com/soundtracks/s/singinintherainlyrics/singin intherainlyrics.html.

Cliff Edwards also popularized "Orange Blossom Time" from *The Hollywood Revue of 1929* with a successful recording. Joe Goodwin furnished the lyrics for Edwards' tune. Hear Paul Whiteman's recording of this song at http://www.redhotjazz.com/pwo.html.

Star Dust (see 1931)

Sunny Side Up

Words: B.G. DeSylva & Lew Brown; Music: Ray Henderson

The Henderson, DeSylva and Brown songwriting team left New York City and Broadway for Hollywood and movie musicals in '29. Their first assignment there was the screen musical *Sunny Side Up*, starring Janet Gaynor and Charles Farrell. The best remembered songs from the score include "(Keep Your) Sunny Side Up" and "If I Had a Talking Picture of You."

"Sunny Side Up" is the title song of a '29 movie musical. Janet Gaynor and Charles Farrell introduced "Sunny Side Up," which became a favorite of the Depression years because of it's positive attitude "Keep your sunny side up."

Earl Burtnett and Johnny Hamp and their orchestras had popular recordings of "Sunny Side Up" in '29. Johnny Hamp's Kentucky Serenaders' version of the song can be heard at http://www.redhotjazz.com/jhks.html.

Variety selected "Sunny Side Up" for its Hit Parade of a Half-Century.

The chorus lyrics begin with the title phrase: "Keep your sunny side up, up!" We're advised to hide our blue side. A particularly clever line is "If you have nine sons in a row, baseball teams make money, you know!" Read the lyrics at http://lirama.net/song/15588.

Two other songs from the film were popular enough to chart: I'm a Dreamer, Aren't We All?" and "Turn on the Heat." Paul Whiteman and his orchestra popularized "I'm a Dreamer, Aren't We All?, while Earl Brutnett and his orchestra popularized "Turn on the Heat." Hear the Charleston Chasers' recording of "Turn on the Heat" at http://www.redhotjazz.com/charleston.html. The sheet music cover and musical score for "I'm a Dreamer, Aren't We All" are available at http://levysheetmusic.mse.jhu. edu/browse.html. Hear Whiteman's recording of "I'm a Dreamer, Aren't We All" at http://www.redhotjazz.com/ pwo.html.

Sweethearts on Parade

Words: Charles Newman; Music: Carmen Lombardo

"Sweethearts on Parade" was composed by Carmen Lombardo, brother of Guy Lombardo, and was introduced by Guy and his Royal Canadians. Carmen played lead saxophone and often sang with the Royal Canadians. The lyricist, Charles Newman, was a songwriter/composer, short story author, and musical director for films.

The song was interpolated into the movie musical of the same name in '30.

The Royal Canadians recording of the song, along with one by Abe Lyman helped popularize the song. Louis Armstrong and his band revived the song with a popular recording in '32. Hear Armstrong's recording of this song at http://www.redhotjazz.com/lao.html.

Tip Toe Through the Tulips
Words: Al Dubin; Music: Joe Burke

The movie musical *Gold Diggers of Broadway* introduced "Tip Toe Through the Tulips." Nick Lucas had a block-buster hit recording of the song in '29; it became one of the decade's biggest selling recordings. Other recorded versions on the market were by the orchestras of Jean Goldkette, Johnny Marvin and Roy Fox.

"Tip Toe Through the Tulips" was also used in the '51 movie musical *Painting the Clouds with Sunshine*.

The song was revived in the late sixties by the "unusual" Tiny Tim. His recording was a big novelty hit. Anyone who has heard Tiny Tim's rendition probably has a strange impression of the song, but it was not taken that way in its original 1920's form. Listen to Nick Lucas' version, it is surprisingly like Tiny Tim's, at http://www.redhotjazz.com/lucas.html.

Dubin's chorus lyrics invite his girl to "Come tip toe through the tulips with me." The singer asks for her pardon if he kisses her in the moonlit garden. Read the lyrics at http://lirama.net/song/19382.

"Tip Toe..." was selected by *Variety* for its *Hit Parade of a Half-Century*. It was nominated for the American Film Institute's list of the greatest songs ever from an American film, but it did not make the final list.

Nick Lucas also popularized "Painting the Clouds with Sunshine" from *Gold Diggers of Broadway*. Hear Lucas' recording of this song at http://www.redhotjazz.com/lucas.html. The song also appeared in the film version of *Little Johnny Jones* ('29) and *Painting the Clouds with Sunshine* ('51).

Wedding Bells (Are Breaking Up That Old Gang of Mine)
Words: Irving Kahal & Willie Raskin; Music: Sammy Fain

It may be difficult not to confuse "Wedding Bells (Are Breaking Up That Old Gang of Mine)" by Irving Kahal, Willie Raskin and Sammy Fain from '29 with "That Old Gang of Mine" by Ray Henderson, Billy Rose and Mort Dixon from '23. However, they are vastly different songs.

The lyrics to "Wedding Bells" complain that nobody is down on the corner as usual, which is a sure sign "that wedding bells are breaking up that old gang of mine." Other "signs" include the boys singing love songs instead of "Sweet Adeline." Read the lyrics at http://www.lyricsandsongs.com/song/255616.html.

Gene Austin had a popular recording of the song in '29. Steve Gibson revived it in '48, as did the Four Aces in '54, both with moderate success, but popular enough to chart.

Variety selected this song for its *Hit Parade of a Half-Century*.

Wedding of the Painted Doll, *and* You Were Meant for Me
Words: Arthur Freed; Music: Nacio Herb Brown

The first authentic movie musical was *The Broadway Melody*. It was the first "100% All-Talking, All-Singing, All-Dancing" screen musical, and it won the Academy Award for best picture of '28. It had its own musical score by Nacio Herb Brown and Arthur Freed, and it was a good one with songs like "Broadway Melody," "Wedding of the Painted Doll" and "You Were Meant for Me." It had an original plot, even though it doesn't seem very original to us now since it has been used in so many movies and musicals, of two stage-struck country girls trying to make careers on the Broadway stage.

WEDDING OF THE PAINTED DOLL
"Wedding of the Painted Doll," introduced in *Broadway Melody*, was an extremely successful recording for Leo Reisman and his orchestra. Broadway and film star Charles King and Earl Burtnett and his Los Angeles Biltmore Hotel Orchestra, with vocalist Paul Gibbons, also had recordings that helped popularize it to the nation.

"Wedding of the Painted Doll" was also used in the classic movie musical *Singin' in the Rain* ('52). It was also featured in *That's Entertainment II* ('74), a second review of many of MGM's highly successful movie musicals and the songs that made them so memorable.

Variety chose this song for its *Hit Parade of a Half-Century*.

YOU WERE MEANT FOR ME
"You Were Meant for Me" was also premiered in *Broadway Melody*. In the film, a vaudeville act, loosely based on the Duncan Sisters, is split because the sisters love the same man. Charles King played the man in the middle. He was fortunate enough to introduce this lovely song that became a standard.

Nat Shilkret and the Victor Orchestra, with a vocal performance by the Four Rajahs, had the most popular recording of "You Were Meant for Me," but Ben Selvin and his orchestra also had a successful release of the song. Connee Boswell and Gordon MacRae both revived it in '48 with moderately successful disks.

"You Were Meant for Me" was performed again in *The Hollywood Revue of 1929*, where Charles King's voice was dubbed for Conrad Nagel, and again in *The Show of Shows* ('29) where Bull Montana and Winnie Lightner performed it. It surfaced again in the '40 movie musical *Hullabaloo*, in *You Were Meant for Me* ('48), and in the classic '52 movie musical *Singin' in the Rain*. The song also appeared in *Sweet and Low Down* ('99) and *Man of the Century* ('99).

Variety also included this song in its *Hit Parade of a Half-Century*.

The lyrics open with the title phrase plus "I was meant for you." The singer, a male, thinks nature rolled up all the sweet things in the world into this girl. He compares her to a melody that he can't get out of his mind. He's convinced the angels sent her and meant her just for him. Read the lyrics at http://www.stlyrics.com/lyrics/singinintherain/youweremeanttome.htm.

Why Was I Born?
Words: Oscar Hammerstein II; Music: Jerome Kern

Sweet Adeline was Kern and Hammerstein's attempt to duplicate the success of their incredible '27 musical *Show Boat*. Although it was not as successful, it was a worthy musical, full of flair, wit, and abundant melody. Described as "a musical romance of the Gay Nineties," it had a backstage setting, a heroine who becomes a singing star, and a hit torch song, "Why Was I Born?" The number is a carbon copy in tone and in theme of "Can't Help Lovin' Dat Man" from *Show Boat*. Helen Morgan, the tragic Julie in *Show Boat*, was also the star of *Sweet Adeline*. The title of the musical, of course, comes from the '03 sentimental ballad that is associated with barbershop quartets.

"Why Was I Born?," a poignant song of despair, became associated with Morgan after her introduction of it, but it also became a part of the tragic lives of blues singer Billie Holliday and also of Judy Garland. The singer ponders why she was born, why she is still living, what she gets out of life and what she is giving to it. She also wonders why she wants things she shouldn't hope for, including a particular man. She realizes she's being foolish, but can't do anything about it. The chorus ends with the question: "Why was I born to love you?" Read the lyrics at http://lirama.net/song/15596.

The most popular recordings of the song in '29 were by torch singers Helen Morgan and Libby Holman. Vic Damone revived it with moderate success in '49.

Warner Bros. filmed a screen version of *Sweet Adeline* in '35. "Why Was I Born?" was performed by Lena Horne in Jerome Kern's screen biography *Till the Clouds Roll By* ('46) and was also featured in *The Helen Morgan Story* ('57).

Variety selected "Why Was I Born?" for its *Hit Parade of a Half-Century*.

With a Song in My Heart

Words: Lorenz Hart; Music: Richard Rodgers

The Rodgers and Hart score for *Spring Is Here* was outstanding, but the musical lasted only a disappointing 104 performances. The most enduring item from the score is "With a Song in My Heart," which was introduced by John Hundley, who played the losing suitor, Stacy. Rarely has such a beautiful song gone to anyone but the hero or heroine.

Richard Rodgers conceived the basic idea for the tune while he was visiting Jules Glaenzer's estate in Westhampton, Long Island. When Rodgers returned to the city, he finished composing the melody and presented it at a party at Glaenzer's city apartment.

Leo Reisman and his orchestra had a popular recording of the song, as did famous tenor James Melton.

A screen version of *Spring Is Here* was released in '30. Perry Como performed "With a Song in My Heart" in Rodgers and Harts' screen biography *Words and Music* ('48). It was also used in the '44 movie musical *This Is the Life*, in *Young Man with a Horn* ('50), *Painting the Clouds with Sunshine* ('51), and *With a Song in My Heart* ('52), the screen biography of Jane Froman, who used the song as her theme song.

Variety included "With a Song in My Heart" on its *Golden 100 Tin Pan Alley Songs*, but not among its *Hit Parade of a Half-Century* list.

The basic idea of the text is summed up in the last couple of musical phrases: "I always knew I would live life through with a song in my heart for you." Read the lyrics at http://www.lorenzhart.org/withsng.htm.

You Do Something to Me

Words & Music: Cole Porter

Cole Porter's second big Broadway hit came with *Fifty Million Frenchmen*. His first stage success was *Paris*, and this musical was also set in Paris. Porter continued his love affair with the "city of light" throughout his entire writing career. The public usually left the theater singing the lovers' duet, "You Do Something to Me." Introduced by

Peter and Looloo, William Gaxton and Genevieve Tobin, the song has been one of Porter's many lasting successes.

Leo Reisman and his orchestra had a reasonably successful recording of "You Do Something to Me" in '30.

It was used in Porter's screen biography, *Night and Day* ('46), *Starlift* ('51), *Because You're Mine* ('52), and *Can-Can* ('60), the film version of a Porter musical that starred Frank Sinatra, Shirley MacLaine, Maurice Chevalier, and Louis Jourdan. The song also appeared in *The Snows of Kilimanjaro* ('52), *Mr. North* ('88), *Scenes from a Mall* ('91) and *Mighty Aphrodite* ('95).

Variety honored the song by including it in its *Hit Parade of a Half-Century*.

The overall idea of this song is in the last musical phrases: "you do something to me that nobody else could do." Read the lyrics at http://lirama.net/song/15599.

You're the Cream in My Coffee

Words: B.G. DeSylva & Lew Brown; Music: Ray Henderson

Henderson, DeSylva, and Brown's *Hold Everything*, a '28 musical comedy that starred Bert Lahr in his first leading role on Broadway, introduced "You're the Cream in My Coffee."

Hold Everything commented on the sport of prizefighting and clean sportsmanship. Bert Lahr was cast as a punch-drunk fighter, Victor Moore was his inept and victimized manager, and Jack Whiting was welterweight champion. Whiting introduced this love duet with Ona Munson, who played the object of his affection.

The primary idea of the song is to point up what a necessity each is for the other. They consider the "necessities" to be a few of the following: cream in coffee, salt in stew, starch in collar, and lace in shoe. The bouncy melody and cute lyrics made the song an irresistible hit. Read the lyrics at http://www.ruthetting.com/songs/youre-the-cream-in-my-coffee.asp.

"You're the Cream in My Coffee" was used in the '30 movie musical *The Cock-Eyed World*.

Ben Selvin and his orchestra, with vocalist Jack Palmer, released the most popular recording of this song. Ted Weems and his orchestra, with a vocal performance by Parker Gibbs, also had a popular recording of the song. Hear Weems' recording at http://www.redhotjazz.com/weems.html. In addition, Broadway star Ruth Etting had a popular version on the market.

Variety selected this song for its *Hit Parade of a Half-Century* representing '28.

Zigeuner

Words & Music: Noel Coward

Bitter-Sweet is Coward's most famous musical in America. Actually, it is part operetta and partly made up of bits and pieces from several different sources.

The song "Zigeuner" was presented in the musical as a piece written by the heroine's husband when he was sixteen years old. On a trip to Germany, the forests, castles and gypsy encampments spurred the youngster's imagination. He wrote this song about a German princess who fell in love with a gypsy.

A '33 movie version of *Bitter-Sweet* starred Anna Neagle.

Variety selected this song for its *Hit Parade of a Half-Century*.

IV

The Depression Years:
1930–1934

The stock market crash on Black Tuesday, October 29, 1929, was the start of the Great Depression. During the early '30s every aspect of life, including popular music, was affected by this catastrophic economic slump.

The '20s were a time to laugh, sing, and dance — an era hell-bent on seeking fun. The '30s were more of a hell: a time of epidemic unemployment, dust storms, soup kitchens and breadlines, the NRA and WPA, living in shanties, scavenging for bits of food, facing eviction for not paying the rent, and lining shoes with cardboard to make them last longer. It was the time of FDR's New Deal, which tried to cure the nation's economic ills.

The people of the United States desperately needed their spirits lifted. For most people, the lift came in the popular songs of the day. The music and lyrics of the decade reflect the attitudes of the people and often comment on their social, economic, and political concerns.

The Musical Theater of the Thirties

The musicals of the '30s were decidedly different from those of the '20s. The Broadway stage began to show its ability to comment on the issues of the day. A lyric, a melody, a dance, or a bit of comedy could often make stronger and more effective comments than any other form of theater. Not all the musicals of the decade were satirical or thought provoking, though the theater was still capable of evenings that were escapes from reality, something the Depression generation desperately needed.

The satirical, intelligent musicals of the era are represented by George and Ira Gershwin's *Strike*

Up the Band ('30) and *Of Thee I Sing* ('31) and by Irving Berlin's *As Thousands Cheer* ('33). More traditional subjects, such as show business, love, marriage, divorce, and college life, were still used for musical comedies, which contained more dance routines than before, dances that featured the fleet feet of Fred Astaire and his contemporaries.

The stage produced some of the best, if not the most popular, songs of the era with hits like "I Got Rhythm," "Embraceable You," "Body and Soul," "Dancing in the Dark," "April in Paris," "Night and Day," "Smoke Gets in Your Eyes," "Easter Parade," "Yesterdays" and "I Get a Kick Out of You."

The quality of the songs that came from the Broadway musicals reflects the genius of the composers and lyricists who were producing the scores. Some of the most illustrious were George and Ira Gershwin, Cole Porter, Jerome Kern, Oscar Hammerstein II, and Irving Berlin.

The decade belonged to the clown because of people's need to laugh in the face of adversity. The clowns poked fun at war and the makers of war; they kidded politicians and governments; they pricked the upper crust and exposed the foibles of all humankind.

The musical theater of the decade tried to raise the spirits of the nation. Americans sang "On the Sunny Side of the Street," "Life Is Just a Bowl of Cherries," "Rise 'n' Shine," and "Get Happy" to shore up their sagging spirits. Songs also voiced the nation's despair with "I Gotta Right to Sing the Blues" and "Brother, Can You Spare a Dime?"

But the theater suffered during the Depression because people could not afford to attend productions. Other media could produce cheaper escapist entertainment.

The Cheapest Form of Entertainment

Radio was the most important entertainment medium of the decade. People could not afford to go out, so they sat at home and got music and other entertainment by twirling the radio dial. Therefore, many hit songs were made through exposure on radio programs as sung or played by radio personalities. Important radio stars included Eddie Cantor, Jack Benny, Will Rogers, Fred Allen, Kate Smith, Bing Crosby, Ed Wynn, Lanny Ross, Fanny Brice, Jessica Dragonette, Rudy Vallee, Will Osborne, Russ Columbo, Morton Downey, Arthur Tracy, Maurice Chevalier, Gene Autry, and the Boswell Sisters. Bands that were popular on radio included those of Ben Bernie, Wayne King, Guy Lombardo, Fred Waring and Paul Whiteman.

Radio could disseminate music to hundreds of thousands of listeners and make a hit overnight, but it also shortened the life of hits. A song's lifespan was smaller because the public heard the songs more often; more exposure equaled shorter life .

The Record and Sheet Music Industry

Record and sheet music sales fell off drastically during the Depression. In the '20s, it was not uncommon for a hit song to sell between 750,000 and a million copies of sheet music. During the early '30s, the maximum sheet music sale was about half a million. The industry never really recovered. Also, the publishers did not seem to be able to print the hits fast enough to keep up with the public's fancy now that radio made and killed hits more quickly.

Record sales were similarly affected. Where an international hit had sold between a million and 1.5 million disks, during the early '30s a big sale now was about 25,000 records. In '34, lower-priced records by popular entertainers entered the marketplace. Not until the end of the decade did record sales become an important part of the popular music industry again.

Dance Bands of the Early Thirties

Several dance bands emerged during the early '30s and most continued into the Swing Era (or the Big Band Era), which started in '35. Joining the bands of the jazz age were those of Hal Kemp, Glen Gray, Wayne King, Guy Lombardo, Ted Weems, and Gus Arnheim.

These bands featured sweet, danceable music, generally not hot jazz. Jazz was kept alive by the African American bands, like that of Fletcher Henderson. Jazz lay semi-dormant, waiting for the nation to emerge from its economic doldrums.

People could not afford to go out much, so the most successful bands were employed in radio or movies. Other bands merely survived with a fierce determination to wait for brighter days.

Movie Musicals

Motion pictures became even more important during the '30s than in the '20s. The screen burst with a plethora of musicals. The cinema offered people a chance to dream and fantasize. The songs from these escapist movie musicals are some of the decade's most enduring hits.

Starring in these classic movie musicals were Dick Powell, Ruby Keeler, Bing Crosby, Alice Faye, Shirley Temple, Maurice Chevalier, and Fred Astaire with his dancing partners, especially Ginger Rogers.

The movie musical of the thirties used dance as it had never been seen before. Fred Astaire and Ginger Rogers emerged as the king and queen of the movie musicals. In films like *Flying Down to Rio*, and *The Gay Divorcee*, their dancing was elegant. Several of their most famous films together came after '34, but during the Depression they established themselves as the most popular dance team since Vernon and Irene Castle.

The Motion Picture Academy of Arts and Sciences had been giving screen awards since '29. The name Oscar was concocted for the awards in '31. But the awards for a song were not made until '34, when the first award went to "The Continental" from *The Gay Divorcee*.

Other memorable songs from the movies of the Depression years include "Beyond the Blue Horizon," "Three Little Words," "Cuban Love Song," "Forty Second Street," "You're Getting to Be a Habit with Me," "Paradise," "Carioca," "It's Only a Paper Moon," "Let's Fall in Love," "Lover," "Shadow Waltz," "We're in the Money," "Temptation," "All I Do Is Dream of You," "I Only Have Eyes for You," "June in January," and "Stay as Sweet as You Are."

The ultimate symbol of these early years of the '30s may be the three little pigs singing "Who's Afraid of the Big Bad Wolf?" Somehow Americans were able to keep smiles on their faces and beat the "big bad wolf" of the Depression.

Some of the loveliest melodies and lyrics ever written and some of the craziest tunes and verses of all time were on the lips of the people as they pulled together to overcome the dark days of the Depression.

1930

Beyond the Blue Horizon

Words: Leo Robin; Music: Richard A. Whiting

Jeanette MacDonald introduced this *Variety Hit Parade of a Half-Century* song in the movie *Monte Carlo*. MacDonald sang the song, which is about looking forward to the future, in a private compartment in a train heading for the Riviera. As the train moves along, shots out the window show peasants working in the fields. As Ms. MacDonald sings, those same peasants harmonize with the song. Such was Hollywood's license for romantic unreality.

Recordings by George Olsen, Jeanette MacDonald and Phil Spitalny helped popularize "Beyond the Blue Horizon" in '30. Hugo Winterhalter revived it successfully in '51.

MacDonald revived the song in the '44 film *Follow the Boys*. The song also appeared in *Dillinger* ('73), in *The Rain Man* ('88), in *The Godfather Part II* ('90) and in a dance sequence in *Stepping Out* ('91).

The chorus lyrics sing about a beautiful day that is waiting "beyond the blue horizon." The singer is confident her life has just begun. Read the lyrics at http://lirama.net/song/15560.

Body and Soul *and* Something to Remember You By

Words & Music: Various

Both "Body and Soul" and "Something to Remember You By" were introduced in the revue *Three's a Crowd*.

BODY AND SOUL

Lyricists Edward Heyman, Robert Sour and Frank Eyton with composer John Green wrote "Body and Soul." The song became a hit in Europe before it came to the United States, where it became one of the biggest hit songs of '30.

"Body and Soul" was written especially for Gertrude Lawrence, who introduced it on British radio. A major London bandleader, Bert Ambrose, heard the broadcast and secured the song for his band's repertoire. The exposure by Ambrose helped make it a hit in England. Max Gordon, a Broadway producer, then bought the American rights to the song to use in his revue *Three's a Crowd*. At first, "Body and Soul" made no impression at all. It wasn't until Howard Dietz convinced composer Ralph Rainger to

write a new arrangement for the song that it was transformed from one of the show's weakest numbers into the smash hit of the score. Torch singer Libby Holman sang "Body and Soul" in the revue and Clifton Webb and Tamara Geva danced to the tune.

"Body and Soul" has become a classic popular song, as shown by its selection to *Variety's Golden 100 Tin Pan Alley Songs* and *Hit Parade of a Half-Century* list. It also became one of the top five most recorded songs of the pre-rock era.

Paul Whiteman and his orchestra continued their success of the '20s with the top recording of "Body and Soul" in '30. Hear Whiteman's recording of this song at http://www.redhotjazz.com/pwo.html. Libby Holman's recording of it was also extremely popular. Several other recorded versions were available including those by Ruth Etting, by Annette Hanshaw, by Helen Morgan, by Ozzie Nelson and his orchestra and by Leo Reisman and his orchestra. Jazz pioneer Louis Armstrong revived it with considerable success in '32, as did "The King of Swing," Benny Goodman and his orchestra in '35. Henry Allen and his orchestra had a moderately successful recorded version in '35. Jazz pianist Art Tatum's version in 1937 did about the same. Trumpeter Ziggy Elman revived it with reasonable success in '47, while vocalist Billy Eckstine had some success with his version in '49. Tenor saxophonist Coleman Hawkins' jazz recording of "Body and Soul" in '39 was inducted into the Grammy Hall of Fame in 1974.

Musically, the chorus begins with a D minor chord in the key of C major, then modulates up a half step to D-flat major, then up a step and a half to E major before modulating back to C to end the song. The bridge section is the part that modulates. The "A" phrase in the AABA form is in C. Such modulations are reasonably uncommon in popular songs.

The chorus lyrics of this torch song indicate the singer is sad and lonely because she is being wronged. She is willing to surrender herself "Body and Soul." Read the lyrics at http://lirama.net/song/15561.

"Body and Soul" was performed in the movie musicals *The Man I Love* ('47), in *Body and Soul* ('47) and *The Helen Morgan Story* ('57). The song also appeared in *Stardust Memories* ('80), *The Color Purple* ('85), *Radio Days* ('87), *One True Thing* ('98) and *Catch Me If You Can* (2002).

SOMETHING TO REMEMBER YOU BY

Libby Holman sang this tender good-bye to Fred MacMurray in *Three's a Crowd* in '30. Howard Dietz and Arthur Schwartz were the lyricist and composer, respectively.

"Something to Remember You By" originated in Britain, as did "Body and Soul." It was called "I Have No Words" when it was first introduced as a fast fox trot in the '29 London musical *Little Tommy Tucker*. Even with a change in lyrics from "I Have No Words" to "Something to Remember You By," Schwartz and Dietz viewed it as a comedy number ("something" referred to a kick in the pants) until Libby Holman urged the writers to change the tempo and mood.

Ms. Holman's recording of the song was the most popular recorded version. Dinah Shore revived it with some success in '43.

Variety selected the song for its *Hit Parade of a Half-Century*.

Fred MacMurray was still an unknown at this time, but his stage work led to a movie contract and starring roles in films by '35.

"Something to Remember You By" was used in the '49 movie musical *Dancing in the Dark*, and in the celebrated movie musical *The Band Wagon* ('53). According to http://www.imdb.com/, this song also appeared uncredited in *Mr. Lucky* ('43).

The singer begs for "something to remember you by, when you are far away." She asks for something to assure her their love will not die. Read the lyrics at http://lirama.net/song/15626.

Chant of the Jungle

Words: Arthur Freed; Music: Nacio Herb Brown

Joan Crawford, as a young chorus girl who takes over top billing from an aging star, introduced "Chant of the Jungle" in the film *Untamed* in '29.

Roy Ingraham and his orchestra recorded "Chant of the Jungle" with another song from the film, "That Wonderful Something," on a Brunswick disk that was terrifically popular in late '29 and early '30. Nat Shilkret and the Victor Orchestra, with a vocal by Frank Munn, also had a very successful disk version of the song. Paul Specht and his orchestra also had a recorded version that sold well; his was actually the first one to chart in late '29. The California Ramblers' recording of "Chant of the Jungle" can be heard at http://www.redhotjazz.com/caramblers.html.

Dancing with Tears in My Eyes

Words: Al Dubin; Music: Joe Burke

First performed by Rudy Vallee over the radio, "Dancing with Tears in My Eyes" had been written for the film *Dancing Sweeties*. It was, however, removed from the final print of the movie musical because some Warner Bros. executives thought the song wasn't good enough. Its eventual success seems to have proved them wrong.

The reason for the tears was the "girl in my arms isn't you." Read the lyrics at http://lirama.net/song/2293.

Variety named the song to its *Hit Parade of a Half-Century*.

Nat Shilkret and the Victor Orchestra had an extremely popular recorded version of "Dancing with Tears in My Eyes." Tenor Lewis James was vocal soloist for the Shilkret disk. Another very successful disk version was released by the Regent Club Orchestra, which was directed by Bob Haring. Ben Selvin and his orchestra's version was also very well received. Ruth Etting also had a recording of the song that sold well in '30. Mantovani and his orchestra revived the song with moderate success in '52. Joe Venuti and his New Yorkers' recording of this song can be heard at http://www.redhotjazz.com/jvny.html.

Get Happy

Words: Ted Koehler; Music: Harold Arlen

Ted Koehler set words to Harold Arlen's music and came up with a song gem that has remained well known long after the revue in which it debuted was forgotten (*9:15 Revue*).

Ruth Etting introduced this rousing hallelujah-type-song in a beach scene at the end of the first act. "Forget your troubles c'mon Get Happy" proved to be the most memorable number from the revue by far. Read the lyrics

and see the sheet music cover at http://www.ruthetting.com/songs/get-happy.asp.

During a break when Harold Arlen was a rehearsal pianist for the Vincent Youmans musical *Great Day*, he began improvising on one of Youmans' themes. Members of the cast and crew encouraged Arlen to turn his improvisation into a song. That's exactly what he did, and "Get Happy" was born.

The most successful recordings of the song were issued by Nat Shilkret and the Victor Orchestra, with vocalists Phil Dewey, Frank Luther, and Leo O'Rourke, and by jazz saxophonist Frankie Trumbauer and his orchestra. Trumbauer also furnished the vocal on his recording. Hear "Get Happy" as recorded by Frankie Trumbauer and his orchestra at http://www.redhotjazz.com/fto.html.

"Get Happy" was also heard in several movie musicals including *Young Man with a Horn* ('50), *Summer Stock* ('50), where Judy Garland performed it, in Jane Froman's screen biography, *With a Song in My Heart* ('52) and in *Cha-Cha-Cha-Boom* ('56). The song also appeared in *Crimes of Passion* ('84).

Variety included "Get Happy" among its *Golden 100 Tin Pan Alley Songs*, but not in its *Hit Parade of a Half-Century*. AFI's *100 Years... 100 Songs* (2004) named "Get Happy" one of the greatest songs from an American film (No. 61) for its performance by Judy Garland in *Summer Stock*.

Happy Days Are Here Again

Words: Jack Yellen; Music: Milton Ager

Milton Ager and Jack Yellen wrote "Happy Days Are Here Again" for *Chasing Rainbows*, a screen musical. It was used in a scene in which World War I soldiers first receive the news that the war has ended.

Before the film was released, the writers published the song and took it to George Olsen for his orchestra to play. As fate would have it, Olsen introduced the song on "Black Tuesday," the day the stock market collapsed. It became the national anthem of those ruined by the crash and helped shore up the spirits of multitudes over the next several years of the Depression. America needed to hear the type of optimism this song offered.

During the '32 presidential election Franklin D. Roosevelt used it as his campaign song to underscore the promise of better times to come with a new administration. It has since been the unofficial anthem of the Democratic party and was used by Harry Truman and John F. Kennedy in their presidential campaigns.

The verse says goodbye to the sad and bad times of the Depression. The singer is happy to be rid of them at last, and says hello to better times ahead. The verse leads into the chorus by stating the cloudy gray times are a thing of the past. Yellen's famous chorus claims that "happy days are here again, the skies above are clear again" (each of the first four lines end with "again," with the interior rhymes being "here," "clear" and "cheer," plus the next three lines end with "it now," with "shout," "doubt" and "about" being the interior rhyme scheme). The chorus continues with the idea that nobody can doubt that our cares and troubles have vanished. We can sing cheerful songs now because "happy days are here again." Read the lyrics at http://ingeb.org/songs/happyday.html.

Recordings by Benny Meroff and his orchestra, with vocalist Dusty Rhodes, by Ben Selvin and his orchestra, and by Leo Reisman and his orchestra, with vocalist L.

Levin, were extremely popular in the early months of thirties. Hear Ben Selvin's recording of this song at http://www.redhotjazz.com/benselvino.html. Barbra Streisand revived the song in '63. Her slow rendition of the normally fast tune helped bring her to national recognition.

In addition to its premier in a movie musical, it was also used by Hollywood in *Thanks a Million* ('35), which starred Dick Powell. The song also appeared in *Slither* ('72) and *Delores Claiborne* ('95).

In 1963, ASCAP selected "Happy Days Are Here Again" as one of sixteen songs on its *All-Time Hit Parade*. *Variety* included the song in its *Golden 100 Tin Pan Alley Songs* and its *Hit Parade of a Half-Century*.

I Got Rhythm *and* Embraceable You

Words: Ira Gershwin; Music: George Gershwin

Girl Crazy was the 1930 Broadway season's best musical and its biggest hit show. The musical was Ginger Rogers' first starring role and introduced an electrifying singing discovery, Ethel Merman, who went on to become Broadway's leading musical comedy star.

The show's plot concerned a New York City playboy whose father sends him to Custerville, Arizona to get him away from fast women and bootleggers. The playboy turns a worthless ranch into a dude ranch complete with fast women and plenty of booze. In the process, he also finds true love.

The '93 Tony Award for Best Musical on Broadway went to *Crazy for You*, a reworking of *Girl Crazy*.

I Got Rhythm

Merman stopped the show with her brassy delivery of "I Got Rhythm," which achieved *Golden 100 Tin Pan Alley Song* status and selection to *Variety's Hit Parade of a Half-Century* representing 1930. "I Got Rhythm" became one of the most recorded songs of the pre-rock era.

George had written the melody some years before in a slow tempo, but with these lyrics, an energetic tempo, and Merman's performance, it became an instant Gershwin classic. When Ethel held a single note in the second chorus for sixteen beats, the audience went wild. Little did they realize they were witnessing her inauguration as queen of the musical theater for the next decade or more. Ethel Merman played the part of Kate Fotheringill, the local saloonkeeper's daughter, and she didn't get on stage until near the end of Act One. Once she appeared, however, she became the show's main attraction.

Red Nichols' Five Pennies issued the most successful recording of "I Got Rhythm." Hear Nichols' recording of this song at http://www.redhotjazz.com/rn5p.html. Dick Robertson was the vocalist on Nichols' recording. Other popular recordings were by blues vocalist Ethel Waters, and by jazz legend Louie Armstrong. The song's highest chart ranking came in '67 when a recording by The Happenings rose to No. 3 on the *Billboard* chart.

Hollywood studios filmed two screen versions of *Girl Crazy*, one in '32, and another in '43. Both featured "I Got Rhythm," but the second one, which starred Judy Garland and Mickey Rooney, had the song played by Tommy Dorsey and his orchestra and was also used as the grand finale. In *Rhapsody in Blue* ('45) the orchestra played "Variations on I Got Rhythm." In *An American in Paris* ('51), Gene Kelly sang and danced the song to a group of French children. It was also used in the '55 movie musical *Sincerely Yours, When the Boys Meet the Girls*, a '66 movie musical, which was a retooling of *Girl Crazy*, had Connie Francis, Harve Presnell, and Louis Armstrong performing the song. The song also appeared in *American Pop* ('81) and *Mr. Holland's Opus* ('95).

AFI's *100 Years ... 100 Songs* (2004) named "I Got Rhythm" as one of the greatest song from an American film even though it did not originate in a film. It was named for its appearance in the '51 film *An American in Paris*, where Gene Kelly performed it.

The title to this song could easily have been "Who Could Ask for Anything More" because the phrase is used often. Ethel Merman sang, "I got rhythm ... music ... my man," so she doesn't think she could ask more. She isn't worried about trouble because she has "starlight" and "sweet dreams." Read the lyrics at http://lirama.net/song/15612.

Embraceable You

Another very well known song from the score of *Girl Crazy* is "Embraceable You," which was introduced by Ginger Rogers and Allen Kearns. Ginger, as Molly Gray, the postmistress of Custerville, was playboy Danny Churchill's, Allen Kearns, love interest. These lyrics are one of four that Ira Gershwin regarded as his best. The others were "The Babbitt and the Bromide," "It Ain't Necessarily So," and "The Saga of Jenny." There are a lot of famous lyrics written by Ira that are left off of that short list. The internal rhymes in the lyrics are especially interesting. Ira rhymes *embraceable* with *irreplaceable, tipsy* with *gypsy, charms* with *arms,* none of which is the end word of a phrase. The last words are you, me, you. Read the lyrics at http://lirama.net/song/15568.

"Embraceable You" had originally been written two years earlier for an Oriental operetta which producer Florenz Ziegfeld had considered but never staged.

Red Nichols helped popularize "Embraceable You" with a recording in '29 and Jimmy Dorsey revived it in '41. Billie Holiday's recording of the song was inducted into the Grammy Hall of Fame in 2005. "Embraceable You" became one of the most recorded songs of the pre-rock era.

The song appeared in the following films: the '43 film version of *Girl Crazy*, plus *Old Acquaintance* ('43), *Taking Sides* (2001) and *Catch Me If You Can* (2002).

A couple of other songs from the score that have remained popular over the years are "Bidin' My Time" and "But Not for Me." The Foursome, most likely the quartet from the Broadway stage, recorded "Bidin' My Time" with some success. Harry James and his orchestra had the most popular recording of "But Not for Me" in '43.

If I Could Be with You One Hour Tonight

Words & Music: Henry Creamer & Jimmy Johnson

Lillian Roth performed "If I Could Be with You One Hour Tonight" in the '30 film *Ladies They Talk About*, where it was an interpolation.

McKinney's Cotton Pickers had a very popular recording of the song during the late summer of '30. Hear the Cotton Pickers' recording of "If I Could Be with You One Hour Tonight" at http://www.redhotjazz.com/cotton.html. George Thomas was featured as vocal soloist on their disk. "Satchmo," Louie Armstrong, also had a successful recorded version on the market.

The lyrics tell us that the singer would like to love you strong and long. He says if he was free to do the things that he'd like to do, he certainly wouldn't be blue. If he could be with you for just an hour he wouldn't go until he had told you why he loves you so much. Read the lyrics at http://kokomo.ca/early_years/if_i_could_be_with_you_lyrics.htm.

The song was used in the '49 Joan Crawford film *Flamingo Road*. It was used as a recurring theme in the film and Ms. Crawford sang the song briefly. It appeared again in the '53 film version of *The Jazz Singer*, where Danny Thomas performed it. It was also used in the Frank Sinatra film *The Joker Is Wild* ('57).

Little White Lies

Words & Music: Walter Donaldson

Walter Donaldson wrote "Little White Lies" for Guy Lombardo and his Royal Canadians. It became one of the top hit songs of '30.

The "little white lies" were those sighs when you said, "I love you." Read the lyrics at http://lirama.net/song/2497.

Fred Waring's Pennsylvanians had a particularly popular record of "Little White Lies" in '30. Hear Waring's recording of the song at http://www.redhotjazz.com/waringspa.html. Other very popular versions were released by Ted Wallace and his Campus Boys, with a vocal performance by Elmer Feldkamp, and by Earl Burtnett and his Los Angeles Biltmore Hotel Orchestra. Dick Haymes revived the song with considerable success in 1948. Dinah Shore also had a '48 disk version of "Little White Lies" that sold very well.

Mama Inez

Words: L. Wolfe Gilbert; Music: Eliseo Grenet

This Cuban number was one of the earliest rumba songs to become a hit in the United States. It was chosen by *Variety* for its *Hit Parade of a Half-Century*.

Adapted from the Cuban song "Ay! Mama-Ines," it was introduced into the States by Maurice Chevalier. Xavier Cugat and his orchestra further popularized the song.

"Mama Inez" was performed on *I Love Lucy*, episode #29, "The Freezer."

The Man from the South (with a Big Cigar in His Mouth)

Words & Music: Rube Bloom & Harry Woods

Ted Weems and his orchestra had an extremely popular recording of "The Man from the South (With a Big Cigar in His Mouth)" in '30. Vocalists Art Jarrett and Parker Gibbs were featured on the recording. Weems' Chicago-based dance band had been recording since the early '20s. Hear Ted Weems' recording of this song at http://www.redhotjazz.com/weems.html.

On the Sunny Side of the Street *and* Exactly Like You

Words: Dorothy Fields; Music: Jimmy McHugh

Lew Leslie's International Revue was a much-anticipated revue with stars Gertrude Lawrence and Harry Richman, but it didn't live up to the hype. The only blessings from the show were a couple of songs by Jimmy McHugh and Dorothy Fields: "On the Sunny Side of the Street" and "Exactly Like You."

ON THE SUNNY SIDE OF THE STREET

Harry Richman introduced "On the Sunny Side of the Street." The lyric points out that if we will walk "on the sunny side of the street," our life will be sweet. It was a great anti-depression song for the Great Depression generation. They needed to hear the optimism espoused by this and several other songs of the era that helped shore up people's spirits. Read the lyrics at http://lirama.net/song/15585.

Ted Lewis's recording of the song was very popular, while Harry Richman's was moderately successful with the record buying public. Hear Ted Lewis' recording of "On the Sunny Side of the Street" at http://www.redhotjazz.com/tlband.html. Tommy Dorsey and his orchestra and Jo Stafford both revived it with some success in '45.

This song is a *Variety Hit Parade of a Half-Century* selection and also made *Variety's Golden 100 Tin Pan Alley Songs* list. "On the Sunny Side of the Street" became one of the most recorded songs of the pre-rock era.

"On the Sunny Side of the Street" has been used in several movie musicals including *Nobody's Darling* ('43), *Is Everybody Happy?* ('43), which starred Ted Lewis, *Swing Parade of 1946*, *Two Blondes and a Redhead* ('47), *Make Believe Ballroom* ('49), *Sunny Side of the Street* ('51) and *The Benny Goodman Story* ('56). The song also appeared in *A League of Their Own* ('92).

EXACTLY LIKE YOU

Gertrude Lawrence and Harry Richman introduced "Exactly Like You," another McHugh and Fields collaboration, in the same revue.

"Someone exactly like you" has finally answered the singer's prayers for a perfect sweetheart. She doesn't see any reason to spend money on a movie, because "no one does those love scenes exactly like you." Read the lyrics at http://lirama.net/song/15569.

Ruth Etting, Harry Richman, and Sam Lanin and his orchestra had moderately successful recordings of "Exactly Like You" in '30. Benny Goodman revived it with good success in '36, which explains why it was used in his screen biography. Don Redman and his orchestra released their version, which did reasonably well, in '37. Hear Louis Armstrong's recording of "Exactly Like You" at http://www.redhotjazz.com/lao.html.

Incidentally, Ethel Merman sang this song, along with "Little White Lies," to audition for George Gershwin for the role in *Girl Crazy* that launched her Broadway career.

This song was one of the *Golden 100 Tin Pan Alley Songs*, and was also chosen for *Variety's Hit Parade of a Half-Century*.

Puttin' on the Ritz *and* There's Danger in Your Eyes, Cherie

Words & Music: Various

The first film in which Irving Berlin played an active role was *Puttin' on the Ritz*, which starred vaudeville singer Harry Richman. The film's plot was the familiar backstage tale in which a washed-up vaudeville star achieves acclaim on Broadway, success goes to his head, but he finally reforms in time to win his girl's affections.

PUTTIN' ON THE RITZ

Harry Richman introduced Irving Berlin's "Puttin' on the Ritz" in his movie debut *Puttin' on the Ritz*. Richman's recording of the song became a big hit with the public. Richman's recording of "Puttin' on the Ritz" was inducted into the Grammy Hall of Fame in 2005. Other recorded versions by Earl Burtnett and his Los Angeles Biltmore Hotel Orchestra and by Leo Reisman and his orchestra, with vocalist Lew Conrad, helped popularize the song nationwide.

"Puttin' on the Ritz" is basically another Irving Berlin "coon" song, with the original lyrics singing about well-dressed "blacks and high browns." Twenty-five years later, Berlin sanitized those "coon" lyrics to more politically correct. Berlin's lyrics ask us if we have seen all the rich people on Park Avenue. Along with their turned up noses, they are wearing high hats, narrow collars, and white spats. They all have plenty of money and seem to be spending it all having a wonderful time. The lyrics recommend that if we're blue, we should try "Puttin' on the Ritz," in other words, we should get all dressed up and try to look super-duper, "like Gary Cooper." Read the lyrics at http://lirama.net/song/8456.

Believe it or not, Clark Gable performed "Puttin' on the Ritz" in *Idiot's Delight* ('39). In *That's Entertainment* ('74), in a sequence about actors who were forced to sing and dance, Gable's efforts were showcased. Fred Astaire performed the song in the '46 movie musical *Blues Skies*, but with new lyrics.

AFI's *100 Years ... 100 Songs* (2004) named "Puttin' on the Ritz" one of the greatest songs ever from an American film (No. 89) for its performance by Gene Wilder and Peter Boyle in *Young Frankenstein* ('74). The song also appeared in *Communion* ('89).

During the early '80s, a disco version of "Puttin' on the Ritz" was released by Taco. It made the Top 5 on *Billboard's* Hot 100.

Hear Fred Astaire's '30 recording of this song at http://www.authentichistory.com/audio/1920s/Fred_-Astaire-Puttin_On_The_Ritz.html. See the sheet music cover and hear a midi musical version at http://www.perfessorbill.com/index1.html.

THERE'S DANGER IN YOUR EYES, CHERIE

Harry Richman also introduced "There's Danger in Your Eyes, Cherie," which he co-wrote with Jack Meskill and Pete Wendling. Did Richman really contribute in the songwriting process? That's difficult to say, however, it was certainly not uncommon for writers to give performers writing credit for performing their songs. It is very possible that Meskill and Wendling realized that having Richman perform their song in a major motion picture musical was well worth giving him co-writing credit.

Even though the singer perceives danger in Cherie's eyes, he doesn't care. He'd even give up paradise if he could share her love. He thinks any sin with her would be worth the cost. He tells her just to tell him when and where and they'll have their love affair.

Variety chose this song for its *Hit Parade of a Half-Century* representing '29, but didn't include "Puttin' on the Ritz"?

Harry Richman also had the most popular recording of the song, but Fred Waring's Pennsylvanians also had a popular version on the market. Hear Waring's recording of this song at http://www.redhotjazz.com/waringspa.html.

Guy Lombardo and his Royal Canadians popularized "With You," another popular song from *Puttin' on the Ritz*. Irving Berlin was the writer of "With You." Hear Fred Waring's recording of this song also at http://www.redhotjazz.com/waringspa.html.

Should I?

Words: Arthur Freed; Music: Nacio Herb Brown

Arthur Freed and Nacio Herb Brown's "Should I?" was introduced in the 1929 movie musical *Lord Byron of Broadway*.

According to Clive Hirschhorn in his *The Hollywood Musical*, "With the central roles so unappealingly cast, and a story ... of only minimal interest, *Lord Byron of Broadway* didn't stand a chance at the box office despite an Arthur Freed–Nacio Herb Brown score which included 'A Bundle of Old Love Letters' and 'Should I?'"

The singer ponders if he should reveal his feelings and confess his love.

The song also appeared in the movie musicals *Thousands Cheer* ('43) and *Singin' in the Rain* ('52).

The Arden-Ohman Orchestra popularized "Should I?" with a reasonably popular recording in 1930. Hear Paul Whiteman's recording of this song at http://www.redhotjazz.com/pwo.html.

Variety chose "Should I?" for its *Hit Parade of a Half-Century* representing 1929.

Stein Song

Words: Lincoln Colcord; Music: E.A. Fenstad & A.W. Sprague

The University of Maine's "Stein Song" began in 1902 while A.W. Sprague was working in Bar Harbor. While there Sprague heard a march called "Opie," written by E.A. Fenstad. While Sprague was a student at the university, he rewrote it and convinced his roommate, Lincoln Colcord, to write lyrics. For years it was the school song of the university and was virtually unknown by those not associated with that institution of higher learning. In '20 NBC bought the rights to the song, which still didn't make much of a splash until Rudy Vallee sang it on his radio program in '30. The collegiate rage of the '20s was still in force, so the song quickly sold several thousand copies of sheet music and approximately half a million copies of Vallee's recording. Other popular versions of the song on the market were by the Colonial Club Orchestra and by Ted Wallace and his Campus Boys with Smith Ballew doing the vocal part of their arrangement. All three versions, but particularly Vallee's, helped the song become one of the biggest hits of the decade.

Variety selected this song for its *Hit Parade of a Half-Century* (listed as "Maine Stein Song).

The '52 film *With a Song in My Heart*, the screen biography of Jane Froman, used the "Maine Stein Song" in the soundtrack.

The song is basically a drinking song. The lyrics encourage us to fill our steins to salute dear old Maine, and drink to all the happy hours and careless days at our alma mater. Toasts are made to the trees, the sky, spring, youth, fire, the girls, in other words, toasts to anything for another drink. Read the lyrics at http://lirama.net/song/15586.

The sheet music is available at the Milton S. Eisenhower

Library of the Johns Hopkins University. The copyright should have expired, since the copyright was 1910, but the sheet music cover and musical score are blocked out at http://levysheetmusic.mse.jhu.edu/otcgi/llscgi60.

Three Little Words

Words: Bert Kalmar; Music: Harry Ruby

The screen biography of Bert Kalmar and Harry Ruby was filmed in '50 and starred Fred Astaire and Red Skelton. Entitled *Three Little Words*, it saluted one of Kalmar and Ruby's greatest hits.

"Three Little Words," a *Variety Hit Parade of a Half-Century* selection, had been introduced by Bing Crosby, backed by Duke Ellington's orchestra, in the Amos and Andy film *Check and Double Check*, the first movie score by Kalmar and Ruby.

Amos 'n' Andy was one of the first serials created for radio. It aired from the '20s through the '50s. The series had such an immense popularity that at its peak it was heard six times a week by an audience of 40,000,000 listeners, one-third of the total U.S. population. The show's creators, Freeman Gosden and Charles Correll, were white actors who were familiar with minstrel traditions. Especially in the early years of the show, Gosden and Correll did all the male voices — 170 different characterizations within the show's first decade.

In 1930, Gosden and Correll went to Hollywood to film an Amos and Andy motion picture. It was titled *Check and Double Check*, which was a catch phrase from their radio show. The cast included a mix of white and black performers with Gosden and Correll playing Amos and Andy in blackface.

Duke Ellington and his orchestra, with a vocal by the Rhythm Boys (Bing Crosby, Al Rinker, and Harry Barris), had a very popular recording of "Three Little Words." Hear Ellington's recording with the Rhythm Boys at http://www.redhotjazz.com/dukeo.html. Other versions on the market included those by Jacques Renard and his orchestra and by the Ipana Troubadours. Ethel Waters released a successful version of it in '31, while Claude Hopkins and his orchestra revived it again in '34.

Those "three little words" are, of course, the three biggest little words in our language: "I love you." Read the lyrics at http://lirama.net/song/603.

Two Hearts (Zwei Herzen in Dreivierteltakt)

English Words: Joe Young; Music: Robert Stolz

This *Variety Hit Parade of a Half-Century* waltz has German origins. Its German title was "Zwei Herzen im Dreivierteltakt." *Zwei Herzen im 3/4 Takt (Two Hearts in Waltz Time)* was the name of the movie from which it came. It was advertised as a German screen operetta, a "100% All-talking & Singing Production."

The original German lyrics were by Walter Reisch and A. Robinson.

Joe Young's chorus lyrics begin with "Two hearts beat with a joy complete ... while waltzing dreamily." The singer wants to share her charms until dawn locked in her lover's arms.

The only charted recording was by Johnny Hamp in '31 entitled "Two Hearts in Waltz Time."

What Is This Thing Called Love?

Words & Music: Cole Porter

Frances Shelley introduced this torchy Porter ballad in the Broadway musical *Wake Up and Dream*.

Porter stated that he derived the idea for this song from the native dance music he heard in Marrakesh, Morocco marketplace on one of his many around-the-world trips. Porter called for a slow blues tempo in the original, but it is better known today in a faster tempo.

The song says it is difficult to understand the mystery of love and why we do the things we do while under its spell. Read the lyrics at http://lirama.net/song/15595.

Recordings by Leo Reisman and his orchestra, with vocalist Lew Conrad, by Ben Bernie and his orchestra, and by Fred Rich and his orchestra, which featured trombonist Tommy Dorsey and trumpeter Bunny Berigan, helped popularize the song in '30. Artie Shaw and his orchestra revived it successfully in '39, in '42 by Tommy Dorsey and his orchestra, and in '48 by Les Paul.

"What Is This Thing Called Love?" was honored with inclusion on both *Variety*'s *Golden 100 Tin Pan Alley Song* and *Hit Parade of a Half-Century* lists. The song became one of the most recorded songs of the pre-rock era.

Lemar performed this song on the soundtrack of the 2004 Porter biopic *De-Lovely*. The song also appeared in *'Round Midnight* ('86).

When It's Springtime in the Rockies

Words: Mary Hale Woolsey & Milton Taggart; Music: Robert Sauer

Very popular recordings by the Hilo Hawaiian Orchestra, with vocal performances by Frank Luther and Carson Robison, and by Ben Selvin and his orchestra established this song as one of 1930's most popular songs. Ray Miller and his orchestra and Ford and Glenn also helped spread its fame nationwide and beyond. Hear Ray Miller's recording of this song at http://www.redhotjazz.com/miller.html.

"When It's Springtime in the Rockies" was used in the Roy Rogers film *Silver Spurs* ('43).

The sheet music describes the song as "a charming waltz song."

The lyrics indicate that the loved one is returning to his "little sweetheart of the mountains" in the spring. Read the lyrics at http://lyricsplayground.com/alpha/songs/w/whenitsspringtimeintherockies.shtml.

You Brought a New Kind of Love to Me

Words: Irving Kahal; Music: Pierre Norman & Sammy Fain

Maurice Chevalier introduced this *Variety Hit Parade of a Half-Century* song in the musical movie *The Big Pond*. This was Sammy Fain's first movie song, but his songs appeared frequently in the next few years. He had songs in three films in '33 and in nine films in '34.

Irving Kahal's lyrics are cleverly written: "If the nightingales could sing like you they'd sing much sweeter ... If the sandman brought me dreams of you I'd want to sleep my whole life thru." Read the complete lyrics at http://lirama.net/song/15598.

Maurice Chevalier's rendition is a classic, remembered as he is for his unique French-accented singing and his novel approach to a popular song. The most popular recordings were by Paul Whiteman, Maurice Chevalier, and the High Hatters. Hear Paul Whiteman's recording of this song at http://www.redhotjazz.com/pwo.html. Helen Ward revived the song with some success in '53.

Paul Whiteman and his orchestra popularized "Livin' in the Sunlight, Lovin' in the Moonlight" from *The Big Pond*. Al Lewis and Al Sherman wrote that song. Hear Whiteman's recording of this song in four different versions at http://www.redhotjazz.com/pwo.html.

You're Driving Me Crazy
Words & Music: Walter Donaldson

Walter Donaldson first named this song "What Did You Do to Me?" but before Guy Lombardo and his Royal Canadians introduced it, Donaldson called him to change the title to "You're Driving Me Crazy." Lombardo introduced it on his radio program and played it every night for the first week. Within three days, with that exposure, it reportedly had sold more than a 100,000 copies of sheet music.

Lombardo's recording of the song was just as successful as the song's sheet music sales. Other successful disks were released by Rudy Vallee and Nick Lucas. Buddy Greco and his orchestra revived it with moderate success in '53. Hear Paul Whiteman's recording of this song at http://www.redhotjazz.com/pwo.html.

To try to help a failing Broadway musical, *Smiles*, "You're Driving Me Crazy (What Did I Do?)" was interpolated into the show, where Adele Astaire and Eddie Foy, Jr. performed it. The show was beyond help, but the song survived.

It was used in the movie musical *Gentlemen Marry Brunettes* ('55).

Donaldson's verse to the song asks why the singer was left sad and lonely. He tells her his heart is only for her, but he blames her for his loneliness. The chorus opens with the title phrase: "Yes, you, you're driving me crazy!" It isn't a compliment. This person has deserted and hurt him. The chorus ends with the question, "What did I do to you?" Read the complete lyrics at http://lirama.net/song/1130.

1931

As Time Goes by (see 1943)

At Your Command
Words & Music: Harry Tobias, Harry Barris & Bing Crosby

The most successful entertainer of the pre-rock era was Bing Crosby. Crosby teamed with Al Rinker and they were hired by Paul Whiteman in '26. Whiteman added Harry Barris to make a trio, the Rhythm Boys. The trio left Whiteman in '30 and got a booking at the Coconut Grove in Los Angeles, where Crosby began to emerge as a soloist. The trio and Bing as a soloist recorded several songs with Gus Arnheim and his orchestra, including "I Surrender, Dear." Its success earned Bing a CBS radio contract. He also began to appear in musical shorts that were filmed by Mack Sennett, the famous filmmaker and inventor of the

Keystone Kops. Over the next thirty years, Crosby sold more than 300,000,000 records and was featured in 50 movies.

His first solo hit recordings came in '31, and "At Your Command" was one of his first big hits on the Brunswick label. Crosby and his singing partners in the Rhythm Boys, Harry Barris, and Harry Tobias, collaborated to write the music and lyrics.

Crosby sang "I Surrender, Dear," "Out of Nowhere," "At Your Command" and the less well-known "A Little Bit of Heaven" in the short two-reel comedy *I Surrender, Dear*. In the twenty-two minute black and white film, Bing mistakes Marion Sayers as his sister and kisses her. Her boyfriend wasn't thrilled by this and he aims to make this point to Bing. When Ms. Sayers learns that Bing is a famous crooner, she is ready to elope.

By the River Sainte Marie (Pres de la Riviere Ste. Marie)
Words: Edgar Leslie; Music: Harry Warren

"By the River Sainte Marie," a Canadian love song, was popularized by Guy Lombardo and his Royal Canadians in a very successful recording in '31. Kate Smith featured it on her first radio program over CBS in May of '31 and her beautiful "Songbird of the South" voice helped spread the song's fame. An audio clip of Tony Bennett singing "By the River St. Marie" can be heard at http://www.harrywarrenmusic.com/realfiles/.

It was interpolated into the '44 film *Swing in the Saddle*.

The singer tells us they pledged their love and after a couple of kisses, he "left her by the River Sainte Marie." She kneeled and said a prayer for him. When spring returns again, he promises to "meet her by the River Sainte Marie." Read the lyrics and hear a midi musical version at http://www.harrywarren.org/songs/0047.htm.

Cuban Love Song
Words: Dorothy Fields; Music: Jimmy McHugh & Herbert Stothart

The first multi-track recording was an over-dubbing of Lawrence Tibbett for the sound track of the MGM movie musical titled *Cuban Love Song*. In the film Tibbett, as a soldier, performed the song with an image of himself as a ghost. Tibbett harmonized with himself, which makes this the first multi-track recording in history. Over-dubbing did not become an important part of the recording industry until Les Paul perfected the technique in the early '50s.

Without the native Cuban rhythms underneath the melody, this triple meter tune would not have a particularly exotic character. Other '31 songs with Cuban influence include "Marta" and "The Peanut Vendor."

The most popular recordings of the song on the market were by Jacques Renard, by Paul Whiteman and his orchestra and by Ruth Etting. Hear Paul Whiteman's recording of "Cuban Love Song" at http://www.redhotjazz.com/pwo.html.

Variety chose "Cuban Love Song" for its *Hit Parade of a Half-Century*.

The chorus begins by telling us the singer's heart is saying "I love you," as the breeze is "playing our Cuban Love Song." In the AABA structure, each "A" line begins with "I love you." Read the lyrics at http://lirama.net/song/15604.

Dancing in the Dark

Words: Howard Dietz; Music: Arthur Schwartz

John Barker introduced Schwartz and Dietz's most famous hit song, "Dancing in the Dark," in the revue *The Band Wagon*. Later in the production, Tilly Losch danced to the tune on a tilted, mirrored stage, illuminated by continually changing lights.

Bing Crosby, and Fred Waring's Pennsylvanians competed with each other for the most popular recorded version of "Dancing in the Dark" in '31. Ben Selvin and his orchestra and Jacques Renard also had successful releases of the song. Artie Shaw and his orchestra revived it in '41 and again in '44, both times with considerable success. "Dancing in the Dark" became one of the most recorded songs of the pre-rock era.

The couple is "dancing in the dark" as new lovers, and are confident they can face the future together. A curiosity in the lyrics is the line "we're waltzing in the wonder of why we're here," but the song is not a waltz; it is not in triple meter, but in cut time (2/2). Read the lyrics at http://lirama.net/song/169.

A '49 film titled *Dancing in the Dark*, of course, used the song. And Fred Astaire and Cyd Charisse danced exquisitely to "Dancing in the Dark" in the film version of *The Band Wagon* ('53).

Variety included "Dancing in the Dark" on both their *Golden 100 Tin Pan Alley Songs* and *Hit Parade of a Half-Century* lists.

Other musical highlights of the revue included "Hoops," where Fred and Adele Astaire played two French children cavorting through Paris causing all sorts of havoc, and "I Love Louisa," with its irresistible oompah beat. A recording by Fred Astaire with Leo Reisman's orchestra of "I Love Louisa" was well received. "New Sun in the Sky," also from the revue, is worthy of mention, in a recording by Fred Astaire with Leo Reisman's orchestra.

Dream a Little Dream of Me

Words: Gus Kahn; Music: Wilber Schwandt & Fabian Andre

Kate Smith featured "Dream a Little Dream of Me" on her first radio program on May 1, 1931. It is difficult to find anything distinctive about the song. The melody and the lyrics are so well known, and the song has been so endearingly popular that it is surprising the tune and lyrics are not particularly novel ("say 'nightie-night' and kiss me"). Read the lyrics at http://lirama.net/song/15606.

Wayne King and his orchestra, with a vocal by Ernie Burchill, had a very popular recording of the song in the early spring of '31. Jack Owens, the former singer on Don McNeill's "Breakfast Club" radio show, and Frankie Laine revived it with moderate success in '50. "Mama" Cass Elliott, formerly a member of the Mamas and Papas, revived the song in a popular solo recording in '68. "Mama" Cass' recording of the song was used in the '95 Meg Ryan film *French Kiss*.

Georgia on My Mind

Words: Stuart Gorrell; Music: Hoagy Carmichael

Hoagy Carmichael, talented composer of such hits as "Star Dust" and "The Nearness of You," first popularized his "Georgia on My Mind." Frankie Trumbauer and his orchestra, with vocalist Art Jarrett, had a popular recorded version in '31. Hear Trumbauer's recording at http://www.redhotjazz.com/fto.html. Jazz singer Mildred Bailey had a reasonably successful version of it in '32. Famous drummer Gene Krupa and his orchestra, with vocalist Anita O'Day, revived it with reasonable success in '41. Hear Hoagy Carmichael and his orchestra's recording of "Georgia on My Mind" at http://www.redhotjazz.com/hoagyo.html.

The song also had considerable success in the '60s, '70s and '90s. In '60, Ray Charles had a number one hit with his soulful version. He also won the Grammy Award for the best male vocal recording and the best pop single performance of the year in '60 with his version of "Georgia..." Country singer Willie Nelson revived it again in '78 and won the Grammy award for the Best Country Vocal Performance, Male, with his rendition. Michael Bolton took it to number one again in '93 and won the Grammy award for Best Male Performance with it, introducing it to a new generation of listeners. "Georgia on My Mind" became one of the most recorded songs of the pre-rock era.

The song is Georgia's state song and the state uses the song on its welcome sign as you enter the state: "We're glad we're on your mind."

The song appeared in the following films: *To Paris with Love* ('55), *Four Friends* ('81), *American Pie 2* (2001). Because of his frequent soulful performances of "Georgia on My Mind," the song was prominently featured in Ray Charles' 2004 screen biography *Ray*.

The lyrics begin with repetitions of "Georgia." Then we learn "an old sweet song keeps" this girl on his mind. This song comes to him "as sweet and clear as moonlight through the pines." Even though other things may lure him away, the road always leads him back to "Georgia." Read the lyrics at http://lirama.net/song/9199. Hear a nice midi musical version at http://www.primeshop.com/midlist3.htm.

Good Night, Sweetheart

Words & Music: Ray Noble, James Campbell & Reg Connelly

Rudy Vallee introduced and helped promote this *Variety Golden 100 Tin Pan Alley Song* on his radio show. The most popular recordings of the song, however, were by Wayne King and his orchestra and by Guy Lombardo and his Royal Canadians. Their recordings were extremely popular in the fall of '31. Other disks that were successful included those by Russ Columbo, by Bing Crosby, and by Ruth Etting. Even though *Variety* honored the song as one of its *Golden 100*, the song was not included in its *Hit Parade of a Half-Century*.

This English song was featured in the '31 edition of the revue *Earl Carroll's Vanities*. It was sung by Milton Watson and Woods Miller, and danced by Irene Ahlberg and Beryl Wallace.

A year or two previously a hit song would have sold between 750,000 and 1,000,000 copies of sheet music. But in the Depression economy of '31 the maximum was about 500,000. The only song to exceed that figure in '31 was "Good Night, Sweetheart," which qualifies it as the top hit of the year.

"Good Night, Sweetheart" was used in the '35 movie musical *The Big Broadcast of 1936*, in *Holiday in Mexico* ('46), and in *You Were Meant for Me* ('48).

The chorus lyrics begin with the title phrase: "Good night, sweetheart, till we meet tomorrow." The singer wants his sweetheart's sleep to chase away her sorrow. The singer continues to reassure her that even though he's not beside her, his love will guide her. He promises to hold her in his dreams and ends the chorus with "Good night, sweetheart, good night." Read the lyrics at http://www.lyricsdepot.com/guy-lombardo/goodnight-sweetheart.html.

Heartaches (see 1947)

I Found a Million Dollar Baby (in a Five and Ten Cent Store)

Words: Mort Dixon & Billy Rose; Music: Harry Warren

Billy Rose's revue *Crazy Quilt* introduced this *Variety Hit Parade of a Half-Century* number. Dressed in top hats and tails, it was sung by Ted Healy, Phil Baker, Lew Brice and Fanny Brice.

Fred Waring's Pennsylvanians had a particularly popular recording of "I Found a Million Dollar Baby" in '31. Hear Waring's recording at http://www.redhotjazz.com/waringspa.html. Bing Crosby and the Boswell Sisters also had very successful releases of the song.

The singer found the million-dollar baby in a five-and-ten-cent store when he ducked in to escape an April shower. Read the lyrics and hear a midi musical version at http://www.harrywarren.org/songs/0183.htm.

The song was used in the '35 film *Million Dollar Baby* and *Funny Lady* ('75), the sequel to movie version of *Funny Girl*. Victor Young and his orchestra's recording of the song was used on the soundtrack of *Paper Moon* ('73). The Boswell Sisters were vocalists on the disk.

I Love a Parade

Words: Ted Koehler; Music: Harold Arlen

Cab Calloway introduced this early Harold Arlen hit at a Cotton Club revue, *Rhythmania*, in Harlem. It was later interpolated into *George White's Music Hall Varieties* ('32), where Harry Richman performed it.

During a walk one cold day, Arlen began to hum a marching tune to pep up his walking partner, lyricist Ted Koehler. It became a composer and lyricist game as they walked; they hummed the melody and constructed lyrics respectively until by the end of the walk, "I Love a Parade" was completed. Read the lyrics at http://www.lyricsvault.net/songs/18081.html.

The Arden-Ohman Orchestra issued the only popular recording of "I Love a Parade" in '32.

The song was used in the film *Manhattan Parade* ('32), which starred Winnie Lightner.

Variety chose "I Love a Parade" for its *Hit Parade of a Half-Century*.

I Surrender, Dear

Words: Gordon Clifford; Music: Harry Barris

"I Surrender, Dear" marks the start of Bing Crosby's solo career. Crosby and the Rhythm Boys were fired by Paul Whiteman and joined Gus Arnheim and his orchestra for some recordings in the early '30s. One of Crosby's first solo recordings was his Rhythm Boys partner Harry Barris's "I Surrender, Dear." The song brought him to the attention of radio executives, and his success on radio led to more recordings and movies that eventually made him a giant of the entertainment world.

The Arnheim recording was the most popular one, but Earl Burtnett and his Los Angeles Biltmore Hotel Orchestra also had a moderately success version. Red Norvo and his orchestra, with Artie Shaw on clarinet and Charlie Barnet on tenor sax, revived it with a reasonable amount of success in '35. Hear Frankie Trumbauer and his orchestra's recording of "I Surrender, Dear" at http://www.redhotjazz.com/fto.html.

Atlantic Pictures filmed a short movie musical directed by Mack Sennett entitled *I Surrender Dear* starring Bing Crosby.

Variety chose "I Surrender, Dear" for its *Hit Parade of a Half-Century*.

Clifford's chorus lyrics begin with "we've played the game of stay away," but the singer surrenders because he can't do without his loved one. He confesses that he may act like he can, but he really can't, so he sings, "I surrender dear." By the end of the chorus, he assures her that she is his love, his life, his all and surrenders to her charms one last time. Read the lyrics at http://lirama.net/song/15613.

Just a Gigolo (Schoner Gigolo)

English Words: Irving Caesar; Music: Leonello Casucci

This Viennese popular song ("Schoner Gigolo") was given English lyrics by Irving Caesar in '30. The German lyrics were by Julius Brammer.

It was first popularized in the United States by Vincent Lopez and his orchestra. Ted Lewis recorded a particularly popular version in '31. Hear Lewis' recording at http://www.redhotjazz.com/tlband.html. Ben Bernie and his orchestra, Bing Crosby, his first record as "Bing Crosby" (not the Rhythm Boys or Gus Arnheim and his orchestra with vocalist Bing Crosby), and Leo Reisman and his orchestra also had recordings that helped popularize the song nationally. Jaye P. Morgan revived it with moderate success in '53. David Lee Roth revived it in a medley that reached No. 12 on *Billboard's* Hot 100 in '85.

"Just a Gigolo" was interpolated into the '46 film *Lover, Come Back*, which starred Lucille Ball and George Brent.

In this sad song's chorus, the singer quickly admits to being a gigolo and says people know what he is. He is "paid for every dance," and sells each romance. He worries what people will say about him once his youth has passed. The song ends with "when the end comes I know, I was just a gigolo, life goes on without me." Read the lyrics at http://www.lyricsdepot.com/yale-whiffenpoofs/just-a-gigolo.html.

Just One More Chance

Words: Sam Coslow; Music: Arthur Johnston

"Just One More Chance" was introduced in the Marx Brothers' film *Monkey Business* ('31).

The song became one of Bing Crosby's first big hit recordings as a soloist. Accompanied by Victor Young's Orchestra, Crosby's version of "Just One More Chance" hit the charts in early June of '31. He had three big hit recordings in '31: "Out of Nowhere," "Just One More Chance," and "At Your Command." Paul Whiteman's recording of the song can be heard at http://www.redhotjazz.com/pwo.html.

"Just One More Chance" was used in the campus movie musical *College Coach* ('33), Dean Martin and Jerry Lewis's *The Stooge* ('53), and *Country Music Holiday* ('58). Crosby's recording of the song was used on the soundtrack of *Paper Moon* ('73), which was set in the '30s.

The singer wants "Just one more chance to prove it's you alone" he cares for. Read the lyrics at http://lirama.net/song/15615.

Life Is Just a Bowl of Cherries

Words: Lew Brown; Music: Ray Henderson

The '31 edition of *George White's Scandals* boasted a lively and melodic collection of Ray Henderson/Lew Brown songs Their writing partner, Buddy DeSylva, had left for Hollywood.

Ethel Merman, who had joined the cast during its pre–Broadway tryouts, lifted everyone's spirits with her rendition of "Life Is Just a Bowl of Cherries." Rudy Vallee, one of the era's most popular recording artists, was also in the cast. Although this song was performed by Ms. Merman in the show, it was Vallee who had the most popular recording of it in '31. Jaye P. Morgan revived it with moderate success in '54.

"Life Is Just a Bowl of Cherries" was used in the '45 movie musical *George White's Scandals of 1945*, where it was performed by Joan Davis and Jack Haley.

This song became one of the most famous Depression philosophy songs of the era. It reasons that one need not work and save because all can be gone in an instant. Whatever we have is a loan, so don't take life too seriously. Laugh at the mysteries of life, and don't worry too much. Read the lyrics at http://lirama.net/song/15616.

"Life Is Just a Bowl of Cherries" was performed by Walt Harrach, Bene Merlino, Vern Rowe, and Robert Tebow in the '82 movie musical *Pennies from Heaven*.

This Henderson/Brown standard was chosen by *Variety* for its *Hit Parade of a Half-Century*.

Rudy Vallee popularized another couple of songs from this edition of the *Scandals*: "My Song" and "The Thrill Is Gone." Kate Smith popularized "That's Why Darkies Were Born."

Love for Sale

Words & Music: Cole Porter

This is one of the few songs in American popular music inspired by the "oldest profession in the world." For years radio banned the song because the words were considered too risqué. Compared with the sexually explicit lyrics of more modern songs, "Love for Sale" now seems tame.

The *Herald Tribune* critic Percy Hammond described its premier in Cole Porter's Broadway musical *The New Yorkers*: "A frightened vocalist, Kathryn Crawford, sings a threnody entitled 'Love for Sale,' in which she impersonates a lily of the gutters, vending her charms in trembling accents, accompanied by a trio of melancholy crooners." Considering the times, it's amazing that Porter got such an explicit song through censorship, even if it was for the more tolerant Broadway stage.

According to www.musicalstonight.org, the plot of *The New Yorkers* revolves around a society girl who falls for a bootlegger. When he innocently ends up in prison, she organizes a successful jailbreak.

Torch singer Libby Holman's delivery fit "Love for Sale," and her recording of the song did remarkably well

during '31. Fred Waring's Pennsylvanians also released a recording of it that did pretty well. Hear Waring's recording of "Love for Sale" at http://www.redhotjazz.com/waringspa.html. Hal Kemp and his orchestra revived the song in '39 with moderate success. "Lady Day," Billie Holiday's recording of the song is now considered a classic. "Love for Sale" became one of the most recorded songs of the pre-rock era.

Porter considered this song and "Begin the Beguine" his favorites out of all of the songs that he wrote. It was used in his screen biography *Night and Day* ('46). The song was also used in *Bride of Chucky* ('98) and *Torch Song Trilogy* ('88). Vivian Green sang "Love for Sale" on the soundtrack of the 2004 Porter film biography *De-Lovely*.

Such lyrics as "appetizing young love for sale" and "who would like to sample my supply" sound out of place in the early '30s. Such blatant sexuality might even raise the voices of many moralists today. This woman of the streets has "been through the mill of love," every kind of love except true love. Read the lyrics at http://lirama.net/song/15617.

Emil Coleman popularized "Where Have You Been?" from *The New Yorkers*.

Love Letters in the Sand

Words: Nick & Charles Kenny; Music: J. Fred Coots

J. Fred Coots happened to read a Nick Kenny poem in the *New York Daily Mirror* that he immediately thought would make a great popular song. He obtained Kenny's permission to set it to music and after four different melodies, composed the one we know. Some authorities have suggested that Coots' song is similar to the 1881 song "The Spanish Cavalier," but there has never been any legal action that charged him with plagiarism.

Russ Columbo was the first singer to show interest in the song. George Hall and his orchestra further popularized the song on their fourteen-broadcasts-per-week radio show. Hall later made it his theme song. Ted Black and his orchestra, with the leader furnishing the vocal, had the most popular recording of the song in '31.

It was much more popular when it was revived in '57 into a million-selling recording by Pat Boone. He also sang it in the film *Bernardine* ('57), in which he starred. It became the biggest hit of the year according to some of the charts, reportedly selling almost 4 million copies.

The singer and his sweetheart "pass the time away writing love letters in the sand," but the tide keeps destroying them. Next the singer accuses the girl of making a vow to be true, but it seemingly meant nothing to her. Now he is broken hearted because her vow was broken as easily as the waves washed away the "love letters in the sand." Read the lyrics at http://lirama.net/song/15618.

Marta

Words: L. Wolfe Gilbert; Music: Moises Simons

Arthur Tracy, known as The Street Singer, made this beautiful song his theme. He was a sentimental singer who achieved recognition over radio. He signed on and off of his three-time-weekly radio show with "Marta," a Cuban song by Moises Simons.

It was popularized in recordings by Roy Fox and Dick Haymes.

Variety listed "Marta (Rambling Rose of the Wildwood)" in its *Hit Parade of a Half-Century*.

The singer had watched Marta grow from childhood and had hoped she'd be his someday. Read the lyrics at http://www.spatty.demon.co.uk/lyrics/marta.htm.

Minnie the Moocher

Words & Music: Irving Mills & Cab Calloway

"Minnie the Moocher" was famed scat singer Cab Calloway's theme. Its "hi-de-ho" singing became his trademark.

Calloway had his first shot at stardom in the revue *Connie's Hot Chocolates* in '29 but did not achieve fame until he fronted a hot band at Harlem's Cotton Club in '31. He became famous for his frantic gyrations and for his vocals on swing and novelty numbers. Calloway's most famous song was the novelty "Minnie the Moocher," which is based on the traditional folk song "Willy the Weeper."

Calloway's recording of "Minnie the Moocher" became phenomenally popular. His recording of the song was inducted into the Grammy Hall of Fame in 1999.

The song's lyrics are almost completely nonsensical, but Calloway's fans didn't seem to notice. His energetic performance and the catchy rhythmic tune were enough to make it a huge hit. Read the lyrics at http://lirama.net/song/22168.

Calloway performed "Minnie the Moocher" in the '32 movie musical *The Big Broadcast*, and in the '80 film *The Blues Brothers*. He was imitated in the film *Cotton Club* ('84). The song was also used in *When You're in Love* ('37).

Mood Indigo

Words: Irving Mills & Albany Bigard; Music: Duke Ellington

Jazz great Duke Ellington first wrote this mellow standard as an instrumental piece entitled "Dreamy Blues." Almost all of Ellington's song began as instrumentals.

With lyrics and a title change the song became one of Ellington's first popular hits. Ellington's recording of the song with his band was inducted into the Grammy Hall of Fame in 1975. Hear Ellington's recording of this song with his Cotton Club Orchestra at http://www.redhot jazz.com/dukecco.html. Other popular recordings of the song were by Jimmie Lunceford in '34, and by the Norman Petty Trio and the Four Freshmen in '54. "Mood Indigo" became one of the most recorded songs of the pre-rock era.

The mood suggests the deep violet-blue of indigo. There are the blues, but there's nothing as blue as "mood indigo." Later in the chorus, the singer laments she's bluer than blue when she gets "that mood indigo." Read the lyrics at http://lirama.net/song/22128.

Out of Nowhere

Words: Edward Heyman; Music: John Green

Green and Heyman published "Out of Nowhere" as an independent number, that is, it was not associated with a musical or movie. This *Variety Hit Parade of a Half-Century* selection was introduced by Guy Lombardo and his Royal Canadians. Leo Reisman and his orchestra, with vocalist Frank Munn, had a popular recorded version of the song. Once the song had begun to gain in popularity, it was interpolated into the '31 film *Dude Ranch*.

"Out of Nowhere" was Bing Crosby's first hit recording as a solo vocalist. His first record release as a soloist was

"Just a Gigolo" backed by "Wrap Your Troubles in Dreams" (actually "Wrap Your Troubles..." did a little better popularity wise than his version of "...Gigolo"). His second release was "Out of Nowhere," and it did much better, climbing quickly in popularity with the public.

Tommy Dorsey popularized a song in '45 titled "You Came Along (From Out of Nowhere)."

"Out of Nowhere" appeared in a couple of movie musicals including *The Joker Is Wild* ('57), the Frank Sinatra film in which he played Joe E. Lewis, and *The Five Pennies* ('57), the screen biography of Red Nichols. In *The Joker Is Wild*, the song had new lyrics by Harry Harris. The song also appear in the short film *I Surrender, Dear* (see "At Your Command" above).

"You came to me from out of nowhere," and if you leave and go "back to your nowhere," the singer vows he'll wait for her return, hoping she'll bring her love back to him. Read the lyrics at http://lirama.net/song/350.

The Peanut Vendor

Words: L. Wolfe Gilbert & Marion Sunshine; Music: Moises Simons

"The Peanut Vendor (El Manisero)" was discovered by Herbert Marks, the son of the famous music publisher Edward B. Marks, when he was on his honeymoon trip to Havana. The younger Marks learned it was written by a local composer, Moises Simons, as "El Manisero." Marks arranged to bring the song back to the United States, where an English lyric was written by Louis Rittenberg. However, the elder Marks decided the Rittenberg lyric was unsuitable, so Marion Sunshine, who was married to the brother of Cuban bandleader Don Azpiazu, wrote another one with lyricist L. Wolfe Gilbert. Azpiazu and his Havana Casino Orchestra introduced the number at Keith's Palace Theater, recorded it, and promoted it into a tremendous hit. The vocalist on Azpiazu's recording was Arturo Machin. Not only was it a huge national hit, it launched a rhumba craze. Their recording was one of the earliest authentically Latin style numbers to be released in the U.S. and it introduced Cuban percussion instruments to American audiences.

Moises Simons composed "El Manicero" late one evening in '28 on a napkin in a Havana tavern. He had been inspired by a passing peanut vendor who was singing a *pregón* (jingle) to sell his *cucuruchos de maní* (paper cones filled with peanuts).

The song was originally what the Cubans referred to as a "son," a slow and dignified dance tune. When the word "son" appeared on the sheet music Americans were confused and thought it might be a typographical mistake. So the publishers decided to call it a rhumba. Of course, "The Peanut Vendor" wasn't a rhumba, but at least the name was familiar to Americans.

Azpiazu had formed his Havana Casino Orchestra in '28. The group recorded the original version of "Green Eyes" in '31 (see '41). A decade later, it was translated into English and became a big hit recording by Jimmy Dorsey and his orchestra. In addition to Azpiazu, the other recordings that were on the market included ones by the California Ramblers, Red Nichols, and Louis Armstrong and his Sebastian New Cotton Club Orchestra. Hear this Armstrong recording at http://www.redhotjazz.com/Sebastian.html. Armstrong released a new recording of the song in '41 that did reasonably well. Hear Paul Whiteman's recording of this song at http://www.redhotjazz.com/pwo.html.

One of the first Latin rhythm numbers to make the big time, "The Peanut Vendor" was featured in the '31 film *Cuban Love Song* (performed by Don Azpiazu's band), *Luxury Liner* ('48), where it was performed by Jane Powell, and in the '54 version of *A Star Is Born*, which starred Judy Garland.

"The Peanut Vendor" was listed in *Variety's Hit Parade of a Half-Century* for '30, but it was most popular in '31.

This song is known more as an instrumental, but it did have lyrics by L. Wolfe Gilbert and Marion Sunshine. Basically, it is the song of the peanut vendor extolling his hot roasted nuts. A funny line in the lyrics is the concluding idea: "If you're looking for a moral to this song, Fifty million monkeys can't be wrong." Read the lyrics at http://lirama.net/song/154.

Prisoner of Love (see 1946)

Sleepy Time Down South

Words & Music: Leon & Otis Rene & Clarence Muse

This *Variety Hit Parade of a Half-Century* selection became a specialty of Louis Armstrong. It is a famous tune, and Armstrong's performance was outstanding, but usually there is a more substantial reason for the song's inclusion in the *Hit Parade of a Half-Century* list. Paul Whiteman's recording of the song was more popular in '31, however. Hear Whiteman's recording of this song at http://www.redhotjazz.com/pwo.html.

The lyrics sing about the dreamy song of the South, and the singer wishes he could go back because he belongs there "when it's sleepy time down south." Read the lyrics at http://www.top50lyrics.com/l/louisarmstrong-lyrics-2389/whenitssleepytimedownsouth-lyrics-283348.html.

Smile, Darn Ya, Smile

Words: Charles O'Flynn & Jack Meskill; *Music: Max Rich*

This *Variety Hit Parade of a Half-Century* song became the theme of Fred Allen's radio show. This nice bit of anti–Depression philosophy in song stayed six weeks in the top ten during '31 and peaked at number three in mid–March of the year.

The *Merrie Melodies* cartoons often showcased songs from Warner Bros. extensive music library. Most of the time, the title of the cartoon was also the title of the song featured in it. There was a *Smile, Darn Ya, Smile!* cartoon. The song was also used in the Disney film *Who Framed Roger Rabbit*.

The lyrics encourage the listener by saying things are never as bad as they seem. Then he says we should "make life worth while come on and smile, darn ya, smile." Read the lyrics at http://www.jbott.com/smildar.html.

Ben Selvin and his orchestra's recording of "Smile, Darn Ya, Smile" was popular in '31. Hear Ben Selvin's recording of this song at http://www.redhotjazz.com/benselvino.html.

Star Dust

Words: Mitchell Parish; Music: Hoagy Carmichael

Composer Hoagy Carmichael made a return visit to his alma mater, the University of Indiana, and during the nostalgic trip came to the "spooning wall" (spooning, in case you're not familiar with that slang word, means dating). As he sat there, he reminisced about a college coed he had loved and lost. A melody suddenly came to mind, and he rushed to the nearest piano to play it before he forgot it. A fellow former student and Hoagy's roommate, Stuart Gorrell, dubbed the piece "Star Dust" because he said "it sounded like dust from the stars drifting down through the summer sky."

The first version was not at all what we know today. It was a fast piano instrumental. Don Redman and his orchestra introduced the fast version, but only had moderate success with it. An arranger, Jimmy Dale, was responsible for suggesting its appeal as a sentimental piece with a slow tempo. In this format, the song was presented in a recording by Emile Seidel and his orchestra with the composer, Hoagy Carmichael, at the piano.

At the insistence of publisher Irving Mills, lyrics were written for the melody by staff writer Mitchell Parish. The introduction of "Star Dust" with lyrics came at the Cotton Club in New York City's Harlem in '29.

Publisher Irving Mills turned recording artist with a version in '30 that did moderately well. Isham Jones and his orchestra probably had the most popular version of "Star Dust" in '31. Hear Jones' recording at http://www.redhotjazz.com/ishamjones.html. Other '31 recordings that helped it become established included releases by Bing Crosby, Louis Armstrong, Wayne King and his orchestra, and jazz saxophonist Lee Sims. Benny Goodman and Tommy Dorsey and their orchestras revived it in '36 with considerable success. Artie Shaw and his orchestra issued another definitive recording of the song in '41. Tommy Dorsey and his orchestra recorded a new version of it in '41, and Glenn Miller and his orchestra also had a recording in '41 that was successful. Tommy Dorsey and his orchestra and Baron Elliott revived it again in '43. Since then it has become one of the most recorded songs of all time; more than 1,000 American disk versions in at least 46 different arrangements. It has been translated into at least 40 different languages. The last really popular version was by Billy Ward in '57.

"Star Dust" is the No. 3 most recorded song of the pre-rock era behind only "Silent Night" and "St. Louis Blues." Two recordings of "Star Dust" have been inducted into the Grammy Hall of Fame: the '27 recording by Hoagy Carmichael and His Pals (inducted 1995), and Artie Shaw and his orchestra's '40 recording (inducted 1988).

In '63 "Star Dust" was selected as one of sixteen songs for ASCAP's *All-Time Hit Parade*. *Variety* included it on its *Golden 100 Tin Pan Alley Songs* list, but inexplicably not among its *Hit Parade of a Half-Century*.

In '55 *Time* magazine said, "In Italy it is called "Polvere di Stelle" and ranks with "O Sole Mio" as an all-time favorite. In Japan it is called "Sutaadasuto, and is one number record stores are not afraid to over order. In England, where professionals call it a 'gone evergreen,' no song has sold more copies. In the U.S. it is called Stardust, and is the nation's most durable hit — comfortable as an old shoe and yet rare as a glass slipper."

Is it "Star Dust" or "Stardust"? According to the sheet music, it's "Star Dust," but it is found spelled both ways.

The lyricist, Mitchell Parish, wrote lyrics that almost perfectly match the story of the song's inception. The singer wonders why he spends "the lonely night dreaming of a song." The melody of this song haunts his reverie. He is once again with a girl from his past. He remembers a garden wall, a starry night and this girl in his arms. He realizes this may be an impossible dream, but the dream will remain in his heart. Read the lyrics at http://lirama. net/song/16208.

"Star Dust" appeared in the movie musical *Hi Buddy* (1943), Nat "King" Cole sang it on the soundtrack of *Sleepless in Seattle* ('93) and Vince Giordano and his Nighthawks Orchestra performed it on the soundtrack of *The Aviator* (2005). In addition, it appeared in *Drug Store Follies* ('37), *Star Dust* ('40), *Stardust Memories* ('80) and *My Favorite Year* ('82).

Sweet and Lovely

Words & Music: Gus Arnheim, Harry Tobias & Jules Lemare

Within a few months after this song's introduction by Gus Arnheim and his orchestra, "Sweet and Lovely" became one of the leading hits throughout the country. Arnheim, Harry Tobias and Jules Lemare collaborated to write this hit while Arnheim's orchestra was appearing at the Cocoanut Grove in Los Angeles. Arnheim and his orchestra's recording was the most popular version on the market in '31, but Guy Lombardo and his Royal Canadians' version was a close second. Donald Novis was vocal soloist on Arnheim's recording. Bing Crosby, Ben Bernie and his orchestra, and Russ Columbo also had recordings of the song that helped popularize it. Crosby revived it in '44 with a moderately successful recording.

"Sweet and Lovely" was used in the '44 movie musical *Two Girls and a Sailor*, where it was performed by June Allyson, Gloria DeHaven, and Harry James and his orchestra.

Variety chose this song for its *Hit Parade of a Half-Century*.

The song sings about a person who is "sweeter than the roses in May." The singer can't think of a nicer surprise than the fact that the girl loves him. Read the lyrics at http://lirama.net/song/152.

(There Ought to Be a) Moonlight Saving Time

Words & Music: Irving Kahal and Harry Richman

Songwriter Irving Kahal teamed up with one of the top vocalists of the late '20s and early '30s, Harry Richman, to pen this song. It's very possible that Kahal gave Richman co-writing credit so he would perform the song and help popularize it. If Richman ever recorded it, his version didn't make much of an impression. His last important recordings were made in '30.

"Moonlight Saving Time" was a big hit recording for Guy Lombardo and his Royal Canadians in '31. It was also a hit for Hal Kemp and his orchestra and the High Hatters in their recordings of the song.

Instead of daylight saving time, the singer wants "Moonlight Saving Time" so he can love his girl all night long. The moon should stay out overtime to keep light on lover's lane.

Time on My Hands (You in My Arms)

Words: Harold Adamson & Mack Gordon; Music: Vincent Youmans

Smiles should have been a smash hit on Broadway in '30. It had a Vincent Youmans score, starred Marilyn

Miller and Fred and Adele Astaire, and was produced by Florenz Ziegfeld. But the show never clicked.

One of Youmans' classic songs, "Time on My Hands," came from the score. This beautiful *Variety Hit Parade of a Half-Century* love song was introduced by Marilyn Miller and Paul Gregory. In the show, Miller played a French waif who was adopted by three American soldiers during the war and afterward was brought to the U.S. Gregory played one of the young doughboys that adopted her.

The singer had time on his hands, a girl in his arms and love in his heart. Obviously the French waif had grown into quite an attractive woman and the soldier had grown quite fond of his adoptee. Read the lyrics at http://lirama.net/song/15633.

Smith Ballew and his orchestra and Leo Reisman and his orchestra, with a Lee Wiley vocal, both had popular recordings of the song in '31.

The tune became the theme of *The Chase and Sanborn Hour* radio variety series. Marilyn Miller's screen biography, *Look for the Silver Lining* ('49), featured the song in its score, as did operatic soprano Grace Moore's screen biography, *So This Is Love* ('53).

Tiger Rag

Words: Harry DeCosta; Music: Original Dixieland Jazz Band

"Tiger Rag" has been attributed to Jelly Roll Morton and also more likely to The Original Dixieland Jazz Band. Most authorities seem to agree that Nick LaRocca's nationally popular jazz band was responsible for "Tiger Rag." The Original Dixieland Jazz Band originally popularized the song in '18. Hear their recording at http://www.redhotjazz.com/odjb.html. Blues vocalist Ethel Waters had released a successful recording of it in '22, and Ted Lewis had popularized it with recordings in both '23 and '27.

In '31, the Mills Brothers performed it in the movie musical *The Big Broadcast*, which was trying to capitalize on the enormous popularity of radio, the cheapest and most popular form of entertainment during the Depression years. The film didn't have much of a plot, it wasn't much more than a '31 MTV, where the music fans could not only hear their favorite performers, and they could see them on the screen.

The Mills Brothers' recording was extremely popular in '31. Ray Noble and his orchestra revived it successfully in '34, Alvino Rey and his orchestra revived it again in '41 and Les Paul and Mary Ford had a very successful release of it in '52; their version reached No. 2 on *Billboard's* chart. "Tiger Rag" became one of the most recorded songs of the pre-rock era.

"Tiger Rag" has been used in several movie musicals beginning with *Is Everybody Happy?* ('29). After the Mills Brothers' performance in *The Big Broadcast* in '31, it was used again in *Birth of the Blues* ('41), a movie musical tribute to the Original Dixieland Jazz Band. In '47 it was used in the Bing Crosby/Bob Hope movie musical *Variety Girl*, and it was used in *Let's Dance* ('50), which starred Betty Hutton and Fred Astaire.

Variety included "Tiger Rag" as one of its *Golden 100 Tin Pan Alley Songs* and in its *Hit Parade of a Half-Century* representing 1917.

Genuine rag or ragtime music was a pianistic development that had an elaborate structure, was notated, and did not employ improvisation. It borrowed its form from the military march and required a great deal of technical virtuosity on the piano to play it well. Scott Joplin was the "Father of Ragtime" and its chief exponent. Joplin's music, most notably "Maple Leaf Rag," and "The Entertainer" were featured on the soundtrack of the '73 award winning *The Sting*. Following that definition of rags, "Tiger Rag" is not an authentic rag.

Many of the high schools, colleges and universities which have a tiger as their mascot use a version of "Tiger Rag" as their fight song.

"Tiger Rag" was recently used in a famous ad — the "Banned Xbox 360 Ad: Best Ad Ever!", advertising an Xbox 360 console from Microsoft

When the Moon Comes Over the Mountain

Words & Music: Kate Smith, Howard Johnson & Harry Woods

"When the Moon Comes Over the Mountain," Kate Smith's theme song, was introduced on her CBS radio show on May 1, 1931. The song was second to "Good Night, Sweetheart" in sheet music sales in '31 with a sale of more than 400,000. At the time, the average hit sold around 200,000 copies.

Variety recognized this song's popularity by selecting it for its *Hit Parade of a Half-Century*.

Called "The Songbird of the South," Kate Smith became a tremendously popular singer. She is best remembered for her radio work and her introduction of Irving Berlin's "God Bless America." Her popular radio program helped many performers get their start. For instance, Abbott and Costello were boosted to fame by their appearances on her program.

Smith was a huge star in a couple of contexts: she was a large person (but over the radio, who knew?), and she also became a mega-star, particularly on radio.

"When the Moon Comes Over the Mountain" was her second Columbia Records release and it was extremely popular with the public. As much as it was associated with Ms. Smith, others released successful recordings of the song, including Nick Lucas, Leo Reisman and his orchestra, with vocalist Ben Gordon, and the Radiolites.

Kate Smith sang "When the moon comes over the mountain ev'ry beam, brings a dream dear of you." She remembers she and her lover strolling beneath the mountain through a rose covered valley. However, she's now alone, only left with her memories. Read the lyrics at http://lirama.net/song/898.

Smith performed the song in the movie musical *The Big Broadcast* ('32), where people got to see as well as hear a large number of their favorite performers perform some of their biggest hits.

When We're Alone (Penthouse Serenade)

Words & Music: Will Jason & Val Burton

Even though it was not a monster hit for any performer, *Variety* chose "When We're Alone" for its *Hit Parade of a Half-Century*.

The chorus lyrics ask us to picture a tall building with a penthouse at the top. It is so high it needed "hinges on

chimneys for stars to go by." The singer and his loved one want to be "heavenly hermits." They are all alone in their little penthouse high above Manhattan. Read the lyrics and hear a midi musical version at http://www.geocities.com/makebelieveballroom2002/easy73/penthous.htm.

The Arden-Ohman Orchestra, Ruth Etting, and Tom Gerun issued the most popular recordings of "(Penthouse Serenade) When We're Alone." The Arden-Ohman Orchestra's version peaked at No. 3 on *Billboard*, making it No. 29 for the year.

When Your Hair Has Turned to Silver

Words: Charles Tobias; Music: Peter DeRose

One day Peter DeRose brought this melody to lyricist Charles Tobias. Tobias wrote the words for the song in fifteen minutes and never changed a word.

Rudy Vallee helped popularize the song over the radio, but Frank Luther and Carson Robison had the most popular recording of it in '31.

Variety included this song in its *Hit Parade of a Half-Century*.

The singer assures his loved one that he will love her just the same when her "hair has turned to silver." Read the lyrics at http://lirama.net/song/15635 to read the lyrics.

When Yuba Plays the Rhumba on the Tuba

Words & Music: Herman Hupfeld

Variety included "When Yuba Plays the Rhumba on the Tuba" in its *Hit Parade of a Half-Century*.

The song premiered in *The Third Little Show*. The first *Little Show* had been in '29, the second in '30. In *The Third Little Show*, Walter O'Keefe introduced this comic song about the tuba player who introduced the oom-pah-pah to the Cubans. One critic said this was one of the dumbest songs of all times.

Rudy Vallee popularized the song with a very successful recording of it in '31.

The song was used in a Merrie Melodies cartoon titled *You're an Education* in '38 and in a Fleischer cartoon titled *When Yuba Plays the Rhumba on the Tuba* in '33 with the Mills Brothers singing the song.

Where the Blue of the Night (Meets the Gold of the Day)

Words: Roy Turk & Bing Crosby; Music: Fred E. Ahlert

"Where the Blue of the Night (Meets the Gold of the Day)" became Bing Crosby's theme song. He performed it in his first major film role in *The Big Broadcast* ('32). In the film's flimsy plot, Crosby, a singer, and a Texas millionaire were in love with the same girl.

Bing used this *Variety Hit Parade of a Half-Century* song as his theme song for his 15-minute radio show, which was broadcast several nights a week. In a short time, the show was expanded to 30-minutes, and eventually, became a weekly program.

Crosby's recording of his theme song was very popular with the record buying public. Brunswick Records reissued it in '40 and it sold moderately well again. Crosby's crooner-competitor, Russ Columbo, also recorded the song; his Victor Records version was actually released before Crosby's. Columbo's disk had "Prisoner of Love" on the flip side. Columbo's version did reasonably well, but not nearly as well as Crosby's.

Crosby's theme song was nominated for the American Film Institute's list of the greatest songs ever from an American film, but it did not make the final list.

Bing sang "Where the blue of the night meets the gold of the day, someone waits for me." This girl has golden hair and blue eyes. He'd be very happy if he could see her again. The last line of the chorus is the same as the first. Read the lyrics at http://ntl.matrix.com.br/pfilho/html/lyrics/w/where_the_blue_of_the_night.txt.

1932

All of Me

Words: Seymour Simons; Music: Gerald Marks

As popular as this standard may be, it has never had the good fortune to be a million-selling recording. Few hits of the '30s became what are now known as gold records. Times were tough economically. People couldn't afford the luxury of buying records, or even perhaps the phonograph to play them on.

Gerald Marks wrote the tune for "All of Me" while playing piano at a summer resort in Harbor Springs, Michigan in '31. Later, he was playing in a gambling house in Detroit when the lyricist Seymour Simons came in. Marks played the music for Simons and he wrote several potential lines that would fit. They picked the ones they thought fit best and took the song to New York City. At first no publisher would touch it because they thought it was risqué, especially the line "Why not take all of me?" They next took the song to Belle Baker, the vaudeville star, who was currently playing at the Fisher Theater. They played the song for her while she put on her makeup. Ms. Baker was so touched by the song that she began to sob, messing up the makeup she was trying to put on. She soon introduced the song at a matinee performance and got seven encores. She also sang it on a radio interview program the following Saturday evening. By Monday every music selling location in New York City was getting calls for "All of Me."

"All of Me" was the theme song of the movie *Careless Lady*, which starred John Boles and Joan Bennett ('32).

Recordings by Louis Armstrong and his orchestra and by Paul Whiteman and his orchestra, with Mildred Bailey featured as vocalist were both equally popular and both sold extremely well in '32. Hear Whiteman's version at http://www.redhotjazz.com/pwo.html. Louis Armstrong's recording of the song was inducted into the Grammy Hall of Fame in 2005. Hear Louis Armstrong and his orchestra's 1932 recording of this song (includes lyrics and photos of Armstrong and his band) at http://www.authentichistory.com/audio/1930s/music/1932-All_Of_Me.html. Ben Selvin and his orchestra also released his version, which sold reasonably well. It was revived by Count Basie and his orchestra in '43, by Frank Sinatra in '48, and by Johnnie Ray in '52. "All of Me" became one of the most recorded songs of the pre-rock era.

Frank Sinatra also sang it in the film *Meet Danny*

Wilson ('51). Gloria DeHaven performed it in the '53 movie musical *Down Among the Sheltering Palms*. It was also featured in Billie Holiday's screen biography, *Lady Sings the Blues* ('72).

"All of Me" furnished the title for, and was played in, a '84 film that starred Steve Martin and Lily Tomlin. Martin played a frustrated lawyer whose body is inadvertently inhabited by the soul of an abrasive and wealthy spinster, who was played by Lily Tomlin. So, in the context of the film, Lily Tomlin's character literally took all of Steve Martin's character by inhabiting his body.

The lyrics say that the loved one has taken "my heart, so why not take all of me?" Read the lyrics at http://lirama.net/song/2566.

April in Paris

Words: E.Y. Harburg; Music: Vernon Duke

Considering Cole Porter's love affair with Paris, we might suspect that he wrote "April in Paris," but instead Vernon Duke composed it to E.Y. Harburg's lyrics. It was premiered in the Broadway revue *Walk a Little Faster*. The revue might have been forgotten if it had not been for the introduction of "April in Paris."

In Vernon Duke's biography, *Passport to Paris*, he explains how the song came about. After auditioning some untalented girls for the revue *Walk a Little Faster*, Duke, Dorothy Parker, Evelyn Hoey, Robert Benchly and Monty Woolley went to a local bar. After several drinks, the group got sentimental. Duke says he can't remember if it was Benchley or Woolley who exclaimed, "Oh to be in Paris now that April's here!" Duke immediately thought "April in Paris" would be an excellent song title. The bar owner had an old upright piano on the second floor, where Duke proceeded to write the song's refrain.

The song describes the atmosphere of Paris in the spring: chestnuts are in blossom, and holiday tables are decked with food under the trees. The vocalist sings that he never understood the charm of spring, never knew his heart could sing until "April in Paris." Read the lyrics at http://lirama.net/song/15878.

Evelyn Hoey introduced the song with laryngitis so bad she could barely be heard. During the run of the show (119 performances), the song began to catch the ear of some of the theatergoers. It wasn't until Freddy Martin and his orchestra, with vocalist Elmer Feldkamp, released a recording of it in late '33 that the rest of the nation began to hear its loveliness. Henry King and his orchestra also helped popularize it with a successful disk.

Doris Day sang the song in the '52 Warner Bros. movie musical titled *April in Paris*. Gogi Grant dubbed the song for Ann Blyth in *The Helen Morgan Story* ('57).

"April in Paris" was selected by *Variety* for both its *Golden 100 Tin Pan Alley Songs* and its *Hit Parade of a Half-Century* lists. Jazz great Count Basie and his orchestra's '55 recording of "April in Paris" was inducted into the Grammy Hall of Fame in 1985. The song became one of the most recorded songs of the pre-rock era.

Brother, Can You Spare a Dime?

Words: E.Y. Harburg; Music: Jay Gorney

"Brother, Can You Spare a Dime?" speaks directly to the facts of life during the Great Depression. The lyrics are very bitter. The verse sketches a portrait of a man who has always done whatever needed to be done from plowing the earth to bearing arms, but he is now "standing in line just waiting for bread." The refrain completes the picture: after having served this country in the war and in peace, this man has been reduced to begging. The music is made up of a verse followed by an AABA thirty-two-bar chorus. Fittingly, it is in a minor key, with harsh chromatic harmonies. Read these great and touching Harburg lyrics at http://lirama.net/song/15645.

Sung by Rex Weber standing in a breadline in a scene in *New Americana*, "Brother, Can You Spare a Dime?" became one of the theme songs for the Depression years. The lyrics illustrate Harburg's social consciousness, but some authorities have suggested that he meant them slightly tongue-in-cheek. Not according to Harburg, as he explained the song: "This man isn't bitter. He's bewildered. Here is a man who had built his faith and hopes in this country ... Then came the crash. Now he can't accept the fact that the bubble has burst. He still believes. He still has faith. He just doesn't understand what could have happened."

Bing Crosby, accompanied by Lennie Heyton's orchestra, and Rudy Vallee and his Connecticut Yankees both had tremendously popular recordings of the song, and both seemed to take it completely seriously. A nation plagued by an economic debacle quickly empathized with it. Because its lyrics spoke of a problem that was on the mind of every person, it probably would have been a hit regardless of who had sung it. Hear Rudy Vallee's '32 recording of this song (includes lyrics & photo of Vallee) at http://www.authentichistory.com/audio/1930s/music/1932-Brother_Can_You_Spare_a_Dime.html or hear Crosby's version at http://www.kcmetro.cc.mo.us/~crosby/brother.html.

"Brother, Can You Spare a Dime?" was chosen by *Variety* for its *Hit Parade of a Half-Century*. Bing Crosby's recording of the song was inducted into the Grammy Hall of Fame in 2005.

It's interesting to notice how often certain writers seem to have hits in streaks. E.Y. Harburg wrote the lyrics for both "April in Paris" and the other songs in *Walk a Little Faster*, and several songs for *New Americana*.

Bugle Call Rag

Words & Music: Jack Pettis, Billy Meyers & Elmer Schoebel

Apparently, there are two "Bugle Call Rag" songs; one written in 1916 by Blake and Morgan and another by Jack Pettis, Billy Meyers and Elmer Schoebel in '23. All the information available is about the '23 song, which was popularized in recordings by Fran Westphal in '23, by Sophie Tucker in '27, by the Mills Brothers in '32, and by Benny Goodman and his orchestra in both '34 and '36. The Mills Brothers' version was the much more popular disk. Hear a '32 recording of "Bugle Call Rag" by the Mills Brothers at http://www.group-harmony.com/Bugle.htm.

Variety chose "Bugle Call Rag" for its *Hit Parade of a Half-Century* representing 1916, but considering the one that is well-known wasn't written until '23, they must have assumed they were honoring the "Bugle Call Rag" that was most popular.

The original recordings of the song were basically Dixieland jazz interpretations.

Benny Goodman and his orchestra performed the song in the movie musicals *Stage Door Canteen* ('43) and *The Benny Goodman Story* ('56). Goodman's version is less Dixieland, more swing.

The sheet music cover can be seen at http://digital.library.ucla.edu/apam/. Abe Lyman and his Ambassador Orchestra are pictured on the cover.

Dinah

Words: Sam M. Lewis & Joe Young; Music: Harry Akst

"Dinah" was introduced by blues singer Ethel Waters in a revue at the Plantation Club in New York City in '24. Eddie Cantor interpolated "Dinah" into *Kid Boots*, which had premiered in '23. That interpolation helped save an otherwise mediocre show.

These lyrics about the South were first set to a bouncy tune that the writers expected to be performed in a corny style, but Waters transformed it into a slow, sentimental classic, however, the lyrics seem to have been written from the male perspective. The chorus lyrics begin with a question: "is there anyone finer in the state of Carolina?" If there is, the singer says, he'd like to see her. He confesses that he shakes with fright at the thought Dinah might change her mind about him. He would even go to China "just to be with Dinah Lee." Read the lyrics at http://www.lyricsdownload.com/waters-ethel-dinah-lyrics.html.

"Dinah" is a *Variety Golden 100 Tin Pan Alley Song* and one of its *Hit Parade of a Half-Century* selections for 1925. Ethel Waters was one of the first authentic blues performers to crossover to the pop mainstream. Her recording of "Dinah" was the most popular version; her recording was inducted into the Grammy Hall of Fame in 1998. "Dinah" became one of the most recorded songs of the pre-rock era.

There were several other recordings on the market, including releases by the Revelers, who became one of the twenties' most famous vocal ensembles, Cliff "Ukulele Ike" Edwards and jazz legend Fletcher Henderson and his band. Hear Cliff Edwards' recording of the song at http://www.redhotjazz.com/ike.html. Ted Lewis revived it in '30, and then Bing Crosby and the Mills Brothers revived it in '32. They performed it in the movie musical *The Big Broadcast*. Their recording became a huge hit. The Boswell Sisters and Fats Waller revived the song again in 1936 when it was featured in the movie musicals *Song and Dance Man* and *Rose Marie*. Once again it was revived in the '42 movie musical *Broadway*. In '44 George Murphy, Constance Moore, Eddie Cantor, and Joan Davis performed it in the movie musical *Show Business.* Then in '46 Sam Donohue revived it again in a successful recording. Andrea McArdle performed the song in *Rainbow* ('78). Therefore, it was a staple of the movie industry and beyond for twenty years or more.

Frances Rose Shore changed her first name to Dinah for her stage name because she used this song as her signature tune over Nashville radio in the late '30s.

How Deep Is the Ocean?

Words & Music: Irving Berlin

A couple of years earlier Berlin had written a song called "To My Mammy" for the film *Mammy*, which contained the lines "How deep is the ocean? How high is the sky?" He resurrected those lines as the main idea for this new song. The lyrics are full of rhetorical questions that reflect on the vastness of love. Read the lyrics at http://www.lyricsfreak.com/i/irving-berlin/68120.html.

There is no substantial proof for this theory, but "How Deep Is the Ocean?" very well could have been written by Berlin pre–'26 during his courtship with his future wife, Ellin MacKay. Between '24 and '26, when they ran away to get married, Berlin wrote some gorgeous love songs, but many of them were sad, lonely, or questioning ("All Alone," "What'll I Do?"). "How Deep Is the Ocean?" seems to fit into his pattern of thinking during that period.

Several successful recordings helped popularize the song to the nation. Guy Lombardo and his Royal Canadians, Paul Whiteman and his orchestra, with vocalist Jack Fulton, and Rudy Vallee and his Connecticut Yankees vied with each other for the most popular recorded version. Ethel Merman also had a reasonably successful recording of the song in '32. Benny Goodman and his orchestra revived it with moderate success in '45. Hear Paul Whiteman's recording of "How Deep Is the Ocean?" at http://www.redhotjazz.com/pwo.html.

Bing Crosby and a female chorus performed "How Deep Is the Ocean?" in the '46 movie musical *Blue Skies* and it was also interpolated into the Frank Sinatra film *Meet Danny Wilson* ('52).

"How Deep Is the Ocean?" was chosen by *Variety* for both its *Hit Parade of a Half-Century* and *Golden 100 Tin Pan Alley Songs* lists.

I'm Gettin' Sentimental Over You

Words: Ned Washington; Music: George Bassman

George Bassman and Ned Washington wrote "I'm Gettin' Sentimental Over You" in '32. The Dorsey Brothers Orchestra first popularized it in '34. After the brothers split in '35, Tommy ordered a new arrangement of the tune for his new band. Tommy's solo trombone opening is a beautiful introduction. It became the theme song for "the Sentimental Gentleman of Swing" and his orchestra. Tommy's recording of the song was inducted into the Grammy Hall of Fame in 1998.

The Dorsey Brothers Orchestra's version was successful, but not nearly as popular as Tommy Dorsey and his orchestras in 1935–36. The Ink Spots revived it in '40 and Jack Leonard recorded it in '41, both with moderate success. Hear the '34 recording by the Dorsey Brothers Orchestra of this song at http://www.redhotjazz.com/dorseybros.html.

Teenagers of the period loved this hauntingly beautiful song and Dorsey's recording of it so much, they made up an acronym (IGSOY) to talk about it.

Tommy Dorsey and his orchestra performed it in the '43 screen version of Cole Porter's Broadway musical *DuBarry Was a Lady* and in *A Song Is Born* ('48). The song also appeared in Abbott and Costello's *Keep 'em Flying* ('41).

The singer never thought he'd fall, but now he's getting sentimental over his girl. He thought he was happy without love. Now, however, love is all he's thinking about, "because I'm sentimental over you." Read the lyrics at http://lirama.net/song/92207.

In a Shanty in Old Shanty Town

Words & Music: Joe Young, John Siras & Jack Little

Radio star Little Jack Little collaborated with Joe Young and John Siras on this song, then introduced it. Ted Lewis and his orchestra had a phenomenally popular recording of the song, one of the biggest hits of the decade. Hear

Lewis' recording of this song at http://www.redhotjazz.com/tlband.html. Ted Black and his orchestra also had an extremely successful release of the song. Johnny Long and his orchestra revived it in '40 with reasonable success.

During the worst years of the Depression, many people lived wherever and in whatever they could find. Many times a house consisted of a few boards, some tin, maybe a piece of cardboard, and some roofing paper, whatever was available to help keep out the elements. The people who were forced to live in these shanties often congregated together for safety and companionship into communities — shanty-towns, hobo havens, or Hoovervilles, as they were sometimes called. "In a Shanty in Old Shanty Town" testifies that poverty or living in a shanty does not exclude happiness and love. Read the lyrics at http://lirama.net/song/16903.

Ted Lewis' recording of "In a Shanty in Old Shanty Town," along with Fred Astaire's recording of "Night and Day," were the biggest hits of '32.

The song can be heard on the soundtracks of the '32 movie musical *Crooner*, and in the '51 movie musical *Lullaby of Broadway*.

Variety honored it by choosing it for its *Hit Parade of a Half-Century*.

It Don't Mean a Thing (If It Ain't Got That Swing)

Words: Irving Mills; Music: Duke Ellington

Duke Ellington originally wrote this tune as an instrumental. Irving Mills added the lyrics later. "It Don't Mean a Thing (If It Ain't Got That Swing)" is one of the earliest uses in popular music of the term "swing," which was to be the byword of the most popular music of the last half of the '30s and into the early '40s.

The lyrics to the song insist that what makes a tune complete is not the melody ("it ain't the music"). It's the rhythm, the most primitive musical element, that makes a song swing, and without it, "it don't mean a thing." Read the lyrics at http://lirama.net/song/22107.

Most people who have grown up since the advent of rock and roll seemed to agree with the sentiment. Teenagers today listen for the beat, the rhythm, first. Is it catchy? Does it make us want to dance or at least tap our feet? Then they may listen to the words. These teenagers have a tough time relating to beautiful love songs like "I'll Be Seeing You" or "I'll Never Smile Again" because they think such songs are too slow and don't have the beat that they expect all songs to possess.

The African American community has always seemed to lead us into new musical territory. This song illustrates their bands were already "swinging" in '32. It took three more years before the rest of the nation began to catch on to the trend.

A Broadway revue *Bubbling Brown Sugar* traced African American contributions to popular music. "It Don't Mean a Thing" was an outstanding part of that show. Broadway also saluted Duke Ellington with *Sophisticated Ladies* ('81), which featured 36 Ellington tunes.

Duke Ellington and the Mills Brothers both had popular recordings of "It Don't Mean a Thing" in '32. Hear Duke Ellington and his orchestra's '32 recording of this song at http://www.authentichistory.com/audio/1930s/music/1932-It_Dont_Mean_a_Thing.html (includes the lyrics and photos of Ellington) or http://www.redhotjazz.com/dukeo.html.

I've Got the World on a String

Words: Ted Koehler; Music: Harold Arlen

Aida Ward introduced "I've Got the World on a String" at the Cotton Club in Harlem. *Variety* selected the song for its *Golden 100 Tin Pan Alley Songs* list. It is a good example of lyrics of the era that tries to convince people that life is great, certainly much better than the alternative. It is a great bit of anti–Depression philosophy. Read the lyrics at http://www.lyricsfreak.com/f/frank-sinatra/552 67.html.

Recordings were issued that helped popularize the song by Cab Calloway in '32, and by Bing Crosby in '33. Frank Sinatra revived it with reasonable success in '53. Hear Louis Armstrong's recording of this song at http://www.redhotjazz.com/lao.html.

Just a Little Street Where Old Friends Meet

Words: Gus Kahn; Music: Harry Woods

Freddie Berrens and his orchestra introduced this *Variety Hit Parade of a Half-Century* song. According to *Variety*, it was the nation's top song during the late summer of '32 for more than a month and stayed among the top ten hits for more than four months.

The singer wants to some day revisit the street that means so much to the people in his hometown. He's sure he will be "as welcome as the flow'rs in May" on this little street where old friends "treat you in the same old way." Read the lyrics at http://lirama.net/song/803.

Just an Echo in the Valley

Words & Music: Harry Woods, Jimmy Campbell & Reg Connelly

Bing Crosby introduced this *Variety Hit Parade of a Half-Century* selection in the movie musical *Going Hollywood*. According to *Variety*, it was the top song of the land for three weeks and stayed among the top ten for more than four months in '32.

Crosby and Rudy Vallee competed for the most popular recording of the song; Crosby barely edged out Vallee. Paul Whiteman's recording of "Just an Echo in the Valley" can be heard at http://www.redhotjazz.com/pwo.html.

For those of you who are "Little Rascals" fans, Alfalfa performed this song. You may remember the film where a frog had climbed into Alfalfa's shirt and croaked at the most inopportune times during his "singing" of this song.

Let's Put Out the Lights (and Go to Sleep)

Words & Music: Herman Hupfeld

"Let's Put Out the Lights," a *Variety Hit Parade of a Half-Century* song, was introduced by Harry Richman, Lili Damita, and Burt Lahr in *George White's Music Hall Varieties* in '32. When Rudy Vallee performed the song as "Let's put out the lights and go to bed" at the Atlantic City Steel Pier, he was amazed that the audience burst into more than usual enthusiastic applause. When he used it on his radio program, the network censors insisted that he change the word "bed" to "sleep," so it is probable that most of us have heard the song as "Let's put out the lights and go to sleep." Most of the people living through the Depression in America didn't have the money to go out, so they stayed home, turned out the lights and went to bed. That may have produced a baby boom, but those people couldn't really afford children either.

By today's moral standards, let's "go to bed" seems rather mild and not worth the censor's time or effort. But Vallee being forced to change the lyrics points up the moral climate of the '30s, at least over the radio. About the same time on Broadway in Cole Porter's *Gay Divorce*, the lyrics to "Night and Day" say "I want to spend the rest of my life making love to you." In '31, Porter's "Love for Sale" also escaped censorship on Broadway. Obviously the same censorship criteria did not apply. Broadway has always been more tolerant in that respect, plus Broadway is not a mass media like radio or television.

The song's title is listed variously as "Let's Put Out the Lights," "Let's Put Out the Lights and Go to Bed," and "Let's Put Out the Lights and Go to Sleep." The sheet music says "Let's Put Out the Lights (and Go to Sleep)."

Recordings by Rudy Vallee and his Connecticut Yankees and by Paul Whiteman and his orchestra, with vocalist Red McKenzie, competed with each other for the most popular version on the market. Both were very successful. Hear Paul Whiteman's recording of this song at http://www.redhotjazz.com/pwo.html. Ben Bernie and his orchestra also had a version out that did very well.

Rudy Vallee's recording of "Let's Put Out the Lights..." was featured in *Pennies from Heaven* ('82), which starred Steve Martin and Bernadette Peters.

The first verse lyrics begin by asking a question about a party the couple has hosted: "Didn't we have a lovely evening?" But by the end of the verse they seem very glad it's over. They decide to leave the cleaning up for another time. Later towards the end of the chorus the lyrics continue with the idea that they don't have any money in the bank or a cute baby. So they ask, "what's to do about it? Let's put out the lights and go to sleep." With the "go to bed" lyrics, this portion of the lyrics would seem more risqué, suggesting the couple should go to bed to at least do something about the baby, since they can't do anything about the money situation. Hear a RealPlayer recording of the song at http://www.carlinamerica.com/titles/titles. cgi?MODULE=LYRICS&ID=327&terms=___terms___ to read the lyrics (it sounds like Bing Crosby and Rosemary Clooney, but the website doesn't reveal who the artists are).

Louisiana Hayride

Words: Howard Dietz; Music: Arthur Schwartz

This song was the jubilant first-act finale of the revue *Flying Colors*. A huge hay wagon was backed up to a moving projection of a country road that gave the impression of movement. Clifton Webb, Tamara Geva, and the chorus introduced this *Variety Hit Parade of a Half-Century* number.

"Louisiana Hayride" was recorded and popularized by Leo Reisman and his orchestra featuring the composer, Arthur Schwartz.

The song was also featured in the '53 movie musical *The Band Wagon*, which starred Fred Astaire, Cyd Charisse, Oscar Levant, Nanette Fabray, and Jack Buchanan.

The singer tries to get everyone to go to the hayride. The lyrics have a large amount of dialect. Dietz must have thought everyone in Louisiana talked in this way (examples: "I like dat sport; sittin' in de hay!" "Start sumpin'"). Read the lyrics at http://www.elyricsworld.com/go/b-/Band-Wagon-lyrics/Louisiana-Hayride-lyrics.html.

Leo Reisman and his orchestra popularized "Alone Together," also from *Flying Colors*. Roger Wolfe Kahn and his orchestra popularized "A Shine on Your Shoes" from *Flying Colors*. Hear Kahn's recording of "A Shine on Your Shoes" at http://www.redhotjazz.com/rwkahno.html.

Lover *and* Isn't It Romantic?

Words: Lorenz Hart; Music: Richard Rodgers

"Lover" and "Isn't It Romantic?" were introduced in the movie musical *Love Me Tonight*. A tailor, Maurice Courtelin, played by Maurice Chevalier, pursues the Vicomte de Vareze, played by Charles Ruggles, to his chateau because the vicomte owes him a great deal of money. The vicomte is afraid his association with a tailor might not be looked upon favorably by his uncle, the duke, so Courtelin is introduced as a baron. Courtelin's charm captivates all the members of the household except for Princess Jeanette, played by Jeanette MacDonald. However, by the end of the film, she has fallen in love with him, even though she says, "the son of a gun is nothing but a tailor."

LOVER

Jeanette MacDonald introduced "Lover," a *Variety Golden 100 Tin Pan Alley Song* and *Hit Parade of a Half-Century* waltz, in the movie musical *Love Me Tonight*. Peggy Lee sang it in the '53 version of *The Jazz Singer*, and her recording of "Lover" was reportedly a million seller. Her recording of the song became the most popular version to date.

Composers generally do not separate syllables of words with rests, but Rodgers placed a rest between the syllables of *lov-er, soft-ly, glanc-ing, danc-ing* and several other key words. The effect was memorable. Read the lyrics and hear a midi musical version at http://www.lorenzhart.org/loversng.htm.

In '33, versions by Paul Whiteman and his orchestra, Guy Lombardo and his Royal Canadians, and Greta Keller were pretty popular. Les Paul revived it in '48 with moderate success. Hear Paul Whiteman's recording of "Lover" at http://www.redhotjazz.com/pwo.html. "Lover" became one of the most recorded songs of the pre-rock era.

"Lover" was also featured in the movie musical *Moonlight in Vermont* ('43), Deanna Durbin sang it in *Because of Him* ('46), in *Words and Music* ('48), Rodgers and Hart's movie biography and Peggy Lee sang it in *The Jazz Singer* ('53).

ISN'T IT ROMANTIC?

Another song from the film's score was "Isn't It Romantic?," which was the opening musical number. Harold Stern popularized it in a recording. AFI's *100 Years ... 100 Songs* (2004) named this song one of the greatest song ever from an American film (No. 73).

What's romantic? Music in the evening, a dream, or just to be young on such a wonderful night. Read the lyrics of "Isn't It Romantic?" at http://www.lorenzhart.org/romanticsng.htm.

Bing Crosby popularized the title song from *Love Me Tonight* with a successful recording. Frankie Trumbauer and his orchestra's recording of "Love Me Tonight" is available at http://www.redhotjazz.com/fto.html. Read the lyrics at http://www.lorenzhart.org/tonightsng.htm.

Another famous song from the film's score is "Mimi,"

a Maurice Chevalier classic. The All Star Trio and Their Orchestra's recording of "Mimi" is available at http://www. redhotjazz.com/bands.html.

Lullaby of the Leaves

Words: Joe Young; Music: Bernice Petkere

George Olsen and his orchestra had a tremendously popular recording of this *Variety Hit Parade of a Half-Century* selection in '32.

According to *Variety*'s list of top hits of '32, "Lullaby of the Leaves" was one of the top ten hits for about five months, beginning in May.

In the chorus, the singer asks the "lullaby of the leaves" to sing him to sleep and let him "dream a dream or two." Read the lyrics at http://lirama.net/song/267.

Masquerade

Words: Paul Francis Webster; Music: John Jacob Loeb

"Masquerade" is a *Variety Hit Parade of a Half-Century* waltz that Paul Whiteman conducted at its introduction at the Lewisohn Stadium concerts in New York City. The song was lyricist Paul Francis Webster's first hit song.

It may be difficult not to confuse 1932's "Masquerade" with 1939's "The Masquerade Is Over," but the '39 song is not a waltz.

More confusion is possible because of George Benson's '76 recording of "This Masquerade," a Leon Russell song that became the Grammy winner as Record of the Year.

Then there's Andrew Lloyd Webber's "Masquerade" from *The Phantom of the Opera* ('87).

Ted Black and his Orchestra popularized 1932's "Masquerade."

Paul Francis Webster's chorus lyrics begin: "Twilight soon will fade, I'll meet you at the Masquerade." The singer wants his lover to unmask her heart so he can love her more completely. The song ends with the Masquerade concluded but his love lives on.

Night and Day

Words & Music: Cole Porter

Cole Porter wrote "Night and Day" for Fred Astaire's limited vocal range. Fred, without his sister, Adele, for the first time, was starring in Porter's *Gay Divorce*. The song's popularity helped the show have a successful run.

Porter said that his inspiration was Muslim calls to prayer in Morocco on one of his around-the-world cruises.

The recording of "Night and Day" by Fred Astaire with Leo Reisman and his orchestra was extremely successful, becoming one of the decade's biggest hits. Along with "In a Shanty in Old Shanty Town," "Night and Day" was the biggest hit song of '32. Pianist Eddy Duchin and his orchestra also had a very successful recording of the song that did well in '33 and '34. Charlie Barnet and his orchestra revived it with moderate success in '40. Frank Sinatra revived it with considerable success in '42 and '44. Bing Crosby's '46 version did reasonably well. "Night and Day" became the No. 10 most recorded song of the pre-rock era. Hear Paul Whiteman and his orchestra's recording of the song at http://www.redhotjazz.com/pwo.html.

"Night and Day" was one of sixteen songs included by ASCAP in its "All-Time Hit Parade" and also a *Variety Hit Parade of a Half-Century* and *Golden 100 Tin Pan Alley Songs* selection.

Porter's lyrics are classic, as his almost always are. The chorus begins with the title phrase: "Night and day you are the one." It continues with the singer assuring his lover that no matter where she is, he is thinking of her "night and day." Then Porter turns the title around to "day and night" and asks why he longs for her wherever he goes. Even in noisy traffic or the silence of his room he thinks of her all the time. The bridge section's three phrases end with "me," but the interior rhymes are "hide" and "inside." It is at bit surprising that Porter didn't get in trouble with the censor over "'Till you let me spend my life making love to you," but this was Broadway, which tended to be more lenient. Read the lyrics at http://lirama.net/song/2208.

Porter's first film biography was titled *Night and Day* and starred Cary Grant as Porter. John Barrowman and Kevin Kline performed "Night and Day" in the 2004 Porter biopic *De-Lovely*. The song also appeared in *What Women Want* (2000).

Of Thee I Sing *and* Love Is Sweeping the Country

Words: Ira Gershwin; Music: George Gershwin

One of the most honored of All-American musical comedies, the first musical awarded the Pulitzer Prize for Drama, and the longest-running musical of the '30s, was George and Ira Gershwin's *Of Thee I Sing*. The show took a barbed, witty, satirical look at a variety of American political and cultural phenomena including presidential campaigns, the Miss America pageant, the Supreme Court, the Vice Presidency, congressional debate, foreign affairs, marriage, and motherhood. Despite the Depression economy, the show lasted 441 performances on Broadway and had a successful road show tour.

OF THEE I SING

"Of Thee I Sing" was John P. Wintergreen's campaign song for the presidency of the United States. William Gaxton and Lois Moran, who starred as Mr. and Mrs. Wintergreen, introduced it. Wintergreen proposed marriage through this song, his campaign song. The bachelor presidential candidate had at first agreed to marry the winner of the Miss America contest, but changed his mind in favor of a girl who made delicious corn muffins.

The lyrics are far more a love song than a campaign song. Love was Wintergreen's platform, but it is a stretch to classify this ditty as anything but a fast love song. The chorus begins with the title phrase: "Of thee I sing, baby." He sings of her every season of the year. He tells Mary that she's his silver lining and his blue sky. Ira Gershwin manages to be slightly patriotic with "shining star and inspiration, worthy of a might nation" to end the chorus. Read the lyrics at http://www.stlyrics.com/lyrics/oftheeising/oftheeising.htm.

Ben Selvin and his orchestra had the only popular recording of "Of Thee I Sing" that was on the market in 1931–32.

LOVE IS SWEEPING THE COUNTRY

Another well-known song from the musical is "Love Is Sweeping the Country." Just before a large political rally in Madison Square Garden, George Murphy, June O'Dea, and the chorus introduced this song. It was a warm-up for the appearance of presidential candidate John P. Wintergreen, who was running on the platform of "Love." It

seems logical that Wintergreen's campaign song would be "Love Is Sweeping the Country," but it wasn't, "Of Thee I Sing" was.

The complete lyrics are rather lengthy; read them at http://www.stlyrics.com/lyrics/oftheeising/loveissweepingthecountry.htm. After the title phrase opens the chorus, we're told that all across the nation there has never been so much love. A particularly clever rhyme comes when the singer tells us every girl and boy "feels that passion'll soon be national."

Gershwin originally intended this tune for the never-produced musical *East Is West*, which had an Oriental setting.

Paradise

Words & Music: Gordon Clifford and Nacio Herb Brown

This waltz was the theme song of the motion picture *A Woman Commands* (it was not a musical). It became one of the theme songs for Russ Columbo. It was chosen by *Variety* for its *Hit Parade of a Half-Century*.

Guy Lombardo and his Royal Canadians and Leo Reisman and his orchestra, with vocalist Frances Maddux, both had extremely successful recordings of "Paradise," but Bing Crosby's and Russ Columbo's may be more interesting to us now.

Clifford and Brown wrote a very clever lyric that allows the listener to join the creative process. After the first phrase, "And then she holds my hand," there is humming, allowing the listener to decide what happened after she took his hand. A similar pattern continues throughout the song. At the end, she takes him to "Paradise." Read the lyrics at http://lirama.net/song/1133.

Russ Columbo's recording of the song substitutes buh, buh, buh's for the humming. Bing Crosby replaced the humming with dah, dah, dah's. It is Crosby who became famous for his buh, buh, buh's, not Columbo. Did Columbo invent them? Did Crosby appropriate them into his singing after Columbo's tragic accidental death in '34? It's interesting to speculate, but no definitive answer is available. Actually, neither the buh, buh, buh's or the dah, dah's are as effective or as suggestive as a hum. Perhaps the censors or the threat of censorship caused both to avoid the more suggestive hums.

Please

Words: Leo Robin; Music: Ralph Rainger

"Please" was one of the songs performed by Bing Crosby in his debut full-length movie, *The Big Broadcast*. He performed it with Eddie Lang on guitar.

The song opens dramatically with the word "Please" on a high note for the first measure. The singer is pleading to be told "that you love me too." Read the lyrics at http://lirama.net/song/352.

Crosby's recording of the song was extremely popular. On his recording he was accompanied by Anson Weeks' orchestra. Crosby released it again in '41 with moderate success. George Olsen and his orchestra also had a very popular version on the market in '32.

Jerry Colonna performed a comic version of the song in movie *College Swing* ('38).

Crosby also popularized "Here Lies Love" from *The Big Broadcast* with a successful recording.

River, Stay 'Way from My Door

Words: Mort Dixon; Music: Harry M. Woods

"River, Stay 'Way from My Door" was popularized by Jimmy Savo in his one-man mime revue *Mum's the Word*. His rendition, with accompanying pantomime, became his most famous routine. Savo also performed that routine in the '37 movie musical *Merry-Go-Round of 1938*.

Kate Smith with Guy Lombardo and his Royal Canadians had a tremendously popular recording of "River, Stay 'Way from My Door" in '32. Ethel Waters also had a successful recording of it.

Variety included this song in its *Hit Parade of a Half-Century* representing '31.

The lyrics ask the river to go its way, while he'll keep goin' his own way. The singer just managed to buy a cabin and wants the river to stay away. The chorus ends with the idea that the singer isn't breaking the river's heart, so the river shouldn't break his; it should just "stay 'way from my door." Read the lyrics at http://www.lyricsdepot.com/kate-smith/river-stay-way-from-my-door.html.

Say It Isn't So

Words & Music: Irving Berlin

"Say It Isn't So" was one of Berlin's first major song successes of the '30s after a number of years of artistic frustration, and it helped restore his self-confidence. Although it is doubtful that the two are connected, Berlin was not very productive musically in the first few years following his marriage to Ellin.

Actually Berlin wasn't particularly happy with "Say It Isn't So," but Max Winslow, head of the professional department of Berlin's publishing company, took the song to radio star Rudy Vallee. The song seemed particularly appropriate for Vallee since he was in the middle of a painful divorce. Vallee later explained his feelings for the song, saying, "The lyrics spoke all I felt. There was I singing that song about my girl seeing someone else and going away — it was all true and happening to me." He was hoping his performance of "Say It Isn't So" on his radio show would persuade his wife, Fay Webb, to reconcile with him. Although the song failed to help Vallee, it became a hit. Vallee's recording of it were largely responsible for its initial popularity. According to *Variety*, it was one of the top three songs of '32 and a *Hit Parade of a Half-Century* selection.

Hear Paul Whiteman's recording of "Say It Isn't So" at http://www.redhotjazz.com/pwo.html.

According to Berlin's lyrics, everyone is telling the singer his girlfriend doesn't love him. People are whispering that she's grown tired of him and has found somebody new. To all of these things he says, "Say it isn't so." Read the lyrics at http://lirama.net/song/1549.

Snuggled on Your Shoulders

Words & Music: Carmen Lombardo & Joe Young

This *Variety Hit Parade of a Half-Century* selection was introduced by Guy Lombardo and His Royal Canadians and further popularized by Eddy Duchin and his orchestra, Kate Smith, Bing Crosby and Isham Jones and his orchestra.

The lyrics say that the singer wants to dance forever and "dream about your charms, snuggled on your shoulder, cuddled in your arms."

Too Many Tears

Words: Al Dubin; Music: Harry Warren

Harry Warren and Al Dubin primarily wrote songs for Hollywood films, but "Too Many Tears" isn't listed in any of their film scores. It was the first hit for this collaboration, but over the next several years, they are unparalleled in their songwriting success.

Guy Lombardo and his Royal Canadians recorded an extremely successful version of "Too Many Tears." Released in the early spring of '32, it became a big hit in a hurry. Without charting services like *Your Hit Parade*, which began in '35, or *Billboard* or *Variety*, which didn't start charting the hits in an organized way until the early '40s, it's difficult to determine exactly how popular a song was, but according to the information available, the public loved it and made Guy Lombardo's recording an instant hit.

The basic idea of Dubin's lyrics is the singer's lover has gone and the souvenir that was left was "Too Many Tears." Read the lyrics and hear a midi musical version at http://www.harrywarren.org/songs/0534.htm. Hear a RealPlayer audio clip by Hal Kemp's Orchestra with Skinney Ennis as vocalist at http://www.harrywarrenmusic.com/realfiles/toomanytears.html.

We Just Couldn't Say Goodbye

Words & Music: Harry Woods

Guy Lombardo and his Royal Canadians and Paul Whiteman and his orchestra, with vocalist Mildred Bailey, competed with each other to see who would have the most popular recorded version of "We Just Couldn't Say Goodbye" in '32. Hear Paul Whiteman's recording of this song with Mildred Bailey singing at http://www.redhotjazz.com/pwo.html.

It was a great year for Lombardo with big hit recordings of "River, Stay 'Way from My Door" with Kate Smith, "Paradise," and "We Just Couldn't Say Goodbye."

Most of the Royal Canadians' vocals between '27 and '40 were performed by Carmen Lombardo's sugary-sweet voice. Evidently, the fans loved his vocals, they certainly bought the records and turned out to hear the band play and Carmen sing live. Lombardo and his Royal Canadians rank near the top (No. 3) of pre-rock era artists (No. 1 was Bing Crosby, No. 2 was Paul Whiteman and his orchestra).

The basic idea of the lyrics is a couple thinks their love is over, but they "just couldn't say goodbye." Finally, they realize, before it's too late, they are happy because they couldn't break up. Read the lyrics at http://www.seeklyrics.com/lyrics/Temple-Shirley/We-Just-Couldn-t-Say-Goodbye.html.

1933

Did You Ever See a Dream Walking?

Words: Mack Gordon; Music: Harry Revel

Jack Haley introduced "Did You Ever See a Dream Walking?" in the movie *Sitting Pretty*. The movie's plot concerned two songwriters, played by Haley and Jack Oakie, hitchhiking to Hollywood.

The lyrics ask several questions: "Did you ever see a dream walking," talking, dancing or romancing? Then the singer exclaims: "Well, I did!" Read the lyrics at http://lirama.net/song/599.

The song became a big hit in '33 for famous pianist Eddy Duchin and his orchestra. Lew Sherwood was Duchin's vocalist on the recording. Practically as popular was Guy Lombardo's recording. Other popular versions included Bing Crosby's and Meyer Davis and his orchestra's. The Pickens Sisters' version was moderately successful in '34.

Bing Crosby's recording of "Did You Ever See a Dream Walking" was featured in *Pennies from Heaven* ('82).

Variety named "Did You Ever See a Dream Walking" to its *Hit Parade of a Half-Century*.

Easter Parade

Words & Music: Irving Berlin

Clifton Webb and Marilyn Miller led a stylish parade down Fifth Avenue in the first-act finale of *As Thousands Cheer* and introduced "Easter Parade," one of Irving Berlin's personal favorites among his compositions. Fifteen years earlier Berlin had used the melody for a lyric entitled "Smile and Show Your Dimple." That song never became a big hit and was quickly forgotten. The sheet music cover and musical score of "Smile and Show Your Dimple" are available at http://levysheetmusic.mse.jhu.edu/browse.html. During the writing of the music for *As Thousands Cheer*, Berlin rediscovered the tune and wrote the new lyrics for the parade scene. The idea was to depict the Easter Parade on New York's Fifth Avenue as it appeared in the sepia-toned newspaper photographs of the era (the rotogravure). The paraders were first seen in a tableau behind a scrim, then as the scrim lifted, they came to life and sang the song. This scene made the entire show a success.

Clifton Webb's recording of the song with Leo Reisman and his orchestra was the most popular version. It remained a Spring favorite for many years with charted singles by Guy Lombardo and his Royal Canadians in '39 and '47, by Harry James and his orchestra in '42 and '46, by Bing Crosby in '47 and '48, and by flamboyant pianist Liberace in '54. Paul Whiteman's recording of "Easter Parade" can be heard at http://www.redhotjazz.com/pwo.html.

"Easter Parade" was featured in the 1938 movie musical *Alexander's Ragtime Band*, where it was performed by Don Ameche, in *Holiday Inn* ('42), where it was performed by Bing Crosby, and *Easter Parade* ('48), where it was performed by Fred Astaire and Judy Garland (more of the female version of the lyrics).

Variety chose "Easter Parade" for both its *Hit Parade of a Half-Century* and *Golden 100 Tin Pan Alley Songs* lists. It was nominated for the American Film Institute's list of the greatest songs ever from American films for its appearance in *Holdiay Inn* ('42), but did not make the final list.

The singer has a date with his girl on Easter morning to promonade in the Easter parade. He compliments her that she will be the "grandest lady in the Easter parade" in her frilly Easter bonnet. He tells her he'll be proud as they walk down Fifth Avenue. He's confident the photographers will want to take their picture to include "in the rotogravure" (rotogravure means "printing by transferring an image from a photogravure plate to a cylinder in a rotary press," in other words, printing their photo in the newspaper.) Read the lyrics at http://www.oldielyrics.com/lyrics/irving_berlin/easter_parade.html.

In the same revue, Ethel Waters introduced "Heat Wave," as a lively and vivacious weather reporter.

Forty Second Street, Shuffle Off to Buffalo, *and* You're Getting to Be a Habit with Me

Words: Al Dubin; Music: Harry Warren

The movie musical really began in '27 with *The Jazz Singer* and the advent of sound. By '29, we were presented the "All-Talking, All-Singing, All-Dancing" films like *The Broadway Melody* and *Hollywood Revue of 1929*. At first the public loved the novelty and supported the musical films with their attendance. But over the next few years, Hollywood overdid a good thing and produced several really poor movie musicals. The public let the studios know they didn't approve by not attending. After a couple of lean years, Warner Bros. decided it was time to try another screen musical. They brought in a Broadway choreographer, and a new songwriting team to collaborate with their screenwriters and a director to film a song and dance story that would bring the audiences back to the theaters. The result was *Forty Second Street*. It was a zestful production that provided good music written by Harry Warren and Al Dubin, memorable dance numbers staged by Busby Berkeley and a believable plot. Although some parts of the film have not aged well, it is still considered one of the movie musical classics. It is available on video in both the original black and white and a colorized version.

Forty Second Street started a movie musical renaissance that led to some of Hollywood's most triumphant musical successes. Depression audiences needed exactly what *Forty Second Street* offered: escapist entertainment that projected a little hope for the future into their lives.

FORTY SECOND STREET

The title song, a *Variety Hit Parade of a Half-Century* selection for '32, is about a street that is filled with happy, dancing feet. New York's theater district was centered on Broadway between 42nd and 50th streets. Ruby Keeler introduced the song in the film.

A recording of the title song was a huge hit for Don Bestor and his orchestra, with Neil Buckley doing the vocal performance in '33. Hear Bestor's recording of "Forty Second Street" at http://www.redhotjazz.com/bestoro.html. Hal Kemp and his orchestra also helped popularize the song with a successful recording.

AFI's *100 Years ... 100 Songs* (2004) named "Forty Second Street" the No. 97 greatest song ever from an American film. The song also appeared the following films: *Virgins in Heat* ('76) and *DuBarry Did All Right* ('37).

There's a street in New York City "that runs into Times Square" called "Forty Second Street." The street is "a crazy quilt that 'Wall Street Jack' built." The singer encourages us to take the time on our visit to go there. In the chorus, we're invited to visit the street and see those dancing feet. The sweet and innocent ladies from the 1850s and the indiscreet ones from the 1880s can be found side by side. Also, here "the underworld can meet the elite." Read the lyrics and hear a midi musical version at http://www.harrywarren.org/songs/0121.htm. An audio clip of Ruby Keeler singing the title song and a short video clip from the film can be heard or seen at http://www.harrywarrenmusic.com/realfiles/.

SHUFFLE OFF TO BUFFALO

"Shuffle Off to Buffalo" was introduced in the film by Ruby Keeler, Clarence Nordstrom, Ginger Rogers, and Una Merkel. The principal singer has gotten married. He and his bride are taking a trip to Niagara Falls via Buffalo for their honeymoon. The chorus lyrics open with words that might have been considered slightly risqué for the time period: "I'll go home and get my panties, you go home and get your scanties." Riding the train to Buffalo was a cheap honeymoon, plus the train went slow so they would have plenty of time together. They hope someday the stork will pay them a visit, but they say they'll worry about that later. They'll spend a quarter to have the lights turned down low as they "shuffle off to Buffalo." Read the lyrics and hear a midi musical version at http://www.harrywarren.org/songs/0460.htm.

"Shuffle Off to Buffalo" was a *Variety Hit Parade of a Half-Century* honoree.

"Shuffle Off to Buffalo" was on the flip side of Don Bestor's recording of "Forty-Second Street." Maurice Cross provided the vocal. It was popular, but not quite as popular as "Forty Second Street." Kemp's recording of "Forty second Street" was on the flip side of "Shuffle Off to Buffalo."

The song also appeared in the following films: *Dead Ringer* ('64), *Canary Row* ('50) and *Secret Service of the Air* ('39).

Forty Second Street opened on Broadway in the early '80s. The Broadway version not only included the songs from the movie musical but several other Warren and Dubin numbers from their other movie musicals of the era. The show has become the second longest running American musical in Broadway history and won The Tony Award for Best Musical.

YOU'RE GETTING TO BE A HABIT WITH ME

Bebe Daniels introduced "You're Getting to Be a Habit with Me" in the film. Doris Day performed it in the '51 movie musical *Lullaby of Broadway*.

Dubin's lyrics are full of drug analogies. The singer tells us her lover's kisses and hugs are addictive as drugs. She's addicted to his charms; she can't do without her supply of his love. She needs him every day, as much as she has become dependent on the caffeine in coffee and tea. Read the lyrics and hear a midi musical version at http://www.harrywarren.org/songs/0636.htm. A short clip of this song by Frank Sinatra can be heard at http://www.harrywarrenmusic.com/realfiles/.

Bing Crosby released an extremely popular recording of "You're Getting to Be a Habit with Me" with Guy Lombardo and his Royal Canadians. Fred Waring's Pennsylvanians also helped popularize the song with a successful recording.

The song also appeared in the film *Fear and Loathing in Las Vegas* ('98).

I Cover the Waterfront

Words: Edward Heyman; Music: John Green

A '33 film titled *I Cover the Waterfront* starred Claudette Colbert and Ben Lyon. Heyman and Green wrote this song after the film was released to capitalize on its popularity.

Ben Bernie and his orchestra featured the song on their radio program and it became such a hit that later prints of the film included the song on the soundtrack.

Eddy Duchin and his orchestra and Joe Haymes had popular recordings of "I Cover the Waterfront" in '33. Hear Louis Armstrong's recording of this song at http://www.redhotjazz.com/lao.html.

The singer is covering the waterfront, watching to see if his loved one will come back. Read the lyrics at http://lirama.net/song/15853.

Variety selected this song for its *Hit Parade of a Half-Century.*

I've Told Ev'ry Little Star

Words: Oscar Hammerstein II; Music: Jerome Kern

Jerome Kern claimed to have heard the basic melody to this song in the song of a finch. With words by Oscar Hammerstein II, this love song was introduced by Walter Slezak as Karl in the musical *Music in the Air* as part of a choral society recital.

Not unlike Kern and Harbach's *Cat and the Fiddle* from the previous year, *Music in the Air* was a modern European tale about the preparation of a musical production. In the plot, Sieglinde and Karl join their local walking club on a hike from Edendorf to Munich. In Munich they meet Frieda, a prima donna, and her lover, Bruno, a librettist. Soon Frieda is flirting with Karl and Bruno is flirting with Sieglinde. After a falling out with Bruno, Frieda refuses to star in Bruno's next operetta, and Sieglinde is given the chance to take over. She proves to be inadequate, however, so Frieda returns to Bruno and Sieglinde and Karl return to their mountain village.

Karl asks why he has told everybody and everything of his love except the one he loves. Read the lyrics at http://www.hartmut.dk/songs/lyrics/lyrics.php?txt=I've%20Told%20Ev'ry%20Little%20Star.

Jack Denny had the most popular recording of the song in '33.

Variety chose this song for its *Hit Parade of a Half-Century* representing 1932.

The film version of *Music in the Air* was filmed in '34.

Jack Denny and his orchestra popularized "The Song Is You," also from *Music in the Air.*

It's the Talk of the Town

Words: Marty Symes & Al J. Neiburg; Music: Jerry Livingston

"It's the Talk of the Town," a *Variety Hit Parade of a Half-Century* song, was popularized by Glen Gray and the Casa Loma Orchestra.

According to *Variety*, the song was number one for one week in '33 and was among the top ten hits for more than a third of the year.

What was the talk of the town? "Everybody knows you left me" just before the wedding day. Read the complete lyrics at http://www.apluslyrics.com/lyrics/71488/Perry_Como/It's_The_Talk_of_The_Town/.

The Last Round-Up

Words & Music: Billy Hill

"The Last Round-up" is a popular song in the style of a cowboy ballad written by Billy Hill. Joe Morrison introduced it at the Paramount Theater in New York City and Don Ross used it in the *Ziegfeld Follies of 1934*. Willie and Eugene Howard offered a comic version of the song in the same *Follies*.

Variety reported that it sold 650,000 copies in various recordings. The most successful versions on the market were by George Olsen and his orchestra with Joe Morrison as soloist and Guy Lombardo and his Royal Canadians with Carmen Lombardo as featured vocalist. Don Bestor and his orchestra with Neil Buckley as soloist also charted highly with their version. It was one of Bing Crosby's earliest successful recordings, and Victor Young and his orchestra with the Songsmiths doing the vocal also had a reasonably popular recording on the market.

The singer is going to saddle his horse, Paint, and head "for the last roundup." The chorus repeats "Git along little doggie, git along, git along" four times. There are three verses. Read the lyrics at http://lirama.net/song/1550.

Roy Rogers' recording of the song was largely responsible for his getting a movie contract. Rogers used the song in his '45 film *Don't Fence Me In*. Gene Autry sang it in *The Singing Hills* ('41) and *The Last Roundup* ('47).

Variety selected it for its *Hit Parade of a Half-Century* for '33.

Lazybones

Words: Johnny Mercer; Music: Hoagy Carmichael

Hoagy Carmichael should be called "the lazy man's songwriter" because he wrote several "lazy" song hits including "Rockin' Chair," "Lazy River," "Two Sleepy People," and "Lazybones."

"Lazybones, loafin' thru the day," should be working, spraying for "tater bugs," but instead, he is "sleeping in the noonday sun." Read the lyrics at http://lirama.net/song/15859.

Carmichael had written the melody earlier and called it "Washboard Blues." Red Nichols and his Five Pennies and Paul Whiteman issued recording of "Washboard Blues" in the late twenties. In the early thirties, Johnny Mercer set these lyrics to the tune.

Ted Lewis and his orchestra had a very successful recording of the lyric version of the song in '33. Hear Lewis' recording at http://www.redhotjazz.com/tlband.html. Don Redman and his orchestra, with vocalist Harlan Lattimore, and Mildred Bailey also had recordings that sold very well.

"Lazybones," sometimes spelled as two words, was chosen by *Variety* for its *Hit Parade of a Half-Century*.

Love Is the Sweetest Thing

Words & Music: Ray Noble

"Love Is the Sweetest Thing" was introduced in the British film *Say It with Music*. It was premiered in the U.S. by Julia Sanderson.

Composer/lyricist Ray Noble and his orchestra had an extremely popular recording of the song during the summer of '33. Hal Kemp and his orchestra's version of the song was also successful. Skinnay Ennis was Kemp's vocalist on their record.

In '45 it was interpolated into the motion picture *Confidential Agent*.

According to *Variety*, it was the nation's biggest hit for three weeks in '33 and *Variety* selected it for its *Hit Parade of a Half-Century*.

Love is not only the sweetest thing, it is also the

strangest and the greatest and it is the only thing that can "bring such happiness to ev'rything." Read the lyrics at http://lirama.net/song/15860.

My Moonlight Madonna

Words: Paul Francis Webster; Music: Zdenko Fibich (adapted by William Scotti)

William Scotti adapted the melody for this song from Zdenko Fibich's "Poeme." Paul Francis Webster added lyrics.

Fibich was a late 19th century Czech composer whose works haven't been performed or recorded very much. His "Poeme" seems to be the most often heard of his compositions.

"My Moonlight Madonna" became the theme song for the radio program *Joyce Jordan, Girl Intern*.

Rudy Vallee introduced this *Variety Hit Parade of a Half-Century* song. It was made popular in a recording by Paul Whiteman and his orchestra. Hear Whiteman's recording of this song at http://www.redhotjazz.com/pwo.html. Others who helped popularize the song include Conrad Thibaut, Jack Fulton and Arthur Tracy.

Play, Fiddle Play

Words: Jack Lawrence; Music: Emery Deutsch

Gypsy violinist Emery Deutsch wrote this song, which *Variety* included in its *Hit Parade of a Half-Century*. It was his radio theme song with the A&P Gypsies.

This waltz sounds rather antiquated today. Ted Lewis and George Olsen and their orchestras helped popularized it in 1932–33 with popular recordings.

The singer wants the fiddle to play a melody for his loved one that sings of his love. Read the lyrics at http://207.44.240.63/~lyricsp/alpha/songs/p/playfiddle play.shtml.

Read about a famous plagiarism suit brought by Ira Arnstein against Jack Lawrence and Emery Deutsch at http://www.ccnmtl.columbia.edu/projects/law/library/cases/case_arnsteinmarks.html. The site includes a midi file and partial score of Arnstein's "I Love You Madly," and a sound recording, a midi file, and a video clip of Lawrence and Deutsch's "Play, Fiddle Play," so we can examine the evidence for ourselves. The district and appellate court ruled for the defendant because the plaintiff could not make a plausible case to shore up his claims of melodic similarities between the works. There is much more about the case at the website.

Shadow Waltz *and* The Gold Diggers' Song (We're in the Money)

Words: Al Dubin; Music: Harry Warren

After the success of Warren and Dubin's musical score for *Forty Second Street*, Warner Bros. hired them to produce music for what became a series of films, *Gold Diggers* (1933–37).

Gold Diggers, a stage play by Avery Hopwood, was first filmed in '23. Next came the '29 musical version called *Gold Diggers of Broadway*. Warner Bros. revived the idea with *Gold Diggers of 1933*, which had the same basic concept as the previous efforts: a group of girls in search of rich husbands. In the '33 version, Dick Powell played a songwriter with wealthy parents. They disapproved of his musical inclinations (being a songwriter was not "working for a living"), and they also strongly opposed his intentions to marry a chorus girl, played by Ruby Keeler.

Shadow Waltz

Powell and Keeler introduced "Shadow Waltz," a *Variety Hit Parade of a Half-Century* song, in *Gold Diggers of 1933*. Busby Berkeley's ingenious staging of the number featured sixty chorus girls playing illuminated violins arranged in patterns until, at the climax, they form an enormous violin.

Bing Crosby's recording of "Shadow Waltz" was exceptionally popular during the summer of '33. Recordings by Rudy Vallee and his Connecticut Yankees and Guy Lombardo and his Royal Canadians also contributed to popularizing the song around the nation. An audio clip of Bing Crosby singing "Shadow Waltz" can be heard at http://harrywarrenmusic.com/realfiles/.

"Shadow Waltz" was also used in the '36 movie musical *Cain and Mabel*.

The singer tells his loved one that he will come in the evening (shadows) and sing her a love song. Read the lyrics and hear a midi musical version at http://www.harrywarren.org/songs/0453.htm.

The Gold Diggers' Song (We're in the Money)

A second hit song from *Gold Diggers of 1933* was "The Gold Diggers' Song," sometimes called "We're in the Money." Introduced by Ginger Rogers, dressed in an outfit made of silver dollars, the song has become a standard.

The lyrics bid goodbye to blues and tears because "old man depression" is through. No more breadlines! No more money problems! Everyone will now be able to pay the rent! Read the lyrics and hear a midi musical version at http://www.harrywarren.org/songs/0140.htm. At http://www.harrywarrenmusic.com/frameset.html you can see Warren's music manuscript of this song.

Ted Lewis and his orchestra, Hal Kemp and his orchestra, with vocalist Skinnay Ennis, and Dick Powell had recordings of the song that were successful in '33. Hear Ted Lewis' recording of this song at http://www.redhotjazz.com/tlband.html.

Variety chose "We're in the Money" for its *Hit Parade of a Half-Century*. This song was nominated for the American Film Institute's list of the greatest songs ever from an American film, but it did not make the final list.

Sophisticated Lady

Words: Mitchell Parish & Irving Mills; Music: Duke Ellington

Duke Ellington's masterpiece, "Sophisticated Lady," as most of his song did, originated as an instrumental composition for his orchestra. When lyrics were added, it became one of Ellington's most successful songs and a *Variety Hit Parade of a Half-Century* honoree.

According to the composer, the song was a portrait of three schoolteachers he remembered who spent nine months teaching and saving their money so they could afford to tour Europe during their summer vacations. To the youngster, Ellington, such a life was the epitome of sophistication. Read the lyrics at http://lirama.net/song/15866.

Ellington and his orchestra had the most popular version of "Sophisticated Lady," but Glen Gray and the Casa Loma Orchestra's version was not far behind. Don Redman and his orchestra also had a recording of the song that was also successful. Billy Eckstine revived it in '48 with moderate success. Hear Ellington's recording of this song at http://www.redhotjazz.com/dukeo.html.

"Sophisticated Lady" was used in the '61 movie musical *Paris Blues*, which starred Diahann Carroll, Joanne Woodward, Sidney Poitier, and Paul Newman.

Stormy Weather

Words: Ted Koehler; Music: Harold Arlen

Jerome Kern's "Smoke Gets in Your Eyes" and "Stormy Weather" seem spiritually kin to each other and to the music Kern wrote for *Show Boat*, especially "Can't Help Lovin' Dat Man." They share a breast beating, down-and-out feeling; great material for torch singers.

"Stormy Weather" was written for Cab Calloway to introduce in a Cotton Club revue, but the writers, Arlen and Koehler, decided it was more suitable for a female singer, so they chose Ethel Waters to premier it. In the interim, Harold Arlen, the composer, recorded the song with Leo Reisman and his orchestra. Their recording sold very well, so that by the time the Cotton Club revue opened the song was already quite a hit. Hear Ted Lewis' recording of "Stormy Weather" at http://www.redhotjazz.com/tlband.html. Ethel Waters sang "Stormy Weather" with all of her soul. She seemed to be expressing the anguish of people who found nothing but gloom and misery in their own lives due to the Depression.

Both recordings by Ethel Waters and by Leo Reisman and his orchestra with a vocal performance by the composer Harold Arlen were extremely popular from the spring into the summer of '33. Guy Lombardo and his Royal Canadians' version was also quite popular, as was Duke Ellington and his orchestra's recording. Ted Lewis and his orchestra also had very good success with their version of the song. "Stormy Weather" and "The Last Round-Up" were probably 1933's most popular songs. Hear Ted Lewis' recording of "Stormy Weather" with vocalist Shirley Jay at http://www.redhotjazz.com/tlband.html.

"Stormy Weather" was featured in the '43 movie musical *Stormy Weather*, where it was sung by Lena Horne and danced by Katherine Dunham and her troupe. Lena Horne's recording of the song in '43 met with reasonable success. Connee Boswell performed it in the '46 movie musical *Swing Parade of 1946*.

Variety selected "Stormy Weather" for its *Hit Parade of a Half-Century* and as a *Golden 100 Tin Pan Alley Song*. AFI's *100 Years ... 100 Songs* (2004) listed "Stormy Weather" as the No. 30 greatest song from an American film even though it did not originate there. It was voted onto the list representing the 1943 film *Stormy Weather* when the song was performed by Lena Horne.

Lena Horne's recording of the song was inducted into the Grammy Hall of Fame in 2000. "Stormy Weather" became one of the most recorded songs of the pre-rock era.

The singer laments that everything is dark and gloomy because she and her man aren't together. Gloom and misery seem to be everywhere. When her man left, the blues walked in and if he doesn't return, the "old rockin' chair will get me." As far as she's concerned, it just "keeps rainin' all the time." Read the lyrics at http://lirama.net/song/645.

Who's Afraid of the Big Bad Wolf

Words & Music: Frank E. Churchill and Ann Ronell

This delightful ditty was introduced in the Walt Disney animated cartoon *The Three Little Pigs*. It is probable that the people of '33 consciously or unconsciously identified with this song because the big bad wolf, the Depression, had them by the throats. It may have dispelled their fears to sing about laughing in the face of danger.

President Roosevelt had reminded the nation in his '33 inaugural address that it had nothing to fear but fear itself. Yet people needed a morale boost and "Who's Afraid of the Big Bad Wolf?" with all its frivolity, did the trick.

Recordings by Don Bestor and his orchestra, with vocalists Florence Case, Charles Yontz, and Frank Sherry, by Victor Young and his orchestra, and by Ben Bernie and his orchestra helped popularize "Who's Afraid of the Big Bad Wolf?" beyond the cartoon.

Variety selected this song for its *Hit Parade of a Half-Century.*

Barbra Streisand made her professional debut with the song in a Greenwich Village nightclub in '61 and had good success with a recorded version. Read the lyrics at http://barbra-streisand.the-lyrics.com/who's-afraid-of-the-big-bad-wolf-336901.html.

You're an Old Smoothie

Words: Bud G. DeSylva; Music: Richard A. Whiting & Nacio Herb Brown

"You're an Old Smoothie" was the hit from the musical *Take a Chance*. Ethel Merman and Jack Haley introduced the song.

The musical *Humpty Dumpty* was completely rewritten and became *Take a Chance*. Two songs were kept from the original, while Vincent Youmans was called in to provide some new songs. Youmans' most important contribution was "Rise 'n Shine."

The basic idea of the lyrics is "you're a smoothie ... I'm a softie ... like putty in the hand of a girl like you." Read the lyrics at http://lyrics.webfitz.com/index.php?option=com_webfitzlyrics&Itemid=27&func=fullview&lyricsid=4904.

Paul Whiteman and his orchestra had the most popular recording of "You're an Old Smoothie" in '33. Hear Whiteman's recording of this song at http://www.redhotjazz.com/pwo.html.

Variety selected this song for its *Hit Parade of a Half-Century* representing 1932.

Ethel Merman popularized "Eadie Was a Lady" from *Take a Chance* with a successful recording. Paul Whiteman's recording of "Eadie Was a Lady" can be heard at http://www.redhotjazz.com/pwo.html.

Paul Whiteman and his orchestra popularized "Rise 'n Shine" from the musical. Hear Whiteman's recording of the song at http://www.redhotjazz.com/pwo.html.

1934

All I Do Is Dream of You

Words: Arthur Freed; Music: Nacio Herb Brown

Gene Raymond introduced "All I Do Is Dream of You" in the '34 Hollywood film *Sadie McKee*. It appeared again in '35 in the Marx Brothers' farce *A Night at the Opera*, where it was played by Chico. Debbie Reynolds' performance of the song in the '52 movie musical *Singin' in the Rain* (she sang it after coming out of a large cake) is probably one of the most famous performances of the song. Debbie Reynolds and Bobby Van performed it in *The Affairs of Dobie Gillis* ('53). The song was also heard in MGM's film version of Sandy Wilson's musical *The Boy Friend* ('71).

Jan Garber and his orchestra had a particularly popular recording of "All I Do Is Dream of You" in '34. Henry Busse and his orchestra and Freddy Martin and his orchestra also helped popularize the song with successful recordings. Johnnie Ray revived it with moderate success in '53.

The singer dreams of his love all day, all night, even if there were "more than twenty-four hours a day," he'd spend them dreaming of her. Read the lyrics at http://lirama.net/song/15876.

Anything Goes, I Get a Kick Out of You *and* You're the Top

Words & Music: Cole Porter

Anything Goes was one of the most successful musicals of the mid–'30s and the toast of Broadway in '34. Producer Vinton Freedley conceived the idea of a show that would present several comic characters in a shipwreck, but the sinking of the S.S. Morro Castle in September of '34 forced him to revise the script. The new plot, though still taking place on a ship, eliminated the wreck. The story revolved around nightclub singer Reno Sweeney, her friend Billy Crocker, who stows away aboard the ship to be near Hope Harcourt, who is traveling to England to marry British nobility, and Moon Face Mooney, currently Public Enemy No. 13, who is disguised as a priest. Ethel Merman became a star of major proportions as Reno.

Anything Goes, Porter's most popular musical score to date, was revived on Broadway in '62 with the addition of several of Porter's most famous songs from other musicals. It was revived again in a splendid Broadway production in '87.

ANYTHING GOES

In the title song, the thirties' moral climate is cataloged. As Reno, the nightclub singer who is posing as an evangelist, Ms. Merman described the decaying moral climate of the times. The list included women's short skirts, authors' four-letter words, nudist parties, and grandmothers going out with gigolos, a rather timeless list of moral decay that is just as current today as it was in '34. Read the libretto and lyrics from a later production of *Anything Goes* when songs were added that were not in the original at http://libretto.musicals.ru/text.php?textid=20&language=1 (Song No. 11).

Paul Whiteman and his orchestra had the only popular recorded version in '34, but Ethel Merman's version has remained a staple over the years. Hear Whiteman's recording at http://www.redhotjazz.com/pwo.html.

"Anything Goes" was nominated for the American Film Institute's list of the greatest songs ever from American films, but did not make the final list. It was nominated for its inclusion in *Indiana Jones and the Temple of Doom* ('84). The song was also used in the movie musical *Anything Goes* ('36), Cole Porter's film biography *Night and*

Day ('46), and the '56 film version of *Anything Goes*, with a revized plot. The song also appeared in *American Pop* ('81), *Indiana Jones and the Temple of Doom* ('84) and *Dancing at Lughnasa* ('98). In *De-Lovely* (2004), another Porter biopic, Caroline O'Connor and the chorus performed "Anything Goes."

I GET A KICK OUT OF YOU

Radio stations refused to play "I Get a Kick Out of You" from *Anything Goes* because of the line "Some get a kick from cocaine." Reno, played by Ethel Merman, claims that the only thing that gives her a kick is the sight of her friend Billy's face. She's bored by such stimulants as champagne, and riding in a airplane. She's also sure that if she took even a sniff of cocaine she'd be bored stiff. The song wasn't a love song; Reno wasn't in love with Billy in the context of the musical's plot. Read the libretto and lyrics at http://libretto.musicals.ru/text.php?textid=20&language=1 (Song No. 2).

Cole Porter never seems content to write a simple love song. This song probably sums up Porter's playboy outlook on life. He had so much money that he may have been bored with life in general.

Cocaine was a legal recreational drug during the early '30s. Its side effects had not yet been documented. Reportedly even Coca-Cola originally had some cocaine in it. Cocaine may have surely been a part of Porter's society life, the lavish parties, the round-the-world cruises, and the clandestine meetings with his "male friends."

Recordings of "I Get a Kick Out of You" were released by Paul Whiteman and his orchestra, by Ethel Merman, and by Leo Reisman and his orchestra, with vocalist Sally Singer. Paul Whiteman's version can be heard at http://www.redhotjazz.com/pwo.html.

"I Get a Kick Out of You" was selected for *Variety*'s *Hit Parade of a Half-Century* and its *Golden 100 Tin Pan Alley Songs* list.

In the '36 film version of *Anything Goes*, Ethel Merman sang "I Get a Kick Out of You." In the '56 version Zizi Jeanmaire performed it. In Porter's film biography, *Night and Day*, Ginny Simms sang it. The song was also used in the '51 movie musical *Sunny Side of the Street* and in the '75 movie musical *At Long Last Love*. According to http://www.imdb.com/, it appeared, but was uncredited, in *Blazing Saddles* ('74). The song was also included in Porter's 2004 screen biography *De-Lovely*.

YOU'RE THE TOP

"You're the Top" was introduced by Reno and Billy in the musical. Porter's clever lyrics itemize the praises of the two for each other. The exchange of compliments is filled with urbane allusions: "from Mickey Mouse to a symphony by Strauss," "Mahatma Gandhi and Napoleon Brandy," and several other lovely bits of wordplay. Read the libretto and lyrics at http://libretto.musicals.ru/text.php?textid=20&language=1 (Song No. 5).

Recordings by Paul Whiteman and his orchestra, with vocalists Peggy Hely and John Hauser, and by the Dorsey Brothers Orchestra, with a vocal performance by Ray McKinley, popularized "You're the Top" beyond the musical in '34. Ethel Merman and Cole Porter's versions were released in '35 and both sold reasonably well. Hear Paul Whiteman's recording of this song at http://www.redhotjazz.com/pwo.html.

In the '36 film edition of *Anything Goes*, Ethel Merman

and Bing Crosby performed "You're the Top." In the '56 screen version, Bing Crosby and Mitzi Gaynor performed it. Ginny Simms sang it in Porter's movie biography, *Night and Day* ('46). "You're the Top" also appeared in the Barbra Streisand film *What's Up, Doc?* ('72). In *De-Lovely* (2004), another Porter biopic, Cole Porter, himself, can be heard singing "You're the Top" on the soundtrack.

Variety selected "You're the Top" for its *Hit Parade of a Half-Century*. "You're the Top" was nominated for the American Film Institute's list of the greatest songs ever from American films, but did not make the final list. It was nominated for its appearance in the '36 film version of *Anything Goes*.

Carioca, Orchids in the Moonlight *and* Flying Down to Rio

Words: Gus Kahn & Edward Eliscu; Music: Vincent Youmans

Vincent Youmans composed his first film score for *Flying Down to Rio* after numerous successful Broadway scores. *Flying Down to Rio* was the movie musical that started the Fred Astaire-Ginger Rogers cycle of singing-and-dancing movies. Astaire was supposed to have performed the song with Dorothy Jordan, but she married the film's executive producer and dropped out of the film. Her replacement was Ginger Rogers.

The primary stars of the film were Delores Del Rio and Gene Raymond, but Astaire and Rogers's charisma together dazzled so brightly they practically upstaged the stars.

CARIOCA

"Carioca," which was introduced in an unforgettable dance routine on top of seven white pianos, was nominated for the first Best Song Academy Award in '34. Since this dance-song was a success, the studio introduced a new dance-song in the next couple of Astaire/Rogers films: "The Continental," and "The Piccolino." "Carioca is not a foxtrot or a polka," the lyrics tell us, it has a "meter that is tricky." Read the lyrics at http://lirama.net/song/15881.

The public loved the song and the dance. A recording by Enric Madriguera and his orchestra, with a vocal by Patricia Gilmore, was extremely popular. Harry Sosnik and his Edgewater Beach Hotel Orchestra, the Castillian Troubadors, and the RKO Studio Orchestra (RKO was the studio that filmed *Flying Down to Rio*) released successful recordings of the song. Super guitarist, Les Paul, revived it with considerable success in '52.

"Carioca" was nominated for the American Film Institute's list of the greatest songs ever from American films for its appearance in *Flying Down to Rio*, but did not make the final list. *Variety* included the song in its *Hit Parade of a Half-Century* representing 1933.

"Carioca" also appeared in Gus Kahn's movie biography *I'll See You in My Dreams* ('52).

ORCHIDS IN THE MOONLIGHT

Another hit from *Flying Down to Rio* was "Orchids in the Moonlight." It was introduced by the newly formed song-and-dance partnership of Fred Astaire and Ginger Rogers.

Kahn and Eliscu's lyrics tell us that the orchids bloom in the moonlight as the lovers vow to be true, but they fade in the sunlight as the vows are shattered. Read the lyrics at http://lirama.net/song/15903.

The principal recording of "Orchids in the Moonlight" was by Rudy Vallee (*"Flying Down to Rio"* was on the flip side). Enric Madriguera and his orchestra also had a popular recording of the song, on the flip side of "Carioca."

All three songs from *Flying Down to Rio* were selected *Variety* for its *Hit Parade of a Half-Century* representing '33.

FLYING DOWN TO RIO

"Flying Down to Rio" was the title song from the movie musical that first matched Fred Astaire and Ginger Rogers. Their magic helped several songs from this and later movie musicals become hits.

Perhaps the public found the exoticism of Rio de Janeiro fascinating, but lyrics like "my Rio by the sea-o" didn't help the song's lasting popularity. The rest of the song's lyrics seem just as contrived and silly, but the Astaire/Rogers magic overcame even that. Read the lyrics to judge for yourself at http://lirama.net/song/15885.

Recordings by Fred Astaire and Rudy Vallee helped popularize *"Flying Down to Rio"* beyond the film soundtrack.

Variety included "Flying Down to Rio" in its *Hit Parade of a Half-Century* representing 1933.

One other song from the film, "Music Makes Me," was recorded and had reasonable success by Fred Astaire.

Cocktails for Two

Words: Arthur Johnston; Music: Sam Coslow

"Cocktails for Two," a *Variety Hit Parade of a Half-Century* song, was introduced in the '34 movie musical *Murder at the Vanities*. It appeared again in Bing Crosby's movie musical *She Loves Me Not* ('34) and again in the '47 movie musical *Ladies' Man*.

Duke Ellington and his orchestra had a very successful recording of the song in '34. Other successful recordings on the market were by Johnny Green and his orchestra, with vocalist Howard Phillips, and by Will Osborne and his orchestra, with Osborne supplying the vocal performance.

However, today it may be best remembered in the Spike Jones and his City Slickers' recording that rose to No. 4 on *Billboard's* chart in early '45. Jones specialized in incorporating strange sounds into songs. In this one, he included the sounds of hiccups and shattering cocktail glasses among others. Jones' recording of "Cocktails for Two" was inducted into the Grammy Hall of Fame in 1995.

The chorus lyrics begin by painting a scene: "In some secluded rendezvous, that overlooks the Avenue" two people are enjoying a chat and "Cocktails for Two." Heads and hearts "go reeling." She hopes they'll have a future together that began with "cocktails for two." Read the lyrics in Duke Ellington's version at http://lirama.net/song/15882.

The Continental

Words: Herb Magidson; Music: Con Conrad

"The Continental" won the first Academy Award for Best Song from Film and was chosen for *Variety's Hit Parade of a Half-Century*. It was introduced in the movie musical *The Gay Divorcee*, which was the film version of Cole Porter's '32 Broadway musical *Gay Divorce*. After acquiring the musical for RKO, the score was gutted except for "Night and Day." The studio commissioned new songs from a variety of composers and changed the title to *The Gay Divorcee*, because the Production Code insisted the term "divorce" wasn't an appropriate subject for Catholics.

Ginger Rogers had the pleasure of singing "The Continental," but then it was sung by several others and danced by Fred Astaire, Ginger Rogers, and a large dance ensemble in a 22-minute production number. When the entire film was less than two hours in length and one production number takes up 22 minutes, there isn't a lot of time left for plot and a half dozen or so other songs.

Herb Magidson's lyrics begin: "Beautiful music! Dangerous rhythm!" A new dance, "The Continental," was about to be born, compliments of Fred, Ginger, and a large troop of dancers. The song's subtitle, "You Kiss While You're Dancing," describes a little of the intent of the song and dance. However, Fred and Ginger did not kiss while they danced to this number. Read the lyrics at http://lirama.net/song/15883.

Fred Astaire's recording with Leo Reisman and his orchestra was a big hit in '34. Jolly Coburn and his orchestra, with vocalists Harold Van Emburgh and Roy Strom, had a recording that competed very well with Astaire's version. Lud Gluskin and his orchestra, with a vocal performance by Joe Host, also had a successful recording of the song.

"The Continental" was nominated for the American Film Institute's list of the greatest songs ever from American films, but did not make the final list.

Fats Waller popularized "Don't Let It Bother You" from *The Gay Divorcee*. Hear Waller's recording at http://www.redhotjazz.com/rhythm.html.

Leo Reisman and his orchestra popularized "A Needle in a Hay Stack" from the film.

Deep Purple (see '39)

Hands Across the Table

Words: Mitchell Parish; Music: Jean Delettre

Lucienne Boyer introduced this *Variety Hit Parade of a Half-Century* selection in the revue *Continental Varieties of 1934*. According to *Variety*, the song was one of the top ten hits of '34 for nine weeks, but it never reached the number one slot.

Lucienne Boyer and Hal Kemp issued the most popular recordings of "Hands Across the Table."

The lyrics tell us about "Hands across the table, while the lights are low." The hands meet tenderly and show "that you belong to me." Read the lyrics at http://lirama.net/song/15886.

I Only Have Eyes for You

Words: Al Dubin; Music: Harry Warren

Harry Warren and Al Dubin were hot commodities in Hollywood. After their success with *Forty Second Street* in '32, and the beginning of the *Gold Diggers* series in '33, they furnished the songs for *Twenty Million Sweethearts* and *Dames* in '34.

In *Dames*, choreographic genius Busby Berkeley set this beautiful song in a dream that the character played by Dick Powell has on a New York City subway. In the sequence, everywhere he looks he sees the face of Ruby Keeler, who played his love interest. Even the advertisements inside the subway become her face. The lyrics say, "I don't know if it's cloudy or bright ... or if we're in a garden: because I only have eyes for you." Read the lyrics and hear a midi musical version at http://www.harrywarren.org/songs/0195a.htm.

Ben Selvin and his orchestra, with vocalist Howard Phillips, had a very popular recording of "I Only Have Eyes for You." Eddy Duchin and his orchestra, with vocalist Lew Sherwood, also had a recording on the market that sold very well. Jane Froman's recording of the song was her first important release and her only one for Decca Records. The song recorded by the Flamingos peaked at No. 11 on *Billboard's* chart in '59, and peaked at No. 18 in '75 in Art Garfunkel's version. The Flamingos '59 recording of the song was inducted into the Grammy Hall of Fame in 2003. "I Only Have Eyes for You" became one of the most recorded songs of the pre-rock era.

The song was also used in the 'movie musicals *Jolson Sings Again* ('49), *Young Man with a Horn* ('50), which starred Kirk Douglas and Doris Day, and Gordon MacRae sang it in *Tea for Two* ('50). The song also appeared in *American Graffiti* ('73), *The Right Stuff* ('83), *In the Line of Fire* ('93), *Pi* ('98), *Eyes Wide Shut* ('99), *Artificial Intelligence: AI* (2001), *The Others* (2001), *Cherish* (2002) and *Something's Gotta Give* (2003).

Variety selected "I Only Have Eyes for You" as a *Hit Parade of a Half-Century* song.

Eddy Duchin and his orchestra popularized the title song from the film, "Dames." Read the lyrics and hear a midi musical verison at http://www.harrywarren.org/songs/0082.htm. The song also appeared in the Broadway version of *42nd Street*.

I Saw Stars

Words & Music: Maurice Sigler, Al Goodhart, & Al Hoffman

Freddy Martin and his orchestra, with a vocal by Elmer Feldkamp, popularized "I Saw Stars" with a very successful recording in '34. According to Joel Whitburn's *A Century of Pop Music*, their disk helped make the song one of the year's top ten hits.

The singer tells us something strange has happened to him when he lost his heart — he saw stars. Read the lyrics at http://lirama.net/song/15888.

Hear Paul Whiteman's recording of "I Saw Stars" at http://www.redhotjazz.com/pwo.html.

I'll Follow My Secret Heart

Words & Music: Noel Coward

This *Variety Hit Parade of a Half-Century* song came from England's Noel Coward. Coward and Yvonne Printemps introduced it in the London musical *Conversation Piece*.

According to *Variety*, "I'll Follow My Secret Heart" was one of the top ten hits of '34 for a month and a half, but it stopped at No. 2 in November, never making it to the top spot.

The singer will follow his secret heart until he finds love. Read the lyrics at http://www.oldielyrics.com/lyrics/frank_sinatra/ill_follow_my_secret_heart.html.

Ray Noble and his orchestra had the most popular recording of the song.

I'll String Along with You

Words: Al Dubin; Music: Harry Warren

Dick Powell and Ginger Rogers introduced this Harry Warren-Al Dubin song in the movie musical *Twenty Million Sweethearts*.

The singer says, in part, that regardless of what human frailties and faults the loved one possesses, "I'll string along with you." The Harry Warren website says the original title was "(You May Not Be an Angel, But) I'll String Along with You." Read the lyrics and hear a midi musical version at http://www.harrywarren.org/songs/0219a.htm.

Ted FioRito and his orchestra were featured in the movie *Twenty Million Sweethearts*, and it was their recording with vocalist Muzzy Marcellino of "I'll String Along with You" that was extremely popular in the late spring and early summer of '34. Tom Coakley and his orchestra, with a vocal performance by Carl Ravazza, also helped popularize the song with a successful recording. An audio clip of this song by Buddy Clark can be heard at http://www.harrywarrenmusic.com/realfiles/.

"(You May Not Be an Angel, But) I'll String Along with You" was also used in the '49 movie musical *My Dream Is Yours*, which starred Doris Day and the '53 version of *The Jazz Singer*, which starred Danny Thomas and Peggy Lee.

Dick Powell popularized "Fair and Warmer" from *Twenty Million Sweethearts* with a successful recording. Read the lyrics and hear a midi musical version of "Fair and Warmer" at http://www.harrywarren.org/songs/0108.htm.

June in January

Words: Leo Robin; Music: Ralph Rainger

The American branch of Decca Records was formed in '34, joining the main companies of the early '30s: RCA Victor, Columbia, and Brunswick. Decca, a European outfit, opened its American branch and quickly pulled off a major coup by luring Bing Crosby away from Brunswick. Crosby's first recording for Decca was "June in January," which he had introduced in the movie musical *Here Is My Heart*.

In this film, Bing played a millionaire crooner, something he would become in a few years, who journeys to Monte Carlo where he falls in love with a princess played by Kitty Carlisle.

Crosby's recording of "June in January" was extremely popular in late '34. Little Jack Little and his orchestra, Ted FioRito and his orchestra, and Guy Lombardo and his Royal Canadians also helped popularize the song with successful recorded releases.

The song also appeared in the '57 movie musical *The Joker Is Wild*, which starred Frank Sinatra.

How can it be June in January? The answer is it's always "spring in my heart ... because I'm in love with you." Read the complete lyrics at http://lirama.net/song/15892.

"June in January" was selected for inclusion in *Variety's Hit Parade of a Half-Century*.

Let's Fall in Love

Words: Ted Koehler; Music: Harold Arlen

After Harold Arlen's "It's Only a Paper Moon" had been interpolated into a film, he got his first assignment for a film score. He wrote "Let's Fall in Love" with lyricist Ted Koehler for the film *Let's Fall in Love*. Ann Sothern introduced the song in the film.

After its premier in *Let's Fall in Love*, it was used again in *Slightly French* ('49), *Sunny Side of the Street* ('51), *The Eddy Duchin Story* ('56), *Juke Box Rhythm* ('59) and *Pepe* ('60).

The song asks, "why shouldn't we fall in love?" Read the lyrics at http://lirama.net/song/15893.

The most popular recordings were by Eddy Duchin with Lew Sherwood furnishing the vocal. Other recordings by Fred Rich and the composer Harold Arlen were also popular. Annette Hanshaw's recording of "Let's Fall in Love" can be heard at http://www.redhotjazz.com/hanshaw.html.

This isn't "Let's Do It (Let's Fall in Love)." That's a Cole Porter song from '28.

Variety selected "Let's Fall in Love" for inclusion in its *Hit Parade of a Half-Century* representing '33.

Little Dutch Mill

Words: Ralph Freed; Music: Harry Barris

Bing Crosby popularized "Little Dutch Mill" with a particularly successful Brunswick recording in '34. According to Joel Whitburn's *A Century of Pop Music*, the song was one of the year's top ten hits.

One of Crosby's former partners in The Rhythm Boys, Harry Barris, was the song's composer.

Read the lyrics at http://www.lyricsvault.net/songs/19459.html.

Little Man, You've Had a Busy Day

Words: Maurice Sigler & Al Hoffman; Music: Mabel Wayne

Variety selected "Little Man, You've Had a Busy Day" for its *Hit Parade of a Half-Century*.

The sheet music cover shows a frightened little boy clinging to a tree limb as if he has climbed the tree and can't get down. The last page of the sheet music includes a recitation that goes along with the song by Bob Rice.

The refrain tells us the little boy is crying because someone took his kiddy car away. Then another boy won his marbles. He also played soldier until the enemy had been defeated. But now it's "time to stop your scheming, time your day was through ... little man, you've had a busy day." Read the lyrics at http://lirama.net/song/15894.

Emil Coleman and his orchestra had a popular recording of the song in '34, while Isham Jones and his orchestra's version was not quite as popular. Hear Isham Jones' recording of this song at http://www.redhotjazz.com/ishamjones.html.

Love in Bloom

Words: Leo Robin; Music: Ralph Rainger

"Love in Bloom" was introduced by Bing Crosby in *She Loves Me Not*. However, it was not in the film or through Crosby's recording of it that the song achieved it greatest exposure. It was to become the theme song for Jack Benny's radio and television shows. This *Variety Hit Parade of a Half-Century* number is most famous today in the "horrible" violin version that began Benny's shows, but of course, that was not the way it was originally popularized.

In Jack Benny's biography, he said that he and his wife, Mary, were in a supper club one evening when the band asked him to join them for a song. He borrowed a "fiddle," as he called a violin, and followed the sheet music as they played "Love in Bloom." The spontaneous performance must have been pretty funny because a wisecracking newspaper columnist wrote "Jack Benny playing 'Love in Bloom' sounded like a breath of fresh air ... if you like fresh air..." The next week, as Benny and his wife visited another club, the orchestra leader started playing "Love in Bloom," having obviously read the newspaper article. Benny said, "The thing just caught on, so I decided to adopt it as my theme song."

In *She Loves Me Not*, Bing played a Princeton student who gives sanctuary to a cabaret dancer who witnessed a murder.

Crosby's recording of "Love in Bloom" was a top hit during the late summer and early fall of '34. Other recordings that helped popularize the song around the nation were issued by Paul Whiteman and his orchestra, Guy Lombardo and his Royal Canadians, and Hal Kemp and his orchestra. Hear Paul Whiteman's recording of "Love in Bloom" at http://www.redhotjazz.com/pwo.html. "Love in Bloom" was also used in the '36 movie musical *College Holiday*, which starred Jack Benny, and in *True to the Army*, the '42 remake of *She Loves Me Not*.

This song was nominated for the American Film Institute's list of the greatest songs ever from an American film, but did not make the final list. It was nominated for its appearance in the '34 version of *She Loves Me Not*.

The lyrics ask if it is the trees that are filling the air with a magic perfume. And they answer, "Oh, no, it isn't the trees, It's love in bloom!" Read the complete lyrics at http://lirama.net/song/15895.

Bing Crosby also popularized "Straight from the Shoulder (Right from the Heart)" from *She Loves Me Not*. That song was written by Mack Gordon and Harry Revel.

Love Thy Neighbor

Words: Mack Gordon; Music: Harry Revel

Bing Crosby was very busy in '34! His movie musicals released in '34 included *She Loves Me Not*, *Here Is My Heart*, and *We're Not Dressing*, in which he introduced "Love Thy Neighbor." He further popularized it in a very successful Decca recording. A recording by Raymond Paige and his orchestra, with a vocal by the Three Rhythm Kings, was moderately successful.

Bing played a sailor ship-wrecked on a desert island in *We're Not Dressing*. Carole Lombard played an aloof millionairess who eventually succumbs to Crosby's charms. Others in the cast included George Burns and Gracie Allen, Ray Milland and Ethel Merman.

According to *Variety*, it was the top song in the nation for a month and spent three months in the Top Ten in '34. *Variety* selected it for its *Hit Parade of a Half-Century*.

This song sounds like Biblical advice: "Love your neighbor as yourself" (Matthew 22:39). The lyrics of this song tell us we should share our neighbor's burden. Now, if that neighbor happened to be a beautiful girl, you should tell her your mother taught you to love your neighbor. The chorus ends with "Life'll be breezier if you love thy neighbor." Read the lyrics at http://www.lyricsdepot.com/bing-crosby/love-thy-neighbor.html.

Bing Crosby also popularized "Goodnight, Lovely Little Lady" and "May I?" from *We're Not Dressing*. Eddy Duchin and his orchestra popularized "She Reminds Me of You" from the film. Hear the Dorsey Brothers Orchestra's recording of "She Reminds Me of You" at http://www.redhotjazz.com/dorseybros.html.

Moonglow

Words & Music: Will Hudson, Eddie DeLange, and Irving Mills

Is it "Moonglow" or "Moon Glow"? It is printed both ways. The sheet music, however, says "Moonglow."

"Moonglow" may be more famous today for its inclusion in the '56 film *Picnic*, which starred William Holden and Kim Novak. Steve Allen and George Duning ingeniously combined "Moonglow" with the theme from the film to create an unforgettable masterpiece. Morris Stoloff, the film's musical director, and his orchestra's recording of "Moon Glow" and Theme from *Picnic* became a No. 1 hit in '56. George Cates and his orchestra's version reached No. 4 on the charts.

Back to '34 — Benny Goodman and his orchestra had an extremely popular recording of "Moonglow." Duke Ellington and his orchestra recorded an almost equally popular version. Other recordings of the song on the market in '34 included those by Cab Calloway and his orchestra, and by Glen Gray and the Casa Loma Orchestra. Benny Goodman and his quartet revived it in '36 with very good success again; Goodman's recording was inducted into the Grammy Hall of Fame in 1998. The song became one of the most recorded songs of the pre-rock era. Joe Venuti and his orchestra's recording of "Moonglow" can be heard at http://www.redhotjazz.com/jvo.html.

Because the song was so successful for Benny Goodman, twice, it was featured in *The Benny Goodman Story*, the film biography of "The King of Swing," which was released in '56. Goodman's recording of the song was used on the soundtrack of *The Aviator* (2005).

The chorus lyric says "it must have been Moonglow ... that led me straight to you." Read the lyrics at http://lirama.net/song/15897.

My Little Grass Shack in Kealakekua, Hawaii

Words & Music: Bill Cogswell, Tom Harrison, and Johnny Noble

Ted FioRito and his orchestra's recording of "My Little Grass Shack in Kealakekua, Hawaii" was a top hit around the nation during the early spring of '34. The vocalist isn't listed for FioRito's recording, but the song is a novelty tune that needs the lyrics, so there probably was a vocal on the recording. Ben Pollack and his orchestra, with vocalists Dorsi Robbins, Nappy Lamare, and Joe Harris, also released a version that sold well. Hear Paul Whiteman and his orchestra's recording of "My Little Grass Shack..." at http://www.redhotjazz.com/pwo.html.

The singer tells us there's a place in Hawaii he wants to go. He wants "to go back to my little grass shack in Kealakekua, Hawaii." This homesick Hawaiian wants his fish and poi that he gets in his little grass shack "where the humuhumunukunukuapuaa goes swimming by." Read the lyrics and see one of the sheet music covers at http://www.squareone.org/Hapa/m1.html. See three different sheet music covers at www.hulapages.com/covers_4.htm.

The Object of My Affection

Words & Music: Pinky Tomlin, Coy Poe, and Jimmie Grier

"The Object of My Affection" became a big hit for co-writer Jimmie Grier and his orchestra right at the end of '34. Jan Garber and his orchestra also released a version that was popular. Then in early '35, a recording by the Boswell Sisters climbed to the top of the charts again. Glen Gray and the Casa Loma Orchestra recorded their version, which did reasonably well in '35.

The song was interpolated into the motion picture *Times Square Lady* in '35. It also appeared in the movie musical *The Fabulous Dorseys* ('47), where it was played by the Dorsey Brothers Orchestra. Jimmie Grier's recording of the song, with Pinky Tomlin performing the vocal, was used on the soundtrack of *Paper Moon* ('73), which starred Ryan and Tatum O'Neal.

The object of the singer's affection can change his "complexion from white to rosy red" anytime she holds his hand and tells him that she's his. Read the lyrics at http://lirama.net/song/15900.

The Old Spinning Wheel

Words & Music: Billy Hill

Boston native, Billy Hill, wrote several nostalgic cowboy ballad songs that reached hit status. He had written "The Old Spinning Wheel" several years earlier, but it had not been published. After the success of 1933's "The Last Round-Up," Hill pulled "The Old Spinning Wheel" out of mothballs. *Variety* reported sales of 800,000 records in '35 and later named it to its *Hit Parade of a Half-Century*.

The British unit, Ray Noble and his orchestra recorded the most popular version of "The Old Spinning Wheel." Their Victor recording was popular from late fall '33 into the early weeks of '34. Al Bowlly was the band's vocalist. Emil Velasco recorded it for Columbia, while Victor Young and his orchestra, with vocalist Scrappy Lambert, recorded it for Brunswick.

The singer treasures the "old spinning wheel in the parlor." It spins old fashioined dreams of a maid and her beau. He thinks he can sometimes hear an organ playing Stephen Foster's "Old Black Joe." Read the lyrics at http://lirama.net/song/15901.

See the sheet music cover at http://www.parlorsongs.com/issues/1998–10/oct98gallery.asp.

One Night of Love

Words: Gus Kahn; Music: Victor Schertzinger

"One Night of Love" was introduced by opera diva, Grace Moore, in the movie musical *One Night of Love* in '34. The film was trying to make operatic singing palatable to an audience who generally regarded opera as entertainment that only nerds could enjoy.

Evidently the audiences found Moore's singing more than palatable, because her recording of the song was a big hit during the fall of '34.

Ms. Moore sang that even when her lover has gone, she'll smile, because she's known "one night of love." Read the lyrics at http://lirama.net/song/15902.

The film won the Academy Award Achievement in Music (Original Score) in '34 for the Columbia Studio Music Department (Thematic Music by Victor Schertzinger and Gus Kahn).

In addition to "One Night of Love," Ms. Moore performed the famous "Ciribiribin," the song that eventually became trumpeter Harry James's theme song, and excerpts from Puccini's *Madame Butterfly*, Bizet's *Carmen*, and Donizetti's *Lucia di Lammermoor*.

Smoke Gets in Your Eyes *and* The Touch of Your Hand

Words: Otto Harbach; Music: Jerome Kern

The basic plot of *Roberta* told an unlikely tale of an All-American football star who finds love and success when he inherits his aunt's dress shop in Paris.

Bob Hope made his first major appearance in *Roberta* and provided its few comic moments.

The screen version of *Roberta* ('35) starred Fred Astaire and Ginger Rogers. The Hollywood version retained four of the original songs from the stage version ("Let's Begin," "Smoke Gets in Your Eyes," "Yesterdays," and "I'll Be Hard to Handle" with a new set of lyrics). "You're Devastating," "The Touch of Your Hand," and "Don't Ask Me Not to Sing" were used only as background music. "Smoke Gets in Your Eyes" was also used in Kern's screen biography *Till the Clouds Roll By*, where it was danced by Cyd Charisse and Gower Champion and *Lovely to Look At*, a remake of *Roberta*, where it was sung by Kathryn Grayson and danced by Marge and Gower Champion.

SMOKE GETS IN YOUR EYES

Tamara introduced "Smoke Gets in Your Eyes" in Jerome Kern's *Roberta*. She performed this lovely ballad, which reflects on love gone up in smoke, seated on an empty stage, accompanying herself on a guitar, and wearing a peasant dress and babushka.

Kern had originally written the melody as a march for the theme of a radio program that never materialized. By slowing the tempo and sentimentalizing the melody, he adapted it for Act II of *Roberta*. The song became a hit even though Harbach's lyrics are rather arcane ("and so I chaffed them and I gaily laughed"). Lyrics to popular songs should be in the vernacular, the way people talk every day. Nobody says "and so I chaffed them." Read the lyrics and judge for yourself at http://lirama.net/song/15905.

Even so, Paul Whiteman and his orchestra's recording, with Bob Lawrence as vocalist, was phenomenally popular in early '34. Hear Whiteman's recording at http://www.red-hotjazz.com/pwo.html. Releases by Leo Reisman and his orchestra, Emil Coleman and his Riviera Orchestra, and Ruth Etting also were successful. Artie Shaw and his orchestra revived it with moderate success in '41. The Platters' recording of "Smoke Gets in Your Eyes" sold more than a million copies and was a No.1 hit in early '59. Blue Haze took it into the Top 30 on *Billboard's* Hot 100 in '73.

Kern's ballad was chosen by *Variety's* Hit Parade of a Half-Century representing 1933 and for its *Golden 100 Tin Pan Alley Songs* lists. "Smoke Gets in Your Eyes" became one of the most recorded songs of the pre-rock era.

Irene Dunne sang "Smoke Gets in Your Eyes" in the '35 film version of *Roberta* (Fred Astaire and Ginger Rogers also danced to it later in the film); while the song was sung by a chorus, Cyd Charisse and Gower Champion danced to it in *Till the Clouds Roll By* ('46), Kathryn Grayson sang it in *Lovely to Look At* ('52) and the Platters' recording of the song was heard on the soundtrack of *La Bamba* ('87). The song was nominated for AFI's list of the greatest songs ever from American films for its appearance in *American Graffiti* ('73), but it did not make the final list.

THE TOUCH OF YOUR HAND

In the musical, Stephanie (played by Tamara) and Ladislaw (played by William Hain) exchange goodbyes in this emotional song. Read the lyrics at http://lirama.net/song/15910.

Leo Reisman and his orchestra also had the most popular recording of "The Touch of Your Hand." Hear Paul Whiteman's recording of this song at http://www.redhot jazz.com/pwo.html.

The critics did not treat *Roberta* kindly, but it had a successful run, thanks largely to the musical score. Kern was reaching the end of his Broadway career, but he was still composing classics.

Variety selected this song for its *Hit Parade of a Half-Century* representing 1933.

Stars Fell on Alabama

Words: Mitchell Parish; Music: Frank Perkins

The state of Alabama has inspired several well-known melodies ("Alabama Jubilee," "Lovin' Sam, the Sheik of Alabam'," "Alabamy Bound," and "Tuxedo Junction," which was in Alabama, for example). Without a doubt, one of the most famous ones is Frank Perkins' composition. "Stars Fell on Alabama" came out about the same time as Carl Carmer's novel of the same title, although there was no official connection between the two works.

Guy Lombardo and his Royal Canadians' recording of "Stars Fell on Alabama" was extremely popular in early '34. Richard Himber and his orchestra 's version of the song was not far behind Lombardo's in popularity. Joey Nash was Himber's vocalist on their record. Jack Teagarden and his orchestra's recording of this song can be heard at http://www.redhotjazz.com/teao.html.

The lyrics say it seemed that "stars fell on Alabama" when we kissed. Read the lyrics at http://lirama.net/song/15906. The State of Alabama currently uses the title phrase on its automobile license plates.

"Stars Fell on Alabama" was selected by *Variety* for its *Hit Parade of a Half-Century* representing 1933.

Stay as Sweet as You Are

Words: Mack Gordon; Music: Harry Revel

In the movie musical *College Rhythm*, Lanny Ross introduced "Stay as Sweet as You Are." Ross's recording of the song did moderately well, but several others were more successful, including those by Little Jack Little and by Guy Lombardo and his Royal Canadians. A release by Jimmie Grier and his orchestra was the most popular version on the market and was particularly successful in the late fall of '34.

The singer pleads with the girl to remain as she is: lovely, charming, and sweet. He hopes no matter if she's young or old, here or somewhere else, she'll "always stay as sweet as you are." Read the lyrics at http://lirama.net/song/15907.

Lanny Ross, who originally introduced the song, became one of the singing stars of *Your Hit Parade* on radio during the late '30s. He was called "The Troubadour of the Moon."

Tumbling Tumbleweeds

Words & Music: Bob Nolan

Bob Nolan's "Tumbling Tumbleweeds" conjures up an image of a group of cowhands singing around a campfire. The song is so well known that many people probably think it is an authentic western folk song, but was written by Bob Nolan, a Canadian, who became fascinated by the desert after he and his family moved to Arizona.

Nolan originally wrote the song on a rainy day in '32 as "Tumbling Leaves." The Sons of the Pioneers introduced it on the radio as "Tumbling Leaves," but later changed it to "tumbleweeds" to more reflect their western image. It became their theme song and was quickly picked up by singers and bands all over the country.

Gene Autry introduced "Tumbling Tumbleweeds" in his first full-length film, *Tumbling Tumbleweeds*. He also performed it in *Don't Fence Me in* ('45).

The Sons of the Pioneers recorded "Tumbling Tumbleweeds" and helped popularize it. Their recording of the song was inducted into the Grammy Hall of Fame in 2002. The group performed the song in the movie musical *Hollywood Canteen* ('45).

Other popular recordings of "Tumbling Tumbleweeds" were issued by Gene Autry in '35, Glen Gray and the Casa Loma Orchestra in '39 and Bing Crosby in '40.

Read the lyrics at http://www.cowboylyrics.com/lyrics/sons-of-the-pioneers/tumbling-tumbleweeds-13413.html.

The Sons of the Pioneers consisted of the song's writer, Nolan, Tim Spencer and Leonard Slye, who achieved celebrity status after '37 as Roy Rogers. Rogers sang "Tumbling Tumbleweeds" in *Silver Spurs* ('43).

The years '33 and '34 were particularly important for songs with a western character. Songs by Billy Hill and Bob Nolan, plus "El Rancho Grande" and "The Cattle Call," which were not as high on the hit list as "Tumbling Tumbleweeds," "Wagon Wheels," "The Last Roundup" or "The Old Spinning Wheel," illustrate the western song mania.

Two Cigarettes in the Dark

Words: Paul Francis Webster; Music: Lew Pollack

Gloria Grafton introduced this *Variety Hit Parade of a Half-Century* selection in the nonmusical motion picture *Kill That Story* ('34).

Smoking was more fashionable in the '30s than it has been since being linked to cancer. Many of the sex symbols of the decade's movie industry were almost always pictured smoking and often with a drink in their hands.

"Two Cigarettes in the Dark" compares striking a match to "the spark that thrilled me" and the glow of the cigarette to love's flame, while "the smoke rings seemed to signify a story old yet new." Read the lyrics at http://lirama.net/song/15911.

Johnny Green and his orchestra, Bing Crosby, Jerry Johnson, Frank Parker, and Glen Gray and their bands all had popular recordings of the song on the market. Ted Lewis' recording of "Two Cigarettes in the Dark" can be heard at http://www.redhotjazz.com/tlband.html.

The Very Thought of You

Words & Music: Ray Noble

British bandleader Ray Noble wrote "The Very Thought of You." He and his orchestra recorded a very popular version of the song that was most successful during the summer of '34. Noble's recording of the song was inducted into the Grammy Hall of Fame in 2005. Bing Crosby's version of the song was successful, but not as popular as Noble's. Vaughn Monroe and his orchestra revived it in reasonable success in '44.

It provided the title for and was featured in a motion picture that starred Eleanor Parker, Faye Emerson and Dennis Morgan in '44. It was sung by Doris Day in the movie musical *Young Man with a Horn* ('50).

Variety selected this song for its *Hit Parade of a Half-Century* for '39, but that must have been a typographical mistake. It was primarily popular in '34 and '44, not '39. "The Very Thought of You" became one of the most recorded songs of the pre-rock era.

When the singer thinks of his loved one, he forgets "to do the little ordinary things that everyone ought to do." Read the lyrics at http://lirama.net/song/15912.

Wagon Wheels

Words: Peter DeRose; Music: Billy Hill

Everett Marshall introduced "Wagon Wheels" in the *Ziegfeld Follies of 1934* (also see "The Last Round Up" in 1933). Its basic two-part form gives the song a folk song feel. The chorus is usually sung first; then comes the verse, followed by the chorus with a slightly different ending. Most folk music and gospel songs have a verse and chorus two-part form pattern.

The lyrics ask the "Wagon wheels" to "keep on a-turning ... roll along, Sing your song ... carry me home." Read the lyrics at http://lirama.net/song/15913.

Paul Whiteman and his orchestra released a particularly popular version of "Wagon Wheels" in '34 that became the top hit in the nation during the early spring of the year. Hear this recording at http://www.redhotjazz.com/pwo.html.

According to *Variety*, "Wagon Wheels" was the top song in the nation for three weeks and spent ten weeks in 1934's Top Ten. *Variety* selected it for its *Hit Parade of a Half-Century*.

What a Diff'rence a Day Made

Words: Stanley Adams; Music: Maria Grever

This popular Spanish song, "Cuando vuelva a tu lado," was written by Maria Grever. The lyrics were translated into English by Stanley Adams in '34.

The difference made by "twenty-four little hours" is romance with you. Read the lyrics at http://lirama.net/song/15914.

A recording by the Dorsey Brothers Orchestra, with a vocal performance by Bing Crosby's brother, Bob, popularized the song in '34. Andy Russell revived it in '44. Dinah Washington revived the number successfully in '58. She won the Best Rhythm and Blues Recording of the Year Grammy for her recording.

Variety selected "What a Diff'rence a Day Made" as a *Golden 100 Tin Pan Alley Song* and its *Hit Parade of a Half-Century* representing '44.

With My Eyes Wide Open, I'm Dreaming

Words: Mack Gordon; Music: Harry Revel

Dorothy Dell and Jack Oakie introduced "With My Eyes Wide Open, I'm Dreaming," a *Variety Hit Parade of a Half-Century* honoree, in the film *Shoot the Works*.

Leo Reisman and his orchestra, with vocalist George Bueler, and Isham Jones and his orchestra, with a vocal performance by Joe Martin, released successful recordings of the song in '34. It was revived in '50 by Patti Page, who reaped her first million seller with her version. It was revived again in '52, when Dean Martin performed it in the movie musical *The Stooge*.

The singer thinks he must be dreaming because "you're with me now sharing a vow never to part." He and his girl are afraid to close their eyes because all this might be "just a silly illusion." They ask to be pinched to prove they're awake, because they can't believe they're lucky enough to have found such a love. Read the complete lyrics at http://lirama.net/song/16574.

Variety reported that the song was the nation's top hit for two weeks, and it spent three months in the Top Ten in '34.

You Oughta Be in Pictures

Words: Edward Heyman; Music: Dana Suesse

Jane Froman introduced "You Oughta Be in Pictures," in the *Ziegfeld Follies of 1934* (see "The Last Round Up"

in 1933 and "Wagon Wheels" above). Mary Martin and Fred MacMurray performed it in the film *New York Town*, in '41. Doris Day next revived it in the '51 film *Starlift*.

Little Jack Little's recording of "You Oughta Be in Pictures" was very popular in '34. Rudy Vallee also had a version that did pretty well, while the Boswell Sisters' version did respectably.

"You Oughta Be in Pictures" is a classic song of the film industry along with "Hooray for Hollywood."

Variety selected it for inclusion in its *Hit Parade of a Half-Century.*

The reason the singer thinks this person he is singing about needs to be in a motion picture is she's wonderful to look at, her voice is thrilling, and her face is adorable. He's convinced if she kissed someone on the big screen "the way you kiss when we're alone," she'd become a star. Read the lyrics at http://lirama.net/song/15916.

V

The Swing Era: 1935–1944

By the middle of the '30s, the country had recovered from the worst of the Depression, but only a few years of relative calm lay between the economic debacle of the early '30s and the holocaust of World War II. By '37, Hitler was in power in Germany, Mussolini had brought fascism to Italy, the Spanish Republic was under attack by Francisco Franco, and Japan had begun systematic attacks upon China. The United States was being inexorably drawn into another major war.

The Big Bands

Swing-style big bands were not the important agents of the year's biggest hits until the last few years of the '30s. The Swing Era, also called the Big Band Era, has been dated variously from '35 to '44 or '39 to '49. No style comes to immediate prominence to the exclusion of all other styles. As one style is beginning, another is declining in popularity. It is impossible, therefore, to pinpoint that the Swing Era began at a particular moment, but Benny Goodman's engagement at the Palomar Ballroom in Los Angeles in August of '35 was one of the early indications that change was happening. Goodman decided to feature his swing repertoire rather than the society style of dance music that his band had been playing. The audience, particularly the youth, gave enthusiastic approval.

Swing was the music of youth, just as much as rock 'n' roll was in the late '50s. In the Swing Era, the adults, not the youth, made the hits. Teenagers did not yet have the buying power they were to acquire by the beginning of rock. Swing had to make inroads into the establishment before it was capable of producing big hits.

The trend toward recognition of the swing consciousness beginning is shown by the '36 movie title *Swing Time*, which starred Fred Astaire and Ginger Rogers.

The roots of swing can be traced to jazz and the sweet bands of the '20s and early '30s. True jazz, as the African American bands played it, was kept alive by aficionados, and the general public knew very little about it. Sweet music was the dominant style on radio and on records. The swing style was a direct result of Goodman, and other white bandleaders, imitating the black bands and using the arrangements of black arrangers like Fletcher Henderson, Don Redman, and Jimmy Mundy. Goodman was able to introduce the swing sound to a broad audience through radio, hotel and ballroom engagements, and recordings. He became "The King of Swing," and danceable jazz became the music of day.

The African American musicians were the innovators and the ones who brought the hot sound of swing into the dance bands, but the white bands sold. Of course, this seems grossly unfair today, but Goodman was also responsible for breaking the color barrier in bands by being the first to have whites and blacks play together in the same band.

Many of the later famous bands, or orchestras as they were called, began about '35. The Dorsey brothers—Jimmy and Tommy—formed theirs in '34. Tommy left in '35 to lead his own group. Clarinetist Artie Shaw formed an orchestra with strings in '36, but disbanded it in the face of Goodman's popularity and formed what he called "the loudest band in the world" in '37. Woody Herman took over the Isham Jones orchestra in '36.

The sweet bands had reigned supreme for

several years, but they began to worry about their continued success as the country became increasingly swing crazy. Some of the major sweet bands included those of Larry Clinton, Eddy Duchin, Sammy Kaye, Hal Kemp, Wayne King, Kay Kyser, Guy Lombardo, Vincent Lopez, Russ Morgan, Ray Noble, Leo Reisman, and Lawrence Welk.

In the swing category, the important bands included those of Jimmy Dorsey, Tommy Dorsey, Benny Goodman, Glen Gray, Harry James, and Artie Shaw. Several of the black bands belong in the swing category. Some of the most famous ones include Louis Armstrong, Count Basie, Duke Ellington, Fletcher Henderson, Earl Hines, and Chick Webb.

There were other bands that featured singers or a leader who could not be identified with either sweet or swing. Glenn Miller may fit in this category. He seemed to specialize in music for dreamy-eyed dancers, but some of his music was definitely swinging. The bands of Ben Bernie, Cab Calloway, Bob Crosby, Little Jack Little, Will Osborne, and Rudy Vallee probably also don't fit exclusively in either category.

The bands demanded exceptional musicianship skills from their players. The players were expected to have extremely advanced technical skills on their instrument and read music fluently. Rhythmic complexities in the band's song arrangements demanded extraordinary reading and playing ability so that the unit played precisely.

Many of the big bands also featured small combos that played more authentic jazz with superb improvisation. Improvisation is not a written arrangement; it is made up on the spot, keeping the song's melody, harmony, and form in mind. A quality big band player did not necessarily possess the most skillful improvisation abilities. While some improvisation was sometimes built into a big band arrangement, it was much easier done by the small combos that became a part of almost all the famous bands.

By the end of the decade the trend toward less boisterous music had become evident. The popularity of Glenn Miller's soft, sweet sound at the beginning of the '40s was an indication that the swing hysteria was calming.

The first peacetime military draft in U.S. history was instituted in '40 because of the war in Europe. The draft caused the bands to juggle their personnel and to look for replacements. Keeping together bands that could play the complex arrangements became more difficult.

A trend toward the bands featuring a vocalist or vocal group began in the early '40s. Important

singers with the bands included Tex Beneke, Doris Day, Bob Eberly, Ray Eberle, Ella Fitzgerald, Helen Forrest, Connie Haines, Kitty Kallen, Helen O'-Connell and Frank Sinatra. Important vocal groups included the Merry Macs, the Mills Brothers, the Modernaires, the Pied Pipers and the Song Spinners. Another important vocal group, but not associated with a band, was the Andrews Sisters.

Wartime shortages, particularly of gasoline, caused problems for the bands. Neither they nor their fans could travel. And a levied amusement tax made it very expensive for people to go out. These, and other factors, contributed to the demise of the big bands. The singers became the important ingredient, leading into the Sing Era.

The Hit Parade

On April 20, 1935, *Your Hit Parade* began broadcasting its weekly program of the top songs in the country. Millions of Americans sat in front of their radios each Saturday evening, waiting for the announcement of the top hits in the nation, especially the number one song. The songs were rated by sheet music and record sales, by the number of performances on jukeboxes, and certain bandleaders were questioned about requests. Radio air play didn't seem to enter into the mix at this time. For the next twenty-five years, the program served as a barometer of the nation's taste in popular music.

The Popularity of Movie Musicals

The movie musicals of the Swing Era are distinctive types: the dance musical, the revue, the operetta, and the animated musical.

The nine films that Fred Astaire and Ginger Rogers made together during the era were filled with incomparable dance routines. They danced to some of the era's most popular music composed by some of its best writers. Their films during the era included *Roberta, Top Hat, Follow the Fleet, Swing Time, Shall We Dance?, Carefree,* and *The Story of Vernon and Irene Castle.* Of course, there were many other movie musicals, and there were important musical stars besides Astaire and Rogers. Some of the most important movie musicals of the era include *Broadway Melody of 1936,* which was nominated for the Best Picture Oscar in '35, *The Great Ziegfeld,* which won the Oscar for Best Picture in '36, *Alexander's Ragtime Band* ('38), *The*

Wizard of Oz ('39), an Academy Award nominee for Best Picture, Crosby, Hope, and Lamour's series of road films [*Road to Singapore* ('40), *Road to Zanzibar* ('41), *Road to Morocco* ('43)], *Yankee Doodle Dandy* ('42), with James Cagney portraying George M. Cohan, Mickey Rooney and Judy Garland's films together, including *Thoroughbreds Don't Cry* ('37), *Andy Hardy Finds Love* ('38), *Babes in Arms* ('39), *Strike Up the Band* ('40), *Babes on Broadway* ('42) and *Girl Crazy* ('43), and the '44 Best Picture Oscar winner, *Going My Way*.

The revue films were nothing new, but several of this type were very popular, especially as the industry began to turn out entertainment for servicemen. After the '41 bombing of Pearl Harbor, most of the movie musicals became patriotic, to aid the war effort, and escapist, to help the country forget the problems the war was creating. A few of the revue type of musical films included *The Big Broadcast of 1936*, *Stars Over Broadway*, *The Goldwyn Follies*, *Hit Parade of 1941*, *Stage Door Canteen*, and *Stars on Parade*.

Jeanette MacDonald and Nelson Eddy teamed up for eight movie versions of operettas beginning with *Naughty Marietta* in '35 and including *Rose Marie*, *Maytime*, *Rosalie*, *Sweethearts*, *New Moon*, *Bitter Sweet*, and *The Chocolate Soldier*. There were other operettas and other performers, but MacDonald and Eddy were the biggest stars of the operetta-style movie musicals.

There also were several movie versions of Broadway musicals including *Roberta*, *Babes in Arms*, *This Is the Army*, *Panama Hattie*, *DuBarry Was a Lady* and *Knickerbocker Holiday*.

Some of the important stars of the movie musicals of the Swing Era were Alice Faye, Frances Langford, Al Jolson, Bing Crosby, Gene Kelly, Eleanor Powell, Betty Hutton, Martha Raye, Betty Grable, Mary Martin, Dan Dailey, Kathryn Grayson, Gloria DeHaven, Dick Haymes, Jane Powell, and June Allyson.

A new kind of movie musical was created during this era: the animated musical, which, of course, was the exclusive product of the Disney studios. Important movie musicals of this type included *Snow White and the Seven Dwarfs*, *Pinocchio*, *Fantasia*, *Dumbo* and *Bambi*.

The Musical Theater

The stage continued to produce many beautiful and enduring popular songs. With composers like Cole Porter, Richard Rodgers and Irving Berlin turning out fabulous scores, Broadway produced more than its share of major hit songs.

The era began with Cole Porter's *Jubilee* and George Gershwin's incredible folk opera *Porgy and Bess*. It also saw the premiers of Porter's *Red, Hot and Blue*, Rodgers and Hart's *Babes in Arms* and Kurt Weill's *Knickerbocker Holiday* and *Lady in the Dark*.

The outstanding musical event of the decade came in '43 with *Oklahoma!*, the first musical collaboration between Richard Rodgers and Oscar Hammerstein II. *Oklahoma!* became one of the greatest Broadway musicals of all time, eventually running for 2,248 performances. The Rodgers and Hammerstein team dominated musical theater for the next ten years.

Some of the most important hits from the Broadway stage during this era include "Begin the Beguine," "Just One of Those Things," "Summertime," "September Song," "All the Things You Are," "Bewitched (Bothered, and Bewildered)," "Oh, What a Beautiful Mornin'," "People Will Say We're in Love," and "I'll Be Seeing You."

The Record Industry

The record industry eventually recovered from the Depression and was booming by the early '40s. But the boom was short-lived. Members of the American Federation of Musicians, the union for instrumentalists, had become worried as recordings and jukeboxes began to replace live musicians on radio and in clubs. They demanded that the record companies establish a fund for unemployed musicians, and they called a strike against the companies to emphasize the point. All-vocal recordings filled the vacuum left by the instrumentalists. Toward the end of '44, the recording companies agreed to pay a royalty on each disk for the benefit of unemployed members, however, the passage of the Taft-Hartley Act in '47 made the agreement illegal. This resulted in another ban on making records, but the companies had stockpiled enough recordings that they were not as vulnerable as they had been the first time.

Record production also declined in the early forties because there was a shortage of shellac, which was used in making records. Shellac was needed for the war effort. The industry launched a drive to get the public to turn in old records that could be melted down and reused to make new records. The drive robbed us of many rare recordings, but fortunately many people kept their records.

The ASCAP Ban

As the '40s opened, before the attack on Pearl Harbor, record sales soared. That prompted ASCAP, the performing rights society, to propose a new contract with radio stations that demanded twice the annual fee the stations had paid under the old contract for playing music written and published by ASCAP members. Radio executives refused to discuss the proposed contract. As a result, all ASCAP music was banned from the airwaves.

To protect its interests, radio formed a new performing rights organization: Broadcast Music Incorporated (BMI), which sought out songwriters and publishers from fields that ASCAP had ignored: foreign music, country and western (then called hillbilly) music, and from places outside the metropolitan areas of New York City and Los Angeles. Within a decade, BMI was licensing 80% of all the music played on radio.

Because of the absence of ASCAP music on radio, public domain songs, like those of Stephen Foster and other older writers, were played on radio. Some imported songs got a hearing, and some relatively unknown songwriters and performers got their big breaks because of the ASCAP ban.

ASCAP retreated in its demands in '41. In the new agreement, it agreed to accept even less each year from the radio stations than under the previous contract.

The End of the Era

The riots caused by Frank Sinatra in the early '40s clearly signaled the end of an era. By '42, Sinatra had decided to break loose from being a band singer and make it as a solo act. For the first few months, he seemed to be going nowhere. Then a series of explosive appearances skyrocketed him to the top. The first came in November of '42, in Newark, New Jersey. The predominantly female teenage audience squealed, screamed, and howled when Sinatra began to sing. A couple of months later, at the Paramount Theater in New York City, he created even more pandemonium among the youngsters in the audience. Then in '44, at the Paramount, the most volcanic riot occurred. Ten

thousand youths waited in line for tickets, and many thousands more wandered in the streets near the theater. When the box office opened, the booth was destroyed by the rush, people were trampled, and a few girls fainted. Sinatra had already become a lead singer on *Your Hit Parade* radio program in '42. His high recognition because of his *Your Hit Parade* appearances and the new fame created by the riots caused his career to soar.

This marked the beginning of the end of the Swing Era. The next several years were dominated by the singers. The drawing power of the bands had declined. Several survived to accompany the singers, but their roles were now secondary.

Determining the Hits

Determining the biggest hits of each year becomes easier during subsequent years. *Your Hit Parade* began featuring the weekly top hits on April 20, 1935. Their charts helped tremendously.

The weekly pop charts of *Variety* and *Billboard* began in the early '40s. Their charts were a great addition. *Variety* published a Top Ten for each year from '41 to '80 in their January 1981 edition that was most valuable.

1935

And Then Some
Words: Tot Seymour; Music: Vee Lawnhurst
Vee Lawnhurst collaborated with lyricist Tot Seymour for a few popular songs in the mid–'30s. Lawnhurst was a staff pianist, and sometimes singer, for a New York City radio station. Tot Seymour became one of the first female lyricists on Tin Pan Alley. "And Then Some" was their only major hit song.

"And Then Some" spent one week at the top spot on *Your Hit Parade* in the late summer of '35.

Ozzie Nelson and his orchestra, with Ozzie himself as vocalist, had a very popular recording of the song. Hear Paul Whiteman's version of "And Then Some" at http://www.redhotjazz.com/pwo.html.

The lyrics, sung by Ozzie Nelson, say he thinks this girl is gorgeous, charming, handsome, perfect "and then some." He'd like to kiss her, caress her, spoil her, "and then some." Read the lyrics at http://lirama.net/song/15920.

Blue Moon
Words: Lorenz Hart; Music: Richard Rodgers
"Blue Moon" is the only Rodgers and Hart song that became a hit without having been introduced in a stage or movie musical. It went through quite a metamorphosis

before it achieved that status. First it was called "The Prayer," and was intended for an M.G.M. film *Hollywood Party*, starring Jean Harlow. Neither the song nor Miss Harlow ending up appearing in the film. Next it was rewritten as the title song for another M.G.M. film, *Manhattan Melodrama*, which starred Clark Gable, William Powell and Myrna Loy. The song was cut from the film before it was released. Its third incarnation was titled "The Bad in Every Man" and was sung by Shirley Ross in the same film, *Manhattan Melodrama*. Finally, in its fourth lyric setting, it became "Blue Moon." Published in this form, it became one of Rodgers and Hart's biggest-selling songs to date.

Glen Gray and the Casa Loma Orchestra, with vocalist Kenny Sargent, had an extremely popular recording of "Blue Moon" in early '35. Other very popular versions were released by Benny Goodman and his orchestra, with vocalist Helen Ward, and by England's top singing sensation, Al Bowlly with Ray Noble and his orchestra. Both Mel Torme and Billy Eckstine successfully revived the song in '49. Rodgers and Hart probably turned over in their graves when the Marcels' '61 version of "Blue Moon" went to No. 1 on *Billboard's* chart. Another noteworthy rendition of the song was Cybill Shepherd's on her television series "Moonlighting." Her recording of the song was released on the television soundtrack album in '87. "Blue Moon" became one of the most recorded songs of the pre-rock era. Frankie Trumbauer and his orchestra's recording of "Blue Moon" can be heard at http://www.redhotjazz.com/fto.html.

The song may not have originally appeared in a movie or Broadway musical, but Hollywood used it in several movie musicals through the years. It appeared in *Hollywood Hotel* ('38), in Marx Brothers' farce *At the Circus* ('39), Perry Como and Cyd Charisse performed it in *Words and Music*, Rodgers and Hart's '49 screen biography, in *With a Song in My Heart*, Jane Froman's '52 movie biography, in *Torch Song* ('53), in *This Could Be the Night* ('57), in *New York, New York* ('77), which starred Liza Minnelli and Robert DeNiro and Sha-Na-Na performed it on the soundtrack of *Grease* ('78).

The "blue moon" saw the singer didn't have a dream in his heart or a love of his own. He was praying for someone he could love. Then suddenly, that certain someone appeared before him and the moon turned to gold. Now, he's no longer alone. Read the lyrics at http://www.lorenzhart.org/moonsng.htm.

Broadway Rhythm *and* You Are My Lucky Star

Words: Arthur Freed; Music: Nacio Herb Brown

Broadway Melody of 1936 was not a sequel to the original *Broadway Melody* in '29. It had a different storyline and a completely different set of characters. As an odious gossip columnist, Jack Benny kept threatening to expose the relationship between handsome producer Robert Taylor and a society girl. Eleanor Powell, in her second screen appearance, was Taylor's childhood sweetheart. Others in the cast included Buddy Ebsen and his sister, Vilma, Una Merkel, June Knight and Frances Langford.

BROADWAY RHYTHM

Eleanor Powell and Frances Langford introduced this *Variety Hit Parade of a Half-Century* song in the movie musical *Broadway Melody of 1936*, an updated imitation of 1929's *Broadway Melody*. Other films in the series followed in '38 and '40. There was to have been another in '44, but the title was changed to *Broadway Rhythm*. In addition to its use in the '36 film, the song was danced by Eleanor Powell in *Broadway Melody of 1938*, Judy Garland sang it in *Babes in Arms* ('39), Garland again sang it with Tommy Dorsey and his orchestra and danced it with Charles Walters in *Presenting Lily Mars* ('43), Gene Kelly belted out "Gotta dance! Gotta dance! Gotta dance!" in the wonderful dance sequence from *Singin' in the Rain* ('52), the song also appeared in *Bloodhounds of Broadway* ('52) and Andrea McArdle sang an excerpt of the song in *Rainbow* ('78).

The *New York Times* reviewer was particularly taken with Eleanor Powell, calling her the distaff Fred Astaire with the most eloquent feet in show business.

Guy Lombardo and his Royal Canadians helped popularize "Broadway Rhythm" with a popular recording in '35.

The lyrics of the chorus open with "Oh that Broadway Rhythm" stated twice. When the singer hears a certain beat he feels like dancing to "that Broadway rhythm." Read the lyrics at http://www.lyricsvault.net/songs/19160.html.

YOU ARE MY LUCKY STAR

Incredible tap-dancer Eleanor Powell introduced this *Variety Hit Parade of a Half-Century* song in the movie musical *Broadway Melody of 1936*.

The *New York Times* reviewer was particularly impressed with the song "Sing Before Breakfast," which did not become a hit, but he was also enchanted with "My Lucky Star" (also called "You Are My Lucky Star"). He practically ignored the hit "Broadway Rhythm."

"You Are My Lucky Star" was subsequently inserted into at least four other Hollywood films through the early '50s, including Betty Jaynes' performance in *Babes in Arms* ('39) Phil Regan's performance in *Three Little Words* ('50) and Gene Kelly and Debbie Reynolds' famous performance of it in *Singin' in the Rain* ('52). This song was nominated for the American Film Institute's list of the greatest songs ever from an American film, but it did not make the final list.

Eddy Duchin and his orchestra had a very popular recording of "You Are My Lucky Star" in '35. Other popular recordings were issued by the Dorsey Brothers Orchestra, by Louis Armstrong, and by Tommy Dorsey and his orchestra with Eleanor Powell as vocalist. Hear Louis Armstrong's recording of this song at http://www.redhotjazz.com/lao.html.

The song stayed at the No. 1 position on *Your Hit Parade* for three weeks in '35.

The singer claims this person has revealed heaven here on earth to him because "you are my lucky star." Read the lyrics at http://lirama.net/song/15963.

Chasing Shadows

Words: Benny Davis; Music: Abner Silver

Jimmy and Tommy Dorsey formed the most famous brother act of the Swing Era. They left Pennsylvania's coal-mining region for New York City in the mid-'20s and for the next decade were some of the busiest studio musicians. Jimmy was an excellent alto saxophonist, while Tommy was a trombone specialist. In '28, they began recording as the Dorsey Brothers Orchestra, but that only lasted until '35 when Tommy left the group. Both brothers then led successful bands for many years.

The Dorsey Brothers' Orchestra's recorded version of "Chasing Shadows," with a vocal performance by Bob Eberly, was a big hit in the early summer of '35. Other record releases by Henry King and his orchestra, with vocalist Joe Sudy, by Enric Madriquera and his orchestra, with vocalist Bob Bunch, and by Louis Prima and his orchestra, with Prima doing the vocal, helped spread the song's fame.

"Chasing Shadows" spent six weeks, between June 22 and August 3, 1935, as the top song on *Your Hit Parade*.

The first verse of the lyrics starts with a simple, but profound statement: "Life without a romance is a life that's sad." In the chorus, the singer is chasing love dreams hoping he'll eventually find his love. Read the lyrics at http://lirama.net/song/15923.

Cheek to Cheek *and* Top Hat, White Tie and Tails

Words & Music: Irving Berlin

Irving Berlin provided the score for the delightful movie musical *Top Hat*, which starred Fred Astaire and Ginger Rogers. The musical score, one of Berlin's best, included "Cheek to Cheek" and "Top Hat, White Tie and Tails," among others.

RKO decreed that Astaire and Rogers' next film would be almost a carbon copy of the successful formula used in their previous film, *The Gay Divorcee*— the same stars, the same director, and practically the same plot.

In the film, Jerry Travers (Fred Astaire) is working on a musical in London. Jerry awakens Dale Tremont (Ginger Rogers) when he is demonstrating some new dance steps late one night in his producer's hotel room. She goes upstairs to complain, but the two feel an immediate mutual attraction. Complications arise when Dale mistakes Jerry for his producer, Horace, played by Edward Everett Horton.

Astaire, the dancing master, and Rogers, whom many felt was his ideal partner, brought all their joyous talent to *Top Hat*, and Berlin contributed some charming songs.

CHEEK TO CHEEK

Astaire and Rogers introduced the romantic adagio "Cheek to Cheek." It got an Academy Award nomination for Best Song and became one of Berlin's greatest commercial successes. It was No. 1 on *Your Hit Parade* for five weeks in the fall of '35. *Variety* selected it for its *Hit Parade of a Half-Century*. AFI's (American Film Institute) *100 Years ... 100 Songs* (2004) listed "Cheek to Cheek" as one of the greatest songs ever from an American film (No. 15).

Fred Astaire's recording of "Cheek to Cheek" became one of the biggest hits of the decade; his recording of the song with Leo Reisman and his orchestra was inducted into the Grammy Hall of Fame in 2000. Eddy Duchin and Guy Lombardo competed with each other for the runner-up position in popularizing the song; both had very successful recordings of it on the market. Phil Ohman and his orchestra and the Boswell Sisters also had recordings of it that sold well.

Actually Berlin had written "Cheek to Cheek," the longest (64 bars, twice the conventional length) and one of the most complex songs he ever wrote, for a never staged musical called *More Cheers*, which was supposed to be the sequel to *As Thousands Cheer*. The song's rhyme scheme was not complicated, it also used the traditional AABA form, but near the end Berlin stuck in an unusual little section — almost another musical idea that added an extra eight measures.

The singer, Fred Astaire in this instance, believes he's in heaven because he and his girl are "together dancing cheek to cheek." Things like mountain climbing or going fishing aren't nearly as thrilling "as dancing cheek to cheek." Read the lyrics at http://lirama.net/song/15924.

The song was also heard in the following films: *The Valachi Papers* ('72), *The English Patient* ('96), *Any Given Sunday* ('99), *Artificial Intelligence* (2001) and *Mr. Deeds* (2002).

TOP HAT, WHITE TIE AND TAILS

Fred Astaire, fortified with a chorus of gentlemen, introduced "Top Hat, White Tie and Tails" in *Top Hat*. A top hat, white tie, tails and Fred Astaire just seem to go together. Ironically, in Astaire's biography, he revealed that he was not particularly fond of the attire.

Recordings of *"Top Hat..."* by Fred Astaire and by Ray Noble and his orchestra helped spread the song's fame beyond the silver screen. Both recordings were fairly popular. The song peaked at No. 2 on *Your Hit Parade*.

Variety chose the song for its *Hit Parade of a Half-Century*. It was nominated for the American Film Institute's list of the greatest songs ever from an American film, but it did not make the final list.

The singer, Astaire in this case, has gotten an invitation to a formal dance so he is dressing in his "top hat, white tie, and tails." Read the lyrics at http://lirama.net/song/15959.

"Top Hat, White Tie and Tails" also appeared in the movie *Billy Elliot* (2000).

Fred Astaire also had a popular recordings of "Isn't This a Lovely Day (to Be Caught in the Rain?)," "No Strings (I'm Fancy Free)," and "The Piccolino" from *Top Hat*. Read the lyrics of "Isn't This a Lovely Day" at http://lirama.net/song/15936. Read the lyrics of "No Strings" at http://www.sing365.com/music/lyric.nsf/No-Strings-I'm-Fancy-Free-lyrics-Irving-Berlin/A5704B3AAAA8A85 C48256970000EEC63.

East of the Sun (and West of the Moon)

Words & Music: Brooks Bowman

"East of the Sun (and West of the Moon)" was introduced in a Princeton University Triangle Club production entitled *Stags at Bay*.

Tom Coakley and his orchestra, with vocalist Carl Ravazza, recorded a very popular version of "East of the Sun." It was particularly popular during the summer of '35. The song was the top hit on *Your Hit Parade* for two weeks.

The singer and his loved one are going to build their dream-house of love "East of the sun and west of the moon." Read the lyrics at http://lirama.net/song/15925.

Jan Garber and his orchestra popularized "Love and a Dime" also from *Stags at Bay*.

I'll Never Say "Never Again" Again

Words & Music: Harry Woods

"I'll Never Say 'Never Again' Again" was featured in the '47 film *The Fabulous Dorseys*, because the tune was the catalyst that brought an abrupt end to the brothers' joint orchestra and launched both brothers on individually successful careers as bandleaders. The band was playing the song at the Glen Island Casino in New Rochelle, New York. When Tommy started the piece at a tempo that Jimmy thought was a little fast, Jimmy's perhaps too vociferous remark was the last straw of the strained partnership. Tommy glared back at his brother, packed his instrument and walked out. Reconciliation failed and within a year each brother had his own musical aggregation.

Harry Woods' song shared the No. 1 spot on *Your Hit Parade* with "Chasing Shadows" on August 3, 1935. Recordings by Ozzie Nelson and his orchestra and by the Dorsey Brothers' Orchestra helped popularize the song. Ozzie furnished the vocal on his recording, while the trio of Don Mattison, Skeets Herfurt, and Roc Hillman vocalized on the Dorsey disk. Benny Goodman and his orchestra revived it with moderate success in '53.

The lyrics of the chorus open with the title phrase. The singer had said he would never again fall in love, but now "here I am ... head over heels in love again with you." Earlier he had walked away from this romance, but now he's reconsidering. Read the lyrics at http://www.mixed-up.com/lyrics/round/show.html?name=never-say-never.

I'm in the Mood for Love

Words: Dorothy Fields; Music: Jimmy McHugh

Jimmy McHugh and Dorothy Fields are the writers of "I'm in the Mood for Love" and "I Feel a Song Comin' On" for the movie musical *Every Night at Eight*. Frances Langford introduced both songs in the film.

By '65, "I'm in the Mood for Love" had been recorded more than 400 times with a total sale of more than 3 million. The song became one of the most recorded songs of the pre-rock era.

The most popular recording of the song appears to have been by Little Jack Little, and it was very successful in the fall of '35. Recordings by Louis Armstrong, by Frances Langford, and by Leo Reisman and his orchestra helped popularize the song. Billy Eckstine revived it in 1946 with good success. Hear Paul Whiteman's recording of this song at http://www.redhotjazz.com/pwo.html or hear Louis Armstrong's version at http://www.redhotjazz.com/lao.html.

"I'm in the Mood for Love" was the top hit on *Your Hit Parade* for the broadcast of September 21, 1935.

The singer is in a loving mood "simply because you're near me." Read the complete lyrics at http://lirama.net/song/15930.

Variety chose the song for its *Hit Parade of a Half-Century* and its list of *Golden 100* songs.

In a Little Gypsy Tea Room

Words: Edgar Leslie; Music: Joe Burke

Jack Denny and his orchestra introduced "In a Little Gypsy Tea Room." Bob Crosby and his orchestra were one of the first to record the song and their recording turned out to be a big hit. Their disk was particularly popular during the summer of '35. Jan Garber, Louis Prima, and Russ Morgan and their orchestras helped popularize the song with successful recordings.

The song spent two weeks at the top of *Your Hit Parade* (June 15 and July 13; "Chasing Shadows" moved it out of the top spot for three weeks in between).

The first time the singer saw this particular person was "in a little Gypsy tea room." A Gypsy read his tea leaves and told him his heart would be stolen away by someone in the tea room. He was surprised by the prediction, but the dream came true as he gave his heart away "in a little Gypsy tea room." Read the lyrics at http://lirama.net/song/15934.

In the Middle of a Kiss

Words & Music: Sam Coslow

Johnny Downs introduced "In the Middle of a Kiss" in the film *College Scandal*. Wendy Barrie reprised it in the same film. Hal Kemp and his orchestra helped popularize the song with a very popular recording. Kemp's vocalist on the recording was Skinnay Ennis.

The song shared the No. 1 spot on *Your Hit Parade* with "Chasing Shadows" on the July 27, 1935 program.

Isle of Capri

Words: Jimmy Kennedy; Music: Will Grosz

The mid-'30s seem to have a fascination with songs about islands. There's "Isle of Capri," "On Treasure Island," and "My Little Grass Shack in Kealakekua, Hawaii."

"Isle of Capri" originated in England, but it became a big hit in America in '35. England's Ray Noble and his orchestra popularized the tune with a very successful recording. Almost as popular as Noble's disk were ones by Freddy Martin and his orchestra, with vocalist Elmer Feldkamp, and by another British band, Lew Stone and his orchestra. England's top vocalist, Al Bowlly, was featured on both Noble's and Stone's recordings.

The song only managed to get to No. 5 on *Your Hit Parade*, but other sources indicate that it was the top hit in the U.S. at the beginning of the year for several weeks.

Variety included "Isle of Capri" in its *Hit Parade of a Half-Century* representing '34.

The singer found a girl he was interested in beneath an old walnut tree on the "Isle of Capri." However, he soon found out that she "wore a plain golden ring on her finger," so he said goodbye to the "Isle of Capri." Read the lyrics at http://lirama.net/song/15935.

Just One of Those Things

Words & Music: Cole Porter

Two hit songs came from Cole Porter's Broadway musical *Jubilee*. One, "Begin the Beguine" wasn't popularized until '38. The other was "Just One of Those Things," which was introduced by June Knight and Charles Walters in the musical.

Porter wrote the song overnight while the show was in pre–Broadway tryouts in Ohio.

The plot of *Jubilee* deals with the Royal Family of a fictional European country who want to find an excuse to abandon the throne so they can pursue their own dreams. Once they find the excuse, an impending revolution, the former King meets a lovely party-giver; the former Queen chases after a swimmer; the former Prince woos a songstress; and the former Princess wins the attention of a playwright, composer and actor. When the revolutionary threat turns out to be a hoax, the Royal Family must return to power, but they arrange to incorporate their new friends into their regal lives.

Richard Himber and his orchestra, with vocalist Stuart Allen, had a reasonably popular recording of "Just One of Those Things" in '35, and Peggy Lee successfully revived it in '52. Frank Sinatra's recording of the tune has become a classic.

"Just One of Those Things" was sung by Lena Horne in the '42 film version of Porter's Broadway musical *Panama Hattie*, Ginny Simms performed it in Cole Porter's first screen biography, *Night and Day* ('46), Doris Day sang it in *Lullaby of Broadway* ('51), in *The Snows of Kilimanjaro* ('52), Peggy Lee performed it in the '53 version of *The Jazz Singer*, Frank Sinatra crooned it in *Young at Heart* ('55), which starred Sinatra and Doris Day, Maurice Chevalier performed it in the film version of Porter's Broadway musical *Can-Can* ('60), and *At Long Last Love* ('70). Diana Krall sang the song on the soundtrack of Porter's 2004 biopic, *De-Lovely*.

The song describes a debonair man's approach to the end of a romance — "it was just one of those things." There are, after all, other worlds to be conquered. Perhaps that was Cole Porter's jaded, playboy outlook coming out in his lyrics. Read the lyrics at http://www.sing365.com/music/lyric.nsf/Just-One-of-Those-Things-lyrics-Frank-Sinatra/8AF5B5163ECCF2164825691F000ACDBB.

Variety chose "Just One of Those Things" for both their *Hit Parade of a Half-Century* and *Golden 100 Tin Pan Alley Songs* lists.

Let's Dance

Words: Fanny Baldridge; Music: Joseph Bonime & Gregory Stone

The date was August 21, 1935. The Palomar Ballroom in Los Angeles was the last stop on the first road tour for a discouraged new dance band. The clarinetist/leader was making a valiant effort to please the crowd with the routine pop tunes that he had been told were what the people wanted to hear. The apathy on the dance floor was as obvious as the band had experienced on other stops of the tour. It looked like this might be the band's last night anywhere. The leader decided to go down swinging — literally. He decided to feature some swing arrangements during the second set. The band came to life, played with new energy and excitement, and the crowd showed its approval. Suddenly the bandstand was surrounded with youngsters with huge smiles on their faces. That was the beginning of the Swing Era. The bandleader, of course, was Benny Goodman.

In Benny Goodman's book, *The Kingdom of Swing*, he explains that in late September of '34, the National Biscuit Company was looking for three bands, a rhumba band, a sweet orchestra and a hot band, for a program on NBC. Some representatives from the company came to hear Goodman and his band. They got the job as the hot band, but they found out later the sponsors had brought the employees from their office to vote for the band they liked. Goodman and his band won by one vote. The three-hour show ran from December '34 to May '35 on 53 stations. Each of the three bands opened its segment with "Let's Dance," a tune that George Bassman arranged from Bonime and Stone's borrowings from German romantic composer Carl Maria von Weber's *Invitation to the Dance*.

The Goodman band recorded the tune and it became their theme song.

The song was used in Goodman's screen biography, *The Benny Goodman Story* ('56). It was also heard in several other films, including *The Powers Girl* ('42), *The Gang's All Here* ('43), and *Sweet and Low Down* ('44).

Let's Swing It

Words: Charles Tobias & Charles Newman; Music: Murray Mencher

Since swing was at first the providence of the young, not many swing hits made it to the top of the charts immediately. The adults had the buying power; they made the hits; they bought the records.

Lillian Carmen performed "Let's Swing It" in *Earl Carroll's Sketch Book* on Broadway in '35.

This tune was more the exception than the rule. Ray Noble and his orchestra's recording of "Let's Swing It" was popular during the early summer of '35. It peaked at No. 6 on *Your Hit Parade*, but then that program always seemed to be a bit conservative. Even when rock 'n' roll was burning up the *Billboard* chart in '56, *Your Hit Parade* tried to ignore it and hoped it would be just a passing fad.

Life Is a Song

Words: Joe Young; Music: Fred Ahlert

Frank Parker introduced "Life Is a Song (Let's Sing It Together)," but it was Ruth Etting who popularized it with a very successful recording. Freddy Martin and his orchestra also issued a popular recording of the song.

"Life Is a Song" stayed at No. 1 for a couple of weeks on *Your Hit Parade* in the early summer of '35.

The chorus opens with the title phrase: "Life is a song, let's sing it together." The singer, Ruth Etting in this instance, hopes the song will last for a long, long time. There's also a reference in the lyrics to Mendelssohn's famous piano piece "Spring Song." Read the lyrics at http://lirama.net/song/15940.

A Little Bit Independent

Words: Edgar Leslie; Music: Joseph A. Burke

"A Little Bit Independent" entered the *Your Hit Parade* chart in late November of '35. It took five weeks before it hit the top spot on the last broadcast of the year. It remained the number one hit on the first broadcast of '36.

African American pianist, singer, composer Fats Waller had a particularly popular recording of the song. Freddy Martin and his orchestra and Bob Crosby and his orchestra also helped popularize the song with successful recordings.

The person this song sings about is "a little bit independent" in her walk, her talk, in the way she dances, and the way she romances. He says "there's nothing like you in Paris or New York." Read the lyrics at http://lirama.net/song/15941.

Lovely to Look At *and* I Won't Dance

Words: Jimmy McHugh & Dorothy Fields; Music: Jerome Kern

Jerome Kern had written the Broadway version of *Roberta* in '33. The movie version in '35 starred Fred Astaire. For the film, Kern wrote two additional hit songs: "I Won't Dance" and "Lovely to Look At."

The film version plot was slightly adapted to showcase the dancing talents of Fred Astaire and Ginger Rogers, even though they played secondary characters to the stars Irene Dunne and Randolph Scott. Ms. Dunne was a deposed White Russian princess, Stephanie, who has become a partner in a famous Parisian fashion establishment with Roberta. Scott was an American football player, John Kent, who inherits his Aunt Roberta's half of the business when she unexpectedly passes away, also establishing the love interest between Stephanie and John. Astaire played bandleader Huck Haines, the character played by Bob Hope in the original Broadway production, while Ms. Rogers was cast as a phony Polish countess who was Huck's former girlfriend.

LOVELY TO LOOK AT

Irene Dunn introduced "Lovely to Look At" as part of the show's fashion parade finale.

The movie's producers felt that "Lovely to Look At" was not hit material because the refrain was only sixteen measures long and the last four measures were unusually complex and subtle. Kern refused to change a note, however, and his confidence in the song proved to be well founded since it became a huge hit, so much so that the second film version of *Roberta* in '52 was titled *Lovely to Look At*. In the '52 film, Howard Keel and the chorus performed it.

Eddy Duchin and his orchestra had an extremely popular recording of "Lovely to Look At" in the spring of '35. Leo Reisman and his orchestra, with vocalist Phil Dewey, and movie actress Irene Dunne, accompanied by Nat Shilkret's Orchestra also released successful recordings of the song in '35.

Variety included "Lovely to Look At" in its *Hit Parade of a Half-Century*. This song was nominated for the American Film Institute's list of the greatest songs ever from an American film, but did not make the final list. It was nominated for it appearance in the '35 film version of *Roberta*.

The person Irene Dunn was singing about was not only "lovely to look at" but delightful and very kissable. Read the lyrics at http://www.lyricsdepot.com/eddy-duchin/lovely-to-look-at.html.

I WON'T DANCE

Fred Astaire introduced "I Won't Dance" in the film version of *Roberta*. Fred requested that Kern write a high-energy dance number and illustrated a few steps to indicated what kind of dynamic rhythm he had in mind. Evidently Kern understood perfectly, because he produced one of his best rhythmic numbers in "I Won't Dance."

Eddy Duchin and his orchestra recorded "I Won't Dance" on the flip side of "Lovely to Look At," and both songs became big hits for him. Lew Sherwood was Duchin's vocalist on both sides. Other recordings of the number were issued by Johnny Green and his orchestra, with vocalists Marjorie Logan and Jimmy Farrell, by Leo Reisman and his orchestra, again with vocalist Phil Dewey, and by George Hall and his orchestra, with vocalists Loretta Lee and Sonny Schuyler.

The song was used in Kern's screen biography, *Till the Clouds Roll By* ('46), where Van Johnson and Lucille Bremer sang it. It was also used in *Lovely to Look At*, the '52 remake of *Roberta*.

The lyrics begin with "I won't dance, don't ask me" twice. And why won't he dance? Because his feet won't do things that they should do when she's in his arms. There's a reference to 1934's Academy Award winning song when he says the girl is charming and gentle especially when she does "the Continental." He says music leads to romance, because if he holds her in his arms he won't dance. Read the complete lyrics at http://lirama.net/song/15928.

Lullaby of Broadway

Words: Al Dubin; Music: Harry Warren

Harry Warren and Al Dubin continued their string of successful movie musicals after *Forty Second Street* with the score for *Gold Diggers of 1935*. They also wrote the music for six other movie musicals in '35.

Famous choreographer/director Busby Berkeley directed *Gold Diggers of 1935*. His masterpiece, "Lullaby of Broadway," was staged as part of a charity show that was produced at a New England summer resort hotel.

Berkeley shows us a slice of life of a "Broadway baby," a woman of the night whose morals are questionable but whose heart is gold. This baby, played by Wini Shaw, sleeps all day and dances all night with her wealthy man, played by Dick Powell. As the sequence begins, Wini Shaw's face is only a small speck on the otherwise black screen. Her face grows larger during the song. After her face reaches close-up size, her profile turns into the Manhattan skyline. Then more than 150 dancers flood the screen in a frenzied sequence. The number ends in reverse, as we watch Shaw's face recede from close-up to speck to black screen. An audio clip of Wini Shaw singing "Lullaby of Broadway" can be heard at http://www.harrywarrenmusic.com/realfiles/. Dick Powell's version of the song was inducted into the Grammy Hall of Fame in 2005.

With "Cheek to Cheek" and "Lovely to Look At" as competition, "Lullaby of Broadway" won the Oscar as the Best Song from Motion Pictures in '35.

"Lullaby of Broadway" was the No. 2 song on the first broadcast of *Your Hit Parade* on April 20, 1935. After two weeks, it became the top song and stayed there for two weeks.

The Dorsey Brothers Orchestra recorded the most popular version of "Lullaby of Broadway," and their disk was extremely popular in the spring of '35. Several other recordings helped popularize the song, including those by pianist/singer Little Jack Little, by pianist Reginald Foresythe, by Hal Kemp, and by Chick Bullock and their orchestras. Bob Crosby was vocalist on the Dorsey recording, while Bob Allen performed the vocal on Hal Kemp's. Chick Bullock was the vocal soloist on his recording.

The song was also heard in a short medley in *The Jolson Story* (1946), in *Young Man with a Horn* ('50), and in *Lullaby of Broadway* ('51), where the song was staged very much like the original Berkeley staging.

Variety included "Lullaby of Broadway" in its *Hit Parade of a Half-Century*.

The singer invites us to "Come on along and listen to the lullaby of Broadway." Part of that lullaby is the subway train's rumble, and the rattle of the taxi cabs. His Broadway baby doesn't say good night until early in the morning. Read the lyrics and hear a midi musical version at http://www.harrywarren.org/songs/0310a.htm.

My Romance

Words: Lorenz Hart; Music: Richard Rodgers

The last production at the Hippodrome before it was torn down was the Rodgers and Hart musical *Jumbo*, which was called a musical extravaganza, and what a spectacle it was, combining a circus with musical comedy, not unlike the first Hippodrome extravaganza, *A Yankee Circus on Mars*, in 1905. Three Rodgers and Hart classics came from the score: "My Romance," "The Most Beautiful Girl in the World," and "Little Girl Blue."

"My Romance" was a duet espousing a love so great it doesn't need romantic trappings. Donald Novis and Gloira Grafton introduced this *Variety Hit Parade of a Half-Century* selection. Doris Day performed the song in the '62 movie adaptation of *Jumbo*.

Paul Whiteman and his orchestra recorded a reasonably successful version of "My Romance." Whiteman's recording of this song can be heard at http://www.red hotjazz.com/pwo.html.

In the context of the lyrics, the singer's romance doesn't need special trappings like the moon, a blue lagoon, or a castle in Spain. His romance "doesn't need a thing but you." Read the lyrics at http://www.lorenzhart.org/romancesng. htm.

On the Good Ship Lollipop
Words: Sidney Clare; Music: Richard A. Whiting

Shirley Temple, at the age of five, was on the set during the shooting of the movie musical *Stand Up and Cheer*. While the music from the film was being recorded, she began to do a number of dance steps. As she danced, the director of the film, Hamilton McFadden, scribbled a dummy lyric to the tune on the back of an envelope. He asked Shirley to learn the lines immediately and to perform them for him. When she performed the song, everyone was so impressed that she was signed to a contract then and there. She was given a role in *Stand Up and Cheer*, and performed the song "Baby, Take a Bow."

Her first starring role came in 1934's *Bright Eyes*. She introduced "On the Good Ship Lollipop" in the film and it helped make her famous. She performed the song aboard an airplane as some of her adult friends took her for a ride.

According to the verse, Shirley has thrown away her toys and now wants to pilot an "aeroplane." The much more famous chorus sounds more like she is singing about an ocean ship rather than an airship, however the lyrics do mention a "happy landing on a chocolate bar." See the sheet music cover, read the lyrics and hear a sound clip at http://www.geocities.com/Hollywood/Hills/8038/1lolipop.htm.

She was presented a Special Academy Award (a miniature statuette) in recognition of her extraordinary contribution to motion picture entertainment in '34. For four years in a row, she was the top box-office attraction.

AFI's (American Film Institute) *100 Years ... 100 Songs* (2004) named "On the Good Ship Lollipop" one of the greatest songs ever from an American film (No. 69). Shirley also performed the song in *Rebecca of Sunnybrook Farm* ('38) as part of the "Au Revoir" sequence. Dan Dailey and Shari Robinson performed it in *You're My Everything* ('49).

As much as we associate "On the Good Ship Lollipop" with Shirley Temple, it was recordings by Rudy Vallee and by Ted FioRito and his orchestra that were the most successful recorded versions on the market. Today, it's difficult for us to imagine anyone but Shirley Temple performing that song.

On Treasure Island
Words: Edgar Leslie; Music: Joe Burke

Tommy Dorsey and his orchestra recorded what appears to have been the most successful version of "On Treasure Island." However, disks by Little Jack Little, by Bing Crosby, by Joe Moss and his Society Dance Orchestra, with vocalist Dick Robertson, and by jazz great Teddy Wilson's piano solo version were also very popular. Hear Louis Armstrong's recording of this song at http://www. redhotjazz.com/lao.html.

Writers Joe Burke and Edgar Leslie had a very successful '35 with "On Treasure Island," "In a Little Gypsy Tearoom," and "A Little Bit Independent" that became big hit songs.

"On Treasure Island" made it to No. 1 on *Your Hit Parade* for the December 21st broadcast, its only week at the top.

The singer has sailed to "Treasure Island" and when he lands, a smile makes his heart stand still. He had come to the island looking for gold, and he found it "when you gave your golden love to me." Read the lyrics at http:// lirama.net/song/15949.

Paris in the Spring
Words: Mack Gordon; Music: Harry Revel

Mary Ellis and Tullio Carminati introduced the title song from the movie musical *Paris in the Spring*. Ellis and Carminati's characters both intend to commit suicide by jumping off the Eiffel Tower, but instead decide to pretend to have an affair with each other to make their respective spouses jealous.

The song was also interpolated into the '36 Carole Lombard and Fred MacMurray film *The Princess Comes Across*.

"Paris in the Spring" was the top song on *Your Hit Parade* for the August 10th broadcast.

Ray Noble and his orchestra and Freddy Martin and his orchestra both had popular recordings of the song, but Noble's was considerably more popular. Noble's vocalists were the Freshmen.

The song begins with the title phrase followed by hums, then "love is in the air" followed by more hums. This pattern repeats itself several times. This writing technique may have been suggested by "Paradise" (see '32), where the hums allowed the listener to fill in the blanks. During the hums each listener's mind could make up whatever they preferred to think happened in "Paris in the Spring," or when love was in the air. Later the lyric says everyone must fall in love there because "ev'ry beating heart becomes a part of Paris in the Spring." Read the lyrics at http://lirama.net/song/15951.

Red Sails in the Sunset
Words: Jimmy Kennedy; Music: Hugh Williams

An English import, "Red Sails in the Sunset" became a big hit in the U.S. in '35, reportedly selling more than a million copies of sheet music and staying at No. 1 on *Your Hit Parade* for four weeks.

The song was written by the British team of Will Grosz, using the pen name Hugh Williams, and Jimmy Kennedy, who also wrote "Isle of Capri."

The inspiration for the lyrics came about one day in Portstewart, Donegal, Ireland, when Jimmy Kennedy and his artist sister were watching a sunset together. The lovely scene was made all the more beautiful by the sight of a graceful sailboat with a bright red sail. In the lyrics, the singer is hoping that those "red sails in the sunset" will bring her loved one safely home to her. Read the lyrics at http://lirama.net/song/15953.

In the Irish community where the lyrics were originally written, the townspeople have erected a ten-foot tall Fishing Boat sculpture and plaque commemorating the song's origin. The boat mentioned in the lyrics (Kitty of Coleraine) has been restored and put on public display in the town.

Englishman Ray Noble and his orchestra introduced the song. It was then interpolated into the revue *The Provincetown Follies.*

Two extremely popular recordings of the song, one by Bing Crosby, the other by Guy Lombardo and his Royal Canadians, competed with each other to be the biggest hit recording. The British orchestras of Mantovani and Jack Jackson also had successful versions of the song on the market. Louis Armstrong released his version in '36 and it sold well. Hear Armstrong's version at http://www.redhotjazz.com/lao.html. Nat "King" Cole's '51 recording of the song may be best remembered by modern audiences.

Bing Crosby's movie career was so successful in '35 that most of the songs he was recording were the ones he was introducing in his films. Although they included some of the best of his entire career, it also meant that he was not getting to release his version of the non-movie songs that were popular. In November of '35, Bing had a recording session in Los Angeles which produced several non-film releases: "Red Sails in the Sunset," "On Treasure Island," and both sides of his enormously successful Christmas single, "Adeste Fidelis" and "Silent Night." Victor Young and his orchestra were Bing's backing for the session.

Variety recognized "Red Sails in the Sunset" by selecting it for its *Hit Parade of a Half-Century.*

Rhythm Is Our Business

Words: Sammy Cahn; Music: Jimmie Lunceford & Saul Chaplin

Only a few swing hits made it to the top of the charts in '35. The teenagers who were swing crazy didn't have the buying power to make their favorite swing songs hits. "Rhythm Is Our Business" was one of the few swing numbers that was really popular in this first year of the nationwide swing craze.

Jimmie Lunceford and his orchestra had a very successful recording of the song. Lunceford, Chaplin, and Cahn devised the song as a means of introducing the members of the band. Willie Smith was Lunceford's vocalist who sang the introductions. Trumpeter Wingy Manone and his orchestra also had a successful recording of the number.

Your Hit Parade ignored "Rhythm Is Our Business" just like they did "Let's Swing It."

She's a Latin from Manhattan

Words: Al Dubin; Music: Harry Warren

Harry Warren and Al Dubin wrote "She's a Latin from Manhattan" and "About a Quarter to Nine" for the musical motion picture *Go Into Your Dance* ('35). Al Jolson introduced both songs in the film. He also sang both songs for the soundtrack of *The Jolson Story* in '46. He sang "About a Quarter to Nine" again for the soundtrack of *Jolson Sings Again* in '49.

The scene for "She's a Latin from Manhattan" was a nightclub. Jolson playfully exposes Ruby Keeler, the sup-

posed "Latin," as a dancer from Tenth Avenue in Manhattan.

Recordings by Victor Young, Johnny Green and Ozzie Nelson helped popularized the song beyond its film origins. Victor Young's recording of "She's a Latin from Manhattan," with vocalists Hal Burke and the Tune Twisters, was a very big hit for him. An audio clip by Al Jolson of this song can be heard at http://www.harrywarrenmusic.com/realfiles/.

The song's verse begins slowly with the lyrics "Fate sent her to me over the sea from Spain." Later the tempo increases as he questions her Spanish origin. By the chorus, he has determined that "she's a Latin from Manhattan" not Spain or Havana. This girl called Dolores was known as Suzy Donahue when she was in a Broadway chorus. Read the lyrics and hear a midi musical version at http://www.harrywarren.org/songs/0457.htm.

Two other popular songs from *Go Into Your Dance* were "About a Quarter to Nine" popularized by Ozzie Nelson and his orchestra with his wife, Harriet Hilliard as vocalist. Read the lyrics and hear a midi musical version of "About a Quarter to Nine" at http://www.harrywarren.org/songs/0001.htm. Johnny Green and his orchestra popularized "The Little Things You Used to Do" from *Go Into Your Dance.* Read the lyrics and hear a midi musical version of "The Little Things You Used to Do" at http://www.harrywarren.org/songs/0288.htm. At http://www.harrywarrenmusic.com/frameset.html you can see Warren's music manuscript of this song.

Soon *and* It's Easy to Remember

Words: Lorenz Hart; Music: Richard Rodgers

The film *Mississippi* was a story of a young man who was against fighting to the point that he refused to defend his sweetheart's honor. After his humiliation at refusing to fight, he joined a Mississippi riverboat troupe and became known a "The Singing Killer." In a plot twist, the "hero," Bing Crosby, falls in love with his former fiancée's sister and finally redeems his own honor enough to win her family's acceptance. Also in the film were W.C. Fields as the owner of the riverboat and Joan Bennett as Bing's romantic interest.

The film's hit songs were "Soon" and "It's Easy to Remember," both introduced by Crosby.

SOON

"Soon (Maybe Not Tomorrow)" was the bigger success of two hit songs from the movie musical *Mississippi.*

"Soon" was the first No. 1 song on the first broadcast of *Your Hit Parade,* but it was only able to maintain the spot for that one week and quickly faded. After a month and a half, it wasn't among the top fifteen hits.

Bing Crosby's recording of "Soon" with Georgie Stoll's orchestra was very popular in the spring of '35. Will Osborne and his orchestra also had a recording of the song that did reasonably well.

The lyrics say the singer's lonely nights will "Soon" end when two hearts will be blended as one. Read the lyrics at http://www.lorenzhart.org/soonsng.htm.

IT'S EASY TO REMEMBER

Crosby's recording of "It's Easy to Remember" with Georgie Stoll's orchestra, the Rhythmettes and Three Shades was also a big hit. *Your Hit Parade's* chart doesn't mention it, but according to *A Century of Pop Music* it was a top hit for a couple of weeks just prior to "Soon" becoming the No. 1 hit.

"It's Easy to Remember" was interpolated into the motion picture *The Blue Dahlia* ('46).

The lyrics begin by enumerating the things that are "easy to remember, but so hard to forget." Read the lyrics at http://www.lorenzhart.org/easysng.htm.

Guy Lombardo and his Royal Canadians popularized "Down by the River" from the film. Read the lyrics of "Down by the River" at http://www.lorenzhart.org/river.htm.

Star Dust (See 1929; named to Variety's Hit Parade of a Half-Century for 1935)

Summertime, Bess, You Is My Woman, I Got Plenty o' Nuttin' *and* It Ain't Necessarily So

Words: Ira Gershwin & DuBose Heyward; Music: George Gershwin

George Gershwin's last Broadway musical was his crowning achievement in the theater. The music, lyrics, and libretto of *Of Thee I Sing* are predictable musical fare, but *Porgy and Bess* is a giant step beyond. The inspired music, lyrics, and book are as unlike other Gershwin musicals as his "Rhapsody in Blue" is unlike other popular instrumental writings of the time. *Porgy and Bess* is now called an American folk opera, not a musical comedy like *Of Thee I Sing*, but nevertheless several of the songs from the score have become very well known.

Gershwin had been planning to write a musical setting of DuBose Heyward's novel *Porgy* since early in '26. In '27, Heyward and his wife, Dorothy, adapted the novel into a play that the Theatre Guild produced. In '28, a capsule musical version of the play was included in the revue *Blackbirds of 1928*. In the early '30s, the Theatre Guild considered a version of *Porgy* starring Al Jolson with music by Jerome Kern and lyrics by Oscar Hammerstein II. Heyward preferred to wait for Gershwin. Finally, in late '33, the project began and eleven months later the score had been written.

The story concerns the people of Catfish Row in Charleston, South Carolina. Porgy, a cripple beggar, and Bess, who is the woman of a brutal man named Crown, fall in love.

SUMMERTIME

"Summertime" is a beautiful lullaby that is sung by Clara, played by Abbie Mitchell, as the folk opera opens. In the '59 adaptation for the screen, Loulie Jean Norman's voice was dubbed for Dorothy Dandridge (Dandridge's character, Bess, was not the one who sang it in the original production).

Many of Gershwin's friends tried to convince him that such a slow, simple song was not an appropriate opening number. The show's opener needed to be flashy, a chorus or production number. Gershwin was convinced it would work, and, of course, he was right.

In addition to its popularity in connection with *Porgy and Bess*, Bob Crosby's band chose it for the theme song for their group, which is rather surprising since the band was known for their Dixieland jazz numbers. Vocal jazz legend Billie Holiday's recording of the song sold well in '36. Paul Whiteman's recording of "Summertime" can be heard at http://www.redhotjazz.com/pwo.html.

Variety selected "Summertime" for its list of *Golden 100* songs, but surprisingly not in its *Hit Parade of a Half-Century*. AFI's *100 Years ... 100 Songs* (2004) named "Summertime" one of the greatest song from an American film for the '59 film version of *Porgy and Bess*. "Summertime" also appeared in the following films: *American Pop* ('81), *Chocolat* (2000) and *Hart's War* (2002).

The song also became the No. 5 most recorded song of the pre-rock era.

Read the lyrics at http://lirama.net/song/13341.

BESS, YOU IS MY WOMAN

"Bess, You Is My Woman" was sung in the original cast by Porgy and Bess (Todd Duncan and Anne Brown, respectively). In the '59 movie version, Robert McFerrin dubbed the song for Sidney Poitier and Adele Addison for Dorothy Dandridge.

Variety selected "Bess, You Is My Woman" for its *Hit Parade of a Half-Century*.

Read the lyrics at http://www.fortunecity.com/tinpan/newbonham/6/bessyouismy.htm.

I GOT PLENTY O' NUTTIN'

Porgy introduced "I Got Plenty o' Nuttin'." The lyrics express Porgy's contentment with the simple things of life. Read the lyrics at http://www.thepeaches.com/music/frank/IGotPlentyoNuttin.htm.

Leo Reisman and his orchestra had a popular recording of both "I Got Plenty o' Nuttin'" and "It Ain't Necessarily So" in late '35.

Variety selected "I Got Plenty o' Nuttin'" for its *Hit Parade of a Half-Century*.

IT AIN'T NECESSARILY SO

Performed by Sportin' Life, the drug dealer, "It Ain't Necessarily So" takes a skeptical view of several biblical tales. Sportin' Life, played by John Bubbles in the original cast and Sammy Davis, Jr. in the screen version, performs the song in high style during a picnic at Kittiwah Island. Read the lyrics at http://www.lyricsfreak.com/b/bronski-beat/24693.html.

Variety selected "It Ain't Necessarily So" for its *Hit Parade of a Half-Century*.

The *Porgy and Bess Original Cast Album* was inducted into the Grammy Hall of Fame in 1990.

Tell Me That You Love Me

Words: Al Silverman; Music: Cesare A. Bixio

This *Variety Hit Parade of a Half-Century* song came to America from Italy. The original lyrics by Ennio Neri were titled "Parlami d'Amore, Mariu." Frank Parker introduced the song, with English lyrics by Al Silverman, in the United States. It was one of the top ten hits on *Your Hit Parade* in '35, but never made it to the top.

Freddy Martin and his orchestra had the most popular recording of the song in '35.

The English lyrics that most people would remember begin: "Tell me that you love me tonight, fill my heart with endless delight." Read both the Italian and English lyrics by Bixio (the English title was "Speak to Me of Love, Mariu") at http://www.ladyofspain.com/Parlami.html.

Truckin'

Words: Ted Koehler; Music: Rube Bloom

Fats Waller recorded a very popular rendition of "Truckin'." The Mills Blue Rhythm Band also had a version of the song that sold rather well.

Truckin' was a dance step and a "hep" expression, as in "truckin' on down." The dance step is difficult to describe in words, but it had an arm extended, elbow bent and index finger wagging, while the feet shuffled forward and sideways with toes turned out. One source suggested that the feet "sloshed." Read the lyrics at http://lirama.net/song/15960.

Unlike "Rhythm Is Our Business" and "Let's Swing It," *Your Hit Parade* didn't completely ignore "Truckin'." It peaked at No. 8 on their chart. *Variety* indicated it was the top hit in the nation during the late fall of '35 and according to *A Century of Pop Music*, it was one of the year's top ten hits.

What's the Reason (I'm Not Pleasin' You)?

Words: Coy Poe & Jimmie Grier; Music: Truman "Pinky" Tomlin & Earl Hatch

Pinky Tomlin introduced "What's the Reason (I'm Not Pleasing You)?" in the film *Times Square Lady*.

It was Guy Lombardo and his Royal Canadians who had a big hit recording of "What's the Reason?" Jimmy Dorsey and his orchestra also released a popular version of the song. Hear Fats Waller's recording of this song at http://www.redhotjazz.com/rhythm.html.

"What's the Reason?" was No. 1 on *Your Hit Parade* for two weeks in May of '35.

The singer questions why everything he does is wrong. He says when he kisses this girl she doesn't ask for another. Even though he continues to try, he doesn't seem to satisfy her, so he asks, "tell me, what's the reason I'm not pleasin' you?" Read the lyrics at http://www.lyricsdepot.com/guy-lombardo/whats-the-reason-im-not-pleasin-you.html.

When I Grow Too Old to Dream

Words: Oscar Hammerstein II; Music: Sigmund Romberg

This *Variety Hit Parade of a Half-Century* selection is one of Sigmund Romberg's most famous waltzes. He wrote it to Oscar Hammerstein II's lyrics for the movie musical *The Night Is Young*. Evelyn Laye and Ramón Novarro introduced it.

The movie and its music were not particularly well received. The only song that attained hit status was "When I Grow Too Old to Dream." Romberg had written much more interesting music; this song seems to have been dashed off without a lot of thought. Perhaps this is because the pressure to provide songs quickly was far greater in Hollywood than on Broadway, with less regard for worth or quality.

The public liked the song, however, and loved Glen Gray and the Casa Loma Orchestra's recording of it. Kenny Sargent was the vocalist on Gray's recording. Movie operetta star Nelson Eddy also had a recording of the song that sold well. Hear Paul Whiteman's recording of this song at http://www.redhotjazz.com/pwo.html. Bob Lawrence was Whiteman's vocalist on the recording.

The song was also used in the '54 movie musical *Deep in My Heart*, which was Sigmund Romberg's screen biography. Jose Ferrer and Helen Traubel performed it in that film.

"When I Grow Too Old to Dream" peaked at No. 2 on *Your Hit Parade*, but other sources indicate that it was the top hit around the nation during the early summer of '35.

The singer is confident that when he grows "too old to dream" he'll have his love to remember. Her love will always live in his heart. Read the lyrics at http://lirama.net/song/15962.

The sheet music cover and musical score are available at http://levysheetmusic.mse.jhu.edu/otcgi/llscgi60.

Glen Gray and the Casa Loma orchestra popularized the title song from *The Night Is Young*. Paul Whiteman's recording of "The Night Is Young" can be heard at http://www.redhotjazz.com/pwo.html.

You and the Night and the Music

Words: Howard Dietz; Music: Arthur Schwartz

Georges Metaxa and Libby Holman introduced "You and the Night and the Music," a *Variety Hit Parade of a Half-Century* song representing 1934, in the musical *Revenge with Music*. Conrad Thibault popularized it on the radio. Recordings by Libby Holman and by Leo Reisman and his orchestra also helped popularize the song.

The MGM Studio Chorus performed the song in the '53 film adaptation of the Broadway musical *The Band Wagon*.

The singer claims the three ingredients that fill him with flaming desire are "you, and the night, and the music." Read the lyrics at http://lirama.net/song/15964.

You're All I Need

Words: Gus Kahn; Music: Bronislau Kaper & Walter Jurmann

Lorraine Bridges introduced "You're All I Need" in the film *Escapade*.

It was popularized in recordings by Eddy Duchin and his orchestra, with vocalist Lew Sherwood. Their recording helped the song become the No. 1 hit on *Your Hit Parade* for two weeks in August of '35. It shared the top spot with "East of the Sun" for one of those two weeks.

Zing! Went the Strings of My Heart

Words & Music: James F. Hanley

Hal LeRoy and Eunice Healey introduced "Zing! Went the Strings of My Heart," a *Variety Golden 100 Tin Pan Alley Song*, in the revue *Thumbs Up*. Judy Garland sang the song in the movie musical *Listen, Darling* ('38), Hal Derwin, dubbing for Gene Nelson, sang it in *Lullaby of Broadway* ('51), used in the film version of *Thumbs Up* ('43), *That Certain Feeling* ('56), which starred Bob Hope and Eva Marie Saint and Andrea McArdle sang it in *Rainbow* ('78). Judy Garland's performance of the number reportedly helped get her a movie contract at MGM.

The singer's heartstrings went "zing" because a certain guy smiled at her. Read the lyrics at http://lirama.net/song/31646.

Judy Garland's recording of the song in '43 became reasonably popular; otherwise, it never made a big splash on the pop charts.

1936

All My Life

Words: Sidney D. Mitchell; Music: Sam H. Stept

"All My Life" was introduced in the movie musical *Laughing Irish Eyes*, a film starring Phil Regan. The song became a big hit recording for Harlem pianist, singer, composer Fats Waller. Waller's rendition is a light, bright, bubbly treatment of the song.

Ain't Misbehavin', a Broadway revue, celebrated the music Waller wrote and performed during his days in Harlem from the late '20s through the early '40s. The show won the Tony Award for the year's best musical for '78. Waller was elected to the Songwriters' Hall of Fame.

Teddy Wilson and his orchestra, with Ella Fitzgerald as vocalist successfully recorded "All My Life," as did Ted FioRito and his orchestra, with vocalist Stanley Hickman.

The song was revived in the '43 movie musical *Johnny Doughboy*, which starred Jane Withers.

On *Your Hit Parade*, "All My Life" peaked at No. 2 in early June of '36.

The singer, Fats Waller in this case, has been waiting for this particular woman all of his life. The first strain is based on "all my life," while the second is built on "all my love," which he freely gives. The lyrics get a little silly with the line "I'm almost afraid to go ga-ga." The third strain goes back to the "all my life" idea of the first strain. Read the lyrics at http://lirama.net/song/15969.

Alone

Words: Arthur Freed; Music: Nacio Herb Brown

Kitty Carlisle and Allan Jones introduced "Alone" in the Marx Brothers' farce *A Night at the Opera*, a '35 MGM movie musical. Harpo Marx played it later in the same film. Judy Garland sang it in *Andy Hardy Meets a Debutante* ('40) and it was also interpolated into *Born to Sing* ('42).

"Alone" became a big hit recording for Tommy Dorsey and his orchestra in early '36. Others who released successful recordings of the song included Hal Kemp and Al Donohue and their orchestras. Dorsey's vocalist on "Alone" was Cliff Weston; Barry McKinley was the singer on Donohue's version.

The singer is "Alone with a heart meant for you," but he seemingly doesn't know exactly whom his heart is meant for ("who ever you are"). Read the lyrics at http://lirama. net/song/15970.

"Alone" spent five weeks at No. 1 on *Your Hit Parade*, and appeared on the program sixteen times between December 28, 1935 and April 11, 1936.

Variety included "Alone" in its *Hit Parade of a Half-Century* representing '35.

Hear a midi musical version of "Alone" at http://www. whyaduck.com/sounds/midi.htm.

A Beautiful Lady in Blue

Words: Sam M. Lewis; Music: J. Fred Coots

Operatic tenor Jan Peerce introduced "A Beautiful Lady in Blue" in '36 over the radio on the Chevrolet Hour.

Jan Garber and his orchestra had a very popular recording of the song. Ray Noble and his orchestra also helped popularize the song with a moderately successful recording. Noble's singer during this time was Al Bowlly. The California Ramblers' recording of "A Beautiful Lady in Blue" can be heard at http://www.redhotjazz.com/caramblers.html.

According to *Your Hit Parade*'s song survey, it peaked at No. 6, but other sources, like *Variety* and *A Century of Pop Music*, indicate that it was the top hit in the nation in late February and early March of '36.

The singer met the "beautiful lady in blue," she kissed him and fled. She thought he was someone else, but to him it was a once in a lifetime moment "with a beautiful lady in blue." Read the lyrics at http://ntl.matrix.com. br/pfilho/html/lyrics/b/beautiful_lady_in_blue.txt.

Did I Remember?

Words: Harold Adamson; Music: Walter Donaldson

An Academy Award nominee in '36, "Did I Remember?" was featured in *Suzy*, which starred Jean Harlow, Cary Grant and Franchot Tone. Virginia Verrill's voice was dubbed into the soundtrack for Harlow's. Cary Grant reprised in a rare attempt at singing for him. Grant's novel attempt at singing was included in *That's Entertainment* ('74), illustrating how the Hollywood studios sometimes forced performers who were more actor than singer to sing. Actually Grant's performance was charming and more than adequate for the scene in the film. He may not have been a "singer," but at least he sang for himself, unlike Jean Harlow.

Harlow was the cinema sex pot of the period, similar to Marilyn Monroe in the future. She wasn't a great singer, so almost all of her vocals were dubbed.

Shep Fields and his Rippling Rhythm Orchestra, with vocalist Charles Chester, recorded an extremely popular rendition of "Did I Remember?" Tommy Dorsey and his orchestra, with singer Edythe Wright, also had a popular version of the song on the market.

The song was No. 1 on *Your Hit Parade* for six weeks.

The singer asks if she has remembered to tell you "I adore you ... I'm lost without you ... and pray forevermore you are mine." Read the lyrics at http://lirama.net/song/15973.

Empty Saddles

Words: J. Keirn Brennan; Music: Billy Hill

1936 was a great year for writer Billy Hill. Bing Crosby introduced his "Empty Saddles" in the movie musical *Rhythm on the Range*. His "Glory of Love," "Lights Out," and "In the Chapel in the Moonlight" all became No. 1 hits on *Your Hit Parade*. "Empty Saddles" only rose to No. 8 and appeared on the program three weeks. Crosby's recording of the song was reasonably popular.

Variety selected "Empty Saddles" for its *Hit Parade of a Half-Century*.

The lyrics tell about a cowboy who is left alone with "Empty saddles in the old corral." He asks if the ghost of the cowboys of the past are "roundin' up the dogies" or are they "on the trail of buffalo?" Read the lyrics at http://lirama.net/song/15975.

The public enjoyed cowboy films and cowboy songs, so Hollywood turned them out. Even stars that had little western inclination sang western songs in films. *Rhythm on the Range* was the first of two westerns starring Crosby. The other was *Stagecoach* ('69).

Crosby introduced another western song in the same film, "I'm an Old Cowhand" (see below).

Variety called the public's apparent enchantment with western songs "hillbilly mania."

Bing Crosby also successfully recorded "I Can't Escape from You" from the soundtrack of *Rhythm on the Range* with Jimmy Dorsey and his orchestra.

The Glory of Love
Words & Music: Billy Hill

This Billy Hill creation was revived in *Guess Who's Coming to Dinner* ('67), where it was featured throughout the film and was sung during the opening titles by a chorus and by Jacqueline Fontaine as a cabaret singer, and in *Pennies from Heaven* ('81), where it was a huge production number, à la Busby Berkeley. Lew Stone and his Band's recording of the song was featured on the soundtrack.

Billy Hill was a famous writer of several western-flavored popular songs particularly during the thirties. His first big hit was "The Last Round-Up;" others include "Wagon Wheels," "Empty Saddles," and "In the Chapel in the Moonlight."

Benny Goodman and his orchestra had a enormously popular recording of "The Glory of Love." Helen Ward was Goodman's vocal soloist on the disk.

"The Glory of Love" made fourteen appearances on *Your Hit Parade*, but could only stay on top for one week (July 4, 1936).

Bette Midler sang "The Glory of Love" in the movie *Beaches* ('88).

Billy Hill's lyrics tell us in love we've got to be willing to give and take and allow our hearts to be broken. As long as lovers have each other they can survive, because "That's the story of, that's the glory of love." Read the lyrics at http://lirama.net/song/15977.

Goody-Goody
Words: Johnny Mercer; Music: Matty Malneck

"Goody-Goody" is a Johnny Mercer and Matt Malneck song that Benny Goodman and his orchestra popularized in '36. Malneck composed several songs during the '30s, mostly with Johnny Mercer as lyricist. After he and Mercer left Paul Whiteman, he led a successful band in the '30s and '40s.

The "King of Swing," clarinetist Benny Goodman's first big hit recording was "Moon Glow" in '34. Their recording of "Blue Moon" was successful, but not a monster hit, in '35. Their next big hit recordings were "It's Been So Long" and "Goody-Goody" in early '36. Both sides of the disk were big hits, although "Goody-Goody" was the larger of the two. Within a few months, Goodman struck paydirt again with his band's recording of "The Glory of Love" (see above). Before the year was out, his versions of "These Foolish Things Remind Me of You," and "You Turned the Tables on Me" were also big hits.

Goodman's female vocalist in '36 was Helen Ward, a singer with a lovely voice as well as an intense rhythmic sense. She was not particularly fond of "Goody-Goody" at first. As a matter of fact, she pleaded with Benny not to make her perform the song, but Goodman's judgment proved to be correct; it became one of her biggest hits with the band. She particularly objected to the song's lyrics which seem to gloat over another person's heartbreak—even if it was a former boyfriend. "I sang it straight,"

Helen Ward said, as she recalled how she used to sing these vindictive lyrics. "I never gimmicked anything; Benny didn't allow me to do that."

The song's writers, Johnny Mercer and Matt Malneck, were still with Paul Whiteman's band (Mercer was vocalist, Malneck played violin). Between sets at the Biltmore Hotel, they often sat around writing songs. Mercer was a friend of Goodman's and played some of his creations for him. The first one Goodman recorded was "The Dixieland Band." Next came "Goody-Goody," which became such a hit the writers were signed to a contract to write for the movies.

Besides Goodman's recording, releases by Freddy Martin and his orchestra and Bob Crosby and his orchestra helped popularize the song.

It was the No. 1 hit on *Your Hit Parade* for four weeks from late March of '36. It spent a total of a dozen weeks on *Your Hit Parade*'s chart.

"Goody-Goody" appeared in Goodman's screen biography, *The Benny Goodman Story* ('56).

The singer seems spitefully pleased. The girl he's singing had her heart broken just as she had broken his. He concludes the chorus with "Hooray and hallelujah! You had it comin' to ya ... And I hope you're satisfied you rascal you." Read the lyrics at http://lirama.net/song/17019.

I Can't Get Started with You
Words: Ira Gershwin; Music: Vernon Duke

Bob Hope sang this song to try to break down Eve Arden's resistance in a scene from the *Ziegfeld Follies of 1936*. Hope is confident that his performance of this song was largely responsible for him landing a film contract.

The singer explains that he has done almost anything anyone could want to do in life, including flying around the world and havin tea with Clark Gable, but he's downhearted because he "can't get started with you." Read the lyrics at http://lirama.net/song/13400.

Hal Kemp and his orchestra, with a vocal performance by Skinnay Ennis, popularized the song in '36, and Bunny Berigan and his orchestra revived it successfully in '38. Berigan was vocalist on his famous disk, which was inducted into the Grammy Hall of Fame in 1975.

"I Can't Get Started with You" became one of the most recorded songs of the pre-rock era.

I'll Sing You a Thousand Love Songs
Words: Al Dubin; Music: Harry Warren

Cain and Mabel was chosen for Marion Davies, whose fading career William Randolph Hurst, her lover, was desperately trying to revitalize by coercing Warner Bros. to hire Clark Gable from MGM as her co-star. Harry Warren and Al Dubin, the supreme movie musical score writers, were hired to furnish the songs. Despite Hurst's best efforts, the film wasn't particularly successful.

However, "I'll Sing You a Thousand Love Songs" from the film's score became a hit song. Bob Page introduced the song in the film. Recordings by both Eddy Duchin and his orchestra and Tempo King and his Kings of Tempo were very popular. Jimmy Newell was Duchin's vocalist, while King was the featured vocalist on all his recordings.

"I'll Sing You a Thousand Love Songs" was the top hit on *Your Hit Parade* for the December 5, 1936 broadcast. It made eleven appearances on the program.

Read the lyrics and hear a midi musical version at http://www.harrywarren.org/songs/0217.htm.

I'm an Old Cowhand

Words & Music: Johnny Mercer

Between movie assignments, Johnny Mercer and his wife took a trip that included crossing Texas. They saw lots of guys wearing spurs and ten-gallon hats and driving cars, not cattle. That struck Mercer's funny bone, so he decided to try to put it into a song.

Bing Crosby performed this *Variety Hit Parade of a Half-Century* song in *Rhythm on the Range* (also see "Empty Saddles" above). His recording with Jimmy Dorsey's Orchestra further popularized the song. Frankie Trumbauer and his orchestra's recording of "I'm an Old Cowhand" is available at http://www.redhotjazz.com/fto.html.

The song is definitely tongue-in-cheek, because even though Bing's character's "legs ain't bowed and his cheeks ain't tanned" and he's never seen a cow or roped a steer, he's "an old cowhand from the Rio Grande." Read the lyrics at http://lirama.net/song/15983.

"I'm an Old Cowhand" peaked at No. 9 on *Your Hit Parade* and made six appearances on their chart. According to another reliable source, it climbed to the No. 2 hit in the country early in '36.

Roy Rogers revived "I'm an Old Cowhand" in *The King of the Cowboys* ('43).

I'm Putting All My Eggs in One Basket

Words & Music: Irving Berlin

This Irving Berlin song was introduced by Fred Astaire in the movie musical *Follow the Fleet* in '36. In the film, Fred played an ex-dancer turned sailor; Ginger Rogers was his former partner, now singing for her supper in a San Francisco dance-hall. They meet up at a dance contest and join forces to put on a fund-raising show for the restoration of a schooner. The setting allowed Fred to dress more casually than his usual top hat, white tie, and tails. Fred introduced "I'm Putting All My Eggs in One Basket" at the piano, then it was danced by both he and Ginger in another of their competitive routines.

Astaire's recording of "I'm Putting All My Eggs in One Basket" was very popular in the spring of '36. Other recordings that helped popularize the song were issued by Jan Garber and his orchestra and Guy Lombardo and his Royal Canadians. Louis Armstrong's recording of this song can be heard at http://www.redhotjazz.com/lao.html.

The song peaked at No. 2 on *Your Hit Parade* and spent nine weeks on the survey.

The singer, Fred Astaire in this case, is "putting all his eggs in one basket" betting everything on this love. He's giving all his love to one person and heaven help him if this girl doesn't return his love. Read the lyrics at http://lirama.net/song/15984.

Other songs from the soundtrack of *Follow the Fleet* that proved to be popular with the public include "I'd Rather Lead a Band," "Let Yourself Go, "We Saw the Sea" and "Let's Face the Music and Dance" which were all popularized by Fred Astaire in recordings. Ozzie Nelson and his orchestra popularized "But Where Are You?" from the film.

I've Got You Under My Skin

Words & Music: Cole Porter

Virginia Bruce introduced this Academy Award nominee in the movie musical *Born to Dance*. Even though the singer knows that the "affair never will go so well," she can't stop seeing her loved one because "I've got you under my skin." Read the lyrics at http://www.lyricsfreak.com/f/frank-sinatra/55638.html.

Cole Porter uses key words to paint the perfect picture he wants, for example, in the phrase "But each time I do, just the thought of you makes me stop." And he puts a rest immediately following the word "stop," so the singer emphasizes it.

Ray Noble and his orchestra, and Hal Kemp and his orchestra both had popular recordings of "I've Got You Under My Skin" that were popular in '36. Stan Freberg did a comic version of the song in '51 that almost made the Top Ten.

"I've Got You Under My Skin" peaked at No. 3 on *Your Hit Parade* in early '37, and made eight appearances on the program between December 12, 1936 and the end of January of '37.

The song was selected by *Variety* for its *Hit Parade of a Half-Century* and as a *Golden 100 Tin Pan Alley Song*. "I've Got You Under My Skin" became one of the most recorded songs of the pre-rock era and was nominated for the American Film Institute's list of greatest songs ever from an American film, but was not on the final list.

Frank Sinatra's '56 recording of "I've Got You Under My Skin" was inducted into the Grammy Hall of Fame in 1998.

"I've Got You Under My Skin" was sung by Ginny Simms in Porter's screen biography, *Night and Day* ('46), while soprano Marina Koshetz performed the song in the '48 movie musical *Luxury Liner*. The song also appeared in *What Women Want* (2003) and *Freaky Friday* (2003).

In the Chapel in the Moonlight

Words & Music: Billy Hill

The famous songsmith Billy Hill wrote this song, which was a big hit recording for Shep Fields and his Rippling Rhythm. Richard Himber and his orchestra also had a popular recording of the song in '36. Mal Hallet and his orchestra, with vocalist Jerry Perkins, and Ruth Etting released successful recordings of it in '37. Kitty Kalen revived it very successfully in '54. Her recording peaked at No. 4 on *Billboard's* chart. The Four Knights' version also did moderately well in '54. During the rock era, it was revived by the Bachelors in '65 and by Dean Martin in '67, both with moderate success.

This is a song of a broken romance, a subject matter like many early country songs. The singer dreams about walking down the aisle for a wedding "in the chapel in the moonlight." Read the lyrics at http://lirama.net/song/15987.

According to *Your Hit Parade*, the song peaked at No. 5 in '54, but was a No. 1 hit for three weeks in late '36 and early '37. *Billboard* listed Kitty Kallen's recording of the song as the No. 28 hit of the year for '54.

Is It True What They Say About Dixie?

Words: Irving Caesar & Sammy Lerner; Music: Gerald Marks

Rudy Vallee and Al Jolson helped popularize this *Variety Hit Parade of a Half-Century* song over radio. Jimmy Dorsey and his orchestra recorded a particularly popular rendition of it in '36. Ozzie Nelson and his orchestra and Willie Bryant and his orchestra helped popularize the song with successful recordings. Both Ozzie and Willie were the vocalists on their versions.

It was *Your Hit Parade*'s top song for five weeks during '36. It appeared on the program a total of fourteen times.

"Does the sun really shine all the time?" it asks; in other words, are all the nice things that one hears about the South really true? In some ways, however, it isn't terribly flattering of the region. For example, it asks if the inhabitants sit around "eating 'possum all the time." Read the lyrics at http://www.songlyrics4u.com/jimmy-dorsey-orchestra/is-it-true-what-they-say-about-dixie.html.

"Is It True What They Say About Dixie?" was performed by Iris Adrian and Robin Raymond in the '53 movie musical *His Butler's Sister* and by Al Jolson in *Jolson Sings Again* ('49).

It's a Sin to Tell a Lie
Words & Music: Billy Mayhew

Kate Smith introduced Billy Mayhew's song on her radio show. Fats Waller had such a big hit recording of it that the song was featured in the Broadway revue *Ain't Misbehavin'*, which saluted Waller and the music he wrote and/or popularized. His recording was particularly popular during the summer of '36. Hear Waller's recording at http://www.redhotjazz.com/rhythm.html. Victor Young and his orchestra, with vocalist Dick Robertson, also helped spread the song's fame with a successful recording. Somethin' Smith and the Redheads took the song to No. 7 on *Billboard's* chart in '55.

"It's a Sin to Tell a Lie" peaked at No. 5 on *Your Hit Parade*. It made sixteen appearances on the program.

The lyrics warn that we should "be sure it's true when you say 'I love you'," because when those words are said when they weren't meant "it's a sin to tell a lie." Read the lyrics at http://lirama.net/song/15988.

Variety selected this song for its *Hit Parade of a Half-Century* for '36.

It's Been So Long
Words: Harold Adamson; Music: Walter Donaldson

Benny Goodman and his orchestra had such a big hit recording of "It's Been So Long" in '36 that it was featured in Goodman's screen biography, *The Benny Goodman Story* ('56). The song had originated in the Academy Award winning film *The Great Ziegfeld*.

Freddy Martin and his orchestra and Bunny Berigan and his orchestra also released successful versions of the song. Helen Ward was Goodman's vocalist on his hit recording of the song.

Most swing bands played lots of pop tunes as well as original material and special arrangements of nostalgic favorites. Making a pop tune sound like a swing number was challenging for both bands and arrangers. David Rose, who later wrote "Holiday for Strings," wrote Goodman's swing arrangement of "It's Been So Long."

Walter Donaldson's tune and Harold Adamson's words make a perfect setting for Helen Ward's appealing voice as Goodman's vocalist on the recording.

"It's Been So Long" and "Goody-Goody" (see above) were on the same single and both sides were very popular with the public.

The song peaked at No. 2 on *Your Hit Parade* (March 28, 1936), and appeared a dozen times on the hit survey.

According to *A Century of Pop Music*, it was the top hit in the nation for a couple of weeks in April of '36.

The chorus lyrics open with "'cause it's been so long since I held you tight when we said good night." The singer has been in a daze for several days because they said goodbye. The Second World War is several years away, but the lyrics sound like something servicemen or others who have been forced to be away from home would say when they return. Read the lyrics at http://lirama.net/song/15989.

Lights Out (Close Your Eyes and Dream of Me)
Words & Music: Billy Hill

This tune by western song writer Billy Hill was popularized by Eddy Duchin and his orchestra in a very popular recording. Victor Young and his orchestra's version was also popular during '36. Lew Sherwood was Duchin's vocal soloist on their recording, while Dick Robertson was Young's soloist.

"Lights Out" began its climb to the number one position on *Your Hit Parade* on the first broadcast of '36 as the No. 13 hit. Nine weeks later it reach the No. 1 spot. The next week it was replaced by "Alone," but regained the top position the next week. It spent a total of sixteen weeks on *Your Hit Parade*'s chart.

"Lights Out" sounds like an expression familiar to soldiers. The singer and his loved one have "reached the hour of parting," so he asks for a tender kiss and asks her to dream of him. Read the lyrics at http://lirama.net/song/15992.

Lost
Words: Johnny Mercer & Macy O. Teetor; Music: Phil Ohman

"Lost" entered *Your Hit Parade*'s chart as the No. 13 hit on the March 21, 1936 broadcast. Five weeks later, it assumed the No. 1 position, which it held for three straight weeks. It was replaced as No. 1 on the May 16th broadcast by "Melody from the Sky" ("Lost" was the No. 2 hit that week), and by "You" on the May 23rd broadcast (it was No. 3), before it regained the top spot for the week of May 30th. It remained on the chart for the month of June, then disappeared.

The sheet music cover says the song was "introduced and featured by Phil Ohman's Music at the Café Trocadero, Hollywood."

Guy Lombardo and his Royal Canadians, Jan Garber and his orchestra and Hal Kemp and his orchestra helped popularize "Lost" with successful recordings. All three groups had popular recording of the song on the market.

A Melody from the Sky
Words: Sidney D. Mitchell; Music: Louis Alter

"A Melody from the Sky" was introduced by Fuzzy Knight (along with Henry Fonda whistling a few bars) in the film *The Trail of the Lonesome Pine* and was nominated for the Oscar for Best Song from films in '36.

The song was popularized by several bands including those of Jan Garber, Eddy Duchin and Bunny Berigan.

The song appeared on *Your Hit Parade* fourteen weeks between April and July of '36. It was No. 1 for only one week: the May 16th broadcast.

The basic idea of the chorus lyrics can be summed up with the first (also the last) couple of lines: "Love is everywhere, it's music fills the air." Read the lyrics at http://lirama.net/song/15995.

Moon Over Miami

Words: Edgar Leslie; Music: Joe Burke

"Moon Over Miami" was introduced by Ted FioRito and his orchestra and it became the theme song for Dean Hudson and his orchestra. Recordings by Eddy Duchin and his orchestra, by Jan Garber and his orchestra, with vocalist Lee Bennett, by Art Karle and his orchestra, with vocalist Chick Bullock, and by one of the Boswell Sisters, Connee, helped popularize the song. Duchin's disk, with a vocal performance by Lew Sherwood, was particularly popular early in '36.

This *Variety Hit Parade of a Half-Century* selection was the top hit on *Your Hit Parade* for one week and stayed in the top ten for more than two months. It reached the top spot for the February 1, 1936 broadcast.

The singer is asking the "moon over Miami" to "shine on my love and me." He says the moon knows they are waiting for a little love and a little kiss. Read the lyrics at http://lirama.net/song/15996.

A '41 movie musical that starred Betty Grable, Don Ameche and Robert Cummings was titled *Moon Over Miami*, but it only used the song during the film's titles and introduction.

The Music Goes 'Round and Around

Words & Music: Ed Farley, Mike Riley & Red Hodgson

"The Music Goes 'Round and Around" became the big novelty hit of the winter of 1935–36. This syncopated music lesson seems to fit the twenties' flapper mentality more than the stark reality of the post-depression era. However, the originators, Mike Riley and Eddie Farley, were famous for their flair for comedy.

At the turn of the century, this type of number was called a "nut song," but as the nation learned to take popular music more seriously, they began to be termed "novelty songs." The type seems to appear in songs of every generation and the thirties were no exception with songs like "Goofus," "A-Tisket, A-Tasket," "Flat Foot Floogee," "Three Little Fishies," "The Hut-Sut Song," "Inka Dinka Doo," and of course, "The Music Goes 'Round and Around."

One day trombonist Mike Riley arrived at the Onyx Club on 52nd Street in New York City with an old, rather battered bass trumpet. Supposedly an inebriated club patron inquired how the funny-looking horn worked and Riley replied: "Well, you blow through here ... The music goes 'round and 'round and it comes out here." Trumpeter, songwriter Red Hodgson, using the chord progression of "Dinah" helped Farley and Riley complete the song. It was introduced, recorded, and popularized by Farley and Riley and their Onyx Club Boys. Their rendition of this song about the mechanics of a brass instrument brought them nationwide popularity. Their recording of the song for the newly formed Decca Records was the first release to show a profit for the company.

The Ritz Brothers performed the song in the '36 film *Sing, Baby, Sing* (see "When Did You Leave Heaven?" below), while Riley and Farley performed it in *The Music*

Goes 'Round ('36). It was also included in *Trocadero* ('44), Ilona Massey and a male chorus sang it in *Holiday in Mexico* ('46), and Danny Kaye and six-year-old Susan Gordon performed it in *The Five Pennies* '50).

It was the nation's top hit on *Your Hit Parade* for three weeks in early '36. *Variety* included the song in its *Hit Parade of a Half-Century* representing '35.

Tommy Dorsey and his orchestra and Riley and Farley competed with each other for the most popular recorded version of "The Music Goes 'Round and Around." Both versions were extremely popular with the public. Hal Kemp and his orchestra and Frank Froeba and his Swing Band, with vocalist Jack Purvis, also had successful recordings of the song on the market. Riley and Farley's version was revived in '38 with good success. Dorsey's recording featured vocalist Edythe Wright, plus some dialogue between Wright and Dorsey. Louis Armstrong's version of the song can be heard at http://www.redhotjazz.com/lao.html.

The lyrics to this novelty song are almost a music lesson in playing a valve instrument like a trumpet: you "blow thru here; the music goes 'round and around" through the tubing "and it comes out here." It goes on to supposedly tell us what happens when we push the first valve, the middle one or the other one. What comes out? Jazz! Read the lyrics at http://lirama.net/song/15997.

Pennies from Heaven

Words: Johnny Burke; Music: Arthur Johnston

Bing Crosby introduced this nominee for the Academy Award for Best Song in the movie musical *Pennies from Heaven,* the story of a wanderer, a disputed legacy and a haunted house. Crosby's character in the film dreamed of becoming a lute-strumming gondolier in Venice. Before he could pursue that dream, he was falsely accused of smuggling and was sentenced to prison for a short period. While in prison, a death-row murderer asked Crosby to look after his family: a ten-year-old daughter and his father. Most of the film revolves around Crosby's attempts to help them.

"Pennies from Heaven" turned out to be one of Bing's biggest records. The song entered *Your Hit Parade*'s chart in mid–November of '36 and made it to No. 1 on the December 19th broadcast. The next two weeks it was replaced at the top by "In the Chapel in the Moonlight," but it returned to the top for the January 9th broadcast. Once again, it was replaced for a week by Cole Porter's "It's De-Lovely," only to return again to the top for the last two programs of January. It was No. 1 for a total of four weeks at the end of '36 and the beginning of '37.

The philosophy expressed in the song seems like Depression era lyrics that were so prevalent during the first three or four years of the '30s. By 1936–37, the country had pulled out of the darkest days of the Depression, so it is a little surprising that this song struck such a responsive chord with the public. The lyrics contend we "must have showers" in our lives if we "want the things we love," but those showers contain "Pennies from Heaven." The Depression left an indelible impression on everyone who lived through it for the rest of their lives, so perhaps it isn't so strange that people found the lyrics reassuring. They could definitely identify; they had lived through the showers and were looking forward to receiving their "pennies from heaven." Read the lyrics at http://lirama.net/song/15998.

The song was interpolated into the '53 film *Cruisin'*

Down the River, From Here to Eternity ('54) and Bing performed it again in *Pepe* ('60). Comedian Steve Martin starred in the '81 film of the same title, but it had no relation to the '36 film. Martin's *Pennies from Heaven* was a salute to the movie musicals of the '30s.

Variety selected "Pennies from Heaven" as a *Golden 100 Tin Pan Alley Song*, but was not among its selections of its *Hit Parade of a Half-Century*. The song became one of the most recorded songs of the pre-rock era. This song was nominated for the American Film Institute's list of the greatest songs ever from an American film, but did not make the final list.

Others songs from the movie score that found enough favor with the public to chart include "Let's Call a Heart a Heart," and "So Do I," popularized by Bing Crosby, plus "One, Two, Button Your Shoe," popularized by Shep Fields.

Say "Si, Si"

Words: Al Stillman and Francia Luban; Music: Ernesto Lecuona

This *Variety Hit Parade of a Half-Century* selection for '36 originated in Cuba with the Spanish title "Para Vigo Me Voy." The original lyrics were by Francia Luban.

The song was introduced in the United States by Xavier Cugat and his orchestra, with Lina Romay doing the vocal. The Andrews Sisters had a best-selling record of "Say 'Si, Si'" in '40, and Gene Autry sang it in the '40 film *Carolina Moon*. According to *Your Hit Parade*, it never made the top ten.

The singer explains how to say "Yes" in Spanish, French, Dutch, and Russian. She would be happy if he would just say "Yes" in any language. Read the lyrics at http://lyrics playground.com/alpha/songs/s/saysisi.shtml.

Sing, Sing, Sing (see 1938)

Take My Heart

Words: Joe Young; Music: Fred H. Ahlert

"Take My Heart" started its chart climb on the June 27th broadcast as the No. 10 hit. After stops at No. 7 and No. 4 in the following weeks, it grabbed the top spot on *Your Hit Parade* for the July 18th broadcast and stayed there for two weeks. It remained on the chart for the rest of July and August and for one week in September before it fell off for good.

Eddy Duchin and his orchestra, with vocalist Jerry Cooper, had a very popular recording of "Take My Heart." Nat Brandywynne and his Stork Club Orchestra, with Buddy Clark as vocalist, also had a popular recording of the song.

There's a Small Hotel

Words: Lorenz Hart; Music: Richard Rodgers

Originally intended for *Jumbo* but dropped from that production, "There's a Small Hotel" resurfaced in *On Your Toes*. Rodgers and Hart's song is a dream of a perfect honeymoon. It was introduced in *On Your Toes* by Ray Bolger and Doris Carson.

On Your Toes was revived on Broadway in '82 starring Leslie Caron.

Hal Kemp and his orchestra recorded a very popular version of "There's a Small Hotel." Paul Whiteman and his orchestra also released a reasonably popular recording of the song. Whiteman's recording of this Rodgers and Hart song can be heard at http://www.redhotjazz.com/pwo. html.

The song peaked at No. 4 on *Your Hit Parade*, but according to other reliable information, it was the nation's biggest hit song for a couple of weeks in July of '36.

Betty Garret sang the song in Rodgers and Hart's film biography, *Words and Music* ('48), while Frank Sinatra sang it in the film version of *Pal Joey* ('57).

The singer wants to go to this small hotel where "there's a bridal suite." They would not be near other people — "who wants people?" Read the lyrics at http://www.lorenzhart.org/hotel.htm.

The title song from the musical was popularized in a successful recording by Ruby Newman. Paul Whiteman's recording of "On Your Toes" can be heard at http://www.redhotjazz.com/pwo.html.

These Foolish Things Remind Me of You

Words: Holt Marvell (pseudonym for Eric Mashwitz); Music: Jack Strachey & Harry Link

Dorothy Dickson introduced this bittersweet nostalgic song comes from the musical *Spread It Abroad*. It was also included in the Olsen and Johnson movie musical *Ghost Catchers* ('44).

Lyricist Eric Maschwitz used the same type of complex rhyme scheme that Cole Porter used in "You're the Top" to enumerate the fleeting memories of young love. Some of the things on the list that call forth memories include "a cigarette that bears a lipstick's traces, An airline ticket to romantic places." All these things and more remind the singer of his love. Read the lyrics at http://lirama.net/song/16004.

The song first appeared on *Your Hit Parade* on the June 27, 1936 broadcast as the No. 9 hit. Five weeks later, it rose to the top spot where it remained for a couple of weeks.

Benny Goodman and his orchestra's recording of the song was particularly popular. Teddy Wilson and his orchestra, with vocalist Billie Holiday, Nat Brandywynne and his Stork Club Orchestra, with vocalist Buddy Clark, pianist Carroll Gibbons and his orchestra, and Joe Sanders and his orchestra also released recordings of the song that sold very well. Red Ingle and the Natural Seven recorded a "hick" version called "Them Durn Fool Things" in '47.

"These Foolish Things" is a *Variety Golden 100 Tin Pan Alley Song* and *Hit Parade of a Half-Century* number. "These Foolish Things" became one of the most recorded songs of the pre-rock era.

Until the Real Thing Comes Along

Words: Sammy Cahn, Mann Holiner & L.E. Freeman; Music: Saul Chaplin & Alberta Nichols

Andy Kirk and his Clouds of Joy had a very popular recording of "Until the Real Thing Comes Along" in late summer of '36. The song became Kirk's theme song. Fats Waller, Jan Garber, and Erskine Hawkins also released recordings of the song that were popular with the public. The Ink Spots revived it in '41 with moderate success. Fats Waller and his Rhythm's recording of this song can be heard at http://www.redhotjazz.com/rhythm.html.

"Until the Real Thing Comes Along" peaked at No. 2

according to *Your Hit Parade*. It appeared on the show eleven broadcasts.

The singer says he'd work or be a slave for this girl; he'd be a beggar or anything else for her. Then he says, "If that isn't love, it will have to do until the real thing comes along." Read the lyrics at http://lirama.net/song/16006.

The Way You Look Tonight *and* A Fine Romance

Words: Dorothy Fields; Music: Jerome Kern

In *Swing Time*, a chronic gambler, Lucky, played by Fred Astaire, is tricked by his magic and dance act into missing his wedding to Margaret, played by Betty Furness. Margaret's incensed father orders Lucky to make $25,000 before he will be allowed to marry her. He goes to New York where he runs into a dancing instructor, Penny, played by Ginger Rogers. She and Lucky form a successful dance partnership, but their romance is thwarted, until the end of the film, by his old attachment to Margaret and hers to a band leader.

THE WAY YOU LOOK TONIGHT

The best remembered song from the movie musical *Swing Time* is the '36 Oscar winner "The Way You Look Tonight." It was the top song on *Your Hit Parade* for a month and a half during the year.

Even though "The Way You Look Tonight" is a love song and as such has become a standard, it was conceived as a comical song. Fred Astaire was kidding Ginger Rogers about her appearance while she was shampooing her hair. Read the lyrics at http://www.lyrics.ly/lyrics.php/Michael+Buble/Lyrics/The+Way+You+Look+Tonight.

In the film, Astaire played a dancer who loved gambling too much. When he was late for his wedding, he was banished until he can raise $25,000 to prove he is no longer an irresponsible gambler. During this banishment, he meets Ginger Rogers and they, of course, dance several dazzling musical numbers. *Swing Time* produced several noteworthy songs including, of course, "The Way You Look Tonight," "A Fine Romance" and "Pick Yourself Up."

Fred Astaire's recording of "The Way You Look Tonight" was extremely popular in the Fall of '36; his recording was inducted into the Grammy Hall of Fame in 1998. Recordings by Guy Lombardo and his Royal Canadians and by Billie Holiday with Teddy Wilson and his orchestra helped popularize the song. Benny Goodman and his orchestra revived it with moderate success in '42.

Variety included this song in its *Hit Parade of a Half-Century* and AFI named it as the No. 43 greatest song from an American film on its *100 Years ... 100 Songs* (2004) list. The song also appeared in the movies *My Best Friend's Wedding* ('97), *Catch Me If You Can* (2002) and *What a Girl Wants* (2003).

"The Way You Look Tonight" became one of the most recorded songs of the pre-rock era.

A FINE ROMANCE

Kern and Fields wrote "A Fine Romance" for Fred Astaire and Ginger Rogers to perform in the movie musical *Swing Time*. Subtitled "A Sarcastic Love Song," it ridicules a romance without kisses and he tells her she's "as cold as yesterday's mashed potatoes." Read the lyrics at http://www.lyricsdepot.com/fred-astaire/a-fine-romance.html.

Rogers first sang this clever song to Astaire during a snowstorm, complaining about his seeming lack of romanticism. He sings his answer.

Astaire's recording of "A Fine Romance" was also very popular in the fall of '36. Recordings by Billie Holiday, Henry King and his orchestra, with vocalist Joe Sudy, and Guy Lombardo and his Royal Canadians also helped popularize the song.

"A Fine Romance" peaked at No. 3 on *Your Hit Parade* and appeared on the program eight times.

"A Fine Romance" was nominated for the American Film Institute's list of the greatest songs ever from American films, but did not make the final list.

Other songs from the *Swing Time* soundtrack that were successfully recorded include "Bojangles of Harlem," "Never Gonna Dance" and "Pick Yourself Up" all popularized by Fred Astarie, plus "Waltz in Swingtime," which was popularized by Johnny Green.

When Did You Leave Heaven? *and* You Turned the Tables on Me

Words & Music: Various

In the movie musical *Sing, Baby, Sing*, nightclub singer Joan Warren's agent, Nicky, puts her into situations designed to advance her career. Alice Faye played Joan Warren, while Gregory Ratoff was her agent, Nicky. In a brief appearance, Tony Martin played Tony Renaldo, an unknown singer who receives his big break on a radio broadcast.

WHEN DID YOU LEAVE HEAVEN?

Tony Martin introduced this Oscar nominated song in the movie musical *Sing, Baby, Sing*. Walter Bullock wrote the words, while Richard Whiting composed the music. The song made the top of *Your Hit Parade* for a couple of weeks. It started its ascent on the September 12th broadcast as the No. 10 hit. After three more weeks among the top ten, it claimed the top spot on the October 10th broadcast. It totaled a dozen appearances on the show.

Alice Faye starred in *Sing, Baby, Sing* as an unknown singer who gets her big break on a radio broadcast. Tony Martin played opposite Ms. Faye and introduced "When Did You Leave Heaven?"

In a major surprise development soon after the filming of *Sing, Baby, Sing*, Tony Martin and Alice Faye were married.

The melody and lyrics to "When Did You Leave Heaven?" seem naive and sentimental by today's standards for songs, but their saccharine sweetness did not turn off the listeners of the mid-'30s. Read the lyrics at http://www.lyricsvault.net/songs/18278.html.

Tony Martin's rendition, his first record for Decca, doesn't sound quite as "mushy" as does the vocal by Carmen Lombardo in Guy Lombardo and his Royal Canadians' version. Lombardo's recording features three hallmarks of Guy Lombardo's band: Lebert Lombardo's muted trumpet, the smooth saxophone section and Carmen Lombardo's overly sweet vocals.

Lombardo's was the most popular version of the song on the market, but Ben Bernie and his orchestra and Henry Allen and his orchestra also contributed to the song's popularity with successful recorded releases.

The film's title song was also a popular recording by Ruby Newman.

YOU TURNED THE TABLES ON ME

Alice Faye introduced "You Turned the Tables on Me" in the movie *Sing, Baby, Sing*. Sidney D. Mitchell wrote the words, while Louis Alter composed the music.

When singer Helen Ward joined Benny Goodman and his band she had just turned 18 but she had experience performing with four different bands and had performed on her own radio show. She was a striking brunette, but when she sang, it was apparent that Goodman had hired her for more than looks. The direct, no-nonsense style which Goodman insisted on from her was ideal for a tune like "You Turned the Tables on Me." In '36, Helen disappointed a lot of her fans by retiring, temporarily, to get married.

The Goodman version of the song was the work of famous black arranger Fletcher Henderson. The arrangement shows off not only the vocalist but also the beautiful blend of saxes in the ensemble, heightened here and there by the clarinet on the melody.

According to *Your Hit Parade*, "You Turned the Tables on Me" peaked at No. 3, but according to other reliable information, it was the nation's top hit for a couple of weeks in November of '36.

ASCAP periodically rewarded unusually creative songs with special awards; this song received such an award for '36.

In the verse the singer confesses he was once the apple of this person's eye, but he always looked the other way. The chorus opens with the tables turned because now he's falling for her. The singer admits he got what was coming to him, "just like the sting of a bee, you turned the tables on me." Read the lyrics at http://webfitz.com/lyrics/index.php?option=com_webfitzlyrics&Itemid=27&func=fullview&lyricsid=5054.

When I'm with You

Words: Mack Gordon; Music: Harry Revel

Shirley Temple introduced "When I'm with You" in the movie musical *Poor Little Rich Girl*. The film was basically a reworking of a 1917 Mary Pickford film about a youngster who teams with two vaudeville performers (Alice Faye and Jack Haley) and becomes a successful radio star. It just so happens that her sponsor is a rival soap company of her father's. Tony Martin also sang "When I'm with You," even though he didn't receive billing. Shirley also performed the song in *Rebecca of Sunnybrook Farm* ('38) in a medley of past hits that also included "On the Good Ship Lollipop" and "Animal Crackers."

"When I'm with You" appeared on *Your Hit Parade* fourteen times between its first appearance in July and mid–October of '36. It claimed the No. 1 spot for two weeks beginning with the August 15th broadcast.

Hal Kemp and his orchestra, with a vocal performance by Skinnay Ennis, had the most popular recorded version of "When I'm with You," but Ray Noble and his orchestra's version was also successful.

When the singer is with his girl every street he walks on becomes a lover's lane. He can see the sun, even though they're out in the rain. Furthermore, "the world is all in rhyme, lovely one, when I'm with you." Read the lyrics at http://ntl.matrix.com.br/pfilho/html/lyrics/w/when_im_with_you1.txt.

You

Words: Harold Adamson; Music: Walter Donaldson

The Ziegfeld Brides and Grooms introduced "You" in 1936's Best Picture Oscar winner, *The Great Ziegfeld*.

"You (Gee but You're Wonderful)" was popularized in recordings by Tommy Dorsey and his orchestra, by Jimmy Dorsey and his orchestra, and by Freddy Martin and his orchestra. Tommy Dorsey's version, with vocalist Edythe Wright, was the most popular one in '36, but brother Jimmy's was a fairly close second. Bob Eberly was Jimmy's vocalist on their disk. Sammy Kaye revived it with a moderately successful recording in '52.

"You" managed a dozen appearances on *Your Hit Parade*, and made it to No. 1 for one week (the May 23rd broadcast).

You are wonderful, lovely and "you completely satisfy." He wants to write a song about "you." Read the lyrics (along with guitar chords) at http://www.theguitarguy.com/you.htm.

1937

The Big Apple

Words: Buddy Bernier; Music: Bob Emmerich

Tommy Dorsey and his Clambake Seven, with alto Edythe Wright as vocalist, popularized "The Big Apple," a song that gives instructions for a dance that "ten can do as easily as two." It was a modified square dance that came out of the Carolinas. After Edythe Wright's vocal, Tommy plays a typically inventive trombone solo. Then we hear a conversation between Tommy and Edythe concerning what this dance is. Several pre–1930 dances are mentioned.

The song didn't make the *Your Hit Parade* survey of hits, which is not uncommon for some of the more lively swing hits. But according to Joel Whitburn's *A Century of Pop Music*, it was the top hit in the nation for a couple of weeks in September of '37.

Other recordings that helped popularize "The Big Apple" were issued by Clyde Lucas and his California Dons and by Hod Williams and his orchestra.

Bob White (Whatcha Gonna Swing Tonight?)

Words: Johnny Mercer; Music: Bernie Hanighen

"Bob White (Whatcha Gonna Swing Tonight?)" was popularized in a duet recording by Bing Crosby and Connee Boswell. Mildred Bailey's version also helped the song become better known around the nation. Benny Goodman also released his rendition that featured vocalist Martha Tilton in her very first appearance on a Goodman record.

Connee Boswell, one of the famed Boswell Sisters, was one of the most popular female vocalists of the period. Her duet with Bing Crosby was accompanied by John Scott Trotter's Orchestra.

According to *Your Hit Parade*, "Bob White" peaked at No. 4 in early '38, but Joel Whitburn's *A Century of Pop Music* indicates that it was the nation's top hit for one week in December of '37.

The singer has been talking to the whippoorwill and the mockingbird about Mister Bob White's "corny trill." Even the owl thinks his lullaby notes are foul. The singer encourages the Bob White to swing it. . Read the lyrics at http://lirama.net/song/16018.

Boo-Hoo!

Words & Music: Carmen Lombardo, John Jacob Loeb & Ed Heyman

A Chicago newspaper columnist is credited with coining the description of the sound of Guy Lombardo's Royal Canadians as "The Sweetest Music This Side of Heaven" back in the '20s. It must have been an apt description; it followed the band through more than fifty years of playing. Over the decades, their sound and style hardly wavered as Guy stuck to his basic philosophy that what the public wanted was good melodies, cleanly played at a danceable tempo. Guy was always the recognized leader among the Lombardo brothers, so, rightfully, he was the leader of the orchestra. It was his business sense, his organizational skills, his ability to administrate, and his sixth sense of what the public wanted to hear that contributed to much of the band's success.

Behind the scenes, however, his brothers played important roles, like Carmen, the saxophone-playing, singing brother, who was the band's musical director, and a talented songwriter as well.

In the early '30s, Carmen wrote a catchy little melody that he tried, unsuccessfully, to promote under several titles including "Cherie;" then to celebrate the end of Prohibition, he rewrote it as "Let's Drink." A year later, he next changed it to "Gay Paree." Finally, prompted by a suggestion from lyricist Ed Heyman, he named the song "Boo-Hoo!" John Jacob Loeb got co-writing credit for suggesting a few musical changes. It was introduced by the Royal Canadians at the Hotel Roosevelt in New York City and it quickly began to catch on.

The Royal Canadians' version of "Boo-Hoo!" is typical of the style of the group on most of its recordings: wheezing saxes, muted brass, very little from the rhythm section and a vocal trio led by Carmen's vibrato (almost tremolo) vocal. It was an easily recognizable sound, one that the radio listening audience could recognize without being announced by an M.C.

Mal Hallet and his orchestra, with vocalist Jerry Perkins, also had a popular version of "Boo-Hoo!" on the market. Fats Waller and his Rhythm's recording of "Boo-Hoo!" can be heard at http://www.redhotjazz.com/rhythm.html.

"Boo-Hoo!" entered the Your Hit Parade survey as the No. 4 hit for the week of March 20th. After a week at the No. 2 slot, it grabbed the No. 1 position and held on for six consecutive weeks. Only "Once in a While," at seven weeks, had more weeks at No. 1 during '37 on Your Hit Parade.

The singer's girl has him crying over her. But the lyrics, at least in some instances, sound childish, like the phrase "I'll tell my mama on you." The chorus ends spitefully with "Someday you'll feel like I do and you'll be Boo-hoo-hoo-in' too." Read the lyrics at http://www.songlyrics4u.com/guy-lombardo/boo-hoo.html.

Carelessly

Words: Charles & Nick Kenny; Music: Norman Ellis

"Carelessly" was a big hit recording for Billie Holiday performing with Teddy Wilson and his orchestra. She was one of the country's all-time great jazz vocalists. The '72 film Lady Sings the Blues, which starred Diana Ross, was roughly based on Billie Holiday's life story, but isn't considered very truthful.

"Carelessly" became the nation's top hit on Your Hit Parade's May 2nd broadcast when it replaced "September in the Rain." It had a two-week run at the top.

The chorus lyrics indicate that the singer's loved one gave her heart to him "carelessly" and the singer broke her heart just as "carelessly" by saying goodbye. Read the lyrics at http://lirama.net/song/13362.

The Dipsy Doodle

Words & Music: Larry Clinton

Larry Clinton was an arranger at the time he came up with this tune. He was hanging out at the Onyx Club, a jazz club on 52nd Street in New York City, where the back of the menus were printed with blank music scores. One evening Clinton wrote the tune on a menu. It wasn't until baseball season rolled around that he came up with the lyrics.

Clinton was a baseball fanatic and he got the idea for this song from New York Giants left-handed pitcher Carl Hubbell. Hubbell had a screwball pitch that had been dubbed the "dipsy doo" for the crazy way it dipped over the plate and befuddled the batters.

Clinton had written the song for Tommy Dorsey. Dorsey made Clinton so well known that he was able to start a band of his own. Then Clinton's band further popularized the song by using it as their theme song. Russ Morgan and his orchestra also released a popular version of the tune. Tommy Dorsey's recording was released in '43 and did moderately well. Honky-tonk pianist Johnny Maddox and the Rhythmasters revived in with decent success in '53.

Every era has its silly songs, and the mid-'30s are no different, with songs like "The Music Goes 'Round and Around" ("whoa-ho-ho-ho-ho-ho and it comes out here"); "The Flat Foot Floogee ("with a floy floy"), "Three Little Fishies" ("Down in the meddy, in a itty bitty poo"), "Mairzy Doats ("dozy doats and liddle lamzy divey"), "The Hut-Sut Song ("Hut-sut rawlson on the rillerah"), plus "The Dipsy Doodle."

These lyrics may be slightly more literate than some of the other novelty hits of the era, however they don't make much sense, but perhaps that's the point. "The Dipsy Doodle" makes us say some pretty crazy things "like rhythm got I and hot am I, That's the way the dipsy doodle works!" Read the lyrics at http://lirama.net/song/16021.

"The Dipsy Doodle" was particularly popular from the latter part of November through December of '37.

Gone with the Wind

Words: Herb Magidson; Music: Allie Wrubel

Hoarce Heidt and his orchestra, with vocalist Larry Cotton, had a particularly popular recording of "Gone with the Wind." Their recording was popular during the summer of '37. Guy Lombardo and his Royal Canadians and Claude Thornhill and his orchestra also released recordings of the song that did rather well. "Gone with the Wind" peaked at No. 5 on Your Hit Parade.

Gone with the Wind, the famous Civil War epic film, was not made until '39, so this popular song has nothing to do with the movie. The book may have suggested the title to the lyric writer Herb Magidson.

The singer's romance has been blown away. His love had burned brightly like a flame, but has now become "an empty smoke dream that has gone, gone with the wind." Read the lyrics at http://lirama.net/song/16026.

Goodnight, My Love
Words: Mack Gordon; Music: Harry Revel

America's dimpled darling, Shirley Temple, introduced "Goodnight, My Love" in the movie musical *Stowaway*. As the orphaned daughter of murdered Chinese missionaries, she stows away aboard a luxury cruise ship. Alice Faye, as the wife of the ship's owner, and Robert Young, also sing the song during the film. It became one of Temple's biggest hits.

Several recordings helped popularize the song, but Benny Goodman's version was the vastly more popular one. Shep Fields, Hal Kemp and Art Kassel and their orchestras also released successful recordings of the tune. Goodman's disk featured the famous Ella Fitzgerald as vocalist. It was also the first hit recording with Harry James on trumpet.

"Goodnight, My Love" entered the *Your Hit Parade* survey on the January 23, 1937 broadcast as the No. 2 hit. The next week it fell to No. 6 before it vaulted into the No. 1 spot for the February 6th broadcast. After two weeks at No. 1, "With Plenty of Money and You" replaced it. However, it regained the No. 1 position the next week and had another two week run at the top. It garnered four weeks at No. 1 and two weeks at No. 2 among its ten appearances on the program.

"Goodnight, My Love" is a sweet love song. The lovers' time together is ending and they hope to meet tomorrow. The singer sings, "Sleep tight, my love, good night, my love, remember that you're mine, sweetheart." Some other parts of the words sound more like they fit the child Shirley Temple, like "Good night, my love, your mommy is kneeling beside you." Read the lyrics at http://lirama.net/song/40457.

It Looks Like Rain in Cherry Blossom Lane
Words & Music: Joe Burke & Edgar Leslie

Guy Lombardo and his Royal Canadians introduced and popularized "It Looks Like Rain in Cherry Blossom Lane." This time it was Lebert Lombardo's vocal that was featured on their recording. Lebert was the band's trumpet soloist and occasional vocalist. The brothers often worked together in choosing the repertoire. It was Lebert who picked "It Looks Like Rain..." and his faith in the tune was vindicated when it became a big hit.

The song made thirteen appearances on *Your Hit Parade*. Of the thirteen, six weeks were spent at the top of the survey (five weeks in July and one week in August). Only "Once in a While," with seven weeks, collected more weeks at No. 1 during the year (Lombardo's "Boo-Hoo!" also garnered six weeks at No. 1).

The reason "it looks like rain in Cherry Blossom Lane" is the loved one's smile is not there and her "golden voice no longer fills the air." Read the lyrics at http://lirama. net/song/16036.

It's De-Lovely
Words & Music: Cole Porter

Cole Porter wrote this tongue-in-cheek chronicle of a young couple's progression from courtship to marriage and parenthood for the '36 musical *Red, Hot and Blue!* Porter's follow-up to *Anything Goes* starred Ethel Merman as a wealthy widow, Bob Hope as her lawyer and boyfriend, and Jimmy Durante as captain of a prison polo team. Durante was released from prison to help Hope and Merman promote a national lottery, but the Supreme Court ruled the lottery was unconstitutional on the grounds that it might actually benefit the country's economy. The show's most famous song was "It's De-Lovely."

Mr. Porter has given two versions of the song's origins: on one of Porter's frequent world tours, while in Java with Monty Woolley and Moss Hart, they were enjoying an exotic fruit, the mangosteen. Mr. Hart said: "It's delightful!" To which Mr. Porter responded: "It's delicious." And Mr. Woolley proclaimed: "It's de-lovely!" On another occasion, Porter claimed to have written it on a trip to Rio de Janeiro. Porter, his wife and Monty Woolley were admiring the landscape as their ship approached the harbor. Porter began with "It's delightful!" His wife followed with "It's delicious!" And Woolley, in a happy state from a night of whiskey, exclaimed, "It's dee-lovely!" Woolley's slightly inebriated exclamation gave Porter the idea for the song.

Porter wrote several clever "de" words in the lyrics, like delectable, delirious, dilemma, delimit, deluxe, divine, and of course, de-lovely. Read the lyrics at http://www. poplyrics.net/waiguo/pop/robbiewilliams/121.htm.

"It's De-Lovely" was a big hit recording for Eddy Duchin and his orchestra. The song's jaunty, danceable beat was the type of music favored by Eddy Duchin, a charming pianist whose fancy keyboard technique and romantic appeal made him the leader of one of the most successful sweet bands of the '30s. Duchin gives this perennial Porter favorite a vigorous keyboard workout, backed neatly by his own orchestra and vocalist Jerry Cooper.

"It's De-Lovely" entered *Your Hit Parade*'s survey on November 28th as the No. 7 hit (this was the first week that only seven hits were listed). After three more weeks, it spent three weeks at No. 2 before assuming the No. 1 spot on the January 16th broadcast.

"It's De-Lovely" was performed by Donald O'Connor and Mitzi Gaynor in 1956's film version of *Anything Goes*. It was also used in the '62 and '87 Broadway revivals of *Anything Goes*, and was featured in 1975's Burt Reynolds-Cybill Shepherd film *At Long Last Love*.

A 2004 movie biography of Cole Porter was titled *De-Lovely*. More than 20 songs Porter wrote during his decades as one of Broadway and Hollywood's most prolific contributors are woven into *De-Lovely*. Robbie Williams performed the song on the film's soundtrack.

Marie
Words & Music: Irving Berlin

This Irving Berlin classic was introduced as a waltz in an early sound film *My Awakening* ('28), which had a music score, but no dialogue. The song was the first Berlin song to appear in a movie. After its premiere, Rudy Valle popularized "Marie" over radio. The most popular recordings of the time were by Rudy Vallee, Nat Shilkret and the Victor Orchestra, and Franklyn Baur.

The Tommy Dorsey band was touring in '36, when they played an African American theater in Philadelphia. The house band was Doc Wheeler's Sunset Royal Orchestra, an all black band that played an arrangement of "Marie." The Dorsey band liked the song and the arrangement, so Tommy traded several arrangements for their version of "Marie." In early '37 Dorsey and his band recorded "Marie" and that recording became the orchestra's first major recording success. In Dorsey's unique and catchy rendition, the bandsmen sang a patter chorus behind the melody (example of their patter: "livin' in a great big way" and almost shouting "Mama!" just before a flashy trumpet solo). The Dorsey version was featured in Tommy and Jimmy Dorsey's screen biography, *The Fabulous Dorseys*, in '47.

The Four Tunes revived "Marie" again in '54.

In the chorus, the singer tells Marie when the dawn breaks she'll awaken with an aching heart. Then she'll cry as she recalls a very tender kiss. The chorus ends with a question: "Will you surrender to me, Marie?" Read the lyrics at http://lirama.net/song/16040.

A trio performed the song in the '54 movie musical *There's No Business Like Show Business*.

Variety listed "Marie" on its *Golden 100 Tin Pan Alley Songs* list, but not one of its *Hit Parade of a Half-Century*.

The Merry-Go-Round Broke Down

Words & Music: Dave Franklin & Cliff Friend

Very popular recordings by both Shep Fields and by Russ Morgan and their orchestras helped push "The Merry-Go-Round Broke Down" up the charts in the early summer of '37. Bob Goday was Fields' vocalist, while Jimmy Lewis was Russ Morgan's singer. Eddy Duchin and his orchestra's version, with vocalist Lew Sherwood, was almost as popular as Fields' and Morgan's. Jimmie Lunceford and his orchestra, with a vocal performance by Sy Oliver, and soft-voiced vocalist Dick Robertson also issued successful recordings of the song.

The song peaked at No. 2 on *Your Hit Parade* and stayed there for three consecutive weeks in July. *A Century of Pop Music* claims "The Merry-Go-Round Broke Down" was No. 1 for a four weeks, Russ Morgan's and Shep Fields' versions were both on top for a couple of weeks each.

The lyrics to this novelty song are not terribly sophisticated. As they rode the merry-go-round the singer would steal a kiss. When "the merry-go-round broke down" they both sighed. They had found love for the cost of the ride ("love for only a dime"). Read the lyrics at http://ntl.matrix.com.br/pfilho/html/lyrics/m/merry_go_round_broken_down.txt.

The Moon Got in My Eyes *and* Smarty

Words & Music: Various

Bing Crosby sang "The Moon Got in My Eyes," by Johnny Burke and Arthur Johnston and "Smarty" by Burton Lane and Ralph Freed, in the movie musical *Double or Nothing*. Crosby, Martha Raye, Andy Devine, and William Frawley were given the chance to make a million dollars by an eccentric philanthropist who wanted to prove to his skeptical brother that most people are honest and enterprising. Bing performed five songs in the film.

THE MOON GOT IN MY EYES

Bing's recording was the most popular version on the market and it was particularly successful in the fall of '37. Shep Fields and his Rippling Rhythm also had a successful recording of the song.

According to *Your Hit Parade*, it peaked at No. 3 in mid–October, but according to Joel Whitburn's *A Century of Pop Music*, it was the nation's biggest hit for four weeks in September and October.

Crosby sang that he was taken by surprise by this girl, Mary Carlisle in the film. He thinks he "should have seen right through" her, "but the moon got in" his eyes. He now believes the ancient adage that those who love are blind. Read the lyrics at http://lirama.net/song/16042.

SMARTY

Bing also sang Burton Lane and Ralph Freed's "Smarty" in the movie musical *Double or Nothing*.

Fats Waller's recording of "(You Know It All) Smarty" was more popular with the public than Bing's. Waller was always a great performer of novelty songs and this one fit his gift.

The song never charted on *Your Hit Parade*, but it may well have been the nation's biggest hit for a couple of weeks in July and early August of '37, according to *Billboard*.

The singer, a male in this case, is trying to prove to "Smarty" that she's not quite as clever as she thinks she is. He tells her she "could learn to be twice as smart" if she had a heart. Read the lyrics at http://lyricsplayground.com/alpha/songs/s/smarty.shtml.

Another song from *Double or Nothing* that was popularized in a successful recording by Bing Crosby was "It's the Natural Thing to Do." Read the lyrics at http://lyrics.-rare-lyrics.com/B/Bing-Crosby/It's-The-Natural-Thing-To-Do.html.

The One Rose (That's Left in My Heart)

Words & Music: Del Lyon & Lani McIntire

Variety selected "The One Rose (That's Left in My Heart)" for its *Hit Parade of a Half-Century*

Larry Clinton and his orchestra, Bing Crosby and Art Kassel and his orchestra each had equally popular recordings of "The One Rose (That's Left in My Heart)" in '37.

The singer is lonesome and blue for the "one rose that's left in my heart." They have parted but he dreams of their reconciliation. Read the lyrics at http://www.sing365.com/music/lyric.nsf/The-One-Rose-That's-Left-In-My-Heart-lyrics-Johnny-Cash/3708411C71D78F4648256DEA000A5888.

Once in a While

Words: Bud Green; Music: Michael Edwards

Trombonist-bandleader Tommy Dorsey introduced this tune as an instrumental entitled "Dancing with You." It had been written by violinist Michael Edwards. Lyricist Bud Green was hired to fit the melody with suitable lyrics, which, of course, he did with outstanding success. Dorsey and his orchestra then recorded the number with Jack Leonard doing the vocal, and it became a big hit. When it began to catch the public's fancy, almost every record company issued their versions. *Metronome* picked Tommy Dorsey's recording of this song as one of the "best sides" of '37. George Simon, *Metronome*'s record reviewer, called it "the band's prettiest side." Hear Louis Armstrong's recording of "Once in a While" at http://www.redhotjazz.com/lao.html.

"Once in a While" has lovely, reflective lyrics. Lyricist Bud Green illustrates how effectively he can write for a variety of circumstances. He is responsible for such diverse lyrics as those for "The Flat Foot Floogee" and "Sentimental Journey." In "Once in a While," the singer asks this particular girl to try to think of him now and then, even though she may be in love with someone else. He says he can be contented with his memories, knowing that he is thought of "Once in a While." Read the lyrics at http://lirama.net/song/16046.

The song was one of the biggest hit songs of '37 and it was quite a hit again when Harry James revived it in the '50 movie musical *I'll Get By*. It was also used in 1977's *New York, New York*.

It was No. 1 on *Your Hit Parade* for seven consecutive weeks. It entered the survey on November 20th as the No. 3 hit and moved to the No. 1 slot the next week. It had more weeks at No. 1 than any other song during '37.

Remember Me?

Words: Al Dubin; Music: Harry Warren

Kenny Baker introduced "Remember Me?" in *Mr. Dodd Takes the Air*. The song won a nomination for the Oscar for Best Song from films in '37, but lost to "Sweet Leilani" from *Waikiki Wedding*. "Remember Me?" was revived in *Never Say Goodbye* ('46), where Errol Flynn and Eleanor Powell sang it and a chorus performed it for the main title sequence.

The most popular recordings of "Remember Me?" were those of Bing Crosby and Teddy Wilson. An audio clip of Crosby's recording can be heard at http://www.harrywarrenmusic.com/realfiles/.

"Remember Me?" entered *Your Hit Parade*'s chart as the No. 7 hit on the broadcast of September 25th. Five weeks later, it had advanced to the No. 1 position for the November 6th program.

The singer asks this girl if she remembers the September afternoon when they got married and went on their honeymoon. He tells her he's still paying the bills on their small cottage. He also reminds her that the child on her knee looks like him. He asks, "Remember me?" Read the lyrics and hear a midi musical version at http://www.harrywarren.org/songs/0428.htm.

A Sailboat in the Moonlight

Words & Music: Carmen Lombardo & John Jacob Loeb

"A Sailboat in the Moonlight" is one of the many songs by Carmen Lombardo that were tailor-made both for the Royal Canadians' style and for Carmen's distinctive singing style. This is the second John Jacob Loeb/Carmen Lombardo collaboration to make the top of *Your Hit Parade* in '37 (see "Boo-Hoo!" above), and one of several hits recorded and popularized by the Royal Canadians this year.

Guy has always been quick to give his brother Carmen a lot of the credit for the band's success. He felt that Carmen's vibrato (instrumentally and vocally) added a "lot of soul" to the group. Other bands tried to imitate the Lombardo sound, but were not very successful and they certainly did not succeed with the number of hits that Lombardo and his band produced.

"A Sailboat in the Moonlight" began its trek up the chart as the No. 8 hit on the June 19th program. Seven weeks later, it replaced "It Looks Like Rain in Cherry Blossom Lane," another Lombardo hit, as the top song. "It Looks Like Rain..." regained the top spot the next week and "A Sailboat in the Moonlight" fell all the way to No. 5. It rebounded the next week to No. 1 and this time stayed for two weeks.

It is amazing that "Boo-Hoo!," "A Sailboat in the Moonlight," and "It Looks Like Rain in Cherry Blossom Lane" were able to attain the top spot on *Your Hit Parade* while songs like Rodgers and Hart's "Where or When" peaked at No. 2, or instrumental numbers like "Sing, Sing, Sing," which entered the Grammy (NARAS) Hall of Fame for the Benny Goodman recording of the number, never made the survey. Every charting service thinks theirs is the most reliable way to gather the information that makes their chart the most accurate. But there are often glaring gaps in *Your Hit Parade*'s survey that are very difficult to explain. Some of it can be blamed on America's listening public and their preferences. Popular taste has never been accused of being highly artistic and the American public often seems to prefer great singing entertainers rather than singers with exceptional voices. However, "Where or When" and "Sing, Sing, Sing" and many others have survived the test of time far better than some of the tunes that did attain *Your Hit Parade*'s pinnacle.

Read the lyrics at http://lirama.net/song/16049.

See the sheet music cover at http://www.parlorsongs.com/issues/1998-10/oct98gallery.asp.

Satan Takes a Holiday

Words & Music: Larry Clinton

Tommy Dorsey and his orchestra popularized this Larry Clinton composition with a very popular recording. The song only made one appearance on *Your Hit Parade*, and that was as the No. 6 hit on the September 14th broadcast. As usual *Your Hit Parade* tended to ignore or almost ignore the really swinging hits that were basically instrumental. *A Century of Pop Music* suggests it was the top hit in the nation for three weeks in September.

"Satan takes a holiday" by dancing to spooky music. Read the lyrics at http://lirama.net/song/16050.

September in the Rain

Words: Al Dubin; Music: Harry Warren

"September in the Rain" was premiered in the '35 movie musical *Stars Over Broadway*, but it was only heard there as instrumental background music. Budget cuts eliminated Busby Berkeley's planned scene for the song.

James Melton, who had starred in *Stars Over Broadway*, re-introduced the song in the '37 movie musical *Melody for Two*.

Master movie musical songsmiths Harry Warren and Al Dubin wrote this reverie of a September that love made worth remembering.

Guy Lombardo and his Royal Canadians' recording of "September in the Rain" was by far the most popular recorded version, but James Melton and the Rhythm Wreckers also had successful versions on the market. Sam Donohue revived the song in '48, as did the George Shearing Quintet in '49. An audio clip of Frank Sinatra singing the song can be heard at http://www.harrywarrenmusic.com/realfiles/.

It was No. 1 on *Your Hit Parade* for five weeks in '37. It claimed the top spot for the May 15th broadcast, but relinquished it to "Carelessly" for the next two weeks. It returned to the top stronger than ever for the June 5th show and remained the top tune for four consecutive weeks.

For more than five decades, "The Sweetest Music This Side of Heaven" was known to more people, including its detractors, than virtually any other. Equally recognizable was the singing of Carmen Lombardo, whose distinctive soft, quavery voice was an important part of the band's attraction. Carmen's voice on "September in the Rain" helped turn this Warren/Dubin favorite into an abiding hit.

The singer asks his loved one to remember when "the leaves of brown came tumbling down ... In September in the rain." Even though it's now spring, to him it's still "that September in the rain." Read the lyrics and hear a midi musical version at http://www.harrywarren.org/songs/0451.htm. See Warren's music manuscript of this song at http://www.harrywarrenmusic.com/frameset.html.

So Rare

Words: Jack Sharpe; Music: Jerry Herst

"So Rare" has been a hit twice since its original success in '37. George Shearing helped popularize it right after the war, and it gave Jimmy Dorsey his last big record just before his death in '57.

Guy Lombardo and his Royal Canadians and Gus Arnheim and his orchestra helped popularize "So Rare" in the late thirties when it was the top hit on *Your Hit Parade* for one week. Lombardo's was by far the most popular version.

Twenty years after its first appearance on the charts, Lee Carlton of Fraternity Records remembered the song and decided it could be popularized again. He hired Lou Douglas to write a new updated arrangement and, even though he had disbanded his orchestra in '53, talked Jimmy Dorsey into recording it. It seems rather strange that a big band would be a hit in the years just preceding rock, but it happened. Douglas's arrangement was rhythmical and danceable and the public loved it.

"So Rare" reentered the *Your Hit Parade* chart as the No. 6 hit for the May 25, 1957 broadcast. This time it peaked at No. 2, but remained there for six consecutive weeks. Counting the '37 and '57 appearances, the song totaled twenty-seven weeks on the *Your Hit Parade* program.

Jerry Herst and Jack Sharpe wrote this song that catalogs the reason why the loved one and their love are "So Rare." Read the lyrics at http://lirama.net/song/16054.

Sweet Leilani

Words & Music: Harry Owens

For the first moment he walked before a movie camera, Bing Crosby seemed destined to become a major motion picture star. *She Loves Me Not* in '34 and *Rhythm on the Range* two years later were both blockbuster successes. Other efforts that added to his star luster, included *Mississippi*, *We're Not Dressing*, and *Pennies from Heaven*.

During a Honolulu vacation, Bing heard Harry Owens and the Royal Hawaiian Hotel Orchestra perform "Sweet Leilani." Crosby inquired about the song and found out that it was written by the band's leader.

Paramount had already planned a tropical musical comedy, *Waikiki Wedding*, starring Bing along with Martha Raye, Bob Burns, and Shirley Ross. The story was fluff—little more than a backdrop for Crosby's singing and the antics of veteran comics Raye and Burns.

The studio wasn't thrilled when Bing insisted that he sing "Sweet Leilani" in the film. However, his persistence earned the studio its first Oscar song and the singer himself his biggest recording success to date.

If you believe *Your Hit Parade*'s survey, "Sweet Leilani" only got to No. 2, but *A Century of Pop Music* claims that it the biggest hit of '37. Hear Don Redman and his orchestra's recording of "Sweet Leilani" at http://www.redhotjazz.com/redmano.html.

"Sweet Leilani" is a *Variety Hit Parade of a Half-Century* song. This song was nominated for the American Film Institute's list of the greatest songs ever from American films, but did not make the final list.

See the sheet music cover at www.hulapages.com/covers_2.htm.

According to the lyrics, "Sweet Leilani" is a "heavenly flower," the singer's "paradise completed," his "dream come true." Read the lyrics at http://lirama.net/song/16056.

Other well-known songs from the score include "Blue Hawaii," which was also popularized by Bing Crosby in a successful recording, but perhaps better known today as the title of an Elvis Presley '62 film, plus "Sweet Is the Word for You" also popularized by Bing Crosby. Read the lyrics to "Sweet Is the Word for You" at http://lirama.net/song/16055. Read the "Blue Hawaii" lyrics at http://lirama.net/song/16017 and hear Paul Whiteman's recording of "Blue Hawaii" at http://www.redhotjazz.com/pwo.html.

"Blue Hawaii" was nominated for the American Film Institute's list of the greatest songs ever from American films for its appearance in the film *Blue Hawaii*, but did not make the final list.

That Old Feeling

Words: Lew Brown; Music: Sammy Fain

An Academy Award nominee for Best Film Song of '37, "That Old Feeling," a *Variety Hit Parade of a Half-Century* song, was introduced by Virginia Verrill in the movie *Walter Wanger's Vogues of 1938*. The words are by Lew Brown, best known as a member of the great 1920's songwriting team of Henderson, DeSylva, and Brown. His colleague this time was Sammy Fain.

When the singer sees his old flame, he realizes he can't love another because "that old feeling is still in" his heart. Read the lyrics at http://lirama.net/song/16058.

The song was revived in Jane Froman's screen biography, *With a Song in My Heart* ('52).

The song was popularized in recordings primarily by Shep Fields. Fields' recording of the song features lots of triplets in the brass and reeds, glissandos on viola, and accordion embellishments. It is a good example of his highly successful "Rippling Rhythm" style. Jan Garber also released a successful version. Hear Fats Waller and his Continental Rhythm's recording of "That Old Feeling" at http://www.redhotjazz.com/continental.html.

"That Old Feeling" made the top spot on *Your Hit*

Parade in '37 for four weeks. It spent two weeks as the runner-up hit to "Whispers in the Dark" before it made the top on the October 9th show. It managed four consecutive weeks at the top spot.

They Can't Take That Away from Me *and* Let's Call the Whole Thing Off
Words: Ira Gershwin; Music: George Gershwin

Shall We Dance? Was Fred Astaire and Ginger Rogers' seventh film together in four years. In this movie musical, Fred, as ballet star Pete "Petroff" Peters, arranges to cross the Atlantic aboard the same ship as the dancer he's fallen for but barely knows, musical star Linda Keene, played by Ginger Rogers. By the time the ocean liner reaches New York, a little white lie has churned through the rumor mill and turned into a hot gossip item: that the two celebrities are secretly married. The primary attraction of the film was the Gershwin songs and Astaire and Rogers' dancing.

THEY CAN'T TAKE THAT AWAY FROM ME

This is what is commonly known in the popular music business as an "Astaire song," one of those classics written expressly for the magical '30s films featuring Fred Astaire and Ginger Rogers and forever identified with Fred. Irving Berlin, George Gershwin, and Jerome Kern wrote some of their finest tunes for these musicals. Consider George and Ira Gershwin's superb score for *Shall We Dance?* ('37) that included "Let's Call the Whole Thing Off," as well as "They Can't Take That Away from Me"—both gems that became a part of the Astaire legend.

"They Can't Take That Away from Me," an Academy Award nominee for Best Song of '37, is a ballad of affectionate reminiscence, full of small images that evoke the intimate side of a relationship now obviously in the past.

The song was also inserted into the '49 Fred Astaire and Ginger Rogers movie musical *The Barkleys of Broadway*.

Jimmy Dorsey and his orchestra were in Los Angeles, backing Bing Crosby on his "Kraft Music Hall" radio shows, when *Shall We Dance?* was released. That's where they recorded several songs from the movie. On this one, Bob Eberly took the vocal in his strong, confident style, and Jimmy contributed his usual fine singing saxophone work.

"They Can't Take That Away from Me" peaked at No. 6 on *Your Hit Parade*, but it well may have been the nation's biggest pop hit for at least one week in May of '37.

This song was nominated for AFI's greatest song from movies list, but did not make the final list. Fred Astaire's recording of "They Can't Take That Away from Me" was inducted into the Grammy Hall of Fame in 2005.

The singer requests permission to list a few of the things "that will keep me loving you." Among them are the way you wear your hat and sip your tea. He also loves your smile and "the way you sing off key." All these things and more that he loved about her can't be taken away. Read the lyrics at http://lirama.net/song/16061.

LET'S CALL THE WHOLE THING OFF

"Let's Call the Whole Thing Off" was also introduced in *Shall We Dance?*

The clever lyrics of "Let's Call the Whole Thing Off" compare American and British pronunciations, like "potayto-potahto, tomayto-tomahto." The song perfectly suited the moment that seems to occur in all Astaire/ Rogers films: the bicker-reconciliation scene. Read the lyrics at http://lirama.net/song/16037.

Fred Astaire, Shep Fields and his Rippling Rhythm and Eddy Duchin and his orchestra popularized "Let's Call the Whole Thing Off" in recordings.

Your Hit Parade's survey says that "Let's Call the Whole Thing Off" made only two appearances on the show and peaked at No. 7.

AFI's *100 Years ... 100 Songs* (2004) named "Let's Call the Whole Thing Off" as the No. 34 greatest song from an American film.

Other songs from the *Shall We Dance* score that charted include "Beginner's Luck," "Shall We Dance?," and "They All Laughed." All recorded and popularized by Fred Astaire. Hear Paul Whiteman's recording of "Shall We Dance?" at http://www.redhotjazz.com/pwo.html.

This Year's Kisses *and* I've Got My Love to Keep Me Warm
Words & Music: Irving Berlin

In *On the Avenue*, Dick Powell stars as Broadway impresario Gary Blake, who is staging his latest Broadway musical starring The Ritz Brothers, appearing as themselves, and musical comedy star Mona Merrick, played by Alice Faye. Mona's role as "The Richest Girl in the World" is a lampoon of Park Avenue millionairess Mimi Caraway. Mimi becomes enraged when she happens to attend a performance. She goes backstage to protest Mona's performance to Gary, who is immediately attracted to Mimi and agrees to tone down Mona's lampooning. Mona, who was once Gary's girlfriend, instead decides to portray Mimi with even more nastiness and self-centeredness. When Mimi and her family attend the show's next performance, they are bewildered to discover Mona's character is even worse than before. In retaliation, Mimi and her family buy out the production and make enormous changes in the show to which Gary objects.

THIS YEAR'S KISSES

Alice Faye introduced "This Year's Kisses" in *On the Avenue*. Ms. Faye was the film's highlight with her performances of Berlin's I've Got My Love to Keep Me Warm" (with Dick Powell) and "This Year's Kisses."

Benny Goodman and Hal Kemp competed with each other for the most popular version of "This Year's Kisses." Both recordings were extremely popular. Shep Fields and his Rippling Rhythm and Teddy Wilson and his orchestra with a vocal performance by Billie Holiday also issued successful recordings of the song.

The song's first appearance among *Your Hit Parade*'s chart was on the February 20th show as the No. 3 tune. After a couple of weeks, it assumed the No. 1 position for the March 13th broadcast and held that status for a three week run. Strangely, it dropped out of the seven featured songs the very next week.

The singer thinks "this year's crop of kisses" aren't as sweet because he still remembers last year's love. Read the lyrics at http://lirama.net/song/16062.

I'VE GOT MY LOVE TO KEEP ME WARM

Irving Berlin wrote "I've Got My Love to Keep Me Warm" for the movie musical *On the Avenue*. The film was a standard backstage musical and would have been exceedingly boring without Berlin's songs. Dick Powell and Alice Faye introduced "I've Got My Love to Keep Me Warm."

Ray Noble and his orchestra, Billie Holiday, Red Norvo and his orchestra, and Glen Gray and the Casa Loma Orchestra popularized the song in recordings in '37. Les Brown and his orchestra took it to No. 1 in '49. Other recordings in '49 that helped popularized it again were issued by the Mills Brothers, by Art Lund and by the Starlighters. See '49 for more.

According to *Your Hit Parade*'s survey, "I've Got My Love to Keep Me Warm" got up to only No. 3 in both '37 and '49.

Even though it is an unusually cold, snowy December, the singer's sure he "can weather the storm," because he has his love to keep him warm. Read the lyrics at http://lirama.net/song/16532.

Two other songs from the *On the Avenue* score were popular with the public: "The Girl on the Police Gazette" (read the lyrics at http://www.oldielyrics.com/lyrics/irving_berlin/the_girl_on_the_police_gazette.html) was popularized by Russ Morgan and "Slumming on Park Avenue" (read the lyrics at http://www.oldielyrics.com/lyrics/irving_berlin/slumming_on_park_avenue.html) was popularized by Red Norvo.

Benny Goodman and his orchestra popularized "He Ain't Got Rhythm" from *On the Avenue*.

Too Marvelous for Words

Words: Johnny Mercer; Music: Richard Whiting

"Too Marvelous for Words" was introduced by Ruby Keeler and Lee Dixon in the movie musical *Ready, Willing and Able*. Keeler and Dixon danced on the keys of a giant typewriter during the production number that followed the vocal.

The singer is trying to find words that are good enough to describe his love, but he can't find any that do her justice. She's beyond description by mere words. She's too special "to ever be in Webster's Dictionary." Read the lyrics at http://lirama.net/song/16063.

The song was interpolated into the Humphrey Bogart film *Dark Passage* ('47), and in the movie musical *Sunny Side of the Street* ('51).

Bing Crosby's recording of "Too Marvelous for Words" with Jimmy Dorsey's orchestra was very popular in the early spring of '37. Leo Reisman and his orchestra released another popular version of the song.

Richard Whiting and Johnny Mercer's song peaked at No. 3 on *Your Hit Parade*, but was more likely the top hit in the nation for at least one week in late April of '37.

Frank Sinatra's recording of the song was used on the soundtrack of the film *What Women Want* (2000), which starred Mel Gibson and Helen Hunt.

Vieni, Vieni

Words: Rudy Vallee; Music: Vincent Scotto

"Vieni, Vieni" came to the U.S. from Corsica. John Royal, then vice-president of NBC, recommended this Corsican tune to Rudy Vallee. Vallee took a liking to it, wrote the English lyrics and introduced it on the "Fleischmann Hour," his popular weekly radio program in '36. He continued to use it periodically on his program for the rest of the year. By that time, he had released a recording of it that began to catch on and made it to No. 1 on *Your Hit Parade* in November of '37.

Many melodies have become world-wide favorites after having been introduced by Vallee through his famous trademark, the megaphone, which he used since his collegiate days to help amplify his soft, crooner's voice. He was the matinee idol of the flappers of the late twenties and continued his popularity into the thirties over radio, in films, and on stage.

"Vieni, Vieni" made a dozen appearances on *Your Hit Parade* between late October '37 and mid–January '38. It made its only appearance as No. 1 on the November 20th broadcast.

Vallee sang, "Vieni, vieni, vieni, vieni, vieni, tusei bella, bella, bella, bella, bella." Part of the lyrics are in English, but most are in Italian. Read the complete lyrics at http://lirama.net/song/16065.

Where or When *and* My Funny Valentine

Words: Lorenz Hart; Music: Richard Rodgers

Richard Rodgers and Lorenz Hart's *Babes in Arms* is surely one of the richest of all the shows written by that distinguished team during the '30s. Just imagine a single score that included "Where or When," "My Funny Valentine," "Johnny One Note" and "The Lady Is a Tramp."

In the musical, a group of teenagers, whose parents are out of work vaudevillians, stage a revue to keep from being sent to a work farm. Unfortunately, the show is a flop. Later, when a transatlantic French flyer lands nearby, they are able to attract enough publicity to put on a successful show and build their own youth center.

Where or When

Billie Smith (Mitzi Green) and Val Lamar (Ray Heatherton) introduced this *Variety Hit Parade of a Half-Century* song in *Babes in Arms*. They sing that this moment seems to have happened before, although neither can recall "where or when." Read the lyrics at http://www.lorenzhart.org/wheresng.htm.

In the '39 film version of the musical, Betty Jaynes and Douglas MacPhail sang it, while Lena Horne sang it in the Rodgers and Hart screen biography, *Words and Music*.

Hal Kemp and his orchestra had a particularly popular recording of "Where or When" on the market. Guy Lombardo and his Royal Canadians' version also help popularize the song.

The song peaked at No. 2 on *Your Hit Parade*, but other information suggests that it was the top hit in the country for at least one week in July of '37. "Where or When" became one of the most recorded songs of the pre-rock era (No. 51).

Dion and the Belmonts revived "Where or When" in '60. Their version peaked at No. 3 on *Billboard*.

My Funny Valentine

Mitzi Green introduced "My Funny Valentine" in Rodgers and Hart's *Babes in Arms*. The song was sung by the character Billie Smith about Valentine ("Val") Lamar whom she loves despite his imperfections. Read the lyrics at http://www.lorenzhart.org/valentinesng.htm.

Judy Garland sang it in the film version in '39, and the song became one of her specialties. It was also inserted into *Gentlemen Marry Brunettes* ('57), *Pal Joey* ('57) and *Words and Music* ('48).

"My Funny Valentine" is such a classic now that it is

surprising that no recordings of the tune were popular in '37. Hal McIntyre revived it with moderate success in '45. It also surprisingly never charted on *Your Hit Parade*.

Variety chose "My Funny Valentine" as one of its *Golden 100 Tin Pan Alley Songs*, but didn't include it among its *Hit Parade of a Half-Century* selections. The song became one of the most recorded songs of the pre-rock era. This song was nominated for the American Film Institute's list of the greatest songs ever from an American film, but did not make the final list. It was nominated for its appearance in '57's *Pal Joey*.

At least two other songs from *Babes in Arms* have sustained their popularity over the years. "Johnny One Note" was popularized in '37 by Hal Kemp and Victor Young and their orchestras. Read the lyrics of "Johnny One Note" at http://www.lorenzhart.org/onenote.htm.

"The Lady Is a Tramp" was popularized in recordings by Tommy Dorsey, Bernie Cummins, Joe Rines and Sophie Tucker in '37. Read the lyrics of "The Lady Is a Tramp" at http://www.lorenzhart.org/trampsng.htm.

Whispers in the Dark
Words: Leo Robin; Music: Fred Hollander

Artists and Models was a large cast movie musical featuring, among others, Jack Benny, Louis Armstrong, Martha Raye, and Connee Boswell. One of the musical numbers in the film, "Whispers in the Dark," was introduced by Connee Boswell with Andre Kostelanetz and his orchestra. The song earned a nomination for the Oscar for Best Song from Films in '37, but lost to "Sweet Leilani."

"Whispers in the Dark" started its *Your Hit Parade* chart history as the No. 7 hit for the week of August 14th. After a couple of weeks, it became the No. 1 hit for the September 4th broadcast. It replaced "A Sailboat in the Moonlight" as the top hit and after only one week on top, it was subsequently replaced by "So Rare." After a week's absence, "Whispers in the Dark" grabbed the No. 1 position again and held it for three consecutive weeks.

Russ Morgan and his orchestra popularized "Stop! You're Breaking My Heart" also from *Artists and Models*. Ted Koehler and Burton Lane wrote this song.

Read the lyrics at http://lirama.net/song/16069.

With Plenty of Money and You (Gold Diggers' Lullaby)
Words: Al Dubin; Music: Harry Warren

By '36, most of the misery of the Depression seemed to have lifted. Franklin D. Roosevelt was President, and his "new deal" promised better times ahead. Even though mass unemployment was still at a dangerous level, the breadlines were gone, and there were new job opportunities for millions through projects of the WPA (Works Progress Administration). For a brief period, the nation's mood was optimistic. The impending tragedy of another world war was still unperceived.

Popular songs reflected the uplifted attitude: songs like "Brother, Can You Spare a Dime?" gave way to "Pennies from Heaven," "Are You Makin' Any Money?," and "With Plenty of Money and You."

Dick Powell, who made it big as a star of several Hollywood musicals, introduced "With Plenty of Money and You" in *Gold Diggers of 1937*. It caught the nation's mood precisely. Powell played the part of an insurance salesman

who becomes the producer of a Broadway show. His love interest in this film was Joan Blondell.

Doris Day sang this song in the movie *My Dream Is Yours* ('49).

Henry Busse had the most popular recording of the song in '37, but Hal Kemp and George Hamilton also had popular versions on the market. Hear an audio clip of Tony Bennett singing "With Plenty of Money and You" at http://www.harrywarrenmusic.com/realfiles/. "With Plenty of Money and You" started its climb to the top of *Your Hit Parade* as the No. 5 hit for the week of January 16, 1937. After two weeks at No. 5, it climbed slowly, one position per week, until it made its only appearance at No. 1 for the February 20th broadcast.

The singer says he's never envied millionaires because they don't seem to be happy. He has his girl, so what does he need with lots of money? However, he admits that even though money may be "the root of all evil," life could be much better "with plenty of money and you." Read the lyrics at http://www.harrywarren.org/songs/0606.htm. See Warren's music manuscript and Dubin's original lyric sheet of this song at http://www.harrywarrenmusic.com/frameset.html.

You Can't Stop Me from Dreaming
Words & Music: Dave Franklin & Cliff Friend

"You Can't Stop Me from Dreaming" started its climb to the top of *Your Hit Parade* as the No. 10 hit for the weeks of October 16th. It fell out of the top ten for the next broadcast, but returned as the No. 8 hit for the last broadcast of October. After another couple of weeks, it made its only appearance at No. 1 on the November 13th program.

Teddy Wilson and his orchestra released a very successful recording of "You Can't Stop Me from Dreaming" in the fall of '37. Other successful recordings were released by Ozzie Nelson and his orchestra, Dick Robertson and his orchestra, and Guy Lombardo and his Royal Canadians.

The lyrics list several things that his girl can stop, like kissing, cuddling, holding hands and romancing, but "you can't stop me from dreaming." Read the lyrics at http://lirama.net/song/16071.

1938

A-Tisket, A-Tasket
Words & Music: Ella Fitzgerald & Van Alexander

"The First Lady of Jazz," Ella Fitzgerald, achieved a major hit with "A-Tisket, A-Tasket," which was the top tune on radio for the year according to *Variety*, and spent six weeks at the head of *Your Hit Parade*. Ella's recording of the song with Chick Webb and his orchestra was inducted into the Grammy Hall of Fame in 1986.

Ella Fitzgerald and Van Alexander adapted an old nursery rhyme into this highly successful song: "A-Tisket, A-Tasket, a green and yellow basket, I wrote a letter to my love and on the way I dropped it." Most of the lyrics are practically unchanged from the nursery rhyme. "She was truckin' on down the avenue" is an example of a swing era phrase that was added by Ella and Van. Read the lyrics at http://www.lyricsdepot.com/Ella-Fitzgerald/a-tisket-a-tasket.html.

Ella Fitzgerald's recording with Chick Webb's Orchestra was phenomenally successful. Its six-week run at the top of *Your Hit Parade* began on the August 20th broadcast and lasted through the September 24th program. It was definitely one of the year's biggest hits. Tommy Dorsey and his orchestra also recorded their version of the song, but theirs was a distant second to Ella's version. Ella performed the song in the '42 Abbott and Costello comedy *Ride 'Em Cowboy*.

Variety listed this song as one of eight in its *Hit Parade of a Half-Century* for '38.

See the sheet music cover at http://www.parlorsongs.com/issues/1998–9/sep98gallery.asp.

Alexander's Ragtime Band

Words & Music: Irving Berlin

For more on the history of "Alexander's Ragtime Band" see 1911.

In '38, 20th Century-Fox released the movie musical *Alexander's Ragtime Band*, which starred Tyrone Power, Alice Faye, and Ethel Merman. It was a magnificent musical with twenty-three Irving Berlin songs. The film's plot revolved around the on and off love affair of a bandleader and a singer. The movie's soundtrack very effectively portrayed the myriad of changes in popular music from the mid–1910s to 1938. Alice Faye had the pleasure of performing the title tune.

As a result of the film, the song became a big hit again. Bing Crosby and Connee Boswell released a very popular duet version of the song. The Boswell Sisters and Ray Noble and his orchestra both also issued popular recordings of the song in '38. A famous '47 recording of the song by Bing Crosby and Al Jolson has them making several remarks in between their singing.

In addition to *Alexander's Ragtime Band*, the song was used as a big production number in *There's No Business Like Show Business* ('55) and in *Titanic* ('97).

According to *Your Hit Parade*'s survey of hits, the song peaked at No. 3, but *A Century of Pop Music* claims that Crosby and Boswell's disk was the nation's top record for a couple of weeks in September of '38.

Tommy Dorsey and his orchestra popularized "Now It Can Be Told" from *Alexander's Ragtime Band*.

Begin the Beguine

Words & Music: Cole Porter

June Knight introduced this Cole Porter classic — an ASCAP *All-Time Hit Parade* selection and *Variety Hit Parade of a Half-Century* and *Golden 100 Tin Pan Alley Song*—in the musical *Jubilee* in '35. The song made little impression at first and it might have been forgotten had it not been for Artie Shaw.

Shaw was playing for a dance at Syracuse University when someone asked him to play "Begin the Beguine." He had never heard the song, but quickly found out that it was a favorite of some of his sidemen. Shaw then asked Jerry Gray to arrange the song for his band. Gray's arrangement retained the beguine rhythm, but Shaw didn't think such a rhythm would go over very well in places like the Waldorf, so he had the band change it to a modified 4/4 beat called "bending the Charleston."

When Shaw was contracted by Bluebird to record his first record for them, which was to be a swing version of Rudolf Friml's "Indian Love Call" from the operetta *Rose Marie*, Shaw signed the contract with the stipulation that he be permitted to record the relatively unknown "Begin the Beguine" on the flip side. As it turned out, "...Beguine" completely overshadowed "Indian Love Call." The disk reportedly sold 2 million copies to become one of the largest-selling instrumental recordings by an American band (the word "reportedly" is used because the Record Industry Association of American did not begin to certify sales figures until '58 when they recognized a Gold Record as 1 million units sold; in '76, they added the Platinum status for 2 million single units sold. Albums are certified Gold for $1 million worth of sales, and Platinum for $2 million in sales. All sales figures prior to '58 are not certified; therefore, they are simply reported figures by the record companies).

In a *Billboard* disk jockey poll, "Begin the Beguine" was voted the No. 3 All-Time Record and the No. 5 All-Time Song. Shaw's recording of "Indian Love Call" was reasonably popular, but "Begin the Beguine" became one of his most successful recordings and his most famous clarinet solo. Shaw's recording of the song was inducted into the Grammy Hall of Fame in 1977.

Porter composed the score for *Jubilee* while he was on a world cruise. The inspiration for "Begin the Beguine" came in Martinique. There he heard a native dance, the beguine (from an old French word meaning flirtation). Porter was like a musical sponge soaking up any new and interesting musical ideas and adapting them to his own uses. That's exactly what he did with the rhythm of the beguine.

"Begin the Beguine" was one of Porter's personal favorites among his plethora of hit songs.

Xavier Cugat and his Waldorf-Astoria Orchestra, with vocalist Don Reid released a recording of the song in '35 that sold reasonably well, but it was not until Artie Shaw's recording became extremely popular in late '38 that the song became a major hit. That '38 recording was inducted into the Grammy Hall of Fame in 1977. The Shaw recording was reissued in '42 and was popular again, but not nearly as much as the first time. Pianist Eddie Heywood revived it in '45 and Frank Sinatra recorded a vocal version of it in '46.

"Begin the Beguine" is one of the most recorded songs of the pre-rock era.

A famous rendition of "Begin the Beguine" was Fred Astaire and Eleanor Powell's extraordinary dance to it in *Broadway Melody of 1940*. The song was also used in the '43 movie musical *Hers to Hold* and in Porter's screen biography, *Night and Day* ('46). In Porter's 2004 biopic, *De-Lovely*, "Begin the Beguine" was performed by Sheryl Crow on the soundtrack.

"Begin the Beguine" was nominated for the American Film Institute's list of the greatest songs ever from American films for its appearance in *Broadway Melody of 1940*, but did not make the final list.

As usual, Cole Porter's lyrics are far more sophisticated than normal. He has the singer reminiscing about a night of tropical splendor as the band played a beguine. He is once more with his love and they are "swearing to love forever, and promising never, never to part." These were divine moments which faded but he hopes they'll be rekindled when they "begin the Beguine." To get the full effect of the lyric, read them at http://www.spiritofsinatra.com/pages/Lyrics/b/Begin_The_Beguine.htm.

Bei Mir Bist du Schon

Words: Sammy Cahn and Saul Chaplin; Music: Sholom Secunda

Sammy Cahn discovered this song in the Yiddish theater, and became so excited about it that he convinced the Andrews Sisters to record it, even though the girls had no idea what the words meant. The record company demanded an English lyric, so Cahn and his partner Saul Chaplin, wrote new, more understandable words. The Andrews Sisters recording reportedly sold a million copies. They were presented the first gold record earned by a female group. The Andrews Sisters' recording of the song was inducted into the Grammy Hall of Fame in 1996.

The original Yiddish lyrics were by Jacob Jacobs.

The title has been printed as both "Bei Mir Bist Du Schon" with an umlaut over the "o," and as "Bei Mir Bist du Schoen." The lyrics explain that "Bei mir bist du Schon means that you're grand ... the fairest in the land." Read the lyrics at http://lirama.net/song/16079..

"Bei Mir Bist du Schon" was No. 1 on *Your Hit Parade* for two weeks and was the No. 3 sheet music seller of '38.

The song was featured in the Warner Bros. film *Love, Honor and Behave* ('38), which starred Priscilla Lane and Wayne Morris.

Variety selected this song as one of only eight in its *Hit Parade of a Half-Century* for '38.

Boogie Woogie

Music: Clarence "Pine-top" Smith

Clarence "Pine-top" Smith wrote "The Original Boogie Woogie" and first recorded it in '28 under the title "Pine-top's Boogie Woogie." He had begun playing the boogie-woogie at rent-parties in the black ghettos of Chicago. "Pine-top" Smith's '28 recording of the song was inducted into the Grammy Hall of Fame in 1983.

Tommy Dorsey and his orchestra had a big hit recording of "Boogie Woogie" in '38. Dorsey's version charted again in '44 and '45.

Boogie woogie style songs became very popular in the late '30s and early '40s. The style inspired several songs including the Andrews Sisters' "Beat Me Daddy, Eight to the Bar" ("eight to the bar" refers to the steady pattern of eighth notes of a boogie bass) and "Boogie Woogie Bugle Boy," Gene Krupa's "Boogie Blues," Louis Jordan's "Boogie Woogie Blue Plate," Glenn Miller's "Booglie Wooglie Piggy," Freddie Slack's "Cow Cow Boogie," and Earl Hines' "Boogie Woogie on St. Louis Blues," to name a few.

In the '50s and '60s, boogie woogie resurfaced as an integral part of some early rhythm and blues and rock 'n' roll songs.

The boogie woogie form is similar to a classic passacaglia, in which a bass melody is repeated over and over while the upper voice melody and chord structure change above it.

See some of the typical boogie bass patterns at http://en.wikipedia.org/wiki/Boogie_woogie_%28music%29.

According to Clarence Williams, piano boogie woogie originated with a pianist from Texas named George W. Thomas. Thomas published one of the earliest pieces of sheet music with a boogie bassline, "New Orleans Hop Scop Blues," in '16, although he had been playing the song in the honky tonks of the deep south for five or six years.

Tap dancer extraordinaire Eleanor Powell danced to "Boogie Woogie" in *Thousands Cheer* ('43).

Cathedral in the Pines

Words & Music: Charles & Nick Kenny

Shep Fields and his "Rippling Rhythm" orchestra, with Jerry Stewart as vocalist, had a very popular recording of "Cathedral in the Pines" in '38. *A Century of Pop Music* was it was the nation's top hit for three weeks in late May and June.

"Cathedral in the Pines" made eight appearances on *Your Hit Parade*, but only rose to No. 5

The lyrics sing about a wedding "in that little old cathedral in the pines." When a baby comes into their lives, they take it to be blessed in that same church. When that baby grew into a young man, he found the love of his life "in a girl who came to pray" in that church. Then another wedding took place in the "cathedral in the pines." Read the lyrics at http://lirama.net/song/16080.

Change Partners

Words & Music: Irving Berlin

After several highly successful "Fred and Ginger" films, Fred Astaire and Ginger Rogers made a few pictures apart, but then reunited for *Carefree* in '38. This time Astaire played a psychiatrist and Ginger was a patient who was sent to him by her boyfriend because she couldn't make up her mind whether to marry him or not. Of course, the patient fell for the analyst and visa versa.

After its introduction in the film, "Change Partners" was popularized in recordings by two particularly successful disks : one by Fred Astaire, the other by Jimmy Dorsey and his orchestra. Ozzie Nelson and his orchestra and Lawrence Welk and his orchestra also released recordings of the song that did very well.

The song was the No. 1 song on *Your Hit Parade* for the October 15th and November 5th broadcasts. It made nine appearances on the program.

The singer is jealous that this girl dances every dance with the same person. He wants her to "change partners" and dance with him. Read the lyrics at http://lirama.net/song/16081.

Cry, Baby, Cry

Words: Jimmy Eaton; Music: Terry Shand

Larry Clinton and his orchestra had a very popular recording of "Cry, Baby, Cry." Kay Kyser and his orchestra and Dick Robertson and his orchestra also released successful recordings of the song.

Clinton's first recordings with his own band came out in late '37. "Cry, Baby, Cry" was the band's first big hit recording. 1938 was a good year for them as they had major hit recordings of "My Reverie," and "Heart and Soul," in addition to "Cry, Baby, Cry."

Songwriters Terry Shand and Jimmy Eaton also had a good year in '38 with two hit songs to their credit: "Cry, Baby, Cry" and "I Double Dare You."

The song made nine appearances on *Your Hit Parade* and managed one week as the top song (June 11th broadcast).

The chorus lyrics begin, "Cry, baby, cry ... just the way

I did the day you broke my heart." Now he's laughing to see her cry. Read the lyrics at http://lirama.net/song/16082.

Don't Be That Way

Words: Mitchell Parish; Music: Edgar Sampson & *Benny Goodman*

Benny Goodman and his orchestra introduced "Don't Be That Way" that was co-written by Goodman and Edgar Sampson. Sampson was Chick Webb's alto saxophonist and arranger. Mitchell Parish, who contributed the words, is one of the most talented and most prolific lyric writers in all of popular music.

Mildred Bailey and Chick Webb and his orchestra also released recordings of the song that the public responded to very well.

"Don't Be That Way" peaked at No. 2 on *Your Hit Parade*, but *A Century of Pop Music* says it was the biggest hit around the country for several weeks in March and April of '38.

Since Goodman was co-writer, the song was used in his screen biography, *The Benny Goodman Story* ('56). It was also used in 1977's *New York, New York*.

The gist of these lyrics can be summed up with the following thought from the lyrics: "don't break my heart, Oh, honey, please don't be that way." Read the lyrics at http://lirama.net/song/16084.

The Flat Foot Floogee

Words & Music: Slim Gaillard, Slam Stewart & Bud *Green*

This "hep" swing era novelty song was introduced and primarily popularized by two of its writers, Slim and Slam. Guitarist Slim Gaillard and bass fiddle player, Slam Stewart, were messing around during an appearance on the WNEW radio show "Jive at Five" when they came up with the basic idea for "The Flat Foot Floogee." Bud Green helped out by providing the lyric.

Other successful recordings of the song were released by Benny Goodman and his orchestra, by Wingy Manone and his orchestra, and by the Mills Brothers.

The word "floogee" is sometimes spelled "floogie" by various authors when they are referring to this song.

We need a jive dictionary to translate the lyrics ("Flat foot floogee with the floy, floy"). The flat foot floogee was a dance to do "when you're feelin' low down." Read the lyrics at http://lirama.net/song/16085.

"The Flat Foot Floogee" peaked at No. 5 on *Your Hit Parade*. It was listed by *Variety* as one of only eight songs in its *Hit Parade of a Half-Century* for '38.

Heart and Soul

Words: Frank Loesser; Music: Hoagy Carmichael

Hoagy Carmichael published "Heart and Soul" as an independent number, that is, it was not intended for a specific movie or Broadway show. Larry Clinton and his orchestra performed it in the '38 movie short *A Song Is Born*. In '39 Gene Krupa and his orchestra used it in the film *Some Like It Hot*. In addition, the song appeared in *I Walk Alone* ('48), *The Touch of Larceny* ('59), *American Graffiti* ('73), *The Godfather, Part Two* ('74), as a dance segment of *Stepping Out* ('91) and *The Heart of Me* (2002).

It was Clinton's recording of the song, with a vocal performance by Bea Wain, which was the most popular version on the market. Eddy Duchin and his orchestra and Al Donohue and his orchestra also released successful editions of the song. Later chartings of the song were had by The Four Aces in '52, Larry Maddox in '57, and by both the Cleftones and Jan and Dean in '61.

Amateur pianists who can play one or two things usually seem to specialize on "Chop Sticks" and the accompaniment to "Heart and Soul."

It is not a slow dreamy love song, which the title might suggest, but rather a lilting love ballad.

"Heart and Soul" made ten appearances on *Your Hit Parade*, but peaked at No. 2. It did, however, manage four consecutive weeks in second place.

The singer fell in love when she was held tightly as a kiss was stolen in the night. Now she is madly in love and has given her "heart and soul." Read the lyrics at http://lirama.net/song/16086.

I Double Dare You

Words: Jimmy Eaton; Music: Terry Shand

Shand and Eaton's second hit song of '38 (see "Cry, Baby, Cry" above) was "I Double Dare You." The song has the lively bounce that Swing Era fans loved to hear.

Of course, Jimmy Eaton capitalized on a popular saying of the time to create the hook for this song. It wasn't "I dare you," it was "I double dare you" to do something that you know you shouldn't do. In this instance, "I double dare you" to fall in love with me.

Popular recordings of the song were issued by Russ Morgan, Larry Clinton, Louis Armstrong, and Woody Herman and their orchestras. Morgan's vocalist was Bernice Parks, Bea Wain was Clinton's singer, while Herman was usually his own vocalist. "I Double Dare You" was Woody Herman's first successful recording.

The song made a dozen appearances on *Your Hit Parade*, but managed only one week as the No. 1 hit (February 26th broadcast).

I Let a Song Go Out of My Heart

Words & Music: Duke Ellington, Irving Mills, John *Redmond & Henry Nemo*

"I Let a Song Go Out of My Heart", a Duke Ellington song, was popularized in big hit recordings by both the composer and his orchestra and Benny Goodman and his orchestra. Connee Boswell, Mildred Bailey and Hot Lips Page also released popular recordings of the song. Martha Tilton was the featured vocalist on the Goodman recording.

"I Let a Song Go Out of My Heart" was the No. 1 hit on *Your Hit Parade* for the July 30th broadcast. The song was on the program a dozen different times.

According to the chorus lyrics, the singer "let a song go out of" his heart. And that melody was really sweet because "you were the song." Read the lyrics at http://lirama.net/song/16088.

I've Got a Pocketful of Dreams

Words: Johnny Burke; Music: James V. Monaco

Bing Crosby introduced "I've Got a Pocketful of Dreams" in the movie musical *Sing, You Sinners*. In the film Crosby played a singer who loves to gamble on the horses.

Crosby also had a very popular recording of the song, which says everything is okay as long as we can dream (that philosophy sounds like it would have been written during the early '30s Depression era). Russ Morgan and his orchestra's recording of the song was almost equally as popular with the public as Bing's.

"I've Got a Pocketful of Dreams" was the No. 1 sheet music seller in '38 and spent four weeks at the top of *Your Hit Parade.*

Bing sings, "I'm no millionaire, but I'm not the type to care, 'cause I've got a pocketful of dreams." He may have an empty purse, but he'd rather calculate his worth in things besides money. Read the lyrics at http://lirama.net/song/16091.

I Won't Tell a Soul (I Love You)

Words & Music: Ross Parker & Hughie Charles

Andy Kirk and his Twelve Clouds of Joy were chiefly responsible for popularizing "I Won't Tell a Soul (I Love You)."

Lawrence Welk and his orchestra and Roy Fox and his orchestra also help popularize the song with successful recordings.

According to *Your Hit Parade*'s hit survey, the song peaked at No. 6, but it may well have closed out '38 as the nation's biggest hit for a couple of weeks.

Love Walked in

Words: Ira Gershwin; Music: George Gershwin

"Love Walked In" and "Love Is Here to Stay" were George Gershwin's last hit songs. He wrote them for the movie musical *The Goldwyn Follies.* He had only partially completed "Love Is Here to Stay" before he collapsed from a brain tumor. He died in '37 following exploratory brain surgery.

Dead at thirty-nine years old, but WOW what he achieved in those years! Had his life not ended at such a young age he surely would have accomplished even more fantastic musical feats. He seemed to be always pushing back the horizons of music.

Kenny Baker introduced "Love Walked In" in *The Goldwyn Follies.* It was on *Your Hit Parade* for fourteen weeks and was No. 1 for four weeks. It was also among the four top sheet music sellers of the year.

Ira's lyrics say everything is sunny since "love walked in" when you appeared. Read the lyrics at http://lirama.net/song/17548.

"Love Walked In" was principally popularized outside the film in recordings by Swing and Sway with Sammy Kaye (that's the way it was listed on the record, instead of Sammy Kaye and his orchestra). Other popular recordings were those released by Jimmy Dorsey and his orchestra, Jan Garber and his orchestra, Kenny Baker, and Louis Armstrong. The Hilltoppers revived it in '53 with considerable success.

"Love Walked In" was also used in Gershwin's screen biography, *Rhapsody in Blue* ('45).

Another well known song from the score of *The Goldwyn Follies* is "Our Love Is Here to Stay," which was popularized in recordings by Larry Clinton and his orchestra and Red Norvo and his orchestra.

Mexicali Rose

Words: Helen Stone; Music: Jack Tenny

Jack Tenny and Helen Stone wrote "Mexicali Rose" in '23. The Clicquot Club Eskimos popularized it on radio

in '26. *Variety* lists the song among its *Hit Parade of a Half-Century* for '38, when Bing Crosby popularized it.

Gene Autry used it in the film *Mexicali Rose* in '39 and also sang it in *Barbed Wire* in '52. Roy Rogers used it in *Song of Texas* in '43. Its frequent use in western films has made it stereotypical of songs about Mexico and its women. The song was used as the theme song for the Barbara Stanwyck film *Mexicali Rose.*

The singer begs "Mexicali Rose" to stop crying because he'll return to her someday. As he says goodbye, he asks for a parting kiss. Read the lyrics at http://lirama.net/song/22390.

Music, Maestro, Please

Music: Allie Wrubel; Words: Herb Magidson

"Music, Maestro, Please" was the No. 2 sheet music seller and was No. 1 on *Your Hit Parade* for four weeks in '38.

Allie Wrubel and Herb Magidson wrote the song over a ping-pong table. They were neighbors as well as collaborators in California in the mid–'30s. Before they began working seriously every day on new songs, they "warmed up" with a game of ping-pong. As they played, they batted lyrical and melodic ideas back and forth as they batted the ball back and forth. By the time they were "warmed up" the song was practically written.

The song was introduced by Frank Parker and Frances Langford on radio.

Variety included the song in its *Hit Parade of a Half-Century* as one of only eight songs it listed for the year.

It was Tommy Dorsey and his orchestra's recording of "Music, Maestro, Please" that was the biggest hit, but Art Kassel and his orchestra and Kay Kyser and his orchestra also released worthy renditions. Frankie Laine revived it with decent success in '50.

The singer does not want to think about a certain girl, so he asks the music leader, the maestro, to play "ragtime, jazztime, swing, any old thing, to help me ease the pain." He also tells the maestro since she liked waltzes, don't play a waltz. Read the lyrics at http://lirama.net/song/16097.

My Reverie

Words & Music: Larry Clinton,

Bandleader/composer Larry Clinton adapted French Impressionist composer Claude Debussy's famous "Reverie" into the popular song "My Reverie" and had one of his first major successes as a recording artist with his version of the song. His first hit recording was "Cry, Baby, Cry," which beat "My Reverie" by about five months.

The song was No. 1 on *Your Hit Parade* for eight weeks at the end of '38 and the beginning of '39. It was among the most played radio tunes and No. 2 in sheet music sales for '38.

The melody is gorgeous, but the lyrics are far less appealing. Phrases like "only a poor fool never schooled in the whirlpool of romance could be so cruel" are not classic examples of the lyricists' art. But then Clinton was more of a musician than a poet. Read the lyrics at http://lirama.net/song/16100 and judge for yourself.

Although Clinton's recording of "My Reverie," with vocalist Bea Wain, was the most popular one, it was not by any means the only one that was popular. Other popular versions were released by Bing Crosby, Mildred Bailey, Glenn Miller and his orchestra and Eddy Duchin and his orchestra. Miller's recording of "My Reverie" was one of his first successful efforts. It really isn't until '39 that his trademark reed sound was developed and he soared to the top among the big bands.

This was not the first popular song that was borrowed from the classics, but within the next few years, it seems to become almost epidemic. The classic music world was not always happy about "their music" being popularized. In a Debussy biography the following comment illustrates the typical response: "In 1938, Debussy joined the immortals that have made the grade in Tin Pan Alley. His salon piece, 'Reverie,' always negligible, lost what little distinction it had in becoming 'My Reverie,' the hit song of the year." Debussy had written the piece early in his composing career and reportedly thought it was terrible.

Nice Work If You Can Get It

Words: Ira Gershwin; Music: George Gershwin

"Nice Work If You Can Get It" was introduced by Fred Astaire in the '37 movie musical A Damsel in Distress. Ginger Rogers wanted a break from the Fred and Ginger partnership, so Joan Fontaine was cast as Fred's partner in this film. This time Fred was an American dancer in England who tries to get Lady Alyce (Ms. Fontaine) to marry him, which he does, of course, after several typical misunderstandings.

Fred introduced "Nice Work If You Can Get It" in a wonderful production number in which he plays a multitude of percussion instruments with his dancing feet.

Fred's recording of the song was particularly popular during early '38. Several others released successful recordings of the song including Shep Fields and his Rippling Rhythm, Maxine Sullivan, the Andrews Sisters, and Teddy Wilson and his orchestra with Billie Holiday's vocal. The song peaked at No. 3 on Your Hit Parade, but may well have been the top hit for at least one week just as the New Year dawned.

Ira Gershwin's chorus lyrics explain what this "nice work" is. He concludes the chorus with, "It's nice work if you can get it and if you get it, won't you tell me how?" Read the lyrics at http://lirama.net/song/16044.

Another outstanding Gershwin song from the film was "A Foggy Day." Read the lyrics at http://www.lyricsfreak.com/f/frank-sinatra/56116.html.

One O'Clock Jump

Music: Count Basie

One of the all-time great jazz pianists and bandleaders, Count Basie wrote "One O'Clock Jump," which became his theme song. His recording with the band was inducted into the Grammy Hall of Fame in 1979. The word "wrote" should probably be in quotes because the song was actually what's called a head arrangement. The song is a riff tune, short musical phrases made up by the band's musicians. These riffs are passed around the band. Basie and some of his sidemen, namely tenor sax players Lester Young and Herschel Evans, trombonist George Hunt and trumpeter Buck Clayton, worked out the head arrangement. So Basie certainly wasn't the "composer" in the traditional sense of the word. Head arrangements, of course, were not written down until much later. Buck Clayton has said the song's title came from the time of day the tune was recorded.

Trumpeter Harry James and his orchestra and clarinetist

Benny Goodman and his orchestra revived the song with reasonably popular recordings in '38.

The Metronome All-Star Band's '41 recording and Basie's '47 recording were also popular.

Forty years after it was written, it was revived by the country group Asleep at the Wheel and earned the 1978 Grammy Award for Best Country Instrumental Performance of the Year.

Please Be Kind

Words: Sammy Cahn; Music: Saul Chaplin

"Please Be Kind" made thirteen appearances on Your Hit Parade, and was its top hit for one week, for the May 7th broadcast.

The most popular recording of the song was by Red Norvo and his orchestra with Norvo's wife, Mildred Bailey, as vocalist. This disk was Norvo's first really big hit recording. He had been with Paul Whiteman in the early '30s before organizing his own group, which featured his wife, the superb jazz vocalist, Mildred Bailey. They had another big hit recording in '38 with "Says My Heart" (see below). Mildred Bailey was elected to the Big Band/Jazz Hall of Fame in 1989 and Red Norvo was elected in 1991.

Bob Crosby and Benny Goodman and their orchestras released moderately successful recordings of the song.

In the chorus lyrics, we learn that this is the singer's "first affair," so he asks "please be kind" and "handle my heart with care." Read the lyrics at http://lirama.net/song/16104.

Rosalie

Words & Music: Cole Porter

"Rosalie" was the seventh rewrite that Cole Porter presented to studio brass when he was writing the score for the movie musical Rosalie. He felt that several of the previous six were better songs than the one finally used, but it nevertheless was good enough to make No. 1 on Your Hit Parade for two weeks. On the January 18th broadcast, "Rosalie" took over the top spot, but was replaced the next two weeks by "Bei Mir Bist du Schon" and "You're a Sweetheart." But "Rosalie" once again rose to the top for the February 8th program.

The lyrics and melody of "Rosalie" do not have the brittle rhymes and haunting melody that are Porter's trademarks. However, he is still the master of the internal rhyme scheme. Read the lyrics at http://lirama.net/song/16105.

Nelson Eddy, playing a college football hero, and Eleanor Powell, playing Princess Rosalie of Romanza, introduced the title song in an elaborate song and dance number (Eddy and the chorus sang, while Ms. Powell danced a famous drum sequence) that seemingly employed every actor, actress and dancer that the studio could find. With wages what they are today for the entertainment industry, such extravagance will likely never be seen again.

Sammy Kaye had a big hit recording of "Rosalie" in '38 and Hoarce Heidt and his band had a popular recording of it also.

"Rosalie" was also used in Porter's biopic, Night and Day ('46). Readers can see part of the number in 1974's That's Entertainment.

Variety included "Rosalie" in its Hit Parade of a Half-Century representing '37.

Another famous song from Rosalie was "In the Still of

the Night." Nelson Eddy had the pleasure of introducing it. Tommy Dorsey and his orchestra and Leo Reisman and his orchestra had popular recordings of "In the Still of the Night" in '37 and '38. It was included in Porter's 2004 screen biography *De-Lovely.*

Says My Heart

Words: Frank Loesser; Music: Burton Lane

Harriet Hilliard (of Ozzie and Harriet fame) introduced "Says My Heart" in the movie musical *The Coconut Grove.* She played a singer who pretends to be a schoolteacher. "Fall in love, says my heart," but the schoolteacher's brain keeps wanting the head to rule the heart. Read the lyrics at http://lirama.net/song/16106.

The song stayed at No. 1 on *Your Hit Parade* for four weeks during the summer of '38 and was the No. 2 sheet music seller and the No. 3 radio tune of the year.

Even though Harriet Hilliard introduced the song, it was Red Norvo's orchestra with his wife, Mildred Bailey, who had the most popular recording of "Says My Heart" (also see "Please Be Kind" above). Hilliard's version with her husband, Ozzie Nelson's band, did very well, but not quite as well as Norvo and Bailey's. Tommy Dorsey and his orchestra, the Andrews Sisters and George Hall and his orchestra each recorded the song and their versions were received well by the public.

Sing, Sing, Sing

Music: Louis Prima

Louis Prima's "Sing, Sing, Sing" was written in '36. He, Bing Crosby, and George Raft were at the race track together. On the way home Prima kept hearing the phrase "Sing, Bing, Sing" run through his mind. He changed it to "Sing, Sing, Sing" for a more commercial title. Prima premiered his song at a Hollywood night spot where he was playing trumpet with a small combo. Prima's publisher convinced Benny Goodman to secure the song for his band to perform.

Goodman's first arrangement of the tune featured Helen Ward, his female singer. But as the band played it in ballrooms and theaters, they began extending some solos and interpolating bits of a tune called "Christopher Columbus." Soon the two tunes had merged. By the time the piece was recorded it had become an exciting succession of solos and ensemble dialogue held together by some brilliant drum passages by Gene Krupa. The song had grown to over eight minutes in length and covered both sides of a 78-rpm record.

Drummer Gene Krupa joined the Benny Goodman band in '35 and was featured on this, the first extended jazz drum solo on a recording. Krupa's performance popularized the drum as a swing solo instrument.

The Goodman recording was inducted into the Grammy Hall of Fame in 1982. Goodman and his orchestra played it in *The Benny Goodman Story* ('56).

Although the lyrics are not all that well known and the song did not originally have lyrics, several versions of the song were recorded with words. There is no lyricist credited; read the lyrics at http://www.lyricsfreak.com/c/chicago/30048.html.

Thanks for the Memory

Words: Leo Robin; Music: Ralph Rainger

Leo Robin and Ralph Rainger weren't at all happy that Bing Crosby insisted on interpolating "Sweet Leilani" into *Waikiki Wedding* in '37. They were even more upset when the song won the Oscar for Best Song. They had written all the other songs for the film. However, they won the Oscar the next year with "Thanks for the Memory." Bob Hope and Shirley Ross sang the song in Hope's first feature film, *The Big Broadcast of 1938.* The song almost immediately became Hope's theme song. He sang it at the end of his television shows, usually with special lyrics to fit the specific occasion.

The tongue-in-cheek lyrics, a catalog of questionable thanks, fit Hope's comic style perfectly. It is about memories of a marriage or relationship that is ending. Hope and Ross performed it in a half-spoken, half-sung delivery. Read the lyrics at http://lirama.net/song/16110.

A recording by Bob Hope and Shirley Ross was popular, but the most popular versions on the market were by Shep Fields and Mildred Bailey. Bob Hope and Shirley Ross' recording of "Thanks for the Memory" was inducted into the Grammy Hall of Fame in 2005.

The song managed three consecutive weeks at No. 1 on *Your Hit Parade* in March of '38. The song was written and released in '37 and appeared on *Variety's Hit Parade of a Half-Century* for '37. AFI's *100 Years ... 100 Songs* (2004) named "Thanks for the Memory" the No. 63 greatest song from an American film.

There's a Gold Mine in the Sky

Words & Music: Charles & Nick Kenny

This *Variety Hit Parade of a Half-Century* selection provided the title for a '38 film that starred Gene Autry, who, of course, performed the song in the movie.

The song was one of the top ten hits on *Your Hit Parade* for fourteen weeks toward the end of '37 and the beginning of '38.

The most popular recordings of "There's a Gold Mine in the Sky" were by Hoarce Heidt and his orchestra, Bing Crosby, and Isham Jones and his orchestra, but none were major hits.

The singer wants to go to the "gold mine in the sky" with his loved one "some sweet day." The "gold mine in the sky" is a western heaven. Read the lyrics at http://www.lirama.net/song/16111.

Ti-Pi-Tin

Words: Raymond Leveen; Music: Maria Grever

"Ti-Pi-Tin" is a Spanish popular song by Maria Grever. English lyrics were added by Raymond Leveen, and it was introduced in America by Horace Heidt's orchestra.

"Ti-Pi-Tin" was the No. 2 radio tune (most plays), was tied for the No. 2 sheet music seller, and was No. 1 on *Your Hit Parade* for six weeks in '38.

Horace Heidt and his orchestra, with vocalists Lysbeth Hughes and Larry Cotton, had the most popular recorded version of "Ti-Pi-Tin." Other successful recordings of the song were released by Guy Lombardo and his Royal Canadians, by Jerry Blaine and his Streamline Rhythm, by George Hall and his orchestra, and by the Andrews Sisters.

According to the lyrics, Rosita met Manuelo one evening. He stole a kiss and was going to leave, but Rosita said he couldn't leave until she knew him better. The chorus begins "Ti-pi-ti-pi-tin ti-pi-tin, Ti-pi-ti-pi-ton ti-pi-ton." Manuelo kept stealing kisses and thought she was satisfied. After a repeat of the "Ti-pi-ti-pi-tin" part, Rosita encouraged him to keep going, so he did. By the end of the song she had become his bride. Read the lyrics at http://www.songlyrics4u.com/guy-lombardo/ti-pi-tin.html.

Two Sleepy People

Words: Frank Loesser; Music: Hoagy Carmichael

Bob Hope and Shirley Ross, who introduced "Thanks for the Memory" in *The Big Broadcast of 1938*, also introduced "Two Sleepy People" in the movie musical *Thanks for the Memory*. The studio wanted to quickly capitalize on the success of the duo after "Thanks for the Memory."

These "two sleepy people" are "too much in love to say goodnight," say the lyrics of this conversational song. Read the lyrics at http://lirama.net/song/16117.

Bob Hope and Shirley Ross's recording of the song was popular with the public but not as popular as Fats Waller's, which was a big hit. Hear Waller's recording of this song at http://www.redhotjazz.com/rhythm.html. Several other individuals and groups recorded the song with varying degrees of success. The others included Sammy Kaye and his orchestra, Kay Kyser and his orchestra, Bob Crosby and his orchestra, Hoagy Carmichael and Ella Logan, and Lawrence Welk and his orchestra.

The song peaked at No. 2 on *Your Hit Parade* (it was No. 2 for two weeks in December of '38), but according to *A Century of Pop Music* was the nation's top hit in mid–December for a couple of weeks.

"Two Sleepy People" has also been heard in *Chocolat* (2000) and *The Curse of the Jade Scorpion* (2001).

Whistle While You Work, One Song *and* Some Day My Prince Will Come

Words: Larry Morey; Music: Frank Churchill

Snow White and the Seven Dwarfs was the first full-length animated feature from the Disney Studios. Its simple story of a charming little princess saved from the evil deeds of her wicked step-mother, the queen, by a group of seven adorable dwarfs made history when it was first released in December, 1937 and has since become an immortal screen classic.

Whistle While You Work

"Whistle While You Work" was introduced by the dwarfs in the Walt Disney animated feature film *Snow White and the Seven Dwarfs*. They found that their work was much easier and less exhausting when they whistled. "Whistle While You Work" peaked at No. 2 on *Your Hit Parade*. The most popular recordings were by the Seven Dwarfs from the soundtrack and by Shep Fields.

Variety selected "Whistle While You Work" for its *Hit Parade of a Half-Century* representing '38. "Whistle While You Work" was one of the songs nominated for AFI's greatest songs in movies list, but was not included in the final list.

Hear Artie Shaw and His New Music's '37 recording of this song (includes lyrics) at http://www.authentichistory.com/audio/1930s/music/1937-Whistle_While_You_Work.html. Read the lyrics at http://lirama.net/song/16120.

One Song

According to *Variety* and *Your Hit Parade* charts, "One Song" may have been one of the year's top hits, but it seems the least popular of the songs from the film in subsequent years. In this love song "my heart keeps singing ... only for you."

The most popular recording of the song was by Artie Shaw and his orchestra.

Read the lyrics at http://www.stlyrics.com/lyrics/snowwhiteandthesevendwarfs/imwishingonesong.htm.

Some Day My Prince Will Come

"Some Day My Prince Will Come" was sung by Snow White while she was dreaming of the day when her knight in shining armor would come to sweep her off her feet. Today Snow White's voice (Adriana Caselotti) isn't as pleasing as it must have been in the late '30s; it's too shrill and rather child-like.

AFI's *100 Years ... 100 Songs* (2004) named "Some Day My Prince Will Come" as the No. 19 greatest song from an American film ever.

Read the lyrics at http://www.stlyrics.com/lyrics/classicdisney/somedaymyprincewillcome.htm.

Another famous part of the film is the seven dwarfs' singing of "Heigh-Ho." Read the lyrics at http://www.stlyrics.com/lyrics/classicdisney/heigh-ho.htm.

The entire score of the film received an Academy Award nomination for Best Score in '37. In '38, the Motion Picture Academy awarded Walt Disney a special Oscar for "significant screen innovation that has charmed millions and pioneered a great new entertainment field for the motion picture cartoon." The original soundtrack recording of *Snow White and the Seven Dwarfs* was inducted into the Grammy Hall of Fame in 1998.

Columnist Westbrook Pegler claimed that this Disney product was the "happiest thing that has happened in the world since the armistice." The pleasing fantasy started the entire nation singing, whistling, and/or humming "Heigh-Ho," "Some Day My Prince Will Come," and "Whistle While You Work."

It also was a blessing to some toy manufacturers, who, along with much of the nation, were suffering a bleak business year because of an economic recession. Top buyers snatched up over three million rubber reproductions of the seven dwarfs from the film. The factory worked twenty-four hours a day and couldn't keep up with the demand.

You Go to My Head

Words: Haven Gillespie; Music: J. Fred Coots

Glen Gray and the Casa Loma Orchestra, with Kenny Sargent doing the vocal, introduced this *Variety Golden 100 Tin Pan Alley Song*.

The song is a little longer than most songs of the day, and the melody jumps around, with several octave intervals, which suggests that it was more instrumentally conceived than lyric born.

The most popular recordings of "You Go to My Head" were by Larry Clinton and his orchestra, by Glen Gray and the Casa Loma Orchestra, and by Teddy Wilson's band with Billie Holiday as vocalist.

The lyrics use analogies of things that go to our heads, like a haunting melody, sparkling Burgundy, or champagne to compare how the loved one intoxicates the singer. Read the lyrics at http://lirama.net/song/16122.

You Must Have Been a Beautiful Baby

Words: Johnny Mercer; Music: Harry Warren

Dick Powell introduced "You Must Have Been a Beautiful Baby," a *Variety Hit Parade of a Half-Century* song representing 1939, in the movie musical *Hard to Get*. The song topped *Your Hit Parade* for one week in '38 and two weeks in '39. Bobby Darin revived the song in a '61 recording.

The lyrics compare present beauty with that of infancy: "you must have been a beautiful baby, 'cause, baby, look at you now." Read the lyrics and hear a midi musical version at http://www.harrywarren.org/songs/0627.htm.

Bing Crosby had a very popular recording of this song in '38. Tommy Dorsey and his orchestra also had a popular version on the market. An audio clip by Nancy LaMott of this song can be heard at http://www.harrywarrenmusic.com/realfiles/.

Doris Day sang the song in the movie *My Dream Is Yours* ('48).

This song was nominated for the American Film Institute's list of the greatest songs ever from an American film, but it did not make the final list.

You're a Sweetheart

Words: Harold Adamson; Music: Jimmy McHugh

George Murphy and Alice Faye introduced "You're a Sweetheart" in the movie musical of the same name. It was interpolated into the '52 movie musical *Meet Danny Wilson*.

Dolly Dawn and her Dawn Patrol's recording of the song was particularly popular in the early months of '38.

"You're a Sweetheart" was Dolly's only big hit recording. Ethel Waters and Jack Owens both released popular recordings of the song.

The central idea of the chorus lyrics can be summed up in the following excerpt: "You're a sweetheart if there ever was one." Read the lyrics at http://www.lirama.net/song/16126.

1939

Address Unknown

Words & Music: Vaughn Horton, Denver Darling and Gene Autry

Even though "Address Unknown" was co-written by Gene Autry, it was the Ink Spots who had the most popular recording of the song.

"If I Didn't Care" in '39 is perhaps the group's most famous record and it was their first recording success; it was inducted into the Grammy Hall of Fame in 1987. Perhaps because the group was still relatively unknown, "If I Didn't Care" didn't rank as high on the charts as "Address Unknown," which is not as well known today.

According to *A Century of Pop Music*, the Ink Spots' "Address Unknown" was the top hit in the country for at least one week in November 1939 (*Variety* and *Billboard* don't start their charts until '40). The song never appeared on *Your Hit Parade*.

In the lyrics, the singer (or in this case, plural) is looking for a long, lost love. They've looked "from the place of your birth to the ends of the earth," but all they have found is "Address Unknown." Read the lyrics at http://lirama.net/song/16128.

And the Angels Sing

Words: Johnny Mercer; Music: Ziggy Elman

Ziggy Elman, a Jewish Cantor's son, grew up listening to the music of his faith. When he played in the Benny Goodman sextet version of "Bei Mir Bist du Schon," a '38 hit derived from Yiddish sources, he loved improvising Yiddish riffs into the arrangement. As a result, he wrote a tune called "Fralich in Swing" ("fralich" means joyous), which became "And the Angels Sing" once Johnny Mercer added lyrics.

Benny Goodman's recording of the tune, which featured Martha Tilton's vocal and Ziggy's trumpet solo, was a very popular hit in the spring of '39. Bing Crosby and Count Basie and his orchestra also released popular versions, but not nearly as popular as Goodman's. Goodman's version was re-released in '44 with moderate success.

As the Goodman recording shows, Johnny Mercer's words couldn't keep the "fralich" feeling out of Ziggy's song. About halfway through, the drum goes into a faster beat and Ziggy, on trumpet, starts his celebrated solo. Eventually, as was the custom, the song reverts back to the swing beat, but for a while, "And the Angels Sing" is all Elman's and it sounds like the joy of an unrestrained Jewish wedding dance.

"And the Angels Sing" was the No. 1 top radio tune for three weeks, the No. 1 jukebox tune for eight weeks, and No. 1 on *Your Hit Parade* for four weeks.

The song was featured in the film *And the Angels Sing* ('44), which starred Betty Hutton, Dorothy Lamour and Fred MacMurray and on the soundtrack of Goodman's screen biography, *The Benny Goodman Story* ('56).

The basic idea of the lyrics is that the loved one is an angel, because when she smiles, the angels sing, when she speaks, the angels sing. When they meet and when they kiss "the angels sing and leave their music ringing in my heart." Read the lyrics at http://lirama.net/song/16130.

At the Woodchopper's Ball

Words: Joe Bishop; Music: Woody Herman

Clarinetist and bandleader Woody Herman wrote and popularized this fast blues. It became his most famous hit. It was re-released in '43 and sold well again. Herman's recording of "...Woodchopper's Ball" was inducted into the Grammy Hall of Fame in 2002.

Beer Barrel Polka

Words: Lew Brown; Music: Jaramir Vejvoda

"Beer Barrel Polka" was a popular Czech song written by Jaromir Vejvoda, which was given English words by Lew Brown in '34. Its original Czech title, "Skoda Lasky," means "lost love." Wladimir A. Timm wrote the Czech lyrics. Will Glahe and his orchestra had a huge hit with the song in '38. The Andrews Sisters also had a very popular version of the song, but they only performed one of the most famous melodies instead for the several that were part of Glahe's arrangement. The Andrews Sisters' version used the lyrics "Roll out the barrel." They performed their version in the '44 movie musical *Follow the Boys*. The other popular version was by Eddie DeLange's Orchestra with vocalist Elisse Cooper. Hear Paul Whiteman's recording of "Beer Barrel Polka" at http://www.redhotjazz.com/pwo.html.

The song was the No. 5 sheet music seller and the No. 2 jukebox song of '39, staying on top of that chart for twenty weeks. The song peaked at No. 2 on *Your Hit Parade*, but made sixteen appearances on the show. It was No. 2 for two weeks. Glahe's version was, most likely, the nation's biggest hit record for about a month in the early summer of '39.

"Beer Barrel Polka" sounds like a drinking song from folk tradition rather than a composed song.

Variety selected "Beer Barrel Polka" for its *Hit Parade of a Half-Century.*

The most famous part of the lyrics begins, "Roll out the barrel, we'll have a barrel of fun." Read the lyrics at http://lirama.net/song/16132.

Blue Orchids

Words & Music: Hoagy Carmichael

"Blue Orchids," a Hoagy Carmichael song popularized by Glenn Miller and his orchestra, featured Tex Beneke on tenor sax and Ray Eberle, who was Miller's male vocalist. Benny Goodman and Bob Crosby and their orchestras also released popular versions of the song.

"Blue Orchids" was No. 1 on *Your Hit Parade* for only the November 4th broadcast. It appeared on the *Hit Parade* survey ten weeks.

Tex Beneke was elected to the Big Band/Jazz Hall of Fame in the class of 1996.

The singer dreamed he had two beautiful blue orchids, but when he met this particular girl, "it was plain to see blue orchids only bloom in your eyes." Read the lyrics at http://lirama.net/song/16134.

Cherokee

Words & Music: Ray Noble

English composer and bandleader Ray Noble wrote this "Indian" song, but Charlie Barnet was chiefly responsible for popularizing it in the U.S. The song, he and his band's first major recording success, became their theme song and was inducted into the Grammy Hall of Fame in 1998.

"Cherokee" was played by Barnet and his band in the movie musical *Jam Session* ('44). The song also appeared in Gene Krupa's screen biography, *The Gene Krupa Story* ('59), where it was played by Krupa's orchestra.

Day in — Day Out

Words: Johnny Mercer; Music: Rube Bloom

"Day in — Day Out" was the No. 1 hit on *Your Hit Parade* for the October 21st broadcast.

A later Johnny Mercer lyric, "Come Rain or Come Shine," is foreshadowed in the lyrics of "Day in — Day Out": "Come rain, come shine, I meet you and to me the day is fine." There's a voodoo enchantment that follows him wherever he goes. When she awakens every morning, she thinks immediately of seeing him. Read the lyrics at http://www.bobbycaldwell.com/discography_lyrics_Day_in_Day_Out.htm.

Bob Crosby and his orchestra, with vocalist Helen Ward, had the most popular recording of "Day In, Day Out." Kay Kyser and Artie Shaw and their orchestra's versions were also reasonably popular. Harry Babbitt was Kyser's vocalist, while Helen Forrest performed Shaw's vocal.

Deep Purple

Words: Mitchell Parish; Music: Peter DeRose

"Deep Purple" originated as a piano solo by Peter DeRose in '34. A year later Domenico Savino arranged it for orchestra. However, it may have reached higher on the hit list when lyrics were added by Mitchell Parish in '39. The melody and lyrics seem inseparable, yet it is doubtful that anyone could detect that the melody came first.

The "deep purple" is the darkness that kindles a memory that brings back thoughts of his loved one. Even though she is gone, she lives on in his "deep purple dreams." Read the lyrics at http://lirama.net/song/16140.

Larry Clinton and his orchestra had the most popular recording of "Deep Purple" in '39. Nino Tempo and April Stevens revived the song in '63 into a No. 1 hit again. Other popular versions included those by Jimmy Dorsey and his orchestra, by Guy Lombardo and his Royal Canadians, by Bing Crosby, and by Artie Shaw and his orchestra in '39. Paul Weston and his orchestra revived it in '49 with decent success. Billy Ward and the Dominos revived it again in '57 and Donny and Marie Osmond covered it again in '76. Hear Paul Whiteman's recording of "Deep Purple" at http://www.redhotjazz.com/pwo.html.

Jimmy Dorsey's recording was on *Metronome*'s best sides of '39, was the No. 1 top radio tune for three weeks, the No. 2 sheet music seller, and the No. 3 jukebox selection of the year. It also spent six weeks on the top of *Your Hit Parade* in February and March of '39.

Variety selected "Deep Purple" for its *Hit Parade of a Half-Century* twice: '35 and '39. The song became one of the most recorded songs of the pre-rock era.

Good Morning

Words: Arthur Freed; Music: Nacio Herb Brown

Mickey Rooney and Judy Garland introduced "Good Morning" in the movie musical *Babes in Arms*. The original *Babes in Arms* was a '37 Broadway musical by Richard Rodgers and Lorenz Hart. Arthur Freed and Nacio Herb Brown's "Good Morning" was interpolated into the film version. Mickey and Judy sing a very jazzy rendition of the song.

Abe Lyman and his orchestra helped popularized the song with a successful '39 recording. However, the most famous rendition of the song is most likely Gene Kelly, Debbie Reynolds and Donald O'Connor's singing and dancing of the number in the '52 movie musical *Singin' in the Rain*. In the film's plot Gene as Don Lockwood, Debbie as Kathy Selden and Donald as Cosmo Brown are sitting together late one evening at Don's house. The film they have been working on, *The Dueling Cavalier*, is a disaster. Then Cosmo suggests making the film into a musical. Once the decision is made, at 1:30 a.m., all three are thrilled and their enthusiasm overflows into a rousing rendition of "Good Morning." Read the lyrics at http://www.stlyrics.com/lyrics/singingintherain/goodmorning.htm.

AFI's *100 Years ... 100 Songs* (2004) named this song the No. 72 greatest song ever from an American film for its inclusion in *Singin' in the Rain*.

Heaven Can Wait

Words: Eddie DeLange; Music: Jimmy Van Heusen

"Heaven Can Wait" replaced "Deep Purple" as the No. 1 song on *Your Hit Parade* on the April 22nd broadcast. It managed two consecutive weeks as the top hit.

Glen Gray and the Casa Loma Orchestra were most responsible for popularizing the song on records. Kay Kyser and his orchestra also had a popular version, but not nearly as popular as Gray's. Clyde Burke was vocalist for the Casa Loma Orchestra on this recording, while Harry Babbitt sang the vocal on Kyser's version.

The basic idea of the lyrics is "Heaven can wait" because this is paradise right here with his loved one. Until its time to die and go to heaven, the love they share is well worth the wait. Read the lyrics at http://www.lirama. net/song/16145.

Jeepers Creepers
Words: Johnny Mercer; Music: Harry Warren

As anyone who loves old films can probably tell you, "Jeepers Creepers" was the name of a horse in the '38 movie *Going Places*. Louis Armstrong introduced this Academy Award nominated song. Although the song wasn't written with Louis in mind, the idea of having him sing it to the horse in the film proved to be inspired. "Jeepers Creepers" became one of his specialties. It was the No. 6 top radio tune and stayed at No. 1 on *Your Hit Parade* for five weeks in '39.

"Jeepers Creepers" lost out to "Thanks for the Memory" for the Academy Award.

Even though Louis (most often pronounced Louie) Armstrong's recording of "Jeepers Creepers" was popular, one by Al Donahue and his orchestra was far more popular in '39. Larry Clinton and his orchestra also had a version on the market that was probably equally as popular as Armstrong's. Paula Kelly was Donohue's vocalist on his disk. Donohue's recording of "Jeepers Creepers" was the most successful recording of his career. Hear Louis Armstrong's recording of "Jeepers Creepers" at http://www.red hotjazz.com/lao.html.

"Jeepers Creepers" was interpolated into the '49 movie musical *My Dream Is Yours*, which starred Doris Day, Jack Carson, and Eve Arden. The song also appeared in the movies *Mr. & Mrs. Bride* ('90), *Sleepless in Seattle* ('93) and *Jeepers Creepers* (2001).

This song was nominated for the American Film Institute's list of greatest songs ever from an American film, but was not on the final list. It was nominated for its appearance in the '38 film *Going Places*.

The most famous part of the lyrics is the opening of the chorus: "Jeepers creepers, where'd ya get those peepers?" Read the lyrics and hear a midi musical version at http:// www.harrywarren.org/songs/0253.htm.

The Man with the Mandolin
Words: James Cavanaugh & John Redmond; Music: Frank Weldon

Glenn Miller and his orchestra, with a vocal performance by Marion Hutton, had a very successful recording of "The Man with the Mandolin" in '39.

1939 was Miller's first big year of success on records. He and his band had No. 1 recordings of "Wishing," "Stairway to the Stars," "Moon Love," "Over the Rainbow," "Blue Orchids," and "The Man with the Mandolin."

Hoarce Heidt and Wayne King and their orchestras also issued popular versions of the song.

According to *A Century of Pop Music*, "The Man with the Mandolin" spent three weeks as the nation's top hit in September 1939, but according to *Your Hit Parade*, it peaked at No. 2.

The idea of the lyric is to describe "the man with the mandolin." This ragged old minstrel man always wears a big grin and all the kids follow him around. A mandolin plays in between several of the lines or phrases. Read the lyrics at http://lirama.net/song/16156.

Moonlight Serenade
Words: Mitchell Parish; Music: Glenn Miller

Glenn Miller wrote the music for this song, which became the orchestra's theme song. The original title was "Now I Lay Me Down to Weep."

As a result of Artie Shaw's illness in '39, several tunes that Shaw was to have recorded were transferred to Miller's band. One was Frankie Carle's theme song, "Sunrise Serenade." Glenn decided to put his own theme on the flip side of the record and, to balance Carle's, renamed his tune "Moonlight Serenade." The song features Miller's distinctive arranging style and Wilbur Schwartz on clarinet.

"Moonlight Serenade" peaked at No. 6 on *Your Hit Parade*, but has remained popular over the years because of its association with Miller and his band as their theme. It was, of course, used in Miller's screen biography, *The Glenn Miller Story* ('54). Miller's recording of the song was inducted into the Grammy Hall of Fame in 1991.

The central idea of the chorus lyrics can be summed up with the following excerpt: "I stand at your gate and I sing you a song in the moonlight ... a Moonlight Serenade." Read the lyrics at http://lirama.net/song/9201.

Moon Love
Words: Mack David & Mack Davis; Music: Andre Kostelanetz

Andre Kostelanetz based this song on a theme from Tchaikovsky's Fifth Symphony. The lyricists added, "Will this be moon love?," meaning will it be gone by dawn or is it really true love? Read the lyrics at http://lirama. net/song/16157.

The marriage of melody and lyrics was No. 1 on *Your Hit Parade* for four weeks in '39 and was one of the top radio tunes of the year.

Tchaikovsky and Chopin are the nineteenth-century classical composers whose melodies have most often been adapted into popular songs.

It was Glenn Miller and his orchestra who recorded the most popular version of the song, but Al Donohue, Paul Whiteman, and Mildred Bailey also recorded successful versions. Ray Eberle was Miller's vocal soloist on "Moon Love." Hear Paul Whiteman's recording of "Moon Love" at http://www.redhotjazz.com/pwo.html.

Our Love
Words: Buddy Bernier & Bob Emmerich; Music: Larry Clinton

Larry Clinton appropriated the theme for this hit song from Tschaikovsky's "Romeo and Juliet." Clinton and his orchestra introduced the song and recordings by Tommy and Jimmy Dorsey and their orchestras helped make it No. 1 on *Your Hit Parade* for two weeks during the year as well as a top radio tune. Tommy's version was slightly more successful than Jimmy's.

The original romantic Tschaikovsky melody was perfect for popular song material.

The chorus lyrics assert "Our love" is everywhere. It is in the breeze, it is like an evening prayer and it's "in every whisper of the trees." Read the lyrics at http://lirama.net/song/16162.

Over the Rainbow

Words: E.Y. Harburg; Music: Harold Arlen

This ASCAP "All-Time Hit Parade" selection and *Variety Hit Parade of a Half-Century* song was the Academy Award winning Best Song in '39. Judy Garland introduced "Over the Rainbow" in *The Wizard of Oz*, and her recording of it with Victor Young and his orchestra was inducted into the Grammy Hall of Fame in 1981. AFI's *100 Years ... 100 Songs* (2004) honored "Over the Rainbow" as the greatest song ever from American films. The song became one of the most recorded songs of the pre-rock era.

But as associated as this song is with Judy Garland today, in '39, hers was not the most popular version (as popular as Garland was in films, she never had a particularly successful recording career). Glenn Miller and his orchestra's version was most popular, followed by Bob Crosby and his orchestra's. Ms. Garland's was the third most popular version, followed by Larry Clinton and his orchestra's version.

"Over the Rainbow" spent six weeks as the No. 1 hit on *Your Hit Parade*. It made fifteen appearances on the program.

See the sheet music cover and musical score at http://lcweb2.loc.gov/cocoon/ihas/loc.natlib.ihas.100004523/.

The lyrics to "Over the Rainbow" are so well known, it probably isn't necessary to remind the reader of them. However, the lyrics do sound a bit like anti–Depression–Era philosophy. It had only been a few years since the worst of the Depression, so that shouldn't be too surprising. The worst may have been over, but in rural America, like Kansas, many families were still "dirt" poor and faced many hardships daily. Dorothy simply wanted to go to the land "Over the Rainbow" where her troubles would "melt like lemon drops." Read the lyrics at http://lirama.net/song/9202.

Judy Garland was only sixteen years old when she starred in this film classic. The film has almost been an annual presentation on television for years so that each new generation has been introduced to Dorothy, Toto, the Tin Man, the Scarecrow, and the Cowardly Lion plus the glorious musical score. *The Wizard of Oz* is probably more successful and far better known today than it was in '39. Its television appearances have made it into one of Hollywood's most famous films.

The first stage production of *The Wizard of Oz* was in 1903. None of the music of the 1903 musical was used in the '39 movie musical version. Another amusing difference between the two is that it was originally Dorothy and her pet cow, Imogene, not Toto, the dog.

Eileen Farrell, dubbing for Eleanor Parker, performed "Over the Rainbow" in *Interrupted Melody* ('55) and Andrea McArdle sang it in *Rainbow* ('78).

Other songs from the *Wizard of Oz* score that were popular recordings include "Ding-Dong! The Witch Is Dead," popularized by Glenn Miller. This song was named the No. 82 greatest song ever from an American film by the American Film Institute in its *100 Years ... 100 Songs* list in 2004. "If I Only Had a Brain/Heart/The Nerve" was nominated for the American Film Institute's list of greatest songs ever from an American film, but did not make the final list.

Penny Serenade

Words: Hal Halifax; Music: Melle Weersma

Guy Lombardo and his Royal Canadians introduced "Penny Serenade." Written in England in '38, it was the first-ranking jukebox tune for eleven weeks during '39. It spent ten weeks in the top ten and stayed in the No. 2 spot for five weeks on *Your Hit Parade* in the spring.

The Royal Canadians' recording was the most popular version, followed closely by Sammy Kaye's. Hoarce Heidt and his orchestra also released a popular version.

Variety listed "Penny Serenade" as one of its *Hit Parade of a Half-Century* songs.

A '42 film entitled *Penny Serenade* refers to this song, which is one of several songs in the film as part of Grant's reminiscences.

The singer is serenading a lovely senorita. "Si, si, si, hear my song for a penny, si, si, si, just a Penny Serenade." Read the lyrics at http://www.lirama.net/song/16163.

Scatter-Brain

Words: Johnny Burke; Music: Kahn Kaene, Carl Bean & Frankie Masters

Kay Kyser and his orchestra performed this novelty song in the '39 movie musical *That's Right, You're Wrong*. It was also a big production number in the Judy Canova film *Scatter-Brain* ('40).

The song stayed at the top spot on *Your Hit Parade* for six weeks at the end of '39 and the beginning of '40. Co-writer Frankie Masters and his orchestra helped popularize the song, which became their theme song. Their recording was most popular in early '40. Freddy Martin and his orchestra's recording was a No. 1 hit in late '39.

The song was one of the top radio tunes of '39. In '40, it was a top sheet music seller and spent a dozen weeks at the number one position on the jukebox chart.

"Scatter-Brain" was probably a big hit song because we all have known a few people that fit the lyrics so perfectly. The singer tells this person they have a delightful smile, but "isn't it a pity that you're such a Scatter-Brain?" He finally admits that it really doesn't matter, because "you're my darling Scatter-Brain." Read the lyrics at http://lirama.net/song/16164.

September Song

Words: Maxwell Anderson; Music: Kurt Weill

"September Song" was one of only sixteen songs selected by ASCAP for its *All-Time Hit Parade* and *Variety* named it to its *Hit Parade of a Half-Century* and its *Golden 100* list. It is quite an honor to be one of only sixteen ASCAP *All-Time Hit Parade* songs from a fifty-year period. "September Song" also became one of the most recorded songs of the pre-rock era.

It was written for *Knickerbocker Holiday*, one of the first musicals on Broadway to be based on a historical subject that commented on contemporary issues. The theme of democracy versus totalitarianism was presented in the reign of Governor Peter Stuyvesant in New Amsterdam in 1647. Walter Huston played the peg-legged Stuyvesant so convincingly, especially when he sang "September Song," that audiences found themselves pulling for the wrong side. Huston more or less movingly spoke the song, and the audiences begged for encores.

In "September Song," Stuyvesant confesses his fears of growing old in this tender ballad sung to the young girl he intends to marry. Read the lyrics at http://lirama.net/song/31571.

Huston had done some singing and dancing in vaudeville as a young man, but by the time he was hired as the lead in *Knickerbocker Holiday*, he was known as a distinguished dramatic actor. When Weill and Anderson wired him inquiring about his vocal range, he replied back, "I have no range." So they wrote "September Song" with his limitations in mind.

The German-born composer Kurt Weill had come to America to escape Nazism. He obviously had very passionate feelings about the democracy versus totalitarianism debate because he had experienced the social and political life of the early days of Nazism.

Huston's recording of the song seems to be the most famous one in the late thirties and today, but Frank Sinatra's '46 recording is also a classic. Huston's recording was inducted into the Grammy Hall of Fame in 1984. Other versions that charted include the Dardanelle Trio's in '46, Stan Kenton and his orchestra's in '51 and Liberace's in '52. Ted Lewis' recording of "September Song" can be heard at http://www.redhotjazz.com/tlband.html.

The film version of *Knickerbocker Holiday* was released in '44. Charles Coburn starred as Stuyvesant and performed the song. Maurice Chevalier performed it in the '60 movie musical *Pepe*.

Stairway to the Stars

Words: Mitchell Parish; Music: Matty Malneck & Frank Signorelli

Matty Malneck, Frank Signorelli and Jimmy Dorsey were three of the talented jazz musicians who gravitated to New York City in the '20s. Malneck played violin and viola in Paul Whiteman's orchestra and got to know Dorsey when he joined the sax section of the band in '27. Signorelli, a freelance pianist, often worked with both Malneck and Dorsey as studio musicians.

The songwriting partnership of Malneck and Signorelli produced "Stairway to the Stars." Initially, the song was part of a more ambitious project, a '35 symphonic work called "Park Avenue Fantasy," which was introduced by Paul Whiteman and his orchestra. The work didn't make them a lot of money, so Malneck and Signorelli reworked their basic melody into a simpler pop song. Lyrics were added by master lyricist Mitchell Parish.

"Stairway to the Stars" was a big hit recording for Glenn Miller and his orchestra, but recordings by Kay Kyser, Jimmy Dorsey, and Al Donohue and their orchestras also contributed to the song's success in '39. Ray Eberle was Miller's vocalist on their recording, while Harry Babbitt was Kyser's vocal soloist. Ray Eberle's brother, Bob Eberly (notice the different spelling of their last name) was the vocalist for Jimmy Dorsey's recording, and Paula Kelly was the soloist on Donohue's version.

The song made a dozen appearances on *Your Hit Parade*, and was the No. 1 hit for four consecutive weeks from mid–July to early August.

Since it was a big Glenn Miller hit, the song was used in his screen biography that was filmed in '54.

The basic idea of the chorus lyrics can be summed up with the following quote: "Let's build a stairway to the stars ... It would be heaven to climb to heaven with you." Read the lyrics at http://lirama.net/song/16167.

Sunrise Serenade

Words: Jack Lawrence; Music: Frankie Carle

Frankie Carle, a great piano soloist and leader of his own highly successful band, also made his mark as a song-writer, especially with the beautiful "Sunrise Serenade," which became his theme song. It was probably Glenn Miller's version that first put "Sunrise Serenade" on the map. He recorded "Sunrise Serenade" on one side of a 78-rpm disk with his own theme song, "Moonlight Serenade" on the flip side.

Perhaps an equally popular version of the song was Glen Gray and the Casa Loma Orchestra's. Miller's version was revived with moderate success in '44.

"Sunrise Serenade" peaked at No. 2 on *Your Hit Parade*, and made fifteen appearances on the program. According to other sources, however, the Casa Loma Orchestra's version was the nation's biggest hit recording for a couple of weeks in August of '39.

Variety selected "Sunrise Serenade" for its *Hit Parade of a Half-Century*.

Jack Lawrence's lyrics are not nearly as familiar as the melody. Because the tune seems so instrumentally conceived, the lyrics aren't very easily sung to the melody as it jumps around in several octave leaps and a few of more than an octave. Triplet figures are also prominent and that doesn't seem to help fit all the words in either. Read the lyrics at http://lirama.net/song/16169.

Thanks for Everything

Words: Mack Gordon; Music: Harry Revel

Adolphe Menjou, Jack Oakie, Jack Haley, Arleen Whelan, Tony Martin, and several others lent their talents to the 20th Century-Fox movie musical *Thanks for Everything* in '38. It was a simple story that had an advertising executive, played by Menjou, together with his public relations man, played by Oakie, conducting a coast-to-coast search for Mister Average Man, who turns out to be Jack Haley from Plainville, Missouri.

Harry Revel and Mack Gordon wrote the film's musical score that included, of course, the title song.

Artie Shaw and his orchestra had a particularly popular recording of the song in '39. Tommy Dorsey and his orchestra's version was also pretty popular. Helen Forrest was Shaw's vocal soloist on "Thanks for Everything."

The song peaked at No. 3 on *Your Hit Parade*, but may well have been the top hit around the nation for a week in January of '39.

The lyrics are thanking the loved one for everything, including "every word, every sigh, every kiss," for making gray skies blue, and for taking her cares away. Read the lyrics at http://lirama.net/song/16171.

They Say

Words: Ed Heyman; Music: Paul Mann & Stephen Weiss

Artie Shaw and his orchestra had a monster hit with their recording of "Begin the Beguine" in '38. By the end of the year, their recording of "They Say" was also a chart-topping hit. Helen Forrest was Shaw's vocal soloist on "They Say."

In '39, Shaw, who seemed to have a running feud with some of his fans, abruptly left his band and went into temporary exile in Mexico. He didn't return until '40.

The Swing and Sway sounds of Sammy Kaye and his orchestra also helped popularize the song with a successful recording.

The song peaked at No. 5 on *Your Hit Parade*, but *A Century of Pop Music* claims that it was the top song in the nation for a couple of weeks right at the beginning of '39.

So what is it "They Say"? "They say" you wouldn't care for me. But the singer says, "I'll always love you no matter what they say." Read the lyrics at http://lirama.net/song/16172.

Three Little Fishies

Words & Music: Saxie Dowell

Anyone who thinks that rock 'n' roll cornered the market on silly nonsense or novelty songs might do well to look at several songs from this period.

Hal Kemp and his orchestra were the first group to popularize this song, which could be subtitled "Boop-Boop Dit-Tem Dot-Tem What-Tem Chu," primarily because the writer, Saxie Dowell, was Kemp's saxophonist. Kemp's recording was popular, but not quite as popular as Kay Kyser and his orchestra's. It reportedly had become Kyser's first million-selling disk by '41. Ginny Simms, Ish Kabibble, and Harry Babbitt were the vocalists on Kyser's version. The venerable Paul Whiteman and his orchestra also had a popular version of the song on the market, which can be heard at http://www.redhotjazz.com/pwo.html.

"Three Little Fishies" peaked at No. 2 on *Your Hit Parade*, but may well have been the nation's biggest hit song for a couple of weeks in May of '39. *Variety* included it in its *Hit Parade of a Half-Century* for '39.

This novelty hit tells about a mama fish and her "three little fishies." A mama fish is teaching her offspring to swim. But by far the most familiar part of the lyric is the subtitle: "Boop-boop dit-tem dat-tem what-tem chu." There are four verses to this novelty. Read all the verses at http://members.tripod.com/~rosemckl/three-little-fishes.html.

The Umbrella Man

Words: James Cavanaugh & Larry Stock; Music: Vincent Rose

Ginny Simms and Harry Babbitt were the vocal soloists on Kay Kyser and his orchestra's very successful recording of "The Umbrella Man."

"The Umbrella Man" was one of the band's first chart topping recordings. Their recording of "Three Little Fishies" (see above) was also a big early hit for the band.

The song peaked at No. 2 on *Your Hit Parade*, but *A Century of Pop Music* claims it was the country's No. 1 hit for one week in February of '39.

Johnny Messner and his orchestra, with a vocal performance by the Three Jacks, also had a popular version of "The Umbrella Man" on the market.

"The Umbrella Man," according to the lyrics, was a repairman who mends umbrellas and parasols. In his spare time, he will also sharpen knives, darn socks, or even mend a broken heart. Read the lyrics at http://lirama.net/song/16176.

When the Saints Go Marching in

Words & Music: Unknown

"When the Saints Go Marching In" has African American spiritual origins, so its history is vague at best. It was most likely a part of oral tradition that was passed down from generation to generation until at some point someone decided it needed to be written down.

Most famously, "When the Saints Go Marching In" (or often just called "Saints") was used as a funeral hymn. In

New Orleans, most of the African Americans belonged to fraternities, societies or burial clubs. When one of their brethren died, these clubs organized a funeral parade. The legitimate mourners were called first liners, while the second liners were often younger people who were attracted to the music and joined the funeral parade just for fun. When the funeral parade left the church headed towards the cemetery, the band would play the tune in a mournful style at a slow tempo. However, once the service was over and they headed back towards town, the tempo increased and the mood became exuberant. This was the part of the funeral the second liners had tagged along to enjoy. They strutted, shook, shouted and high-stepped all the way back.

The first recording of the song that was popular enough to chart was Louis Armstrong's in '39. Hear Armstrong's recording of "...Saints..." at http://www.redhotjazz.com/lao.html. However, all the New Orleans jazz bands mostly likely played it for many years prior to '39. The only other recordings popular enough to chart on *Billboard* were by the Weavers in '51 and by Percy Faith and his orchestra in '51.

The song has certainly been a favorite of movie musicals for many years. It appeared in the great all-black film *Green Pastures* ('36), and Mario Lanza, imitating Louis Armstrong, sang it in *The Seven Hills of Rome* ('58), Louis Armstrong and Danny Kaye sang it in *The Five Pennies* ('59; new lyrics written by Danny Kaye's wife, Sylvia Fine), *Hey Boy, Hey Girl* ('59), and Elvis Presley and the Jordanaires performed it in *Frankie and Johnny* ('66; once again with new lyrics).

Wishing (Will Make It So)

Words & Music: Buddy DeSylva

B.G. "Buddy" DeSylva, one of the most prolific lyricists of popular music, wrote both the words and music for "Wishing," which topped *Your Hit Parade* for four weeks. It was introduced in the motion picture *Love Affair*. The song was nominated for the Oscar, but lost to "Over the Rainbow."

"Wishing (Will Make It So)" was chiefly popularized by Glenn Miller and his orchestra in a very successful recording in '39. Russ Morgan, Skinnay Ennis, and Orrin Tucker and their orchestras also issued popular recordings of the song. Miller's version was the fourth best-selling record and the third best sheet music seller of the year. Ray Eberle was Miller's vocal soloist on their version.

The singer is convinced that "wishing will make it so," because our wishes are just daytime dreams. Read the lyrics at http://www.lyricsdepot.com/glenn-miller/wishing.html.

DeSylva had been a very successful lyricist with the Henderson, DeSylva, Brown team. This was one of the rare occasions when he wrote both words and music.

Variety included "Wishing" in its *Hit Parade of a Half-Century*.

1940

All the Things You Are

Words: Oscar Hammerstein II; Music: Jerome Kern

During the first two months of '40, "All the Things You Are" was the top song on *Your Hit Parade* for a couple of weeks. It originated in the '39 Broadway musical *Very Warm for May*, where it was introduced by Hollace Shaw, Frances Mercer, Hiram Sherman, and Ralph Stuart. Composer Jerome Kern was convinced the song was too sophisticated to be popular, but he was mistaken. It was the top hit for two weeks (January 27th and February 10th) in early '40 and stayed in the top ten for almost three months at the end of '39 and the beginning of '40.

"All the Things You Are" seems too much in the operetta style for the swing era, but for seven weeks it was the top jukebox song in recordings by Tommy Dorsey and his orchestra with Jack Leonard's vocal, plus Artie Shaw and Frankie Masters and their orchestras. In a poll conducted by the *Saturday Review* in 1964, more composers picked this song as their favorite than any other. "All the Things You Are" was selected by *Variety* for its *Hit Parade of a Half-Century* representing 1939. It also became one of the most recorded songs of the pre-rock era. Hear Paul Whiteman's recording of this song at http://www.redhotjazz.com/pwo.html.

The singer compliments his loved one telling her she is "the promised kiss of springtime." He yearns for the day when his arms will hold her and "when all the things you are, are mine!" Read the lyrics at http://www.metrolyrics.com/lyrics/154647/Ella_Fitzgerald/All_The_Things_You_Are.

Ginny Simms sang "All the Things You Are" in the '41 movie musical *Broadway Rhythm*, Judy Garland sang it in Jerome Kern's screen biography, *Till the Clouds Roll By* ('46). Mario Lanza sang it in movie musical *Because You're Mine* in '52 and an excerpt in *The Seven Hills of Rome* ('58). The song also appeared in *Tin Men* ('87) and *The Rookie* ('90).

At the Balalaika
Words: Bob Wright & George "Chet" Forrest; Music: George Posford

This *Variety Hit Parade of a Half-Century* selection representing 1939 originated in England. The original music by George Posford was adapted by Herbert Stothart, and the original lyrics by Eric Maschwitz were discarded for new ones by Bob Wright and Chet Forrest. Ilona Massey and the Russian Art Choir introduced the revised version of "At the Balalaika" in the film *Balalaika* ('39). British composer George Posford had written the song in '36 for an English musical *The Gay Hussar*.

The song spent nine weeks among the top ten on *Your Hit Parade* in '40 but never reached No. 1; its highest rank was No. 3 in mid–February of '40.

The most popular recordings of the song were by Orrin Tucker and his orchestra and by Abe Lyman and his Californians.

The balalaika is one of a family of Central Asian lutes; it has a unique triangular body shape. The balalaika became one of the most important plucked stringed instruments in Eastern Europe, and is particularly associated with Russia and the Ukraine.

However, in the context of this song, the Balalaika is a bar or restaurant. The singer is having a rendezvous "At the Balalaika." There is sparkling wine, candlelight and a haunting melody played on a gypsy violin and the singer wants to stay until daybreak. Read the lyrics at http://www.lyricsxp.com/lyrics/a/at_the_balalaika_orrin_tucker.html.

Back in the Saddle Again
Words & Music: Ray Whitley and Gene Autry

Gene Autry was the first really famous singing cowboy movie star. By the end of his career, in the early '50s, he had made about 100 films, which often grossed ten times their production costs. His own company produced his TV series *The Gene Autry Show*, *The Adventures of Champion*, and *Annie Oakley* in the '50s. In addition, he was the star of the radio show *Melody Ranch* from the early '40s through the early '50s.

He was also the writer or co-writer of several hits; he wrote over 200 songs. "Back in the Saddle Again" is one example of his writing, which he introduced in the '41 film *Back in the Saddle*. The song was one of the American Film Institute's 400 nominated songs for its *100 Years ... 100 Songs* list that was published in 2004. Autry's recording of "Back in the Saddle Again" was inducted into the Grammy Hall of Fame in 1997. The song was also featured on the soundtrack of *Sleepless in Seattle*.

One morning Ray Whitley got a call from his bosses at RKO. They wanted him to write a song for a new western film they were starting to film that day. As he explained the call to his wife, he said to her, "Well, I'm back in the saddle again." She told him that would make a good title for the song and he agreed. He wrote the song almost immediately. He performed it for his bosses the next day at the shooting location. When Gene Autry heard the song he thought it fit his character perfectly. He and Whitley rewrote it slightly before Autry sang it in his next film. It became Autry's signature song.

"Back in the Saddle Again" is a fairly typical song that appeared in many of the singing cowboy films of the era. A man's horse, his dog and his gun were his most valuable possessions. He sleeps out under the stars every night and the law is always right. Read the lyrics at http://www.stlyrics.com/lyrics/sleeplessinseattle/backinthesaddleagain.htm.

Bewitched (Bothered and Bewildered) (see 1950)

Dick Rodgers and Larry Hart wrote "Bewitched (Bothered and Bewildered)," a *Variety Golden 100 Tin Pan Alley Song*, for the 1940 musical *Pal Joey*, but it became more popular in '50.

Blueberry Hill
Words & Music: Al Lewis, Larry Stock & Vincent Rose

Most people who were born after the early forties probably think that Fats Domino wrote "Blueberry Hill" because he popularized it in the mid-fifties. Those who remember the song from recordings by Glenn Miller, Kay Kyser, and Russ Morgan's orchestras from the early forties know differently. It was the top jukebox song for eleven weeks. Ray Eberle was Miller's vocal soloist on their very popular recording. Hear "Blueberry Hill" recorded by Paul Whiteman and his orchestra at http://www.redhotjazz.com/pwo.html.

Singing cowboy Gene Autry interpolated "Blueberry Hill" into the '41 film *The Singing Hill*.

The song peaked at No. 2 on *Your Hit Parade* in '40 and at No. 4 in early '57, but, according to *Variety*, it was the nation's biggest hit song for at least one week in November of '40.

Of course, Fats Domino did record the song and introduced it to a whole new generation with his popular rhythm and blues version. His version peaked at No. 2 on *Billboard's* chart in early '57, and according to *Billboard*, it was the biggest hit of Domino's illustrious recording career.

The singer found his "thrill on Blueberry Hill" when he found this girl. And even though they are now away from each other, "you're part of me still." Read the lyrics at http://lirama.net/song/9196.

The Breeze and I

Words: Al Stillman; Music: Ernesto Lecuona

Jimmy Dorsey and his orchestra made an important recording of "The Breeze and I," which was adapted from Ernesto Lecuona's "Andalucia." *Variety* listed the song as one of the top ten of '40 but other information makes it appear not quite so important. *Billboard* reported that recordings by Jimmy Dorsey's, Charlie Barnet's, and Freddy Martin's orchestras made the song the No. 1 jukebox record for seven weeks during the year. The song that stayed the longest in that category stayed there for twenty-one weeks, and twenty-seven songs were on top longer than "The Breeze and I."

The song peaked at No. 2 on *Your Hit Parade*, where it made thirteen appearances. However, Dorsey's recording, according to *Variety*, was the top one around the nation for one week in September of '40.

Bob Eberly was Jimmy Dorsey's vocalist on their very popular disk. Another popular recording of "The Breeze and I" was by Xavier Cugat and his orchestra. Vic Damone revived it in '54 and had decent success with his vocal version.

Organist Ethel Smith played the song in the '46 movie musical *Cuban Pete*.

Variety included "The Breeze and I" in its *Hit Parade of a Half-Century.*

The chorus lyrics open with "The breeze and I are saying ... that you no longer care." Even though the singer and his loved one's attraction seemed solid, it ended "in a strange, mournful tune." Read the lyrics at http://lirama. net/song/16776.

Careless

Words & Music: Dick Jurgens, Eddy Howard & Lew Qualding

"Careless" was a big hit recording for Glenn Miller and his orchestra with vocalist Ray Eberle in the early part of '40. Co-writer, Dick Jurgens and his orchestra also had a popular recording of the song.

The song was No. 1 on *Your Hit Parade* for five weeks. Out of an eight-week period in February and March, "Careless" was No. 1 for five of those weeks.

The singer, Ray Eberle in this case, sings that his love is "Careless" after she got him to fall in love with her. He finally asks "Are you just careless ... or do you just care less for me?" What a clever lyricist idea to turn "careless" into "care less." Read the lyrics at http://www.lyrics depot.com/glenn-miller/careless.html.

Darn That Dream

Words: Eddie DeLange; Music: James Van Heusen

Benny Goodman and his orchestra introduced "Darn That Dream" in the musical *Swingin' the Dream*, a swing

version of Shakespeare's *A Midsummer Night's Dream*. Goodman's recording of the song, with Mildred Bailey as vocalist, was the most popular version on the market, but disks by the Blue Barron and his orchestra and by Tommy Dorsey and his orchestra were also popular with the public. "Darn That Dream" as recorded by Paul Whiteman and his orchestra can be heard at http://www.redhotjazz. com/pwo.html.

"Darn That Dream" was No. 1 on *Your Hit Parade* for the March 16th broadcast. It only made half a dozen appearances on the program.

The singer dreams of her beloved, but when she awakes, he is not there, and she curses the dream. Read the lyrics at http://www.lyricsfreak.com/b/billie-holiday/18018. html.

Ferryboat Serenade (La Piccinina)

Words: Harold Adamson; Music: Eldo di Lazzaro

The Andrews Sisters' recording of this Italian song helped it stay nine weeks at No. 1 on the jukebox charts and rate among the top fifteen sheet music sellers for the year.

Kay Kyser and his orchestra, Gray Gordon and his orchestra, Frankie Masters and his orchestra, and Leo Reisman and his orchestra released important recordings of "Ferryboat Serenade."

The feud between ASCAP and broadcasting interests in the early forties caused foreign music to become much more important. BMI, Broadcast Music Incorporated, the new performing rights organization formed by radio interests, was forced to seek out music from areas that ASCAP had ignored. One of those areas was foreign writers and their music.

The singer loves to ride the ferry because the music is good, couples are dancing and romancing, and everyone is happy. Read the English or Italian lyrics at http://lyrics playground.com/alpha/songs/f/ferryboatserenade.shtml.

Fools Rush In

Words: Johnny Mercer; Music: Rube Bloom

Johnny Mercer set words to Rube Bloom's composition "Shangri La" to make "Fools Rush In." The second-strain lyrics are "Fools rush in where wise men never go, but wise men never fall in love, so how are they to know?"

"Fools Rush in (Where Angels Fear to Tread)" was the top jukebox song for eight weeks in '40. It was made popular through recordings by Glenn Miller and his orchestra, with Ray Eberle's vocal, by Tommy Dorsey and his orchestra, with a Frank Sinatra vocal performance, and by singer Tony Martin, with Ray Sinatra's Orchestra. Ricky Nelson revived it in 1963 in a successful recording.

The song was No. 1 for only one week, the July 20th broadcast, on *Your Hit Parade*.

The most famous part of Johnny Mercer's lyric is probably "Fools rush in" where they know there's no chance of love. He further reminds us "wise men never fall in love so how are they to know?" Read the lyrics at http://lirama. net/song/15692.

Frenesi (Cancion Tropical)

Words: Ray Charles & S.K. Russell; Music: Alberto Dominguez

"Frenesi" was the first song by a Mexican writer to sell a million records. The song was popularized chiefly by

Artie Shaw and his orchestra. His recording became one of the biggest hits of the decade. Shaw's recording of "Frenesi" was inducted into the Grammy Hall of Fame in 2000.

In '39 Artie Shaw was in exile in Acapulco reportedly recuperating from a blood disease, but more likely, according to the press, escaping his bobby-soxer fans or protesting the jitterbug dance. While he was there, he heard "Frenesi" played by a mariachi band. When he returned to the U.S. in '40, he brought "Frenesi" back to the states with him and recorded it, using the string and woodwind treatment he called "the sound of a small symphony orchestra with a jazz band buried in it." The tremendous success of his recording of the song thrust him back into the national spotlight even though he had been gone for a year.

The song stayed at No. 1 on *Your Hit Parade* for three weeks, but made nineteen appearances on the show. According to *Billboard*, "Frenesi" spent thirteen weeks at No. 1, which makes it one of the decade's biggest hits, and the No. 3 hit of the pre-rock era.

Shaw's recording was by far the most successful one, featuring Shaw's wonderful clarinet solos and his strings, which were rather uncommon in most big bands. Woody Herman and Glenn Miller also released successful versions.

Variety included "Frenesi" in its *Hit Parade of a Half-Century* representing 1940.

The English lyrics of the chorus tell us "Frenesi" means "please love me." Read the English or Spanish lyrics at http://www.azlyrics.us/17359.

The flip side of Artie Shaw's "Frenesi" was "Adios, Marquita Linda," which was popular enough to chart. *Variety* also listed it in its *Hit Parade of a Half-Century* representing 1939.

God Bless America

Words & Music: Irving Berlin

Irving Berlin wrote "God Bless America" in 1918 for a production number in the all-soldier revue *Yip, Yip, Yaphank*, but decided to delete it from the show. Berlin's unashamed patriotism is amply evident as he wrote about prairies and mountains and oceans white with foam. Songwriter Harry Ruby convinced Berlin that every songwriter was pouring out patriotic songs at the time and another one was not needed, so Berlin cut it from the score and placed it in his trunk of musical ideas.

In '38, with the horror of war looming, Berlin decided to write a peace song. He felt writing about peace was "hard to do, because you have trouble dramatizing peace." He wrote "Thanks, America," but didn't like it. Then he came up with "Let's Talk About Liberty," but didn't get far with that idea. Then he remembered "God Bless America," the song deleted from the score of *Yip, Yip, Yaphank* over twenty years before. He changed a couple of lyrics, which necessitated a slight melodic change. One line in the original said, "Stand beside her and guide her to the right with a light from above." Back in '18, "to the right" had no political connotation, but in '38 it did, so he changed the line to read "Through the night with a light from above." Another original line was "Make her victorious on land and foam," but since Berlin didn't want this to be a war song he changed it to "From the mountains to the prairies to the oceans white with foam." This long line altered the meter and demanded a melodic change.

Kate Smith's manager, Ted Collins, was looking for a patriotic song for Kate to perform on her Armistice Day radio show. He was looking for a peace song, so Berlin thought his new and improved "God Bless America" was the appropriate song. Kate introduced it on November 11, 1938, the last peacetime Armistice Day in America prior to the beginning of World War II in Europe.

Within days the song began to acquire the status of our unofficial national anthem. As the country drew closer to war, the song seemed like a heart-felt prayer. On Memorial Day 1939, when the song was played at the Brooklyn Dodgers game at Ebbets Field the crowd stood and the men removed their hats as if they were hearing the national anthem. Kate Smith performed the song at the '39 New York World's Fair. By this time, the sheet music had sold over 400,000 copies and royalties had exceeded $40,000.

Both major political parties used the song as the key song for the presidential nominating conventions of '40.

Berlin, always proud of his adopted country, refused to capitalize on patriotism, so he copyrighted the song in the names of boxer Gene Tunney, politician Theodore Roosevelt, Jr., and Herbert Swope, an old friend of Berlin's, making them a committee to administrate a "God Bless America" fund. Berlin was also concerned that a careful balance of religions were represented: Tunney was Catholic, Swope was Jewish, and Roosevelt was Protestant. All proceeds were assigned to the Boy and Girl Scouts of America. By 1981, more than a million dollars had been turned over to the scouts.

As strange as it may seem today, there was some reaction against "God Bless America." Its critics fumed that a mere creature of commerce—a Tin Pan Alley songwriter—not a classically trained musician, had written the nation's unofficial national anthem. They were also upset that the son of Russian Jewish immigrants, not a native-born American, had composed the song.

In a national poll in the late '50s, "God Bless America" was second to the national anthem as the nation's favorite patriotic song. It was chosen an ASCAP *All-Time Hit Parade* selection, one of only sixteen songs from a fifty-year period. It was also among the songs *Variety* selected for its *Hit Parade of a Half-Century* representing 1940. "God Bless America" was nominated for the American Film Institute's list of the greatest songs ever from American films for its appearance in the 1978 film *The Deer Hunter*, but did not make the final list.

Berlin considered "God Bless America" one of his five best songs, along with "Always," "Easter Parade," "There's No Business Like Show Business," and "White Christmas."

Kate Smith's version of the song is now considered *the* definitive one; her recording of "God Bless America" was inducted into the Grammy Hall of Fame in 1982. Her recording also charted in '39, '40 and '42. Bing Crosby's '39 recording was also popular.

Ms. Smith performed the song in the screen version of Berlin's World War II all-soldier revue, *This Is the Army* ('43). Opera star Lotte Lehmann performed it in *Big City* ('48). The song also appeared in *It's a Big Country* ('51), *The Deer Hunter* ('78) and *Once Upon a Time in America* (84).

During the last several years since the 9/11 catastrophe, major league baseball has "God Bless America" performed, and the crowd sings along, during a break in the action.

Just as "Take Me Out to the Ball Game" has been performed during the seventh inning stretch, now "God Bless America" is also performed. The song has become almost like a second national anthem to many people in this country. Read the lyrics and hear a midi musical version at http://www.scoutsongs.com/lyrics/godblessamerica.html.

I'll Never Smile Again

Words & Music: Ruth Lowe

The tale concerning the origin of "I'll Never Smile Again" may be apocryphal, but it is interesting. Supposedly Ruth Lowe, a pianist with Ina Ray Hutton's all-girl orchestra, wrote the song while mourning the death of her husband a few months after they had been married.

Percy Faith and his orchestra introduced the number on Canadian radio. Tommy Dorsey and his orchestra, with a Frank Sinatra vocal, made the song an outstanding hit, the No. 1 jukebox tune for sixteen weeks in '40. It was the first No. 1 song on the first *Billboard* bestseller chart in '40. It was also Sinatra's first monster hit recording.

Up to this time a big band usually limited the singer to one chorus, but in this recording, Sinatra was featured, backed by Tommy Dorsey's Orchestra. More and more over the next few years, bands featured the singers, leading to the end of the swing era and the opening of the Sing era, when the vocalists, not the bands and their leaders, were the kings of popular music.

"I'll Never Smile Again" was No. 1 on *Your Hit Parade* for seven weeks and made sixteen appearances on their hit survey. According to *Billboard*, it managed a dozen weeks at No. 1, making Miller's recording one of the decade's biggest hits. It ranks among the top twenty for the entire pre-rock era. This Miller recording was inducted into the Grammy Hall of Fame in 1982. *Variety* included "I'll Never Smile Again" in its *Hit Parade of a Half-Century*.

The Four Aces revived "I'll Never Smile Again" with reasonable success in '53.

The singer says he'll "never smile again until I smile at you." Many of the service men during the approaching war felt exactly that way towards their loved one back home. Read the lyrics at http://lirama.net/song/17729.

Imagination

Words: Johnny Burke; Music: James Van Heusen

Fred Waring's Pennsylvanians introduced "Imagination," but recordings by Glenn Miller and his orchestra, with vocalist Ray Eberle, by Tommy Dorsey and his orchestra, with Frank Sinatra as vocalist, by jazz legend Ella Fitzgerald, by Harry Reser's Orchestra, and by Ted Straeter and his orchestra helped popularize the song. Hear Roger Wolfe Kahn and his orchestra's recording of "Imagination" at http://www.redhotjazz.com/rwkahno.html.

"Imagination" was No. 1 on *Your Hit Parade* for three weeks in June and July 1940. It made thirteen appearances on the show. It was on top of the jukebox charts for seven weeks.

Johnny Burke's chorus lyrics tell us "Imagination" is funny, crazy and silly. The singer finds himself wanting this girl but he can't imagine that she would want him too. Read the lyrics at http://lirama.net/song/67059.

A different song, "Imagination," written by Michael Sembello, Michael Boddicker, Jerry Hey and Phil Ramone, was in the movie *Flashdance* ('83).

Indian Summer

Words: Al Dubin; Music: Victor Herbert

The tune to "Indian Summer" originated in 1919 as a piano composition by Victor Herbert. But not until Al Dubin furnished it with lyrics in '39 did it become a hit.

Recordings by Tommy Dorsey and his orchestra and by Glenn Miller and his orchestra helped the song become the No. 1 music machine recording for twelve weeks in '40. It was No. 1 on *Your Hit Parade* for only the February 24th broadcast, but made fourteen appearances on the survey.

One of operetta's great composers, Victor Herbert, wrote this melody, which has a wide range in comparison to most other popular songs of the period.

"Indian Summer" is a time when summer's normal heat is cooled unexpectedly. And in the context of the lyric, a love that was hot in June has faded far too soon. Read the lyrics at http://www.sing365.com/music/lyric.nsf/Indian-Summer-lyrics-Frank-Sinatra/37AE8457BD0CF53748256920002887B9.

In the Mood

Words: Andy Razaf; Music: Joe Garland

Glenn Miller's biggest hit, "In the Mood," which sold millions of records, isn't a Miller original. It was based on a very old jazz riff previously used in "Tar Paper Stomp," recorded by trumpeter Wingy Manone in '30, and used in a Fletcher Henderson tune called "Hot and Anxious." Arranger Joe Garland embellished the riff into an eight-minute piece that he copyrighted as "In the Mood" in '38. It was first recorded as such by the Edgar Hayes Orchestra. Miller, a gifted arranger himself, pared the number down to fit on one side of a 78-rpm disk.

The Bluebird label recording called "In the Mood" a "fox-trot," but the youth of the early '40s danced the jitterbug to it. The tempo direction in the score reads "In the Groove," which means "cool, with it" in swing era jive talk.

The charting services really disagreed on this number. *Your Hit Parade* claimed it peaked at No. 9 (but *Your Hit Parade* seemed to shy away from strictly instrumental hits; they preferred songs with lyrics that their singers could perform on the weekly radio show), while *Billboard* reported that it was No. 1 for thirteen weeks, making it one of the biggest hits of the decade, and one of the top fifteen of the pre-rock era. It was the top jukebox tune of '40, spending twenty-one weeks at the top of that chart. In retrospect, it is easier to believe *Billboard*. Miller's recording of "In the Mood" was inducted into the Grammy Hall of Fame in 1983.

Miller and his band played "In the Mood" in the '41 movie musical *Sun Valley Serenade*. The song was also featured in Miller's screen biography, *The Glenn Miller Story* ('54).

Although Glenn Miller's version of the number is an instrumental, the song does have words. Read the lyrics at http://www.lyricsdepot.com/glenn-miller/in-the-mood.html.

Make-Believe Island

Words & Music: Nick & Charles Kenny, Will Grosz & Sam Coslow

"Make-Believe Island" spent nine weeks at the top of the music machine (jukebox) charts in '40. The public in the early '40s was just as interested in unreality as later generations were with the television series *Fantasy Island*.

The song was widely heard in recordings by the orchestras of Mitchell Ayres, Jan Savitt, Dick Todd, Dick Jurgens, and Sammy Kaye. Mary Ann Mercer was Mitchell Ayres' vocalist on their recording.

"Make-Believe Island" was No. 1 on *Your Hit Parade* for two weeks in '40. *Billboard* reported that Mitchell Ayres' recording was the nation's biggest hit for a couple of weeks.

This "Make-Believe Island" is a "wonderful island where broken dreams come true." Read the lyrics at http://ntl.matrix.com.br/pfilho/html/lyrics/m/make_believe_island.txt.

Maybe

Words & Music: Allan Flynn & Frank Madden

The Ink Spots may have been the most widely copied vocal group in show business, but in the early '40s, they were so hot they didn't care. They were enjoying their success: one hit record after another; individual salaries of approximately $15,000 a week; and an entourage that included a valet, a private barber, and a masseur.

The Ink Spots' records were usually made to the same formula: Bill Kenny would sing the melody in his high, beautiful falsetto voice; then Orville "Hoppy" Jones would recite the same lyrics in his deep bass voice. However, there's no "Hoppy" lyrics recitation in this song.

"Maybe" lends itself well to the Ink Spots' touch. Like "If I Didn't Care" and "Address Unknown," it was a big hit.

In addition to the Ink Spots, "Maybe" was recorded successfully by Bobby Byrne in '40. Perry Como and Eddie Fisher revived it very successfully in '52 in a duet recording.

"Maybe" topped *Your Hit Parade* three weeks in '40, beginning with the September 28th broadcast. The next week it fell to No. 3, but reclaimed the No. 1 spot for the next two weeks. On *Billboard*, it peaked at No. 2, but stayed there for six weeks.

There are a lot of maybes in a romance: "Maybe you'll think of me when you are all alone," for instance. By the end of the chorus, the singer tells his girl that she may want him back again some day, but "maybe I'll say maybe." Read the lyrics at http://lirama.net/song/16625.

My Prayer

Words: Jimmy Kennedy; Music: Georges Boulanger

Another tune based on a work by a classical composer, "My Prayer" was based on Georges Boulanger's "Avant de Mourir." The famous English songwriter Jimmy Kennedy was the adapter and lyricist.

The song was on *Your Hit Parade* for fourteen weeks in '39, reaching the No. 2 spot by the end of the year, and it was one of the top radio tunes of the year.

Glenn Miller and his orchestra and the Ink Spots were the chief agents for popularizing the song in '39 and '40.

In '56, the Platters revived the song; they reportedly had a million-selling recording that was the No. 10 hit of the year and spent twenty-three weeks on the best-sellers chart.

What is the singer's prayer? "To linger with you at the end of the day in a dream that's divine." He is praying to his girl that she will answer positively and will continue to

answer the same for as long as they live. Read the lyrics at http://lirama.net/song/16159.

The Nearness of You

Words: Ned Washington; Music: Hoagy Carmichael

Hoagy Carmichael considered "The Nearness of You" one of his best songs, along with "Star Dust," "Rockin' Chair," and "One Morning in May." He collaborated with Ned Washington to write it for the movie musical *Romance in the Dark*.

Glenn Miller and his orchestra were responsible for the most popular recording of "The Nearness of You" in '40. In '53, Bob Manning accompanied by Monty Kelly and his orchestra successfully revived it.

Variety included "The Nearness of You" on its "Golden 100 Tin Pan Alley Songs" list.

The singer is trying to convince his loved one that things like the moon or her delightful conversation don't thrill him; it is simply "the nearness of you" that excites him. Read the lyrics at http://lirama.net/song/29573.

The song appeared in the following films: Stella Stevens, back by the Jordanaires, performed it in *Girls, Girls, Girls* ('62), *Flashdance* ('83), *A League of Their Own* ('92), *The Impostors* ('98) and *Two Weeks Notice* (2002).

Oh Johnny, Oh Johnny, Oh! (See 1917)

Only Forever

Words: Johnny Burke; Music: James V. Monaco

In *Rhythm on the River*, Bing Crosby was cast as a composer of popular songs who much preferred owning a boat to writing music. To make ends meet, he agrees to become ghost composer for a famous songwriter with writer's block. Mary Martin was the famous writer's ghost lyricist. After an uneasy courtship, when neither knew that they were collaborating with the other, Crosby and Martin finally get together, and of course, by the end of the film, they get the recognition that they deserve for writing the music and lyrics of a hit song.

The film's big hit song, written by James V. Monaco and Johnny Burke, was "Only Forever." Crosby's recording of the song was very popular. Tommy Dorsey and Eddy Duchin and their orchestras also issued successful recordings of the song.

"Only Forever" managed three consecutive weeks at No. 1 on *Your Hit Parade*, while *Billboard* reported it was No. 1 on their chart for nine weeks.

Variety included "Only Forever" in its *Hit Parade of a Half-Century*.

Another potential title for this song might have been "that's puttin' it mild" because the phrase was used at the end of each strain. Burke's chorus lyrics open with a question: "Do I want to be with you as the years come and go?" And the answer is "Only forever." Read the lyrics at http://www.lyricsdepot.com/bing-crosby/only-forever.html.

Playmates

Words & Music: Saxie Dowell

Novelty songwriter Saxie Dowell wrote "Playmates." He also wrote "Three Little Fishies" (see '39).

Recordings by Kay Kyser and his orchestra and by

Mitchell Ayres and his orchestra made it No. 1 on the juke-box chart for eleven weeks and sixth biggest hit of the year on the jukebox chart. According to *Billboard*, Kyser's recording made it to No. 2.

Dowell's song sounds much older than '40. It sounds like it came from the 1890s and there was a song by Harry Dacre titled "Playmates" in 1889, but it isn't at all like Dowell's.

Dowell's lyrics are very childish, but that isn't meant as criticism. The singer wants her playmate to come out and play with their dolls. Among other things, they'll climb an apple tree, look down a rain barrel and slide down her cellar door. They'll remain "friends forever more." Read the lyrics at http://www.niehs.nih.gov/kids/lyrics/playmate.htm.

See the sheet music cover and hear a midi musical version of this song at http://www.parlorsongs.com/issues/1998–9/sep98feature.asp.

Practice Makes Perfect

Words & Music: Don Roberts & Ernest Gold

"Practice Makes Perfect" was the No. 1 song on *Your Hit Parade* for a couple of weeks in October, 1940. According to *Billboard*, Bob Chester and his orchestra's recorded version of the song peaked at No. 3. Al Stuart was Chester's vocal soloist on the disk. Al Kavelin and his orchestra also released a successful version of the song that featured Bill Darnel's vocal performance.

The lyrics suggest that the lovers practice more embraces and kissing, but "We're not doing bad right now." Read the lyrics at http://lyrics.rare-lyrics.com/B/Billie-Holiday/Practice-Maker-Perfect.html.

Sierra Sue

Words & Music: Joseph Buell Carey

"Sierra Sue" was written in '16. Elliott Shapiro revised the lyrics in '40, when Bing Crosby sang the new version. Glenn Miller and his orchestra also helped popularize the song with a popular recording of it. In '41, Gene Autry sang it in the film *Sierra Sue*. It probably was revived because of the popularity of other western-style songs in the late '30s.

The song was No. 1 on *Your Hit Parade* for one week, the August 17th broadcast. It made fourteen appearances on the program. According to *Billboard*, Crosby's recording was the nation's biggest hit recording for four weeks.

"Sierra Sue" is another western song. The singer is "sad and lonely," as are the "rocks and rills," for this girl called "Sierra Sue." Read the lyrics at http://ntl.matrix.com.br/pfilho/html/lyrics/s/sierra_sue.txt.

South of the Border

Words: Jimmy Kennedy; Music: Michael Carr

English songwriters Jimmy Kennedy and Michael Carr wrote "South of the Border" for Gene Autry, whose recording reportedly sold 3 million copies in two years. It was No. 1 on *Your Hit Parade* for five weeks toward the end of '39. It was also the top-ranking sheet music seller and the fifth best-selling record of the year. It continued to be popular into '40, selling enough sheet music to be the top seller, and it was the top jukebox tune for twelve weeks as well.

Shep Fields and his Rippling Rhythm made a success-ful recording of this song. Hal Derwin was Fields vocal soloist on "South of the Border." Other popular recordings were those by Guy Lombardo and his Royal Canadians, by Ambrose, by Gene Autry, and by Tony Martin. Frank Sinatra revived it with moderate success in '53.

The song was performed by Bing Crosby in the '60 movie musical *Pepe*.

"South of the Border" was selected by *Variety* for its *Hit Parade of a Half-Century* representing 1939. This song was nominated for the American Film Institute's list of the greatest songs ever from an American film, but did not make the final list. It was nominated for it appearance in *South of the Border* ('39).

The singer wants to go "South of the border down Mexico way," because that's where he fell in love with a girl dressed "in old Spanish lace." They had intended to meet "Manana," but tomorrow never came. He returned one day but felt he shouldn't stay "South of the border." Read the lyrics at http://lirama.net/song/16165.

Trade Winds

Words: Charles Tobias; Music: Cliff Friend

"Trade Winds" was another big hit recording for Bing Crosby in '40. According to *Billboard* it was the nation's biggest hit for four weeks in November. It was No. 1 for only the November 30th broadcast of *Your Hit Parade*.

Crosby's recording prominently featured a steel guitar to give it the appropriate tropical feel. In addition to Crosby's popular version, the other successful disk on the market was by Tommy Dorsey and his orchestra.

The lyrics are about a guy finding a beautiful girl "down where the trade winds play." They exchanged vows the night he sailed away, but he questions if the vows were only made to be broken. Read the lyrics at http://www.lyricsdepot.com/bing-crosby/trade-winds.html.

Tuxedo Junction

Words: Buddy Feyne; Music: Erskine Hawkins, William Johnson & Julian Dash

Erskine Hawkins was the first to record "Tuxedo Junction," but Glenn Miller made it lastingly famous. The composers, Hawkins, Johnson, and Dash, were students together at Alabama State College. They worked up this tune from a musical idea Dash had originated. After college, Dash joined Hawkins' new band. The band improvised a head arrangement. They played it at Baltimore's Royal Theater to accompany a vaudeville act, and began using it at Harlem's Savoy Ballroom as their last number of the evening. Audiences seemed to like it, so they decided to record it as the B-side of "Gin Mill Special."

Hawkins named the tune "Tuxedo Junction" after a streetcar junction in the Tuxedo section of his native Birmingham. The lyrics tell us it is "an old place where people go to dance the night away." Read the lyrics at http://lirama.net/song/9204.

Glenn Miller picked up the tune after he heard Hawkins' band play it when they worked a double-header at the Savoy. His recording was such a hit that he called his California ranch Tuxedo Junction. His version is slower than the Hawkins' original.

According to *Billboard*, Miller's recording was No. 1 for nine weeks in '40, and as usual, the more conservative, less instrumentally conscious, *Your Hit Parade* never recognized the song as a hit. It was one of the top three on the jukebox chart for the year. It stayed on the top of that chart for fifteen weeks during the year. In addition to Miller and Erskine's popular recordings of the song, Jan Savitt and his orchestra also released a successful version.

We Could Make Such Beautiful Music

Words: Robert Sour; Music: Henry Manners

Variety included "We Could Make Such Beautiful Music" in its *Hit Parade of a Half-Century* for 1940, one of only ten songs listed for the year. However, the song never appeared on *Your Hit Parade*.

Vaughn Monroe and his orchestra popularized the song, but their recording never charted on any of the charting services.

Judy Garland performed the song with her daughter, Liza Minnelli, as part of a medley with "Bob White (Whatcha Gonna Swing Tonight)" on the "Live" at the London Palladium concert in 1964. The song's title on that program was listed as "We Could Make Such Beautiful Music Together," but Sour and Manners were listed as the writers. Fred Waring's music collection at Penn State University also includes the song as "We Could Make Such Beautiful Music Together" with Sour and Manners as the writers.

The chorus lyrics begin, "We could make such beautiful music together," followed by a measure of hums on a C minor arpeggio (hums, like in "Paradise" in '32 and "Paris in the Spring" in'35) which may have been to allow each listener to be part of the composition process by deciding what was happening during the humming. The singer says, "You and I and love are the blending of true notes — not blue notes" (Is this suggesting blue notes are not true notes?).

We Three

Words & Music: Sammy Mysels, Dick Robertson & Nelson Cogane

The Ink Spots and Tommy Dorsey and his orchestra made recordings of "We Three (My Echo, My Shadow, and Me)" that helped it stay at the top of the jukebox chart for eight weeks during the year. *Your Hit Parade* top ten listed it on top in the last month of '40 with sales in the "going strong" category into '41.

This singer is living all alone with his echo, his shadow and himself. He doesn't see much good in the moonlight because he is without the one he loves. He says he'll wait for her until eternity. In the Ink Spots version, there is the usual spoken chorus interspersed into the recording. Read the lyrics at http://www.lirama.net/song/16214.

When You Wish Upon a Star

Words: Ned Washington; Music: Leigh Harline

Cliff "Ukulele Ike" Edwards sang this Academy Award winner on the sound track of the Walt Disney full-length animated film *Pinocchio*. "When You Wish Upon a Star" was among the top sheet music sellers of '40 and was on top of the jukebox charts for eight weeks. Cliff Edwards recording from the soundtrack was inducted into the Grammy Hall of Fame in 2002. The American Film Institute's list of the greatest songs in American films, which came out in 2004, included "When You Wish Upon a Star" as No. 7.

It was popularized on records by Glenn Miller and his

orchestra, by Guy Lombardo and his Royal Canadians, by Cliff Edwards, and by Hoarce Heidt and his orchestra. Ray Eberle was Miller's vocalist on their very popular recording. Tex Beneke was also featured as saxophone soloist. According to *Billboard*, Miller's disk was the top hit for five weeks. The song was No. 1 on *Your Hit Parade* for five consecutive weeks between the end of March and the end of April.

The chorus lyrics tell us that when we "wish upon a star" anything our heart desires will come to us and our dreams will come true (a fantastic but perhaps dangerous idea if children really believe this). Read the lyrics and hear a rather upbeat midi musical version at http://www. niehs.nih.gov/kids/lyrics/wishstar.htm.

Another song from the *Pinocchio* score that was popular was "Give a Little Whistle," which was popularized in a recording by Cliff "Ukulele Ike" Edwards, the voice of Jiminy Cricket. Read the lyrics and hear a midi musical version at http://www.niehs.nih.gov/kids/lyrics/give whistle.htm. The song is also the theme song for the *Wonderful World of Disney* television series.

Where Was I?

Words: Al Dubin; Music: W. Franke Harling

"Where Was I?" was premiered in the film *Till We Meet Again* ('40), which starred Merle Oberon and George Brent. Charlie Barnet and his orchestra with vocalist Mary Ann McCall had a very popular recording of the song. According to *Billboard*, it was the nation's biggest hit recording for a couple of weeks in August. The song peaked at No. 2 on *Your Hit Parade*.

Other popular recordings of "Where Was I?" were released by Sammy Kaye and Jan Savitt and their orchestras.

The singer questions where he was "the night that you surrendered to a sigh." He was afraid she "would melt in someone's arms some night" and he was right. He thinks it's a shame that someone wasn't him. Read the lyrics at http://www.webfitz.com/lyrics/index.php?option=com_ webfitzlyrics&Itemid=27&func=fullview&lyricsid=5286.

The Woodpecker Song

Words: Harold Adamson; Music: Eldo di Lazzaro

This Italian import shouldn't be confused with 1947's "Woody Woodpecker." A host of recordings by Glenn Miller and his orchestra with vocalist Marion Hutton, by the Andrews Sisters, by Will Glahe and his orchestra and by Kate Smith helped make this song a hit. It was on top of the jukebox chart for sixteen weeks, tied with "I'll Never Smile Again," and second to "In the Mood" for the year. It was also among the top sellers of sheet music and spent seven weeks at the top spot on *Your Hit Parade*. Miller's recording was *Billboard's* No. 1 hit also for seven weeks.

Eldo di Lazzaro's original Italian song was titled "Reginella Campagnola."

These "tick-a-tick-tick, tick-a-tick-tick" lyrics were almost as contagious as the hand-clapping chorus of 1941's "Deep in the Heart of Texas." Read the lyrics at http:// www.alsimmons.com/lyrics/cwl_thewoodpeckersong. html.

Eldo di Lazzaro and Harold Adamson had a good year with this hit and "Ferryboat Serenade" both being popular.

You Walk by

Words: Ben Raleigh; Music: Bernie Wayne

Variety selected "You Walk By" for its *Hit Parade of a Half-Century* for 1940, one of only ten songs listed for the year. However, very little can be found about the song, especially who wrote it.

Pianist Eddy Duchin, Blue Barron and Tommy Tucker had popular recordings of the song that all peaked around No. 6 or 7 on *Billboard* in 1941. Kenny Baker, Wayne King and Bobby Byrne's recordings of the song also charted in '41, but weren't nearly as popular.

The song peaked at No. 2 on *Your Hit Parade*, but managed sixteen appearances on that survey of hits.

The lyrics begin, "You walk by, enchanting as a dream."

1941

Amapola

Words: Albert Gamse; Music: Joseph M. Lacalle

Until "Amapola" became a big hit, saxophonist Jimmy Dorsey had experienced only moderate success as a bandleader, especially compared to that of this younger brother, Tommy. His luck began to change in '41: Jimmy's group was performing on a radio show for Twenty Grand cigarettes which closed with a spot featuring Jimmy and two singers, Bob Eberly and Helen O'Connell. Trumpeter-arranger Tutti Camarata suggested a routine that would first introduce Bob singing a song in a slow, romantic tempo, then double the tempo for Jimmy to play some jazz licks around the tune, and finally bring on Helen to sing the lyric with a swing. The formula worked, and the hits started.

"Amapola," Spanish for "poppy," was a Latin tune that had been around since '24, but Deanna Durbin reintroduced it in the film *First Love* in '39. Jimmy and his band's version of the song shot to the top and reportedly became their first million seller. They interpolated their version of the song into the '42 movie musical *The Fleet's In*. Hear Dorsey's recording at http://cfelt.com/0601_4.html. The Castillians had charted with their recording of "Amapola" in '34.

According to *Billboard*, Jimmy's version of "Amapola" was the biggest hit in the nation for ten weeks, which makes it one of the top fifty hits of the entire pre-rock era. The song was No. 1 for six weeks on *Your Hit Parade*, and made nineteen appearances on the program. It was *Variety's* No. 6 hit of the year. The song is one of *Variety's Hit Parade of a Half-Century* selections.

Over the next several years, Jimmy's band had success with several Latin-flavored songs.

It's rather surprising that the song was not used in the '47 screen biography of the Dorsey brothers, *The Fabulous Dorseys*.

Bob Eberly begins to sing at the very opening of the recording, which is rather unusual for band recordings. His singing chorus is in a slow tempo, but when Helen O'Connell's chorus begins, the tempo increases. The chorus lyrics begin with the definition of "Amapola," as "my pretty little poppy." Read the lyrics at http://lirama.net/song/16178.

The Anniversary Waltz

Words: Al Dubin; Music: Dave Franklin

Bing Crosby was chiefly responsible for popularizing "The Anniversary Waltz." This song is often confused with Al Jolson's "Anniversary Song" ('46), but Jolson's song is in cut time while this waltz is, of course, in triple time.

Dave Franklin and Al Dubin's waltz was included in *Variety's Hit Parade of a Half-Century*.

The singer wants a promise that he and his loved one will always dance "the Anniversary Waltz" together. Read the lyrics and hear a midi musical version at http://www.geocities.com/SunsetStrip/Stage/1430/Jbrenner/anniv lyric.html.

The Band Played On

Words: John E. Palmer; Music: Charles B. Ward

John E. Palmer wrote this song, inspired by the German brass bands that played in the streets of New York City before the turn of the 20th century, in 1895. Palmer sold his rights to the song to a vaudevillian, Charles B. Ward. As was the custom, once a person had paid for the song, it was theirs; they could publish it and take full credit. When Ward published it, he claimed to have written the music, but he did give Palmer credit for the words.

Dan Quinn helped popularize "The Band Played On" in 1895 with an early recording.

In '41, the song was interpolated into the James Cagney and Rita Hayworth film *The Strawberry Blonde*. That public exposure of the song prompted new recordings to be made and issued by Guy Lombardo and his Royal Canadians and by the Jesters. Lombardo's disk was particularly popular, claiming two weeks at No. 1 according to *Billboard*.

Since the copyright is 1895, the famous chorus lyrics are printed below: *Casey would waltz with the strawberry blonde and the band played on. / He'd glide 'cross the floor with the girl he'd adore and the band played on. / But his brain was so loaded It nearly exploded / The poor girl Would shake with alarm / He'd ne'er leave the girl with the strawberry curl and the band played on.*

Read the lyrics and hear a midi musical version at http://www.niehs.nih.gov/kids/lyrics/strawberry.htm. See the sheet music cover and musical score at http://levysheetmusic.mse.jhu.edu/otcgi/llscgi60 or see the sheet music cover and hear a midi musical version at http://www.parlorsongs.com/issues/2002–1/thismonth/featurea.asp.

A 1993 television film was titled "And the Band Played On."

Blue Champagne

Words & Music: Grady Watts and Frank Ryerson

1941 was probably the best single year of Jimmy Dorsey's career. He and his orchestra had big hit recordings of "Amapola," "Green Eyes," "High on a Windy Hill," "I Hear a Rhapsody," "Maria Elena," "My Sister and I," and "Blue Champagne."

Bob Eberly was vocalist for Jimmy Dorsey and his orchestra on "Blue Champagne," which was No. 1 on *Billboard* for one week, but never made the hit survey of *Your Hit Parade*.

As most big band recording usually did, the band plays a chorus or two before the vocalist sings.

The bubbles in the champagne are suddenly crystallizing to form a vision of his beloved, but the singer is left with "memories and Blue Champagne to toast the dream that was you." Read the lyrics at http://lirama.net/song/16181.

Boogie Woogie Bugle Boy
Words: Hughie Prince; Music: Don Raye

The Andrews Sisters introduced this song in the Abbott and Costello film *Buck Privates*. This famous World War II vintage number was an Academy Award nominee, but surprisingly was not listed among the top songs of the year. However, when people think back to the war years, "Boogie Woogie Bugle Boy" as performed by the Andrews Sisters, is one of the songs they recall. The Andrews Sisters also performed the song in the '43 movie musical *Swingtime Johnny*. The sisters also sang the song in the '44 film *Follow the Boys*. Their recording of "Boogie Woogie Bugle Boy" was inducted into the Grammy Hall of Fame in 2000.

According to *Billboard*, the song peaked at No. 6 and it never charted on *Your Hit Parade*. Bette Midler revived it in '73, when her version peaked at No. 8 on *Billboard*.

"Boogie Woogie Bugle Boy" was nominated for the American Film Institute's list of the greatest songs ever from American films for its appearance in *Buck Privates*, but did not make the final list.

Hear the Andrews Sisters' V-Disk recording of this song at http://www.authentichistory.com/audio/ww2/ww2music05.html.

The trumpeter they are singing about is "from out Chicago way" and he could play in a boogie style like no one else. His draft number came up and he was inducted into the army, where he now blows reveille instead of jammin' with his musician buddies. The captain of his unit understood his plight and drafted a band so that now "the company jumps when he plays reveille." Read the lyrics at http://lirama.net/song/12919.

Chattanooga Choo Choo
Words: Mack Gordon; Music: Harry Warren

The top song of '41, according to *Variety*, was Harry Warren and Mack Gordon's "Chattanooga Choo Choo." It was featured in the movie musical *Sun Valley Serenade*, in which Glenn Miller and his orchestra shared top billing with ice skating star Sonja Henie. Not only was the song played by Miller's band and sung by Tex Beneke and the Modernaires, but it was danced in a splendid production number by the Nicholas Brothers and Dorothy Dandridge. The song also won an Academy Award nomination for Best Song, but it lost out to "The Last Time I Saw Paris."

Miller's recording reportedly had sold a million copies by '42. The first gold disk ever given was presented to him by RCA Victor for his recording of "Chattanooga Choo Choo" on their Bluebird label. The presentation was made over the Chesterfield radio program on February 10, 1942; the recording had sold 1.2 million copies by then. Miller's recording of "Chattanooga Choo Choo" was inducted into the Grammy Hall of Fame in 1996. An audio clip of Miller's recording of this song can be heard at http://www.harrywarrenmusic.com/realfiles/.

According to *Billboard*, Miller's version of the song spent nine weeks at No. 1, second to "Amapola," which collected ten weeks at the top in '41. Amazingly, it only managed two weeks at No. 1 on *Your Hit Parade*. *Variety* included the song in its *Hit Parade of a Half-Century*.

"Chattanooga Choo Choo" was also performed by Carmen Miranda in the '42 movie musical *Springtime in the Rockies*, in '49's *You're My Everything*, and, of course, in *The Glenn Miller Story* ('54), where it was performed by Frances Langford, the Modernaires and the Miller Orchestra. The song also appeared in *Don't Bother to Knock* ('52), *Patch Adams* ('98), *Babe: Pig in the City* ('98) and *Last Orders* (2001).

This song was nominated for the American Film Institute's list of the greatest songs ever from American films for its appearance in *Sun Valley Serenade*, but did not make the final list.

Mack Gordon's famous chorus lyrics begin: "Pardon me boy is that the Chattanooga Choo Choo?" "Boy" is unfortunately the way African American males were often addressed during this time. The singer is expecting "a certain party at the station," a girl he "used to call funny face." He's going to tell her that he's home to stay. Read the lyrics and hear a midi musical version at http://www.harrywarren.org/songs/0058.htm.

Glenn Miller and his orchestra popularized "I Know Why (And So Do You)"also from *Sun Valley Serenade*. Read the lyrics and hear a midi musical version at http://www.harrywarren.org/songs/0189.htm.

Miller and his orchestra also popularized "It Happened in Sun Valley" from the film. Read the lyrics and hear a midi musical version at http://www.harrywarren.org/songs/0235.htm.

Daddy
Words & Music: Bobby Troup

Sammy Kaye and his orchestra (or Swing and Sway with Sammy Kaye) had a big hit recording of "Daddy," which had been introduced in the '41 movie *Two Latins from Manhattan* by Joan Davis and Jinx Falkenburg.

This is another "gold digger" song, not unlike "My Heart Belongs to Daddy." The "Daddy" referred to is definitely more like a "sugar daddy" than any girl's father.

The most memorable part of Kaye's version of the song is the all male vocal by the band members singing words that seem more appropriately sung by a female. The verse explains that the guy is singing about what his girl said to him. She wanted her "daddy" to buy her diamond rings, bracelets, sables, clothes from Paris, and a brand new car, in other words, the best of everything. Read the words at http://lirama.net/song/16184.

Joan Merrill and Frankie Masters and his orchestra released other popular recordings of "Daddy" in '41.

Variety listed "Daddy" as the No. 5 hit of the year. *Billboard* says that it spent eight weeks at No. 1, while it spent six weeks at No. 1 on *Your Hit Parade*.

Do I Worry?
Words & Music: Stanley Cowan & Bobby Worth

"Do I Worry?" was introduced in the movie musical *Pardon My Sarong*. The film's title sounds like a Bing Crosby and Bob Hope caper, but it starred Bud Abbott and Lou Costello instead. Nan Wynn, who was most often used as Rita Hayworth's singing voice, got to act and sing for herself in this film. The Ink Spots also put in a personal appearance.

Tommy Dorsey and his orchestra helped popularize "Do I Worry?" beyond the Hollywood film with a popular recording in '41. The Ink Spots and Bea Wain also had recordings of the song that charted in '41.

Variety included "Do I Worry?" in its *Hit Parade of a Half-Century* representing '40.

The singer asks, "Do I worry 'cause you're stepping out?" The answer? "You can bet your life I do." Read the lyrics at http://www.sing365.com/music/lyric.nsf/Do-I-Worry-lyrics-Frank-Sinatra/BB1A41ED731D92CA 4825691F00160887.

Dolores

Words: Frank Loesser; Music: Louis Alter

Frank Sinatra introduced "Dolores" in his film debut in *Las Vegas Nights*. He performed it with Tommy Dorsey and his orchestra. The song was nominated for the Oscar for Best Song from Film, but lost out to "The Last Time I Saw Paris."

Recordings by Tommy Dorsey and his orchestra and by Bing Crosby backed by the Merry Macs were both very popular. Dorsey's version, with Sinatra doing the vocal was *Billboard's* top hit for a week in June of '41, but never even made *Your Hit Parade*'s top ten.

The singer, Sinatra in this case, wants Dolores; "Not Marie or Emily or Doris." He asks us to imagine her charms, including "eyes like moonrise, a voice like music, lips like wine." He wants to make Dolores all his. Read the words at http://www.songlyrics4u.com/frank-sinatra/dolores.html.

Dream Valley

Words: Charles and Nick Kenny; Music: Joe Burke

According to *Billboard*, Sammy Kaye's recording of "Dream Valley" was the biggest hit in the nation for the week of March 1, 1941, but it peaked at No. 9 on *Your Hit Parade*. It only made two appearances on *Your Hit Parade*: No. 10 on November 16, and No. 9 on November 23, 1940.

Sammy Kaye and his orchestra had the only popular version of the song in '41, although Eddy Duchin and his band had a version that charted in '40.

"Dream Valley" is at the end of the rainbow, a land of "let's pretend." The lyricists tell us that his and his loved one's dreams will come true in "Dream Valley." Read the lyrics at http://lirama.net/song/16187.

Elmer's Tune

Words & Music: Elmer Albrecht, Sammy Gallop and Dick Jurgens

The seventh-ranking top tune of '41 according to *Variety* was "Elmer's Tune," obviously named for co-writer Elmer Albrecht. Another co-writer, Dick Jurgens, and his orchestra introduced the song, but it was Glenn Miller and his orchestra, with Ray Eberle and the Modernaires doing the vocal, that had the most popular version on the market in '41. Glenn Miller's version of the song was the No. 1 hit on *Billboard* for one week in December of '41, but it topped the *Your Hit Parade* survey for three weeks (two weeks in December, 1941, and one week in January, 1942).

Country pianist Del Wood revived the song in '53 with moderate success.

"Elmer's Tune" was interpolated into the '42 movie musical *Strictly in the Groove*.

The chorus lyrics ask several questions concerning why unusual things happen, like "What makes a lady of eighty go out on the loose?" The answer? "It's just Elmer's tune." Read the lyrics at http://lirama.net/song/9198.

Green Eyes (Aquellos Ojos Verdes)

Words: E. Rivera and Eddie Woods; Music: Nilo Menendez

Several of the song hits of '41 were BMI tunes that were discovered during the ASCAP ban. "Ferryboat Serenade" and "The Woodpecker's Song" from Italy, "Frenesi," "Maria Elena," "Tangerine," and "Green Eyes" from Latin American sources are good examples. Nilo Menendez and Adolfo Utrera had written "Aquellos Ojos Verdes". E. Rivera and Eddie Woods translated it into "Green Eyes" in '29.

Jimmy Dorsey and his orchestra, with vocal performances by Helen O'Connell and Bob Eberly, popularized the song and reportedly had a million-selling recording of it. According to *Variety*, their version of the song was the year's No. 3 record. Dorsey's version was No. 1 on *Billboard* for four weeks in August and September, but the song only reached No. 3 on *Your Hit Parade* (it was No. 3 for three weeks). *Variety* included the song in its *Hit Parade of a Half-Century*.

Other popular recordings of the song were released by Xavier Cugat and his orchestra and Tony Pastor and his orchestra.

Since "Green Eyes" was a big hit for Jimmy Dorsey, it was featured in movie musical *The Fabulous Dorseys* in '47.

The opening of "Green Eyes" might be described as a rocket launch covering an octave and a half in the first seven notes. Such a range suggests that the song was conceived as an instrumental number.

The singer, Bob Eberly sings, "Green eyes with their soft lights." Later Helen O'Connell's rendition of the lyrics "those cool and limpid green eyes" is particularly memorable as she emphasizes the words "cool" and "limpid." Those eyes will haunt and taunt the singer for the rest of their life, but they wonder if those eyes will ever want them. Read the lyrics at http://lirama.net/song/16189.

High on a Windy Hill

Words & Music: Alex Kramer and Joan Whitney

Today this song title recalls a line from the '55 motion picture title song "Love Is a Many Splendored Thing": "Once on a high and windy hill..."

The '41 "High on a Windy Hill" was a song by Alex Kramer and Joan Whitney that was popularized by several groups, particularly including Jimmy Dorsey and his orchestra, with a vocal performance by Bob Eberly. Other popular versions were released by Gene Krupa and his orchestra, by Will Bradley and his orchestra, and by Vaughn Monroe and his orchestra.

Billboard has the song at No. 1 for two weeks in April, while *Your Hit Parade* has it peaking at No. 3.

Alex Kramer and his wife, Joan Whitney, had a good year in '41 with this hit song and "My Sister and I," which was also popularized by Jimmy Dorsey's band.

The singer's heart is standing still because he can hear his loved one calling his name. He goes in search of her, but she eludes him. Read the lyrics at http://lirama.net/song/16190.

The Hut-Sut Song

Words & Music: Leo Killian, Ted McMichael and Jack Owens

"The Hut-Sut Song (A Swedish Serenade)" is a novelty song with tongue-twisting lyrics: "Hut-sut Rawlson on the rillerah and a brawla brawla soo it." It later explains that the "Rawlson" is a town in Sweden, "rillerah" is a stream, while "brawla" represents a boy and girl, and "Hut-sut" is the dream they share. Read the lyrics at http://www.song lyrics4u.com/horace-heidt/hut-sut-song.html.

The song had been written in '39, but in '41 it was interpolated into the movie musical *San Antonio Rose* (the title of a '40 country-western hit song by Bob Wills). The Merry Macs performed the song in the film.

We might say that Freddy Martin and his orchestra went from the sublime of Tchiakovsky's "Tonight We Love" (see below) to the ridiculous with "The Hut-Sut Song." Although there were several popular versions of the song, Martin's was the most popular.

The song was No. 1 on *Your Hit Parade* for three weeks, while it only reached No. 2 on *Billboard*. Other versions of the song on the market were by Hoarce Heidt and his orchestra, by the King Sisters, and by the Merry Macs.

Variety included "The Hut-Sut Song" in its *Hit Parade of a Half-Century*.

I Don't Want to Set the World on Fire

Words & Music: Bennie Benjamin, Eddie Durham, Eddie Seiler, and Sol Marcus

"I Don't Want to Set the World on Fire" was written three years before its publication in '41, but once it was published, it became one of the year's leading songs.

The lyrics say, in part, that the singer is not interested in setting the world on fire but he just wants to start a flame in his girlfriend's heart. Read the lyrics at http://lirama.net/song/16192.

This ardent love song was introduced by Harland Leonard and his Kansas City Rockets, but was principally popularized on records by Hoarce Heidt and his orchestra, by the Ink Spots, by Tommy Tucker and his orchestra, and by Mitchell Ayres and his orchestra. Heidt's vocalists on this song were Larry Cotton, Donna Wood, and the Don Juans.

Hoarce Heidt's version of "I Don't Want to Set the World on Fire" topped the *Billboard* hit chart for three weeks late in '41, while the song was No. 1 on *Your Hit Parade* for four weeks and was picked by *Variety* for its *Hit Parade of a Half-Century*.

I Hear a Rhapsody

Words & Music: George Fragos, Jack Baker, and Dick Gasparre

"I Hear a Rhapsody" was featured in several motion pictures and was a best-selling recording by Jimmy Dorsey and his orchestra.

His lover's call, her sparkling eyes, and whispers of love make music of rhapsodic sweetness. Read the words at http://lirama.net/song/16194.

This song is another example of an early BMI property that achieved hit status, in this instance *Variety*'s No. 10 hit of '41. Jimmy Dorsey's recording topped the *Billboard* chart for two weeks, but it was a much bigger hit according to the *Your Hit Parade* survey; it was No. 1 for ten

weeks on that program. Eleven other songs managed ten weeks at No. 1 and two others collected more than ten weeks at the top in the history of *Your Hit Parade*; that puts "I Hear a Rhapsody" in really classy company.

Variety included "I Hear a Rhapsody" in its *Hit Parade of a Half-Century* representing '41.

The song's only movie musical appearance was in '51's *Casa Manana*.

Intermezzo (A Love Story)

Words: Robert Henning; Music: Heinz Provost

Heinz Provost's "Souvenir de Vienne" became known as "Intermezzo" in the United States in '41 when Robert Henning added English lyrics and it appeared in the Ingrid Bergman film *Intermezzo*.

Guy Lombardo and his Royal Canadians' recording of the song was *Billboard*'s No. 1 tune for one week in early August. The song made twenty appearances on *Your Hit Parade* and topped its survey of hits for two weeks.

Numerous other recordings of this beautiful song helped popularize it around the world. Other successful releases of the song were issued by Wayne King, Freddy Martin, Benny Goodman, Charlie Spivak, Toscha Seidel, Clyde Lucas, Enric Madriguera, and Xavier Cugat and their orchestras.

Read the lyrics at http://lirama.net/song/16195.

The Last Time I Saw Paris

Words: Oscar Hammerstein II; Music: Jerome Kern

The Nazis occupied Paris in June, 1940. This invasion inspired Oscar Hammerstein II to write the lyrics to "The Last Time I Saw Paris," remembering the beautiful city and wondering what awful damage the German soldiers were inflicting on its famous landmarks. Hammerstein shared the lyric with Jerome Kern, who wrote the tune. Read the lyrics at http://www.stlyrics.com/lyrics/tillthe cloudsrollby/thelasttimeisawparis.htm. It is the only Jerome Kern song for which the lyric came before the music and which was not written for the stage or screen.

"The Songbird of the South," Kate Smith, introduced the song on her radio program, and because she had a six-week option on the song, nobody else could perform it. By the time the option ended, the ASCAP ban had started, keeping it off the airwaves. Therefore, it was next heard in the nightclub acts of performers like Hildegarde, Noel Coward, and Sophie Tucker. Kate Smith's recording of the song was the only really popular version on the market.

Director/producer Arthur Freed insisted that "The Last Time I Saw Paris" be interpolated into his screen version of Gershwin's *Lady, Be Good!* in '41 because of its relevance to World War II. Ann Sothern's performance of the song was very poignant, but it really didn't belong in *Lady, Be Good!* even though the film version bore absolutely no resemblance to the original '24 Gershwin Broadway musical.

"The Last Time I Saw Paris" won the Academy Award for Best Song from Film, but many people, including Kern, felt that the song should not have been eligible for the Oscar since it was not written specifically for the film. As a result of this incident, the rules were changed so that subsequent songs were supposed to be expressly written for the motion picture in which they appeared to be eligible for the award (however, it seems doubtful that the rule has always been enforced).

Jerome Kern's screen biography, *Till the Clouds Roll By* ('46), featured Dinah Shore performing the song.

This song was nominated for the American Film Institute's list of the greatest songs ever from an American film, but did not make the final list. It was nominated for its appearance in *Lady Be Good* ('41).

Maria Elena

Words: S.K. Russell; Music: Lorenzo Barcelata

"Maria Elena" is a 1933 Spanish song that was popularized in '41 by Jimmy Dorsey and his orchestra. Hear Dorsey's recording at http://cfelt.com/0601_1.html. Dorsey's recording of "Green Eyes" had "Maria Elena" on the flip side. Both songs were very popular, so it would be difficult to say that either song was the "B" side of the disk. "Maria Elena" was more popular on both *Billboard* and on *Your Hit Parade*, so that probably makes it the "A" side. Dorsey's version of the song, with Bob Eberly's vocal, was No. 1 on *Billboard* for six weeks beginning in mid–June, 1941. "Maria Elena" collected twenty-two appearances on *Your Hit Parade*, but was their No. 1 hit for only two weeks. *Variety* ranked "Maria Elena" backed by "Green Eyes" their No. 3 hit of the year.

Other popular versions of "Maria Elena" on the market were those by Wayne King, Tony Pastor, and Lawrence Welk and their orchestras. The song reached No. 6 on the charts in '63 in a recording by Los Indios Tabajaras.

The lady of the title was the wife of Mexico's chief executive, Mrs. Pontes Gil, to whom the song was originally dedicated.

Read the English and Spanish lyrics at http://lirama.net/song/16198.

My Sister and I

Words & Music: Alex Kramer and Joan Whitney

According to *Billboard* and *Your Hit Parade*, Jimmy Dorsey and his orchestra's recording of "My Sister and I" was the top hit song in the nation for a couple of weeks in June, '41. Bob Eberly was Dorsey's vocalist on "My Sister and I."

Other popular recordings of the song were issued by Bea Wain, Larry Clinton's former vocalist, by Bob Chester and his orchestra, and by Benny Goodman and his orchestra.

Alex Kramer and Joan Whitney had a good year in '41 with this hit song and "High on a Windy Hill," which was also popularized by Jimmy Dorsey's band.

The singer sings about "My Sister and I" remembering a tulip garden by an old Dutch mill, and their home, "but we don't talk about that." The title of the song could have been "But We Don't Talk About That," because it is a common phrase in the lyrics. The singer and the sister left their home because of the war; now they're almost happy in this country, but sometimes they wake up at night and cry for their friends who stayed behind, but they don't talk about it. Read the lyrics at http://lirama.net/song/16199.

Variety included "My Sister and I" in its *Hit Parade of a Half-Century.*

Oh! Look at Me Now

Music: Joe Bushkin; Words: John DeVries

Variety's No. 9 hit of '41 was "Oh! Look at Me Now," which was introduced and recorded by Tommy Dorsey and his orchestra, with the vocal by Frank Sinatra and Connie Haines. The song didn't fare so well on *Billboard* or *Your Hit Parade*. It peaked at No. 6 on *Your Hit Parade* and at No. 2 on *Billboard*.

The singer, a guy, has never cared about love before, but "Oh! look at me now!" He didn't know about the technique of kissing, or the thrill he could get from this girl's touch. Read the lyrics at http://lirama.net/song/16202.

Song of the Volga Boatmen

Words & Music: Russian Folk Song

"Song of the Volga Boatmen, a Russian folk song, was revived in '41 by Glenn Miller and his orchestra. Arranged by Bill Finegan, the band members sound like they are shivering from the cold right at the beginning of their recording.

The song had first become familiar to Americans through the concerts and recordings of Feodor Chaliapin, the legendary Russian bass. Chaliapin had once worked as a stevedore on the river and had heard the boatmen chanting "Ei Ukhneim, Ei Ukhneim."

In mid–March, 1941, "Song of the Volga Boatmen" was the No. 1 hit on *Billboard* for one week, but it never charted on *Your Hit Parade* (at the time they were presenting the top ten hits each week; at other times the number varied from seven to fifteen).

There I Go

Words: Hy Zaret; Music: Irving Weiser

Vaughn Monroe and his orchestra's recording of "There I Go" was the No. 1 hit on *Billboard* for three weeks in February, 1941. It was distinctive singer, trumpeter, and bandleader Monroe's first hit recording. It established his national reputation after he had built quite a following in the Boston area. The song was No. 1 on *Your Hit Parade* for four weeks.

Tommy Tucker and his orchestra, Kenny Baker, Will Bradley and his orchestra and Woody Herman and his orchestra also released popular recordings of "There I Go" in '41.

Hy Zaret's chorus lyrics begin: "There I go, leading with my heart again." A particularly insightful line in the lyric goes, "There's no golden rule to guide a fool in love." Read the lyrics at http://www.lyricsdepot.com/vaughn-monroe/there-i-go.html.

There'll Be Some Changes Made

Words & Music: Billy Higgins and W.B. Overstreet

Co-writer, Billy Higgins, introduced this tune in vaudeville in the early '20s. Blues singer Ethel Waters was the first to record the song in '22. *Variety* chose this song for its *Hit Parade of a Half-Century* for '23. Ted Lewis also had a popular recording during the mid-twenties, as did Marion Harris. Then Sophie Tucker revived it in '28. The most popular recorded versions of the song came in the early '40s. Releases by Benny Goodman, Ted Weems, Gene Krupa, Vaughn Monroe and their orchestras introduced the song to a new generation. Ted Lewis' recording of "There'll Be Some Changes Made" can be heard at http://www.redhotjazz.com/tlband.html, while Marion Harris' version is available at http://www.redhotjazz.com/marionharris.html.

The changes mentioned in the title may have referred to the changes in popular music as well as in the social scene during the jazz era of the flapper and her beau. The chorus lyrics tell us everything about the singer is changing, including her walk, her talk and even her name. Nothing about her "is goin' to be the same." And why is she willing to make all these changes? Because "nobody wants you when you're old and gray." Read the lyrics at http://www.mp3lyrics.org/b/billie-holiday/therell-be-some-changes-made/. See the sheet music cover with Ruth Etting picture on the cover at http://www.ruthetting.com/songs/changes-made.asp.

"There'll Be Some Changes Made" became even more famous in '41. The song was used in the '41 film *Playgirl*, which starred Kay Francis. Such national exposure in a motion picture often seems to re-popularize songs. Such was the case for "There'll Be Some Changes Made."

The song was acquired by BMI, so it was one that could be played on radio during the ASCAP ban of the airwaves in the early forties.

Recordings in the '20s had been popular, but not nearly as successful as Benny Goodman's version in '41. Louise Tobin was Goodman's singer on their popular disk. Goodman's recording was *Billboard's* No. 1 hit for four weeks in April and May 1941, while the song peaked at No. 2 on *Your Hit Parade*.

Several other successful recordings helped popularize the song; they included those by Ted Weems, Gene Krupa, and Vaughn Monroe and their orchestras. Weems' version was revived in '47 with moderate success.

"There'll Be Some Changes Made" was used in the soundtrack of *All That Jazz* ('79).

This Love of Mine

Words: Frank Sinatra; Music: Sol Parker and Henry Sanicola

Variety's No. 8 hit of '41 was Tommy Dorsey and his orchestra's recording of "This Love of Mine" with lyricist Frank Sinatra performing the vocal. It didn't chart so well on *Billboard* and *Your Hit Parade*, only reaching No. 3 and No. 4 respectively.

The singer insists his love will continue even though his lover is gone. Read the lyrics at http://www.lyricsfreak.com/f/frank-sinatra/56142.html.

'Til Reveille

Words: Bobby Worth; Music: Stanley Cowan

In the last months before the tragic bombing of Pearl Harbor by the Japanese, Americans were very conscious of the war already raging in Europe. The ghastly memories of World War I were revived. Most people in our country felt deep sympathy for our allies who were valiantly trying to fend off Hitler's advances.

The few songs that related or alluded to the hostilities were decidedly pro–Allies: examples would be "The White Cliffs of Dover," and "The Last Time I Saw Paris." Even the patriotism of Irving Berlin's "God Bless America" ('39) was a part of the pre-war American psyche.

"(Lights Out) 'Till Reveille" was popularized by Kay Kyser and his orchestra with the bombing of Pearl Harbor still several weeks into the future. The Selective Service Act of 1940, the first peacetime draft in our history, had been extended, so many American men were already in the services, going through basic training, and/or otherwise preparing for what seemed like inevitable war. The song is a soldier saying to his girl that he dreams about her "from taps 'till reveille."

"'Till Reveille" was No. 1 on *Billboard's* chart for a couple of weeks in late October and early November of '41 (Pearl Harbor was bombed on December 7th, "the day that will live in infamy"). The song peaked at No. 2 on *Your Hit Parade*.

Harry Babbitt, Ginny Simms, Max Williams, and Jack Martin were the vocalists on Kay Kyser version of the song. Bing Crosby, Wayne King and his orchestra, and Freddy Martin and his orchestra each released successful recorded versions of this song.

Bobby Worth's lyrics tell us that the singer dreams of his sweetheart the entire night — "from taps 'till reveille." Read the lyrics at http://lirama.net/song/16210.

Tonight We Love

Words: Bobby Worth; Music: Ray Austin and Freddy Martin

Most people who know Montague Street in the Brooklyn Heights section of New York City may not realize that the Bossert Hotel there was a once-elegant feature of a very fashionable neighborhood. The hotel's Marine Roof was once the home base for Freddy Martin's orchestra and was one of the city's most romantic spots for an evening of dining and dancing. In those years, a Martin highlight was his arrangement of Tchaikovsky's famed *Piano Concerto No. 1 in B Flat Minor*, which spotlighted the dazzling piano technique of Jack Fina pitted against the orchestra. Words were added later to make the song "Tonight We Love." The vocal version featured Clyde Rogers.

Variety lists "Tonight We Love" as its No. 4 hit of '41, while *Billboard* claims that the instrumental version titled "Piano Concerto in B Flat" (not minor?) was No. 1 on their chart for eight weeks. *Your Hit Parade* doesn't mention the instrumental title, but has "Tonight We Love" in the No. 1 spot for four weeks. *Billboard* claims the vocal version peaked at No. 5 in '41 in a version by Tony Martin and at No. 8 in 1942 in Freddy Martin's version with Clyde Rogers' vocal.

This song was selected by *Variety* for its *Hit Parade of a Half-Century* representing '42.

This number was primarily known as an instrumental, but it did have words. Read the lyrics at http://lirama.net/song/16212.

The Wise Old Owl

Words & Music: Joe Ricardel

"The Wise Old Owl" was No. 1 on *Your Hit Parade* for one week, the April 19th broadcast. The song made ten appearances on the program. The *Billboard* chart claims that the song topped out at No. 3.

Popular recordings of the song were released by Al Donohue and his orchestra, with vocalist Dee Keating, by Teddy Powell and his orchestra (his first chart single), with Ruth Gaylor's vocal performance, and by Kay Kyser and his orchestra.

Joe Ricardel's orchestra played society music for New York City's society elite. He played violin, sang with his orchestra, and wrote popular songs. One of his best known works is the jazz piece, "Frim Fram Sauce," which he wrote for Nat "King" Cole.

You and I

Words & Music: Meredith Willson

"You and I" was Meredith Willson's first major success as a songwriter. Willson would find considerable fame when he wrote the Broadway musicals *Music Man*

('57), *The Unsinkable Molly Brown* ('60), and *Here's Love* ('63).

In addition to being featured by Glenn Miller and his orchestra, "You and I" was the theme for the *Maxwell House Coffee Hour* radio program.

Glenn Miller's version of "You and I" was *Billboard's* top hit for five weeks during the later months of '41. It was also No. 1 on *Your Hit Parade* for five weeks and made nineteen appearances on the survey of hits.

The reason the summer skies are blue, that birds sing, and romance is so sweet is "You and I." Read the lyrics at http://lirama.net/song/16216.

You Are My Sunshine

Words & Music: Jimmie Davis & Charles Mitchell

Jimmie Davis used the popularity of this song to launch a film and political career. He made several films even after he had become Governor of Louisiana. "You Are My Sunshine" was introduced in the film *Take Me Back to Oklahoma* by cowboy star Tex Ritter. In '42 it was added to *In the Groove*, a film that starred Donald O'Connor and Martha Tilton. Jimmy Davis' recording of "You Are My Sunshine" was inducted into the Grammy Hall of Fame in 1999.

Because Davis' musical background was in gospel music, he used the verse/chorus form (also called two-part or AB form) that is prevalent in gospel music but very rare during this period of the AABA (three-part) form in popular songs. Many of the songs from the '70s and '80s are two-part (verse/chorus) form.

The most famous part of the lyric, the chorus, begins, "You are my sunshine, my only sunshine." She makes him happy even when gray skies appear. He tells her she'll never know how much he loves her and begs "please don't take my sunshine away." Read the complete lyrics and hear a midi musical version at http://www.niehs.nih.gov/kids/lyrics/sunshine.htm.

Yours (Quiereme Mucho)

Words: Jack Sherr; Music: Gonzalo Roig

Variety included "Yours" in its *Hit Parade of a Half-Century*.

Jimmy Dorsey and his orchestra had a very popular recording of "Yours" in '41. Other recordings that charted in '41 include those by Xavier Cugat and his orchestra, Vaughn Monroe, and Benny Goodman and his orchestra. Vera Lynn revived it successfully in '52. Dick Contino's '54 revival was moderately successful.

Augustin Rodriguez wrote the original Spanish lyrics.

The singer tells his lover he will be "Yours till the stars lose their glory" and until the birds stop singing. He says he was born to be her loved one. Read both the Spanish and English lyrics at http://www.ioctv.zaq.ne.jp/daaacl02/querememucho.htm.

1942

Blues in the Night

Words: Johnny Mercer; Music: Harold Arlen

The mood and style of this song are as true to the blues as any Tin Pan Alley song. Arlen and Mercer had written

the number for a jail sequence for a film called *Hot Nocturne*. The song proved to be so successful that the producers decided to change the name of the film to *Blues in the Night*. William Gillespie introduced the song in the film backed up by Jimmie Lunceford's orchestra.

Several recordings helped the song become popular. The most popular version was Woody Herman and his orchestra's, with Woody himself doing the vocal. Other popular versions were released by Jimmie Lunceford and his orchestra, by Dinah Shore in her first hit recording, by Cab Calloway, by Artie Shaw and his orchestra and by Benny Goodman and his orchestra. Rosemary Clooney revived the song with decent success in '54.

Woody Herman's version of "Blues in the Night" was *Billboard's* top hit for four weeks beginning in February, 1942, while the song was No. 1 on *Your Hit Parade* for two weeks.

When "The Last Time I Saw Paris" won the Academy Award for Best Song over "Blues in the Night," Oscar Hammerstein II told Robert E. Dolan to tell Johnny Mercer he was robbed.

John Garfield performed it in the '43 movie musical *Thank Your Lucky Stars*, a Warner Bros. montage designed to entertain the soldiers overseas and their families left here at home.

"Blues in the Night" was nominated for the American Film Institute's list of the greatest songs ever from American films for its appearance in *Blues in the Night*, but did not make the final list.

Johnny Mercer's wonderful chorus lyrics open, "My mama done tol' me," then spells out some of the thing his mama told him, including a woman can sweet talk a man into doing almost anything. She also can be two-faced, a lot of worry and she'll cause you to sing "the blues in the night." Read the lyrics at http://lirama.net/song/16234.

Deep in the Heart of Texas

Words: June Hershey; Music: Don Swander

"Deep in the Heart of Texas" is the song that helped establish Alvino Rey and his orchestra as important hit makers. Their recording also provides a glimpse of Rey's unusual "talking" guitar. Rey's version of "Deep in the Heart of Texas" was *Billboard's* top hit for one week in May, while *Your Hit Parade's* survey of hits has it with five weeks at No. 1.

Other successful recordings of the song were released by Bing Crosby, by Hoarce Heidt and his orchestra, by the Merry Macs, and by Ted Weems and his orchestra.

Audiences loved this song because they got to participate by clapping several times during the song, like "The stars at night are big and bright, (clap, clap, clap, clap) deep in the heart of Texas." The lyrics glorify the state. Read the lyrics at http://lirama.net/song/16237.

Variety included "Deep in the Heart of Texas" in its *Hit Parade of a Half-Century* representing 1941.

The song has been interpolated into numerous films including *Heart of the Rio Grande* ('42), where it was sung by Gene Autry, *Hi, Neighbor* ('42), *Thirty Seconds Over Tokyo* ('44), *I'll Get By* ('50), Jane Powell, Wendell Corey and the ensemble performed the song in *Rich, Young and Pretty* ('51), Howard Keel and the chorus performed it in *Texas Carnival* ('51), Jane Froman sang the song for film star Susan Hayward in *With a Song in My Heart* ('52),

Froman's screen biography, *How to Marry a Millionaire* ('53), and *Teahouse of the August Moon* ('57).

"Deep in the Heart of Texas" was nominated for the American Film Institute's list of the greatest songs ever from American films for its appearance in the 1942 film *Deep in the Heart of Texas*, but did not make the final list.

Don't Sit Under the Apple Tree

Words: Lew Brown & Charles Tobias; Music: Sam H. Stept

Composer Sam Stept first wrote this tune for a lyric entitled "Anywhere the Bluebird Goes," but Charles Tobias and Lew Brown wrote new words for it. The new lyric version was interpolated into the '39 Broadway musical *Yokel Boy*. When America went to war in late '41, "Don't Sit Under the Apple Tree" seemed particularly timely to the servicemen and their loved ones.

In '42, the Andrews Sisters sang it in the movie musical *Private Buckaroo*. In the film the sisters joined Harry James and his orchestra to put on a show for servicemen. The Andrews Sisters' skillfully harmonized trio rendition of "Don't Sit Under the Apple Tree (With Anyone Else but Me)" was one of the musical highlights of the film.

Glenn Miller and his orchestra had by far the most popular recording of the song, but the Andrews Sisters' version is also very memorable. Miller's version was the top hit on *Billboard* for two weeks in July, while the song was No. 1 on *Your Hit Parade* for five weeks. Hear a radio program recording of this song at http://www.authentic history.com/audio/ww2/ww2music06.html.

Variety included this song in its *Hit Parade of a Half-Century.*

Eileen Farrell, dubbing for Eleanor Parker, sang the song in the film *Interrupted Melody* ('55).

The singer asks his girl to remain faithful by not sitting "under the apple tree with anyone else" until he comes back from the war. Such lyrics were particularly popular with the servicemen and their loved ones during the war. Read the lyrics at http://lirama.net/song/16238.

This song was selected by *Variety* for its *Hit Parade of a Half-Century.*

The Andrews Sisters also popularized "Three Little Sisters" from the film. Irving Taylor and Vic Mizzy wrote the song.

He Wears a Pair of Silver Wings

Words: Eric Maschwitz; Music: Michael Carr

Since music is such a basic element in our lives, the songs about our involvement in World War II are very nostalgic.

In '42, it looked like the Axis forces were dominating. Things weren't going well for the Allies on most fronts. However, an air raid on Tokyo was led by Lieutenant Colonel James H. Doolittle, the first American offensive action in the Pacific.

Several war songs began to be heard: Irving Berlin's "This Is the Army, Mr. Jones," Elton Britt's "There's a Star-Spangled Banner Waving Somewhere," and "He Wears a Pair of Silver Wings," which was, of course, talking about our servicemen who flew during the war.

Kay Kyser and his orchestra's recording of the song was the No. 1 hit on *Billboard* for four weeks. The song topped the *Your Hit Parade* survey for four consecutive weeks beginning with the August 29th broadcast.

Variety included this song in its *Hit Parade of a Half-Century* representing 1941.

The guy in the song "wears a pair of silver wings" indicating he is member of the Air Force. The girl singing the song adores this crazy guy who taught her happy heart to "wear a pair of silver wings." Read the lyrics at http://lirama.net/song/16242.

1942 was a really good year for Kay Kyser and his orchestra. They had big hit recordings of "The White Cliffs of Dover," "Who Wouldn't Love You," "Jingle Jangle Jingle," "He Wears a Pair of Silver Wings," "Strip Polka," and "Praise the Lord and Pass the Ammunition."

Dinah Shore also released a popular recording of "He Wears a Pair of Silver Wings."

I Don't Want to Walk Without You

Words: Frank Loesser; Music: Jule Styne

Jule Styne and Frank Loesser became hot properties in Hollywood with this song about a broken romance, which they wrote for the movie musical *Sweater Girl*. The film was a typical campus frolic that involved a group of collegians producing a musical revue. "I Don't Want to Walk Without You" was introduced by Johnnie Johnston in the film (it was later reprised by Betty Jane Rhodes).

On the surface "I Don't Want to Walk Without You" doesn't appear to be a war song, but there were several popular songs of the time that sang about the loneliness of those left at home, of romantic fantasy, and of forced optimism that can be attributed to the war. "I Don't Want to Walk Without You" is one of the songs about loneliness. Read the lyrics at http://lirama.net/song/20918.

Harry James and his orchestra's version of the song was *Billboard's* top hit for two weeks, while it topped the *Your Hit Parade* survey for only one week. Other popular recordings of the song were available by Bing Crosby and by Dinah Shore.

The song reappeared in 1944's movie musical *You Can't Ration Love*, and was revived by Barry Manilow in '80 (his version made *Billboard's* Top 40).

Alvino Rey and his orchestra popularized "I Said No!," another song from the score of *Sweater Girl*.

(I've Got a Gal in) Kalamazoo

Words: Mack Gordon; Music: Harry Warren

Sun Valley Serenade was such a big success that 20th Century Fox decided to shoot another film starring Glenn Miller and his orchestra. They also brought back Harry Warren and Mack Gordon to write the songs for the film that was titled *Orchestra Wives*. The songs that have continued to be remembered from the score are "At Last," "Serenade in Blue" and "(I've Got a Gal in) Kalamazoo."

Miller's band with Tex Beneke, Marion Hutton, and the Modernaires really captured America's musical tastes in the early forties with their performance of "(I've Got a Gal in) Kalamazoo" in the film.

Miller's recording of the song was No. 1 on *Billboard* for eight weeks in the fall of '42, and was *Variety's* No. 3 hit of the year. According to *Your Hit Parade*, however, the song was No. 1 for only the October 10th broadcast.

Benny Goodman and his orchestra performed the song in the '43 film *The Gang's All Here*.

The verse begins as the Modernaires question Tex (Beneke) about his new romance. He tells them "she's the toast of Kalamazoo." This "freckle-faced kid" is "a real pipperoo." Read the complete lyrics and hear a midi musical version at http://www.harrywarren.org/songs/0247. htm.

Hear Paul Whiteman's recording of this song at http://www.redhotjazz.com/pwo.html or hear an audio clip of Glenn Miller's recording of the song at http://www.harry warrenmusic.com/realfiles/.

Glenn Miller and his orchestra popularized "At Last," from the film's score. Read the lyrics and hear a midi musical version at http://www.harrywarren.org/songs/0015. htm. "At Last" has appeared in several films, including *How to Make an American Quilt* ('95), *Father of the Bride Part II* ('95), *The Other Sister* ('99) and *American Pie* ('99).

Glenn Miller also popularized "Serenade in Blue" from the film. Hear Paul Whiteman's recording of "Serenade in Blue" at http://www.redhotjazz.com/pwo.html. Read the lyrics and hear a midi musical version at http://www.harrywarren.org/songs/0452.htm. See Warren's music manuscript of this song at http://www.harrywarren music.com/frameset.html.

Jersey Bounce

Words & Music: Bobby Plater, Tiny Bradshaw, Edward Johnson & Robert B. Wright

"Jersey Bounce" was originally a successful instrumental composition written in '41; lyrics were not added until '46. Very few people know the lyrics or have ever heard them. As an instrumental, the most successful recordings were by Benny Goodman, Jimmy Dorsey, and Shep Fields and their orchestras. The song became the No. 9 hit in *Variety*'s Top Ten for '42.

At a moderate tempo and with chords changing every couple of measures, some improvisation was possible in songs like "Jersey Bounce" even within the context of a big band arrangement.

Benny Goodman's version of "Jersey Bounce" was *Billboard*'s No. 1 hit for four weeks, while the song peaked at No. 4 on *Your Hit Parade*.

The chorus lyrics begin, "They call it the Jersey bounce, a rhythm that really counts." The singer tells us this rhythm started on Journal Square, then someone played it on the radio and now people are hearing it everywhere. We're encouraged to go to "some Jersey spot" and even if we aren't hep the song will make us swing. Read the lyrics at http://lirama.net/song/16272.

Jingle Jangle Jingle

Words: Frank Loesser; Music: Joseph J. Lilley

A group of horseback riders in the film *The Forest Rangers* introduced "Jingle Jangle Jingle." The lyrics are definitely anti-marriage, which was a stereo-typical cowboy trait. The singer is glad to be single and hopes to remain that way. The song has a decidedly western feel to it. Read the lyrics at http://lirama.net/song/16277.

Kay Kyser and his orchestra, Gene Autry, Freddy Martin and his orchestra and the Merry Macs released the most popular recordings of the song .

Kyser's version of the song was the No. 1 hit on *Billboard* for eight weeks, and the song claimed the top spot on *Your Hit Parade* for five weeks. It was *Variety*'s No. 2 hit for the year.

"Jingle Jangle Jingle" was picked by *Variety* for its *Hit Parade of a Half-Century*.

Johnny Doughboy Found a Rose in Ireland

Words: Kay Twomey; Music: Al Goodhart

Variety included "Johnny Doughboy Found a Rose in Ireland" in its *Hit Parade of a Half-Century*.

Kay Kyser and his orchestra had the most popular recording of this song in '42, but by far not the only one available. Others who issued popular recordings in '42 include Guy Lombardo and his Royal Canadians, Kenny Baker, Freddy Martin and his orchestra, Sammy Kaye and his orchestra and Tommy Tucker and his orchestra.

The song made sixteen appearances on *Your Hit Parade*, peaking at No. 2.

The lyrics tell us this soldier sailed to Ireland. There he found a rose, "the fairest flow'r that Erin ever grew." He told her it was his duty to make an American beauty rose of her. Read the lyrics at http://www.digitaltimes.com/karaoke/singers/patriotic/johnnydoughboy_found.html.

Mister Five by Five

Words: Don Raye; Music: Gene DePaul

Harry James and his orchestra's recording of "Mister Five by Five" was No. 1 on *Billboard* for two weeks in late January and early February of '43. However, the song only climbed to No. 2 on *Your Hit Parade*.

"Mister Five by Five" had been introduced in the '42 movie musical *Almost Married*. It was used again in '42 in *Behind the Eight Ball*, and in '43 in *Always a Bridesmaid*. Being heard in three movie musicals in two years was enough national exposure to ensure the song would be very successful.

The Andrews Sisters had starred in *Always a Bridesmaid* and their recording of the song was also popular, as was one by Freddie Slack and his orchestra.

Someone would certainly claim discrimination today concerning the words to this song. They describe a guy who is five feet tall and five feet wide. Even though he has fifteen chins, he "can really jump it for a fat man." Read the lyrics at http://lirama.net/song/16316.

Moonlight Cocktail

Words: Kim Gannon; Music: Lucky Roberts

The No. 4 song in *Variety*'s Top Ten for '42 was "Moonlight Cocktail." The piece was adapted from Harlem pianist Lucky Roberts' ragtime piece called "Ripples in the Nile." Glenn Miller and his orchestra had the most successful recording of it. Their version was No. 1 on *Billboard* for ten weeks, making it one of the biggest hits of the era and among the top fifty of the pre-rock era. *Your Hit Parade* disagrees. Their survey says the song topped out at No. 4. Since *Variety* and *Billboard* claim it was a big hit, we'll go with the majority.

This song gives us the recipe for a mixed drink that combines a "coupla jiggers of moonlight," a star, a June night, a guitar, a couple of dreamers, flowers, and a drop of dew. Stir for a couple of hours; then serve it under starlight. Read the lyrics at http://ntl.matrix.com.br/pfilho/html/lyrics/m/moonlight_cocktail.txt.

Ray Eberle and the Modernaires were the vocalists on Miller's recording. On a video compilation titled *Best of the Big Bands*, the Miller band does "Moonlight Cocktail" in a style very similar to today's MTV or VH1 music videos. Music video may have begun long before most people would have believed.

My Devotion

Words & Music: Roc Hillman & Johnny Napton

"My Devotion" was No. 1 on *Your Hit Parade* for four weeks between September 26 and October 24, 1942. *Billboard* has Charlie Spivak and his orchestra's version of the song peaking at No. 2. Hear Spivak's recording of "My Devotion" with vocalist Garry Stevens at http://cfelt.com/0506_2.html.

Jimmy Dorsey and his orchestra, Vaughn Monroe and his orchestra, and the King Sisters also had successful releases of the song.

The singer says his devotion "is endless and deep as the ocean," and he assures her his affection "is not just a sudden emotion." Read the lyrics at http://lyricsplayground.com/alpha/songs/m/mydevotion.shtml.

One Dozen Roses

Words: Roger Lewis & Country Washburne; Music: Dick Jurgens & Walter Donovan

"One Dozen Roses" has a "country" feel to it.

The song was primarily popularized by the co-lyricist Dick Jurgens and his orchestra. Their disk peaked at No. 3 on *Billboard*, but the song topped *Your Hit Parade* for a couple of weeks (July 4th and July 11th broadcasts).

Other successful recordings of the song were released by Harry James and his orchestra, by Glen Gray and the Casa Loma Orchestra, and by Dinah Shore.

Walter Donovan was also co-writer of 1914's "The Aba Daba Honeymoon" that was revived in 1950.

Joe "Country" Washburne and his orchestra were regulars on Roy Rogers' radio program.

The singer wants a dozen roses so he can put his "heart in beside them and send them to the one I love." Read the lyrics at http://lirama.net/song/16286.

Praise the Lord and Pass the Ammunition!

Words & Music: Frank Loesser

"Praise the Lord and Pass the Ammunition" was supposedly inspired by an exclamation of Navy chaplain William Maguire during the Japanese attack on Pearl Harbor, but Maguire denies the story. Maguire's phrase was printed in the newspapers and when Frank Loesser read it, he thought it would make a great "hook" for a song. Loesser wrote the lyrics and, as was his habit, furnished the text with a dummy tune to try it out. When he sang the song for some friends, they insisted that he keep the folk-like melody rather than get another composer to write a new one. It was the first, but not the last, hit for which Loesser wrote both words and music.

Loesser called Kay Kyser in Hollywood where Kyser and his band were in a recording session. Loesser sang the song to Kyser over the phone. Kyser liked it so much that he put an arranger on the phone to write down the words and music as Loesser sang them. After a quick arrangement was completed, the band rehearsed and recorded it on July 31, 1942, the last recording session before the musicians' union strike against the record companies took effect.

The lyrics for the chorus are extremely repetitive, very much like a children's song or folk song. The first three lines are "Praise the Lord and pass the ammunition!" The punch line is "And we'll all stay free!" Read the lyrics at http://www.authentichistory.com/audio/ww2/praiselord.html.

The song's up-tempo beat and its assumption that God was on America's side in the war certainly contributed to its appeal.

Kyser's recording reportedly became a million seller. The song, in various recorded versions, sold more than 2 million, and also sold a million copies of sheet music. It was *Variety*'s No. 10 hit for '42. The song was No. 1 on *Billboard* for three weeks just as '43 dawned, but *Your Hit Parade* has it peaking at No. 2 on their survey. Hear Kay Kyser and his orchestra's recording of this song at http://www.authentichistory.com/audio/ww2/ww2music03.html.

This song was selected by *Variety* for its *Hit Parade of a Half-Century* representing 1942.

Remember Pearl Harbor

Words: Don Reid; Music: Don Reid & Sammy Kaye

Variety included "Remember Pearl Harbor" in its *Hit Parade of a Half-Century*.

Sammy Kaye and his orchestra (Swing and Sway with Sammy Kaye) had the most popular recording of "Remember Pearl Harbor" in '42. It peaked at No. 3 on the *Billboard* chart. Hear Carson Robison's recording of this song at http://www.authentichistory.com/audio/ww2/ww2music01.html.

December 7, 1941 became a defining moment in history when the Japanese attacked Pearl Harbor. The raid was planned to remove the U.S. Navy as a threat to Japan.

The Japanese planes hit early on December 7th. Within an incredibly short time five of eight battleships were sunk or sinking, with the rest of the U.S. fleet damaged. Most Hawaii-based combat planes were also knocked out and over 2400 Americans were killed.

America was unprepared, and though considerably weakened, was abruptly brought into World War II full force. The public was outraged and definitely wanted to "Remember Pearl Harbor."

The singer asks his listeners to "Remember Pearl Harbor ... as we did the Alamo" and always remember those who died for the cause of Liberty. Now on to victory. Read the lyrics at http://lirama.net/song/16288.

Rose O'Day

Words: Charles Tobias; Music: Al Lewis

"Rose O'Day" is subtitled "The Filla-Da-Gusha Song." The song might be considered the Irish answer to the Swedish "The Hut-Sut Song."

Freddy Martin and his orchestra's recording of the song was *Billboard*'s top hit for two weeks in late March of '42. It peaked at No. 2 on *Your Hit Parade*.

Other recordings of the song include versions by Kate Smith, by Woody Herman and his orchestra, and by the King Sisters.

Variety included "Rose O'Day" in its *Hit Parade of a Half-Century*.

This song sounds like one of the Irish songs from the turn-of-the-century. According to the lyrics, "Johnny McCarthy loved Rosie O'Day" and every night he'd sing "You're my filla-da-gusha, filla-ma-rusha, bah-da-rah-da-bomm-foo-dee-ay." Read the lyrics at http://lirama.net/song/16289.

Sleepy Lagoon

Words: Jack Lawrence; Music: Eric Coates

This 1930 song became a major hit in '42, when it was popularized by Harry James and his orchestra. James's version was No. 1 for four weeks on *Billboard's* chart. The song made nineteen appearances on *Your Hit Parade* and collected three weeks at the top of their hit survey. It was *Variety's* No. 6 hit of the year.

Dinah Shore's version of "Sleepy Lagoon" also charted; her recording of it peaked at No. 12.

A Judy Canova movie in '43 bore the *Sleepy Lagoon* title.

This song is another example of a melody that has lyrics but is by far better known without them. The lyrics are reminiscent of the fascination during the late '20s and early '30s for faraway places. "A tropical moon, a sleepy lagoon and you!" sums up the text. Quite a few of our servicemen were fighting in the Pacific on tropical islands. Perhaps this could be one of their dreams. Read the lyrics at http://lirama.net/song/16293.

See the sheet music cover at www.hulapages.com/covers_5.htm (look in 1940).

Somebody Else Is Taking My Place

Words & Music: Dick Howard, Bob Ellsworth & Russ Morgan

Benny Goodman and his orchestra's version of "Somebody Else Is Taking My Place" was *Billboard's* top hit for three weeks in the early summer of '42. Peggy Lee was Goodman's vocalist on the disk, and Billy Butterfield was featured on trumpet. The song managed three weeks at No. 1 on *Your Hit Parade.*

Russ Morgan and his orchestra's version of the song peaked at No. 5 on *Billboard* in 1942. In '48, Goodman's recording was re-released and made the top thirty.

Howard, Ellsworth and Morgan had written the song back in '37.

The basic idea of the chorus lyrics can be summed up in the following quote from the lyrics: "My heart is aching, my heart is breaking, for somebody's taking my place." Read the lyrics at http://www.lirama.net/song/16294.

A String of Pearls

Words: Eddie DeLange; Music: Jerry Gray

Glenn Miller and his orchestra's version of "A String of Pearls" topped the *Billboard* hit chart for a couple of weeks right at the beginning of '42. Benny Goodman also had a popular version of the song on the market. Miller's version was re-released in '44, when it again made the top thirty.

"A String of Pearls" was *Variety's* No. 8 hit of '42, but in another case of tremendous disparity, it never charted on *Your Hit Parade,* another example of *Your Hit Parade* discriminating against an instrumental hit. Two of the three charts rank it as a big hit.

A beautiful, graceful cornet solo by Bobby Hackett turned what might have been just another Glenn Miller instrumental into a hit. Hackett was actually Miller's guitarist at the time, but in this instance, he contributed a classic 12-bar blues chorus on his horn. Other featured soloists on the record included Hal McIntyre on alto sax, Tex Beneke and Al Klink on tenor saxes, and Chummy MacGregor on piano.

Jerry Gray was young and single, living at home in Somerville, outside Boston, when he wrote the music for this song. His parents had gone to a movie, so he sat down at the piano in the dark. The idea just came to him — the whole thing — the introduction, the melody, and the arrangement. By the time his folks returned that evening, he had the whole thing mapped out in his head. It took just a couple of hours. Gray took his song to Glenn Miller, who made a few insignificant changes. With the song's success, Gray was promoted from arranger to composer by Miller.

The text is less familiar than the melody, but it is interesting to note that the string of pearls was "a la Woolworth," from a five-and-ten-cent store, not a very cultured type of pearl.

Strip Polka

Words & Music: Johnny Mercer

Johnny Mercer is primarily known as a lyricist, one of the most prolific of all time. In this instance, however, he wrote both the words and the music, and recorded it himself on his new record label, Capitol Records. Mercer's version of the song peaked at No. 7 on *Billboard.*

The most popular recorded version of the song was Kay Kyser's. Jack Martin was Kyser's vocalist on the song. His disk was No. 1 on *Billboard* for a couple of weeks near the end of '42. The song may have been a little too risqué for *Your Hit Parade;* the song never charted among its top ten hits. Other popular versions of the song were released by the Andrews Sisters and by Alvino Rey and his orchestra.

The song became a particularly big hit on jukeboxes around Army bases and GI hangouts. The number was just sexy enough for the guys. The lyrics are, of course, a play on words: "Strip Polka" instead of the card game "Strip Poker." Queenie, the burlesque cutie, insists on stripping to a polka. The guys are urging her to "take it off," but she always stops just in time. Read the lyrics and see the melody at http://sniff.numachi.com/~rickheit/dtrad/pages/tiSTRPOLKA;ttSTRPOLKA.html (the entire lyrics are printed below the first verse lyrics and melody).

Tangerine

Words: Johnny Mercer; Music: Victor Schertzinger

The pattern that Jimmy Dorsey had established with past hits like "Green Eyes" and "Amapola" — a slow, romantic vocal by Bob Eberly, the band featured in the middle section, and Helen O'Connell's swinging vocal to close — seemed to work for one hit record after another in the early '40s.

"Tangerine," unlike "Maria Elena," "Green Eyes," and others, was not of Latin American origin, even though it is about a girl from Argentina. It came from the '42 movie musical *The Fleet's In,* and had a lyric by Johnny Mercer to a melody composed by movie director Victor Schertzinger. The song was introduced by Dorsey and his orchestra with Helen O'Connell and Bob Eberly doing the vocal in the film.

Their recording of the song was *Variety's* No. 7 hit in '42. Dorsey's version of the song was No. 1 on *Billboard* for six weeks, while *Your Hit Parade* says the song peaked at No. 2 on their survey of hits. Once again, two of the three charts agree that it was a big hit.

Vaughn Monroe's recording of the song also charted, but didn't crack *Billboard's* top ten.

The lyrics describe a girl named "Tangerine." She's extremely beautiful, but her heart belongs only to herself. All the guys are attracted to her, but "she's only fooling one girl, she's only fooling Tangerine!" Read the lyrics at http://lirama.net/song/67101.

Another popular song from the score of *The Fleet's in* was "Arthur Murray Taught Me Dancing in a Hurry," which was popularized by Jimmy Dorsey and his orchestra.

Jimmy Dorsey and his orchestra also popularized "I Remember You" from *The Fleet's In*.

This Is the Army, Mr. Jones *and* I Left My Heart at the Stage Door Canteen

Words & Music: Irving Berlin

The entertainment industry played an important role with their efforts during World War I and World War II. Irving Berlin had written an all-soldier revue for World War I called *Yip, Yip, Yaphank* (he was stationed at Camp Upton at Yaphank, Long Island). Songs like "Mandy," and "Oh, How I Hate to Get Up in the Morning" came from that revue. When World War II erupted, Berlin again wrote an all-soldier revue, *This Is the Army*, which benefited the Army Emergency Relief Fund.

This Is the Army, Mr. Jones

"This Is the Army, Mr. Jones," a cheerful introduction to military life, was premiered in Berlin's World War II all-soldier revue by a group of new inductees. Berlin wrote a musical score for the revue that was a nonstop succession of various views of army life as seen from the soldiers' point of view. Read the lyrics at http://www.ostlyrics.com/read.php?sid=9423.

"This Is the Army, Mr. Jones" was selected by *Variety* for its *Hit Parade of a Half-Century*.

I Left My Heart at the Stage Door Canteen

Among the scenes from *This Is the Army* was a show at the Stage Door Canteen, where "I Left My Heart at the Stage Door Canteen" was introduced by Earl Oxford.

The Stage Door Canteen, located in the basement of the 44th Street Theater in New York City, was one of the most famous canteens where off-duty service personnel could eat, relax, write letters home, dance with the hostesses, and in general, unwind. Operated by the American Theatre Wing exclusively for the Allied forces, the canteen offered both free food and the world's greatest entertainers. Not only did the entertainers perform, but they served food, washed dishes, and talked to the GIs — whatever would help the war effort and boost the morale of the soldiers. Many of the female stars and starlets danced with the guys, but all the women who worked at the canteen were forbidden to date servicemen.

The popularity of the canteen was proven by the number of men lined up on the sidewalk trying to get in each evening. The canteen served 200 gallons of coffee and 5,000 cigarettes were smoked every evening between 5 p.m. and midnight.

"I Left My Heart at the Stage Door Canteen" speaks of the fleeting love that many of the men felt when they had to leave the canteen, never to see these beautiful women again. Read the lyrics at http://lirama.net/song/16254.

The most popular recordings of the song were released by Sammy Kaye and Charlie Spivak and their orchestras. Kaye's disk peaked at No. 3 on *Billboard*, while the song topped out at No. 2 on *Your Hit Parade*. Don Cornell was Sammy Kaye's vocalist, while Garry Stevens did the vocal for Spivak's recording.

Earl Oxford, the person who introduced "I Left My Heart at the Stage Door Canteen" in the original Broadway production, also sang it in the screen version of *This Is the Army*.

Hear Kenny Baker's recording of the song at http://www.authentichistory.com/audio/ww2/ww2music03.html.

Another song from the score that was popular with the public was "I'm Getting Tired So I Can Sleep," which was popularized in a recording by Jimmy Dorsey and his orchestra. Read the lyrics at http://www.ostlyrics.com/read.php?sid=9419.

When the Lights Go on Again

Words & Music: Eddie Seiler, Sol Marcus & Bennie Benjamin

In some respects, '42 was one of the gloomiest years of the war. We were at war in both Europe and in the Pacific, and the tide of battle had not yet turned in our favor. The mood at home was one of hope and stoicism. No song reflected that feeling better than "When the Lights Go on Again (All Over the World)," which looked forward to an end to the nightmare.

The song's title refers to the practice of having to turn off all the lights (black out) at possible bombing targets and to avoid backlighting torpedo targets for offshore U-boats. Read the lyrics at http://lirama.net/song/16330.

Vaughn Monroe's recording of the song spent three weeks at No. 1 on *Billboard* in mid–February, 1943, but the song peaked at No. 2 on *Your Hit Parade*.

Variety included this song in its *Hit Parade of a Half-Century*.

White Christmas

Words & Music: Irving Berlin

Irving Berlin stockpiled show ideas as well as song ideas in his trunk. He had been considering a revue for twenty years or more about a successful, but lazy entertainer who retired from the stage to open a country inn that was only operated on holidays. He had chosen the name *Holiday Inn*. With the threat of war on the horizon, Berlin was convinced holidays would take on even more significance.

He had already written "Easter Parade" and he quickly devised songs for other national holidays. At first he had difficulty writing the song for Christmas. The problem wasn't his Jewish faith; he had celebrated the holiday since childhood on New York's Lower East Side. He thought the Christmas song would be the high point of the production and it needed to be a great song like his "Alexander's Ragtime Band" or "God Bless America." It needed to be simple, universal, but unforgettable. He began reminiscing about being stranded in Los Angeles during one holiday season, which made him nostalgic for the Christmases in New York. The palm trees and warm temperatures didn't fit his idea of Christmas. What he wanted, and he thought what everyone wanted, was a white Christmas. Almost everyone knows the lyrics of this song, but not many know the verse that begins, "The sun is shining, the grass is green, the orange and palm trees sway." Read the lyrics, including the verse, at http://www.ostlyrics.com/read.php?sid=4076.

Irving Berlin's classic "White Christmas" became the second most popular Christmas song next to "Silent Night" ("Silent Night" is the most recorded song of the pre-rock era, "White Christmas" is No. 8). Bing Crosby introduced it in the movie musical *Holiday Inn*. Crosby's recording with the Ken Darby Singers and John Scott Trotter's orchestra reportedly sold 1 million copies in four years. By 1968, it had established a world record for sales for a single disk: 30 million. Bing's recording of "White Christmas" spent eleven weeks at the top of *Billboard's* chart and was *Variety's* No. 1 hit of the year. The song topped the *Your Hit Parade* survey for ten consecutive weeks from the October 31st broadcast until the January 2, 1943 broadcast.

Crosby's recording of the song was inducted into the NARAS (Grammy) Hall of Fame in 1974. Crosby's version charted on *Billboard* in '42, twice in '44 (once in early January and again in December); it reached No. 1 again in '45 and '47; charted again in '48, '49, twice again in '50 and '52; '53, '54, '55, 57, 60, '61 and '62.

Crosby's was not the only version of the song that was popular in '42 or since. Others that charted with successful versions in '42 include Charlie Spivak, Gordon Jenkins, and Freddy Martin and their orchestras (Martin's version charted again in '45). Frank Sinatra's version charted in '44, and twice in '46. Jo Stafford's version charted in '46, while Eddy Howard's and Perry Como's made the chart in '47. Mantovani and his orchestra's version was popular enough to chart in '52. The Drifters' version is one of the top ten Christmas hits of the rock era. Sales of all recordings by the end of '70 added up to the astronomical total of 68 million. By the end of the '70s, the total had grown to more than 90 million.

Concerning the song, Berlin said, "Not only is it the best song I ever wrote, it's the best song anybody ever wrote." The "White Christmas" copyright is the world's most valuable song property because the song returns every year to sell an average of 300,000 copies of sheet music and almost innumerable versions on Christmas records. It has been translated into numerous languages and had reportedly sold 43,000,000 disks and 5,500,000 copies of sheet music by the end of the '70s (according to http://www.classicbands.com/bestsellers.html, it had sold 30 million in the U.S. as of November, 2003). The seventy-two weeks that the song spent on the best-seller chart in the U.S. is still a record. In the first ten years of its existence, it sold three million copies of sheet music. Isn't it ironic that a descendant of Russian Jewish parents wrote the most famous Christmas song, the Christian holiday that celebrates the birth of Jesus?

In 1963 ASCAP selected "White Christmas" as one of sixteen numbers in its *All-Time Hit Parade*. Irving Berlin considered it one of his greatest creations. *Variety* included it in its *Hit Parade of a Half-Century*. AFI's *100 Years ... 100 Songs* (2004) listed "White Christmas" as the No. 5 greatest song from an American film. It was included in the list for its debut in *Holiday Inn* not for its inclusion in *White Christmas* ('54).

In addition to all its other honors, "White Christmas" won the Academy Award in '42 for Best Song from a film. In addition to *Holiday Inn*, "White Christmas" also appeared in *Blue Skies* ('46), *White Christmas* ('54), *Home*

Alone ('90), *Mixed Nuts* ('94), *The Santa Clause* ('94), *Green Dragon* (2001), *Love Actually* (2003) and *The Polar Express* (2004).

A couple of other songs from the *Holiday Inn* score became popular with the public: "Be Careful! It's My Heart," which was popularized in recordings by Bing Crosby and by Tommy Dorsey and his orchestra and "Let's Start the New Year Right," which was popularized by Bing Crosby. Read the lyrics of "Be Careful! It's My Heart" at http://www.stlyrics.com/lyrics/holidayinn/becarefulitsmyheart.htm. Read the lyrics for "Let's Start the New Year Right" at http://www.stlyrics.com/lyrics/holidayinn/letsstartthenewyearright.htm. Supposedly the cast of *Holiday Inn* expected "Be Careful, It's My Heart," the song about Valentine's Day in the film, to become the film's big hit song. "Abraham," yet another song from the score, charted and was popularized by Freddy Martin and his orchestra. Read these lyrics at http://www.stlyrics.com/lyrics/holidayinn/abraham.htm. Another song from the film score, "Happy Holidays," was never popular enough to chart, but has remained more well known during the holiday season than some other songs from the movie. Read these lyrics at http://www.stlyrics.com/lyrics/holidayinn/happyholiday.htm.

The White Cliffs of Dover

Words: Nat Burton; Music: Walter Kent

Before our involvement in World War II, Americans were very conscious of the problems being faced by Britain, France, and our other friends in Europe. England was taking a courageous stand against Nazi Germany.

One of the first "war" songs of the period was an optimistic one that dreamed of the day when England's difficulties would be over. There would be blue birds over those white cliffs instead of bombers, the shepherds could tend their sheep again, and things in general could return to some sort of normalcy. Read the lyrics at http://lirama.net/song/16300.

"The White Cliffs of Dover" was probably inspired by a long poem, "The White Cliffs of Dover," by Alice Duer Miller, which had become a best seller in '40 and furnished the basis of a successful film that starred Irene Dunne.

"The White Cliffs of Dover" was written in '41 and was recorded by a number of bands and vocalists. The most popular version was by Kay Kyser and his orchestra. Their recording was No. 1 on *Billboard* for one week in mid–March of '42, but the song was No. 1 on *Your Hit Parade* for six weeks.

Glenn Miller and his orchestra, Kate Smith, Sammy Kaye and his orchestra and Jimmy Dorsey and his orchestra each released popular recordings of the song.

A 1944 film, which starred Irene Dunne, was titled *The White Cliffs of Dover*.

Variety included "The White Cliffs of Dover" in its *Hit Parade of a Half-Century*.

Who Wouldn't Love You?

Words: Bill Carey; Music: Carl Fischer

Kay Kyser and his orchestra's recording of "Who Wouldn't Love You?" was the No. 1 hit on *Billboard* for a couple of weeks in the late summer of '42., but the song peaked at No. 3 on *Your Hit Parade*. *Variety* listed it as the No. 5 hit of the year.

A slow ballad, "Who Wouldn't Love You?" speaks of a loved one who is so enchanting, so much like a breath of spring, so much the answer to a prayer, that no one could keep from falling in love with her or him. Read the lyrics at http://www.mixed-up.com/lyrics/round/show.html?name=who-wouldnt.

The whistling part of Kyser's recording is very catchy and is one of the disk's most intriguing aspects.

1943

All or Nothing at All
Words & Music: Jack Lawrence & Arthur Altman
Frank Sinatra recorded "All or Nothing at All" with Harry James and his orchestra in '40, but it didn't stir any enthusiasm when it was first released. Sinatra's meteoric rise to fame in '43 and the American Federation of Musicians recording ban caused the record to be re-released, and it became a big hit.

According to *Billboard*, Sinatra's disk was the nation's biggest hit for a couple of weeks in the fall of '43. The song was only No. 1 on *Your Hit Parade* for the September 25th broadcast.

Sinatra was a vocalist on *Your Hit Parade* from February '43 until December '44. The national exposure he got on the program made him a household name.

The singer pleads not to be tempted by lips, a kiss, a touch of a hand. He wants "all or nothing at all." Read the lyrics at http://lirama.net/song/16301.

Variety selected this song for its *Hit Parade of a Half-Century*.

As Time Goes By
Words & Music: Herman Hupfeld
Frances Williams introduced Herman Hupfeld's best-remembered song, "As Time Goes By," in the musical *Everybody's Welcome* in '31. The musical's plot dealt with the ups and downs of married life of a Greenwich Village couple. The show is chiefly remembered today for introducing this song.

When Rudy Vallee and Jacques Renard recorded the song in '31, it became moderately popular. However, when Dooley Wilson performed it in the Humphrey Bogart/Ingrid Bergman classic *Casablanca* in '42, its popularity skyrocketed and it achieved the status of a standard.

Wilson played a singer/pianist employed by nightclub owner Rick. He performed several songs for the nightclub audience, including "It Had to Be You." But it was "As Time Goes By" that really figures into the plot. Bergman's character, Ilsa, regards the song as "their song." Because of their breakup and Ilsa's marriage to someone else, Rick has forbidden the song to be played in the club. When Ilsa requests Sam to play it, he eventually gives in. Hearing Sam sing the song makes Rick aware that Ilsa is there and that she still cares for him.

Ironically, Wilson was a singer and drummer, not a pianist. The piano playing in the film was by Elliott Carpenter, while Wilson faked the hand movements.

A new recording could not be made using instrumentalist members of the American Federation of Musicians

because of a strike that the union had called against the record companies. Vallee and Renard's '31 recordings were re-released and soared up the charts. Vallee's version was No. 1 on the *Billboard* chart of hits for four weeks beginning in late June '43. "As Time Goes By" collected twenty-one appearances on *Your Hit Parade*, with four weeks at No. 1. Ray Anthony and his orchestra revived the song in '52, when their version made *Billboard's* top ten.

It seems strange that Dooley Wilson's version, the guy at the piano who sang it in the film, was not popular. Was it not released? If not, why? Did that also fall under the AFM ban or was it racial? His version in the film is what caused the song to regain popularity. He certainly didn't get the recognition that he deserved.

Jimmy Durante's recording of the song was featured on the soundtrack of the romantic film *Sleepless in Seattle* ('93).

The lyrics champion romantic love and claim that whatever new there may be or whatever comes in the future, love will last "as time goes by." Read the lyrics and hear an audio clip of Dooley Wilson singing the song at http://www.reelclassics.com/Movies/Casablanca/astimegoesby-lyrics.htm.

Variety listed the song on its *Hit Parade of a Half-Century* for 1931 and 1943 and as a *Golden 100 Tin Pan Alley Song*. AFI's *100 Years ... 100 Songs* (2004) listed "As Time Goes By" as the No. 2 greatest song from an American film behind only "Over the Rainbow." "As Time Goes By" became one of the most recorded songs of the pre-rock era.

Brazil
Words: Bob Russell; Music: Ary Barroso
This Brazilian samba was composed by Ary Barroso in '39 as "Aquarela do Brasil." Bob Russell added the English lyrics later. The song was interpolated into Walt Disney's full-length animated film *Saludos Amigos* ('42) and *The Gang's All Here* ('43), which may have set the stage for its popularity on the pop charts in '43.

The samba beat is the most distinguishing and intriguing feature of the song. Although many varieties of the samba existed in various parts of Brazil, it was the dance from Rio de Janeiro that became internationally famous.

Recordings by Xavier Cugat and his orchestra and Jimmy Dorsey and his orchestra popularized the song in '43. According to *Billboard*, Cugat's recording peaked at No. 2, but the song garnered three weeks at No. 1 on *Your Hit Parade*. It was *Variety's* No. 5 hit in '43's Top Ten.

Les Paul revived the song in a recording in '48 that almost made *Billboard's* top twenty.

"Brazil" was also interpolated into *Jam Session* ('44), *Brazil* ('44), and *The Eddie Duchin Story* ('56).

"Brazil" was selected by *Variety* for its *Hit Parade of a Half-Century*.

The chorus lyrics tells us that two people "kissed and clung together" in Brazil, only to find themselves parted the next day. He promises to return "to old Brazil." Read the lyrics at http://www.seeklyrics.com/lyrics/Frank-Sinatra/Brazil.html.

Comin' in on a Wing and a Prayer
Words: Harold Adamson; Music: Jimmy McHugh
In late '42, composer Jimmy McHugh received a letter from a young Army pilot, a former football star named

Sonny Bragg. He told McHugh about a close call he'd had on a flying assignment in North Africa. He had cheated death by coming in, in his own words, "on a wing and a prayer." For McHugh, the phrase was tailor-made for a song. He and lyricist Harold Adamson turned out the song that seemed to capture the mood of America's airmen in the heat of combat. "Comin' in on a Wing and a Prayer" is a vivid reminder of the spirit of our pilots and other airmen during the war. Read the lyrics at http://lirama. net/song/16305.

Because of the AFM ban, the most successful recording of the song was an a cappella version by the Song Spinners. This was their only really successful recording, except they backed up Dick Haymes on "It Can't Be Wrong" and "You'll Never Know." The song was No. 1 on both *Billboard* and *Your Hit Parade* for three weeks.

Willie Kelly and his orchestra and the Four Vagabonds also released successful recordings of the song.

Hear Bobby Sherwood and his orchestra's recording of this song at http://www.authentichistory.com/audio/ww2/ ww2music05.html.

Variety chose this song for its *Hit Parade of a Half-Century.*

Don't Get Around Much Anymore

Words: Bob Russell; Music: Duke Ellington

Duke Ellington's instrumental composition "Never No Lament" furnished the melody for Bob Russell's lyric "Don't Get Around Much Anymore" (it was a good year for Russell, who wrote the lyrics for this hit song and "Brazil"). Ellington and his band introduced the song and made a successful recording of it (No. 8 on *Billboard*).

The most popular version of the song was put out by the Ink Spots. Their version peaked at No. 2 on *Billboard*. Another successful version was recorded by Glen Gray and the Casa Loma Orchestra. The song, however, managed three weeks at No. 1 on *Your Hit Parade*, with sixteen total weeks on the program.

In the lyrics, the person doesn't go to the Saturday dance, to the club, or out on dates, because they are without their loved one. Such sentiments were popular among the servicemen and their loved ones at home. Read the lyrics at http://lirama.net/song/16306.

This song was chosen by *Variety* for its *Hit Parade of a Half-Century.*

I Had the Craziest Dream

Words: Mack Gordon; Music: Harry Warren

"I Had the Craziest Dream" was introduced by Harry James and his orchestra in the '42 movie musical *Springtime in the Rockies*. With a vocal performance by Helen Forrest, their recording of the song had reportedly sold a million copies by '43. James's disk was *Billboard's* top hit for two weeks in February '43. The song peaked at No. 2 on *Your Hit Parade*. It was *Variety's* No. 7 hit of the year. An audio clip of Helen Forrest with Harry James and his orchestra singing "I Had the Craziest Dream" can be heard at http://www.harrywarrenmusic.com/realfiles/.

The GI's favorite pin-up girl, Betty Grable, married bandleader Harry James in '43. She also starred in *Springtime in the Rockies*, sharing the musical spotlight with her future husband.

What was the crazy dream? The singer dreamed a particular girl was in love with him. At the end of the strain, he begs that she will "make my craziest dream come true." Read the lyrics and hear a midi musical version at http://www.harrywarren.org/songs/0186.htm.

I'll Be Home for Christmas

Words & Music: Walter Kent, Kim Gannon & Buck Ram

Bing Crosby introduced this traditional Tin Pan Alley Christmas favorite; he also had the most popular recorded version. His recording charted on *Billboard* in '43 and '44, with its highest ranking in '43 at No. 3. The song also reached No. 3 on *Your Hit Parade* in early '44. Crosby's recording became a million seller.

The song has always been especially appealing to those in the military and others who must be away from home for the holidays. It was especially touching during this World War II period. The text says they will be home for Christmas even if it is only in their dreams. Read the lyrics at http://lirama.net/song/16309.

See the musical score at http://lcweb2.loc.gov/cocoon/ ihas/loc.natlib.ihas.100010539/.

I've Heard That Song Before

Words: Sammy Cahn; Music: Jule Styne

Jule Styne and Sammy Cahn began their successful partnership with "I've Heard That Song Before." The song was introduced by Bob Crosby and his orchestra in the '42 movie musical *Youth on Parade*. Harry James and his orchestra recorded the tune in Hollywood in July '42, and reportedly had a million seller by '43. Helen Forrest was the vocalist on the disk.

The lyrics comment on how certain songs help us reminisce about an old flame, which is very similar to the idea of "One of Those Songs," which was popularized in the mid-'60s. Read the lyrics at http://lirama.net/song/16310.

"I've Heard That Song Before" was an Academy Award nominee for '42, but lost to "You'll Never Know." The song collected four weeks at No. 1 on *Your Hit Parade* and it was *Variety's* No. 2 hit of '43. *Billboard* ranks it even higher, with thirteen weeks at No. 1, making it one of the biggest hits of the decade and one of the top six of the entire pre-rock era. There's no doubt that it was a big hit, but *Billboard's* ranking seems too far out of line with the other charts to be completely reliable.

This song was nominated for the American Film Institute's list of greatest songs ever from an American film, but was not on the final list.

In the Blue of Evening

Words: Tom Adair; Music: Alfonso D'Artega

Tommy Dorsey and his orchestra's recording of "In the Blue of Evening" was the No. 1 hit on *Billboard* for three weeks in the late summer of '43. It was also *Variety's* No. 8 hit of the year. The song appeared on *Your Hit Parade* eighteen times, peaking at No. 2.

Variety included "In the Blue of Evening" in its *Hit Parade of a Half-Century.*

"In the blue of the evening" is dusk. It was at this time of day the singer met his dear one. They had found romance "in the blue of evening." Read the lyrics at http:// www.seeklyrics.com/lyrics/Frank-Sinatra/In-The-Blue-of-The-Evening.html.

It Can't Be Wrong

Words: Kim Gannon; Music: Max Steiner

"It Can't Be Wrong" was introduced in the '42 motion picture *Now, Voyager*, which starred Bette Davis and Paul Henreid.

Kim Gannon furnished lyrics for several popular hits including this one and "I'll Be Home for Christmas" in '43.

Dick Haymes had sung with several bands during the early forties, but "It Can't Be Wrong" was his first hit recording as a solo act. Since the AFM ban was in effect, Haymes was accompanied by the Song Spinners in this all-vocal or a cappella recording. Even though '43 was Haymes first as a soloist, it was his most successful. With No. 1 singles of "It Can't Be Wrong" and "You'll Never Know" in '43, he never found that much of success in one year again. The nearest he came was with a couple of duets with Helen Forrest in '44 and '45.

According to Joel Whitburn's *Pop Memories*, "It Can't Be Wrong" was a *Billboard* No. 1 hit, but in *A Century of Pop Music*, it appears as a No. 2 hit for four weeks.

Allen Miller also had a popular recording of the song on the market in '43.

The lyrics to "It Can't Be Wrong" are basically several questions trying to determine why it would be wrong. Questions include: would it be wrong to kiss, would it be wrong to stay here in your arms, and why am I content to be with you forever? The song ends with more of an affirmation: "It must be right, it can't be wrong." That sentiment is reminiscent of the '70s hit song "(If Lovin' You Is Wrong) I Don't Want to Be Right." Read the lyrics at http://lirama.net/song/16312.

Let's Get Lost

Words: Frank Loesser; Music: Jimmy McHugh

Vaughn Monroe's recording of "Let's Get Lost" was the No. 1 hit on *Billboard* for three weeks in July and August of '43. The song managed only one week at the top of *Your Hit Parade*, the June 12th broadcast.

"Let's Get Lost" had been introduced in the '43 movie musical *Happy Go Lucky*, which starred Mary Martin, Dick Powell, Betty Hutton and Eddie Bracken. Mary Martin introduced the song in the film.

The basic idea of this song is now that "we have found each other Darling, let's get lost." Read the lyrics at http://lirama.net/song/16315.

Variety included "Let's Get Lost" in its *Hit Parade of a Half-Century*.

Although it wasn't as popular on the charts as "Let's Get Lost," Betty Hutton's exuberant singing of "Murder, He Says" is a classic performance from the film. Read the lyrics at http://www.yessaid.com/lyrics/murderhesays.html.

Moonlight Becomes You *and* Road to Morocco

Words: Johnny Burke; Music: Jimmy Van Heusen

How many "road" films did Bing Crosby, Bob Hope, and Dorothy Lamour make? There must be as many or more than the *Rocky* films of Sylvester Stallone. There are four films: *Road to Morocco, Road to Singapore, The Road to Utopia*, and *Road to Zanzibar. Road to Morocco* is one of the better ones from the series. In this one, Bing sells Bob into slavery in exotic Morocco.

Moonlight Becomes You

One of the few songs from the series of films that became a big hit came from this film: "Moonlight Becomes You."

Crosby's Decca recording helped popularize the song beyond the silver screen. Glenn Miller and Harry James' orchestras also had successful recordings of the song. Bing's recording came out in late '42 and by mid–April was the No. 1 hit on *Billboard*. It stayed on top for a couple of weeks on both *Billboard* and *Your Hit Parade*.

The singer, Bing Crosby in this case, sings, "Moonlight becomes you, it goes with your hair." He hopes they will have a romantic evening. He tells the girl it is her not the moonlight that would cause him to say, "I love you." Read the lyrics at http://lirama.net/song/16317.

Variety included "Moonlight Becomes You" in its *Hit Parade of a Half-Century*. This song was nominated for the American Film Institute's list of the greatest songs ever from an American film, but did not make the final list.

Road to Morocco

"Road to Morocco" was the title song from the third Bing Crosby-Bob Hope "road" film.

Bing recorded this tune without the aid of his co-star, Bob Hope, in '42. Two years after the release of the film Bing and Bob recorded a duet version accompanied by the Vic Schoen Orchestra. Their duet recording spent one week in the pop charts in '45 at the No. 21 spot.

AFI's *100 Years ... 100 Songs* (2004) named "Road to Morocco" the No. 95 greatest song ever from an American film, but "Moonlight Becomes You" didn't make the final list? It doesn't make much sense that the more popular song wouldn't make the list.

Read Johnny Burke's clever lyrics at http://www.kcmetro.cc.mo.us/pennvalley/biology/lewis/crosby/RoadToMorocco.html.

Oh, What a Beautiful Mornin', People Will Say We're in Love, *and* The Surrey with the Fringe on Top

Words: Oscar Hammerstein II; Music: Richard Rodgers

When Richard Rodgers and Oscar Hammerstein II teamed up for the first time, the result was the blockbuster musical *Oklahoma!* in '43. The idea for the musical came from Therea Helburn of the Theatre Guild, who suggested to Rodgers that Lynn Riggs' play *Green Grow the Lilacs* could be developed into an excellent musical. When Rodgers presented the idea to Larry Hart, his writing partner since 1919, Hart wasn't interested, so Rodgers turned to master lyricist Oscar Hammerstein II.

Oklahoma! is one of the most important productions in Broadway theater history: a literate, believable story (although today it seems a little bit shallow and naive), enhanced by a gorgeous musical score that does not interrupt the action. It also makes use of ballet in the development of the plot.

The story of the musical is set in the Oklahoma Territory a few years before statehood in 1907. Two ranch hands, Curly and the menacing Jud, are rivals for their boss's niece, Laurey. To spite Curly, Laurey goes to the box social with Jud. To prove his affection, Curly bids all he owns on the picnic basket that Laurey has made. Curly and Laurey marry. Jud challenges Curly to a fight and is accidentally killed by his own knife. Curly is quickly tried, but is just as quickly acquitted. Curly and Laurey ride off into the sunset to happiness in a brand new state.

The exceptional score spawned several hit songs.

OH, WHAT A BEAUTIFUL MORNIN'

"Oh, What a Beautiful Mornin'" is the lazy waltz that opens the musical. Alfred Drake, who played Curly, had the pleasure of introducing the song.

Variety chose "Oh, What a Beautiful Mornin'" for its *Hit Parade of a Half-Century*. This song was nominated for the American Film Institute's list of the greatest songs ever from an American film, but did not make the final list. It was nominated for the '55 film version of *Oklahoma*.

Bing Crosby's recording of the primary love song, "People Will Say We're in Love," with "Oh, What a Beautiful Mornin'" on the flip side, was *Variety*'s No. 10 hit of '43. Trudy Erwin and the Sportsmen Glee Club were Bing's helpers on these recordings. "People Will Say We're in Love" peaked at No. 2 on *Billboard*, but managed three weeks at No. 1 on *Your Hit Parade*. "Oh, What a Beautiful Mornin'" made it to No. 4 on *Billboard*, and to No. 2 on *Your Hit Parade*.

Read the lyrics (Song #1) at http://libretto.musicals.ru/text.php?textid=244&language=1.

PEOPLE WILL SAY WE'RE IN LOVE

"People Will Say We're in Love" is the principal love song of the musical. Curly (Alfred Drake) and Laurey (Joan Roberts) want to convince other people and themselves that they are not in love. Of course, they are, but are hesitant to admit it. Read the lyrics (Song #9) at http://libretto.musicals.ru/text.php?textid=244&language=1.

The song appeared on *Your Hit Parade* for thirty times and hit No. 1 on the October 30, 1943 broadcast. It managed three weeks at the top (again on November 20th and December 4th).

Bing Crosby, Frank Sinatra and Hal Goodman had popular recordings of the song in '43.

Variety chose the song for its *Hit Parade of a Half-Century*.

THE SURREY WITH THE FRINGE ON TOP

Another song from the score that charted on *Billboard* was "The Surrey with the Fringe on Top." Alfred Drake described this imaginary vehicle to Joan Roberts. Read the lyrics (Song #4) at http://libretto.musicals.ru/text.php?textid=244&language=1.

Variety included this song in its *Hit Parade of a Half-Century*.

Another well-known song from the score is the title song, "Oklahoma," which has become the official song of the state of Oklahoma (Song #16). Other outstanding songs from the musical include "Kansas City" (Song #5), "I Cain't Say No" (Song #6), "Pore Jud Is Daid" (Song #10), "Out of My Dreams" (Song #12), "The Farmer and the Cowman" (Song #13) and "All er Nothin'" (Song #14), {all of these can be accessed at http://libretto.musicals.ru/text.php?textid=244&language=1}. The title song was also nominated for the American Film Institute's list of the greatest songs from American films, but did not make the final list.

The score of *Oklahoma!* was put on 78-rpm disks , the first time an entire score of a Broadway musical was put on

record. The original cast album, which is still available, has sold more than 3 million copies, with the soundtrack album made from the '55 movie version selling more than 1 million copies.

The birth of the Rodgers and Hammerstein partnership was fortunate for the musical theater, for their own success, and for all of us who love their wonderful Broadway musicals. Their collaboration gave us not only *Oklahoma!*, but also several other Broadway classics, including *Carousel, South Pacific, The King and I,* and *The Sound of Music.*

One for My Baby (and One More for the Road)

Words: Johnny Mercer; Music: Harold Arlen

"One for My Baby (And One More for the Road)" premiered in the '43 movie musical *The Sky's the Limit*. Fred Astaire introduced the song. Frank Sinatra sang it in the '55 movie musical *Young at Heart*. Sinatra's recording of "One for My Baby" was inducted into the Grammy Hall of Fame in 2005. The song was sung by Ida Lupino in *Roadhouse* ('48) and by Jane Russell in *Macao* ('52).

Lena Horne had a popular recording of the song that charted in '45, the only version that managed to chart.

The song is rather long, as popular songs generally go (48 measures) and it changes key, which is not unheard of, but not completely normal for popular material.

Johnny Mercer's wonderfully creative lyrics are dramatic as they tell the story of a guy sitting in a bar at 2:45 in the morning. He tells the story of his failed romance to the bartender, Joe. He tells Joe to "make it one for my baby and one more for the road." Read the lyrics at http://lirama.net/song/28201.

Paper Doll

Words & Music: Johnny S. Black

"Paper Doll" was copyrighted in 1915 by Johnny S. Black, the same writer who wrote the piano rag, "Turkish Tom Tom," that was plagiarized by Fred Fisher for the big '20 hit "Dardanella."

The Mills Brothers' '43 recording of "Paper Doll" reportedly sold more than 6 million copies over the next several years. Some writers have suggested that this song's success signaled the beginning of the end for the big bands. The Mills Brothers' recording of "Paper Doll" was inducted into the Grammy Hall of Fame in 1998.

"Paper Doll," as recorded by the Mills Brothers, was, according to *Variety*, 1943's biggest hit, and with twelve weeks at No. 1 on *Billboard*, it was one of the biggest hits of the decade and No. 11 of the pre-rock era. It appeared on *Your Hit Parade* for twenty-three weeks, a record eventually topped by only seven other songs, but surprisingly, only managed three weeks at No. 1 on that survey.

The brothers want to buy a paper doll so they can have a woman of their own and not bother with the real-live types, who are, in their opinion, too fickle. Hear the song and read the lyrics at http://www.geocities.com/dferg5493/paperdoll.htm.

Most big hit songs have several versions of it available on the market. Every record company seemed to release at least one version of all the big hits, but "Paper Doll" was the exception. The Mills Brothers had "the" authoritative version. The Mills Brothers' recording of the song was heard on the soundtrack of *The Majestic*, a 2001 film starring Jim Carrey.

The Delta Rhythm Boys performed "Paper Doll" in the movie musical *Hi Good Lookin'* ('44) and Lena Horne sang it in *Two Girls and a Sailor*.

"Paper Doll" was selected by *Variety* for its *Hit Parade of a Half-Century*.

Pistol Packin' Mama

Words & Music: Al Dexter

A big novelty hit of '43 was Al Dexter's "Pistol Packin' Mama." Two recordings of the song were very popular: Al Dexter and his Troopers, the original country-western version, and Bing Crosby with the Andrews Sisters and Vic Schoen's orchestra. Al Dexter's recording of the song was inducted into the Grammy Hall of Fame in 2000.

The song was inspired by a tale about a Texas roadside cafe owner, Molly Jackson. In earlier days Molly, with a pistol for protection, would ride out into the Kentucky hills to bring her bootlegger husband home for the weekends. When she approached the still, she would call out to her husband to come down. He would call back, "Lay your pistol down, Ma, or we ain't comin'." Dexter frequently ate at Molly's and she often treated him to meals when he was broke. He repaid her by writing this song inspired by her tale. Read the lyrics at http://bing-crosby-lyrics.wonderlyrics.com/Pistol-Packin-Mama.html.

The song was banned from both the Blue and NBC radio networks because of the line "drinkin' beer in a cabaret." The publisher had a radio version prepared after it was banned, by changing the lyrics to "singin' songs in a cabaret."

Billboard lists Dexter's version of the song as the most popular version with eight weeks at No. 1. If that's really true, it is one of the first country-western recordings to cross-over into the pop mainstream. However, the Crosby/Andrews Sisters disk was *Variety*'s most popular version, their No. 9 hit of the year. *Billboard* has Crosby's version peaking at No. 2, but staying there for four weeks. The song only managed to get to No. 2 on *Your Hit Parade*.

Variety named "Pistol Packin' Mama" to its *Hit Parade of a Half-Century*.

Hear a V-Disk version of this song at http://www.authentichistory.com/audio/ww2/ww2music04.html.

Sunday, Monday, or Always

Words: Johnny Burke; Music: James Van Heusen

Bing Crosby sang "Sunday, Monday, or Always" in the '43 movie musical *Dixie*. Crosby played Daniel Decatur Emmett, a singer in the Virginia Minstrels who composed such classics as "Dixie," "The Blue Tail Fly," and "Old Dan Tucker." The fictional plot was about the transformation of Emmett's "Dixie" from a slow ballad to the rousing song we know today.

Crosby's recording with the Ken Darby Singers of "Sunday, Monday, or Always" is another all-vocal disk. His disk was No. 1 on *Billboard* for seven weeks and eventually became a million seller. The song made eighteen appearances on *Your Hit Parade* and collected six weeks at No. 1. It was *Variety*'s No. 4 hit in 1943's Top Ten. Frank Sinatra's version of the song peaked at No. 9 on *Billboard*.

"Sunday, Monday, or Always" was interpolated into the '44 movie musical *Take It Big*.

Variety selected "Sunday, Monday or Always" for its *Hit Parade of a Half-Century*.

The singer, Bing Crosby in this instance, asks his loved one to tell him when they will meet again, "Sunday, Monday or always." He tells her if she's satisfied, he'll be by her side always. Read the lyrics at http://lirama.net/song/16324.

Taking a Chance on Love

Words: John Latouche; Music: Vernon Duke

The '40 Broadway musical *Cabin in the Sky* became a great triumph for Ethel Waters. The story concerned a battle between the Lawd's general and Lucifer, Jr., for the soul of Little Joe Jackson. Waters played Petunia, Joe's wife.

The title song and "Taking a Chance on Love" are the show's most remembered songs. Ms. Waters introduced both songs.

In '43, MGM filmed the screen version of the musical starring Ethel Waters again. With a renewal of interest in the music from the musical, a recording of "Taking a Chance on Love" by Benny Goodman and his orchestra, with Helen Forrest's vocal performance, became a big hit. Goodman's disk was No. 1 on *Billboard* for three weeks in June. The song only reached No. 5 on *Your Hit Parade*.

Sammy Kaye and his orchestra also released a popular version of the song.

Lena Horne sang "Taking a Chance on Love" as an interpolation in *I Dood It* ('43), June Haver and Gloria DeHaven performed it in *I'll Get By* ('50), and the song also appeared in 1957's *This Could Be the Night* and in 1977's *New York, New York*.

Ethel Waters was hesitant, but now she's "all aglow again taking a chance on love." She sees a rainbow that will lead to a happy ending. Read the lyrics at http://lirama.net/song/16057.

That Old Black Magic

Words: Johnny Mercer; Music: Harold Arlen

"That Old Black Magic" was introduced by Johnnie Johnston (and danced by Vera Zorina) in the movie musical *Star Spangled Rhythm*, which was one of Paramount's contributions to the war effort. Its chief purpose was to entertain the servicemen at home and abroad.

Composer Arlen has given Mercer's lyrics credit for the song's success, contending that the words sustain the listener's interest, make sense, contain memorable phrases, and tell a story. Such ingredients add up to a successful lyric. The lyric describes the spell of "that old black magic called love." Read the lyrics at http://lirama.net/song/16326.

Glenn Miller and his orchestra's version of "That Old Black Magic" was No. 1 on *Billboard* for one week in late May of '43. Skip Nelson and the Modernaires provided the vocals on this record. The song topped out at No. 2 on *Your Hit Parade*. Freddie Slack and Hoarce Heidt and their orchestras also released successful recordings of the song. Although it doesn't seem to have charted, a version of the song often played on the radio is a fast version by Louis Prima and Keely Smith.

Bing Crosby sang the song in *Here Come the WAVES* ('44).

Variety included "That Old Black Magic" in its *Hit Parade of a Half-Century*. This song was nominated for the American Film Institute's list of the greatest songs ever from an American film, but did not make the final list. It was nominated for its inclusion in *Bus Stop* ('56).

There Are Such Things

Words: Abel Baer & Stanley Adams; Music: George W. Meyer

The recording of "There Are Such Things" by the Tommy Dorsey Orchestra, with Frank Sinatra and the Pied Pipers, reportedly took two years to become a million seller. Dorsey's disk topped the *Billboard* chart for six weeks and the song topped the *Your Hit Parade* chart for six weeks in early '43. *Variety* had it ranked as the No. 3 hit of the year.

The lyrics strike a note of optimism: two people can fulfill their dreams even though the world is torn apart by war. A particularly philosophical phrase from the lyrics is "not caring what you own but just what you are." Read the lyrics at http://lirama.net/song/16327.

Variety selected this song for its *Hit Parade of a Half-Century*.

There's a Star Spangled Banner Waving Somewhere

Words & Music: Paul Roberts & Shelby Darnell

"There's a Star Spangled Banner Waving Somewhere" was one of the timeliest hits of the early war years. Country singer Elton Britt—billed as "the world's highest yodeler"—recorded the song which reportedly sold four million disks by '44 and was reportedly the first country recording to receive an official gold record.

According to the lyrics, the place the star spangled banner is waving is in a U.S. heaven for heroes: "Only Uncle Sam's great heroes get to go there." The singer wants to volunteer to help protect our freedom: "can't the U.S. use a mountain boy like me?" However, this person has a crippled leg, but doesn't want to be judged unworthy for military service and become a hero so he can live in that hero heaven when he dies. Read the lyrics at http://lirama.net/song/16328.

The song was named by *Variety* to its *Hit Parade of a Half-Century* representing 1942.

Warsaw Concerto

Music: Richard Addinsell

Variety included "Warsaw Concerto" in its *Hit Parade of a Half-Century* representing 1942.

Composer Richard Addinsell is probably most famous for the "Warsaw Concerto." It was written for a wartime film titled *Dangerous Moonlight*. The music was heard only in small doses before being played at a concert near the end of the film.

A concerto is a classical composition form for solo instrument and orchestra. That's exactly what this piece is and it is in the flamboyant style of late 19th Century composers like Sergei Rachmaninoff and Franz Lizst.

The concerto captured the public's attention immediately and became a successful recording for Freddy Martin and his orchestra. Claude Thornhill and his orchestra revived it with some success in '48 and Ralph Marterie and his orchestra did the same in '53. *Your Hit Parade* ignored the song, as they usually tended to do with strictly instrumental numbers.

You'd Be So Nice to Come Home To

Words & Music: Cole Porter

Cole Porter wrote this number for the movie musical *Something to Shout About*. Janet Blair and Don Ameche introduced it in the film. "You'd Be So Nice to Come Home To" is a slow ballad, not as inventive and special as most of Porter's Broadway songs. The final line of the song sums up the lyric's intent: "You'd be so nice, you'd be paradise to come home to and love."

The most popular recordings of the song were by Dinah Shore and by Six Hits and a Miss.

The song made sixteen appearances on *Your Hit Parade*, peaking at No. 2.

The song was picked by *Variety* for its *Hit Parade of a Half-Century*.

See the sheet music cover at http://parlorsongs.com/issues/1998-7/jul98gallery.asp.

Porter's chorus lyrics open with "You'd Be So Nice to Come Home To" and he affirms this girl would be his heart's desire by the fire. Read the lyrics at http://lirama.net/song/16332.

You'll Never Know

Words: Mack Gordon; Music: Harry Warren

The Academy Award winner for '43 and the year's No. 6 hit in *Variety*'s Top Ten was Harry Warren and Mack Gordon's "You'll Never Know." It was written for the movie musical *Hello, Frisco, Hello*, and was sung by Alice Faye in the film. Dick Haymes and the Song Spinners all-vocal recording, due to the musicians' strike (see The Recording Industry section of the introduction to the Swing Era), was the most popular version on the market. It was seven weeks at No. 1 on *Billboard*. The song made twenty-four appearances on *Your Hit Parade* and garnered nine weeks at the top of that chart.

Frank Sinatra, and Willie Kelly and his orchestra also released successful recordings of the song in '43. Rosemary Clooney with Harry James and his orchestra revived the song in '53 with moderate success. An audio clip of Bobby Darin singing "You'll Never Know" can be heard at http://www.harrywarrenmusic.com/realfiles/.

The idea behind the lyric is that with all the things done and said to prove love, if the loved one doesn't know they are loved by now, they never will. Read the lyrics and hear a midi musical version at http://www.harrywarren.org/songs/0631.htm. See Warren's music manuscript of this song at http://www.harrywarrenmusic.com/frameset.html.

Betty Grable performed "You'll Never Know" in the '45 movie musical *Billy Rose's Diamond Horseshoe*. The song also appeared in *Since You Went Away* ('44), *Boarding House Blues* ('48), *Dreamboat* ('52), *Alice Doesn't Live Here Anymore* ('74), *Radio Days* ('87) and *Enigma* (2001).

Variety chose "You'll Never Know" for this *Hit Parade of a Half-Century*. It was nominated for the American Film Institute's list of the greatest songs ever from an American film, but it did not make the final list.

1944

Amor

Words: Sunny Skylar; Music: Gabriel Ruiz

"Amor" is, of course, "love" in Spanish. The song was introduced by Ginny Simms in the '44 movie musical *Broadway Rhythm*. Ms. Simms performed the song in

Spanish. Before the year was out, it was used in another movie musical entitled *Swing in the Saddle*.

This song of love was popularized in recordings by Bing Crosby, by Andy Russell, and by Xavier Cugat and his orchestra. The Four Aces revived the song in '54 with a moderately successful recording.

"Amor" made nineteen appearances on *Your Hit Parade* and collected two weeks at No. 1. According to *Billboard*, Crosby's recordings, the most popular version on the market, peaked at No. 2. In the early '60s the song charted twice: by Ben E. King and by Roger Williams.

1944 was a good year for lyricist Sunny Skylar, who wrote the words for two big hit songs: "Amor" and "Besame Mucho."

Variety included "Amor" in its *Hit Parade of a Half-Century*.

The lyrics quickly define "amor" as "I adore you" (actually Amor was the god of love and the word is most often defined as "love"). The singer tells his loved one "when you're away there is no day, and nights are lonely." Read the lyrics at http://lirama.net/song/16335.

Babalu

English Words: Bob Russell; Spanish Words & Music: Marguerita Lecuona

Marguerita Lecuona wrote "Babalu" in '39; Bob Russell added English lyrics in '42, but it became popular when Xavier Cugat introduced it in the U.S. in '44 and when Cugat and his orchestra played the song in the movie musical *Two Girls and a Sailor* in '44. The song surfaced again in the '45 movie musical *Pan-American*.

However, the song may be most famous as Desi Arnaz's theme song. He performed it on at least six episodes of *I Love Lucy*. Arnaz and his orchestra recorded the song in '46.

Variety included the song in its *Hit Parade of a Half-Century*.

Babalu is a god that can bring back the love he has taken. Read both the Spanish and English lyrics at http://members.tripod.com/TropicanaNightclub/babalu.html.

Besame Mucho

Words: Sunny Skylar; Music: Consuelo Velazquez

There's quite a Spanish influence in the songs of '44. The first three songs listed this year all had Spanish titles.

Originally composed in '41 by Consuelo Velazquez for a Mexican opera, *Goyescas*, this song received English lyrics by Sunny Skylar in '44. A recording by Jimmy Dorsey and his orchestra, with Kitty Kallen and Bob Eberly, caught on immediately and reportedly sold a million or more copies. It was No. 7 on *Variety*'s Top Ten for '44. It managed seven weeks at No. 1 on *Billboard*, and three weeks at No. 1 on *Your Hit Parade*.

This song was on *Variety*'s *Hit Parade of a Half-Century*.

Andy Russell's recordings of both "Amor" and "Besame Mucho" were well received. "Besame Mucho" was his first chart single, while "Amor" was his second.

Abe Lyman and his California Orchestra also had a successful recording of "Besame Mucho" in '44.

"Besame Mucho" translates as "kiss me much," but the English lyrics' only reference to kissing is "each time I cling to your kiss I hear music divine." Read both the English and Spanish lyrics at http://lirama.net/song/16336.

Dance with a Dolly

Words: Jimmy Eaton & Mickey Leader; Music: Terry Shand

The melody for this '44 hit song was adapted from a hundred year old song "Lubly Fan." The song's writer, Cool White, introduced it in a minstrel show not too many years before the Civil War. Its second reincarnation was as the song "Buffalo Gals" (it frequently took on the title of different locales). Mark Twain mentioned this song in his *Tom Sawyer*.

Its third reincarnation came in '44 as "Dance with a Dolly (With a Hole in Her Stocking)." Recordings by Russ Morgan and his orchestra, with vocalist Al Jennings, Evelyn Knight with Camarata's Orchestra, and Tony Pastor and his orchestra, with Tony himself providing the vocal, helped popularized the song.

The song managed No. 1 on *Your Hit Parade* for only one week. *Billboard* has Russ Morgan's disk, the most popular version, only getting to No. 3.

"Dance with a Dolly" was interpolated into two '45 movie musicals: the Andrews Sisters performed it in *Her Lucky Night* and it also appeared in *On Stage Everybody*.

"Buffalo Gals," mentioned earlier, was nominated for the American Film Institute's list of the greatest songs ever from American films for its appearance in the 1946 film *It's a Wonderful Life*, but did not make the final list.

An alternate title for the song might have been "Dance by the Light of the Moon" because the phrase is used several times. As the singer was walking down the street he met a girl and asked if they might talk for a while. All the other fellows were jealous. One of the most familiar lines from the song is "Gonna dance with a dolly with a hole in her stockin', while her knees keep a-knockin' and her toes keep arockin'." Read the lyrics at http://www.lirama.net/song/16337.

Don't Fence Me in

Words & Music: Cole Porter

"Don't Fence Me in" is far too plebeian to have been written by Cole Porter. It just doesn't have the sophistication of most of his lyrics, "Friendship" not withstanding, nor does it seem especially clever or debonair. Porter did "write" it for a never-released film, *Adios Argentina*.

As it turns out, Porter bought the rights to the song from a Montana cowboy, Robert H. Fletcher. Porter used the title and a few phrases from the original in writing "Don't Fence Me in." That probably explains the un–Porter-like character of the lyrics.

The song lay forgotten until Roy Rogers and the Sons of the Pioneers and the Andrews Sisters performed it in the '44 movie musical *Hollywood Canteen*. A recording by Bing Crosby and the Andrews Sisters was the most popular version on the market. Their disk ended '44 and began '45 as No. 1 on both *Billboard* and *Your Hit Parade*. It topped both charts for eight weeks. *Variety* ranked it No. 4 for '45.

Bing Crosby and the Andrews Sisters' recording of "Don't Fence Me In" was inducted into the Grammy Hall of Fame in 1998.

The number is a cowboy folk-style song that repeats "Don't Fence Me in" four different times. The singer is a footloose and fancy-free kind of person and wants to stay that way. It is as anti-marriage as '42's "Jingle, Jangle,

Jingle," another cowboy number. The stereotypical cowboy loves women, but refuses to be tied down. Read the lyrics at http://lirama.net/song/16339.

The song was also featured in Porter's screen biography, *Night and Day* (1946).

Variety included "Don't Fence Me In" in its *Hit Parade of a Half-Century*. This song was nominated for the American Film Institute's list of the greatest songs ever from American films for its appearance in the 1945 film *Don't Fence Me In*, but did not make the final list. The song also appeared in the movie *The Bachelor* ('99).

G. I. Jive
Words & Music: Johnny Mercer

According to Dave Dexter, who was then Capitol Records' publicity director, A&R man, and talent scout, this cute wartime ditty was written by Johnny Mercer in practically no time at all. Mercer got the idea while stopped at a traffic light at Sunset and Vine in L.A. Several servicemen were at the busy intersection, which started Mercer's initial thoughts. He drove another block to his office, went in, sat down at the typewriter, and wrote the entire lyric in a few minutes. It turned out to be Mercer's biggest hit of the year.

Mercer's clever lyrics are full of abbreviations that our servicemen knew all too well. There's P.V.T., M.P., and K.P., among others. There are also some "jive" phrases like "Root-tie-tee-toot, Jump in your suit, Make a salute (Voot!)." Mercer definitely captured the real soldier, but dealt with his frustrations with military life in a comical way. See if you can understand this jive talk at http://lirama.net/song/16341.

Louis Jordan and his Tympany Five's recording of the song was No. 1 on *Billboard's* chart for a couple of weeks in August of '44. The song never charted on *Your Hit Parade*. Johnny Mercer's version of the song made it to No. 11 on *Billboard*.

Hear a V-Disk (with introduction by Glenn Miller) of this song: http://www.authentichistory.com/audio/ww2/ww2music03.html.

Holiday for Strings
Music: David Rose

This brilliant and original composition and orchestral scoring by David Rose made him famous and gave him his first hit recording.

"Holiday for Strings" was the No. 9 hit of '44 according to *Variety* and was selected by *Variety* for its *Hit Parade of a Half-Century*.

The song appeared in the '47 film *The Unfinished Dance*.

(There'll Be) a Hot Time in the Town of Berlin (When the Yanks Go Marching in)
Words: John DeVries; Music: Joe Bushkin

Bing Crosby and the Andrews Sisters' recording of "(There'll Be) a Hot Time in the Town of Berlin (When the Yanks Go Marching In)" was No. 1 for six weeks in '44, according to *Billboard*. However, none of the other charts mention the song.

The song sounds like a cross between "Hot Time in the Old Town Tonight" from 1896; a song that was popular during the Spanish American War, and "When the Saints Go Marchin' In." Read the lyrics of this World War II song at http://www.lyricsvault.net/songs/19426.html.

I Couldn't Sleep a Wink Last Night
Words: Harold Adamson; Music: Jimmy McHugh

Higher and Higher was a Richard Rodgers/Lorenz Hart musical that did moderately well on Broadway in '40. The musical went through several changes including a new musical score for the '43 film version. Frank Sinatra performed five songs in the film including "I Couldn't Sleep a Wink Last Night" and "A Lovely Way to Spend an Evening."

Sinatra's all-vocal recording of the song, due to the musicians' strike (see The Record Industry section of the introduction to the Swing Era), was with the Bobby Tucker Singers. It only made it to No. 4 on *Billboard*, but topped *Your Hit Parade* for one week.

The song was interpolated into the '45 movie musical *Radio Stars on Parade* and *Beat the Band* in '47.

This McHugh and Adamson's song was an Academy Award nominee, losing out to "Swinging on a Star."

Adamson's chorus lyrics indicate the guy "couldn't sleep a wink last night" because he had a silly fight with his girl. The first thing the next morning, the guy called the girl to make certain everything was all right. Read the lyrics at http://lirama.net/song/16344.

I Love You
Words & Music: Cole Porter

There were two songs titled "I Love You" in '44. One was Robert Wright and Chet Forrest's "I Love You" which they had adapted from Edvard Grieg's "Ich Liebe Dich" for the Broadway musical *Song of Norway*.

This "I Love You" came from Cole Porter's Broadway musical *Mexican Hayride*. Porter wrote the song when a friend bet him he could not write a successful song with such a trite title as "I Love You." Porter accepted the challenge, wrote this song, and won the bet. He maintained, however, that it was the song's melody, not the lyrics, which made it popular. However, it is interesting how Porter built the lyrics: the April breeze, the echoing hills, and the birds sing "I love you." Read the lyrics at http://lirama.net/song/16346.

Bing Crosby's recording of Porter's "I Love You" collected five weeks at No. 1 on *Billboard*, and three weeks on top of *Your Hit Parade*.

Variety included Porter's "I Love You" in its *Hit Parade of a Half-Century*.

I'll Be Seeing You
Words: Irving Kahal; Music: Sammy Fain

Tamara introduced this torch ballad in the '38 Broadway musical *Right This Way*. Bing Crosby sang "I'll Be Seeing You" in the '44 movie musical *I'll Be Seeing You*. Martha Wainwright sang it on the soundtrack of *The Aviator* (2005).

The song spoke eloquently of the sentiments of millions of servicemen and their loved ones who had been rather abruptly and painfully torn apart by the war. Neither the men nor their loved ones knew if they'd ever see each other again. Read the lyrics at http://lirama.net/song/16347.

With ten weeks at No. 1, "I'll Be Seeing You" was *Your Hit Parade*'s biggest hit of the year. It also ranked No. 1 for the year for *Variety*. Crosby's recording with John Scott Trotter's Orchestra topped *Billboard*'s chart for four weeks.

Tommy Dorsey and his orchestra also had a popular version of the song on the market. Frank Sinatra was Dorsey's vocalist on the disk.

In the fifties, Liberace used the song as the closing theme for his television show.

Variety selected the song for its *Golden 100 Tin Pan Alley Songs* and *Hit Parade of a Half-Century* lists.

I'll Get By

Words: Roy Turk; Music: Fred E. Ahlert

"I'll Get By" was a leading song hit of the late twenties, reportedly selling more than a million copies of sheet music and approximately a million copies of various recordings. Unlike our day, when a song is identified with a particular performer, in this period it was generally the song, not a specific performance by a singer or group that sold. Still, "I'll Get By" is often closely identified with Ruth Etting, who had the most popular recorded version of the song in '29. Nick Lucas and Aileen Stanley also helped popularize it with success releases at the time.

A recording of "I'll Get By (As Long as I Have You)" by Harry James and his orchestra with vocalist Dick Haymes topped the *Billboard* chart for six weeks in '44. *Variety* ranked it at No. 3 for the year. It peaked at No. 2 on *Your Hit Parade*. Other popular versions that charted were by the Ink Spots and the King Sisters.

"I'll Get By" was used in several movie musicals beginning with 1930's *Puttin' on the Ritz*, Harry Richman's talking film debut. It was used as a background theme in the '43 film *A Guy Named Joe* and in the 1944 movie musical *Follow the Boys*. It was used in 1948's *You Were Meant for Me*, which was set in the twenties. A '50 movie musical was titled *I'll Get By*. It also appeared in Judy Garland's '54 remake of *A Star Is Born*. *The Helen Morgan Story* ('57) also used "I'll Get By" in its score. Don Murray, and later Andrea McArdle, sang it in *Rainbow* ('78).

Roy Turk's chorus lyrics open with "I'll get by as long as I have you." The singer sings that even though he is far away he'll get by as long as he has her love. Read the lyrics at http://lirama.net/song/16348.

I'll Walk Alone

Words: Sammy Cahn; Music: Jule Styne

"I'll Walk Alone" was nominated for the Academy Award, but lost to "Swinging on a Star," after it was introduced by Dinah Shore in the '44 movie musical *Follow the Boy*. Her recording of the song was No. 1 on *Billboard* for four weeks in the fall of '44. The song made twenty-one appearances on *Your Hit Parade*, and collected eight weeks at No. 1.

Other popular recordings of "I'll Walk Alone" were released by Martha Tilton and Mary Martin in '44.

The song was also used in Jane Froman's screen biography, *With a Song in My Heart*, in '52. Her recording of the song rose to No. 14 on *Billboard*, but Don Cornell's version made it to No. 5. Other '52 versions that charted included those by Richard Hayes, and Margaret Whiting.

The song had great success during the war years because of its lyrics, which suggest that the lovers who are separated will "walk alone" until they can walk together.

Those parted by military service found this idea very appealing. Read the lyrics at http://lirama.net/song/16349.

Variety included "I'll Walk Alone" in its *Hit Parade of a Half-Century*. This song was nominated for the American Film Institute's list of greatest songs ever from an American film, but was not on the final list. It was nominated for its appearance in *Follow the Boys*.

I'm Making Believe

Words: Mack Gordon; Music: James V. Monaco

Ella Fitzgerald combined with the Ink Spots to record "I'm Making Believe" and "Into Each Life Some Rain Must Fall." Both recordings made it to No. 1 on *Billboard* for two weeks. "I'm Making Believe" peaked at No. 2 on *Your Hit Parade*.

"I'm Making Believe" was nominated for the Academy Award for Best Song from Film in '44 after it had been introduced in the movie musical *Sweet and Low Down*.

Hal McIntyre and his orchestra's version of the song did pretty well on the charts in '45.

Ella Fitzgerald sang she is making believe her lover is in her arms even though she knows he's far away. She says, "making believe is just another way of dreamin'." Read the lyrics at http://lirama.net/song/16350.

Into Each Life Some Rain Must Fall

Words & Music: Allan Roberts & Doris Fisher

The flip side of Ella Fitzgerald and the Ink Spots' "I'm Making Believe" was "Into Each Life Some Rain Must Fall." "Into Each Life..." topped the *Billboard* chart for the first week of December, while "I'm Making Believe" was No. 1 for the second week of the month. Both songs eventually topped that chart for two weeks. "Into Each Life..." never charted on *Your Hit Parade*.

Allan Roberts and Doris Fisher were the writers of two big hit songs in '44: "Into Each Life..." and "You Always Hurt the One You Love."

The lyrics tell us that we expect rain, a metaphor for bad things, to dampen our lives, but too much rain is falling in the singer's life. It continues by saying that some people can shake the blues, but every time the singer thinks of this person, "another shower starts." Read the words at http://lirama.net/song/16666.

Is You Is, or Is You Ain't My Baby?

Words & Music: Louis Jordan & Billy Austin

"Is You Is, or Is You Ain't My Baby?" was interpolated by co-writer Louis Jordan into the '44 movie musical *Follow the Boys*. It was also sung by the Delta Rhythm Boys in the '45 film *Easy to Look At*.

Jazz critic Leonard Feather has suggested that if we trace rock 'n' roll back to its roots, we'd find Louis Jordan. The rhythmic character of his band definitely had a tremendous influence on the course of popular music. Just a sample of their '49 recording of "Saturday Night Fish Fry" is enough to hear rock 'n' roll's roots (some historians consider it "the first" rock 'n' roll record).

Jordan was honored in 1992 by the Broadway musical *Five Guys Named Moe*. All of the songs in the show were either written or popularized by Jordan. "Is You Is..." was one of the songs used in the show. Other songs featured include "Ain't Nobody Here but Us Chickens" and "Caldonia," which is certainly a forerunner of Little Richard's style of singing.

Songwriter Billy Austin worked as a lumberjack, a sailor and in construction before he had any success in the music business. This song was his most successful song on the charts.

Both Louis Jordan and his Tympany Five's and Bing Crosby and the Andrews Sisters' recordings of "Is You Is..." peaked at No. 2 on the *Billboard* chart. The song also reached No. 2 on *Your Hit Parade*.

The singer asks, "Is you is or is you ain't my baby?" He tells her the way she's been acting makes him doubt her. He thinks she may have found somebody new. Read the lyrics at http://lirama.net/song/16351.

It's Love, Love, Love

Words & Music: Alex Kramer, Joan Whitney & Mack David

Guy Lombardo and his Royal Canadians' recording of "It's Love, Love, Love" was *Billboard's* No. 1 hit for a couple of weeks in the spring of '44. The song managed three weeks at No. 1 on *Your Hit Parade*.

Skip Nelson was the vocalist on Lombardo's recording. This was the group's first big hit record since '41. The King Sisters also released a popular version of the song that charted on *Billboard*.

The song had been introduced in the '44 movie musical *Stars on Parade*.

The lyrics are basically trying to tell us the symptoms of love. "If your heart goes bumpety-bump ... your throat comes up with a lump ... your knees go knockety-knock" then "it's love, love, love!" Read the lyrics at http://lirama.net/song/16354.

Long Ago (and Far Away)

Words: Ira Gershwin; Music: Jerome Kern

Jerome Kern collaborated with Ira Gershwin to write "Long Ago (And Far Away)" for the movie musical *Cover Girl*. Gene Kelly and Rita Hayworth (voiced by Martha Mears) introduced the song. The number was set in a dingy Brooklyn nightclub. The film concerned a nightclub dancer, played by Rita Hayworth, who deserts her lover, played by Kelly, to become a model. In a series of flashbacks, we find that Hayworth's grandmother had followed the same course. That's where the song "Long Ago (And Far Away)" fits into the plot. Read the lyrics at http://www.stlyrics.com/lyrics/tillthecloudsrollby/longagoandfaraway.htm.

In addition to receiving an Academy Award nomination, the song climbed to the top of *Your Hit Parade*, where it stayed for six weeks. The most popular recording was a duet by Helen Forrest and Dick Haymes, which peaked at No. 2 on *Billboard*. Other versions that charted on *Billboard* included Bing Crosby's, Jo Stafford's, Perry Como's, Guy Lombardo and his Royal Canadians', and the Three Suns'.

This was Kern's last big hit song; he died in '45. His screen biography, *Till the Clouds Roll By*, was filmed in '46, where Kathryn Grayson performed "Long Ago (And Far Away)."

AFI's *100 Years ... 100 Songs* (2004) named "Long Ago (And Far Away)" the No. 92 greatest song ever from an American film.

Mairzy Doats

Words & Music: Milton Drake, Al Hoffman & Jerry Livingston

Every era has its crazy, novelty songs, and the war years are no different. The craziness probably gave the public something to laugh about so they wouldn't cry. Such was the case of several lighthearted songs during the Great Depression of the early thirties.

The novelty song hit of '44 was "Mairzy Doats." Several popular recordings of the song helped spread its fame from coast to coast and beyond. The Merry Macs' version was the most successful one, topping the *Billboard* chart for five weeks beginning in mid–March of '44. This crazy ditty was No. 1 on *Your Hit Parade* for one week, the March 11th broadcast, with eleven appearances on the program.

Other popular recordings of "Mairzy Doats" were those by Al Trace and his orchestra, the Pied Pipers, Lawrence Welk and his orchestra, and the King Sisters.

Milton Drake got the idea for this song when his four-year-old daughter came home from kindergarten one day jabbering "Cowzy tweet and sowzy tweet and liddle sharsky doisters." Little children often make up words that they think they hear adults uttering, but they come out as gibberish. Drake's lyrics actually explain the meaning: "Mares eat oats and does eat oats and little lambs eat ivy." Read these crazy lyrics at http://lirama.net/song/16357.

Variety named "Mairzy Doats" to its *Hit Parade of a Half-Century*.

My Heart Tells Me

Words: Mack Gordon; Music: Harry Warren

Betty Grable introduced "My Heart Tells Me" in the movie musical *Sweet Rosie O'Grady* ('43). The film was about Madeleine Marlowe, a famous musical comedy star, who was really Rosie O'Grady, a former singer at Flugelman's Beer Garden in the Bowery, not the high-born lady she had been portrayed to be. The song was filmed with Betty Grable, the GI's favorite pinup girl, in a bathtub. Read the lyrics at http://www.harrywarren.org/songs/0352.htm (no midi musical version this time).

Most of the songs in the film were old songs from the 1880s, but Harry Warren and Mack Gordon furnished the new ones.

"My Heart Tells Me (Should I Believe My Heart?)" was a big hit for Glen Gray and the Casa Loma Orchestra, their first big success since '39. Eugenie Baird was Gray's vocalist on this recording. Their version of the song was No. 1 on *Billboard* for five weeks in early '44. The song was *Variety*'s No. 6 hit in 1944's Top Ten. The song appeared on *Your Hit* Parade nineteen times and ranked No. 1 nine weeks. Jan Garber and his orchestra, with vocalist Bon Davis, also released a popular version of the song. Warren and Gordon's song can be heard in an audio clip at http://www.harrywarrenmusic.com/realfiles/ as sung by Nat "King" Cole.

Variety included "My Heart Tells Me" in its *Hit Parade of a Half-Century* representing '43.

New York, New York

Words: Betty Comden and Adolph Green; Music: Leonard Bernstein

"New York, New York" was introduced in the Broadway musical *On the Town*. In the musical's plot three sailors have a 24-hour leave in New York City. They discover many of the city's landmarks and meet three girls. In the original cast the three sailors were played by Adolph Green, John Battles and Cris Alexander, while the three girls were portrayed by Ivy Smith, Nancy Walker and Betty Comden.

The song is the opening number of the musical as the guys disembark and talk about all they want to do in the scant hours they have in the Big Apple. The original lyrics were, "New York, New York, a helluva town." "Helluva" was changed to "wonderful" for the '49 film version.

AFI's *100 Years ... 100 Songs* (2004) named this song the No. 41 greatest song ever from an American film for its includion in the '49 film version of the Broadway musical, which starred Gene Kelly, Frank Sinatra and Jules Munshin as the sailors with Vera- Ellen, Ann Miller and Betty Garrett was their love interests.

San Fernando Valley
Words & Music: Gordon Jenkins

Bing Crosby's recording of Gordon Jenkins' "San Fernando Valley" topped the *Billboard* chart for five weeks in the spring of '44. The song peaked at No. 2 on *Your Hit Parade*.

The rush for California land had begun during the Depression years. Many of the Dust Bowl states lost population to the Golden State's larger metropolitan areas like Los Angeles. However, as those population centers became increasingly crowded, a lot of people looked for more space with the same great weather. They found what they were looking for in the San Fernando Valley. Jenkins' song put the area on the map nationally. His song makes it sound like this would be the greatest place on earth to live and he never wants to leave. Read the lyrics at http://www.lyricsdepot.com/bing-crosby/san-fernando-valley.html.

Shoo-Shoo Baby
Words & Music: Phil Moore

Phil Moore was employed at the MGM studios in Hollywood, where he had the habit of using the expression "shoo-shoo." At a rehearsal with Lena Horne, which had not gone particularly well, he kept trying to relax her by saying "shoo, shoo, Lena, take it easy." After several days of this, he decided to improvise a lyric around the phrase and then set it to music. Read the lyrics at http://www.lyricsdepot.com/the-andrews-sisters/shoo-shoo-baby.html.

The song was introduced by Ms. Horne and was used by Georgia Gibbs in her nightclub act before it was published.

In '44, it was interpolated into the movie musicals *Trocadero*, where Ida James sang it, *Follow the Boys*, where it was performed by the Andrews Sisters, *Beautiful but Broke,* and *South of Dixie*. In '45 Betty Grable sang it in *Billy Rose's Diamond Horseshoe*. It resurfaced again in the '48 movie musical *Big City*.

The Andrews Sisters, who had performed the song in *Follow the Boys* (also known as *Three Cheers for the Boys*) , had the biggest hit with their recording. Their version was No. 1 on *Billboard* for nine weeks, the most weeks at the top of any hit of the year, except "Swinging on a Star," which also collected nine weeks at No. 1. The song managed seventeen appearances on *Your Hit Parade*, but only two weeks at the top.

Ella Mae Morse and Jan Garber and his orchestra also had versions of the song that charted on *Billboard*.

"Shoo-Shoo Baby" was selected by *Variety* for its *Hit Parade of a Half-Century*.

Speak Low
Words: Ogden Nash; Music: Kurt Weill

This love duet came from *One Touch of Venus*, Kurt Weill's longest-running Broadway musical. The story was a fantasy about a statue of Venus that comes to life and falls in love with a barber named Rodney. Mary Martin played Venus, in her first starring Broadway role. Ms. Martin and Kenny Baker introduced "Speak Low" in the musical.

Ogden Nash got the idea for the lyrics from a line in Shakespeare's *Much Ado About Nothing*: "Speak low, if you speak love." Read the lyrics at http://www.lyricsdepot.com/guy-lombardo/speak-low.html.

Eileen Wilson sang the song for Ava Gardner in the film version of *One Touch of Venus* ('48).

Guy Lombardo and his Royal Canadians popularized the song with a popular recording. It was selected by *Variety* for its *Hit Parade of a Half-Century* representing '43.

Swinging on a Star
Words: Johnny Burke; Music: Jimmy Van Heusen

The winner of the '44 Academy Award for the best song from a film went to James Van Heusen and Johnny Burke's "Swinging on a Star." Bing Crosby introduced it in the film *Going My Way*, one of Crosby's best and most remembered performances. He was cast as Father O'Malley, a young Catholic priest, who has been sent to replace Father Fitzgibbon, played by Barry Fitzgerald. Crosby performed "Swinging on a Star" with a group of children at St. Dominic's Church.

One of the most lastingly popular songs of the era, this whimsical ditty may also owe its birth to Crosby. Burke and Van Heusen were visiting in Crosby's home when one of the Crosby sons misbehaved. Bing reprimanded him for acting "like a mule." Burke expanded the incident into the lyrics "By the way, if you hate to go to school, you may grow up to be a mule." Read the lyrics at http://www.lyricsdepot.com/bing-crosby/swinging-on-astar.html.

This song was selected by *Variety* for its *Hit Parade of a Half-Century*. AFI's *100 Years ... 100 Songs* (2004) named "Swinging on a Star" as the No. 37 greatest song from an American film.

Crosby's recording with John Scott Trotter's Orchestra became a gold disk (one million single units sold). His recording of the song was No. 1 on *Billboard* for nine weeks (the only other song that managed nine weeks at No. 1 on *Billboard* in '44 was "Shoo-Shoo Baby"). Very surprisingly, the song only reached No. 2 on *Your Hit Parade*. The song was No. 2 in *Variety*'s Top Ten for '44. Tied for No. 1 on *Billboard* and No. 2 on *Variety*, but never made it to No. 1 on *Your Hit Parade*. Who do we believe? In this instance, take the two out of three. Crosby's recording of "Swinging on a Star" was inducted into the Grammy Hall of Fame in 2002.

"Swinging on a Star" has an interesting side note. The vocal background for Bing's recording was by the Williams Brothers, who included future singing star Andy Williams.

Another song from the film that found favor with the public was the title song, "Going My Way," also popularized by Bing Crosby.

They're Either Too Young or Too Old
Words: Frank Loesser; Music: Arthur Schwartz

In World War II the only men left at home were "either too young or too old" for military service. This song, a female's wartime lament about that problem (especially a dilemma for marriageable women), was introduced by Bette Davis in the '43 movie musical *Thank Your Lucky Stars*. Read the lyrics at http://www.songlyrics4u.com/jimmy-dorsey-orchestra/ theyre-either-too-young-or-too-old.html.

The film was typical of the seemingly hundreds of motion pictures that were turned out in assembly line fashion for one purpose: entertain the soldiers and those left behind during the war.

Jimmy Dorsey and his orchestra, with vocalist Kitty Kallen, had the most popular recording of the song in '44. Their recording peaked at No. 2 on *Billboard*. The song appeared on *Your Hit Parade* a dozen times, peaking at No. 2.

In Jane Froman's film biography, *With a Song in My Heart* ('52), Froman sang the song for the film's star, Susan Heyward.

Variety selected the song for its *Hit Parade of a Half-Century* representing '43.

Too-Ra-Loo-Ra-Loo-Ral (see 1914)

"Too-Ra-Loo-Ra-Loo-Ral (That's an Irish Lullaby)," a hit from the Bing Crosby film *Going My Way* (also see "Swinging on a Star," above), was actually a revival of a popular song from 1914.

The Trolley Song *and* Have Yourself a Merry Little Christmas

Words: Ralph Blane; Music: Hugh Martin

The movie musical *Meet Me in St. Louis* is set in 1903. The well-to-do Smith family has four beautiful daughters, including Esther, played by Judy Garland, and little Tootie, played by Margaret O'Brien. Esther, now 17-years old, has fallen in love with the boy next door. He barely notices her at first. The family is totally surprised when Mr. Smith announces that he has been transfered to a nice position in New York City, which means that the family has to leave St. Louis and the approaching St. Louis Fair.

THE TROLLEY SONG

Ralph Blane and Hugh Martin wrote "The Trolley Song" for the '44 movie musical *Meet Me in St. Louis*. Judy Garland introduced the song in the film and also had a popular recording of it. Garland played Esther, the Smith sister who has developed a crush on the boy next door. She sang about the crush in two of the film's best-remembered songs: "The Trolley Song" and "The Boy Next Door."

The song won an Academy Award nomination for the year's best song, but lost to "Swinging on a Star." AFI's *100 Years ... 100 Songs* (2004) listed "The Trolley Song" as the No. 26 greatest song ever from an American film. "The Boy Next Door" was one of the songs nominated for the list, but was not one on the final list.

The Pied Pipers had the most popular recorded version of the song. Their version reached No. 2 on *Billboard*. "The Trolley Song" collected five weeks at No. 1 on *Your Hit Parade*, with fourteen appearances on their hit survey. Garland's version reached No. 4 on *Billboard*, but she was always much more popular in films than on records. The King Sisters' recording also charted in '44, as did Vaughn Monroe's and Guy Lombardo's in '45.

The song tells of Esther's meeting a young man of the trolley who makes her heart go "zing, zing, zing." The "clang, clang, clang" in the lyric imitating the trolley bell is one of the most distinctive features of the song.

Read the lyrics at http://www.hugelyrics.com/lyrics/102205/Garland_Judy/Trolley_Song.

Variety picked "The Trolley Song" for its *Hit Parade of a Half-Century*.

HAVE YOURSELF A MERRY LITTLE CHRISTMAS

Another famous song from the score of the film was "Have Yourself a Merry Little Christmas." Judy Garland introduced this seasonal favorite in the film. AFI's *100 Years ... 100 Songs* (2004) named this holiday song the No. 76 greatest song ever from an American film.

In the film, Judy Garland's St. Louis family was moving to New York, against the wishes of everyone in the family except the father. Judy Garland's character had recently discovered that she was in love with the boy next door (another song from the film, "The Boy Next Door"). Judy's younger sister, played by Margaret O'Brien, was afraid Santa wouldn't be able to find her in a different town. Blane and Martin wrote the first version of the song to capitalize on the sadness of the impending move. The lyrics opened, "Have yourself a merry little Christmas; it will be your last. Next year we will be living in the past."

Judy refused to perform the song because it was too somber, too full of pain. She may have also been thinking about all the soldiers fighting in World War II and the effect such a song would have had on them. Nevertheless, Blane and Martin revised the lyrics to contain a more encouraging message.

The lyrics of the song mention our troubles, most likely referring to troubles at home and abroad. "Have yourself a merry little Christmas ... from now on, our troubles will be out of sight." There's another mention of troubles in the next strain. After that, the lyrics are reminiscing about happier days and relishing the presence of friends and family. Read the lyrics at http://www.carols.org.uk/have_yourself_a_merry_little_christmas.htm.

What a Diff'rence a Day Made (see 1934)

Variety selected "What a Diff'rence a Day Made" as a *Golden 100 Tin Pan Alley Song* and its *Hit Parade of a Half-Century* representing '44, however, it was more popular in '34.

You Always Hurt the One You Love

Words & Music: Allan Roberts & Doris Fisher

The Mills Brothers popularized "You Always Hurt the One You Love," and reportedly their recording eventually sold more than a million disks. The Mills Brothers' recording of this song, with "Till Then" on the flip side, was *Variety*'s No. 5 hit of '44. Their disk topped the *Billboard* chart for five weeks in the fall. The song never charted on *Your Hit Parade* (the program was charting nine hits each week since mid–August, 1943).

The tender lyric and the Mills Brothers' rendition caught the fancy of the public. "You Always Hurt the One You Love" was the Brothers' follow-up to their enormously successful '43 recording of "Paper Doll."

The chorus lyrics remind us that we often hurt the people we love, the very ones we shouldn't hurt. So, the singer says, "if I broke your heart last night, it's because I love you most of all." Read the lyrics at http://www.lyricsvault.net/songs/20670.html.

Sammy Kaye and his orchestra also had a popular recording of the song that charted on *Billboard*.

VI

The Sing Era:
1945–1955

As World War II ended, the people of the United States found far too often that the lives they had known before the war did not exist anymore.

The big bands had suffered during the war years because most of the musicians had been drafted or had enlisted in the military services. Once these bandsmen reentered civilian life, they found that the popular music scene had changed drastically. The bands were no longer the major hit makers. The top tunes now came from singers like Frank Sinatra, Dinah Shore, Perry Como and Doris Day.

During the war, because rationing of gasoline and tires made traveling difficult, numerous clubs and ballrooms where the bands had once played had been forced to close. In addition, a twenty percent amusement tax had been imposed wherever there was dancing. That caused many clubs to cover their dance floors. Therefore, the bands that re-formed after the war had fewer places to perform. The era of the big bands became a memory. The singers were now the giants of the entertainment world.

The Expanding Record Industry

By the end of World War II there were several new record companies and the recording industry was growing into the giant of today.

The records that were sold during the late '40s were 78-rpm disks. In '49, the Victor and Columbia record companies argued over the merits of the 45 and 33⅓-rpm speeds. Columbia unveiled the 33⅓-rpm long-playing record. Victor, however, favored the smaller 45-rpm disks and brought out a new three-speed player (78, 45, and 33⅓-rpm)

in the early '50s. Capitol and Decca switched to the new speeds. In a few years, the 78-rpm record practically disappeared from the market.

The number of million-selling records more than doubled from '45 to '55 and that was only the beginning of the big boom in record sales. In '45, twenty-one records that would eventually sell a million copies were released. It usually took three to five years for a disk to become a million-seller. In '55, fifty records became million-sellers, and the disks usually reached gold within their first year of release.

Some of the most successful sellers of records during this period were Perry Como, Bing Crosby, Frankie Laine, Jo Stafford, Nat "King" Cole, Patti Page, Teresa Brewer, Rosemary Clooney, Eddie Fisher, Doris Day, early rhythm and blues artist Fats Domino, and country singer Eddy Arnold.

The Movies Spawn Hits

The fiftieth anniversary of motion pictures was observed in '44, and movies were more popular than ever. Some very ambitious movie musicals premiered during the late '40s and early '50s.

Several screen biographies of songwriters or performers were made in Hollywood. These included *The Jolson Story*, the Cole Porter biopic *Night and Day*, the screen bio of Jerome Kern *Till the Clouds Roll By*, *Words and Music*, about Richard Rodgers and Lorenz Hart, *Three Little Words*, with Fred Astaire and Red Skelton portraying Burt Kalmar and Harry Ruby, and *The Great Caruso*, with Mario Lanza playing Enrico Caruso, the fabled opera tenor.

Several nostalgic musicals were produced in

the late '40s and early '50s. These included *Look For the Silver Lining, In the Good Old Summertime, Take Me Out to the Ball Game, On Moonlight Bay* and *By the Light of the Silvery Moon.*

The Broadway stage was the source of several movie musicals, such as *Annie Get Your Gun, Show Boat, The Merry Widow, Roberta* (retitled *Lovely to Look At*), *The Band Wagon, Kiss Me, Kate, Call Me Madam, Rose Marie, The Student Prince in Heidelberg, Brigadoon, Kismet, Guys and Dolls, Hit the Deck* and *Oklahoma!*

Singin' in the Rain is perhaps one of the most enduring movie musicals ever made. Gene Kelly, Debbie Reynolds, and Donald O'Connor starred in this classic film musical released in the early '50s.

Some of the most honored (by Academy Award nominations) and top moneymaking movie musicals of the last half of the '40s include *Anchors Aweigh, Rhapsody in Blue, A Song to Remember, The Jolson Story, Night and Day, Till the Clouds Roll By, The Harvey Girls, Road to Utopia, Blue Skies, Ziegfeld Follies, Good News, The Perils of Pauline, Road to Rio, Easter Parade, Words and Music, Jolson Sings Again, Look For the Silver Lining, In the Good Old Summertime, Take Me Out to the Ball Game, Neptune's Daughter* and *The Barkley's of Broadway.*

Top moneymaking and Academy Award–nominated movie musicals of the first half of the '50s include *Annie Get Your Gun, Cinderella, Three Little Words, An American in Paris, Show Boat, The Great Caruso, Royal Wedding, Here Comes the Groom, On Moonlight Bay, Son of Paleface, Singin' in the Rain, With a Song in My Heart, Stars and Stripes Forever, I'll See You in My Dreams, Lili, Peter Pan, Gentlemen Prefer Blondes, Scared Stiff, The Stooge, Road to Bali, Seven Brides for Seven Brothers, White Christmas, A Star Is Born, There's No Business Like Show Business, The Glenn Miller Story, Love Me or Leave Me,* and *The Lady and the Tramp.*

A few of the era's most popular songs that were introduced in the movie musicals include the '45 Oscar winner, "It Might As Well Be Spring," the '46 Academy Award winner, "On the Atchison, Topeka and the Santa Fe," '47's winner, "Zip-a-Dee-Doo-Dah," the '48 Academy Award winner, "Buttons and Bows," '49's Oscar winner "Baby, It's Cold Outside," the '50 winner, "Mona Lisa," '51's Oscar winner, "In the Cool, Cool, Cool of the Evening," the '52 theme song from the western classic *High Noon,* '53's "Secret Love," '54's "Three Coins in the Fountain," and '55's "Love Is a Many-Splendored Thing."

As the decade closed, television was capturing

much of the movie audience. That situation was worsened when McCarthy accused many in the motion-picture industry of Communist associations, which caused public skepticism about the movies in general.

Postwar Broadway Musicals

The '30s are often called the heyday of the musical theater, while the '40s marked a transition from musical comedy to a more serious dramatic musical. There were no earthshaking musical developments on Broadway during the early '50s, but the theater did its share of producing hit musicals.

Richard Rodgers and Oscar Hammerstein II were the most important writers of hit musicals for the Broadway stage during the '45-'55 period. As the era opened, their *Oklahoma!* was still running on Broadway and on the road, and they had a new hit with *Carousel.* In '49, *South Pacific* opened and broke all kinds of records and was awarded a Pulitzer Prize. Rodgers and Hammerstein returned to Broadway in '51 with *The King and I.*

The Antoinette Perry Awards (the Tonys) for "distinguished achievement in the theater" began honoring musicals of the year in '49. Those honored during this period were *Kiss Me, Kate, South Pacific, Guys and Dolls, The King and I, Wonderful Town, Kismet, The Pajama Game* and *Damn Yankees.*

Other significant musicals that were not selected for Tony Awards (partially because they didn't begin until '49) include *Annie Get Your Gun, Finian's Rainbow, Brigadoon, Where's Charley?* and *Paint Your Wagon.*

Broadway was not the hit-making medium for popular songs that it had been, but it produced a few genuine hits and some songs that have become standards. Some of the biggest hit songs from musicals of the period include "They Say It's Wonderful" from *Annie Get Your Gun,* "Some Enchanted Evening" from *South Pacific,* "Wish You Were Here" from the musical of the same name, and "Stranger in Paradise" from *Kismet.* "Hey, There" and "Hernando's Hideaway" from *The Pajama Game* became big hits.

Some great songs that weren't major hits came from the period's musicals. They include "You'll Never Walk Alone" from *Carousel,* " Doin' What Comes Natur'lly" and "There's No Business Like Show Business" from *Annie Get Your Gun,* "Almost Like Being in Love" from *Brigadoon,* "How Are

Things in Glocca Morra" from *Finian's Rainbow*, "Another Op'nin', Another Show" from *Kiss Me, Kate*, "Once in Love With Amy" from *Where's Charley?*, "A Bushel and a Peck" from *Guys and Dolls*, "Hello, Young Lovers" from *The King and I*, "Steam Heat" from *The Pajama Game* and "Heart" from *Damn Yankees*.

The Foreign Influence

The popular music industry in the '40s and early '50s imported more songs, particularly Latin American ones. The practice had started during the ASCAP ban in the early '40s and the trend continued in the mid-'40s and early '50s with the English song "The Gypsy," the French "La Vie en Rose" and "C'est Si Bon," the Australian "Now Is the Hour," the German songs "You, You, You," "You Can't Be True, Dear" and "Glow Worm," the Swiss songs "Oh! My Pa-Pa," and "Forever and Ever," the Brazilian song "Delicado," the Italian song "Botch-a-Me," the Bahamian calypso trend of the early '50s and the Austrian song "The Happy Wanderer." The industry was definitely becoming more international.

Country-Western Crossovers

In addition to embracing foreign popular music, the industry began to recognize the country artists and their songs. Eddy Arnold and Hank Williams reportedly collected several million-selling records during this period. Other country stars who were able to crossover and have mainstream hits during the era were Jimmy Wakely, who had a hit duet with Margaret Whiting in '49, Tex Williams, who had a top ten hit with "Smoke! Smoke! Smoke! (That Cigarette)" in '47, and Red Foley, who had a mainstream hit with "Chattanoogie Shoe Shine Boy" in '50. Mainstream pop singers released "cover versions" of country songs just as they did of rhythm and blues songs just prior to the birth of rock 'n' roll. Examples of covers of country material include Patti Page's "Tennessee Waltz," Tony Bennett's cover of Hank Williams' "Cold, Cold Heart" and Perry Como's "Don't Let the Stars Get in Your Eyes."

There were several other hits that had a definite country feel, if not origin. Some of these include songs performed by Tennessee Ernie Ford, Guy Mitchell, Les Paul and Mary Ford, and even Frankie Laine.

The inroads that country music made during these years laid the foundation for the astronomical success of former country performers like Bill Haley, Elvis Presley and the Everly Brothers in the last half of the '50s.

TV—A New Medium of Entertainment

A new medium of entertainment began to challenge the supremacy of radio by the mid-'50s. By the end of the '40s, fifty stations were broadcasting to 700,000 home television sets with a potential audience of approximately 4 million.

Still, not until the last years of the '40s and the first few years of the '50s was radio seriously threatened. By that time, TV had begun to take over the variety shows, the quiz programs, the soap operas and the big stars.

Radio as we know it today, primarily dedicated to the dissemination of news and the playing of music, originated when television usurped its place in the entertainment world. Now the disk jockey began to rule the radio airwaves. He became a power in the pop music industry, especially in the metropolitan areas. A disk jockey could make or break a record, make unknown singers overnight sensations or send them into oblivion.

Rock 'n' Roll's Ancestry

Rock 'n' roll is an amalgam of several divergent musical styles. A lot of its development can be attributed to the music of African Americans, just as they were instrumental in the birth of the blues, of ragtime, of jazz and of swing. Their rhythm and blues music became one of the chief ingredients of rock 'n' roll.

In '51, Alan Freed, a disk jockey in Cleveland, coined the term rock 'n' roll (or rock and roll) to disguise the blackness of the rhythm and blues music that he played on his radio program so that a wider audience would accept it. When he moved to New York City in '54, his rock and roll programming became even more influential, but most of the white audience was still hesitant to accept this new sound.

Some of the early rhythm and blues performers who became rock 'n' roll pioneers include Fats Domino, Ivory Joe Hunter, Hank Ballard and the Midnighters, Joe Turner and LaVern Baker.

Another ingredient that contributed to the birth of rock 'n' roll is country music (or country and western). This area if often ignored by historians. In '54, a white country combo headed by Bill Haley gave new impetus to rock 'n' roll. Haley and his Comets had combined elements of rhythm and blues with their country and western sound to produce a type of rock 'n' roll music that quickly caught on. Their first big hit was "Shake, Rattle, and Roll," a cover of Joe Turner's original rhythm and blues version. "Rock Around the Clock" had been written in '53, Bill Haley and his Comets recorded it in '54, and it was included in the '55 film *The Blackboard Jungle*. That gave rock 'n' roll the national publicity it needed to unify the nation's teens behind this new musical trend.

Various historians argue about what the first rock 'n' roll recording was but most will agree that The Crew Cuts' cover version of the Chords' "Sh-Boom" was the first really big rock 'n' roll hit, even though today it doesn't sound particularly rock. Its success proved to record executives that cover recordings of rhythm and blues songs could be profitable. Soon many white, mainstream singers or groups made covers of rhythm and blues songs.

As the rock 'n' roll craze picked up momentum, new stars emerged. Out of country (or rockabilly) came Buddy Holly, Jerry Lee Lewis and Carl Perkins. The rhythm and blues tradition contributed Chuck Berry, Little Richard and the Platters. A few whites began to have hits with rock material: Pat Boone with Fats Domino's "Ain't That a Shame!," and the McGuire Sisters with The Moonglows' "Sincerely" for instance.

But what rock needed was a charismatic superstar and it found that in '56 in the person of Elvis Presley. Elvis personally combined the styles of country, gospel, and rhythm and blues into one individual who had an enormous amount of sexuality and showmanship. But that is a subject not covered by this book.

1945

Ac-cent-tchu-ate the Positive

Words: Johnny Mercer; Music: Harold Arlen

1945 was a great year for Johnny Mercer, not only as a lyricist, but also as a singer. He wrote the lyrics for "Ac-cent-tchu-ate the Positive," "Laura," "On the Atchison, Topeka, and the Santa Fe," and the music and lyrics for "Dream." He had big hit recordings of "Ac-cent-tchu-ate

the Positive," "Candy," and "On the Atchison, Topeka, and the Santa Fe."

Bing Crosby introduced "Ac-cent-tchu-ate the Positive" in the '44 movie musical *Here Come the WAVES*. Crosby played a singing idol, a parody of the crooners like Sinatra and himself. Bing's recording of the song with the Andrews Sisters was very popular, but not as popular as Johnny Mercer's version, which hit No. 1 on *Billboard* and stayed there for two weeks in March. Crosby and the Andrews Sisters' version peaked at No. 2 on *Billboard*. Artie Shaw and Kay Kyser and their orchestras also had versions that charted on *Billboard*. The song spent four weeks at No. 1 on *Your Hit Parade*. *Variety* chose this song for its *Hit Parade of a Half-Century.*

Johnny Mercer and the Pied Pipers' recording was inducted into the Grammy Hall of Fame in 1998.

"Ac-cent-tchu-ate the Positive" was nominated for the American Film Institute's list of the greatest songs ever from American films, but did not make the final list.

The title came about, according to one account, from a newspaper clipping that quoted a Harlem revival preacher with the title phrase. Another account says that it was advice given to Johnny Mercer by a psychologist. Wherever the idea came from, the song crystallized one day while composer Harold Arlen and Mercer were driving. Mercer reminded Arlen of a spiritual-sounding tune Arlen had been humming almost constantly. When Arlen began singing it again, Mercer remarked rather disgustedly, "You've got to accentuate the positive." Arlen then went about fitting the line into his melody. By the time they arrived at the studio, they practically had the song written.

Bing Crosby was always clowning around with a minstrel-show dialect, so the preaching spirit of this song was ideal for him. The sheet music suggests the tempo should be slow and "sermon-like." The preacher feels a sermon coming on and he wants everyone to gather around to listen. He tells them they need to "Accent-tchu-ate the positive," eliminate ("elim-my-nate") the negative, grab ("latch on to") the affirmative. Read the lyrics at http://www.lyricsvault.net/songs/18719.html.

It became such a hit that it received an Academy Award nomination, but lost to Rodgers and Hammerstein's "It Might As Well Be Spring."

Bell Bottom Trousers

Words & Music: Moe Jaffe

Navy trousers during World War II had belled cuffs. Moe Jaffe set new lyrics to a sea chantey for this popular song. There were several recordings of the song that were popular with the public: Guy Lombardo and Tony Pastor's orchestras competed for the most popular version, but Kay Kyser's was extremely close. Louis Prima, Jerry Colonna, and the Jesters each had successful versions on the market. Pastor's version made it to No. 2 for two weeks, while Guy Lombardo's version, with a vocal by Jimmy Brown, also peaked at No. 2, with only one week at that position. Kay Kyser's version, with Ferdy and Slim as vocalists, peaked at No. 3. The song collected a dozen appearances on *Your Hit Parade*, peaking at No. 3.

It's not uncommon for many versions of the same song to find favor with pre-rock audiences. In most instances, it was the song they liked, not a particular, definitive performance. That's a phenomenon of the rock era. Pre-rock buyers of recordings, players of jukeboxes, radio listeners seemed to pick their personal favorite among numerous versions of any particular song.

This song was included in *Variety's Hit Parade of a Half-Century* representing '44.

According to the lyrics, a girl who lived next door to the singer loved a sailor who was only three years old. This sailor, now grown big and strong, is on a battleship. She thinks he's really cute in his "bell bottom trousers, coat of navy blue." She loves him and he loves her too. Read the several verses at http://lirama.net/song/16376.

Hear Connee Boswell & the V-Disk Men's recording of this song at http://www.authentichistory.com/audio/ww2/ww2music05.html.

Candy

Words & Music: Joan Whitney, Alex Kramer & Mack David

"Candy" is best known through a recording by Johnny Mercer, Jo Stafford, and the Pied Pipers. Their version was No.1 on *Billboard* for a week at the end of March and the beginning of April. The song collected four weeks at No.1 on *Your Hit Parade*.

Other charting versions of "Candy" were by Dinah Shore, by Johnny Long and his orchestra, by the King Sisters, and by Jerry Wald and his orchestra.

The song is often sung by a male vocalist, with "Candy" being a female, but the original lyrics are from the female perspective. She wishes there were four of him so she could love him that much more. She's looking forward to the day she can have "Candy" all to herself. Read the lyrics at http://lirama.net/song/16377.

Chickery Chick

Words: Sylvia Dee; Music: Sidney Lippman

"Chickery Chick" is another novelty song in the same genre as '43's "Mairzy Doats" and '41's "The Hut-Sut Song."

Sammy Kaye's version became *Variety's* No. 8 hit of '45. His recording topped *Billboard's* chart for four weeks. However, the song peaked at No. 4 on *Your Hit Parade*. Kaye's disk featured the vocal performances of Nancy Norman and Billy Williams. Other popular recordings were released by Gene Krupa and his orchestra, by George Olsen and his orchestra, and by Evelyn Knight with Three Jesters and Bob Haggart's Orchestra.

One day a chicken got tired of just clucking, so he found a new song to sing, which was "Chickery chick cha-la, cha-la, check-a-la romey in a bananika." Later the lyrics advise us if we're bored we should try something new. Read the lyrics at http://lirama.net/song/16378.

Dream

Words & Music: Johnny Mercer

Johnny Mercer wrote both the words and music to "Dream"; in the past, he had most often written only the lyrics. He said he was doodling around on the piano and came up with a series of chords that appealed to him. Mercer and Paul Weston and his orchestra were on the Chesterfield Show on radio together for six months. Johnny played his chord progression for Weston and suggested they use it for the theme song for the show. It became his closing theme for the program. The lyrics "Dream, while the smoke rings rise in the air" was almost like a commercial for Chesterfield cigarettes.

A recording by the Pied Pipers backed by Paul Weston's orchestra became particularly popular. Their version topped the *Billboard* chart for one week, while the song managed five weeks at No. 1 on *Your Hit Parade*.

Other popular versions were those by Frank Sinatra, by Freddy Martin and his orchestra, and by Jimmy Dorsey and his orchestra. The Four Aces revived the song in '54 with a moderately successful version.

Variety listed "Dream, Dream, Dream" in their *Hit Parade of a Half-Century* representing 1947. There is a song titled "Dream, Dream, Dream" that charted on *Billboard* in '54, but Percy Faith and his orchestra's recording only made it to No. 25. *Variety* must have meant this song, which ends, "Dream, Dream, Dream," even though the dates don't match (the *Variety* list is only titles, with no other information about writers, performers, etc.).

"Dream" was interpolated into the '55 movie musical *Daddy Long Legs*.

The chorus lyrics tell us when we're blue we should "Dream." The lyrics reassure us things aren't quite as bad as they seem, so we should just "Dream." Read the lyrics at http://lirama.net/song/16382.

I Can't Begin to Tell You

Words: Mack Gordon; Music: James V. Monaco

The '45 movie musical *The Dolly Sisters* introduced "I Can't Begin to Tell You." First Betty Grable sang it; then it was reprised in the final scene by Grable and John Payne. The song was an Academy Award nominee in '46, but lost to "On the Atchison, Topeka, and the Santa Fe."

Bing Crosby's recording with pianist Carmen Cavallaro was *Billboard's* top hit for six weeks toward the end of the year. Harry James and his orchestra's version featuring his wife, Betty Grable's vocal performance, was also pretty popular in '46. Andy Russell's and Sammy Kaye's versions also charted in '46.

The song only managed one week at the top of *Your Hit Parade*.

Bing sang, "I can't begin to tell you how much you mean to me." He can't seem to tell his girl exactly how he feels, so he tells her to think of all the sweetest things lovers say to each other, then she should make believe he's saying all of them to her. Read the lyrics at http://lirama.net/song/16387.

If I Loved You, You'll Never Walk Alone *and* June Is Bustin' Out All Over

Words: Oscar Hammerstein II; Music: Richard Rodgers

Hungarian playwright Ferenc Molnar's robust but tender fantasy *Liliom*, about a carnival barker who marries a factory girl, is killed in a robbery attempt, and then is allowed to return to earth for a brief time, was transformed by Rodgers and Hammerstein into the highly successful Broadway musical *Carousel*.

IF I LOVED YOU

The main romantic duet, "If I Loved You," was sung by Billy Bigelow and Julie Jordan (played by John Raitt and Jan Clayton respectively). The dialogue that precedes the song prompted the Hammerstein lyric. In the scene, Billy asks Julie, "But you wouldn't marry a rough guy like me — that is — uh — if you loved me?" Julie answers, "Yes, I would — if I loved you." Read the lyrics at http://libretto. musicals.ru/text.php?textid=69&language=1 (Song #5).

Perry Como's recording of "If I Loved You" reportedly sold two million copies. Como's disk peaked at No. 3 on *Billboard*. The song made nineteen appearances on *Your Hit Parade*, and collected three weeks at No. 1. Other popular recordings of the song were released by Frank Sinatra, Bing Crosby, and Harry James and his orchestra in '45. Roy Hamilton revived it with some success in '54.

Variety chose "If I Loved You" for its *Hit Parade of a Half-Century*.

Gordon MacRae and Shirley Jones played Billy Bigelow and Julie Jordan in the '56 film version of the musical and they performed "If I Loved You." This song was nominated for the American Film Institute's list of greatest songs ever from an American film, but was not on the final list. It was nominated for its appearance in the '56 film version of the musical.

You'll Never Walk Alone

"You'll Never Walk Alone" is an inspirational number from Rodgers and Hammerstein's *Carousel*. It was introduced by Nettie, played by Christine Johnson, as she was trying to give Julie courage after her husband, Billy, was killed in a robbery attempt. In the musical's finale, the entire ensemble reprised the song as Billy, on a visit to earth after death, watches his daughter graduate from high school. Read the lyrics at http://libretto.musicals.ru/text. php?textid=69&language=1 (Song #16).

The most popular versions were by Frank Sinatra and by Judy Garland in 1945–46. Roy Hamilton revived it with reasonable success in '54.

Claramae Turner and Shirley Jones performed the song in the '56 film version. This song was also nominated for the American Film Institute's list of greatest songs ever from an American film, but was not on the final list. It was nominated for its appearance in the '56 film version of the musical.

Variety selected "You'll Never Walk Alone" as a *Golden 100 Tin Pan Alley Song*, but not its *Hit Parade of a Half-Century*.

June Is Bustin' Out All Over

"June Is Bustin' Out All Over" was the announcement of the arrival of summer in *Carousel*. The song was introduced by Nettie Fowler (played by Christine Johnson), Carrie Pipperidge (played by Jean Darling), and the chorus. Pearl Lang and the chorus also danced it. Read the lyrics at http://libretto.musicals.ru/text.php?textid=69& language=1 (Song #7).

This song is in *Variety's Hit Parade of a Half-Century*. This song was also nominated for the American Film Institute's list of greatest songs ever from an American film, but was not on the final list. It was nominated for its appearance in the '56 film version of the musical.

There are several other noteworthy songs from the score including "Carousel Waltz," "Mister Snow," "Soliloquy," "When the Children Are Asleep," and "What's the Use of Wond'rin'?"

The original Broadway cast album of *Carousel* was inducted into the Grammy Hall of Fame in 1998.

I'll Buy That Dream
Words: Herb Magidson; Music: Allie Wrubel

"I'll Buy That Dream" was introduced by Anne Jeffreys in the movie musical *Sing Your Way Home*.

The war brought about a multitude of changes, even changes in attitude about dreams and love. During the war, a lot of the songs were about the prospect of reuniting with a loved one, of living happily-ever-after once the catastrophic war ended. When the end finally came in '45, this song was there expressing the ideas of many of the GIs. They all wanted to buy into the American dream. Read the lyrics at http://lirama.net/song/16392.

The most popular recording of the song was a duet by Helen Forrest and Dick Haymes. Their disk only reached No. 2 on *Billboard*, but the song managed two weeks at the top of *Your Hit Parade*. Harry James' recording, with his vocalist Kitty Kallen, also peaked at No. 2 on *Billboard*, but stayed there only a single week. Hal McIntyre and his orchestra also released a popular recording of the song in '45.

I'm Beginning to See the Light
Words & Music: Don George, Johnny Hodges, Duke Ellington & Harry James

Harry James and his orchestra introduced and popularized "I'm Beginning to See the Light." It was one of the first recordings James made after the musicians' strike ended in November of '44. James' recording, with vocalist Kitty Kallen, topped the *Billboard* chart for two weeks. Other popular versions were issued by Ella Fitzgerald and the Ink Spots, and by co-writer Duke Ellington and his orchestra, with Joya Sherrill's vocal.

Ellington's recording of this song was one of his first commercial successes on the pop market.

Four men are listed as the song's co-writers. According to *The Swing Era: 1944–1945*, the tune probably originated with Johnny Hodges, Duke Ellington's saxophonist. Hodges took the tune to Ellington for his approval and any constructive ideas. Don George got the idea for the lyrics from a short being shown at the Paramount Theater on Times Square. The film was about a preacher's congregation in the Deep South who were getting carried away by the spirit. One large woman in the film shouted, "I'm beginning to see the light." George quickly left the theater with his lyric idea. Harry James' contribution is a mystery.

The singer never cared much for moonlight, but now that he sees the stars are in his girl's eyes he's "beginning to see the light." Now he's catching on to several things concerning love. Read the lyrics at http://lirama.net/ song/22119.

It Might as Well Be Spring, It's a Grand Night for Singing *and* That's for Me
Words: Oscar Hammerstein II; Music: Richard Rodgers

In *State Fair*, the Frake family head for the Iowa State Fair. On the first day, the discontented daughter, Margy, and her brother, Wayne, meet attractive love interests. Their father, Abel Frake, has a prize hog, Blue Boy; he also finds a love interest. As the fair proceeds, the romances flourish, but the lovers must separate when the fair closes.

IT MIGHT AS WELL BE SPRING

The Academy Award winner in '45 was "It Might As Well Be Spring" from the Rodgers and Hammerstein movie musical *State Fair*. It was sung on the soundtrack by Louanne Hogan for the film's star, Jeanne Crain. The film was a musical remake of a '33 nonmusical that had starred Will Rogers and Janet Gaynor.

Lyricist Hammerstein wanted the girl, Marty, to appear to have spring fever, but the state fair was in the fall, so he had her sing that even though it was autumn, "it might as well be spring." Read the lyrics at http://libretto.musicals.ru/text.php?textid=325&language=1 (Song No. 1).

Dick Haymes' recording of this song only reached No. 3 on *Billboard*, but collected three weeks at No. 1 on *Your Hit Parade*. Paul Weston and his orchestra and Sammy Kaye and his orchestra also released popular recordings of "It Might As Well Be Spring."

In '62 20th Century Fox filmed another version of *State Fair* that starred Pat Boone, Bobby Darin, Ann-Margret and Pamela Tiffin. Anita Gordon dubbed Pamela Tiffin's singing in the '62 film version.

Variety picked this song for its *Hit Parade of a Half-Century* representing '46. This song was nominated for the American Film Institute's list of greatest songs ever from an American film, but was not on the final list. It was nominated for its appearance in the '45 film version of the musical.

IT'S A GRAND NIGHT FOR SINGING

Another well-known song from the score of the film is "It's a Grand Night For Singing."

In the '45 film the song was sung by the ensemble, but in the '62 remake, it was sung by Pat Boone, Anita Gordon (dubbed for Pamela Tiffin), and Bobby Darin.

This fast waltz-meter tune was one of the songs the audiences left the theaters humming.

Read the lyrics at http://libretto.musicals.ru/text.php?textid=325&language=1 (Song No. 10).

Variety picked the song for its *Hit Parade of a Half-Century* and as a *Golden 100* representing '45.

THAT'S FOR ME

"That's For Me" is another hit song from the movie musical *State Fair*. It was introduced in the film by Vivian Blaine and Dick Haymes. In the '62 remake it was sung by Pat Boone.

Recordings by Jo Stafford, by Dick Haymes, and by Kay Kyser helped popularize the song beyond the film.

"That's for Me" made fifteen appearances on *Your Hit Parade* peaking at No. 3 in the fall of '45.

Variety named the song to its *Hit Parade of a Half-Century* representing '45.

The singer is enumerating several things that he likes about his girl: her charms, and the tilt of your chin when she chuckles or grins. "That's for me," he says. Read the lyrics at http://libretto.musicals.ru/text.php?textid=325&language=1 (Song No. 4).

It's Been a Long, Long Time

Words: Sammy Cahn; Music: Jule Styne

"It's Been a Long, Long Time" was introduced on the radio by Phil Brito, but Harry James and his orchestra, with Kitty Kallen's vocal, and Bing Crosby both had top ranked recordings of the song.

Crosby's recording was *Variety*'s No. 9 hit of '45. His recording with Les Brown and his orchestra spent two weeks at No. 1 on *Billboard*, while James's version spent three weeks at No. 1. That's five weeks total for the song counting both versions. It also collected five weeks at the top of *Your Hit Parade*.

Other popular versions on record were by Charlie Spivak and by Stan Kenton and their orchestras.

The most famous line of the song is "Kiss me once, then kiss me twice, Then kiss me once again," because it had been a long time since they had been able to kiss each other. Those sentiments were most likely those of every serviceman as they returned from their wartime posts to their loved ones back home. Read the lyrics at http://lirama.net/song/16397.

"It's Been a Long, Long Time" appeared in the movie musical *I'll Get By* ('50), which starred June Haver.

Variety named the song to its *Hit Parade of a Half-Century*.

Laura

Words: Johnny Mercer; Music: David Raskin

Randy Newman, who narrated an American Movie Classics special titled *The Hollywood Soundtrack Story*, said "the most famous song to emerge from a movie was 'Laura' from the classic 1944 murder mystery of the same name." It wasn't originally written as a song. "David Raskin wrote it as the haunting main theme for the film, and if ever a theme haunted a movie this one surely does," said Newman.

The lyrics were added by Johnny Mercer a few months after the film's release. Johnny Johnston first sang the song on radio, and Woody Herman's band had the most successful recording of the song. Herman's version peaked at No. 4 on *Billboard*, but managed one week at No. 1 on *Your Hit Parade*.

Other famous '45 recordings of "Laura" were by Johnnie Johnston, by Freddy Martin and his orchestra, by Jerry Wald and his orchestra, and by Dick Haymes. Stan Kenton and his orchestra revived it successfully in '51.

"Laura" was chosen by *Variety* for its *Hit Parade of a Half-Century*. The song became one of the most recorded songs of the pre-rock era.

The singer see Laura's face in the night, hears her footsteps, or sees her on a passing train. However, "Laura" is just a dream. Read the lyrics at http://lirama.net/song/16398.

A Little on the Lonely Side

Words & Music: Dick Robertson, James Cavanaugh & Frank Weldon

"A Little On the Lonely Side" was No. 1 on *Your Hit Parade* for one week in mid–March of '45. Frankie Carle and his orchestra's recording of the song, with vocalist Paul Allen, peaked at No. 4 on *Billboard*.

Other successful recordings of the song include those by Guy Lombardo and his Royal Canadians and by the Phil Moore Four.

The singer is "a little on the lonely side" because he is away from his girl. He tells her if anyone sees him with someone else, it's just a dance partner. Read the lyrics at http://www.lyricsvault.net/songs/19567.html.

The More I See You

Words: Mack Gordon; Music: Harry Warren

Dick Haymes introduced Harry Warren and Mack Gordon's "The More I See You" in the '45 movie musical *Billy Rose's Diamond Horseshoe*. His recording of the song only reached No. 7 on *Billboard*, but the song was No. 1 on *Your Hit Parade* for one week, the July 28th broadcast.

Harry James and his orchestra's recording of the song also charted.

The song also appeared in the movies *Don't Bother to Knock* ('52), *I Shot Andy Warhol* ('96) and *Anywhere But Here* ('99).

The more often the singer sees this particular girl, the more he wants her. He asks her to imagine how much he'll love her "as years go by." Read the lyrics at http://lirama.net/song/16400.

My Dreams Are Getting Better All the Time

Words: Mann Curtis; Music: Vic Mizzy

Les Brown and his orchestra's recording of "My Dreams Are Getting Better All the Time," with his vocalist Doris Day, was *Variety*'s No. 7 hit of '45. Brown's disk topped the *Billboard* chart for seven weeks, and the song collected three weeks at the top of the *Your Hit Parade* survey.

Marion Hutton introduced the song in the Abbott and Costello '44 film *In Society*.

Johnny Long and his orchestra with Dick Robertson and the Phil Moore Four also had recordings of the song that peaked at No. 3 on *Billboard*.

The girl vocalist sings that a particular guy smiled at her in a dream last night, so she thinks her "dreams are getting better all the time." Now she wants the dream to become reality. Read the lyrics at http://lirama.net/song/16402.

My Heart Sings

Words: Harold Rome; Music: Philippe Herpin

Harold Rome adapted a '44 French popular song, "Ma Mie," into "My Heart Sings," which Kathryn Grayson introduced in the '45 movie musical *Anchors Aweigh*. It was also used in the '46 movie musical *Junior Prom*. French words were by Jean Marie Blanvillain.

Johnnie Johnston and Martha Stewart both helped popularize this song with recordings that sold well.

Variety listed the song among its *Hit Parade of a Half-Century* songs. Paul Anka's '59 recording of the song peaked at No. 15, and Mel Carter's '65 recording barely made the Top 40.

The singer is remembering all the things that cause her heart to sing. Some of those things include the way he holds her hand, his embrace, his laugh, the way he dances and the way he kisses her. Read the lyrics at http://lirama.net/song/17305.

On the Atchison, Topeka, and the Santa Fe

Words: Johnny Mercer; Music: Harry Warren

The No. 3 hit in *Variety*'s Top Ten for '45 and the '46 Academy Award winner was "On the Atchison, Topeka, and the Santa Fe." Harry Warren and Johnny Mercer wrote the song for the '46 movie musical *The Harvey Girls*. The Harvey girls were actually a group of refined waitresses taken to the Wild West by restaurateur Fred Harvey.

In the film, "On the Atchison, Topeka, and the Santa Fe" was performed by Judy Garland, Ray Bolger, and a train full of Harvey girls.

Johnny Mercer and the Pied Pipers were primarily responsible for popularizing the song; their recording spent eight weeks at No. 1 on *Billboard*. Bing Crosby's version peaked at No. 3 on *Billboard*.

The song's subject is very unusual for a popular song hit. Most popular songs are love songs, but this is a song about anticipating the arrival of a train. The train does carry a valuable cargo: women, beautiful, young women; something the west didn't have in abundance. Read the lyrics and hear a midi musical version at http://www.harrywarren.org/songs/0385.htm (both the sheet music version and Judy Garland's entrance in the film version are available at this site). Hear an audio clip of this song from the film score at http://www.harrywarrenmusic.com/realfiles/.

Variety picked the song for its *Hit Parade of a Half-Century*. This song was nominated for the American Film Institute's list of the greatest songs ever from an American film, but did not make the final list.

It's also amazing how many popular songs there are about train travel: "Sentimental Journey," "Chattanooga Choo, Choo," "Blues in the Night" and "Tuxedo Junction," to name only a few. Generally, those songs have a romantic view of traveling by train that is very seldom found in more current songs about other means of transportation. There must have been something extremely romantic about traveling by train.

Rum and Coca-Cola

Words: Morey Amsterdam; Music: Lionel Belasco

The No. 5 hit in *Variety*'s Top Ten for '45 was the Andrews Sisters' recording of "Rum and Coca-Cola." Their disk spent ten weeks at No. 1 on *Billboard* beginning in early February. The song only managed to reach No. 4 on *Your Hit Parade*. Maybe their survey was a little prejudiced toward a song about an alcoholic drink.

Morey Amsterdam, who later would star with Rose Marie and Dick Van Dyke as writers on *The Dick Van Dyke Show*, heard this calypso-style melody during a vacation to Trinidad. He assumed it was a folk melody, which would be in the public domain, so he had Jeri Sullivan and Paul Baron adapt it for American audiences. He then published it with his own lyrics. It was introduced by Sullivan at a New York City nightclub.

The Andrews Sisters recording of the song with Vic Schoen and his orchestra became a big hit. Abe Lyman and Vaughn Monroe also released popular versions of the song.

When the song became famous, it was involved in a plagiarism suit. The song, it turned out, was not in the public domain, but was Lionel Belasco's "L'Annee Pasee," which he had written in Trinidad in 1906.

The chorus lyrics tell us that when we visit Trinidad, the people will make us very glad we came. We are guaranteed to have a fine time as we drink "Rum and Coca Cola." Read the lyrics at http://www.lyricsvault.net/songs/17584.html.

Saturday Night (Is the Loneliest Night of the Week)

Words: Sammy Cahn; Music: Jule Styne

Jule Styne and Sammy Cahn wrote "Saturday Night (Is the Loneliest Night of the Week") in '44.

It was introduced and popularized by Frank Sinatra, however, there were several successful recordings of the song on the market. Other important versions were released by Sammy Kaye, by Frankie Carle, by Woody Herman and by the King Sisters. Sinatra's version peaked at No. 2 on the *Billboard* chart.

The song made ten appearances on *Your Hit Parade*, peaking at No. 2.

Saturday night is lonely because that's the night the singer, Sinatra in this case, and his sweetie used to dance. He has other things to occupy him on the other nights of the week, but until his girl is in his arms again, "Saturday night is the loneliest night of the week." Read the lyrics at http://www.lyricsfreak.com/f/frank-sinatra/557 04.html.

Variety chose it for its *Hit Parade of a Half-Century*.

Sentimental Journey

Words: Ben Homer; Music: Bud Green & Les Brown

Variety's top hit of '45 was a recording of "Sentimental Journey" by Les Brown and his orchestra. Doris Day was Brown's vocalist for the record. Brown's disk registered nine weeks at No. 1 on *Billboard*, and five weeks at the top of *Your Hit Parade*. *Variety* chose the song for its *Hit Parade of a Half-Century*.

Hal McIntyre and his orchestra, with vocalist Frankie Lester, had their version of "Sentimental Journey" peak at No. 3 on *Billboard* , while the Merry Macs' version topped out at No. 4. In '51, a recording by the Ames Brothers with Les Brown's Orchestra did moderately well.

Along with songs like "Star Dust" and "My Blue Heaven," "Sentimental Journey" is one of those songs of a generation. Most people who were alive in '45, and especially those people who began dating their future spouse while this song was popular, identify the song with fond memories. It could probably be termed the theme song of that generation, but especially of '45.

Les Brown's recording of "Sentimental Journey" was inducted into the Grammy Hall of Fame in 1998.

"Sentimental Journey" is another famous song about traveling by train. The singer is taking "a sentimental journey to renew old memories." She's all packed and is excited to hear the conductor call "All aboard." One slightly unusual word comes in the following line: "never thought my heart could be so yearny." Ben Homer needed a word to rhyme with "journey," so he created "yearny." Read the lyrics at http://lirama.net/song/16408.

There! I've Said It Again

Words: Dave Mann; Music: Redd Evans

In '41 Redd Evans and Dave Mann wrote the words and music to "There! I've Said It Again." Evans convinced the still-unknown Boston bandleader Vaughn Monroe to use the song, but it was not until '45 that Monroe popularized it. It turned out to be a huge hit for him and established him as a star.

"There! I've Said It Again" was *Variety*'s No. 6 hit in '45's Top Ten. Monroe's recording was No. 1 on *Billboard*

for six weeks. The song didn't fare so well on *Your Hit Parade*; it peaked at No. 2 on that hit survey.

Other popular '45 recordings of the song were those of Jimmy Dorsey and his orchestra, and the Modernaires with Paula Kelly.

The song was picked by *Variety* for its *Hit Parade of a Half-Century*.

"There! I've Said It Again" was revived in '64 by Bobby Vinton, whose recording of the song became a No. 1 hit on *Billboard*'s chart again, this time for four weeks.

The lyrics open with the singer declaring, "I love you." He had tried to come up with a phrase that would tell the girl how he felt about her, but couldn't come up with anything better than "I love you." He concludes by telling her that he has loved her "since heaven knows when." Read the lyrics at http://lirama.net/song/16415.

There Must Be a Way

Words & Music: Sammy Gallop, David Saxon & Robert Cook

Variety included "There Must Be a Way" in its *Hit Parade of a Half-Century*.

Johnnie Johnston and Charlie Spivak and his orchestra had recordings of the song that charted in '45, but neither rose above No. 9 on the *Billboard* chart. The song appeared three times on *Your Hit Parade*, but its highest ranking was at No. 8.

The singer says "there must be a way" he can forget his romance with his girl is over and "there must be a way" he can stop dreaming about her. He also says, "There must be a song" that doesn't remind him of her. He thinks "there must be a way" to go on without her and find someone new, but he's finding that difficult. Read the lyrics at http://lirama.net/song/17445.

Tico-Tico

Words: Ervin Drake; Music: Zequinha Abreu

Disney's *Saludos Amigos* introduced "Tico-Tico," a Brazilian popular song, to American audiences. Xavier Cugat and his orchestra helped popularize the tune through a recording and in nightclub appearances. The most popular recordings of the song were by Charles Wolcott, by the Andrews Sisters and by organist Ethel Smith.

Maxine Barrat and Don Loper danced to "Tico-Tico" in the '43 film *Thousands Cheer*, organist Ethel Smith played it in *Bathing Beauty* ('44) and Sonja Henie skated to it in *It's a Pleasure* ('45).

The English lyrics to this samba identify Tico as a cuckoo in a clock that advises in matters of amour. Read the lyrics at http://lirama.net/song/25863. In the original Brazilian version, the Tico-tico bird was in the cornmeal.

"Tico-Tico" was chosen by *Variety* for its *Hit Parade of a Half-Century* representing '44.

Till the End of Time

Words & Music: Buddy Kaye & Ted Mossman

Buddy Kaye and Ted Mossman adapted Frederick Chopin's melody from "Polonaise in A Flat Major" for "Till the End of Time." Perry Como's recording with the Russ Case orchestra was No. 1 on *Billboard* for ten weeks. It topped the *Your Hit Parade* survey of hits for seven weeks, and was *Variety*'s No. 2 hit of the year. Les Brown and his orchestra, and Dick Haymes also issued successful versions of "Till the End of Time." Both Les Brown's recording, with Doris Day as his vocalist, and Dick Haymes' version peaked at No. 3 on *Billboard*.

A rhythmic version of the same polonaise by pianist Carmen Cavallaro and his orchestra was *Variety*'s No. 10 hit of the year. Cavallaro's version reached No. 3 on *Billboard* and stayed there ten weeks.

Concert pianist Jose Iturbi, who played the polonaise for the '44 film *A Song to Remember*, a motion picture based on the life of Chopin, the great Polish composer, also charted on *Billboard*.

The lyrics for the song insist that as "long as stars are in the blue, long as there's a spring," in other words, "till the end of time," you will be loved.

Perry Como's recording of "Till the End of Time" was inducted into the Grammy Hall of Fame in 1998. *Variety* selected the song for its *Hit Parade of a Half-Century*.

The singer is telling his loved one that he will love her "till the end of time." The rest of the lyric mentions several other things that may last that long, like mountains and birds singing. Read the lyrics at http://lirama.net/song/16416.

White Christmas (see 1942)

Crosby's recording hit No. 1 again on *Billboard* in '45.

You Belong to My Heart (Solamente una vez)

Words: Ray Gilbert; Music: Augustin Lara

The Spanish-Cuban influence in songs continued in '45 with "You Belong to My Heart," among others. It was introduced by Dora Luz in the '45 Walt Disney production *The Three Caballeros*.

Recordings by Bing Crosby with Xavier Cugat, by Charlie Spivak, and by Phil Brito helped popularized the song.

The song managed six appearances on *Your Hit Parade*, peaking at No. 4 during the summer of '45.

Ezio Pinza, Trudy Erwin (dubbing for Lana Turner) and the Guadalajara Trio performed the song in *Mr. Imperium* ('51).

Variety included "You Belong to My Heart" in its *Hit Parade of a Half-Century*.

The singer tells his loved one she will belong to his heart "now and forever." He told her he loved her "while a million guitars played" their love song. Read the lyrics at http://lirama.net/song/16418.

1946

All Through the Day

Words: Oscar Hammerstein II; Music: Jerome Kern

Jerome Kern and Oscar Hammerstein II wrote "All Through the Day" for the '46 movie musical *Centennial Summer*. Larry Stevens, Cornel Wilde, and Louanne Hogan, who dubbed the singing for film star Jeanne Crain, introduced the song. Kern's music was the highlight of an otherwise lackluster film. The composer died shortly after completing this project.

Kern's melody for this song is not as operatic as many of his earlier songs had been. Even such a master as Kern had difficulty spanning the gap between the operettas he had written in his youth and maturity and the music that was now fashionable.

Kern and Hammerstein's song was one of the nominated songs for the '46 Academy Award for Best Song, which was captured by "On the Atchison, Topeka, and the Santa Fe."

"All Through the Day" made eighteen appearances on *Your Hit Parade* and collected two weeks at No. 1 (May 11th and 18th broadcasts). It didn't fare as well on *Billboard*; Frank Sinatra's version, the most popular one, only reached No. 7. Perry Como and Margaret Whiting's versions also charted.

"All Through the Day" the singer dreams about the night he will spend with his girl. As night falls he runs to meet her so he can receive the kiss he dreamed of "all through the day." Read the lyrics at http://lirama.net/song/16419.

The Christmas Song

Words: Robert Wells; Music: Mel Torme

Singer, songwriter Mel Torme went to visit lyricist Robert Wells one sweltering California summer day. Wells was trying to keep cool by thinking of winters he'd spent in New England. Torme noticed that he had jotted down a few lines, not as a lyric, but as part of his thought process to "think cool." Wells had scribbled the lines "Chestnuts roasting ... Jack Frost nipping ... Yuletide carols ... Folks dressed up like Eskimos." In less than an hour, Torme and Wells had converted Wells' few lines into "The Christmas Song." They quickly drove to Nat Cole's L.A. home to demonstrate their new song. Cole loved it immediately and cut his recording of the song within a few days.

Nat "King" Cole's version became the most popular recording. Cole's version peaked at No. 3 in '46, but charted again in '47, '49, '53, and '54. Cole's recording was inducted into the Grammy (NARAS) Hall of Fame in 1974. The song only reached No. 10 on *Your Hit Parade*. Les Brown and his band's recording of the song charted in '47.

The lyrics conjure up lovely images of chestnuts roasting, a choir singing carols and children's eyes aglow with anticipation of the gifts they'll receive. Read the lyrics at http://www.carols.org.uk/the_christmas_song_chestnuts_roasting.htm.

The song has remained an important seasonal song. No authoritative sales figures are available, but since the song returns year after year and is included on numerous Christmas albums, it either is, or will be, one of the world's best sellers. "The Christmas Song" became one of the most recorded songs of the pre-rock era.

Come Rain or Come Shine

Words: Johnny Mercer; Music: Harold Arlen

"Come Rain or Come Shine," a love duet from the stage musical *St. Louis Woman*, was written by Harold Arlen and Johnny Mercer. Ruby Hill and Harold Nicholas introduced the song at the opening of Act II. The melody and lyrics have a distinctly blues feel.

St. Louis Woman had an all-black cast that included Pearl Bailey and Rex Ingram.

The most popular recording of the song were issued by Margaret Whiting and a duet recording by Helen Forrest and Dick Haymes.

The song only managed three weeks on *Your Hit Parade* survey of hits, peaking at No. 8.

Variety chose the song for its *Golden 100 Tin Pan Alley Songs* list, but not one of its *Hit Parade of a Half-Century*.

The singer tells her lover she's going to love him like nobody's loved him "come rain or come shine." Then she turns things around to demand he love her the same way. She tells him every day may not be sunny, and they may not have money, but she'll stay with him "come rain or come shine." Read the lyrics at http://lirama.net/song/16424.

Doctor, Lawyer, Indian Chief

Words: Paul Francis Webster; Music: Hoagy Carmichael

"Doctor, Lawyer, Indian Chief" was introduced by Betty Hutton in the movie musical *Stork Club*. Her recording of the song was also very popular, topping *Billboard's* chart for two weeks. The song only managed to reach No. 4 on *Your Hit Parade*.

Les Brown and his orchestra and the song's composer, Hoagy Carmichael, also had recordings of the song that charted.

The lyrics assert that neither doctor, lawyer nor Indian Chief "could love you anymore than I do." Read the lyrics at http://lirama.net/song/16429.

Five Minutes More

Words: Sammy Cahn; Music: Jule Styne

The No. 6 hit in *Variety's* Top Ten for '46 was Jule Styne and Sammy Cahn's "Five Minutes More." The song was first published independently, that is, it was not written for a musical or movie, but it was later interpolated into the '46 movie musical *The Sweetheart of Sigma Chi*, where it was performed by Phil Brito.

Frank Sinatra's recording helped the song reach the top of both *Billboard* and *Your Hit Parade* for four weeks. According to *Top Pop Singles of the Year* published by *Billboard Publications* (1982), Sinatra's version ranked No. 4 for the year. The same publication had Tex Beneke and the Glenn Miller Orchestra's version at No. 25 for the year.

Other charting singles of the song were those by the Three Suns, by Skitch Henderson and his orchestra, and by Bob Crosby and his orchestra.

The singer is begging for "five minutes more" in his lover's arms to enjoy her charms. He's been dreaming of their Saturday date all week long and reminds her that she can sleep late on Sunday morning. Read the lyrics at http://lirama.net/song/16431.

For Sentimental Reasons

Words & Music: William Best & Deek Watson

"For Sentimental Reasons" was popularized by a very successful recording by Nat "King" Cole at the end of '46 and the beginning of '47. Cole's disk collected six weeks at No. 1 on *Billboard* and the song managed seven weeks at the top of *Your Hit Parade*. *A Century of Pop Music* has it at No. 8 for the year, but *Billboard's Top Pop Singles of the Year* had Cole's disk ranked No. 41 for '46 and tied for

No. 25 in '47, but its weeks at No. 1 seem to deserve a higher ranking.

Deek Watson, an original member of the Ink Spots, is credited as co-writer of this song, but later research indicates that William Best most likely wrote both words and music.

Other versions of "(I Love You) for Sentimental Reasons" that were successful in '46 and '47 were released by Eddy Howard, by Dinah Shore, by Charlie Spivak and his orchestra, by Ella Fitzgerald, and by Art Kassel and his orchestra. In '58, Sam Cooke charted with his version and in '61 the Cleftones recording was only reasonably successful.

This ballad begins "I love you for sentimental reasons." He hopes his girl believes him, because he's given her his heart. Read the lyrics at http://lirama.net/song/16432.

A Gal in Calico

Words: Leo Robin; Music: Arthur Schwartz

"A Gal in Calico" was written for the '46 movie musical *The Time, The Place and the Girl*. An Academy Award nominee, "A Gal in Calico" was introduced by Jack Carson, Dennis Morgan, and Martha Vickers in the film.

Johnny Mercer had the most popular recording of the song, which managed one week at No. 1 on *Your Hit Parade* in early '47. Mercer's disk only made it to No. 5 on *Billboard*. Other versions of the song that charted included those by Tex Beneke and his orchestra, by Benny Goodman and his orchestra, and by Bing Crosby.

This song has a decidedly western flavor. The singer met this "gal in calico" in Santa Fe, where he was working in a rodeo that traveled from town to town. He plans to buy "a bolt of calico" to make a wedding dress for her. Read the lyrics at http://lirama.net/song/16434.

The Gypsy

Words & Music: Billy Reid

English songwriter Billy Reid wrote "The Gypsy" in '45, and it was popularized in the U.S. in '46 by two extremely popular recordings, one by the Ink Spots and one by Dinah Shore. The Inks Spots' disk was *Variety's* No. 1 and *Billboard's* No. 3 hit of the year, while Shore's recording was No. 8 in *Variety's* Top Ten and *Billboard's* No. 9 hit of '46. The Ink Spots version spent thirteen weeks at the top of the *Billboard* chart making it one of the top five hits of the decade, and one of the top ten of the pre-rock era. Dinah Shore's version racked up eight weeks at No. 1 on *Billboard*. The total of twenty-one weeks at No. 1 on *Billboard* means that this one song spent 40% of the weeks of the year at No. 1. The song also earned eight weeks at No. 1 on *Your Hit Parade*.

And that's not all. There were other successful recordings on the market including versions released by Sammy Kaye and his orchestra with vocalist Mary Marlow, by Hildegarde with Guy Lombardo's Royal Canadians, and by Jan Garber and his orchestra.

The song seemed tailor-made for the Ink Spots: a smooth melody that could be crooned in Bill Kenny's high tenor, and a sugary sweet lyric.

The singer is seeking a Gypsy fortuneteller's advice on romance. Read the lyrics at http://lirama.net/song/16435.

Variety chose this song for its *Hit Parade of a Half-Century*.

I'm a Big Girl Now

Words & Music: Al Hoffman, Jerry Livingston & Milton Drake

"I'm a Big Girl Now" is a novelty song that became a No. 1 hit on *Billboard* in the spring of '46 for one week. Sammy Kaye and his orchestra with Betty Barclay's vocal had a very popular recording of the song.

The song never appeared on *Your Hit Parade*.

A little girl who thinks she's grown sings this song. No age is confirmed, but she's old enough to want to have some adventures with the opposite sex that she can write in her diary. She also hates it when her father makes her leave the room to tell a dirty joke. She claims she could tell some jokes "that would curl his hair."

Laughing on the Outside (Crying on the Inside)

Words: Ben Raleigh; Music: Bernie Wayne

"Laughing On the Outside, Crying On the Inside" tries to cover up the singer's sad feelings with a lighthearted air. Read the lyrics at http://lirama.net/song/16440.

The song was popularized in a recording by Dinah Shore; the song was on the flip side of her extremely popular recording of "The Gypsy."

"Laughing On the Outside, Crying On the Inside" earned one week at No. 1 on *Your Hit Parade* (May 25th broadcast). Dinah's disk peaked at No. 3 on *Billboard*. Other popular recordings of the song that charted on *Billboard* were by Andy Russell with Paul Weston's Orchestra, by Sammy Kaye and his orchestra with Billy Williams as vocalist, by Teddy Walters accompanied by Lou Bring and his Orchestra, and by the Merry Macs. The Four Aces revived the song in '53 with a moderately successful recording.

Let It Snow! Let It Snow! Let It Snow!

Words: Sammy Cahn; Music: Jule Styne

Jule Styne and Sammy Cahn wrote this seasonal hit in '45. Vaughn Monroe popularized the song with a very popular recording in '46. It tied with "Symphony" for the No. 10 hit in *Variety's* Top Ten of '46. Monroe's disk topped the *Billboard* chart for five weeks. The song was No. 1 on *Your Hit Parade* for two weeks.

Other successful recordings of the song that charted on *Billboard* were those by Woody Herman and his orchestra, by Connee Boswell, and by Bob Crosby and his orchestra.

The Vaughn Monroe recording of the song was played on the soundtrack of Bruce Willis' *Die Hard II*.

According to *Billboard*, it is the second biggest Christmas hit of the 1935–1954 era.

The lyrics say that even though the weather is unbearable outside, two can keep cozy and warm together by the fire, so why go out? Read the lyrics at http://lirama.net/song/16441.

Variety selected this song for its *Hit Parade of a Half-Century*.

Oh! What It Seemed to Be

Words & Music: Frankie Carle, Bennie Benjamin & George Weiss

"Oh! What It Seemed to Be," as recorded by Frankie Carle and his orchestra with Marjorie Hughes as vocalist

and by Frank Sinatra gained the top spot on *Billboard* in February of '46. Co-writer Carle's disk racked up eleven weeks at No. 1, while Sinatra's version collected eight weeks at No. 1. Nineteen total weeks at the top of the *Billboard* chart means that the song occupied the top spot for 35% of the weeks in the year. Carle's version ranks at No. 22 of the pre-rock era, while Sinatra's doesn't quite make the Top 100, but the combination is more weeks than any other except for "The Gypsy."

The song collected nineteen appearances on the *Your Hit Parade* survey of hit songs, with eight weeks at No. 1.

The song expresses the thought that some rather insignificant things, like a high school dance, can take on added meaning when our loved one is involved. Read the lyrics at http://lirama.net/song/16442.

"Oh! What It Seemed to Be" was selected by *Variety* for its *Hit Parade of a Half-Century*.

The Old Lamp-Lighter

Words: Charles Tobias; Music: Nat Simon

There was a time, not so long ago, that the lamplighter was a common job in urban America. With his matches and ladder, he would make his rounds from lamppost to lamppost, lighting gas lamps at dusk and putting them out at dawn.

Charles Tobias got the idea for this song from his memories of boyhood days in Worcester, Massachusetts, and the lamplighter there.

Recordings by Sammy Kaye and his orchestra with vocalist Billy Williams and the Kaye Choir, Kay Kyser and his orchestra with vocalist Michael Douglas, Hal Derwin, Kenny Baker, and Morton Downey were very successful in '46 and '47. The Browns revived it with a '60 recording that made it to No. 5 on *Billboard*.

Sammy Kaye's disk spent seven weeks at No. 1 on *Billboard* toward the end of the year. His recording was *Variety's* No. 4 hit of '46. The song peaked at No. 2 on *Your Hit Parade*.

"The old lamplighter" makes his nightly rounds, lighting the lamps in the park, but he will leave a lamp unlit near lovers sitting on a park bench, because of his memories of his own loved one from long ago. Read the lyrics at http://www.lyricstrax.com/sammy-kaye/old-lamplighter.html.

Ole Buttermilk Sky

Words: Jack Brooks; Music: Hoagy Carmichael

It had been six years since Hoagy Carmichael created a big hit, but in '46, he and Jack Brooks collaborated to produce the Academy Award nominee "Ole Buttermilk Sky." Carmichael himself introduced the song in the film *Canyon Passage*.

Kay Kyser and his orchestra with Michael Douglas as vocalist had the most successful recording of the song. Their version topped the *Billboard* chart for two weeks and stayed at No. 1 on *Your Hit Parade* for six weeks.

Hoagy Carmichael's version was also very popular, reaching No. 2 on *Billboard*. Other popular recordings of the song were released by Paul Weston and his orchestra, Helen Carroll, Danny O'Neil, and Connee Boswell. Bill Black's Combo revived the song with a moderately successful recording in '61.

The singer asks the "ole buttermilk sky" to make a lovely setting for a rendezvous with the one he loves. The song is in the style of a cowboy ballad. Read the lyrics at http://ntl.matrix.com.br/pfilho/html/lyrics/o/ole_butter milk_sky.txt.

"Ole Buttermilk Sky" was included in *Variety*'s *Hit Parade of a Half-Century*.

Personality

Words: Johnny Burke; Music: Jimmy Van Heusen

There have been two tunes with the title "Personality." James Van Heusen and Johnny Burke wrote one in '45 and Harold Logan and Lloyd Price wrote the second one in '59.

Lloyd Price's song reached No. 2 on *Billboard* in the late '50s. Its most memorable words are: "She's got personality, walk, personality, talk, personality..."

The Van Heusen-Burke song was introduced by Dorothy Lamour in the '46 movie musical *Road to Utopia*, another Crosby, Hope, and Lamour "road film."

Road to Utopia was one of the zaniest and most successful of the series. This one took the trio to Alaska during the days of the gold rush.

Johnny Mercer, a songwriter himself, made the song popular in a recording with the Pied Pipers. Mercer's disk was *Variety*'s No. 9 and according to *Billboard's* publication *Top Pop Singles of the Year*, No. 7 hit of the year. The song reached No. 2 on *Your Hit Parade*.

Other recordings of the song that charted on *Billboard* were by Bing Crosby and Dinah Shore.

The song lyrics begin by saying all the gentlemen could easily tell that Madam Pompadour had "the cutest personality." The lyrics also question what made Madame DuBarry the toast of Paris. The answer was it was her "well-developed personality," of course. Salome's dancing entranced all the men because "she knew how to use her personality." Have you ever wondered why a particular girl is offered things like sable coats and wedding rings? It's her "personality." To conclude, he tells his girl she has "the cutest personality!!" Read the lyrics at http://lirama. net/song/16444.

Put the Blame on Mame

Words & Music: Doris Fisher & Allan Roberts

"Put the Blame on Mame" premiered in the film *Gilda*, where it was sung in a seductive striptease fashion by Rita Hayworth. It became one of her most famous roles. In the film Rita is in her bedroom singing along to a phonograph recording of "Put the Blame on Mame," which was actually Anita Ellis singing for Ms. Hayworth. In the striptease segment she actually only removes her long black gloves.

Read the lyrics at http://lyricsplayground.com/alpha/ songs/p/puttheblameonmame.shtml.

AFI's *100 Years ... 100 Songs* (2004) named this song the No. 84 greatest song ever from an American film.

Also in '46, the song appeared in the film *Betty Co-Ed*.

In '46, a pin-up of Rita Hayworth and the name *Gilda* rode on the side of the atomic bomb tested at Bikini Atoll in the Pacific.

In *The Big Heat* ('53), when Lee Marvin first sees Glenn Ford face to face, the music in the background is "Put the Blame on Mame," a sly reference to Ford's performance in *Gilda*.

Prisoner of Love

Words: Leo Robin; Music: Russ Columbo & Clarence Gaskill

Co-composer Russ Columbo and his orchestra introduced "Prisoner of Love" in '31 (performers were often given writing credit to get them to perform and popularize the song, but in this case, it's impossible to tell if Columbo really contributed to the composition). Columbo became one of the early '30s top male vocalists. Columbo's recording of the song with Nat Shilkret's Orchestra was only moderately popular.

In '46, Perry Como's relaxed, effortless style of crooning seemed to fit the song (however, the song actually has more passion, more intensity than many from this period) and his recording of it became a big hit. *Billboard* ranked it No. 1 for the year, while *Variety* had it at No. 3. The song only reached No. 3 on *Your Hit Parade*, however. Other successful '46 recordings of the song were by the Ink Spots and by Billy Eckstine. The Ink Spots and Eckstine's versions both reached the Top 10.

Even though he is not famous today, Russ Columbo was a strong competitor of Bing Crosby and Rudy Vallee for the top male singer during the early '30s. The crooning of Crosby and Columbo was so similar that it was difficult to identify which one was singing. Columbo might have become a huge star, but a fatal accident cut his career short in '34.

The singer tells us that he's alone every night because he's "a prisoner of love." Even though his loved one has found someone else, he isn't free to love again because she's haunting his dreams whether he's awake or asleep. Read the lyrics at http://www.oldielyrics.com/lyrics/frank_sinatra/ prisoner_of_love.html.

(Get Your Kicks on) Route 66

Words & Music: Robert Troup

There were two popular recordings of "Route 66" in '46, one by Bing Crosby and the Andrews Sisters and a slightly more popular one by Nat "King" Cole. Cole's recording of the song was inducted into the Grammy Hall of Fame in 2002.

Bandleader Bobby Troupe wrote "(Get Your Kicks on) Route 66," as he and his wife traveled across country to California. When Troupe arrived in California, he took the tune to Nat "King" Cole, who liked the idea and asked Troupe to finish it and bring it back. So Troupe hurried to the old NBC studios where he went from one rehearsal studio to another looking for a piano that wasn't being used. When he found one, he'd use it until some musicians came along to run him out; then he'd find another empty studio. He also carried a map along to help him remember the names of the towns along the route. Cole liked the final product and recorded it almost immediately.

The lyrics tells us the best highway to take us west is Route 66. "It winds from Chicago to L.A. more than 2,000 miles all the way." The lyrics also name many of the towns we'll see along the way, like St. Louis (St. Louie), Joplin, Missouri, Oklahoma City, Amarillo, Gallup, New Mexico, Flagstaff, Arizona, Winona, Kingman, Barstow, and San Bernardino.

An advertising copywriter called U.S. Highway 66 "America's Main Street" even before the entire highway was completed. Once the road was finished Route 66 became the path that led poor farmers out of the Dust Bowl states that were plagued by drought and towards what they hoped was salvation in California. The road acquired many nicknames; John Steinbeck called it "the Mother Road" in his *Grapes of Wrath*.

Jane Powell and Pat Hyatt (dubbing for Ann Todd) performed "Route 66" in *Three Darling Daughters* ('46). Jose Iturbi also contributed a boogie piano solo of the song in the same film. The 2006 Pixar film *Cars* has a lot to do with the highway and the song is prominently featured in recordings by Chuck Berry and John Mayer.

The song has been a favorite with jazz bands and jazz (scat) vocalists for many years. According to *Missouri Life Magazine*, more than 200 different artists have recorded the song.

Read the lyrics at http://lirama.net/song/22923.

Rumors Are Flying

Words & Music: Bennie Benjamin & George Weiss

Frankie Carle and his orchestra's recording, with Marjorie Hughes doing the vocal, of "Rumors Are Flying" was a huge hit in '46, staying at No. 1 on *Billboard* for nine weeks. It was No. 5 for the year on both *Variety* and *Billboard*. It also managed two weeks at No. 1 on *Your Hit Parade*.

Other recordings of the song that charted include those by the Andrews Sisters with Les Paul's Trio, by Betty Jane Rhodes, by Billy Butterfield and his orchestra, by the Three Suns, by Tony Martin, and by Harry Cool and Mindy Carson.

It seems "rumors are flying" that the singer is in love. Rumors aren't often based on fact, but in this particular case, the rumors are true. Read the lyrics at http://lirama.net/song/16445.

Seems Like Old Times

Words & Music: Carmen Lombardo & John Jacob Loeb

Guy Lombardo and his Royal Canadians and Vaughn Monroe both had recordings of "Seems Like Old Times" that rose to No. 7 on the *Billboard* chart in '46. Kate Smith's version only made it to No. 12 on that chart. The song only appeared on *Your Hit Parade* for one week in May of '46 and that was at No. 8.

AFI's *100 Years ... 100 Songs* (2004) named this song the No. 90 greatest song ever from an American film for its performance by Diane Keaton in *Annie Hall* ('77).

A 1980 Neil Simon film was titled *Seems Like Old Times*. Read the lyrics at http://lirama.net/song/16447.

Shoo-fly Pie and Apple Pan Dowdy

Words: Sammy Gallop ; Music: Guy Wood

"Shoo-fly Pie and Apple Pan Dowdy," a novelty song, became a hit in '46 in recordings by Stan Kenton and his orchestra with June Christy's vocal, by Guy Lombardo and his Royal Canadians, and by Dinah Shore. All those disks were pretty evenly matched in popularity.

The song made eight appearances on *Your Hit Parade*, peaking at No. 3 in May of '46.

Variety chose the song for one of its *Hit Parade of a Half-Century* songs.

There really is such a thing as Shoo-fly Pie and also

Apple Pan Dowdy. Shoo Fly Pie is a traditional Pennsylvania Dutch dessert. The ingredients are all non-perishable, so they could survive the long trip to America made by German immigrants. The pie's unusual name is said to have come from the fact the cook would constantly have to shoo the flies away from the pies as they set on windowsills to cool. Apple Pandowdy (sometimes spelled together and sometimes separately) is known in different parts of the world as cobblers, duffs, grunts, slumps and pandowdies. The exact origin of the name Pandowdy is unknown, but it is thought to refer to the dessert's plain or "dowdy" appearance.

The song lyrics tell us to go to New England if we're fussy about our food because "Shoo-fly Pie and Apple Pan Dowdy" will put us in a happy mood. We're told it's so wonderful we'll never get enough. Read the lyrics at http://lirama.net/song/16448 to read the lyrics.

Sioux City Sue

Words: Max C. Freedman; Music: Dick Thomas

Written in '45, "Sioux City Sue" was introduced by Gene Autry in the '46 film *Sioux City Sue*.

The most popular recordings were by Bing Crosby and the Jesters, by Tony Pastor, and by Dick Thomas.

The song garnered sixteen weeks on *Your Hit Parade*, but only got up to No. 4 on the survey in early June of '46. Crosby's recording with the Jesters collected four weeks at No. 3 on *Billboard*.

"Sioux City Sue" is in *Variety's Hit Parade of a Half-Century*.

A cowboy's greatest possession was his horse and his dog. In this song, the singer is willing to swap his horse and dog for Sioux City Sue." This cowboy had driven a herd of cattle from Nebraska to Iowa where he met "Sioux City Sue." Read the lyrics at http://ntl.matrix.com.br/pfilho/html/lyrics/s/sioux_city_sioux.txt.

South America, Take It Away

Words & Music: Harold Rome

Harold Rome wrote this song two years before it was introduced in the musical *Call Me Mister*. A satirical look at the Latin American dances like the rumba and samba that were invading the U.S., it became the hit of the show. Betty Garrett introduced the song in a serviceman's canteen scene. Bing Crosby and the Andrews Sisters accompanied by Vic Schoen and his orchestra had the most popular recorded version of the song.

Variety selected "South America, Take It Away" for its *Hit Parade of a Half-Century*.

The lyrics ask South America to take back their dances like the Conga, the Samba, and the Rumba. These dances are too strenuous and are causing too many back problems for the dancers. Read the lyrics at http://www.lirama.net/song/16451.

Another song from the *Call Me Mister* score was popular with the public: "Along With Me," which was popularized by Margaret Whiting in a successful recording.

Surrender

Words & Music: Bennie Benjamin & George Weiss

1946 was a very good year for Bennie Benjamin and George Weiss. They wrote "Oh! What It Seemed to Be,"

"Rumors Are Flying" and "Surrender," all very popular songs during the year.

"Surrender" was a No. 1 hit on *Billboard's* chart in Perry Como's version. According to *Billboard's Top Pop Singles of the Year*, Como's recording ranked No. 11 for the year. The song didn't do quite as well on *Your Hit Parade*; it only reached No. 2.

Woody Herman and his orchestra also had a successful recording of the song.

The idea of the song may have come from the end of World War II when Germany and Japan surrendered. Benjamin and Weiss made a connection between that type of surrender and lovers surrendering to each other. Read the lyrics at http://lirama.net/song/16452.

Symphony

Words: Jack Lawrence; Music: Alex Alstone

The ugly American syndrome had something to do with the version of this popular song that became a hit in the United States. Mark Twain wrote about Americans as "Innocents Abroad." In this instance, the innocents were American servicemen in Europe misunderstanding a French song. The French song was "C'est Fini," which meant "It's Over." Johnny Desmond performed the song with Glenn Miller's American Air Force Band and it became a big hit with our fighting men. The GIs mistakenly thought that the song was "Symphony," instead of "C'est Fini." The original French words were by Andre Tabet and Roger Bernstein. When the song was brought to this country, Jack Lawrence wrote English lyrics to fit the misunderstanding.

"Symphony" does sound a lot like "c'est fini," but the meaning is considerably different. According to the lyrics, a "symphony of love" begins when his lover walks in. Read the words at http://lirama.net/song/16453.

Freddy Martin and his orchestra, with a Clyde Rogers' vocal, had the most popular recording of the song. Their disk was *Variety's* No. 10 hit of the year, tied with "Let It Snow! Let It Snow! Let It Snow!." Martin's version spent two weeks at the top of *Billboard's* chart. The song racked up seven weeks at No. 1 on *Your Hit Parade*. Four recordings of the song made *Billboard's* Top Forty for the year: Martin's, Bing Crosby's, Benny Goodman and his orchestra's with vocalist Liza Morrow, and Jo Stafford's. Guy Lombardo and his Royal Canadians also had a successful recording of the song on the market.

Variety picked "Symphony" for its *Hit Parade of a Half-Century*.

Doin' What Comes Natur'lly, The Girl That I Marry, They Say It's Wonderful, Anything You Can Do, I Got the Sun in the Morning *and* There's No Business Like Show Business

Words & Music: Irving Berlin

Annie Get Your Gun is based on the life of female sharpshooter Annie Oakley. The idea originated with Dorothy Fields, who intended to write the lyrics for composer Jerome Kern, but Kern died before the project began. Rodgers and Hammerstein had agreed to be the producers, the only musical they produced that was not their own. After Kern's death, Rodgers and Hammerstein signed Irving Berlin to write both words and music. The show became the second book musical to exceed the magical 1,000-performance figure on Broadway (*Oklahoma!* had been the first).

Most people probably thought that Berlin was past his prime, since his last Broadway project had been *This Is the Army*, the all-soldier revue of '42. Not only was he alive and well, he wrote a score like none other he had produced. The number of hit songs set a record for Berlin; neither he, nor anyone else, had ever written a Broadway musical with more hit songs than *Annie Get Your Gun* contained.

The Broadway musical starred Ethel Merman as Annie. The film version of the musical was released in '50. It starred Betty Hutton and Howard Keel. The show was revived on Broadway in '99 starring Bernadette Peters as Annie and Tom Wopat as Frank Butler.

The story traces the rise of Annie Oakley from uneducated hillbilly to the star of Buffalo Bill's Wild West Show. It also involves the shooting rivalry and eventual love between Annie and Frank Butler.

DOIN' WHAT COMES NATUR'LLY

"Doin' What Comes Natur'lly" is a comic number that introduces the earthy, crude Annie Oakley. It expresses her idea of the way life should be — natural. She claims we don't need special training to attract the opposite sex, nor do we need any education to create children; we don't need to learn to write our names even to cash checks (her wealthy uncle signs his checks with an "X" but they still cash them). Read the lyrics at http://www.stlyrics.com/lyrics/anniegetyourgun/doinwhatcomesnaturlly.htm.

The most popular recordings of "Doin' What Comes Natur'lly" were by Freddy Martin and his orchestra, with vocalist Glenn Hughes, Dinah Shore with Spade Cooley, and Jimmy Dorsey and his orchestra. Freddy Martin's version is too corny and makes fun of the "hillbilly" character of the song. His disk made it to No. 2 on *Billboard*, so most of the public didn't agree that it was too corny.

Variety chose "Doin' What Comes Natur'lly" for its *Hit Parade of a Half-Century*.

THE GIRL THAT I MARRY

Frank Butler, played by Ray Middleton, introduced "The Girl That I Marry." He sang the number to illustrate to country hick Annie that she definitely was not the kind of girl he intended to marry. Read the lyrics at http://www.stlyrics.com/lyrics/anniegetyourgun/thegirlthatimarry.htm.

Recordings by Frank Sinatra and Eddy Howard helped popularize this song outside the musical.

"The Girl That I Marry" was chosen for *Variety's* *Hit Parade of a Half-Century*.

THEY SAY IT'S WONDERFUL

The biggest hit from the musical, in terms of chart performance, would be "They Say Its Wonderful." This song is Annie and Frank's contemplation of what they have heard love is supposed to be. Ray Middleton introduced the song, which Ethel Merman reprised. Read the lyrics at http://www.stlyrics.com/lyrics/anniegetyourgun/theysayitswonderful.htm.

Recordings by Frank Sinatra, Perry Como, Andy Russell, Bing Crosby, and Ethel Merman helped popularize the song. The song racked up four weeks at No. 1 on *Your Hit*

Parade. The most popular recording, Frank Sinatra's version, peaked at No. 2 on *Billboard.*

"They Say It's Wonderful" appeared in the movie *The Next Best Thing* (2000).

Variety chose "They Say It's Wonderful" for its *Hit Parade of a Half-Century.*

ANYTHING YOU CAN DO

When Annie and Frank finally get around to a shootout to decide once and for all who the best marksman was, they sing the comic challenge song, "Anything You Can Do." Each one tries to think of something that they can do better than the other one. Read the lyrics at http://www.stlyrics.com/lyrics/anniegetyourgun/anythingyoucando.htm.

Although the song never charted, it is one of the musical's biggest crowd pleasers.

Berlin wrote the song in a taxicab in fifteen minutes. He may well have been thinking of his own rivalry with Richard Rodgers. Whether he admitted it or not, Berlin felt challenged by Rodgers' enormous success with *Oklahoma!* and *Carousel.*

"Anything You Can Do" was nominated for the American Film Institute's list of the greatest songs ever from American films, but did not make the final list. It was nominated for the 1950 film version of *Annie Get Your Gun.*

I GOT THE SUN IN THE MORNING

Annie Oakley, played by Ethel Merman, introduced "I Got the Sun in the Morning." She sang it to enumerate some of life's simple pleasures. She doesn't have diamonds or pearls, but still she thinks she's a lucky girl, because she has the "sun in the morning and the moon at night." Read the lyrics at http://www.stlyrics.com/lyrics/anniegetyourgun/igotthesuninthemorning.htm.

Recordings by Les Brown and Artie Shaw and their orchestras helped popularize "I Got the Sun in the Morning."

Variety picked "I Got the Sun in the Morning" for its *Hit Parade of a Half-Century.*

THERE'S NO BUSINESS LIKE SHOW BUSINESS

"There's No Business Like Show Business" has become one of the unofficial anthems of the theater. It was introduced by Annie, Frank, Buffalo Bill Cody, and Charlie Davenport. Annie actually sings only toward the end of the song, after the other three have convinced her how great their Wild West Show is going to be. Read the lyrics at http://www.stlyrics.com/lyrics/anniegetyourgun/theresnobusinesslikeshowbusiness.htm.

A recording of "There's No Business Like Show Business" by Bing Crosby, the Andrews Sisters, and Dick Haymes made *Billboard's* chart in '47.

"There's No Business Like Show Business" was nominated for the American Film Institute's list of the greatest songs ever from American films for the 1950 film version of *Annie Get Your Gun,* but did not make the final list. The song also appeared in *There's No Business Like Show Business* ('54), *Noises Off* ('92) and *Lucky Break* (2001).

How can "They Say It's Wonderful," "Doin' What Comes Natur'lly," "The Girl That I Marry" and "I Got the Sun in the Morning" make the *Variety Hit Parade of Half-Century* listing, but not "There's No Business Like Show Business," or for that matter, "Anything You Can Do"?

Another well-known song from *Annie Get Your Gun* is "You Can't Get a Man With a Gun."

The original Broadway cast album of *Annie Get Your Gun* was inducted into the Grammy Hall of Fame in 1998.

To Each His Own
Words: Ray Evans; Music: Jay Livingston

The first major success for the songwriting team of Jay Livingston and Ray Evans was "To Each His Own," which reportedly sold three million recordings in '46. Eddy Howard's version climbed to the No. 1 spot on *Billboard* and stayed there for eight weeks. His recording was *Billboard* and *Variety's* No. 2 hit of the year. The song also spent eight weeks at No. 1 on *Your Hit Parade.*

In the film *To Each His Own,* set during World War I, a small-town girl, Josephine, played by Olivia DeHavilland has an illegitimate son by an itinerant pilot, played by John Lund.

"To Each His Own" is included in *Variety's Hit Parade of a Half-Century.* Five different recordings of "To Each His Own" made *Billboard's* Top 40 for the year. Besides Eddy Howard's recordings, others were Freddy Martin and his orchestra with vocalist Stuart Wade, the Ink Spots, the Modernaires with Paula Kelly and Tony Martin. According to *A Century of Pop Music,* Eddy Howard's, Freddy Martin's and the Ink Spots' recordings made it to No. 1 on *Billboard.* Collectively, the song collected eleven weeks at No. 1 among these recordings.

According to David Ewen in *American Popular Songs,* the song "was written to publicize the non-musical motion picture of the same name ... but was not used there." However, the sheet music cover for the song seems to indicate, but does not specifically say, it was used in the film. The sheet music cover advertises the film and pictures the film's stars, Olivia DeHavilland and John Lund.

The beautiful lyrics say that for everything or everyone there must be something or someone to make them complete. The singer has found the love that made him complete, his "one and only you." Read the lyrics at http://lirama.net/song/16457.

White Christmas (see 1942)

Crosby's recording of "White Christmas" made it to No. 1 again in '46 with one week at the top of the *Billboard* chart.

1947

Anniversary Song
Words & Music: Saul Chaplin & Al Jolson

This song became an international hit because it was included in the extremely popular '46 movie musical *The Jolson Story.* Saul Chaplin adapted the melody of Josef Ivanovici's "Waves of the Danube," and Chaplin and Al Jolson probably contributed the words. (I say "probably" because it is extremely difficult to tell if Jolson really helped write any of the songs that he was credited for as co-writer. Often in the past at least, Jolson was given co-writing credit just to get him to perform the song, which, back a few decades, meant an almost certain hit song, but by the late '40s that was definitely not the case. Therefore, it is at least probable that Jolson contributed to this song.) Jolson's recording from the film's soundtrack reportedly sold more than a million copies.

With the release of *The Jolson Story* in '46 and *Jolson Sings Again* in '49, "The World's Greatest Entertainer" was introduced to a new generation and experienced a remarkable comeback. Many of his old hits were re-recorded with much better fidelity, and many of them sold very well. Examples include Jolson and Bing Crosby's duet recording of Irving Berlin's "Alexander's Ragtime Band," "April Showers" was revived in '47 by Guy Lombardo and by Jolson, and Jolson's version of "My Mammy" charted again. *The Jolson Story* soundtrack album and *Songs He Made Famous* also were big sellers.

Be careful not to confuse Jolson's "Anniversary Song" with 1941's "The Anniversary Waltz." Jolson's song speaks of a couple dancing on the night of their wedding and vowing their love would remain true.

Jolson's recording was No. 9 among *Variety*'s Top Ten for 1947 and No. 8 on *Billboard* for the year. It topped the *Billboard* chart for two weeks and the song topped *Your Hit Parade* for six weeks.

Other popular versions of "Anniversary Song" include Guy Lombardo's, Dinah Shore's, Tex Beneke and the Glenn Miller Orchestra's and Andy Russell's. Kenny Gardner was Lombardo's vocalist on their recording. Garry Stevens was vocalist on the Tex Beneke version.

Variety chose this song for its *Hit Parade of a Half-Century.*

The singer and his bride danced on their wedding night and pledged their true love. Read the lyrics at http://lirama.net/song/16461.

Ballerina

Words: Bob Russell; Music: Carl Sigman

By '48, "Ballerina (Dance, Ballerina, Dance)," recorded by Vaughn Monroe, had reportedly sold a million copies. His recording of the song was '47's No. 2 hit for *Variety*. It spent ten weeks at No. 1 on *Billboard*, but was only ranked No. 11 for the year (those figures don't make sense). Those ten weeks at the top qualifies it as the No. 39 hit of the pre-rock era. The song also collected five weeks at the top of *Your Hit Parade*.

Other recorded versions that charted in '47 or '48 include those by Buddy Clark, by Bing Crosby, and by Jimmy Dorsey and his orchestra. Nat "King" Cole's recording in '57 made *Billboard's* top twenty.

The lyrics encourage the ballerina to dance her best even though her heart is breaking. It's breaking because the man she loves is not sitting out front to watch her steal the show. She had said she wanted fame before love, now she must accept the consequences of her choice. Read the words at http://lirama.net/song/16462.

Variety picked this song for its *Hit Parade of a Half-Century* representing 1948.

Chi-Baba, Chi-Baba (My Bambino Go to Sleep)

Words & Music: Jerry Livingston, Al Hoffman & Mack David

Perry Como's recording of "Chi-Baba, Chi-Baba," with 1898's "When You Were Sweet Sixteen" on the flip side,

was *Variety*'s No. 6 hit of the year. It was tied for No. 14 on *Billboard*, where it was No. 1 for three weeks. The song peaked at No. 3 on *Your Hit Parade*. The Satisfiers backed Como on his recording of "Chi-Baba, Chi-Baba."

Peggy Lee, Blue Barron and his orchestra, and the Charioteers also had recordings of "Chi-Baba, Chi-Baba" that charted.

The lyrics to this song make about as much sense as those of "Mairzy Doats" ('44). A sampling of the words includes "Chi-baba, chi-baba, chi-wawa, Enja-lawa, cook-ala-goomba." Sounds like Italian gibberish, but it's supposed to be a lullaby. Read the words at http://lirama.net/song/16463.

Civilization

Words: Bob Hilliard; Music: Carl Sigman

Carl Sigman followed his success with "Ballerina" with "Civilization," which he wrote with Bob Hilliard. It was interpolated into the Broadway revue *Angel in the Wings*, where Elaine Stritch introduced it.

A missionary tells some natives how fine civilization is. However, the natives don't want any part of bright lights, false teeth, door bells or landlords, etc. Read the words at http://lirama.net/song/16497.

The most popular version of the song was by the Andrews Sisters and Danny Kaye. Other charted versions included those by Ray McKinley and his orchestra, by Louis Prima, by Jack Smith, and by Woody Herman and his orchestra.

"Civilization (Bongo, Bongo, Bongo)" was No. 1 on *Your Hit Parade* for one week, but it only made it to No. 3 on *Billboard*.

Louis Prima's recording of "Civilization" appeared on the soundtrack of the 1998 film *Lolita*.

Variety chose "Civilization" for its *Hit Parade of a Half-Century* representing 1948.

Feudin' and Fightin'

Words: Al Dubin; Music: Burton Lane

This comic, hillbilly song was introduced by Pat Brewster in the Broadway revue *Laffing Room Only* in '44, but didn't become well known until '47 because the producers of the revue were involved in a bitter dispute with ASCAP and refused to release the broadcasting rights to the musical score from the show. Composer Burton Lane acquired the rights in '47 and gave permission to Dorothy Shay to sing and record "Feudin' and Fightin'." She introduced her version on a Bing Crosby radio program.

Ms. Shay was known as "the Park Avenue Hillbillie" because she often performed decidedly country-flavored songs, but she was dressed in the finest gowns and was backed by an orchestra not a country-western band.

"Feudin' and Fightin", actually "feudin' and fussin' and a-fightin'" in the song, managed only one week at No. 1 on *Your Hit Parade*, and Dorothy Shay's recording only reached No. 4 on *Billboard*. However, it made *Billboard's* Top Forty for the year, at No. 38.

Jo Stafford and Bing Crosby also had successful recordings of the song.

This hillbilly-sounding lyric tells us the singer was feuding with her "ornery neighbors down by the creek." Somebody shot Grandma. Now they want to get the funeral over quickly so they can start the feuding again. Read the lyrics at http://lirama.net/song/16465.

Heartaches

Words: John Klenner; Music: Al Hoffman

Al Hoffman and John Klenner wrote "Heartaches" in '31. Only a recorded version by Guy Lombardo and his Royal Canadians did very well in '31. Ted Weems and his orchestra recorded it in '33, but their version was not particularly popular at the time.

Then fourteen years after it was recorded (in '47), a Charlotte, North Carolina, disk jockey pulled the Weems record off the shelf and played it on his show. He liked it, and he got favorable response from his listeners, so he played it every day for a week. Record dealers in the South were suddenly swamped with requests for the record. Victor reissued the disk on its Bluebird label and Weems' version of "Heartaches" became a huge hit and eventually sold more than two million copies. Weems' record racked up thirteen weeks at No. 1 on *Billboard*, and was *Billboard* and *Variety's* No. 3 hit of '47. Those thirteen weeks at the top of *Billboard* makes it the No. 6 hit of the decade and No. 10 of the pre-rock era. The song topped the *Your Hit Parade* survey for two weeks.

The arrangement was, according to Weems, a "corny sort of half-rumba rhythm and with all those effects." One of the highlights of Weems' recording is Elmo Tanner's whistling. Hear the '33 recording or the '38 recording with Elmo Tanner's whistling at http://www.redhotjazz.com/weems.html.

With the success of Weems' disk, others recorded "Heartaches," including Harry James, Jimmy Dorsey, and Eddy Howard and their orchestras.

The lyrics tell us "loving you meant only heartaches." The singer knows he should find someone new, but his "heart aches for you." Lyricist John Klenner cleverly turned "heartaches" into "heart aches." Read the lyrics at http://lirama.net/song/16468.

How Are Things in Glocca Morra?

Words: E.Y. Harburg; Music: Burton Lane

Finian's Rainbow, a fantasy musical, introduced the wistful "How Are Things in Glocca Morra?. Sharon McLonergan, played by Ella Logan in the original cast, sang the song. Sharon is in the United States wondering about her homeland, Ireland. The song of a bird prompts her reminiscence, "the same skylark music we have back in Ireland." Read the lyrics at http://lirama.net/song/16469.

Burton Lane and E.Y. Harburg wrote *Finian's Rainbow*. Harburg wanted to satirize the American economic system. Finian, a simple Irish immigrant, believes that a pot of gold he buried at Fort Knox will grow and make him incredibly rich. Also included in the plot are comments on union versus labor, the Social Security system, and integration. In many respects, the musical was far ahead of its time.

The '68 film version starred Fred Astaire as Finian, Petula Clark as Sharon, his daughter, and Tommy Steele as the leprechaun, Og. In the original, Finian did not sing or dance, but Astaire was given songs to sing and to feature his dancing. This song was nominated for the American Film Institute's list of greatest songs ever from an American film, but was not on the final list. It was nominated for its appearance in the '68 film version of *Finian's Rainbow*.

Recordings by Buddy Clark, by Martha Tilton, by Tommy Dorsey and his orchestra, and by Dick Haymes helped popularize "How Are Things in Glocca Morra" beyond the Broadway stage.

The song was included in *Variety's Hit Parade of a Half-Century.*

Other reasonably well-known songs from the musical's score include "Old Devil Moon," which was popularized in recordings by Margaret Whiting and by Gene Krupa and his orchestra; "If This Isn't Love," "Look to the Rainbow," and "When I'm Not Near the Girl I Love." Find the lyrics to most of these songs at http://www.ostlyrics.com/movie.php?sid=501&movie=Finian's%20Rainbow.

Huggin' and Chalkin'

Words & Music: Clancy Hayes & Kermit Goell

Master songwriter, singer and actor Hoagy Carmichael had his biggest personal hit recording in '47 with a song he didn't write. The novelty song, "Huggin' and Chalkin'," was written by Clancy Hayes and Kermit Goell.

The backing group on Carmichael's recording was the Chickadees and Vic Schoen's Orchestra.

The singer has a girl friend that tips the scales at over 300 pounds (perhaps not unlike Arthur Godfrey's "Too Fat Polka," which was also popular in '47). When he hugs her, he needs a piece of chalk to mark where he began so he'll know when he has returned to the place he started. The girl was so fat, that he met another guy "huggin' and chalkin'" coming around the other way. Such lyrics would probably be deemed politically incorrect today. Read these hilarious lyrics at http://lirama.net/song/16470.

As silly as the song may sound, it was No. 1 on *Billboard* for two weeks in '47, and among *Billboard's* top thirty hits of the year. Carmichael wasn't the only one who recorded the song either. Other versions were released by Johnny Mercer, and by Kay Kyser and his orchestra, with Jack Martin and the Campus Kids.

I Wish I Didn't Love You So

Words & Music: Frank Loesser

Frank Loesser's "I Wish I Didn't Love You So" was introduced by "The Blonde Bombshell," Betty Hutton, in the '47 movie musical *The Perils of Pauline*.

Both Dinah Shore and Vaughn Monroe had very popular recordings of the song; both reached No. 2 on *Billboard*. Monroe's version was *Billboard's* No. 6 hit of the year. The song topped the *Your Hit Parade* survey of hits for two weeks. Betty Hutton's recording with Joe Lilley's Orchestra was also popular, as were releases by Dick Haymes and by Dick Farney.

The singer wishes she didn't love this person so much and she thinks their romance should have already ended. But when she tries someone new, she still can only say "I Wish I Didn't Love You So." Read the lyrics at http://lirama.net/song/16471.

I Wonder, I Wonder, I Wonder

Words & Music: Darwin Frank Hutchins

Bandleader and singer Eddy Howard, formerly vocalist with the Dick Jurgens Orchestra, continued the success that he had experienced with "To Each His Own" in '46 with "I Wonder, I Wonder, I Wonder" in '47. Howard sang the lead vocal with the backing of a vocal trio, the same formula that had worked in his previous hit.

The song was No. 1 for one week on *Your Hit Parade.* Howard's version peaked at No. 2 on *Billboard.* Other renditions on the market were by Guy Lombardo and his Royal Canadians with vocalist Don Rodney, by Martha Tilton, and by Tony Pastor and his orchestra.

Eddy Howard's recording of "I Wonder, I Wonder, I Wonder" appeared on the soundtrack of the 1998 film *Lolita.*

I Wonder Who's Kissing Her Now (see 1909)

Linda

Words & Music: Jack Lawrence & Ann Ronell

"Linda" was introduced in the '45 film *The Story of G.I. Joe.* Then Buddy Clark with Ray Noble and his orchestra had a '47 hit recording of the song that topped *Billboard's* chart for a couple of weeks. Clark's disk was tied for No. 4 for the year according to *Billboard,* and No. 7 for *Variety.* The song collected four weeks at No. 1 on *Your Hit Parade.*

Charlie Spivak and his orchestra, with vocalist Tommy Mercer, Paul Weston and his orchestra, with vocalist Matt Dennis, and Larry Douglas with Ray Bloch's Radio Seven also had recordings of "Linda" that were popular with the public.

To help him go to sleep, the singer doesn't count sheep, he counts "all the charms about Linda." Read the lyrics at http://lirama.net/song/22328.

Variety chose "Linda" for its *Hit Parade of a Half-Century.*

Mam'selle

Words: Mack Gordon; Music: Edmund Goulding

"Mam'selle" was introduced in a French cafe scene in the '46 film of Somerset Maugham's *The Razor's Edge,* which was set during World War I. Art Lund and Frank Sinatra popularized the song with successful recordings that topped the *Billboard* chart for two and one week respectively. The song was No. 1 on *Your Hit Parade* for three weeks in mid–'47.

Other popular recordings of the song included those by Dick Haymes, by the Pied Pipers, by Ray Dorey, by Dennis Day, and by Frankie Laine.

British movie director Edmund Goulding and American lyricist Mack Gordon collaborated on "Mam'selle."

The lyrics speak of a rendezvous in a small cafe between the singer and "Mam'selle," but there is a hint of sadness because the singer feels she will say good-bye. Read the lyrics at http://www.lyricsdir.com/frank-sinatra-mamselle-lyrics.html.

"Mam'selle" is one of the songs in *Variety's Hit Parade of a Half-Century.*

Managua, Nicaragua

Words: Albert Gamse; Music: Irving Fields

Two versions of "Managua, Nicaragua" hit No. 1 on *Billboard:* Freddy Martin and his orchestra's recording spent three weeks at the top, while Guy Lombardo and his Royal Canadians' disk topped the chart for one week. Stuart Wade and some of the band members were the vocalists on Martin's version, while Don Rodney was the singer on Lombardo's. The song peaked at No. 2 on *Your Hit Parade.*

Kay Kyser and his orchestra, with Gloria Wood and the Campus Kids, also had a successful recording of the song on the market.

The song claims that "Managua, Nicaragua" is a beautiful town and a heavenly place. The lyrics kiddingly call Brooklyn a foreign tropical port. Read the lyrics at http://lirama.net/song/16477.

Variety included "Managua, Nicaragua" in its *Hit Parade of a Half-Century.*

Misirlou

English Words: Bob Russell, Fred Wise & Milton Leeds; Music: Nick Roubanis

"Misirlou," a *Variety Hit Parade of a Half-Century* selection, most likely originated in Athens, Greece among the refugees from Smyrna (now Ismir, Turkey) during the '20s. The first known recording was in Greece around 1930.

In '41, Nick Roubanis, a Greco-American music instructor released a jazz instrumental arrangement of the song, crediting himself as composer and lyricist (he is still officially credited as the composer, since his claim was never challenged in court). S.K. "Bob" Russell, Fred Wise and Milton Leeds later wrote the English lyrics.

"Misirlou" is a woman who is "a dream of delight." The singer is confident Allah will bless their love.

Harry James and his orchestra recorded a popular version of the song in '41, but the most popular version was by Jan August and his orchestra in '46. Leon Berry charted with his version in '53. The Beach Boys included the song in their '63 album "Surfin' USA."

In '94, Dick Dale's (a guitarist) version of "Misirlou" was heard on the soundtrack of *Pulp Fiction.* The Athens Olympic Organizing Committee felt the song was one of the most influential Greek songs of all time, so, it was heard during the closing ceremony, performed by Greek singer Anna Vissi.

My Adobe Hacienda

Words & Music: Louise Massey & Lee Penny

Variety included "My Adobe Hacienda" in its *Hit Parade of a Half-Century* representing '47.

The song had been popularized in '41 with a recording by Louise Massey that only reached No. 23 on the *Billboard* chart. Five recordings of the song helped popularize it in '47, with Eddy Howard's version being the most successful, reaching No. 2 on the *Billboard* chart. Other successful recordings were by the Dinning Sisters, the Billy Williams Quartet, and Kenny Baker. Louise Massey's version surfaced again in '47 and made it to No. 16 this time.

"My Adobe Hacienda" made ten appearances on *Your Hit Parade,* peaking at No. 2 for two weeks in May and once again in mid–June of '47.

In the singer's adobe hacienda his life and love are complete. Read the lyrics at http://www.lyricsvault.net/songs/18835.html.

Near You

Words: Kermit Goell; Music: Francis Craig

The No. 1 hit of '47 on both *Billboard* and *Variety* was pianist Francis Craig's "Near You," which reportedly sold two and a half million disks. Craig's recording spent seventeen weeks at No. 1 on *Billboard.* That makes it the top hit of the pre-rock era in terms of weeks at No. 1, however, the No. 2 hit, "White Christmas," deserves the top hit honor due to its lasting popularity and all of the records it holds for sales of a single disk. No other song had ever lasted more than fourteen weeks at No. 1 on *Billboard*, including all of the rock era until the mid-'90s ("One Sweet Day" by Mariah Carey and Boyz II Men collected 16 weeks at No. 1 on *Billboard* in '95). "Near You" also topped *Your Hit Parade*'s survey for six weeks.

There were also several other successful recordings of the song, notably those by the Andrews Sisters, by Larry Green, by Alvino Rey and his orchestra with vocalist Jimmy Joyce, by Elliott Lawrence, and by Two-Ton Baker. "Near You" also became Milton Berle's theme song for his tremendously successful *Texaco Star Theater* television show.

Craig's recording of "Near You" was more or less a happenstance. He had organized a band after World War I and had played for more than twenty years at Nashville's Hermitage Hotel. Craig was one of the family that controlled Nashville radio station WSM and the Grand Ole Opry; he was a staff member there for twenty-five years and was on NBC for twelve years. Jim Bulleit, owner of Bullet Records, began a pop music series to compliment his country, gospel, and rhythm and blues releases. One of his first releases was a recording of Craig's theme song, "Red Rose." Before the recording session, Bulleit reminded Craig that he needed two songs for the record. Craig selected "Near You" for the "B" side.

Craig had retired, but he regrouped his band for the recording session. The recording was made in WSM's Studio C and piped by telephone line to the recording studio.

A Georgia disk jockey was the first one who flipped the record over and played "Near You," sung by Craig's sightless vocalist, Bob Lamm. It became a phenomenal success. At one point, Bullet Records had to hire forty record pressing plants to try to meet the demand for the disk.

"Near You" was selected by *Variety* for its *Hit Parade of a Half-Century* representing '48.

There's only one place the singer wants to be and that's "near you." He never wants to be more than two lips away. He concludes by begging this girl to allow him to spend the rest of his days near her. Read the lyrics at http://lirama.net/song/16480.

Open the Door, Richard

Words: Dusty Fletcher & John Mason; Music: Jack McVea & Dan Howell

Count Basie and his orchestra had been one of country's premier jazz ensembles since the late thirties. Ironically, their only No. 1 hit was the novelty song "Open the Door, Richard." The number was "sung" by trumpeter Harry "Sweets" Edison and trombonist Bill Johnson. It had been written by saxophonist Jack McVea with Dan Howell. "Dusty" Fletcher and John Mason had used the phrase as part of a comedy routine in the thirties and forties. They expanded it into the words for this hit song.

Actually, two versions, Count Basie's and one by the rhythm and blues trio, the Three Flames, hit No. 1 on *Billboard*. Basie's topped the chart for one week in late February, and the Flames' version followed it into the top spot for one week in early March. The song didn't fare as well on *Your Hit Parade*; it only reached No. 7 (it was probably a bit to ethnic for that survey of hits).

Five other artists released successful recordings of the song that charted. There were versions by co-lyricist "Dusty" Fletcher, by co-composer Jack McVea, by the Charioteers, by Louis Jordan and his Tympany Five, and by the Pied Pipers.

The song was so popular that the title phrase became a cliché and a common expression whenever anyone knocked on a door. There's a lot of talking in Basie's recording, but the part that is sung, and the most famous part, is the chorus, which goes like this: "Open the door, Richard, Open the door and let me in." Read the words at http://lirama.net/song/16482.

Jack McVea's recording of "Open the Door, Richard" appeared on the soundtrack of the 1998 film *Lolita*.

Variety chose "Open the Door, Richard" for its *Hit Parade of a Half-Century*.

Peg o' My Heart

Words: Alfred Bryan; Music: Fred Fisher

Jose Collins introduced "Peg o' My Heart" in the *Ziegfeld Follies of 1913* as an interpolation (for more see 1913).

"Peg o' My Heart" was a big hit song in '47. Three versions hit No. 1 on *Billboard*: the Harmonicats', the Three Suns', and Buddy Clark's. Jerry Murad's Harmonicats' instrumental version collected eight weeks at the top; a trio consisting of guitar, accordion, and organ, the Three Suns' version, managed four weeks on top; while Buddy Clark's vocal version reportedly racked up six weeks at No. 1. However, only the Harmonicats and the Three Suns's versions placed in *Billboard's* yearly Top Ten. The harmonica group's recording was No. 2, while the Three Suns' disk was No. 7. They were No. 4 and No. 10 respectively on *Variety* for the year. The song collected nine weeks at No. 1 on *Your Hit Parade*.

Other recorded versions that charted in '47 included those by Art Lund, by Ted Weems and his orchestra, and by Clark Dennis.

In '33, the song was featured in the film *Peg o' My Heart*. It was also prominent in Fred Fisher's '49 screen biography, *Oh, You Beautiful Doll*.

The Harmonicats' recording of "Peg o' My Heart" was inducted into the Grammy Hall of Fame in 1999.

Lyrics are available at http://lirama.net/song/16483.

Smoke! Smoke! Smoke! That Cigarette

Words & Music: Merle Travis & Tex Williams

With all the hoopla in recent years concerning smoking and its health hazards, it's surprising that "Smoke! Smoke! Smoke! That Cigarette" hasn't been revived into popularity.

There have been a few country songs that have been covered by mainstream pop singers that have become big hits, but very few have made it to the top of the pop charts in the original country version. Al Dexter's '43 hit "Pistol Packin' Mama" may be an exception, and evidently so was "Prisoner's Song" by Vernon Dalhart (1925–26). Elton Britt's recording of "There's a Star-Spangled Banner Waving Somewhere" was a popular World War II song. However, they are few and far between. This song is another of the genre; one of the few that climbed to the top of the national pop charts to date (there'll be a few more in the next several years).

Tex Williams and Merle Travis wrote this comic patter

song, which Tex Williams recorded with his band, the Western Caravan. His recording became Capitol Records' first million seller, reportedly selling more than 2.5 million copies. It was No. 1 on *Billboard* for six weeks. Williams' disk was tied for No. 4 for the year on *Billboard*, and was No. 5 on *Variety*. *Your Hit Parade* ignored it.

Phil Harris also had a version of the song that charted, and the song was featured in the 2005 film *Thank You for Smoking*. The anti-smoking lyrics tell us when we smoke ourselves to death we will beg St. Peter to wait so we can have one more cigarette. Read the lyrics at http://www.stlyrics.com/songs/j/jimmydean6735/smokesmokesmoket hatcigarette468780.html.

That's My Desire

Words: Carroll Loveday; Music: Helmy Kresa

Irving Berlin's publishing company issued this song in '31, but it remained reasonably forgotten until Mills Music, Inc., acquired the copyright sixteen years later. Frankie Laine revived the number in his nightclub act, and it was heard by a Mercury Records executive who signed him to record it. The disk brought commercial success to both Laine and Mercury.

Laine's recording was popular, but according to *Billboard*, Sammy Kaye's version, with vocalist Don Cornell, was a bit more successful. Kaye's disk peaked at No. 2, while Laine's only reached No. 4. Kaye's version was *Billboard's* No. 10 hit of the year. The song's popularity was strong enough to garner one week at No. 1 on *Your Hit Parade*.

Martha Tilton and Woody Herman and his orchestra also had recordings of the song that were successful in '47.

Frankie Laine's recording of "That's My Desire" was inducted into the Grammy Hall of Fame in 1998.

The singer's desire is to spend one night with his girl in their old rendezvous where they will dance until dawn. He wants to hear her whisper "Darling, I love you." That's his desire! Read the words at http://lirama.net/song/16488.

Tim-Tayshun (Temptation)

Words: Arthur Freed; Music: Nacio Herb Brown

Bing Crosby introduced "Temptation" in the movie musical *Going Hollywood* in 1933. With this film, Crosby rose to the Top Ten box-office attractions list. The song became one of his biggest hits to date.

"Temptation" normally is played with a beguine beat. The "temptation" is a woman who came when he was alone, and now he's a slave to her. Read the lyrics at http://www.lyricsdownload.com/bing-crosby-temptation-lyrics.html.

Bing Crosby, Ted FioRito and his orchestra and Paul Whiteman's pianist/arranger, Ferde Grofe and his orchestra popularized "Temptation" in recordings in '34. Artie Shaw and his orchestra revived it with some success in '44, while Perry Como's recording of the song charted on *Billboard* in '45 and '46. Then in '47, Jo Stafford, as Cinderella G. Stump, released a version pronounced "Tim-tayshun," with Red Ingle and the Natural Seven that climbed to No.1 on *Billboard's* chart. Their hick version almost ruins a beautiful song, but it tied for *Billboard's* No. 14 spot for the year.

Jo Stafford's spoofs didn't stop there! She and her husband, Paul Weston, recorded a few albums as Jonathan and Darlene Edwards. They are purposefully bad! Really

bad! They are performing like a singer and pianist who think they are great, but are actually horrible.

Red Ingle had played saxophone for both Ted Weems and Spike Jones. This farcical recording was likely influenced by his time with Spike Jones. It is his only major hit.

"Temptation" was used in the '48 movie musical *A Date With Judy* and in *The Seven Hills of Rome* ('58), which starred Mario Lanza.

You Do

Words: Mack Gordon; Music: Josef Myrow

"You Do," an Academy Award nominee, was introduced in the '47 movie musical *Mother Wore Tights*, which starred Betty Grable and Dan Dailey.

"You Do" was popularized in recordings by Dinah Shore, by Vaughn Monroe, by Margaret Whiting, by Vic Damone and by Bing Crosby. Shore's recording peaked at No. 4 on *Billboard's* chart, but the song managed one week at No. 1 on *Your Hit Parade*.

The lyrics ask several questions that are all answered with "you do," like "Who knows how much I love you?" Read the words at http://www.lyricsvault.net/songs/18847.html.

Zip-A-Dee-Doo-Dah

Words: Ray Gilbert; Music: Allie Wrubel

"Zip-A-Dee-Doo-Dah" is the Academy Award winner of '47 from Disney's '46 cartoon-live action feature *Song of the South*. The song was sung in the film by Uncle Remus, played by James Baskett. It was popularized on the pop charts in recordings by Johnny Mercer and the Pied Pipers, by Sammy Kaye and his orchestra, and by the Modernaires with Paula Kelly.

It's amazing how a lyricist can come up with such an unusual phrase as "zip-a-dee-doo-dah," that expresses so precisely the jollity and carefree spirit of the scene in the film. Wrubel's bright, bouncy melody helped the lyrics project the idea of a wonderful, sunshiny day when "ev'rything is 'satisfactch'll.'" Read the lyrics and hear an audio clip of James Baskett singing the song at http://www.songofthe-south.net/movie/lyrics/zip-a-dee-doo-dah.html.

Variety chose this song for its *Hit Parade of a Half-Century*. AFI's *100 Years ... 100 Songs* (2004) named "Zip-a-Dee-Doo-Dah" as the No. 47 greatest song from an American film ever.

1948

All I Want for Christmas (Is My Two Front Teeth)

Words & Music: Don Gardner

Don Gardner's wife, Doris, was a music teacher in a New York elementary school. One day in '44, Gardner filled in for his wife. When he said something funny, the children laughed. He was immediately struck by their teeth, or lack thereof. Sixteen out of the twenty-two students were missing their front teeth. That evening he wrote "All I Want for Christmas Is My Two Front Teeth" in less than half an hour. It wasn't published, however, until '48, when the Satisfiers introduced the song on Perry Como's radio show.

Spike Jones and his City Slickers had a No. 1 hit with the song on *Billboard* for three weeks during the '48 Christmas season. George Rock was Spike Jones' vocalist on their recording of the song. It also charted in early '50.

A little boy's Christmas wish is to get his two front teeth back so he can wish us "Merry Christmas." It's very difficult to say words that contain "s" when those teeth are gone. For example, he has difficulty saying "Sister Susie sitting on a thistle" and it is almost impossible for him to whistle. Read the lyrics at http://www.carols.org.uk/all_i_want_for_christmas_is_my_two_front_teeth.htm.

Another Op'nin', Another Show
Words & Music: Cole Porter

Cole Porter wrote the musical *Kiss Me Kate*, transforming Shakespeare's *Taming of the Shrew* into a modern tale. The musical is a play within a play. A group of actors are performing the Shakespearean play, but offstage a modern "taming" is in progress as a husband tries to tame his former wife. The actors play two roles: the Shakespeare characters and their offstage persons. Porter's sophisticated lyrics and beautiful melodies were never better, mixing Elizabethan dialogue and American slang to create a unique and colorful production.

"Another Op'nin', Another Show" is the show's first musical number. It was introduced in the musical by the maid, Hattie (played by Annabelle Hill). In some later productions, a male butler performed the song. To seasoned performers this is just "another op'nin', another show" in any of many towns. It's another job that they hope will make the future brighter than their past. They rehearsed for weeks and the show didn't seem to be getting any better, then suddenly it's opening night. Everyone's excited again as the curtain rises. Read the lyrics at http://www.lyricsondemand.com/soundtracks/k/kissmekatelyrics/anotheropninanothershowlyrics.html.

Along with Irving Berlin's "There's No Business Like Show Business," "Another Op'nin', Another Show" is the best-known ode to show business and the theater.

Kiss Me Kate won the first Tony Award for Best Musical that was awarded in '49. The New York theater season runs from April 1 to March 31. The award often comes in the year after a musical opens.

Other noteworthy songs from the score include "Always True to You in My Fashion," "So In Love," "Too Darn Hot," "Why Can't You Behave?," "Wunderbar," and "Brush Up Your Shakespeare."

"Too Darn Hot" was nominated for the American Film Institute's list of the greatest songs ever from an American film, but it did not make the final list. It was nominated for the '53 film version of *Kiss Me Kate*.

Buttons and Bows
Words & Music: Jay Livingston & Ray Evans

Bob Hope and Jane Russell introduced this Academy Award winner in '48 in the movie *The Paleface*; that's the second Oscar winner introduced by Bob Hope; the first one was his theme song "Thanks For the Memory." Dinah Shore's recording was a No. 1 hit for ten weeks on *Billboard* and the song also managed ten weeks at No. 1 on *Your Hit Parade*. The song was *Variety*'s No. 1 hit of the year, and stayed longer at No. 1 on *Billboard* and *Your Hit Parade* than any other song during the year.

Other popular recordings of the song were released by the Dinning Sisters, by Betty Garrett, by Betty Jane Rhodes, by Evelyn Knight, and by Gene Autry.

"Buttons and Bows" has a distinct western flavor in lyrics and melody. The lyrics make several allusions to Hope's character in the film, an eastern dude dentist. He isn't fond of people who "tote a gun" and his bones ache from riding the bouncing buckboards. Read the lyrics at http://www.lyricsdepot.com/Dinah-Shore/buttons-and-bows.html.

Jane Russell, Roy Rogers, Bob Hope and the chorus girls performed the song with new lyrics in *Son of Paleface* ('52).

Variety chose "Buttons and Bows" for its *Hit Parade of a Half-Century*. AFI's *100 Years ... 100 Songs* (2004) named this song the No. 87 greatest song ever from an American film.

Cool Water
Words & Music: Bob Nolan

Water is a necessity of life. That statement seems even more true in desert regions where water is particularly precious. Seventy-five percent of the human body is water. The brain is 85% water, human blood is 90% water, muscles are 75% water, the liver is 82% water and our bones are 22% water. Every part of the human body is dependent on water. If our glands and organs are not nourished with good, clean water, their functions begin to deteriorate.

The song "Cool Water" was written in '41 by Bob Nolan, one of the original Sons of the Pioneers. It is about a man, his mule and a mirage. The man and his mule, Dan, are traveling across the barren waste of the desert and both thirst for the taste of cool, clear water. Read the lyrics at http://www.cowboylyrics.com/lyrics/sons-of-the-pioneers/cool-water-13406.html.

The most popular recorded version was by Vaughn Monroe and The Sons of the Pioneers in '48. The recording was released by RCA Victor Records. The record was on the Billboard magazine chart for 13 weeks, peaking at No. 9. The Sons of the Pioneers' version charted in '41. Their recording of the song was inducted into the Grammy Hall of Fame in 1986.

The song was sung by the Sons of the Pioneers in *Ding Dong Williams* ('46). The group appeared in several films and sang in almost all of them, but exactly what songs they performed are not always listed in the film's synopsis.

Golden Earrings
Words: Jay Livingston & Ray Evans; Music: Victor Young

Marlene Dietrich introduced this '46 song in the '47 movie *Golden Earrings*. Peggy Lee's recordings of the song was No. 1 on *Your Hit Parade* for one week, but peaked at No. 2 on *Billboard*. Dinah Shore also had a recorded version that charted on *Billboard*.

The song was included in the *Variety Hit Parade of a Half-Century*.

The lyrics to this song should be very interesting to all the people today, both male and female, who wear earrings. The gypsies say "when your love wears golden earrings, she belongs to you." Also, love will come to you if you wear golden earrings. Read the lyrics at http://lirama. net/song/16500.

Hair of Gold, Eyes of Blue

Words & Music: Sunny Skylar

Jack Emerson introduced this folk song-style piece, but it was Gordon MacRae who had the most popular recording of the song. There were numerous recordings of the song on the market, including the Harmonicats, Jack Emerson, Jack Lathrop, Art Lund, John Laurenz and Bob Eberly.

"Hair of Gold, Eyes of Blue" appeared on *Your Hit Parade* fourteen times, peaking at No. 3. According to *Pop Memories*, Gordon MacRae's recording of the song peaked at No. 7 on *Billboard*, with the other charting singles ranging from No. 15 to No. 25.

The song was included in *Variety*'s *Hit Parade of a Half-Century*.

The singer tells us that he came from Butte, Montana and stopped in Santa Fe, where he met a pretty girl with "hair of gold, eyes of blue, lips like cherry wine." He thinks she's the prettiest girl he's ever seen and he intends to make her his girl. Read the lyrics at http://www.sing 365.com/music/lyric.nsf/Hair-Of-Gold-Eyes-Of-Blue-lyrics-Frank-Sinatra/ EF9D516AD76578C4825692100102 186.

How Soon?

Words: Carroll Lucas; Music: Jack Owens

"How Soon (Will I Be Seeing You?)" spent two weeks at No. 1 on *Your Hit Parade*, but peaked at No. 2 on *Billboard*. The most popular recording was by the composer, Jack Owens, with Eddie Bellantyne's Orchestra. Owens had been a featured singer on Don McNeill's "Breakfast Club" network radio show.

Other charted versions were by Vaughn Monroe, Bing Crosby, and Dinah Shore.

The lyrics open with the title: "How soon will I be seeing you?" Later he asks how soon he will be close to her so they can dance the way they once did? Read the lyrics at http://lyricsplayground.com/alpha/songs/h/howsoon. shtml.

I'll Dance at Your Wedding

Words by Herb Magidson; Music by Ben Oakland

Variety included "I'll Dance at Your Wedding" in its *Hit Parade of a Half-Century*.

Tony Martin's recording of this song peaked at No. 23 on the *Billboard* chart in late '47, while Buddy Clark's recording with Ray Noble and his orchestra climbed to No. 3 in '48. Peggy Lee's version only made it to No. 11.

The song made eight appearances on *Your Hit Parade* peaking at No. 2 in mid–February of '48.

Herb Magidson's lyrics start very simply, "I'll dance at your wedding" repeated three times. The singer then says he'll drink to her father and mother then have another drink "for Auld Lang Syne." He's going to kiss all the ladies, have another drink and kiss them again. At the end of the lyrics, we find out that this was his own wedding. It sounds like he needed some liquor fortification to make it through the affair.

I'm Looking Over a Four Leaf Clover

Words: Mort Dixon; Music: Harry Woods

Harry Woods and Mort Dixon wrote this song hit, one of their most famous collaborations in 1927.

In '27, "The Singing Troubador" Nick Lucas, who was also famous for playing banjo, guitar, and ukulele, Ben Bernie and his orchestra and Jean Goldkette and his orchestra had recordings of "I'm Looking Over a Four Leaf Clover" that helped popularize the song nationwide. Hear Nick Lucas' recording at http://www.redhotjazz.com/ lucas.html or hear Jean Goldkette's recording at http:// www.redhotjazz.com/goldo.html. It was perhaps even more popular in '48, when it became a reported million seller for Art Mooney and his orchestra, featuring banjoist Mike Pingatore. Art Mooney and his orchestra revived it in '48 to a No. 1 hit on *Billboard* for five weeks and the song became No. 1 on *Your Hit Parade* for two weeks. Mooney's disk was *Variety*'s No. 7 hit of the year. Mooney's recording featured the banjo playing of Mike Pingatore, who had played with Paul Whiteman and his orchestra in the '20s. In addition to Mooney's chart topping recording, there were several other successful ones including Russ Morgan and his orchestra, Alvino Rey and his orchestra, the Three Suns, the Uptown String Band and radio personality Arthur Godfrey with the Mariners.

The only movie musicals that included the song in its score were *Jolson Sings Again* ('49) and *The Jazz Singer* ('53), where it was included as part of a medley sung by Danny Thomas.

The singer is looking over a lucky four-leaf clover that he had overlooked in the past. He explains what each leaf signifies to him: sunshine, rain, roses and somebody he adores. Read the lyrics and hear a midi musical version at http://www.fourleafclover.com/words.html.

It's Magic

Words: Sammy Cahn; Music: Jule Styne

Doris Day's first film, *Romance on the High Seas*, produced this hit and made her an internationally known singer and actress. Her recording of "It's Magic" managed one week at No. 1 on *Your Hit Parade*, but peaked at No. 2 on *Billboard*.

Other charted versions in order of popularity were by Dick Haymes, Gordon MacRae, Tony Martin, Sarah Vaughan, and Vic Damone.

What's magic? The fantastic things that happen when she is in her lover's arms are magic and her love for him is also magic. Read the lyrics at http://lirama.net/song/ 16504.

Variety chose "It's Magic" for its *Hit Parade of a Half-Century*. This song was nominated for the American Film Institute's list of greatest songs ever from an American film, but was not on the final list.

Love Somebody

Words & Music: Alex Kramer & Joan Whitney

A duet recording of "Love Somebody" by Doris Day and Buddy Clark was No. 1 for five weeks on *Billboard*, but it only rose to No. 5 on *Your Hit Parade*.

Ms. Day and Mr. Clark also teamed up for a duet of Frank Loesser's "My Darling, My Darling" from the Broadway musical *Where's Charley?*, which made it to No. 7 on *Billboard* in '48. The song will be a No. 1 hit in '49 in a duet recording by Jo Stafford and Gordon MacRae.

The chorus to this song is really simplistic: "Love somebody, yes I do" is sung three times. Then the chorus concludes with the singer refusing to tell who it is she loves. Read the lyrics at http://lirama.net/song/16506.

Manana

Words & Music: Peggy Lee & Dave Barbour

This Latin number was written by singer Peggy Lee and her then-husband, guitarist Dave Barbour. It became one of the year's biggest hits, staying at No. 1 on *Billboard* for nine weeks, but only one week on *Your Hit Parade*. It was *Variety*'s No. 3 hit of the year.

"Manana (Is Soon Enough for Me)" would probably never have become popular if it had been released in today's market. Its lyrics make fun of Latin Americans, particularly accusing them of being lazy and wanting to put off any work until tomorrow ("manana"). Such ethnic humor is frowned upon and viewed as politically incorrect today. Read the lyrics at http://www.lyricsdepot.com/peggy-lee/manana.html.

Variety picked "Manana" for its *Hit Parade of a Half-Century*.

My Happiness

Words: Betty Peterson; Music: Borney Bergantine

This song was written in '33, but it was first popularized in '48 by a duet recording by Jon and Sandra Steele, which peaked at No. 2 on *Billboard*, according to *A Century of Pop Music*. However, *Billboard's Top Pop Singles of the Year* has the Steele's recording listed as the No. 5 hit of the year. It also rose to No. 2 on *Your Hit Parade*.

Other versions that charted included those by the Pied Pipers, Ella Fitzgerald, the Marlin Sisters, and John Laurenz. The Mulcays revived it in '53, when their version climbed to No. 26 on *Billboard's* chart. Connie Francis revived it again in '59, taking it to No. 2 on *Billboard*.

According to the lyrics, the singer is blue every evening because he longs to be with his girl, who is his happiness. He misses her kisses and thinks it seems like a million years since they have been together. He claims he could stand gray skies any where in the world as long as his girl was with him. Read the lyrics at http://lirama.net/song/17397.

Nature Boy

Words & Music: eden ahbez

The year '48 saw Nat "King" Cole become a major recording personality. "Nature Boy" became *Variety*'s No. 5 hit of the year, was No. 1 on *Billboard* for eight weeks and the song managed six weeks at the top of *Your Hit Parade*. This hit made him internationally famous.

Cole's recording of "Nature Boy" was inducted into the Grammy Hall of Fame in 1999. This song was nominated for the American Film Institute's list of the greatest songs ever from an American film, but did not make the final list. It was nominated for its appearance in *The Boy With Green Hair* ('48).

A Brooklyn yogi, eden ahbez, who believed that only divinities deserved capital letters, wrote "Nature Boy." He left the song at the stage door of a California theater where Cole was playing. Cole recorded it, and it leaped into immediate popularity.

The song has a Yiddish-sounding melody. The publishers of the Yiddish song "Schwieg Mein Hertz" thought it had too much similarity to their song. They later settled out of court with ahbez after the tune became a hit.

Cole tried it out a few times in his show and finally decided to record it.

The "Nature Boy" of the song was a strange and enchanted lad who espoused this beautiful philosophy to the singer one day: "The greatest thing you'll ever learn is just to love and be loved in return." Read these thoughtful lyrics at http://lirama.net/song/16510.

Variety selected "Nature Boy" for its *Hit Parade of a Half-Century*.

Now Is the Hour

Words & Music: Maewa Kaihau, Dorothy Stewart & Clement Scott

Variety's No. 6 hit in 1948's Top Ten originated in New Zealand. In Australia in 1913, "Swiss Cradle Song" by Clement Scott was published. In New Zealand Maori lyrics were added to this tune. In '20, Maewa Kaihau added more words to make a song now titled "Haere Ra Waltz Song." Over the next decade the song became a wharfside farewell song for passenger ships and eventually gained worldwide popularity as "Now Is the Hour."

Gracie Fields heard the song on a trip to New Zealand and recorded it once she was back in Great Britain.

Words for the English version were written by Dorothy Stewart.

The most popular version in the U.S. was by Bing Crosby and the Ken Darby Choir. Crosby's disk was No. 1 on *Billboard* for three weeks, while the song topped *Your Hit Parade*'s chart for ten weeks.

Other charted versions in order of popularity were by Margaret Whiting, Gracie Fields, Buddy Clark, Eddy Howard, Kate Smith, and Charlie Spivak and his orchestra.

Variety chose "Now Is the Hour" for its *Hit Parade of a Half-Century*.

Bing Crosby sang, "Now is the hour when we must say goodbye." Soon his loved one will be sailing away. He hopes he'll be remembered while she's away, because he will be waiting for her return. Read the lyrics at http://lirama.net/song/16511. See the original Maori lyrics and tune at http://folksong.org.nz/poatarau/index.html.

On a Slow Boat to China

Words & Music: Frank Loesser

This Frank Loesser number was *Variety*'s No. 9 hit of their Top Ten for the year. Kay Kyser and his orchestra's version climbed to No. 2 on *Billboard*, but spent two weeks at No. 1 on *Your Hit Parade*. Harry Babbitt and Gloria Wood were Kyser's vocalists for "On a Slow Boat to China."

Other charted versions were released by Freddy Martin and his orchestra with vocalist Glenn Hughes, by Eddy Howard, by Benny Goodman and his orchestra, by Art Lund, by Snooky Lanson, and by Larry Clinton and his orchestra.

The singer wants to get his love "on a slow boat to China," all to himself. He feels he must get the girl away from other suitors so he can melt her stone heart. Read the lyrics at http://lirama.net/song/16512.

Variety named "On a Slow Boat to China" to its *Hit Parade of a Half-Century*.

The year '48 was a great one for Frank Loesser, with this song topping *Your Hit Parade* and his "My Darling, My Darling" from his very successful Broadway musical, *Where's Charley?*, making it to No. 2. "Once in Love with Amy" from the same musical has remained very popular over the years, even though it only made it to No. 16 on *Billboard's* chart in '48.

A Tree in the Meadow

Words & Music: Billy Reid

Written by England's Billy Reid, "A Tree in the Meadow" was Margaret Whiting's first No. 1 hit—it topped the *Billboard* chart for five weeks. The song did even better on *Your Hit Parade* with ten weeks at the top. It was *Variety's* No. 4 hit in the Top Ten for the year.

Other charted versions in order of popularity were by Joe Loss, John Laurenz, Paul Fennelly with the Ames Brothers, Monica Lewis, Sam Browne, and Buddy Johnson.

The song's lyrics explain that the "tree in the meadow" is special because her lover carved "I love you till I die" on that tree. However, she saw him kissing someone else on lover's lane. Still, she wants him to know she will love him until she dies. Read the lyrics at http://lirama.net/song/16515.

Variety chose "A Tree in the Meadow" for its *Hit Parade of a Half-Century.*

Twelfth Street Rag

Words: Andy Razaf; Music: Euday L. Bowman

This ragtime classic was published as a piano rag in 1914. Lyrics were added to the music in 1916 by James S. Sumner. New lyrics were added by Spencer Williams in '29 and again by Andy Razaf in '42.

Pee Wee Hunt and his orchestra decided to do the number during one of their Capitol recording dates. When it was released, it became one of the biggest hits Capitol had released to date. It reportedly sold a million copies by '51 and was No. 2 on *Variety's* Top Ten of '48. Hunt's recording was a rousing Dixieland rendition of this ragtime number. According to *Top Pop Singles of the Year*, Pee Wee Hunt's recording of "Twelfth Street Rag" was *Billboard's* No. 1 hit of the year.

Frankie Carle and his orchestra also had a popular recording of "Twelfth Street Rag" in '48. In '54, Liberace's version peaked at No. 23 on *Billboard's* chart.

Variety named "Twelfth Street Rag" to its "Hit Parade of a Half-Century," listing it in 1914. The song became one of the most recorded songs of the pre-rock era. Five recordings of "Twelfth Street Rag" are available for listening at http://www.redhotjazz.com/bands.html: All Star Trio, Earl Fuller's Rector Novelty Orchestra, Ted Lewis and his Band, Fats Waller and his Rhythm and Paul Whiteman and his orchestra.

The sheet music cover and musical score are available at http://levysheetmusic.mse.jhu.edu/browse.html or at http://digital.library.ucla.edu/apam/. Hear a midi musical version at http://www.primeshop.com/midlist3.htm.

The song appeared in the '29 movie musical *Close Harmony.*

Woody Woodpecker

Words & Music: George Tibbles & Ramez Idriss

The infectious "ho ho ho ho ho" phrase, for which the cartoon character Woody Woodpecker is famous, is the principal ingredient of this hit song. It was introduced in the '48 cartoon *Wet Blanket Policy*. Kay Kyser and his orchestra's recording reportedly sold a million copies and was No. 1 on *Billboard* for six weeks. Gloria Wood was the vocalist on Kyser's recording. The song only managed two weeks at No. 1 on *Your Hit Parade*, but was No. 10 for *Variety* for the year. The song was also nominated for the Academy Award for the year's best song from film (it lost to "Buttons and Bows").

The voice of numerous cartoon characters, Mel Blanc, and the Sportsmen's version peaked at No. 2 on *Billboard*, while the Andrews Sisters and Danny Kaye's version made the Top 20.

By far the most memorable part of this song is Woody Woodpecker's infectious laugh. Read the lyrics at http://lirama.net/song/16516.

You Call Everybody Darling

Words & Music: Sam Martin, Ben Trace, & Clem Watts

Written in '46, "You Call Everybody Darling" was a big hit for Al Trace and his orchestra with vocalist Bob Vincent in '48. It was No. 1 on *Billboard* for six weeks and No. 1 on *Your Hit Parade* for one week.

Several other versions of the song charted on *Billboard*, including renditions by Anne Vincent, by the Andrews Sisters, by Jack Smith with the Clark Sisters, by Jerry Wayne, by Bruce Hayes, by Art Lund, and by Jack Lathrop. Al Trace released a second version of the song with vocalist Bob Vincent that peaked at No. 21 on *Billboard*.

Variety included "You Call Everybody Darlin'" in its *Hit Parade of a Half-Century.*

In the lyrics, instead of "Darling," it's "Darlin'." The singer is fussing at this girl because she calls "everybody Darlin' and everybody calls" her "Darlin'" also. He tells her if she continues doing this she will not find true love. Read the lyrics at http://lirama.net/song/16517.

You Can't Be True, Dear

Words: Hal Cotton; Music: Hans Otten & Ken Griffin

A recording of this song by organist Ken Griffin and vocalist Jerry Wayne was a first. Griffin made the recording originally in early '48, primarily as music to accompany ice skaters on public rinks. It became so popular with the skaters that the publisher Dave Dreyer decided to dub in a vocal. He signed Jerry Wayne to do the singing. The lyrics were written while Wayne was waiting to do the recording. The resulting disk was the first big success for a recording made by superimposing a voice on an already existing recording.

"You Can't Be True, Dear" became one of the top sellers of '48 (reportedly eventually selling 3 million) and was No. 8 in *Variety's* Top Ten. The original instrumental version peaked at No. 2 on *Billboard*. but the vocal version went to No. 1 and stayed there for seven weeks. The song managed three weeks at No. 1 on *Your Hit Parade.*

Other charted versions in order of popularity were by the Sportsmen, Dick Haymes, Vera Lynn, Will Glahe and his orchestra, Dick James, and the Marlin Sisters.

The song was originally written in '35 in Germany; its original title was "Du Kannst Nicht Treu Sein"; Hans Otten and Gerhard Ebeler wrote it.

The singer accuses his girl of being untrue. He tells her

that her kisses reveal to him they are through. Even though she can't be true, he says he'll continue loving her. Read both the English and the German lyrics at http://lirama.net/song/16518.

You Were Only Fooling (While I Was Falling in Love)

Words: William E. Faber & Fred Meadows; Music: Larry Fotine

Variety included "You Were Only Fooling (While I Was Falling in Love)" in its *Hit Parade of a Half-Century.*

The song began as a country hit for Patsy Cline.

Kay Starr's recording of the song was the only one that charted on *Billboard* and it peaked at No. 16 in '48.

The song managed thirteen appearances on *Your Hit Parade*, but only made it to No. 3 in late November of '48.

The title and subtitle give an excellent hint to this song's intent lyrically. A particularly pertinent thought from the lyric goes, "I was making love but you were making believe." Read the lyrics at http://lirama.net/song/18722.

1949

"A" — You're Adorable

Words & Music: Buddy Kaye, Fred Wise & Sidney Lippman

"'A' — You're Adorable," sometimes called "The Alphabet Song," was written in '48, and became a No. 1 hit through a recording by Perry Como with the Fontane Sisters. Their disk was No. 1 on *Billboard* for two weeks; the song only got up to No. 3 on *Your Hit Parade*.

"A" is adorable; "B" is beautiful; "C" is a cutie full of charms, etc. The lyrics itemize what, alphabetically speaking, his loved one means to him. Read the lyrics at http://www.metrolyrics.com/lyrics/28168/Sesame_Street/, _You're_Adorable (as you can tell from address of this website, Sesame Street has used the song to help children learn their alphabet).

Jo Stafford and Gordon MacRae, Tony Pastor and his orchestra, and the Buddy Kaye Quintet also released successful recordings of the song.

Variety selected the song for its *Hit Parade of a Half-Century* representing '47, which must have been a mistake, since it was only popularized in '49.

Again

Words: Dorcas Cochran; Music: Lionel Newman

Ida Lupino originally sang this song in the '48 film *Road House*. The song climbed to No. 1 on the *Your Hit Parade* chart, stayed there for a couple of weeks in the late spring of '49, and was among *Variety*'s Top Ten hits of the year, No. 10, tied with the Blue Barron's recording of "Cruising Down the River."

The most popular recorded versions were by Gordon Jenkins and his orchestra with Joe Graydon as vocalist and by Doris Day. Both versions peaked at No. 2 on *Billboard*, while Mel Torme's recording climbed to No. 3. Other versions include those by Vic Damone, Tommy Dorsey and

his orchestra, Art Mooney and his orchestra, and Vera Lynn. *Variety* listed Gordon Jenkins' version as tied for No. 10, while *Billboard* ranked his version No. 13 for the year.

The lyrics say that this once-in-a-lifetime thrill, that you're suddenly mine, couldn't possibly happen again, and if it doesn't, we'll have this moment to remember forever. Read the lyrics at http://lirama.net/song/16520.

"Again" is one of the songs in *Variety*'s *Hit Parade of a Half-Century*, one of only eight songs chosen for the year.

Baby, It's Cold Outside

Words & Music: Frank Loesser

Frank Loesser wrote this clever song to perform at parties, never thinking it would become a hit. However, in '48, he decided to allow it to be used in the Esther Williams film *Neptune's Daughter*. It was first sung by Esther Williams and Ricardo Montalban, then reprised, comically, by Red Skelton and Betty Garrett. The song won the Academy Award in '49. "Baby, It's Cold Outside" was nominated for the American Film Institute's list of the greatest songs ever from American films, but did not make the final list.

In the duet, the woman tells the man that she can't stay, but he says it's too cold to go out. For every reason she finds to leave, he finds a reason for her to stay. Read the lyrics at http://lirama.net/song/16522.

Several recordings charted, but Johnny Mercer and Margaret Whiting's version, which peaked at No. 3 on *Billboard*, and Dinah Shore and Buddy Clark's version, which topped out at No. 4, were the most popular ones. Other versions that charted include a duet by Ella Fitzgerald and Louis Jordan, Sammy Kaye and his orchestra's rendition, and a comical country parody by Homer and Jethro with June Carter.

The song peaked at No. 4 on *Your Hit Parade*, but appeared on the program seven times.

Leon Redbone and Zooey Deschanel performed this song on the soundtrack of the 2003 film *Elf.*

Careless Hands

Words & Music: Bob Hilliard & Carl Sigman

Mel Torme was primarily responsible for popularizing "Careless Hands"; his recording topped the *Billboard* chart for one week in the spring of '49. Sammy Kaye and his orchestra's version with vocalist Don Cornell peaked at No. 3 on *Billboard*, but they list his recording as the No. 32 hit of the year, while Torme's is not listed among the year's top hits. The song only managed to reach No. 4 on *Your Hit Parade*. Other versions were released by Bing Crosby, and by Bob and Jeanne.

The singer let his "heart fall into careless hands," and he gets his heart broken. Read the lyrics at http://lirama.net/song/16524.

Variety chose "Careless Hands" for its *Hit Parade of a Half-Century*, one of only eight songs chosen for 1949.

Cruising Down the River

Words: Eily Beadell; Music: Nell Tollerton

Two middle-aged British women wrote this popular song in '45. It won a nationwide song contest in Great Britain.

Two recordings in '49 made it to No. 1 on *Billboard*: Russ Morgan and his orchestra's version with the Skylarks and Blue Barron and his orchestra's version, both stayed at No. 1 for seven weeks. Morgan's version was No. 4 for the year for *Billboard*, and No. 6 for *Variety*. Barron's version was No. 5 for *Billboard*, and tied for No. 10 with Gordon Jenkins' "Again" for *Variety*. The song held the top spot on *Your Hit Parade* for eight weeks.

Other recordings that charted include those by Jack Smith and the Clark Sisters, Frankie Carle and his orchestra, the Three Suns, Primo Scala, the Ames Brothers, and Helen Carroll.

This waltz seems out of place in the late '40s. Its style is reminiscent of songs written forty to fifty years earlier. The carefree Sunday afternoon spent cruising down the river is a scene associated with the 1890s and early 1900s. Very few waltz meter (3) songs have made a big impact since the early days of this century on the pop song market. In that sense, the song could be considered a nostalgic hit. Read the lyrics at http://www.lirama.net/song/16525.

We must remember that in '49 it was the adults, not the youth, who still made the hits. Adults might very likely have felt sentimental about a more uncomplicated time. Several songs from the '10s and '20s were being revived into popularity during this time, so nostalgia was an important factor. Only with the coming of rock 'n' roll in the mid-'50s did the making of hit songs become the province of the young.

"Cruising Down the River" was included in the *Variety Hit Parade of a Half-Century*, one of only eight songs chosen for 1949.

Don't Cry, Joe

Words & Music: Joe Marsala

"Don't Cry, Joe (Let Her Go, Let Her Go, Let Her Go)" was the No. 1 hit on *Your Hit Parade* for three weeks in '49. Gordon Jenkins and his orchestra's recording with Betty Brewer as vocalist peaked at No. 3 on *Billboard*.

Other recordings that charted include those by Ralph Flanagan and his orchestra, by Frank Sinatra, by Johnny Desmond, and by Juanita Hall.

The lyrics are urging Joe to let this girl go and not to cry over her. The singer is advising Joe that he'll feel much better once he makes up his mind to break off this romance. Read the lyrics at http://lirama.net/song/16527.

Far Away Places

Words & Music: Joan Whitney & Alex Kramer

"Far Away Places" was featured on popular recordings by Bing Crosby with the Ken Darby Choir, by Margaret Whiting with the Crew Chiefs, by Perry Como, and by Dinah Shore. It was No. 1 on *Your Hit Parade* for three weeks in early '49. Margaret Whiting version was No. 18 for the year on *Billboard*. Crosby's version peaked at No. 2 on *Billboard*, but was No. 20 for the year on their chart.

This song may have been a hit because of servicemen who yearned to return to places they saw during World War II, or because of people at home who have learned about many places they never knew existed from their loved ones who served there or from news reports from war zones.

The singer dreams of seeing the "far away places with the strange sounding names" that are calling him. Read the lyrics at http://lirama.net/song/16529.

Variety chose "Far Away Places" for its *Hit Parade of a Half-Century* representing '48 and '49.

Forever and Ever (Fliege mit Mir in die Heimat)

Words: Malia Rosa; Music: Franz Winkler

"Forever and Ever" originated in Switzerland. The song's original German title, "Fliege mit Mir in die Heimat," meant "Fly with me to the home-land." Many people thought it was an old German folk song. Whatever its origin, it became a public domain song and became popular in the concentration camps after the war.

London Records discovered its German-language recording selling so well, it decided the song would sell even faster in English. Lyricist Malia Rosa, really May Singhi ("Ukulele Lady") Breen and Mrs. Peter DeRose, thought up simple words to match the simple tune ("Forever and ever, My heart will be true," etc.). Within days "Fliege mit Mir" became a hit in the U.S.

Variety picked "Forever and Ever" for its *Hit Parade of a Half-Century*, one of only eight songs chosen for 1949.

Gracie Fields recorded it first, but it was Russ Morgan and his orchestra with the Skylarks and Perry Como who both had recordings of the song that helped popularized it around the nation. Morgan's version spent three weeks at No. 1 on *Billboard* and ranked No. 14 for the year. Como's version peaked at No. 2 on *Billboard* and ranked No. 9 for the year. The song never made it to No. 1 on *Your Hit Parade*. Other versions that charted on *Billboard* included those by Margaret Whiting, and by Dinah Shore.

In this waltz, the singer promises to always be true. Read the lyrics at http://www.lirama.net/song/16530.

I've Got My Love to Keep Me Warm

Words & Music: Irving Berlin

"I've Got My Love to Keep Me Warm" is another revival of an old song. Irving Berlin wrote it for the '37 movie musical *On the Avenue*, where Dick Powell introduced it. Ray Noble and his orchestra were chiefly responsible for popularizing it in '37. See 1937 for more.

In '46, Les Brown and his band were in a recording session. With twenty minutes studio time left, they decided to record "I've Got My Love to Keep Me Warm." The record company decided not to release the song, so it lay around for several years. Brown and the band were playing on a Bob Hope radio show in '48 when they played the song. One of the Columbia record company executives heard the show and wired Brown to record the song immediately. Brown wired him back to look in the company files; it was already recorded. So the company released it in '49. Their version caught the public's fancy and it topped *Billboard's* chart for one week in the early spring of '49. The song only reached No. 3 on *Your Hit Parade*.

The Mills Brothers, Art Lund, and the Starlighters all released important versions of the song in '49.

The chorus lyrics present evidence that the weather is definitely unusually cold. The singer "can't remember a worse December." However, he says he doesn't need his overcoat and gloves, because he's "burning with love." He can weather any storm since he has his love to keep him warm. Read the lyrics at http://lirama.net/song/16532.

A Little Bird Told Me

Words & Music: Harvey Brooks

The No. 7 hit in *Variety*'s Top Ten of '49 and No. 3 for the year on *Billboard* was "A Little Bird Told Me." Paula

Watson introduced it, but Evelyn Knight with the Star dusters made it well known with a disk that topped the *Billboard* chart for seven weeks. The song was No. 1 on *Your Hit Parade* for three weeks.

And what did the little bird tell the singer? The bird told her that her lover loved her and that they'd be happy. Read the lyrics at http://lirama.net/song/16535.

Other charted versions were by Blu Lu Barker, by Paula Watson, and by Jerry Wayne.

Mule Train

Words & Music: Johnny Lange, Hy Heath & Fred Glickman

Frankie Laine hit the million sales figure with this rugged, western-flavored number that became *Variety*'s No. 9 hit of the year. His recording was No. 1 on *Billboard* for six weeks, and the song topped the *Your Hit Parade* survey of hits for one week. Laine's version was No. 6 for the year on *Billboard* and No. 9 on *Variety*, and No. 4 in '50 on *Cash Box*, another charting service that started in '50.

The song is the mule driver singing about his mule train's cargo, things like a "plug o'chaw tobacky," a gheetar," and a "dress of calico." Read the lyrics at http://lirama.net/song/16537.

The song provided the title for and was sung by Gene Autry in a '50 film. Vaughn Monroe sang it in *Singing Guns*, also in '50. Even though it was not specifically written for the film in which it appeared, "Mule Train" was nominated for the Academy Award for best song from film for its appearance in *Singing Guns* (it lost to "Mona Lisa").

Other recorded versions that charted include those by Bing Crosby, Tennessee Ernie Ford, Vaughn Monroe, and Gordon MacRae.

My Darling, My Darling *and* Once in Love with Amy

Words & Music: Frank Loesser

Frank Loesser wrote the musical *Where's Charley?*, which premiered in '48. One of the theater's most durable farces, *Charley's Aunt*, furnished the story. The action takes place at Oxford in 1892, when two undergraduates, Jack and Charley, wish to entertain their women friends, Amy and Kitty, but have to have a chaperone. Charley disguises himself as his aunt to fit the bill. Complications develop.

MY DARLING, MY DARLING

The show's hits were "My Darling, My Darling" and "Once in Love With Amy." "My Darling, My Darling" was Jack's salutation on a letter to his beloved Kitty. It was introduced by Byron Palmer and Doretta Morrow in the musical.

Jo Stafford and Gordon MacRae's duet version topped the *Billboard* chart for one week in early '49. The song peaked at No. 2 on *Your Hit Parade*. Doris Day and Buddy Clark also had a very popular duet version in late '48. Other charted versions were by Peter Lind Hayes and by Jack Lathrop and Eve Young.

The lyrics begin with the title and continue by declaring he has wanted to call her "my darling" for a long time. Then the singer tells his girl since she kissed him she should "get used to that name of my darling." Read the lyrics at http://lirama.net/song/11428.

ONCE IN LOVE WITH AMY

Another song from *Where's Charley?* that was popular with the public was "Once in Love With Amy," which was introduced and popularized in a recording by Ray Bolger.

Bolger's singing and dancing to "Once in Love With Amy" was an audience favorite. They often sang along as he sang, "Once in love with Amy, always in love with Amy." He is telling other guys how they might woo Amy, but in the end he tells them she'd rather stay in love with him. Read the lyrics at http://www.spiritofsinatra.com/pages/Lyrics/o/Once_in_Love_with_Amy.htm.

Powder Your Face With Sunshine

Words: Stanley Rochinsky; Music: Carmen Lombardo

Stanley Rochinsky (or Rochinski) brought Carmen Lombardo this lyric. Lombardo found it fascinating, so he set it to music. Guy Lombardo and his Royal Canadians introduced and helped popularize it. Evelyn Knight, who also had considerable success with "A Little Bird Told Me" in '49, had the most popular recording of "Powder Your Face with Sunshine." Her disk spent one week at the top of the *Billboard* chart in the early spring. The song also topped the *Your Hit Parade* survey for two weeks. Gene Autry interpolated the song into the '50 film *Cow Town*.

Dean Martin, Sammy Kaye and his orchestra, Doris Day and Buddy Clark, and Blue Barron and his orchestra released popular recordings of "Powder Your Face With Sunshine."

The song sounds like the anti–Depression songs of the early '30s. The cheerful lyrics promise that if we smile, others will smile too. As a matter of fact, the song's subtitle is "Smile! Smile! Smile!" Read the lyrics at http://lirama.net/song/16539.

Variety chose the song for its *Hit Parade of a Half-Century* representing 1948.

Red Roses for a Blue Lady

Words & Music: Sid Tepper & Roy Brodsky

Vaughn Monroe and Guy Lombardo and his Royal Canadians first popularized "Red Roses for a Blue Lady" in '49. John Laurenz also had a recording of the song that was fairly popular in '49.

Bert Kaempfert and his orchestra revived it in '65. Other recordings by Wayne Newton and by Vic Dana were also well received during the mid–'60s.

The song peaked at No. 2 on *Your Hit Parade*, but managed a dozen appearances on the hit survey.

Variety chose the song for its *Hit Parade of a Half-Century*, one of only eight songs chosen for 1949.

The singer wants the florist to take his order for red roses that will help chase his girl's blues away. He tells the florist if these flowers do their job, he will be back soon to pick out a white orchid for her wedding gown. Read the lyrics at http://lirama.net/song/16540.

Riders in the Sky

Words & Music: Stan Jones

The biggest hit song of '49 was "Riders in the Sky." This haunting Western number, subtitled "A Cowboy Legend," is evidence of country-western music's impact on the popular music scene. The composer, Stan Jones, was a park ranger. He gave the song to Bob Nolan of the Sons of the Pioneers singing group. Nolan and the group recorded the song for RCA, but their version didn't catch on with the public. Another RCA artist, Vaughn Monroe, recorded a more dramatic version that reached No. 1. His version was No. 1 on *Billboard* for a dozen weeks, while the song managed three weeks at No. 1 on *Your Hit Parade*. It was the No. 1 hit of the year on both *Billboard* and *Variety.*

"Riders in the Sky," "That Lucky Old Sun," and "Mule Train" gave 1949's songs a rustic, outdoors atmosphere.

Other recordings of the song that charted include those by Peggy Lee, by Bing Crosby, and by Burl Ives. The song was revived again in '61 and in '81 as "Ghost Riders in the Sky." The Ramrods versions in '61 peaked at No. 30, the Baja Marimba Band got to #52 in '66, while the Outlaws' '81 version peaked at No. 31.

According to Michelle Sundin from conversations with Stan Jones' wife, the story of the writing of "Riders in the Sky" is as follows: "An impressionable 12 year old rode to the top of an Arizona hill one afternoon with an old Cowboy friend to check a windmill. A big storm was building and they needed to lock the blades down before the wind hit. When finished, they paused to watch the clouds darken and spread across the sky. As lightning flashed, the Cowboy told the boy to watch closely and he would see the devil's herd, their eyes red and hooves flashing, stampede ahead of phantom horsemen. The Cowboy warned the youth that if he didn't watch himself, he would someday be up there with them, chasing steers for all eternity. The terrified boy jumped on his horse and took off for the safety of home. Years later, he recalled that scary, dark afternoon and on his 34th birthday, Stan Jones sat outside his Death Valley home and wrote '(Ghost) Riders in the Sky'" (http://www.westernmusic.org/HallOfFamefiles/StanJones.html). Read the lyrics at http://lirama.net/song/16541.

Room Full of Roses
Words & Music: Tim Spencer

"Room Full of Roses" is another song with country-western origins. Tim Spencer, the writer, was one of the Sons of the Pioneers. Gene Autry sang the song in the '50 film *Mule Train.*

In the pop music market place, the song was primarily popularized by Sammy Kaye and his orchestra, with Don Cornell as vocalist. Their version peaked at No. 2 on *Billboard*, but ranked No. 23 for the year on that chart. The song spent two weeks at No. 1 on *Your Hit Parade.*

Other versions include those by Eddy Howard, by Dick Haymes, by Jerry Wayne, by the Starlighters, by country singer George Morgan, and by the Sons of the Pioneers.

The singer tells his girlfriend if he sent a rose to her for every time she made him blue, she'd have "a room full of roses." Finally, he tells her if she thought about sending roses to him, he doesn't want them. He just wants his arms full of her. Read the lyrics at http://lirama.net/song/16542.

Slipping Around
Words & Music: Floyd Tillman

Country music was making inroads into the pop field, but generally it was by "cover" versions. If a song began to have success on the country-western chart, then some mainline popular artist would re-record the song in a "pop" version.

Country-western singer and writer Floyd Tillman got the idea for this song when he stopped at a diner and happened to overhear a woman in a phone booth say "If a man answers, hang up." Tillman assumed that the woman was "slipping around" on her husband. He wrote this song as a result of the incident and his recording of it was a hit on the country-western charts.

Capitol Records decided to record a duet version combining pop vocalist Margaret Whiting, and country-western singer and cowboy movie personality, Jimmy Wakely. Their version topped both the pop and country-western charts. The *Billboard* chart has their recording at No. 1 for three weeks and as its No. 10 hit of the year. *Variety* ranked it at No. 8 for the year.

"Slipping Around" is one of the earliest songs to tackle the subject of adultery. Perhaps because of the subject matter or because of its country-western flavor, the song only made it to No. 6 on *Your Hit Parade.* Read the lyrics at http://lirama.net/song/16543.

Someday
Words & Music: Jimmie Hodges

"Someday (You'll Want Me to Want You)" was a No. 1 hit on *Billboard* for Vaughn Monroe. His recording was No. 11 for the year on that chart. The song only made it to No. 2 on *Your Hit Parade.* The Mills Brothers version of the song peaked at No. 5 on *Billboard.*

Jimmie Hodges had written the song back in '46, when the Hoosier Hot Shots had a recording of the song that made it to No. 12 on the *Billboard* chart.

The idea of the song is that when you get around to wanting me, I may not want you. I may be in love with somebody else by then. Read the lyrics at http://lirama.net/song/16546.

Some Enchanted Evening *and* A Wonderful Guy
Words: Oscar Hammerstein II; Music: Richard Rodgers

The next colossal Rodgers and Hammerstein musical success, *South Pacific*, opened in '49. Hammerstein and Joshua Logan adapted a couple of the short stories from James A. Michener's Pulitzer prize-winning novel, *Tales of the South Pacific*, for the musical's plot. They combined "Fo' Dolla," a short story about U.S. Captain Joe Cable's romance with a Polynesian girl, with "Our Heroine," which dealt with the unlikely love between Emile de Becque, a worldly French planter, and Nellie Forbush, a naive navy nurse from Little Rock, Arkansas. The common ingredient of both stories is the power of love to break down prejudice. The musical was also built around World War II, which was still very much in the minds of Americans.

The South Pacific Original Cast album was inducted into the Grammy Hall of Fame in 1987.

SOME ENCHANTED EVENING

"Some Enchanted Evening" was introduced by Ezio Pinza, as the French planter Emile de Becque. Emile sings this passionate love song when he discovers that he has fallen in love with the navy nurse.

Perry Como's recording of the song was very successful. It climbed to No. 1 on *Billboard* and stayed there for five weeks. It was No. 7 for the year on *Billboard*, and No. 2

for the year on *Variety*. The song spent ten weeks at the top on *Your Hit Parade*.

Other recordings of the song that charted included those by Bing Crosby, by Jo Stafford, by Frank Sinatra, by Ezio Pinza, by Paul Weston and his orchestra, and by John Laurenz. It charted again in '65, when Jay and the Americans' version peaked at No. 13 on *Billboard*.

Variety selected "Some Enchanted Evening" as a *Golden 100 Tin Pan Alley Song* and included it in its *Hit Parade of a Half-Century*, one of only eight songs chosen for 1949. AFI's *100 Years ... 100 Songs* (2004) included "Some Enchanted Evening" as the No. 28 greatest song from an American film even though it was not originally from a motion picture. It was named for the 1958 film version of *South Pacific*, when Giorgio Tozzi sang for Rossano Brazzi.

See two sheet music covers at www.hulapages.com/covers_5.htm.

The basic idea of these lyrics can be summed up with the following idea: on some special evening when we feel love call we need to take advantage of the opportunity. If we don't then we may "dream all alone" for the rest of our lives. Read the lyrics at http://libretto.musicals.ru/text.php?textid=315&language=1 (Song #5).

A Wonderful Guy

Mary Martin introduced this exuberant song. She is telling the world she has found "A Wonderful Guy" to love. Read the lyrics at http://libretto.musicals.ru/text.php?textid=315&language=1 (song #10).

Margaret Whiting, Fran Warren and Dinah Shore helped popularize the song beyond the Broadway stage with successful recordings.

Variety included "A Wonderful Guy" in its *Hit Parade of a Half-Century*, one of only eight songs chosen for 1949.

Other popular songs from the score include "Bali Ha'i," "I'm Gonna Wash That Man Right Outa My Hair," "There Is Nothin' Like a Dame," "This Nearly Was Mine," and "Younger Than Springtime." Lyrics for all the above songs can be found at http://libretto.musicals.ru/text.php?textid=315&language=1.

That Lucky Old Sun

Words: Haven Gillespie; Music: Beasley Smith

Frankie Laine had two songs in *Variety*'s Top Ten of '49: "That Lucky Old Sun" was No. 6, and "Mule Train" was No. 9. "That Lucky Old Sun" spent eight weeks at the top of the *Billboard* chart and three weeks on top of *Your Hit Parade*. *Billboard* had it ranked No. 2 for the year, while *Cash Box* had it as No. 10 for 1950.

The song made a dozen appearances on *Your Hit Parade*, and collected three weeks at No. 1.

Nashville jazz pianist and bandleader Beasley Smith had composed the melody.

This song speaks of a man who is tired of working, of fussing with his woman and who longs for the day when the Lord will take him out of this life so he can be like "that lucky old sun" that just rolls around heaven all day. Read the lyrics at http://lirama.net/song/16549.

You're Breaking My Heart

Words & Music: Pat Genaro & Sunny Skylar

"You're Breaking My Heart" was based on "Mattinata ('Tis the Day)" from Ruggiero Leoncavallo's opera *I Pagliacci*. Vic Damone's record made it the No. 8 hit of the year for *Billboard* and the No. 4 for the year on *Variety*'s chart. Damone's version topped the *Billboard* chart for four weeks. The song was No. 1 on *Your Hit Parade* for six weeks.

Other charted versions in order of popularity were by Buddy Clark, by the Ink Spots, by Ralph Flanagan and his orchestra, by Jan Garber and his orchestra, and by Russ Case and his orchestra.

The lyrics tell us that the singer's heart is breaking because his lover is leaving. Read the lyrics at http://lirama.net/song/16552.

1950

All My Love

Words: Mitchell Parish; Music: Maurice Ravel; Adapted by Paul Durand

Once again a popular song is borrowed from the classics, this time "Bolero" by French composer Maurice Ravel. Patti Page's recording of the song was No.1 on *Billboard* for five weeks and *Cash Box* for three weeks. *Billboard*'s year-end chart ranked it at No. 9. The song collected five weeks at No. 1 on *Your Hit Parade*. *Variety* selected it for its *Hit Parade of a Half-Century*.

Other charted versions in order of popularity were by Percy Faith and his orchestra, by Guy Lombardo and his Royal Canadians, by Bing Crosby, and by Dennis Day.

The very distinctive bolero rhythm of Ravel's composition has probably been the key to the original's continuing popularity. The same melodic idea is repeated over and over, beginning very softly. With each repetition instruments are added, until the sound is almost deafening.

The basic idea of the text is, "I've waited all my life to give you all my love." Read the lyrics at http://lirama.net/song/16553.

"Bolero" found new popularity when the character played by Bo Derek in the highly successful movie *10* said it was her favorite lovemaking music.

Bewitched (Bothered and Bewildered)

Words: Lorenz Hart; Music: Richard Rodgers

Richard Rodgers and Larry Hart wrote "Bewitched (Bothered and Bewildered)," a *Variety Golden 100 Tin Pan Alley Song*, for the 1940 musical *Pal Joey*. Vivienne Segal introduced the song as a middle-aged woman who is cynical about falling in love again. The song was not an immediate hit, probably because it could not be played on the radio because of the ASCAP ban. Or perhaps it was due to the subject matter of the musical *Pal Joey*, which was a bit questionable for 1940 audiences.

In this song, the middle-aged woman was questioning falling in love again with a much younger man. Lines like "Couldn't sleep and wouldn't sleep until I could sleep where I shouldn't sleep" and "Horizontally speaking he's at his very best" were too risqué for the moral climate of the early '40s. Even the '50s versions most often revised the more suggestive lyrics. Read the lyrics at http://www.lorenzhart.org/bewitchedsng.htm.

In '50, the Bill Snyder Orchestra revived the song into popularity with a recording that peaked at No. 3 on

Billboard and *Cash Box* for three weeks. The song topped the *Your Hit Parade* hit survey for five weeks. This recording was Snyder's only chart single.

Other recorded versions that were popular enough to chart included those by Gordon Jenkins and his Orchestra with vocalist Bonnie Lou Williams, by Jan August, by the Harmonicats, by Mel Torme, by Doris Day, by Larry Green, and by Roy Ross.

The screen version of *Pal Joey* was released in 1957. The film starred Frank Sinatra, Rita Hayworth, and Kim Novak. Rita Hayworth was dubbed by Jo Ann Greer for her singing in the film, including "Bewitched."

A Bushel and a Peck *and* Luck Be a Lady

Words & Music: Frank Loesser

Guys and Dolls garnered several outstanding honors, including the Tony Award for the best Broadway musical of 1950. Based on Damon Runyan stories about Broadway nightlife, the show was an outstanding success. The *Guy and Dolls* Original Cast Album was inducted into the Grammy Hall of Fame in 1998.

The plot revolves around Sarah Brown, a Salvation Army Sergeant at the Save a Soul Mission in Times Square, Sky Masterson, a cool, high roller gambler, Nathan Detroit, the organizer of the "oldest established floating crap game in New York," and Adelaide, Nathan's girlfriend and showgirl at the Hot Box nightclub. Ms. Brown is desperately trying to spread the Word and make some difference in the sinful streets of the city. Adelaide is trying to get Nathan to marry her after a fourteen year engagement. Nathan is trying to find a new location for his floating dice game. Sky will bet on almost anything if it will turn him a profit. These and sundry other tipsters, gamblers, con men, and showgirls are some of the characters in this Runyan story.

A Bushel and a Peck

Vivian Blaine and the Hot Box girls squeaked out this satirical song during a floorshow scene in Frank Loesser's Broadway musical, *Guys and Dolls*.

This two-part song is made up of several verses and a chorus, a form that is more characteristic of gospel songs and songs of the late '70s, '80s, and '90s than of the '50s. Ms. Blaine sings, "I love you a bushel and a peck." Read the lyrics at http://lirama.net/song/36612.

The most popular recorded version of "A Bushel and a Peck" was a duet by Perry Como and Betty Hutton, which peaked at No. 3 on *Billboard*, and at No.4 on *Cash Box*, but the song managed to top the *Your Hit Parade* survey for one week.

Other charted versions included those by Margaret Whiting and Jimmy Wakely, by Doris Day, by the Andrews Sisters, and by Johnny Desmond.

Variety included the song in its *Hit Parade of a Half-Century* representing 1951.

Luck Be a Lady

Robert Alda, as Sky Masterson, introduced "Luck Be a Lady" in *Guys and Dolls*. He is pleading with Lady Luck to be on his side in Nathan Detroit's floating dice game. Read the lyrics at http://lirama.net/song/92253. Marlon Brando performed the song in the film version ('55).

No recordings fared well enough to chart according to *Pop Memories*.

However, "Luck Be a Lady" was named the No. 42 greatest song from an American film in AFI's 2004 list *100 Years ... 100 Songs*, even though it did not originate in a film.

Other songs from the Broadway score include "If I Were a Bell," which was popularized by Frankie Laine in a recording, plus "Adelaide's Lament," "Guy and Dolls," "I'll Know" and "Sit Down, You're Rockin' the Boat," which was nominated for AFI's list, but did not make the final list.

Chattanoogie Shoe Shine Boy

Words & Music: Harry Stone and Jack Stapp

One of the biggest country and western disks of '50 became *Variety*'s No. 9 hit of the year. Red Foley's recording of "Chattanoogie Shoe Shine Boy" was the Country Music Hall of Famer's only No. 1 hit on the *Billboard* pop music chart. Foley's disk was No. 1 on *Billboard* for eight weeks, No. 1 on *Your Hit Parade* for six weeks and peaked at No. 3 on *Cash Box*. It was No. 7 for the year on *Billboard*, and No. 9 on *Variety*. The song made nine appearances on *Your Hit Parade*, six of them at No. 1. Foley's recording reportedly was an eventual million-seller.

Variety honored the song by including it in its *Hit Parade of a Half-Century*.

Other recordings of "Chattanoogie Shoe Shine Boy" that charted on *Billboard* included those by Bing Crosby, by Phil Harris, by Frank Sinatra, by Bradford and Romano, and by Bill Darnel. Freddy Cannon revived it in 1960, when his version peaked at No. 34 on *Billboard*.

Harry Stone and Jack Stapp, employees at WSM radio in Nashville, wrote the song. The song's tune is basically a boogie-woogie bass turned into a melody.

Even though the title is spelled "Chattanoogie," Foley sounded like he pronounced it "Chattanooga." "The Chattanoogie Shoe Shine Boy" pops his shoe shine rag to a boogie woogie beat. Read the lyrics at http://lirama.net/song/16557.

The Cry of the Wild Goose

Words & Music: Terry Gilkyson

Frankie Laine's recording of "The Cry of the Wild Goose" became his third No. 1 hit on *Billboard*. It topped the *Billboard* chart for two weeks in the early spring of '50. *Your Hit Parade* ignored it.

The song was interpolated into the 1950 film *Saddle Tramp*.

"The Cry of the Wild Goose" continued the style with which Laine had experienced considerable success in the late '40s with songs like "Mule Train" and "That Lucky Old Sun."

Tennessee Ernie Ford also had a recording of "The Cry of the Wild Goose" that made it to *Billboard's* top twenty.

Frankie Laine sang about a guy who had a bad case of wanderlust. Read the lyrics at http://lirama.net/song/16558.

Dear Hearts and Gentle People

Words: Bob Hilliard; Music: Sammy Fain

The title of this song came from a phrase that early American songwriter, Stephen Foster, had scribbled on a piece of paper but never used. Like 1949's "Cruising Down the River," it sounds like a nostalgic hit.

The song's lyrics tell of the love the singer has for the "dear hearts and gentle people" who live in his/her home town. Read the lyrics at http://lirama.net/song/16526.

Bing Crosby, accompanied by Perry Botkin's String Band, had the most popular recording of "Dear Hearts and Gentle People." Crosby's disk peaked at No. 2 on the *Billboard* chart, but the song managed seven weeks at No. 1 on *Your Hit Parade*.

Other charted versions were by Dinah Shore, by Dennis Day, by Benny Strong, by Gordon MacRae, and by Ralph Flanagan and his orchestra.

Diamonds Are a Girl's Best Friend

Words: Leo Robin; Music: Jule Styne

Carol Channing introduced "Diamonds Are a Girl's Best Friend" in the musical *Gentlemen Prefer Blondes* ('49). Marilyn Monroe and Jane Russell performed this materialistic song in the film version of the musical in '53. AFI's *100 Years ... 100 Songs* (2004) listed this song as the No. 12 greatest song from an American film.

The plot of the musical centered around two gold-diggers, Lorelei Lee, played by Carol Channing, and her chum Dorothy Shaw, played by Yvonne Adair. They are tycoon hunting aboard the Ile de France during the '20s. In the film version, Marilyn Monroe was Lorelei and Jane Russell was Dorothy. The film version had a new musical score except for three songs from the original Broadway version: "Bye, Bye, Baby," "Diamonds Are a Girl's Best Friend" and a slightly changed "A Little Girl from Little Rock," which became "Two Little Girls from Little Rock."

Jo Stafford's recording of the song peaked at No. 30 on the *Billboard* chart in '50. The song never appeared on *Your Hit Parade*.

Read the lyrics and hear a sound clip of the song at http://marilynmonroepages.com/page9.html#q1.

Enjoy Yourself (It's Later Than You Think)

Words: Herb Magidson; Music: Carl Sigman

Sigman and Magidson wrote this song in '48, but it was not popular until Guy Lombardo and his Royal Canadians popularized it in a '50 recording. Another popular recording of the song was by Doris Day. According to *Pop Memories*, Lombardo's recording peaked at No. 10, while Doris Day's only made it to No. 24.

The song only made seven appearances on the *Your Hit Parade* survey and peaked at No. 7.

The lyrics encourage us to enjoy ourselves because life is much shorter than we imagine. Read the lyrics at http://www.songlyrics4u.com/guy-lombardo/enjoy-yourself.html.

Variety selected "Enjoy Yourself" as a *Hit Parade of a Half-Century* song.

Goodnight, Irene

Words & Music: Huddie Ledbetter and John Lomax

"Goodnight, Irene" is an adaptation by John Lomax of a folk song recorded by Huddie "Leadbelly" Ledbetter in 1936. The Weavers recorded the song with Gordon Jenkins and his orchestra in '50. Their disk was No. 1 on *Billboard* for thirteen weeks, which makes it the No. 7 hit of the pre-rock era. The Weavers disk was also No. 1 on *Cash Box* for ten weeks, tied with "Because of You" for the

longest stay at No. 1 on that chart. It was No. 1 for the year on *Variety*, and *Cash Box* and No. 2 on *Billboard*. The song made fifteen appearances on *Your Hit Parade* in the fall of 1950, claiming four weeks at No. 1.

Other charted recordings of "Goodnight, Irene" were by Jo Stafford, by country-western singer Red Foley, and by country-western singer Ernest Tubb.

"Goodnight, Irene" has a two-part (verse and chorus) framework. Such a form is more common of songs from the late '70s to the present than it was in the '50s. The song is incredibly simple melodically and chordally and has simplistic lyrics. In addition to being simplistic, the lyric sense is sometimes obscure, like the singer says sometimes he lives in the country, and sometimes in town, and then sometimes he has "a big notion to jump into the river and drown." However, the public seemed to thrive on the song's amateurish melody and chord structure and didn't mind, or didn't really listen to, the inane words. Read these lyrics and judge for yourselves at http://lirama.net/song/16560.

Variety selected "Goodnight, Irene" for its *Hit Parade of a Half-Century.*

Harbor Lights

Words: Jimmy Kennedy; Music: Hugh Williams

Although this song was written by English tunesmiths Will Grosz (under the pen name Hugh Williams) and Jimmy Kennedy in '37, it had its greatest fame when it was revived in '50. Sammy Kaye and his orchestra with Tony Alamo as vocalist had the most successful recording of the song. Their disk topped the *Billboard* chart for four weeks, and *Cash Box* for three weeks. Kaye's version was No. 11 for the year on *Billboard*, and No. 6 on *Variety*. The song managed two weeks at No. 1 on *Your Hit Parade*. It is a *Variety Hit Parade of a Half-Century* selection.

Other versions that charted include those by Guy Lombardo and his Royal Canadians with vocalist Kenny Gardner, by Ray Anthony and his orchestra, by Ralph Flanagan and his orchestra, by Bing Crosby, by organist Ken Griffin, and by Jerry Byrd and Jerry Murad's Harmonicats. "Harbor Lights" was revived by the Platters in '60; their version peaked at No. 8 on *Billboard*.

The lyrics say the "harbor lights" that once brought his girl to him are now taking her away because she was on a ship and he was on the shore. Read the words at http://lirama.net/song/16561.

Hoop-Dee-Doo

Words: Frank Loesser; Music: Milton DeLugg

This novelty polka was a No. 1 hit on the *Billboard* chart for a couple of weeks during the early summer of '50. Perry Como's recording of the song with the Fontane Sisters was the most popular version. His disk peaked at No. 4 on *Cash Box* and the song only made it to No. 3 on *Your Hit Parade*. *Variety* thought enough of it to include it in its *Hit Parade of a Half-Century.*

Other versions that charted were those by Kay Starr, by Russ Morgan and his orchestra, and by Doris Day.

The singer hears a polka and his troubles are over, because this type of music is like heaven to him. He wants someone to "hand me down my soup and fish" (a typical Polish lunch usually consisted of soup and salmon or herring), because he is getting his wish to "Hoop-Dee-Doo it tonight." There isn't an explanation of exactly what "hoop-dee-doin'" means, but it can be assumed to be celebrating. Read the words at http://ntl.matrix.com.br/pfilho/html/lyrics/h/hoop-dee-doo.txt.

I Can Dream, Can't I?

Words: Irving Kahal; Music: Sammy Fain

Sammy Fain and Irving Kahal wrote "I Can Dream, Can't I?" in '37 and it was introduced by Tamara in the '38 musical *Right This Way*.

"I Can Dream, Can't I?" was listed on *Variety's Hit Parade of a Half-Century* for '50 because of the very popular Andrews Sisters' recording of the song, which was released in '49 and had reportedly sold a million copies by '50. The song had originally been a hit recording for Tommy Dorsey in '38, but was much more popular in '50. In addition to the Andrews Sisters' disk which went to No. 1 on *Billboard*, recordings by Toni Arden and by Tex Beneke were also popular.

"I Can Dream, Can't I?" had only three appearances on *Your Hit Parade* in '38, peaking at No. 4, but it collected 17 weeks in late '49 and early '50, with two weeks at the top of the hits survey.

The girl sings about a guy who will never belong to her, but she says, "I can dream, can't I?" She's aware that her dream is disillusioned. Read the lyrics at http://lirama.net/song/120.

I Wanna Be Loved

Words: Billy Rose and Edward Heyman; Music: John Green

"I Wanna Be Loved" was introduced in '32 in Billy Rose's Casino de Paree in New York City. A '50 recording by Patty Andrews of the Andrews Sisters brought it back to the public's attention. Her recording of the song climbed to the top of both the *Billboard* and *Cash Box* charts and stayed there on both for two weeks. It was No. 7 for the year on *Cash Box*, and No. 13 on *Billboard*. The song fizzled at No. 2 on *Your Hit Parade*'s hit survey.

Other recordings of "I Wanna Be Loved" that charted were those by Billy Eckstine, by Hugo Winterhalter and his orchestra, by Dinah Washington, by Dottie O'Brien, and by Jan Garber and his orchestra.

"I Wanna Be Loved" is a *Variety Hit Parade of a Half-Century* song.

This girl wants to be loved and tells the guy "instead of merely holding conversation hold me tight." She says she wants to do more than "turtledoving." Read the lyrics at http://lirama.net/song/16563.

If I Knew You Were Comin' I'd've Baked a Cake

Words & Music: Al Hoffman, Bob Merrill, and Clem Watts

An obscure Chicago publisher of hymns, Maurice Wells, bought this *Variety Hit Parade of a Half-Century* song for $300 and persuaded some friends to sing it on the *Breakfast Club Radio Show*, which was broadcast early each morning. Before the day was over several publishers were seeking publishing rights to the song. Brooklyn-born Eileen Barton got to record the song, and it brought her her only No.1 hit.

Barton's version of the song topped the *Billboard* chart for ten weeks, while the song managed three weeks at No.

1 on both *Your Hit Parade* and *Cash Box*. Her disk was No. 5 for the year on *Billboard*, and No. 8 on *Cash Box*. Other versions that charted include those by Georgia Gibbs, by Benny Strong, by Ethel Merman and Ray Bolger, and by Art Mooney and his orchestra.

Like a folk song, parts of the text repeat, and the melody has a limited range and stepwise movement. A distinctive lyric in the song is "How ja do," which is repeated twice. It has a contagious down-home friendliness about it that the American public found interesting. Read the words at http://ntl.matrix.com.br/pfilho/html/lyrics/i/if_i_knew_you_were_comin.txt.

It Isn't Fair

Words & Music: Richard Himber, Frank Warshauer, and Sylvester Sprigato

This '33 oldie was revived in '50 by Sammy Kaye and his orchestra with vocalist Don Cornell. Their disk peaked at No. 2 on *Billboard* and the song topped out at No. 2 on *Your Hit Parade*, but it managed one week at No. 1 on *Cash Box*. *Cash Box*'s year-end chart had it at No. 2, which seems strange with only one week at the top, while *Billboard* had it ranked No. 18 for the year.

Other recordings of "It Isn't Fair" that charted were those by Benny Goodman and his orchestra, by Bill Farrell, and by Les Brown and his orchestra.

What isn't fair? It isn't fair for the girl to want him and taunt him "if it's just for a day." Read the lyrics at http://lirama.net/song/15855.

Variety chose "It Isn't Fair" for its *Hit Parade of a Half-Century*.

La Vie en Rose

Words: Edith Piaf; Music: Louiguy

Louiguy and Edith Piaf wrote this French song in '46. Frank Eyton wrote an English lyric in '47, while Mack David authored another in '50.

Edith Piaf's recording of "La Vie en Rose" has reportedly sold more than 3 million copies globally through the years. Her recording was inducted into the Grammy Hall of Fame in 1998.

In '50, Tony Martin had a successful recording of the song with Mack David's English lyrics. His version peaked at No. 4 on *Cash Box*, and at No. 9 on *Billboard*, but the song managed one week at No. 1 on *Your Hit Parade*.

Other recordings of the song that charted were those by Paul Weston and his orchestra, by Bing Crosby, by Edith Piaf, by Ralph Flanagan and his orchestra, by Victor Young and his orchestra, and by Louis Armstrong.

Variety selected "La Vie en Rose" as one of the songs of 1950 for its *Hit Parade of a Half-Century*.

The singer wants her loved one to hold her fast. The "magic spell you cast ... is la vie en rose." "La vie en rose" is French for "life in pink." Read Edith Piaf's French version at http://lirama.net/song/32000 or the English version at http://lirama.net/song/24204.

Mona Lisa

Words & Music: Jay Livingston and Ray Evans

"Mona Lisa" was introduced in the '49 film *Captain Carey, U.S.A.* It was heard only in fragments and in Italian on the soundtrack, but it won the Oscar for the Best Song from a film in '50.

Nat "King" Cole agreed to record the song only after the writers almost begged. His recording topped the *Billboard* chart for eight weeks, and the song was No. 1 on the *Cash Box* chart for four weeks, and the *Your Hit Parade* survey for eight weeks. His disk was No. 6 for the year on *Billboard*, and No. 3 on both *Variety* and *Cash Box*. Cole's recording stayed on the best-seller chart for twenty-seven weeks, reportedly sold more than three million copies and was inducted into the Grammy Hall of Fame in 1992.

Leonardo da Vinci's "Mona Lisa" was the inspiration for the song. The Mona Lisa of the song has a mystic smile. The lyrics ask if that smile is to tempt a lover or is it hiding a broken heart. The singer asks if Mona Lisa is "just a cold and lonely, lovely work of art?" He was, of course, comparing his love one to the painting's Mona Lisa. Read the lyrics at http://lirama.net/song/16565.

Several other recordings of "Mona Lisa" were popular with the public and charted on *Billboard*. Among those were versions by Victor Young and his orchestra with vocalist Don Cherry, by Harry James and his orchestra with vocalist Dick Williams, by Art Lund, by Ralph Flanagan and his orchestra with vocalist Harry Prime, by Charlie Spivak and his orchestra, and by Dennis Day.

"Mona Lisa" was selected by *Variety* for its *Hit Parade of a Half-Century*. This song was nominated for the American Film Institute's list of the greatest songs from American films, but it did not make the final list.

Music! Music! Music!

Words & Music: Stephen Weiss and Bernie Baum

Singer Teresa Brewer had her first major hit recording with "Music! Music! Music!" This disk became *Billboard* and *Cash Box*'s No. 6 hit of the year, and *Variety*'s No. 5. It was No. 1 on *Billboard* for four weeks and *Cash Box* for five weeks. The song peaked at No. 2 on *Your Hit Parade*.

This peppy tune requests us to put a nickel in the nickelodeon, the jukebox, because all she wants is "loving you and music, music, music." Read the lyrics at http://lirama.net/song/16568.

Other recordings of this *Variety Hit Parade of a Half-Century* song that charted include those by pianist Carmen Cavallaro, by Freddy Martin and his orchestra with later talk-show host and eventual multi-millionaire Merv Griffin as vocalist, by the Ames Brothers, by Hugo Winterhalter and his orchestra with a vocal performance by the Five Gems, plus Mickey Katz and his orchestra's humorous version. Katz, the father of actor Joel Grey, had previously played with Spike Jones and his City Slickers.

See the sheet music cover at http://www.perfessorbill.com/index2.htm.

My Foolish Heart

Words: Ned Washington; Music: Victor Young

My Foolish Heart was the title song of a '49 film. Susan Hayward sang the title song on the soundtrack; it was an Academy Award nominee, but lost to "Mona Lisa."

Gordon Jenkins and his orchestra with vocalist Sandy Evans had the most popular recording of the song. Their version peaked at No. 3 on *Billboard*, but topped the *Cash Box* chart for three weeks. The song collected nine weeks at No. 1 on *Your Hit Parade*. Jenkins' version was No. 34 for the year on *Billboard*, while Billy Eckstine's version was in the top thirty.

In addition to those two recordings, others that charted

include those by Mindy Carson, by Margaret Whiting, by Richard Hayes, and by Hugo Winterhalter and his orchestra.

Variety selected "My Foolish Heart" for its *Hit Parade of a Half-Century*.

Ned Washington's lyrics begin, "The night is like a lovely tune, beware my foolish heart!" The lyrics remind us that the line between love and fascination is often difficult to determine, especially when we're lost in a passionate kiss. The singer is confident this is love, not merely fascination. Read the lyrics at http://www.oldielyrics.com/lyrics/frank_sinatra/my_foolish_heart.html.

Nevertheless

Words: Bert Kalmar; Music: Harry Ruby

Quite a few songs that were hits in the late forties and early fifties were revivals. "Nevertheless" was written by Ruby and Kalmar in '31. Jack Denny and his orchestra with vocalist Rob May had popularized the song in the early thirties with a popular recording. Johnny Hamp and his orchestra's recording of the song can be heard at http://www.redhotjazz.com/hampo.html.

When Ruby and Kalmar's screen biography, *Three Little Words*, was released in '50; "Nevertheless (I'm in Love With You)" found new life. It was performed in the film by Anita Ellis (her voice was dubbed for Vera-Ellen) and Fred Astaire. The song climbed to No. 1 on *Your Hit Parade* for one week in December 1950.

Actually, in '49, the Mills Brothers released their version, which peaked at No. 4 on *Billboard*. In '50, Paul Weston and his orchestra with the Norman Luboff Choir had their recording reach No. 2 on *Billboard*; it could only manage No. 4 on *Cash Box*.

Other recordings of "Nevertheless" that charted in '50 include those by Ray Anthony and his orchestra with Ronnie Deauville and the Skyliners, by Ralph Flanagan and his orchestra with vocalist Harry Prime, by Frankie Laine, and by Frank Sinatra.

Even though it was written in '31, "Nevertheless" was chosen by *Variety* for its *Hit Parade of a Half-Century* representing '50.

The most familiar part of Kalmar's lyrics is the singer singing he may be right or wrong, weak or strong, but "nevertheless" he's in love. Read the lyrics at http://www.elyrics4u.com/n/nevertheless_the_mills_brothers.htm.

The Old Master Painter

Words: Haven Gillespie; Music: Beasley Smith

This *Variety Hit Parade of a Half-Century* song, published in '49, was introduced by Snooky Lanson and popularized by Richard Hayes in a popular recording in '50

Hayes' recording climbed to No. 2 on *Billboard*. Other versions that charted include those by Dick Haymes, by Peggy Lee and Mel Torme, by Phil Harris, by Snooky Lanson, and by Frank Sinatra.

"The Old Master Painter" collected eight weeks on the *Your Hit Parade* survey, peaking at No. 2 in early '50.

In the context of the lyrics, "the old master painter" is analogous to God or the Supreme Being, because he created the beauty of nature. In addition to natural wonders, his masterpiece was when "he smiled down from heaven and he gave me you." Read the lyrics at http://lirama.net/song/16567.

Play a Simple Melody *and* Sam's Song
Words & Music: Various

PLAY A SIMPLE MELODY

In another revival of an oldie, Bing and Gary Crosby, father and son, recorded Irving Berlin's "Play a Simple Melody," which was originally introduced by Sallie Fisher and Charles King in the '14 Broadway revue *Watch Your Step*. The '14 sheet music cover indicates the title was "(Won't You Play) A Simple Melody," but the '50 recording was titled "Play a Simple Melody."

Variety chose this song for its *Hit Parade of a Half-Century* representing 1914. Walter Van Brunt and Mary Carson and Billy Murray and Elsie Baker helped popularize the song in 1915–16.

The Crosby disk read "by Gary Crosby and Friend," and with "Sam's Song" on the flip side, the record became No. 4 in *Variety*'s top ten for the year. The father and son version peaked at No. 2 on *Billboard*. Other versions that charted in '50 include those by Jo Stafford, by Georgia Gibbs and Bob Crosby, and by Phil Harris.

According to *Your Hit Parade*, the song appeared eleven times on their hit survey, peaking at No. 2.

In *Watch Your Step* back in '14 the song was introduced in a scene where one man, Algy Cuffs played by Charles King, asks his friend Kilgobbin if he had been to the theater that evening. Kilgobbin said he had been to the opening of *The Onion Girl*. He thought there was one crackerjack song in the production, but couldn't remember exactly how it went. Algy's girlfriend picked up the cue and proceeded to sing a syncopated tune about a "musical demon." Then Kilgobbin complained that "this new music gives me a pain." Then Stella (Sallie Fisher) agreed with Kilgobbin and sang what seemed to be a completely different tune. Later, the two melodies are performed simultaneously. It was pure musical propaganda, suggesting that traditional popular fare could coexist with ragtime.

In Bing and Gary Crosby's version of this delightful song the father (Bing) sings, "Play a simple melody," like those that were popular when I was young. The son (Gary) then sings, "No! Play a tune that is snappy." In '14, Berlin was talking about ragtime, but in every age there has existed that generation gap, whether it was during the roaring '20s, the early rock 'n' roll years of the mid–'50s or today. When the two melodies are combined to make beautiful contrapuntal harmonies it signifies that the different musical generations can make beautiful music together. Read the lyrics at http://www.lyricsfreak.com/i/irving-berlin/68134.html.

The sheet music cover and musical score are available at http://levysheetmusic.mse.jhu.edu/browse.html.

Ethel Merman and Dan Dailey sang "Play a Simple Melody" in the '54 movie musical *There's No Business Like Show Business*.

SAM'S SONG

The flip side of the record was "Sam's Song" with lyrics by Jack Elliott and music by Lew Qualding. Gary and Bing's recording made it to No. 3 on the Billboard chart in '49. Ragtime pianist Joe "Fingers" Carr's recording of the song made it to No. 7 in '50. The song made a dozen appearances on the *Your Hit Parade* survey of hits and peaked at No. 2 in mid–August 1950.

Variety included "Sam's Song" in its *Hit Parade of a Half-Century* representing 1950.

This happy, catchy tune will help you forget your troubles and you'll wear a smile if you sing it. The first time through the song was sung straight, but on the repeat Bing interpolated faster pace lyrics (patter) between the original lines. Read the lyrics at http://www.oldielyrics.com/lyrics/bing_crosby/sams_song.html.

Rag Mop
Words & Music: Johnnie Lee Wills and Deacon Anderson

This bouncy, rhythmical song uses only six different notes. It throws in a few nonsense syllables for variety, and *voila* a big hit! The Ames Brothers' recording, backed with "Sentimental Me," was No. 1 for two weeks on *Billboard*. The song only rose to No. 2 on *Cash Box* and No. 4 on *Your Hit Parade*. The Ames Brothers' disk was No. 10 for the year on *Variety* and No. 14 on *Billboard*.

Other versions that charted included those by Ralph Flanagan and his orchestra, by Lionel Hampton and his orchestra, by Johnnie Lee Wills, by the Starlighters, by Jimmy Dorsey and his orchestra, and by Eddy Howard.

These rather simplistic lyrics basically spell "Rag Mop," beginning with "Mop," then "Rag." Read these lyrics at http://lirama.net/song/16570.

Rudolph, the Red-Nosed Reindeer
Words & Music: Johnny Marks

This Christmas favorite became Columbia Records' all-time bestseller in the early '50s. The lyrics were based on Robert L. May's book. Gene Autry introduced and recorded the song with the Pinafores. His disk reportedly had reached a million in sales by '50 and went on to sell more than seven million. Autry's version was No. 1 on *Billboard* for one week, while the song topped the *Your Hit Parade* survey for two weeks. The song charted on *Billboard* at the beginning of '50 (the end of the '49 Christmas season), and at the end of '50, in '51, '52, and '53. Autry's recording was voted into the Grammy (NARAS) Hall of Fame in 1985.

During the pre-rock era, there is hardly ever a definitive version of any song, but Gene Autry's version comes close. The only other recordings that charted were by Spike Jones and his City Slickers, and by Bing Crosby.

Sales of more than 450 versions in the United States rose to more than 75 million by the end of the seventies, and the song continues to sell more every Christmas. Foreign sales have contributed another 36 million.

"Rudolph..." is the runner-up to "White Christmas" as the top seasonal song in sales during the pre-rock era. ASCAP selected it in 1963 as one of sixteen songs to appear in its "All-Time Hit Parade." The song became one of the most recorded songs of the pre-rock era.

Just about everyone knows the story and the song about "Rudolph, the Red-Nosed Reindeer" and his leading Santa's sleigh on a foggy night. Read the words at http://www.carols.org.uk/rudolf_the_red_nosed_reindeer.htm.

Sentimental Me
Words: Jimmy Cassin; Music: Jim Morehead

"Sentimental Me" was first popularized by Ben Selvin and his orchestra and by the Arden-Ohman Orchestra in

'25 and '26 respectively. In '50, the Ames Brothers had back to back hits with "Rag Mop" and "Sentimental Me." Both songs made it to No. 1 on *Billboard*; "Sentimental Me" topped the chart for one week in early summer. It peaked at No. 3 on both *Your Hit Parade* and *Cash Box*. *Variety* listed the Ames Brothers' "Rag Mop/Sentimental Me" as its No. 10 hit of the year.

Ray Anthony and his orchestra and Russ Morgan and his orchestra also had versions of "Sentimental Me" that were popular enough with the public to chart.

The singer he is so in love that he'll always be sentimental. Read the lyrics at http://www.lirama.net/song/16571.

Tennessee Waltz
Words & Music: Redd Stewart & Pee Wee King
Redd Stewart and Pee Wee King wrote this song in '48, when it was popularized on the country-western chart. Pee Wee King's recording of the song made *Billboard's* Top 30 in '48, but the song became phenomenally successful after Patti Page recorded it in '50. Her recording of "Tennessee Waltz" reportedly sold more than six million copies during the next twenty years. It was No. 1 on *Billboard* for thirteen weeks, No. 1 for '50. Those thirteen weeks rank the song No. 5 for the pre-rock era for *Billboard*. Patti Page's disk was No. 1 on *Cash Box* for six weeks, and their No. 1 of '51. It was *Variety*'s No. 2 hit of the year. Her recording was one of the earliest multi-track recordings. Multi-tracking allowed her to harmonize with her own voice. The song was No. 1 on *Your Hit Parade* for six weeks.

Guy Lombardo and his Royal Canadians' version with Kenny Gardner as vocalist was No. 1 on *Cash Box* for one week. Their recording was No. 40 in '51 on the *Billboard* chart. Other versions that charted included those by Les Paul and Mary Ford, by Jo Stafford, a comical version by Spike Jones and his City Slickers, by the Fontane Sisters, and by Anita O'Day. Sam Cooke revived the song in '64 with some success.

In '65, the state of Tennessee chose "Tennessee Waltz" as its official state song. Patti Page's recording of the song was inducted into the Grammy Hall of Fame in 1998. *Variety* selected "Tennessee Waltz" for its *Hit Parade of a Half-Century* representing '51.

The singer was dancing with her sweetheart when she noticed an old friend. She introduced this friend to her loved one and she lost her darling as her friend and loved one danced to "the beautiful Tennessee Waltz." Read the lyrics at http://lirama.net/song/18486.

The Thing
Words & Music: Charles R. Grean
Charles R. Grean adapted an old Rabelaisian song, "The Tailor's Boy," into "The Thing," which became a *Variety Hit Parade of a Half-Century* selection.

The words never specify what "the thing" is; there is a period of silence followed by three booms on the drum, instead, allowing each listener to determine what this horrible thing was. Read the lyrics at http://www.oldielyrics.com/lyrics/phil_harris/the_thing.html. There was a horror film released in '51 titled *The Thing*, but the two do not seem to be related in any way.

Phil Harris's recording of "The Thing" was No. 1 on *Billboard* for three weeks and on *Cash Box* for two weeks.

The song rose to No. 2 on *Your Hit Parade*. It was No. 8 for the year on *Variety* and was No. 10 on *Billboard*.

Arthur Godfrey and the Ames Brothers were the only others who recorded the song with enough success that their versions charted, and both versions never made the Top Twenty.

The Third Man Theme
Words & Music: Anton Karas
Anton Karas, a zither player from Vienna, was hired to furnish the soundtrack music for Orson Welles's *The Third Man*, which needed music appropriate to postwar Vienna. Karas composed the theme, which is variously called "The Third Man Theme" or "The Harry Lime Theme," for the main character in the film. Karas's recording from the soundtrack reportedly sold four million copies, and total disk sales for the song were estimated to have reached more than 40 million.

Karas's disk was No. 1 on *Billboard* for eleven weeks, *Cash Box* for two weeks. Guy Lombardo and his Royal Canadians' version also topped *Billboard* for eleven weeks. The song didn't fare quite as well on *Your Hit Parade*; it only made it to No. 2. Karas' version was No. 3 for the year on *Billboard* and *Cash Box*, No. 2 on *Variety*. Lombardo's version was No. 4 for the year on *Billboard* and No. 7 on *Variety*. Karas' version ranks No. 19 of the pre-rock era.

Variety chose "The Third Man Theme" for its *Hit Parade of a Half-Century*.

Other recordings of the song that sold well enough to chart include those by Freddy Martin and his orchestra, by Hugo Winterhalter and his orchestra, by Victor Young and his orchestra, and by Owen Bradley and his orchestra.

Although this song is primarily known as an instrumental, read the lyrics at http://lirama.net/song/16573.

Tzena, Tzena, Tzena
Words: Mitchell Parish; Music: Issachar Miron & Yehiel Haggiz
The Weavers sparked a rebirth of interest in folk music that culminated in the folk song craze of the early '60s. Their recording of this Jewish song was almost as popular as the "A" side of the record "Goodnight Irene." "Tzena, Tzena, Tzena" was, most likely, the first Hebrew folksong to become a popular song hit.

"Tzena, Tzena, Tzena" went through a metamorphosis before it got to this recording. The song dates from the pre-independence days of Israel. Written in '41, it was rewritten by Julius Grossman in '47 and arranged by Spencer Ross to lyrics by Gordon Jenkins. That version was forced off the market by legal action. The '50 version had lyrics by Mitchell Parish and was recorded by the Weavers with Gordon Jenkins and his orchestra.

The Weavers' recording made it to No. 2 on *Billboard*. Other versions that charted include those by Mitch Miller, by Vic Damone, and by Ralph Flanagan and his orchestra. The song only managed three appearances on *Your Hit Parade*, peaking at No. 5.

Variety chose "Tzena..." for its *Hit Parade of a Half-Century*.

Read the Hebrew lyrics and an English translation ("Go Forth, Daughters") at http://www.hebrewsongs.com/song-tzenatzena.htm.

1951

Be My Love

Words: Sammy Cahn; Music: Nicholas Brodszky

Variety's No. 6 hit in 1951's Top Ten was "Be My Love" as recorded by Mario Lanza. Lanza and Kathryn Grayson introduced the song in the '50 movie musical *Toast of New Orleans*. Lanza's recording only managed one week at No.1 on *Billboard*, and the song peaked at No. 2 on both *Your Hit Parade* and *Cash Box*. It was No. 4 for the year on *Cash Box*, however, and No. 9 on *Billboard*. The song was nominated for the Academy Award for Best Song, but lost to "Mona Lisa."

Ray Anthony and his orchestra and Billy Eckstine also had versions of the song that were popular enough to chart, but their recordings were far behind Lanza's in popularity.

Most of the score for the film consisted of excerpts from operas, but the audiences seemed to be most impressed with "Be My Love." Lanza's operatic tenor voice was the perfect style for this song. The melody is dramatic and shows off Lanza's vocal agility, range, and power.

Lanza passionately sang, "Be my love for no one else can end this yearning." He promises if she will be his love they will "find love's promised land." Read the lyrics at http://lirama.net/song/16577.

Doretta Morrow performed the song in *Because You're Mine* ('52) and Connie Francis performed it in *Looking for Love* ('64).

"Be My Love" is a *Variety Hit Parade of a Half-Century* song. "Be My Love" was nominated for the American Film Institute's list of the greatest songs ever from American films, but did not make the final list.

Because of You

Words: Arthur Hammerstein; Music: Dudley Wilkinson

"Because of You," a 1940 song, became popular in '51 when it was featured in the film *I Was an American Spy*. It was also used as incidental music in the '51 Claudette Colbert film *Let's Make It Legal*.

Tony Bennett had his first million seller with his recording of "Because of You," which stayed on top of *Your Hit Parade* for eleven weeks in '51. That's the second longest stay at No. 1 on *Your Hit Parade*, next to the twelve weeks that "Too Young" spent there. Bennett's disk spent ten weeks at No. 1 on both *Billboard* and *Cash Box*. The ten weeks at No. 1 on *Cash Box* is tops for that chart, tied with "Goodnight, Irene." Ten weeks at No. 1 on *Billboard* ranks No. 33 of the pre-rock era. It was No. 1 for the year on *Variety*, No. 2 on *Billboard*, and No. 5 on *Cash Box*.

Other versions that were popular enough with the public to chart include those by Les Baxter and his orchestra, by Gloria DeHaven with Guy Lombardo and his Royal Canadians, by Jan Peerce, by Johnny Desmond, by Tab Smith, and by Ray Barber. Larry Clinton and his orchestra had recorded the song back in '41, but their version didn't make much of an impact.

The lyrics say that "because of you" there's a song in the singer's heart. Also because of her his life will now be worthwhile and he can smile. Read the lyrics at http://lirama.net/song/16579.

Lyricist Arthur Hammerstein was the uncle of famed lyricist Oscar Hammerstein II.

"Because of You" was selected for *Variety*'s *Hit Parade of a Half-Century*.

Cold, Cold Heart

Words & Music: Hank Williams

In the early fifties, a few country music stars like Eddy Arnold began to bridge the gap between country and western music and main-line popular music, and a few songs transcended their country music origin to become top popular songs. Such a song was Hank Williams' "Cold, Cold Heart."

Tony Bennett's cover version stayed at the top of the *Billboard* chart for six weeks in the early winter of '51, which qualified it to be No. 7 for the year for *Billboard*. It was No. 1 on *Cash Box* for two weeks. The song never made it to the top of *Your Hit Parade*, even though it stayed on the program for eleven weeks. It peaked at No. 2. It was No. 5 for the year on *Variety*.

The Fontane Sisters, Eileen Wilson, Hank Williams, and Tony Fontane also had recordings of the song that charted.

Variety selected "Cold, Cold Heart" for its *Hit Parade of a Half-Century*.

When Hank Williams died in a tragic car accident in '53 he became a country music legend. He was named to the Country Music Hall of Fame in '61 and his screen biography, *Your Cheating Heart*, was filmed in '64. His son, Hank, Jr., has also become a country music star.

The most famous line from the lyric is, "Why can't I free your doubtful mind and melt your cold, cold heart?" Read the lyrics at http://lirama.net/song/16581.

Come on-a My House

Words & Music: Ross Bagdasarian and William Saroyan

"Come on-a My House" is an adaptation of an Armenian folk song that playwright William Saroyan and his cousin, Ross Bagdasarian, remembered from their childhoods. On an automobile trip through the western states in '49, the two devised the song, which Saroyan used in his '49 off–Broadway play *Son*. Kay Armen recorded it at that time. Mitch Miller, then recording director of popular music at Columbia, decided to have Rosemary Clooney record the song. Released in '51, it became her first No. 1 hit. It was No. 1 on *Billboard* for eight weeks, which qualified it to be *Billboard*'s No. 6 hit of the year. It was No. 1 on *Cash Box* for four weeks, their No. 9 hit of the year. *Variety* ranked it as its No. 8 hit of 1951. The song peaked at No. 2 on *Your Hit Parade*.

Other versions of the song that were popular enough to chart included those by Kay Starr, by Richard Hayes, and a comical version by Mickey Katz and his orchestra.

In the recording an unusual effect suggested by Miller, was the use of a harpsichord to accompany Clooney.

"Come on-a My House" was chosen by *Variety* for its *Hit Parade of a Half-Century*.

The singer invites us to "Come on-a my house." If we come she promises to give us candy and more ("I'm gonna give you everything"). Read the words at http://ntl.matrix.com.br/pfilho/html/lyrics/c/come_on_a_my_house.txt.

Ross Bagdasarian was later responsible for the famous "Chipmunk" recordings, which began in '58.

Cry

Words & Music: Churchill Kohlman

Johnnie Ray cried himself to fame and fortune in the early '50s with two hits: "Cry" backed by "The Little White Cloud That Cried" (see '52). This disk was both *Cash Box*'s and *Variety*'s biggest hit of the year, plus "Cry" was *Billboard*'s No. 1 hit for '51. It stayed at No. 1 on *Billboard* for eleven weeks, on *Cash Box* for eight weeks, and the song was the top hit on *Your Hit Parade* for five weeks. "Cry" was a much bigger hit than "The Little White Cloud...," but both songs did very well. With eleven weeks at No. 1, "Cry" ranks as the No. 21 hit of the pre-rock era for *Billboard*.

Churchill Kohlman, a Pittsburgh dry cleaning plant watchman, entered "Cry" into an amateur songwriting contest at the Copa Night Club in Pittsburgh. It was eliminated in the first round, while another Kohlman song made it to the finals. "Cry" didn't make much of an impression until Johnnie Ray recorded it. Johnnie's recording of the song was inducted into the Grammy Hall of Fame in 1998.

Three other recordings of the song charted. The others were by Eileen Barton, by the Four Knights, and by Georgia Gibbs.

"Cry" was a *Variety Hit Parade of a Half-Century* song representing 1952.

Johnnie Ray tells us if our sweetheart sends us a goodbye letter, we'll feel better if we cry. And Ray really milked the word "cry," with lots of emphasis on the first consonant. Read the lyrics at http://www.lyricsdepot.com/johnnie-ray/cry.html.

Down Yonder

Words & Music: L. Wolfe Gilbert

The composer, L. Wolfe Gilbert, introduced "Down Yonder" at the Orpheum Theater in New Orleans in 1921. Several important singers of the time used it in their acts, but when Gilbert published it, it never sold very well. Recordings by Ernest Hare and Billy Jones and by the Peerless Quartet popularized the song in 1921.

The song lay practically forgotten for a dozen years, when in '34, Gid Tanner and his Skillet Lickers, a hillbilly quartet, revived it.

Once again it disappeared for several years until country pianist Del Wood recorded it in '51. The disk rose to No. 4 on the *Billboard* chart. The song appeared on the *Your Hit Parade* survey of hits fourteen weeks, peaking at No. 2 for the January 19, 1952 broadcast.

There were quite a few other recorded versions on the market in 1951. Other recordings were by Joe "Fingers" Carr, by Freddy Martin, by Ethel Smith, by Champ Butler, by Lawrence (Piano Roll) Cook, and by the Frank Petty Trio.

Variety chose "Down Yonder" to appear on its *Hit Parade of a Half-Century* for 1951.

Since the song was copyrighted in 1921, the chorus lyrics follow: *Down yonder someone beckons to me, Down yonder someone reckons to me. / I seem to see a race in memory, Between the Natchez and the Robert E. Lee, / Swanee shore, I miss you more and more Ev'ry day, my Mammy land, you're simply grand. / Down yonder when the folks get the news, Don't wonder at the hullabaloos. / There's Daddy and Mammy, There's Ephraim and Sammy, Waitin' down yonder for me."*

Read the verse and chorus lyrics at http://www.geocities.com/dferg5493/downyonder.htm.

Hello, Young Lovers *and* We Kiss in a Shadow

Words: Oscar Hammerstein II; Music: Richard Rodgers

Rodgers and Hammerstein's giant Broadway success after *South Pacific* was 1951's *The King and I*. Set in Bangkok in the 1860s, the musical centers on an English governess, Anna, and the King of Siam. It is about mutual understanding between people of different cultures.

The King and I, based on Margaret Landon's novel *Anna and the King of Siam*, ran for 1,246 performances on Broadway. Landon's novel had been based on Anna Leonowens' diaries, *The English Governess at the Siamese Court*. The film version of the musical in '56 was also quite successful. The Original Cast Album was inducted into the Grammy Hall of Fame in 1998.

HELLO, YOUNG LOVERS

Anna, played by Gertrude Lawrence, introduced "Hello, Young Lovers" as she counseled the young lovers, Tuptim and Lun Tha, to be brave, faithful and true. She begins by reminiscing about her husband, Tom. Since she has been in love, she has only good wishes for Tuptim and Lun Tha. Read the lyrics at http://lirama.net/song/16585.

Perry Como's recording of "Hello, Young Lovers" helped introduce the song and the musical to a national audience.

WE KISS IN A SHADOW

"We Kiss in a Shadow" was sung by the young lovers, Tuptim and Lun Tha, played by Doretta Morrow and Larry Douglas in the original cast. The young people are afraid to show their love openly because Tuptim has been given to the King by her country as a present. Read the lyrics at http://www.stlyrics.com/lyrics/thekingandi/wekissinashadow.htm. Once their love is discovered, the King gets extremely angry and threatens to kill Tuptim.

Frank Sinatra's recording of "We Kiss in a Shadow" popularized the song beyond the Broadway stage.

Although there are many wonderful songs in the score of *The King and I*, only "Hello, Young Lovers" and "We Kiss in a Shadow" charted. Other great songs from the score include "I Whistle a Happy Tune," "March of the Siamese Children," "Getting to Know You," "Something Wonderful," and "Shall We Dance?" These song lyrics are available at http://www.stlyrics.com/t/thekingandi.htm. "Shall We Dance" and "Getting to Know You" were nominated for the American Film Institute's list of the greatest songs ever from American films for the '56 film version of *The King and I*, but did not make the final list.

How High the Moon

Words: Nancy Hamilton; Music: Morgan Lewis

Frances Comstock and Alfred Drake introduced "How High the Moon" in the 1940 revue *Two For the Show*. Benny Goodman and his orchestra and Mitchell Ayres and his orchestra helped popularized the song with successful recordings in '40. Stan Kenton and his orchestra revived it again with some success in '48.

In '51, Les Paul and Mary Ford revived it again with great success. Their version topped the *Billboard* chart for nine weeks, making it No. 3 for the year on that chart. *Variety* ranked it No. 4 for the year. It topped the *Cash Box* chart for five weeks, which was good enough for the No. 2 spot for the year on that chart. The song only made it to No. 3 on *Your Hit Parade*.

Les Paul and Mary Ford's recording of the song was inducted into the Grammy Hall of Fame in 1979.

"How High the Moon" became one of the most recorded songs of the pre-rock era. Hear Paul Whiteman's recording with Joe Venuti of "How High the Moon" at http://www.redhotjazz.com/pwo.html.

The singer is searching for music and heaven but will be unable to find them until he loves her as she loves him. Read the lyrics at http://lirama.net/song/16586.

I Get Ideas

Words: Dorcas Cochran; Music: Julio C. Sanders

An Argentine tango, entitled "Adios Muchachos," was transformed into the popular song "I Get Ideas." The singer gets ideas when he's dancing with his love. Read the words at http://www.lyricsvault.net/songs/17728.html.

Tony Martin popularized the English version with a very popular recording that rose to No. 3 on *Billboard*, making it the No. 19 hit of the year on that chart. The song made fifteen appearances on the *Your Hit Parade* survey of hits, peaking at No. 2 (it spent four weeks at No. 2 in October and November 1951).

Louis Armstrong and Peggy Lee released recordings of "I Get Ideas" that were also popular in '51.

Variety selected "I Get Ideas" for its *Hit Parade of a Half-Century.*

If

Words: Robert Hargreaves and Stanley J. Damerell; Music: Tolchard Evans

Perry Como's ninth million-selling record was "If" by the English writing team of Hargreaves, Damerell, and Evans. It was one of many revivals during the period; the song had been written in '34. The song spent ten weeks on the top of *Your Hit Parade*, and became the year's No. 7 hit for both *Variety* and *Cash Box* (it had topped that chart for six weeks). Como's disk was No. 1 on *Billboard* for eight weeks and their No. 5 hit of the year.

Several other recordings were popular with the public. Those included versions by Jo Stafford, by Billy Eckstine, by Dean Martin, by Guy Lombardo and his Royal Canadians, by the Ink Spots, by Jan Garber and his orchestra, and by Vic Damone.

Variety chose "If" for its *Hit Parade of a Half-Century.* Another "If" song was a hit by the group Bread in '71, but the two songs are not at all alike. This "If" is a waltz song that says life would not be worth anything if it were not for loving and being loved. Read the lyrics at http://www.lyricsvault.net/songs/17727.html.

In the Cool, Cool, Cool of the Evening

Words: Johnny Mercer; Music: Hoagy Carmichael

"In the Cool, Cool, Cool of the Evening," the Academy Award winner, was introduced by Bing Crosby in a duet with Jane Wyman in the movie musical *Here Comes the Groom*. Another title for the song might be "Tell 'Em I'll Be There," because the phrase is heard often in the lyrics.

"In the Cool, Cool, Cool of the Evening," when the party really gets heated up, "and music fills the air," I'll be there. Read the lyrics and hear a midi musical version at http://www.smickandsmodoo.com/oldcodgers/oldcodgers.shtml.

Crosby and Wyman's duet from the soundtrack of the film was the most popular recording of the song, but Frankie Laine and Jo Stafford's version was also successful.

This song was nominated for the American Film Institute's list of greatest songs ever from an American film, but, even though it was an Academy Award winner, it did not make the final list.

It Is No Secret

Words & Music: Stuart Hamblen

Stuart Hamblen promoted this religious song to hit status in '51. It was popularized in recordings by Jo Stafford and by Bill Kenny.

By today's standards, this openly religious song wouldn't have much chance on the pop market. The song's statement of faith is, "there is no secret what God can do." Read the lyrics at http://lirama.net/song/22337.

It was selected for *Variety*'s *Hit Parade of a Half-Century.*

The Loveliest Night of the Year

Words: Paul Francis Webster; Music: Juventino Rosas

Mario Lanza's second big hit of '51 (see "Be My Love") was "The Loveliest Night of the Year" from the movie musical *The Great Caruso*. Lanza also sang the song in *The Seven Hills of Rome* ('58).

Irving Aaronson adapted Juvenito Rosas' "Sobre las Olas," a waltz composed in the late 19th century, for this hit song.

Enrico Caruso was one of the world's most famous operatic tenors, and Lanza played the Caruso part well, both dramatically and vocally. Ann Blyth sang "The Loveliest Night of the Year" in the film, but Lanza recorded it. Lanza's recording peaked at No. 3 on the *Billboard* chart, making it their No. 21 hit of the year. The song collected 23 weeks on the *Your Hit Parade* survey of hits, but peaked at No. 2 in the fall of 1951.

The lyrics say that when we're in love "it's the loveliest night of the year." Read the lyrics at http://www.oldie lyrics.com/lyrics/mario_lanza/loveliest_night_of_the_year.html.

Variety selected the song for its *Hit Parade of a Half-Century.*

Mockin' Bird Hill

Words & Music: Vaughn Horton

Les Paul and Mary Ford's recording of "Mockin' Bird Hill" was the first multi-track recording. Guitarist Les Paul had developed this new recording technique. Multi-track recording allows each instrument, and each singer to be recorded on a different track. The same singer can be recorded several times, and stacked on top of themselves to produce a richer sound.

This disk peaked at No. 2 on *Billboard*, but was No. 1 on *Cash Box* for two weeks, and the song topped the *Your Hit Parade* survey for three weeks. "Mockin' Bird Hill" was No. 10 for the year for *Cash Box*, No.12 for *Billboard*.

Patti Page's version also made it to No. 2 on *Billboard*. The Pinetoppers and Russ Morgan and his orchestra also had recordings of the song that were popular enough to chart.

Variety selected "Mockin' Bird Hill" for its *Hit Parade of a Half-Century*.

This waltz tune is a verse and chorus type of song that has a simple, easy chord structure (only three chord: G, C, and D7). It has a folk song character about it. The lyrics describe the pleasure of living on "Mockin' Bird Hill." Read the lyrics at http://lirama.net/song/16594.

My Heart Cries for You

Words: Carl Sigman; Music: Percy Faith

In '50 Carl Sigman and Percy Faith adapted the melody of "Chason de Marie Antoinette" for the hit song "My Heart Cries for You." The original tune had supposedly been written by France's eighteenth-century queen Marie Antoinette.

Guy Mitchell's recording of the song became *Variety*'s No. 9 hit of the year, No. 11 on *Billboard* (it only rose to No. 2 on that chart, but stayed there seven weeks). His disk was No. 1 on *Cash Box* for six weeks. The song collected two weeks at No. 1 on *Your Hit Parade*.

Several other versions charted including those by Dinah Shore, by Vic Damone, by Jimmy Wakely, by Bill Farrell, by Al Morgan, by Red Foley, by Evelyn Knight, and by Victor Young and his orchestra.

Because of its eighteenth-century origins, "My Heart Cries for You" was also reasonably simple, as were other songs of the year like "Mockin' Bird Hill" and "On Top of Old Smoky."

The first verse basically says the singer will follow his loved one wherever she goes because his love is endless. The chorus opens with "My heart cries for you," and he begs her to come back. Read the lyrics at http://lirama.net/song/16597.

Variety chose "My Heart Cries For You" for its *Hit Parade of a Half-Century*.

On Top of Old Smoky

Words & Music: Traditional

Folk singer Pete Seeger adapted this Appalachian folk song into one of 1951's big hit songs. The song was No. 1 on *Your Hit Parade* for a couple of weeks. It didn't fare quite as well on the other charts, peaking at No. 2. However, *Cash Box* year-end charts had it at No. 6, while *Billboard* had it at No. 10.

The most successful recorded version in '51 was one by the Weavers and Terry Gilkyson with a chorus and orchestra conducted by Vic Schoen. Other charted versions were by Vaughn Monroe, and by Percy Faith and his orchestra. Folk singer Burl Ives had charted with his version of the song in '49.

Gene Autry sang the song in the '51 film *Valley of Fire*.

"On Top of Old Smokey" was chosen for *Variety*'s *Hit Parade of a Half-Century*. The title is sometimes spelled "On Top of Old Smoky" and sometimes "On Top of Old Smokey."

There are far too many verses to this folk song to quote them all, but what follows below is enough to remind the reader of the gist of the song: *On top of Old Smoky, All covered with snow, / I lost my true lover, For courting too slow. / For courting's a pleasure, But parting is grief, / And a false-hearted lover, Is worse than a thief."*

Read the complete original lyrics at http://www.kiddiles.com/mouseum/o036.html.

Children have sometimes sung the melody to a lyric entitled "On Top of Spaghetti."

Shrimp Boats

Words & Music: Paul Mason Howard and Paul Weston

"Shrimp boats is a-comin', there's dancin' tonight," sang Jo Stafford in this charming bayou song. Stafford's recording of the song peaked at No. 2 on the *Billboard* chart, making it the No. 15 hit of the year. Delores Gray also had a popular recording of "Shrimp Boats" on the market. The song appeared on the *Your Hit Parade* survey for ten weeks, peaking at No. 3 in February of 1952.

Variety chose it for its '52 list in its *Hit Parade of a Half-Century*.

Jo Stafford was singing about the shrimp boats returning to shore and the celebration that will follow. Read the words at http://www.lyricsvault.net/songs/19052.html.

(It's No) Sin

Words: Chester R. Shull; Music: George Hoven

Two very popular recordings of "Sin" or "It's No Sin" propelled it to Top Ten status for '51. The most popular version was by Eddy Howard. His disk was No. 1 on *Billboard* for eight weeks, and on *Cash Box* for one week. His version of the song was *Billboard*'s No. 4 hit of the year, while *Variety* had it ranked at No. 10. The Four Aces featuring Al Alberts recording of the song topped *Cash Box* for two weeks, and was their No. 8 hit of the year; their version came in at No. 31 on *Billboard* for the year.

The song appeared on *Your Hit Parade* seventeen times, making seven appearances as the No. 1 hit.

Other recordings of "Sin" that charted include those by Savannah Churchill (*Billboard*'s No. 39 hit of the year), by the Four Knights, by Sammy Kaye and his orchestra, and by the Billy Williams Quartet.

"Sin" lists several things that the writers think would be sinful. Some of those things include taking away flowers, April showers or taking the violins from a lovely symphony. The catch at the end is the singer will keep loving this person forever for "it's no sin." Read the lyrics at http://lirama.net/song/16600.

"Sin" was chosen for *Variety*'s *Hit Parade of a Half-Century*.

Sound Off

Words & Music: Willie Lee Duckworth

"Sound Off" was originally used for close-order drill training by the U.S. armed forces. It was first published in *The Cadence System of Teaching Close Order Drill* by Colonel Bernard Lentz.

In '51 a recording by Vaughn Monroe propelled the song onto the hit list. Monroe's disk peaked at No. 3 on the *Billboard* chart, which means it was that chart's No. 23 hit of the year. *Your Hit Parade* ignored it.

Variety chose it for its *Hit Parade of a Half-Century*.

The lyrics are almost endless because the soldiers concocted new ones constantly as they drilled. Read the words at http://www.oldielyrics.com/lyrics/vaughn_monroe/sound_off.html.

Sparrow in the Tree Top

Words & Music: Bob Merrill

Even though a group known as the Pinetoppers first recorded this Bob Merrill song, it was not until Guy Mitchell teamed with Mitch Miller to record the song and

Bing Crosby and the Andrews Sisters did the same that it made much impact on the pop music charts. Both Mitchell's and Crosby and the Andrews Sisters' versions peaked at No. 8 on the *Billboard* chart. The song collected five weeks on the *Your Hit Parade* hit survey, peaking at No. 4 in the spring of '51.

Rex Allen also had a popular recording of the song on the market.

Variety selected "Sparrow in the Tree Top" for its *Hit Parade of a Half-Century.*

The chorus of this song is almost as simplistic as "My Heart Cries For You" (see above). Basically, the chorus says, even though the sparrow in the treetop loves his mate, he's afraid to go home because "it's too darn late." Read the complete lyrics at http://ntl.matrix.com.br/pfilho/html/lyrics/s/sparrow_in_the_treetop.txt.

The Merrill, Mitchell, and Miller team was heard often on the airwaves during the spring of '51 with "Sparrow in the Tree Top" and "My Truly, Truly Fair" both becoming popular.

Too Young

Words: Sylvia Dee; Music: Sidney Lippman

Nat "King" Cole's Capitol recording of "Too Young" moved to the No. 3 position in *Variety*'s '51 Top Ten. Johnny Desmond had introduced the song, but it was Cole's performance that caused it to climb to the top of the *Your Hit Parade* and stay there for a record twelve weeks. No other song ever collected more weeks at No. 1 on that hit survey. Cole's disk topped the *Billboard* chart for five weeks and was that chart's No. 8 hit of the year. It was No. 1 on *Cash Box* for eight weeks, and that chart's No. 3 hit of the year.

Toni Arden, Patty Andrews, Fran Allison, and Richard Hayes each had recordings of "Too Young" that were popular enough with the public to chart during '51.

Variety selected "Too Young" for its *Hit Parade of a Half-Century.*

Several songs about the young were in vogue, and teenagers, even pre-teenagers, began to have more influence on the making of hit songs. It was probably the popularity of "Too Young" that convinced record producers and record company executives that the youth had the buying power to make hits which led to the rock 'n' roll music of the youngsters of the mid-'50s.

The lyrics sing that adults try to tell young people they are "too young to really be in love," but, of course, that is not the opinion of young lovers. Read the lyrics at http://lirama.net/song/16603.

1952

Any Time

Words & Music: Herbert Lawson

"Any Time" was written by Herbert "Happy" Lawson and published in the early '20s, when it was a minor success. Country star Eddy Arnold had a successful recording of the song in '48, but Eddie Fisher's '52 recording of it made it to No. 2 on the *Billboard* chart.

"Any Time" made 17 appearances on *Your Hit Parade*

beginning in late January 1952. It peaked at No. 2, but it held that position for six weeks between late March and mid–May.

Perhaps because Arnold's successful recording of the song predated Fisher's, the song seems to be remembered today as a country hit.

The song definitely fits the stereotype of the country song about a broken romance. The singer will take his girl back "any time" she'll say she wants him back again. Read the lyrics at http://www.lyricsvault.net/songs/19046.html.

Variety included "Any Time" in its *Hit Parade of a Half-Century.*

Auf Wiederseh'n, Sweetheart

Words: Geoffrey Parsons and John Turner; Music: Eberhard Storch

Total sales of this 1949 German publication reportedly went over the 2 million mark. Eberhard Storch wrote the melody to which English lyrics were added in '52. Vera Lynn, a British songstress, had her most famous U.S. hit with the song. Her recording popularized the song to the No. 4 position on *Variety*'s Top Ten, *Cash Box*'s No. 10 and *Billboard*'s No. 4 hit of '52. It spent six weeks at No. 1 on *Cash Box* and nine weeks at No. 1 on *Billboard*.

America's war wounds must have mended by the early fifties. During World War I and II, German operas were either banned or seldom, if ever, performed, German was eliminated from the curriculum of most schools, and in general, there was quite a lot of anti–German sentiment. Those feelings must have abated to the point that a German song could make it to No. 1 on *Your Hit Parade*. "Auf Wiederseh'n, Sweetheart" appeared on the program sixteen weeks, and spent three weeks at the top of that hit survey.

Other versions of the song that charted included those by Eddy Howard, by the Ames Brothers, by Guy Lombardo and his Royal Canadians, and by Les Baxter and his orchestra.

Even though the war was over, this certainly sounds like a wartime song about separated lovers. Could it have been a wartime romance between a German girl and an Allied soldier? Vera Lynn sang, "Auf wiederseh'n ... we'll meet again, sweetheart." She and her loved one must part, but they are confident they'll kiss again. She tells him she'll wait for him. Read the lyrics at http://www.lyricsdepot.com/vera-lynn-chorus/auf-wiedersehn.html.

Variety selected "Auf Wiederseh'n, Sweetheart" for its *Hit Parade of a Half-Century.*

Other "Auf Wiedersehn" songs include Sigmund Romberg's "Auf Wiedersehn" in 1915, and "Auf Wiedersehn, My Dear" in 1932.

Be Anything (But Be Mine)

Words & Music: Irving Gordon

Eddy Howard popularized this *Variety Hit Parade of a Half-Century* song. Howard's recording of "Be Anything (But Be Mine)" peaked at No. 7 on *Billboard*. The song collected eleven weeks on *Your Hit Parade*. It entered their top ten at No. 7 in May and peaked at No. 2 in June.

Other popular recordings of the song were released by Peggy Lee, by Champ Butler, and by Helen O'Connell.

The lyrics tell the singer's loved one they can be a beggar, a thief, a wise man, a fool, an angel, or the devil. They can be whatever they want to be as long as their love continues.

Blue Tango

Words: Mitchell Parish; Music: Leroy Anderson

Leroy Anderson generally writes what might be termed "semi-classical" music and he is noted for his works that feature unusual effects. His "The Syncopated Clock," with its tick-tocks that become a little jazzy, "Sandpaper Ballet," with the sound of sandpaper scraped together as if it were a dancer's feet, and "The Typewriter," with its typing effects, are good examples.

Both the tango and the blues are of African origin. Leroy Anderson had the inspired idea of combining these two traditional African themes, spicing them up with his own ingenious ideas. The shuffling tango rhythm may be heard under the melody, while little blues figures decorate the theme. The result is a fresh and original work by a brilliant composer.

"Blue Tango" is Anderson's biggest hit, as a composer and as an orchestra leader. He and his orchestra's recording of his song was *Billboard's* top hit for five weeks and *Billboard's* No. 7 hit of the year; it was No. 1 on *Cash Box* for two weeks and No. 2 hit of the year. It was also No. 2 for the year on *Variety*. The song topped the *Your Hit Parade* hit survey for two weeks.

Most of the songs on *Your Hit Parade* are at least partially vocals. Even during the era of the big bands, the instrumentalists were dominant, but the vocalists usually got to sing a chorus or two. Several of the purely instrumental hits of the Swing Era did not make *Your Hit Parade's* chart. "Blue Tango" is one of only a few instrumentals to reach the No. 1 position on *Your Hit Parade*.

Other basically instrumental No. 1 hits on *Your Hit Parade* include "Song from *Moulin Rouge*" ('53), "Canadian Sunset" ('56), "Melody of Love" ('55), "The Poor People of Paris" ('56), "Lisbon Antigua" ('56), "Autumn Leaves" ('55, Roger Williams' piano version, but the vocal version was also popular), "Frenesi" ('40), "Picnic/Moonglow" ('56), "April in Portugal" ('53), "Heartaches" ('47, Ted Weems' version) and "Intermezzo" ('41).

Other versions of "Blue Tango" that were popular enough to chart include those by Hugo Winterhalter and his orchestra, by Guy Lombardo and his Royal Canadians, and by Les Baxter and his orchestra.

The studio orchestra played "Blue Tango" in the film *La Bamba* ('87).

Variety picked "Blue Tango" for its *Hit Parade of a Half-Century*.

Delicado

Words: Jack Lawrence; Music: Waldyr Azevedo

Percy Faith and his orchestra popularized this Brazilian song, a *Variety Hit Parade of a Half-Century* selection. His recording was No. 1 on *Billboard* for one week; it reached No. 2 on *Your Hit Parade*, and No. 3 on *Cash Box*. It was the No. 15 hit of the year on *Billboard*, No. 4 for *Cash Box*.

Stan Kenton and his orchestra, Ralph Flanagan and his orchestra, and Dinah Shore also had recordings of the song that were popular enough with the public to chart, but none of them even made the Top 20.

Many songs are remembered when we hear them, but we may not always remember them by their title or by who performed them. Such is the case of "Delicado."

The Glow Worm

Words: Johnny Mercer; Music: Paul Lincke

"The Glow Worm," originally published in Germany in 1902, became a big seller at that time in Europe and the United States. (For more, please see 1908).

Publisher Edward Marks signed Johnny Mercer to write new lyrics, which the Mills Brothers recorded and ultimately made into 1952's No. 9 hit in *Variety's* Top 10 and No. 8 for the year for *Billboard*. The Mills Brothers' disk was No. 1 on *Billboard* for three weeks, but it only reached No. 2 on *Cash Box*. The song topped the *Your Hit Parade* survey for two weeks.

Johnny Mercer's version of "The Glow Worm" only made it to No. 30 on the *Billboard* chart.

One might not consider a song about a bug whose tail lights up to be the best popular song material, but the singer is requesting the "glow worm" to light the path that will lead the singer and his girl to love. Read the lyrics at http://ntl.matrix.com.br/pfilho/html/lyrics/g/glow_worm.txt.

"The Glow Worm" was named to *Variety's* *Hit Parade of a Half-Century* for 1907.

A Guy Is a Guy

Words & Music: Oscar Brand

"A Guy Is a Guy" was adapted from an old seaman song by folk artist Oscar Brand. While he was in the service he learned the original bawdy version. Several years later, he cleaned up the lyrics, added a bridge, and changed the title.

It became a No. 1 for one week on both *Billboard* and *Cash Box*. The song peaked at No. 2 on *Your Hit Parade*. Doris Day's recording of the song was most popular.

The title to this song could have been "like a good girl should," because of the number of times the phrase is used in the song. The singer, a girl, walks down the street "like a good girl should" and a guy follows like she knew he would. How did she know? "Because a guy is a guy." By the end of the song, she has agreed to marry this guy. Read the lyrics at http://www.oldielyrics.com/lyrics/doris_day/guy_is_a_guy.html.

Half As Much

Words & Music: Curley Williams

Rosemary Clooney had three big hit recordings in 1952: the beautiful '46 waltz "Tenderly," "Botch-a-me," and this Curley Williams song, that had been popularized on the country and western charts by Hank Williams.

Ms. Clooney's recording of the song was No. 1 for three weeks on *Billboard*, and for four weeks on *Cash Box*. Her disk was No. 9 for the year on *Billboard's* year-end chart. The song only reached No. 2 on *Your Hit Parade*.

Guy Lombardo and his Royal Canadians' version of the song only made it to No. 20 on *Billboard*.

Variety chose "Half As Much" for its *Hit Parade of a Half-Century*.

The chord structure of the song is definitely simpler than that of music in the '40s. The tune uses the tonic chord (D) for the first six and a half measures, then the dominant seventh (A7) for two measures before returning to tonic for the cadence. Only two other chords are used in the song. Music was gravitating toward amateurism, a trend even more apparent in the later part of the decade and over the next several years.

Rosemary Clooney tells her guy if he loved her "half as much" as she loved him, he wouldn't worry her as much as he does. Her guy is only nice to her when nobody else is around and that makes her feel blue. Read the lyrics at http://lirama.net/song/16615.

Here in My Heart

Words & Music: Pat Genaro, Lou Levinson, and Bill Borrelli

Al Martino's first big hit record was "Here In My Heart." It ranked No. 8 in *Variety's* Top Ten for 1952, No. 10 on *Billboard* and No. 9 on *Cash Box*. His recording spent three weeks at the top of the *Billboard* chart, and four weeks at No. 1 on *Cash Box*. It never made it to the top of the *Your Hit Parade* survey, peaking at No. 2. Martino's tenor voice suited the musical and lyrical style of song very well.

Vic Damone and Tony Bennett also had recordings of "Here In My Heart" that were popular enough to chart.

Al Martino sings "Here in my heart, I'm alone." He yearns for this girl and pledges his heart, his life and his all to her. Read the words at http://lirama.net/song/16617.

High Noon (Do Not Forsake Me)

Words: Ned Washington; Music: Dimitri Tiomkin

The classic western film *High Noon* introduced this song as its theme. It won the Oscar for the best song from films in '52 and was chosen for *Variety's* *Hit Parade of a Half-Century*.

It was sung on the soundtrack by cowboy movie star and singer Tex Ritter, the father of actor John Ritter, who starred for several years on the TV sitcoms *Three's Company* and *Eight Simple Rules*. At previews neither the film nor its music found favor. Tiomkin asked for and received publication rights to the song, and since Ritter refused to record the theme song, Tiomkin talked Frankie Laine into it. The recording was released four months before the film and became such a hit that interest was heightened in the film. Once the Laine disk had become successful, Tex Ritter reconsidered and recorded the song.

The film turned out to be profitable and achieved classic status among westerns perhaps because of its theme song, which is subtitled "Do Not Forsake Me."

Frankie Laine's recording of the song peaked at No. 5 on *Billboard*, making it that charts No. 36 hit of the year. *Your Hit Parade* ignored the song.

AFI's *100 Years ... 100 Songs* (2004) listed "High Noon" as the No. 25 greatest song ever from an American film.

The singer (or the movie character) doesn't know what fate has in store for him. He only knows he has to be brave as he faces a hateful man in a gunfight. He certainly doesn't want to be a coward. Read the lyrics at http://lirama.net/song/16618.

I Saw Mommy Kissing Santa Claus

Words & Music: Tommie Connor

Jimmy Boyd's recording of "I Saw Mommy Kissing Santa Claus" broke records for Columbia, selling 248,000 copies in one day, 700,000 in ten days in early December, and more than 1 million before Christmas of '52. Columbia reported total sales exceeded 2.5 million.

Boyd's recording was No. 1 on *Billboard* for two weeks,

but only reached No. 4 on *Cash Box*. The song managed one week at No. 1 on *Your Hit Parade*. It was *Billboard's* No. 13 hit of the year.

Spike Jones and His City Slickers' comic version made it to No. 4 on *Billboard*, making it the No. 34 hit of the year. Molly Bee also had a recording of the song that charted in '53.

British songwriter Tommie Connor wrote the song, which had sold more than 11 million disks in all versions by the mid-sixties.

"I Saw Mommy Kissing Santa Claus" was selected for *Variety's* *Hit Parade of a Half-Century*.

A small child saw his "Mommy kissing Santa Claus" and he wonders what his Daddy would do if he had seen them. Read the lyrics at http://41051.com/xmaslyrics/isaw mommy.html.

I Went to Your Wedding

Words & Music: Jessie Mae Robinson

"I Went to Your Wedding" was the No. 6 hit in '52's Top 10 for *Variety*. Patti Page's recording of the song spent ten weeks at No. 1 on *Billboard* and six weeks at No. 1 on *Cash Box*. The song only made it to No. 3 on *Your Hit Parade*.

Steve Gibson also had a recording of the song that charted in '52. Spike Jones and His City Slickers' comedy version charted in '53.

Jessie Mae Robinson's song is a bore! Its slow tempo and "oom-pah-pah" guitar accompaniment are simplistic and amateurish, but the public seemed to love it. Such simplistic amateurism seemed to be the wave of the future, and it was beginning to catch on with the record-buying public.

The singer went to the wedding of the girl he thought he would be marrying. Not only were her mother and father crying, but he was crying too because he had lost her to someone else. Read the words at http://lirama.net/song/16621.

I'm Yours

Words & Music: Robert Merrill

Don Cornell, who had been a singer with Sammy Kaye's orchestra, had one of his biggest hits with "I'm Yours" in '52. His recording of the song reportedly became a million seller. "I'm Yours" and '54's "Hold My Hand" were his biggest successes as a solo recording artist. He had been the vocalist on "It Isn't Fair," a '50 hit for Sammy Kaye's band.

Eddie Fisher, the Four Aces, and Toni Arden also had recordings of "I'm Yours" that did well enough with the record buying public to chart. As a matter of fact, *Billboard* ranked Eddie Fisher's version above Don Cornell's for the year: Fisher's was No. 25, Cornell's was No. 27 (both versions peaked at No. 3 on *Billboard*). Cornell's version was No. 8 for the year on *Cash Box*. The song was No. 1 on *Your Hit Parade* for three weeks.

The chord structure of this hit is complicated, more similar to the hits of the past than to the majority of those in the future. Chords like B flat diminished, F7, C diminished, and B flat augmented in the key of E flat make for variety, interest, and a lush harmonic scheme.

Don Cornell sang to his girl that he was hers with all his heart and soul. And he hopes and prays someday he'll hear her say 'I'm yours.'" Read the lyrics at http://www.oldie lyrics.com/lyrics/don_cornell/im_yours.html.

Variety included "I'm Yours" in its *Hit Parade of a Half-Century*.

It's in the Book

Words & Music: Johnny Standley and Art Thorsen

"It's in the Book" is not a song in the strict sense, it is a comedy recording, but it collected two weeks at No. 1 on *Billboard* and was the year's No. 10 hit according to *Variety*.

Comedian Johnny Standley's parody of a fundamentalist preacher sermonizing on "Little Bo Peep" produced a comedy classic. Standley wrote the routine in collaboration with Art Thorsen and recorded it with Horace Heidt and his orchestra.

Read this hilarious "sermon" at http://www.songlyrics.com/song-lyrics/Johnny_Standley/Miscellaneous/It_s_In_The_Book_%28parts_1_and_2%29/198842.html.

Jambalaya

Words & Music: Hank Williams

The Louisiana Cajun dish jambalaya furnished the title for this Hank Williams song about bayou culture and the language of the Creoles. Several Cajun dishes are mentioned in addition to "Jambalaya," including "crawfish pie and file' gumbo." The singer is excited because that evening he's going to see his "ma cher amio," which is Cajun-French for "my dear." Read the lyrics at http://lirama.net/song/6499.

The song is similar to "Grand Texas," which was a Cajun-French song about life, parties and Cajun cuisine. Hank Williams was accused of buying several of his songs from other writers, a practice that was fairly prevalent during the time in the country song market, but no proof has ever surfaced.

Jo Stafford's recording of the song peaked at No. 3 on *Billboard*. Hank Williams' more country version only made it to No. 20 on *Billboard*, but his recording was inducted into the Grammy Hall of Fame in 2002.

Hank Williams' song appeared on *Your Hit Parade* fourteen times, peaking at No. 2.

"Jambalaya" was selected for *Variety*'s Hit Parade of a Half-Century.

Kiss of Fire

Words: Lester Allen and Robert Hill; Music: A.G. Villoldo

An Argentine tango, "El Choclo," written by A.G. Villoldo in 1913, was adapted by Lester Allen and Robert Hill into the hit song "Kiss of Fire." The song spent seven weeks on the top of *Your Hit Parade* in the late spring and early summer of '52. Georgia Gibbs' recording of it was No. 1 on *Billboard* for seven weeks, and No. 1 on *Cash Box* for six weeks. It was No. 5 for the year on both *Billboard* and *Cash Box*.

Other recordings of the song that charted include those by Tony Martin, by Toni Arden, by Billy Eckstine, by Louis Armstrong, and by Guy Lombardo and his Royal Canadians.

Ms. Gibbs's sultry rendition of the lyrics burned up the airwaves and jukeboxes, making it one of '52's biggest hits. She can't resist his "kiss of fire" even though she knows he is lying. Read the lyrics at http://lirama.net/song/16623.

Lady of Spain

Words: Erell Reaves; Music: Tolchard Evans

British writers Evans and Reaves wrote this song in 1931, but it was put back into circulation in '52 when Eddie Fisher's recording of the song became a hit. His version peaked at No. 6, while Les Paul's recordings of it made it to No. 8. Back in '31 Ray Noble and his orchestra had popularized the song with a popular recording. Noble's version resurfaced on the charts in '49.

According to *Your Hit Parade*, the song peaked at No. 5.

"Lady of Spain" was selected for *Variety*'s Hit Parade of a Half-Century representing 1952.

Most of the song is simply a repetition of a musical phrase at different pitches. The key ingredient in "Lady of Spain" is its catchy, spirited Spanish rhythm.

The singer adores the "Lady of Spain." His heart has been yearning for her from the first night he saw her. Read the lyrics at http://www.lyricsvault.net/songs/17796.html.

The Little White Cloud That Cried

Words & Music: Johnnie Ray

Johnnie Ray wrote and popularized this *Variety* Hit Parade of a Half-Century song. It was the flip side of "Cry," which made the disk the No. 1 record of '52 for *Variety*. *Billboard* had "Cry" as the top hit of '51, while "The Little White Cloud That Cried" peaked at No. 2 on that chart and came in at No. 20 for '52. "The Little White Cloud..." made eight appearances on *Your Hit Parade*, peaking at No. 4 in early '52.

Ray's voice broke with emotion as he crooned that he would remember forever "the little white cloud, that sat right down and cried." The cloud cried because it was lonesome and it felt that no one cared what happened to it. Then the cloud offered this Depression era-sounding philosophy, we should remain faithful in all circumstances, because things will get better in time. Read the lyrics at http://lirama.net/song/16592.

Please, Mr. Sun

Words: Sid Frank; Music: Ray Getzov

Johnnie Ray, Perry Como and Tommy Edwards popularized this *Variety* Hit Parade of a Half-Century selection that was composed in '51. Ray's version was the highest on the charts, but it only managed No. 6 on *Billboard*, making it the No. 39 hit of the year. *Variety* claims it rose to No. 2 on their chart in the early spring of '52 and stayed on the best-seller chart for 14 weeks.

The song collected a dozen weeks on the *Your Hit Parade* survey of hits, peaking at No. 2 in April '52.

The singer asks several things of Mr. Sun, a tree, the wind, and a robin. He wants Mr. Sun to speak to his loved one on his behalf. He wants the trees to take her under their branches, the wind to whisper to her and the robin to sing to her. Read the lyrics at http://lirama.net/song/16631.

Singin' in the Rain (see '29) *and* Make 'Em Laugh

The wonderful movie musical *Singin' in the Rain* was released in '52. It may well be the greatest movie musical ever filmed. Most of the songs from the score were Arthur Freed and Nacio Herb Brown numbers from earlier MGM films. Included were "All I Do Is Dream of You," "I've Got a Feelin' You're Foolin'," "You Are My Lucky Star," "Broadway Rhythm," "The Wedding of the Painted Doll," "You Were Meant For Me," "Good Morning,"

"Broadway Melody," and especially the title song, among others.

One of the film's many highlights was Donald O'Connor singing, dancing, and clowning to Freed and Brown's "Make 'Em Laugh." AFI's *100 Years ... 100 Songs* (2004) named "Make 'Em Laugh" the No. 49 greatest song ever from an American film.

As the filming of *Singin' in the Rain* progressed it became evident that Donald O'Connor needed a solo number to showcase his talents. Freed and Brown were instructed to write a song for him like Cole Porter's "Be a Clown." They followed orders, but, being the talented songwriters they were, made "Make 'Em Laugh" distinctive and a completely different song, although there are some similarities.

Read the lyrics of "Make 'Em Laugh" at http://www.reelclassics.com/Musicals/Singin/lyrics/makeemlaugh-lyrics.htm.

Slow Poke

Words & Music: Pee Wee King, Redd Stewart, and Chilton Price

Chilton Price was a broadcast-station record librarian from Louisville, Kentucky, who became friends with country-western bandleader Pee Wee King. Price started bringing song ideas to King, and in '52, two of the ideas produced hit songs: "Slow Poke" and "You Belong to Me."

Co-writer King recorded "Slow Poke" with a vocal by co-writer Redd Stewart. It made it to No. 1 on the country charts, then crossed over and climbed to No. 1 on *Billboard* for three weeks, No. 1 on *Cash Box* for two weeks. The song was No. 1 on *Your Hit Parade* at the end of 1951 for one week, and the beginning of 1952 for six weeks.

Other recordings of "Slow Poke" that did well enough to chart include those by Ralph Flanagan and his orchestra, by Helen O'Connell, by Arthur Godfrey, by Roberta Lee, and by country singer Hawkshaw Hawkins.

The singer waits and worries but his girl never seems to hurry. He finally decides he'll "have to learn to be a slow poke, too." Read the lyrics at http://ntl.matrix.com.br/pfilho/html/lyrics/s/slow_poke.txt.

Tenderly

Words: Jack Lawrence; Music: Walter Gross

"Tenderly" is one of the most beautiful romantic ballads ever written. Sarah Vaughan first popularized it in '47. Next the Hope Quintet revived it in '50. Rosemary Clooney revived it once again in '52. Bert Kaempfert and his orchestra revived it yet again in '61.

The lyrics express feelings with which most lovers readily identify. The singer tells us her loved one's arms opened wide and closed her inside; he took her lips and her love very "tenderly." Read the lyrics at http://lirama.net/song/16634.

Variety selected "Tenderly" as a *Golden 100 Tin Pan Alley Song*. "Tenderly" became one of the most recorded songs of the pre-rock era.

Unforgettable

Words & Music: Irving Gordon

"Unforgettable" has been popular several times over the years. Nat "King" Cole popularized it with his beautiful rendition in '51-'52. His disk was inducted into the Grammy Hall of Fame in 2000.

The Dick Hyman Trio revived it successfully in '54. In '59 Dinah Washington revived it. Although her recording never charted, it was inducted into the Grammy Hall of Fame in 2001.

Then in '91, Nat "King" Cole's daughter, Natalie, released an album of standards titled *Unforgettable* that sold nine million copies and which won seven Grammy awards. Through the marvel of modern engineering, Natalie sang "Unforgettable" with her father.

To the singer, his lover is definitely "Unforgettable." Read the lyrics at http://www.romantic-lyrics.com/lu2.shtml.

Walkin' My Baby Back Home

Words & Music: Roy Turk, Fred E. Ahlert, and Harry Richman

Harry Richman collaborated on, introduced and helped popularize "Walkin' My Baby Back Home" in '30. The most popular recordings of the song, however, were by Nick Lucas and by Ted Weems and his orchestra, with vocalist Parker Gibbs in '31. The Charleston Chasers and Lee Morse, with accompaniment by Tommy Dorsey on trombone, Benny Goodman on clarinet, and Eddie Lang on guitar, helped popularize the song with popular recordings in '31. Three recordings of "Walkin' My Baby Back Home" can be heard at http://www.redhotjazz.com/bands.html: Louis Armstrong's, the Charleston Chasers' and Annette Hanshaw's.

Johnnie Ray revived it in '52 and made it a big hit again. The song spent three weeks at No. 1 on *Your Hit Parade*, but only made it to No. 4 on both *Billboard* and *Cash Box*. Johnnie Ray's recording was *Billboard's* No. 29 hit of the year.

Nat "King" Cole also had a recording of the song that charted in '52.

The singer is walking his baby back home one evening. As they walk, they harmonize on a song or he recites a poem. Once they stop to pet she gets powder on his vest. He straightens his tie and she borrows his comb before they continue their walk. Read the lyrics at http://lirama.net/song/16639.

Wheel of Fortune

Words: George Weiss; Music: Bennie Benjamin

"Wheel of Fortune" was the No. 3 hit on *Variety*'s Top Ten for '52. Kay Starr's recording of the song spent ten weeks at No. 1 on *Billboard*, six weeks at the top of both *Cash Box* and *Your Hit Parade*. Her disk was No. 2 for the year on *Billboard*, and No. 6 on *Cash Box*. Starr's ten weeks at No. 1 on *Billboard* makes her recording of this song No. 36 of the pre-rock era for that charting service.

Kay Starr's recording of "Wheel of Fortune" was inducted into the Grammy Hall of Fame in 1998.

Other recordings of "Wheel of Fortune" that charted include those by Bobby Wayne, by the Bell Sisters, and by Eddie Wilcox with Sunny Gale.

"Wheel of Fortune" suggests that love is a game of chance; if the wheel lands on our number, love will come our way. Read the lyrics at http://www.oldielyrics.com/lyrics/kay_starr/wheel_of_fortune.html.

Variety chose "Wheel of Fortune" for its *Hit Parade of a Half-Century*.

Why Don't You Believe Me?

Words & Music: Lew Douglas, King Laney & Roy Rodde

Joni James had her first big hit recording with "Why Don't You Believe Me?" Her recording reached the No. 6 position in *Billboard's* top ten for '52. The song collected 14 weeks on the *Your Hit Parade* survey of hits and spent five weeks at No. 1 there at the end of '52 and the beginning of '53.

James actually paid for the recording session herself, but the disk was purchased and released by MGM.

Other popular recordings of the song were released by Patti Page and by Margaret Whiting. Their versions were more popular in '53.

Variety named it to its *Hit Parade of a Half-Century* for 1952.

Joni James sang, "Why don't you believe me?" She tells this guy she adores him whether he believes her or not. Read the lyrics at http://www.lyricsdownload.com/joni-james-why-don-t-you-believe-me-lyrics.html.

Wish You Were Here

Words & Music: Harold Rome

Jack Cassidy, the father of later teenage heartthrob David Cassidy, a singer and TV star of *The Partridge Family*, introduced the title song of the Broadway musical *Wish You Were Here*.

The hero longs for his absent heroine in this *Variety Hit Parade of a Half-Century* selection. He tells her the skies aren't as blue, the leaf colors are all wrong, and the birds aren't singing the same song as when she was with him. Read the lyrics at http://lirama.net/song/602.

Eddie Fisher's recording of the song made it to No. 1 on *Billboard* and stayed there for one week, but it only made it to No. 2 on *Cash Box*. The song managed three weeks at No. 1 on *Your Hit Parade*. Fisher's recording of "Wish You Were Here" was *Billboard's* No. 14 hit of the year.

You Belong to Me

Words & Music: Pee Wee King, Redd Stewart, and Chilton Price

The same writers that produced "Slow Poke" also wrote "You Belong to Me," although the two songs have very little in common. "Slow Poke" is decidedly country, but "You Belong to Me" doesn't sound country at all.

Jo Stafford recorded this song, which not only turned out to be the No. 1 hit of the year on *Billboard*, and the No. 5 hit on *Variety*, but also proved its durability when the Duprees took it to the Top 10 with their version in '62. Ms. Stafford's version of the song spent a dozen weeks at No. 1 on *Billboard*, and four weeks at No. 1 on *Cash Box*. The song collected nine weeks at No. 1 on *Your Hit Parade*. Ms. Stafford's twelve weeks at No. 1 with this song ranks at No. 14 of the pre-rock era for *Billboard*. According to *Variety*, Jo Stafford's recording of "You Belong to Me" was No. 5 for the year, while Patti Page's version was No. 6 for the year. Both versions in the year's Top Ten is quite an accomplishment.

Jo Stafford's recording of "You Belong to Me" was inducted into the Grammy Hall of Fame in 1998.

Dean Martin also had a recording of the song that charted.

The lyrics say that a loved one may travel all around the world and see many of the most famous sights, but she asks him to remember until he's back home again, he belongs to her. Read the lyrics at http://lirama.net/song/16647.

Variety included "You Belong to Me" in its *Hit Parade of a Half-Century*.

See another "You Belong to Me" in 1916.

1953

April in Portugal

Words: Jimmy Kennedy; Music: Raul Ferrao

1953 was a good year for instrumental hits. Basically non-vocal hits included "April in Portugal," "Song from *Moulin Rouge*," and "Ebb Tide," plus the instrumental successes "Ruby," the theme from the movie *Ruby Gentry*, "Anna," the theme from the television series "Dragnet," and Charlie Chaplin's composition "Terry's Theme" from *Limelight* (also called "Limelight" or in the lyric version "Eternally").

Songs about months are not particularly numerous. The only *Your Hit Parade* No. 1 hits that have months in their titles were "September in the Rain," "April in Portugal," and "April Love." The only other song with a month in the title to ever make *Your Hit Parade's* hit survey was "Sleighride in July," which made it to No. 6. There are other well-known songs that have months in their title. A few include "September Song," "April in Paris," "April Showers," "I'll Remember April," "June Is Busting Out All Over," and "June in January."

"April in Portugal," popularized by Les Baxter and his orchestra, was among *Variety's*, *Billboard's*, and *Cash Box's* top hits of '53 (tied at No. 10 on *Variety*, No. 13 on *Billboard*, No. 3 on *Cash Box*). The song originated as a '47 Portuguese song by Raul Ferrao titled "Coimbra," a city in Portugal. Georgia Carr introduced it in the U.S. as "The Whispering Serenade." It became "April in Portugal" when Chappell Publishing Company hired Jimmy Kennedy to write a new lyric for the tune in '53. Baxter's version, however, did not use the lyrics. Read the lyrics at http://lirama.net/song/16648.

Baxter's recording of the song only reached No. 2 on both *Billboard* and *Cash Box*, but the song collected two weeks at No. 1 on *Your Hit Parade*.

Other recordings of the tune that charted include those by Vic Damone, by Richard Hayman, by Freddy Martin and his orchestra, and by Tony Martin.

Variety named "April in Portugal" to its *Hit Parade of a Half-Century*.

Changing Partners

Words: Joe Darion; Music: Larry Coleman

"Changing Partners" became Patti Page's tenth million seller, however, her recording only made it to No. 3 on the *Billboard* chart in early '54. The song only managed one appearance on *Your Hit Parade* and that was at the No. 4 position in mid–December '53.

Joe Darion, the lyricist, later became famous as the lyricist for the Broadway stage, notably for *Man of La*

Mancha in '64-'65, and for the Academy Award-winning song "Never on Sunday" in '60.

This *Variety Hit Parade of a Half-Century* waltz tells the sad tale of a lover who danced away when the bandleader called out "change partners." The singer is certain the lovers will continue changing partners until they have their loved one again and then they'll "never change partners again!" Read the lyrics at http://lirama.net/song/16652.

Crying in the Chapel

Words & Music: Artie Glenn

According to Larry Glenn, the writer's son, the chapel referred to in the song was Loving Avenue Baptist Church in Fort Worth, Texas. His father had gone there to pray and repent. Glenn had recently under gone spinal surgery. While in the hospital, he had promised God a closer relationship. The lyrics directly reflect his mood: he was crying tears of joy.

The song first was recorded in '53 by the songwriter's son, Darrell, when he was 17. Darrell's recording made it to No. 6 on *Billboard*. Country and western vocalist Rex Allen had success with it on both the country and pop charts, and the rhythm and blues group, the Orioles, featuring Sonny Til, had good success with their Jubilee disk. However, June Valli had the most successful version on the pop charts. Her version was No. 1 for one week on *Cash Box*, but only managed No. 3 on *Your Hit Parade* and No. 4 on *Billboard*.

Ella Fitzgerald and Art Lund also had recordings of "Crying in the Chapel" that charted in '53.

Elvis Presley recorded the song on an album in '60, but it wasn't released as a single until '65, when his recording of the song peaked at No. 3 on the *Billboard* chart.

In the song's lyrics, a person searches for peace, and once it has been found, he thanks the Lord with tears of joy. Read the lyrics at http://www.lyricsdepot.com/june-valli/crying-in-the-chapel.html.

Variety named "Crying in the Chapel" to its *Hit Parade of a Half-Century.*

Don't Let the Stars Get in Your Eyes

Words & Music: Slim Willet, Cactus Pryor, and Barbara Trammel

When country singer Slim Willet recorded his version of "Don't Let the Stars Get in Your Eyes" in late '52, he felt that he and his collaborators had written a good song that had hit potential on the country charts, but he had no idea that it would be so successful on the pop charts. Two other country singers, Ray Price and Skeets McDonald, recorded their versions of the song and all three were successful on the country charts. Then Red Foley released a rendition in early '53, which began to climb the national pop charts, so it was covered by Perry Como. Como's version became a national hit.

As rhythm and blues becomes rock and roll in the next few years, "cover" recordings became extremely common. When some black singer released a rhythm and blues song that began to show hit potential in the black market, some mainline pop singer would record what was called a "cover" version. The cover version was almost always the most popular one on the national scene. Before cover version were made of rhythm and blues song, covers were being made of country music song hits.

Perry Como's version of "Don't Let the Stars Get in Your Eyes" with Hugo Winterhalter and his orchestra and

the Ramblers was *Billboard's* No. 8 hit for the year and No. 4 on *Variety's* Top Ten. It spent five weeks each at the top of *Billboard*, *Cash Box*, and *Your Hit Parade*.

Gisele MacKenzie and Eileen Barton also released recordings of the song that charted.

The song is based on the irregular meter and form of a Mexican ranchera, a type of Tex-Mex song. The chorus is sung first with two verses interspersed between choruses. Two chords, the tonic and dominant seventh, comprise the sparse harmonic scheme.

The singer is afraid he will be gone too long and his girl will change her mind about him. He's cautioning her to not allow the stars to get in her eyes or the moon to break her heart. He also reminds her that the love that blooms at night often dies in the daylight, so she should keep her heart only for him until he returns. Read the lyrics at http://www.twin-music.com/azlyrics/c_file/songs/como/dont.html.

"Don't Let the Star Get in Your Eyes" is a *Variety Hit Parade of a Half-Century* selection.

Ebb Tide

Words & Music: Carl Sigman & Robert Maxwell

"Ebb Tide" is another of '53's instrumental hits. The beautiful "Ebb Tide" was most popular in a recording by Frank Chacksfield's Orchestra. His disk opened with a solo oboe against a background of recorded waves hitting the shore. The song was surprisingly No. 1 on *Your Hit Parade* for four weeks in '53 and one week in '54 (surprisingly because *Your Hit Parade* often ignored instrumental hits, but perhaps the performers on the show got to use the lyric version). It reached No. 2 on *Billboard* and No. 3 on *Cash Box*. *Variety* had it tied for No. 10 for the year, while *Billboard* ranked it No. 12.

Vic Damone and Roy Hamilton also released versions of the song that were popular enough to chart in '53 or '54. Lenny Welch revived the song with mediocre success in '64, while the Righteous Brothers' '66 version reached No. 5 on *Billboard*.

Sigman's lyrics draw a clever analogy between the sea and love: "Like the tide at its ebb, I'm at peace in the web of your arms." Read the lyrics at http://www.oracleband.net/Lyrics/ebb_tide.htm.

Variety selected "Ebb Tide" for its *Hit Parade of a Half-Century* representing '53.

I Believe

Words & Music: Ervin Drake, Irvin Graham, Jimmy Shirl, and Al Stillman

Frankie Laine's version of "I Believe" helped popularize the song to hit status (No. 14 on *Billboard*, No. 9 on *Variety*, and No. 6 on *Cash Box*). It eventually sold three million copies. The song was No. 1 on *Your Hit Parade* for three weeks; it topped the *Cash Box* chart for a couple of weeks. It peaked at No. 2 on *Billboard*.

Jane Froman's recording of the song peaked just outside *Billboard's* top ten. The vocal trio the Bachelors revived the song again in '64.

According to Songwriters' Hall of Fame website, "I Believe" has sold a total of 20 million copies, however according to Ervin Drake's website, it has sold over 100 million copies.

The lyrics allude to a belief in God but never actually say so. The nearest the song comes to a reference to actual religious belief is his conviction that "the smallest pray'r will still be heard." Read the lyrics at http://www.oldielyrics.com/lyrics/frankie_laine/i_believe.html.

"I Believe" was chosen by *Variety* for its *Hit Parade of a Half-Century.*

I'm Walking Behind You
Words & Music: Billy Reid

British songwriter and bandleader Billy Reid wrote this song that was popularized by Eddie Fisher. It was *Variety*'s No. 8 hit of the year; it was No. 5 on *Cash Box* and No. 7 on *Billboard.* The song spent three weeks as the No. 1 hit on *Your Hit Parade.*

The subtitle of the song is a line that precedes the title: "Look over your shoulder." The lyrics sing about watching the one you love get married to someone else. The singer wishes the bride well, but promises if things go wrong, he'll be there for her. Read the lyrics at http://ntl.matrix.com.br/pfilho/html/lyrics/i/im_walking_behind_you.txt.

Eddie Fisher's recording collected seven weeks at No. 1 on *Billboard,* while Frank Sinatra's recording of the song only made it to No. 7 on *Billboard.*

Variety selected "I'm Walking Behind You" for its *Hit Parade of a Half-Century* representing both '53 and '54.

Keep It a Secret
Words & Music: Jessie Mae Robinson

This *Variety Hit Parade of a Half-Century* song was a hit by Jo Stafford and by Bing Crosby (Stafford's was most popular in '53, Crosby's in '52). Country star Slim Whitman also had a recording of the song that was popular on the country charts and somewhat popular on the pop charts.

The song was one of the top ten songs on *Your Hit Parade* for fourteen weeks in 1953, but never made it to the top spot.

The singer tells us if we see his or her sweetheart with someone else, we're to "keep it a secret." Read the lyrics at http://www.lyricsvault.net/songs/17800.html.

Patti Page popularized Jessie Mae Robinson's "I Went to Your Wedding" in '52.

Many Times
English Words: Jessie Barnes (pseudonym for Carl Sigman); Music: Felix Stahl

This *Variety Hit Parade of a Half-Century* number was a Belgian song that was introduced in the U.S. by Percy Faith and his orchestra. The song was on *Your Hit Parade*'s top ten for eleven weeks at the end of '53 and the beginning of '54, but it never made it past the No. 3 spot.

Eddie Fisher popularized the song in a recording that peaked at No. 4 on *Billboard.* Percy Faith and his orchestra's version also charted.

"Many Times" the singer has wanted his girl's kisses. He had often dreamed he'd hold her and they'd be kissing. To him this was heaven and he wants to be taken there by her "Many Times" again.

No Other Love
Words: Oscar Hammerstein II; Music: Richard Rodgers

Richard Rodgers first used this melody as a tango in the "Beneath the Southern Cross" section of the television documentary *Victory at Sea* in '52. Then he and lyricist Oscar Hammerstein II transformed it into "No Other Love," which was introduced by Bill Hayes and Isabel Bigley in the Broadway musical *Me and Juliet.*

The song pledges undying faithfulness. Read the lyrics at http://www.songlyrics4u.com/perry-como/no-other-love.html.

Perry Como popularized the song to No. 1 for two weeks in the fall of '53 on *Your Hit Parade.* It also topped the *Cash Box* chart for two weeks, and the *Billboard* chart for four weeks. It was *Billboard*'s No. 9 hit of the year.

Variety selected "No Other Love" for its *Hit Parade of a Half-Century.*

Pretend
Words & Music: Lew Douglas, Cliff Parman, and Frank Lavere

Nat "King" Cole popularized "Pretend" to the top spot on *Your Hit Parade* for three weeks in the spring of '53. It only reached No. 2 on *Billboard* and *Cash Box,* but ranked No. 18 for the year on *Billboard,* and No. 10 for *Cash Box.*

Ralph Marterie and his orchestra and Eileen Barton also had recordings of "Pretend" that charted.

The singer encourages us to "Pretend" we're happy even if we're blue. Read the lyrics at http://www.lyricsdepot.com/nat_king_cole/pretend.html.

Rags to Riches
Words & Music: Richard Adler and Jerry Ross

Billboard's No. 4 hit, with eight weeks at No. 1, was Tony Bennett's recording of "Rags to Riches." Bennett's recording was *Variety*'s No. 6 hit and it topped the *Cash Box* chart for four weeks. Bennett's disk reportedly sold almost two million copies. The song collected two weeks at No. 1 on *Your Hit Parade.*

The writers of the musicals *Pajama Game* and *Damn Yankees,* Richard Adler and Jerry Ross, wrote this song as an independent song, that is not for a Broadway musical or Hollywood movie, prior to their Broadway associations.

Bennett sang that he would go from "rags to riches" if only the object of his affection would say she cared for him. Read the lyrics at http://www.lyricsvault.net/songs/17783.html.

Variety selected "Rags to Riches" for its *Hit Parade of a Half-Century.*

Richocet
Words & Music: Larry Coleman, Joe Darion, and Norman Gimbel

Teresa Brewer had a big hit with this song that has a country flavor.

The song collected one week at No. 1 on both *Your Hit Parade* and *Cash Box.* It peaked at No. 2 on *Billboard.*

Ms. Brewer sang in her shrill, high-pitched voice that she did not want a guy that would ricochet from one girl to another. If so, she would gladly set him free.

Variety chose "Richocet" for its *Hit Parade of a Half-Century.*

Teresa Brewer performed the song in the '53 film *Those Redheads from Seattle.*

The Song from Moulin Rouge (Where Is My Heart?)

Words: William Engvick; Music: Georges Auric

The screen biography of Toulouse-Lautrec, *Moulin Rouge*, produced *Cash Box*'s No. 1 hit and *Billboard*'s and *Variety*'s No. 2 hit of 1953. Percy Faith and his orchestra's recording of the song spent ten weeks at No. 1 on *Billboard*, nine weeks at No. 1 on *Cash Box*. The song collected eight weeks at No. 1 on *Your Hit Parade*.

The song was performed on the film's soundtrack by Muriel Smith singing for Zsa Zsa Gabor.

Even though this was one of the year's biggest hit songs that had film origins, the song was ignored by the Academy when nominations for the Oscar were made, which shouldn't be too surprising since the nominations generally tend to ignore basically instrumental numbers. Surprisingly, it was not ignored by the *Your Hit Parade* survey; they also often bypass basically instrumental hits. However, towards the end of Percy Faith and his orchestra's recording Felicia Sanders does sing, so it was not completely instrumental.

Other versions that charted were those by Mantovani and his orchestra and by Henri Rene and his orchestra with vocalist Alvy West.

The tune was by composer Georges Auric. The original French title was "Le Long de la Seine" with French words by Jacques Larue.

The song's subtitle is "Where Is Your Heart?" The singer tells her lover his lips may be near, but she questions where his heart is. Read the lyrics at http://homepage.ntlworld.com/gary.hart/lyricsm/mantovani.html.

Variety named "The Song from Moulin Rouge" to its *Hit Parade of a Half-Century*.

There have been six films titled *Moulin Rouge* (in '28, '34, '40, '41, '52 and 2001) according to the Internet Movie Database website. The plot of the '52 film revolves around Henri de Toulouse-Lautrec, who frequently visits the Moulin Rouge, where he draws sketches of the dancers and singers. Henri's personal life is often unhappy due to his legs being badly deformed by a childhood fall. As he is heading home one night, a young woman of the streets named Marie, asks him for help. Henri, the son of a count, falls in love with her, and the two become involved. Toulouse-Lautrec, played by Jose Ferrer, increasingly finds it more difficult to balance his personal feelings, his artistic abilities, and maintain his family name and position. In the more recent 2001 film, the plot line was completely different and it was a musical. In its plot, Christian, a young Scottish poet living in 1899 Paris, becomes involved with Satine, the star attraction of the Moulin Rouge. This film starred Nicole Kidman and Ewan McGregor.

St. George and the Dragonet

Words: Stan Freberg; Music: Walter Schumann

Stan Freberg's comedy routine "St George and the Dragonet" was No. 1 on *Billboard* for four weeks in '53; it ranked No. 10 for the year. It only made it to No. 8 on *Cash Box*, and was snubbed by *Your Hit Parade* and *Variety*, perhaps because it was not really or completely a song; it was more of a comedy routine. However, it did use the *Dragnet* theme music.

This comic routine is a spoof that combines the story of "St. George and the Dragon" with the modern televi-

sion show *Dragnet*. Walter Schumann's *Dragnet* theme music is an integral part of the recording. Read the "lyrics" to this spoof at http://lirama.net/song/16684.

The early fifties seem to have been the heyday of comedy recordings. In '52 Johnny Standley's "It's in the Book" made it to No. 1 on *Billboard*, and in '53, this Stan Freberg classic also topped the chart. Others from the time period that have become comedy classics include Andy Griffith's "What It Was, Was Football" and "Romeo and Juliet," Yogi Yorgesson's "The Bees and the Birds" and "The Object of My Affection," Harry Kari's "Yokohama Mama," and Stan Freberg's "Little Blue Riding Hood" and "John and Marsha," among others.

That's Amore

Words: Jack Brooks; Music: Harry Warren

This Academy Award nominee for '53 was introduced in *The Caddy*, which starred Dean Martin and Jerry Lewis.

Dean Martin's recording of the song rose to No. 2 on *Billboard*, making it that chart's No. 11 hit of the year. The song became Martin's first million seller and sold more than four million copies over the next decade. The song made a dozen appearances on the *Your Hit Parade* hit survey, peaking at No. 2 in early 1954.

Martin sings in a slight Italian accent as the lyrics sing about several Italian delicacies, like "a big pizza pie" and "pasta fazool." "That's amore" literally means "that's love," but according to the lyrics it means "you're in love." Read the lyrics and hear a midi musical version at http://www.harrywarren.org/songs/0508.htm. See Harry Warren's original manuscript at http://www.harrywarrenmusic.com/frameset.html.

"That's Amore" was selected by *Variety* for its *Hit Parade of a Half-Century*. This song was nominated for the American Film Institute's list of the greatest songs ever from an American film, but did not make the final list. It was nominated for its inclusion in *Moonstruck* ('87). The song also appeared in *Rear Window* ('54), *Bye Bye Love* ('95), *Grumpier Old Men* ('95), *Money Talks* ('97), *Babe: Pig in the City* ('98) and *Cotton Mary* ('99).

(How Much Is) That Doggie in the Window

Words & Music: Bob Merrill

Bob Merrill wrote this novelty song in '52; Patti Page recording of it was released in '53. Her recording reportedly sold over three million copies over the next fourteen years. Ms. Page's disk garnered the No. 3 spot in *Variety*'s and No. 5 on *Billboard*'s Top Ten for the year; it was No. 8 on *Cash Box* for the year. It collected eight weeks at No. 1 on *Billboard* and five weeks on *Cash Box*. The song topped *Your Hit Parade*'s chart for one week in April '53, but it appeared on the hit survey for a dozen weeks.

Patti Page introduced "That Doggie in the Window" on a children's album, but there was such demand by disk jockeys for its release as a single, the company acquiesced.

According to the sheet music cover, the correct title for the song is "(How Much Is) That Doggie in the Window," not simply "Doggie in the Window."

"How much is that doggie in the window?" sang Page and the nation showed its empathy by buying the record. Read the words at http://www.lyricsvault.net/songs/19786.html.

Variety included "That Doggie in the Window" on its *Hit Parade of a Half-Century.*

That's Entertainment
Words: Howard Dietz; Music: Arthur Schwartz

Fred Astaire, Oscar Levant, Jack Buchanan and Nanette Fabray performed "That's Entertainment" in the film version of the Broadway revue *The Band Wagon.* Producer Arthur Freed asked Schwartz and Dietz to write a "There's No Business Like Show Business" kind of song for the film. In approximately thirty minutes, they came up with another pean to show business, which will probably continue to rival Berlin's "There's No Business Like Show Business" and Cohan's "Give My Regards to Broadway" as the most famous show business song for many years. AFI's *100 Years ... 100 Songs* (2004) named this song the No. 45 greatest song ever from an American film.

There have been three compilation films of excerpts from MGM movie musicals titled *That's Entertainment, That's Entertainment II* and *That's Entertainment III.* The song also appeared in the Elvis Presley film *Viva Las Vegas* ('64) as background music for a plate-spinning act.

Read the lyrics at http://www.stlyrics.com/lyrics/the bandwagon/thatsentertainment.htm.

Till I Waltz Again with You
Words & Music: Sidney Prosen

Teresa Brewer recorded this *Variety Hit Parade of a Half-Century* song in '52 and popularized it to No. 1 in '53. It was No. 1 on *Billboard* for seven weeks, on *Cash Box* for five weeks, and the song was No. 1 on *Your Hit Parade* for four weeks. It was No. 2 for the year on *Cash Box*, No. 5 for *Variety*, and No. 6 for *Billboard.*

Other recordings of the song that were popular enough to chart include those by Dick Todd, by Russ Morgan and his orchestra, and by the Harmonicats.

The song suggests that the loved one waltz alone until they waltz again together. However, the song is not a waltz. Read the lyrics at http://lirama.net/song/16635.

Vaya Con Dios
Words & Music: Larry Russell, Inez James, and Buddy Pepper

Variety's and *Billboard*'s No. 1 hit and *Cash Box*'s No. 4 hit of the year was Les Paul and Mary Ford's recording of "Vaya Con Dios." Their disk spent eleven weeks at No. 1 on *Billboard* and three weeks at the top of *Cash Box*'s chart. The song managed five weeks at No. 1 on *Your Hit Parade.*

In late '52, jazz singer Anita O'Day was in a recording session when her orchestra leader Larry Russell showed her a song he had co-written named "Vaya Con Dios." O'Day cut the song and released it for the independent Clef label. She was supposed to perform the song on the TV show *Juke Box Jury* in early '53, but the night before her appearance, she was arrested on a heroin charge. By the time she resolved this issue, her chance to promote her recording of the song had passed, because Les Paul and Mary Ford had heard her recording on the radio, loved it, and immediately recorded their own version. It became the biggest of Les Paul and Mary Ford's hits. Their recording of the song was inducted into the Grammy Hall of Fame in 2005.

"Vaya Con Dios" is a salutation meaning "God be with you," which was the singer's wish as she said goodbye to her loved one. Read the lyrics at http://lirama.net/song/16687.

"Vaya Con Dios" was named to *Variety*'s *Hit Parade of a Half-Century.*

You, You, You
Words: Robert Mellin; Music: Lotar Olias

Billboard's No. 3 and *Variety*'s and *Cash Box*'s No. 7 hit of '53 was the Ames Brothers' recording of "You, You, You" by German composer Lotar Olias. Robert Mellin had furnished the English lyrics in '52. The Ames Brothers' disk spent eight weeks at No. 1 on *Billboard*, six weeks at the top of *Cash Box*, and the song was No. 1 for four weeks on *Your Hit Parade.*

The repetition of the "You, You, You" ("Du, Du, Du" in German) of the title five times in the song is its most distinctive characteristic. Read the lyrics at http://ntl.matrix.com.br/pfilho/html/lyrics/y/you_you_you.txt.

Variety named "You, You, You" to its *Hit Parade of a Half-Century* representing '53.

Your Cheating Heart
Words & Music: Hank Williams

Country legend Hank Williams had four million selling recordings in '52-'53: "Jambalaya," "Honky Tonk Blues," "I'll Never Get Out of This World Alive" (which may have been prophetic since he died in '53), and "Your Cheating Heart." Williams' recording of "Your Cheating Heart" was inducted into the Grammy Hall of Fame in '83.

The song has a stereotypical country subject, a broken romance, but the song transcended the boundaries of country to become a major hit. Joni James' recording of the song was the most popular version on the pop chart, peaking at No. 2 on *Billboard.* Frankie Laine and Hank Williams' versions also charted on *Billboard.*

The song made thirteen appearances on *Your Hit Parade*, topping out at No. 4 on the show for the second week of May of '53.

The basic idea of the song can be summed up in the line, "Your cheating heart will tell on you." Read the words at http://www.oldielyrics.com/lyrics/joni_james/your_cheating_heart.html.

1954

Cross Over the Bridge
Words & Music: Bennie Benjamin & George Weiss

Patti Page had another million seller with Bennie Benjamin and George Weiss' "Cross Over the Bridge." Page's hit peaked at No. 2 on *Billboard.* The song managed nine weeks on *Your Hit Parade*, peaking at No. 3 in the spring of 1954.

The singer advises us to leave our fickle past behind us and "cross over the bridge" to true romance. Read the lyrics at http://lirama.net/song/16699.

The song was named to *Variety*'s *Hit Parade of a Half-Century.*

The Happy Wanderer (Der Frohliche Wanderer)

English Words: Antonia Ridge; Music: Friedrich-Wilhelm Moller

"The Happy Wanderer" is easily mistaken as a folk song, but it was a composed song by Friedrich-Wilhelm Moller, with lyrics by his sister, Edith, and Florenz Siegesmund. Edith Moller was the conductor of an amateur children's choir. That choir won an international choir festival in North Wales in '53. The BBC broadcast the festival, where the children sang "Der Frohliche Wanderer" as their encore. The song quickly became a hit, rising to No. 2 on the UK singles chart in early '54.

The amateur choir toured internationally as Obernkirchen Children's Choir. They performed on *The Ed Sullivan Show* twice.

The song's German lyrics by Florenz Siegesmund and Edith Moller were translated into English by Antonia Ridge.

Frank Weir and his orchestra, Henri Rene and his orchestra, and Tommy Leonetti popularized the song with successful recordings.

The song appeared on *Your Hit Parade* eight times, but only made it to No. 4.

The "val-de-ri, val-de-ra" of the chorus is very distinctive and memorable; it is the song mountain hikers' sang to express their joy. Read the lyrics at http://lirama.net/song/16706.

Hey There *and* Hernando's Hideaway

Words & Music: Richard Adler and Jerry Ross

The musical was based on Richard Bissell's novel *7½ Cents*, about a small town pajama factory that is threatened by a strike.

HEY THERE

"Hey There," from *Pajama Game*, is the first Broadway song since '49's "Some Enchanted Evening" to make it to No. 1 on *Your Hit Parade*; it was No. 1 for ten weeks. It also was No. 1 on *Billboard* for six weeks, and No. 1 on *Cash Box* for eight weeks (seven weeks for Rosemary Clooney's recording, and one week for Sammy Davis, Jr.'s version). It was No. 1 for the year on *Variety*, No. 2 for *Cash Box*, and No. 7 for *Billboard*.

John Raitt, playing Sid Sorokin, the new superintendent of the Sleep Tite Pajama Factory, introduced "Hey, There" as a memo to himself via a Dictaphone. He then plays it back while he interpolates comments and ends by singing a duet with himself.

Rosemary Clooney's recording of "Hey There," coupled with the flip side recording of "This Ole House," reportedly became a two and a half million seller. Her recording also used the singer singing a duet with herself through one of the earlier uses of multitrack recording. Her recording of the song was inducted into the Grammy Hall of Fame in 1999.

The singer is talking to herself, reminding herself that love never had made a fool of her, she was too wise. She's telling herself to forget this man. However, she doesn't seem to be heeding her self-advice. Read the lyrics at http://lirama.net/song/16709.

Johnnie Ray also had a recording of the song that charted on *Billboard*.

Variety included "Hey, There" in its *Hit Parade of a Half-Century*. This song was nominated for the American Film Institute's list of greatest songs ever from an American film, but was not on the final list. It was nominated for the 1957 film version of *Pajama Game*.

HERNANDO'S HIDEAWAY

"Hernando's Hideaway" is a comic tango from the same Broadway musical. Gladys, played by Carol Haney, introduced this slinky tune, which was popularized in the popular music marketplace by Archie Bleyer and his orchestra. His recording was No. 1 on *Cash Box* for two weeks, and reached No. 2 on *Billboard*. *Billboard* ranked it No. 13 for the year. The song was No. 1 on *Your Hit Parade* for one week

Guy Lombardo and his Royal Canadians and Johnnie Ray also had recordings of the song that charted on *Billboard*.

The singer knows a dark secluded club where no one knows you. They don't care how late it gets at "Hernando's Hideaway." At this club, you are free to gaze at the singer and talk to her of love. Read the words at http://lirama.net/song/16708.

Variety chose "Hernando's Hideaway" for its *Hit Parade of a Half-Century*.

Another famous song from *Pajama Game* is "Steam Heat."

The film version of *Pajama Game*, starring John Raitt and Doris Day, was released in 1957. Carol Haney performed "Hernando's Hideaway" and "Steam Heat" while Raitt reprised his Broadway performance of "Hey There."

The High and the Mighty

Words: Ned Washington; Music: Dimitri Tiomkin

Dimitri Tiomkin had great success with the theme from the film *The High and the Mighty*. He had composed the 1952 Academy Award winner, "High Noon," with lyricist Ned Washington also. This song also copped an Oscar nomination, but lost to "Three Coins in the Fountain."

In the film John Wayne whistled the melody, so whistling was prominent in the popular recordings. The most popular recording was by Les Baxter and his orchestra, which peaked at No. 4 on *Billboard*, while Victor Young and his orchestra's recording rose to No. 6. Leroy Holmes and his orchestra, Johnny Desmond and the composer Dimitri Tiomkin also released popular recordings of the song.

The song made a dozen appearances on *Your Hit Parade*, but only managed to get to No. 2.

The singer admits when he was "high and mighty" he laughed at love. Then along came a girl that taught his heart to love. Now he's not cynical because he has a love that is "worth all the gold on earth." Read the lyrics at http://lirama.net/song/16710.

"The High and the Mighty" was chosen for *Variety*'s *Hit Parade of a Half-Century*.

I Get So Lonely (When I Dream About You)

Words & Music: Pat Ballard

Variety included this song (as "Oh, Baby Mine") in its *Hit Parade of a Half-Century*.

The Four Knights recording of "I Get So Lonely (When I Dream About You)" peaked at No. 2 on the *Billboard* chart in '54.

The song managed fourteen appearances on *Your Hit Parade*, but only rose to No. 4 by mid–May, 1954.

"Oh, Baby Mine" is a prominent part of the lyric, especially as the introduction and by the background singers. The lead singer tells his baby he'll give her "kisses without number," but it is only in his dreams. Read the lyrics at http://www.oldielyrics.com/lyrics/the_four_knights/i_get_so_lonely_when_i_dream_about_you.html.

I Need You Now

Words & Music: Jimmie Crane and Al Jacobs

It was an extraordinary year for the songwriting team of Jimmie Crane and Al Jacobs. They had two big hits: "If I Give My Heart to You" and "I Need You Now." The second one was No. 1 for three weeks on both *Billboard* and *Cash Box*, but only collected one week at No. 1 on *Your Hit Parade*.

Eddie Fisher's recording of the song was No. 10 for the year on *Billboard*, No. 7 on *Variety*.

Fisher sang, "If I ever needed you, I need you now." He feels all alone and doesn't know what to do about it. Only this girl knows how to ease his aching heart. Read the lyrics at http://lirama.net/song/16715.

If I Give My Heart to You

Words & Music: Jimmie Crane, Al Jacobs, and Jimmy Brewster

"If I Give My Heart to You" was popularized by Doris Day. Her recording boosted the song to the No. 1 spot on both *Cash Box* and *Your Hit Parade* for two weeks. It only made it to No. 3 on *Billboard*, but came in at No. 22 for the year.

Denise Lor, Connee Boswell, the Wright Brothers, and Dinah Shore had recordings of "If I Give My Heart to You" that sold well enough to chart.

The singer asks, "If I give my heart to you, will you handle it with care?" Read the lyrics at http://www.lyricsdepot.com/doris-day/if-i-give-my-heart-to-you.html.

Variety selected "If I Give My Heart to You" for its *Hit Parade of a Half-Century*.

Little Things Mean a Lot

Words & Music: Edith Lindeman and Carl Stutz

Billboard's and *Cash Box's* No. 1 hit of the year was Kitty Kallen's recording of "Little Things Mean a Lot." It was No. 2 in *Variety's* Top Ten for 1954. It collected nine weeks at No. 1 on *Billboard*, six weeks at the top of both *Cash Box* and *Your Hit Parade*.

A Richmond, Virginia disk jockey, Carl Stutz, and the amusement editor for the Richmond *Times-Dispatch*, Edith Lindeman, wrote this song that reportedly became a million seller for Ms. Kallen, her first No. 1 hit as a solo artist. She had been a singer with several big bands including stints with Jack Teagarden, Jimmy Dorsey, and Harry James.

The song itemizes some of those little things that women appreciate men doing for them, including blowing her a kiss, saying she looks nice even when she really doesn't, and giving her his arm as they cross the street. Read the lyrics at http://ntl.matrix.com.br/pfilho/html/lyrics/l/little_things_mean_a_lot.txt.

"Little Things Mean a Lot" is one of the songs included in *Variety's Hit Parade of a Half-Century*.

Make Love to Me

Words: Bill Norvas and Allan Copeland; Music: New Orleans Rhythm Kings and Walter Melrose

"Make Love to Me" seems too sexually suggestive to have been popular in the relatively conservative fifties. Perhaps its roots in jazz explain its suggestiveness since many jazz lyrics are full of sexual innuendoes. But the song was extremely popular and was reportedly a million seller for Jo Stafford. It became *Billboard's* No. 5 hit of the year, with seven weeks at No. 1, and *Variety's* No. 8 hit of the year. It managed only one week at the top of the *Cash Box* chart. Perhaps its suggestive nature kept it off the *Your Hit Parade* survey.

The song began in 1923 as "Tin Roof Blues," written by five players in the New Orleans Rhythm Kings plus Walter Melrose, a composer, author, and publisher during the twenties. Melrose wrote the original lyrics, but Bill Norvas and Allan Copeland contributed the present version in 1953.

The song's tempo marking calls for a moderately slow shuffle with a beat. The predominance of dotted eighth- and sixteenth-note patterns gives the tune a bounciness that's catchy.

Jo Stafford wants her lover to take her in his arms and never let her go. She provocatively tells him to "Come a little closer, make love to me." Read the lyrics at http://lirama.net/song/16729.

Make Yourself Comfortable

Words & Music: Bob Merrill

Variety included "Make Yourself Comfortable" in its *Hit Parade of a Half-Century*.

Recordings by Sarah Vaughan, Andy Griffith and Jean Wilson and by Peggy Lee helped popularized the song in '55. Vaughan's was the highest ranked version, peaking at No. 6 on the *Billboard* chart.

The song appeared twice on *Your Hit Parade*, peaking at No. 5 in early February of '55.

The singer wants her lover to get comfortable by taking his shoes off and loosening his tie. She says they hurried through dinner, the dance and a movie ("picture show") to save time for hugging and kissing. Read the lyrics at http://www.lyricsdepot.com/sarah-vaughan/make-yourself-comfortable.html.

Mambo Italiano

Words & Music: Bob Merrill

Rosemary Clooney collected three gold records in '54: "Hey There," "This Ole House," and "Mambo Italiano." However, "Mambo Italiano" only made it to No. 10 on the *Billboard* chart and it never appeared on *Your Hit Parade*.

The mambo is a type of rumba that originated in Cuba. It has a quadruple (4) meter with a syncopated (accented) third beat. Its Spanish origins make "Mambo Italiano" sound like a misnomer.

According to the lyrics, the singer returned to Napoli because she missed the city's scenery, the native Italian dances and their charming songs. Then, she abruptly halts this tale and declares something was not right; after the halt, the song changes to "Hey, mambo! Mambo italiano!" There are several Italian words and phrases which help its authenticity, including "sicialiano," "paisano," "mozzarella," and a fish enchilada (Italian dish?). Read the lyrics at http://lirama.net/song/16731.

Variety thought enough of the song to include it in its *Hit Parade of a Half-Century*.

The Man That Got Away

Words: Ira Gershwin; Music: Harold Arlen

Judy Garland introduced "The Man That Got Away" in the movie musical *A Star Is Born* ('54). The song was nominated for the '54 Academy Award for Best Song, but lost to "Three Coins in the Fountain." However, AFI's *100 Years ... 100 Songs* (2004) listed "The Man That Got Away" as the No. 11 greatest song from an American film.

Frank Sinatra's recording of the song as "The Gal That Got Away" peaked at No. 21 on *Billboard*, while Judy Garland's female version came in at only No. 22.

The song is rather long for a pop song, extending 62 measures. It is sometimes considered a blues, but it is not a blues in the traditional sense, although it might be considered a Tin Pan Alley blues. It might actually be more of was called a "torch song" back in the '30s.

The singer bemoans the bitter night, the stars with no glitter, and the colder winds. She even feels suddenly a lot older, because her lover left ("got away"). Read the lyrics as Sinatra sang them at http://franksinatra.lyrics.info/thegalthatgotaway.html.

Mister Sandman

Words & Music: Pat Ballard

The No. 6 hit in 1954's top ten on the *Billboard* chart was the Chordettes' recording of "Mister Sandman." It collected seven weeks at No. 1 on that chart. The song collected eighteen appearances on *Your Hit Parade*, including eight weeks at No. 1 (four weeks at the end of 1954 and four at the beginning of 1955).

Pat Ballard, the music editor of *College Humor*, wrote the song.

The Chordettes were the prototype of many groups that became famous in the next several years. The Chordettes' recording of the song was inducted into the Grammy Hall of Fame in 2002.

Buddy Morrow and the Lancers issued popular recordings of the song in '54, while the Four Aces' recording was most popular in '55.

The singers are begging the sandman to bring them a dream of the cutest guy they have ever seen. Most of the melody is sung staccato. Read the words at http://www.lyricsvault.net/songs/17899.html.

Variety included "Mister Sandman" in its *Hit Parade of a Half-Century*.

Oh! My Pa-Pa

Words: John Turner and Geoffrey Parsons; Music: Paul Burkhard

This song was a fantastic hit in '54: it was No. 4 for the year on *Variety*, No. 4 on *Billboard*, and No. 8 on *Cash Box*. Eddie Fisher's recording of "Oh! My Pa-Pa" collected eight weeks at No. 1 on *Billboard* and five weeks at the top of the *Cash Box* chart. The song never made it to No. 1 on *Your Hit Parade*, peaking at No. 2.

Paul Burkhard wrote the song, with German lyrics, in '48; it was published in Switzerland, and was used in a musical in Zurich (*Schwarze Hecht*). The show was re-

vived in Hamburg, Germany, as *Feuerwerke* (Fireworks) in '53, when the song began to gain attention. Britain's John Turner (pen name for Jimmy Phillips) and Geoffrey Parsons translated the original into English.

Eddie Calvert, a trumpet player from Preston, England, had his recording of the song rise to No. 6 on *Billboard*, while Ray Anthony and his orchestra's version made it to No. 15.

Eddie Fisher's recording with Hugo Winterhalter's orchestra and chorus was far more popular in the United States. The singer sang with heartfelt passion about his late father. Read the lyrics at http://www.songlyrics4u.com/eddie-fisher/oh-my-papa.html.

Variety chose "Oh! My Pa-Pa" to represent 1953 in its *Hit Parade of a Half-Century*.

Secret Love

Words: Paul Francis Webster; Music: Sammy Fain

The Oscar for the best song from films in '53 went to the song "Secret Love" from the movie musical *Calamity Jane*, which starred Doris Day in the title role. The film was released in '53, as was the recording of "Secret Love" by Doris Day. Her recording racked up four weeks at No. 1 on *Billboard*, five weeks at the top of *Cash Box*'s chart, and seven weeks at No. 1 on *Your Hit Parade*. Her disk was No. 8 for the year on *Billboard*, No. 9 on *Cash Box*, No. 10 on *Variety* for '54.

Calamity Jane sings about the love she feels for Wild Bill Hickock, that has been a secret, perhaps even to herself, until this moment. She was always too rough and tough to allow herself to be so vulnerable as to let love enter her life. Read the lyrics at http://www.lyricsdepot.com/doris-day/secret-love.html.

Doris Day's recording of the song was inducted into the Grammy Hall of Fame in 1999.

Tommy Edwards, Ray Anthony and his orchestra, Billy Stewart and Freddy Fender also had recordings of "Secret Love" that charted.

Variety chose "Secret Love" for its *Hit Parade of a Half-Century*. This song was nominated for the American Film Institute's list of the greatest songs ever from an American film, but did not make the final list.

Shake, Rattle and Roll

Words & Music: Charles Calhoun

"Shake, Rattle and Roll" along with "Rock Around the Clock" ('55) launched the rock and roll craze that dominated popular music for the second half of the 20th century.

Joe Turner originally recorded a rhythm and blues version of "Shake, Rattle and Roll." His version made it to No. 22 on *Billboard*. Turner's recording of the song was inducted into the Grammy Hall of Fame in 1998.

Then Bill Haley and his Comets recorded it, cleaned up the lyrics a little to be more palatable to WASP (white, Anglo-Saxon, Protestant) ears, and had a much bigger hit with their cover version. It peaked at No. 7 on *Billboard*, but showed that there was a market for cover versions of rhythm and blues material.

Arthur Conley revived "Shake, Rattle and Roll" in 1967, when his version only made it to No. 31 on *Billboard*.

Read the lyrics from Bill Haley's version at http://www.oldielyrics.com/lyrics/bill_haley_and_the_comets/shake_rattle_and_roll.html or read Joe Turner's version, Charles

Calhoun's original lyrics, at http://www.harptab.com/lyrics/ly2648.shtml.

Variety included "Shake, Rattle and Roll" in its *Hit Parade of a Half-Century.*

Sh-Boom

Words & Music: The Chords

The Crew Cuts' version of "Sh-Boom" is one of the first rock 'n' roll hits and one of a flood of cover versions of rhythm and blues songs. "Sh-Boom" was written and originally recorded by the Chords for Cat Records. The Chords' version sold well among blacks, so the Crew Cuts, a white group with the closely cropped hair, covered the song for Mercury. Their version zoomed to the top of the charts. The Crew Cuts' disk was No. 1 on *Billboard* for nine weeks and No. 1 on *Cash Box* for four weeks. The Chords' version topped the *Cash Box* chart for five weeks, but only made it to No. 5 on *Billboard*. "Sh-Boom" was *Billboard's* No. 4 hit of the year, and *Variety* and *Cash Box's* No. 5. The Crew Cuts' version was *Billboard's* No. 2 hit of the year. The song didn't fare quite as well on *Your Hit Parade*, but it did make that chart for a dozen weeks, peaking at No. 3.

Stan Freberg's comic version peaked at No. 14 on *Billboard*, while the recording by the Billy Williams Quartet only made it to No. 21.

The 2006 Pixar film *Cars* uses The Chords' recording of "Sh-Boom" on the soundtrack.

The song opens with nonsense lyrics: "Hey nonny ding dong alang alang alang." The song's subtitle is "Life could be a dream." But the most memorable part of the song is an interlude of "sh-boom, sh-boom, ya-da-da" nonsense words. Even though it is considered one of the first rock 'n' roll hits, it doesn't seem particularly rock by today's standards. Read the lyrics at http://www.oldielyrics.com/lyrics/the_crew_cuts/sh-boom.html.

Variety selected "Sh-Boom" for its *Hit Parade of a Half-Century.*

Stranger in Paradise

Words: George "Chet" Forrest; Music: Robert Wright

"Stranger in Paradise," the most popular excerpt from the Broadway musical *Kismet*, was based on a theme from the "Polovtsian Dances" from Alexander Borodin's opera *Prince Igor*. Other important songs from *Kismet* include "Baubles, Bangles and Beads" and "And This Is My Beloved."

"Chet" Forrest and Robert Wright teamed on writing several popular songs, but they are best known for adapting classical material for the popular market. *Kismet* was their most famous adaptation, but they also adapted Norwegian composer Edvard Grieg's music for 1944's *Song of Norway*.

Kismet was an Arabian Nights fable of romance and intrigue in Old Bagdad. The Caliph, Richard Kiley, and Marsinah, Doretta Morrow, sang this lovely song as a duet when they first met. Read the lyrics at http://www.lyricsdepot.com/tony-bennett/stranger-in-paradise.html.

Tony Bennett's recording of the song collected four weeks at No. 1 on *Cash Box*, but only made it to No. 2 on *Billboard*. The song lasted six weeks at the top of *Your Hit Parade*. Bennett's disk was *Billboard's* No. 14 hit of the

year. The Four Aces' recording peaked at No. 3 on *Billboard*, and ranked No. 23 for the year.

Other recordings of "Stranger in Paradise" that charted include those by Tony Martin and by Gordon MacRae.

Variety selected "Stranger in Paradise" for its *Hit Parade of a Half-Century.*

The screen version of *Kismet* was released in 1949. It starred Alfred Drake, Ann Blyth, and Vic Damone. It was Damone who sang "Stranger in Paradise" in the film. This song was nominated for AFI's list of the greatest songs ever from American films, but it did not make the final list.

1954 was a good year for Broadway songs. "Hey There," "Hernando's Hideaway" and "Stranger in Paradise" all did well that year.

Teach Me Tonight

Words: Sammy Cahn; Music: Gene DePaul

This *Variety Hit Parade of a Half-Century* song was the first collaboration between Gene DePaul and Sammy Cahn. Cahn had to give Warner Bros. first chance at the song because he was under contract to them. The studio turned it down, and Cahn got it published by a small company owned by several songwriters.

The first recording, according to Cahn, was by "some young lady," and it sold three copies: the girl bought one, Cahn and DePaul bought the other two. The song became a hit when the DeCastro Sisters recorded it on Abbott Records. Their version peaked at No. 2 on *Billboard*, but was the No. 18 hit of the year in 1954. Other recordings that charted include those by Jo Stafford, by Janet Brace, by Dinah Washington, and by Helen Grayco. Dinah Washington's version was inducted into the Grammy Hall of Fame in 1999.

The song made ten appearances on *Your Hit Parade*, reaching No. 1 for one week.

The lyrics of the song are asking a person to teach the other about love. They want to start at the beginning of the alphabet and continue right through to the end. The person questions if the teacher should stand so near. Along with "Make Love to Me," and this song, lyrics are getting more suggestive. Read the lyrics at http://www.lyricsvault.net/songs/19787.html.

This Ole House

Words & Music: Stuart Hamblen

Stuart Hamblen was inspired to write this song when he discovered a dilapidated hunter's hut while on a hunting trip in Texas. Inside the house a man was dead. Moved by what he had seen, Hamblen wrote the song, published it and introduced it himself. Hamblen's recording only made it to No. 25 on *Billboard*, but Rosemary Clooney's recording collected three weeks at No. 1 on *Billboard*, making it the No. 9 hit of the year on that chart.

The song peaked at No. 2 on *Your Hit Parade*, but appeared on the program eleven times.

The singer tells us his house once was filled with the laughter of his children and his wife. In the chorus, we learn that he doesn't need the house any longer because he's "a-getting' ready to meet the saints." Read the lyrics at http://lirama.net/song/16754.

Variety honored Hamblen by selecting two of his songs for its *Hit Parade of a Half-Century*: "This Ole House" in 1954 and "It Is No Secret" in 1951.

Three Coins in the Fountain

Words: Sammy Cahn; Music: Jule Styne

The Academy Award winner for best song from the movies in 1954 went to the theme song from the non-musical film *Three Coins in the Fountain*. Frank Sinatra sang the song on the soundtrack, but it was the Four Aces' recording that made it to No. 1. Their disk topped the *Cash Box* chart for two weeks, and the *Billboard* chart for one week. The song collected four weeks at No. 1 on *Your Hit Parade*. The Four Aces' version was *Cash Box*'s No. 6 hit of the year; it was No. 11 for *Billboard*. Frank Sinatra's version only reached No. 4, while Julius LaRosa's stalled at No. 21.

The inspiration for the song came from the legend that whoever throws a coin into the water of the Fountain of the Trevi in Rome will return to that Eternal City. The three coins were for the three couples featured in the film: Clifton Webb and Dorothy McGuire, Jean Peters and Louis Jourdan, and Maggie McNamara and Rossano Brazzi.

Each of the three couples threw a coin in the fountain seeking happiness. One of the key lines from the song is the question: "Which one will the fountain bless?" Supposedly only one of the wishes will be granted. Which will it be? Read the lyrics at http://lirama.net/song/16755.

Variety chose "Three Coins in the Fountain" for its *Hit Parade of a Half-Century*. This song was nominated for the American Film Institute's list of the greatest songs ever from an American film, but did not make the final list.

The song is featured in the show *Forever Plaid*.

Wanted

Words & Music: Jack Fulton and Lois Steele

Perry Como's recording of "Wanted" collected eight weeks at No. 1 on *Billboard*, and seven weeks at the top of both *Your Hit Parade* and *Cash Box*. His disk was No. 3 for the year on *Billboard*, *Variety* and *Cash Box*.

"Wanted" is used in the song as if it were a police most-wanted list warning to be on the lookout for some suspicious character. In this case, the singer seeks the person who kissed him and held him closely, then stole his heart. Several words in the song hint at criminal-police jargon: "hiding out," "jury may find her guilty," and "a signed confession." Read the lyrics at http://www.lyricsdepot.com/perry-como/wanted.html.

Variety selected "Wanted" for its *Hit Parade of a Half-Century*.

Young at Heart

Words: Carolyn Leigh; Music: Johnny Richards

The tune for this song originated in '39 as "Moonbeam" by Johnny Richards. Carolyn Leigh added new lyrics in '53. Frank Sinatra's recording helped popularize the song to the No. 1 spot on *Your Hit Parade* for two weeks in the spring of 1954. The song never made it to the top of either *Billboard* or *Cash Box*, peaking at No. 2.

The song was then used as the title and theme song for a '54 film starring Sinatra and Doris Day.

Sinatra sang that if we are among the "young at heart" we can laugh when our dreams fall apart. Read the words at http://www.lyricsfreak.com/f/frank-sinatra/55277.html.

"Young at Heart" was selected by *Variety* for its *Hit Parade of a Half-Century*.

1955

Ain't That a Shame

Words & Music: Fats Domino and Dave Bartholomew

New Orleans rhythm and blues pianist and singer Antoine "Fats" Domino is estimated to have sold more than 65 million records, among the top dozen recording artists in recording history. Domino had a string of hits beginning with "The Fat Man" in 1948. By 1960, he had twenty-three gold records. He was one of the pioneers in the evolution of rhythm and blues to rock 'n' roll.

Today Fats' recording of "Ain't That a Shame" is considered one of the early classics, but in 1955, it was Pat Boone's cover version that was the big hit. Nevertheless, Fats' recording was inducted into the Grammy Hall of Fame in 2002. As with other rhythm and blues songs of the period, when Fats' version began to climb up the charts, a record executive called in some mainline pop artist to cover the song so that his company would have a national hit. Today such a practice appears to be grossly unfair to the original artist, and many people are convinced that it was racist. The social climate of the nation during the '50s was racial, of course, but other factors were also pertinent. Mainline pop artists were covering country songs at the same time, but that doesn't seem to bother people as much as covering the rhythm and blues tunes. It was usually a white singer covering a rhythm and blues song, so it takes on racial implications. A song recorded by an African American artist usually did not become a national hit, mainly because they were recording for a small independent record label that did not have the funds to promote the record nationally. Pat Boone was signed to a recording contract with Dot Records of Gallatin, Tennessee. If the owner of the company, Randy Wood, told him to record Fats Domino's "Ain't That a Shame," or Little Richard's "Tutti Frutti," or any other song, Pat was not in a position to refuse, not if he wanted to continue to make records.

Covering is still practiced today, although we don't hear much about it. Whitney Houston's "I Will Always Love You" was a cover of Dolly Parton's original, All 4 One's "I Swear" was a cover of country singer John Michael Montgomery's original, Garth Brooks' "Shameless" was a cover of the Billy Joel original. Even Elvis Presley covered songs; his "Hound Dog" had been a rhythm and blues success for Big Mama Thornton. So was Elvis racist? Was Whitney Houston being racist by covering a white country singer's song? Of course not!

Domino's recording of "Ain't That a Shame" is full of soul, while, to our ears today, Boone's version sounds pretty square. His recording of the song doesn't have the "soul" that Domino's had. But in 1955, while Fats' version only reached No. 10 on *Billboard*, Pat Boone's climbed to No. 1 and stayed there for two weeks on *Variety* and one week on *Cash Box*. *Your Hit Parade* was a little more conservative, so the song peaked at No. 2 on their survey. Boone's recording was No. 6 for the year on *Cash Box*, and No. 14 for *Billboard*.

In 1963, the Four Seasons revived the song, but their version only reached No. 22 on *Billboard*, then in 1979, Cheap Trick's revision peaked at No. 35.

The singer thinks it's a shame his girl left and broke his heart, but he says, "You're the one to blame." Read the lyrics at http://lirama.net/song/16769.

Autumn Leaves

English Words: Johnny Mercer; Music: Joseph Kosma

The No. 2 hit in *Variety*'s Top Ten for 1955 began as a French popular song, "Les Feuilles Mortes," by Joseph Kosma in 1947. Johnny Mercer supplied the song with English lyrics in 1955. In the first few years of the '50s, Bing Crosby and Jo Stafford were among a dozen or so recording artists who released not particularly successful recordings of this song. However, when pianist Roger Williams recorded "Autumn Leaves" in 1953 (released in 1954), it reportedly sold more than 2 million copies globally.

Roger Williams' instrumental version was No. 1 for four weeks on *Billboard*, and three weeks at No. 1 on both *Cash Box* and *Your Hit Parade*. His disk was *Billboard*'s No. 8 hit of the year.

Pianist and television personality Steve Allen was the only other person whose recording of the song was popular enough to chart in '55.

Nat "King" Cole sang it in the 1956 film *Autumn Leaves* as the film's theme song at the beginning and end of the film.

Now that the autumn leaves are falling, the singer is remembering the kisses of summer. Since his woman went away the days have grown long. The following is a quote from the French version: "C'est une chanson, qui nous ressemble." Read the lyrics at http://www.lyricsfreak.com/n/nat-king-cole/98011.html.

Variety selected "Autumn Leaves" for its *Hit Parade of a Half-Century*.

The Ballad of Davy Crockett

Words: Tom Blackburn; Music: George Bruns

Three versions of "The Ballad of Davy Crockett" made *Billboard*'s Top 40 during '55: Bill Hayes' version was No. 7, Tennessee Ernie Ford's version ranked No. 33 and Fess Parker, the star of the TV series *Davy Crockett*, recorded a version that became No. 37 for the year. The song spent nine weeks at the top of *Your Hit Parade*, and five weeks at No. 1 on *Billboard*, three weeks at the top of the *Cash Box* chart. *Cash Box* ranked it No. 2 for the year, while *Variety* claimed it was No. 7. The Voices of Walter Shumann, a choral ensemble, had their recording of the song also make the *Billboard* chart during the year.

A ballad typically tells a story, and indeed, this ballad chronicles some of the exploits of the legendary Crockett, who was "king of the wild frontier." The song sounds like a folk song, with a narrow range, reasonably simple chord structure, and an easily singable tune. Read the lyrics at http://lirama.net/song/16772.

The country group The Kentucky Headhunters resurrected the song with good success on the country chart in the early '90s.

Variety selected "Ballad of Davy Crockett" for its *Hit Parade of a Half-Century*.

Cherry Pink and Apple Blossom White

English Words: Mack David; Music: Louiguy

"Cherry Pink and Apple Blossom White" had been written by Louiguy and Jacques Larue and published in

Paris in 1950 as "Cerisier Rose et Pommer Blanc." In 1951, Mack David wrote the English lyrics. Perez Prado and his orchestra had recorded the song in 1951, but when the song was selected for inclusion in the 1955 film *Underwater*, Prado cut a new version for the film.

Cuban Perez Prado formed his own band in Mexico in 1948 and began to popularize the mambo beat. The mambo began to get attention in the U.S. in 1954 with hits like "Mambo Italiano," "They Were Doin' the Mambo," and "Papa Loves Mambo." Prado and his group followed their success with "Cherry Pink and Apple Blossom White" with 1958's "Patricia."

There was something about Prado's recording that captured the listening public. Perhaps it was the sliding glissando on the trumpet that opened the song. This brief moment of musical suspension of time never failed to create the same effect each time it was heard. Whatever the psychological explanation, it proved to be a fascinating and ingenious musical idea.

With ten weeks at No. 1, Prado's disk was No. 1 for the year on *Billboard* and *Variety*. It was No. 1 on *Cash Box* for three weeks, and their No. 3 hit of the year. The song also collected one week at the top of the *Your Hit Parade* survey (*Your Hit Parade* never did justice to strictly instrumental hits). Prado's recording was the second longest at No. 1 on *Billboard* during the second half of the fifties. Only Elvis Presley's "Don't Be Cruel/Hound Dog" in 1956, with eleven weeks at No. 1, beat it for weeks at the top of the chart. The McGuire Sisters' recording of "Sincerely" in 1955 and Guy Mitchell's "Singing the Blues" in 1956 tied "Cherry Pink and Apple Blossom White" with ten weeks at No. 1 on *Billboard*. In light of those figures, a mambo was the second biggest hit of the rock 'n' roll fifties. What a shock! Even more shocking is the fact that only 1977's "You Light Up My Life" by Debby Boone, and Olivia Newton-John's "Physical" in 1981 also collected ten weeks at No. 1 until the 1990s. Whitney Houston's recording of "I Will Always Love You" collected thirteen weeks at No. 1 making it the top hit ever on *Billboard*, and Boyz II Men's "The End of the Road" stayed a dozen weeks at the top, becoming the No. 2 hit of all-time on *Billboard*. That makes Elvis' "Don't Be Cruel/Hound Dog" No. 3, and "Cherry Pink..." No. 4 in weeks at No. 1 during the entire rock era. Recently *Billboard* has stopped counting any hits of 1955 prior to July 9th, when "Rock Around the Clock" took over the No. 1 spot, as part of the rock era. Figuring it as a part of the pre-rock era, it would rank approximately No. 34, and would be No. 9 for the pre-rock fifties.

Alan Dale's vocal version of the song peaked at No. 14 on the *Billboard* chart.

Although the most popular version of the song was an instrumental, there were lyrics. Read them at http://ntl.matrix.com.br/pfilho/oldies_list/top/lyrics/cherry_pink_and_apple_blossom_white.txt.

Variety included "Cherry Pink and Apple Blossom White" in its *Hit Parade of a Half-Century*.

Cry Me a River

Words & Music: Arthur Hamilton

Julie London popularized "Cry Me a River" in '55 with her first successful Liberty recording. Her recordings peaked at No. 9 on the *Billboard* chart. She also sang it in the '58 20th Century–Fox film *The Girl Can't Help It*. Her recording of the song was inducted into the Grammy Hall of Fame in 2001.

Joe Cocker's recording of the song peaked at No. 11 on *Billboard* in '70.

The singer wants the person who has wronged her to be lonely and to cry throughout the night, because she has already cried a river over him. Even though he now says he loves her, she wants him to prove it by crying a river. Read the words at http://www.oldielyrics.com/lyrics/julie_london/cry_me_a_river.html.

Earth Angel

Words & Music: Jesse Belvin, Curtis Williams & Gaynel Hodge

One of the great rhythm and blues songs of the '50s was "Earth Angel" co-written by Curtis Williams, the lead singer of the quartet that popularized the song, the Penguins.

The Penguins' smooth harmony as they sang "Earth angel, will you be mine?" made this one of the classic early rhythm and blues hits. The Penguins' recording was inducted into the Grammy Hall of Fame in 1998.

"Earth Angel (Will You Be Mine)" by The Penguins has sold in the millions over the last 50+ years and is still one of the most popular records of all time.

In the beginning, Curtis Williams was credited with writing the song. Later a lawsuit was taken to court to prove that Belvin and Hodge also had a hand in writing it.

The song's subtitle "Will You Be Mine" was lyrically and melodically copied from The Swallows' '51 R&B song, "Will You Be Mine."

"Earth Angel," like many doo-wop ballads, was structured on the chord changes of Rodgers & Hart's "Blue Moon," beginning with what musicians call the I or tonic chord, then changing to the vi chord, which is minor, next came the IV chord (called sub-dominant), the V chord (called dominant), and back to tonic (I). This chord progression (I, iv, IV, V, I) came to be known as "Blue Moon changes" or "ice cream changes" and formed the basis for many '50s songs.

As popular as the song and recording seem in retrospect, it only rose to No. 3 on *Billboard* and *Your Hit Parade* ignored it, as it did most R&B songs.

The singer wants "Earth Angel" to be his and love him all the time. He realizes he's just a fool to love her. Read the lyrics at http://www.oldielyrics.com/lyrics/the_penguins/earth_angel.html.

Heart

Words & Music: Richard Adler & Jerry Ross

Damn Yankees was a Broadway musical about a man, Joe Hardy, who loves baseball so much he sells his soul to the devil for the opportunity to play for his beloved Washington Senators, a team in our nation's capital from 1901 until 1960. The devil, Mr. Applegate, is assisted by a lovely temptress, Lola.

Damn Yankees was the Tony Awarding winning Best Musical in 1956. Gwen Verdon won for Best Actress for her portrayal of Lola, while Ray Walston won the award for Best Actor for his wonderful portrayal of Mr. Applegate, the devil. The show collected several other Tony awards in '56. It also received several Tony awards when it was revived on Broadway in '94.

The show's most popular song was "Heart," which was sung in the musical by several of the baseball players. They are convinced by the team's manager, Van Buren, that all the team needs to be successful is "Heart." Read the lyrics at http://www.stlyrics.com/lyrics/damnyankees/heart.htm.

Eddie Fisher's recording of the song was popular in the mid–'50s, maxing out at No. 6 on *Billboard*, while the Four Aces recording peaked at No. 13.

The song made seven appearances on *Your Hit Parade*, peaking at No. 3 on the June 25th broadcast.

Another well known song from *Damn Yankees* is "Whatever Lola Wants."

Hearts of Stone

Words: Eddy Ray; Music: Ruby Jackson

First popularized around the nation by Otis Williams and the Charms, a rhythm and blues quintet in late '54, "Hearts of Stone" was covered by the Fontane Sisters. The Charms' version only made it to No. 15 on *Billboard*, but the Fontane Sisters' cover version ascended to the top of the chart and enjoyed three weeks at No. 1 on both *Billboard* and *Cash Box*. The song attained No. 2 on *Your Hit Parade*. The Fontane Sisters' disk was *Billboard's* No. 11 hit of the year, another example of a cover version doing much better on the charts than the original R&B version.

Actually the Charms' recording was also a cover of an obscure West Coast group called the Jewels, who had been the first to record "Hearts of Stone."

"Hearts of Stone" charted again in 1961 when Bill Black's Combo made the Top 20 with the song, and again in 1973, when the Blue Ridge Rangers' version barely made the Top 40.

The singers tell us "hearts of stone" never break and will only cause us pain. Read the lyrics at http://lirama.net/song/16792.

How Important Can It Be?

Words & Music: Bennie Benjamin & George Weiss

"How Important Can It Be?" became Joni James' fourth gold record. The song spent fifteen weeks on the bestseller chart. Joni's recording peaked at No. 2 on *Billboard*, but came in as the No. 22 hit of the year. On *Your Hit Parade*, the song only made it to No. 4.

Sarah Vaughan also had a successful recording of the song.

The singer asks if it is important she loved someone else when she was young and foolish, but thinks she's much wiser now. The only important thing, she said, is the present and she assures him their love is here to stay. Read the lyrics at http://www.oldielyrics.com/lyrics/joni_james/how_important_can_it_be.html.

Variety chose "How Important Can It Be?" for its *Hit Parade of a Half-Century.*

Ko Ko Mo (I Love You So)

Words & Music: Forest Wilson, Jake Porter, and Eunice Levy

The original rhythm and blues version of this *Variety Hit Parade of a Half-Century* number was by Gene and Eunice for Combo No. 64 Records. However, as often occurred, the cover version by Perry Como sold better. On *Billboard*, it peaked at No. 2, but ranked No. 18 for the year. The Crew Cuts' version only made it to No. 6 on *Billboard*.

The song made seven appearances on *Your Hit Parade*, rising to No. 2 in early March 1955.

Other artists who released versions of "Ko Ko Mo" include the Dooley Sisters, Louis Armstrong and Gary Crosby.

Como's recording opens with a dozen repetitions of "Kokomo." He urges her to come closer, and to not be afraid. Read these simplistic lyrics at http://www.lyricsvault.net/songs/17565.html.

Learnin' the Blues

Words & Music: Dolores Vicki Silvers

"Learnin' the Blues" became another No. 1 hit for Frank Sinatra. His recording collected two weeks at No. 1 on *Billboard* and one week at No. 1 on *Your Hit Parade*. It peaked at No. 2 on *Cash Box*. "Learnin' the Blues" was *Billboard's* No. 13 hit of the year.

"Ole Blue Eyes" had some success during the rock era, but not nearly as much as earlier. "Learnin' the Blues" was his last No. 1 hit on *Billboard* until '66 when "Strangers in the Night" made it to the top. In '67, he and his daughter, Nancy, made it to No. 1 with "Somethin' Stupid." In '55, his recordings of "Love and Marraige" and "(Love Is) The Tender Trap" were also popular. Otherwise, his biggest hit of the period was 1957's "All the Way," which peaked at No. 2.

Rather surprisingly, Sinatra was only the No. 14 artist of the '40s, No. 21 of the '50s and No. 36 of the '60s. From his fame, one would assume that he was one of the top recording artists of all time.

The singer paints a picture of loneliness: empty tables, deserted dance floor, and playing the same love song on the juke box for the tenth time. That is the "first lesson in learnin' the blues."

"Learnin' the Blues" was a *Variety Hit Parade of a Half-Century* song.

Let Me Go, Lover

Words & Music: Jenny Lou Carson & Al Hill

Jenny Lou Carson originally wrote this song in 1953 under the title "Let Me Go, Devil" as a song about addiction to alcohol. Mitch Miller suggested that the lyrics be revised. Al Hill got co-writing credit for the revised version.

Eighteen-year-old Joan Weber recorded the revised version and gained her only major hit. It was No. 1 on *Billboard* for four weeks, and on *Cash Box* and *Your Hit Parade* for two weeks. Her recording was No. 10 for the year on *Variety*, and No. 9 on *Billboard*.

Teresa Brewer, Patti Page, the Lancers and Sunny Gale also had recordings of "Let Me Go, Lover" that were popular enough to make the pop charts.

When you listen to the words of the song, you can hear that they could just as easily be talking about alcohol, or drugs, or any other addiction, as they could about a lover. Read the lyrics at http://lirama.net/song/16801.

"Let Me Go, Lover" was selected as one of *Variety's* Hit Parade of a Half-Century songs representing 1954.

Love Is a Many-Splendored Thing

Words: Paul Francis Webster; Music: Sammy Fain

The Academy Award winning song for 1955 was the theme song from the motion picture *Love Is a Many-Splendored Thing*. This passionate song defines love as nature's way of giving us a reason to live, then it describes a scene from the film when high on a windy hill "two lovers kissed and the world stood still." The lyrics name some of the things that make love such a special thing. Read the lyrics at http://www.webfitz.com/lyrics/Lyrics/1955/71955.html.

Based on the autobiography of Han Suyin, *Love Is a Many-Splendored Thing* was a romantic film about a Eurasian female physician who fell in love with an American journalist in Hong Kong at the time of the Korean War.

The Four Aces were about the only ones willing to record the song; most artists and record producers felt it was too heavy for wide popularity. The Four Aces recording spent six weeks at No. 1 on *Billboard*, five weeks at No. 1 on *Cash Box*, and two weeks at No. 1 on *Your Hit Parade*. Their disk was No. 6 for the year on *Variety*, and No. 5 for *Billboard*.

Don Cornell was the only other artist whose recording of the song was popular enough to make the charts.

An instrumental version of the song appeared on the soundtrack of the film version of *Grease* ('78).

Variety chose "Love Is a Many-Splendored Thing" for its *Hit Parade of a Half-Century*. This song was nominated for the American Film Institute's list of the greatest songs ever from an American film, but did not make the final list.

Melody of Love

Words: Tom Glazer; Music: H. Engelmann

"Melody of Love" was adapted from "Melodie d'Amour" which had been written in 1903. Billy Vaughn and his orchestra's recording of the song was the most popular one, but versions by the Four Aces, by David Carroll, by Frank Sinatra and Ray Anthony and his orchestra, and by Lou Diamond also helped popularize the song.

"Melody of Love" sounds like the turn-of-the-century song it is. It is a slow tempo waltz. It must have been a nostalgia-type of hit, causing the adults to remember a slower, more serene era. Read the lyrics at http://www.lyricsdepot.com/the-four-aces-featuring-al-alberts/melody-of-love.html.

"Melody of Love" was orchestra leader Billy Vaughn's first big hit recording. Vaughn was musical director for Dot Records, so he was the arranger and conductor for most of Pat Boone's recordings. Vaughn's recording of "Melody of Love" topped the *Cash Box* chart for four weeks and the *Your Hit Parade* hit survey for six weeks. It only reached No. 2 on *Billboard*. It was *Cash Box's* No. 4 hit of the year, No. 19 for *Billboard*.

Variety chose "Melody of Love" for its *Hit Parade of a Half-Century*.

Only You

Words & Music: Buck Ram and Ande Rand

The Platters popularized "Only You" with a successful recording of the song in '55. Perhaps because it was one of the Platters' first hits, it didn't chart as high as many of their subsequent hits. It only reached No. 5 on the *Billboard* chart. However, their recording of the song was inducted into the Grammy Hall of Fame in 1999.

The Hilltoppers' version peaked at No. 8 in '55, Franck Pourcel's French Fiddlers' recording made it to No. 9 in '59, while Ringo Starr's '75 recording rose to No. 6 on *Billboard*.

The song made a couple of appearances on *Your Hit Parade*, charting at No. 7 on both the December 3rd and December 17th broadcasts.

"Only You" can make the singer's dreams of love come true. Read the lyrics and hear the Platters' recording of the song at http://peachpatch.com/onlyyou.html.

Rock Around the Clock

Words & Music: Max C. Freedman and Jimmy DeKnight

"Rock Around the Clock" was written in 1953, recorded by Bill Haley and his Comets in 1954, and included in the 1955 film *The Blackboard Jungle*. A reasonably inauspicious beginning for what turned out to be such a phenomenal song and hit recording. As we look back from the perspective of years, we credit Haley's recording of the song with launching rock 'n' roll nationally. Of course, there were evidences of it earlier, but the song's appearance in a major motion picture brought this new musical fad to national prominence.

The actual birth of rock 'n' roll is debatable. Fats Domino, the singer-pianist from New Orleans, said that what became known as rock 'n' roll was what he had been playing for fifteen years. Some pop music historians suggest that the first rock 'n' roll recording was "Rocket 88" recorded by Ike Turner's band with vocalist Jackie Brenston in 1951 for the small independent Chicago label Chess Records (incidentally, Bill Haley's first record for a small independent company was "Rocket 88" backed with "Rock the Joint"). At this point, though, the independent labels were not considering anything but the black market. At some point prior to 1954, these companies began to realize that whites, particularly white high school and college kids, were buying their records. They suddenly discovered that they could sell far more records because a new audience was opening up. The entire white audience was not totally ready to accept this new sound, however.

Disk jockey Alan Freed is given credit for inventing the term "rock and roll" to cover up rhythm and blues' blackness in 1947 when he was working in Cleveland, but the term did not come into general use until 1955 after Freed moved his radio show to New York City. Prior to the term's acceptance, this music had been called "cat music."

The film *The Blackboard Jungle* would probably be forgotten by now had it not showcased Haley's version of "Rock Around the Clock," where it was heard under the film's opening credits. Glenn Ford played a young teacher who gets through to some tough students in an inner-city school. Young Sidney Poitier was one of his rebellious students.

Decca Records re-released Haley's recording of the song when the film began to cause a sensation. It zoomed up the charts! It collected eight weeks at No. 1 on *Billboard*, five weeks at the top of *Cash Box*'s chart. The song even managed two weeks at No. 1 on the conservative *Your Hit Parade* hit survey. It was No. 1 for the year on *Cash Box*, and No. 2 for the year on *Variety* and No. 3 on *Billboard*. Haley's disk reentered the *Billboard* chart in 1974.

Haley's recording was inducted into the Grammy Hall of Fame in 1982.

Haley counts down the hours from one to twelve indicating "we're gonna rock around the clock tonight." Read the lyrics at http://www.webfitz.com/lyrics/Lyrics/1955/91955.html.

Variety included "Rock Around the Clock" for its *Hit Parade of a Half-Century*. AFI's *100 Years ... 100 Songs* (2004) named "Rock Around the Clock" as the No. 50 greatest song from an American film for its appearance in *Blackboard Jungle*.

Sincerely

Words & Music: Harvey Fuqua and Alan Freed

The three-sister singing group, the McGuire Sisters, had their first No. 1 hit single with "Sincerely." The Moonglows had recorded the original rhythm and blues version. The Moonglows' version peaked at No. 20 on *Billboard*, while the McGuire Sisters' version spent ten weeks at No. 1. It also collected three weeks at No. 1 on *Cash Box*. The song peaked at No. 2 on *Your Hit Parade*. It was No. 2 for the year on *Billboard*, No. 7 for the year on *Cash Box*, and No. 8 on *Variety*.

The Moonglows' recording of "Sincerely" was inducted into the Grammy Hall of Fame in 2002.

The co-writer, Alan Freed, was most famous as a disk jockey and for originating the term "rock and roll" in the late forties for his "Moon Dog's Rock and Roll Party" radio program in Cleveland. However, he occasionally contributed material to the rock milieu as he did with "Sincerely." It may very well be that the writer, Harvey Fuqua, gave Freed writing credit because he knew of Freed's connections with the rhythm and blues groups and knew he would get one of them to record the song.

The Moonglows' version was used on the soundtrack of the 2002 film *Confessions of a Dangerous Mind*.

Even though the most popular recordings were by groups, the lyrics are singular, not plural. The singer wonders why she loves this fellow so much, because he doesn't return her feelings. She isn't willing to let him go, however. She begs him to say he will be hers. Read the lyrics at http://www.stlyrics.com/lyrics/confessionsofadangerousmind/sincerely.htm.

Variety named "Sincerely" to its *Hit Parade of a Half-Century*.

Sixteen Tons

Words & Music: Merle Travis

Tennessee Ernie Ford's biggest hit came in 1955 with "Sixteen Tons," a cover of country singer-writer Merle Travis' song. It reportedly sold more than one million copies in three weeks, becoming the fastest selling single to date. It became *Variety*'s No. 3 hit of the year, and *Billboard*'s No. 4. Ford's disk spent eight weeks at No. 1 on *Billboard*, four weeks at the top of *Cash Box* in '55 and three weeks in '56. The song was No. 1 for five weeks in '55 on *Your Hit Parade*.

Tennessee Ernie Ford's recording of "Sixteen Tons" was inducted into the Grammy Hall of Fame in 1998.

"Sixteen Tons" was written by Merle Travis, a Kentucky coal miner's son, in '47. Travis wrote the song to include on his own "Folk Songs of the Hills" album. The lyrics' homey cynicism struck a chord with the record buying public. People empathized with working hard but not really getting ahead, getting older and never getting out of debt. Getting "deeper in debt" was a favorite saying of Travis' father. Read the lyrics at http://www.lyrics.ly/lyrics.php/Tennessee+Ernie+Ford/Lyrics/Sixteen+Tons.

Johnny Desmond also had a recording of the song that charted.

Something's Gotta Give

Words & Music: Johnny Mercer

"Something's Gotta Give" was introduced by Fred Astaire in the movie musical *Daddy Long Legs*. He sang it on a hotel balcony, and then danced it with his co-star Leslie Caron. The song won a nomination for the Oscar for best song from films in '55. *Daddy Long Legs* had been written as a novel in 1912 by Jean Webster and had been filmed twice: in 1919 and 1931. The third film version was a '55 movie musical starring Fred Astaire and Leslie Caron.

A problem arose during the script preparation for the film over what to do about an older man being in love with a much younger woman, and she in love with him. The problem was solved by Johnny Mercer's song "Something's Gotta Give." In other words, Astaire's character fought the inevitable with all his might, but when the "irresistible force," Ms. Caron, met the "immovable object," Astaire, something gave! Read the lyrics at http://lirama.net/song/16835.

The most popular recording of the song was by the McGuire Sisters. Their disk only made it to No. 3 on *Cash Box* and No. 5 on *Billboard*, but the song managed one week at No. 1 on *Your Hit Parade*.

Sammy Davis, Jr. also released a recording of "Something's Gotta Give" that charted.

That's All I Want From You

Words & Music: M. Rotha

Fritz Rotta, using the pseudonym M. Rotha, wrote this *Variety Hit Parade of a Half-Century* song in 1954. Jaye P. Morgan popularized the song in '55. Her recording rose to No. 3 on *Billboard*, coming in at No. 29 for the year.

The song managed ten weeks on the *Your Hit Parade* survey of hits, peaking at No. 3.

So what is it that the singer wants? Among other things, she wants a love that will slowly grow and grow, not one that comes and goes. Read the lyrics at http://lirama.net/song/16750.

Tweedle Dee

Words & Music: Winfield Scott

Georgia Gibbs's "Tweedle Dee" was a cover version of the original rhythm and blues version by LaVern Baker. Baker's disk only made it to No. 14 on the *Billboard* chart, while Gibbs's reached No. 2 on both *Billboard* and *Cash Box*. The song did manage to reach the No. 1 position on *Your Hit Parade* for one week.

"Tweedle Dee" is a catchy, peppy, dance number that was a favorite with the teenagers. Read the lyrics at http://lirama.net/song/16842.

"Tweedle Dee" was chosen by *Variety* to represent 1955 in its *Hit Parade of a Half-Century*.

Unchained Melody

Words: Hy Zaret; Music: Alex North

This song was the theme for the film *Unchained* (surely they could have come up with a more original title for such a beautiful song). Two versions made *Billboard's* year-end charts: Les Baxter and his orchestra's recording was No. 12, while Al Hibbler's vocal version was No. 25, his version reached No. 3 on *Billboard*. However, Hibbler's disk was *Cash Box's* No. 8 hit of the year, and Baxter's was *Variety's* No. 9. The song collected eight weeks at No. 1 on *Cash Box*, seven weeks at the top of the *Your Hit Parade* survey.

Roy Hamilton and June Valli also had recording of the song that made the *Billboard* chart in 1955. In 1965, the Righteous Brothers revived the song; their version peaked at No. 4 on *Billboard*. The Righteous Brothers' version found new life in '90 when it was included in the soundtrack of the movie *Ghost*. The Righteous Brothers' recording was inducted into the Grammy Hall of Fame in 2000.

"Unchained Melody" became one of the most recorded songs of the 20th century, perhaps over 500 recorded versions.

The film's plot concerned a convict in a medium-security prison who was torn between finishing his sentence so he could get back to his wife and family, but also his passionate desire to escape from prison. Leonard Maltin, in his *1995 Movie Guide*, contended that jazz legend Georgie Auld played the film's theme on sax instead of Dexter Gordon, but Gordon was also a well-respected jazz saxophonist. Gordon was serving a heroin conviction in the prison where the film was shot.

The song begins with the chorus, followed by the verse. The song is about someone who has waited a long time for their lover's return. Read the lyrics at http://www.geocities.com/Paris/Parc/9842/unchain.html.

Variety selected "Unchained Melody" for its *Hit Parade of a Half-Century*. It was nominated for the American Film Institute's list of the greatest songs ever from an American film, but it did not make the final list. It was nominated for its appearance in *Ghost* ('90).

Wallflower (Dance with Me, Henry)

Words & Music: Johnny Otis, Hank Ballard, and Etta James

Hank Ballard had decent success with a song he had co-written called "Work with Me, Annie" in 1954, but the lyrics were deemed too suggestive, so many radio stations would not play it. Etta James recorded the tune as "Roll with Me, Henry," but her version was still too raunchy for most listeners of the reasonably innocent mid-'50s. Georgia Gibbs's cover version altered the suggestive lyrics and was marketed as "Wallflower," with the subtitle, "Dance with Me, Henry." Her disk collected three weeks at No. 1 on *Billboard*, and was that chart's No. 10 hit of the year. The song didn't fare so well on the other charts, only making it to No. 3 on *Cash Box*, and No. 4 on *Your Hit Parade*.

Read the lyrics of Georgia Gibbs' version at http://lirama.net/song/16784 or read Etta James' more suggestive version at http://www.stlyrics.com/songs/e/ettajames7412/wallflower918879.html.

The Yellow Rose of Texas

Words & Music: J.K.

"The Yellow Rose of Texas" was *Billboard's* No. 6 hit of 1955, *Variety's* No. 4, and *Cash Box's* No. 5. That's not bad for a song written in 1853.

The song had probably originated on the Northern minstrel show circuit before it became a favorite of Civil War soldiers. Its composer is anonymous, known only as "J.K."

Composer-arranger Don George took this old Civil War campfire song, eliminated some of its racial overtones, and set it to an exciting march beat. George's arrangement first appeared on an album of Civil War songs, where Mitch Miller discovered it. Miller, Artist and Repertoire Director at Columbia, gave it a new arrangement, particularly adding an exciting snare drum part. If Miller had not been an executive with the company, the record would probably never have been released, but he insisted. His confidence was vindicated when it topped the *Billboard* chart for six weeks, the *Cash Box* chart for four weeks, and *Your Hit Parade* for nine weeks. Miller and his gang of male singers' version of the song was No. 3 for the year on *Billboard*, No. 4 on *Variety*, and No. 5 on *Cash Box*.

Miller became very famous for his "Sing-along with Mitch" series of albums and his television series of the late fifties and early sixties.

Johnny Desmond also had a recording of "The Yellow Rose of Texas" that made the pop charts. Stan Freberg's comic treatment also charted.

Since the song was written in 1853, the lyrics are now in the public domain. The following is an excerpt: *There's a yellow rose of Texas That I am going to see, / No other fellow knows her, No other, only me. / She cried so when I left her, It like to break my heart, / And if I ever find her We never more will part.*

Read the complete lyrics at http://www.civilwarhome.com/yellowrose.htm.

A 1944 Roy Rogers film bore the same title. Although the soundtrack music was unavailable, chances are the song was included. Elvis Presley performed the song as part of a medley in his '64 film *Viva Las Vegas*.

"The Yellow Rose of Texas" was chosen for *Variety*'s *Hit Parade of a Half-Century*.

Biographies

Irving Aaronson (1895–1963) Irving Aaronson began his professional music career playing piano for the silent movies at age 11. His recording career began in '26 with a band called the Crusaders. The group's name was changed to Commanders soon after he joined. At various times, the band included Tony Pastor, Artie Shaw, Claude Thornhill and Gene Krupa. In '28 the band appeared in Cole Porter's Broadway show *Paris*. The show's Parisian star, Irene Bordoni recorded four songs from the show for Victor using the Commanders as the band. Bing Crosby used Aaronson's Commanders on four songs he recorded from his movie, *She Loves Me Not*. One of them, "Love in Bloom," became a big hit record for Crosby (see '34). In '52, after disbanding the Commanders, Aaronson found work as a musical supervisor for MGM, a position he kept until his death. Aaronson co-wrote "The Loveliest Night of the Year" with lyricist Paul Francis Webster. Mario Lanza popularized the song (see '51). Aaronson's most popular recordings with his Commanders include "Let's Do It" from *Paris* with vocal performances by Phil Saxe and Jack Armstrong in '29 and "Pardon My Southern Accent" with Ernie Mathias doing the vocal in '34.

Maurice Abrahams (1883–1931) Maurice Abrahams was a composer, publisher, author and a charter member of ASCAP. He wrote special material for vaudeville singers, including Belle Baker, who became his wife. His most famous popular songs were "Ragtime Cowboy Joe" (see '12) and "Hitchy-Koo" (see '13). He also composed "He'd Have to Get Under — Get Out and Get Under (to Fix Up His Automobile)" and "When the Grown-up Ladies Act Like Babies (I've Got to Love 'Em, That's All)," among others.

Zequinha Abreu (1880–1935) Zequinha Abreu became one of the most successful Brazilian songwriters of the modern era. Disney's *Saludos Amigos* introduced his "Tico-Tico" to American audiences (see '45).

Tom Adair (real name: Thomas Montgomery Adair; 1913–1988) Tom Adair was the lyricist of "In the Blue of Evening" (see '43). Among others, Adair also wrote "Let's Get Away from It All" and "The Night We Called It a Day." He wrote for several radio shows, including *Duffy's Tavern*. Adair wrote the music for several television series, including *The Ann Sothern Show* and *Hazel*. Then he teamed with James B. Allardice to write a couple of *Hazel* episodes, plus scripts for *My Three Sons, F Troop, I Dream of Jeannie* and *Gomer Pyle*.

A. Emmett Adams A. Emmett Adams contributed the music for "The Bells of St. Mary's" (see '17).

Frank R. Adams (1883–1963) Frank Adams was educated at the University of Chicago, and worked as a reporter for the Chicago Tribune, Daily News, and Examiner. He penned several books and contributed lyrics for five stage productions, particularly including *The Prince of Tonight*. His chief musical collaborators included Joe Howard, Harold Orlob and Will Hough. By far his most famous song credit is "I Wonder Who's Kissing Her Now" (see '09).

Stanley Adams (1915–1977) Stanley Adams was lyricist of "What a Diff'rence a Day Made" (see '34) and co-lyricist of "There Are Such Things" (see '43).

Harold Adamson (1906–1980) Harold Adamson grew up in New York City before attending the University of Kansas and Harvard University. After college, he began to seriously pursue a songwriting career. By the early '30s he had contributed to Broadway shows such as *Smiles*, for which he wrote "Time on My Hands" (see '31), *Earl Carroll's Vanities*, and *The Third Little Show*. In '33, Adamson moved to Hollywood and signed a contract with MGM, where he spent the rest of his career writing music for the movies. Over the years, he collaborated with composers Burton Lane, Jimmy McHugh, Walter Donaldson, Victor Young, and Duke Ellington. Others of Adamson's most famous songs are "Did I Remember?" (see '36), "It's Been So Long" (see '36), "You" (see '36), "You're a Sweetheart" (see '38), "Ferryboat Serenade" (see '40), "The Woodpecker Song" (see '40), "Comin' in on a Wing and a Prayer" (see '43) and "I Couldn't Sleep a Wink Last Night" (see '44). In the '50s, he began to write scores and/or songs for non-musical movies, including *Around the World in 80 Days, An Affair to Remember,* and *The Incredible Mr. Limpit*, among others. Other Adamson songs include "Everything I Have Is Yours," "A Lovely Way to Spend an Evening," "It's a Most Unusual Day," "An Affair to Remember" and "It's a Wonderful World." Adamson also provided the lyrics to Eliot Daniel's music for the theme to the *I Love Lucy* TV series. At http://www.songwritershalloffame.org/exhibit_audio_video.asp?exhibitId=38 hear audio clips of Gene Austin performing "Everything I Have Is Yours" and Nat "King" Cole singing "An Affair to Remember."

Richard Addinsell (1904–1977) English composer Richard Addinsell wrote "Warsaw Concerto" for the wartime film *Dangerous Moonlight* (see '43). Addinsell studied law at Oxford, but took some classes in music at the Royal College of Music in London. He came to Hollywood where he wrote film scores for movie studios.

Richard Adler (1921–)   Richard Adler is a Jewish-American lyricist, composer and producer of several Broadway musicals. Adler was born in New York City. Since his father was a concert pianist, he had a childhood that was surrounded with music. After a stint in the navy he began his career as a lyricist, teaming up with Jerry Ross at the beginning of the '50s. Prior to their Broadway success, Adler and Ross wrote "Rags to Riches" (see '53). Adler and Ross are best known for two Broadway musicals: *The Pajama Game* ('54) and *Damn Yankees* ('55). After those Broadway successes, Ross died in '55, but Adler continued writing alone. "Hey There" from *The Pajama Game* was a top hit (see '54). "Heart" was the biggest hit song from *Damn Yankees* (see '55). Adler was inducted into the Songwriters' Hall of Fame in '84. Adler's autobiography, *You Gotta Have Heart*, was published in '90.

Milton Ager (1893–1979)   Composer Milton Ager was an important writer of popular songs during the '20s and '30s. He began his music career as a movie house intermission pianist for the silent movie theaters, became a vaudevillian, a song plugger and furnished accompaniment for the Orpheum Vaudeville Circuit. In '13, he began working for the publishing company Waterson, Berlin and Snyder until World War I when he joined the U.S. Army's Morale Division. After the war, Ager went back to songwriting. In the early '20s his first successes came with "Nobody's Baby" and "Who Cares." In '22 he became a partner in his own music publishing company, Ager, Yellen and Bornstein. Some of Ager's most famous songs include "Lovin' Sam" (see '23), "I Wonder What's Become of Sally" (see '24), "Ain't She Sweet?" (see '27), "Forgive Me" (see '27) and "Happy Days Are Here Again" (see '30). In '30, Ager moved to Hollywood, where he contributed to several film scores. Songs in these movies include "Happy Feet," and "If I Didn't Care." His chief collaborators include George Meyer, Grant Clarke, Benny Davis, Lester Santly, Joe Young, Jack Yellen, Jean Schwartz, Stanley Adams and Joe McCarthy. Ager was elected to membership in the Songwriters' Hall of Fame in '72. At http://www.songwritershalloffame.org/exhibit_audio_video.asp?exhibitId=205 hear Ben Selvin and his orchestra with the Crooners perform "Happy Days Are Here Again" and Miss Patricola with the Virginians perform "Lovin' Sam."

eden ahbez (real name: Alexander Aberle; 1908–1995)   This Brooklyn yogi was one of the really unique characters of pre-rock popular music. He believed that only divinities deserved capital letters, so he refused to use them in his name. He reportedly led a beatnik life style, wearing sandals, camping out beneath the Hollywood sign above Los Angeles, ate only vegetables, fruits and nuts, wore a beard and shoulder-length hair, lived on only three dollars per week, and practiced Oriental mysticism. His only famous song is "Nature Boy" (see '48), which became a huge hit for Nat "King" Cole.

Fred Ahlert (1892–1953)   Composer Fred E. Ahlert spent his career in Manhattan. After graduating from the City College of New York and Fordham Law School, he got a job with Waterson, Berlin and Snyder Publishers creating arrangements for Irving Aaronson and his Commanders orchestra and then for the Fred Waring Glee Club. In the early '20s he had his first songwriting successes with "I'd Love to Fall Asleep and Wake Up in My Mammy's Arms" and "I Gave You Up Before You Threw Me Down." Ahlert's collaboration with lyricist Joe Young created several hit songs including "Life Is a Song" (see '35), "Take My Heart" (see '36), "I'm Gonna Sit Right Down and Write Myself a Letter" and "It Can Happen to You." In '28, Ahlert met lyricist Roy Turk and they discovered they had a most successful writing chemistry. They wrote "Where the Blue of the Night (Meets the Gold of the Day)" (see '31), "I'll Get By" (see '44), "Walkin' My Baby Back Home" (see '52), plus "Mean to Me," "I Don't Know Why (I Just Do)," and "Love, You Funny Thing!" In '33, Ahlert became a Director of ASCAP, a position he would hold for 20 years (except for the '48–'50 when he was elected to the position of President). He also contributed songs for inclusion in some of the first Hollywood musicals including "Puttin' on the Ritz" (see '30). Ahlert has been a member of the Songwriters' Hall of Fame since its inception in '70. At http://www.songwritershalloffame.org/exhibit_audio_video.asp?exhibitId=34 hear Maurice Chevalier sing "Walkin' My Baby Back Home" and Layton and Johnstone perform "I Don't Know Why, I Just Do."

Harry Akst (1894–1963)   Harry Akst was an accomplished pianist and conductor as well as one of the most prolific composers of his era. He spent his early music career as a pianist and accompanist. In '16 he enlisted in the U.S. Army. While at Camp Upton, Akst became friends with another young composer, Irving Berlin. Together, the two would create "Home Again Blues." During World War II, he again joined the war effort, this time as an accompanist and bandleader for Al Jolson's overseas tours. In '25, Akst, in collaboration with Sam M. Lewis and Joe Young, wrote one of the most recorded songs from the '20s and '30s, "Dinah" (see '32). Other notable collaborators were Benny Davis, Jack Yellen, Grant Clarke, Sidney Clarke and Al Jolson. Akst, with various collaborators, produced "Baby Face" (see '26) and "Am I Blue" (see '29), among others. Akst collaborated on the '27 Broadway production *Artists and Models* and moved to Hollywood in the late '20s to work on Hollywood movie musicals. He was admitted into the Songwriters' Hall of Fame in '83. At http://www.songwritershalloffame.org/exhibit_audio_video.asp?exhibitId=35 hear Bing Crosby perform "Dinah."

Elmer Albrecht   Elmer Albrecht was one of the co-writers of "Elmer's Tune" (see '41). However, the song most likely was almost solely Albrecht's, but the more famous Sammy Gallop and Dick Jurgens helped him polish it for publication and got co-writing credit. Albrecht worked next door to Chicago's Aragon Ballroom and received permission to use one of their pianos on his lunch hours. It was there he perfected his tune.

Robert Alda (1914–1986)   Robert Alda, as Sky Masterson, introduced "Luck Be a Lady" in *Guys and Dolls* (see '50). He also appeared in the Broadway musical *What Makes Sammy Run*. Alda's career began in vaudeville as a singer and dancer. His film debut was playing George Gershwin in *Rhapsody in Blue* ('45). He is the father of actor Alan Alda.

Joseph R. Alden   Joseph R. Alden was co-lyricist with Raymond B. Egan on "Sleepy Time Gal" (see '26).

Cris Alexander (real name: Alan Smith; 1920–)
Cris Alexander, Adolph Green and John Battles introduced "New York, New York" in the Broadway musical *On the Town* (see '44). Alexander grew up in Tulsa, Oklahoma, where he and Tony Randall performed on a weekly radio show in the late '30s. After his performance in *On the Town*, he played in *Present Laughter*, *Wonderful Town* and *Auntie Mame*. The multi-talented Mr. Alexander was also a gifted photographer. He became the official photographer for the New York City Ballet.

Van Alexander (1915–) Van Alexander collaborated with Ella Fitzgerald on "A-Tisket, A-Tasket" (see '38). Van Alexander has enjoyed an extraordinary career as a successful composer, arranger, songwriter, author, conductor and bandleader for over six decades. Alexander was an arranger for Chick Webb's band while they were performing at the Savoy Ballroom in New York City. It was during this time that he collaborated with Ella on the hit. He later arranged for Benny Goodman, Paul Whiteman, Les Brown and many other bandleaders. In the late '30s, he formed his own orchestra. He and his band appeared on radio and toured all the famous ballrooms and theaters along the east coast and as far west as Chicago. He and his band recorded for the Victor Bluebird label and the Varsity label. In the mid-'40s, he moved to California and scored more than twenty full length feature films and hundreds of television shows. He also arranged and conducted for Dinah Shore, Doris Day, Dean Martin, Kay Starr, Peggy Lee, Dakota Staton, Patty Andrews and Gordon MacRae. His credits include scores for five films starring Mickey Rooney and the scores to classic television shows such as *Hazel*, *The Farmer's Daughter*, *Bewitched*, *I Dream of Jeannie* and *Dennis the Menace*. Alexander was awarded The ASCAP Foundation Lifetime Achievement Award in 2002.

Janet Allen Janet Allen, a member of the vaudeville team of Allen and McShane, introduced "Will You Love Me in December as You Do in May?" (see '06).

Lester Allen (1891–1949) Lester Allen was co-lyricist of "Kiss of Fire" (see '52).

Thomas S. Allen (1876–1919) Boston violinist Thomas S. Allen wrote the hit song "Any Rags?" (see '03).

Thornton W. Allen Thornton Allen composed additional music for the verses of Washington and Lee University's fight song, "Washington and Lee Swing" (see '10).

Alex Alstone (1910–) French composer Alex Alstone wrote the music for "Symphony" (see '46). Alstone also wrote "More," which was popularized in '56 by Perry Como.

Louis Alter (1902–1980) Composer Louis Alter began playing the piano in his Massachusetts hometown movie houses for silent pictures at age 13. He later enrolled at the New England Conservatory. For four or five years in the mid- to late '20s, Alter was the accompanist and touring partner to entertainer Nora Bayes. In '28, he began composing and had his first hit with "Manhattan Serenade," originally an instrumental that would later become the theme song for the Easy Aces Radio Show in the '30s. The song would have another incarnation in '42 when Harold Adamson would add lyrics. Alter wrote music for a few Broadway musical productions including

Ballyhoo, Earl Carroll's Vanities 1925 and 1928, Americana, Sweet and Low, Crazy Quilt and Hold Your Horses. He moved to Hollywood in the late '20s to write for films, but he also continued accompanying singers including Irene Bordoni, Helen Morgan and Beatrice Lillie. The most famous films he worked on include *Hollywood Revue, Rainbow on the River, The Trail of the Lonesome Pine, Sing, Baby, Sing, Make a Wish, Las Vegas Nights and New Orleans.* In '41, Alter entered World War II in the U.S. Air Force, entertaining troops. Alter collaborated with several lyricists including Joe Goodwin, Jo Trent, Sidney Mitchell, Edward Heyman, Frank Loesser, Paul Francis Webster, Eddie Delange, Harold Adamson, Ray Klages, Bob Russell, Milton Drake, Oscar Hammerstein II, Lew Brown and Stanley Adams. Highlights from Alter's popular catalog of songs include "A Melody from the Sky" (see '36), "You Turned the Tables on Me" (see '36), and "Dolores" (see '41), plus "Do You Know What It Means to Miss New Orleans?" Alter also wrote several instrumentals and full orchestral works. Alter has been a member of the Songwriters' Hall of Fame since '75. At http://www.songwritershall offame.org/exhibit_audio_video.asp?exhibitId=207 hear an audio clip of "Do You Know What It Mean to Miss New Orleans?"

Arthur Altman (1910–1994) Arthur Altman was co-writer of "All or Nothing at All" (see '43).

Don Ameche (real name: Dominic Felix Amici; 1908–1993) Don Ameche was a popular film star of the '30s and '40s. Ameche and Janet Blair introduced Cole Porter's "You'd Be So Nice to Come Home to" in the movie musical *Something to Shout About* (see '43). He was also a popular radio master of ceremonies during the same era. As his film career faded in the '50s, he turned to theater and television. He managed somewhat of a comeback in the '80s in *Trading Places* ('83) and *Cocoon* ('85).

American Quartet Billy Murray (tenor, see his biographical sketch), John Bieling (tenor, see his biographical sketch), Steve Porter (baritone, see his biographical sketch), William F. Hooley (bass). The American Quartet was a highly successful vocal group during the second decade of the 20th Century. The group was formed in '09. Billy Murray had been singing with the Haydn Quartet, but it was decided he needed to be in a quartet in which he was the star. John Bieling and William Hooley were borrowed from the Haydn Quartet (although they continued to sing in that quartet) and baritone Steve Porter was brought in from the Peerless Quartet. Bieling left the group in '14 and was replaced by John Young. When Hooley died in late '18, Donald Chalmers succeeded him. In '20, a revamped American Quartet featured Billy Murray, Albert Campbell, John Meyer and Frank Croxton. While some of the individual members, particularly Billy Murray, enjoyed solo recording successes, the quartet is responsible for some of the most successful recordings of the 1910s including "Casey Jones" (see '10), "Call Me Up Some Rainy Afternoon" (see '10) and "Come, Josephine, in My Flying Machine" (see '11), both with Ada Jones, "Moonlight Bay" (see '12), "Everybody Two-Step" (see '12), "Oh, You Beautiful Doll" (see '12), "Rebecca of Sunny-brook Farm" (see '14), "It's a Long, Long Way to Tipperary" (see '15), "Chinatown, My Chinatown" (see '15), "Over There" (see '17), "Oh Johnny, Oh Johnny, Oh" (see '17) and "Good-bye Broadway, Hello France" (see '17). The quartet became the No. 3 recording artist of the 1910s and the No. 16 top recording artist of the first half of the 20th Century. Five recordings by the American Quartet are available at http://www.collectionscanada.ca/gramophone/ including "When You Wore a Tulip and I Wore a Big Red Rose," "Everybody Loves an Irish Song" and "Along the Rocky Road to Dublin." The Vocal Group Hall of Fame awarded their Pioneer Award to the American Quartet.

Ames Brothers (real name: Urick) Ed (1927–), Joe (1921–), Gene (1923–), Vic (1925–1978). The Ames Brothers were a popular quartet in the late '40s and early '50s. They broke up in the late '50s, and Ed continued as a single. Ed is particularly remembered for his role as the Indian on the Daniel Boone television series. His recording of "Try to Remember" is probably his most well known recording as a solo artist. The brothers were sons of Russian Jewish immigrants from the Ukraine. All four brothers pursued careers other than singing: Gene became a painter and semi-pro baseball player, Vic became an actor and professional boxer, Ed became a table tennis champ and Joe studied engineering at UCLA and music at Boston College. He eventually starred at the Montreal Metropolitan Opera. The group's most popular recordings were "Rag Mop" (see '50), "Sentimental Me" (see '50) and "You, You, You" (see '53) all in the early '50s. Other remembered recordings include "Undecided" with Les Brown and his Band of Renown, "The Man with the Banjo" and "The Naughty Lady of Shady Lane." The Ames Brothers rank as the No. 13 top recording artist of the '50s. They were inducted into the Vocal Group Hall of Fame in '98.

Morey Amsterdam (1908–1996) Morey Amsterdam, who later starred with Rose Marie and Dick Van Dyke as writers on *The Dick Van Dyke Show*, heard a calypso-style melody during a vacation to Trinidad. He assumed it was a folk melody, which would be in the public domain, so he had Jeri Sullivan and Paul Baron adapt it for American audiences. He then published it with his own lyrics as "Rum and Coca-Cola" (see '45). Amsterdam started performing in vaudeville at age 14, as a straight man for his brother, who played piano. In another couple of years, he was working in Chicago speakeasies owned by Al Capone. When he got caught up in a shootout one night, Morey determined to find safer employment. He moved to California, where he became a joke writer for such stars as Fanny Brice, Jimmy Durante and Will Rogers. Next came jobs on the radio during the '30s and '40s. It was there he began to gain fame. He later performed on TV in his own variety show from the late '40s into the early '50s. He was also host of a talk show that developed into NBC's *The Tonight Show*. After his extremely successful years on *The Dick Van Dyke Show*, he made guest appearances on television and took some small roles in films.

Deacon Anderson Deacon Anderson was a co-writer with Johnnie Lee Wills of "Rag Mop" (see '50).

Leroy Anderson (1908–1975) Leroy Anderson showed musical talent as a youngster and studied piano at the New England Conservatory at age 11. He graduated from Harvard University with a Bachelor of Arts and later a Masters degree in music. He began his music career as a church organist; later he served on the faculty at Radcliffe College, played double bass and conducted orchestras in the Boston area, became director of the Harvard University Band and served as guest conductor of the famed Boston "Pops" Orchestra and other symphonies. During World War II, he served in military intelligence. After the war, Anderson returned to music and wrote several well-known compositions in the '40s and '50s. His most famous composition was "Blue Tango" (see '52). Most of his works might be labeled semi-classical. Some of those compositions include "Fiddle Faddle," "Sleigh Ride," "Jazz Pizzicato," "The Syncopated Clock," "A Trumpeter's Lullaby," "Sandpaper Ballet," "The Bugler's Holiday," "The Typewriter," and "Plink, Plank, Plunk." He collaborated with several lyricists including Mitchell Parish, Walter and Jean Kerr and Joan Ford. Anderson has been a member of the Songwriters' Hall of Fame since '88. Anderson's most famous recording, with his Pops Concert Orchestra, was "Blue Tango" in '52.

Maxwell Anderson (1888–1959) Playwright and lyricist Maxwell Anderson is best known in popular music for writing the libretto and lyrics for *Knickerbocker Holiday*, which premiered "September Song" (see '39), but he also wrote the book and lyrics for *Lost in the Stars* ('44), also with Kurt Weill as composer. As a playwright, he had several plays produced on Broadway, including *What Price Glory?*, *Saturday's Children, Key Largo*, and *The Bad Seed*.

Fabian Andre (1910–1960) Fabian Andre was co-composer of "Dream a Little Dream of Me" (see '31).

Andrews Sisters LaVerne (1911–1967), Maxene (1916–1995), Patty (1918–). The Andrews Sisters got their start in Minneapolis by winning a children's talent contest. The girls sang with bands and appeared in vaudeville and in nightclubs, but it was not until their recording of "Bei Mir Bist du Schoen" (see '37) that the trio became famous. Their other big hit recordings included "Ferryboat Serenade" (see '40), "Shoo-Shoo Baby" (see '44), "Don't Fence Me in" with Bing Crosby (see '44), "(There'll Be a) Hot Time in the Town of Berlin (When the Yanks Go Marching in)" with Bing Crosby (see '44), "Rum and Coca-Cola," which became their biggest hit (see '45), "I Can Dream, Can't I?" (see '50) and "I Wanna Be Loved," which was really a Patty solo recording (see '50). They recorded often with Bing Crosby and had several other hit recordings with him. Today we remember them and associate them with "Boogie Woogie Bugle Boy" (see '41), which they performed in the Abbott and Costello film *Buck Privates*, but it wasn't a gigantic hit when it was first released. The sisters' collective disk sales through the years have been estimated at 60 million. They also appeared in seventeen films. The Andrews Sisters are ranked as the No. 3 top recording artist of the '40s and No. 23 top recording artist of the first half of the 20th century. The sisters were inducted into the Vocal Group Hall of Fame in '98 and the Popular Music Hall of Fame in 2003. The Andrews Sisters' official website is http://www.cmgww.com/music/andrews/home.php.

Harry Archer (real name: Harry Auracher; 1888–1960) Composer Harry Archer became an important bandleader and occasional composer during the '20s and '30s. He wrote the scores for several Broadway musicals, but by far his greatest success was *Little Jesse James*. His most popular song, "I Love You" (see '24), came from that musical.

Harold Arlen (real name: Hymen Arluck; 1905–1986) Harold Arlen became one of the greatest of American composers and songwriters, writing extraordinarily complex melodies and harmonies that remained accessible to a broad popular audience. By age 7 he was singing in his father's Buffalo, N.Y. synagogue choir and by age 15 he had become a professional pianist and entertainer in nightclubs and on lake steamers. In his late teens he organized a trio that eventually took him to New York City to perform in vaudeville. In Manhattan, Arlen found a home as a singer, pianist and arranger with dance bands and eventually with Arnold Johnson's pit orchestra for the Broadway revue *George White's Scandals of 1928*. Arlen appeared at the Palace Theatre in New York City, the best of vaudeville theaters, and did several tours with Loew's vaudeville circuit. He also began to write songs for Broadway revues in the early '30s, including *9:15 Revue*, which introduced "Get Happy." Later he wrote for *Earl Carroll's Vanities* and wrote the complete scores for several successful Broadway musicals. Arlen collaborated with the greatest of the Tin Pan Alley lyricists, including E.Y. "Yip" Harburg, Johnny Mercer, Ted Koehler, Leo Robin, Ira Gershwin, Dorothy Fields and Truman Capote. Arlen was also active in Hollywood producing the music for several movie musicals. The standout of his career is the unforgettable score for the film *The Wizard of Oz*. The film score includes a collection of outstanding songs, most notably the celebrated "Over the Rainbow" (see '39). The Harold Arlen song catalog boasts such well-known songs as "Get Happy" (see '30), "I Love a Parade" (see '31), "Stormy Weather" (see '33), "I've Got the World on a String" (see '32), "Let's Fall in Love" (see '34), "Blues in the Night" (see '42), "That Old Black Magic" (see '43), "One for My Baby" (see '43), "Ac-cent-tchu-ate the Positive" (see '45), "Come Rain or Come Shine" (see '46) and "The Man That Got Away" (see '54). Others include "Between the Devil and the Deep Blue Sea," "I Gotta Right to Sing the Blues," "It's Only a Paper Moon," "Happiness Is a Thing Called Joe," and "My Shining Hour." As a singer, Arlen's recording of "Stormy Weather" (see '33) with Leo Reisman and his orchestra was particularly popular. Arlen has been a member of the Songwriters' Hall of Fame since '71. He was inducted into the Popular Music Hall of Fame in 2005. At http://www.songwritershall offame.org/exhibit_audio_video.asp?exhibitId=53 hear Arlen's "Down with Love" performed by Judy Garland, "Happiness Is a Thing Called Joe" by Ella Fitzgerald, "It's Only a Paper Moon" by Ella Fitzgerald, "Over the Rainbow" by Ella Fitzgerald, "Ding-Dong! The Witch Is Dead" by Harry Connick, Jr., and "Ain't It the Truth" by Lena Horne.

Henry W. Armstrong (1879–1951) Henry W. (Harry) Armstrong was an American boxer, booking agent, producer, singer, pianist and composer. He was born in Sommerville, Massachusetts and died in New York. During World War I, he performed in hospitals and went on to appear in night clubs, radio and near the end of his life, even on TV. His greatest hit was "Sweet Adeline" (see '04) with Richard H. Gerard. Harry Armstrong and Billy Clark wrote "I Love My Wife; but Oh, You Kid!" (see '09).

Louis Armstrong (real name: Daniel Louis Armstrong; 1900–1971) Louis "Satchmo" Armstrong was born in New Orleans around the turn of the 20th Century.

He became one of the most important and influential jazz trumpeters. He learned to read music and play several instruments in the Colored Waif's Home for Boys in New Orleans. He got his professional start with King Oliver in '22, joined Fletcher Henderson in New York in '24 and played in several other bands including Clarence Williams' Blue Five until '27, when he formed his own band. Armstrong introduced "Jeepers Creepers" in the movie *Going Places* (see '39). Louie's biggest recording successes came in the early '30s with "All of Me" (see '32) and "You Can Depend on Me," plus the title song from the Broadway musical *Hello, Dolly!* in '64. In jazz circles, Armstrong has been a staple since the '20s and many of his trumpet solos and vocal renditions have become jazz classics. "Satchmo," an abbreviation for "Satchelmouth," was elected to the Big Band/Jazz Hall of Fame in the original class of '78. Armstrong was voted by *Time* as one of the most influential people in the world. Several of Armstrong's most famous recordings are available at http://www.redhotjazz. com/bands.html. Satchmo's official website is http://www. satchmo.net/.

Felix Arndt (1889–1918) Felix Arndt was an American pianist and composer of popular music. Born in New York with an aristocratic background (his mother was supposedly related to Napoleon III). He wrote for a number of vaudeville troupers including Nora Bayes, Jack Norworth and Gus Edwards. He recorded some 3000 piano rolls for Duo-Art, QRS and other companies over a three-year period. His only major hit was "Nola" (see '16), which he dedicated to his wife Nola Locke, herself a composer, singer, and teacher. The orchestra leader Vincent Lopez made it his theme song.

Gus Arnheim (1897–1955) Pianist Gus Arnheim was the leader of a band which was most popular during the late '20s and '30s. They toured the U.S. and Europe and appeared in the '29 film *The Street Girl*. Russ Columbo sang with the band from '29 through early '31. Bing Crosby, as a member of the Rhythm Boys, recorded with the band in early '31. Band members at various times included saxophonist and future bandleader Jimmie Grier, future movie actor Fred MacMurray on clarinet and tenor sax, and future bandleaders clarinetist Woody Herman and pianist Stan Kenton. Arnheim also composed several popular songs, including "I Cried for You" and "Sweet and Lovely." His most famous recording was of his "Sweet and Lovely" (see '31) with vocalist Donald Novis. He retired from the band after the mid-'40s but returned in the mid-'50s for a brief time. Gus Arnheim ranks as the No. 35 top recording artist of the '30s.

Eddy Arnold (1918–) Eddy Arnold became one of the top country and western singers in the business and also one of the first to bridge the gap between country and main line popular music. Arnold worked with Pee Wee King and his band in the early '40s and with them began to attract attention at the Grand Ole Opry. By the mid-'40s he had begun to work as a single, but it was not until '47 that he had his first big hit, "I'll Hold You in My Heart." This Country Music Hall of Fame singer had several hit recordings including "Any Time" (see '52), "Bouquet of Roses," "I Wanna Play House with You," "Cattle Call," "I Really Don't Want to Know" and "Make the World Go Away." Eddy Arnold's website is at http://www. eddyarnold.com/. You can hear Arnold's recordings of

"Have I Told You Lately That I Love You?," "I Really Don't Want to Know" and "Somebody Like Me" at his website.

George Asaff (see George Henry Powell)

Sam Ash (1884–1951)   Sam Ash was a popular tenor who appeared in several Broadway operettas and later in some Hollywood films. He is not the person who founded the Sam Ash music store chain. A couple of his most popular recordings included "Hello, Frisco!" with Elida Morris (see '15) and "Give Me the Moonlight, Give Me the Girl" (see '18). He primarily recorded for Columbia.

Adele Astaire (real name: Adele Marie Austerlitz; 1896–1981)   Adele Astaire was a singer and dancer, the sister of Fred (see below). When she was five years old, she and her younger brother, Fred, began a successful vaudeville act. They developed into very prominent Broadway entertainers. Early in their Broadway career, she was the bigger star. Adele and Fred introduced Gershwin's "Fascinating Rhythm" in *Lady, Be Good!* (see '24). "The Man I Love" (see '24) was originally written for Adele to sing in *Lady, Be Good!*, but the song was dropped from the show. "'S Wonderful" was introduced by Ms. Astaire and Allen Kearns in *Funny Face* (see '28). In the early '30s, after a successful run with her brother in *The Band Wagon* on Broadway, Adele retired from show business to marry Lord Charles Arthur Francis Cavendish, and moved to Ireland, where they lived at Lismore Castle.

Fred Astaire (real name: Frederick Austerlitz; 1899–1987)   Fred Astaire began his show business career in '16 with his sister, Adele, as a dancing couple, much like the famous Castles, Vernon and Irene, who had been popular in the '10s. The Astaires started in vaudeville and climbed to Broadway stardom. Adele retired from the act when she married Lord Cavendish in '32. Fred appeared as a solo dancer and with numerous dancing partners, but his most famous partner was Ginger Rogers, with whom he made several Hollywood movie musicals. Astaire is the acknowledged King of the Movie Musicals, and was unrivaled as an elegant, sophisticated, virtuoso dancer. His small, limited voice never hindered him or the musicals or films in which he appeared. He had a style with popular songs that was irresistible. Fred's most popular recordings came in the '30s and included "Night and Day" (see '32), "Cheek to Cheek" (see '35), "Top Hat, White Tie, and Tails" (see '35), "The Way You Look Tonight" (see '36), "A Fine Romance" (see '36), "I'm Putting All My Eggs in One Basket" (see '36), "They Can't Take That Away from Me" (see '37), "Change Partners" (see '38) and "Nice Work If You Can Get It" (see '38). Astaire is ranked as the No. 8 top recording artist of the '30s. Astaire starred in more than thirty movie musicals and in about a dozen Broadway musicals. A few of the most famous Broadway productions in which he appeared include *Lady, Be Good!*, *Funny Face*, *The Band Wagon* and *Gay Divorce*. Some of the most famous movie musicals in which he starred include *Flying Down to Rio* (see "The Carioca" in '34), *Top Hat*, *The Gay Divorcee*, *Roberta* (where he introduced "I Won't Dance," see '35), *Follow the Fleet*, *Swing Time*, *Shall We Dance*, *Damsel in Distress*, *The Story of Vernon and Irene Castle*, *Broadway Melody of 1940*, *Holiday Inn*, *Blue Skies*, *The Barkleys of Broadway*, *Easter Parade*, *Three Little Words*,

Royal Wedding, *The Band Wagon* (where he and others introduced "That's Entertainment" see '53), *Daddy Long Legs* (where he introduced "Something's Gotta Give" see '55), *Funny Face* and *Finian's Rainbow*. The Fred Astaire website is http://www.fredastaire.net/.

Harold R. Atteridge (1886–1938)   Harold R. Atteridge wrote the lyrics for the highly successful popular song "By the Beautiful Sea" (see '14).

Georges Auric (1899–1983)   French composer Georges Auric wrote "The song from *Moulin Rouge* (Where Is Your Heart?)" (see '53). The original French title was "Le Long de la Seine" with French words by Jacques Larue. Auric had his first compositions published at age 15. He had orchestrated and written incidental music for several ballets and stage productions before he was twenty. He studied at the Paris Conservatory in '20, and began writing for films in the early '30s.

Billy Austin (1896–1964)   Billy Austin is listed as a co-writer of "Is You Is or Is You Ain't My Baby?" (see '44). In addition to being a songwriter, Austin at one time or another worked as a lumberjack, a sailor and in construction.

Gene Austin (real name: Lemeul Eugene Lucas; 1900–1972)   Gene Austin took the name of his stepfather Jim Austin, who was a blacksmith. During World War I, at age 17, Gene enlisted in the Army hoping to be sent to Europe. Because of his blacksmithing experience, he was instead assigned to the cavalry and sent to Mexico with the Pancho Villa Expedition. He was awarded the Mexican Service Medal. After his discharge in '19, Austin attended a vaudeville act in Houston, Texas where, on a dare from some friends, Gene took the stage and sang. The audience response was enthusiastic, so the vaudeville company offered him a spot in their show. Austin is often given credit for inventing the "crooner" style of singing. He had established himself as a major star before the end of the '20s. By the early '30s, however, his fame began to fade primarily because his soft voice could not compete with the bands that were becoming fashionable and microphones had not developed enough to compensate. Austin's most famous recordings came between the mid– '20s and the very early '30s. His biggest hit recordings include "Yes Sir, That's My Baby" (see '25), "Five Foot Two, Eyes of Blue" (see '26), "Bye Bye Blackbird" (see '26), "My Blue Heaven" (see '27), "Tonight You Belong to Me" (see '27), "Forgive Me" (see '27), "Ramona" (see '28), "Jeannine (I Dream of Lilac Time)" (see '28), and "Carolina Moon" (see '29). Other popular recordings by Austin include "Sleepy Time Gal," "My Melancholy Baby." "Yearning (Just for You)," "When My Sugar Walks Down the Street" with Aileen Stanley, "Girl of My Dreams," "She's Funny That Way," and "Please Don't Talk About Me When I'm Gone." His recording of "My Blue Heaven" was the biggest hit of the '20s. Austin was the third most successful artist of the '20s behind Paul Whiteman and Al Jolson. He also ranks as the No. 24 top recording artist of the first half of the 20th century. In addition to his performing, he composed several popular songs including "How Come You Do Me Like You Do?," "When My Sugar Walks Down the Street," and "The Lonesome Road." Austin also appeared in three films, *Belle of the Nineties* ('34), *Klondike Annie* ('36) and the Mae West film

My Little Chickadee ('40). In '78, Gene Austin was posthumously awarded a Grammy Hall of Fame Award for his '28 recording of "Bye, Bye, Blackbird," and in 2005, he was admitted to the Grammy Hall of Fame.

Lovie Austin (real name: Cora Calhoun; 1887–1972) Lovie Austin was a popular figure in the '20s Chicago jazz and blues scene. Her early career was in vaudeville where she played piano and performed in variety acts. Throughout the '20s, she was the musical director at the Monogram Theatre in Chicago. Lovie Austin is best remembered today as the composer of "Down Hearted Blues" (see '23).

Ray Austin Ray Austin teamed with Freddy Martin to adapt Tschaikovsky's *Piano Concerto in B-flat Minor* into a big band instrumental. With Bobby Worth's lyrics and Clyde Rogers' vocal, it became "Tonight We Love" (see '41).

Gene Autry (real name: Orvon Gene Autry; 1907–1998) Gene Autry became the first big singing cowboy movie star. In '28 he began singing on a radio station, and three years later he had his own show and was making his first recordings. In '31, his film debut was in Ken Maynard's *In Old Santa Fe*. The following year, he starred in a 13-part serial, *Phantom Empire*. His first starring movie role came in the '35 film *Tumbling Tumbleweeds*. By the end of his career, in the early '50s, he had made about 100 films, which often grossed ten times their production costs. His own company produced his TV series *The Gene Autry Show*, *The Adventures of Champion*, and *Annie Oakley* in the '50s. In addition, he was the star of the radio show *Melody Ranch* from the early '40s through the early '50s. He collaborated with Vaughn Horton and Denver Darling on "Address Unknown" (see '39). Autry introduced "There's a Gold Mine in the Sky" in a film of the same title (see '38) and "Sioux City Sue" in the film of the same name (see '46). "Mule Train" provided the title for and was sung by Autry in a '50 film (see '49). He also sang "Room Full of Roses" in *Mule Train* (see '49). He recorded extensively and made several hit records, particularly "Rudolph the Red-Nosed Reindeer" (see '50), "Peter Cottontail," "Here Comes Santa Claus" and "Frosty the Snowman." He was also the writer or co-writer of several hit songs; he wrote over 200 songs. "Back in the Saddle Again" is one example of his writing (see '40). His recording of "Back in the Saddle Again" was inducted into the Grammy Hall of Fame in '97. He was also the composer or co-composer of several hits in the country and western market, some of which became national hits. His most famous compositions include "That Silver-Haired Daddy of Mine," "Have I Told You Lately That I Love You?," and "Here Comes Santa Claus." In his latter years he became less active in show business, concentrating instead on his considerable business empire, which included radio and television stations, recording and publishing firms, movie studios, and the California (or Anaheim) Angels baseball team. Autry received many honors and awards, but a few of the most significant ones are, he was voted the No. 1 western film star every year from '37 to '42 and again from '46 to '53; in '55, he was voted Favorite Western Star on Radio; he was inducted into the Country Music Hall of Fame in '69, in '73, the Country Music Association presented him with the Pioneer Award in recognition of his contributions to films and music since

the early '30s. Gene Autry's official website is http://www.autry.com.

Nat D. Ayer (1887–1952) Nat Ayer composed the music for "Oh, You Beautiful Doll" (see '12) and "If You Were the Only Girl in the World" ('25), which was revived by Perry Como in '46.

Mitchell Ayres (real name: Mitchell Agress; 1910–1969) Mitchell Ayres was a bandleader who gained most of his fame when he and his band backed Perry Como on Como's radio and television shows. During the '30s and '40s Ayres led a popular sweet band, which appeared in a few minor films and recorded occasionally. "Make-Believe Island" (see '40) was their only big hit recording. His group was called Mitchell Ayres and his Fashions in Music. When Perry Como folded his TV show, Ayres moved to the Hollywood Palace TV program, where he worked until his death.

Waldyr Azevedo Brazilian composer Waldyr Azevedo wrote the music for "Delicado" (see '52).

Don Azpiazu (1893–1943) Cuban bandleader, Don Azpiazu, had a very popular recording of "The Peanut Vendor" (see '31). Not only did this become a huge national hit, launching a decade of rumbamania, it was also the first U.S. recording with an authentic Latin style (i.e. Latin music, not U.S. music to a Latin beat). Azpiazu's "The Peanut Vendor" also introduced many of the Cuban percussion instruments to the U.S. Azpizau and his Havana Casino Orchestra were also the first to record "Green Eyes" in '31, which became much more popular in the early '40s.

Abel Baer (1893–1976) Abel Baer was a composer, pianist and author. He was educated at the College of Physicians and Surgeons, giving up dentistry to join a New York City music publisher in '20. He accompanied the famous singer Nora Bayes. He moved to Hollywood in '29 to write songs for sound films. His chief musical collaborators were L. Wolfe Gilbert, Stanley Adams, Cliff Friend, Sam Lewis, and Mabel Wayne. His most famous popular song compositions were "June Night" (see '24) and "There Are Such Things" (see 43). Some of his other popular-song compositions include "I Miss My Swiss," "Lucky Lindy," "Mama Loves Papa," and "When the One You Love, Loves You."

Ross Bagdasarian (1919–1972) Ross Bagdasarian and his cousin, playwright William Saroyan, were on an automobile trip in '49, during which they adapted an old Armenia folk song into "Come on-a My House" (see '51). Ross Bagdasarian was later responsible for the famous "Chipmunk" recordings, which began in '58. It used the name David Seville. The "Chipmunk" recording of "The Witch Doctor" became a No. 1 hit in '58. Their "The Chipmunk Song (Christmas Don't Be Late)" also made it to No.1 in '58. Seville and the Chipmunks had a successful animated television series in the early '60s. Bagdasarian was a pianist, songwriter, actor and record producer. He appeared in a minor role in Hitchcock's *Rear Window*, plus parts in *Stalag 17, Viva Zapata!* and *The Greatest Show on Earth*.

Mildred Bailey (real name: Mildred Rinker; 1907–1951) Mildred began her music career on a Los Angeles radio station. In the late '20s, she was hired by Paul Whiteman to sing with his orchestra. She also sang with Glen Gray and the Casa Loma Orchestra in '33, when she married bandleader Red Norvo. They became known as "Mr. and Mrs. Swing." Her most popular recordings came with Norvo and his band: "Says My Heart" (see '38) and "Please Be Kind" (see '38). She was the sister of Al Rinker, who sang with Whiteman's orchestra as one of the Rhythm Boys. As a matter of fact, she was instrumental in getting them the job with Whiteman.

Faye Bainter (1891–1968)   "Chinese Lullaby" (see '19) originated in the musical production *East Is West*. According to the sheet music cover, Fay Bainter performed the song in that production. A person named Fay Bainter was also active in Hollywood films between '34 and the late '60s. She received an Oscar for Best Supporting Actress for *Jezebel* ('38). Fay or Faye Bainter also starred opposite Charles Winninger in *State Fair* ('45).

Belle Baker (1893–1957)   Belle Baker was an actress and singer. She appeared on stage, in vaudeville, in motion pictures and on television. Ms. Baker introduced "Blue Skies" in the Irving Berlin musical *Betsy* (see '27).

Bonnie Baker (real name: Evelyn Nelson; 1918–1990)   Wee Bonnie Baker is primarily remembered as vocalist for Orrin Tucker's band. She rose to prominence as the band's tiny soloist after she joined in '36. In '40, she was voted the most popular female band vocalist in a *Billboard* poll among college students.She and the band were featured in the '41 film *You're the One*. In the late '40s, she worked as a single for a while, but her career gradually declined. She may be most remembered for her vocal on Tucker's recording of "Oh Johnny, Oh Johnny, Oh!" in '40 (see '17).

Elsie Baker (1892–1958)   Elsie Baker sometimes recorded under the pseudonym Edna Brown. She was also a member of the Victor Light Opera Company. Ms. Baker's most famous recordings include "I Love You Truly" (see '12), and "Missouri Waltz" (see '17). A recording of "Mysterious Moon" by Edna Brown and Billy Murray is available in an MP3 download at http://www.publicdo main4u.com/html/moon.htm.

Jack Baker   Jack Baker was one of the co-writers of "I Hear a Rhapsody" (see '41). Baker was also a noted choreographer.

Kenny Baker (real name: Kenneth Laurence Baker; 1912–1985)   Kenny Baker introduced "Remember Me?" in *Mr. Dodd Takes the Air* (see '37) and "Love Walked in" in *The Goldwyn Follies* (see '38). Mr. Baker and Mary Martin introduced "Speak Low" in the musical *One Touch of Venus* (see '44). Kenny Baker and his beautiful tenor voice are best known for work in films, beginning with *King of Burlesque* ('36) and concluding with *Calendar Girl* ('47). From '35 through the remainder of the decade, he was a regular on the popular Jack Benny radio show. He appeared on the *Texaco Star Theater* radio program in the late '30s and with Fred Allen on his popular radio show in the early '40s. He had his own radio show in '44.

Phil Baker (1896–1963)   Phil Baker is best known as a comedian and radio emcee, but he was also a vaudeville actor, songwriter, accordionist and author. He, Ted Healy, Fanny Brice and her brother Lew introduced "I Found a Million Dollar Baby" in Billy Rose's revue *Crazy Quilt* (see '31).

Fanny Baldridge   Fanny Baldridge was the lyricist of "Let's Dance" (see '35).

Ernest R. Ball (1878–1927)   In '05, composer Ernest Ball was in New York City when he was given a few verses written by the then State Senator, James J. Walker, who later became famous as Jimmy Walker, Mayor of New York City. Ball put one of the verses to music, and "Will You Love Me in December as You Do in May?" became a hit (see '06). Beginning in '06, Ball had a dual career: writing songs and singing them on the vaudeville stages. At first he worked alone, but later shared billing with his second wife, Maude Lambert. In '07 he was a charter member of the American Society of Composers, Authors and Publishers (ASCAP) and signed a contract with Witmark Music as a demonstrator and house composer. Ball's most famous songs include "Love Me, and the World Is Mine" (see '06), "My Dear" (see '08), "As Long as the World Rolls On" (see '08), "To the End of the World with You" (see '09), "I Love the Name of Mary" (see '11), "Mother Machree" (see '11), "When Irish Eyes Are Smiling" (see '13), "Isle o' Dreams" (see '13), "Till the Sands of the Desert Grow Cold" (see '13), "A Little Bit of Heaven (Shure, They Call It Ireland)" (see '15), "Goodbye, Good Luck, God Bless You (Is All That I Can Say)" (see '16), and "Turn Back the Universe (andGive Me Yesterday)" (see '16). Ball has said that he became a successful composer when he learned to write songs that came from his heart and were about things that he knew. He collaborated with several lyricists including Chauncey Olcott, George Graff, Darl MacBoyle, J. Kiern Brennan, James J. Walker, Arthur Penn, Annelu Burns and David Reed. Ernest Ball was inducted into the Songwriters' Hall of Fame at its inception in '70.

Hank Ballard (1927–2003)   Hank Ballard was cowriter, with Johnny Otis and Etta James, of "Wallflower (Dance with Me, Henry)" (see '55). Ballard was an R&B singer and is now a member of the Rock and Roll Hall of Fame. Originally from Detroit, Ballard grew up in Alabama, but returned to Detroit, where he formed a doo wop group. He soon joined an R&B group called The Royals. Their first major success was "Work with Me Annie." "Wallflower," see above, was a reworking of "Work with Me Annie." The Royals soon changed its name to the Midnighters. Ballard also wrote "The Twist," which Chubby Checker took to No. 1 in the rock 'n' roll era.

Pat Ballard (real name: Francis Drake Ballard; 1897–1958)   Pat Ballard wrote the words and music for "Mister Sandman" (see '54) and "I Get So Lonely (When I Dream About You)" (see '54). Both of those hit songs came after Ballard had supposedly retired from the music business and had returned to his hometown of Troy, Pennsylvania. Ballard played drums in a college Dixieland jazz band at the University of Pennsylvania. Ted Weems was the trombone player in that band. Pat wrote music for two editions of the Mask and Wig Varsity Shows during college. Ballard's first songwriting success was in '25 with "Any Ice Today, Lady?" "I Get So Lonely" was recorded in California by the Four Knights for Capitol Records early in '53. It was finally released just before the Christmas rush of holiday songs that year. By April it was one of the nation's biggest hits. The success of "I Get so Lonely" prompted Ballard to write again. He finished

"Mister Sandman" in the late summer of '54. Vaughn Monroe recorded it on the "B" side of "Mambo." Then Archie Bleyer decided to have the Chordettes record the song. It became an immediate smash hit. Ballard was an original member of ASCAP. In addition to songwriting, Ballard was music editor for *College Humor* for several years and wrote film scripts for Hollywood. In the early '50s, he wrote many children's songs for a series called "Little John Records," which sold over five million copies.

Dave Barbour (real name: David Michael Barbour; 1912–1965) Jazz guitarist and bandleader, Dave Barbour may be most famous as singer Peggy Lee's husband. He began his music career as a banjo player, but switched to guitar. His first professional job was with Wingy Manone in '34, but transferred to Red Norvo's band in '36. In the late '30s, he worked as a studio musician. He joined Benny Goodman in '42, where he met and in '43 married Peggy Lee. Ms. Lee quit the music business to raise their daughter, but Capitol Records eventually convinced her to return. Barbour formed his owned band and backed his wife on several recordings. Barbour also co-wrote several songs; particularly noteworthy was "Manana" (see '48). He suffered for several years with severe stomach ailments that forced his early retirement.

Lorenzo Barcelata (real name: Lorenzo Barcelata y Castro; 1898–1943) Lorenzo Barcelata was born in Mexico into a family of musicians and fandango dancers. He is best known in the U.S. as the composer and lyricist for the waltz "Maria Elena" (see '41). In the early '30s, Barcelata contributed music for some Paramount films and later did the same for Mexican film studios.

John Barker John Barker introduced "Dancing in the Dark," in the revue *The Band Wagon* (see '31).

F.J. Barnes F.J. Barnes was co-lyricist with R. P. Weston for "I've Got Rings on My Fingers" (see '09).

Paul Barnes Paul Barnes' only major contribution to popular music was as composer for "Good-bye, Dolly Gray" (see '01).

Charlie Barnet (1913–1991) In addition to being a bandleader, Charlie Barnet was a millionaire playboy. He played in his first band at age 16, and formed his own group in '33. They first achieved recognition in the late '30s with their recording of "Cherokee" (see '39), which was inducted into the Grammy Hall of Fame in '98. The song became his theme song. Barnet and his orchestra's best success in recordings came in the first couple of years of the '40s. "Where Was I?" (see '40) became their biggest hit recording on the pop charts. At a time when most bands were segregated, Barnet hired several African American instrumentalists and singers, including Lena Horne in the early '40s. His hiring practices may have hurt his overall popularity because several popular hotels and ballrooms that were "for whites only" would not hire his band. Barnet became a member of the Big Band/Jazz Hall of Fame in '84. He was ranked as the No. 38 top recording artist of the '40s.

Harry Barris (1905–1962) After composer Harry Barris grew up in Denver, he began to gain fame in '26 when he joined Bing Crosby and Al Rinker to form the Rhythm Boys. They soon were contracted to sing with Paul Whiteman's orchestra. After they appeared in the movie musical *King of Jazz*, they left Whiteman to join Gus Arnheim's band at the Los Angeles Cocoanut Grove. About that time Crosby began to do more solo work so the trio faded in importance and eventually broke up. During the '30s and '40s Barris often appeared in bit parts as a rehearsal pianist, jive-talking band musician, or bandleader in some of Crosby's films. He also composed or helped write a few all-time pop standards — namely "At Your Command" (see '31), "Mississippi Mud" (see '31), "I Surrender, Dear" (see '31) and "Little Dutch Mill" (see '34), most of those primarily popularized by his pal, Bing Crosby.

Blue Barron (real name: Harry Friedland; 1913–2005) Harry Friedland attended Ohio State University, where he played violin in a campus band, and started his career as an agent, booking bands around the Cleveland area. In '36 he formed his own sweet-style band, taking the stage name Blue Barron. He and his band were billed as "Music of Yesterday and Today, styled the Blue Barron Way." His style featured the trombone and sax sections. His band's first big success came in '38 when he got a contract at the Green Room in the Taft Hotel (NY) that included three radio broadcasts each week. During World War II, he served in an Airborne Division. His band continued to work under the leadership of singer Tommy Ryan. His only major hit recording was "Cruising Down the River" (see '49).

Ary Barroso (1903–1964) Ary Barroso was a very influential Brazilian composer, who wrote the popular song "Brazil" (see '43). Barroso's "No Baixa de Sapateiro" was included in the Disney film *The Three Caballeros* and popularized as "Baia." He received an Academy Award nomination for his score for the '44 film *Rio de Janeiro*. Barroso was a multi-talented person: a lawyer, radio announcer, writer, humorist, reporter, producer, emcee, interviewer and soccer commentator.

Dave Bartholomew (1920–) Dave Bartholomew is famous as a bandleader and songwriter. He co-wrote "Ain't That a Shame?" with Fats Domino (see '55). Bartholomew was active in the New Orleans music scene from the mid-'20s until the present. He played rhythm and blues, big band swing, rock 'n' roll, jazz and Dixieland. He arranged several of Fats Domino's hits of the '50s, including "Blueberry Hill." Bartholomew was inducted into the Rock and Roll Hall of Fame in 2006.

Eileen Barton (1929–) Eileen Barton joined her parents' vaudeville dance team at age four. By the late '30s, she was a featured child performer with stars such as Eddie Cantor, Rudy Vallee and Milton Berle. In the early '40s, she appeared on radio with Frank Sinatra and had a standby role in the Broadway musical *Best Foot Forward*. She also sang in nightclubs in New York and other locations in the Northeast. In late '40s, she was recording for a New York City independent label that specialized in rhythm and blues performers. In late '49, Eileen recorded a novelty tune that was introduced on the *Breakfast Club* radio show called "If I Knew You Were Comin' I'd've Baked a Cake" (see '50). The record was an instant sensation. The independent label, National, couldn't keep up with the demand for the record, so they contracted for national distribution by Mercury Records which also put the record out on their label in certain parts of the country not covered by National. The numbers for this tune were phenomenal. It became one of the highest selling records on an independent label in recording history. For the next several years Barton struggled to keep her career going. By '54, Barton had moved to network radio with a program for CBS, but network radio was no longer what it had been. As rock 'n' roll began to emerge, Barton's career faded.

Count Basie (real name: William Basie; 1904–1984) Pianist William "Count" Basie was one of the most famous bandleaders of the '30s and '40s. Basie and his band remained active into the '70s. Basie began playing piano in New York in the early '20s and toured for several years in the vaudeville circuits. He played with Bennie Moten's band from '29 until Moten's death in '35. Basie began to form his own band in '36, but it did not achieve popularity until '38 at New York City's Savoy Ballroom. Basie's theme song, "One O'Clock Jump," became one of the most famous big band themes (see '38). His orchestra's only "mainstream" hit recording was "Open the Door, Richard" (see '47). Basie was elected to the Big Band/Jazz Hall of Fame in '81. For more, go to http://www.countbasie.com/.

James Baskett (1904–1948) James Baskett, as Uncle Remus, introduced "Zip-A-Dee-Doo-Dah" in Disney's cartoon-live action feature *Song of the South* (see '47). Baskett won a special Academy Award for his wonderful performance in *Song of the South*, the first African American male to be awarded an Academy Award. Ironically, his performance could not be seen in the United States for many years because the Walt Disney Co. would not release the film on the home video market due to the NAACP denouncing it as racist when it premiered. It is available on some internet sites, however, these may not be official copies. There is a petition circulating to request Disney to officially release it. Mr. Baskett appeared in the role of Gabby Gibson on the *Amos 'n' Andy* radio show.

Billy Baskette Composer Billy Baskette wrote or co-wrote the music for the World War I hit "Good-bye Broadway, Hello France" (see '17), plus "Everybody Wants a Key to My Cellar."

Paul Bass Paul Bass and Margaret Simms introduced "Ain't Misbehavin'" in *Connie's Hot Chocolates* (see '29).

George Bassman (1914–1997) George Bassman was the composer of "I'm Gettin' Sentimental Over You" (see '32). Composer George Bassman was born to Russian Jewish emigrants in New York City. His family later moved to Boston and he studied music at the Boston Conservatory while he was still very young. He left home in his teens to play piano in a touring jazz band; he later worked as an arranger for Fletcher Henderson's band. He later worked as an arranger for Andre Kostelanetz. Then, he moved to Hollywood in the mid-'30s. One of his first Hollywood assignments was orchestrating Gershwin songs for the Fred Astaire film *A Damsel in Distress* for RKO. He also composed music for the Marx Brothers films *A Day at the Races, Go West* and *The Big Store*, as well as writing and/or arranging music for *Lady, Be Good!* and *Cabin in the Sky*. He also worked on the Judy Garland films *The Wizard of Oz*, where he wrote several musical sequences, *Babes in Arms* and *For Me and My Gal*. Bassman also worked on a few film dramas, including *The Clock* and

The Postman Always Rings Twice. Bassman's career was in serious jeopardy in the '50s during the House Un-American Activities Committee hearings. His family had been Communists in the 1910s. Since he was virtually black-listed by the studios, he returned to New York City where he worked on some Broadway musicals, including orchestrating *Guys and Dolls*. He also found work in television in its infancy as composer and conductor. In the mid- to late '50s he began to compose for films again.

John Battles John Battles, Adolph Green and Cris Alexander introduced "New York, New York" in the Broadway musical *On the Town* (see '44).

Bernie Baum (1928–1993) Bernie Baum was a co-writer of "Music! Music! Music!" (see '50). He also wrote several songs for Elvis Presley films.

Les Baxter (1922–1996) Les Baxter started his musical career as a teenage concert pianist. Later he was a member of the vocal group Mel Torme and the Mel Tones. After that, he began concentrating on arranging and conducting. In the late '40s he became musical director for Bob Hope's and Abbott and Costello's radio shows. In the '50s he was a producer and recording artist for Capitol Records. Les Baxter and his orchestra's most productive period was the '50s. Their most popular recordings include "Because of You" (see '51), "April in Portugal" (see '53), "The High and the Mighty" (see '54), "Unchained Melody" (see '55) and "The Poor People of Paris" in '56. Baxter ranks as the No. 22 top recording artist of the '50s. The official Les Baxter website is http://www.lesbaxter.com/.

Nora Bayes (real name: Dora Goldberg; 1880–1928) Nora Bayes became known as the "Queen of the Two-a-Days" because of her fame on the vaudeville circuit. She also starred in several Broadway musicals from the early 1900s into the early '20s. She and her second husband, Jack Norworth, wrote the popular classic "Shine On, Harvest Moon" (see '09), as well as a few other popular songs. Ms. Bayes introduced "Down Where the Wurzburger Flows" at the Orpheum Theater in Brooklyn (see '03). The song became such a success for her that she was often identified as "The Wurzburger Girl." Bayes also introduced her husband's song "Take Me Out to the Ball Game" (see '08) in vaudeville. Ms. Bayes and Henry Lewis introduced "Oh Johnny, Oh Johnny, Oh!" as an interpolation into the musical *Follow Me* (see '17). Bayes had a successful recording career from approximately '10 into the early '20s. Her most famous recordings were "Over There" (see '17) and "Make Believe" (see '21). Other popular recordings by Nora Bayes include "Has Anybody Here Seen Kelly?," "The Good Ship Mary Ann," "How Ya Gonna Keep 'Em Down on the Farm," "Goodbye, France," "Just Like a Gypsy," "Lovin' Sam (The Sheik of Alabam') and "All Over Nothing at All." Ms. Bayes became the No. 20 top recording artist of the 1910s.

Eily Beadell Two middle-aged British women, Eily Beadell and Nell Tollerton, wrote "Cruising Down the River" in '45. It won a nationwide song contest in Great Britain. The song became a big hit in the U.S. in '49.

Carl Bean Carl Bean collaborated on the music of "Scatter-Brain" (see '39).

Nellie Beaumont According to the sheet music cover, Nellie Beaumont sang "Everybody Two-Step" in *A Lucky*

Hoodoo (see '12). Ms. Beaumont and her sister, Rose, had appeared for many years in vaudeville as the Beaumont Sisters. She married Billy V. Van, an actor, comedian, dancer, and singer/songwriter.

Carl Beck Carl Beck, a former University of Wisconsin student, supplied the lyrics for "On Wisconsin" (see '09).

Lionel Belasco (1881–1967) Pianist, composer and bandleader Lionel Belasco is best known for his calypso music. He was leading his own band by '02 and made his first recordings in Trinidad in '14. About that time, he traveled to New York City, where he made more recordings and set up a publishing business. His most famous popular song in the U.S. is "Rum and Coca Cola" (see '45).

Joe Belmont (real name: Joseph Walter Fulton; 1876–1949) Belmont was famous as a member of the Columbia Male Quartet and as a whistling soloist. He was called "The Human Bird." He also recorded with Ada Jones and Billy Murray. In '01, Belmont joined Byron Harlan, Frank Stanley and the Florodora Girls to record "Tell Me, Pretty Maiden" from the Broadway musical *Florodora*. Their Columbia recording was very successful (see '01). His whistling recordings of birds were also well received.

Jesse Belvin (1933–1960) Jesse Belvin was a cowriter of "Earth Angel" (see '55). For more on Belvin, see http://elvispelvis.com/jessebelvin.htm.

Tex Beneke (real name: Gordon Lee Beneke; 1914–2000) Tex was tenor saxophonist and sometimes vocalist with Glenn Miller's orchestra from '38 to '42. Beneke's most famous vocal was on Miller's recording of "Chattanooga Choo Choo" (see '41). When Miller joined the Army Air Force in '42, he disbanded his band. Beneke worked some with the Modernaires, Jan Savitt and Horace Heidt during the war. Once the war ended, Glenn Miller's widow, Helen, asked Beneke to reform the Miller band and front the group. The band was then known as Tex Beneke and the Glenn Miller Orchestra.

Bennie Benjamin (real name: Claude A. Benjamin; 1907–1989) Bennie Benjamin was born in Christiansted, St. Croix, Virgin Islands. He moved to New York City at age 20 where he studied the banjo and guitar. Benjamin spent several years performing in vaudeville and various orchestras before becoming a staff composer and music publisher. Benjamin's prolific output began in '41 when he collaborated with Sol Marcus, Ed Durham and Ed Seiler, to produce the songs "I Don't Want to Set the World on Fire" (see '41) and "When the Lights Go on Again" (see '42). In '46, Benjamin teamed with George David Weiss to produce the following hit songs: "Oh! What It Seemed to Be" (see '46), "Rumors Are Flying" (see '46), "Surrender" (see '46), "Wheel of Fortune" (see '52), "Cross Over the Bridge" (see '54) and "How Important Can It Be" (see '55). Other Benjamin/Weiss songs include "Can Anyone Explain? (No, No, No)," and "I'll Never Be Free." Benjamin formed his own publishing company in '68. In addition to his enormous catalog, Benjamin also collaborated on music and theme songs for movies including *Fun and Fancy Free* and *Melody Time*. Benjamin was inducted into the Songwriters' Hall of Fame in '84. At http://www.songwritershalloffame.org/exhibit

_audio_video.asp?exhibitId=320 hear Frankie Carle and his orchestra with vocalist Marjorie Hughes perform Benjamin's "Rumors Are Flying" and Horace Heidt and his Musical Knights with vocalists Larry Cotton, Donna and her Don Juans perform his "I Don't Want to Set the World on Fire."

Tony Bennett (real name: Anthony Dominick Benedetto; 1926–) Singer Tony Bennett was most popular in the '50s, but he has continued to perform into the 21st century. Bennett's most famous recordings came in the early '50s with "Because of You" (see '51), "Cold, Cold Heart" (see '51), and "Rags to Riches" (see '53). A church minstrel show gave him his first public appearance at age seven, but he did not begin to make an impact until he appeared on an *Arthur Godfrey's Talent Scouts* show. That led to a television contract that helped Bennett become nationally famous. Bennett was inducted into the Big Band/Jazz Hall of Fame in '96. He was inducted into the Popular Music Hall of Fame in 2004. Tony became the No. 18 top recording artist of the '50s. He is also a talented painter. The Tony Bennett website is http://www. tonybennett.net/.

Wilda Bennett (1893–1967) Wilda Bennett introduced "When You're Away" in the Victor Herbert musical *The Only Girl* (see '15). In the '21 edition of the *Music Box Revue*, Ms. Bennett and Paul Frawley introduced "Say It with Music."

David Berg David Berg's sole contribution to popular music was as lyricist for "There's a Quaker Down in Quaker Town" (see '16).

Borney Bergantine Borney Bergantine was the composer of "My Happiness" (see '48).

Henry Bergman (1868–1946) Born in San Francisco, Henry Bergman made his Broadway debut in 1899. Bergman and Gladys Clark introduced Irving Berlin's "Remember" in vaudeville (see '25) and "Always" (see '26). Bergman is most remembered today for his long association with Charlie Chaplin. He began working with Chaplin in '16. He appeared in several Chaplin shorts and features, including *The Gold Rush*, *The Immigrant*, *The Circus*, and *Modern Times*. Bergman later assisted Chaplin in directing some of his films. Chaplin helped Bergman finance a Hollywood restaurant that later became a popular spot for celebrities.

Busby Berkeley (real name: William Berkeley Enos; 1895–1976) Choreographer Busby Berkeley came to national prominence when he directed the musical numbers for *Forty Second Street* for Warner Bros. in '32. He had begun his career as a soldier in '18 when he directed Army parades, and after World War I, staged camp shows for soldiers. Berkeley appeared in several Broadway musicals, beginning with *Holka-Polka* ('25). He graduated to staging extravagant dance routines for Broadway productions, like *A Connecticut Yankee in King Arthur's Court* ('27). He introduced the song "You Took Advantage of Me" in *Present Arms* ('28). Following a decade as a Broadway dance director, he moved to Hollywood, where he found he wanted to control the camera for the dance sequences. He gained considerable fame in the movie business as a choreographer and eventually as a director. He created almost all of the musical numbers for the movie musicals Warner Bros. produced from '33 to '37. His overhead kaleidoscopic shots became his signature. After interest in movie musicals declined in the late '30s, he directed some non-musical pictures. He moved from Warner's to MGM where he worked as choreographer and director for several famous movie musicals. He directed his last film, *Take Me Out to the Ball Game*, in the late '40s, but the choreography for that film was by Gene Kelly. By the end of the '50s he was practically forgotten, but during the late '60s and early '70s interest in his choreography was resurrected. He served as supervisor for an early '70s revival of *No, No, Nanette* on Broadway.

Irving Berlin (real name: Israel Baline or Beilin; 1888–1989) Irving Berlin became perhaps the greatest writer of popular songs in the history of America's popular music industry. His career stretches from just after the turn of the century into the '60s. He was most assuredly elected to the Songwriters' Hall of Fame. He was inducted into the Popular Music Hall of Fame in 2000. Born Israel Baline in Mogilyov, Russia (now Belarus), he came to the United States as a youngster when his family immigrated and settled in New York City in 1893. When his father died, Berlin, just 13 years old, left home to earn a living. He worked as a busker singing for pennies, then as a singing waiter. Part of his early music career was spent as a song plugger for publishing firms. He changed his name to Irving Berlin and began his composing career shortly before '10 with "That Mesmerizing Mendelssohn Tune" and "My Wife's Gone to the Country (Hurrah! Hurrah!)." His first monster hit song, "Alexander's Ragtime Band," came in '11 (see both '11 and '38). Over the next fifty years, Irving Berlin produced an amazing amount of ballads, dance numbers, novelty tunes and love songs. He was equally at home writing for Broadway revues and musicals and for Hollywood films. Berlin's hit list is extensive, but the most famous early ones include "Call Me Up Some Rainy Afternoon" (see '10), "Everybody's Doin' It Now" (see '12), "Somebody's Coming to My House" (see '13), "When I Lost You" (see '13), "When That Midnight Choo-Choo Leaves for Alabam'" (see '13), "Play a Simple Melody" ('14, see '50, when it was most popular), "That International Rag" (see '14), "He's a Devil in His Own Home Town" (see '14), "This Is the Life" (see '14), "I Want to Go Back to Michigan (Down on the Farm)" (see '14), "He's a Rag Picker" (see '15), "My Bird of Paradise" (see '15), "When I Leave the World Behind" (see '15), "The Girl on the Magazine" (see '16), "I Love a Piano" (see '16), "Oh, How I Hate to Get Up in the Morning" (see '18), "Mandy" (see '19) and "A Pretty Girl Is Like a Melody" (see '19), which became one of the theme songs for Ziegfeld's *Follies*. Berlin continued his string of hits in the '20s with "I've Got My Captain Working for Me Now" (see '20), "You'd Be Surprised" (see '20), "All by Myself" (see '21), "Say It with Music" (see '21), "Lady of the Evening" (see '23), "Crinoline Days" (see '23), "What'll I Do?" (see '24), "All Alone" (see '25), "Remember" (see '25), "Always" (see '26), "Blue Skies" (see '27), "Russian Lullaby" (see '27), "Marie" (see '37, when it was most popular). Some of Berlin's most popular songs of the '30s include "Puttin' on the Ritz" (see '30), "How Deep Is the Ocean?" (see '32), "Say It Isn't So" (see '32), Easter Parade" (see '33), "Cheek to Cheek" (see '35), "Top Hat, White Tie and Tails" (see '35), "I'm Putting All My Eggs in One Basket" (see '36), "This Year's Kisses" (see '37), "I've Got My Love to Keep Me Warm" (see '37 and '49), "Change Partners"

(see '38) plus "Let's Have Another Cup of Coffee," "Heat Wave," and "Let's Face the Music and Dance." Berlin's hits in the '40s include "God Bless America" (see '40). "I Left My Heart at the Stage Door Canteen" and "This Is the Army, Mr. Jones" from *This Is the Army* (see '42), plus "There's No Business Like Show Business," and several others from *Annie Get Your Gun*, including "They Say It's Wonderful," "Doin' What Comes Natur'lly," "Anything You Can Do," "The Girl That I Marry," "I Got the Sun in the Morning," and the incredibly famous "White Christmas" (see '42). Berlin's last well-known songs came in the mid-'50s from the movie musical *White Christmas*. "Count Your Blessings Instead of Sheep" and "Sisters" are from that film. Berlin's last composing venture was the Broadway musical *Mr. President* in '62. His song "Puttin' on the Ritz" was revived and charted in '83. Berlin's personal favorites among his hit songs were "Easter Parade," "Always," "God Bless America," "There's No Business Like Show Business," and "White Christmas." When ASCAP selected its *All-Time Hit Parade* on the organization's fiftieth anniversary in '63, Berlin was honored with three songs on the list of only sixteen songs: "Alexander's Ragtime Band," "God Bless America," and "White Christmas." Berlin was a co-founder of ASCAP (American Society of Composer, Authors and Publishers), founder of his own extremely successful publishing company, and with producer Sam Harris, built his own Broadway theater, The Music Box. Berlin died in '89 at age 101. At http://www.songwritershalloffame.org/exhibit_audio_video.asp?exhibitId=3 hear Bing Crosby sing "White Christmas," Irving Berlin sing "Oh! How I Hate to Get Up in the Morning," Irving Berlin also performs "God Bless America," "Just One Way to Say I Love You," "Sing a Song of Sing Song," "Alexander's Ragtime Band," "Follow the Crowd," and "What Can a Songwriter Say?," Bing Crosby's recordings of "You Keep Coming Back Like a Song" and "Count Your Blessings Instead of Sheep," Ella Fitzgerald's recordings of "How Deep Is the Ocean" and "Cheek to Cheek," Frank Sinatra singing "Blue Skies," Louis Armstrong and Ella Fitzgerald performing "I've Got My Love to Keep Me Warm," Sarah Vaughan and Billy Eckstine performing "Easter Parade," Fred Astaire singing "Puttin' on the Ritz," Billie Holiday performing "Always," Frank Sinatra singing "It Only Happens When I Dance with You," Sarah Vaughan's recording of "Say It Isn't So," and Al Jolson's recording of "Let Me Sing and I'm Happy."

Felix Bernard (real name: Felix William Bernhardt; 1897–1944) Felix Bernard was a composer, conductor and pianist. His early musical studies were with his father, and Bernard became a professional pianist from childhood. He toured the U.S. and abroad for the Orpheum and Keith vaudeville circuits. After working as a pianist for music publishers and dance orchestras, he formed his own band. He wrote professional one-act musical comedies for vaudeville and special musical material for such stars as Sophie Tucker, Nora Bayes, Marilyn Miller, Al Jolson and Eddie Cantor. Bernard also had his own radio show. His chief musical collaborators were Johnny Black, Richard Smith, L. Wolfe Gilbert, and Sam Coslow. "Dardenella" (see '20) may be his most famous song, but he almost didn't get credit for it. After the song had become successful, Bernard claimed he had written the tune but had renounced his rights for a cash settlement of $100.

After a court fight, later sheet music publications carried Fred Fisher's name as lyricist and Johnny S. Black and Bernard as composers. Bernard's "Winter Wonderland" is also quite well known.

Ben Bernie (real name: Benjamin Anzelwitz; 1891–1943)   Ben Bernie was a jazz violinist, a radio personality, a popular bandleader and sometimes composer in the late '20s and '30s. He was known as the Ol' Maestro. By his mid-teens, he was teaching violin. He dropped out of music for a period of time, but returned to perform in vaudeville. In '22, he joined his first orchestra and would later have his own band called "the lads." By '29 his musical career had declined and he suffered financially and professionally due to the Great Depression. A few years later he became a radio personality noted for using the word "yowsah" (a southern "yes sir"). He wrote "Sweet Georgia Brown" (see '25) with Maceo Pinkard and Kenneth Casey. Bernie and his orchestra had several popular recordings between '23 and the early '30s including "Sweet Georgia Brown" (see '25), "Sleepy Time Gal" (see '26), and "Ain't She Sweet" (see '27). Ben Bernie and his orchestra became the No. 11 top recording artists of the '20s. His band appeared in the movies *Shoot the Works* ('34) and *Stolen Melody* ('35).

Buddy Bernier   Buddy Bernier was lyricist of "The Big Apple" (see '37) and co-lyricist of "Our Love" (see '39). Bernier also wrote "Poinciana."

Leonard Bernstein (1918–1990)   Leonard Bernstein became a huge force in American music as a great and famous conductor, an admired composer of serious (classical) music, and an innovative music educator with television broadcasts that profoundly influenced a generation. He was also a songwriter of enormous distinction. He was born into a family of Russian Jewish immigrants. He graduated from Harvard University and the Curtis Institute of Music. In '44 he teamed up with choreographer Jerome Robbins for the ballet *Fancy Free*. That ballet spawned the idea of doing a Broadway musical about three sailors on leave in New York City. The result, *On the Town*, opened in late '44, and was a hit. The most famous song from the score was "New York, New York" (see '44). Bernstein returned to Broadway in '53, this time with the Tony Award winning *Wonderful Town*. Then in '57 Bernstein wrote his Broadway masterpiece, the brilliant *West Side Story*, with lyrics by the young Stephen Sondheim, amazing choreography and direction by Jerome Robbins, and songs that included "Something's Coming," "Maria," "Tonight," "I Feel Pretty," and "One Hand, One Heart." Leonard Bernstein was inducted into the Songwriters' Hall of Fame in '72. At http://www.songwritershalloffame. org/exhibit_audio_video.asp?exhibitId=4 hear Barbra Streisand's recording of "Somewhere" from *West Side Story*. For more, see Bernstein's official website: http://www. leonardbernstein.com/.

William Best (1913–1962)   Composer William Best was widely known as Pat Best. During the '30s and '40s, Best was a Hollywood actor; he appeared in 118 films. He most often appeared as a shuffling, illiterate, superstitious porter, stable boy, or chauffeur. If he received screen credit, it was as Willie Best or "Sleep 'n' Eat." Today, Best is most famous for writing "For Sentimental Reasons" (see '46), which became a big hit song for Nat "King" Cole. He

reportedly wrote both words and music at age 14 (Deek Watson is credited as co-writer, but had no part in writing the song). Best also wrote songs for the vocal group The Brown Dots, which included as members Best, Deek Watson (formerly of the Ink Spots), Jimmy Gordon and Jimmie Nabbie. They later changed the group's name to the Sentimentalists and later to The Four Tunes.

Don Bestor (1889–1970)   Don Bestor began his show business career in vaudeville as a pianist He formed his own band in the early '20s, disbanded it to lead the Benson Orchestra of Chicago, and reorganized it again in the mid-'20s. The group became more famous in the '30s when they popularized "Forty Second Street" (see '33) and when they appeared on Jack Benny's radio program. Bestor is also responsible for the famous Jell-O jingle: "J-E-L-L-O." He remained active with the band until he retired in '43. Bestor became the No. 30 top recording artist of the '30s. Several of Don Bestor and his orchestra's recordings are available at http://www.redhotjazz.com/bands.html.

Irving Bibo (1889–1962)   Irving Bibo wrote several college songs including some for UCLA, Stanford and Michigan State University. He was also a popular songwriter, author and publisher. He wrote songs for Broadway, and USO acts for Marlene Dietrich, Billy Gilbert, Jim Burke, and Ann Sheridan. His musical collaborators were Al Piantadosi, Leo Wood, and Don R. George. Bibo's most famous song was "Cherie" (see '21).

John Bieling (1869–1948)   Bieling was a member of the Manhansett Quartet in the 1890s, but later became a member of the very famous Haydn and American quartets. As a soloist, he had a very popular Victor recording of "In the Sweet Bye and Bye" (see '03).

Big Four Quartet   The Big Four Quartet consisted of Arthur Collins, Byron Harlan, Joe Natus, and A. D. Madeira. They had a particularly popular recording of "Good-bye, Dolly Gray" (see '01).

Albany Bigard (real name: Alban Leon Bigard; 1906–1980)   Albany Bigard was co-lyricist of "Mood Indigo" (see '31).

Isabel Bigley (1928–)   Isabel Bigley originated the role of Sarah Brown, the Salvation Army doll, in *Guys and Dolls* ('50). She and Bill Hayes introduced Rodgers and Hammerstein's "No Other Love," in the Broadway musical *Me and Juliet* (see '53).

Henry Rowley Bishop (1786–1855)   Sir Henry Rowley Bishop was a distinguished English opera conductor, composer and arranger of dramatic works. Bishop is most famous today for composing the song "Home Sweet Home" in 1823. The song was popularized again in '15. Bishop was also professor of music at Oxford College until his death in 1855.

Joe Bishop (1907–)   Joe Bishop was the lyricist of "At the Woodchopper's Ball" (see '39).

Cesare A. Bixio (1896–1978)   Cesare A. Bixio was the composer of "Tell Me That You Love Me" (see '35). The song began in Italy as "Parlami d'Amore, Mariu."

Ben Black (1889–1950)   Ben Black was a British composer of popular songs. Born in Dudley, England, Black worked as music director in Paramount Pictures' cinemas across the U.S., before moving on to theatrical productions. Ben Black is principally known today as the composer of "Hold Me" (see '20), which was introduced in the *Ziegfeld Follies of 1920*. His "Moonlight and Roses" (see '25) was adapted from an organ piece by Edwin H. Lemare.

Johnny S. Black Johnny S. Black, wrote a piano rag entitled "Turkish Tom Tom," which Fred Fisher wrote lyrics for, then published it himself as "Dardenella" (see '20). As lyricist and publisher of "Dardanella," Fisher is believed to have earned more than $1 million. After the song had become successful, Felix Bernard, a vaudevillian, claimed he had written the tune but had renounced his rights for a cash settlement of $100. After a court fight, later sheet music publications carried Fred Fisher's name as lyricist and Black and Bernard shared composer credit. Black also wrote "Paper Doll" in '15, but it wasn't popular until the Mills Brothers recorded it in the early '40s (see '43).

Tom Blackburn (real name: Thomas W. Blackburn) Tom Blackburn was the lyricist for "The Ballad of Davy Crockett" (see '55). Blackburn contributed to several Disney films of the era.

Vivian Blaine (real name: Vivian Stapleton; 1921–1995) Vivian Blaine is especially associated with her portrayal of Miss Adelaide in the Broadway and film version of *Guy and Dolls*, where she introduced "A Bushel and a Peck" (see '50); however, she also originated roles on Broadway in *Say Darling* and *Enter Laughing*. She also starred on Broadway in *Hatful of Rain*, *Company* and *Zorba*. She also appeared in several national touring productions. Before her Broadway successes, Ms. Blaine appeared in several musical films. For instance, she and Dick Haymes introduced "That's for Me" in the movie musical *State Fair* (see '45).

Janet Blair (real name: Martha Jean Lafferty; 1921–) Janet Blair and Don Ameche introduced Cole Porter's "You'd Be So Nice to Come Home to" in the movie musical *Something to Shout About* (see '43).

Eubie Blake (real name: James Hubert Blake; 1883–1983) Eubie Blake was active in the popular music field for more than seventy years, beginning as a teenager playing the piano wherever he could find work and continuing well into the '70s, when he was still performing at age 90. The '78 Broadway production *Eubie* was a tribute to him. Blake's first successful popular song, "Charleston Rag," came in 1899 (not to be confused with the Charleston dance of the '20s). In '15 he joined with Noble Sissle for a vaudeville act, and they wrote songs for their performances. By far their most successful venture was the Broadway production *Shuffle Along*, with songs like "I'm Just Wild About Harry" (see '22), "Shuffle Along" and "Bandana Days." For more on Blake, see Noble Sissle's biographical sketch. Blake's most popular recording was his Victor recording of "Bandana Days" in '21. Several Eubie Blake recordings are available at http://www.redhotjazz.com/bands.html.

Mel Blanc (real name: Melvin Jerome Blank; 1908–1989) Mel Blanc became known as "the Man of 1,000 Voices." He was also an accomplished bassist, violinist and sousaphone player. Early in his career he played in the NBC Radio Orchestra. He voiced almost every major Warner Bros. cartoon character, except Elmer Fudd. His most famous voices included those of Bugs Bunny and Daffy Duck. Blanc and the Sportsmen had a popular recording of "Woody Woodpecker" (see '48). Although not quite as popular, he also had a popular recording of "I Taut I Taw a Puddy Tat" with Billy May and his orchestra in '51. He also recorded some with Spike Jones and his City Slickers. His autobiography is *That's Not All, Folks!* was published in '88.

James A. Bland (1854–1911) James Bland is the composer of the great minstrel show tunes, "Carry Me Back to Old Virginny" (written in 1878, see '15), "In the Evening by the Moonlight," "De Golden Wedding" and "Oh Dem Golden Slippers." Bland was born in 1854 in Flushing, New York. Bland's father was one of the first African Americans to receive a college education. He was appointed examiner in the U. S. Patent Office, the first African American to hold that post and the family moved to Washington D.C., where James attended school. As a teenager, he became a page in the House of Representatives and often performed before members of the Manhattan Club, and at homes of Washington society notables. After high school, James enrolled in Howard University to study Liberal Arts. He graduated at age 19 and wanted to become a stage performer. He applied for positions with some minstrel groups but was turned down, because they preferred white men in blackface. In 1875, he got his first job with Billy Kersands' all-black minstrel group. For the next several years he toured the U.S. with Kersands' group and other companies. In 1881, James traveled to England as a member of the Callender-Haverly Minstrels. They were very popular and performed before Queen Victoria and the Prince of Wales. At that time, he was making about $10,000 a year, which was quite a bit of money for that period, but Bland was not frugal. He returned to the U.S. penniless. A friend got him a job in Washington, D.C. From there he moved to Philadelphia where he died from tuberculosis in '11. James Bland was buried in an unmarked grave in a part of the African American cemetery in Merion, PA. In '39 ASCAP found his gravesite, landscaped it and erected a monument. In '40, the Virginia State Legislature made "Carry Me Back to Old Virginny" the official state song.

Ralph Blane (real name: Ralph Uriah; 1914–1995) Ralph Blane left Oklahoma to study music at Northwestern University, then moved to New York City where he appeared in the Broadway musical *Hurray for What?* He organized a vocal quartet, The Martins, with close friend Hugh Martin. They became a songwriting team. Blane wrote the scores for the Broadway musicals *Best Foot Forward* and *Three Wishes for Jamie*. His most remarkable film score was *Meet Me in St. Louis*, which premiered the songs "Trolley Song" and "Have Yourself a Merry Little Christmas" (see '44). Blane also contributed to the films *My Blue Heaven*, *Athena*, *The Girl Most Likely* and *The French Line*. Some of Martin and Blane's best-known songs include "The Trolley Song," which was nominated for an Academy Award for Best Song in '45. Other Martin and Blane well-known songs include "Buckle Down, Winsocki," "The Boy Next Door," and "Pass That Peace Pipe," which was nominated for an Academy Award for Best Song in '48. Blane also collaborated with Harry Warren, Harold Arlen and Roger Edens. Blane was inducted into the Songwriters' Hall of Fame in '83.

Rube Bloom (real name: Reuben Bloom; 1902–1976) Rube Bloom, a self-taught pianist, began his music career in '19 when he found work as an accompanist for vaudeville shows. He played for dance bands and jazz groups throughout the '20s, as well as arranging songs for numerous publishing companies. From '24 until '31 he recorded with performers including the Sioux City Six, the Cotton Pickers, Frankie Trumbauer's Orchestra, the Tennessee Tooters, the Hottentots, Joe Venuti's All Star Rhythm Boys, Ethel Waters, Noble Sissle, Annette Hanshaw, Seger Ellis, and Red Nichols' Redheads. Bloom was a significant novelty ragtime composer and pianist who recorded 23 piano solos during '26–'28 and four additional ones in '34. In '28, one of his compositions, "Song of the Bayou," won a Victor Records song contest and the following year, he wrote the music and Harry Woods wrote the lyrics for "The Man from the South" (see '30), which Ted Weems recorded successfully in '30. In '30 Bloom recorded six more of his tunes including "The Man from the South," with his own group the Bayou Boys (which included Tommy Dorsey and Benny Goodman). Bloom collaborated with lyricist Ted Koehler on several hits including "Truckin'" (see '35). For the stage show *The Cotton Club Parade* in '39, Bloom and Koehler wrote "Don't Worry 'Bout Me." Collaborations with Johnny Mercer produced "Day in — Day Out" (see '39) and "Fools Rush in" (see '40). For the '46 movie *Wake Up and Dream* he teamed again with Harry Ruby to write "Give Me the Simple Life." Rube Bloom was inducted into the Songwriters' Hall of Fame in '82.

Henry Blossom (real name: Henry Martyn Blossom, Jr.; 1866–1919) Henry Blossom was a lyricist, author and insurance salesman. He collaborated musically with Victor Herbert and Alfred Robyn. Blossom's most famous Broadway productions include *The Only Girl, The Red Mill, Mlle. Modiste, Eileen* and *The Yankee Consul*. His most famous songs were "Kiss Me Again" (see '05), "I Want What I Want When I Want It" (see '05), "The Streets of New York" (see '06), "Every Day Is Ladies Day with Me" (see '06), "Because You're You" (see '06), "When You're Away" (see '15), and "Thine Alone" (see '17).

Ray Bolger (real name: Raymond Wallace Bulcao; 1904–1987) Ray Bolger is so closely identified with his role as the rubbery-legged scarecrow in the '39 film *The Wizard of Oz* that it may have hindered his career. He is primarily known as a dancer who specialized in comic routines, but he occasionally sang and introduced a number of hits. His first supporting role on Broadway came in '29, and his first starring role was in '34. *On Your Toes* was his second leading role, but the first that introduced a hit, "There's a Small Hotel" (see '36). His other most notable Broadway performance was in *Where's Charley?*, in which he introduced "Once in Love with Amy" (see '49). In Hollywood productions, he first appeared in *The Great Ziegfeld* ('36), followed by *Dancing Lady* ('33), *Rosalie* ('37) and *Sweethearts* ('38), before he found immortality in *The Wizard of Oz* ('39). That wasn't the end, of course. He made *Four Jacks and a Jill* ('42) and performed opposite Judy Garland in *The Harvey Girls* (see "On the Atchison, Topeka, and the Santa Fe" in '45), before he starred as Charley in the film version of *Where's Charley?* ('52). In '53, he turned to TV and starred in his own sitcom series. After the TV series ended, he made

several guest appearances on TV and had a few small roles in films.

Guy Bolton (real name: Guy Reginald Bolton; 1884–1979) Guy Bolton was born in England, but became an American citizen. Bolton was a playwright, librettist and lyricist who was best known for his witty and articulate librettos, on which he collaborated with such notables as P. G. Wodehouse, George Middleton, and Fred Thompson. Bolton studied architecture before he began writing plays. His first play appeared on Broadway in '11, but it was not until he began contributing to Broadway musicals that he became hugely successful. In collaboration with Wodehouse and others, Bolton turned out scripts that were enhanced with music by composers such as Jerome Kern, George Gershwin, and Cole Porter. Among his finer works are *Oh, Boy!* ('17), *Oh, Lady! Lady!* ('18), *Sally* ('20), *Lady, Be Good!* ('24), *Oh, Kay!* ('26), and *Anything Goes* ('34). Bolton also wrote for a number of London productions. He is considered a major contributor to the development of the musical. Guy Bolton was co-lyricist with P. G. Wodehouse for "Till the Clouds Roll By" (see '17).

Joseph Bonime Joseph Bonime was a co-composer of Benny Goodman's famous "Let's Dance" (see '35).

Nat Bonx (real name: Nathan Bonx; 1900–1950) Nat Bonx was a lyricist, composer, author and lawyer. He was educated at the University of Pennsylvania Law School. His chief musical collaborator was Moe Jaffe, but he also wrote with Lew Brown and Jack Fulton. Bonx's most familiar song is "Collegiate" (see '25), which he wrote with fellow lawyer Moe Jaffe.

Pat Boone (real name: Charles Eugene Boone; 1934–) Pat Boone was a very popular singer during the early years of rock 'n' roll, probably the biggest singing star next to Elvis Presley. He became the No. 5 top recording artist of the '50s. Boone was the clean-cut alternative to Elvis Presley. Even though he performed soft rock or R&B songs, '50s parents did not object to Boone nearly as much as they did to the blatant sexuality and greasy-haired, black-jacket image that Presley presented. During the early years of his popularity, Boone was still attending college, earning his master's degree in English. This ambitious, married, educated young man was much less of a threat to the values of the older generation than most of the early rock personalities. Boone won the *Original Amateur Hour* and *Arthur Godfrey's Talent Scout* shows and signed with Dot Records before he finished college. He married Shirley Foley, the daughter of famous country-western legend Red Foley. Boone appeared in several films, including *April Love, Mardi Gras*, the '62 edition of *State Fair* and *Journey to the Center of the Earth*. He also had his own television show. Boone's most popular recordings were "Ain't That a Shame" (see '55), "I Almost Lost My Mind" (both covers of R&B songs), "Love Letters in the Sand" (see '31, when it was most popular), "April Love," the title song from one of his films, "Don't Forbid Me" and "Moody River." Other popular recordings include "I'll Be Home," "Friendly Persuasion," another film song, and "A Wonderful Time Up There." His daughter, Debby, has also become a famous singer; she had fantastic success with "You Light Up My Life" in '77. For more, go to http://www.patsgold.com or http://www.patboone.com/.

Irene Bordoni (1895–1953) Irene Bordoni, born in Corsica, was a charming singer and actress who made her Paris debut in '07. Her first appearance in the United States was in *Broadway to Paris* ('12) at age 17. Bordoni's most famous Broadway appearances include introducing "Do It Again" in *The French Doll* (see '22), and introducing Cole Porter's "Let's Do It" in *Paris* (see '28). She made one of her few film appearances in the '30 screen version of that musical. She had a couple of moderate recording successes with "So This Is Love" from the Broadway musical *Little Miss Bluebeard* ('24) and "This Means Nothing to Me" from the Broadway musical *Naughty Cinderella* ('26).

Bill Borrelli Bill Borrelli was one of the co-writers of "Here in My Heart" (see '52).

The Boswell Sisters Connee (1907–1976), Martha (1905–1958), Vet (1911–1988). The Boswell Sisters were a very popular trio in the early to mid–'30s. These New Orleans natives began to make records in '31, and that led to appearances in several movie musicals, including *The Big Broadcast of 1932*, plus *Moulin Rouge* and *Transatlantic Merry-Go-Round* (both in '34). The sisters disbanded the act in late '35, but Connee continued as a single even though she performed from a wheelchair as the result of a handicap. The Boswell Sisters' most famous contribution to popular music was their recording with Bing Crosby and the Mills Brothers of several hits from *George White's Scandals of 1931* (Gems from "George White's Scandals"). This was one of the earliest efforts to reproduce the most important songs from the score of a Broadway musical on record. Otherwise, their most successful recording was "The Object of My Affection" (see '35). Connee had further success with a '37 duet with Bing Crosby of "Bob White" (see '37) and her recording with Bing of Irving Berlin's "Alexander's Ragtime Band" (see '38). Connee also introduced "Whispers in the Dark" in the movie musical *Artists and Models* (see '37). The Boswell Sisters were inducted into the Vocal Group Hall of Fame in '98. For more on the Boswell Sisters, go to http://www.boswellmuseum.org/.

Phil Boutelje (1895–1979) Phil Boutelje was co-writer with Dick Winfree for "China Boy" (see '22). Boutelje was a pianist, songwriter, author and conductor. He was educated at the Philadelphia Music Academy. He became the pianist and arranger for the Paul Whiteman orchestra. He served in World War I as a military bandmaster. Later, he became the music director for Paramount Pictures and United Artists Studios. His main collaborators were Ned Washington, Dick Winfree, Harry Tobias, and Al Dubin.

Frederick V. Bowers Frederick V. Bowers most popular composition was "Because" (see '00). His "Because" is not the famous wedding song by Edward Teschemacher and Guy d'Hardelot from '02.

Robert Hood Bowers (1877–1941) Between '04 and '34, Robert Hood Bowers was involved with approximately fifteen Broadway productions either as composer, lyricist, librettist, orchestra director or music director. Bowers wrote the words and music for "Chinese Lullaby" which premiered in the musical *East Is West* (see '19).

Brooks Bowman Brooks Bowman was the writer of "East of the Sun (and West of the Moon)" (see '35). The song was introduced in a Princeton University Triangle Club production entitled *Stags at Bay*.

Elmer Bowman Elmer Bowman's only major contribution to popular music was as co-composer with Chris Smith for "Good Morning, Carrie!" (see '02).

Euday L. Bowman (1887–1949) Texan Euday Bowman's music career began as an arranger for popular orchestras. His most popular composition was "Twelfth Street Rag," one of the most popular rags ever (see '48 when it was most popular). Bowman was most likely the last of the early ragtime composers. Bowman first published the song himself, then sold the rights for $100 to a Kansas City publisher. In '37, the song's rights reverted back to him and were subsequently transferred to Shapiro-Bernstein Music Publishers, the current owners of the copyright. Unfortunately, Bowman was not able to make a living in music during his later years. He had a paper salvage business in his native Fort Worth, Texas.

Jimmy Boyd (1939–) Jimmy Boyd is primarily famous as the thirteen-year-old singer of "I Saw Mommy Kissing Santa Claus" (see '52). Jimmy, aged 12 years, 11 months, had signed with Columbia Records and recorded "I Saw Mommy Kissing Santa Claus," which to date has sold over 60 million records. In '41 his father moved his wife and their two sons from Mississippi to Riverside, California in hopes of a better life. When Jimmy sang and played guitar at a country and western dance one evening, the audience went wild. He was invited to appear every Saturday night and to sing on a local radio show. On a trip to Los Angeles Jimmy auditioned for the Al Jarvis Talent Show on KLAC-TV. Jarvis was so impressed with Jimmy that he put him on the show that evening. Jimmy won. Jarvis quickly made Jimmy a regular on his *Make-Believe Ballroom* radio show. Next came an appearance on *the Frank Sinatra Show* on CBS. Boyd made several appearances on the *Ed Sullivan Show* and also appeared on several TV series and a few films. Boyd also developed a form of puppetry called Aniforms. In '71, the Children's Television Workshop (now *Sesame Street*) contacted Jimmy about using his creations in a television show that became known as *The Electric Company*. During the first season, Boyd voiced the character J. Arthur Crank, an unseen character until season two, when he became a regular cast member, appearing on-camera until the show stopped production in '77. For his contribution to the recording industry, Jimmy Boyd has a star on the Hollywood Walk of Fame.

Lucienne Boyer (real name: Emilienne-Henriette Boyer; 1903–1983) When Lucienne Boyer lost her father in World War I, she had to work in a munitions factory to help her family survive, but by age 16 she became a part-time model and began to sing in the cabarets in the Montparnasse quarter of Paris. She was soon singing in the major music halls of Paris. In '27, Ms. Boyer was singing at a concert where she was heard by one of the famous Shubert brothers of Broadway fame, who offered her a contract. For the next several years, she performed in New York, Paris and also in South America. Ms. Boyer introduced "Hands Across the Table" in the revue *Continental Varieties of 1934* (see '34). During World War II, Ms. Boyer performed primarily in France. After the war, she continued her cabaret career for thirty more years.

Tiny Bradshaw (1905–1958) Tiny Bradshaw was a co-writer of "Jersey Bounce" (see '42). Bradshaw played swing during the Big Band Era and also was an early rhythm and blues artist. He had majored in psychology at Wilberforce University, but ended up with a music career. He played drums and sang with several small bands. When he organized his own band in '34, they recorded eight songs for Decca. After a decade of struggling, his band recorded again in '44, but this time his music was more jump-oriented, leading towards R&B.

Oscar Brand (1920–) Canadian folksinger/composer Oscar Brand adapted an old seamen's song into "A Guy Is a Guy" (see '52). In his lenghty career Brand composed at least 300 songs and released nearly 100 albums.

Jim Brennan Jim Brennan was co-lyricist with Al Wilson on "Song of India" (see '21). They wrote the words to Rimsky-Korsakoff's famous melody.

J. Keirn Brennan (1873–1948) Brennan's chief musical collaborator was Ernest R. Ball, but he also wrote with Rudolf Friml, Billy Hill, Karl Hajos, Harry Akst, Walter Donaldson, Werner Janssen, and Maurice Rubens. His most famous lyrics are "A Little Bit of Heaven (Shure They Call It Ireland)" (see '15), "Goodbye, Good Luck, God Bless You" (see '16), "Turn Back the Universe and Give Me Yesterday" (see '16) and "Empty Saddles" (see '36).

Ernest Breuer Composer Ernest Breuer wrote the music for "Oh! Gee, Oh! Gosh, Oh! Golly, I'm in Love" (see '23) with the comedy team Olsen and Johnson. He also wrote another of the novelty song hits of the '20s "Does the Spearmint Lose Its Flavor on the Bedpost Over Night?"

Teresa Brewer (real name: Theresa Breuer; 1931–) Teresa Brewer was an important singing star in the '50s. Her start came at the age of two when she auditioned for a radio program in Toledo. From age 5 to 12, she toured with the *Major Bowes' Amateur Hour*. She spent the next several years touring with the *Amateur Hour* troupe. Then she joined the *Pick and Pat* radio show. In '48 the 16-year-old Teresa won a local competition, and along with three other winners, was sent to New York to appear on a talent show called *Stairway to the Stars*. It was at approximately this time she changed the spelling of her name from Breuer to Brewer. Richie Lisella became her agent and soon got her a contract with London Records. In '49 she recorded a record called "Copenhagen" with the Dixieland All-Stars. The B-side of the record was a song called "Music! Music! Music!" As it turned out "Music! Music! Music!" was the song that became a big hit, selling over a million copies, and became Teresa's signature song (see '50). Her next big hit recording came with "Till I Waltz Again with You" (see '53). Other popular recordings include "Ricochet" (see '53) and "A Tear Fell," which was popular in '56. She became the No. 24 recording artist of the '50s. By the '60s her singing career began to wane, but she continued to perform. A revival of interest in the music of the '50s caused her to make a comeback in the early '70s. During her career, she recorded nearly 600 song titles. For her contribution to the recording industry, Teresa Brewer has a star on the Hollywood Walk of Fame.

Jimmy Brewster Jimmy Brewster is listed as one of the co-writers of "If I Give My Heart to You" (see '54).

Pat Brewster Pat Brewster introduced "Feudin' and Fightin'" in the Broadway revue *Laffing Room Only* in '44, but the song didn't become popular until '47.

Donald Brian (1877–1948) Donald Brian began performing with a vocal quartet in his mid-teens. He soon joined a theatrical troupe and toured extensively before he went to New York City, where he won major roles in more than 20 Broadway musicals. He got his first break in replacement casts, including leading roles in *On the Wabash* (1899) and the long-running *Florodora* ('02). He was also featured in Cohan's *Little Johnny Jones* ('04) and *45 Minutes from Broadway* ('06). He portrayed Prince Danilo in the first Broadway production of Franz Lehar's *The Merry Widow* ('07). After starring in *The Dollar Princess* ('09), Brian co-starred with soprano Julia Sanderson in *The Siren* ('11). Their chemistry clicked so well they were re-teamed for *The Girl from Utah*, where they introduced Jerome Kern's "They Didn't Believe Me" (see '15). Sanderson and Brian's last appearance together was in *Sybil* ('16). Brian starred in a revival of *The Chocolate Soldier* ('21), *Up She Goes* ('22) and the national tour of *No, No, Nanette* ('26). After joining the cast of Kern's *Music in the Air* ('33), Brian made his final musical stage appearance in Kern's last Broadway musical, *Very Warm for May* ('39).

Elizabeth Brice (?–1965) Elizabeth Brice was featured in several Broadway musicals between '06 and the early '20s. She was not related to Fanny Brice. Ms. Brice introduced "Row, Row, Row" in the *Ziegfeld Follies of 1912* (see '13). Her most popular recording was of "My Own Iona" for Columbia (see '16), but her duet recording of "Oh, Johnny! Oh, Johnny! Oh!" with Charles King in '17 was also well received.

Fanny Brice (real name: Fania Borach; 1891–1951) Fanny Brice became a star comedienne of several *Ziegfeld Follies* and was immortalized in the '64 Broadway musical *Funny Girl*, which was based on her life. The film version of *Funny Girl* was released in '68 starring Barbra Streisand as Ms. Brice. Then in '75, a sequel, *Funny Lady*, was released again starring Barbra Streisand as Fanny. Born on New York City's Lower East Side in 1891, Fania Borach was the third of four children of immigrant saloonowners. Fania decided early in life she wanted to be a performer. In '08, she dropped out of school and found work as a chorus girl in a burlesque revue. She also changed her name to Brice, perhaps to escape the Jewish stereotype. A year later, she would made her first Broadway musical comedy appearance in *The College Girls*, singing Irving Berlin's "Sadie Salome, Go Home" with a put-on Yiddish accent, while dancing a parody of the seductive veil dance from Richard Strauss' opera *Salome*. Her act was a sensation. As her fame increased, so did her notoriety. In '18, she married Jules "Nicky" Arnstein, a handsome con man and thief she had lived with for six years. Despite his infidelity and a stretch in Sing Sing Prison for illegal wiretapping, Ms. Brice stayed with him, had two children and basically supported him. This tumultuous relationship was highlighted in her famous rendition of "My Man" in the *Ziegfeld Follies of 1921*. In '24, when Arnstein was charged with Wall Street bond theft, Ms. Brice funded his legal defense. Arnstein was convicted and sentenced to the

Federal penitentiary at Leavenworth. Once he was released in '27, Arnstein disappeared from Brice's life and that of his two children. Reluctantly, Fanny divorced him. Ms. Brice, her brother, Lew, Phil Baker and Ted Healy introduced "I Found a Million Dollar Baby" in Billy Rose's revue *Crazy Quilt* (see '31). After a failed marriage to Broadway impresario Billy Rose and starring roles in Hollywood film, in '38 Ms. Brice turned to radio. Her character was Baby Snooks, a precocious, bratty toddler. She had a very successful tenure on radio. Ms. Brice's most popular recordings were of "My Man" (see '21) and "Second Hand Rose" (see '21).

Lew Brice (1893–1966)   Lew Brice, his sister Fanny, Phil Baker and Ted Healy introduced "I Found a Million Dollar Baby" in Billy Rose's revue *Crazy Quilt* (see '31).

Lorraine Bridges (1906–1993)   Lorraine Bridges introduced "You're All I Need" in the film *Escapade* (see '35). According to http://www.imdb.com/, Bridges was the singing voice of Ozmite, Glinda and part of the Lullaby League in *The Wizard of Oz* ('39).

Phil Brito (real name: Philip Colombrito; 1915–2005)   Phil Brito introduced "It's Been a Long, Long Time" on the radio (see '45) and sang ""Five Minutes More" in the movie musical *The Sweetheart of Sigma Chi*, where it was an interpolation (see '46). Brito was a singer, songwriter, and author. After high school, he became a singer with the dance bands of Jan Savitt and Lloyd Huntley. He appeared often on radio, in films, on stage, television and in nightclubs.

Elton Britt (real name: James Britt Baker; 1913–1972)   Elton Britt began playing guitar and singing around his Arkansas hometown while he was still in his teens. In '30 he won a talent contest for a job with The Beverly Hill Billies. After three years, he moved to New York City where he signed a recording contract with RCA's Bluebird label and met songwriter/producer Bob Miller. Miller wrote almost all of Britt's early recordings as Shelby Darnell including his most famous one, "There's a Star-Spangled Banner Waving Somewhere" (see '43). President Franklin Roosevelt invited Britt to the White House in '42 to perform the song.

James Brockman (1878–1967)   Composer, lyricist and comedian James Brockman was a comedian in vaudeville and musicals in the early 1900s and moved to Hollywood as a songwriter for films. Brockman collaborated with James Kendis, Nat Vincent, L. Wolfe Gilbert, Ted Snyder, Nat Osborne, Eddie Dowling, Howard Johnson, James Hanley, Ted FioRito, John Kellette, Ray Brown, Will Oakland, Ira Schuster, Vincent Lopez, Irving Bibo and Abe Olman. Jean Kenbrovin was the pseudonym for James Kendis, James Brockman, and Nat Vincent when they co-wrote the lyrics for "I'm Forever Blowing Bubbles" (see '19). Kendis, Brockman, and Vincent had separate contracts with publishers that led them to merge their names into Jean Kenbrovin for credit on "I'm Forever Blowing Bubbles." Brockman's biggest hit songs "I'm Forever Blowing Bubbles (see '19 and "Down Among the Sheltering Palms" (see '15), plus "Feather Your Nest" and "I Faw Down and Go Boom." James Brockman was inducted into the Songwriters' Hall of Fame when it was organized in '70.

Roy Brodsky   Roy Brodsky was a co-writer of "Red Roses for a Blue Lady" (see '49).

Nicholas Brodszky (1905–1958)   Russian composer Nicholas Brodszky wrote "Be My Love" (see '51). Brodszky began writing for German and Austrian films in the early '30s. His first film project in the U.S. was *French Without Tears* ('40). He continued to write film scores and individual songs for films until his death in '58.

Harvey Brooks (1899–1968)   Composer Harvey Brooks wrote several songs for films. His most famous compositions were "Ain't Misbehavin'" (see '29), which he composed with Fats Waller and "A Little Bird Told Me" (see '49).

Jack Brooks (1912–1971)   British-American Jack Brooks was the lyricist for "Ole Buttermilk Sky" (see '46) and "That's Amore" (see '53).

Shelton Brooks (1886–1975)   Shelton Brooks, from Detroit, began his entertainment career as a ragtime pianist, initially entertaining the public in Detroit, and later Chicago, cafes and nightclubs. Brooks began to compose his own songs around '09. By this time he was an accomplished vaudeville entertainer, touring the U.S., Canada and the British Isles. Brooks established himself as a songwriter when he wrote "Some of These Days" in '10 (see '27 when it was most popular). "The Darktown Strutters' Ball" (see '18) became Brooks' next big hit. Brooks continued performing on stage, in movies and on the radio after he stopped composing. He appeared in the cast of *Lew Leslie's Plantation Revue*, in '22.

A. Seymour Brown (1885–1947)   A. Seymour Brown was a songwriter, author, composer and actor. He wrote songs for the *Ziegfeld Follies of 1909*. He appeared in vaudeville between '11 and '14, then joined a music publisher's staff, where he worked into '26. He wrote at least three Broadway stage scores. His most well known popular songs were "Oh, You Beautiful Doll" (see '12), and "Rebecca of Sunny-brook Farm" (see '14).

Anne Brown (real name: Anne Wiggins Brown; 1912–)   Soprano Anne Brown, as Bess, helped introduce "Bess, You Is My Woman" in George Gershwin's folk opera *Porgy and Bess* (see '35). Ms. Brown was trained at Morgan College in Baltimore and at the New Institute of Musical Art, which is now known as Juilliard School, in New York City. After originating the role of Bess in *Porgy and Bess*, she appeared in the Broadway play *Mamba's Daughters* and in the film *Rhapsody in Blue*. She toured as a concert artist during the '40s, then settled in Oslo, Norway, met and married a Norwegian Olympic ski-jumper Thorleif Schjelderup. She also taught; one of her students was actress Liv Ullmann.

Les Brown (1912–2001)   Famed bandleader, composer, author, arranger and conductor, Les Brown was educated at Ithaca College, the New York Military Academy, and Duke University, where he led the dance orchestra. He worked as a freelance arranger, and formed the Band of Renown in '38, touring until '47. He and his band were one of only a few that survived the decline of the big bands in the mid–'40s. In '96, the Guiness Book of World Records recognized Les Brown for being the leader of the longest lasting musical organization in the history of popular music. Brown and his band's biggest hits were "Sentimental Journey" (see '45), "My Dreams Are Getting Better All the Time" (see '45) and "I've Got My Love to Keep Me Warm" (see '49). Brown also wrote several popular songs with Ben Homer and Bud Green, most notably "Sentimental Journey." Brown was the conductor on the Bob Hope radio and television shows from '47 through '62. He was elected to the Big Band/Jazz Hall of Fame in '99. Brown and his band became the No. 17 top recording artists of the '40s. Brown's most famous vocalist was Doris Day. His band also accompanied the Ames Brothers and Teresa Brewer on some of their recordings.

Lew Brown (real name: Louis Brownstein; 1893–1958)

Lyricist Lew Brown was born in Odessa, Russia. His first writing success came in '12, when he wrote the lyrics to a melody by Albert Von Tilzer. Brown collaborated with Harry Akst, Sam Stept and Albert Von Tilzer. He achieved his greatest success when he teamed with Ray Henderson in the early '20s. They were joined by Buddy DeSylva in '25. The partnership lasted until the early '30s. After DeSylva left, Brown and Henderson continued their collaborations. Brown's most famous songs include "I'm the Lonesomest Gal in Town" (see '12), "Give Me the Moonlight, Give Me the Girl" (see '18), "Annabelle" (see '23), "Last Night on the Back Porch" (see '24), "Birth of the Blues" (see '26), "Black Bottom" (see '26), "The Best Things in Life Are Free" (see '27), "Varsity Drag" (see '27), "Just a Memory" (see '27), "Sonny Boy" (see '28), "Together" (see '28), "Button Up Your Overcoat" (see '29), "Little Pal" (see '29), "Sunny Side Up" (see '29), "You're the Cream in My Coffee" (see '29), "Life Is Just a Bowl of Cherries" (see '31), "That Old Feeling" (see '37), "Beer Barrel Polka" (see '39) and "Don't Sit Under the Apple Tree" (see '42). Other well known songs include "If You Were the Only Girl," "Don't Bring Lulu," "That's Why Darkies Were Born," "The Thrill Is Gone," "If I Had a Talking Picture of You," "It All Depends on You," and "Lucky in Love." With DeSylva and Brown collaborating on the lyrics, and Henderson writing the music, the threesome contributed songs to several Broadway shows including George White's Scandals of 1925 and 1926, Good News, Hold Everything!, Follow Thru, and Flying High. In '29, De Sylva, Brown and Henderson sold their publishing firm they had founded in '25 and moved to Hollywood under contract with Fox studios. Their first film was The Singing Fool, starring Al Jolson, and included "Sonny Boy" and "It All Depends on You." Say It with Songs, another Jolson film, including the songs "Little Pal" and "Sunny Side Up" and Just Imagine, the film version of Follow Thru, were both released in '30. In '31, De Sylva left the team to work with other composers, and Brown and Henderson continued working together producing "Life Is Just a Bowl of Cherries" and "The Thrill Is Gone." Brown collaborated with other composers, including Con Conrad, Moe Jaffe, Sidney Clare, Harry Warren, Cliff Friend, Harry Akst, Jay Gorney, Louis Alter, Sammy Fain and Harold Arlen. In '56, Hollywood produced a biographical film about the legendary threesome of DeSylva, Brown and Henderson, entitled The Best Things in Life Are Free. Lew Brown was inducted into the Songwriters' Hall of Fame at its inception in '70. At http://www.song writershalloffame.org/exhibit_audio_video.asp?exhibitId= 55 hear a recording of "Life Is Just a Bowl of Cherries."

Nacio Herb Brown (1896–1964)

Nacio Herb Brown was an important composer of music for the movies from the early days of sound through the early '50s. After attending UCLA, he became a tailor and made a fortune in Beverly Hills real estate. He began to try his hand at composing in the early '20s, but success was scarce until '29, when he became a top composer for the early movie musicals. In the early days of sound films, Brown signed with MGM where he produced some of the greatest film scores ever written. He wrote complete scores for films such as Broadway Melody of 1929, 1936 and 1937, Going Hollywood, Sadie McKee, Student Tour, Greenwich Village and The Kissing Bandit. Other films with Brown songs include Hollywood Revue, A Night at the Opera, San Francisco and Babes in Arms. His greatest success would come with the score and title song entitled Singin' in the Rain. Brown wrote "The Wedding of the Painted Doll" (see '29), "Pagan Love Song" (see '29), "Singin' in the Rain" (see '29), "You Were Meant for Me" (see '29), "Chant of the Jungle" (see '30), "Should I?" (see '30), "Paradise" (see '32), "Temptation" (written in '33, see '47 as "Tim-Tayshun"), "You're an Old Smoothie" (see '33), "All I Do Is Dream of You" (see '34), "Broadway Rhythm" (see '35), "You Are My Lucky Star" (see '35), "Alone" (see '37), "Good Morning" (see '39) and "Make 'Em Laugh" (see '52), plus "I've Got a Feelin' You're Foolin'," "Broadway Melody," "A New Moon Is Over My Shoulder," "You Stepped Out of a Dream" and "Love Is Where You Find It." Brown collaborated with Arthur Freed, Buddy DeSylva, Gus Kahn, Leo Robin and Gordon Clifford. Nacio Herb Brown was inducted into the Songwriters' Hall of Fame in '70. At http://www.songwritershalloffame.org/ex hibit_audio_video.asp?exhibitId=79 hear the Everly Brothers perform "Temptation" and Angelo Ferdinando with His Hotel Great Northern Orchestra with vocalist Dick Robertson perform Brown's "All I Do Is Dream of You."

Virginia Bruce (real name: Helen Virginia Briggs; 1910–1982)

Virginia Bruce was particularly active in films of the '30s and '40s. She began her Hollywood career in extra roles and bit parts, but graduated to lead roles in B-films or as the "other woman" in more famous productions. Virginia Bruce introduced the Academy Award nominee "I've Got You Under My Skin" in the movie musical Born to Dance (see '36).

George Bruns (1914–1983)

George Bruns was the composer of "The Ballad of Davy Crockett" (see '55). Bruns contributed several melodies for various Disney projects.

Alfred Bryan (1871–1958)

Lyricist Alfred Bryan, born in Brantford, Ontario, Canada, moved to New York City in the late 1880s where he developed his talent for songwriting. Bryan worked as a staff arranger for several New York publishing firms and was a charter member of ASCAP in '14. He collaborated on several Broadway scores including The Shubert Gaieties of 1919, The Midnight Rounders of 1920 and 1921, The Century Revue and A Night in Spain. In the '20s Bryan moved to Hollywood and wrote songs for film scores. Bryan collaborated with composers like Fred Fisher, Al Piantadosi, George Meyer, Larry Stock, Albert Gumble, Joe McCarthy and John Klenner. Bryan's best-known songs include "Are You Sincere?" (see '08), "Come, Josephine in My Flying Machine" (see '11), "Peg O' My Heart" (see '13 and '47), "I Didn't Raise My Boy to be a Soldier" (see '15), "I'm on My Way to Mandalay" (see '14) and "Sweet Little Buttercup" (see '18). Others of Bryan's popular songs were "Oui, Oui,

Marie," "Daddy, You've Been a Mother to Me" and "Madelon." Alfred Bryan was inducted into the Songwriters' Hall of Fame when it was organized in '70.

Vincent P. Bryan (1878–1937) Vincent Bryan was born in St. John's, Newfoundland. He wrote the lyrics for several popular songs, including "Down Where the Wurzburger Flows" (see '03) and "In the Sweet Bye and Bye" (see '03) with Harry Von Tilzer and "Hurrah for Baffin's Bay" (see '03) with Theodore F. Morse. In '05, he wrote "In My Merry Oldsmobile" (see '05) with Gus Edwards. He also contributed the lyrics for "He Goes to Church on Sunday" and "The Cubanola Glide."

John Bubbles (real name: John William Sublett; 1902–1986) John Bubbles, as Sportin' Life, introduced "It Ain't Necessarily So" in George Gershwin's folk opera *Porgy and Bess* (see '35). John Sublett was a vaudeville performer, singer, dancer and entertainer. When his family moved from Kentucky to New York City, John, then age 10, began performing with Ford L. Buck in an act called "Buck and Bubbles." They appeared in the *Ziegfeld Follies of 1931.* John became known as the "Father of Rhythm Tap," a form of tap dancing. In the early '20s, Sublett taught Fred Astaire tap dancing. Astaire reportedly considered Sublett the finest tap dancer of his era. Sublett appeared in a few Hollywood films of the late '30s and '40s, including *Varsity Show* ('37), *Cabin in the Sky* ('43) and *A Song Is Born* ('48).

Jack Buchanan (1891–1957) Jack Buchanan, born in Scotland, was often called "the British Fred Astaire" because of his excellent dancing ability, but the comparison probably isn't very fair since Buchanan was around long before Astaire. He got his start in Scottish music halls and graduated to a London Broadway–type production in '15. His American Broadway debut came in *Andre Charlot's Revue*. In total Buchanan appeared in more than two-dozen London musicals, as well as four Broadway productions. Buchanan starred in a couple of early Hollywood movie musicals: *Paris* ('29) and *Monte Carlo* ('30), but American movie producers and audiences didn't seem particularly enthused. His most famous Hollywood musical was in the MGM classic *The Band Wagon*, where he performed "I Guess I'll Have to Change My Plan" with Fred Astaire (see '29) and help introduced "That's Entertainment" (see '53).

Gene Buck (1885–1957) Gene Buck was a songwriter, producer, author, director and artist. He was educated at the University of Detroit and the Detroit Art School. He was an early designer of sheet music covers. In '07 he moved to New York, and designed and directed an act for Lillian Russell. In '12, he became the chief writer and assistant to Florenz Ziegfeld, lasting to '26. He composed Broadway stage scores and sketches for thirteen editions of the *Ziegfeld Follies* and two editions of *Ziegfeld's 9 O'Clock Revue*, and he originated and directed eleven editions of the *Ziegfeld Midnight Frolics*. Buck's chief musical collaborator was David Stamper, but he also worked with Rudolf Friml, Jerome Kern, Mischa Elman, Augustus Thomas, Werner Janssen, James Hanley, Ray Hubbell, Victor Herbert and Louis Hirsch. His most famous song is "Hello, Frisco" (see '15).

Richard Henry Buck Richard Henry Buck was lyricist for "Dear Old Girl" (see '04).

Walter Bullock (1907–1953) Walter Bullock was lyricist of "When Did You Leave Heaven?" (see '36). Bullock, a DePauw University alumni, was a songwriter and author. His principal collaborators were Harold Spina, Alfred Newman, Richard Whiting and Abraham Ellstein.

Johnny Burke (1908–1964) Johnny Burke was the songwriter of such legendary songs as "Pennies from Heaven" (see '36), "Swinging on a Star" (see '44) and "I've Got a Pocketful of Dreams" (see '38). He graduated from the University of Wisconsin. In '26, he moved to Chicago and worked as a pianist and song salesman for Irving Berlin Publishing Co. He was transferred to the New York City office in the early '30s and there he began his career as one of the most prolific songwriters from the era. At Irving Berlin, Inc., Burke teamed up with Harold Spina, his first major collaboration and the team produced such songs as "Shadows on the Swanee," "Annie Doesn't Live Here Anymore," and "Beat o' My Heart." In '36, Burke moved to Hollywood under contract with Paramount Pictures. At Paramount, Burke collaborated with new composers including Arthur Johnston, Jimmy Monaco and most notably Jimmy Van Heusen. Films that included Burke scores and songs included *Pennies from Heaven, Double or Nothing, Doctor Rhythm, Sing, You Sinners, East Side of Heaven, The Star Maker, Road to Singapore, If I Had My Way, Rhythm on the River, Love Thy Neighbor, Playmates, Road to Zanzibar, Road to Morocco, Dixie, Going My Way, Welcome Stranger, A Connecticut Yankee in King Arthur's Court, Riding High, Mister Music*, and many others. In total, Burke worked on over 50 films, including 25 starring Bing Crosby. The '56 film, *The Vagabond King*, was Johnny Burke's last Hollywood work. Other popular Burke songs include "The Moon Got in My Eyes" (see '37), "Scatter-Brain" (see '39), "Only Forever" (see '40), "Moonlight Becomes You" and "Road to Morocco" (see '43), "Sunday, Monday or Always" (see '43) and "Personality, (see '46), plus "Sleigh Ride in July," "The Day After Forever," "Aren't You Glad You're You?," "But Beautiful," "What's New?" and "Misty." Johnny Burke was inducted into the Songwriters' Hall of Fame since its inception in '70. At http://www.songwritershalloffame.org/exhibit _audio_video.asp?exhibitId=81 hear Louis Armstrong's recording of "What's New?"

Joseph A. Burke (1884–1950) Joseph A. "Joe" Burke was the composer of several hit songs from the late '20s through the '40s. Burke first appeared in the entertainment business in Hollywood films, where he acted in several films. Burke composed for films such as *Gold Diggers of Broadway 1929, Hearts in Exile, Little Johnny Jones, She Couldn't Say No, Hold Everything, Dancing Sweeties, Oh Sailor Behave, Top Speed, Sweethearts on Parade, Sally, Big Boy* and *Palooka*. Burke's most famous songs include "Oh, How I Miss You Tonight" (see '25), "Carolina Moon" (see '29), "Tip Toe Through the Tulips" (see '29), "Dancing with Tears in My Eyes" (see '30), "On Treasure Island" (see '35), "A Little Bit Independent" (see '35), "In a Little Gypsy Tearoom" (see '35), "Life Is a Song (Let's Sing It Together)" (see '35), "Moon Over Miami" (see '36), "It Looks Like Rain in Cherry Blossom Lane" (see '37), "Dream Valley" (see '41) and "Who Wouldn't Love You" (see '42). A composer and pianist, Burke collaborated with several lyricists most notably Edgar Leslie, Al Dubin, Benny Davis, Mark Fisher and Charles Tobias.

Joseph A. Burke was inducted into the Songwriters' Hall of Fame in '70. At http://www.songwritershalloffame.org/exhibit_audio_video.asp?exhibitId=80 hear Ben Selvin and his orchestra with vocalist Ruth Etting perform "Dancing with Tears in My Eyes."

Paul Burkhard (1911–1977) Paul Burkhard wrote "Oh! My Pa-Pa," (see '54) with German lyrics, ("O mein Papa") in '48; it was published in Switzerland, and was used in a musical in Zurich (*Schwarze Hecht*). The show was revived in Hamburg, Germany, as *Feuerwerke* (Fireworks) in '53, when the song began to gain attention.

Ernie Burnett (1884–1959) Composer, pianist and publisher, Ernie Burnett was educated at the Charlottenberg Conservatory and also studied music in Italy and Austria. He returned to the U.S. in '01 and became a vaudeville pianist and entertainer. During World War I, he served in the 89th Division of the Allied Expeditionary Forces. He led dance orchestras, and was active in music for three years throughout the Panama Canal Zone. He formed his own publishing company after the war. Burnett collaborated musically with George Norton and Paul Cunningham. His most famous song is "My Melancholy Baby" (see '28).

Robert Burns (1759–1796) Robert Burns, also known as Rabbie Burns, Robbie Burns, Scotland's favourite son, the Ploughman Poet, the Bard of Ayrshire, and in Scotland simply as The Bard, was born in Alloway, South Ayrshire, Scotland, the son of William Burnes or Burns, a small farmer. Burns is widely regarded as the national poet of Scotland, and is the best known of the poets who have written in the Scots language, although much of his writing is also in English or in a "light" Scots dialect which would have been accessible to a wider audience. Burns became a cultural icon in Scotland and among Scots who have relocated to other parts of the world. Burns also collected folk songs from across Scotland, often revising or adapting them. His poem (and song) "Auld Lang Syne" (see '07) is often sung on New Year's Eve (Hogmanay), and his "Scots Wha Hae" has served as the unofficial national anthem of the country.

Henry Burr (real name: Harry McClaskey; 1882–1941) Henry Burr became the most prolific recording artist of his time, with more than 12,000 recordings to his credit. Burr began his solo recording career for Columbia Records around '02 and recorded with the Columbia Male Quartet (they also recorded for Victor as the Peerless Quartet) and several other ensembles. He, like many other artists of the time, recorded under various names, including his real name, Henry Burr, and Irving Gillette. He also recorded numerous duets with Albert Campbell and Frank Stanley. In the mid-'20s he became program director for the Columbia Broadcasting Company. Burr's most famous recordings were "Come Down, Ma Ev'ning Star" (see '03), "In the Shade of the Old Apple Tree" as Irving Gillette (see '05), "Love Me, and the World Is Mine" (see '06), "To the End of the World with You" (see '09), "I Wonder Who's Kissing Her Now" (see '09), "Meet Me Tonight in Dreamland" (see '10), "When I Lost You" (see '13), "Last Night Was the End of the World" (see '13), "The Song That Stole My Heart" (see '14), "M-O-T-H-E-R (A Word That Means the World to Me)" (see '16), "Goodbye, Good Luck, God Bless You (Is All That I Can Say)" (see '16), "Just a Baby's Prayer at Twilight (for

Her Daddy Over There)" (see '18), "I'm Sorry I Made You Cry" (see '18), "Beautiful Ohio" (see '19), "Oh! What a Pal Was Mary" (see '19) and "My Buddy" (see 22). His most famous duet recordings with Albert Campbell include "When I Was Twenty-One and You Were Sweet Sixteen" (see '12), "The Trail of the Lonesome Pine" (see '13), "I'm on My Way to Mandalay" (see '14, also with Will Oakland), ""Close to My Heart" (see '15), "There's a Quaker Down in Quaker Town" (see '16), "Lookout Mountain" (see '17), "Till We Meet Again" (see '19) and "I'm Forever Blowing Bubbles" (see '19). Burr became the No. 7 top recording artist of the first decade of the 20th Century and the No. 1 recording artist of the second decade, qualifying him as the No. 4 top recording artist of the first half of the 20th Century. At the time of his death in '41, he was a regular on NBC's *National Barn Dance* radio show. Numerous recordings by Henry Burr as a soloist and with Joe Belmont, Albert Campbell, Helen Clark, the Columbia Mixed Quartet, the Columbia Stellar Quartet, Frances Fisher, Ada Jones, the Peerless Quartet, the Sterling Trio and others are available at http://www.collectionscanada.ca/gramophone/ in RealAudio or MP3 files for listening or downloading.

James Henry Burris James Henry Burris wrote the lyrics for Chris Smith's music for "Ballin' the Jack" (see '14) and "Brighten the Corner Where You Are."

Earl Burtnett (1896–1936) Earl Burtnett was a songwriter, bandleader, arranger, pianist, composer and author. He was pianist and arranger for the Art Hickman orchestra, and became its leader after Hickman's death. He played in hotels and ballrooms throughout the country. Burtnett's band was called Earl Burtnett and his Los Angeles Biltmore Hotel Orchestra. They recorded for the Columbia and Brunswick labels. Their biggest hit recording was "So Beats My Heart for You" in '30. He collaborated musically with Adam Geibel. The writer of "Sleep" (see '24) is listed as Earl Lebieg, but the writers were really Earl Burtnett and Adam Geibel. They used Burtnett's first name with Geibel spelled backwards for their pseudonym.

Nat Burton Nat Burton was the lyricist of "The White Cliffs of Dover" (see '42). The Dover, U.K. website chides Burton for putting "blue birds over the white cliffs of Dover," but they surmise since he was an American who had never been within 3,000 miles of the White Cliffs he was only being poetic.

Val Burton (1899–?) Val Burton was co-writer of "When We're Alone (Penthouse Serenade)" (see '31). Burton's chief collaborator was Will Jason. In addition to being a songwriter, Burton was a producer, screenwriter and author. He wrote the scripts for the "Henry Aldrich" radio series.

Joe Bushkin (1916–2004) Joe Bushkin, a swing and jazz pianist, was playing keyboard for the Tommy Dorsey band when he wrote "Oh, Look at Me Now" (see '41). In the mid-'30s, Bushkin landed a piano job at the Famous Door Club in New York City. He soon joined Eddie Condon's band, then transferred to Joe Marsala's sextet. It was in '40 that Bushkin moved to the Tommy Dorsey band. He also composed the tune for "(There'll Be a) Hot Time in the Town of Berlin (When the Yanks Go Marching in)" (see '44). After serving in the Army during World War II, he joined Benny Goodman, where he wrote several songs for the band. In the early '50s he formed his own band and recorded several albums featuring his jazz piano style.

Henry Busse (1894–1955) Trumpeter Henry Busse is particularly remembered for his theme song, "Hot Lips," a showcase tune for trumpet. He played with Paul Whiteman and later with his own band. Busse, who was born in Germany, immigrated to the United States in '16 where he found work playing trumpet in a movie theatre pit band. He formed his own band and toured the country ending up in San Francisco where they disbanded. In '17 he was playing trumpet with the Frisco Jass Band and in '18 he joined the Paul Whiteman Orchestra. Busse was a major contributor to Whiteman's Orchestra. He composed or co-composed several of the band's early hit songs including "Wang Wang Blues" (see '21) and "Hot Lips" (see '22). Busse stayed with Whiteman until '28 when he left to form the Henry Busse Orchestra. This group was more of a sweet dance band than a jazz group. They continued to record and perform up until Busse's death. Busse's most famous recordings were of "Hot Lips" (see '22) and "With Plenty of Money and You" (see '37). Busse's soft, muted trumpet styling was his trademark. Several recordings by Busse's Buzzards are available at http://www.redhotjazz.com/bands.html.

Irving Caesar (1895–1996) Irving Caesar was an important lyricist, author, and publisher who wrote several songs that became popular primarily during the '20s. Early in his career, he was a singer/performer in vaudeville. Caesar left college to volunteer for a pre–World War I effort to help the Europeans. When he returned from Europe, he became a regular on Tin Pan Alley, where he met George Gershwin. That fortunate meeting resulted in "Swanee," one of Gershwin and Caesar's earliest hits. Another working relationship, this time with composer, Vincent Youmans, was due to an urgent need for some new songs for the Broadway show, No, No, Nanette. Two famous Caesar lyrics, "Tea for Two" and "I Want to Be Happy" (see '25), were introduced after the show had an unimpressive debut in Detroit. The songs were greatly responsible for the show's success. Another of his famous Broadway musicals is Hit the Deck in '27. Caesar's most famous contributions to popular music were "Swanee" (see '20), "Tea for Two" and "I Want to Be Happy" (see '25), and "Sometimes I'm Happy" (see '27). Also well-known are "Just a Gigolo" (see '31), and "Is It True What They Say About Dixie" (see '36). Irving Caesar was inducted into the Songwriters' Hall of Fame in '72. At http://www.songwritershalloffame.org/exhibit_audio_video.asp?exhibitId=56 hear Eddie Cantor perform Caesar's "I Love Her — She Loves Me (I'm Her He — She's My She)."

Marie Cahill (1874–1933) Marie Cahill interpolated "Under the Bamboo Tree" into Sally in Our Alley (see '02), "Navajo" into the musical Nancy Brown after it had opened (see '04), and introduced "He's a Cousin of Mine" in the musical Marrying Mary (see '07). According to Stanley Green in Encyclopedia of the Musical Theatre, Marie Cahill was "a plump, pugnacious comedienne." She appeared in approximately twenty Broadway shows between 1894 and '30.

Sammy Cahn (real name: Samuel Cohen; 1913–1993) Sammy Cahn was born into a Jewish immigrant family from Polish Galicia. His childhood was spent on the Lower East Side of New York City, where he learned to play the violin. By age 14 he was playing in local Bar Mitzvah bands. While still in his teens, Cahn began playing in pit bands of burlesque houses. He became friends with fellow band-member, pianist Saul Chaplin. They became a songwriting partnership that first wrote specialty numbers for vaudeville acts. In '35 they wrote "Rhythm Is Our Business" (see '35), which Jimmy Lunceford and his band popularized; it became the band's theme song. In '36 they scored another success with "Until the Real Thing Comes Along" (see '36). They adapted a Yiddish song, "Bei Mir Bist Du Schoen," for the Andrews Sisters (see '38), who were still unknowns. Cahn also teamed with Chaplin to write "Please Be Kind" (see '38). In '40, Cahn and Chaplin moved to Hollywood to write for films, but they soon parted ways. In '42, Cahn began writing with Jules Styne. For the next decade, Cahn and Styne would write songs for 19 films. Among their most popular songs were "I've Heard That Song Before" (see '43), "I'll Walk Alone" (see '44), "It's Been a Long, Long Time" (see '45), "Saturday Night (Is the Loneliest Night of the Week") (see '45), "Five Minutes More" (see '46), "Let It Snow, Let It Snow, Let It Snow" (see '46), "It's Magic" (see '48) and "Put 'Em in a Box, Tie 'Em with a Ribbon" for Doris Day's first film, and the title song of the film Three Coins in the Fountain (see '54). In '47, Styne and Cahn wrote the successful Broadway musical High Button Shoes. Other songs from Cahn's collaboration with Styne include "Time After Time," "There Goes That Song Again," "The Things We Did Last Summer" and "Guess I'll Hang My Tears Out to Dry." Cahn wrote "Be My Love" with composer Nicholas Brodszky (see '51). He wrote the lyrics for "Teach Me Tonight" (see '54) with composer Gene DePaul. In '55, longtime friend, Frank Sinatra, introduced Cahn to composer Jimmy Van Heusen. Cahn and Van Heusen began collaborating together and wrote the title song for the '55 Sinatra film The Tender Trap. They also wrote a TV musical version of Our Town, which starred Sinatra. The score included "Love and Marriage." In '57, Cahn and Van Heusen wrote "All the Way" for the Sinatra film The Joker Is Wild, which won Cahn his second Oscar. In '59 came A Hole in the Head, another Sinatra film. For that film, they wrote "High Hopes," which won Cahn his third Oscar. With a revised lyric, the song became John F. Kennedy's campaign song. In '60, Sinatra recorded their "The Second Time Around." Cahn won his fourth Oscar, and Van Heusen his third, in '63 for "Call Me Irresponsible" from Papa's Delicate Condition. They also wrote "My Kind of Town" for Sinatra's '64 film Robin and the 7 Hoods. Sammy Cahn was nominated for more than 30 Oscars, and won four times. He became a member of the Songwriters' Hall of Fame in '72. At http://www.songwritershalloffame.org/exhibit_audio_video.asp?exhibitId=5 hear audio clips of Al Jolson's performance of "It's Been a Long, Long Time," Dean Martin sing "The Things We Did Last Summer," Keely Martin perform "It's Magic," Bing Crosby's version of "Second Time Around," Nat "King" Cole sing "Teach Me Tonight," the Andrews Sisters perform "Bei Mir Bist du Schon," Lena Horne's recording of "All the Way," June Christy sing "I Should Care," Dean Martin's recording of "Ain't Love a Kick in the Head," Nancy Wilson perform "I'll Only Miss Him When I Think of Him," Peggy Lee singing "Please Be Kind,"

Lena Horne's recording of "Let It Snow!...," Louis Armstrong performing "I Still Get Jealous," Ella Fitzgerald performing "If You Ever Should Leave," plus Frank Sinatra's recordings of "The Last Dance," "My Kind of Town," "I Fall in Love Too Easily," and "Time After Time."

Georgia Caine (1876–1964) Georgia Caine was a Broadway musical star from the 1890s through the early 1900s, who played character roles in '30s and '40s Hollywood films. Ms. Caine and Victor Morley introduced Jerome Kern's "How'd You Like to Spoon with Me?" in *The Earl and the Girl* (see '06).

Anne Caldwell (real name: Anne Caldwell O'Dea; 1867–1936) Lyricist Anne Caldwell began her career as a singer with the Juvenile Opera Co. Ms. Caldwell was one of only four female songwriters active in the early 1900s. A charter member of the American Society of Composer, Authors and Publishers (ASCAP), Caldwell's output as a lyricist and librettist in the years '07 through '28 focused mainly on Broadway scores. She was the main lyricist for several Broadway productions including *Good Morning Dearie, Hitchy Koo of 1921, The Bunch and Judy, Stepping Stones, Criss Cross* and *Oh, Please!*, among others. From '00 through the mid–'20s Caldwell mainly collaborated with composer Jerome Kern. Beginning in '26 she teamed with other composers including Vincent Youmans, Dave Stamper, Harry Tierney, Raymond Hubbell, Otto Harbach and Hugo Felix. Her most popular hit song was "I Know That You Know" (see '27). Anne Caldwell was inducted into the Songwriters' Hall of Fame in '70.

Charles Calhoun (alias Jesse Stone; 1901–1999) Calhoun or Stone was a rhythm and blues musician. Duke Ellington helped his band get a booking at the Cotton Club in '36. He joined the staff of Atlantic Records as a producer, songwriter and arranger in the late '40s. Calhoun was inducted into the Blues Hall of Fame.

J. Will Callahan (1874–1946) J. Will Callahan's principal contribution to pop music history was as the lyricist for "Smiles" (see '18). His chief musical collaborator was Max Kortlander. He was a songwriter, singer and author. He became an accountant after he graduated from high school, then became a singer.

Cab Calloway (1907–1994) Cab Calloway achieved phenomenal success in the mid–'30s as the "King of Hide-ho." Calloway introduced "I Love a Parade" (see '31) at a Cotton Club revue, *Rhythmania*, in Harlem. Calloway's most famous recordings include "Minnie the Moocher" (see '31) which he co-wrote, "St. James' Infirmary" and "(Hep-Hep) Jumpin' Jive," a dance disk that was particularly popular during World War II. He received an award for his work in the '43 film *Stormy Weather*, was outstanding in the role of Sportin' Life in George Gershwin's *Porgy and Bess* in the early '50s and appeared in the '80 movie *The Blues Brothers*, in which he performed "Minnie the Moocher." Calloway was elected to the Big Band/Jazz Hall of Fame in '87. Calloway became the No. 39 top recording artist of the '30s.

Albert Campbell (1873–1947) Tenor Albert Campbell began his recording career on Berliner Records in 1897. As a soloist, his most popular recordings were "My Wild Irish Rose" (see '00), "My Blushin' Rosie" (see '01) and "Love Me, and the World Is Mine" (see '06). Campbell's greatest recording success came when he collaborated with Henry Burr on several popular duets, including "When I Was Twenty-One and You Were Sweet Sixteen" (see '12), "The Trail of the Lonesome Pine" (see '13), "I'm on My Way to Mandalay" (see '14) also with Will Oakland, "Close to My Heart" (see '15), "There's a Quaker Down in Quaker Town" (see '16), "Lookout Mountain" (see '17), "Till We Meet Again" (see '19) and "I'm Forever Blowing Bubbles" (see '19). Campbell also sang with the Columbia Male Quartet, the Peerless Quartet and the Sterling Trio between '04 and '25. Campbell ranked as the No. 15 recording artist of the first decade of the 20th Century and No. 8 for the second decade, qualifying him as the No. 15 top recording artist of the first half of the 20th Century.

Jimmy Campbell Jimmy Campbell was one of the co-writers of "Show Me the Way to Go Home" (see '26), "Good Night, Sweetheart" (see '31) and "Just an Echo in the Valley" (see '32). Other famous Campbell songs include "Try a Little Tenderness." British native Jimmy Campbell was one half of a songwriting partnership with fellow Londoner Reginald Connelly. They primarily concentrated on writing lyrics. They sometimes wrote under the pseudonym Irving King. Connelly and Campbell also ran their own music publishing company.

Hughie Cannon (1877–1912) Hughie Cannon, an American popular songwriter, was a pianist for many vaudeville performers. His biggest hit song was "Bill Bailey, Won't You Please Come Home" (see '02).

Eddie Cantor (real name: Eddie Israel Iskowitz; 1892–1964) Eddie Cantor became a world-famous entertainer. He began his show business career as a child when he appeared in Gus Edwards' vaudeville act, which featured young performers. Cantor made the leap to stardom in '16 when Florenz Ziegfeld first signed him. He performed "Oh! How She Could Yacki Hacki Wicki Wachi Woo" (see '16) in his Broadway debut in a Ziegfeld production on the Midnight Roof of the New Amsterdam Theater. He became a full-fledged Ziegfeld star when he appeared in the 1917 edition of the *Ziegfeld Follies*. He appeared in the next several editions of the *Follies*. Cantor also performed in *The Midnight Rounders of 1921* and *Make It Snappy* ('22). He was a featured performer in the '24 musical *Kid Boots* and the '28 musical *Whoopee*. Cantor began his movie career in the Depression years and made several popular films during the '30s and '40s. He also had considerable radio and television work until the early '50s, when a heart attack caused him to retire Cantor is famous for his stage demeanor: his "banjo eyes" practically popping out of their sockets through large white horn-rimmed spectacles (with no glass), clapping his hands as he jumped like a kangaroo around the stage. He is associated with several songs because he either introduced them or helped popularize them with his extroverted performances. Some of his most popular recordings were of "You'd Be Surprised" (see '20), "Margie" (see '21), "No! No! Nora!" (see '23), and "If You Knew Susie" (see '25). Other popular Cantor recordings were "They Go Wild, Simply Wild Over Me," "Mandy," "Oh! Gee, Oh! Gosh, Oh! Golly, I'm in Love," "Yes Sir, That's My Baby," and "Makin' Whoopee!" Cantor became the No. 10 top recording artist of the '20s.

June Caprice According to the sheet music cover Helen Carrington introduced "I'm Forever Blowing

Bubbles" in the revue *The Passing Show of 1918* (see '19). However, other sources credit June Caprice with introducing it. June Caprice was a Hollywood actress during the silent era; she took her name from her first film, *Caprice of the Mountains* in '16. She became the first female lead to appear nude in a feature film in *The Ragged Princess* ('16). She appeared in a nude swimming sequence

Bill Carey (1916–2004) Bill Carey was the lyricist of "Who Wouldn't Love You?" (see '42). Carey was a songwriter, actor, singer and author. After high school in San Francisco, he became a vocalist with dance bands, then acted in films and stage. During World War II he served in the Army.

Frankie Carle (real name: Francis Nunzio Carlone; 1903–2001) Frankie Carle became a well-known pianist, composer, and bandleader. He was leading his band by the late '30s, but disbanded that group to join Horace Heidt and remained with him until '43. He reorganized his own band in '44 and was very successful for the rest of the decade and into the early '50s. His theme song, "Sunrise Serenade" (see '39), is his best-known composition. He and his band's biggest hit recordings were "Oh! What It Seemed to Be" (see '46) and "Rumors Are Flying" (see '46). Carle was inducted into the Big Band/ Jazz Hall of Fame in '89. Carle and his band were the No. 23 top recording artists of the '40s.

Bob Carleton (real name: Robert Louis Carleton; 1896–1956) The sheet music cover of "Ja-Da" identifies the writer as "Bob Carleton, U.S.N.R.F.," which meant that Carleton was in the U.S. Navy Reserve (see '19). He actually served in the Navy during World War I and wrote musicals for the Great Lakes Naval Training Center in Illinois. Carleton was a pianist and songwriter.

Kitty Carlisle (1910–) Kitty Carlisle was particularly active as a singer onstage, in movies, and on radio during the '30s and '40s. She costarred with Bing Crosby in two important films and with Allan Jones in *A Night at the Opera*, where she and Jones introduced "Alone" (see '36). She is primarily remembered today for her television work, especially as a panelist on *To Tell the Truth* in the '50s and later. Her recording output was slim, but she did sing occasionally in her films. She was married to playwright Moss Hart, who wrote the book and lyrics for three Broadway musicals.

Lillian Carmen Lillian Carmen performed "Let's Swing It" in *Earl Carroll's Sketch Book* on Broadway (see '35).

Hoagy Carmichael (real name: Hoagland Carmichael; 1899–1981) Hoagy Carmichael was a composer, author and entertainer. He collaborated with some major lyricists, including Mitchell Parish, Johnny Mercer, Paul Francis Webster, Ned Washington, and Irving Mills, to name just a few. Carmichael was a very inventive songwriter. Much of his best work reflects his love of the jazz of the '20s. Carmichael showed an early interest in music. In Indianapolis in '16, he took lessons from an African American pianist, Reginald DuValle. During his undergraduate studies at Indiana University he organized his own jazz band. When the great jazz cornetist Bix Beiderbecke visited the university in '24, he and Carmichael became friends. Carmichael wrote his first piece, "Riverboat

Shuffle," for Beiderbecke, which he and the Wolverines recorded. He graduated with a law degree in '26 (he evidently didn't attend Law School after graduating from Indiana University) and began his law practice in West Palm Beach, Florida. However, when his "Washboard Blues" was recorded he decided to abandon law for music. In '29 he arrived in New York City, where he resumed his friendship with Beiderbecke, who introduced Carmichael to some of the most talented young musicians of the day, including Louis Armstrong, the Dorsey Brothers, Benny Goodman, and Jack Teagarden. Another important friendship during this time was also established with lyricist Johnny Mercer. Gradually, musicians heard Carmichael's songs and he became increasingly well known as a songwriter. In addition, his performing career flourished and he made many recordings. In '36 he moved to Hollywood where he continued to write both independent songs and songs for movies. In '37 he began what was to become a significant secondary career as an actor, appearing in a bit part in the film *Topper*. Roles, which usually involved singing, followed in many other movies, including *To Have and Have Not* ('42), *Canyon Passage* ('45), *The Best Years of Our Lives* ('46) and *Young Man with a Horn* ('50). In the late '50s and early '60s, he became a regular on TV in the western series *Laramie*. Also in the '40s, he was a popular radio personality. Carmichael's most famous compositions include "Star Dust," (see '31), "Georgia on My Mind" (see '31), "Lazybones" (see '33), "Two Sleepy People" (see '38), "Heart and Soul" (see '38), "Blue Orchids" (see '39), "The Nearness of You" (see '40), "Doctor, Lawyer, Indian Chief" (see '46), "Ole Buttermilk Sky" (see '46), and "In the Cool, Cool, Cool of the Evening," which was awarded the Academy Award for Best Song (see '51). Other well-known Carmichael songs include "Rockin' Chair," "Small Fry," "I Get Along Without You Very Well," "Skylark," and "Lazy River." Hoagy was also a recording artist who had hit recordings of "Ole Buttermilk Sky" (see '46) and "Huggin' and Chalkin'" (see '47). He was inducted into the Songwriters' Hall of Fame in '71 and the Popular Music Hall of Fame in 2002. At http://www.songwritershalloffame.org/exhibit_audio_ video.asp?exhibitId=57 hear audio clips of Nat "King" Cole's recording of "Star Dust," and Mel Torme's performance of "One Morning in May." Some of Hoagy Carmichael's recordings (Hoagy Carmichael and his orchestra and Hoagy Carmichael and his Pals) are available for listening at http://www.redhotjazz.com/bands.html.

Tullio Carminati (1894–1971) Italian born singer and actor Tullio Carminati and Mary Ellis introduced the title song from the movie musical *Paris in the Spring* (see '35).

Constance Carpenter (1904–1992) British singer/ actress Constance Carpenter and William Gaxton introduced "My Heart Stood Still" and "Thou Swell" in the musical *A Connecticut Yankee* (see '28).

Michael Carr (1900–1968) British composer Michael Carr was the co-writer of "South of the Border" (see '40) and composer of "He Wears a Pair of Silver Wings" (see '42).

Helen Carrington (1894–?) According to the sheet music cover, Helen Carrington introduced "I'm Forever Blowing Bubbles" in the revue *The Passing Show of 1918* (see '19).

Nell Carrington Nell Carrington and a chorus of girls introduced "Smiles" in the revue *The Passing Show of 1918*.

Harry Carroll (1892–1962) Composer Harry Carroll was a self-taught musician. He began his career playing piano in movie houses while he was still in elementary school. After high school, he moved to New York City where he found work as an arranger on Tin Pan Alley. In the evening after his Tin Pan Alley job, he moonlighted by entertaining patrons at the Garden Café and also played piano for various vaudeville shows. The Schubert brothers hired him as a writer in '12; his first show for them was entitled *On the Mississippi*. In '14, Carroll became a charter member of the American Society of Composers, Authors and Publishers (ASCAP) as well as one of its first directors. He also collaborated with Harold Atteridge on one of his biggest hits, "By the Beautiful Sea" (see '14). Carroll's first complete Broadway musical, *Oh, Look!*, was produced in '18 and featured the hit song "I'm Always Chasing Rainbows" (see '18). Other Broadway scores Carroll collaborated on include *The Passing Show of 1914, Dancing Around, Maid in America, The Little Blue Devil, Ziegfeld Follies* ('20 and '21) and *Greenwich Village Follies*. Carroll's best known song, in collaboration with lyricist Ballard MacDonald, was "Trail of the Lonesome Pine" (see '13). Carroll was married to singer Anna Wheaton and they performed as a vaudeville act for several years. In his later career, he toured various cafes performing his own hits. Harry Carroll was inducted into the Songwriters' Hall of Fame in '70.

Doris Carson (1912–1995) Doris Carson was the granddaughter of a popular 19th century vaudeville team and the daughter of character actor James B. Carson. Ms. Carson was understudy for Ruby Keeler in the musical *Show Girl* ('29). That led to more important roles in Gershwin's *Strike Up the Band* ('30), Jerome Kern's *The Cat and the Fiddle* ('31) and Rodgers and Hart's *On Your Toes*, where she and Ray Bolger introduced "There's a Small Hotel" (see '36).

Jack Carson (real name: John Elmer Carson; 1910–1963) Jack Carson, Dennis Morgan, and Martha Vickers introduced "A Gal in Calico" in the movie musical *The Time, the Place and the Girl* (see '46). Carson began his entertainment career as a Hollywood extra at RKO in '37. He eventually developed into a popular character actor. When he transferred to Warner Bros. in '41, he began to get more quality supporting roles and after a few years began to receive starring roles. Later, Carson became a radio comedian and, in the '50s, transitioned into TV.

Jenny Lou Carson (real name: Virginia Lucille Overstake; 1915–1978) Jenny Lou Carson first found fame on WLS and the Barn Dance radio show in the mid–'40s. She wrote most of her own songs, and eventually earned a spot in the Nashville Songwriters Hall of Fame in '71. Her primary fame in the pop field is for writing "Let Me Go, Lover" (see '55).

Emma Carus (1879–1927) "Alexander's Ragtime Band" was first popularized by the German-born singer Emma Carus in vaudeville (see '11). The sheet music cover of "Curse of an Aching Heart" advertises the song as "Emma Carus' wonderful hit," but there is no other evidence to suggest that Ms. Carus was primarily responsible for popularizing the song (see '13). Read more about

Ms. Carus at http://theanachronist.blogspot.com/2005/11/who-was-emma-carus_15.html.

Enrico Caruso (1873–1921) Enrico Caruso was one of the greatest operatic tenors of his generation. His powerful voice was a natural gift, developed by vocal training. He became one of the most legendary singers of all time. Caruso was born in Naples, Italy and sang in the churches of the city as a child. He began serious vocal study at age eighteen. He made his debut in Naples in 1894. He came to the United States in '03, where he found almost immediate fame. It's difficult to imagine today how popular Caruso was during the first two decades of the 20th century. Opera has never been as popular in the U.S. as it is in Europe, but Caruso became famous and introduced operatic arias to many people who would not have heard them except through his charismatic performances. His most popular recordings were of "Vesti la giubba" from *I Pagliacci* (see '07), "Love Is Mine" (see '12) and "Over There" (see '17). Caruso became the No. 18 top recording artist of the first decade of the 20th Century and the No. 19 recording artist of the second decade. Mario Lanza played Caruso in his extremely fictionalized screen biography *The Great Caruso* in '51.

Ivan Caryll (real name: Felix Tilkins; 1861–1921) Felix Tilkins, better known by his pen name Ivan Caryll, was a composer of musical comedy and operetta in the English language. Among his works are the musicals *Chin-Chin, A Runaway Girl* and *The Pink Lady*. His "Goodbye Girls, I'm Through" from *Chin-Chin* is his most famous song (see '15). Tilkins was born in Belgium and studied at the Liege Conservatoire. He moved to London in 1882 and served as the musical director for the Gaiety and Lyric Theaters.

Mose Case Mose Case was one among several credited with writing "Arkansas Traveler" (see '02).

Adriana Caselotti (1916–1997) Andriana Caselotti was the voice of Snow White in Disney's *Snow White and the Seven Dwarfs*. Her voice introduced "One Song" and "Some Day My Prince Will Come" (see '38). Caselotti was born into an operatic family. When she was 18 years old, Walt Disney chose her for the voice of Snow White. Under contract and jealously guarded by Disney, she was not allowed in any other films, except a bit part in *The Wizard of Oz* ('39). Disney wouldn't even allow her to appear on Jack Benny's radio show. Ms. Caselotti sang some opera, but mostly invested in real estate and the stock market.

Kenneth Casey (1899–1965) Kenneth Casey was a lyricist, composer, conductor, publisher, author, producer and child actor. He studied piano with Vincent Lopez, and organized his own band, later conducting on radio and records. He was the president of publishing firms and theatrical production companies, and wrote several stage scores and special material. He received a United States Navy commendation for his work on the radio show *Winnie the Wave*. He collaborated musically with Kenneth Sisson, Ben Bernie, Maceo Pinkard, and George Briegel. Casey's most famous song is "Sweet Georgia Brown" (see '25), which he co-wrote with Ben Bernie and Maceo Pinkard.

Jack Cassidy (real name: John Joseph Edward Cassidy; 1927–1976) Jack Cassidy was the father of later teenage heartthrob David Cassidy, a singer and TV star of *The Partridge Family*, and husband of Shirley Jones.

Cassidy introduced the title song of the Broadway musical *Wish You Were Here* (see '52). He won the '64 Tony Award as Best Supporting or Featured Actor (Musical) for *She Loves Me*. This was followed with three other Tony nominations. He became one of the most Tony-nominated musical actors in Broadway history.

Jimmy Cassin Jimmy Cassin was the lyricist of "Sentimental Me" (see '50). "Sentimental Me" was first popularized by Ben Selvin and his orchestra and by the Arden-Ohman Orchestra in '25 and '26 respectively, but it was revived into popularity by the Ames Brothers in '50.

Leonello Casucci Leonello Casucci was the composer of "Schoner Gigolo," which became "Just a Gigolo" (see '31).

Walter Catlett (1889–1960) According to Stanley Green in *Encyclopedia of the Musical Theatre*, "Catlett usually played the affable, derby-wearing, cigar-chomping blusterer." Catlett began his stage career in his hometown of San Francisco. After college, he moved to New York City and in '11 appeared in the musical *The Prince of Pilsen*. He later starred in several editions of the *Ziegfeld Follies*, and in the Ziegfeld musical *Sally*. His biggest Broadway success was in *Oh, Lady Be Good!*, where he introduced the title song. He appeared in a few silent films, but was more successful in talking pictures. His first movie musical role was in *Married in Hollywood* ('29). He may be most remembered for his role as the local constable in the Katharine Hepburn film *Bringing Up Baby* ('38) and as the stage manager in *Yankee Doodle Dandy* ('42). Near the end of his film career, he appeared in *Friendly Persuasion* ('56) and played New York governor Al Smith in *Beau James* ('57). He retired from films in the mid-'50s.

Carmen Cavallaro (1913–1989) Pianist Carmen Cavallaro formed his orchestra in '39 and featured a sweet sound with numerous piano solos. His biggest hit recordings include "I Can't Begin to Tell You" with Bing Crosby (see '45), plus his rhythmic version of Frederic Chopin's "Polonaise in A-flat," which became the song "Till the End of Time" (see '45). He also gained a great deal of attention with the piano recordings for the '56 movie *The Eddy Duchin Story*.

J. M. Cavanass J. M. Cavanass is a one hit wonder in the popular music field. He contributed the lyrics for "By the Waters of Minnetonka" (see '15).

James Cavanaugh James Cavanaugh was one of the co-writers of "The Man with the Mandolin" (see '39), "The Umbrella Man" (see '39) and "A Little on the Lonely Side" (see '45). He also wrote "The Gaucho Serenade." Cavanaugh began his songwriting career after high school, writing material for vaudeville acts.

Frank Chacksfield (1914–1995) Frank Chacksfield is a British arranger and orchestra leader who had a couple of popular recordings in the U.S. in the early '50s. His versions of "Ebb Tide" (see '53) and "Terry's Theme" from *Limelight* were quite popular in '53. For more on Chacksfield, see http://www.rfsoc.org.uk/fchacksfield.shtml.

Carol Channing (1921–) Carol Channing, the wide-eyed, gravel-voiced actress, became a Broadway star in *Gentlemen Prefer Blondes* ('49). She introduced "Diamonds Are a Girl's Best Friend" in that musical (see '50).

Her biggest triumph came in *Hello, Dolly!* ('64), in which she starred as Dolly Gallagher Levi. Ms. Channing also appeared in several Hollywood movie musicals most notably *Gentlemen Prefer Blondes* ('53) and *Thoroughly Modern Mille* ('67). For more, see Ms. Channing's official website: http://www.carolchanning.net/.

Saul Chaplin (real name: Saul Kaplin; 1912–1997) Saul Chaplin attended New York University's School of Commerce with the intention of becoming an accountant. A self-taught pianist, he earned money while in school by playing with local bands. One night in '33 another band member, Sammy Kahn, suggested they try writing songs together. They soon were writing as many as ten songs a day. The songwriting team first made money as writers of special material for entertainers at resorts in the Catskills. In '34 they had their first song published, "Rhythm Is Our Business" (see '35), which became a hit for bandleader Jimmy Lunceford. About the same time, they changed their names to Sammy Cahn (instead of Kahn) and Saul Chaplin (instead of Kaplin). During the next few years they produced several well-known songs including "Until the Real Thing Comes Along" (see '36), and "Please Be Kind" (see '38). When the then-unknown Andrews Sisters recorded and popularized Cahn and Chaplin's English version of "Bei Mir Bist Du Schoen," adapted from a Yiddish theater song, it firmly established the careers of Chaplin, Cahn, and the Andrews Sisters (see '38). In '40, Chaplin and Cahn moved to Hollywood where they wrote songs for Columbia Pictures. In '42, Cahn ended the partnership with Chaplin to write with other songwriters. Although Chaplin continued writing songs, he focused more and more on scoring and arranging music for films. He also toured with Frank Sinatra and Phil Silvers to entertain the troops during World War II. In '47, Chaplin's collaboration with Al Jolson, "Anniversary Song" from *The Jolson Story*, was a big hit. In '49, Chaplin transferred to MGM, where he was the vocal arranger and uncredited co-musical director of *On the Town*. He was co-musical director of *Summer Stock* and of *An American in Paris*, for which he won his first Academy Award, sharing it with co-musical director Johnny Green. He was co-musical director of *Kiss Me Kate*, which resulted in an Academy Award nomination for Chaplin and co-music director Andre Previn. He was co-musical director with Adolph Deutsch of *Seven Brides for Seven Brothers*, which won him his second Academy Award. Next, he was co-musical director of Cole Porter's *High Society*, winning another Academy Award nomination for himself and co-musical director Johnny Green. He continued his association with Cole Porter as Associate Producer and music supervisor of *Les Girls*. His final MGM film was *Merry Andrew* ('58), which starred Danny Kaye. Chaplin also wrote the songs for *Merry Andrew*, working with Johnny Mercer. Chaplin left MGM in '59 to work as a free-lance songwriter. In '60, he was Associate Producer and Music Supervisor of another musical with a Cole Porter score, *Can Can*. Then he became Associate Producer of *West Side Story* ('61), which won Chaplin his third Academy Award, shared with Johnny Green, Sid Ramin, and Irwin Kostal. He signed on again with director Robert Wise to be Associate Producer of *The Sound of Music*, starring Julie Andrews, and he was Producer of *That's Entertainment, Part 2* in '76. Saul Chaplin was inducted into the Songwriters' Hall of Fame in '85. At http://www.songwrit

ershalloffame.org/exhibit_audio_video.asp?exhibitId=58 hear audio clips of Dinah Shore singing "Anniversary Song," the Andrews Sisters' recording of "Bei Mir Bist du Schon," Peggy Lee singing "Please Be Kind" and Ella Fitzgerald performing "If Ever You Should Leave."

Hughie Charles Hughie Charles was a co-writer of "I Won't Tell a Soul (I Love You)" (see '38). Ross Parker and Charles also wrote "There'll Always Be England," referring to England's World War II problems, and "We'll Meet Again," which became a popular Vera Lynn recording.

The Charms The R&B group, the Jewels, was the first to record "Hearts of Stone," but Otis Williams and the Charms, a rhythm and blues quintet, began to spread the song around the nation in late '54. The Fontane Sisters popularized the song in '55. For more on the Charms, see http://www.destinationdoowop.com/charms.htm.

Thurland Chattaway (1872–1947) Thurland Chattaway was a popular music composer, active from the late 1890s into the early 1910s. Chattaway is most famous for writing the words and music for "Mandy Lee" (see '00) and the words to the popular hit "Red Wing" (see '07).

Ruth Chatterton (1893–1961) Ruth Chatterton began her show business career as a chorus girl at age 14. She became a Broadway star in *Daddy Long Legs* in '14. She appeared in *Mary Rose* and starred as Jane Ellen in *Come Out of the Kitchen*, which premiered "L'il Liza Jane" (see '16). She moved to Hollywood in '25. Once her film career faded in the late '30s, she returned to the stage, but also worked on radio and TV. She began a successful writing career in the '50s.

Maurice Chevalier (1888–1972) French entertainer Maurice Chevalier made his United States debut in the last midnight revue produced by Ziegfeld on the roof of the New Amsterdam Theater in '29. His popularity declined slightly from the mid–'30s until he starred in the '58 movie musical *Gigi*. In the following decade, he was very busy with a dozen films and frequent television appearances. His most popular recording was undoubtedly "Louise" (see '29). His most famous American films include *The Love Parade, Paramount on Parade, One Hour with You, The Smiling Lieutenant, The Merry Widow, Love Me Tonight, Folies Bergere de Paris, Can Can* and *Gigi*.

The Chordettes Jinny Osborn (real name: Virginia Cole; 1927–2003), Janet Ertel (1913–1988), Carol Bushman (or Buschman), Dorothy Schwartz (replaced by Lynn Evans in '51). Jinny Osborn formed the Chordettes in '49. Her father had been tremendously involved in barbershop quartet singing. The girl's quartet won a spot on Arthur Godfrey's prestigious *Talent Scouts* daily TV show. The girls stayed four years as Godfrey regulars, sticking to a traditional a cappella barbershop repertoire and even cutting some records for Columbia. They also became the new stars of the barbershop convention circuit. Dorothy left the group in '51 and was replaced by Lynn Evans. Godfrey's musical director, orchestra leader Archie Bleyer, thought the girls should break away from the barbershop mold. When Bleyer quit Godfrey's show to concentrate on his new record company Cadence, he was dating Janet Ertel. Therefore the Chordettes signed with Cadence and left Godfrey. The Cadence/Chordettes bond strengthened when Archie and Janet wed. The group's second single, "Mister Sandman" (see '54), rocketed them to major chart success. Some other popular recordings include "Born to Be with You" and "Lollipop." They were the No. 36 top recording artists of the '50s. The Chordettes were inducted into the Vocal Group Hall of Fame in 2001.

The Chords Carl Feaster, lead; Claude Feaster, baritone; Jimmy Keyes, first tenor; Floyd "Buddy" McRae, second tenor; Ricky Edwards, bass. The Chords formed in '51 in the Bronx. They eventually signed a contract with Atlantic Records. The group is credited as the writers of "Sh-Boom" (see '54). For more on The Chords, see http://www.history-of-rock.com/dootwo.htm.

The Christy Minstrels The original Christy Minstrels were a group of blackfaced minstrel singers who crossed the country between 1842 and '21, popularizing many Stephen Foster tunes, particularly "Old Folks at Home." Later members included Al Jolson and Eddie Cantor. A group called the New Christy Minstrels was organized by Randy Sparks in '61, but they had nothing, except the name, in common with the original group.

Frank Churchill (1901–1942) Composer Frank Churchill was active during the '30s and early '40s. His most famous songs include "Who's Afraid of the Big Bad Wolf?" (see '33), and his songs from the '38 feature length cartoon *Snow White and the Seven Dwarfs*, especially including "Whistle While You Work," "One Song" and "Some Day My Prince Will Come" (see '38). He also wrote the scores for *Dumbo* ('41) and *Bambi* ('42). His chief lyricists were Ann Ronell, Larry Morey, and Ned Washington.

Ina Claire (real name: Ina Fagan; 1892–1985) Ina Claire introduced "Hello, Frisco" in the *Ziegfeld Follies of 1915* (see '15). Ms. Claire was a vaudeville comedienne in pre–World War I days. She also made a few films during the silent era and was featured in the *Ziegfeld Follies* of '15 and '16. She developed into a Broadway favorite in the '20s. She returned to films in *The Awful Truth* ('29). She appeared in a few other movies in the '30s and '40s; her last appearance was as Dorothy McGuire's courageous, doomed mother in *Claudia* ('43). She retired from the stage in '54. She was married to screen star John Gilbert from '29–'31. Read more about Ina Claire at http://broadway.cas.sc.edu/index.php?action=showPerformer&id=29.

Sidney Clare (1892–1972) Sidney Clare performed in vaudeville as a dancer and comedian. He eventually became a writer of special material for vaudeville acts. His principal fame would come, however, in the music he wrote for over 50 films. In '33, Clare moved to Hollywood and wrote the entire score for the first RKO film, *Street Girl*. Films that followed include *Tanned Legs, Transatlantic Merry-Go-Round, Sing and Be Happy, Hit the Deck, Jimmy and Sally, Bright Eyes, The Littlest Rebel* and *Rascals*. His main collaborators were Con Conrad, Cliff Friend, Lew Pollack, Sam Stept, Lew Brown, Richard Whiting, Jay Gorney, Harry Warren, Vincent Youmans, Oscar Levant, Jimmy Monaco and Buddy De Sylva. Some of Clare's well-known songs include "Ma (He's Making Eyes at Me)" (see '21), "Miss Annabelle Lee" (see '27), "On the Good Ship Lollipop" (see '35), plus "Then I'll Be Happy," and "Please Don't Talk About Me When I'm Gone." Sidney Clare was a member of the Songwriters' Hall of Fame. At http://www.songwritershalloffame.org/exhibit_audio_video.asp?exhibitId=82 hear an audio clip of Isham Jones and his orchestra performing "Ma! (He's Making Eyes at Me)."

Billy Clark   Billy Clark and Harry Armstrong wrote "I Love My Wife; but Oh, You Kid!" (see '09).

Buddy Clark (real name: Samuel Goldberg; 1912–1949)   Buddy Clark was an important radio personality in the '30s and '40s. He appeared on *Your Hit Parade* from '36 to '38. He was the vocalist for Benny Goodman on two recordings and on Goodman's *Let's Dance* radio show. Even though Clark performed on radio often and on numerous recordings, often without label credit, he was not very well known until the '40s. His biggest selling recordings were "Peg o' My Heart" (see '47), "Linda" (see '47) and "Love Somebody" with Doris Day (see '48). Clark became the No. 16 top recording artist of the '40s.

Edward Clark (1878–1954)   Edward Clark was an actor, songwriter composer, author, director and producer. He came to the U.S. from Russia in 1891, and became a vaudeville comedian. He composed the Broadway stage score and libretto for *Little Miss Charity*, and co-wrote the lyrics for *You're in Love* (the title song was very popular in '17). He wrote the librettos for several other musicals and plays. His chief musical collaborators included Rudolf Friml, Otto Harbach, and Albert Von Tilzer. In Hollywood, he operated his own acting school for seventeen years, and was a contract film writer. His most successful song was "You're in Love" (see '17).

Gladys Clark   Gladys Clark and Henry Bergman introduced Berlin's "Remember" in vaudeville (see '25). They also introduced Berlin's "Always" (see '26).

Helen Clark   Helen Clark was a member of the Victor Light Opera Company. She and Walter Van Brunt had a very successful duet recording of "Sympathy" from *The Firefly* (see '13).

Grant Clarke (1891–1931)   Grant Clarke was a songwriter, author and publisher. When he graduated from Akron (OH) High School, he became an actor in stock companies. Later he became a staff writer for New York City music publishing firms. He wrote special material for Bert Williams, Fanny Brice, Eva Tanguay, Nora Bayes, and Al Jolson, and also the Broadway stage score for *Dixie to Broadway* and songs for *Ziegfeld Follies of 1921* and *Bombo*. He collaborated musically with George Meyer, Harry Akst, James Monaco, Fred Fisher, Harry Warren, Al Piantadosi, Milton Ager, Archie Gottler, Arthur Johnston, James Hanley, and Lewis Muir. His most famous popular song lyrics include "Ragtime Cowboy Joe" (see '12), "He's a Devil in His Own Home Town" (see '14), "I Love the Ladies" (see '14), "Second Hand Rose" (see '21), and "Am I Blue?" (see '29). Other well-known popular songs from his pen include "He'd Have to Get Under — Get Out and Get Under to Fix Up His Automobile," "When You're in Love with Someone Who Is Not in Love with You," "Beatrice Fairfax, Tell Me What to Do!," "There's a Little Bit of Bad in Every Good Little Girl," "You Can't Get Along with 'Em or Without 'Em," "Everything Is Peaches Down in Georgia," "Mandy, Make Up Your Mind," "Birmingham Bertha," and "Weary River."

Jan Clayton (1917–1983)   Jan Clayton and John Raitt introduced "If I Loved You" in Rodgers and Hammerstein's musical *Carousel* (see '45).

N. J. Clesi   Clesi's only important contribution to the history of popular music was as composer and lyricist for "I'm Sorry I Made You Cry" (see '18).

Gordon Clifford (1902–1968)   Gordon Clifford was co-writer of "I Surrender Dear" (see '31) and "Paradise" (see '32). In addition to being a songwriter, Clifford was also an actor and author.

Larry Clinton (1909–1985)   Larry Clinton became an outstanding bandleader, arranger, and composer during the '30s and '40s. He was particularly noted for adapting classics to popular music. Clinton arranged for many of the best big bands — namely Isham Jones, Glen Gray, and Tommy and Jimmy Dorsey. Clinton's most successful recordings were "My Reverie" (see '38), "Cry, Baby, Cry" (see '38), "Heart and Soul" (see '38) and "Deep Purple" (see '39). Clinton wrote "Dipsy Doodle" (see '37), "Satan Takes a Holiday" (see '37), My Reverie (see '38), and "Our Love" (see '39), among others. His career began to wane after '41, and although he tried a comeback in the late '40s, he never regained his former popularity. Clinton and his orchestra were the No. 17 top recording artists of the '30s.

Rosemary Clooney (1928–2002)   Rosemary Clooney began her career as half of the Clooney Sisters' singing act with Tony Pastor's band in '46. In '49 she got her solo break when Mitch Miller helped her towards a career in records, television, nightclubs and films. She became particularly known for her roles in the films *Here Come the Girls* with Bob Hope and *White Christmas* with Bing Crosby. Clooney's most successful recording career was in the pre-rock '50s. Her first big recording success was with "Come on-a My House" (see '51). Other famous recordings include "Half as Much" (see '52), "Hey, There" (see '54) and "This Ole House" (see '54). Ms. Clooney became the No. 11 top recording artist of the '50s. Ms. Clooney was inducted into the Popular Music Hall of Fame in 2000. Rosemary Clooney's website is http://www. rosemaryclooney.com/.

Arthur Clough   Arthur Clough was a frequent performer in vaudeville and musical comedies. He and the Brunswick Quartet had a very popular recording of "Down by the Old Mill Stream" (see '11).

Tom Coakley (1905–1995)   Tom Coakley had played in instrumental groups since the eighth grade. After college at the University of California, he entered law school, but in the late '20s organized a band to play for college dances and at Yosemite National Park during summer vacations. Next came a two-year engagement in Oakland and Hollywood. The group's only hit recording was "East of the Sun" (see '35). The name on the label was Tom Coakley and his Palace Hotel Orchestra. The name came from their engagement at the Palace Hotel in San Francisco, where they gained exposure on a radio program broadcast from the hotel's Rose Room. In '36 Coakley turned the band over to vocalist Carl Ravazza and started a law practice. In '53, he was appointed judge and in '69, he began serving as Associate Justice of the California Court of Appeal. He retired from the bench in '72.

Eric Coates (1886–1957)   English composer Eric Coates wrote "Sleepy Lagoon" (see '42). Coates, a viola player and composer, studied music at the Royal Academy of Music in London. In the early 1910s he began playing in the Queen's Hall Orchestra. By the end of that decade he was concentrating on composing.

Will D. Cobb (1876–1930) Will Cobb was a famous lyricist and composer of the early 1900s. He had a partnership with Ren Shields that produced many popular songs and musical productions, but he also collaborated with other writers, including Gus Edwards. Some of Cobb's most famous songs include "Good-Bye, Dolly Gray" (see '01), "Waltz Me Around Again, Willie" (see '06), "School Days" (see '07), "I Just Can't Make My Eyes Behave" (see '07), "Sunbonnet Sue" (see '08), "Yip-I-Addy-I-Ay" (see '09) and "If I Was a Millionaire" (see '10).

Dorcas Cochran (circa 1909–1991) Dorcas Cochran was primarily a Hollywood studio writer, but is also credited with writing lyrics for a few hit tunes. Cochran wrote the lyrics for "Again" (see '49). She wrote new English lyrics for an Argentine tango entitled "Adios Muchachos." It was transformed into "I Get Ideas" (see '51).

Bill Cogswell (1900–1977) Bill Cogswell was one of the co-writers of "My Little Grass Shack in Kealakekua, Hawaii" (see '34). According to the Livingston Enterprise News Digest, the local newspaper in Cogswell's home state, Montana, "The humuhumunukunukuapuaa (pronounced HOO moo HOO moo NOO koo NOO koo Ah poo AH ah) was recently reinstated as Hawaii's state fish because it was featured in a popular song, 'My Little Grass Shack.'" Cogswell attended the journalism school at the University of Montana. After college he accepted a reporting job with the Honolulu Star Bulletin.

George M. Cohan (1878–1942) George Michael Cohan, often called "America's original song-and-dance man," made his first professional appearance at the age of 9 in Little Georgie, as a member of the famous vaudeville team The Four Cohan's, with his sister, Josephine, and their parents. In '04 he produced his first successful musical play *Little Johnny Jones*, in which he played the character The Yankee Doodle Boy. As a songwriter, he was a charter member of the American Society of Composers, Authors and Publishers (ASCAP). His popular song catalog includes "The Yankee Doodle Boy" (see '05), "Give My Regards to Broadway" (see '05), "Mary's a Grand Old Name" (see '06), "So Long, Mary" (see '06), "Forty-Five Minutes from Broadway" (see '06), "You're a Grand Old Flag" (see '06), the patriotic song and 2002 Towering Song Award winner, "Harrigan" (see '07), "When We Are M-a-double-r-i-e-d" (see '07), "Under Any Old Flag at All" (see '08), "That Haunting Melody" (see '12), and "Over There," *the* song of World War I, which earned Cohan the Congressional Medal of Honor (see '17). Other Cohan favorites include "I Guess I'll Have to Telegraph My Baby," "You Remind Me of My Mother," "Life's a Funny Proposition After All," "Nellie Kelly, I Love You," and "Molly Malone." Cohan wrote, produced, directed and starred in over 40 musicals on Broadway. To name only a few of the most famous ones, they include *Forty-Five Minutes from Broadway, Little Johnny Jones, George Washington, Jr., Fifty Miles from Boston, Little Nellie Kelly, Ah, Wilderness!* and *I'd Rather Be Right.* Surprisingly, Cohan was a well known recording artist. He recorded "Life's a Funny Proposition, After All" from his musical *Little Johnny Jones*, and "The Small-Town Gal" from his *Fifty Miles from Boston* for

Victor. Both of those recordings were fairly popular in '11. In the '50s his life was documented in the film *Yankee Doodle Dandy,* where James Cagney starred as George. The '68 Broadway musical, *George M,* was based on Cohan's life and music; Joel Grey starred as Cohan. In '59, Oscar Hammerstein II presented an eight-foot high, bronze statue of Cohan that stands in the heart of Times Square on Broadway. George M. Cohan was inducted into the Songwriters' Hall of Fame when it was organized in '70. At http://www.songwritershalloffame.org/exhibit_audio_video.asp?exhibitId=213 hear a '05 audio clip of Billy Murray performing "The Yankee Doodle Boy."

Irving Cohn (1898–1961) Irving Cohn co-wrote one of the '20s' biggest novelty hits, "Yes! We Have No Bananas" (see '23).

Lincoln Colcord (1883?) Lincoln Colcord was lyricist of "Stein Song," sometimes called "Maine Stein Song" (see '30). A.W. Sprague reworked a tune by E.A. Fenstad and gave it to his roommate, Lincoln Colcord, who wrote the words. Colcord graduated in '06. Colcord was born at sea off the coast of Cape Horn, South Africa. His father and mother were on a two-year voyage.

Bob Cole (1868–1911) Bob Cole was born in Athens, Georgia. His earliest published songs were issued in 1893, and one of his earliest stage jobs was with Sam T. Jack's *Creole Show,* the first African American show to break from the strict minstrel tradition of all male performers. Cole also performed as an actor and directed the All Star Stock Company at Worth's Museum in New York, the first such company organized by African Americans. When he was in his mid-twenties and performing with Black Patti's Troubadours, Cole was engaged to write an entire show with Billy Johnson, his first collaborator. After a dispute over ownership of his music, Cole left the Troubadours to organize his own company. He created a full-length musical, *A Trip to Coontown,* which was performed off–Broadway in New York City during the 1898-99 season. It was the first musical entirely written, performed, produced, and owned by African Americans. Unlike other black entertainments of the time, Cole's production had a book and lyrics that could sustain a dramatic subplot. After the show closed, Cole and his partner, Billy Johnson, broke off their working relationship, and Cole met the Johnson brothers, Rosamond and James Weldon, with whom he was to create his most successful songs. Cole and the Johnson Brothers' "Under the Bamboo Tree" was very popular in '02.

Nat "King" Cole (1919–1965) Nat Cole was the son of an ordained minister in Montgomery, Alabama, but he attended school and received his music training in Chicago. His first professional job was in the tour band for the revue *Shuffle Along* in '36. Otherwise, he worked primarily as a nightclub jazz pianist. He formed the King Cole Trio in '39 with guitarist Oscar Moore and bassist Wesley Prince. Johnny Miller later replaced Prince in the trio. Cole's singing career started by accident. On a particular evening an over-enthusiastic patron insisted that he sing "Sweet Lorraine." At first he refused, but after he had complied, his relaxed style of singing became a major asset. For a while he performed in what was billed as the Nat Cole Trio, and he added the "King" to his name in '40. The trio signed with Capitol Records in '43, and Cole began to emerge as a solo attraction. In '58 Cole starred in the film *St. Louis Blues* as the famous blues composer W.C. Handy. Cole's outstanding recording career began in earnest in with "For Sentimental Reasons" (see '46) and "The Christmas Song" (see '46). The next big hit recording came with "Nature Boy" (see '48). Other big hits include "Mona Lisa" (see '50), "Too Young" (see '51) and "Pretend" (see '53). He continued to have chart hits into the '60s. Cole became the No. 27 top recording artist of the '40s and No. 19 for the '50s. In the '50s, he was the first black performer to have his own television series. Cole was elected to the Big Band/Jazz Hall of Fame in '93. He was inducted into the Popular Music Hall of Fame in 2003. At the time of his death, Cole had sold $50,000,000 worth of records for Capitol, which had 29 of his albums on the market at once. He had seven gold records — records that had sold more a million copies. His income was almost a million dollars per year. Nat's daughter, Natalie, has also had a very successful recording career.

Larry Coleman Jr. Larry Coleman Jr. was the composer of "Changing Partners" (see '53) and "Richocet" (see '53).

Arthur Collins (1864–1933) Arthur Collins became the leading minstrel-style dialect singer of the early years of the 20th Century. His solo hits, led by the famous "Preacher and the Bear," were plentiful; however, he achieved his greatest success in his duet partnership with tenor Byron Harlan. He was also a member of the Peerless Quartet from '06 until '18. Collins' most popular recordings include "Ma Tiger Lily" (see '00), "Mandy Lee" (see '00), "Bill Bailey, Won't You Please Come Home" (see '02), "Under the Bamboo Tree" (see '02), "Any Rags?" (see '03), "Good-bye, Eliza Jane" (see '03) and "The Preacher and the Bear" (see '05). His most popular duet recordings with Byron Harlan include "Down Where the Wurzberger Flows" (see '03), "Hurrah for Baffin's Bay" (see '03), "Camp Meetin' Time" (see '07), "You're in the Right Church, but the Wrong Pew" (see '09), "Alexander's Ragtime Band" (see '11), "Under the Yum Yum Tree" (see '11), "Put Your Arms Around Me, Honey" (see '11), "When That Midnight Choo Choo Leaves for Alabam'" (see '13), "I Love the Ladies" (see '14), "The Aba Daba Honeymoon" (see '14), "Oh How She Could Yacki Hacki Wicki Wachi Woo" (see '16) and "Dark Town Strutters' Ball" (see '18). And that does not include his recordings with the Peerless Quartet! Collins was the No. 4 recording artist of the first decade of the 20th Century and No. 2 of the second decade, making him the No. 6 top recording artist of the first half of the 20th Century. Collins' solo recording of "Nobody" and his duet recording with Byron Harlan of "With Her do-re-mi-fa-sol-la-si-do and do" are available for listening or downloading in RealAudio or MP3 files at http://www.collectionscanada.ca/gramophone/.

Jose Collins (real name: Josephine Charlotte Collins; 1887–1958) British singer Jose Collins introduced "Peg o' My Heart" in the *Ziegfeld Follies of 1913* as an interpolation (see '13). Ms. Collins helped popularize "Rebecca of Sunny-Brook Farm" by interpolating it into the *Ziegfeld Follies of 1913* (see '14). Jose Collins was born into an entertainment family. Her mother, Lottie Collins, was a music hall singer who helped popularize "Ta-ra-ra-boom-de-ay" in England. Jose made her West End debut in *The Antelope* ('08). She came to the U.S. and starred

on Broadway in *Vera Violetta* ('11), *The Merry Countess* ('12) and sang a duet with the famous Al Jolson in *The Whirl of Society* ('12). By 1917, she returned to London and was a stage favorite for several years.

Columbia Mixed Double Quartet The Columbia Mixed Double Quartet recorded a particularly popular version of "America" (see '16). The personnel of this double quartet are not listed in the Columbia Records files.

Columbia Stellar Quartet Charles Harrison (see his biographical sketch), John Barnes Wells, Frank Croxton, Andrea Sarto. In '15 Henry Burr replaced Wells, but he was soon replaced by Reed Miller. The group had a very successful recording of "The Battle Hymn of the Republic" (see '18). The record label read Charles Harrison and Columbia Stellar Quartet.

Russ Columbo (1908–1934) Russ Columbo died tragically young when he was at a friend's home in Hollywood. The friend was using a set of ancient dueling pistols as paperweights. Believing them to be unloaded, the friend struck a match against one pistol to light a cigarette. The gun fired, a bullet ricocheted off a desk and struck Columbo in the head. Even though he is not nearly as famous today, Russ Columbo was a strong competitor of Bing Crosby and Rudy Vallee for the top male singer during the early '30s. The crooning of Crosby and Columbo was so similar that it was almost difficult to identify which one was singing. Columbo might have become a huge star had not that fatal accident cut his career short. Columbo appeared in three films and had a hand in writing several songs he featured in his brief but spectacular career. His best-known recordings were "Goodnight, Sweetheart" (see '31) and "Prisoner of Love" (see '46 when it was most popular) but he was also famous for his theme song, "You Call It Madness" and he recorded many of the most popular songs of the early '30s, including "Time on My Hands," "All of Me," "You're My Everything," "Paradise," and "Sweet and Lovely." Go to http://www.russcolumbo.com/ for more on Russ Columbo.

Betty Comden (real name: Elizabeth Cohen; 1919–) Betty Comden graduated from New York University, where she studied drama. Shortly after graduation, she started looking for a theatrical agent. While she didn't find an agent, she did get acquainted with Adolph Green. The team of Betty Comden and Adolph Green began writing and performing their own satirical comic material in a group called The Revuers, which also included Judy Holliday. They collaborated with Leonard Bernstein and Jerome Robbins on what was the first show for all of them, *On the Town*. They also wrote the lyrics for Bernstein's *Wonderful Town*. They wrote the book and/or lyrics with Jule Styne for *Bells Are Ringing, Hallelujah, Baby, Do Re Mi, Subways Are for Sleeping, Peter Pan*, and others. They wrote the book for *Applause*, and book and lyrics for *On the Twentieth Century*. Four of these, *Applause, Hallelujah, Baby, Wonderful Town*, and *On the Twentieth Century*, won them five Tony Awards. Film musicals that included their songs include *Singin' in the Rain, The Band Wagon, On the Town, Bells Are Ringing, It's Always Fair Weather, Good News*, and *The Barkleys of Broadway*. Two of these, *The Band Wagon* and *It's Always Fair Weather*, received Academy Award nominations, and those two plus *On the Town* won the Screen Writer's Award. As performers, both Comden and Green appeared in *On the Town*. Comden appeared in the film *Garbo Talks*, and on the stage in Wendy Wasserstein's *Isn't It Romantic?* Highlights from the Comden-Green catalog include "Just in Time," "The Party's Over," "Make Someone Happy" and "New York, New York" (see '44). In '91, Comden and Green reunited with Cy Coleman to write the lyrics for the Tony Award winning Broadway success, *The Will Rogers Follies*. Comden was inducted into the Songwriters' Hall of Fame in '80.

Perry Como (real name: Pierino Como; 1912–2001) Perry Como was one of the most dominant performers in the recording field from the mid-'40s through the '50s. His amazingly popular career extended into the '70s, but his prime popularity came from the end of the big band era into the early years of rock. Como became the No. 5 top recording artist of the '40s and the No. 2 recording artist of the '50s. He also was the No. 33 recording artist of the first half of the 20th Century and the No. 8 recording artist of the second half of the 20th Century. Como was an established barber in his hometown before he successfully auditioned for Freddie Carlone's band and traveled with it and Ted Weems' band for several years. He signed a solo recording contract in '43 and had his first big hit with "Till the End of Time" in '45. His collective disk sales by the end of the '60s were estimated at more than 50 million. Perry was elected to the Big Band/Jazz Hall of Fame in 2004. Como's most productive period for really successful recordings runs from '45 until '58. Mr. C's biggest hit recordings include "Till the End of Time" (see '45), "Prisoner of Love" (see '46), "Surrender" (see '46), "Chi-Baba, Chi-Baba" (see '47), "Some Enchanted Evening" (see '49), "A — You're Adorable" (see '49), "Hoop-Dee-Doo" (see '50), "If" (see '51), "Don't Let the Stars Get in Your Eyes" (see '53), "No Other Love" (see '53), "Wanted" (see '54), "Round and Round" ('57) and "Catch a Falling Star" ('58.) Other popular recordings for Como include "If I Loved You," "They Say It's Wonderful," "Forever and Ever," "A Bushel and a Peck" with Betty Hutton, "Ko Ko Mo," and several revivals of oldies including "I Wonder Who's Kissing Her Now" with Ted Weems and his orchestra, "When You Were Sweet Sixteen," and "Because," plus "I'm Gonna Love That Gal," "Dig You Later," "A Dreamer's Holiday," You're Just in Love," "Maybe" with Eddie Fisher, "Say You're Mine Again," "Papa Loves Mambo," "Tina Marie," and "More." Como appeared in several Hollywood films, but he was much more successful on television. He hosted an extremely successful weekly hour-long variety show from '55 to '63. Also his annual Christmas TV show became a holiday tradition. His relaxed singing style and his informality with his audience on TV or in live performances became his trademark. Perry was inducted into the Popular Music Hall of Fame in 2004. Perry Como's website is http://www.perrycomo.net/.

Frances Comstock Frances Comstock and Alfred Drake introduced "How High the Moon" in the '40 revue *Two for the Show* (see '51).

Zez Confrey (real name: Edward Elzear Confrey; 1895–1971) Zez Confrey wrote several solo piano pieces that became very popular in the '20s. His best-known works include "Kitten on the Keys," "Dizzy Fingers," and "Stumbling" (see '22). He was pianist for many piano rolls for player pianos.

Reginald Connelly Reginald Connelly was one of the co-writers of "Show Me the Way to Go Home" (see '26), "Good Night, Sweetheart" (see '31) and "Just an Echo in the Valley" (see '32). Another famous Connelly song was "Try a Little Tenderness." This British native was the songwriting partner of fellow Londoner Jimmy Campbell. They primarily concentrated on writing lyrics. They sometimes wrote under the pseudonym Irving King. Connelly and Campbell also ran their own music publishing company.

Tommie Connor British songwriter Tommie Connor wrote "I Saw Mommy Kissing Santa Claus" (see '52). Connor's song had sold more than 11 million disks in all versions by the mid-'60s.

Con Conrad (real name: Conrad K. Dober; 1891–1938) Con Conrad became a composer, pianist, and publisher who wrote several popular songs from the '20s through the '30s. Conrad briefly attended a military academy where he was introduced to the piano. At 16, he left high school and started working in a Harlem movie house, playing songs to accompany the silent films. Later, he would perform in vaudeville, working for the Keith circuit shows, which toured the United States and overseas. In '12, Conrad had his first song published, "Down in Dear Old New Orleans." The following year, he produced a show on Broadway, *The Honeymoon Express*, which starred the still unknown Al Jolson. In '18, Conrad settled into the career of professional songwriting and publishing, forming a partnership with publisher Henry Waterson. In '20, Conrad had his first big hit, "Margie." In '23, Conrad's emphasis reverted back to creating scores for Broadway shows. Loosing his entire fortune on an unsuccessful Broadway show, Conrad moved to Hollywood in '29 where he worked on several successful films. In '34, Conrad, with collaborator Herb Magidson, was awarded the first Academy Award for Best Song for "The Continental." In addition to Herb Magidson, Conrad also collaborated with Joe Young, Sidney Clare, Billy Rose, Buddy DeSylva, Benny Davis, Leo Robin, J. Russel Robinson, Vincent Rose, Archie Gottler, Sidney Mitchell and William Friedlander. Conrad's most famous compositions include "Palesteena" (see '20), "Margie" (see '21), "Ma! (He's Making Eyes at Me)" (see '21), "Barney Google" (see '23), "You've Got to See Mamma Ev'ry Night" (see '23), "Memory Lane" (see '24), Prisoner of Love" (see '46, when it was most popular), and the first Academy Award winning song, "The Continental" (see '34). Other Conrad well-known songs include "You Call It Madness (but I Call It Love)," and "Singin' the Blues." Conrad was elected to the Songwriters' Hall of Fame in '70. At http://www.songwritershalloffame.org/exhibit_audio_video.asp?exhibitId=83 hear audio clips of "Ma (He's Making Eyes at Me)" by Isham Jones and his orchestra and "The Continental" by Sam Browne with George Scott Wood and The London Piano–Accordion Band.

Olga Cook Olga Cook and Bertram Peacock introduced "Song of Love" in the Broadway musical *Blossom Time* (see '22).

Robert Cook Robert Cook was a co-writer of "There Must Be a Way" (see '45).

Leonard Cooke Songwriter Leonard Cooke contributed the lyrics for "The Sunshine of Your Smile" (see '16).

Leslie Cooke Leslie Cooke was lyricist for "Love Sends a Little Gift of Roses" (see '23).

J. Fred Coots (real name: John Frederick Coots; 1897–1985) J. Fred Coots was taught to play the piano by his mother. After leaving high school, he got a job in a bank on Wall Street, but, in '14, he heard a song plugger in a music shop demonstrating new songs, and decided to change careers. His first job in music was as a pianist and stock boy in a music shop, but by '17 he had his first song published. He then went into vaudeville, playing the piano and writing songs tailored to specific performers like Sophie Tucker. In '22 he wrote the music for a Broadway show called *Sally, Irene, and Mary* with lyrics by Raymond Klages. His last Broadway score was *Sons o' Guns*, in '29. Coots then left New York for Hollywood. Throughout his career, Coots wrote songs for the Cotton Club revues ('36, '38 and '39) primarily working with lyricist Benny Davis. Coots continued to perform, first in vaudeville and later in nightclubs. J. Fred Coots was a prolific songwriter. In the course of his long career he wrote over 700 songs. Among his most successful songs were "Precious Little Thing Called Love" (see '29), "Love Letters in the Sand" (see '31), "You Go to My Head" (see '38) and "Beautiful Lady in Blue" (see '36), plus "I Still Get a Thrill (Thinking of You)" and "Santa Claus Is Comin' to Town." He collaborated with lyricists Benny Davis, Sam M. Lewis, Dorothy Fields, Lou Davis and Haven Gillespie. Coots was inducted into the Songwriters' Hall of Fame in '72. At http://www.songwritershalloffame.org/exhibit_audio_video.asp?exhibitId=45 hear an audio clip of Louis Armstrong performing "You Go to My Head."

Allan Copeland Allan Copeland was co-lyricist of "Make Love to Me" (see '54). The song began in '23 as "Tin Roof Blues," written by five players in the New Orleans Rhythm Kings plus Walter Melrose, a composer, author, and publisher during the '20s. Melrose wrote the original, more risqué, lyrics, but Bill Norvas and Allan Copeland contributed the present version in '53.

Sam Coslow (1902–1982) Sam Coslow began writing songs while he was still a teenager. His first success came in '20, with a song called "Grieving for You." He had a number of hit songs over the next few years. Together with composer Larry Spier, he founded his own publishing company, the Spier & Coslow Music Company and also had a minor career as a recording artist for RCA Victor, Decca and Columbia Records. In '29, Spier and Coslow sold their publishing firm to Paramount Pictures. Spier continued in publishing, while Coslow became the first Broadway songwriter to be hired by Paramount. During his decade with Paramount, he wrote songs for many of their films, including most of the early Bing Crosby pictures. His most remembered songs from this period include "Just One More Chance" (see '31), "Cocktails for Two" (see '34), "In the Middle of a Kiss" (see '35), plus "Learn to Croon," and "My Old Flame." In '40, Coslow joined with Herbert Mills, of Mills Novelty, and with James Roosevelt, son of then–President Franklin Roosevelt, to found RCM Productions in order to produce "soundies" for the Panoram machine, a coin operated machine like a jukebox that showed 3-minute music films. Over the next few years, they placed some 10,000 Panorams in bars, diners, and soda shops, wherever one might find a jukebox. They produced "soundies" in every popular music style of the day, and many of them featured African American performers who were often neglected by Hollywood. They were producing at least one reel of eight soundies every week. From the late '40s through the '50s Coslow produced a number of films. A short film, *Heavenly Music*, produced by Coslow for MGM, won the Academy Award for Best Short in '43. He also produced and wrote screenplays for full-length musical feature films, including *Out of This World* ('45) and *Copacabana* ('47). In the mid–'50s, he lived in London, where he wrote for film and stage musicals. Coslow also collaborated with Hoagy Carmichael, Sigmund Romberg, J. Fred Coots, Fred Hollander, and Will Grosz. Sam Coslow was inducted into the Songwriters' Hall of Fame in '70. At http://www.songwritershalloffame.org/exhibit_audio_video.asp?exhibitId=52 hear an audio clip of Bing Crosby singing "Just One More Chance."

Hal Cotton Hal Cotton wrote the English lyrics for "You Can't Be True, Dear" (see '48).

Stanley Cowan (1918–1991) Stanley Cowan was co-writer of "Do I Worry?" (see '41) and "'Til Reveille" (see '41). Cowan was a songwriter, author, publicist and director. After high school, he went to Hollywood, where he became an assistant film director and wrote music for films, including the westerns of "Hopalong" Cassidy, for musicals and for some of the dance orchestras. During World War II, he produced shows for the U.S. Air Force. By the end of the '40s, he was active in radio and television production. By the early '50s, he was a publicist, organizing his own company, Rogers and Cowan in '60. His chief collaborators included his father Rubey Cowan, Bobby Worth, and Sidney Miller.

Noel Coward (1899–1973) Composer, lyricist, librettist, actor, director Noel Coward became an extremely successful writer for the London stage. He contributed several distinctively smart, satirical revues and musicals as well as a few operettas. Coward often appeared in his own musical productions. Most of his musicals and his witty songs were so British, their success in the U.S. was limited. His "Zigeuner" was popular in the U.S. in '29 and his "I'll Follow My Secret Heart" was also quite popular (see '34). Coward is a member of the Songwriters' Hall of Fame.

Francis Craig (real name: Francis Jackson Craig; 1900–1966) Pianist and bandleader Francis Craig was the ninth of ten children of a Tennessee Methodist minister. Craig attended Vanderbilt University and formed a dance band in '20 to help pay his college expenses. After he graduated in '22, he decided to try a career in music. In '24, he and his band were hired for a two-week engagement at the Hermitage Hotel in downtown Nashville. That two week contract stretched until '46. From '25 to '47, the band's performances were broadcast live over WSM radio in Nashville and were carried nationally. In '46, Craig decided to retire from performing and take a position as a disk jockey at WSM. His last recording before his retirement, however, became his biggest hit and led to two more years of touring and personal appearances. "Near You," on the small Bullet label, became the first recording recorded in Nashville to sell over a million copies; it reportedly eventually sold in excess of two and a half million. After more touring for a couple of years,

Craig returned to Nashville to work for the radio station. Craig's success with "Near You" (see '47) and "Beg Your Pardon" in '48 boosted him to the No. 31 top recording artist of the '40s.

Jimmie Crane Jimmie Crane was co-writer of "I Need You Now" (see '54) and "If I Give My Heart to You" (see '54).

Allene Crater (1876–1957) A native of Denver, Colorado, Allene Crater first appeared in local productions before she was recruited for a tour of *Sinbad* starring Eddie Foy. A couple of years later she starred in *The Ballet Girl* (1897) and in *Miss Simplicity* (1898). Ms. Crater appeared in the successful musical *A Trip to Chinatown* (1899) before she toured Australia and New Zealand. Back in the United States, Crater's next engagement in the summer of '03 was as the Lady Lunatic during the second season of the original run of *The Wizard of Oz*. The stars of this show were Dave Montgomery and Fred Stone appearing respectively as The Tin Woodsman and The Scarecrow. Fred Stone married Ms. Crater in '04. Allene Crater and Neal McCay introduced "Because You're You" in *The Red Mill*, another Montgomery and Stone production.

Joan Crawford (real name: Lucille Fay LeSueur; 1904–1977) Lucille LeSueur's parents separated and divorced before she was born. By her teens, she had known several fathers, one, a vaudeville theater manager, had given her the stage name Billie Cassin. In '15, she and her mother lived in Kansas City, where she worked in a laundry to help pay school tuition. She won an amateur dance contest in '23, which led to some chorus work in Chicago, Detroit and New York. In '25, she headed for Hollywood, where she became Joan Crawford. She had a string of successes at MGM. She introduced the song "Chant of the Jungle" in the film *Untamed* (see '30). After she signed with Warner Bros. in '43, she won an Oscar for her role in *Mildred Pierce* ('45). She married the Chairman of the Board of the Pepsi-Cola Co. After her husband died, she made a come back starring with Bette Davis in *What Ever Happened to Baby Jane?* ('62). She retired in '74.

Kathryn Crawford (1908–1980) Kathryn Crawford introduced Cole Porter's "Love for Sale" in the Broadway musical *The New Yorkers* (see '31).

Henry Creamer (1879–1930) Henry Creamer, songwriter, composer, author, publisher and singer, was educated in New York public schools. He toured the U.S. and Europe in vaudeville. His chief musical collaborator was Turner Layton. His most famous popular songs include "That's A-Plenty" (see '09), "After You've Gone" (see '19), "Way Down Yonder in New Orleans" (see '22), and "If I Could Be with You One Hour Tonight" (see '30).

The Crew Cuts Rudi Maugeri (1931–2004), Pat Barrett (1933–), Roy Perkins (1932–), Johnnie Perkins (1931–). The Crew Cuts had their biggest hit recording with their cover version of the Chords' original R&B version of "Sh-Boom" in '54. The Crew Cuts' recording of "Sh-Boom" is considered by some to be the first rock and roll hit (see '54). They also had a popular cover recording of the Penguins' "Earth Angel" in '55.

Bing Crosby (real name: Harry Lillis Crosby; 1904–1977) Crosby acquired the nickname "Bing" in his childhood because of his attachment to the character

Bingo in the comic *The Bingville Bugle*. During his college days at Gonzaga University, he teamed with Al Rinker to form a small band. In '24 they quit school and went to Los Angeles to see if Rinker's sister, Mildred Bailey, could help them get started in show business. In '27, after several jobs on the West Coast, Paul Whiteman hired them and took them to New York City. There, Harry Barris joined the group, forming the Rhythm Boys. After three on and off years with Whiteman, the trio got a booking at the Cocoanut Grove in Los Angeles, where Crosby began to emerge as a soloist. In '31 he signed a contract with CBS and began his radio career, which eventually brought him a film contract. His extraordinary fame in films, on recordings, and on radio and television continued for many years. Crosby made more than 2,600 recordings, which had amassed a total disk sales figure by '75 of 400 million. Twenty-one of these recordings were million-selling singles, and he had one gold album. Bing is the No. 1 recording artist of the first half of the 20th Century, because he was the top artist of both the '30s and the '40s. Crosby was elected to the Big Band/Jazz Hall of Fame in 2004. His biggest hit recordings of the '30s include "Out of Nowhere" (see '31), "At Your Command" (see '31) which he help write, "Just One More Chance" (see '31), "Please" (see '32), "Dinah" (see '32), "Brother, Can You Spare a Dime?" (see '32), "You're Getting to Be a Habit with Me" (see '33), "Shadow Waltz" (see '33), "June in January" (see '34), "Love in Bloom" (see '34), "Little Dutch Mill" (see '34), "It's Easy to Remember" (see '35), "Red Sails in the Sunset" (see '35), "Soon" (see '35), "Pennies from Heaven" (see '36), "Sweet Leilani" (see '37), "The Moon Got in My Eyes" (see '37), "Remember Me?" (see '37), "Too Marvelous for Words" (see '37), "Bob White" (see '37), "I've Got a Pocketful of Dreams" (see '38), "You Must Have Been a Beautiful Baby" (see '38) and "Alexander's Ragtime Band" (see '38). Unusually successful recordings of the '40s include "Only Forever" (see '40), "Sierra Sue" (see '40), "Trade Winds" (see '40), "White Christmas" (see '42), "Moonlight Becomes You" (see '43), "Sunday, Monday or Always" (see '43), "Swinging on a Star" (see '44), "Don't Fence Me in" (see '44), "(There'll Be a) Hot Time in the Town of Berlin (When the Yanks Go Marching in)" (see '44), "San Fernando Valley" (see '44), "I Love You" (see '44), "I'll Be Seeing You" (see '44), "I Can't Begin to Tell You" (see '45), "It's Been a Long, Long Time" (see '45) and "Now Is the Hour" (see '48). Bing collaborated with Roy Turk and Fred Ahlert on the song that became his theme song, "Where the Blue of the Night (Meets the Gold of the Day)" (see '31). At Gonzaga University in Spokane, Washington, the Student Center is named after Harry "Bing" Crosby, a former Gonzaga student. The Center houses the Crosbyana Room, where about 200 pieces of the world's largest public collection of Bing Crosby memorabilia is displayed. The remainder of the immense collection is housed in the Foley Center's Rare Book vault. Bing was inducted into the Popular Music Hall of Fame in 2000. The Bing Crosby Internet Museum is at http://www.kcmetro.cc.mo.us/pennvalley/biology/lewis/crosby/bing.htm.

Bob Crosby (1913–1993) Bob Crosby was Bing's younger brother. He began his career as a singer with various bands, including the Dorsey Brothers. When Ben Pollack retired in '34, several of the bandsmen reorganized as a corporation and hired Bob as the front man and singer. The band had a Dixieland style, which was unusual for a big band. Their theme song was Gershwin's "Summertime," which was an unusual choice for a Dixieland group. A combo within the band, the Bob Cats, played even more Dixieland. The Crosby orchestra was very successful until the early '40s, when it disbanded. After that Crosby worked in several movies and led military big bands during World War II. After the war he worked on radio and early television. He remained active in the '60s and into the early '70s. Bob Crosby and his orchestra introduced "I've Heard That Song Before" in the movie musical *Youth on Parade* (see '43). Bob Crosby and his orchestra's most famous recordings include "In a Little Gypsy Tea Room" (see '35), "Whispers in the Dark" (see '37), and "Day in — Day Out" (see '39). Their most productive period was the mid–'30s through the early '40s.

Xavier Cugat (1900–1990)

Xavier Cugat, born in Spain, is particularly associated with the rumba and other Spanish and Latin American dances. He organized his band in the late '20s. They gained popularity in the early '30s and continued into the late '40s. Cugat's family moved from Spain to Cuba when he was young. He came to the U.S. as a violinist to play in symphony orchestras. In the early '20s "Cugie" decided to abandon classical music for popular music. After several years of various engagements, he formed his own group in the early '30s. Cugat was married five times, including two of his vocalists. The young Desi Arnez got his big break in show business in Cugat's band. "Cugie" was also a talented caricaturist, whose work appeared in newspapers and magazines all over the world. He retired from show business in the early '70s and settled in Barcelona before his death. Cugat's biggest hit recordings came in the early to mid–'40s, but none made it to No. 1 on the charts. His biggest hit was "Brazil," which peaked at No. 2 in '43. He became, however, the No. 35 top recording artist of the '40s.

Mann Curtis (real name: Emanuel Kurtz; 1911–1984)

Mann Curtis was lyricist of "My Dreams Are Getting Better All the Time" (see '45). Curtis also wrote "In a Sentimental Mood."

Catherine Chisholm Cushing (1874–1952)

Catherine Chisholm Cushing was a lyricist, composer and author. She was educated at girls' schools. She wrote the Broadway stage librettos for a couple of shows. Her chief musical collaborators were Rudolf Friml and Hugo Felix. Cushing's most popular songs were "Love's Own Sweet Song" (see '14), and "L'Amour, Toujours, L'Amour" (see '22).

Ford Dabney (1883–1958)

Ford Dabney, songwriter, composer, conductor and pianist, is primarily remembered as the composer of "That's Why They Call Me 'Shine'" (see '10). He was educated at Armstrong Manual Training School. He studied music with his father and also with a few other teachers. In '04, he became the official court musician for the president of Haiti. He returned to the U.S. in '07 to lead his own quartet. He was owner-operator of his own film and vaudeville theatre in Washington, and in '13 he organized the Tempo Club (an African American talent bureau) in New York City. He helped create some of the original dance numbers for Vernon and Irene Castle, and conducted the Ziegfeld

Midnight Frolics orchestra for eight years. His chief musical collaborators included Joe Trent, Lew Brown and Cecil Mack, with whom he wrote "That's Why They Call Me 'Shine'."

Vernon Dalhart (real name: Marion Try Slaughter; 1883–1948)

Vernon Dalhart took his stage name from two towns near his hometown (Vernon and Dalhart, Texas). After receiving formal music training, he went to New York City to sing light opera. After hearing the Okeh recording of "The Wreck of the Old 97" by Henry Whittier, Dalhart concluded that there was big money to be made in hillbilly music. He imitated the Whittier recording of "Wreck of the Old 97" for Edison Records and then recorded it again, coupled with "The Prisoner's Song" for Victor. Dalhart sang for 30 or more record companies and recorded "The Prisoner's Song" for at least 28 labels under 70 various names for an estimated total of 25 million records sold. Dalhart's most popular recording was by far "The Prisoner's Song" (see '25). Dalhart became the No. 17 top recording artist of the '20s.

Stanley J. Damerell

Stanley J. Damerell was co-lyricist of "If" (see '51). Ian Whitcomb, a highly respected performer, composer, and music historian, claims on his website (http://www.picklehead.com/ian/uncle.html) that his uncle wrote "Lady of Spain." He also claims that Stanley J. Damerell is one of many names his uncle used to write his songs. Damerell was also lyricist of "Let's All Sing Like the Birdies Sing" in '32.

Lili (Lili) Damita (real name: Liliane Marie Madeleine Carré; 1906–1994)

Lili Damita was educated in convents and ballet schools in France, Spain and Portugal. By age 14, she was a dancer in the Opera de Paris. At age 16, she was performing in Paris music halls. By the early '20s, she was appearing in several French and German silent films. In the late '20s, she was signed by Samuel Goldwyn and came to Hollywood. She appeared in several early talkies, including *The Bridge of San Luis Rey* ('29) and *Fighting Caravans* ('31). Lili, Harry Richman and Bert Lahr introduced "Let's Put Out the Lights" in *George White's Music Hall Varieties* in '32 (see '32). In '35, she married Errol Flynn. Their marriage only lasted until '42.

Vic Damone (real name: Vito Rocco Farinola; 1928–)

Vic Damone had a distinguished career as a singer in recordings, radio, television, and movies. Comedian Milton Berle helped him land his first singing job at the La Martinique club. He graduated to the Paramount Theater and radio appearances and, in the late '40s, to his own radio program. He began his recording career in the late '40s and had his only No. 1 hit with "You're Breaking My Heart" (see '49). That success led to network radio spots, more prestigious nightclub dates, and his film debut in *Rich, Young and Pretty* ('51). After two years of military service, Damone resumed his singing career. He did some radio work, recorded occasionally, and appeared in several films, notably *Hit the Deck* and *Kismet* (both released in '55). For more, visit Vic Damone's official website: http://www.vicdamone.com/.

Bebe Daniels (1901–1971)

Bebe Daniels was the singing star of several movie musicals in the late '20s and early '30s. She began her movie career in the silent era but, unlike many silent movie actors, made the transition to talkies. She is especially remembered for her appearances with Harold Lloyd in several of his films and for her starring roles in the movie musicals *Rio Rita* and *Forty Second Street*. She introduced "You're Getting to Be a Habit with Me" in that film (see '33). She and her husband, film executive Ben Lyon, remained active in the entertainment business into the '60s, when Ms. Daniels suffered a stroke and had to retire.

Hart Pease Danks (1834–1903) Hart Pease Danks was born in New Haven, Connecticut. His family moved to Saratoga Springs, N.Y. when Hart was 8 years old, where he began to study music. At age 19, he was earning his living as a carpenter, in Chicago, where his father had a construction business, but soon gave it up to fulfill a career as a composer. His first composition was included in William Bradley's *Jubilee*, entitled "Lake Street." In 1856, Danks' "The Old Lane" was published and he would go on to produce songs for stage shows such as *Anna Lee*. He returned to New York City in 1864 and his first operetta *Pauline* was published in 1872. His second operetta, *Conquered by Kindness* was published in 1881. As a choirmaster, Danks produced several hymns and secular compositions. In his lifetime, over 1300 hymns and popular songs were published, but today he is primarily remembered for "Silver Threads Among the Gold," with lyrics by Eben E. Rexford (see '04). Hart P. Danks died in poverty in Philadelphia in '03. His last written words were "It's hard to die alone." Danks was inducted into the Songwriters' Hall of Fame in '70.

Joe Darion (1917–2001) Joe Darion was lyricist for "Changing Partners" (see '53) and "Ricochet" (see '53). Joe Darion later became famous as the lyricist for the Broadway stage, notably for *Man of La Mancha* in '65, and for the Academy Award–winning song "Never on Sunday" in '60.

Denver Darling (1909–1981) Denver Darling was a co-writer with Gene Autry and Vaughn Horton of "Address Unknown" (see '39).

Jean Darling (real name: Dorothy Jean LeVake; 1922–) Jean Darling, as Carrie Pipperidge, and Christine Johnson, as Nettie Fowler, introduced "June Is Bustin' Out All Over" in the Rodgers and Hammerstein musical *Carousel* (see '45). This is the same Jean Darling who appeared in the Our Gang films of the late '20s. She is one of the last surviving cast members of the silent film era. She appeared in other films after leaving Our Gang, including Laurel and Hardy's '34 adaptation of *Babes in Toyland*. She later moved to Ireland and became a radio actress.

Shelby Darnell (see Bob Miller)

Alfonso D'Artega (1907–?) Mexican composer Alfonso D'Artega wrote "In the Blue of Evening" (see '43). D'Artega was a songwriter, conductor, arranger and pianist. He came to the U.S. in '18, after he had studied at Strassburger Conservatory of Music. He often conducted orchestras on radio, theaters, films, recordings and symphony concerts; he originated the "pops" concerts at Carnegie Hall. According to http://www.imdb.com, he composed the NBC chimes theme.

Lee David Lee David was the composer of "Tonight You Belong to Me" (see '27).

Mack David (1912–1993) Mack David was an important lyric writer from the early '30s through the '60s.

David originally intended to become an attorney. He attended Cornell University and St. John's University Law School. When his younger brother Hal David was considering a career, Mack advised him to seek a more stable profession than songwriting. However, he failed to follow his own advice. David and Mack Davis teamed up to write the lyrics of "Moon Love" (see '39). While primarily a lyricist, David wrote both words and music for "Sunflower" ('48) Years later, he filed an infringement of copyright lawsuit against Jerry Herman for similarities between "Sunflower" and "Hello, Dolly." He won the suit. In '48, David moved to Hollywood, where he became active in film and television. He was nominated for eight Academy Awards, including "The Hanging Tree" ('59), "Bachelor in Paradise" ('61), "Walk on the Wild Side" ('62), "It's a Mad, Mad, Mad, Mad World" ('61), "Hush ... Hush, Sweet Charlotte" ('64), {all of the above songs were title songs}, "The Ballad of Cat Ballou" ('65, from *Cat Ballou*), and "My Wishing Doll" ('66, from *Hawaii*). His best-known songs include "Moon Love" (see '39), "It's Love, Love, Love" (see '44), "Candy" (see '46), "Chi-Baba Chi-Baba" (see '47), the lyrics for the Disney feature cartoon *Cinderella*, particularly including "Bibbidi Bobbidi Boo" which was nominated for the Academy Award in '50, "I Don't Care If the Sun Don't Shine," the English lyrics for "La Vie en Rose" (see '50), the lyrics for Max Steiner's "Tara's Theme" from *Gone with the Wind* ("My Own True Love"), and "Cherry Pink and Apple Blossom White" (see '55). And in '61, the Shirelles had a hit with his song "Baby, It's You." In addition to words for popular songs, he wrote the lyrics for the themes of several television shows, including *Casper, the Friendly Ghost*, *77 Sunset Strip*, *Bourbon Street Beat*, and *Hawaiian Eye*. His theme song, "This Is It," for *The Bugs Bunny Hour* is also very well known. He collaborated with several of the best composers in the business, notably Jerry Livingston, Burt Bacharach, Ernest Gold, Elmer Bernstein, Henry Mancini, John Green, Jimmy Van Heusen, Alex Kramer, Joan Whitney, Count Basie and Franz Waxman. Mack David was inducted into the Songwriters' Hall of Fame in '75.

Benny Davis (1895–1979) Lyricist Benny Davis had a significant output of songs that became hits. His most productive years were in the '20s, but he was still producing in the '60s. Davis started performing in vaudeville acts when he was a teenager and later performed as Blossom Seeley's accompanist. By the early '20s, he began his professional songwriting career and had his first hit songs with "Margie" (see '21) and "Make Believe" (see '21). In the late '20s, Davis returned to the theater producing scores for a couple of Broadway shows and several editions of the Cotton Club revues. Davis collaborated with several other songwriters including Milton Ager, Harry Akst, Con Conrad, Nathaniel Skilkret, J. Fred Coots, Billy Baskette, Arthur Swanstrom, Ted Murray and J. Russel Robinson. Davis was one of the most prolific writers of his era and produced such hits as "Good-bye Broadway, Hello France" (see '17), "Angel Child" (see '22), "Oh, How I Miss You Tonight" (see '25), "Baby Face" (see '26), "Carolina Moon" (see '29), "Chasing Shadows" (see '35). Benny Davis was inducted into the Songwriters' Hall of Fame in '75. At http://www.songwritershalloffame.org/exhibit_audio_video.asp?exhibitId=84 hear audio clip of Al Jolson singing Davis' "Angel Child."

Bette Davis (real name: Ruth Elizabeth Davis; 1908–1989) Bette Davis' chief musical contribution was introducing "They're Either Too Young or Too Old" in the movie musical *Thank Your Lucky Stars* (see '44). Ms. Davis' outstanding career is far too broad to do justice in a biographical sketch. The highlights include the Best Actress Academy Awards for *Dangerous* ('35) and *Jezebel* ('38). After many weak films in the '40s, she rebounded with Oscar nominations for *All About Eve* ('50) and *What Ever Happened to Baby Jane?* ('62). In '77, she received AFI's Lifetime Achievement Award. In '79, she won a Best Actress Emmy for the television production *Strangers: The Story of a Mother and Daughter.*

Jessie Bartlett Davis (1860–1905) Jessie Bartlett Davis introduced "Oh, Promise Me" in the musical *Robin Hood* in 1890 (see '07). The temperamental Ms. Davis played Alan-a-Dale in the production.

Jimmie Davis (real name: James Houston Davis; 1899–2000) Jimmie Davis had a remarkable life. He was a country-western singer, a songwriter, an actor in western films and Louisiana's governor for two terms. One of his films, *Louisiana* ('47) mirrored his life: a country boy becomes a singer and then a governor. Davis was elected to the governor's office in '44 and again in '60. He was 'the singing governor," often performing music for his campaigns. In his later years he devoted most of his time to the gospel music field, where he and his wife, Anna Gordon Davis, sang with "The Chuck Wagon Gang." His best-known song is "You Are My Sunshine," which became the official state song of Louisiana in '77 (see '41). Davis, however, supposedly purchased the song from its composer and copyrighted it under his name. He also wrote "Worried Mind." Davis was also a recording artist. Most of his recordings were in the gospel field, but he had a couple of reasonably successful recordings in the popular music market. Davis was inducted into the Country Music Hall of Fame in '72 and the Southern Gospel Music Association Hall of Fame in '97.

Joan Davis (real name: Madonna Josephine Davis; 1907–1961) Joan Davis and Jinx Falkenburg introduced "Daddy" in the movie *Two Latins from Manhattan* (see '41). Ms. Davis was a popular comedienne in '40s' radio and on early TV. Her *I Married Joan* TV series was very popular.

Lou Davis (1881–1961) Lou Davis was co-writer with Henry Lange and Henry Busse for "Hot Lips" (see '22). Davis wrote the lyrics for "A Precious Little Thing Called Love" (see '29). Davis was a songwriter, author, and businessman. He was in the wholesale meat business. His primary collaborators were Abel Baer, Henry Busse, Harold Arlen, Henry Lange and J. Fred Coots.

Mack Davis (1898–1947) Mack Davis and Mack David teamed up to write the lyrics for "Moon Love" (see '39). Davis also conducted his own orchestra and was an executive on the staff of CBS' Artist Bureau and MCA. His songwriting collaborators included Sammy Stept, Mack David, Don George and Walter Kent.

Dolly Dawn (real name: Theresa Maria Stabile; 1916–2002) In '35 Dolly Dawn became the singer for George Hall's Arcadians. The diminutive teenager changed her name to Dolly Dawn and immediately became a crowd favorite. The band (and Dolly) got a lot of exposure when they broadcast six days a week over the CBS radio network from noon to 12:30. In '36, she began recording under the name Dolly Dawn and her Dawn Patrol, but the musicians were still members of Hall's band. Although "You're a Sweetheart" was labeled Dolly Dawn and her Dawn Patrol, it wasn't until '41 that Hall publicly turned over his band's leadership to Dolly and the band was officially renamed. That arrangement only lasted a few months when World War II caused many of the group's musicians to be drafted. In '98 Dolly Dawn was inducted into the Big Band Hall of Fame. "You're a Sweetheart" (see '38) was her only big hit recording.

Hazel Dawn (1891–?) According to the sheet music cover, Hazel Dawn was the star of the Victor Herbert musical *The Debutante.* "The Springtime of Life" (see '14) premiered in that production.

Doris Day (real name: Doris Mary Ann Kappelhoff; 1924–) Doris Day had studied dance, but turned to singing after she broke her leg in a car accident at age 14. She was offered her first job by bandleader Barney Rapp, who suggested she change her name. She was christened Day because of her rendition of the song "Day After Day," which she used to audition for Rapp. She continued to be known primarily as a band singer until '48, when she began her movie career that led to 39 films in 20 years, almost all of them big hits. She became one of the top female movie box-office attractions in both musicals and non-musicals. Her biggest hit recordings include "Love Somebody" with Buddy Clark (see '48) and "It's Magic" from her first film, *Romance on the High Seas* (see '48), "A Guy Is a Guy" (see '52) and "Secret Love," the Academy Award winner from *Calamity Jane* (see '54). She also introduced "Que Sera, Sera (Whatever Will Be, Will Be)" in Alfred Hitchcock's *The Man Who Knew Too Much* ('56). As her film career waned, she turned to television. The very popular *The Doris Day Show* ran from '68 to '72. She appeared on occasional TV specials over the next several years, but returned with *Doris Day's Best Friends* in '85. Ms. Day became the No. 32 top recording artist of the '40s and No. 26 for the '50s. The following website particularly features Ms. Day's films: http://www.dorisday.net/.

Edith Day (1896–1971) Edith Day became one of the most famous musical ingénues on Broadway when she was cast in the title role of *Irene.* She also starred in the '20 London production and was so well received that she made England home. She became known as "The Queen of Drury Lane Theatre" because of the productions she starred in there over the next two decades. During the mid–'40s she retired from the stage, but returned briefly in the early '60s. Edith Day had popular recordings of "Alice Blue Gown" and "Irene" from *Irene* (see both songs in '20).

Arthur Deagon (circa 1871–1927) Arthur Deagon and Dennis King introduced the title song from Rudolf Friml's *Rose Marie* (see '25). Deagon appeared in ten Broadway productions between '02 and the mid–'20s, including the *Ziegfeld Follies* of 1908, 1909 and 1914. He also was in *Little Nellie Kelly* in '22 and, as mentioned above, *Rose Marie.*

Claude Debussy (1862–1918) Achille-Claude Debussy was a composer of classical-style music. He developed the style commonly referred to as impressionism, a term which he disliked. Debussy was not only one of the most important French composers but was also one of the most important figures in music at the turn of the last century; his music represents the transition from late-romantic music to 20th century modernist music. Debussy's "Clair de Lune" was very popular (see '05). His "Reverie" was turned into the popular song "My Reverie" and popularized by Larry Clinton and his orchestra (see '38).

Harry DeCosta (1895–1964)   Harry DeCosta is credited as the writer of the super simplistic words of "Tiger Rag" (see '31). DeCosta was a songwriter, author and pianist.

Sylvia Dee (real name: Josephine Moore; 1914–) Sylvia Dee was the lyricist of "Chickery Chick" (see '45) and "Too Young" (see '51). Although not quite as popular, she also wrote "My Sugar Is So Refined," which was popularized by Johnny Mercer in a '46 recording. She was educated at the University of Michigan. She worked as a copywriter for a Rochester, New York newspaper and wrote several short stories.

Jimmy DeKnight (see James E. Myers)

Reginald DeKoven (real name: Henry Louis Reginald; 1859–1920)   Composer Reginald De-Koven's family moved to England when he was 11. DeKoven graduated from St. John's College, Oxford, England in 1879. After graduation, DeKoven studied music with the best European instructors of his day. In 1882, DeKoven returned to the US. He settled in Chicago, worked in a brokerage firm, married Anna Farwell and started a dry-goods business that became very successful and supplied him with a steady income that allowed him to return to music. From 1890 through '20, DeKoven introduced over 450 popular songs through his operas and operettas. By far his most successful song was "Oh, Promise Me" from *Robin Hood* (see '07). DeKoven was also a famous music critic. In '02, he organized and conducted the Washington D.C. Symphony. Reginald DeKoven was inducted into the Songwriters' Hall of Fame when it was organized in '70. At http://www.songwritershalloffame. org/exhibit_audio_video.asp?exhibitId=242 hear "O Promise Me" performed by Edward Franklin.

Countess Ada DeLachau   Countess Ada DeLachau's only contribution to popular music was "Li'l Liza Jane" (see '16).

Tom Delaney   Tom Delaney was composer of the jazz classic "Jazz Me Blues" (see '21).

Eddie DeLange (1904–1949)   Eddie DeLange was a lyricist and bandleader during the '30s and '40s. In the opening years of the '30s, he joined composer/arranger Will Hudson to form one of the earliest swing bands, the Hudson-DeLange Orchestra. One of Hudson and De-Lange's very first collaborations was the very popular "Moonglow" (see '34). About '34, after several years in show business, including bit parts in several movies, De-Lange began to concentrate on writing lyrics. "What Are Little Girls Made of?" won him a contract with a famous music publishing house. During this period, he put words to Duke Ellington's "Solitude" and wrote "I Wish That I Were Twins," with Frank Loesser and Joseph Meyer. Between "35 and '38, the Hudson-DeLange band recorded more than 50 songs for Brunswick Records, many of them

composed by the two men fronting the group. The Hudson-DeLange partnership broke up in '38, when Eddie DeLange formed his own band. The DeLange Orchestra was also featured for a time on CBS Radio's *Dole Pineapple Show*. During this period, DeLange met composer Jimmy Van Heusen which resulted in a productive partnership which produced such hit songs as "Heaven Can Wait" (see '39) and "Darn That Dream" (see '40). During a 41-week run between '37 and '39, there was at least one Eddie DeLange song at the top of *Your Hit Parade*, every week but one. During the earlier years of World War II, he continued to turn out important hit tunes, among them the immortal "String of Pearls" (see '42). After the war Hollywood beckoned, and in '44, DeLange moved to L.A., where he wrote songs for such films as *The Bishop's Wife, Captain from Castille, The Kissing Bandit* and *Along the Navajo Trail* and *New Orleans*, which produced "Do You Know What It Means to Miss New Orleans." Eddie DeLange was inducted into the Songwriters' Hall of Fame in '89. At http://www.songwritershalloffame. org/exhibit_audio_video.asp?exhibitId=46 hear an audio clip of Mildred Bailey, accompanied by Benny Goodman's orchestra, singing DeLange's "Darn That Dream."

Vaughn DeLeath (real name: Leonore Vonderleath; 1896–1943)   Vaughn DeLeath was one of the first women singers to gain recognition on radio and one of several people who are credited with originating the crooning style of singing. She was very popular on radio during the late '20s and early '30s, appeared occasionally on Broadway and in vaudeville, and recorded frequently. She was also composer or lyricist for several songs, none of which were especially successful. Her most popular recordings were "Ukulele Lady" (see '25) and "Are You Lonesome Tonight?" in '27.

Jean Delettre   Jean Delettre was composer of "Hands Across the Table" (see '34).

Dorothy Dell (real name: Dorothy Dell Goff; 1915–1934)   After Dorothy Dell won the title "Miss New Orleans," she became a successful vaudeville act. In '31, she moved to New York City and appeared on Broadway in the *Ziegfeld Follies*. She became closely associated with singer Russ Colombo before his tragic, early death. In '33, she moved to Hollywood and signed a contract with Paramount Studios. Dell and Jack Oakie introduced "With My Eyes Wide Open, I'm Dreaming" in the film *Shoot the Works* (see '34). She also appeared in the Shirley Temple film *Little Miss Marker*. In '34, she was killed in an automobile accident.

Milton DeLugg (1918–)   Composer Milton DeLugg wrote "Hoop-Dee-Doo" (see '50). Although not quite as popular, he also penned "Orange-Colored Sky," "Shanghai," "Be My Life's Companion" and the theme song for *What's My Line*. DeLugg was also an accordionist, pianist, conductor and author. He studied music at UCLA. After college he became a staff musician at a Hollywood radio station and at some of the film studios. During World War II, he served in the Army Air Force in the Radio Production Unit.

C.M. Denison   Denison is primarily remembered as the composer of "My Rosary of Dreams" (see '11). He wrote with lyricist E.F. Dusenberry.

Lucien Denni (1886–1947) Lucien Denni was a composer, songwriter and conductor. He was educated at Columbia. He was a pianist in vaudeville and night club orchestras, and later, conductor of the Kansas City Symphony Orchestra and music director of the New Amsterdam Theatre in New York. He wrote one stage score, *Happy Go Lucky*, and composed for films, including cartoons. By far his most famous popular song composition was "Oceana Roll" (see '12).

Jack Denny (1895–1950) Orchestra leader Jack Denny started his musical career in Montreal in the early '20s. He and his band were especially successful during the early '30s. Denny and his orchestra were the first to introduce "In a Little Gypsy Tea Room" (see '35).

Will Denny (1860–1908) Will Denny, a recording industry pioneer, had a very popular Gram-o-Phone recording of "Any Old Place I Hang My Hat Is 'Home Sweet Home' to Me" (see '01).

Gene DePaul (1919–1988) During his early professional years, Gene DePaul trained as a classical pianist, performed as a pianist in dance bands and toured theaters as a singer and arranger for vocal groups. He also served in the U.S. Army during World War II. During the '40s and '50s, DePaul was under contract to Hollywood studios where he contributed to several films, including *Keep 'Em Flying, When Johnny Comes Marching Home, I Dood It, Broadway Rhythm, A Date with Judy, A Song Is Born, So Dear to My Heart, They Live by Night*, and *Seven Brides for Seven Brothers*. DePaul also wrote the Broadway score for *Li'l Abner*, with lyricist Johnny Mercer. DePaul collaborated with such famous lyricists as Johnny Mercer, Don Raye, Carolyn Leigh, Bob Russell and Charles Rinker. His most famous songs include "Mister Five by Five" (see '42), "Teach Me Tonight" (see '54), plus "Cow Cow Boogie," "If I Had My Druthers" and "I'll Remember April." Gene De Paul was inducted into the Songwriters' Hall of Fame in '85.

Lois Deppe Lois Deppe and Russell Wooding's Jubilee Singers introduced "Without a Song," in the Broadway musical *Great Day* (see '29). Deppe was a singer and saxophonist. His band was very popular in Pennsylvania and included the great jazz artist Earl Hines.

Peter DeRose (1900–1953) Peter DeRose's older sister taught him music. After high school, DeRose found work at a famous publishing firm. He also appeared with his wife, May Singhi Breen, on the NBC show *Sweethearts of the Air* for over 16 years ('23–'39). While performing on radio, DeRose was collaborating with lyricists like Carl Sigman, Jo Trent, Harry Richman, Charles Tobias, Billy Hill, Mitchell Parish, Bert Shefter, Benny Davis, Al Stillman, Sammy Gallop, Sam Lewis and Stanley Adams on songs. He contributed songs to Broadway productions like *Earl Carroll's Vanities of 1928* and *Ziegfeld Follies of 1934* plus the film scores for *Song of Love* and *The Fighting Seabees*. His most famous songs include "When Your Hair Has Turned to Silver" (see '31), "Wagon Wheels" (see '34), "Deep Purple" (see '39), plus "The Lamp Is Low," "Somebody Loves You," "I Heard a Forest Praying," and "A Marshmellow World." Peter DeRose was inducted into the Songwriters' Hall of Fame in '70. At http://www.songwritershalloffame.org/exhibit_audio_video.asp?exhibitId=257 hear an audio clip of Nino Tempo and April Stevens performing DeRose's "Deep Purple."

B.G. DeSylva (real name: George Gard DeSylva; 1895–1950) B.G. "Buddy" DeSylva became one of the most prolific and successful popular song lyricists. DeSylva was born in New York City, but grew up in California, where he graduated from the University of Southern California. In '18 Al Jolson discovered DeSylva in California and took him back to New York City. Jolson interpolated several of DeSylva's songs into the Broadway show *Sinbad*. DeSylva teamed up with Lew Brown and Ray Henderson in '25, and that trio produced several outstanding hits for the rest of the decade. After leaving the team in the early '30s, DeSylva collaborated with several other outstanding composers and occasionally wrote both words and music for songs. He became a Broadway show and film producer (he produced several Shirley Temple films) and wrote songs for several films. After that he became a music publisher and an executive in Capitol Records. Other than Brown and Henderson, De Sylva worked with several composers and lyricists including Gus Kahn, Al Jolson, George Gershwin, Jerome Kern, Vincent Rose, Louis Silvers, Joe Meyer, Victor Herbert, Emmerich Kalman, Ira Gershwin, Ballard MacDonald, Lewis Gensler, James Hanley, Nacio Herb Brown, Richard Whiting and Vincent Youmans. A partial list of DeSylva's well-known songs include "I'll Say She Does" (see '19), "Look for the Silver Lining" (see '21), "April Showers" (see '22), "Do It Again" (see '22), "A Kiss in the Dark" (see '22), "I'll Build a Stairway to Paradise" (see '23), "California, Here I Come" (see '24), "Memory Lane" (see '24), "Somebody Loves Me" (see '24), "Alabamy Bound" (see '25), "If You Knew Susie" (see '25), "Birth of the Blues" (see '26), "Black Bottom" (see '26), "The Best Things in Life Are Free" (see '27), "Just a Memory" (see '27), "The Varsity Drag" (see '27), "Sonny Boy" (see '28), "Together" (see '28), "Sunny Side Up" (see '29), "You're the Cream in My Coffee" (see '29), "Button Up Your Overcoat" (see '29), "Little Pal" (see '29), "You're an Old Smoothie" (see '33) and "Wishing" (see '39). Other well known DeSylva songs include "Just a Cottage Small," "When Day Is Done," "Lucky Day," "It All Depends on You," "Good News!," "Lucky in Love" and "If I Had a Talking Picture of You." He was an original member of the Songwriters' Hall of Fame in '70. At http://www.songwritershalloffame.org/exhibit_audio_video.asp?exhibitId=101 hear an audio clip of Marion Harris, accompanied by Isham Jones and his orchestra, perform DeSylva's "Look for the Silver Lining."

Emery Deutsch (1907–1997) Emery Deutsch was born in Budapest, Hungary and came to the U.S. in '15. He became a prominent bandleader in the U.S. in the '30 and '40s. He was particularly famous for his Gypsy violin style of playing. He composed and helped popularize "Play, Fiddle, Play" (see 33). He also wrote his theme song: "When a Gypsy Makes His Violin Cry." After Deutsch graduated from Julliard School of Music, he became Music Director of a small Queens's radio station. When the station was purchased by William Paley and turned into the new CBS network, Deutsch became Music Director for the new venture. His orchestra became popular greatly due to their exposure on CBS.

John DeVries (1915–1992) John DeVries was lyricist of "Oh! Look at Me Now" (see '41) and "(There'll Be) a Hot Time in the Town of Berlin (When the Yanks Go Marching in)" (see '44).

Al Dexter (real name: Clarence Albert Poindexter; circa 1902–1984) Dexter was primarily a country singer, songwriter and guitarist. His OKEH recording of "Pistol Packin' Mama," which he also wrote, was a big No. 1 hit on the pop charts (see '43). He was billed as Al Dexter and his Troopers. He had a few other recordings that charted on *Billboard*, but most of his recordings were much more popular with the country-western market. Dexter was inducted into the Nashville Songwriters Foundation Hall of Fame in '71. The Nashville Songwriters Foundation Hall of Fame website says Dexter was the first country artist to play on Broadway. Different sources disagree on his birth date; '02, '03, and '05 were given in various sources.

Guy d'Hardelot (see Helen Rhodes)

Dorothy Dickson (1893–1995) Dancer and actress Dorothy Dickson made her first appearance on Broadway as a dancer. She moved to London in '21 and became a musical star there. Her major claim to fame in the U.S. was introducing "These Foolish Things" in the musical *Spread It Abroad* (see '36).

Marlene Dietrich (real name: Maria Magdalene Dietrich von Losch; 1901–1992) German-born Marlene Dietrich was a very successful star of American movies in the '30s and '40s. Her half-talking, low, raspy singing voice was deemed extremely sexy. One of her most famous roles was in the '30 German film *The Blue Angel*, in which she introduced "Falling in Love Again." Her first film in the U.S. was *Morocco* ('31). She is especially remembered for her rendition of "See What the Boys in the Back Room Will Have" from the '39 movie *Destry Rides Again*. She introduced "Golden Earrings" in the movie *Golden Earrings* (see '48).

Howard Dietz (1896–1983) Howard Dietz was an important lyricist from the late '20s into the '60s. Dietz studied journalism at Columbia University, and then began working in advertising. After a stint in the Navy during World War I, he returned to advertising, doing ad and publicity work for several movie firms. In '19, he joined Goldwyn Pictures as publicity director. In '24, he became director of advertising and publicity for MGM, a position he held for over 30 years, eventually becoming a vice-president. It was Dietz who devised the MGM symbol, Leo the Lion, and its slogan, "Ars Gratia Artis." In the early years of his career, he collaborated primarily with composer Arthur Schwartz on Broadway shows like *The Little Show, Three's a Crowd* and *Between the Devil*. Later he wrote with Jerome Kern, Vernon Duke, Jimmy McHugh, and Ralph Rainger. After '38, Dietz and Schwartz dissolved their partnership for over a decade and Dietz concentrated on his work for MGM and writing material for radio and television. In '48, Dietz again teamed with Schwartz to write the score for *Inside U.S.A.*, which featured the song "Rhode Island Is Famous for You." Dietz and Schwartz again worked together to write the song "That's Entertainment" for the movie version of *The Band Wagon* (see '53). Dietz's best-known lyrics include "I Guess I'll Have to Change My Plan" (see '29), "Moanin' Low" (see '29), "Something to Remember You By" (see '30), "Dancing in the Dark" (see '31), "Louisiana Hayride" (see '32), "You and the Night and the Music" (see '35), "That's Entertainment" (see '53) plus "I Love Louisa," "A Shine on Your Shoes," "If There Is Someone Lovelier Than You" and "I See Your Face Before Me." His autobiography is entitled *Dancing in the Dark*. Dietz was admitted into the Songwriters' Hall of Fame in '72.

Herbert Dillea Herbert Dillea's only major contribution to popular music was as composer for "Absence Makes the Heart Grow Fonder" (see '01).

William Dillon (1877–1966) William Dillon was an American songwriter and vaudevillian. He is best known for his song "I Want a Girl (Just Like the Girl That Married Dear Old Dad)" (see '11). He was born in Cortland, New York and performed in vaudeville with his brothers, John and Harry.

Lee Dixon (1914–1953) Lee Dixon and Ruby Keeler introduced "Too Marvelous for Words" in the movie musical *Ready, Willing and Able* (see '37). Lee Dixon was an actor in vaudeville, stage and film. Alcoholism ruined his career and his life.

Mort Dixon (1892–1956) Lyricist Mort Dixon was an important writer during the '20s and '30s. Dixon served in the Army during World War I and directed the Army show, *Whiz Bang*, which toured France after the war. When he returned to New York, he started his music career as a vaudeville actor and had his first songwriting success with his first published song, "That Old Gang of Mine." His chief composer collaborators were Billy Rose, Ray Henderson, Harry Warren, Harry Woods, and Allie Wrubel. Dixon contributed to several stage scores and nearly 20 film scores. Dixon's most famous songs include "That Old Gang of Mine" (see '23), "Bye, Bye Blackbird" (see '26), "I'm Looking Over a Four Leaf Clover" ('27, see '48 when it was most popular), "I Found a Million Dollar Baby (in a Five and Ten Cent Store)" (see '31), "River, Stay 'Way from My Door" (see '32), plus "Bam Bam Bamy Shore," "You're My Everything," "Would You Like to Take a Walk?," "Mr. and Mrs. Is the Name," and "The Lady in Red." Mort Dixon entered the Songwriters' Hall of Fame in '70. At http://www.songwritershalloffame.org/exhibit_audio_video.asp?exhibitId=86 hear an audio clips of Benny Goodman and his orchestra with vocalist Annette Hanshaw perform Dixon's "Would You Like to Take a Walk?" and Nat "King" Cole perform Dixon's "I Found a Million Dollar Baby."

Gilbert Dodge Gilbert Dodge was co-writer with Harry Pease and Ed. G. Nelson on "Peggy O'Neil" (see '21).

Dolly Sisters Jennie (real name: Janszieka Deutsch; 1892–1941), Rosie (real name: Roszika Deutsch; 1892–1970). The Hungarian born Dolly Sisters were dancing headliners in vaudeville before Ziegfeld hired them for his 1911 *Follies*. They introduced "Be My Little Baby Bumble Bee" in those *Follies* (see '12). One internet source claimed the girls were identical twins. *The Dolly Sisters* ('45) is the Hollywood version of Jennie and Rosie's entertainment career.

Fats Domino (real name: Antoine Domino; (1928–) Fats Domino's estimated record sales are more than 65 million, which, if true, would rank him among the top dozen recording stars of all time. Domino was the first of the New Orleans rhythm and blues personalities to break into the national limelight. His first national success came in '48 with "The Fat Man." Over the next several years he collected some successful recordings, but nothing like his "Ain't That a Shame" (see '55). It was Pat Boone's recording of the song that was the biggest hit nationally, but the song's success brought more attention to Fats. Fats' most popular recordings were "I'm in Love Again" in '56 and his revival of the '40 song "Blueberry Hill" in '57. Most of Fats' songs were written with Dave Bartholomew. For more on Fats Domino, visit http://www.fatsonline.nl/.

Al Donahue (1903–1983) Boston-born bandleader Al Donahue was also a songwriter and arranger. Singer Paula Kelly was the most famous singer with his band primarily during the mid- to late '30s. Donahue's most popular recording was of "Jeepers Creepers" (see '39). Otherwise, his recording of "The Wise Old Owl" with vocalist Dee Keating (see '41) was his next most popular disk.

Walter Donaldson (1893–1947) Composer Walter Donaldson was one of the top writers of popular songs, with a long list of famous hits. He was particularly active from the early to mid–'20s through '28. Donaldson was a son of a piano teacher and showed an early talent for composition, writing songs for plays during high school. After high school, he worked as a clerk in a Wall Street brokerage house, but soon became a demonstrator for music publishers. He lost that job when the bosses caught him writing his own songs during business hours. Donaldson's first success came in '15 with the song "Back Home in Tennessee." Next came "You'd Never Know the Old Home Town of Mine," with a lyric by Howard Johnson. From '16 through '19, he wrote "The Daughter of Rosie O'Grady," and "How Ya Gonna Keep 'Em Down on the Farm?," among others. During World War I while he was entertaining troops at Camp Upton he met Irving Berlin. After the war, he joined Berlin's publishing firm and wrote hits such as "My Mammy" (see '21), "My Buddy" (see '22), "Carolina in the Morning" (see '23), "Yes Sir, That's My Baby" (see '25), "At Sundown" (see '27), and "My Blue Heaven" (see '27). Donaldson left Irving Berlin, Inc. in '28 to form his own publishing company, Donaldson, Douglas & Gumble. Under contract with film studios, Donaldson moved to Hollywood in '29. He would contribute songs to many film musicals. Donaldson worked with such lyricists as Edgar Leslie, Sam Lewis, Joe Young, Gus Kahn, Cliff Friend, Harold Adamson and Johnny Mercer. After Donaldson formed his own publishing company, he wrote "Makin' Whoopee" (see '29), "Love Me or Leave Me" (see '29), "Little White Lies" (see '30), "You're Driving Me Crazy" (see '30), "Did I Remember?" (see '36), "It's Been So Long" (see '36), "You" (see '36), and many others. Walter Donaldson was inducted into the Songwriters' Hall of Fame when it was organized in '70. At http://www.songwritershalloffame.org/exhibit_audio_video.asp?exhibitId=102 hear audio clips of "Little White Lies" performed by Waring's Pennsylvanians with Clare Hanlon and the Waring Girls, "Sweet Indiana Home" performed by Marion Harris with Isham Jones and his orchestra, and "You're Driving Me Crazy" performed by Guy Lombardo and his Royal Canadians with vocalists Carmen Lombardo.

Dorothy Donnelly (1880–1928) Lyricist and librettist, Dorothy Donnelly, began her entertainment career as an actress. She was, however, most noted for her operettas written with composer Sigmund Romberg. They wrote together on *Blossom Time*, *The Student Prince in Heidelberg*, and *My Maryland*. Her most famous songs include "Song of Love" from *Blossom Time* (see '22), and "Serenade" from *The Student Prince in Heidelberg* (see '24).

Walter Donovan (1888–1964) Walter Donovan composed the music for Arthur Fields lyrics of "Aba Daba Honeymoon" (see '14). Donovan was also co-composer of "One Dozen Roses" (see '42). After high school, Donovan became a member of a vaudeville piano and vocal act. Later, he was manager of some music publishing firms. His musical collaborators were Dick Jurgens, Don Bestor, Roger Lewis and Country Washburne.

Dorsey Brothers Orchestra Tommy and Jimmy Dorsey were very successful session musicians in the late '20s and early '30s. During that period they also recorded as the Dorsey Brothers Orchestra, but in '34, they formed the group as a permanent band. Glenn Miller was their arranger. They split in '35 and both were extremely successful with their own bands over the next several years. The most popular recording of the Dorsey Brothers Orchestra were "Lullaby of Broadway" (see '35) and "Chasing Shadows" (see '35). Bob Crosby was vocalist on "Lullaby of Broadway," while Bob Eberle was the vocal soloist on "Chasing Shadows." The brothers reunited in '53. They hosted a summer television show in '54 and '55–'56. Recordings by the Dorsey Brothers Orchestra are available at http://www.redhotjazz.com/bands.html.

Jimmy Dorsey (1904–1957) Jimmy Dorsey was one of the great bandleaders of the swing era. His primary instrument was the alto saxophone, but he was also a facile performer on the clarinet. Jimmy and his brother, Tommy, formed a joint band in '28. They stayed together until '35, when they broke up to form separate units. Jimmy's band was immediately successful and remained so until the early '50s. The band built a faithful following in the '30s and hit its peak in the early '40s. Their most popular recordings include "Is It True What They Say About Dixie" (their first No. 1 single in '36), "Change Partners" (see '38), "The Breeze and I" (see '40), "I Hear a Rhapsody" (see '41), "High on a Windy Hill" (see '41), "Green Eyes" (see '41), "Amapola" (see '41), "Maria Elena" (see '41), "My Sister and I" (see '41), "Blue Champagne" (see '41), "Tangerine" (see '42) and "Besame Mucho" (see '44). Jimmy was inducted into the Big Band/Jazz Hall of Fame in '83. Dorsey was the No. 6 top recording artist of the '40s and No. 16 for the '30s, making him the No. 20 recording artist of the first half of the 20th Century. Recordings by Jimmy Dorsey accompanied by the Dorsey Brothers Orchestra are available at http://www.redhotjazz.com/bands.html.

Tommy Dorsey (1905–1956) Tommy Dorsey became one of the most famous bandleaders and trombonists of the swing era. When the Dorsey brothers split up in '35, Jimmy kept the nucleus of the band, while Tommy took over the Joe Haymes band, renamed Tommy Dorsey and his orchestra. Over the next fifteen years they recorded extensively. From '40 to '42 Frank Sinatra was the star vocalist with Tommy's band. Other famous vocalists who sang with the group included Connie Haines, Jo Stafford, the Pied Pipers, and Dick Haymes. Tommy's major hits included "I'm Getting Sentimental Over You" (Tommy's theme song, see '32), "On Treasure Island" (see '35),

"Alone" (see '36), "The Music Goes 'Round and Around" (see '36), "You" (see '36), "Once in a While" (see '37), "Dipsy Doodle" (see '37), "Satan Takes a Holiday" (see '37), "Marie" (see '37), "The Big Apple" (see '37), "Music, Maestro, Please" (see '38), "Our Love" (see '39), "Indian Summer" (see '40), "All the Things You Are" (see '40), "I'll Never Smile Again" (see '40), "Dolores" (see '41), "There Are Such Things" (see '43) and "In the Blue of Evening" (see '43). And that names only the biggest hits! He was inducted into the Big Band/Jazz Hall of Fame in '81 and into the Popular Music Hall of Fame in 2003. Dorsey became the No. 3 top recording artist of the '30s and No. 7 for the '40s, making him the No. 12 recording artist of the first half of the 20th Century.

Larry Douglas (real name: Lipman Duckat; 1914–1996) Larry Douglas and Doretta Morrow introduced "We Kiss in a Shadow" in *The King and I* (see '51). Douglas appeared in eleven Broadway musicals between the mid-'30s and the early '70s, including *Jumbo, Panama Hattie, The Music Man,* and *Here's Love.*

Lew Douglas Lew Douglas was one of the co-writers of "Why Don't You Believe Me?" (see '52) and "Pretend" (see '53).

Mike Douglas (real name: Michael Delaney Dowd; 1925–2006) Michael Douglas was the featured male vocalist with Kay Kyser's band from '45 until '50. He was vocalist on Kyser's recordings of "Ole Buttermilk Sky" (see '46) and "The Old Lamp-Lighter" (see '46). Douglas dubbed the voice of Prince Charming in *Cinderella* ('50). In '66, he had a popular recording of "The Men in My Little Girl's Life" that reached No. 6 on the *Billboard* chart. In later years he became famous as a syndicated television talk show host.

Saxie Dowell (1904–1974) Saxie Dowell played saxophone and occasionally sang with Hal Kemp's band during the '20s and '30s. He organized his own band in '39 and helped popularize two novelty songs, which he wrote: "Three Little Fishies" (see '39) and "Playmates" (see '40). He remained in the business after a stint in the service during World War II and also worked in the music publishing business.

Johnny Downs (1913–1994) Johnny Downs introduced "In the Middle of a Kiss" in the film *College Scandal* (see '35). Downs was the host of a San Diego, California TV series, *The Johnny Downs Show* during the early '50s.

Alfred Drake (real name: Alfred Capurro; 1914–1992) Singer Alfred Drake is famous for his starring roles in three Broadway musicals: *Oklahoma!* (see '43), in which he introduced "Oh, What a Beautiful Mornin'," "People Will Say We're in Love," "Surrey with the Fringe on Top" and "Oklahoma!," *Kiss Me, Kate* ('49), in which he introduced "Wunderbar" and "So in Love," and *Kismet* ('53), in which he introduced "And This Is My Beloved." He also introduced "How High the Moon" in *Two for the Show* ('40, see '51 when it was most popular).

Ervin Drake (real name: Ervin Maurice Druckman; 1919–) Composer and lyricist Ervin Drake had a varied career, including work as a producer in television and as activist on behalf of songwriters. Drake graduated from City College of New York, where he studied social

sciences and graphic arts. It was many years later, during the '60s, that Drake formally studied music at the Julliard School of Music. His first success came in '42 when he wrote the English lyric for "Tico-Tico" (see '45). Drake's other successes include "I Believe" (see '53), "Perdido," and "It Was a Very Good Year." Collaborators included Irvin Graham, Jimmy Shirl, Al Stillman, Johnny Hodges, Ernesto Lecuona, Max Steiner, Paul Misraki, Robert Stolz, A. Donida, and Tony Renis. Between '48 and '62, he worked primarily in television, where he wrote, composed, and produced some 700 prime time network programs. He also wrote the lyrics and music for the Broadway musical *What Makes Sammy Run?* From '73 to '82, he was President of the American Guild of Authors and Composers, where he led a successful campaign to pass the US Copyright Law of '76. Drake was inducted into the Songwriters' Hall of Fame in '83.

Milton Drake (1912–) Milton Drake was a songwriter, composer, lyricist, author and market researcher. He began performing in vaudeville, radio and films as a child. Drake studied at the Baruch School of Business Administration, but also studied violin privately. He later wrote special material for theater and nightclub revues. Drake most often collaborated with Oscar Levant, Al Hoffman, Jerry Livingston, Louis Alter, Con Conrad, Ben Oakland, Milton Berle, Fred Spielman, Al Frisch, Artie Shaw and Morris Charlap. Some of Drake's most famous songs include "Mairzy Doats" (see '44) and "I'm a Big Girl Now" (see '46). He also co-wrote "Java Jive."

Paul Dresser (real name: John Paul Dreiser, Jr.; 1858–1906) Paul Dresser became one of the most important composers of the 1890s. Dresser was the fourth of thirteen children and the older brother of famous author Theodore Dreiser. He changed his name from Dreiser to Dresser after he left his hometown of Terre Haute at 16 to join a medicine show in Indianapolis. He also toured in vaudeville as a singer and monologist. In the late 1880s, Dresser moved to New York City and found work in the Billy Rice Minstrels and was a founding member of the music-publishing firm Howley, Haviland & Dresser. As a songwriter, Dresser relied heavily on the sentimental themes of home, boyhood, mother, patriotism, and romance. By the late 1890s, he was one of the most successful songwriters producing such hits as "My Gal Sal," "On the Banks of the Wabash, Far Away" (which became Indiana's state song), and "The Blue and the Gray." He composed and published his more than 100 songs. His "Way Down in Old Indiana" was also very popular (see '02). His last big hit, "My Gal Sal" (see '07), inspired a '42 movie of the same name, which was based loosely on his life. Paul Dresser was inducted into the Songwriters' Hall of Fame in '70.

Dave Dreyer (1894–1967) Composer Dave Dreyer wrote several successful songs during the '20s and '30s. He began his career as accompanist for such stars as Al Jolson and Sophie Tucker. In '23, he was hired as a staff pianist at Irving Berlin Music Company where he stayed until the late '40s. From '29 to '40, he contributed several songs to film scores. He became the head of the music department at RKO Radio. In '47, Dreyer left Irving Berlin's company to start his own publishing firm. Collaborating with lyricists such as Billy Rose, Ballard MacDonald, Herman Ruby and others, Dreyer wrote such songs as "Cecilia" (see '25), "Me and My Shadow" (see '27), "There's a Rainbow 'Round My Shoulder" (see '28), and "You Can't Be True, Dear" (see '48), plus "Back in Your Own Back Yard." Dave Dreyer was inducted into the Songwriters' Hall of Fame in '70.

Jack Drislane   Jack Drislane was lyricist for "The Good Old U.S.A." (see '06) and "Nobody's Little Girl" (see '07).

Al Dubin (1891–1945)   Al Dubin was born in Zurich, Switzerland; his family, originally from Russia, moved to Philadelphia when he was very young. Neither of his parents wanted him to pursue a music career, but by his teen years, he was cutting classes to attend Broadway shows and was spending a lot of time around Tin Pan Alley, where he tried to sell special material to vaudeville entertainers. During high school, Dubin excelled in athletics, however, his love of late nights, booze and girls often resulted in suspensions. Just before graduation, he was expelled from the private high school he attended. He enrolled in med school, but was expelled from there also. After that he found work as a staff writer at Witmark, a famous music-publishing firm. In '16, he wrote his first song "Twas Only an Irishman's Dream," but other successes didn't follow. He next worked as a singing waiter, until he entered the Army in World War I. After the war, he resumed songwriting, working with various composers. A couple of his early hits were "Just a Girl That Men Forget" (see '23), and "A Cup of Coffee, a Sandwich and You" (see '26). During the mid-'20s, he wrote music to promote silent films, and he was one of the first songwriters hired for talking pictures. He wrote many songs with Joseph Burke, such as "Tip Toe Through the Tulips" (see '29), "Dancing with Tears in My Eyes" (see '30), "Painting the Clouds with Sunshine" and "The Kiss Waltz." In the early '30s, he teamed with Harry Warren. They collaborated together for the remainder of the decade, often writing as many as 60 songs per year. Some of their famous songs include "Too Many Tears" (see '32), "Shadow Waltz" (see '33), "The Gold Digger's Song (We're in the Money)" (see '33), "Forty Second Street" (see '33), "Shuffle Off to Buffalo" (see '33), "You're Getting to Be a Habit with Me" (see '33), "I'll String Along with You" (see '34), "I Only Have Eyes for You" (see '34), "She's a Latin from Manhattan" (see '35), "I'll Sing You a Thousand Love Songs" (see '36), "Remember Me?" (see '37), "With Plenty of Money and You" (see '37), "September in the Rain" (see '37), and their Academy Award winner, "Lullaby of Broadway" (see '35). Other Dubin well-known songs from this period include "The Boulevard of Broken Dreams," "About a Quarter to Nine," and "Lulu's Back in Town." After '39, Dubin wrote with many other composers, including Jimmy McHugh and Will Grosz. Big hit songs from those collaborations include "South American Way" and "Along the Santa Fe Trail." Dubin provided the lyrics to the song "Indian Summer," set to music written in '19 by composer Victor Herbert (see '40). Dubin's lifestyle excesses began to cause health problems in the early '40s, and he died of barbiturate poisoning and pneumonia. However, his collaboration with Dave Franklin, "The Anniversary Waltz," was a hit in '41 and his lyric "Feudin' and Fightin'" was a hit in '47. Dubin and Burton Lane had written that song in '44. Dubin was inducted into the Songwriters' Hall of Fame in '70. At http://www.songwritershalloffame.org/ex

hibit_audio_video.asp?exhibitId=68 hear audio clips of Ben Selvin and his orchestra with vocalist Ruth Etting performing "Dancing with Tears in My Eyes," Anne Richards performing "Lullaby of Broadway," Rosemary Clooney singing "We're in the Money," Dakota Stanton performing "September in the Rain," Fats Waller performing "Lulu's Back in Town," Dinah Shore singing "I Only Have Eyes for You," Al Jolson performing "She's a Latin from Manhattan," Peggy Lee singing "You're Getting to Be a Habit with Me," and Denny Dennis with Roy Fox and his band performing "Keep Young and Beautiful."

Eddy Duchin (1910–1951)   Eddy Duchin became most famous as a piano showman. He began his career in the late '20s with Leo Reisman's orchestra. His flashy stage personality quickly elevated him to star status with the group. In the early '30s he took over Reisman's role as leader of the band. In the late '30s, Duchin updated the band's sound to reflect the nation's preference for swing. During World War II, Duchin served in the Navy in a non-musical role. After the war, he formed a new band. By the late '40s, he contracted leukemia, which worsened until his death in '51. His son, Peter, became a pianist and society bandleader also. Hollywood filmed *The Eddie Duchin Story* in '56. Duchin's biggest hit recordings were "Did You Ever See a Dream Walking?" (see '33), "Let's Fall in Love" (see '34), "Lovely to Look At" (see '35), "I Won't Dance" (see '35), "You Are My Lucky Star" (see '35), "Moon Over Miami" (see '36), "Take My Heart" (see '36), "Lights Out" (see '36), "I'll Sing You a Thousand Love Songs" (see '36) and "It's De-Lovely" (see '37). Duchin became the No. 5 top recording artist of the '30s, qualifying him as the No. 30 recording artist of the first half of the 20th Century.

Willie Lee Duckworth   Willie Lee Duckworth is credited with writing "Sound Off" (see '51). "Sound Off" was originally used for close-order drill training by the U.S. armed forces. It was first published in *The Cadence System of Teaching Close Order Drill* by Colonel Bernard Lentz.

S.H. Dudley (real name: Samuel Holland Rous; 1866–1947)   Dudley started his music career singing opera (1886–1898). By the end of the 1890s, he was the second tenor (usually the melody singer) in the Edison Male Quartet and the Haydn Quartet. He later became an executive at Victor, and then returned to recording under his own name. Dudley's most popular recording as a soloist was "When Reuben Comes to Town" (see '01).

Vernon Duke (real name: Vladmir Dukelsky; 1903–1969)   Vernon Duke was a composer of popular songs principally in the '30s and '40s. Even though his family was among the Russian nobility and he was a respected serious music composer, he and his family fled the country during the Russian Revolution. They settled for a while in '20 in Constantinople, where the teenaged Vladmir played the piano in cafes. In '21, the family traveled to New York City, where the young Dukelsky's classical compositions began to receive attention. It was around this time that Vladmir met George Gershwin. Gershwin encouraged him to write popular songs and also suggested a name change to fit better into his new American culture. Dukelsky accepted Gershwin's suggestion and became Vernon Duke, although he continued to use

Dukelsky for his classical compositions. In '24, he moved to Paris, where he wrote music for the ballet, his first symphony and other classical works He visited London often and contributed some songs to British musical comedies. In the late '20s, Duke returned to the U.S., and began to establish himself as a popular songwriter. By the early '30s, he had written his first complete Broadway score, a revue called *Walk a Little Faster*, which introduced his "April in Paris" (see '32). Duke wrote the music for "What Is There to Say" for the *Ziegfeld Follies of 1934*. He wrote both words and music for "Autumn in New York," which was introduced in a Broadway revue called *Thumbs Up* ('35). *The Ziegfeld Follies of 1936* introduced Duke and Ira Gershwin's "I Can't Get Started" (see '36). Duke's *Cabin in the Sky* came to Broadway in '40. It featured an African American cast and introduced "Taking a Chance on Love" (see '43). He became an American citizen and, during World War II, was a Lieutenant Commander in the U.S. Coast Guard. He wrote the score for a Coast Guard revue that starred the then-unknown Sid Caesar. After the war, he lived in France for a while where he wrote French popular songs, and also composed some classical works. In the late '40s, he returned to the U.S., living first in New York and later in California. By the mid-'50s, he had dropped the name Dukelsky, so that both his classical and popular compositions were credited to Vernon Duke. Duke's most famous popular song is "April Showers" (see '22) but some of his other successes include "Autumn in New York," "I Can't Get Started" and "Taking a Chance on Love." Vernon Duke was elected to the Songwriters' Hall of Fame in '70. At http://www.songwritershalloffame.org/exhibit_audio_video.asp?exhibitId=64 hear audio clips of "Autumn in New York" performed by Louis Armstrong and Ella Fitzgerald and "April in Paris" sung by Sarah Vaughan.

Todd Duncan (1903–1998) Todd Duncan, as Porgy, introduced several songs in George Gershwin's folk opera *Porgy and Bess* including "Bess, You Is My Woman," and "I Got Plenty o' Nuttin'" (see '35). Duncan was Gershwin's personal choice to portray Porgy. He played the role over 1,800 times. He also originated the role of Stephen Kumalo in Kurt Weill's *Lost in the Stars*. In addition to his Broadway roles, Duncan appeared on the concert stage and taught voice at Howard University in Washington, D.C. for over fifty years. Duncan had obtained his musical training at Butler University in Indianapolis and from Columbia University Teachers College. During the '30s and '40s, he appeared in operas with several major opera companies.

Irene Dunn (1898–1990) Irene Dunn began her stage career in Louisville, Kentucky when she appeared in *A Midsummer Night's Dream* at age 5. After her father died when she was 12, the family moved from Kentucky to Indiana. There she studied voice and piano. After she graduated from high school, she studied music at a music conservatory in Indianapolis. Upon graduation she accepted a position as a music and art teacher in East Chicago, Indiana. On the way to the job, she read a newspaper ad for a scholarship contest. Irene won the contest and studied at the Chicago Music College for a year. She then headed for New York City. She auditioned for the Metropolitan Opera Company, but wasn't accepted. She did get the leading role in a road theater company and that led to several plays. In '28, Irene married Francis Dennis Griffin, a

dentist. They remained together until his death in '65. Her performance in an east coast production of *Show Boat* caught Hollywood's attention. She signed a contract with RKO in the early '30s. In '31, she received the first of five Academy Award nominations for her appearance in *Cimarron*. Ms. Dunn introduced "Lovely to Look At" in the film version of *Roberta* (see '35). Her second Oscar nomination came from her appearance in *Theodora Goes Wild* ('36). She received a third nomination for *The Awful Truth* ('37). Next came nominations for *Love Affair* ('39) and *I Remember Mama* ('48). Her last major movie was *It Grows on Trees* in '52. After that she appeared occasionally as a guest on television. President Eisenhower appointed her as a special U.S. delegate to the United Nations in '57.

Paul Durand Paul Durand adapted French composer Maurice Ravel's "Bolero" into the popular song "All My Love" (see '50).

Jimmy Durante (1893–1980) Jimmy Durante, nicknamed "the Schnoz" or "schnozzola" because of his large nose, was one of the most popular performers in show business. He appeared in seven Broadway productions, most memorably in *Jumbo* ('35) and *Red, Hot and Blue!* ('36). His first starring role in films was *Palooka* ('34), where he performed his famous "Inka Dinka Doo." He was particularly funny performing "Toscanini, Iturbi and Me" in *Music for Millions* ('44); he teamed with Frank Sinatra for a duet of "The Song's Gotta Come from the Heart" in *It Happened in Brooklyn* ('47) and he was prominent in the screen version of *Jumbo* ('62). His raspy, half-talking singing style was one of his trademarks. Another part of his act consisted of his slaughtering the English language. Some recordings from '20 by Jimmy Durante's Jazz Band are available at http://www.redhotjazz.com/bands.html.

Deanna Durbin (real name: Edna Mae Durbin; 1921–) Deanna Durbin starred in several movie musicals from '37 through the late '40s. Her first film was a short with Judy Garland. Because of her young age, she played teenage roles, but later she matured into more romantic roles. She married a French film director in the late '50s and retired from the business to live in France. She introduced "Amapola" in the '39 film *First Love* (see '41). Her operatic soprano voice was best suited for dramatic songs and popular songs derived from the classics.

Eddie Durham (1906–1987) Eddie Durham was one of the co-writers of "I Don't Want to Set the World on Fire" (see '41). Durham was one of the first to use the electric guitar in jazz. He also played trombone and was a swing-era arranger. He and his brothers organized a family band. He later played with Bennie Moten, Jimmie Lunceford and Count Basie. Durham wrote arrangements for Artie Shaw and Glenn Miller (he was the arranger of Miller's "In the Mood"). He led his own band for a couple of years in the early '40s and led an all-female, except for himself, group.

E.F. Dusenberry Dusenberry is primarily remembered for collaborating with C. M. Denison on "My Rosary of Dreams" (see '11) and "Have You Forgotten, Marguerite." He also furnished the lyrics for Edward Elgar's "Land of Hope and Glory."

D. Eardley-Wilmot D. Eardley-Wilmot wrote the lyrics for the popular song "Little Grey Home in the West" (see '14).

Mary Earl (real name: Robert A. King; 1862–1932) Mary Earl is a pseudonym for Robert A. "Bobo" King of New York City. In '18, he went to work for Shapiro-Bernstein Music Publishers under a contract to produce four songs per month. One of the songs he produced during that period was "Beautiful Ohio" (see '19).

R.A. Eastburn (see J. E. Winner)

Jimmy Eaton (1906–1979) Songwriter Jimmy Eaton was also a guitarist in various bands until the late '30s when he was hired by a famous publishing house to write songs. His best-known songs were written with Terry Shand. They were "Cry, Baby, Cry" (see '38), "I Double Dare You" (see '38), "Blue Champagne" (see '41) and "Dance with a Dolly" (see '44). His chief musical collaborators included Terry Shand, Larry Wagner, and Grady Watts.

Ray Eberle (1919–1979) Ray Eberle was the featured male vocalist with the Glenn Miller band at the zenith of the big bands. His older brother, Bob Eberly (notice the different spelling of the last name; Bob changed the spelling, Ray kept the original family spelling), was the male vocalist for the Jimmy Dorsey orchestra. In '40 and again in '42, Ray was voted the No. 1 male band singer, edging out Frank Sinatra, in *Billboard's* college survey. Eberle's voice was featured on dozens of the Miller band's recordings and on their radio show. He was featured on "Over the Rainbow" (see '39), "Moon Love" (see '39), "Wishing" (see '39), "Stairway to the Stars" (see '39), "Blue Orchids" (see '39), "Careless" (see '40), "When You Wish Upon a Star" (see '40), "Blueberry Hill" (see '40), "Imagination" (see '40), "Fools Rush in" (see '40), "My Prayer" (see '40), "Elmer's Tune" (see '41), "You and I" (see '41), "Moonlight Cocktail" (see '42) and "The White Cliffs of Dover" (see '42), among others. He left the band shortly before Miller entered military service in '42 and worked as a single. In the late '40s and '50s, after Miller's death, he led the Miller band.

Bob Eberly (1916–1981) Bob Eberly was the featured male vocalist of the Jimmy Dorsey band in the heyday of the big bands. His brother, Ray Eberle (different spelling of last name), was the featured male vocalist with the Glenn Miller band. Bob began singing with the Dorsey Brothers Orchestra just before their split. At the separation, Eberly stayed with Jimmy. Bob was featured on several of Jimmy Dorsey's famous recordings including "Chasing Shadows" (see '35), "Is It True What They Say About Dixie?" (see '36), "Change Partners" (see '38), "Deep Purple" (see '39), "The Breeze and I" (see '40), "Amapola" (see '41), "Green Eyes" (see '41), "Maria Elena" (see '41), "My Sister and I" (see '41), "Blue Champagne" (see '4), "Yours" (see '41), "I Hear a Rhapsody" (see '41), "Tangerine" (see '42), and "Besame Mucho" (see '44). Eberly left the band for military service in '43 and never regained his popularity after the war. In the '50s he and Helen O'-Connell appeared with Ray Anthony's band on a TV series. Bob was elected to the Big Band/Jazz Hall of Fame in 2003. Bob ranked No. 3 for three straight years in the early '40s in *Billboard's* college poll.

Nelson Eddy (1901–1967) Nelson Eddy was a star of several operetta movies during the '30s and '40s. When he teamed up with Jeanette MacDonald in a series of operetta-style musicals, they became top box-office attractions. His most famous movie roles came in *Naughty Marietta* ('35), *Rose Marie* ('36), *Rosalie* ('37), *Girl of the Golden West* and *Sweethearts* ('38), *Bitter Sweet* and *New Moon* ('40) and *Knickerbocker Holiday* ('44). Eddy's recordings weren't especially popular, but his Victor recordings of "Ah! Sweet Mystery of Life" and "I'm Falling in Love with Someone" from *Naughty Marietta* (see '10), "When I Grow Too Old to Dream" from *The Night Is Young* (see '35) and "Indian Love Call" with Jeanette MacDonald from *Rose Marie* (see '25) were well received. Eddy and Eleanor Powell introduced the title song of the movie musical *Rosalie* (see '38). A Nelson Eddy Archive has been established at the American Music Research Center, College of Music, at the University of Colorado at Boulder. This archive will house donations of collections of his music and memorabilia.

Cliff Edwards (1895–1971) Cliff "Ukulele Ike" Edwards was a very popular singer in the '20s and '30s. He appeared in the Broadway musicals *Lady Be Good!* ('24), *Sunny* ('25), *Ziegfeld Follies of 1927* and *George White's Scandals of 1936*. He had roles in more than twenty movies in the late '20s and early '30s. Through the rest of the '30s and into the '40s he appeared in an additional forty-seven films, mostly musicals. Edwards' most famous recordings were "I Can't Give You Anything but Love" (see '28) and "Singin' in the Rain" (see '29). Edwards appeared in over fifty early movie musicals. His voice is probably most familiar to modern audiences as the squeaky-voiced Jiminy Cricket in the feature-length Disney cartoon *Pinocchio*, where he performed "When You Wish Upon a Star" (see '40). Recordings by Cliff Edwards (accompanied by the Californians, Cliff Edwards and the Eton Boys, Cliff Edwards and his Hot Combination, and accompanied by Andy Iona and his Islanders) are available at http://www.redhotjazz.com/bands.html.

Gus Edwards (1879–1945) Songwriter and vaudeville legend Gus Edwards was born in Hohensalza, Prussia. When he was 7 years old, the family immigrated to the U.S. and settled in Brooklyn. As a child, Edwards worked in the family cigar store and attended school until he found jobs as a singer in various lodge halls, ferryboat lounges, saloons and athletic clubs. Edwards was later hired as a song plugger for a music publisher. He also worked at the Bowery Theater and performed in several variety shows. In 1896, vaudeville agent, James Hyde formed Newsboys Quintet with Edwards and four other boys for a nation-wide tour. While on tour, Edwards wrote his first song "All I Want Is My Black Baby Back." While the Newsboys Quintet was entertaining soldiers during the Spanish-American War, Edwards met Will Cobb. The two began collaborating on songs. Their collaboration lasted two decades. In '05, Edwards formed his own publishing company in New York City and began work on his own vaudeville revue entitled *School Boys and Girls*, which opened in '07. The act was so successful that it ran for over twenty years. Some of the young talent Edwards' discovered for his revue included Groucho Marx, Eddie Cantor, Walter Winchell, Elsie Janis, Sally Rand, Ray Bolger, Ina Ray Hutton, Lila Lee, George Jessel, the Duncan Sisters and Georgie Price. Edwards introduced so many stars that he became known as "The Star Maker." The revue featured music written by Gus Edwards, mainly with Will Cobb. One of Edwards' biggest hits was "School Days

(When We Were a Couple of Kids)," which sold millions of copies of sheet music. "School Days" became one of the most recorded songs in the pre-rock era (see '07). Other Edwards-Cobb songs include "I Just Can't Make My Eyes Behave" (see '07), "Sunbonnet Sue" (see '08) and "If I Was a Millionaire" (see '10). Edwards also collaborated with Vincent Bryan on "In My Merry Oldsmobile" (see '05) and with Edward Madden on "By the Light of the Silvery Moon" (see '10) and "Look Out for Jimmy Valentine" (see '11). While writing, directing, producing and starring in his own revue, Edwards also found time to write music for other Broadway productions, including some music for Florenz Ziegfeld and for Weber and Fields. Edwards also became a charter member of the new performing rights organization, ASCAP (American Society of Composers, Authors and Publishers) in '14. In '28, Edwards moved to Hollywood to write for films. He wrote film scores with Joe Goodwin, most notably *Orange Blossom Time* and appeared in a couple of films. However, in '30, he left the film industry and returned to the vaudeville where he continued to write and introduce his own songs on stage. Edwards retired in '39, the same year Paramount Pictures released a biographical movie of Edwards' life, *The Star Maker*, starring Bing Crosby. Gus Edwards was inducted into the Songwriters' Hall of Fame in '70. At http://www.songwritershalloffame.org/exhibit_audio_video.asp?exhibitId=229 hear audio clips of "By the Light of the Silv'ry Moon" and "In My Merry Oldsmobile" both performed by Billy Murray.

Michael Edwards (1893–1962) Michael Edwards was the composer of "Once in a While" (see '37). Edwards was a composer, arranger and music editor for Mills Music. The Michael Edwards Collection is available at Stony Brook University.

Raymond B. Egan (1890–1952) Lyricist Raymond Egan was born in Windsor, Ontario, Canada. Egan's family moved to Michigan in 1892 where he attended college at the University of Michigan. After graduation, Egan worked as a bank clerk and later as a staff writer for a music publisher in Detroit. Egan moved to New York City in the early '20s where he wrote songs for several Broadway musicals and a few films, but his primary focus was writing song lyrics without the restrictions of a storybook or a preexisting musical score. Throughout the '20s and into the '30s, Egan collaborated with several composers including Walter Donaldson, Ted FioRito, Harry Tierney, Richard Whiting and Gus Kahn. Some of Egan's most remembered songs include "Till We Meet Again" (see '19), "Japanese Sandman" (see '20), "Ain't We Got Fun?" (see '21), "I Never Knew I Could Love Anybody the Way I'm Loving You" (see '21) and "Sleepy Time Gal" (see '26). Raymond Egan was elected into the Songwriters' Hall of Fame in '70. At http://www.songwritershalloffame.org/exhibit_audio_video.asp?exhibitId=241 hear an audio clip of "Ain't We Got Fun?" performed by Van and Schenck.

Edward Eliscu (1902–1998) Lyricist, playwright, producer and actor, Edward Eliscu developed a love for music and acting as a young boy. After receiving his degree from the City College of New York, he began his show business career performing in Broadway plays. Eliscu wrote his first Broadway score, *Great Day!*, with composer Vincent Youmans and co-lyricist Billy Rose. Well-known songs from the score include "Great Day," "More Than

You Know" and "Without a Song" (see '29). Eliscu wrote several other Broadway scores, but none were as famous as *Great Day!* He also contributed to the revues *9:15 Revue*, the '30 *Garrick Gaieties* and *The Little Show*. In the early '30s, Eliscu began writing songs for films as well as writing screenplays. He produced songs for over 40 films, the most notable being the Fred Astaire movie musical *Flying Down to Rio* ('34). "Carioca" (see '34) from the film earned Eliscu an Academy Award nomination for Best Song. Other popular songs from the film score were the title song and "Orchids in the Moonlight" (see '34). Eliscu's talent as a playwright and screenwriter was widely recognized. One of his screenplays was for *The Gay Divorcee*, another famous Fred Astaire and Ginger Rogers' movie musical. Eliscu collaborated with several famous songwriters including Vincent Youmans, Billy Rose, Jay Gorney, John Green, Gus Kahn, Vernon Duke and Billy Hill. Edward Eliscu was inducted into the Songwriters' Hall of Fame in '75. At http://www.songwritershalloffame.org/exhibit_audio_video.asp?exhibitId=251 hear an audio clip of Connie Boswell singing "Carioca" accompanied by Victor Young and his orchestra.

Duke Ellington (real name: Edward Kennedy Ellington; 1899–1974) Duke Ellington became one of America's musical giants: a composer, a bandleader and an arranger. Most of his compositions were jazz works, but several that started as instrumental jazz compositions became lastingly popular songs. Ellington began by leading a small band in '18 in Washington, D.C., and he had a highly successful career for the next half-century and more. His band recorded a large catalog of disks and appeared in seven motion pictures. In '27, Ellington's band was hired to play regularly at the Cotton Club; they stayed five years and were heard regularly on broadcasts from the club. By the early '30s they were well known and Ellington was beginning to be recognized as a composer. After World War II, big bands weren't as fashionable. Nevertheless, Ellington kept his band together, often subsidizing it from his royalties as a composer. Most of Ellington's songs were written as instrumental pieces, with words added at some later date. Some of his best-known songs include "Mood Indigo" (see '31), "It Don't Mean a Thing" (see '32), "Sophisticated Lady" (see '33), "I Let a Song Go Out of My Heart" (see '38), "Don't Get Around Much Any More" (see '43), "I'm Beginning to See the Light" (see '45) plus "In a Sentimental Mood," "I Got It Bad (andThat Ain't Good)," "Do Nothin' Till You Hear from Me," and "Satin Doll." The Ellington band's theme song was Billy Strayhorn's "Take the 'A' Train." Their recording of the tune was inducted into the Grammy Hall of Fame in '76. Ellington and his band's most popular recordings include "Three Little Words" (see '30) with the Rhythm Boys, "Cocktails for Two" (see '34) and "I Let a Song Go Out of My Heart" (see '38). Other not quite so popular recordings include "Stormy Weather," "Moonglow," "Solitude," "Cotton," "Caravan," "Don't Get Around Much Anymore" and "I'm Beginning to See the Light." Duke was elected to the Songwriters' Hall of Fame in '71. He is also a member of the Big Band/Jazz Hall of Fame. Ellington became the No. 15 top recording artist of the '30s. At http://www.songwritershalloffame.org/exhibit_audio_video.asp?exhibitId=9 hear audio clips of "Sophisticated Lady" performed by Rosemary Clooney, "It Don't Mean a Thing" performed by Louis Armstrong, "Drop Me Off in Harlem" performed by Louis Armstrong, "Solitude" performed by Billie Holiday, "I Got It Bad (andThat Ain't Good)" performed by Ella Fitzgerald, "Prelude to a Kiss" performed by Sarah Vaughan, "I'm a Lucky So-and-So" performed by Al Hibbler, "Me and You" performed by Ivie Anderson, "Just Squeeze Me" performed by Ray Nance, and "Do Nothing Till You Hear from Me" performed by Billie Holiday. Recordings by Ellington (Duke Ellington and his Cotton Club Orchestra, Duke Ellington and his Kentucky Club Orchestra, Duke Ellington and his Memphis Men, and Duke Ellington and his orchestra) are available at http://www.redhotjazz.com/bands.html.

Jack Elliott (1914–)   Jack Elliott was lyricist of "Sam's Song" (see '50).

Zo Elliott (1891–1964)   Zo Elliott was a songwriter, composer and author. Elliott was educated at Yale, Trinity College (Cambridge, England), Columbia Law School, the American Conservatory in Fontainebleau, France and in private music study with famous teachers like Nadia Boulanger and Leonard Bernstein. His chief musical collaborator was Stoddard King. Together they wrote the World War I classic "There's a Long, Long Trail" (see '16).

Anita Ellis (1926–)   Anita Ellis, singing for Rita Hayworth, introduced "Put the Blame on Mame" in the film *Gilda* (see '46). She also sang for Vera-Ellen in *Three Little Words* ('50).

Mary Ellis (real name: May Belle Elsas; 1897–2003)   Mary Ellis was a member of the Metropolitan Opera Company from '18–'22. There she sang with Enrico Caruso, the famous tenor, before switching to the Broadway stage. After a few dramatic roles, she garnered the title role in *Rose Marie*. The show's most lasting song, "Indian Love Call," was introduced by Mary Ellis and Dennis King. She helped introduced "Paris in the Spring" in *Paris in the Spring* (see '35). Ellis relocated to London in the mid–'30s.

Norman Ellis   Norman Ellis was the composer of "Carelessly" (see '37).

Bob Ellsworth (real name: Robert H. Ellsworth; 1895–?)   Bob Ellsworth was one of the co-writers of "Somebody Else Is Taking My Place" (see '42). Ellsworth was a songwriter, author, and publisher. He was educated at the Boston Conservatory of Music. After serving in the military during World War I, he managed the offices of a couple of New York music publishers, then became a publisher himself.

Ziggy Elman (real name: Harry Finkelman; 1914–1968)   Ziggy Elman was one of the leading trumpeters of the big band era. Elman joined the Benny Goodman band in the fall of '36. When trumpet star Harry James left at the end of '38, Elman became the leading trumpet soloist. He in turn left the Goodman band in '40 and joined Tommy Dorsey. He remained with Dorsey, except for military service and a short stint leading his own band, for most of the '40s. Elman is particularly famous for his trumpet solo on the Goodman band's recording of Elman's composition "And the Angels Sing" (see '39).

Ida Emerson   Joe E. Howard and Ida Emerson met while they were performing in vaudeville. Ms. Emerson became Howard's second of nine wives. She and Howard are credited with writing "Hello, Ma Baby" (see '00), which she helped to popularize. She also helped popularize "Good-Bye, My Lady Love" ('04). Ms. Emerson appeared on Broadway in *In New York Town* ('05) and *The District Leader* ('06).

Bob Emmerich (real name: Robert D. Emmerich; 1905–1988)   Bob Emmerich was the composer of "The Big Apple" (see '37) and co-lyricist of "Our Love" (see '39). Emmerich, a pianist and composer, played with the Tommy Dorsey band. According to his New York Times obituary, Emmerich's wife, Miriam, said of the song "The Big Apple," "Walter Winchell liked it so much he started calling New York 'the Big Apple.'"

H. Engelmann   H. Engelmann was the composer of "Melodie d'Amour" ('03), which became "Melody of Love" (see '55).

William Engvick   William Engvick was the lyricist for "The song from *Moulin Rouge* (Where Is Your Heart?)" (see '53).

John Valentine Eppell   "Missouri Waltz" was originally published as a piano instrumental in '14 (see '17 when it was most popular). Frederick Knight Logan was credited as the "arranger" on the original sheet music, which claimed that the song had come from "an original melody procurred by John Valentine Eppell." The Missouri State Archives website lists a number of individuals variously credited for the original melody; all are African American. Several websites now credit the music to Eppell, with Logan as the arranger.

Ernie Erdman (1879–1946)   Composer and lyricist Ernie Erdman was the pianist in the New Orleans Original Jazz Band. He also was on the staff of several Chicago music publishers. His chief musical collaborators included Gus Kahn, Ted FioRito, Robert King, Elmer Schoebel, and Billy Meyers. Erdman's most well known compositions include "No! No! Nora!" (see '23), "Toot Toot Tootsie" (see '23) and "Nobody's Sweetheart" (see '24). Erdman was co-lyricist with Gus Kahn for "Nobody's Sweetheart" and "Toot Toot Tootsie." He was co-composer with Ted FioRito on "No! No! Nora!"

Ralph Erwin (real name: Ralf Erwin; 1896–1943)   Polish composer Ralph Erwin composed the music for "I Kiss Your Hand, Madame" (see '29).

D.A. Esrom (see Dorothy Terriss)

Ruth Etting (1907–1978)   Ruth Etting was a major singing star of the '20s and '30s, first in nightclubs and then on Broadway. She was known as a torch singer. She got her big break in the *Ziegfeld Follies of 1927*. Other Broadway musicals in addition to *Whoopee* were *Simple Simon* ('30) and the *Ziegfeld Follies of 1931*. Ms. Etting introduced "Get Happy" in the *9:15 Revue* (see '30). She also appeared often on radio during the '30s and occasionally in movies, but by the late '30s her career began to wane. Ruth Etting's most prosperous period in the recording industry came between the mid–'20s and the mid–'30s. Her most popular recording was "Life Is a Song" (see '35), but several others did well including "Love Me or Leave Me" (see '29), "I'll Get By" (see '44), "Lonesome and Sorry," "'Deed I Do," "Shaking the Blues Away," "Mean to Me," and "Ten Cents a Dance." Etting's film biography was the '55 movie *Love Me or Leave Me*, which starred

Doris Day. Go to http://www.ruthetting.com/ for more on Ruth Etting. Some of her music is offered in RealAudio files.

George Evans (1870–1915) Renowned minstrel George "Honey Boy" Evans, a Welshman, wrote the music for "In the Good Old Summer Time" (see '02). Evans, his future wife, singer Blanche Ring and comedian-lyricist Ren Shields were all involved in the writing and introduction process. Jack Norworth and Albert Von Tilzer wrote a song titled "Honey Boy" in '07 that was a tribute to Evans.

Ray Evans (1915–2007) Ray Evans was a lyricist of several popular songs from the '40s and '50s. Most of his lyrics have been written for songs from movies. After graduating from high school, Evans attended the University of Pennsylvania. It was there he met a fellow student named Jay Livingston who had formed a dance band. Evans joined the band playing reed instruments. The band played for various college functions, in local nightclubs and on cruise ships. Evans and Livingston began writing songs and after their graduation from Penn in '37, they moved to New York City to work as Tin Pan Alley songwriters. Their first hit song was "G'bye Now." Evans and Livingston moved to Hollywood in the mid–'40s and, under contract to Paramount Studios, stayed for the next decade. Around the mid–'50s, the team began free-lancing for various movie studios, sometimes contributing only a song or two and sometimes writing the complete score. Their film credits include *My Friend Irma, Here Come the Girls, All Hands on Deck, The Stork Club, Sorrowful Jones, The Lemon Drop Kid, Fancy Pants, Here Comes the Groom, Somebody Loves Me, Son of Paleface* and *The Man Who Knew Too Much*. Recognizing their contribution to films, Livingston and Evans were presented with a star on the Hollywood Boulevard Walk of Fame in '95. The team returned to New York City in the late '50s, where they wrote a couple of Broadway musicals, neither of which proved to be very successful. Evans and Livingston also produced the theme or title songs for television shows such as *Bonanza, Ed* and *Mr. Lucky*. They also wrote special material for several famous stars for their nightclub acts and television specials. They have written material for Bob Hope since '47 (they had written songs for several of Hope's films). Some of Evans' most famous lyrics include "To Each His Own" (see '46), "Golden Earrings" (see '48), 1949's Academy Award winner "Buttons and Bows" (see '48), 1950's Academy Award winner "Mona Lisa" (see '50), "Silver Bells," 1956's Academy Award winner "Que Sera, Sera," and "Tammy" ('57). According to the Livingston and Evans website, they have 26 songs that have sold a million or more records. They report the total record sales of their songs to be over 400 million. Ray Evans was elected into membership of the Songwriters' Hall of Fame in '77.

Redd Evans (1912–1972) Lyricist Redd Evans began his career as a hillbilly act, but later wrote words and sometimes music for popular songs. He eventually became a publisher. He collaborated with David Mann on the smash hit "There! I've Said It Again" (see '45). Other hit songs include "Ballerina" (see '47) and "Too Young" (see '51).

Tolchard Evans (?–1978) Tolchard Evans was the composer of "If" (see '51) and "Lady of Spain" (see '52).

British writers Evans and Erell Reaves wrote "Lady of Spain" in '31, but it was put back into circulation in '52 when Eddie Fisher's recording of the song became a hit. Ian Whitcomb is a highly respected performer, composer, and music historian, claims on his website (http://www.picklehead.com/ian/uncle.html) that his uncle wrote "Lady of Spain." He also claims that the name Erell Reaves was an amalgam of the last five letters of Damerell (he claims his uncle also wrote using the name Stanley J. Damerell) and the last six letters of Robert Hargreaves (listed as co-lyricist). So that, he claims Tolchard Evans and Erell Reaves is the same person, his uncle.

Frank Eyton (1894–1962) British lyricist Frank Eyton was co-lyricist of "Body and Soul" (see '30).

William E. Faber William E. Faber was a co-lyricist of "You Were Only Fooling (While I Was Falling in Love)" (see '48).

Nanette Fabray (real name: Ruby Bernadette Nanette Fabares; 1920–) Nanette Fabray began her show business career as a child vaudevillian. At age 7, she appeared in some of the Our Gang film shorts. She gained considerable fame on Broadway in *High Button Shoes* and *Love Life*. Ms. Fabray, Fred Astaire, Oscar Levant, and Jack Buchanan performed "That's Entertainment" in the film version of the Broadway revue *The Band Wagon* (see '53). She also performed "Louisiana Hayride" (see '32) in the film and with Astaire and Buchanan performed the hilarious "Triplets." In the '50s she became a TV star, winning three Emmy Awards for her appearances on the Sid Caesar show. She had replaced Imogene Coca on the program.

Sammy Fain (real name: Samuel Feinberg; 1902–1989) Sammy Fain became an important composer of popular song melodies whose career spans from the '20s into the '70s. He collaborated with several lyricists, notably Paul Francis Webster, E.Y. Harburg, Jack Yellen, Mitchell Parish and Lew Brown. Fain taught himself to play the piano and began composing popular songs while he was still in high school. He sent some of these to publishers, but they were rejected. After completing high school, Fain went to New York City to pursue songwriting. His first job in the city was in the stockroom of Mills Music Publishing. One day his boss caught Fain playing some of his own songs in the audition room, which landed him a job as a song plugger. He worked as a song plugger for several different publishers. During this period, he met singer Artie Dunn, and they formed a singing team that was popular in vaudeville and on radio. Fain continued writing songs, and in '25 he collaborated with Irving Mills and Al Dubin on his first published song, "Nobody Knows What a Red-Headed Mama Can Do." About this time, Fain met lyricist Irving Kahal; they formed a songwriting team that lasted until Kahal's death in '42. Their first successful song was "Let a Smile Be Your Umbrella" in '27. Another early success for the team was "Wedding Bells (are Breaking Up That Old Gang of Mine)" (see '29). In '30, Paramount Pictures signed Fain and Kahal to write a song for the Maurice Chevalier movie *The Big Pond*. A popular hit from that film was "You Brought a New Kind of Love to Me" (see '30), written with Pierre Norman. They adopted L.A. as their base of operations and worked for several movie studios, providing one or two songs for many films. Some of their better-remembered movie tunes include: "When I Take My Sugar to Tea" from the Marx Brothers movie *Monkey Business*, "By a Waterfall" from *Footlight Parade*, and the title song from *Easy to Love*. Fain and Lew Brown's "That Old Feeling" was nominated for the Best Song Oscar (see '37). The duo also wrote for the Broadway stage. A '38 Broadway musical *Right This Way* included two of Fain and Kahal's most famous songs: "I'll Be Seeing You" (see '44) and "I Can Dream, Can't I?" (see '50) Following Kahal's death, Fain worked with numerous lyricist including Ralph Freed, Bob Hilliard, E.Y. Harburg, Sammy Cahn, and Paul Francis Webster. In '45 he wrote "The Worry Song," to which Gene Kelly and the animated Jerry the Mouse danced in the movie *Anchors Aweigh*. In '49 Fain wrote "Dear Hearts and Gentle People" (see '50). Fain also wrote the Broadway musical *Flahooley*, but it wasn't particularly successful. Fain collaborated on the scores to two Walt Disney animated features: *Alice in Wonderland* and *Peter Pan*. Fain composed the score for Doris Day's movie *Calamity Jane*, for which he won the Academy Award for Best Song for "Secret Love" (see '54). The following year he collaborated on the score for another Doris Day movie, *Lucky Me*, which included the song "I Speak to the Stars." In '55, he won another Academy Award for Best Song for the title tune to *Love Is a Many Splendored Thing* (see '55). Other movie songs include the title songs from *April Love* and *A Certain Smile*. Throughout the '60s and '70s, Fain continued to write for the movies. His last contribution to films was the '77 Disney animated feature *The Rescuers*. He is a member of the Songwriters' Hall of Fame since '72. At http://www.songwritershalloffame.org/exhibit_audio_video.asp?exhibitId=50 hear audio clips of "Once Upon a Dream" performed by Barbra Streisand, "When I Take My Sugar to Tea" sung by the Boswell Sisters accompanied by the Dorsey Brothers Orchestra, and "You Brought a New Kind of Love to Me" performed by Maurice Chevalier.

George Fairman (1881–1962) George Fairman is most remembered as the writer of "The Preacher and the Bear" (see '05), "'Way Down South" (see '12) and "I Don't Know Where I'm Going, but I'm on My Way" (see '18).

Percy Faith (1908–1976) Percy Faith's orchestra specialized in beautiful, interesting arrangements of popular tunes, but occasionally they had hits of their own. Faith held the post of musical director at Columbia Records and recorded with its studio orchestra. In the early '50s Faith and his orchestra backed Tony Bennett on some of his big hit recordings. Percy Faith and his orchestra's biggest hit recordings include "Delicado" (see '52), "The Song from Moulin Rouge" (see '53), which was one of the biggest hits of the '50s and "The Theme from 'A Summer Place,'" which was the second biggest hit of the '60s behind the Beatles' "Hey Jude." In addition, Faith arranged and conducted the music for the '55 Doris Day film *Love Me or Leave Me*, which was Ruth Etting's film biography. His song, "My Heart Cries for You," written with Carl Sigman, was a hit for Guy Mitchell (see '51). He also composed the theme for the television series *The Virginian* and remained active in studio recording work into the '70s.

Jinx Falkenburg (real name: Eugenia Lincoln Falkenburg; 1919–2003) Jinx Falkenburg and Joan Davis introduced "Daddy" in the movie *Two Latins from Manhattan* (see '41). Ms. Falkenburg was raised in Chile.

Her first exposure to the entertainment business was as a very successful model. She and her husband, Tex McCrary, hosted a radio and later TV series, *The Tex and Jinx Show*.

Richard Fall (1882–1945) German composer Richard Fall wrote the music for "O, Katharina" (see '25). The song premiered in a revue, *Chauve Souris*, conceived in Russia, revived in Paris, and brought to Broadway in '22.

Ed Farley (circa 1904–1983) Ed Farley was a trumpeter and singer. He is best known for co-writing "The Music Goes 'Round and Around" (see '36). He was partnered with Mike Riley. Farley's first professional job was with Bert Lown and his Hotel Biltmore Orchestra in the late '20s. Farley and Riley split in '36.

Charles Farrell (1901–1990) Charles Farrell became a leading man in some silent films and at the beginning of the talkies. He teamed with Janet Gaynor for a dozen screen romances between '27 and '34. Farrell and Gaynor introduced "Sunny Side Up" (see '29) in the movie musical of the same name. Farrell retired from films in the early '40s, but became Gale Storm's widower dad in her popular television series *My Little Margie* in the early '50s.

Marguerite Farrell (1889–1951) Marguerite Farrell was a popular vaudeville star who had a very popular recording of "If I Knock the 'L' Out of Kelly (It Would Still Be Kelly to Me) (see '16).

Alice Faye (real name: Alice Jeanne Leppert; 1915–1998) Alice Faye was a star performer in the movies from the mid-'30s to the mid-'40s. She was in the chorus line at the Capitol Theater by age 14. She met Rudy Vallee when they appeared together in *George White's Scandals of 1931*, and he took charge of her career. He helped her get a role in his '34 movie *George White's Scandals*. After three minor roles she shot to stardom in three '35 films. She was married first to singer Tony Martin, then to bandleader and singer Phil Harris. In the mid-'40s, she retired but made occasional appearances in films, radio, and television. Alice Faye introduced or co-introduced "You Turned the Tables on Me" in the movie *Sing, Baby, Sing* (see '36), "This Year's Kisses" and "I've Got My Love to Keep Me Warm" in *On the Avenue* (see '37), "You're a Sweetheart" in the movie of the same name (see '38) and "You'll Never Know" in the movie musical *Hello, Frisco, Hello* (see '43).

E.A. Fenstad E.A. Fenstad wrote a march named "Opie," which A.W. Sprague reworked into the tune for "Stein Song," or as it is sometimes called "Maine Stein Song" (see '30). Fenstad and Sprague are listed as co-composers.

Carl Fenton (real name: Walter Gustave Haenschen; 1889–1980) Actually, there was no such person as Carl Fenton. It was pianist, composer, arranger, and record producer Walter Gustave "Gus" Haenschen . Haenschen recorded extensively for Brunswick Records as Walter G. Haenschen, Gus Haenschen and as the Carl Fenton Orchestra. He used the Carl Fenton name during the '20 to '27 period. Haenschen's family had emigrated from Germany and settled in St. Louis, where he was born. By his teenage years, Gus was providing piano accompaniment for silent films in St. Louis theaters. Augustus Busch, the owner of the Budweiser brewing company, was instrumental in helping Haenschen find jobs at country club dances and other St. Louis social events, even including his band playing between innings of Busch's St. Louis Cardinals baseball games. In '19, Haenschen was hired by the new Brunswick record label to manage their popular records department. He was to Brunswick what Nat Shilkret was to Columbia. Haenschen invented the Carl Fenton Orchestra when he joined Brunswick. German names were not very popular in the era following World War I so instead of Haenschen, he became Carl Fenton. "Love Sends a Little Gift of Roses" (see '23) was the only big hit recording for Carl Fenton and his orchestra.

Raul Ferrao "April in Portugal" originated as a '47 Portuguese song by Raul Ferrao titled "Coimbra," a city in Portugal. It was later introduced in the U.S. as "Avril au Portugal (The Whisp'ring Serenade)." English lyrics were furnished by Jimmy Kennedy, when it became "April in Portugal" (see '53).

Buddy Feyne (1912–1998) During the early '30s Buddy Feyne worked as a song plugger until he proved to publishers that he could write excellent lyrics for popular songs. His most famous lyrics include "Tuxedo Junction" (see '40), and "Jersey Bounce" (see '42), using the name Robert B. Wright.

Zdenko Fibich (1850–1900) Czech composer Zdenko Fibich's "Poeme" was adapted by William Scotti into the popular song "My Moonlight Madonna" (see '33). Paul Francis Webster added lyrics.

Arthur Fields (1889–1953) Fields started his professional career as a child singer at age eleven. He performed in vaudeville, radio and made recordings. He also became a songwriter, co-writing such popular songs as "Aba Daba Honeymoon" (see '14). His most popular recording was of Irving Berlin's World War I song "Oh, How I Hate to Get Up in the Morning" (see '18).

Dorothy Fields (1905–1974) Dorothy Fields, the daughter of Lew Fields of the famous comedy team Weber and Fields, was an important lyricist of popular songs from the late '20s into the '70s. Dorothy wanted to become an actress, but her father disapproved. After graduating from a New York City high school, she met composer Jimmy McHugh. Since she was not allowed to become a performer, she found her talent as a lyricist. Fields and McHugh began writing for revues at Harlem's Cotton Club, and soon moved to Broadway. They scored a big hit with "I Can't Give You Anything but Love," and "Diga Diga Doo" (see '28) written for *Blackbirds of 1928*. Next came "On the Sunny Side of the Street" and "Exactly Like You" (see '30), written for the *International Revue*. In the early '30s, they began writing songs for Hollywood movies. They wrote the title song for *Cuban Love Song* (see '31)and "I'm in the Mood for Love" (see '35) for *Every Night at Eight*. Fields worked with several other composers, including Jerome Kern. She and Kern wrote some wonderful songs for the Fred Astaire film *Swingtime*, including "A Fine Romance," the Academy-award winning "The Way You Look Tonight" (see '36) and "I Won't Dance" and "Lovely to Look At" (see '35) for the film version of *Roberta*. In '46, she and her brother, Herbert Fields, wrote the book for the blockbuster Irving Berlin musical *Annie Get Your Gun*. In '59, she wrote book and lyrics for the Broadway musical *Redhead*, which won six Tony awards. Fields teamed up with Cy Coleman to write the songs for the '66 Broadway musical *Sweet Charity*, which included such songs as "Big Spender" and "If My Friends Could See Me Now." Dorothy Fields became the first woman elected to the Songwriters' Hall of Fame in '71. At http://www.songwritershalloffame.org/exhibit_audio_video.asp?exhibitId=65 hear audio clips of "Cuban Love Song" performed by Laurence Tibbett and "On the Sunny Side of the Street" performed by Louis Armstrong.

Irving Fields (1915–) Irving Fields, composer of "Managua, Nicaragua" (see '47), was also a pianist, arranger and bandleader. Fields was educated at the Eastman School of Music and the Masters Institute. For more, see http://www.irvingfields.com/bio.html.

Shep Fields (1910–1981) Shep Fields intended to be a lawyer but earned his way through school playing in bands. He decided to stay with music and organized his first professional band at age 19. Fame came only after he had created his "rippling rhythm" style; each number opened with the effect of blowing through a straw into a glass of water near a microphone. In '43 Fields pioneered another style: an all-reed (no brass) ensemble, but he never recaptured the success he had in the '30s. By the mid-'50s he had retired to Houston, where he worked as a disc jockey and occasionally as a bandleader. Shep Fields' biggest hit recordings include "Did I Remember?" (see '36), "In the Chapel in the Moonlight" (see '36), "That Old Feeling" (see '37), "The Merry-Go-Round Broke Down" (see '37), "Thanks for the Memory" (see '38), "Cathedral in the Pines" (see '38) and "South of the Border" (see '40). Shep Fields became the No. 16 top recording artist of the '30s.

Dick Finch (1898–1955) Dick Finch co-wrote the lyrics of "Jealous" with Tommie Malie (see '24). Finch also wrote "Along the Rocky Road to Dublin."

Henry Fink Henry Fink was lyricist, composer, author and comedian. He was educated at the Foster School and Goodrich School in Chicago. After he began his entertainment career as a vaudeville comedian, he switched to musical comedies. He was a restaurateur for a time, owned and operated a tourist hotel in Mexico and eventually returned to the stage. He also wrote songs for nightclub revues. His chief musical collaborators included Al Piantadosi and Abner Silver. His most famous lyric was "The Curse of an Aching Heart" (see '13).

Ted FioRito (1900–1971) Ted FioRito (some times written Fiorito) was a pianist and bandleader who occasionally composed popular songs. Film star Betty Grable sang with his band briefly in the early '30s, as did June Haver in the early '40s. His band's most popular time was the mid-'30s, when he had a great deal of exposure on radio, records, and movies. FioRito and his orchestra's most popular recordings came with "I'll String Along with You" (see '34) and "My Little Grass Shack in Kealakekua, Hawaii" (see '34). FioRito collaborated with several celebrated lyricists including Gus Kahn, Ernie Erdman, Dan Russon, Albert Von Tilzer, Sam Lewis, Joe Young and Cecil Mack. His songwriting credits include "Toot, Toot Tootsie!" (see '23), "Charley, My Boy" (see '24), "No! No! Nora!" (see '23), and "Laugh, Clown, Laugh" (see '28). In the '40s his fame began to diminish. In the '50s and '60s he led bands in Chicago and Arizona. FioRito was inducted into the Songwriters' Hall of Fame in '70. At http://www.songwritershalloffame.org/exhibit_audio_video.asp?exhibitId=87 hear an audio clip of "Charley, My Boy" sung by Billy Murray.

Carl Fischer (1912–1954) Carl Fischer was the composer of "Who Wouldn't Love You?" (see '42). Carl T. Fischer was a songwriter based in Los Angeles. Of approximately 40 published songs by Fischer listed on the ASCAP website, only "Who Wouldn't Love You?" was recognizable. This Carl Fischer is not related to the Carl Fischer of music publishing fame.

Doris Fisher (1915–2003) Songwriter Doris Fisher, the daughter of composer Fred Fisher, wrote a few hits with Allan Roberts. She also sang in nightclubs, on radio and with Eddy Duchin's orchestra in the early '40s. She organized her own group called Penny Wise and her Wise Guys, but they only had limited success. Her most remembered songs include "You Always Hurt the One You Love" (see '44), "Into Each Life Some Rain Must Fall" (see '44) and "Put the Blame on Mame" from the movie *Gilda* (see '46).

Eddie Fisher (real name: Edwin Jack Fisher; 1928–) Eddie Fisher was one of the nation's singing idols of the early '50s until the arrival of Elvis Presley. He had his first successful recording with "Wish You Were Here" in '52. Fisher became the protégé of Eddie Cantor at age twenty-one. Cantor had heard him at Grossinger's, the Catskills resort in New York. Cantor featured him on his radio show in the late '40s and promoted him toward a successful singing career. Fisher was very popular for the first few years of the '50s, but his career was interrupted by military service in '52 and '53. After his discharge he began to reach stardom once again. According to his autobiography, *Eddie: My Life, My Loves*, Fisher was not able to cope with the fishbowl existence of a celebrity. By his account, the press forced him into his first marriage to actress Debbie Reynolds. From that marriage came his daughter, Carrie, who starred as Princess Leia in the *Star Wars* films. Fisher divorced Debbie Reynolds to marry Elizabeth Taylor. The public seemed to turn against him, never forgiving him for dumping Debbie for Liz. Fisher later married Connie Stevens. Fisher attempted comebacks but was never able to regain the popularity he had in the early '50s. Fisher's biggest recording successes were "Wish You Were Here" (see '52), "I'm Walking Behind You" (see '53), "Oh! My Pa-Pa" (see '54) and "I Need You Now" (see '54). Other popular recordings include "Any Time," "I'm Yours," "Maybe" with Perry Como, "Tell Me Why," "Many Times," and "Count Your Blessings (Instead of Sheep)." Fisher became the No. 4 top recording artist of the '50s, behind only Elvis Presley, Perry Como and Patti Page.

Fred Fisher (1875–1942) Fred Fisher became one of America's best-known songwriters from the early years of the 20th Century through the '40s. He was born and educated in Germany and served in the German Imperial Navy and in the French Foreign Legion. He came to the United States in 1900. He claims to have learned to play the piano in one lesson given by a pianist in a Chicago southside bar. Fisher eventually established his own publishing firm. He was the father of Doris Fisher, who also became a songwriter (see above). In the early 1900s, Fisher wrote background music for silent films and when sound came to the movies in the late '20s, he wrote songs for "talkies." He also often wrote special material for vaudeville and nightclub acts. Collaborating with such songwriters as Grant Clarke, Joe McCarthy, Billy Rose, Alfred Bryan, Billy Hill, and his daughter Doris Fisher, Fred Fisher wrote such songs as "Any Little Girl That's a Nice Little Girl" (see '10), "Come, Josephine in My Flying Machine" (see '11), "Gee, but It's Great to Meet a Friend from Your Home Town" (see '11), "Peg o' My Heart" (see '13 and '47), "I'm on My Way to Mandalay" (see '14), "Ireland Must Be Heaven" (see '16), "There's a Broken Heart for Every Light on Broadway" (see '16), "They Go Wild, Simply Wild, Over Me" (see '17), "Dardanella" (see '20), and "Chicago" (see '22). Fisher also wrote "Daddy, You've Been a Mother to Me," "Oui, Oui, Marie," "Fifty Million Frenchmen Can't Be Wrong," "Your Feet's Too Big," and "Siam." The '49 movie musical *Oh, You Beautiful Doll* was a Hollywood fictionalized biography of Fred Fisher and featured many of his songs. Fred is an original member of the Songwriters' Hall of Fame ('70).

Mark Fisher Mark Fisher teamed up with Benny Davis to write the lyrics for "Oh, How I Miss You Tonight" (see '25) and with Joe Goodwin and Larry Shay for "When You're Smiling" (see '28).

Ella Fitzgerald (1917–1996) Ella Fitzgerald was only sixteen years old when she won an amateur talent night at the Harlem Opera House. As a result, Chick Webb hired her as vocalist for his band that was headquartered at the Savoy Ballroom in Harlem. Webb eventually legally adopted her. After Webb died from tuberculosis in '39, Ella ran the band for a while before embarking on a solo career in the early '40s. Ella became one of the most famous jazz singers in the world, and she has also made her mark in popular music. She was inducted into the Big Band/Jazz Hall of Fame at its inception in '78. She appeared in several movies and performed often on television from the late '50s through the '70s. Ella's most popular recordings include "A-Tisket, A-Tasket" (see '38), with Chick Webb and his orchestra, plus "Into Each Life Some Rain Must Fall" (see '44) and "I'm Making Believe" with the Ink Spots (see '44). Otherwise, her recordings were better known in the jazz field. Ella Fitzgerald's website is http://www.ellafitzgerald.com/. Real Audio clips of "A-Tisket A-Tasket," "Someone to Watch Over Me," "Mack the Knife," "Blue Skies," "They Can't Take That Away from Me," and "Misty" are available at this site.

Neville Fleeson Neville Fleeson was a lyricist, pianist and author. He began his entertainment career writing vaudeville sketches, then served with the U.S. Army during World War I. He was a member of the cast of Irving Berlin's service musical *Yip, Yip, Yaphank*. Later he worked on the staff of a music publishing company. He wrote a couple of reasonably successful Broadway stage scores and wrote songs for Hollywood films. His chief musical collaborators included Albert Von Tilzer, Mabel Wayne, and Alec Templeton. By far his most famous lyric was "I'll Be with You in Apple Blossom Time" (see '20).

Dusty Fletcher (circa 1896–1954) Dusty Fletcher was co-lyricist of "Open the Door, Richard" (see '47). Fletcher and John Mason had used the title phrase in their vaudeville act during the '30s and '40s. Fletcher also acted in a few Hollywood films.

The Florodora Girls The original *Florodora* sextet of chorines — Daisy Green, Marjorie Relyea, Vaughn Texsmith, Margaret Walker, Agnes Wayburn, and Marie Wilson — teamed with Byron Harlan, Frank Stanley and Joe Belmont to record "Tell Me, Pretty Maiden" (see '01), which they had helped introduce in the musical.

John H. Flynn John H. Flynn was the composer for "Yip-I-Addy-I-Ay!" (see '09). Flynn also wrote "Sweet Annie Moore" for the musical *The Casino Girl* ('01).

Marie Flynn Marie Flynn, Lawrence Wheat and the chorus introduced the title song of the musical *You're in Love* (see '17).

Red Foley (real name: Clyde John Foley; 1910–1968) Red Foley is one of the most famous country singers of all time. He was particularly popular in the '40s and '50s. His daughter, Shirley, married singer Pat Boone. Foley had a big national hit recording with "Chattanoogie Shoe Shine Boy" (see '50). He owned a publishing firm, composed many country songs, and appeared regularly on Nashville's *Grand Ole Opry*. Foley is a member of the Country Music Hall of Fame.

Fontane Sisters Bea Rosse, Geri Rosse, Margi Rosse. The Fontane Sisters were a vocal trio who were often featured on Perry Como's radio and TV programs. The girls' biggest hit recording was "Hearts of Stone" (see '55).

Lena Guilbert Ford (1870–1916) Poet Lena Guilbert Ford penned the lyric for "Keep the Home Fires Burning (Till the Boys Come Home)," a popular World War I song (see '16).

Mary Ford (1924–1977) Mary Ford began singing and playing guitar on country-western radio shows as a child. She joined Les Paul in '42 for a radio show. They married in '48 but later divorced. During their time together they had several major hit recordings, including "How High the Moon" (see '51), "Mockin' Bird Hill" (see '51), "The World Is Waiting for the Sunrise" (see '20), "Just One More Chance" (see '31), "Tiger Rag" (see '31), "Vaya Con Dios" (see '53), one of the top five hits of the '50s. Most of their biggest hits seem to have been revivals of older songs except for "Vaya Con Dios." Les Paul and Mary Ford became the No. 6 top recording artists of the '50s.

Tennessee Ernie Ford (real name: Ernest Jennings; 1919–1991) The "ole pea picker," Tennessee Ernie Ford was popular as a singer and television personality during the '50s and '60s. Ford had studied voice at the Cincinnati Conservatory of Music, intending to sing "serious" music, but made his living for several years as a disk jockey. That work caused him to gravitate towards country music. He signed his first record contract after a Capitol Records executive heard him singing along with a record on the radio. His first recording success came in '49 with his version of "Mule Train," which made *Billboard's* Top 10. His duet with Kay Starr of "I'll Never Be Free" in '50 peaked at No. 3 on *Billboard*. His recording of "The Ballad of Davy Crockett" in early '55 made it to No. 5 on *Billboard*, but "Sixteen Tons" was the blockbuster success that really brought him national recognition (see '55). He ranks as the No. 35 top recording artist of the '50s. He hosted a very popular television variety show

from '55 to '65. Later in his singing career, he seemed to concentrate on gospel singing. Ford is a member of the Country Music Hall of Fame ('90). For more on Ford, see http://www.ernieford.com/Bio.htm.

George Forrest (1915–1999) George "Chet" Forrest teamed with Robert Wright on the music and lyrics for several popular songs, but they are best known for adapting classical material to popular songs. Their most famous adaptation was Aleksandr Borodin's music for the '53 Broadway musical *Kismet*. They also adapted Norwegian composer Edvard Grieg's music for *Song of Norway* ('44). One of their first transformations was Rudolf Friml's "Chansonette" into "Donkey Serenade" in '37. Other well-known songs that were Forrest-Wright collaborations are "At the Balalaika" (see '40) and "It's a Blue World." Songs from *Kismet* include "Stranger in Paradise" (see '54), "Baubles, Bangles and Beads" and "And This Is My Beloved." Songs from *Song of Norway* include "Strange Music" and "I Love You."

Helen Forrest (1917–1999) Helen Forrest was a leading female vocalist during the big band era. She was a singer with Artie Shaw, Benny Goodman, and Harry James. By the late '50s she was less active in the music business, but she continued to perform occasionally into the '70s. She also recorded several duets with Dick Haymes in the mid-'40s. Some of her recordings with big bands include "They Say" and "Thanks for Everything," with Artie Shaw (see '39), "I Don't Want to Walk Without You" (see '42), "Mister Five by Five" (see '42), "I've Heard That Song Before" (see '43), and "I Had the Craziest Dream" (see '43) with Harry James, plus "Taking a Chance on Love" with Benny Goodman (see '43). Others of her most famous recordings include "Long Ago (and Far Away)" (see '44), "Together," "It Had to Be You," "I'll Buy That Dream" (see '45), all duets with Dick Haymes. Ms. Forrest was inducted into the Big Band/Jazz Hall of Fame in 2001. She was the No. 26 top recording artist of the '40s.

Stephen C. Foster (1826–1864) Stephen Collins Foster was the pre-eminent American songwriter of the era just prior to the Civil War. Many of his songs, such as "Oh! Susanna," "Camptown Races," "Old Folks at Home" (see '00), "My Old Kentucky Home" (see '03) and "Beautiful Dreamer," are still very well known over 150 years after their composition. Foster was born in Lawrenceville, Pennsylvania, which later became a suburb of Pittsburgh. His education included little formal music training, only a little by Henry Kleber, a music store owner in Pittsburgh. Despite his lack of musical knowledge, he had written several songs before he was twenty years old. His first published song, "Open Thy Lattice Love," appeared when he was eighteen. In 1846 when he moved to Cincinnati, Ohio to work as a bookkeeper with his brother's steamship company, Foster had his first really important song published, "Oh! Susanna," which was to serve as the anthem of the California gold rush in the late 1840s. By 1849 he returned to Pennsylvania and formed a contract with the Ed Christy and his minstrel company. During this period most of his best-known songs were written: "Camptown Races" (1850), "Nelly Bly" (1850), "Old Folks at Home" (1851, see '00), "My Old Kentucky Home" (1853, see '03), and "Jeannie with the Light Brown Hair" (1854), which was written for his wife, Jane McDowall. Foster tried to make a living as a professional songwriter, which was quite uncommon for the period. Consequently, Foster saw very little of the profits which his works generated for sheet music printers. Multiple publishers often printed their own competing editions of Foster's tunes, paying Foster nothing. He received only $100 for "Oh! Susanna" for instance. He moved to New York City just prior to the Civil War. In approximately 1861 his wife and daughter abandoned him to return to Pittsburgh. His musical fortunes soon began to decline. And the Civil War practically ruined the music and entertainment market. Stephen Foster died in poverty at age 37. In his pocket was a scrap of paper with "dear friends and gentle hearts" written on it. The '50 hit "Dear Hearts and Gentle People" was inspired by Foster's last written words. One of his most famous songs, "Beautiful Dreamer," was published shortly after his death.

Larry Fotine (real name: Lawrence Constantine Fotinakis; 1911–1990)   Larry Fotine was the composer of "You Were Only Fooling (While I Was Falling in Love)" (see '48). Fotine's father emigrated from Smyrna, Turkey to the U.S. in '07. By the '30s, he was an insurance salesman in the Camden, New Jersey area. Larry began to study piano at age 14. Around '35, he organized a band that played in the New Jersey area. He became Sammy Kaye's arranger in '40, then arranged for the Blue Barron and Art Mooney bands from '45 to '47. He organized his own group in '48. They disbanded in '55. Fotine moved to California, where he joined the Lawrence Welk orchestra as an arranger in '58. Larry Fotine wrote and published over 300 songs.

The Four Aces   Al Alberts (real name: Al Albertini; 1922–), Dave Mahoney, Lou Silvestri, Sol Vocarro. Al Alberts organized The Four Aces in '49. At first they sang only part time, but later they graduated to full-time work and recording. Their first successful disk was "Sin" (see '51), which they paid to record. Their biggest hit recordings were "Three Coins in the Fountain" (see '54) and "Love Is a Many-Splendored Thing" (see '55). Other popular recordings included "Tell Me Why," "Stranger in Paradise," "Mister Sandman" and "Melody of Love." They rank as the No. 9 top recording artists of the '50s. The group was inducted into the Vocal Group Hall of Fame in 2001.

The Four Lads   Frank Busseri, Bernard Toorish (real name: John Bernard Toorish; 1931–), James Arnold (1932–2004), Connie Codarini (real name: Corrado Codarini). The Four Lads, a Toronto, Canada quartet, backed Johnnie Ray in '51 on his big back-to-back hits "Cry" and "The Little White Cloud That Cried" (see '51). After that success, they began to record on their own. Their biggest hit recordings include "Moments to Remember," "No, Not Much!" and "Standing on the Corner." They rank as the No. 17 top recording artists of the '50s. They were inducted into the Vocal Group Hall of Fame in 2003.

Harry Fox (real name: Arthur Carringford; 1882–1959)   According to http://www.imdb.com/, Fox's 1913 *Ziegfeld Follies* act included a trotting step that became later the popular ballroom dance "fox-trot." Harry Fox introduced Irving Berlin's "I Love a Piano" in the musical *Stop! Look! Listen!* (see '16). Fox also introduced "I'm Always Chasing Rainbows" in the musical *Oh, Look!* (see '18).

Charley Foy (1898–1984)   Gus Kahn and Ted FioRito dedicated "Charley, My Boy" (see '24) to Charley Foy, the famous vaudevillian. After the death of their mother, Foy's father, Eddie, formed the brothers and sisters into a vaudeville act known as "The Seven Little Foys."

George Fragos   George Fragos was one of the co-writers of "I Hear a Rhapsody" (see '41).

W. T. Francis   W. T. Francis was the co-composer with John Stromberg for "Come Down Ma Evenin' Star" (see '03).

Sid Frank   Sid Frank was the lyricist of "Please, Mr. Sun" (see '52).

Dave Franklin (1895–?)   Dave Franklin usually served as lyricist for composer Cliff Friend, but he wrote "The Anniversary Waltz" with Al Dubin (see '41). Among Franklin and Friend's well-known songs are "The Merry-Go-Round Broke Down" and "You Can't Stop Me from Dreaming" (see '37). Franklin also wrote "When My Dream Boat Comes Home."

Paul Frawley (1889–1973)   In the '21 edition of the *Music Box Revue,* Paul Frawley and Wilda Bennett introduced Irving Berlin's "Say It with Music." Paul was the brother of William Frawley (see below). They performed together in vaudeville before William joined Franz Rath and went to the west coast.

William Frawley (1887–1966)   William Frawley began singing in his church and at a local opera house in his hometown of Burlington, Iowa. His first job was as a stenographer for the Union Pacific Railroad. He performed in vaudeville with his brother Paul, then joined pianist Franz Rath in an act that took them to the west coast. In '14 he formed a comedy act with his new wife, Edna Louise Broedt. They toured the Orpheum and Keith circuits until they divorced in '27. Frawley was the first to introduce "My Mammy" in his vaudeville act (see '21). He eventually moved to Broadway and then, in the early '30s, to Hollywood with Paramount Pictures. By the early '50s, when he became Fred Mertz on Lucille Ball's TV show, he had performed in over 100 films. After *I Love Lucy* ended, he performed five years on *My Three Sons.*

Stan Freberg (1926–)   Stan Freberg became one of the best at producing parodies of hit songs in the early days of rock 'n' roll. He had a number of comedy records that were very popular in the early '50s. Stan began his entertainment career at age 11 in his uncle's magic show. In '43 he began doing voice impersonations on Cliffie Stone's radio show. After World War II, Freberg did cartoon voices for some of the major animated film studios. In '50, Stan put together his first satirical record for Capitol. "John and Marsha" was a take-off on radio soap operas. In '53 he turned his attention to the radio/television show *Dragnet* with "St. George and the Dragonet," which became a *Billboard* No. 1 hit (see '53). Next, Freberg wrote parodies of well-known pop songs of the day. His '55 version of "The Yellow Rose of Texas," which had been a big hit for Mitch Miller, was well received, as were his send-ups of the Platters' "The Great Pretender," and Harry Belafonte's "Banana Boat [Day-O]." By the early '60s, Freberg turned his attention to the advertising business. He produced several commercials that were very funny. In '61 the concept album "Stan Freberg Presents the United States of America" charted on *Billboard*.

Alan Freed (1922–1965) Disk jockey Alan Freed is particularly famous for originating the term "rock 'n' roll" in '51 for his *Moon Dog's Rock and Roll Party* over radio station WWJ in Cleveland. Freed moved to New York City's WINS in '54, where his fame spread. Within a year he was earning high pay promoting rock records and selling the products that sponsored his program. In addition to his disk jockeying, Freed occasionally contributed material for songs, such as "Sincerely" (see '55). However, there is some question that Freed really helped Moonglows member Harvey Fuqua write the song. Fuqua might have been happy to give Freed writing credit so Freed would help promote the song on his radio show. The '78 film *American Hot Wax* chronicled Freed's career.

Arthur Freed (real name: Arthur Grossman; 1894–1973) Arthur Freed was an important song lyricist who collaborated chiefly with composer Nacio Herb Brown. After graduation from high school, Arthur Freed worked as a pianist and song plugger for a Chicago music publisher. In Chicago, he met Minnie Marx, the mother of the Marx Brothers. That meeting led to his touring the vaudeville circuit with the Marx Brothers as a singer and writer of musical material. He also performed with Gus Edwards and with Louis Silvers. In '21, he collaborated for the first time with composer Nacio Herb Brown on the song "When Buddha Smiles," but Freed's first big success as a songwriter came in '23, when he wrote "I Cried for You" with Gus Arnheim and Abe Lyman. After a few years of touring the nightclub circuit and staging some plays in Los Angeles, Freed joined MGM as a lyricist and was assigned to work with his former collaborator, Nacio Herb Brown. They wrote many of the songs heard in the studio's early musicals including the film *Broadway Melody*, which featured the songs "You Were Meant for Me" (see '29), and "The Wedding of the Painted Doll" (see '29). The team contributed "Singin' in the Rain" for *Hollywood Revue of 1929* (see '29), and for the film *The Pagan*, they wrote "Pagan Love Song" (see '29). Throughout the '30s, Freed continued to write songs and movie scores, mostly with Brown. Songs written during this period included "Chant of the Jungle" (see '30), "Should I?" (see '30), "Temptation" (written in '33, see "Tim-Tayshun" in '47), "All I Do Is Dream of You" (see '34), "Broadway Rhythm" (see '35), "You Are My Lucky Star" (see '35), "Alone" (see '36), and "Good Morning" (see '39). He also contributed the lyrics for "Make 'Em Laugh" (see '52). Following an assignment as associate producer on *The Wizard of Oz* in '39, Freed began his second career as a film producer. Freed produced nearly 50 movies for MGM, including *Babes in Arms* ('39), *Strike Up the Band* ('40), *Lady Be Good* ('41), *Cabin in the Sky* ('43), *Meet Me in St. Louis* ('44), *The Harvey Girls* ('46), *The Ziegfeld Follies* ('46), *Good News* ('47), *The Pirate* ('48), *Easter Parade* ('48), *Words and Music* ('48), *The Barkleys of Broadway* ('49), *Take Me Out to the Ball Game* ('49), *On the Town* ('49), *Annie Get Your Gun* ('50), *An American in Paris* ('51), *Show Boat* ('51), *Singin' in the Rain* ('52), *The Band Wagon* ('53), *Brigadoon* ('54), *Kismet* ('55), *It's Always Fair Weather* ('55), *Silk Stockings* ('57), *Gigi* ('58) and *Bells Are Ringing* ('60). After retiring from filmmaking, Freed served as president of the Academy of Motion Picture Arts and Sci-

ences, and applied his showmanship skills to the annual Academy Award telecast. Freed was inducted into the Songwriters' Hall of Fame in '72. At http://www.song writershalloffame.org/exhibit_audio_video.asp?exhibitId= 63 hear an audio clip of "All I Do Is Dream of You" performed by Angelo Ferdinando with His Hotel Great Northern Orchestra with vocalist Dick Robertson.

Ralph Freed (1907–1973) Ralph Freed collaborated with Harry Barris to write "Little Dutch Mill" (see '34) and with Burton Lane to write "Smarty" (see '37). He also helped write "How About You?" and "Hawaiian War Chant." Freed was a songwriter, author and producer. He was a contract writer for Paramount, Universal and MGM studios. In the mid-'50s, he began producing television shows and films. Freed's chief musical collaborators included Sammy Fain, Burton Lane, and Harry Barris.

Max C. Freedman (1893–1962) Max C. Freedman was lyricist for "Sioux City Sue" (see '46) and co-writer with James E. Myers (aka. Jimmy DeKnight) on "Rock Around the Clock" (see '55).

L.E. Freeman L.E. Freeman was one of the lyricists of "Until the Real Thing Comes Along" (see '36).

Martin Fried Martin Fried was a composer, lyricist, and longtime accompanist and arranger for Al Jolson. He conducted many Jolson musicals. Fried's most well known popular song composition is "Broadway Rose" (see '21), which he co-wrote with Otis Spencer.

Anatol Friedland (1881–1938) Anatol Friedland was a composer, songwriter, author and pianist. He was educated at the Moscow Conservatory and Columbia University, where he received an architecture degree. He wrote special material for the *Passing Show* revues, was a vaudeville pianist, and had his own nightclub, Club Anatole. His chief musical collaborators included L. Wolfe Gilbert and Harold Atteridge. His most popular songs were "My Little Dream Girl" (see '15) and "My Own Iona" (see '17).

Leo Friedman (1869–1927) Leo Friedman is primarily remember as the composer of "Meet Me Tonight in Dreamland" (see '10) and "Let Me Call You Sweetheart" (see '11). His chief musical collaborator was Beth Slater Whitson.

Cliff Friend (1893–1974) Cliff Friend was a songwriter, author and pianist. He was educated at the Cincinnati College and Conservatory. He was also a test pilot at Wright Field. After three years as accompanist to Harry Richman in vaudeville, he was featured in English music halls, and later throughout the world. He wrote song for several Broadway stage productions including *George White's Scandals of 1929*, *Bombo* and *The Passing Show of 1921*. His chief musical collaborators were Lew Brown, Sidney Clare, Billy Rose, Irving Caesar, Dave Franklin, Abel Baer, and Charles Tobias. Friend's most famous songs include "June Night" (see '24), "The Merry-Go-Round Broke Down" (see '37), "You Can't Stop Me from Dreaming" (see '37), and "Trade Winds" (see '40). His other popular-song compositions include "You Tell Her, I Stutter," "Then I'll Be Happy "When My Dream Boat Comes Home," "We Did It Before, and We Can Do It Again," and "Don't Sweetheart Me."

Rudolf Friml (1879–1972) Composer Rudolf Friml was born in Prague, Czechoslovakia in 1879. Living in

Czechoslovakia, he attended the Prague Conservatory and studied piano with composers Dvorak and Jiranek. In his 20s, Friml toured throughout Europe and the United States as a concert pianist with violinist Jan Kubelik. Soon after his last American tour in '06, Friml moved to New York City where he began contributing his compositions to stage productions. In '12, he replaced the legendary Victor Herbert as the composer for the Broadway musical *The Firefly*. From '12 through the early '30s, Friml would work on several other stage scores including *High Jinks, The Peasant Girl, Katinka, You're in Love, Sometime, Glorianna, Tumble In, The Little Whopper, June Love, The Blue Kitten, Rose Marie, The Vagabond King, No Foolin', The Wild Rose* and *The Three Musketeers*. In '34, Friml moved to Hollywood to work on film musicals. He worked on several, but the most famous ones include *The Vagabond King, Rose Marie* and *The Firefly*. While Friml worked alone on more than half of his compositions he also collaborated with many of the greatest lyricists of his time including Otto Harbach, P.G. Wodehouse, Rida Johnson Young, Oscar Hammerstein II, Brian Hooker, Cliff Grey, Catherine Chisholm Cushing and Harold Atteridge. Friml's most famous songs include "Sympathy" (see '13), "Giannina Mia" (see '13), "You're in Love" (see '17), "L'Amour, Toujours, L'Amour" (see '22), "Rose Marie" (see '25), "Indian Love Call" (see '25), and "Song of the Vagabonds" (see '25). Rudolf Friml was a charter member of the American Society of Composers, Authors and Publishers. Friml was inducted into the Songwriters' Hall of Fame in '71.

Jane Froman (1907–1980) Jane Froman was a well-known singer in the '30s and '40s. She starred in several Broadway musicals, notably *Ziegfeld Follies of 1934*, where she introduced "You Oughta Be in Pictures," *Keep Off the Grass* ('40) and *Artists and Models* ('43), and in the Hollywood movies *Stars Over Broadway* ('35) and *Radio City Revels* ('38). Froman was seriously injured in a '43 plane accident while entertaining the U.S. military overseas. The '52 movie *With a Song in My Heart* was a tribute to Froman and her life; Susan Hayward played the starring role. By the mid-'50s Froman's career was more or less over. "More Than You Know" became a Froman specialty (see '29), as did, "With a Song in My Heart" (see '29), and "That Old Feeling" (see '37).

Tom Frost Tom Frost collaborated with John Philip Sousa on the lyrics of "El Capitan" (see '09).

Jack Fulton (real name: John Collins Fulton; 1903–1993) Jack Fulton was a co-writer of "Wanted" (see '54). Fulton was a member of the Paul Whiteman Orchestra for eight years and played with the group on radio for twenty-two years. Fulton's chief collaborator was Lois Steele. Fulton also wrote "Ivory Tower," which was popularized by Cathy Carr in '56.

Harvey Fuqua (1929–) Harvey Fuqua was co-writer with Alan Freed of "Sincerely" (see '55). Fuqua was a member of the Moonglows, the R&B group who first popularized the song.

Douglas Furber (real name: Lewin Michael Sultan; 1885–1961) Englishman Douglas Furber wrote the lyrics for "The Bells of St. Mary's" (see '17), "Limehouse Blues," and for the musical *Me and My Girl* ('37). *Me and My Girl* became London's longest running musical of the '30s. In '87, Furber was posthumously nominated for two

Tony Awards for *Me and My Girl*: as Best Score, his lyrics with music by Noel Gay, and other lyrics by L. Arthur Rose; and as Best Book (Musical), with Rose.

Zsa Zsa Gabor (real name: Sari Gabor; 1917–) Zsa Zsa Gabor, actually Muriel Smith singing for her, introduced the title song from *Moulin Rouge*, which is sometimes called "Where Is Your Heart?," but most often titled "The Song from *Moulin Rouge*" (see '53). The Hungarian born Ms. Gabor and her sister, Eva, became Hollywood celebrities. Ms. Gabor's first film was *Lovely to Look At* ('52), followed closely by *We're Not Married!* ('52). It was also in '52 that she starred opposite Jose Ferrer in *Moulin Rouge*. She has continued in films, mostly in supporting roles or as herself, through the end of the century.

Slim Gaillard (real name: Bulee Gaillard; 1911–1991) Slim Gaillard was an African-Cuban jazz singer, songwriter, pianist and guitarist. He was noted for his scat singing. Gaillard's first taste of success in the entertainment field was in the late '30s with Slam Stewart as the novelty act Slim and Slam. They collaborated with Bud Green to write "Flat Foot Floogee" (see '38). Another well known Slim and Slam creation was "Cement Mixer (Put-Ti, Put-Ti)." They appeared in the '41 movie *Hellzapoppin'*. Gaillard also appeared in the TV series *Roots: The Next Generations* in the '70s and in '86 he appeared the movie musical *Absolute Beginners*. Gaillard's daughter, Janis Hunter, married singer Marvin Gaye.

Gallagher and Shean Ed Gallagher (1873–1929), Al Shean (1868–1949). Gallagher and Shean were a famous comedy team who starred on vaudeville and the musical stages of the '20s. They composed the song "Mister Gallagher and Mister Shean" (sometimes listed as "Oh, Mister Gallagher and Mister Shean" or "Mr. Gallagher and Mr. Shean," see '22), which they premiered in the *Ziegfeld Follies*. Their recording of the song was very popular in '22. The team split permanently in '25. Al Shean was an uncle of the Marx Brothers.

Sammy Gallop (1915–1971) Sammy Gallop was a songwriter in the '40s and '50s. His best-known songs were "Elmer's Tune" (see '41), "Holiday for Strings" (see '44), "There Must Be a Way" (see '45) and "Shoo-fly Pie and Apple Pan Dowdy" (see '46). Gallop also wrote "Wake the Town and Tell the People," which was popularized in '55.

Albert Gamse Albert Gamse was lyricist of "Amapola" (see '41) and "Managua, Nicaragua" (see '47).

Kim Gannon (real name: James Kimble Gannon; 1900–1974) Kim Gannon was a popular song lyricist during the '40s and '50s. His best-known lyrics are "Moonlight Cocktail" (see '42), "It Can't Be Wrong" (see '43) and "I'll Be Home for Christmas" (see '43).

Jan Garber (1897–1977) Bandleader Jan Garber became violinist in the Philadelphia Symphony Orchestra after attending the University of North Carolina. Garber began his popular music career in a quartet following World War I. This group morphed into a hot band of the '20s, a sweet band during the early '30s, a swing band during World War II, and back to a sweet band after the war. His band became a popular attraction on the Burns and Allen radio show. Garber's biggest hit recordings include "Baby Face" (see '26), "All I Do Is Dream of You" (see '34), "Melody from the Sky" (see '36) and "A Beautiful Lady in Blue" (see '36). Garber became the No. 15 top recording artist of the '30s.

Don Gardner (1910–) Don Gardner wrote "All I Want for Christmas Is My Two Front Teeth" (see '48). Don Gardner's wife, Doris, was a music teacher in a New York elementary school. One day in '44, Gardner filled in for his wife. When he said something funny, the children laughed. He was immediately struck by their teeth, or lack thereof. Sixteen out of the twenty-two students were missing their front teeth. That evening he wrote "All I Want for Christmas Is My Two Front Teeth" in less than half an hour. It wasn't published, however, until '48, when the Satisfiers introduced the song on Perry Como's radio show. Spike Jones and his City Slickers took it to No. 1.

William H. Gardner William H. Gardner co-wrote "Can't Yo' Heah Me Callin' Caroline?" with Caro Roma (see '14).

Joe Garland (1903–1977) Joe Garland is famous for composing a couple of jazz-oriented tunes for big bands. He composed "In the Mood" (see '40) and Les Brown's theme song, "Leap Frog." Otherwise, Garland was known as a sideman, musical director, and arranger.

Judy Garland (real name: Frances Gumm; 1922– 1969) During her teenage years, Judy Garland was the darling of several movie musicals, quite a few costarring Mickey Rooney. One of her first important movie songs was singing "Dear Mr. Gable (You Made Me Love You)" to a photo of Clark Gable in *Broadway Melody of '38*. Ms. Garland and Mickey Rooney introduced "Good Morning" in the film version of the musical *Babes in Arms* (see '39). Judy was only sixteen years old when she starred in the film classic *The Wizard of Oz* and introduced "Over the Rainbow" (see '39). Ms. Garland's most popular recordings came in the early '40s. They include "The Trolley Song," which she introduced in *Meet Me in St. Louis* (see '44) and "For Me and My Gal" in a duet with Gene Kelly from the '42 film *For Me and My Gal* (see '17 when it was most popular). Judy and Ray Bolger introduced "On the Atchison, Topeka, and the Santa Fe" in *The Harvey Girls* (see '45). Ms. Garland introduced "The Man That Got Away" in the movie musical *A Star Is Born* (see '54). Unfortunately perhaps because of the huge amount of fame and success she experienced so early in life, Judy led a troubled and turbulent life, particularly in the '50s and '60s, when she was in ill health, reportedly due to overuse of alcohol and drugs. She died of a reported drug overdose in London. Perhaps surprisingly, Ms. Garland was never particularly successful as a recording artist, even for songs like "Over the Rainbow." Judy was inducted into the Popular Music Hall of Fame in 2001. Liza Minnelli, Garland's daughter by director Vincente Minnelli, also became a major star on Broadway and in films. Judy Garland's website is http://www.thejudyroom.com/. There are several MP3 files available at this site.

Betty Garrett (1919–) Betty Garrett introduced "South America, Take It Away" in the musical *Call Me Mister* (see '46). She was a Broadway regular during the mid-'40s. Ms. Garrett had a promising career in MGM musicals cut short by McCarthy-era blacklisting. Her husband Larry Parks confessed to a prior affiliation with the Communist party. She appeared in *Words and Music, On the Town, Take Me Out to the Ball Game* and *Neptune's Daughter*, among others. She appeared often on television during the '70s, particularly in *All in the Family* and *Laverne and Shirley*.

Joe Garron Joe Garron's chief claim to fame in the popular music field is he was the composer for "Just a Girl That Men Forget" (see '23).

Clarence G. Gartner Clarence Gartner is primarily remembered today for writing the music for "Love Is Mine" (see '12).

Clarence Gaskill (1892–1947) Clarence Gaskill had a very limited output of songs, but now and then he composed a hit. His most remembered songs are "Sweet Adeline" (see '04) and "Prisoner of Love" (see '46).

George J. Gaskin (1850s–1920) George Gaskin was called "The Silver-Voiced Irish Tenor." Born in Belfast, Ireland, he became one of the leading pioneers in the recording industry. He had numerous very popular recordings from 1891 through the very early years of the 20th Century. His most important recordings in the years covered by this book include "When Chloe Sings a Song" (see '00), "When You Were Sweet Sixteen" (see '00) and to a slightly less degree "Absence Makes the Heart Grow Fonder" (see '01) and "Bedelia" (see '04). He recorded those four songs for Columbia. For more on Gaskin, see http://www.songwritershalloffame.org/artist_bio.asp?artist Id=70.

Dick Gasparre Dick Gasparre was one of the co-writers of "I Hear a Rhapsody" (see '41). Gasparre, a pianist, led a society-style orchestra during the '30s and '40s.

William Gaxton (real name: Arturo Antonio Gaxiola; 1893–1963) William Gaxton starred in several Broadway musicals in the '30s and early '40s. Among them were *A Connecticut Yankee, Fifty Million Frenchmen, Of Thee I Sing, Let 'Em Eat Cake, Anything Goes, Leave It to Me* and *Louisiana Purchase*. Gaxton and Constance Carpenter introduced "My Heart Stood Still" and "Thou Swell" in the musical *A Connecticut Yankee* (see '28). Gaxton and Genevieve Tobin introduced "You Do Something to Me" in Cole Porter's *Fifty Million Frenchmen* (see '29), while Gaxton and Lois Moran introduced the title song in *Of Thee I Sing* (see '32).

Janet Gaynor (real name: Laura Gainer; 1907– 1984) Janet Gaynor sang and danced in several movie musicals including *Sunny Side Up* (see '29), *Happy Days, Society Blues* and *Delicious*. Gaynor and Charles Farrell became the top movie team of the early '30s. Gaynor demanded more serious roles in later years.

Adam Geibel (1855–1933) Though blinded by an eye infection at age eight, Adam Geibel was a successful composer, conductor, and organist. He studied at the Philadelphia Institute for the Blind, and wrote a number of gospel songs, anthems, cantatas, and popular songs. He founded the Adam Geibel Music Company, later evolved into the Hall-Mack Company, and later merged to become the Rodeheaver Hall-Mack Company. In the popular music field, Geibel collaborated musically with Earl Burtnett. The writer of "Sleep" (see '24) is listed as Earl Lebieg, but the writers were really Earl Burtnett and Adam

Geibel. They used Burtnett's first name with Geibel spelled backwards for their pseudonym.

Pat Genaro   Pat Genaro was one of the co-writers of "You're Breaking My Heart" (see '49) and "Here in My Heart" (see '52).

Don George (1909–1987)   Don George was an artist and lyricist. Some of his work became very well known. After his education, he began to write special material for such stars as Fran Warren, Nat "King" Cole, and Patti Page. Among his musical collaborators were Mabel Wayne, Duke Ellington, Steve Allen, Bee Walker, Oscar Levant, Peter DeRose and Harry James. His most famous compositions are such tunes as "I'm Beginning to See the Light" (see '45) and "Yellow Rose of Texas" (see '55).

Richard H. Gerard (real name: Richard Gerard Husch; 1876–1948)   Richard Gerard's chief contribution to popular music was as lyricist for "Sweet Adeline" (see '04). Gerard (or Husch) was employed at the New York City Post Office.

George Gershwin (real name: Jacob Gershvin; 1898–1937)   George Gershwin (his father, a Russian immigrant, was Gershovitz, but Americanized the name) became one of the greatest composers of the first half of the 20th Century in both serious and popular music. In the history of music many geniuses have died at young ages, cutting their productive lives short. Such was the case of Gershwin. He died at age thirty-eight, having composed for only a little more than twenty years. His accomplishments in those brief years are absolutely remarkable. Gershwin is, of course, in the Songwriters' Hall of Fame and was inducted into the Popular Music Hall of Fame in 2003. He grew up in New York City and his considerable musical talent was evident early. He began at age 15 as a pianist, an accompanist for Nora Bayes and Louise Dresser, and as a song plugger. He became staff composer for the Harms Publishing Company in '17 and produced his first major hit, "Swanee" (see '20). He collaborated with several lyricists, but most often with his brother, Ira. In the early part of his career, his songs were inserted into other people's shows, but in '19 he wrote his first complete Broadway musical, *La La Lucille*. Gershwin became extremely successful from '24 when he wrote the Broadway musical *Lady Be Good!* His Broadway musicals to follow in the '20s, the majority written with his brother Ira, included *Oh, Kay!* ('26), *Funny Face* ('27), *Rosalie* ('28) and *Show Girl* ('29). During the '30s he continued his success on Broadway with *Strike Up the Band* ('30), *Girl Crazy* ('30) and *Of Thee I Sing* ('31). Then George and Ira turned their attention to movie musicals and produced *Shall We Dance* ('37) and *A Damsel in Distress* ('37). At the time of George's tragically early death during a brain operation in '38, they were working on *The Goldwyn Follies*. George was ambitious in the realm of artistic (classical) music also. In that genre he wrote "Rhapsody in Blue" (see '24) and "An American in Paris" ('28) among others, plus the American folk-opera *Porgy and Bess* ('35), especially including "Summertime," "Bess, You Is My Woman," "I Got Plenty o' Nuttin'" and "It Ain't Necessarily So." Gershwin was a tremendously social person, but never married. He also was a gifted painter. Some of Gershwin's most famous popular songs of the pre-'30s were "Swanee" (see '20), "Do It Again" (see '22), "I'll Build

a Stairway to Paradise" (see '23), "Somebody Loves Me" (see '24), "Oh, Lady Be Good!" (see '24), "Fascinating Rhythm" (see '24), "The Man I Love" (see '24), and "'S Wonderful" (see '28). In the '30s Gershwin contributed "I Got Rhythm" (see '30), "Embraceable You" (see '30), "Love Is Sweeping the Country" (see '32), "Of Thee I Sing" (see '32), "Summertime" (see '35), "Bess, You Is My Woman," (see '25), "I Got Plenty o' Nuttin'" (see '35), "It Ain't Necessarily So" (see '35), "Let's Call the Whole Thing Off" and "They Can't Take That Away from Me" (see '37), "Nice Work If You Can Get It" and "Love Walked in" (see '38). Hear numerous examples of Gershwin's songs performed by some of the most notable artists at http://www.gershwin.com/.

Ira Gershwin (real name: Israel Gershwin; 1896–1983)   Ira Gershwin was George Gershwin's brother. Ira met "Yip" Harburg during high school and they began writing lyrics together. Ira started his career in '18 under the pen name Arthur Francis. It was not until '24 that Ira and George began collaborating. His outstanding lyrics became an integral part of many of the most popular songs of the '20s and '30s. George and Ira's first collaborations include the following Broadway shows and the most famous songs from them: *George White's Scandals*, which included "I'll Build a Stairway to Paradise" (see '23), *Lady, Be Good!*, which included "Fascinating Rhythm," the title song and, although it was cut from the show, "The Man I Love" (see '24), *Tip Toes*, which introduced "Sweet and Low Down," *Oh, Kay!*, which premiered "Clap Yo' Hands," "Do-Do-Do," "Maybe" and "Someone to Watch Over Me," *Funny Face*, which included "'S Wonderful" (see '28). *Rosalie*, which introduced "How Long Has This Been Going On?," *Show Girl*, which premiered "Liza," *Strike Up the Band*, which included "I've Got a Crush on You" and "Soon," *Girl Crazy*, with "But Not for Me," "Embraceable You," "Bidin' My Time" and "I Got Rhythm," *Of Thee I Sing*, the first musical to win the Pulitzer Prize, which included "Of Thee I Sing" and "Love Is Sweeping the Country" (see '32). In '31, the brother team headed to Hollywood to produce film scores for Fox Studios. After a couple of years, they returned to Broadway producing *Pardon My English* and *Let 'Em Eat Cake*. In '35, Ira collaborated with Dubose Heyward on the words for *Porgy and Bess*, an American folk-opera that includes such wonderful songs as "Summertime," "Bess, You Is My Woman Now," "It Ain't Necessarily So" and "I Got Plenty O' Nuthin'." Of course, brother George was the composer (see '35). In '37, Ira and George headed back to Hollywood to write for RKO. Among the movies they scored were *Shall We Dance?*, which included such songs as "Let's Call the Whole Thing Off" and "They Can't Take That Away from Me" (see '37) and *A Damsel in Distress*, which included "A Foggy Day" and "Nice Work If You Can Get It" (see '38). While the brothers were working on the score for the *Goldwyn Follies of '38*, George died from a brain tumor. The score they were writing produced "Love Walked in" (see '38) and "Our Love Is Here to Stay." After George's death, Ira continued to write with many of the best composers of the day, including Jerome Kern, Harold Arlen, Harry Warren, Burton Lane, Kurt Weill, and Aaron Copland. Ira's most famous song lyrics with these composers include "I Can't Get Started with You" (see '36), "The Man That Got Away" (see '54) and "Long Ago (and Far Away)," the biggest hit he ever had in any one year (see

'44). Although Ira was associated with some of Hollywood's most famous songs, only three of his lyrics won Oscar nominations: "They Can't Take That Away from Me," "Long Ago and Far Away," and "The Man That Got Away," but he never won the award. Ira's personal favorites among his lyrics were "Embraceable You," "The Babbitt and the Bromide," "It Ain't Necessarily So," and "The Saga of Jenny." Ira, like his brother, is a member of the Songwriters' Hall of Fame. Hear numerous examples of Gershwin's songs performed by some of the most notable artists at http://www.gershwin.com/.

Ray Getzov   Ray Getzov was the composer of "Please, Mr. Sun" (see '52).

Tamara Geva (real name: Sheversheieva Gevergeva; 1908–1997)   Tamara Geva married choreographer George Balanchine in Europe when she was dancing with the Monte Carlo Ballet. She came to Broadway in the Russian revue *Chauve Souris*. Geva is most remembered for her role in the '36 Broadway musical *On Your Toes*, but she also helped introduce "Louisiana Hayride" in *Flying Colors* (see '32). She should not be confused with the Tamara who starred in *Roberta* ('33). That Tamara did not use a surname.

Georgia Gibbs (real name: Fredda Gibson, changed from Gibbons; 1920–)   Georgia Gibbs was a popular singer from the late '30s through the '50s. She sang on *Your Hit Parade* in '37 and '38 and again in the early '40s under the name Gibson. In '42 she adopted the name Georgia Gibbs. She recorded often in the late '40s and '50s, scoring hits with "Kiss of Fire" (see '52), "Wallflower (Dance with Me Henry)" (see '55) and "Tweedle Dee" (see '55). She became the No. 15 top recording artist of the '50s.

L. Wolfe Gilbert (1886–1970)   L. Wolfe Gilbert, born in Odessa, Russia, was a popular lyricist from the '10s into the early '30s. Gilbert's career began as a vaudeville entertainer when he toured with the famous boxer John L. Sullivan and later with The Ragtime Octet. Gilbert had his first songwriting success with "Waiting for the Robert E. Lee" (see '12). Gilbert's chief collaborators were Lewis Muir, Mabel Wayne, Abel Baer, Ben Oakland, Jay Gorney, Nat Shilkret, Richard Fall and Anatole Friedland. His other best-known songs include "Ragging the Baby to Sleep" (see '12), "Hitchy Koo" (see '13), "By Heck" (see '15), "My Little Dream Girl" (see '15), "My Own Iona" (see '17), "Down Yonder" ('22, see '51, when it was most popular), "O, Katharina" (see '25), "Ramona" (see '28), "Jeannine, I Dream of Lilac Time" (see '28), "Mama Inez" (see '30), "Marta" (see '31), "The Peanut Vendor" (see '31), and "Green Eyes" (see '41). He was a founding member of the Songwriters' Hall of Fame in '70. At http://www.songwritershalloffame.org/exhibit_audio_video.asp?exhibitId=11 hear an audio clip of "Waiting for the Robert E. Lee" performed by the Heidelberg Quintet.

Ray Gilbert (1912–1976)   Academy Award–winning songwriter, composer and author, Ray Gilbert began his career as a writer of special material for show business legends like Sophie Tucker, Harry Richman and Buddy Rogers. He went to Hollywood in the late '30s and after a few years signed with the Walt Disney Company. Gilbert's chief collaborators have included Hoagy Carmichael, Ted FioRito, and Allie Wrubel. Some of his most famous songs include "You Belong to My Heart" (see '45), "Cuanto le Gusta," "All the Cats Join In," "Casey at the Bat," but "Zip-a-Dee-Doo-Dah" is by far the most famous (see '47), all for Disney films.

Terry Gilkyson (1919–1999)   Terry Gilkyson studied music at the University of Pennsylvania. After graduation he worked as a folk singer on armed forces radio. His first success as a recording artist was with the Weavers in '51 on their recording of "On Top of Old Smoky" (see '51). He composed "Cry of the Wild Goose" (see '50), which was a hit for Frankie Laine and "Marianne," a calypso song, recorded by Gilkyson and the Easy Riders in '57. In the folk world, Gilkyson's "Greenfields" has become a modern classic. "The Bare Necessities," from the '67 Disney film *The Jungle Book*, earned Gilkyson an Oscar nomination. He also contributed music to Disney's *Swiss Family Robinson*, *Thomasina* and *Aristocats*.

Arthur Gillespie   Arthur Gillespie's only major contribution to popular music was as lyricist for "Absence Makes the Heart Grow Fonder" (see '01).

Haven Gillespie (1888–1975)   Haven Gillespie was a songwriter, primarily a lyricist, who was most active in the '20s and '30s. Gillespie left high school at the age of 16 to work as a typesetter for the Cincinnati newspaper. In his early 20s, he moved to New York City and found work as a journalist at one of the city's most prestigious newspapers. He also started working as a song plugger and wrote lyrics for vaudeville acts. Gillespie collaborated with J. Fred Coots, Henry Marshall, Henry Tobias, Charles Tobias, Neil Moret, Peter DeRose, Egbert Van Alstyne, Victor Young, Jack Little, Richard Whiting, Peter Wendling, Seymour Simons, Byron Gay, Rudy Vallee, Larry Shay and Lee David. His best known songs include "Breezin' Along with the Breeze" (see '26), "Honey" (see '29), "You Go to My Head" (see '38), "That Lucky Old Sun" (see '49) and "The Old Master Painter" (see '50). Other particularly well known Gillespie songs are "Drifting and Dreaming," and "Santa Claus Is Comin' to Town." He was elected to the Songwriters' Hall of Fame in '72. At http://www.songwritershalloffame.org/exhibit_audio_video.asp?exhibitId=260 hear audio clips of "You Go to My Head" performed by Louis Armstrong and "Whose Honey Are You?" performed by Fats Waller.

William Gillespie   William Gillespie introduced the title song of the film *Blues in the Night* (see '42).

Norman Gimbel (1927–)   Norman Gimbel is a graduate of Baruch School of Business and the Teachers College of Columbia University. His first music job was office boy for Edwin H. Morris music publishing company. It wasn't long before he became a contract songwriter. Gimbel was a co-writer of "Ricochet" (see '53). In '56, he and Eddie Heywood had success with "Canadian Sunset." In the early '60s, Gimbel became associated with a group of young Brazilian composers. Gimbel wrote the English lyrics of Carlos Jobim's "The Girl from Ipanema," which won him a Grammy award. He also wrote the English lyrics for Michel Legrand's music from the '64 film *The Umbrellas of Cherbourg*. In the late '60s he moved to Hollywood, where he became active in film and television. In the early '70s, Gimbel experienced another very successful song when Roberta Flack recorded his (and composer Charles Fox) "Killing Me Softly with His Song" in '73. He won an Academy Award for "Best Original Song" for "It Goes Like It Goes" from *Norma Rae* (with composer David Shire) in '79. With composer Charles Fox, Gimbel has written several TV series theme songs, including those for *Laverne and Shirley* and *Happy Days*. He was inducted into the Songwriters' Hall of Fame in '84.

Will Glahe (1902–1989)   Glahe was a German accordionist and bandleader. He had an especially popular recording of the Czechoslovakian song "Skoda Lasky" titled "Beer Barrel Polka" (see '39). Otherwise, his Victor recordings were only moderately successful.

Tom Glazer (1914–)   Folksinger and songwriter Tom Glazer was lyricist on "Melody of Love" (see '55).

Artie Glenn   Artie Glenn was the writer of "Crying in the Chapel" (see '53). Artie Glenn played guitar and bass fiddle in many bands, including a stint with the Light Crust Doughboys. He wrote many other songs, some of which were recorded by Bob Wills and others. And he wrote a gospel album for TV evangelist Kenneth Copeland.

Fred Glickman (1903–1981)   Fred Glickman was one of the co-writers of "Mule Train" (see '49). Glickman was a composer, songwriter, author, violinist, violist and publisher. He was educated at the Columbia School of Music and at the Chicago Musical College. After stints with dance bands and symphony orchestras, Glickman joined the NBC staff in New York. He was often violinist for Broadway musicals and for film-studio orchestras.

Alma Gluck (1884–1938)   Ms. Gluck was born in Bucharest, Romania, but was raised in the United States. Her first success came with the New York Metropolitan Opera, but from '11 through the rest of the decade, she recorded several popular songs. The most successful was a recording of "Carry Me Back to Old Virginny" (1878, see '15 when it was popular again). Other not quite so successful recordings include "The Old Folks at Home," "Listen to the Mocking Bird" and "My Old Kentucky Home." She is the mother of Efrem Zimbalist, Jr. who starred in some television series and the grandmother of Stephanie Zimbalist who was featured in the *Remington Steele* television series.

Kermit Goell (circa 1915–1997)   Lyricist Kermit Goell was the lyric writer for two '47 hit songs: "Near You" (see '47) and "Huggin' and Chalkin'" (see '47). Goell was a composer, author, and archeologist who was educated at Cornell University in agriculture. He had a myriad of professions: diary farm operator, real estate and construction, and after World War II service, was an archeologist in Turkey.

E. Ray Goetz (real name: Edward Ray Goetz; 1886–1954)   E. Ray Goetz was co-lyricist of "For Me and My Gal" (see '17) and "Yaaka Hula Hickey Dula," which was a famous Al Jolson song. In addition to being a lyricist, Goetz also composed, was an author and a producer. He wrote several Broadway musical scores, including *Roly-Poly, The Pleasure Seekers, The George White's Scandals of '22* and *Hitchy-Koo*. He was the producer of the Broadway musicals *The French Doll, Paris, Fifty Million Frenchmen* and *The New Yorkers*. His primary musical collaborators were Silvio Hein, A. Baldwin Sloane, Raymond

Hubbell, George Meyer, Pete Wendling, Jean Schwartz, George Gershwin and Edgar Leslie.

Ernest Gold (1921–1999)   Ernest Gold was a violin and piano child prodigy in his native Austria. His family left Austria to escape the Nazis in '38, settling in the mid-'40s in Hollywood, where Ernest found employment writing music at Columbia Pictures. His song "Practice Makes Perfect" became a No. 1 hit on *Your Hit Parade* (see '40). Some of the famous films he wrote music for include *On the Beach, Inherit the Wind* and *Judgment at Nuremberg*. In '60, he won an Academy Award for "Exodus," the theme song for the film of the same name. In addition to his film work, Gold has worked on such TV series as *Hawaii Five-O*. His first marriage in '50 to Marni Nixon ended in divorce in '69. Nixon (real name: Marni McEathron) was the dubbed voice behind several famous stars in movie musicals. Her voice was dubbed for Audrey Hepburn in *My Fair Lady*, for Natalie Wood in *West Side Story* and for Deborah Kerr in *The King and I*. When the American Film Institute collected nominations for its *100 Years ... 100 Songs* list, eight songs that Marni Nixon had introduced in films were nominated. Gold's second marriage to Jan Keller lasted until his death in '99.

John Golden (1874–1955)   John Golden wrote lyrics for "Goodbye Girls, I'm Through" for the musical *Chin-Chin* (see '15) and "Poor Butterfly," which premiered in *The Big Show* (see '17).

Al Goodhart (1905–1955)   Al Goodhart was the composer of "I Saw Stars" (see '34) and the World War II song "Johnny Doughboy Found a Rose in Ireland" (see '42). Goodhart was a pianist composer. After high school, he became a radio announcer, a vaudeville pianist, and wrote special material of entertainers. His chief musical collaborators were Mann Curtis, Maurice Sigler, Ed Nelson, Kay Twomey, Allan Roberts, Sammy Lerner and Al Hoffman. Some of his other well known songs include "I Apologize," "Serenade of the Bells," "Auf Wiedersehn, My Dear," "Fit as a Fiddle" and "She Shall Have Music."

Benny Goodman (1909–1986)   Benny Goodman, one of the all-time great clarinetists and big band leaders, became known as the "King of Swing." In the summer of '34 Goodman formed a big band to play in Billy Rose's Music Hall. After mediocre success playing "society music" for dancing, Goodman made a fortunate decision. While playing at the Palomar Ballroom in Los Angeles in '35, he decided to feature his swing sound rather than the society style. The audience, particularly the young people, responded enthusiastically. By early '36 the swing craze was under way, thanks in large part to Benny Goodman. When he was ten, his father sent him to learn music on a borrowed clarinet at Hull House in Chicago. Within two years he was playing the clarinet professionally. In '25 he was hired by Ben Pollack for his orchestra and played with him for four years. The next few years Goodman freelanced in New York City with various studio-recording groups, in pit bands for Broadway shows, and in radio bands. Goodman enjoyed great commercial success, particularly between '36 and '42, with his trio (Goodman, pianist Teddy Wilson and drummer Gene Krupa), quartet (Goodman, Wilson, Krupa and vibraphonist Lionel Hampton), combos (various combinations of quintet, sextet and septet) and the big band. Several of the great jazz instrumentalists played with the Goodman band and then became famous bandleaders themselves. In addition to Krupa, Wilson, and Hampton, Harry James is a notable example; he joined the band in '37 and left in late '38. Goodman's big hit recordings started with "Moonglow" (see '34) and continued with "Goody-Goody" (see '36), "The Glory of Love" (see '36), "These Foolish Things Remind Me of You" (see '36), "It's Been So Long" (see '36), "You Turned the Tables on Me" (see '36), "Goodnight, My Love" (see '37), "This Year's Kisses" (see '37), "Don't Be That Way" (see '38), "I Let a Song Go Out of My Heart" (see '38), "And the Angels Sing" (see '39), "Darn That Dream" (see '40), "There'll Be Some Changes Made" (see '41), "Somebody Else Is Taking My Place" (see '42), "Jersey Bounce" (see '42) and "Taking a Chance on Love" (see '43). *Metronome* nominated the Goodman band the best band of '35. Goodman holds the all-time record of 27 awards in *Down Beat*'s annual readers' poll: top swing band in each year from '36 through '41 and then in '43, top or favorite soloist from '36 through '41 and again from '43 through '47 and '49, top clarinetist from '37 through '39, top quartet in '38, and top small combo from '39 through '42. Goodman was one of five original inductees into the Big Band/Jazz Hall of Fame in '78. Benny was inducted into the Popular Music Hall of Fame in 2002. Goodman rank as the No. 4 top recording artist of the '30s and No. 18 of the '40s, making him the No. 17 top recording artist of the first half of the 20th Century. Some '29 recordings by Benny Goodman's Boys are available at http://www.red hotjazz.com/bands.html.

J. Cheever Goodwin (1850–1912) J. Cheever Goodwin penned the lyrics for the popular song "When Reuben Comes to Town" (see '01). Goodwin wrote for several Broadway productions including *Wang* (1871), *Evangeline* (1874) and *In Central Park* ('00).

Joe Goodwin (1889–1943) Lyricist Joe Goodwin was a charter ASCAP member in '14. He became a songwriter during World War I when he wrote songs for the 81st Wildcats. After the war, he was a monologist in vaudeville and a professional manager for music publishers. He later wrote lyrics for Hollywood films and for London revues. His chief musical collaborators included Nat Ayer, Louis Alter, Gus Edwards, George Meyer, Al Piantadosi, Mark Fisher, and Larry Shay. Goodwin's most famous lyrics were "Baby Shoes" (see '16), "They're Wearing 'Em Higher in Hawaii" (see '17) and "When You're Smiling" (see '28).

Irving Gordon (1915–1996) Irving Gordon was the writer of "Be Anything (but Be Mine)" (see '52) and "Unforgettable" (see '52). Another of his well known songs is "Mister and Mississippi." Gordon studied violin as a child. After high school, he worked in the Catskill Mountain resort hotels. In the '30s, he went to work for Irving Mills' music publishing firm. At first he only wrote lyrics, but later wrote both words and music.

Mack Gordon (real name: Morris Gittler; 1904–1959) Mack Gordon, born in Warsaw, Poland, is particularly remembered as the lyricist of several popular songs from the movies of the '30s and '40s. In the '30s he teamed with Harry Revel, but he did write with other composers. When he and his family immigrated to New York City in '08, his name got Americanized. He began his

show business career as a boy soprano in a minstrel show. Over time, he developed comedy routines and became a singing comic on the vaudeville circuit. He teamed with English immigrant pianist Harry Revel to write songs for the '31 *Ziegfeld Follies*. Later Gordon and Revel were offered a contract by Paramount Pictures. His lyrics were first heard in motion pictures in '29. He wrote and collaborated on nearly 50 film scores. Gordon won the Academy Award for Best Song for "You'll Never Know." He collected nine other Oscar nominations for Best Song. Through the '30s and early '40s, Gordon collaborated with several composers including Harry Warren, Josef Myrow, Jimmy Van Heusen, Vincent Youmans, James Monaco and Edmund Goulding. Gordon's most famous songs include "Time on My Hands" (see '31), "Did You Ever See a Dream Walking?" (see '33), "Love Thy Neighbor" (see '34), "Stay as Sweet as You Are" (see '34), "With My Eyes Wide Open, I'm Dreaming" (see '34), "Paris in the Spring" (see '35), "Goodnight, My Love" (see '37), "When I'm with You" (see '36), "Thanks for Everything" (see '39), "Chattanooga Choo Choo" (see '41), "(I've Got a Gal in) Kalamazoo" (see '42), "I Had the Craziest Dream" (see '43), "You'll Never Know" (see '43), "I'm Making Believe" (see '44), "My Heart Tells Me" (see '44), "The More I See You" (see '45), "I Can't Begin to Tell You" (see '45), "Mam'selle" (see '47) and "You Do" (see '47). Gordon also wrote "At Last," "My Heart Is an Open Book," "Lookie, Lookie, Lookie, Here Comes Cookie," "Without a Word of Warning," "From the Top of Your Head (To the Tip of Your Toes)," "I Feel Like a Feather in the Breeze," "There Will Never Be Another You," "Serenade in Blue," "On the Boardwalk in Atlantic City," and "You Make Me Feel So Young." Gordon was inducted into the Songwriters' Hall of Fame in '70. At http://www.song writershalloffame.org/exhibit_audio_video.asp?exhibit Id=220 hear audio clips of "There Will Never Be Another You" performed by Chet Baker, "Chattanooga Choo Choo" performed by Ray Anthony and his orchestra, "You'll Never Know" performed by Dick Haymes and the Song Spinners, "The More I See You" performed by Nancy Wilson, "Serenade in Blue" performed by Ethel Ennis, "Stay as Sweet as You Are" performed by Sam Browne with Ambrose and his orchestra, and "At Last" performed by Eva Cassidy.

Jay Gorney (real name: Daniel Jason Gorney; 1896–1990) Composer Jay Gorney, born in Bialystok, Russia, wrote "Brother, Can You Spare a Dime?" (see '32) and not a lot else that is very well known. He wrote the music for several Hollywood movies from the mid–'30s through the '40s, but most of the songs never became particularly important hits. "Baby, Take a Bow" from the '34 movie *Stand Up and Cheer* is one song that escaped anonymity. In the '50s, Gorney worked as a producer-composer for CBS-TV, and also worked with the faculty of the American Theater Wing. In '61, Gorney and E.Y. Harburg adapted the music of Jacques Offenbach for the Broadway show *The Happiest Girl in the World*. Also in '61, Gorney and lyricist John W. Block wrote a group of original scores for NBC-TV, entitled *Frontiers of Faith*.

Stuart Gorrell Stuart Gorrell, Hoagy Carmichael's roommate, was the lyricist of "Georgia on My Mind" (see '31). The website http://en.wikipedia.org says he wrote this lyric for Georgia, Hoagy's sister. It was also Gorrell who dubbed Carmichael's masterpiece "Star Dust," because he said "it sounded like dust from the stars drifting down through the summer sky."

Edmund Goulding (1891–1959) Edmund Goulding was a well-known actor, playwright, and director for the London stage. He emigrated to the U.S. after World War I. He became a screenwriter in Hollywood, wrote a novel, *Fury*, in '22 and directed the film version of his novel. He became a screenwriter and director at MGM in '25. Goulding's only well-known song was "Mam'selle," which was introduced in the film *The Razor's Edge* (see '47).

Betty Grable (real name: Ruth Elizabeth Grable; 1916–1973) Betty Grable was the number one pinup girl for servicemen during World War II. Almost two million copies of her famous picture in a white bathing suit were sent to men in the military all over the world. She was a singing and dancing star of several movie musicals in the '40s and '50s. Her fabled legs were often displayed in her movies and on pinup calendars. She married Jackie Coogan in '37 (divorced in '40) and received her first real acclaim in the '39 Broadway musical *DuBarry Was a Lady*. She became a Hollywood star in the '40s. Ms. Grable introduced "My Heart Tells Me" in the movie musical *Sweet Rosie O'Grady* (see '44). She married bandleader Harry James in '43 (divorced in '65). Despite her extensive musical activities, there is an odd lack of recordings by her. After she introduced "I Can't Begin to Tell You" in *The Dolly Sisters*, she helped popularized it with the Harry James band under the name Ruth Haag (see '45).

George Graff, Jr. (1886–1973) George Graff, Jr. co-wrote several popular songs with Ernest R. Ball and Chauncey Olcott, most notably "I Love the Name of Mary" (see '11), "Isle o' Dreams" ('13), and "When Irish Eyes Are Smiling" (see '13). He also wrote "As Long as the World Rolls On" (see '08), "To the End of the World with You" (see '09) and "Till the Sands of the Desert Grow Cold" (see '13) with Ball.

George Grafton George Grafton was co-lyricist with Harry Lauder for "I Love a Lassie" (see '07). Another co-lyricist with Lauder is listed as Gerald Grafton ("A Wee Deoch-an-Doris"). Are they really the same person or brothers?

Gloria Grafton (1909–1994) Gloria Grafton introduced "Two Cigarettes in the Dark" in the nonmusical motion picture *Kill That Story* (see '34). Ms. Grafton and Donald Novis introduced "My Romance" in the Rodgers and Hart musical *Jumbo* (see '35).

Irvin Graham (1909–2001) Irvin Graham was one of the co-writers of "I Believe" (see '53). Graham was a composer, actor, author, writer and singer. He was educated at Zeckwer Hahn Musical Academy.

Roger Graham Roger Graham was the lyricist for "I Ain't Got Nobody" (see '16).

Bert Grant (1878–1951) Bert Grant was the composer of "If I Knock the 'L' Out of Kelly (It Would Still Be Kelly to Me)" (see '16). Mr. Grant was a pianist/songwriter. Grant's other songs include "When the Angelus Is Ringing" and "Along the Rocky Road to Dublin." Grant claimed to have performed the first musical broadcast from Roselle Park in New Jersey.

Glen Gray (real name: Glen Gray "Spike" Knob-laugh; 1906–1963) The Orange Blossom Band was renamed the Casa Loma Orchestra after it had played an engagement at the Casa Loma Hotel in Toronto in '28. The band was reorganized in '29 and Glen Gray became president and leader, but he did not actually front the group until '37. Pee Wee Hunt, Kenny Sargent, Red Nichols, and Bobby Hackett were members of the band at various times. The band began to attract considerable attention in the early '30s and had their biggest hit recordings with "When I Grow Too Old to Dream" (see '35), "Blue Moon" (see '35), "Heaven Can Wait" (see '39), "Sunrise Serenade" (see '39) plus "My Heart Tells Me" (see '44). The Big Band/Jazz Hall of Fame honored Glen Gray's Casa Loma Orchestra with induction in 2002. The members are generally individuals, but in this instance, the entire group was honored. Gray is listed as the No. 20 top recording artist of the '30s.

Jerry Gray (real name: Jerry Graziano; 1915–1976) Jerry Gray composed some of the Glenn Miller orchestra's biggest hits. He began arranging for the Artie Shaw band in the late '30s and for Miller in the early '40s. He was responsible for the arrangement of "Begin the Beguine" that was Shaw's first major hit. Gray's most famous compositions were "A String of Pearls" (see '42) and "Pennsylvania 6-5000."

Thomas J. Gray (1888–1924) Thomas J. Gray was an author and lyricist. He was educated at Holy Cross School and a charter member of ASCAP. He served overseas during World War I, and later wrote songs for Broadway and London revues, plus special material for Bert Williams, Blossom Seeley, and Mae West. His chief musical collaborators included Fred Fisher and Ray Walker. His most famous popular song was "Any Little Girl That's a Nice Little Girl Is the Right Little Girl for Me" (see '10).

Kathryn Grayson (real name: Zelma Kathryn Elisabeth Hedrick; 1922–) Singer Kathryn Grayson starred in several movie musicals in the '40s and '50s. Her operatic soprano voice was particularly suited for the songs from *Show Boat, Rio Rita, The Desert Song, The Vagabond King, The Toast of New Orleans* and as opera singer Grace Moore in *So This Is Love*. Ms. Grayson introduced "My Heart Sings" in the movie musical *Anchors Aweigh* (see '45). She and Mario Lanza introduced "Be My Love" in the movie musical *Toast of New Orleans* (see '51). As beautiful as her clear voice was for operatic numbers, she was also very capable on popular numbers.

Charles R. Grean (1913–2003) Charles R. Grean adapted an old Rabelaisian song, "The Tailor's Boy" into "The Thing" (see '50). Mr. Grean worked with Glenn Miller, Artie Shaw, Nat King Cole and others. His first solo recording was "Quentin's Theme" from the TV series *Dark Shadows*. Mr. Grean composed the score for the documentary *Two Men of Karamoja*. For more on Grean, please see http://www.geocities.com/Nashville/1845/grean.htm.

Adolph Green (1914–2002) Adolph Green was a songwriter, author, actor and singer. He met his writing partner, Betty Comden, when they were members of the Revuers. His Broadway score for *Wonderful Town* won a Tony Award in '53. His other stage scores include *Peter Pan* and *Do Re Mi*. He was co-librettist and co-lyricist for

On the Town and *Bells Are Ringing*, among others. Green, John Battles and Cris Alexander introduced "New York, New York," for which Green co-wrote the lyrics, in the Broadway musical *On the Town* (see '44).

Bud Green (1897–1981) Lyricist Bud Green was particularly active from the early '20s through the late '40s. He had come to this country from his native Austria. As a young adult, Green began writing special material for vaudeville shows. Working as a staff writer for music publishers from '20 through '27, he wrote Broadway stage scores and songs for such renowned performers as Sophie Tucker. Green collaborated with such songwriters as Les Brown, Buddy De Sylva, Al Dubin, Ella Fitzgerald, Slim Gaillard, Ray Henderson, Ben Homer, Raymond Scott, Sam Stept and Harry Warren. Bud Green's most famous songs include "Alabamy Bound" (see '25), "That's My Weakness Now" (see '28), "Once in a While" (see '37), "Flat Foot Floogee" (see '38) and "Sentimental Journey" (see '45). Bud Green was elected to the Songwriters' Hall of Fame in '75.

Jane Green Jane Green inserted "I Never Knew I Could Love Anybody Like I'm Loving You" into the revue *The Century Revue* and also into the *Midnight Rounders of '21* (see '21).

Johnny Green (1908–1989) Johnny Green is important as a composer, an arranger, a conductor, and musical director for several significant Hollywood films. Green graduated from Harvard University in '28. During his early career, he arranged for the Guy Lombardo Orchestra and contributed to various revues, including *Three's a Crowd*. For a few years during the early '30s, he was an arranger and conductor for Paramount studios and accompanist for several famous singers. He also conducted the orchestra for the Jack Benny and Philip Morris radio shows. In the late '40s, Green was hired as the Music Director at MGM, a position he would hold until the late '50s. Green wrote film scores for some of MGM's most celebrated films including *Raintree County, Easter Parade, Bathing Beauty, Summer Stock, The Toast of New Orleans,* and *Royal Wedding,* among others. From the late '50s through mid-'60s, Green conducted various orchestras throughout the country. Green collaborated with several famous lyricists including Gus Kahn, "Yip" Harburg, Edward Heyman, Paul Francis Webster, Mack David, Billy Rose and Johnny Mercer. Johnny Green's most famous songs include "Body and Soul" (see '30), "Out of Nowhere" (see '31), "I Cover the Waterfront" (see '33), "I Wanna Be Loved" (see '50). Others of Green's songs include "Coquette," "Easy Come, Easy Go" and "The Song of Raintree County." He was inducted into the Songwriters' Hall of Fame in '72. Green also had a successful recording career from '34 through '36. His most popular recordings were of "Two Cigarettes in the Dark" with Ethel Merman and "The Little Things We Used to Do." Both made it to No. 2 on the *Billboard* chart.

Mitzi Green (real name: Elizabeth Keno; 1920–1969) Mitzi Green and Ray Heatherton introduced "Where or When" in *Babes in Arms*. Ms. Green also introduced "My Funny Valentine," in the same musical (see '37). "Little Mitzi," as she was known early in her career, was the first child Paramount Pictures ever signed to a multi-picture contract.

Clay M. Greene (1850–1933) Clay M. Greene's contribution to popular music was as lyricist for "Ma Tiger Lily" (see '00).

Paul Gregory (circa 1904–1942) Paul Gregory and Marilyn Miller introduced "Time on My Hands" in the Broadway musical *Smiles* (see '31).

Eliseo Grenet (1893–1950) Cuban composer Eliseo Grenet wrote "Mama Inez" (see '30). Grenet is primarily known in the U.S. as the composer of this song. He also directed a theatrical group, toured Mexico and Central America, and organized a group to perform his compositions. He later scored films in France, Mexico and Cuba.

Maria Grever (real name: María Joaquina de la Portilla Torres; 1894–1951) Spanish composer Maria Grever wrote the popular songs "What a Diff'rence a Day Made" (see '34) and "Ti-Pi-Tin" (see '38). She was a songwriter, singer and pianist. Her chief collaborators were Stanley Adams, Irving Caesar and Raymond Leveen.

Clifford Grey (real name: Percival Davis; 1887–1941) Lyricist and author, Clifford Grey was educated in his hometown of Birmingham, England. He began as an actor, then wrote for the Broadway stage on productions such as *Sally, Vogues of '24, Artists and Models* ('24 and '25 editions), *Gay Paree, Great Temptations, Hit the Deck,* and *The Three Musketeers.* His chief musical collaborators included J. Fred Coots, Jay Gorney, Jerome Kern, Sigmund Romberg, Rudolf Friml, Lewis Gensler, Johnny Green, Oscar Levant, Leo Robin, Richard Myers, Victor Schertzinger, Herbert Stothart, Vincent Youmans, Werner Janssen, Al Goodman, Maurie Rubens, William Cary Duncan, and Jean Schwartz. Grey's most popular songs were "Look for the Silver Lining" from *Sally* (see '21), the English lyrics for "Valencia" (see '26), "Hallelujah!" From *Hit the Deck* (see '27), and "Sometimes I'm Happy" (see '27). His other popular-songs include "If You Were the Only Girl in the World" and "Got a Date with an Angel."

Jimmie Grier (1902–1959) Jimmie (or Jimmy) Grier played clarinet and saxophone. He got his start as arranger for Gus Arnheim's Cocoanut Grove Orchestra. When Arnheim's group left the Cocoanut Grove, Grier was hired. Some of the vocalists with Grier's band at various times included Harry Barris, one of the original Rhythm Boys, Larry Cotton, who later was vocalist for Horace Heidt's band, and Pinky Tomlin. Some of Grier's most popular recordings include "Stay as Sweet as You Are" (see '34), "The Object of My Affection" (see '34) and "What's the Reason (I'm Not Pleasin' You)" (see '35). Grier and his band became the No. 32 top recording artists of the '30s. Grier also co-wrote "The Object of My Affection" (see '34) and "What's the Reason?" (see '35).

Ken Griffin (1909–1956) Organist Ken Griffin taught himself to play the organ and accompanied silent films during the '20s. During the '30s he played hotels in the mid-west. After military service during World War II, he began recording mostly waltzes and nostalgic tunes, many of which were played at ice skating rinks. A recording of "You Can't Be True, Dear" (see '48) by Griffin and vocalist Jerry Wayne was a first. Griffin originally recorded it in early '48, primarily as music to accompany ice skaters. It became so popular with the skaters that the publisher Dave Dreyer decided to dub in a vocal. He signed Jerry

Wayne to do the singing. The lyrics were written while Wayne was waiting to do the recording. The resulting disk was the first big success for a recording made by superimposing a voice on an already existing recording. Both the vocal version and the non-vocal version charted. Griffin became the No. 40 top recording artist of the '40s. Griffin was also given composing credit, sharing it with Hans Otten, the original composer. It's difficult to ascertain what Griffin contributed to receive credit.

Merv Griffin (1925–)   Griffin started his show business career as a big band singer with such groups as Freddy Martin. He was with Martin from '48 until '51. He then appeared in a few Warner Bros. films. He later turned to TV and hosted a long-running talk show. By the mid–'60s, Griffin founded Merv Griffin Productions, which produced television shows. Most notably, Griffin and his company are the producers of *Wheel of Fortune* and *Jeopardy*.

Louise Groody (1897–1961)   Louise Groody began her show business career as a dancer. She gained considerable fame on Broadway in *No, No, Nanette* and *Hit the Deck*. Groody and John Barker introduced "Tea for Two" in *No, No, Nanette* (see '25), while she and Charles Winninger introduced "I Want to Be Happy" in the same production (see '25). Ms. Groody and Charles King introduced "Sometimes I'm Happy" in *Hit the Deck* (see '27).

Walter Gross (real name: Walter Lloyd Gross; 1909–1967)   Songwriter, composer, pianist, conductor, author and publisher, Walter Gross gave his first piano recital at age 10. He later became pianist with Paul Whiteman, Andre Kostelanetz and Tommy Dorsey. He served in the Army during World War II. After the war, he became the music director for CBS and Musicraft records. He also conducted for Gordon MacRae, Sarah Vaughan, Mel Torme, Frank Sinatra and Buddy Clark. Gross was the composer of "Tenderly" (see '52).

Will Grosz (real name: Wilhelm Grosz; 1894–1939)   Composer Will Grosz was born in Vienna, Austria. In '34 he emigrated to the U.S., where he composed operas, ballets, and popular music. Some of his melodies include "Isle of Capri" (see '35), "Red Sails in the Sunset" (see '35) and "Harbor Lights" (see '50), written under the pseudonym Hugh Williams.

Albert Gumble (1883–1946)   Albert Gumble was an American composer of popular music who worked in various music-publishing houses. Although he published several of his own compositions, most of his work was done arranging pieces by people such as Percy Wenrich, Vincent Bryan, Alfred Bryan, Gus Kahn, Edward Madden, Buddy DeSylva, George Whiting, Jack Yellen and many others. His "Are You Sincere?" which he wrote with Alfred Bryan, was very popular in '08. His "Rebecca of Sunny-brook Farm" was popular in '14.

Yehiel Haggiz   Yehiel Haggiz was co-writer of "Tzena, Tzena, Tzena" (see '50). Haggiz was a friend of Issachar Miron. Miron was 19 years old, while Haggiz was 30 years old when they wrote the tune to this song. American folksinger Pete Seeger helped Haggiz and Miron develop the song into what became the '50 hit song.

William Hain   William Hain and Tamara introduced "The Touch of Your Hand" in *Roberta* (see '34).

Connie Haines (real name: Yvonne Marie Jamais; 1922–)   Connie Haines is best remembered as vocalist with the Tommy Dorsey orchestra. She began singing as a child and worked with bands in Miami in the late '30s before her break into the big time. She sang with Harry James for a few months, and about this time she changed her name. She joined the Dorsey band in '40 and stayed for two years. After she left the band, she sang as a single and recorded occasionally. She was one of the featured vocalists on Tommy Dorsey's hit recording of "Oh, Look at Me Now" (see '41).

Bill Haley (1925–1981)   Bill Haley was one of the most famous of the early rock 'n' roll personalities. He is often given credit for starting the rock 'n' roll craze with his recordings of "Shake, Rattle and Roll" (see '54) and "Rock Around the Clock" (see '55). Haley and his Comets had sold more than 60 million records by the beginning of the '70s. The collective sales of "Rock Around the Clock" alone have been estimated to be more than 22 million. However, Haley was not listed among the top recording artists of the '50s. Haley's only other really popular recording was "See You Later, Alligator" in '56.

Jack Haley (1901–1979)   Jack Haley was a member of the vaudeville team of Crofts and Haley before he made his Broadway debut in *Follow Thru*. He also appeared in *Take a Chance* ('32) and *Inside USA* ('48) on Broadway, but today he is better known for his film roles. Haley introduced "Did You Ever See a Dream Walking?" in the movie *Sitting Pretty* (see '33). Haley and Ethel Merman introduced "You're an Old Smoothie" in the musical *Take a Chance* (see '33). Haley, who became almost immortal for his role as the Tin Man in the '39 movie musical *The Wizard of Oz*, was particularly adept at playing the bewildered, inept, reluctant hero. Movie musicals with Haley in the cast include *Alexander's Ragtime Band, Moon Over Miami, Poor Little Rich Girl* and *Wake Up and Live*, among others.

Hal Halifax   Hal Halifax was the lyricist of "Penny Serenade" (see '39).

Adelaide Hall (1895–1993)   Adelaide Hall appeared in several all-black revues, including *Shuffle Along* ('21), *Runnin' Wild* ('23) and *Blackbirds of 1928*. She introduced "Diga Diga Doo" in her first starring role on Broadway in *Blackbirds of 1928* (see '28). After extensive touring she settled in Europe in '36. She came back to Broadway in '57 for a role in *Jamaica*. Ms. Hall worked with many wonderful performers including Bill "Bojangles" Robinson, Ethel Waters, Josephine Baker, Louis Armstrong, Lena Horne, and Cab Calloway among others. She adopted England as her home in the late '30s and during the '40s became one of that country's highest paid entertainers.

Owen Hall (real name: James Davis; 1853–1907)   Owen Hall was the pen name of 19th and early 20th century theatre critic James Davis, who was born in Dublin. He wrote the librettos for several very successful shows, most notably *Florodora* (see "Tell Me, Pretty Maiden" in '01), but also including *A Gaiety Girl, An Artist's Model, The Geisha, A Greek Slave, The Silver Slipper, The Girl from Kay's, The Medal and the Maid* and *Sergeant Brue*. Davis became a librettist after he had written a review of a George Edwardes production; the producer challenged Davis to do better. The result was *A Gaiety Girl*. He was a keen gambler. It has been reported that his pen name,

Owen Hall, was chosen as irony ("owing all") because of his extensive gambling debts. Another of his pseudonyms was Payne Nunn ("paying none").

Wendell Hall (1896–1969) Songwriter, composer, singer, ukulele player and author, Wendell Hall was educated at the Chicago Preparatory School. He served in the military during World War I. Afterwards, he sang and played ukulele on radio beginning in '22. He was known as the "Red-Headed Music Maker." He became broadcasting director for the CBS *Majestic Theatre of the Air* in '29, and was a featured performer on the NBC *Fitch Band Wagon* between '32 and '35. Later he was the song leader on the *Original Community Sing* over CBS in '36 and '37. From '41 through '48 he was an advertising executive. His chief musical collaborators included Haven Gillespie, Carson Robison, Harry Woods, and Peter De Rose. By far his most famous song was "It Ain't Gonna Rain No Mo'" (see '24).

Robert Halliday (1893–1975) Robert Halliday, the hero of *The Desert Song* and *The New Moon*, immigrated to the United States from Scotland. Halliday appeared in fourteen Broadway musicals from '21 to '52. Halliday helped introduce "Lover, Come Back to Me" and several other songs in *The New Moon* (see '29). He married Evelyn Herbert, who was his co-star in three Broadway productions. After the early '50s, Halliday and Herbert enjoyed their retirement at their "New Moon" ranch in California, dying within months of each other.

Edith Hallor (1896–1971) Edith Hallor introduced the title song of the musical *Leave It to Jane* (see '17).

Stuart Hamblen (1908–1989) Stuart Hamblen became one of the first singing cowboys on radio in '26. Between '31 and '52 Hamblen had a series of radio shows on the West Coast. He also composed music and acted in a few films with such other stars as Gene Autry, Roy Rogers and John Wayne. His most famous songs were "It Is No Secret" (see '51) and "This Ole House" (see '54). In the late '40s he had a religious conversion at an L.A. revival meeting. He soon gave up his secular radio and film career to enter religious broadcasting with his radio show, *The Cowboy Church of the Air*. Hamblen supported the temperance movement and agreed to run as the Prohibition Party's candidate for President in the '52 national election. Hamblen was inducted into the Nashville Songwriters Hall of Fame in '70, the Academy of Country and Western Music honored him with its prestigious Pioneer Award for being the "first singing Country and Western Cowboy in the history of broadcasting" in '72, and he was inducted into the Western Music Hall of Fame in '99.

Arthur Hamilton Arthur Hamilton wrote the words and music for "Cry Me a River" (see '55). Hamilton was a songwriter, author and publisher. He composed some Hollywood film scores, including *The Girl Can't Help It* and *Pete Kelly's Blues*. In addition to his film and television work, he became a music publisher in '58.

Nancy Hamilton (1908–1985) Nancy Hamilton was the lyricist of "How High the Moon" (see '51). The song had been introduced originally in '40. Hamilton was a songwriter, singer, actress and author. She had been educated at the Sorbonne in Paris and at Smith College. She appeared in several Broadway productions and wrote a play that was produced there. She wrote the Broadway

scores for *One for the Money, Two for the Show* and *Three to Make Ready*.

Arthur Hammerstein (circa 1873–1955) Lyricist Arthur Hammerstein was the uncle of famed lyricist Oscar Hammerstein II. He penned the words to "Because of You" (see '51).

Oscar Hammerstein II (1895–1960) Other than Irving Berlin, Oscar Hammerstein II is the most prolific lyricist of all time. Hammerstein collaborated with several excellent composers, but his association with Richard Rodgers from the early '40s until his death is best known. He had previously collaborated with Jerome Kern, Sigmund Romberg, Rudolf Friml, George Gershwin and Vincent Youmans. He is, of course, a member of the Songwriters' Hall of Fame. Hammerstein was born into a show business family. His father was manager of the historic Victoria vaudeville theater in New York City, and his grandfather had been an important opera impresario and theater builder. The list of hit songs credited to Oscar Hammerstein II is filled with some of the greatest lyrics written from the '20s through the '50s. Some of his best-known songs of the '20s include "Bambalina" (see '23), "Rose Marie" (see '25), "Indian Love Call" (see '25), "Who?" (see '26), "The Desert Song" (see '27), "One Alone" (see '27), "Riff Song" (see '27), "Can't Help Lovin' Dat Man" (see '28), "Make Believe" (see '28), "Ol' Man River" (see '28), "Why Do I Love You?" (see '28), "Lover, Come Back to Me" (see '29), "Softly, as in a Morning Sunrise" (see '29), and "Why Was I Born?" (see '29). In the '30s Hammerstein continued to produce numerous hit songs, as yet without Richard Rodgers. Some of his biggest hit songs of the decade include "I've Told Ev'ry Little Star" (see '33), "When I Grow Too Old to Dream" (see '35), and "All the Things You Are" (see '40). One of his pre–Rodgers hit songs of the early '40s was "The Last Time I Saw Paris" (see '41). The first Broadway musical for the Rodgers and Hammerstein team was the fantastically successful *Oklahoma!* ('43). Through the rest of the '40s Hammerstein's most famous song lyrics include the songs from *Oklahoma!,* particularly including "People Will Say We're in Love," "Oh, What a Beautiful Mornin'," and "The Surrey with the Fringe on Top" (see '43), several well-known songs from *Carousel*, particularly including "If I Loved You" (see '45), "You'll Never Walk Alone" (see '45) and "June Is Bustin' Out All Over," the songs from *State Fair*, including "It Might as Well Be Spring," "It's a Grand Night for Singing" and "That's for Me" (see '45), *Allegro*, and the wonderful songs from *South Pacific*, especially including "Some Enchanted Evening" and "A Wonderful Guy" (see '49). Hammerstein and Jerome Kern collaborated on "All Through the Day" for the movie musical *Centennial Summer* (see '46), Hammerstein's most memorable lyrics from Broadway musicals of the '50s include the songs from *The King and I, Me and Juliet, Pipe Dream, Flower Drum Song* and *The Sound of Music. The King and I* had several songs that are still remembered, but the two that were most popular on the charts were "Hello, Young Lovers" and "We Kiss in a Shadow" (see '51). He also produced the lyrics for the television musical *Cinderella*. At http://www.songwritershalloffame.org/exhibit_audio_vide o.asp?exhibitId=13 hear audio clips of "All the Things You Are" performed by Sarah Vaughan, "Lover, Come Back to Me" as recorded by Billie Holiday, "Can't Help Lovin'

Dat Man," "Why Was I Born?," and "Bill" performed by Lena Horne, "A Kiss to Build a Dream On" performed by Louis Armstrong, "Oh, What a Beautiful Mornin'!," "If I Loved You," "You'll Never Walk Alone," and "Some Enchanted Evening" sung by Frank Sinatra, "Do-Re-Mi" and "Edelweiss" sung by Harry Connick, Jr., "Getting to Know You" performed by Gertrude Lawrence, "June Is Bustin' Out All Over" performed by Celeste Holm and "Oklahoma!" performed by the original cast of the musical.

Lou Handman (1894–1956) In his early show business career, composer Lou Handman toured the vaudeville circuit, mostly throughout Australia and New York. After serving in the U.S. Army during World War I, he resumed his career as a pianist and accompanist to vaudeville singers. Handman primarily collaborated with Roy Turk, but he also wrote with Archie Gottler and Harry Harris. Handman and Turk collaborated on "My Sweetie Went Away" (see '23) and "One Night of Love" (see '34). Another well known Handman song is "Are You Lonesome Tonight." Lou Handman was inducted into the Songwriters' Hall of Fame in '75.

W.C. Handy (real name: William Christopher Handy; 1873–1958) Known as the Father of the Blues, W.C. Handy was born in Florence, Alabama. Handy performed as a cornetist with a touring quartet that played at Chicago's World Fair in 1893. He moved around from Chicago to Texas and eventually to Mississippi, where he was a bandmaster and music teacher. In '13, Handy became the first African American to own his own publishing company. "Memphis Blues" (see '14), "Beale Street Blues" (see '16) and "St. Louis Blues" (see '20) are by far his most well known compositions, but he also wrote "Loveless Love," which became the song "Careless Love." Others of his compositions include "Yellow Dog Blues," "Joe Turner Blues," "Hesitating Blues," "Aunt Hagar's Blues" and "John Henry." Handy was inducted into the Songwriters' Hall of Fame in '70 and the Big Band/Jazz Hall of Fame in '81. At http://www.song writershalloffame.org/exhibit_audio_video.asp? exhibitId=263 hear an audio clip of "St. Louis Blues" performed by Paul Robeson with Ray Noble and the New Mayfair Orchestra. Some recordings by W.C. Handy (Handy's Orchestra of Memphis, Handy's Memphis Blues Band, Handy's Orchestra, W.C. Handy and Orchestra) are available at http://www.redhotjazz.com/bands.html.

Carol Haney (1924–1964) Carol Haney introduced "Hernando's Hideaway" in the Broadway musical *Pajama Game* (see '54). Haney was primarily a dancer. She opened a dance studio in her hometown of New Bedford, MA before she graduated from high school. During World War II, she went to Hollywood and became a protégée of Gene Kelly. After *Pajama Game*, she was primarily a choreographer for such Broadway hits as *Flower Drum Song, She Loves Me* and *Funny Girl*.

Bernie Hanighen (real name: Bernard D. Hanighen; 1908–1976) Bernie Hanighen was the composer of "Bob White (Whatcha Gonna Swing Tonight?)" (see '37). Hanighen and Clarence Williams turned Thelonious Monk's "'Round About Midnight" into "'Round Midnight."

James F. Hanley (1892–1942) Composer James Frederick Hanley attended Champion College and the Chicago Musical College. In '14, he joined the Army and served during World War I in the 82nd division. After the war, Hanley found work as an accompanist for vaudeville shows and soon began writing a succession of Broadway stage scores. Working with collaborators such as B.G. De Sylva, Edward Madden, Eddie Dowling, Percy Wenrich, Theodore Morse and Ballard MacDonald, Hanley produced such well-known songs as "Indiana" (see '17), "Rose of Washington Square" (see '20), "Second Hand Rose" (see '21), and "Zing! Went the Strings of My Heart" (see '35). James Hanley has been a member of the Songwriters' Hall of Fame since '70. At http://www.songwriters halloffame.org/exhibit_audio_video.asp?exhibitId=255 hear an audio clip of "Second Hand Rose" performed by Fanny Brice.

Bert Hanlon (1890–1972) Bert Hanlan, composer, songwriter, actor, author and director, was educated at City College of New York. He appeared in vaudeville, in Broadway musicals and Hollywood films and wrote special material for films, as well as serving as dialogue director. His chief musical collaborators included Walter Donaldson, James Hanley, Al Bryan, Harry Tierney, Harry Akst, and Milton Ager. His most remembered song is "M-I-S-S-I-S-S-I-P-P-I" (see '17).

Otto Harbach (real name: Otto Abels Hauerbach; 1873–1963) Although lyricist Otto Harbach did not begin writing songs until his mid-thirties, he produced lyrics for several important Broadway musicals. Many of his greatest successes were in collaboration with Oscar Hammerstein II. He also wrote with some of popular music's greatest composers, including Jerome Kern, George Gershwin, Rudolf Friml, Vincent Youmans, and Karl Hoschna. After graduating from Knox College in 1895, Harbach embarked on several careers. From 1895 through '01, he served as a Professor of English at Columbia University and Whitman College; during '02 and '03, he was a New York City newspaper writer; and from '03 through '10, he worked for advertising agencies. When Harbach met composer Karl Hoschna, they began collaborating on songs for vaudeville and minstrel acts. When they began to achieve some success, Harbach decided to devote himself to writing for Broadway productions. Harbach worked as lyricist and often librettist on many Broadway productions, including *Roberta, Rose Marie, No, No, Nanette, Sunny, The Desert Song, Kid Boots, Oh, Please!, Good Boy,* among others. In '14, Harbach was a charter member of ASCAP and remained actively involved serving as a director, vice president and president. Harbach collaborated with some the best songwriters of his time, including Oscar Hammerstein II, Rudolf Friml, Jerome Kern, L. Wolfe Gilbert, Louis Hirsch, Herbert Stothart, Vincent Youmans, George Gershwin and Sigmund Romberg. Highlights of Harbach's most famous songs include "Cuddle Up a Little Closer, Lovey Mine" (see '08), "Yama Yama Man" (see '09), "Every Little Movement" (see '10), "Sympathy" (see '13), "Giannina Mia" (see '13), "You're in Love" (see '17), "The Love Nest" (see '20), "Bambalina" (see '23), "Indian Love Call" (see '25), "Rose Marie" (see '25), "Who?" (see '26), "The Desert Song" (see '27), "Riff Song" (see '27), "One Alone" (see '27), "Smoke Gets in Your Eyes" (see '34), "The Touch of Your Hand" (see '34) and "I Won't Dance" (see '35). Otto A. Harbach was inducted into the Songwriters' Hall of Fame in '70. At http://www.songwritershalloffame.org/exhibit_audio_video.asp?exhibitId=105 hear an audio clip of "Smoke Gets in Your Eyes" performed by Irene Dunne with Victor Young and his orchestra.

E.Y. Harburg (real name: Isidore Hochberg; 1898–1981)

E.Y. "Yip" Harburg became an important lyricist of popular songs, especially in the '30s and '40s. He wrote for several important Broadway musicals and independently. His chief collaborators were composers Harold Arlen and Jay Gorney. Harburg's nickname was "Yipsel," the Yiddish word for squirrel, because he was constantly clowning and had unlimited energy. The nickname was later shortened to "Yip." As a youngster, he worked at many jobs, including putting pickles in jars at a small pickle factory, selling newspapers, and lighting street lamps along the docks of the East River. He attended high school at an experimental school for talented children, where he worked on the school newspaper with Ira Gershwin. After graduation from City College of New York in '21, Harburg worked for a few years as a journalist in South America. When he returned to the U.S., he became co-owner of an electrical appliance company that went out of business as a result of the '29 stock market crash. Harburg's high school friend, Ira Gershwin loaned him some money and introduced him to a number of talented songwriters. Harburg's first venture into songwriting was writing lyrics for music by Jay Gorney, a former lawyer. In '29 they supplied six songs for *Earl Carroll's Sketch Book*, and they wrote the Depression era classic "Brother, Can You Spare a Dime?" for the revue *Americana* (see '32). During the next few decades, Harburg wrote lyrics for the music of many composers including Harold Arlen, Vernon Duke, Jerome Kern, Jule Styne, and Burton Lane. The Harburg-Arlen team's pinnacle came in '39, when they wrote the score for the movie *The Wizard of Oz*, which was approached as a Depression fantasy. The film included several famous songs, most notably "Over the Rainbow" (see '39), the Academy Award winner. They wrote the score for the movie *Cabin in the Sky*, which featured "Happiness Is a Thing Called Joe" (see '43). Harburg and Arlen's '44 Broadway musical, *Bloomer Girl* addressed slavery, the woman's reform movement and the horrors of war. Harburg and Burton Lane collaborated on what is considered the masterpiece of Harburg's career, the Broadway musical *Finian's Rainbow*, which dealt with issues of race and prejudice. The score included "How Are Things in Glocca Morra?" (see '47). Others of Harburg's best-known songs are "April in Paris" (see '32) and "It's Only a Paper Moon." Harburg was elected to the Songwriters' Hall of Fame in '72. At http://www.songwritershalloffame.org/exhibit_audio_video.asp?exhibitId=14 hear audio clips of "Brother, Can You Spare a Dime?" performed by Rudy Vallee, "Old Devil Moon" sung by Judy Garland, "Happiness Is a Thing Called Joe," "It's Only a Paper Moon" and "Over the Rainbow" performed by Ella Fitzgerald, "Down with Love" performed by Judy Garland, "April in Paris" performed by Sarah Vaughan, "Ding-Dong! The Witch Is Dead" performed by Harry Connick, Jr., "If This Isn't Love" as recorded by Sarah Vaughan, and "Ain't It the Truth" performed by Lena Horne.

Ernest Hare (real name: Thomas Ernest Hare; 1983–1939)

Ernest Hare recorded often with Billy Jones. Hare began his recording career in '18. He was Al Jolson's understudy in the Broadway show, *Sinbad*, for a couple of years. Hare recorded with other duet partners and as a soloist. He, like other recording artists of the period, recorded under various names: Bob Thomas, Wallace Daniels, Arthur Grant, Henry Jones, Robert Judson, Walter Lang, Walter Leslie, Roy Roberts, Bob Thompson, "Hobo" Jack Turner, and Frank Mann. He also recorded at various times with the Cleartone Four, the Crescent Trio, the Harmonizers Quartet, and the Premier Quartet. He and Jones became a very famous duo, becoming the highest paid radio singers by the late '20s. Hare's biggest hit recording was a duet with Billy Jones of "Mr. Gallagher and Mr. Shean" (see '22) but "Barney Google" (see '23) was also very popular. Hare became the No. 26 top recording artist of the '20s.

Robert Hargreaves

Robert Hargreaves was the co-lyricist of "If" (see '51).

Bob Haring (1896–?)

Bob Haring's orchestra was one of three "housebands" for Cameo Records. The group recorded often under a number of various names. On Cameo and the company's affiliate labels the band was known as Bob Haring and his Velvetone Orchestra, the Society Night Club Orchestra and the Copley Plaza Orchestra. On the Brunswick label, Haring recorded under his own name and as the Colonial Club Orchestra. He had a big hit with his recording of "Pagan Love Song" (see '29).

Byron Harlan (real name: George Byron Harlan, 1861–1936)

Harlan is famous as half of the comic duo Collins (Arthur Collins) and Harlan. However he made many records without Collins. As a tenor soloist he specialized in sentimental ballads. Harlan was the No. 3 recording artist of the first decade of the 20th Century and No. 4 for the second decade, ranking him the No. 5 top recording artist of the first half of the 20th Century. Some of Harlan's most popular recordings include "Hello Central, Give Me Heaven" (see '01), "Tell Me, Pretty Maiden" with Frank Stanley, Joe Belmont and the Florodora Girls (see '01), "The Mansion of Aching Hearts" (see '02), "Blue Bell" with Frank Stanley (see '04), "All Aboard for Dreamland" (see '04), "Where the Morning Glories Twine Around the Door" (see '05), Wait Till the Sun Shines, Nellie" (see '06), "The Good Old U.S.A." (see '06), "School Days" (see '07), "My Gal Sal" (see '07), "Nobody's Little Girl" (see '07) and "Tramp! Tramp! Tramp!" (see '10) with Frank Stanley. His most popular duet recordings with Arthur Collins include "Down Where the Wurzberger Flows" (see '03), "Hurrah for Baffin's Bay" (see '03), "Camp Meetin' Time" (see '07), "You're in the Right Church, but the Wrong Pew" (see '09), "Alexander's Ragtime Band" (see '11), "Under the Yum Yum Tree" (see '11), "Put Your Arms Around Me, Honey" (see '11) "When That Midnight Choo Choo Leaves for Alabam'" (see '13), "I Love the Ladies" (see '14), "The Aba Daba Honeymoon" (see '14), "Oh How She Could Yacki Hacki Wicki Wachi Woo" (see '16) and "Dark Town Strutters' Ball" (see '18). And those are only the most popular ones!

W. Frank Harling (1887–1958)

British lyricist W. Frank Harling was particularly active in popular song writing in the '20s and '30s. He contributed songs to over 150 films, although he was often not credited on the screen. He wrote "Where Was I?" (see '40) with lyricist Al Dubin.

Harmonicats Jerry Murad (real name: Jerry Muradian, ?–1996), Al Fiore (real name: Al Fiorentino, 1923–1996), Don Les (real name: Dominic Leshinski, 1914–1994). Jerry Murad organized this harmonica group, which was originally called "The Harmonica Madcaps." The first group consisted of Murad on chromatic lead harmonica, Bob Hadamik on bass harmonica, Pete Pedersen on chromatic, and Fiore on chord harmonica. The group was later re-formed as a trio with Murad, Fiore, and bassist Don Les. Pederson remained connected with the group throughout its existance; working on arrangements and occasionally recording. Their recording of "Peg o' My Heart" sold over a million copies and reached No. 1 on the *Billboard* chart (see '47). They had other charted hits, but they were only moderately successful.

Edward "Ned" Harrigan (1844–1911) Edward "Ned" Harrigan was a famous performer in the Harrigan and (Tony) Hart partnership. Harrigan and Hart presented a series of farces with music back in the early 1890s. Many of these shows were about the Mulligan Guards, which dealt with Irish, German, Italian and Jewish immigrants. Their humor and their songs were topical, but would probably be considered too caustically racial today. George M. Cohan's song, "Harrigan," was a tribute to Ed Harrigan (see '07).

Charles K. Harris (1867–1930) Charles K. Harris began his career as a banjo player, wrote special material for vaudeville acts and later for silent films. He was one of the first songwriters to establish his own publishing company. By far, Harris' biggest songwriting success was "After the Ball," which was popularized in the early 1890s. Another well-known Harris songs were "Hello Central, Give Me Heaven" (see '01), and "The Lights of My Home Town" (see '16). Charles K. Harris was elected to the Songwriters' Hall of Fame when it was organized in '70. At http://www.songwritershalloffame.org/exhibit_audio_video.asp?exhibitId=264 hear an audio clip of "Break the News to Mother" from an 1899 recording by George Gaskin.

Marion Harris (real name: Marion Ellen Harrison; 1896–1944) Marion Harris became a popular singer of the early 20th century in vaudeville, Broadway musicals, Hollywood films, and in recordings. Dancer Vernon Castle reportedly discovered her, and took her to New York City, where she got her first Broadway role in *Stop! Look! Listen!* ('15). She began her recording career with the Victor label in '20, but transferred to Columbia allegedly because Victor wouldn't allow her to record "St. Louis Blues" (she recorded it for Columbia). She tended to record blues and jazz tunes, but occasionally recorded other material like "Look for the Silver Lining." Ms. Harris' most popular recordings include "After You've Gone" (see '19), "St. Louis Blues" (see '20), "Look for the Silver Lining" (see '21), and "Tea for Two" (see '25). The most productive part of her recording career was between '16 and '25. She became the No. 24 top recording artist of the 1910s and No. 7 of the '20s, making her the No. 32 top recording artist of the first half of the 20th Century. In the late '20s and early '30s she appeared in several Hollywood movie musicals. She moved to England in the mid-'30s and retired from show business in the late '30s.

Phil Harris (real name: Wonga Phil Harris; 1904–1995) Phil Harris is particularly associated with novelty songs that he made famous. He was also a bandleader and a radio, movie and television personality. He joined the Jack Benny radio show in '36 and stayed with it for ten years. From '47 through '54 he co-starred with his wife, Alice Faye, on a radio show. Harris' only really big hit recording was "The Thing" (see '50). He may be best known today as the voice in some Disney cartoons, most notably as Baloo the Bear in *The Jungle Book*, in which he sang the Academy Award nominee "The Bare Necessities."

Will J. Harris (1900–?) Will J. Harris was lyricist for "Sweet Sue — Just You" (see '28).

Charles Harrison (1891–1974) Harrison was a tenor in the Columbia Stellar Quartet and the Columbia Mixed Quartet. He also recorded as a soloist. His most popular recordings include "Peg o' My Heart" (see '13), "Ireland Must Be Heaven, for My Mother Came from There" (see '16) and "I'm Always Chasing Rainbows" (see '18).

James F. Harrison (real name: Frederick Wheeler; 1878–1951) James Harrison was a member of the Knickerbocker Quartet and other groups that recorded for Edison. As a soloist, his most popular recording was of "Keep the Homes Fires Burning (Till the Boys Come Home)" (see '16). Popular duet recordings with tenor James Reed were "My Little Dream Girl" (see '15) and "There's a Long, Long Trail" (see '16). James F. Harrison and the Knickerbocker Quartet had a very popular recording of "Pack Up Your Troubles in Your Old Kit Bag and Smile, Smile, Smile" (see '17).

Tom Harrison Tom Harrison was one of the co-writers of "My Little Grass Shack in Kealakekua, Hawaii" (see '34).

James Harrod James Harrod and Anna Wheaton recorded a particularly successful version of "Till the Clouds Roll By" from *Oh, Boy!* (see '17).

Orville Harrold Orville Harrold, as Capt. Dick, and Emma Trentini, as Marietta, introduced "Ah, Sweet Mystery of Life" in the operetta *Naughty Marietta* (see '10). Harrold also introduced "Tramp! Tramp! Tramp!" and "I'm Falling in Love with Someone" in that same production (see '10).

Charles Hart (1884–1965) Charles Hart was the first tenor of the Shannon Four from '17 until '23, but he also recorded as a soloist and in duets, plus performing in opera and vaudeville. By far Hart's most popular recording was of "Till We Meet Again" (see '19). He recorded the song with Harry MacDonough and Nicholas Orlando's Orchestra and in a duet with Lewis James. Both recordings were very popular. In later years he appeared as an actor opposite Mae West and Katharine Hepburn. For more on Hart, see http://www.garlic.com/~tgracyk/charles hart.html.

Lorenz Hart (1895–1943) Lorenz "Larry" Hart became one of the greatest lyricists for Broadway musicals, particularly in his partnership with Richard Rodgers from '19 until just before his death in '43. Hart had already been writing when he met Rodgers, then a student at Columbia University. Hart's life-style always conflicted with that of Rodgers, but somehow they managed to work together to produce some of the most sophisticated lyrics and the most brilliant music that the Broadway stage had seen to that date. A mutual friend introduced Hart to the much younger Richard Rodgers. They began writing musical scores for amateur productions presented as charity benefits and for Columbia University shows. Hart, who spoke fluent German, also supported himself by translating operettas and plays for the famous Shubert Brothers. The Rodgers and Hart team's first songwriting success came with the score for the '25 revue *Garrick Gaieties*. For the next decade or more, Rodgers and Hart wrote an astonishing array of musical comedies for Broadway. During their most productive period, they were writing an average of four new shows a year. In '30 the team moved to Hollywood to contribute songs to several movie musicals, including *Love Me Tonight, Hallelujah, I'm a Bum,* and *Mississippi.* Hart also provided the translation for a '34 MGM version of Lehar's *The Merry Widow.* In '35, Rodgers and Hart were lured back to New York City by Billy Rose to write the songs for his circus musical spectacular, *Jumbo.* From '36 to '43 Rodgers and Hart wrote a series of Broadway musical comedies. Each one seemed to top the one before in terms of innovation and box office success. Some of Hart's most famous song lyrics from the '20s include "Manhattan" (see '25), "The Blue Room" (see '26), "The Girl Friend" (see '26), "My Heart Stood Still" (see '28), "Thou Swell" (see '28) and "With a Song in My Heart" (see '29). His most remembered lyrics from the '30s include "Isn't It Romantic?" (see '32), "Lover" (see '32), "My Romance" (see '35), "Blue Moon" (see '35), "Soon" and "It's Easy to Remember" (see '35), "There's a Small Hotel" (see '36), "Where or When" (see '37), and "My Funny Valentine" (see '37). Little happened in the early '40s before Rodgers and Hart split, but Hart's famous lyrics from the '40s include "Bewitched (Bothered and Bewildered)" (see '50). Always the eccentric as far as life-style was concerned, Hart's health weakened, he caught pneumonia and died. The '48 film *Words and Music* was based on Rodgers and Hart's partnership. Hart is also an original member of the Songwriters' Hall of Fame in '70. At http://www.songwritershalloffame.org/exhibit_audio_video.asp?exhibitId=66 hear an audio clip of "Ten Cents a Dance" by Ruth Etting. At http://www.lorenzhart.org/ many of Hart's lyrics are posted and most of them have midi musical versions for listening.

Morton Harvey (1886–1961)

Morton Harvey was an American vaudeville performer and singer who had a moderately successful recording career during the 1910s. Harvey was born in Omaha, Nebraska. His family wanted him to become a minister, but he had musical and theatrical ambitions. He eventually gained a recording contract, just a few years after records began to become popular. Though most of his recordings were not best sellers, he is notable for being the first singer to record a blues song, the "Memphis Blues" by W.C. Handy (see '14). He is also notable for recording the antiwar protest song "I Didn't Raise My Boy to Be a Soldier" (see '15). Harvey continued performing in vaudeville until the mid–'20s, often in duets. After his retirement from show business, he moved to Oklahoma where he managed a radio station. In '41 after the outbreak of World War II, he moved to San Francisco where he served as director of job relations at the War Manpower Commission, and then as personnel director of an army hospital. In '46 he opened a photography studio in Las Gatos, California. He continued to write songs until his death in '61.

Earl Hatch (1919–)

Earl Hatch was co-composer with "Pinky" Tomlin of "What's the Reason (I'm Not Pleasin' You)" (see '35).

Jean Havez (1869–1925)

Jean Havez was a songwriter, author and agent who also wrote special material for musical comedy and vaudeville. Havez also wrote scenarios for Charlie Chaplin, Buster Keaton, and Harold Lloyd, and was press agent for Lew Dockstader's Minstrels. Havez' most famous song was "Everybody Works but Father" (see '06).

Alice Hawthorne (see Septimus Winner)

Haydn Quartet

John Bieling (tenor, see his biographical sketch), Harry MacDonough (tenor, see his biographical sketch), S.H. Dudley (baritone, see his biographical sketch), William F. Hooley (bass) Along with the Peerless and American Quartets, the Haydn Quartet was one of the three great vocal groups in the early years of the 20th Century. The Haydn Quartet was the No. 5 recording artist of the first decade of the 20th Century and No. 29 for the second decade, making them the No. 13 top recording artist of the first half of the 20th Century. The Edison record label formed this quartet in the late 1890s. When Dudley left the group, baritone Reginald Werrenrath replaced him. That group stayed together until they disbanded in '14. Some of the quartet's most popular recordings include "Because" (see '00), "In the Good Old Summer Time" (see '02), "Bedelia" with Harry MacDonough as lead vocalist (see '04), "Blue Bell" with Harry MacDonough as lead vocalist (see '04), "Toyland" with Corrine Morgan (see '04), "Sweet Adeline" with John Bieling and S.H. Dudley as lead vocalists (see '04), "Dearie" with Corrine Morgan (see '05), "How'd You Like to Spoon with Me? with Corrine Morgan (see '06), "Take Me Out to the Ball Game" with Billy Murray as lead vocalist (see '08), "Sunbonnet Sue" with Harry MacDonough as lead vocalist (see '08), "Put on Your Old Grey Bonnet" (see '09), and "By the Light of the Silvery Moon" with Billy Murray as lead vocalist (see '10).

Bill Hayes (1926–)

Bill Hayes had appeared on comedian Sid Caesar's '50s TV series *Your Show of Shows.* Hayes and Isabel Bigley introduced Rodgers and Hammerstein's "No Other Love" in the Broadway musical *Me and Juliet* (see '53). His recording of "The Ballad of Davy Crockett" went to the top of the charts (see '55). Hayes also played Doug Williams on the NBC TV soap opera *Days of Our Lives.*

Clancy Hayes (real name: Clarence Leonard Hayes; 1902–1972)

Clancy Hayes was a co-writer of "Huggin' and Chalkin'" (see '47). Hayes was a vocalist and a banjoist in Dixieland bands.

Grace Hayes (1895–1989)

Grace Hayes introduced "Lovin' Sam (the Sheik of Alabam')" (see '23) in the musical *The Bunch and Judy,* where it was an interpolation. Ms. Hayes was a singer, actress and vaudeville headliner. She was the mother of actor Peter Lind Hayes.

Dick Haymes (1916–1980)

Dick Haymes was born in Buenos Aires, Argentina. He became one of the most popular male singers in the '40s and '50s. He began his singing career at age 16. When he was hired by Harry James in '40 to replace Frank Sinatra, he began to achieve recognition. He switched to the Benny Goodman band in '42 and toured with the Tommy Dorsey band in '43, once again following Sinatra. His biggest boost came in '43, when he replaced Buddy Clark on a network radio program and began to rival Bing Crosby and Sinatra for popularity. During his big band days, he sang on the hit recording "I'll Get By (as Love as I Have You)" with Harry James (see '44). "You'll Never Know" was his biggest hit recording (see '43), but several others were very popular including "It Can't Be Wrong" (see '43). He also recorded several duets with Helen Forrest in the '40s. His career received another boost in '44 when he played composer Ernest R. Ball in *Irish Eyes Are Smiling*, his film debut. He and Vivian Blaine introduced "That's for Me" in the movie musical *State Fair* (see '45). He also introduced Harry Warren and Mack Gordon's "The More I See You" in the movie musical *Billy Rose's Diamond Horseshoe* (see '45). In the next few years he made several movies, appeared often on network radio, especially *Your Hit Parade,* and had other successful recordings. Haymes became the No. 15 top recording artist of the '40s. Haymes formed his own production firm in the mid–'50s and continued to perform in nightclubs and on television. Dick Haymes website is http://www.dickhaymes.com/. Two songs are available on RealAudio: "When I Write My Song" and "Thanks for the Memory" with Martha Tilton.

Susan Hayward (real name: Edythe Marrener; 1918–1975) After high school in Brooklyn, New York, Susan Hayward began modeling. In '37, she went to Hollywood during a nationwide search for someone to play Scarlett O'Hara in *Gone with the Wind*. She didn't get the role of Scarlett, but she did get a big part in *Hollywood Hotel* ('37). In '39, she finally got a better part in *Beau Geste*. Later films include *Among the Living, Reap the Wild Wind, The Forest Rangers, And Now Tomorrow,* and *Deadline at Dawn*. In '47 she received the first of five Academy Award nominations for *Smash-Up: The Story of a Woman*. In '49 she was nominated again for *My Foolish Heart,* where she introduced the title song (see '50). Her next nominations came in '53 for *With a Song in My Heart* and in '55 for *I'll Cry Tomorrow*. Finally, in '58, she won an Oscar for *I Want to Live!*

Rita Hayworth (real name: Margarita Carmen Cansino; 1918–1987) Margarita had been trained as a dancer by her Spanish dancer father, Eduardo Cansino. She joined his stage act at age 12. At age 16, she made her film debut in *Dante's Inferno* ('35). It wasn't until Columbia signed her that her name was changed. Her first big successes came in *The Strawberry Blonde* ('41) and *You'll Never Get Rich* with Fred Astaire ('41). *Gilda* made her a superstar. Ms. Hayworth premiered "Put the Blame on Mame" in the film *Gilda,* however, it was Anita Ellis who sang for Ms. Hayworth (see '46). In '49, she married Prince Aly Khan. After they divorced, she starred in *Miss Sadie Thompson* ('53) and *They Came to Cordura* ('59). Although it wasn't diagnosed until '80, Rita began to experience the onset of Alzheimer's in the early '60s.

Eunice Healey Eunice Healey and Hal LeRoy introduced "Zing! Went the Strings of My Heart" in the revue *Thumbs Up* (see '35).

Ted Healy (real name: Ernest Lee Nash; 1896–1937) In '23 Ted Healy founded a stage act known as "Ted Healy and His Stooges." His Stooges were Moe and Shemp Horwitz (later Howard) plus Larry Feineberg (later Fine). In '34, Moe, Shemp, and Larry left to form "The Three Stooges." Ted Healy, Phil Baker, Fanny Brice and her brother, Lew, introduced "I Found a Million Dollar Baby" in Billy Rose's revue *Crazy Quilt* ('31).

Bobby Heath (1889–1952) Composer, songwriter, author, pianist and producer, Bobby Heath was a vaudeville accompanist first, and then later a vaudeville producer. His most notable popular song is "My Pony Boy" (see '09).

E.P. Heath Heath co-wrote the lyrics of "Love's Own Sweet Song" (see '14) with C.C.S. Cushing.

Hy Heath (real name: Walter Henry Heath; 1890–1965) Hy Heath was a comedian in musical comedy, vaudeville, minstrel and burlesque shows. As a songwriter, his chief musical collaborators were Johnny Lange and Fred Rose. Heath's most well known song is "Mule Train" (see '49).

Ray Heatherton (1909–1997) Ray Heatherton and Mitzi Green introduced "Where or When" in *Babes in Arms* (see '37). Heatherton made his vocal debut with a jazz band in Floral Park, Long Island, New York. He made his professional debut with Paul Whiteman's *Old Gold Show* on the CBS radio network. Heatherton then performed in Ziegfeld's *Midnight Frolics*. He also performed in nightclubs, on radio, and in Broadway musicals. After he served in the U.S. Marine Corps, he hosted the TV program, *Heatherton House,* a weekday morning talk and variety show on a local New York City station. In '50, he began a new kids TV show titled *The Merry Mailman*. His daughter, Joey, also became a popular performer.

Heidelberg Quintet Billy Murray (tenor; see his biographical sketch), John Bieling (tenor; see his biographical sketch), Steve Porter (baritone; see his biographical sketch), William F. Hooley (bass), Will Oakland (countertenor; see his biographical sketch). The Heidelberg Quintet was basically the American Quartet plus countertenor Will Oakland. A countertenor is a man who uses either falsetto or can sing in the alto range. The Quintet's biggest recordings were of "Waiting for the Robert E. Lee" (see '12) and "By the Beautiful Sea" (see '14).

Horace Heidt (1901–1986) Horace Heidt was a popular bandleader in the '30s and '40s. His band, billed both as Horace Heidt and his Musical Knights and as the Brigadiers, was at its peak of popularity in the late '30s and early '40s. In the late '50s Heidt retired from music. Heidt and his Musical Knights had big hit recordings of "Gone with the Wind" (see '37) and "Ti-Pi-Tin" (see '38) and to a slightly lesser degree "Once in a While" and "The Man with the Mandolin." They helped popularize some songs in the early '40s particularly including "I Don't Want to Set the World on Fire" (see '41). Heidt was the No. 31 top recording artist of the '30s, but not listed among the top 40 of the '40s.

Silvio Hein (1879–1918) Silvio Hein was an American composer of popular music who was born and died in New York. Probably his best-known and most popular work was "He's a Cousin of Mine" (see '07).

Anna Held (real name: Helene Anna Held; 1872–1918) Anna Held was born in Warsaw, Poland, the daughter of a Jewish glove maker and his French-Jewish wife. In 1881, anti-semitic pogroms forced the family to flee to Paris. When her father's glovemaking business failed, he found work as a janitor, while her mother operated a kosher restaurant. Anna began working in the garment industry, then found work as a singer in Jewish theaters in Paris and later in London. Her vivacious and animated personality proved popular, and her career as a stage performer gained momentum. She was soon known for her risque songs and willingness to show her legs on stage. Around this time, she became the wife of a much-older Uruguayan playboy. While she was appearing in London in 1896 she met Broadway impresario Florenz Ziegfeld. Ziegfeld wanted her to come to New York City to star in some of his productions; she agreed. By the time they arrived in New York, thanks to Ziegfeld's talent for creating publicity, she was already the subject of intense public speculation. When she finally performed, the critics weren't particularly impressed, but the public was enamored. From '05 Held enjoyed several successes on Broadway which apart from bolstering Ziegfeld's fortune, made her a millionaire in her own right. Ms. Held was the one who suggested to Ziegfeld the format for what would become the famous Ziegfeld Follies in '07. In '09 Ziegfeld apparently lost interest in her and began an affair with the actress Lilliane Lorraine and then with another actress, Billie Burke. Anna Held interpolated her sensational eye song, "I Just Can't Make My Eyes Behave," in the musical *A Parisian Model* (see '07). Ms. Held, who wrote the English lyrics, introduced "It's Delightful to Be Married," a French song by Vincent Scotto, also in *The Parisian Model* (see '07). Ms. Held spent the years of World War I working in vaudeville, touring France, and performing for French soldiers. She came to be regarded as a war heroine for her contributions, and was highly regarded for her courage in performing near the front lines. After the war ended, she returned to America and made two films in Hollywood but by then her health was failing. In '18, she collapsed onstage and died a few months later. Ms. Held was credited as co-writer of a few popular songs, most notably "It's Delightful to Be Married" with Vincent Scotto (see '07). The film *The Great Ziegfeld* ('36) tells an often glamorized story of the Ziegfeld, Held and Billie Burke triangle. Actress Luise Rainer won an Academy Award for her performance as Ms. Held.

Charles Henderson (1907–1970) Composer, conductor, pianist, arranger and author, Charles Henderson was educated at Roxbury Latin School and Harvard University. He was a pianist, arranger and vocal arranger for orchestras, musicals and radio. Between '49 and '51 he was a composer, arranger and musical director for film studios and television productions, and he created and conducted Las Vegas nightclub acts. His chief musical collaborators included Rudy Vallee, Tom Waring, Edward Heyman, Mack Gordon, and Alfred Newman. Henderson's most famous composition is "Deep Night" (see '29), which he wrote with Rudy Vallee.

Ray Henderson (1896–1970) Ray Henderson was an important composer of popular songs, particularly in the '20s and '30s, especially when he teamed with Lew Brown and Buddy DeSylva from '26 through '30. Henderson studied piano and composition at the Chicago Conservatory, where he cultivated a melodic style that would help his pop songs become standards. After the Conservatory, Henderson moved to New York City where he began doing song arrangements for vaudeville acts and for Tin Pan Alley publishing companies. In '22, Henderson was introduced to lyricist Lew Brown, and in the mid–'20s, they teamed with lyricist Buddy DeSylva to create the most successful songwriting-publishing trio from the mid–'20s until the beginning of the '30s. In collaboration with DeSylva and/or Brown, Henderson wrote "Annabelle" (see '23), "That Old Gang of Mine" (see '23), "Alabamy Bound" (see '25), "Birth of the Blues" (see '26), "Black Bottom" (see '26), "Just a Memory" (see '27), "The Best Things in Life Are Free" (see '27), "The Varsity Drag" (see '27), "Together" (see '28), "Sonny Boy" (see '28), "You're the Cream in My Coffee" (see '29), "Button Up Your Overcoat" (see '29), "Little Pal" (see '29), "Sunny Side Up" (see '29) and "You Are My Lucky Star" (see '35). In '29, DeSylva, Brown and Henderson sold their publishing firm and moved to Hollywood under contract with Fox studios. Their first films were *The Singing Fool* and *Say It with Songs* both starring Al Jolson. The film version of their Broadway musical *Follow Thru*, retitled *Just Imagine*, was also released in '30. Henderson also worked with lyricists Mort Dixon, Sam Lewis, Joe Young, Billy Rose, Ted Koehler, Jack Yellen and Irving Caesar. Other Henderson collaborations include "Five Foot Two, Eyes of Blue" (see '26), "Bye Bye Blackbird" (see '26), and "I'm Sitting on Top of the World" (see '26). In '31 DeSylva left the team to work with other composers, but Henderson and Brown continued together for several years. Henderson's only major song after '30 was "Life Is Just a Bowl of Cherries" (see '31). Although he wrote consistently through the early '40s, he did not experience the success he had enjoyed earlier. Henderson became a member of the Songwriters' Hall of Fame when it was organized in '70. At http://www.songwritershalloffame.org/exhibit_audio_video.asp?exhibitId=106 hear audio clips of "That Old Gang of Mine" performed by Billy Murray and "Life Is Just a Bowl of Cherries" performed by Hutch.

Robert Henning Robert Henning was the lyricist of "Intermezzo (a Love Story)" (see '41).

S.R. Henry S. R. Henry wrote the music for the popular song "By Heck" (see '15). L. Wolfe Gilbert contributed the lyrics.

Evelyn Herbert (real name: Evelyn Houstellier; 1898–1975) Evelyn Herbert had an operatic career in Chicago and New York City before her Broadway debut in *Stepping Stones* ('23). Her greatest success came in *The New Moon*, where she helped introduce "Lover, Come Back to Me" (see '29). She married Robert Halliday, who was her co-star in three Broadway productions. After the early '50s, Herbert and Halliday enjoyed their retirement at their "New Moon" ranch in California, dying within months of each other.

Victor Herbert (1859–1924) Victor Herbert became one of the greatest operetta composers for the New York stage. He was trained in classical music in Europe and was a virtuoso cellist. He and his wife, an operatic soprano, came to the U.S. in 1886. She sang at the Met briefly, and he played in pit orchestras and performed as a cello soloist. His first composing success came with the 1897 Broadway production *The Serenade*, and his first song to become well known was "Gypsy Love Song" from *The Fortune Teller* (1898). Herbert's best-known songs prior to the '20s include "Toyland" (see '04), "A Good Cigar Is a Smoke" (see '05), "Kiss Me Again" (see '05), "I Want What I Want When I Want It" (see '05), "The Streets of New York" (see '06), "Because You're You" (see '06), "Every Day Is Ladies Day to Me" (see '06), "Ah! Sweet Mystery of Life" (see '10), "I'm Falling in Love with Someone" (see '10), "Tramp! Tramp! Tramp!" (see '10), "Italian Street Song" (see '10), "Sweethearts" (see '13), "The Angelus" (see '13), "When You're Away" (see '15), "You Belong to Me" (see '16), "The Springtime of Life" (see '14), and "Thine Alone" (see '17). His most memorable songs from the '20s were "A Kiss in the Dark" (see '22). "Indian Summer," which Herbert wrote as a piano piece in '19, was reworked and achieved considerable popularity in '40. Herbert also recorded occasionally on Victor with his orchestra. He had less than ten recordings between '11 and '19 that were fairly popular, the most successful being "March of the Toys." In '17, his suit against Shanley's Restaurant in New York City resulted in the U.S. Supreme Court's decision to uphold the right of a copyright owner to receive royalties from public performances. That decision led to the founding of the performing rights organization, ASCAP. As one of the nine founders, Herbert served the organization as a director and as vice president. Victor Herbert was elected to the Songwriters' Hall of Fame when it was organized in '70. At http://www.songwritershalloffame. org/exhibit_audio_video.asp?exhibitId=290 hear an audio clip of "Naughty Marietta."

Woody Herman (1913–1987)   Woody Herman became one of the top bandleaders from the mid–'30s into the '70s. By the age 8 he was a vaudeville trouper. At 9 he was billed as "The Boy Wonder of the Clarinet." At 14 he began working in local Milwaukee bands. Stints with the bands of Tom Gerun, Harry Sosnick, and Isham Jones followed. When Jones retired in '38, Woody conducted the group until he assumed complete control in '41. His band became one of the most important groups of the '40s. Although they recorded often and experienced some hits, "Blues in the Night" (see '42) was their biggest success. Woody is particularly associated with "At the Woodchopper's Ball" (see '39); that recording was inducted into the Grammy Hall of Fame in 2002. He and his band also recorded the theme song of the film *Laura* in '45. His band, sometimes called "Herman's Herd," was voted the best band of '49 and appeared in several movies during the '40s. Herman was inducted into the Big Band/Jazz Hall of Fame in '81. Herman became the No. 28 top recording artist of the '40s.

Philippe Herpin   French composer Philippe Herpin wrote "My Heart Sings" (see '45).

June Hershey (1909–2000)   June Hershey was lyricist of "Deep in the Heart of Texas" (see '42).

Jerry Herst   Jerry Herst was the composer of "So Rare" (see '37).

Wallie Herzer   Wallie Herzer was the composer of "Everybody Two-Step" (see '12). Herzer had written an instrumental version of this song in '10. His only other fairly well known song is "Aloha Land" ('16).

Edward Heyman (1907–1981)   Edward Heyman is famous as a lyricist of several popular song hits from the

'30s and '40s. Heyman attended the University of Michigan where he started writing college musicals. After college, he moved to New York City where he began collaborating with Vincent Youmans, Victor Young, Dana Suesse, Morton Gould, Nacio Herb Brown, Johnny Green, Rudolf Friml, Sigmund Romberg, Arthur Schwartz, Ray Henderson, Oscar Levant and Richard Myers. Heyman wrote some scores for Broadway and contributed songs for some Hollywood productions. In '41, Heyman joined the United States Air Force and served during World War II. Some of Edward Heyman's most famous songs include "Body and Soul" (see '30), "Out of Nowhere" (see '31), "I Cover the Waterfront" (see '33), "You Oughta Be in Pictures" (see '34), "Boo-Hoo" (see '37), "They Say" (see '39) and "I Wanna Be Loved" (see '50). Heyman was elected to the Songwriters' Hall of Fame in '75. At http://www.songwritershalloffame.org/exhibit_audio_video.asp?exhibitId=265 hear audio clips of "Love Letters" performed by Diana Krall and "Body and Soul" performed by Jack Fulton with Paul Whiteman and his orchestra.

DuBose Heyward (1885–1940)   DuBose Heyward was chiefly responsible for the concept of *Porgy and Bess*. George Gershwin had been planning to write a musical setting of Heyward's novel *Porgy* since early in '26. In '27, Heyward and his wife, Dorothy, adapted the novel into a play that the Theatre Guild produced. In '28, a capsule musical version of the play was included in the revue *Blackbirds of 1928*. In the early '30s, the Theatre Guild considered a version of *Porgy* starring Al Jolson with music by Jerome Kern and lyrics by Oscar Hammerstein II. Heyward preferred to wait for Gershwin. Finally, in late '33, the project began and eleven months later the score had been written (see '35). Heyward and Ira Gershwin worked on the libretto and lyrics. In addition to *Porgy and Bess*, Heyward also wrote the screen play of Eugene O'Neill's *Emperor Jones*.

Art Hickman (1886–1930)   Art Hickman was one of the better-known West Coast dance bandleaders of the '20s. He and his orchestra had started in San Francisco in '13. In '19, Hickman and his band journeyed to New York City to play at the Biltmore Hotel and to record with Columbia Records. They returned to the West coast briefly, but were offered the chance for a part in the *Follies* and returned to New York. After several months, they returned again to California where they played major hotels in L.A. and San Francisco. By the late '20s, Hickman's health began to fail. Hickman's band was often described as a jazz band, but like Paul Whiteman's group, were not really authentic wild and crazy jazz units. They might more likely be described as playing "white jazz" or in Whiteman's words, as "trying to make a lady out of jazz." Hickman was also a songwriter, penning the lyrics for "Hold Me" (see '20). His orchestra recorded the most popular version of the song also. He and his orchestra had a very popular recording of "The Love Nest" (see '20). The majority of his popular recordings came in '20 and '21. Hickman became the No. 16 top recording artist of the '20s. Recordings by Hickman (Art Hickman and his orchestra and Art Hickman's New York London Five) are available at http://www.redhotjazz.com/bands.html.

Mina Hickman   Mina Hickman's Columbia recording of "Come Down, Ma Evening Star" was very popular in '03. She had a few other popular recordings between '01 and '04.

Billy Higgins   Co-writer, Billy Higgins, introduced "There'll Be Some Changes Made" in vaudeville in the early '20s. It was more popular in '41 when Benny Goodman recorded it.

Al Hill   Al Hill was co-writer on "Let Me Go, Lover" (see '55).

Annabelle Hill   Annabelle Hill, as Hattie the maid, introduced "Another Op'nin', Another Show" in Cole Porter's musical *Kiss Me Kate* (see '48).

Billy Hill (real name: William Joseph Hill; 1899–1940)   Billy Hill, a famous writer of several western-flavored popular songs, was surprisingly born in Boston. He studied the violin at the New England Conservatory. At 17, he traveled to the west coast where he worked as a surveyor in Death Valley and as a violinist and pianist in dance halls. He formed his own jazz band in Salt Lake City. Hill moved to New York City in '30, where he worked a series of odd jobs while he continued to pursue a music career. His first hit arrived with a song called "The Last Round-Up" (see '33). After that, Billy Hill became one of Tin Pan Alley's most successful writers. Collaborating with an array of songwriters including Peter De Rose, his wife Dedette Hill, Victor Young, William Raskin, Edward Eliscu and J. Keirn Brennan, Billy Hill produced such hit songs as "Wagon Wheels" (see '34), "The Old Spinning Wheel" (see '34), "Empty Saddles" (see '36), "In the Chapel in the Moonlight" (see '36), "Lights Out" (see '36), and "The Glory of Love" (see '36). Hill has been a member of the Songwriters' Hall of Fame since '70.

Robert Hill   Robert Hill was co-lyricist of "Kiss of Fire" (see '52).

Ruby Hill (1922–)   Ruby Hill and Harold Nicholas introduced "Come Rain or Come Shine" in the musical *St. Louis Woman* (see '46).

Bob Hilliard (1918–1971)   Bob Hilliard was an important lyricist of popular songs from the mid-'40s into the '60s. Throughout his career, Hilliard collaborated with many composers and lyricists including Carl Sigman, Jule Styne, Mort Garson, Sammy Mysels, Dick Sanford, Milton Delugg, Philip Springer, Lee Pockriss and Sammy Fain. Some of his best-known songs are "Civilization (Bongo, Bongo, Bongo)" (see '47), "Careless Hands" (see '49), and "Dear Hearts and Gentle People" (see '50). Hilliard also wrote "Be My Life's Companion," "Somebody Bad Stole de Wedding Bell (Who's Got de Ding Dong)," "In the Wee Small Hours of the Morning," "Moonlight Gambler," "Seven Little Girls," "My Little Corner of the World," "Any Day Now" and "Our Day Will Come." Hilliard may be most remembered as the lyricist for the film score of *Alice in Wonderland*. Bob Hilliard was inducted into the Songwriters' Hall of Fame in '83.

Harriet Hilliard (real name: Peggy Lou Snyder; 1909–1994)   Singer and actress Harriet Hilliard was from Des Moines, Iowa. She was performing in vaudeville when she met the saxophonist Ozzie Nelson. He hired her as vocalist for his band. Ms. Hilliard introduced "Says My Heart" in the movie musical *The Coconut Grove* (see '38). Ozzie and Harriet married three years later. They and their children, Ricky and David, starred in the highly successful radio and television series *The Adventures of Ozzie and Harriet* between '44 and '66. See more under Ozzie Nelson.

Roc Hillman (1910–)   Roc Hillman was a guitarist and composer. He had played with the Dorsey Brothers Orchestra and stayed with Jimmy Dorsey when the brothers split. He also played guitar with Kay Kyser's band. After a stint in the Army during World War II, he returned to Kyser's orchestra. After his band days, he continued to write and teach in California. Hillman wrote or co-wrote several songs, but only "My Devotion" was particularly popular (see '42).

Hilo Hawaiian Orchestra   Orchestra director Nat Shilkret's Hilo Hawaiian Orchestra had a very popular recording of "When It's Springtime in the Rockies" (see '30). Also see the biographical sketch of Nat Shilkret.

Richard Himber (real name: Herbert Richard Imber; 1900–1966)   Richard Himber was a bandleader, composer, violinist, magician and practical joker. He was born in Newark, New Jersey to the owner of a chain of meat stores. His parents gave him violin lessons, but when they found him performing in a seedy Newark dive, they took the instrument away from him and sent him to military school. In '15, he stole away into New York City, where Sophie Tucker heard him play and hired him as a novelty act to play with her and the Five Kings of Syncopation where Himber was the highlight of the cabaret act. He performed in vaudeville and eventually worked his way to Tin Pan Alley. In '33 he composed the hit song "It Isn't Fair." He managed Rudy Vallee's orchestra and organized his first band for an engagement at New York City's Essex House in '34, where they were heard on radio. His group was voted the best band of '38. His band's theme song was "It Isn't Fair," which became a hit (see '50). Himber and his orchestra's biggest hit recording was "Stars Fell on Alabama" (see '34). Himber was also a magic enthusiast, and invented many magic tricks including the Himber Wallet and the Himber Milk Pitcher. Although he is now remembered primarily for his musical legacy, his contemporaries recall his incessant practical joking. Himber was the publisher of the R-H Log, a weekly survey of the most popular tunes on radio and television. To the annoyance of most music publishers, he refused to accept payola.

Louis A. Hirsch (real name: Louis Achille Hirsch; 1887–1924)   Louis A. Hirsch was a songwriter, composer and publisher, one of the nine founders of ASCAP in '14. He was educated at the City College of New York and the Stern Academy in Berlin. His career began as a staff pianist with the Gus Edwards, and Shapiro & Bernstein music companies, and later he wrote songs for the Lew Dockstader Minstrels. Between '12 and '14 he was a staff composer for the Shubert brothers, where he wrote several Broadway scores including *Vera Violeta*, *Passing Show of 1912*, four editions of the *Ziegfeld Follies*, and the '22 and '23 editions of the *Greenwich Follies*. His chief musical collaborators included Otto Harbach, Edward Madden, Irving Caesar, Harold Atteridge and Gene Buck. Hirsch's most well known songs are "Hello, Frisco" from the *Ziegfeld Follies of 1915* (see '15) and "The Love Nest" from *Mary* (see '20). His other popular-song compositions include "'Neath the Southern Moon" and "The Gaby Glide."

Gaynel Hodge (1937–) Gaynel Hodge was a co-writer of "Earth Angel" (see '55). At first Curtis Williams was credited with writing the song, but a lawsuit proved that Jesse Belvin and Gaynel Hodge also had a hand in writing the song. For more on Hodge, see http://gaynel hodge.tripod.com/.

Jimmie Hodges (1885–1971) Jimmie Hodges wrote "Someday" in '46, but it was most popular in '49. Hodges was a songwriter, composer, author, producer and publisher. During World War I, Hodges appeared in some Liberty Theater shows and produced his own shows. During World War II, he entertained in hospitals, camps and for the USO.

Johnny Hodges (real name: John Cornelius Hodges; 1906–1970) Johnny Hodges was lead alto sax player in Duke Ellington's band for more than forty years. Hodges was a co-writer of "I'm Beginning to See the Light" (see '45).

Red Hodgson Red Hodgson was a co-writer of "The Music Goes 'Round and Around" (see '36).

Evelyn Hoey (circa 1910–1935) Evelyn Hoey began her stage career at age 10 in Minneapolis. She appeared on Broadway in *Yours Truly* ('28), then traveled to London where she appeared in *Good News*. In '29 she was performing in a Paris night club when E. Ray Goetz heard her and offered her a contract to perform in *Fifty Million Frenchmen*. Next, she introduced "April in Paris" in the Broadway revue *Walk a Little Faster* (see '32). She was killed in '35.

Al Hoffman (1902–1960) Al Hoffman, born in Minsk, Russia, composed several excellent popular songs during the '30s, '40s, and '50s. He grew up in Seattle, but moved to New York City in '28. There he found work as a drummer in nightclubs while he tried to get his songwriting career started. He began collaborating with songwriters such as Al Goodhart, Maurice Sigler, Ed Nelson, Sammy Lerner, Dick Manning, Jerry Livingston, Milton Drake, Mack David, Mann Curtis, Leo Corday, Leon Carr, Bob Merrill and Walter Kent in the early '30s. With those songwriters, Hoffman produced several hit songs including "I Saw Stars" (see '34), "Little Man, You've Had Busy Day" (see '34), "Mairzy Doats" (see '44), "I'm a Big Girl Now" (see '46), "Chi-Baba, Chi-Baba" (see '47), "Heartaches" (see '47), and "If I Knew You Were Comin' I'd 'ave Baked a Cake" (see '50). In '34, Hoffman moved to England and wrote for the London stage. He returned to the U.S. in '37, and continued to write musical scores for Broadway. He also wrote the score for the film *Cinderella*. Other highlights from Hoffman's catalog of songs include "Goodnight, Wherever You Are," "Bibbidi-Bobbidi-Boo," "Takes Two to Tango," "Allegheny Moon," "Hot Diggity," "Papa Loves Mambo," "Hawaiian Wedding Song," "I Apologize," "Auf Wiedersehn, My Dear" and "Fit as a Fiddle." Hoffman was inducted into the Songwriters' Hall of Fame in '84. At http://www.song writershalloffame.org/exhibit_audio_video.asp?ex-hibitId=273 hear an audio clip of "Little Man, You've Had a Busy Day" performed by Paul Robeson with Ray Noble and the New Mayfair Orchestra.

Louanne Hogan (1918–2006) Louanne Hogan was the singing voice for Jeanne Crain in introducing "It Might as Well Be Spring" in the Rodgers and Hammerstein movie musical *State Fair* (see '45). Ms. Hogan, who again dubbed the singing for film star Jeanne Crain, Larry Stevens and Cornel Wilde introduced "All Through the Day" in the movie musical *Centennial Summer* (see '46). Ms. Hogan was a member of the Pied Pipers during the '50s.

Billie Holiday (real name: Elinore Harris or Eleanor Gough; 1915–1959) Billie Holiday is regarded one of the greatest, if not *the* greatest, of the singers of jazz. She was inducted into the Big Band/Jazz Hall of Fame in '79. She left her hometown, Philadelphia, in '27 for New York City where she worked in Harlem clubs. Her recording debut was with the Benny Goodman orchestra in '33, but it was with Goodman's pianist, Teddy Wilson, that she recorded several classic renditions of songs in the mid- to late '30s. Her recording output in the '30s was rather extensive, but by the '40s, her considerable talent was deteriorating due to alcohol and drug abuse. After a jail sentence, she returned in the early '50s, but bad health never allowed her to return to her former glory. Billie Holiday's biggest hit recording was "Carelessly" (see '37). Although not as highly ranked, her recording of "God Bless the Child" in '41 is one of her most famous. That recording was selected for the NARAS (Grammy) Hall of Fame. The '72 film *Lady Sings the Blues*, which starred Diana Ross, was roughly based on Billie Holiday's life story, but isn't considered very factual.

Mann Holiner (1897–1958) Mann Holiner was one of the lyricists of "Until the Real Thing Comes Along" (see '36). Holiner as a songwriter, actor and author. He studied at Cornell University and the American Academy of Dramatic Arts. He also acted on Broadway, in stock productions and in vaudeville. During World War II, he served in the Army, earning the rank of Major. After the war, he became a radio advertising executive.

Fred Hollander (real name: Frederick Hollander; 1896–1976) Fred Hollander was the composer of "Whispers in the Dark" (see '37). Hollander was born in England, while his father was employed in London. The family returned to Germany, where he was educated at the Berlin Conservatory of Music. He became an associate conductor at the Prague Opera House by age 18. He composed the scores for several German films, most notably *Der Blaue Engel* (*The Blue Angel*). Once Hollander came to the U.S., he composed for Hollywood films before returning to Germany in the mid-'50s.

Libby Holman (1906–1971) Torch singer Libby Holman is particularly identified with a quartet of songs: "Moanin' Low" (see '29), "Body and Soul" (see '30), "Something to Remember You By" (see '30) and "You and the Night and the Music" (see '35). She appeared in nine Broadway productions, but the two most famous ones were *The Little Show, Three's a Crowd*, and to a degree *Revenge with Music*. Ms. Holman introduced "Can't We Be Friends?" in *The Little Show* (see '29). By the end of the '30s her career had faded. Her most popular recording was of "Body and Soul" (see '30).

Ben Homer (1917–) Ben Homer was the lyricist of "Sentimental Journey" (see '45). Although not as popular, his "Joltin' Joe DiMaggio" is a baseball fan classic. Homer was sometimes a lyricist, sometimes a composer. He was educated at the New England Conservatory of Music. He arranged for Benny Goodman, Tommy Dorsey, Jimmy Dorsey and Les Brown and their bands. He also wrote for films and television.

Brian Hooker (1880–1946) Brian Hooker is most remembered as the librettist and lyricist for *The Vagabond King*. Rudolf Friml composed the music for the operetta. The most memorable song from the production was "Song of the Vagabonds" (see '25). Hooker also collaborated with George Gershwin, Hugo Felix, William Daly and Franklin Hauser. He produced the libretto and/or only lyrics for six other Broadway productions.

Bob Hope (real name: Leslie Townes Hope; 1903–2003) Bob Hope became an American institution even though he was born in England. He grew up in Cleveland, experimented with boxing as a career, and became, instead, a song-and-dance man in vaudeville. His first roles on Broadway were bit parts before he attracted attention in *Roberta* ('33). Greater success followed when he introduced "I Can't Get Started with You" (see '36) in the Ziegfeld *Follies* of 1936. He also appeared as Bob Hale in *Red, Hot and Blue!*, where he sang "It's De-Lovely" (see '37). He began his incredible career in films in *The Big Broadcast of 1938*, where he and Shirley Ross introduced the song that was to become his theme, "Thanks for the Memory" (see '38). Hope and Ross also introduced "Two Sleepy People" in *Thanks for the Memory* (see '38). Hope and Bing Crosby starred with Dorothy Lamour in a series of "Road" films. In addition to "Thanks for the Memory," he is remembered for the Academy Award winner "Buttons and Bows," which he and Jane Russell performed in *The Paleface* (see '48). Hope is especially known for his tours overseas to entertain servicemen. His TV appearances since the '50s have been numerous, mostly in specials, often recounting Christmas tours to entertain the troops. He, of course, is noted as a comedian, but he sang creditably in his many movies. Hope's website is http://www.bobhope.com/.

Lena Horne (1917–) Singer Lena Horne became very popular in the '40s and continued to perform into the '80s. In '81 a Broadway revue, *Lena Horne: The Lady and Her Music Live on Broadway*, honored her and the music associated with her. Ms. Horne was inducted into the Big Band/Jazz Hall of Fame in '91. However, she was not a particularly popular recording artist in the pop field. "Stormy Weather," which became her theme song, was probably her most famous pop recording. She started her singing career at age sixteen in the chorus at the famous Harlem nightclub the Cotton Club. Her first Broadway appearance came in *Lew Leslie's Blackbirds of 1939*. In the early '40s she was a singer with Charlie Barnet and his orchestra. Her first movie role was a small part in *Panama Hattie* ('42), but the recognition she gained there led to other movies (still mostly small parts or cameo appearances). In '43 she appeared in the movie version of *Cabin in the Sky, Stormy Weather*, which starred many of the country's top African American entertainers, *I Dood It*, in which she played herself and sang "Taking a Chance on Love," *Thousands Cheer*, a revue of big-name stars to entertain the soldiers in which she performed "Honeysuckle Rose" and *Swing Fever*. Horne was featured in *Broadway*

Rhythm and in *Two Girls and a Sailor* (both in '44). She had cameo roles in *Ziegfeld Follies* ('46) and *Till the Clouds Roll By* ('47), in which she sang Jerome Kern's "Can't Help Lovin' Dat Man" and "Why Was I Born?" and *Words and Music*, in which she performed "The Lady Is a Tramp" and "Where or When." She was a guest star in *Duchess of Idaho* ('50) and *Meet Me in Las Vegas* ('56). She was also seen in non-musical film *Death of a Gunfighter* ('69). Horne returned to Broadway in '57 to star in the musical *Jamaica*.

Vaughn Horton (1911–1988) Vaughn Horton collaborated with Gene Autry and Denver Darling on "Address Unknown" (see '39). He also was the writer of "Mockin' Bird Hill" (see '51). Horton wrote the song in Pennsylvania, his home state, in the late '20s. For more on Horton, see http://www.nashvillesongwritersfoundation.com/fame/horton.html.

Charles Horwitz Charles Horwitz' most popular lyric was "Because" (see '00). His "Because" is not the famous wedding song by Edward Teschemacher and Guy d'Hardelot from '02.

Karl Hoschna (1877–1911) Hoschna was born in Bohemia and studied oboe at the Vienna Conservatory of Music. After graduating with honors, he played oboe in the Austrian Army Band. He came to the U.S. in 1895 and played oboe in Victor Herbert's orchestra. Hoschna became convinced that the double-reed vibrations of the oboe were affecting his mind, so he gave up the instrument and became a copyist at Witmark, the famous music publishing company. He was soon writing arrangements. In '02, Hoschna met Otto Harbach and they began to collaborate on music for the Broadway stage. They finally scored big with *The Three Twins*, which introduced "Cuddle Up a Little Closer" (see '08) and "The Yama Yama Man" (see '09). They had another hit show with *Madame Sherry*, which introduced "Every Little Movement" (see '10). Hoschna died suddenly at the age of 34, just at the peak of his success.

Will M. Hough (1882–1962) Will M. Hough was a songwriter and author, who was educated at the University of Chicago. He wrote special material for vaudeville acts and for Broadway and Chicago stage shows. His chief musical collaborators included Joe Howard, Frank Adams and Harold Orlob. By far his most famous song, written for *The Prince of Tonight*, was "I Wonder Who's Kissing Her Now" (see '09).

George Hoven (1913–1974) George Hoven was composer of "(It's No) Sin" (see '51). Hoven owned a music store in Chester, PA. He played and taught piano and accordion. Due to his Polish background, he often wrote polkas, obereks, and waltzes.

Dick Howard (1890–1981) Dick Howard was one of the co-writers of "Somebody Else Is Taking My Place" (see '42). In addition to his songwriting, Howard was an entertainer and author. After high school, he became a minstrel and performed in vaudeville for several years, often writing his own material. He served in the U.S. Navy during World War I.

Eddy Howard (1914–1963) Singer Eddy Howard first drew national attention when he sang with Dick Jurgens' band in the late '30s. During his work with

Jurgens, he popularized two of his own compositions: "My Last Goodbye" and "Careless" (see '40). He led his own band in the '40s and '50s. Howard's first big hit recording came with "To Each His Own" (see '46). His only other No. 1 hit was "Sin" (see '51). Howard became the No. 21 top recording artist of the '40s. Ill health caused him to retire for a few years in the early '50s, but he rebounded with a reorganized band in '54 and remained active into the early '60s.

Joseph E. Howard (1867–1961) Joe Howard ran away from home, wound up in an orphanage, ran away from the orphanage, then sang in St. Louis pool halls and saloons to make enough money to exist. By age eleven he was acting in St. Louis vaudeville, billed as Master Joseph, Boy Soprano. Later he toured the vaudeville circuit, but was stranded in St. Joseph, Missouri. He continued to perform in dance halls and saloons in Denver, Dodge City and Tombstone, Arizona. At age seventeen, Howard teamed up with Ida Emerson to form a vaudeville team (she became one of his nine wives). Howard and Emerson eventually made it to New York City and played the famous Tony Pastor's Music Hall. Howard wrote his first big hit song, "Hello, Ma Baby" in 1899 (see '00). Between '05 and '15, he produced a great many shows in Chicago. Most of the shows were written in collaboration with Will M. Hough and Frank R. Adams. Howard produced such hit songs as "I Wonder Who's Kissing Her Now" (see '09) and "Good-Bye, My Lady Love." Howard's screen biography was *I Wonder Who's Kissing Her Now* ('47). Joe Howard was elected to the Songwriters' Hall of Fame when it was organized in '70. At http://www.songwritershall offame.org/exhibit_audio_video.asp?exhibitId=262 hear an audio clip of "Hello, Ma Baby" performed by Arthur Collins.

Paul Mason Howard (1909–1975) Paul Mason Howard was co-writer of "Shrimp Boats" (see '51). Howard was a songwriter, bandleader, entertainer, composer and author. He lead a jazz band in the mid-'20s and appeared in vaudeville and in nightclubs. Later he wrote for newspapers and advertising agencies. He also composed the music for some commercials.

Julia Ward Howe (1819–1910) Julia Ward Howe was a prominent American abolitionist, social activist, and poet. Julia Ward was born in New York City, the third of six children of a wealthy banker. In 1843 she married a fellow abolitionist, physician Dr. Samuel Gridley Howe. The couple made their home in Boston and were the parents of six children. Howe is most famous for writing the poem that became "Battle Hymn of the Republic" (1862, see '18), which became very popular in the U.S. during World War I. After the Civil War ended she was an active Pacifist and a fervent supporter of women's suffrage.

Dan Howell Dan Howell is credited as co-composer of "Open the Door, Richard" (see '47).

Raymond Hubbell (real name: John Raymond Hubbell; 1879–1954) Raymond Hubbell composed the music for the hit song "Poor Butterfly" (see '17). According to www.grainger.de/music/composers/wv_hubbell r.html, Hubbell had almost fifty published songs.

Will Hudson (1908–1981) Will Hudson was one of the co-writers of "Moonglow" (see '34). Songwriter/conductor Will Hudson studied at Juilliard. He was later an arranger for bands and co-bandleader with Eddie De-Lange between '36 and '38. He then directed his own band in '39 and '40. During World War II, he served in the Army Air Force.

John Hundley (1899–1990) John Hundley appeared in several Broadway musicals during the late '20s. He introduced "With a Song in My Heart" in the Rodgers and Hart musical *Spring Is Here* (see '29). He appeared in *Walk a Little Faster* in '32. In the late '30s, he became an announcer for CBS radio. That led to other positions in programming and sales. He eventually became an executive in charge of censorship until his retirement in '65.

Pee Wee Hunt (real name: Walter Hunt; 1907–1979) Pee Wee Hunt came from a musical family (his father was a violinist and his mother played banjo). Hunt also learned banjo. After graduation from Cincinnati Conservatory of Music and Ohio State University, he began playing in local groups. He played trombone and banjo in several bands in the late '20s, but began to find fame when he became an original member of the group that became the Casa Loma Orchestra. He was featured vocalist, trombonist, and vice-president of the group for 16 years. He left the band in '43 and, after a few years of different jobs, organized his own band, a Dixieland outfit, in '46. He and his orchestra had a fantastic hit with their revival of "Twelfth Street Rag" (see '48). Hunt's only other best selling recording was a revival of 1919's "Oh" in '53.

Alberta Hunter (1895–1984) According to http://www.redhotjazz.com, "at age twelve Alberta Hunter ran away from her hometown of Memphis to go to Chicago to become a Blues singer. She had a somewhat hard time at first but gradually, achieved her goal and became one of the most popular African American entertainers of the 1920s." Alberta got her professional start in '11 at a Southside Chicago club. In '15 Hunter got a singing engagement at the Panama Cafe, which was a fancy place that catered to whites. Alberta then worked at the Dreamland Café, where King Oliver's band played. There she became a full-fledged star, billed as the "Sweetheart of Dreamland." In '21 Alberta moved to New York City and launched her recording career with the Black Swan label with Fletcher Henderson's Novelty Orchestra, but she switched to Paramount in '22 where Fletcher Henderson continued to accompany her on the piano. Hunter wrote a lot of her own material and her song "Down Hearted Blues," became Bessie Smith's first record (see '23). That same year she became the first African American singer to be backed up by a white band, when the Original Memphis Five supported her on "Tain't Nobody's Biz-ness If I Do." While in New York City, Hunter performed in several African American musical revues. Ms. Hunter recorded under several pseudonyms during the '20s in an attempt to keep record companies she had signed exclusive contracts with from finding out about her extra income sources. She recorded as Alberta Prime, Josephine Beatty and as Alberta Hunter. She left for Europe in '27 and became a hit in Paris. She continued to perform in Europe, the Middle East and Russia throughout the '30s. During World War II, Alberta entertained troops throughout Asia, the South Pacific Islands and Europe. After the war she returned to America and at age of 59 enrolled in a practical nursing course. For the next twenty years she worked in a New York City hospital. You can hear several Alberta

Hunter recordings at http://www.redhotjazz.com/hunter.html.

Herman Hupfield (1894–1951)   Herman Hupfield did not write a large number of hits, but he managed to produce at least one quality song that will likely survive for many years to come: "As Time Goes by" (see '43). His other well-known songs are "Let's Put Out the Lights" (see '32) and "When Yuba Plays the Rhumba on the Tuba" (see '31).

Walter Huston (real name: Walter Houghston; 1884–1950)   Walter Huston, not particularly known for his singing ability, introduced "September Song" in the Broadway musical *Knickerbocker Holiday* (see '39). His Brunswick recording of the song sold very well. Huston became a powerful performer in talking films. His film debut came in *Gentlemen of the Press* ('29). He quickly followed with *The Virginian* ('29) and *Abraham Lincoln* ('30). He was very busy in films for the next several years. He was nominated for an Oscar in '36 for his work in *Dodsworth*. He was next nominated for *All That Money Can Buy* ('41). His directorial debut was *The Maltese Falcon* ('41). Huston's first Oscar nomination for Best Supporting Actor was for the role of George M. Cohan's father in *Yankee Doodle Dandy* ('42). He finally won an Oscar for *The Treasure of the Sierra Madre* ('48).

Darwin Frank Hutchins   Darwin Frank Hutchins was the writer of "I Wonder, I Wonder, I Wonder" (see '48).

Betty Hutton (real name: Elizabeth June Thornburg; 1921–)   Singer/actress Betty Hutton was a prominent star of several movies in the '40s. Her forte was comedy and novelty numbers. She started out with her sister, Marion Hutton, singing with Vincent Lopez and his orchestra in the late '30s. In '40, Betty starred in the Broadway musical *Two for the Show* and had a small part in *Panama Hattie*, but it was not until her first movie musicals, *The Fleet's in* and *Star Spangled Rhythm*, in '42 that she became a national star. She stole the show in *Happy Go Lucky* in '43 performing the novelty song "Murder He Says." Her most important role to this point in her career came in *Incendiary Blonde* in '45, in which she portrayed entertainer and speakeasy owner Texas Guinan. She garnered her biggest hit record with "Doctor, Lawyer, Indian Chief" after she introduced it in *Stork Club* (see '46). Her next really important role came when she starred in *The Perils of Pauline*, where she introduced "I Wish I Didn't Love You So" (see '47). Perhaps Hutton's juiciest role came in the '50 film version of Irving Berlin's Broadway musical *Annie Get Your Gun*.

Marion Hutton (real name: Marion Thornburg; 1919–1987)   Marion Hutton is the older sister of Betty Hutton. After the sisters had worked with Vincent Lopez's band, Marion joined Glenn Miller in '38. She stayed with the Miller band until it disbanded in '42. After that she worked as a single in clubs, theaters, radio and films. She remained active until the '50s, when she appeared only occasionally. She married bandleader Vic Schoen and settled in California.

Ramez Idriss (1911–1971)   Ramez Idriss was a cowriter of "Woody Woodpecker" (see '48). The song was nominated for an Oscar. Idriss, nicknamed Ramey, was a songwriter, author and musician. He attended Los Ange-

les Community College. In addition to playing in dance bands on radio, recordings and films, he wrote television scripts.

Red Ingle (real name: Ernest Jansen Ingle; 1906–1965)   Red Ingle was tenor saxophonist and singer with Ted Weems and his orchestra from '31 until the beginning of the '40s. He then perfected his comic talents with Spike Jones and his City Slickers. A hillbilly recording of "Temptation" called "Tim-Tayshun" was a big hit for Red Ingle and his Natural Seven with a vocal by Cinderella G. Stump, who was really Jo Stafford (see '47). They tried the same formula with a few other pop songs like "Them Durn Fool Things" (based on "These Foolish Things"), "Nowhere" (based on "You Came Along") and "Serutan Yob (a Song for Backward Boys and Girls Under 40)" (based on "Nature Boy"). They also had a charted hit with "Cigarettes, Whusky and Wild, Wild Women." But those efforts paled in comparison with the success of "Tim-Tayshun."

Herbert Ingraham (1883–1910)   Herbert Ingraham was an American composer of popular music born in Aurora, Illinois. He headed his own theatrical company and conducted an orchestra while he was still a child in the Chicago area. Once he moved to New York City to write for Shapiro, Bernstein and Co., he started a promising career which was tragically cut short dying of tuberculosis. His most remembered song is probably "Don't Wake Me Up, I'm Dreaming," which he wrote with Beth Slater Whitson (see '10).

Roy Ingraham (1893–?)   Roy Ingraham and his orchestra had a particularly popular recording of "Chant of the Jungle" from the movie *Untamed* (see '30). In addition to being a bandleader, Ingraham was also a composer, author, and singer. His first song was published at age 17. He wrote special material for entertainers like Sophie Tucker and wrote for several motion pictures. Roy is the brother of Herbert Ingraham (see above).

Ink Spots   Orville "Hoppy" Jones (1902–1944), Jerry Daniels (1916–1995; replaced by Billy Kenny in '36), Charlie Fuqua (1910–1971; replaced by Bernie MacKay when Fuqua was drafted in '44), Ivory "Deek" Watson (1909–1969). The Ink Spots had been porters at New York City's Paramount Theater when an agent discovered them and arranged for them to record. They became famous for their talking choruses in several of their recordings. The Ink Spots' most productive recording period was from the late '30s to '46. Their most popular recordings include "Address Unknown" (see '39), "We Three" (see '40), "The Gypsy" (see '46), "To Each His Own" (see '46), plus "Into Each Life Some Rain Must Fall" (see '44) and "I'm Making Believe" (see '44) with Ella Fitzgerald. Although it was not a No. 1 hit, "If I Didn't Care," one of their first recordings, is very closely associated with the group. The Ink Spots became the No. 12 top recording artists of the '40s. They were inducted into the Vocal Group Hall of Fame in '99. The original group split in the mid-'40s.

Wallace Irwin (1875–1959)   Wallace Irwin is important in the popular music realm as lyricist and librettist for the Broadway musical *A Yankee Tourist* ('07). "Wouldn't You Like to Have Me for a Sweetheart?" from that production was very popular in a recording by Billy Murray and Ada Jones (see '08). He was also a poet, writing "Love Sonnets of a Hoodlum," among other works.

Jose Iturbi (1895–1980) Concert pianist Jose Iturbi played the Chopin polonaise that became "Till the End of Time" in *A Song to Remember*, a motion picture based on the life of Chopin (see '45). For more on Iturbi, see http://en.wikipedia.org/wiki/Jose_Iturbi.

Ruby Jackson Ruby Jackson wrote the melody for "Hearts of Stone" (see '55). Jackson was a member of the Jewels, a rhythm and blues vocal group from San Bernardino, CA. The Jewels recorded "Hearts of Stone" in '54 before it became famous in '55 by the Charms and by the Fontane Sisters.

Tony Jackson (real name: Anthony Jackson; 1876–1921) Tony Jackson's only contribution to popular music was as co-composer with Egbert Van Alstyne on "Pretty Baby" (see '16). Although there is no proof, it appears that the unknown Jackson took his tune to the established composer, Van Alstyne, who polished the tune and secured Gus Kahn to furnish lyrics. Then it was published as a joint effort.

Al Jacobs (1903–) Al Jacobs was co-writer of "I Need You Now" and "If I Give My Heart to You" (see '54). Jacobs was also a contributor to "This Is My Country." After college, Jacobs became a piano salesman and taught piano. He managed several music companies over the years, including the Sherman Clay music publishing company, the Miller Music Company, Crawford Music, Melrose Music and Stasny Music companies.

Carrie Jacobs-Bond (1862–1946) Composer, lyricist, poet Carrie Jacobs-Bond was the first woman to establish a music publishing firm in America. Ms. Jacobs-Bond formed the Bond Shop in 1894 to publish her compositions which included "I Love You Truly" (see '12), "A Perfect Day," and "Just A-Wearyin' for You." During her early career, she appeared in vaudeville acts touring throughout this country. In '05 she performed for President Teddy Roosevelt at the White House and during World War I, she performed at U.S. Army camps throughout Europe. Carrie Jacobs-Bond was elected into the Songwriters' Hall of Fame in '70. At http://www.songwritershalloffame.org/exhibit_audio_video.asp?exhibitId=274 hear an audio clip of "I Love You Truly" performed by Elsie Baker.

Moe Jaffe (real name: Moses Jaffe; 1901–1972) Over three decades, starting in the late '20s, Moe Jaffe contributed more than 250 songs to the American Songbook. "Collegiate" (see '25) and "Bell Bottom Trousers" (see '45) are Jaffe's most famous songs. Jaffe was born in Vilna, Russia, now Vilnius, Lithuania. His family left for America almost immediately. His family settled in Keyport, New Jersey, where his father peddled dry goods and owned a stable. After graduating from high school, Moe worked his way through the University of Pennsylvania's Wharton School and Law School by playing piano and leading a campus dance band called Jaffe's Collegians. The band's theme song was "Collegiate." From the late '20s through the mid–'40s, Moe's songwriting credits made Moe Jaffe and His Orchestra a Philadelphia favorite. Their dance music was broadcast live from the Georgian Room of the Benjamin Franklin Hotel. They received marquee billing at Atlantic City's Steel Pier. And for many summers, he led the band north to Poland Spring, Maine, where they served as the house orchestra at the fashionable Poland Spring House. Between gigs, he continued to pursue his songwriting career, primarily as a lyricist, although he also wrote the music for some songs. In '44, Jaffe took credit for words and music on "Bell Bottom Trousers " (see '45), although he would freely admit that it wasn't an entirely original concept. For a hundred years or more, sailors sang a much bawdier version of the tune, much too "blue" for the times. With hits like that under his belt Moe move to New York City and established an office in the famous Brill Building, the spiritual heart of Tin Pan Alley, but he never produced another huge hit. Jaffe's chief musical collaborator was Nat Bonx, but he also wrote with several others including Ted Weems, Fred Waring, Jack Fulton, Henry Tobias, and Larry Vincent.

Etta James (real name: Jamesetta Hawkins; 1938–) Etta James is famous as an American rhythm and blues singer. She began singing at the St. Paul Baptist Church in Los Angeles at a very early age. After her family moved to San Francisco in the early '50s, she sang in a trio called the Creolettes. Johnny Otis took notice, changed her name (he took her first name Jamesetta) and turned it around to become Etta James and got her a recording contract. Her first record became a hit in '55. It was "Wallflower (Dance with Me, Henry)" (see '55) a reworking of Hank Ballard's "Work with Me, Annie." She is listed as co-writer with Johnny Otis and Hank Ballard. Ms. James may be most famous today for her soulful recording of "At Last." In 2003 she received a Grammy Lifetime Achievement Award. She was inducted into both the Rock 'n' Roll and Blues Hall of Fames.

Harry James (1916–1983) Harry James came from a circus family. His father, the circus bandmaster, taught him the trumpet. The family finally quit the circus and settled in Beaumont, Texas, where Harry attended school. At age 15 he left home for a job in a band. His first important band post came with Ben Pollack in '35. Then, in '37, he joined the Benny Goodman band as featured trumpet soloist. After only a year Goodman lent James $42,000 to organize his own band. The James orchestra specialized in the blues, boogie-woogie, and, of course, trumpet showpieces. James was elected to the Big Band/Jazz Hall of Fame in '83. James' theme song was the 1898 Italian tune "Ciribiribin" arranged in big band style with a flashy trumpet solo. His first big hit recordings were "I Don't Want to Walk Without You" (see '42) and "Sleepy Lagoon" (see '42). Other James recordings that ranked equally high were "Mister Five by Five" (see '42), "I Had the Craziest Dream" (see '43), "I've Heard That Song Before" (see '43), "All or Nothing at All" with Frank Sinatra (see '43), a revival of 1928's "I'll Get By" (see '44), "I'm Beginning to See the Light" (see '45), and "It's Been a Long, Long Time" (see '45). James became the No. 4 top recording artist of the '40s, No. 31 of the first half of the 20th Century. Vocalist at different times for the band included Helen Forrest, John McAfee, Frank Sinatra, and Dick Haymes. James and the band signed a movie contract in the '40s and appeared in *Springtime in the Rockies, Private Buckaroo*, and *Syncopation* in '42. Other film appearances included *Do You Love Me?* and *If I'm Lucky* in '46. James married the popular film star Betty Grable in '43; she was his second wife (Louise Tobin had been the first). They divorced in '65. After the decline in popularity of the big bands, James and his group continued to perform occasionally. In the early '50s James had a short-lived TV show.

Inez James (1919–1993)   Inez James was one of the co-writers of "Vaya Con Dios" (see '53). Songwriter Inez James was educated at the Hollywood Conservatory. She has written for film and television. One of her film songs was "Pillow Talk," written for the Doris Day film with the same title.

Joni James (real name: Joan Carmello Babbo; 1930–)   Joni was born in Chicago of Italian extraction. She studied drama and ballet as a youngster and began her show business career as a dancer. However, she finally decided to pursue a singing career. Her break came when some executives at Metro-Goldwyn-Mayer (MGM) spotted her in a television commercial, and she was signed in '52. Her first hit, "Why Don't You Believe Me?" (see '52) sold over a million copies. She had a number of hits following that one, including "Your Cheatin' Heart," a cover of Hank Williams' song and "Have You Heard." She was reportedly the first American to record at London's Abbey Road Studios, and recorded five albums there. In '64 she retired from music, in part because her husband was in bad health and needed her attention. For many years she was out of the public eye, but began touring again in the mid-'90s following her husband's death. In '97 she married retired Air Force General Bernard Adolph Schriever, 20 years her senior. Gen. Schriever passed away in 2005. For her contribution to the recording industry, Joni James has a star on the Hollywood Walk of Fame.

Lewis James (1893–1959)   Lewis James recorded with several groups including the Shannon Four, the Revelers and the Criterion Trio between '17 and the late '20s. He reportedly sold almost 3,000 recordings during that time period. His most popular recording was a duet with Charles Hart of "Till We Meet Again" (see '19).

Paul James (see James Paul Warburg)

Will Jason (real name: William Jacobson; 1899–1970)   Will Jason was co-writer of "When We're Alone (Penthouse Serenade)" (see '31). Jason held a variety of positions in the film industry, beginning when he was only 13 years old. He scored several films and eventually became a director. Jason collaborated with Val Burton on the songs he wrote.

Anne Jeffreys (real name: Anne Carmichael; 1923–)   Anne Jeffreys began vocal training at an early age to prepare for an operatic career. She later became a junior model for the John Robert Powers agency in New York City. In the early '40s, she obtained a role in a Hollywood musical revue, *Fun for the Money*. The exposure got her a role in Rodgers and Hart's movie musical *I Married an Angel* ('42). She signed film contracts with both Republic and RKO. For the next several years, she appeared in "B" westerns and crime films. Jeffreys introduced "I'll Buy That Dream" in the movie musical *Sing Your Way Home* (see '45). She also appeared in some regional operas and the Broadway musical *My Romance* and succeeded Patricia Morison as Lilli Vanessi in *Kiss Me Kate* on Broadway. It was during her performances in *Kiss Me Kate* that she met her husband Robert Sterling. They became a successful club act in the early '50s. Ms. Jeffreys played Marion Kirby in the *Topper* TV series of the early '50s. By the

'60s, she semi-retired, but took occasional musical roles on Broadway and in regional productions. In the '70s, she returned to TV for roles in soap operas like *General Hospital*. She also appeared as the mother of David Hasselhoff on the *Baywatch* TV series in the late '80s.

Gordon Jenkins (1910–1984)   Composer, arranger, and conductor Gordon Jenkins is probably best known as conductor of his orchestra, which has made numerous recordings and has backed many illustrious artists on recordings. Jenkins was the son of a movie theater organist. While he was still a child, he would sometimes accompany his father on the organ at the theater. During Prohibition, he worked at a speakeasy piano player in St. Louis. In the early '30s, he played banjo and piano for a St. Louis radio station. Isham Jones hired him to play the piano and write arrangements for his band. When Jones's band became the Woody Herman band in '36, Jenkins stayed on as the band's arranger. He also wrote arrangements for Paul Whiteman, Benny Goodman, and Andre Kostelanetz. In '38, he moved to California to work for Paramount Pictures. In '39, he became music director for the west coast division of NBC. During the mid- to late '40s, he worked on Dick Haymes' radio show. In '45, he became a staff conductor for Decca Records. Jenkins eventually became Decca's musical director, and was responsible for signing the folk singing group, the Weavers to the label. Jenkins also began recording successfully for Decca under his own name. He worked for NBC-TV as a producer for a couple of years in the mid- to late '50s. Jenkins' first big success in the recording field came with "Maybe You'll Be There" in '48 that he and his orchestra and chorus recorded with a vocal by Charles LaVere. The next year brought recordings of "Again" (see '49) and "Don't Cry Joe" (see '49) that also did well on the charts. Jenkins and his orchestra's only monster hit recording was "Goodnight Irene" with the Weavers (see '50), but "Tzena Tzena Tzena," also with the Weavers (see '50), wasn't far behind. Jenkins became the No. 37 top recording artist of the '40s and No. 16 of the '50s. He worked often with Nat "King" Cole, Judy Garland, Peggy Lee, the Weavers and Frank Sinatra. For his songwriting career, he worked primarily with lyricists Tom Adair and Johnny Mercer. His most famous popular song is "San Fernando Valley" (see '44). Others include "Blue Prelude," "Blue Evening," "P.S. I Love You," "When a Man Loves a Woman" and "This Is All I Ask." Jenkins was inducted into the Songwriters' Hall of Fame in '82.

M.K. Jerome (1893–1977)   M.K. Jerome was a songwriter, composer and publisher. While in high school, he was a vaudeville pianist and accompanist in film theaters, then became a staff pianist for the publishing company of Waterson, Berlin and Snyder. He moved to Hollywood in '29, and wrote theme songs for early film musicals. He was under contract to Warner Bros. for eighteen years. His chief musical collaborators included Ted Koehler, Joe Young, Sam Lewis and Jack Scholl. His most famous composition was "Just a Baby's Prayer at Twilight," one of World War I's biggest hit songs (see '18).

William Jerome (1865–1932)   William Jerome collaborated with Jean Schwartz on several songs and Broadway productions in the 1900s and early 1910s. Some of his most famous songs include "Any Old Place I Can Hang My Hat Is Home Sweet Home to Me" (see '01), "Bedelia" (see

'04), "The Green Grass Grew All Around" (see '13), "Row, Row, Row" (see '13) and "Chinatown, My Chinatown" (see '15). He was an early member and one of the first directors of ASCAP, the American Society of Authors, Composers and Publishers.

Leon Jessel (1871–1942) German composer Leon Jessel is most famous in the popular music genre for composing the music for "Parade of the Wooden Soldiers" (see '23). Being a Jew, Jessel suffered greatly during Hitler's reign. He died after being tortured by the Gestapo.

Buster Johnson Buster Johnson was co-lyricist with Gus Mueller on "Wang Wang Blues" (see '21). Johnson played trombone for Paul Whiteman's Orchestra.

Chic Johnson (real name: Harold Ogden Johnson; 1891–1962) With Ole Olsen, Chic Johnson was half of that lunatic comedy team from vaudeville. The pair made several films, among which the most successful was *Hellzapoppin'* ('41).Olsen and Johnson were lyricists for "Oh! Gee, Oh! Gosh, Oh! Golly, I'm in Love" (see '23). Olsen and Johnson performed the song in *Hellzapoppin'*.

Christine Johnson Christine Johnson introduced "You'll Never Walk Alone" and "June Is Bustin' Out All Over" in the Rodgers and Hammerstein musical *Carousel* (see '45).

Edward Johnson (1910–1961) Edward Johnson was a co-writer of "Jersey Bounce" (see '42). Johnson was a trombonist, composer and arranger.

Howard Johnson (1887–1941) Lyricist Howard Johnson began his music career as a pianist in Boston stage and film theaters. In '14, he joined the United States Navy and served during World War I. After the war, Johnson moved to New York City where he worked as a staff writer for publishing companies on Tin Pan Alley. He began collaborating with lyricists and composers such as Milton Ager, Walter Donaldson, George Meyer, Joe Meyer, Joe Davis, Percy Wenrich, James Kendis, Harry M. Woods, James Brockman, Archie Gottler and W. Edward Breuder. Johnson produced such songs as "Ireland Must Be Heaven for My Mother Came from There" (see '16), "M-O-T-H-E-R" (see '16), "There's a Broken Heart for Every Light on Broadway" (see '16), and "When the Moon Comes Over the Mountain" (see '31). Johnson also wrote "I Scream, You Scream, We All Scream for Ice Cream," "I Don't Want to Get Well," "Siam," and "Feather Your Nest." Howard Johnson was an original member of the Songwriters' Hall of Fame when it was opened in '70.

J. Rosamond Johnson (1873–1954) John Rosamond Johnson, like his brother James Weldon Johnson, was born in Jacksonville, Florida. By the age of four, Rosamond was already an accomplished pianist. He was trained at the New England Conservatory and then studied in London. He returned to Jacksonville and taught public school. He began his show business career along with his brother and Bob Cole. As a songwriting team, they wrote "Under the Bamboo Tree" (see '02). J. Rosamond Johnson was active in various musical roles during his career. He toured in vaudeville and, after Cole's death, began a successful tour with Charles Hart and Tom Brown. In London, he wrote music for a theater revue. After returning to the United States, New York's Music School Settlement for Colored — founded by the New York Symphony

Orchestra's David Mannes — appointed him as director where he served from '14 to '19. With his own ensembles — the Harlem Rounders and the Inimitable Five — he toured as well, and performed in Negro spiritual concerts with Taylor Gordon. The London production of Lew Leslie's *Blackbirds of 1936* engaged Johnson as musical director. During the '30s, Johnson also sang the Lawyer in the original production of Gershwin's *Porgy and Bess*, taking roles in other productions as well.

James P. Johnson (1891–1955) Composer and pianist James P. Johnson, the father of stride piano, was the composer of "Charleston" (see '24). In the early 1910s, Johnson worked as a pianist in summer resorts, theaters and nightclubs before forming his own band in the early '20s called the Clef Club. Johnson and his band toured Europe with a vaudeville show. Returning to the U.S., Johnson became accompanist for such renowned singers as Bessie Smith and Ethel Waters. Johnson's stride piano style influenced performers like Duke Ellington and Fats Domino. Johnson's most famous song other than "Charleston" was "If I Could Be with You One Hour Tonight" (see '30). He also wrote "Runnin' Wild." Johnson wrote primarily by himself but did collaborate with lyricists Mike Riley, Nelson Cogane and Cecil Mack. Johnson was elected to membership in the Songwriters' Hall of Fame in '70 and to the Big Band/Jazz Hall of Fame. Some '21 recordings by James P. Johnson's Harmony Eight are available at http://www.redhotjazz.com/bands. html.

James Weldon Johnson (1871–1938) Lyricist, lawyer, activist, diplomat and educator James Weldon Johnson was educated at Atlanta University where he received his bachelor and masters degrees. He also passed the Florida bar exam. In the early 1900s, Johnson moved to New York City and began writing songs, collaborating with his brother, J. Rosamond Johnson (see below). Johnson's most famous song is "Under the Bamboo Tree" (see '02). Actually, songwriting was a minor part of Johnson's life. He worked as a school principal, was the founder and editor of the first African American daily newspaper in this country, was appointed to the U.S. consul in Venezuela and later in Nicaragua, worked as an assistant editor of a New York magazine, was a visiting professor of creative literature at Boston's Fisk University, was a trustee at Atlanta University, served as a director for the American Fund for Public Service, was the author of several books on African American life and was the National Secretary of the NAACP. James W. Johnson was inducted into the Songwriters' Hall of Fame in '70.

Jimmy Johnson (1896–?) Jimmy Johnson was co-writer of "If I Could Be with You One Hour Tonight" (see '30).

Arthur Johnston (1898–1954) Arthur Johnston is primarily remembered for the songs he composed for movie musicals in the '30s. In his early career, Johnston performed as a pianist in film theaters and later was a pianist and music director for Irving Berlin's Broadway productions. Johnston moved to Hollywood in the late '20s and wrote the scores for such hit films as *College Humor, Murder at the Vanities, Pennies from Heaven* and *Double or Nothing*. During World War II, Johnston served in the 351st infantry. Johnston collaborated with several lyricists including Sam Coslow, Gus Kahn and Johnny Burke. Johnston's most well-known songs include "Just One More Chance" (see '31), "Cocktails for Two" (see '34), "Pennies from Heaven" (see '36), and "The Moon Got in My Eyes" (see '37). Arthur Johnston was inducted into the Songwriters' Hall of Fame in '70. At http://www.songwriters halloffame.org/exhibit_audio_video.asp?exhibitId=90 hear an audio clip of "Just One More Chance" performed by Bing Crosby with Victor Young and his orchestra and "Moon Song" performed by Louis Armstrong.

Johnny Johnston (1915–1996) Johnny Johnston introduced "I Don't Want to Walk Without You" in the movie musical *Sweater Girl* (see '42) and "That Old Black Magic" in the movie musical *Star Spangled Rhythm* (see '43). He began his career as a singer with Art Kassel and his band. He also appeared on radio often during the late '30s. Johnston became a nightclub singer and a leading man in a few Hollywood movie musicals of the '40s. In '42, he signed with Capitol Records, becoming one of the first four artists signed by the label. Johnston's most popular recording was of "Laura" in '45.

Al Jolson (real name: Asa Yoelson; 1886–1950) Al Jolson was born Asa Yoelson in Russia. His father trained him to become a synagogue cantor, but he gave up that career to sing popular music. He became known as "The World's Greatest Entertainer" and was a very charismatic personality in show business from the early '10s through the mid–'30s. After a few years of relative obscurity his career zoomed again with release of two motion pictures: *The Jolson Story* ('46) and *Jolson Sings Again* ('49). Jolson starred in the first part-sound film, *The Jazz Singer*, in which he performed several of his favorite songs. The first words he uttered in the film were his famous expression: "Folks, you ain't heard nothin' yet." He was in several other films, most notably *The Singing Fool* ('28), *Hallelujah, I'm a Bum* ('33), *Wonder Bar* ('34), *Go Into Your Dance* ('35) and *Rhapsody in Blue* ('45). Some of the famous pre–'20s hits identified with Jolson (generally because he introduced and popularized them) include "Raggin' the Baby to Sleep" (see '12), "That Haunting Melody" (see '12), "You Made Me Love You (I Didn't want to Do It)" (see '13), "The Spaniard That Blighted My Life" (see '13), "I Sent My Wife to the Thousand Isles" (see '16), "Rock-a-Bye Your Baby with a Dixie Melody" (see '18), "I'm All Bound 'Round with the Mason Dixon Line" (see '18), "Hello Central, Give Me No Man's Land" (see '18) and "I'll Say She Does" (see '19). The string continued into the '20s with "Swanee" (see '20), "I've Got My Captain Working for Me Now" (see '20), "Avalon" (see '21), "O-HI-O" (see '21), "April Showers" (see '22), "Angel Child" (see '22), "Toot, Toot, Tootsie!" (see '23), "California, Here I Come" (see '24), "I Wonder What's Become of Sally" (see '24), "All Alone" (see '25), "I'm Sitting on Top of the World" (see '26), "When the Red, Red, Robin Comes Bob, Bob, Bobbin' Along" (see '26), "Sonny Boy" (see '28), "There's a Rainbow 'Round My Shoulder" (see '28) and "Little Pal" (see '29). Jolson also was credited as writer or co-writer of several hit songs including "I'll Say She Does" (see '19), "I'll Sing You a Thousand Love Songs" (see '19), "Avalon" (see '21), "California, Here I Come" (see '24), "Me and My Shadow" (see '27), and "There's a Rainbow 'Round My Shoulder" (see '28). In '47, Jolson's collaboration with Saul Chaplin, "Anniversary Song" from

The Jolson Story, was a big hit. Al was inducted into the Popular Music Hall of Fame in 2001. Jolson became the No. 9 top recording artist of the '10s and No. 2 for the '20s, which makes him the No. 7 top recording artist of the first half of the 20th Century. Jolson's website is http://www.jolson.org/.

Ada Jones (1873–1922) Alto Ada Jones, born in Lancashire, England, became the most popular female singer of the pre-twenties era. Jones was a versatile singer; she sang in vaudeville sketches, performed sentimental ballads, rags and Irish songs equally well. However, she was most adept at comic songs. Her family moved from England to Philadelphia in 1879. After her mother died, her new stepmother encouraged her to pursue music. As early as 1882, "Little Ada Jones" began appearing on the cover of sheet music. Her earliest recordings were brown wax cylinders for Edison Recording Company in the early 1890s, which are among the earliest commercial recordings of a female singer. She did not record extensively, however, until '04. Some of Ms. Jones' most popular recordings include "I Just Can't Make My Eyes Behave" (see '07), "The Yama Yama Man" with the Victor Light Opera Co. (see '09), "I've Got Rings on My Fingers" (see '09), "Call Me Up Some Rainy Afternoon" with the American Quartet (see '10), "Come, Josephine, in My Flying Machine" with Billy Murray and the American Quartet (see '11), "Row, Row, Row" (see '13) and "By the Beautiful Sea" with Billy Watkins (see '14). Ms. Jones also teamed with Billy Murray for several popular duet recordings. Some of their most popular disks include "Let's Take an Old-Fashioned Walk" (see '07), "When We Are M-A-Double-R-I-E-D" (see '07), "Cuddle Up a Little Closer, Lovey Mine" (see '08), "Wouldn't You Like to Have Me for a Sweetheart?" (see '08), "Shine on, Harvest Moon" (see '09) and "Be My Little Baby Bumble Bee" (see '12). Contractual obligations caused the duo to split in '13. She also recorded duets with Len Spencer, but they were not quite as successful. By '16, her popularity declined. Her career suffered when popular music changed in the World War I era toward the novelty jazz songs.

Allan Jones (1908–1992) Singer Allan Jones starred in several movie musicals and appeared on radio often during the '30s and '40s. He gained national attention in the mid–'30s when he appeared in the Marx Brothers film *A Night at the Opera* and introduced the song "Alone" (see '36). He also costarred with Jeanette MacDonald in the movie version of Rudolf Friml's *The Firefly* in '37. In the late '30s and '40s he remained active on radio. His career waned during the '50s, and he became a dentist. His son, Jack, is also a popular singer.

Billy Jones (real name: William Reese Jones; 1889–1940) Billy Jones tried several occupations before making his recording debut in '18. He recorded under numerous names: Billy Jones, Harry Blake, Billy Clarke, Lester George, Duncan Jones, John Kelley, Dennis O'-Malley, William Rees, Victor Roberts, Billy West, William West, and Carlton Williams. He also recorded with the Cleartone Four, the Crescent Trio, the Harmonizers Quartet and the Premier Quartet. But he actually may be best known for his duets with Ernest Hare (billed as Jones and Hare or the Happiness Boys). The Happiness Boys name came from the Happiness Candy Stores, who were their radio sponsors. By the late '20s they were the highest paid radio singers. Billy Jones' biggest hit recording came in the early '20s with "Yes! We Have No Bananas" (see '23). Jones became the No. 13 top recording artist of the '20s.

Earl C. Jones   Earl C. Jones was the lyricist for the hit song "Everybody Two-Step" (see '12).

Isham Jones (1894–1956)   Composer and orchestra leader, Isham Jones learned as a youngster to play the saxophone and piano. In his early career, he was a saxophonist in dance bands and eventually began his own orchestra. Jones and his band became the pride of Chicago and a very popular band around the nation. Jones' band was one of the most successful during the '20s. His biggest hit recordings include "Wabash Blues" (see '21), "On the Alamo" (see '22), "Swingin' Down the Lane" (see '23), "It Had to Be You" (see '24), "Spain" (see '24), "I'll See You in My Dreams" (see '25), "Remember" (see '25) and "Stardust" (see '31). Jones and his orchestra became the No. 4 top recording artists of the '20s, No. 22 of the first half of the 20th Century. Jones collaborated with Gus Kahn, Jack Yellen, Charles Newman, Gordon Jenkins and other lyricists on some of the biggest hits of the day. The most famous songs Jones had a hand in writing include "On the Alamo" (see '22), "Swingin' Down the Lane" (see '23), "It Had to Be You" (see '24), "Spain" (see '24), "I'll See You in My Dreams" (see '25), plus "The One I Love Belongs to Somebody Else." Isham Jones has been a member of the Songwriters' Hall of Fame since '70 and is also a member of the Big Band/Jazz Hall of Fame. Some recordings by Isham Jones and his orchestra and Isham Jones and his Rainbo Orchestra are available at http://www.redhotjazz.com/bands.html.

John Price Jones   John Price Jones and Mary Lawlor introduced "The Best Things in Life Are Free" in *Good News* (see '27).

Spike Jones (real name: Lindley Armstrong Jones; 1911–1964)   "The King of Corn," Spike Jones was famous for his novelty band. They often performed parodies of popular hits, using pistols, cowbells, saws, whistles, cheers, clinking glasses, etc. to create their zany arrangements. Jones and his crew gained national attention in '42 with their rendition of "Der Fuehrer's Face," which made fun of Adolf Hitler. Their only No. 1 hit was "All I Want for Christmas (Is My Two Front Teeth)" (see '48), but they also had considerable success with "I Saw Mommy Kissing Santa Claus" (see '52).

Stan Jones (1914–1963)   Stan Jones was the writer of "Riders in the Sky" (see '49). Jones grew up in southeastern Arizona. He moved to California for college, but soon traveled all over the West and Pacific Northwest. He also worked for the National Park Service in Death Valley. It was there he wrote many of his songs, including "Riders in the Sky." The Park Service made Stan their representative when Hollywood film crews came to Death Valley. On one occasion, the cast and crew listened to Stan's songs and stories. They encouraged him to get them published. Burl Ives was the first to record Stan's "Riders in the Sky." Soon after Vaughn Monroe cut his version and actually released it before Ives' version. Later, Jones wrote the music for the films *Wagonmaster, Rio Grande* and *The Searchers.* Stan also got to appear in *Rio Grande* as a sergeant who presented the Regimental Singer, actually the Sons of the Pioneers, to John Wayne and Maureen O'Hara. Disney

hired Jones to write music for many of their movies and TV shows. He sometimes appeared on *The Wonderful World of Color* singing a western song. He also wrote the theme for the TV series *Cheyenne.*

Scott Joplin (1868–1919)   Scott Joplin was one of the most important developers of ragtime music. As a youngster, Joplin taught himself to play the piano, but he learned classical music from a neighbor, Louis Chauvin. In his teens he became a pianist in the low-life districts that would hire African American musicians. In 1893 he played piano at the World's Columbian Exposition in Chicago, and when the fair closed, he moved to Sedalia, Missouri. It was there that he wrote "Maple Leaf Rag" in 1899 (see '07). He moved to New York City in '07. In '11, he published his opera *Treemonisha,* which was the first original African American opera. It was not the success Joplin expected. Joplin's music drew new interest after his rag "The Entertainer" was used in the '73 film *The Sting,* which enabled *Treemonisha* to be re-staged with considerable success in '75 by the Houston Grand Opera. Scott Joplin was an original member of the Songwriters' Hall of Fame in '70. Go to the following website for more on Joplin: http://www.scottjoplin.org/.

Louis Jordan (1908–1975)   Louis Jordan became one of the few African American rhythm and blues musicians to find success in the mainstream of popular music during and immediately after the swing era. In the early '30s, Jordan played saxophone with Chick Webb and Clarence Williams. By the late '30s he organized his Tympany Five. In the '40s Jordan released dozens of records, some which did quite well on the charts. Some of Jordan's most successful recordings include "Is You Is or Is You Ain't My Baby?" (see '44), and "G.I. Jive" (see '44). Other Jordan successes include "Choo Ch' Boogie," "Caldonia," and "Ain't Nobody Here but Us Chickens." The Broadway musical *Five Guys Named Moe* honored Jordan in '92. All of the songs in the show were either written or popularized by Jordan. Jordan was elected to the Big Band/Jazz Hall of Fame in '98.

Richard Jose (1869–1941)   Richard Jose had a particularly popular Victor recording of "Silver Threads Among the Gold" (see '04). Jose also helped popularize "Dear Old Girl" (see '04). He was a British-born countertenor who had performed in vaudeville since the 1890s.

Jubilee Singers (see Russell Wooding's Jubilee Singers)

Jack Judge (1872–1938)   Jack Judge was a British music-hall entertainer and composer of popular songs. He is famous for writing "It's a Long, Long Way to Tipperary" in '12 (see '15).

Dick Jurgens (1910–1993)   Dick Jurgens was a trumpeter, bandleader and composer. He formed his first band in '28. One of the vocalists for his band was Eddy Howard, who became famous as a solo recording artist in the early '50s. Jurgens co-wrote "Careless" (see '40), "Elmer's Tune" (see '41), and "One Dozen Roses" (see '42). As a recording artist, Jurgens and his band had reasonable success with "Careless," "In an Old Dutch Garden," and "One Dozen Roses." He entertained our troops during World War II. After the war, he formed another band and continued to lead the group into the '70s.

Walter Jurmann (1903–1971) Austrian-born composer Walter Jurmann was co-composer of "You're All I Need" (see '35). Jurmann came to the U.S. to write for the movie studios. He began studying medicine, but in '24 decided to pursue a career in music instead. He moved to Berlin and was soon writing film music for German movies. When the Nazis came to power in '33, Jurmann fled to Paris, where he continued composing. In '34 he was offered a seven-year contract with MGM. He and his Polish-born composing partner, Bronislaw Kaper, left for Hollywood. Jurmann's successful films include *Mutiny on the Bounty, San Francisco*, and *Presenting Lily Mars*. In the early '40s Jurmann left the film business.

Kahn Kaene Kahn Kaene was one of the co-composers of "Scatter-Brain" (see '39).

Irving Kahal (1903–1942) Irving Kahal wrote several successful popular song lyrics in the '20s and '30s. Kahal was performing in vaudeville when he met composer Sammy Fain. They began a songwriting partnership that lasted until Kahal's death. Their first song, written with lyricist Francis Wheeler, was "Let a Smile Be Your Umbrella" in '27. In the early '30s, Kahal and Fain signed with Paramount Pictures to write a song for the Maurice Chevalier movie *The Big Pond*. The resulting song was "You Brought a New Kind of Love to Me" (see '30), written with Pierre Norman. Kahal and Fain. He continued to furnish songs for various movie studios, focusing on providing individual songs rather than complete scores. Other well-known Kahal songs include "Wedding Bells (Are Breaking Up That Old Gang of Mine)" (see '29), "Moonlight Saving Time" (see '31), "I'll Be Seeing You" (see '44), and "I Can Dream, Can't I?" (see '50). Kahal has been a member of the Songwriters' Hall of Fame since '70. At http://www.songwritershalloffame.org/exhibit_audio_video.asp?exhibitId=49 hear audio clips of "You Brought a New Kind of Love to Me" performed by Maurice Chevalier and "When I Take My Sugar to Tea" performed by the Boswell Sisters with the Dorsey Brothers Orchestra.

Gus Kahn (1886–1941) Lyricist Gus Kahn, born in Coblenz, Germany, became one of the most important writers of popular songs from the early years of the 20th Century through the '20s. Kahn's family immigrated to the U.S. in 1891 and settled in Chicago. After his high school years, he worked in a mail order business before launching his successful and prolific career as a songwriter. He got his first song, "My Dreamy China Lady," published at age 20. Kahn contributed to several Broadway musical scores including *Whoopee, Sinbad, Passing Show of 1922* and *Greenwich Village Follies of 1923*. At the same time, he was writing for films, primarily for MGM. By the early '30s, Kahn had become a full-time songwriter for the movies contributing to such films as *Flying Down to Rio, Thanks a Million, One Night of Love, Three Smart Girls, San Francisco* and *Ziegfeld Girl*. Kahn's primary collaborator was Walter Donaldson, but he also worked with his wife, Grace LeBoy Kahn, Egbert Van Alstyne, Richard Whiting, Buddy DeSylva, Al Jolson, Raymond Egan, Ted FioRito, Isham Jones, Ernie Erdman, Neil Moret, Vincent Youmans, George Gershwin, Ira Gershwin, Harry Akst, Harry M. Woods, Edward Eliscu, Victor Schertzinger, Arthur Johnston, Bronislau Kaper, Walter Jurmann, Sigmund Romberg and Harry Warren. Some of Kahn's most famous lyrics include "The Good Ship Mary

Ann" (see '14), "Memories" (see '16), "Pretty Baby" (see '16), "I'll Say She Does" (see '19), "My Buddy" (see '22), "Carolina in the Morning" (see '23), "No! No! Nora!" (see '23), Toot, Toot, Tootsie" (see '23), "Swingin' Down the Lane" (see '23), "It Had to Be You" (see '24), "Charley, My Boy" (see '24), "Nobody's Sweetheart" (see '24), "Spain" (see '24), "I'll See You in My Dreams" (see '25), "Yes, Sir, That's My Baby!" (see '25), "Ukulele Lady" (see '25), "Chloe" (see '28), "Makin' Whoopee" (see '29), "Love Me or Leave Me" (see '29), "Dancing in the Dark" (see '31), "Dream a Little Dream of Me" (see '31), "Just a Little Street Where Old Friends Meet" (see '32), "Flying Down to Rio" (see '34), "The Carioca" (see '34), "Orchids in the Moonlight" (see '34), "One Night of Love" (see '34), "You're All I Need" (see '35) and "I'll Sing You a Thousand Love Songs" (see '36). Other well known Kahn lyrics include "San Francisco," "You Stepped Out of a Dream," "Side by Side," "The One I Love Belongs to Somebody Else," "That Certain Party," "You Tell Me Your Dreams, I'll Tell You Mine," "Coquette," "Liza," "The Waltz You Saved for Me," "My Baby Just Cares for Me," and "I'm Through with Love." Kahn was elected to the Songwriters' Hall of Fame in '70. At http://www.songwritershall offame.org/exhibit_audio_video.asp?exhibitId=91 hear audio clips of "My Buddy" performed by Henry Burr, "Carioca" performed by Connee Boswell with Victor Young and his orchestra, "Ain't We Got Fun?" performed by Van and Schenck and "Makin' Whoopee" performed by Louis Armstrong.

Roger Wolfe Kahn (1907–1962) In '23, Otto Kahn, a wealthy millionaire banker, indulged his teenage son's hobby by buying him the Arthur Lange Orchestra. He also bought some good musicians for the band: Jack Teagarden, Gene Krupa, Red Nichols, Eddie Lang, and Joe Venuti among them. Roger Wolfe Kahn began studying the violin at age 7, but eventually mastered 18 different instruments. In the mid-'20s he had his own booking office and owned his own nightclub. Roger Wolfe Kahn and his orchestra's only major hit recording was "Russian Lullaby" (see '27). By the mid-'30s, Kahn transferred his interest to aviation and gave up his band. In the early '40s, he became a test pilot. Some recordings by Roger Wolfe Kahn and his orchestra and Roger Wolfe Kahn and his Hotel Biltmore Orchestra are available at http://www.redhot jazz.com/bands.html.

Maewa Kaihau (real name: Emira Maewa Kaihau; 1879–?) Maewa Kaihau was born Louisa Flavell in New Zealand. She married Henare Kaihau, a member of Parliament representing Western Maori. Maewa played the piano, sang, and wrote poetry. She took a tune by Clement Scott, Maori lyrics, and added some new words for a song titled "Haere Ra Waltz Song." Over the next decade the song became a wharfside farewell song for passenger ships and eventually gained worldwide popularity as "Now Is the Hour" (see '48). Dorothy Stewart wrote the English lyrics.

Henry Kailimai (1882–1948) Henry Kailimai was born in the Kohala District on the Big Island of Hawaii, the son of William Henry and Kaaipelana Kailimai (notice he took his father's last name as his first, and his mother's last name as his last name; since Hawaii was a matriarchal society, his taking his mother's maiden name is not surprising). He soon became an accomplished musician and eventually a music teacher. He moved to Oahu where he became a member of the Mormon Church and played organ for church services. He also became a protégé of Ernest Kaai, the first important Hawaiian talent agent, and worked as one of Kaai's musicians. Over the years, Henry's talent for writing songs and making music brought him fame in the islands. When he was invited to perform at an exposition in San Francisco, Henry's Royal Hawaiians were listed as a star attraction. One of the many people captivated by Kailimai's musical talents was Henry Ford who invited him to Detroit to become a resident musician providing music for Ford Motor Company entertainment functions. Kailimai accepted Ford's offer. Today, Kailimai is primarily remembered as the composer of "On the Beach at Waikiki" (see '15).

Kitty Kallen (real name: Genevieve Agostinello; 1922–) Singer Kitty Kallen was particularly active in the '40s and '50s. Her most famous big band jobs were with Jimmy Dorsey and Harry James. She did the vocals on Jimmy Dorsey's recordings of "Besame Mucho" (see '44), and "They're Either Too Young or Too Old" (see '44) and on Harry James' recordings of "It's Been a Long, Long Time" (see '45), "I'm Beginning to See the Light" (see '45) and "I'll Buy That Dream" (see '45). During the late '40s and early '50s her singing career faltered for a while, but it was revived with the hit "Little Things Mean a Lot" (see '54).

Emmerich Kalman (1882–1953) Hungarian composer Emmerich Kálmán is best remembered for his operettas. He was born in the Hungarian town of Siófok on Lake Balaton. He began studying piano as a teenager but was sidelined by a stress injury in his hands. To continue pursuing his musical interests, he studied composition at the Budapest Academy of Music. In '07, he had his first success with operetta, which led him to Vienna. During his years there, he composed more than eight operettas, often mixing elements of Viennese and Hungarian musical styles with libretti of Hungarian themes. Because of the Nazi takeover of Austria in '38, he left Vienna for Paris and then the United States, where he obtained citizenship. About a decade later, Kalman returned to Paris, where he remained until his death in '53. Today Kalman is primarily remembered for "Love's Own Sweet Song" from the operetta *Sari* (see '14).

Bert Kalmar (1884–1947) Lyricist Bert Kalmar collaborated primarily with composer Harry Ruby. They wrote several hit songs for Hollywood movies and also contributed to some Broadway musicals in the '20s. As a child growing up in Manhattan, Kalmar began his show business career performing as a magician in tent shows and then as a comedian in vaudeville acts. In addition to Ruby, Kalmar collaborated with composers Ted Snyder, Oscar Hammerstein II, Fred Ahlert, Harry Akst, Con Conrad, Herbert Stothart, Harry Tierney, Pete Wendling and Edgar Leslie. Some of Kalmar's most famous songs include "Where Did You Get That Girl?" (see '13), "Hello, Hawaii, How Are You?" (see '16), "Oh! What a Pal Was Mary" (see '19), "Three Little Words" (see '30), "I Wanna Be Loved by You" (see '28) and "Nevertheless" (see '50). Other well-know Kalmar lyrics include "So Long, Oo-Long (How Long You Gonna Be Gone)," "Who's Sorry Now?," "Thinking of You," "My Sunny Tennessee," "I Love You So Much," and "Take Your Girlie to the Movies

(If You Can't Make Love at Home)." Kalmar even had a hit in '51 with "A Kiss to Build a Dream on," which came four years after his death and twenty years after his previous hit. *Three Little Words* ('50) was a Hollywood movie musical biography of Kalmar and Ruby starring Fred Astaire and Red Skelton. Bert Kalmar has been a member of the Songwriters' Hall of Fame since '70. Surprisingly, his partner, Harry Ruby, wasn't listed among the members of the Songwriters' Hall of Fame. At http://www.song writershalloffame.org/exhibit_audio_video.asp? exhibitId=266 hear audio clips of "My Sunny Tennessee" performed by the Peerless Quartet and "A Kiss to Build a Dream on" performed by Louis Armstrong.

Helen Kane (real name: Helen Schroder; 1904–1966) Helen Kane, born to a poor family in the Bronx, became star stuck at an early age. By the time she was 15, Helen was onstage professionally, touring the Orpheum Circuit with the Marx brothers in their pre-movie days. Helen spent the early and mid–'20s trouping in vaudeville as a singer. She then married department store buyer Joseph Kane and took his name professionally; however they divorced by '28. When Helen interpolated the lyrics "boop-boop-a-doop" into "That's My Weakness Now" the audience went crazy (see '28). Seemingly overnight, the world changed for Helen. Her agent got her $5,500 a week for appearing in *Good Boy*, where she introduced her big hit, "I Want to Be Loved by You" (see '28), again inserting her "boop-boop-a-doops." In mid–'29, Paramount signed Helen to make a series of film musicals. In '30, animators Dave, Max, and Louis Fleischer decided to cash in on Helen's popularity. They assigned staff animator Grim Natwick to come up with a girlfriend for Bimbo the Dog; the result was a caricature of Helen Kane, with droopy dog ears and a squeaky, boop-a-doop singing voice. They called the character Betty Boop and Betty became an instant hit with audiences. By '32, the character lost its dog features and became human. In '32, Helen filed a $250,000 suit against Max Fleischer, his studio, and Paramount Publix Corporation, charging unfair competition and wrongful appropriation in the Betty Boop cartoons. Amazingly, the judge ruled against Helen in '34. By '35, Helen Kane dropped out of show business.

Bronislau Kaper (1902–1983) Bronislau Kaper was co-composer of "You're All I Need" (see '35). Composer/conductor Bronislau Kaper studied music at the Warsaw Conservatory in his native Poland. He worked as a film composer, arranger and conductor in Warsaw, Berlin, Vienna, London and Paris. Kaper came to Hollywood in the mid–'30s to write for films. He composed several background scores for MGM films including *San Francisco, Gaslight, Our Vines Have Tender Grapes, The Stranger, Mrs. Parkington, Green Dolphin Street, Invitation, Lili.* for which he won the Academy Award for Best Score in '53, *The Glass Slipper,* and *Mutiny on the Bounty.* He wrote the full score for *A Day at the Races.* His chief collaborators were Sammy Cahn, Walter Jurmann, Gus Kahn, and Paul Francis Webster.

Anton Karas (1906–1985) Karas was an Austrian zither player who had a megahit recording in '50 with the theme song from the film *The Third Man.* His London recording of "The Third Man Theme" (see '50) sold over two million copies and stayed at the top of the *Billboard* pop chart for eleven weeks. Karas wrote the entire score for the film. He used his earnings from the film and recordings to buy a wine bar in Grinzing, Austria called, quite naturally, "The Third Man Theme." He played at the bar and made occasional recordings, mostly for the Austrian and German market.

Irving Kaufman (1891–1976) New Yorker Irving Kaufman was a member of the Avon Comedy Four. He also recorded as a soloist between '14 and the end of the '20s. His most popular recording was of "Hail! Hail! The Gang's All Here" with the Columbia Quartet (see '18).

Buddy Kaye (real name: Jules Leonard Kaye; 1918–2002) Songwriter Buddy Kaye was particularly active in the '40s and '50s. He wrote hits for several famous singers, including Perry Como, and Frank Sinatra. His most famous songs include "Till the End of Time" (see '45), "'A'— You're Adorable" (see '49), and "Full Moon and Empty Arms," the first and last mentioned songs were adapted from famous classical composers: Chopin and Rachmaninoff. He often wrote special material for nightclub acts for several stars, wrote for cartoon series, and later became a record producer. He was the co-writer of the theme song for the TV show *I Dream of Jeannie*.

Sammy Kaye (1910–1987) Bandleader Sammy Kaye led a very successful sweet-style band during the '30s and '40s. They continued to thrive into the '50s and '60s, but not quite to the earlier extent. A few of his hits tended toward the novelty variety. Kaye was inducted into the Big Band/Jazz Hall of Fame in '92. Kaye's major hit recordings were "Love Walked in" (see '38), "Rosalie" (see '38), "Dream Valley" (see '41), "Daddy" (see '41), "Chickery Chick" (see '45), "The Old Lamp-Lighter" (see '46), "I'm a Big Girl Now" (see '46) and "Harbor Lights" (see '50). Kaye became the No. 34 top recording artist of the '30s and No. 9 of the '40s, making him the No. 27 top recording artist of the first half of the 20th Century. Sammy also helped Don Reid compose the music for the World War II hit "Remember Pearl Harbor" (see '42).

Allen Kearns (1894–1956) Canadian actor, singer, dancer Allen Kearns and Adele Astaire introduced "'S Wonderful" in the Gershwin musical *Funny Face* (see '28)

Ruby Keeler (real name: Ethel Hilda Keeler; 1909–1986) Ruby Keeler was born in Halifax, Nova Scotia. Her Irish family were accomplished ballroom dancers. Ruby became a talented tap-dancer, but by later standards, Fred Astaire, Eleanor Powell, Gene Kelly, etc., she was not particularly adept. On Broadway, she appeared in the chorus of *The Rise of Rosie O'Reilly* ('23) at age thirteen and had featured roles in three different short-lived musicals in '27. Her only other Broadway role besides Dixie Dugan in *Show Girl* was in a '71 revival of *No, No, Nanette*. After she married Al Jolson, she became particularly famous when she starred opposite Dick Powell in the movie musical *Forty Second Street* (see '33). She followed that gigantic success with starring roles in *The Gold Diggers of 1933* (see "Shadow Waltz" in '33). She and Lee Dixon introduced "Too Marvelous for Words" in the movie musical *Ready, Willing and Able* (see '37). She starred in several other movie musicals by the early '40s. She divorced Jolson in '39, remarried, and went into semi-retirement. She was honored with a star on the Hollywood Walk of Fame.

John W. Kellette (1873–1922) John W. Kellette was active in the Hollywood silent film industry. In the pop music genre, he was the composer of "I'm Forever Blowing Bubbles" (see '19).

Gene Kelly (real name: Eugene Curran Kelly; 1912–1996) Gene Kelly became one of the most famous and gifted dancers Hollywood ever featured. His acrobatic dance routines were some of the best ever filmed. Although he was not a great singer, he, like fellow dancer Fred Astaire, had a distinctive singing style that could sell a song. His early training in his family's dance studio led him to Broadway in the early '40s. After starring in *Pal Joey* ('41), he began his movie career in '42. Over the next several years, he starred in more than 30 movies, notably *Cover Girl*, in which he introduced "Long Ago and Far Away" (see '44), *Anchors Aweigh* ('45), *On the Town* ('49), *An American in Paris* ('51), *Singin' in the Rain* ('52) and *Brigadoon* ('54). Kelly's most popular recordings were made in duets with Judy Garland. "For Me and My Gal" in '43 was most popular (see '17 when it was most popular), however, his recording of "Singin' in the Rain" has remained a fan favorite for over 50 years (see '52).

Patsy Kelly (real name: Sarah Veronica Rose Kelly; 1910–1981) Patsy Kelly introduced "I Can't Give You Anything but Love" in the '27 revue *Harry Delmar's Revels* (see '28), her Broadway debut. After she preformed for producer Earl Carroll in his *Sketches* and *Vanities* musicals, she headed to Hollywood to make films. She became a popular film comedienne. She returned to Broadway in '73 in a revival of *No, No, Nanette*. She won the Tony Award for Best Actress in a Musical for her performance in that production. The following year, she starred in a revival of *Irene* and received a second Best Actress Tony. In '76, she appeared in the film *Freaky Friday*.

Hal Kemp (real name: James Harold Kemp; 1905–1940) Hal Kemp led a sweet-style band during the '30s. He had organized a band while he was in college, and most of the members had continued with the group when it went professional in '27. Kemp was killed in an auto accident on the way to an engagement in San Francisco in late '40. Kemp's most famous hits were "When I'm with You" (see '36), "There's a Small Hotel" (see '36), "This Year's Kisses" (see '37) and "Where or When" (see '37). Kemp's band was also known for vocals by drummer Skinnay Ennis and saxman Saxie Dowell's nonsense songs: "Three Little Fishies" (see '39) and "Playmates" (see '40). Kemp was elected to the Big Band/Jazz Hall of Fame in '92. Kemp and his band became the No. 13 top recording artists of the '30s.

Jean Kenbrovin (see James Kendis, James Brockman and Nat Vincent)

James Kendis (1883–1946) Jean Kenbrovin was the pseudonym for James Kendis, James Brockman, and Nat Vincent when they co-wrote the lyrics for "I'm Forever Blowing Bubbles" (see '19). Kendis, Brockman, and Vincent had separate contracts with publishers that led them to merge their names into Jean Kenbrovin for credit on "I'm Forever Blowing Bubbles." Kendis also wrote the music for "If I Had My Way" (see '14).

Jimmy Kennedy (1902–1984) Songwriter Jimmy Kennedy was born in Omagh, County Tyrone, Ireland. During his career, Kennedy wrote over 2,000 songs. Kennedy is best known for the songs he produced in the mid-'30s and '40s. His biggest hits include "Isle of Capri" (see '35), "Red Sails in the Sunset" (see '35), "Harbor Lights" (see '50), "South of the Border" (see '40), "My Prayer" (see '40) and "April in Portugal" (see '53). Kennedy was inducted into the Songwriters' Hall of Fame in '97. At http://www.songwritershalloffame.org/exhibit_audio_vide o.asp?exhibitId=227 hear an audio clip of "Isle of Capri" performed by Gracie Fields with Percival MacKey and the New Mayfair Dance Orchestra.

Nick Kenny (1895–1975) and Charles Kenny (1898–1978)   Nick Kenny and Charles Kenny were brothers who collaborated to write several popular songs in the '30s and '40s. Nick was also a well-known poet and radio columnist for newspapers. Their most famous songs include "Love Letters in the Sand" (see '31), "Carelessly" (see '37), "Cathedral in the Pines" (see '38), "There's a Gold Mine in the Sky" (see '38) and "Dream Valley" (see '41).

Billy Kent   Billy Kent and Jeanette Warner introduced "Ballin' the Jack" in vaudeville (see '14). Kent and Warner are credited with being the creators of the fox trot dance.

Walter Kent (1911–1994)   Walter Kent studied music at the prestigious Julliard School of Music in New York City. His first songwriting success came with "Pu-Leeze Mister Hemingway" in '32. He began working in the Hollywood film industry during the late '30s, where he wrote several songs for westerns. He wrote "The White Cliffs of Dover" (see '42). He also wrote the music for the classic film *For Whom the Bell Tolls*. He joined Kim Gannon to write the Christmas classic "I'll Be Home for Christmas," which was particularly poignant for our GIs overseas (see '43). He and Gannon continued to collaborate on film songs. They wrote three songs for the Disney animated short *Johnny Appleseed* in '46.

Jerome Kern (1885–1945)   Jerome Kern became one of the most important composers in popular music history. Kern's first music teacher was his mother, followed by studies at the New York College of Music and further musical studies in Heidelberg, Germany. Returning to New York City, he began working as a pianist for a music publisher, and soon began contributing songs to various musical shows. He wrote his first complete Broadway musical score in '11. His first hit song was "They Didn't Believe Me" from *The Girl from Utah* (see '15). Kern, along with P.G. Wodehouse and Guy Bolton, experimented with contemporary, integrated, comical libretto, with songs that tried to fit the characters and situations. Most of those shows had American subjects and were staged in the small Princess Theater in New York City. The best known Princess Theater shows include *Very Good Eddie* ('15), *Oh, Boy!* ('17) and *Oh, Lady! Lady!* ('18). Several other shows in the late 1910s and early '20s led the way for the tremendously important *Show Boat* in '27 and then for *Roberta* in '33. By the end of the '30s Kern had composed his last Broadway musical. In the mid-'30s, Kern went to Hollywood, where he spent most of the rest of his career, writing some of his very best music. Kern's hit output was prolific. A few of his most famous hit songs include "How'd You Like to Spoon with Me" (see 1907), "Leave It to Jane" (see '17), "Look for the Silver Lining" (see '21), "Who?" (see '26), "Ol' Man River" (see '28), "Can't Help Lovin' Dat Man" (see '28), "Make Believe" (see '28),

"Why Do I Love You?" (see '28), "Why Was I Born?" (see '29), "I've Told Ev'ry Little Star" (see '33), "Smoke Gets in Your Eyes" (see '34), "The Touch of Your Hand" (see '34), "I Won't Dance" (see '35), "Lovely to Look At" (see '35), "A Fine Romance" (see '36), "The Way You Look Tonight," which won the Academy Award for Best Song (see '36), "Lovely to Look At" (see '35), "All the Things You Are" (see '40), "The Last Time I Saw Paris" (see '41), "Long Ago and Far Away" (see '44), and "All Through the Day" (see '46). Kern was inducted into the Songwriters' Hall of Fame in '70. He was inducted into the Popular Music Hall of Fame in 2004. The movie musical biography of Kern was *Till the Clouds Roll By* in '46. At http://www.songwritershalloffame.org/exhibit_audio_vide o.asp?exhibitId=67 hear audio clips of "Smoke Gets in Your Eyes" performed by Irene Dunne with Victor Young and his orchestra, "All the Things You Are" performed by Sarah Vaughan, "Bill," "Can't Help Lovin' Dat Man," and "Why Was I Born" performed by Lena Horne.

Grace Kerns (1886–1936)   Grace Kerns helped popularize "Song of Songs" with a popular Columbia recording in '15. Her most popular recording was a duet with John Barnes Wells of "Chinatown, My Chinatown" in '15. Ms. Kerns was a popular concert soprano. She became a college music professor after she retired from the stage.

Albert William Ketelbey (1875–1959)   Albert William Ketelbey, the British composer, was born in Birmingham, England, the son an engraver. Piano lessons must have started at an early age. By the age of thirteen he won a scholarship to Trinity College of Music in London. Although he tried his hand at several instruments, composition took an ever-increasing role. While he was still at the College, Ketèlbey managed to have many short pieces published. The more serious ones appeared under his real name, but the salon pieces and mandolin music appeared under the pseudonym of Raoul Clifford. His breakthrough into the popular market came when his "In a Monastery Garden" was published (see '15).

Francis Scott Key (1779–1843)   Francis Scott Key was an American lawyer and amateur poet who wrote the United States national anthem, "The Star-Spangled Banner," which became very popular as World War I began to cause grave concerns for U.S. citizens (see '16). For more on Key, visit http://en.wikipedia.org/wiki/Francis_Scott_ Key.

Gilbert Keyes   Gilbert Keyes was a lyricist and later a music publisher. Gilbert and Joe Lyons were co-lyricists on "On the Alamo" (see '22).

Richard Kiley (1922–)   Richard Kiley and Doretta Morrow introduced "Stranger in Paradise" in the Broadway musical *Kismet* (see '54). Kiley also starred in *Redhead, No Strings, Here's Love* and, especially, *Man of La Mancha*.

Leo Killian   Leo Killian was one of the co-writers of "The Hut-Sut Song (a Swedish Serenade)" (see '41).

Charles King (1889–1944)   Charles King began his show business career in vaudeville with his singing partner Elizabeth Brice. He was in the chorus of his first Broadway musical, *The Yankee Prince* ('08). He appeared in over fifteen Broadway musicals through the late '30s, but by far his biggest success was in *Hit the Deck*. King and

Louise Groody introduced "Sometimes I'm Happy" in *Hit the Deck* (see '27). He also introduced "Play a Simple Melody" in *Watch Your Step* in '14 (see '50 when it was most popular). He was in the first original film musical, *The Broadway Melody*, where he introduced "You Were Meant for Me" (see '29).

Charles E. King (1874–1950) Charles E. King was a composer, author, Hawaiian legislator and educator. He was a native Hawaiian who became a leader in musical education in Hawaii, an authority on Hawaiian songs and conductor of the Royal Hawaiian Band. In the early '20s, he served as a senator in the Hawaiian legislature. By far his most familiar song is "Song of the Islands (Na Lei O Hawaii)" (see '15). Almost all of the information about King and his song spelled the state "Hawai'i." Another of his popular-song compositions was "Ke Kali Nei Au (Hawaiian Wedding Song)."

Dennis King (real name: Dennis Pratt; 1897–1971) Englishman Dennis King was a classically trained singer and actor. King and Mary Ellis introduced "Indian Love Call" in *Rose Marie*, while he and Arthur Deagon introduced the musical's title song (see '25). He also created the role of Fancois Villon in Rudolf Friml's *The Vagabond King*, where he introduced "Song of the Vagabonds" (see '25). He recreated the role in his film debut opposite Jeanette MacDonald. Even though he was primarily known as a stage actor, he made a few other films and was active on early television

Irving King Irving King wrote the words and music for "Show Me the Way to Go Home" (see '26).

Pee Wee King (real name: Julius Frank Anthony Kuczynski; 1914–2000) Pee Wee King is most famous in the country music field. However, he co-wrote some songs that were covered by mainline pop artists and became major hits. His own recording of "Slow Poke" was a big hit (see '52). His other songs that became big hits were "Tennessee Waltz" (see '50) and "You Belong to Me" (see '52). King was inducted into the Nashville Songwriters Hall of Fame in '70 and into the Country Music Hall of Fame in '74.

Stoddard King (1889–1933) Stoddard King's contribution to popular music was as lyricist for the World War I classic "There's a Long, Long Trail" (see '16).

Wayne King (1901–1985) Bandleader Wayne King became known as "The Waltz King." Prior to his full-time music career he worked as a mechanic and for an insurance company. When the Aragon Ballroom opened in '27, King was hired to lead a band there. Chicago became his home base. He also landed a weekly radio spot where he catered to older listeners. Buddy Clark was one of the vocalists with the band just prior to World War II. Over the years King invested wisely and became wealthy. King's biggest hit recordings were "Good-Night, Sweetheart" (see '31) and "Dream a Little Dream of Me" (see '31). King became the No. 21 top recording artist of the '30s.

Rudyard Kipling (1865–1936) Rudyard Kipling is a famous English short-story writer, novelist and poet. As far as popular music is concerned, composer Oley Speaks turned his "On the Road to Mandalay" into a very successful popular song (see '13). Harry B. Smith's lyrics for "A Good Cigar Is a Smoke" (see 1905) were inspired by a Rudyard Kipling quote from *The Betrothed*: "A woman is only a woman, but a good cigar is a smoke." He wrote *The Jungle Book*, which became a hugely successful Disney film.

Andy Kirk (real name: Andrew Dewey Kirk; 1898–1992) Andy Kirk was raised in Colorado. As a youngster, he learned to play several instruments, and even studied for a while with Paul Whiteman's father. In '27, he joined Terrence Holder's band, the Dark Clouds of Joy. In '29, Kirk took over leadership of the group and changed its name to Andy Kirk and his Clouds of Joy. Vocalist Pha Terrell became one of the band's greatest assets. His voice was featured on "Until the Real Thing Comes Along" (see '36). They also had considerable success with "I Won't Tell a Soul" (see '38). The band remained particularly popular in the Kansas City area for many years until it folded in '48. Kirk was elected to the Big Band/Jazz Hall of Fame in '91. Kirk became the No. 28 top recording artist of the '30s. Some recordings by Andy Kirk and his Twelve Clouds of Joy are available for listening at http://www.redhotjazz.com/bands.html.

Lou Klein Lou Klein wrote the lyrics for "If I Had My Way" (see '14).

Manuel Klein (1876–1919) British Manuel Klein is primarily remembered for writing the words and music for "It's a Long Lane That Has No Turning" (see '17).

John Klenner (1899–1955) John Klenner's first published song came in '28. His most well known songs are "Heartaches" (see '47) and "That's My Desire" (see '47).

Olive Kline Olive Kline was first famous as a concert soprano, as a member of the Victor Light Opera Company and as a member of the Lyric Quartet. She also recorded several popular songs between '13 and the early '20s. Her most popular recordings were "Hello, Frisco!" (see '15) and "They Didn't Believe Me" (see '15) both with Harry MacDonough (on both recordings she was listed as Alice Green).

Knickerbocker Quartet John Young (tenor), George M. Stricklett (tenor), Frederick Wheeler (baritone), Gus Reed (bass). James F. Harrison and the Knickerbocker Quartet, led by Lewis James, had a very popular recording of "Pack Up Your Troubles in Your Old Kit Bag and Smile, Smile, Smile" (see '17). After '12 there were no consistent personnel. Edison lists several different people participating in various sessions including Robert D. Armour, John Finnegan, Royal Fish, Harvey Hindermeyer, William F. Hooley, Reinald Werrenrath, Frederick Wheeler, and John Young.

Evelyn Knight (1929–) Evelyn Knight was born in Reedsville, Virginia, and got her start as a singer on Washington D.C. radio. It was during the mid-'40s that she had her first taste of success with her Decca recording of "Dance with a Dolly" with Camarata's Orchestra (see '44). In early '46 "Chickery Chick," originally recorded by the Gene Krupa Orchestra, was recorded with Knight's vocal backed up by the Three Jesters and the Bob Haggart band (see '45). Knight then was absent from the hit lists for a few years. In late '48 Knight covered a tune originally recorded by Paula Watson for Supreme Records. The song, "A Little Bird Told Me," was recorded with the Stardusters (see '49). It rose quickly to the top of the pop charts and remained in the number one position in the country for seven weeks. "A Little Bird..." was the subject of a lawsuit brought by Supreme Records against Decca, claiming that they stole the arrangement from the Paula Watson original. The court found that the Decca release did not violate any copyright law. "Powder Your Face with Sunshine" on Decca recorded with the Stardusters sold in huge numbers going all the way to number one (see '49). Evelyn Knight's impressive feat of two number ones, "A Little Bird Told Me" and "Powder Your Face with Sunshine," in a couple of months was quite an accomplishment.

Fuzzy Knight (real name: John Forrest Knight; 1901–1976) Fuzzy Knight introduced "A Melody from the Sky," along with Henry Fonda whistling a few bars, in the film *The Trail of the Lonesome Pine* (see '36). Knight began his show business career singing in vaudeville and in stage musicals. He also led his own band. He also appeared in a couple of Mae West films: *She Done Him Wrong* ('33) and *My Little Chickadee* ('40). Knight was the comic sidekick for Tex Ritter and Johnny Mack Brown in several "B" westerns of the late '30s and '40s.

June Knight (real name: Margaret Rose Valliquietto; 1913–1987) June Knight was a singer-dancer-actress who appeared in seven Broadway musicals. By far her most famous role came in *Jubilee* where she introduced "Just One of Those Things" (see '35) and "Begin the Beguine" (see '38). She got her first Broadway exposure in the chorus of *Fifty Million Frenchmen* ('29).

Ted Koehler (1894–1973) Lyricist Ted Koehler was very active in the '30s and '40s. Koehler began his career as a pianist in motion picture theaters. That led to writing special material for vaudeville singers, which then led him to produce his own nightclub shows. In Manhattan in the '20s and early '30s, Koehler contributed to Broadway musicals such as *9:15 Revue, Earl Carroll Vanities* of '30 and '32, *Americana*, and others. Koehler moved to Hollywood in early '30s, where he worked on several successful film musicals including *Let's Fall in Love, Artists & Models, Springtime in the Rockies, Hollywood Canteen* and *Summer Stock*, among others. Koehler collaborated most notably with Harold Arlen, but he also wrote with Harry Barris, Duke Ellington, Rube Bloom, Sammy Fain, Jay Gorney, Ray Henderson, Burton Lane, Jimmy McHugh, Jimmy Monaco, Sammy Stept and Harry Warren. Some of Koehler's most memorable songs include "Dreamy Melody" (see '23), "Get Happy" (see '30), "I Love a Parade" (see '31), "I've Got the World on a String" (see '32), "Stormy Weather" (see '33), "Let's Fall in Love" (see '34), "Truckin'" (see '35) and "Linda" (see '47). Other well known Koehler songs include "Between the Devil and the Deep Blue Sea," "Kickin' the Gong Around," "I Gotta Right to Sing the Blues" "Some Sunday Morning," "Wrap Your Troubles in Dreams," "Don't Worry 'Bout Me," and "Animal Crackers in My Soup." Koehler has been a member of the Songwriters' Hall of Fame since '72. At http://www.songwritershalloffame.org/exhibit_audio_video.asp?exhibitId=92 hear an audio clip of "Stormy Weather" performed by Louis Armstrong.

Churchill Kohlman (1906–1983) Churchill Kohlman, a Pittsburgh dry cleaning plant watchman, entered "Cry" (see '51) into an amateur songwriting contest at the Copa Night Club in Pittsburgh. It was eliminated in the first round, while another Kohlman song made it to the finals. "Cry" didn't make much of an impression until Johnnie Ray recorded it.

Joseph Kosma (1905–1969) Hungarian Joseph Kosma was the composer of "Autumn Leaves" (see '55).

Andre Kostelanetz (1901–1980) Andre Kostelanetz was most famous as an orchestra conductor. He came to the U.S. from Russia in '22 and worked as an accompanist for and a coach of opera singers. He appeared on radio as a conductor in the early '30s. In more recent years he concentrated on recording work, composing, and arranging. Kostelanetz also wrote "Moon Love" (see '39), which he based on a melody from Tchaikovsky's Fifth Symphony.

Alex J. Kramer (1903–1998) Alex J. Kramer was a Tin Pan Alley songwriter who worked as a staff composer for one of the famous publishing firms, Bourne. A native Canadian, Kramer began his music career as a teenage pianist in a Montreal silent-film theater. In the early '20s he conducted some bands for radio shows and worked as an accompanist in vaudeville and in nightclubs. He also coached some young vocalists in singing techniques. Joan Whitney was one of his pupils. They married and began a songwriting partnership. Their first success was "High on a Windy Hill" (see '41). Others among their best-known songs include "My Sister and I" (see '41), "It's Love, Love, Love" (see '44), "Candy" (see '45), "Love Somebody" (see '48) and "Far Away Places" (see '49). Kramer also co-authored the closing theme for the *Your Hit Parade* radio show: "So Long for a While."

Helmy Kresa (1905–1991) Helmy Kresa was a songwriter, orchestrator, and principal arranger for Irving Berlin's publishing company. He began working for Berlin in '26 and eventually became the general professional manager of the Irving Berlin Music Company. Kresa composed the music for "That's My Desire" (see '47).

Gene Krupa (1909–1973) Gene Krupa was a famous, energetic and flamboyant big band drummer, perhaps the most influential drummer of the 20th Century. He began playing professionally in the mid-'20s. By the late '20s, he had moved to New York City and worked in Red Nichols' band. In '34 he joined Benny Goodman's band, where he became a featured performer. After four years he left Goodman to lead his own group, which he fronted until '43. After returning to Goodman for a few months, he transferred to Tommy Dorsey's band, and then organized a new big band. Krupa and his band's best-known recordings were released in the early '40s. The most popular one was "High on a Windy Hill" (see '41). One of his most famous recordings was "Sing, Sing, Sing" with Benny Goodman's orchestra. It was a drummer's showpiece (see '38). Krupa was arrested for drug possession in the mid-'40s and was under suspicion of drug use for the rest of his career. By the late '60s, Krupa had retired, although he occasionally played in public until his death from leukemia. *The Gene Krupa Story* was filmed in '59. The film chronicles his life in the fast lane, with drugs, alcohol, women and parties. After Krupa hits rock bottom, he faces reality and takes charge of his life.

Clare Kummer (real name: Clare Rodman Beecher; 1873–1958) Composer, songwriter, playwright, and author, Clare Kummer was educated at the Packer Institute and in private music study. She wrote several Broadway stage scores. Her chief musical collaborators included Sigmund Romberg and Jerome Kern. She is primarily remembered for the song "Dearie" (see 1905).

Kay Kyser (1905–1985) Kay Kyser became one of the most successful bandleaders in the '30s and '40s. He formed his first band while he attended the University of North Carolina. By the mid–'30s his band had become firmly established as one of the most popular groups. His radio show, *Kay Kyser's Kollege of Musical Knowledge*, in the late '30s and '40s was particularly popular. Kyser and his band appeared in several movies from the late '30s through the mid–'40s, including *That's Right, You're Wrong* ('39), *You'll Find Out* ('40), *Playmates* ('41), *My Favorite Spy* ('42), *Swing Fever* and *Carolina Blues* ('44). The band also played one number in both *Stage Door Canteen* and *Thousands Cheer* ('43). Kyser and his orchestra performed "Scatter-Brain" in the movie musical *That's Right, You're Wrong* (see '39). Kyser and his orchestra's most popular recordings include "Three Little Fishies" (see '39), "The Umbrella Man" (see '39), "(Lights Out) 'Til Reveille" (see '41), "The White Cliffs of Dover" (see '42), "Who Wouldn't Love You" (see '42), "Jingle Jangle Jingle" (see '42), "He Wears a Pair of Silver Wings" (see '42), "Strip Polka" (see '42), "Praise the Lord and Pass the Ammunition!" (see '42), "Ole Buttermilk Sky" (see '46) and "Woody Woodpecker" (see '48). Kyser and his band became the No. 8 top recording artists of the '40s, No. 30 of the first half of the 20th Century. Kyser's most well known singers were Harry Babbitt, Ginny Simms and trumpeter Ish Kabibble. Ish Kabibble's real name was Merwyn Bogue.

Joseph M. Lacalle (real name: Jose Maria Lacalle Garcia; circa 1868–1937) Spanish composer Joseph M. Lacalle wrote the music for "Amapola" as a tango in '24 (see '41).

Bert Lahr (real name: Irving Lahrheim; 1895–1967) Bert Lahr is famous as a comedian in Broadway musicals and in Hollywood films. He began his comic career in vaudeville and burlesque. He graduated to Broadway in *Harry Delmar's Revels* ('27). He appeared in 14 Broadway productions from '27 through '64. In *Hold Everything*, his first Broadway leading role, Lahr introduced "You're the Cream in My Coffee" (see '29). Lahr, Lily Damita and Harry Richman introduced "Let's Put Out the Lights" in *George White's Music Hall Varieties* (see '32). He is probably best known today for his role as the Cowardly Lion in *The Wizard of Oz* ('39). He also appeared in the film version of *Flying High* ('31), where he repeated the role he had originated on Broadway in '30, *Merry-Go-Round of 1938*, where he sang "The Woodman's Song," which he had introduced in the Broadway musical *The Show Is On* ('36); he and Ethel Merman introduced "Friendship" in Cole Porter's Broadway musical *DuBarry Was a Lady* and he also appeared in the '53 film version of *Rose Marie*, to name his more "musical" film performances.

Frankie Laine (real name: Frank Paul LoVecchio; 1913–2007) Singer Frankie Laine got his big break in show business in early '46 and gained national attention with his '47 recording of "That's My Desire." In the '30s and early '40s he had worked at odd jobs and had a few minor singing jobs. Laine also appeared in a few low-budget films in the late '40s and early '50s. Laine's biggest hit recordings include "That Lucky Old Sun" (see '49), "Mule Train" (see '49) and "The Cry of the Wild Goose" (see '50). Laine became the No. 8 top recording artist of the '50s.

Arthur J. Lamb (1870–1928) Arthur J. Lamb was born in Somerset, England. He is perhaps most famous as the lyricist for "A Bird in a Gilded Cage" (see 1900), "The Mansion of Aching Hearts" (see '02) and "Any Old Port in the Storm" (see '08).

Maude Lambert Vaudevillian Maude Lambert, composer Ernest Ball's second wife, helped popularize her husband's "Love Me, and the World Is Mine" (see '06). Ms. Lambert also appeared in several Broadway musical productions between 1899 and '15.

Dorothy Lamour (real name: Mary Leta Dorothy Slaton; 1914–1996) Dorothy Lamour was "Miss New Orleans" in '31. Later, she worked as a Chicago elevator operator, band vocalist with her first husband, bandleader Herbie Kaye's band, and as a radio performer before her Hollywood career. In '36 she wore her soon-to-be-famous sarong in her film debut at Paramount, *The Jungle Princess*. Perhaps her most famous roles were in the Bing Crosby and Bob Hope "Road" films. She introduced "Personality" in *Road to Utopia* (see '46).

Art Landry (1890–?) Art Landry started his band in the early '20s. His Call of the North Orchestra toured the nation from coast to coast. They originally recorded on the Gennett label, but later signed with RCA Victor. Landry's group thrived until the onset of the big band era in the mid–'30s. The group's only major hit recording was of "Dreamy Melody" (see '23). One of Landry's sidemen was Ted Mack, who later hosted the famous Major Bowes Amateur radio program. Landry celebrated his 100th birthday in 1990. Some recordings of Art Landry and his orchestra are available for listening at http://www.redhotjazz.com/bands.html.

Burton Lane (1912–1985) Composer Burton Lane was an important writer of popular songs for Broadway shows and Hollywood movies from the early '30s through the mid–'60s. Burton's music career began in '27, while in his mid-teens, he signed a contract with music publisher Remick Music Company. At age 17, he got the chance to perform some of his music for the Gershwin brothers and they were very encouraging. During the '30s, Lane worked on several musical revues, collaborating with Howard Dietz on two songs for *Three's a Crowd*, and with Harold Adamson on one song for *The Third Little Show* and wrote virtually the entire score for the ninth edition of *Earl Carroll's Vanities*. In '33, Lane collaborated with Harold Adamson on "Everything I Have Is Yours," for MGM's *Dancing Lady*. Lane is credited with discovering the then 11-year-old, Frances Gumm, who he brought to MGM's attention; he even played for her audition. MGM signed her almost immediately and changed her name to Judy Garland. Over the next two decades, with the exception of a few interruptions for Broadway assignments, Lane focused on movie music, writing for more than 30 motion pictures. Lane received his first Oscar nomination for the song "How About You," introduced in *Babes on Broadway*. Lane collaborated with E.Y. Harburg on the score for the Broadway musical *Finian's Rainbow*, which introduced the world to "How Are Things in Glocca Morra" (see '47). Not long after the success of *Finian's Rainbow*, Lane collaborated with Alan Jay Lerner on the score for the Fred Astaire movie musical *Royal Wedding*, which produced Lane's second Oscar nomination, for the song "Too Late Now." In '63, Lane and Lerner teamed again to write the score for the Broadway musical *On a Clear Day You Can See Forever*, which won a Grammy for Best Original Cast Album. A few of Lane's well-known songs that have not been mentioned above are "Smarty" (see '37), "Says My Heart" (see 38) and "Feudin' and Fightin'" (see '47). Lane has been a member of the Songwriters' Hall of Fame since '72. At http://www.songwritershalloffame.org/exhibit_audio_video.asp?exhibitId=71 hear audio clips of "On a Clear Day" sung by Barbra Streisand, "Everything I Have Is Yours" as recorded by Gene Austin, and "If This Isn't Love" performed by Sarah Vaughan.

King Laney   King Laney was one of the co-writers of "Why Don't You Believe Me?" (see '52).

Henry Lange (1895–?)   Henry Lange was co-writer with Henry Busse and Lou Davis for "Hot Lips" (see '22). Lange was a songwriter, conductor and pianist. He was the pianist for the Paul Whiteman Orchestra in the early '20s. By the mid-'20s, he formed his own orchestra. He became the music director for the Baker Hotels in Texas and toured the vaudeville circuit. By the mid-'30s, he was the music director of a radio station.

Johnny Lange (1905–2006)   Johnny Lange's best-known song is "Mule Train" (see '49). Lange was a songwriter, author and publisher. He got a music staff job at a film studio in '37, then after several years away, resumed his film career in the mid-'40s. He wrote several songs for films into the '60s. He also wrote music for the Ice Capades in the '50s. His principal collaborators were Archie Gottler and Jack Meskill.

Frances Langford (real name: Frances Newbern; 1913–2005)   Frances Langford was a popular singer/actress, sometimes called "The Florida Thrush," in the '30s and '40s on radio, in the movies, and on recordings. She got her break when Rudy Vallee heard her sing on a Tampa, Florida radio show and helped her get started in big-time show business. Her biggest successes came in '35 in *Every Night at Eight*, in which she introduced "I'm in the Mood for Love" (see '35). She appeared in thirty Hollywood movies, including *Broadway Melody of 1926*, where she helped introduce "Broadway Rhythm" (see '35), *Yankee Doodle Dandy* and *The Hit Parade*. She played herself in her final film, *The Glenn Miller Story* ('54). She became an integral part of Bob Hope's USO tours during World War II entertaining service men around the globe. She also entertained a new generation of soldiers in Korea and Vietnam. She became known as the "Sweetheart of the Fighting Fronts" for entertaining the troops.

Mario Lanza (real name: Alfred Arnold Cocozza; 1921–1959)   Mario Lanza was most famous for "Be My Love" (see '51), which he had introduced in the Hollywood movie musical *Toast of New Orleans* and for his portrayal of Enrico Caruso in the '51 film *The Great Caruso*. Lanza's only other popular recording was "The Loveliest Night of the Year" (see '51), which he introduced in *The Great Caruso*. He sang primarily operatic arias or popular song in that style. His voice was dubbed for Edmund Purdom's in the movie version of *The Student Prince*

('54). Lanza succumbed to weight problems and died of a heart attack.

Augustin Lara (1909–1969)   Mexican composer Augustin Lara wrote "Solamente una vez," which became "You Belong to My Heart" (see '45). It was used in the Walt Disney production *The Three Caballeros*.

Grace LaRue (real name: Stella Gray; 1882–1956)   American stage actress and vocalist Grace LaRue began her theatrical career at the age of eleven. Her first real success came in '06 when she appeared in New York musical play *The Blue Moon*. Next came a number of New York productions, including the *Follies* of '07 and '08, *The Troubadour,* and *Betsy*. In '13 Ms. LaRue made her first trip to London, where she made quite an impact singing "You Made Me Love You (I Didn't Want to Do It)." Ms. LaRue then appeared in the musical, *The Girl Who Didn't,* in London. She returned to the U.S. in '14 where she appeared in vaudeville and in a number of other musicals and revues, both in New York and Chicago. She interpolated "M-I-S-S-I-S-S-I-P-P-I" into the revue *Hitchy Koo* in '17, after Frances White introduced the song in the Ziegfeld revue *Midnight Frolics* in '16. In '22 and '23 she appeared in Irving Berlin's second *Music Box Revue*. Ms. LaRue introduced Berlin's "Crinoline Days" in the second *Music Box Revue*. Over the next several years, she was back and forth between London and New York. She appeared in some productions in the late '20s such as *The Greenwich Village Follies*. But by the early '30s she was living in retirement in California. She appeared in Mae West's film *She Done Him Wrong* ('33).

Jacques Larue   Jacques Larue wrote the original French lyrics for "Cherry Pink and Apple Blossom White" (see '55).

Edward Laska (1894–1959)   Edward Laska was a composer and lyricist. He is probably most famous for his collaboration with Jerome Kern on "How'd You Like to Spoon with Me" (see '06) and with Albert Von Tilzer on "Alcoholic Blues (Some Blues)" during the Prohibition Era.

John Latouche (1913–1956)   John Latouche's first big success came with the 13-minute musical, "Ballad for Americans," a tribute to American democracy. It gained national recognition when Paul Robeson recorded it. Next came writing the lyrics for the Broadway musical *Cabin in the Sky*, which included the hit song "Taking a Chance on Love" (see '43). Next, he wrote the lyrics for two unsuccessful operettas, then three critically acclaimed but unsuccessful musicals. One of the musicals, *Golden Apple*, produced the song "Lazy Afternoon." His best-known work may be the '56 opera *The Ballad of Baby Doe*.

Harry Lauder (real name: Henry Lauder; 1870–1950)   Harry Lauder was a famous Scottish entertainer of the early years of the 20th century. He was tremendously popular as a music hall and vaudeville performer. Over his forty years of touring the world, he made over twenty U.S. appearances. Harry also entertained the troops in France during World War I. After the war, King George V knighted him. Even though he was getting up in years, he also entertained troops during World War II. Sir Harry wrote most of his own songs. His most famous ones include "I Love a Lassie" (see '07), his most famous recordings in America, and "Roamin' in the Gloamin'" (see '12). Lauder became the No. 35 top recording artist of the first decade of the 20th Century. For more, see http://www.sirharry lauder.com/.

Frank Lavere Frank Lavere was one of the co-writers of "Pretend" (see '53).

Mary Lawlor (1911–) Mary Lawlor began her stage career at age four. Her greatest Broadway success came in Henderson, DeSylva and Brown's *Good News*, where she and John Price Jones introduced "The Best Things in Life Are Free" (see '27). She recreated her role as Connie in the screen version in '30.

Vee Lawnhurst (real name: Laura Lowenherz; 1905–1992) Vee Lawnhurst was a top notch pop pianist, singer, a pioneer on radio, and recorder of numerous piano rolls. Lawnhurst and Tot Seymour were advertised as "the first successful team of girl songwriters in popular music history." See "And Then Some" (p. 208).

Gertrude Lawrence (real name: Gertrude Alexandria Dagmar Lawrence-Klasen; 1898–1952) Gertrude Lawrence began entertaining in music halls of her native England as a youngster. She made her Broadway debut in *Charlot's Revue* ('24). A starring role followed in *Oh, Kay!* ('26), but her biggest roles came in *Lady in the Dark* ('41) and *The King and I* ('51). She introduced "Hello, Young Lovers" in *The King and I* (see '51). "Body and Soul" (see '30) was written especially for Gertrude Lawrence. She introduced it on British radio. Ms. Lawrence and Harry Richman introduced "Exactly Like You," in *Lew Leslie's International Revue* (see '30). The '68 movie musical *Star!*, starring Julie Andrews as Ms. Lawrence, was based on her career. Ms. Lawrence had a popular recording of "Someone to Watch Over Me" in '27.

Jack Lawrence (1912–) Jack Lawrence primarily wrote lyrics but occasionally composed the music as well. Most of his songs were produced from the early '30s to the '50s. Lawrence was also a good singer and appeared on several radio shows. He received his degree from Long Island University before he served in the U.S. Coast Guard during World War II. During the war, Lawrence organized service bands that entertained the troops in our bases in Europe. After the war, Lawrence began collaborating with other songwriters such as Louis Alter, Hoagy Carmichael, Clara Edwards, Stan Freeman and Walter Gross. Some of Jack Lawrence's most famous songs include "Play, Fiddle, Play" (see '33), "Sunrise Serenade" (see '39), "Sleepy Lagoon" (see '42), "All or Nothing at All" (see '43), "Symphony" (see '46), "Linda" (see '47), "Tenderly" (see '52), and "Delicado" (see '52). Lawrence was inducted into the Songwriters' Hall of Fame in '75. At http://www.song-writershalloffame.org/exhibit_audio_video.asp?exhibitId=298 hear audio clips of "Handful of Stars" performed by Dinah Washington and "Sleepy Lagoon" performed by Harry James and his orchestra. For more, see http://www.jacklawrencesongwriter.com/mybio.html.

Herbert Lawson Herbert "Happy" Lawson wrote "Any Time" and published in the early '20s, when it was a minor success. The song found major success in '52.

Evelyn Laye (real name: Elsie Evelyn Lay; 1900–1996) British actress Evelyn Laye and Ramon Novarro introduced "When I Grow Too Old to Dream" in the movie musical *The Night Is Young* (see '35). Ms. Laye began her musical career in '15. In the first part of her career she appeared primarily in musical comedies. She made her Broadway debut in '29 in Noel Coward's *Bitter Sweet*. She also appeared in the Hollywood movie musical *One Heavenly Night* ('31).

Turner Layton (1894–1978) Pianist and singer Turner Layton's chief contribution to popular music was as composer of "After You've Gone" (see '19) and "'Way Down Yonder in New Orleans" (see '22). Layton also became a popular entertainer in '20s and '30s in England with his partner Clarence Johnstone. Layton and Johnstone were radio favorites. They sold an estimated 10 million records, principally in Britain. The duo split in the wake of Johnstone's society divorce scandal. Layton continued to perform and had a successful solo career lasting until the late '40s.

Eldo di Lazzaro (1902–1968) Italian composer Eldo di Lazzaro wrote "La Piccinina" that became the U.S. hit "Ferryboat Serenade" (see '40) and "Reginella Campagnola" that became "The Woodpecker Song" (see '40).

Mickey Leader Mickey Leader was co-lyricist of "Dance with a Dolly" (see '44).

Earl Lebieg (see Earl Burtnett & Adam Geibel)

Grace LeBoy (1908–1932) Grace LeBoy, the daughter of a tailor, took music courses at Elgin High before leaving for Chicago in '05. Grace later married Gus Kahn, an aspiring lyricist, and collaborated with him on "The Good Ship Mary Ann" (see '14).

Ernesto Lecuona (1895–1963) Cuban-born Ernesto Lecuona became a major influence helping Latin music become an important force in the world music marketplace. Lecuona's style influenced all subsequent Latin music, even including the salsa. His musical talent was already discernible at an early age. Following piano studies with his sister, Ernestina, he studied at the Conservatorio Peyrellade. At 17 he graduated from the National Conservatory of Havana with a gold medal in performance. His fine pianistic talents were displayed in the U.S. for the first time when he appeared at Aeolian Hall in New York City in '16. Lecuona produced a plethora of music including a number of major pop songs, such as "Malaguena," "Siboney" (see '29), and "Andalucia," but he may perhaps be better remembered for its Americanized version, "The Breeze and I" (see '40). He also composed the music for "Say 'Si, Si'" (see '36). The song originated in Cuba with the Spanish title "Para Vigo Me Voy." Lecuona was inducted into the Songwriters' Hall of Fame in '97.

Marguerita Lecuona (1910–1981) Marguerita Lecuona wrote "Babalu" (see '44).

Huddie Ledbetter (real name: Huddie William Ledbetter; circa 1889–1949) John Lomax adapted a folk song recorded by Huddie "Leadbelly" Ledbetter in '36 into "Goodnight, Irene" (see '50). Lomax discovered Ledbetter at the Louisiana State Penitentiary at Angola, where Ledbetter was serving time. Ledbetter was inducted into the Songwriters' Hall of Fame in '70, but from a popular music perspective, he wasn't particularly significant. Besides "Goodnight, Irene," his "Rock Island Line," "Midnight Special," "Pick a Bale of Cotton" and "Cottonfields" are well known. For more on Leadbelly, see http://www.songwritershalloffame.org/exhibit_bio.asp?exhibitId=16.

Peggy Lee (real name: Norma Deloris Engstrom; 1922–2002) Peggy Lee began singing on radio in her home state of North Dakota at age 16. Her big break came when she sang with Will Osborne's band in late '40. In '41 she joined Benny Goodman's band and adopted her stage name. Before she left the Goodman band in '43, she appeared in a couple of films and recorded several hit songs with the band. She married guitarist Dave Barbour in '43 (divorced '52), and they teamed up to write "Manana." They also wrote "It's a Good Day" in '47, but it wasn't quite as successful. During her Goodman years, she sang on several hit recordings including "I Got It Bad and That Ain't Good" and "Why Don't You Do Right?," which she and the band performed in *Stage Door Canteen* ('43). Her biggest recording, and only No. 1 hit, was "Manana" (see '48). Ms. Lee became the No. 30 top recording artist of the '40s. In later years she appeared in several films, recorded steadily, often with considerable jazz influence, and appeared frequently on TV. Some modern readers may remember her best as the voice of Lady in Disney's *Lady and the Tramp* ('55). She also starred opposite Jack Webb in *Pete Kelly's Blues* ('55), for which she received an Academy Award nomination for Best Actress. Ms. Lee was elected to the Big Band/Jazz Hall of Fame in '92. Peggy Lee's official website is http://www.peggylee.com/.

Milton Leeds (1909–2005) Milton Leeds was one of the co-lyricists of "Misirlou" (see '47).

Franz Lehar (1870–1948) Franz Lehár was a Hungarian composer, mainly known for his operettas. Lehár was born in Komárno, now Slovakia, as the eldest son of a bandmaster in the Austro-Hungarian army. He studied violin and composition at the Prague Conservatory but was advised by Antonin Dvorak to focus on composing music. After graduation in 1899 he joined his father's band in Vienna, as assistant bandmaster. In '02 he became conductor at the Vienna Theater an der Wien, where his first opera was performed. He is most famous for his operettas, the most successful of which is *The Merry Widow* (see '07); however, he also wrote sonatas, symphonic poems, marches and a number of waltzes.

Carolyn Leigh (1926–1983) Carolyn Leigh was lyricist for "Young at Heart" (see '54). After attending Queens College in her hometown of New York City, Ms. Leigh worked as a copyrighter for radio stations and advertising agencies. She principally collaborated with Cy Coleman, but also wrote with Johnny Richards. Ms. Leigh wrote the lyrics for the Broadway productions of *Peter Pan, Wildcat* and *Little Me*. In addition to "Young at Heart," some of her most familiar songs include "How Little We Know," "I'm Flying," "I Gotta Crow," "Hey, Look Me Over," "Real Live Girl," and "Pass Me by." She also contributed to some film scores, including *The Cardinal* and *Father Goose*. Ms. Leigh was inducted into the Songwriters' Hall of Fame in '85.

Jules Lemare Jules Lemare was one of the co-writers of "Sweet and Lovely" (see '31).

Jean Lenox Jean Lenox's only major contribution to popular music was as lyricist for "I Don't Care" (see '05).

Eddie Leonard (1870–1941) One of the last great minstrels, Eddie Leonard, wrote "Ida! Sweet as Apple Cider" in 1903 (see '27).

Ruggero Leoncavallo (1857–1919) Ruggero Leoncavallo was an Italian opera composer. Leoncavallo was educated at the Conservatorio San Pietro a Majella in Naples. After some years spent teaching and in frustration in getting his works performed, he produced his own opera, *I Pagliacci*. *I Pagliacci* was performed in Milan in 1892 with immediate success; today it is the only work by Leoncavallo in the standard operatic repertory. Its most famous aria "Vesti la giubba" (see '07) was recorded by Enrico Caruso and reportedly became the world's first records to sell a million copies.

Sammy Lerner (real name: Samuel Manuel Lerner; 1903–1989) Sammy Lerner was co-lyricist of "Is It True What They Say About Dixie?" (see '36). Lerner also wrote "I'm Popeye, the Sailor Man." Lerner was a songwriter, author and publisher. He came to the U.S. from Romania in '10. After Wayne University, he wrote special material for vaudeville singers including Sophie Tucker. He became a music publisher in '28. He moved to London in '36, where he wrote for the stage and for British films. In '38, he came back to the U.S. His chief collaborators were Hoagy Carmichael, Jay Gorney, Al Hoffman, and Al Goodhart.

Hal LeRoy (real name: John LeRoy Schotte; 1913–1985) Hal LeRoy began his entertainment career in '28 in *Hoboken Heroes* in a Hoboken, New Jersey theater. In '31, he appeared in the Broadway show *The Gang's All Here*. He also appeared with his partner Mitzi Mayfair in the *Ziegfeld Follies of 1931*. Other Broadway productions in which he appeared include *Thumbs Up* ('35) and Rodgers and Hart's *Too Many Girls* ('39). LeRoy and Eunice Healey introduced "Zing! Went the Strings of My Heart" in the revue *Thumbs Up* (see '35). He made his first Hollywood film for RKO, *Was My Face Red*, in '32. LeRoy continued to appear in occasional films throughout the '30s. He also appeared in vaudeville in the '30s and '40s, and with Woody Herman and Clyde McCoy's bands. In later years, he appeared on television and in summer stock productions.

Edgar Leslie (1885–1976) Lyricist Edgar Leslie was most active in the popular music field during the '20s and '30s. His first published song, "Lonesome," came in '09. Leslie also wrote songs for vaudeville acts. Leslie collaborated with writers such as Irving Berlin, Joe Burke, Fred Ahlert, James Monaco, Walter Donaldson, Archie Gottler, Maurice Abrams, Joe Young, Harry Warren, Pete Wendling, George Meyer, Ray Goetz and Horatio Nicholls (pseudonym for publisher Lawrence Wright). In '14, Leslie was a charter member of ASCAP and he formed his own publishing firm in the mid-'20s. He was lyricist or co-lyricist for "Hello, Hawaii, How Are You?" (see '16), "For Me and My Gal" (see '17), "Oh! What a Pal Was Mary" (see '19), "Among My Souvenirs" (see '28), "By the River Sainte Marie" (see '31), "On Treasure Island" (see '35), "A Little Bit Independent" (see '35), "In a Little Gypsy Tearoom" (see '35), "Moon Over Miami" (see '36), and "It Looks Like Rain in Cherry Blossom Lane" (see '37). Other well-known Leslie lyrics include "He'd Have to Get Under — Get Out and Get Under (to Fix Up His Automobile)," "When the Grown Up Ladies Act Like Babies (I've

Got to Love 'Em, That's All)," "Take Your Girlie to the Movies (If You Can't Make Love at Home)," "Take Me to the Land of Jazz," "On the Gin Gin Ginny Shore," "Rose of the Rio Grande," and "Home in Pasadena." Edgar Leslie was elected to the Songwriters' Hall of Fame in '72. At http://www.songwritershalloffame.org/exhibit_audio_ video.asp?exhibitId=93 hear an audio clip of Billy Murray performing "He'd Have to Get Under — Get Out and Get Under (to Fix Up His Automobile)."

Will Letters   Will Letters was co-writer with C. W. Murphy, John Charles Moore and William C. McKenna for "Has Anybody Here Seen Kelly?" (see '10).

Oscar Levant (1906–1972)   Oscar Levant, Fred Astaire, Jack Buchanan and Nanette Fabray performed "That's Entertainment" in the film version of the Broadway revue *The Band Wagon* (see '53). Levant is primarily known as a fine pianist, but he was also a composer and a witty performer in films, radio and television. He appeared in several well-known movie musicals, including *You Were Meant for Me* ('48), *Romance on the High Seas* ('48), *The Barkleys of Broadway* ('49) and *An American in Paris* ('51). He was a close friend of George Gershwin. Levant often performed and/or recorded Gershwin's piano works.

Raymond Leveen   Raymond Leveen wrote the English lyrics of "Ti-Pi-Tin" (see '38).

Maurice Levi   Very little is known about Maurice Levi except he wrote for Broadway shows including those for the Rogers Brothers productions *In Central Park* (1900), *In Washington* ('01) and *In Harvard* ('02). He also wrote for the famous Ziegfeld revues of '08, '09 and '11. His "When Reuben Comes to Town" from *In Central Park* was very popular in '01.

Lou Levinson   Lou Levinson was one of the co-writers of "Here in My Heart" (see '52).

Eunice Levy (1931–2002)   Eunice Levy was a co-writer on "Ko Ko Mo" (see '55). The original rhythm and blues version of "Ko Ko Mo" was by Gene and Eunice (Eunice being Eunice Levy and Gene being Forest Gene Wilson, also a co-writer of the song). For more on Gene and Eunice, see http://www.electricearl.com/dws/gene &eunice.html.

Al Lewis (1901–1967)   Al Lewis, who wrote mostly lyrics and occasionally music, is best known for the songs he wrote from the '20s to the '50s. His most famous songs include "Blueberry Hill" (see '40) and "Rose O'Day" (see '42).

Henry Lewis   Henry Lewis and Nora Bayes introduced "Oh Johnny, Oh Johnny, Oh!" as an interpolation, into the musical *Follow Me* (see '17).

Morgan Lewis (real name: William Morgan Lewis, Jr., 1906–)   Morgan Lewis was the composer of "How High the Moon" (see '51). The song had premiered in '40.

Roger Lewis   Roger Lewis was the lyricist for the hit song "Oceana Roll" (see '12). A Roger Lewis was co-lyricist of "One Dozen Roses" (see '42). Is this the same person thirty years apart?

Sam M. Lewis (1885–1959)   Sam Lewis was a lyricist who wrote several popular hits from the early 1900s

through the '30s. Lewis began his show business career singing in cafes around New York City. He began his songwriting career around '12 and from '16 into the '30s his principal lyric collaborator was Joe Young. Besides Young, Lewis collaborated with Fred Ahlert, Walter Donaldson, Bert Grant, Harry Warren, Jean Schwartz, George Meyer, Ted FioRito, J. Fred Coots, Ray Henderson, Victor Young, Peter DeRose and Harry Akst. Lewis' most famous lyrics include "When You're a Long, Long Way from Home" (see '14), "If I Knock the 'L' Out of Kelly" (see '16), "Where Did Robinson Crusoe Go with Friday on Saturday Night?" (see '16), "I'm All Bound 'Round with the Mason-Dixon Line" (see '18), "Hello, Central, Give Me No Man's Land" (see '18), "Just a Baby's Prayer at Twilight (for Her Daddy Over There)" (see '18), "Rock-a-bye Your Baby with a Dixie Melody" (see '18), "My Mammy" (see '21), "Tuck Me to Sleep in My Old 'Tucky Home" (see '22), "Five Foot Two, Eyes of Blue" (see '26), "I'm Sitting on Top of the World" (see '26), "In a Little Spanish Town" (see '27), "Laugh, Clown, Laugh" (see '28), "I Kiss Your Hand, Madame" (see '29), "Dinah" (see '32), and "A Beautiful Lady in Blue" (see '36). Other Lewis songs that are well-known include "Arrah Go on, I'm Gonna Go Back to Oregon," "How Ya Gonna Keep 'Em Down on the Farm (After They've Seen Paree)?," "Cryin' for the Carolines," "Street of Dreams," "Lawd, You Made the Night Too Long," and "For All We Know." Sam Lewis was a charter member of ASCAP in '14. He was inducted into the Songwriters' Hall of Fame in '70. At http://www. songwritershalloffame.org/exhibit_audio_video.asp? exhibitId=95 hear audio clips of "Dinah" sung by Bing Crosby, "For All We Know" performed by Barbara Streisand, "Street of Dreams" as recorded by Sarah Vaughan, "Crying for the Carolines" performed by Waring's Pennsylvanians, and "Tuck Me to Sleep in My Old 'Tucky Home" performed by Vernon Dalhart.

Ted Lewis (real name: Theodore Leopold Friedman; 1892–1971)   Clarinetist, bandleader, and entertainer Ted Lewis enjoyed a successful sixty-year career in show business. His trademarks were a worn and battered hat and his opening line: "Is ev'rybody happy?" Lewis' most popular recordings were "When My Baby Smiles at Me" (see '20, Lewis was also co-lyricist), "All by Myself" (see '21), "O, Katharina!" (see '25), "Some of These Days" (see '27) with Sophie Tucker, "Just a Gigolo" (see '31), "In a Shanty in Old Shanty Town" (see '32) and "Lazybones" (see '33). Lewis became the No. 6 top recording artist of the '20s and No. 9 for the '30s, making him the No. 19 top recording artist for the first half of the 20th Century. Several recordings by Ted Lewis and his Band are available for listening at http://www.redhotjazz.com/bands.html.

Thurlow Lieurance (1878–1963)   Thurlow Lieurance is a one hit wonder in the popular music field. He contributed the music for "By the Waters of Minnetonka" (see '15). According to a typewritten account from Lieurance's estate papers "By the Waters of Minnetonka" was inspired by a Sioux love song recorded by Lieurance in '11 on the Crow Reservation in Montana. He copied the tune as sung by Sitting Eagle, a Sioux. The song's lyrics were based upon a Sioux legend.

Winnie Lightner (real name: Winifred Reeves; 1899–1972)   Winnie Lightner was an actress, singer and dancer. As did most entertainers of her era, Lightner began her career in vaudeville. On Broadway, Winnie Lightner introduced "I'll Build a Stairway to Paradise" in *George White's Scandals of 1922* (see '23) and George Gershwin's "Somebody Loves Me" in *George White's Scandals of 1924* (see '24). She began her film career in the late '20s and soon became a Warner Bros. star. Her first major screen role was in *Gold Diggers of Broadway* ('29).

Joseph J. Lilley (1913–1971) Joseph J. Lilley was the composer of "Jingle Jangle Jingle" (see '42). Lilley was musical director, arranger, choreographer and sometimes vocalist on numerous Hollywood films, including *The Forest Rangers*, which premiered "Jingle Jangle Jingle."

Beatrice Lillie (real name: Constance Sylvia Gladys Munston; 1894–1989) Comedienne Beatrice Lillie was the daughter of a Canadian government official. She sang in a family trio act with her mother and her piano-playing older sister. In the early 1910s, the ambitious mother took the girls to England seeking success. In '14 Beatrice made her solo debut on London's West End and was a huge hit. She eventually became known as "The Funniest Woman in the World." In New York, she introduced "Ja-Da" in the stage musical *Bran Pie* (see '19). She experienced even more success in subsequent Broadway productions. Lillie and Charles Purcell introduced "I Know That You Know" in Vincent Youmans' *Oh, Please!* (see '27). She also became a top radio and comedy recording artist. Her success in films was surprisingly limited however. During World War II, Bea became a favorite performer with the troops, and in her post-war years toured with her own show *An Evening with Beatrice Lillie*. In '58 she replaced Rosalind Russell as the lead in *Auntie Mame*. In '64, she appeared in her last musical, *High Spirits*. She faded from public view after an appearance in the movie musical *Thoroughly Modern Millie* ('67).

Paul Lincke (1866–1946) Paul Lincke was a German composer. The operetta, *Berliner Luft*, seems to be his most well known piece. The march "Berliner Luft" is the hymn of Berlin. Other Lincke operettas include *Reich des Indra* and *Lysistrata*. The latter includes the song "Gleuhwuermchen," translated as "Glow Worm" (see '08). Johnny Mercer wrote new lyrics for it in the early '50s when the Mills Brothers popularized it (see '52).

Edith Lindeman (1898–?) Edith Lindeman and Carl Stutz wrote "Little Things Mean a Lot" (see '54). Lindeman was the amusement editor for the Richmond Times-Dispatch. Her married name was Calisch.

Harry Link Harry Link teamed with Thomas "Fats" Waller to compose the music for "I've Got a Feeling I'm Falling" (see '29). Link collaborated with Jack Strachey on the music for "These Foolish Things (Remind Me of You)" (see '36).

Sidney Lippman (1914–2003) Composer Sidney Lippman produced his most famous songs during the '40s and '50s. He most often collaborated with lyricist Sylvia Dee. His biggest hit songs were "Chickery Chick" (see '46), "'A'— You're Adorable" (see '49) and "Too Young" (see '51).

Jack Little (real name: John Leonard; 1900–1956) Jack Little was born in London at the beginning of the 20th Century. He was especially popular as a radio singer during the '20s, one of the first performers to become popular because of his exposure on that medium. In addition to his singing, he composed several songs, notably "Jealous" (see '24) and "In a Shanty in Old Shanty Town" (see '32). In the '30s he led a band, and in the '40s he worked as a single. After that he became a disk jockey, then disappeared from the public eye. Little Jack Little and his orchestra's biggest recording success came with "I'm in the Mood for Love" (see '35).

Jay Livingston (1915–2001) Jay Livingston produced several popular song hits, particularly for the movies. He most often collaborated with lyricist Ray Evans. Livingston studied piano in Pittsburgh as a child and while attending the University of Pennsylvania. While he was a student at Penn, he organized a dance band that played for various college functions and eventually played in local nightclubs and on cruise ships. Ray Evans, a fellow Penn student, joined the band and the two began a lifelong songwriting partnership. After their graduation from Penn in '37, they moved to New York City. At first, they wrote special material for Broadway stars like Ole Olsen and Chic Johnson. Their first successful song was "G'bye Now." Livingston served in the U.S. Army during World War II. After the war, he and Evans moved to Hollywood to write for Paramount Pictures, where they stayed for the next decade. Their first film was *To Each His Own*, which earned the team their first Academy Award nomination for the title song. After they left Paramount, the team freelanced for several studios, contributing some individual songs and some complete scores. Returning to New York City in the late '50, Livingston and Evans produced their first Broadway scores: *Oh Captain* and *Let It Ride!*, but neither was especially successful. Livingston and Evans were the recipients of three Academy Awards for Best Song and received nearly 10 other Oscar nominations. Some of the films they worked on include *My Friend Irma, Here Come the Girls, All Hands on Deck, The Stork Club, Monsieur Beaucaire, Sorrowful Jones, The Lemon Drop Kid, Fancy Pants, Here Comes the Groom, Somebody Loves Me, Son of Paleface* and *The Man Who Knew Too Much*. Livingston and Evans were honored with a star on the Hollywood Boulevard Walk of Fame in '95 for their musical contribution to films. The team also produced theme songs for the TV shows *Bonanza* and *Mr. Lucky*. They also wrote special material for nightclub acts and TV specials. They had a particularly long relationship with Bob Hope. Livingston and Evans wrote all of his personal appearance material since '47. Some of Livingston's most famous songs include "To Each His Own" (see '46), "Golden Earrings" (see '48), the '49 Academy Award winner "Buttons and Bows" (see '48), the '50 Academy Award winner "Mona Lisa" (see '50), the '56 Academy Award winner "Que Sera, Sera," plus "Tammy" and "Dear Heart." According to their official website, the team has twenty-six songs that have sold over a million records or more, and the total record sales of their songs has exceeded 400 million. Livingston was elected to the Songwriters' Hall of Fame in '77.

Jerry Livingston (real name: Jerry Levinson; 1909–1987) Composer Jerry Livingston wrote several popular hits from the '30s into the '50s. He formed his own publishing company in the '40s and began writing for Hollywood films in the late '40s. In the late '50s he composed several successful TV show theme songs, including

"Casper, the Friendly Ghost" and the "Bugs Bunny theme." Livingston attended the University of Arizona, where he formed his own orchestra. He became the first freshman to write for the University's annual musical. Livingston moved to New York City in the early '30s and worked as a pianist in dance orchestras, before organizing his own band in '40. He moved to Hollywood in the late '40s, where he wrote film scores for several different studios. Some of the famous films he wrote for include *Cinderella*, *At War with the Army*, *Sailor Beware* and *Jumping Jacks*. Livingston also wrote title songs for TV shows like *77 Sunset Strip*, *Bourbon Street Beat*, *Hawaiian Eye* and *Surfside 6*, in addition to the ones mentioned above. Livingston collaborated with songwriters such as Mack David, Al Hoffman, Al Neiburg, Marty Symes, Milton Drake, Paul Francis Webster, Dan Shapiro, Ralph Freed, Mann Curtis, Helen Deutsch, Mitchell Parish, Milton Berle, Allen Roberts and Bob Merrill. His most famous hit songs include "It's the Talk of the Town" (see '33), "Bibbidi Bobbidi Boo" from *Cinderella*, "Mairzy Doats" (see '44), "I'm a Big Girl Now" (see '46), and "Chi-Baba Chi-Baba" (see '47). Livingston was elected to the Songwriters' Hall of Fame in '81.

Eugene Lockhart (1891–1957) Eugene Lockhart was born in London, Ontario, Canada. His father had studied singing and Eugene displayed an early interest in drama and music. His father joined a band as a Scottish tenor and the family accompanied the group to England. While his father toured, Eugene studied at the Brompton Oratory School in London. When they returned to Canada, Gene began singing in concert, often on the same program with Beatrice Lillie. His mother encouraged his career, urging him to try for a part on Broadway and he got his first part in a New York City play in '17. Between acting engagements, he wrote for the stage. His first production was *The Pierrot Players* for which he wrote both book and lyrics. *Heigh-Ho* (1920), a musical fantasy with book and lyrics by Lockhart, followed. It had a short run, but introduced "The World Is Waiting for the Sunrise" (see '20), which Lockhart wrote with composer Ernest Seitz. Most of Lockhart's future fame was as an actor on Broadway and in Hollywood films.

John Jacob Loeb (1910–) John Jacob Loeb is most famous as the writer of "Masquerade" (see '32), "Boo-Hoo" (see '37), "A Sailboat in the Moonlight" (see '37) and "Seems Like Old Times" (see '46). He most often collaborated with Carmen Lombardo, and Guy Lombardo and his Royal Canadians often introduced his songs.

Frank Loesser (1910–1969) Frank Loesser became one of this country's major hit writers. In the early part of his career he primarily wrote lyrics, but later he contributed both words and music. Even though Frank's father was a well-known pianist and teacher and his older half-brother, Arthur, became a famous pianist and music educator, Frank never studied music formally. Nevertheless, he became a very famous songwriter for films and musicals. Loesser wrote his first song at the age of six and as a child taught himself to play the harmonica and the piano. He left college in '30 and held diverse jobs in newspaper advertising, as a process server and as a newspaper editor until he began to write songs and sketches for radio scripts. Loesser's first published song was "In Love with the Memory of You," with music by William Schuman. In the mid-'30s, Universal Pictures put Loesser under contract to write songs for film musicals. For Universal and later for Paramount Pictures, Loesser wrote the scores for more than sixty films over the next thirty years. The wartime hit "Praise the Lord and Pass the Ammunition" was the first song for which Frank wrote both the words and music (see '42). After World War II, Loesser moved back to New York City to write the Broadway musical *Where's Charley?* Loesser followed that success with *Guy and Dolls*, which opened in '50. With a score full of wonderful songs, *Guys and Dolls* swept the Tony Awards that year, including the coveted Best Musical trophy. In '52, Loesser returned to Hollywood to write the score for *Hans Christian Andersen* that included "Thumbelina," which was nominated for the Best Song Oscar in '52. Returning to Broadway in '56, Loesser wrote the score and book for *The Most Happy Fella*, which included the song "Standing on the Corner." Another success came in '61 with the Broadway production *How to Succeed in Business Without Really Trying*, which won the Pulitzer Prize and seven Tony Awards. Loesser collaborated with several famous Tin Pan Alley composers, including Burton Lane, Hoagy Carmichael, Jimmy McHugh, Jule Styne, Victor Schertzinger and Arthur Schwartz. Loesser's biggest hit songs, in addition to the ones mentioned above, include "Heart and Soul" (see '38), "Says My Heart" (see '38), "Two Sleepy People" (see '38), "Dolores" (see '41), "I Don't Want to Walk Without You" (see '42), "Jingle Jangle Jingle" (see '42), "Let's Get Lost" (see '43), "They're Either Too Young or Too Old" (see '44), "I Wish I Didn't Love You So" (see '47), "On a Slow Boat to China" (see '48), "Once in Love with Amy" and "My Darling, My Darling" (see '49), the Academy Award winning song "Baby, It's Cold Outside" (see '49), "A Bushel and a Peck" and "Luck Be a Lady" (see '50) and "Hoop-Dee-Doo" (see '50). Loesser has been a member of the Songwriters' Hall of Fame since '70. At http://www.songwritershalloffame. org/exhibit_audio_video.asp?exhibitId=230 hear an audio clip of Barbra Streisand singing "I'll Know" from *Guys and Dolls*.

Ella Logan (real name: Ina Allan; 1913–1969) Scottish Ella Logan, as Sharon McLonergan, introduced "How Are Things in Glocca Morra?" in the musical *Finian's Rainbow* (see '47). Ms. Logan began her career as a child singing star in British music halls. She was appearing in London's West End by age 17. She toured Europe in the early '30s. After she married an American tap-dancer, she moved to the U.S. She then appeared in a couple of Hollywood films including *52nd Street* ('37) and *The Goldwyn Follies* ('37), however, her greatest success came on Broadway. Ms. Logan entertained the troops during World War II.

Frederick Knight Logan (1871–1928) "Missouri Waltz" (see '17) was originally published as a piano instrumental in '14. Frederick Knight Logan was credited as the "arranger" on the original sheet music, which claimed that the song had come from "an original melody procurred by John Valentine Eppell." The Missouri State Archives website lists a number of individuals variously credited for the original melody; all are African American. Several websites now credit the music to Eppell, with Logan as the arranger.

Fritz Lohner (?–1942) German Jewish lyricist Fritz Lohner collaborated with L. Wolfe Gilbert on the lyric for "O, Katharina" (see '25). The song premiered in a revue conceived in Russia, revived in Paris, and brought to Broadway in '22. Fritz Lohner died in a Nazi concentration camp in '42.

Hermann Lohr (1871–1943)   In the popular music field, Hermann Lohr is primarily remembered for composing the music for "Little Grey Home in the West" (see '14).

John Lomax (1867–1948)   John Lomax adapted a folk song recorded by Huddie "Leadbelly" Ledbetter in '36 into "Goodnight, Irene" (see '50). Lomax is primarily known as a musicologist and folk music collector. He discovered Huddie "Leadbelly" Ledbetter, a twelve-string guitar player, at the Louisiana State Penitentiary at Angola where Ledbetter was serving time.

Carmen Lombardo (1903–1971)   Carmen Lombardo, Guy's younger brother, was the lead saxophonist and the featured vocalist on almost all of the Guy Lombardo and his Royal Canadians' recordings from '27 until the early '40s. Carmen also wrote or co-wrote several popular songs, including "Sweethearts on Parade" (see '29), "Snuggled on Your Shoulders" (see '32), "Boo-Hoo" (see '37), "A Sailboat in the Moonlight" (see '37), "Seems Like Old Times" (see '46), and "Powder Your Face with Sunshine" (see '49).

Guy Lombardo (1902–1977)   Guy Lombardo and his Royal Canadians were phenomenally successful, eventually selling over 100,000,000 records, making them one of the top artists of the pre-rock era. The Lombardo brothers, Carmen, Guy, Lebert, and Victor, formed their group in '25 and selected Guy as the front man or leader. Carmen, the second most visible of the brothers, was lead saxophonist and vocalist. For more than five decades, "The Sweetest Music This Side of Heaven" was known to more people, including its detractors, than virtually any other. Lombardo's list of hit recordings is extensive. The band's most productive time for hits covers the period from the late '20s into the early '50s. The most popular ones were "Charmaine" (see '27), "Sweethearts on Parade" (see '29), "You're Driving Me Crazy" (see '30), "By the River Sainte Marie" (see '31), "Moonlight Saving Time" (see '31), "Good Night, Sweetheart" (see '31), "We Just Couldn't Say Goodbye" (see '32), "Paradise" (see '32), "Too Many Tears" (see '32), "River, Stay 'Way from My Door" with Kate Smith (see '32), "You're Getting to Be a Habit with Me" with Bing Crosby (see '33), "The Last Round-Up" (see '33), "Stars Fell on Alabama" (see '34), "Red Sails in the Sunset" (see '35), "What's the Reason (I'm Not Pleasin' You?)" (see '35), "When Did You Leave Heaven?" (see '36), "Lost" (see '36), "It Looks Like Rain in Cherry Blossom Lane" (see '37), "Boo-Hoo" (see '37), "September in the Rain" (see '37), "A Sailboat in the Moonlight" (see '37), "So Rare" (see '37), "Penny Serenade" (see '39), "The Band Played on" (see '41), "Intermezzo" (see '41), "It's Love, Love, Love" (see '44), "Managua, Nicaragua" (see '47) and "The Third Man Theme" (see '50). Lombardo and the Royal Canadians were the No. 33 top recording artists of the '20s, No. 2 for the '30s, No. 24 for the '40s, and No. 31 for the '50s, culminating in the No. 9 recording artists of the first half of the 20th Century. Guy was inducted into the Big Band/Jazz Hall of Fame in '92. Numerous recordings between '19 and '77 by Guy Lombardo

and his Royal Canadians are available for listening at http://www.redhotjazz.com/bands.html.

Julie London (1926–2000)   Julie London popularized "Cry Me a River" in '55 with her first successful Liberty recording. She also sang it in the '58 20th Century–Fox film *The Girl Can't Help It*. Her recording of the song was inducted into the Grammy Hall of Fame in 2001. Ms. London became an actress and sultry singer in several movies of the '40s and '50s. After playing small roles in the early '40s and being a pin-up girl for the service men of World War II, Julie married Jack Webb prior to his *Dragnet* fame. After she and Webb divorced, she married jazz musician, songwriter and actor Bobby Troup (see "Route 66" in '46). Her most productive period as a singer and recording artist was the mid- to late '50s. To modern fans, she may be remembered for her role as Nurse Dixie McCall in the TV series *Emergency!* during the '70s.

Vincent Lopez (1898–1975)   Pianist Vincent Lopez led a sweet-style band that was popular in the '20s and early '30s. He and his band's most notable hit recording was "Always" (see '26), but they had several other popular records between '22 and '28. Lopez and his band were the No. 15 top recording artists of the '20s. Even after the sweet bands had waned in popularity, Lopez continued to appear on radio, television, and in ballrooms. He is credited with discovering singer Betty Hutton. Recordings by Vincent Lopez and his Hotel Pennsylvania Orchestra, Vincent Lopez and his Casa Lopez Orchestra and Vincent Lopez and his orchestra between '20 and '61 are available at http://www.redhotjazz.com/bands.html.

Ange Lorenzo (1894–1971)   Ange Lorenzo was co-composer with Richard A. Whiting on "Sleepy Time Gal" (see '26).

Lillian Lorraine (real name: Eulallean de Jacques; 1892–1955)   Lillian Lorraine introduced "My Pony Boy" in the musical *Miss Innocence* (see '09), she interpolated "By the Light of the Silvery Moon" into the *Ziegfeld Follies of 1909* (see '10), and "Row! Row! Row!" in the *Ziegfeld Follies of 1912* (see '13). Ms. Lorraine appeared in several Broadway production between '09 and '22. She became particularly famous as one of Florenz Ziegfeld's beautiful mistresses.

Louiguy (real name: Louis Guglielmi; 1916–1991)   Born in Barcelona, Louiguy is most famous for writing the melody to Edith Piaf's words for "La Vie en Rose" (see '50) and for composing the Latin jazz composition that Perez Prado recast as a mambo, "Cherry Pink and Apple Blossom White" (see '55).

Carroll Loveday   Carroll Loveday was lyricist of "That's My Desire" (see '47).

Royal Lovell   In '26, Royal Lovell, a Midshipman, added verses to "Anchors Aweigh" (see '06).

Francia Luban   Cuban Francia Luban was lyricist of "Para Vigo Me Voy," which became "Say 'Si, Si'" (see '36).

Carroll Lucas   Carroll Lucas wrote the lyrics for "How Soon (Will I Be Seeing You?)" (see '48).

Clarence Lucas (1866–1947)   Clarence Lucas was a Canadian composer, lyricist, conductor and music professor. Lucas was born at Six Nations Reserve, Ontario. He taught at the Toronto College of Music, taught in

Utica, New York, and was the musical director at Wesleyan Ladies College in Hamilton, Ontario. He later lived and taught in London and in Sevres, just outside Paris. In the popular music realm, Lucas is remembered as the English lyricist for "The Song of Songs" (see '15).

Jimmy Lucas Jimmy Lucas is famous for writing the lyrics for "I Love, I Love, I Love My Wife, but Oh! You Kid! to Harry Von Tilzer's music (see '09).

Nick Lucas (real name: Dominic Nicholas Anthony Lucanese; 1897–1982) At an early age Nick Lucas learned how to play the guitar, mandolin and banjo. His older brother taught him the solfeggio system and to play the mandolin. The brothers began playing on street corners and for Italian weddings. After his brother joined a vaudeville troupe, Nick got a job at the Johnson's Cafe in Newark, playing guitar in a band. Because the guitar was too soft, he got a banjorine, which has a banjo body but the neck of a mandolin. After a few years at the Johnson's Café Nick went to another Newark nightclub, the Iroquois. After high school, Lucas formed a group called the "Kentucky Five," which included Ted FioRito, and did his first touring in vaudeville. After Nick's marriage in '17, he moved his family to New York City and got a job working with Sam Lanin's orchestra at the Roseland Ballroom. Nick then joined the Russo-FioRito Orchestra at the Edgewater Beach Hotel in Chicago in '22. They went into the Edgewater Beach Hotel for two weeks, and stayed there for two years. The Russo-FioRito Orchestra's broadcast over Chicago's WEBH were heard across the country, and Lucas would occasionally do a solo broadcast, singing and playing guitar. This led to a recording contract with Brunswick, and eighty-weeks on the prestigious Orpheum vaudeville circuit, plus the creation of the Gibson's Nick Lucas model guitar. During his career, he sold some 84 million recordings, the bulk of them in the '20s. His first recording success was with "My Best Girl," in '25. His biggest hit was by far "Tip-Toe Through the Tulips" (see '29). Nick became the No. 12 recording artist of the '20s. Lucas appeared in the following movie musicals: *Gold Diggers of Broadway* ('29), where he introduced "Tip-Toe Through the Tulips with Me" and "Painting the Clouds with Sunshine," *The Show of Shows* ('29) and *Disk Jockey* ('51).

Gustav Luders (1865–1913) Gustav Luders was a German-born composer of popular music and wrote several Broadway operettas. Born in Bremen, Germany, Luders studied in Europe before immigrating to Milwaukee, Wisconsin in 1888. After establishing himself as an arranger at Witmark Publishing in Chicago, he wrote his first operetta *Little Robinson Crusoe* (1899). This was followed by *King Dodo* ('01), *The Prince of Pilsen* ('03), *Woodland* ('04), *The Sho Gun* ('04), *The Grand Mogul* ('07), *Marcelle* ('08), *The Fair Co-ed* ('08), *The Gypsy on Broadway* ('12) and *Somewhere Else* ('13). His "Tale of a Bumble Bee" from *King Dodo* was very popular in '01. Luders' "Heidelberg Stein Song," from *The Sho Gun*, was enormously popular with male quartets at that time throughout America.

Jimmie Lunceford (1902–1947) Jimmie Lunceford gave up a job as athletic director of a Memphis, Tennessee high school to form a band in the late '20s. It became one of the great hot jazz bands of the '30s and '40s.

Lunceford was on the road with the band in Seaside, Oregon when he suffered a fatal heart attack in '47. Jimmie Lunceford and his orchestra's most famous recording was "Rhythm Is Our Business" (see '35). Their most productive period was from the mid–'30s through the early '40s. He was inducted into the Big Band/Jazz Hall of Fame in '87.

Art Lund (real name: Art London; 1915–1990) Art Lund gained fame as a vocalist with the Benny Goodman band in the early '40s. He left Goodman in '42, but returned in '46. He recorded his only major hit, "Mam'selle" (see '47). He had a starring role in the U.S. and London productions of *The Most Happy Fella* (U.S. '56, London '60), but after that his career began to fade.

Ida Lupino (1918–1995) Ida Lupino was born into a show business family in London. She came to Hollywood in '34, where she starred opposite some of the biggest leading men of the era, including Humphrey Bogart, Ronald Colman, John Garfield and Edward G. Robinson. Ms. Lupino introduced "Again" in the film *Road House* (see '49). Later, she turned to TV where she directed episodes of *The Untouchables* and *The Fugitive* in the late '50s and early '60s.

Dora Luz South American singer Dora Luz introduced "You Belong to My Heart" in the Walt Disney production *The Three Caballeros* (see '45).

Tommy Lyman Cabaret singer Tommy Lyman co-wrote "Montmartre Rose" (see '25) with C.E. Wheeler.

Vera Lynn (real name: Vera Margaret Welch; 1917–) Vera Lynn was England's sweetheart during World War II. She began singing in London clubs at age seven and joined a children's dance troupe at age eleven. At age fifteen, she began singing with Howard Baker's orchestra. Her first radio broadcast came in '35 with the Joe Loss Orchestra. She also sang with Charlie Kunz and Ambrose. In '40, she became the host of the BBC radio program *Sincerely Yours*; the show became popular with many servicemen who missed their girlfriends. During the war years, she made some films, appeared in a stage revue and entertained troops. She retired briefly at the end of the war. Her retirement only lasted a couple of years. She returned to the spotlight in '47, touring the variety circuit and hosting another BBC radio program. In '48, her record label, Decca, released some of her material in the U.S. during a musicians' strike that seriously weakened the American music industry. Her first stateside chart single was "You Can't Be True, Dear." In '52, she became the first British artist to hit No. 1 on the American charts with "Auf Wiederseh'n Sweetheart" (see '52), which spent nine weeks at the top spot of the *Billboard* chart. After that success, she moved from radio/variety work to television spots. She recorded occasionally during the '60s and '70s. In '76, Lynn added the title Dame of the British Empire to her credits.

Del Lyon Del Lyon was co-writer of "The One Rose (That's Left in My Heart)" (see '37).

Joe Lyons Joe Lyons was co-lyricist with Gilbert Keyes on "On the Alamo" (see '22).

Darl MacBoyle Darl MacBoyle was lyricist for "Forever Is a Long, Long Time" (see '16).

Ballard MacDonald (1882–1935) After graduating from Princeton University, Ballard MacDonald began writing lyrics for vaudeville acts. His work there led to Broadway, where he worked as a lyricist and librettist on several scores, including some Ziegfeld productions. MacDonald is most remembered as the lyricist for "The Trail of the Lonesome Pine" (see '13), "Indiana" (see '17), "Beautiful Ohio," the official state song for the state of Ohio (see '19), "Rose of Washington Square" (see '20), "Second Hand Rose" (see '21), "Parade of the Wooden Soldiers" (see '23), and "Somebody Loves Me" (see '24). Among the composers he collaborated with were Harry Carroll, Con Conrad, Joe Meyer, Sigmund Romberg, Albert Von Tilzer, George Gershwin, Jesse Greer, James Hanley, Victor Herbert, Lewis Muir and Walter Donaldson. MacDonald was a charter member of ASCAP in '14. He was inducted into the Songwriters' Hall of Fame in '70.

Christine MacDonald (1875–1962) Nova Scotian Christine MacDonald introduced "Sweethearts" and "The Angelus" in the operetta *Sweethearts*. She is primarily known for her appearance in this operetta, but she appeared in several productions on Broadway from 1894 to '20.

Jeanette MacDonald (1901–1965) Singing star Jeanette MacDonald is most famous for the operetta-style movie musicals she made with Nelson Eddy in the '30s. She began costarring with Eddy in *Naughty Marietta* ('35), but their most famous collaboration was *Rose Marie* ('36). Ms. MacDonald introduced "Beyond the Blue Horizon" in the movie *Monte Carlo* (see '30) and "Lover" in the movie musical *Love Me Tonight* (see '32). Perhaps a bit surprisingly, her recordings did not sell particularly well. MacDonald was married to actor Gene Raymond.

Glen MacDonough (1870–1924) Glen MacDonough was the lyricist for the famous musical *Babes in Toyland*. Several well-known songs came from that production, namely "Toyland" (see '04).

Harry MacDonough (real name: John S. MacDonough; 1871–1931) Canadian born tenor, Harry MacDonough became one of the great ballad singers of the early years of the 20th Century. In addition to his solo recordings, he was a member of the Edison, Haydn, Lyric and Orpheus Quartets and also a member of the Victor Light Opera Co. MacDonough began his singing career as a church soloist. He made his first recordings in 1898. In 1899, he was invited to sing second tenor for the Haydn Quartet. By '20, MacDonough retired from singing and focused on the business side of music, eventually rising to top executive level at Victor Records. MacDonough's most popular recordings include "Tell Me, Pretty Maiden" with Grace Spencer (see '01), "The Tale of a Bumble Bee" (see '01), "Absence Makes the Heart Grow Fonder" (see '01), "The Mansion of Aching Hearts" (see '02), "In the Sweet Bye and Bye" with John Bieling (see '03), "Hiawatha" (see '03), "Because You're You" with Elise Stevenson (see '07), "My Dear" (see '07), "Shine on, Harvest Moon" with Miss Walton (see '09), "Where the River Shannon Flows" (see '10), "Every Little Movement" with Lucy Isabelle Marsh (see '10), "In the Valley of Yesterday" (see '10), "Down by the Old Mill Stream" (see '11), "They Didn't Believe Me" with Alice Green (see '15) and "The Girl on the Magazine" (see '16). And that does not include

his recordings with the various quartets and the Victor Light Opera Co. MacDonough became the No. 2 recording artist of the first decade of the 20th Century and No. 7 for the second decade, making him the No. 8 top recording artist of the first half of the 20th Century. Numerous recordings by Harry MacDonough as a soloist and with Joseph Belmont, John H. Bieling, S.H. Dudley, the Haydn Quartet, the Lyric Quartet, Lucy Isabelle Marsh, the Orpheus Quartet, Grace Spencer, Frank Stanley, and others are available in RealAudio and MP3 for listening or downloading at http://www.collectionscanada.ca/gramophone/.

George MacFarlane (1878–1932) Canadian-born George MacFarlane recorded a very popular version of "A Little Bit of Heaven (Shure, They Call It Ireland)" (see '15). MacFarlane also performed on Broadway and in some Gilbert and Sullivan operettas.

Cecil Mack (real name: Richard C. McPherson; 1883–1944) Cecil Mack was an African American lyricist for several popular songs of the early 1900s and 1910s. Mack often collaborated with Chris Smith. His first songwriting success came with "Good Morning, Carrie" (see '01), which he wrote for Bert Williams and his vaudeville partner, George Walker. Other famous songs by Cecil Mack include "Down Among the Sheltering Palms" (see '15), "He's a Cousin of Mine" (see '07), "You're in the Right Church, but the Wrong Pew" (see '09), "That's Why They Call Me 'Shine'" (see '10) and, perhaps most famous of all, "Charleston," the dance of the '20s (see '24).

Dermot MacMurrough (1868–1937) Dermot MacMurrough shared his name with the ancient King of Leinster. However, this Dermot MacMurrough is relatively unknown except for writing the music for "Macushla" (see '10).

Gordon MacRae (1921–2004) Singer Gordon MacRae is particularly remembered for the movie musicals he made in the '50s. His break into the big time came in '42, when be began singing with Horace Heidt's band. MacRae had a featured part in the '46 Broadway musical *Three to Make Ready*, but he is more remembered for his movie roles in *Oklahoma!* ('55) and *Carousel* ('56). He remained active in several phases of show business into the '70s. His only really important popular song recording was "My Darling, My Darling" (see '49), a duet with Jo Stafford, however, they recorded several duets together in the late '40s.

Edward Madden (1878–1952) Lyricist Edward Madden grew up in New York City and graduated from Fordham University. He started his songwriting career supplying special material for various vaudeville acts. That eventually led to the Broadway stage. Madden collaborated with composers such as his wife Dorothy Jardon, Ben Jerome, Joseph Daly, Gus Edwards, Julian Edwards, Louis Hirsch, Theodore Morse, Percy Wenrich and Jerome Kern. Madden produced the lyrics for such well-known songs as "Blue Bell" (see '04), "By the Light of the Silvery Moon" (see '10), "Look Out for Jimmy Valentine" (see '11) and "Moonlight Bay" (see '12). His work on Broadway produced the scores for several musicals and several Madden songs were included in films of the '30s, '40s and '50s including *Babes in Arms, Tin-Pan-Alley, Birth of the Blues, Ship Ahoy, On Moonlight Bay* and *By the Light of the Silvery Moon*. Edward Madden was a charter member of

ASCAP. He was elected into the Songwriters' Hall of Fame in '70. At http://www.songwritershalloffame.org/exhibit_audio_video.asp?exhibitId=254 you can hear audio clips of "Moonlight Bay" performed by the American Quartet and "By the Light of the Silv'ry Moon" performed by Billy Murray.

Enric Madriguera (1904–1973) Violinist, composer, arranger, and bandleader Enric Madriguera immigrated to South America from Spain. He traveled to New York City in the late '20s where he formed his first band. He was a pioneer of Latin-American music in the U.S. His orchestra became the inspiration for many of the Latin bands that followed. Madriguera disbanded the group in the early '50s. Enric was also a composer. Among his songs were "Adios," "Minute Samba" and "The Language of Love." His most famous recording in the U.S. was "Carioca" (see '34).

Herb Magidson (1906–1986) Herb Magidson wrote lyrics for some important songs in the '30s and remained active in the music industry into the '50s. After graduating from the University of Pittsburgh, Magidson moved to New York City in the late '20s where he began to write songs for Tin Pan Alley publishers. He very quickly caught the attention of the Hollywood film studios and Magidson moved to the west coast at the end of the decade to work on movie musicals such as *The Great Ziegfeld, No, No, Nanette, The Gay Divorcee,* and *Hers to Hold.* Magidson collaborated with songwriters like Con Conrad, Allie Wrubel, Ben Oakland, Carl Sigman, Michael Cleary, Jule Styne, Sam Stept and Sammy Fain. His best-known hits include the first Academy Award winning song, "The Continental" (see '34), "Gone with the Wind" (see '37), "Music, Maestro, Please" (see '38), "I'll Buy That Dream" (see '45), "I'll Dance at Your Wedding" (see '48) and "Enjoy Yourself (It's Later than You Think)" (see '50). Magidson was elected to the Songwriters' Hall of Fame in '80. At http://www.songwritershalloffame. org/exhibit_audio_video.asp?exhibitId=94 you can hear an audio clip of "The Continental" performed by Sam Browne with George Scott Wood and the London Piano-Accordion Band.

Frank Magine Frank Magine's most famous contribution to popular music was being co-lyricist on "Dreamy Melody" (see '23).

Jack Mahoney (real name: Ruben Kusnitt; 1882–1945) Jack Mahoney's greatest lyric was "When You Wore a Tulip and I Wore a Big Red Rose," with composer Percy Wenrich (see '15).

Jere Mahoney A member of the Edison Male Quartet form 1896 until '00, Jere Mahoney recorded a couple of very successful solo recordings for Edison in '00. His versions of "When You Were Sweet Sixteen" (see '00) and "A Bird in a Gilded Cage" (see '00) were both very well received.

Tommie Malie Tommie Malie co-wrote the lyrics of "Jealous" with Dick Finch (see '24).

Matty Malneck (1903–1981) Matty Malneck was a violinist, songwriter, and bandleader. He was primarily active during the '30s and '40s. Most of his songs were written to Johnny Mercer lyrics. He composed "Goody Goody" (see '36) and "Park Avenue Fantasy," which later became "Stairway to the Stars" (see '39).

David Mann (real name: David Freedman; 1916–2002) David Mann began playing the piano by ear at a very early age. By his early teen years, he was playing in bands around his hometown of Philadelphia. After he graduated from the famous Curtis Institute at the end of the '30s, he moved to New York City, where he worked as a session musician for Decca Records, played in Charley Spivak's band and was accompanist for singer Gordon MacRae. He spent his spare time composing. During World War II, Mann joined the Army, where he was pianist with Artie Shaw and Jimmy Dorsey's bands. Upon his discharge in '45, he became personal pianist to President Truman. Mann can be seen in several films, including *Twenty Grand, I Dood It, Four Jills and a Jeep, Pin-Up Girl,* and *Second Chorus.* In the '50s, he composed the scores for three Disney Nature Series films: *The Living Desert, Water Birds,* and *Seal Island.* His most well known song is "There! I've Said It Again" (see '45).

Paul Mann (1910–1983) Paul Mann collaborated with Stephen Weiss as co-composers of "They Say" (see '39).

Audrey Maple Audrey Maple and Melville Stewart introduced "Sympathy" in *The Firefly* (see '13).

Sol Marcus (1913–1976) Sol Marcus was one of the co-writers of "I Don't Want to Set the World on Fire" (see '41) and "When the Lights Go on Again" (see '42).

Arthur Margetson (1887–1951) Englishman Arthur Margetson and Irene Bordoni introduced "Let's Do It" in Cole Porter's first Broadway show, *Paris* (see '28). In the '30s and '40s, Margetson appeared in several films.

Gerald Marks (1900–1997) Gerald Marks was the composer of "All of Me" (see '32) and "Is It True What They Say About Dixie?" (see '36). Marks published 400 songs. His first composition was performed publicly when he was age 11. He dropped out of school and left Michigan for New York City to become a professional songwriter.

Johnny Marks (1909–1985) Johnny Marks graduated from Colgate and Columbia Universities and studied in Paris. During World War II, he served as a Captain in the 26th Special Service Company. In '49, he formed St. Nicholas Music. Marks is probably the "King of Christmas Songs." His most famous songs include "Rudolph, the Red-Nosed Reindeer" (see '50), the No. 3 Christmas hit of the pre-rock era, and "Rockin' Around the Christmas Tree" the No. 2 Christmas hit of the rock era, plus "When Santa Claus Gets Your Letter," "I Heard the Bells on Christmas Day," "A Holly Jolly Christmas," "The Night Before Christmas Song," and "Silver and Gold." Marks wrote a few non–Christmas songs, most notably "Address Unknown" (see '39). Johnny Marks was inducted into the Songwriters' Hall of Fame in '81.

James C. Marlowe (circa 1865–1926) James C. Marlowe appeared in several Broadway productions between '06 and '23. His most famous contribution was introducing George M. Cohan's "Harrigan" in *Fifty Miles from Boston* (see '07).

Joe Marsala (1907–1978) Joe Marsala played clarinet and sax. He and his drummer brother played in local Chicago bands in the late '20s. Later, during prohibition, he played in Chicago speakeasies. Marsala worked several different stints with jazz great Wingy Manone. In the late '40s, Joe opened a music publishing business. As a songwriter, he wrote "Don't Cry Joe" (see '49).

Lucy Isabelle Marsh (1879–1956) Ms. Marsh was a popular concert soprano and a member of the Victor Light Opera Company. Her Columbia recording of "The Glow Worm" (see '08) was very popular, as was her Victor recording of "Every Little Movement" with Harry MacDonough (see '10).

Roy Marsh Roy Marsh was co-writer with Tom Pitts and Ray Egan on "I Never Knew I Could Love Anybody the Way I'm Loving You" (see '21).

Everett Marshall (1901–1965) Everett Marshall was a baritone at the Metropolitan Opera for four seasons ('27–'31). He made his film debut in '30 in the movie musical *Dixiana*. Marshall introduced "Wagon Wheels" in the *Ziegfeld Follies of 1934* (see '34).

Henry I. Marshall Henry Marshall is primarily remembered today as the composer of the tune for "Be My Little Baby Bumble Bee" (see '12).

Dean Martin (real name: Dino Crocetti; 1917–1995) Singer and actor Dean Martin was singing in nightclubs when he teamed up with comedian Jerry Lewis in the mid–'40s. They became stars of several movies, with Martin playing straight man to Lewis. The pair broke up in '57. Martin achieved wide recognition with his *Dean Martin Show* on television in the '70s. Martin's most popular pre-rock recording was "That's Amore," which he sang in the Martin and Lewis film *The Caddy* (see '53). Other popular recordings include "Memories Are Made of This" in '55, "Return to Me" and "Volare" in '58 and "Everybody Loves Somebody" in '64. Dean was inducted into the Popular Music Hall of Fame in 2005.

Freddy Martin (1907–1983) Freddy Martin learned to play the drums in an orphanage band and added the saxophone while he was a student at Ohio State University. He formed his own professional band in '32. Martin's biggest hit recordings were "I Saw Stars" (see '34), "Tonight We Love (Piano Concerto in B Flat)" (see '41), "Rose O'Day" (see '42), "To Each His Own" (see '46), "Symphony" (see '46) and "Managua, Nicaragua" (see '47). Martin became the No. 36 top recording artist of the '30s and No. 13 for the '40s. Merv Griffin was his band's singer in the late '40s.

Hugh Martin (1914–) Hugh Martin and Ralph Blane became very successful popular songwriting team. They created the Broadway musical *Best Foot Forward* ('41), which introduced "Buckle Down, Winsocki" and the '48 nominee for the Academy Award for Best Song "Pass That Peace Pipe." They also wrote the songs from *Meet Me in St. Louis*, which include "The Trolley Song" and "Have Yourself a Merry Little Christmas" (see '44). Martin sometimes supplied his own lyrics, but also worked with lyricist Timothy Gray. Martin also served as Judy Garland's and Eddie Fisher's accompanist on occasion. He was also music director of the '79 Broadway musical *Sugar Babies*, which starred Mickey Rooney. Martin was elected to the Songwriters' Hall of Fame in '83.

Mary Martin (1913–1990) Broadway star Mary Martin is most famous for her leading roles in the musicals *South Pacific* and *The Sound of Music*. She first came to prominence when she introduced "My Heart Belongs to Daddy" in *Leave It to Me!*. Other Broadway successes include *One Touch of Venus* and *I Do! I Do!* ('66). Ms. Martin and Kenny Baker introduced "Speak Low" in the musical *One Touch of Venus* (see '44). She introduced "A Wonderful Guy" and other songs as Nellie Forbush in *South Pacific* (see '49). Ms. Martin also appeared in several films, including *Birth of the Blues* ('41), *Star Spangled Rhythm* ('42), *Happy Go Lucky* ('43) and *Night and Day* ('46). Martin introduced "Let's Get Lost" in the movie musical *Happy Go Lucky* (see '43). Her son, Larry Hagman, starred as J.R. Ewing in the long-running TV series *Dallas*.

Sam Martin Sam Martin was one of the co-writers of "You Call Everybody Darling" (see '48).

Tony Martin (real name: Alfred Norris, Jr.; 1913–) Pop singer Tony Martin occasionally acted in Hollywood films. He introduced "When Did You Leave Heaven?" in the movie musical *Sing, Baby, Sing* (see '36). He also appeared in *Here Come the Girls* ('53) and *Hit the Deck* ('55). Early in his career he played sax in a band headed by Tom Gerun. Martin married actress Alice Faye and, after their divorce, married dancer and actress Cyd Charisse. Tony had several charting singles between '38 and '54. His most successful disks were "It's a Blue World" in '40 and "There's No Tomorrow" in '49.

Al Martino (real name: Alfred Cini; 1927–) Singer Al Martino had his first No. 1 hit with "Here Is My Heart" (see '52). Eleven years later, in '63, he charted with "I Love You Because." Martino also had some success with "Spanish Eyes." Martino became more successful in Europe than he was in America. For more, go to http://www.almartino.com/.

Johnny Marvin (1897–1944) Johnny Marvin was one of the most popular band singers in the '20s. He later wrote several songs for Gene Autry films. His Columbia recording of "Breezin' Along with the Breeze" (see '26) became very popular.

Marx Brothers Chico (real name: Leonard; 1887–1961), Harpo (real name: Adolph; 1888–1964), Groucho (real name: Julius Henry; 1890–1977), Gummo (real name: Milton; 1892–1977), Zeppo (real name: Herbert; 1901–1979). The Marx Brothers were a team of comedian brothers. They appeared in vaudeville, stage plays, films and television. The Marx Brothers introduced "Just One More Chance" in the film *Monkey Business* ('31). For more of these famous brothers, see http://www.marx-brothers.org/.

Eric Maschwitz (1901–1969) British lyricist Eric Maschwitz began his career on the English stage and in the mid–'20s joined the BBC. In the late '30s he was signed by MGM and moved to Hollywood. His work at the studio included writing the screenplays for films such as *Goodbye Mr. Chips*. After serving in the British Intelligence Service and the 21st Armed Forces during World War II, he returned to writing. Among the most memorable Maschwitz lyrics are "These Foolish Things" (see '36), "At the Balalaika" (see '40), and "He Wears a Pair of Silver Wings" (see '42).

John Mason John Mason was co-lyricist of "Open the Door, Richard" (see '47). Mason and Dusty Fletcher had used the title phrase as part of their vaudeville routine in the '30s and '40s.

Guy Massey   According to Novie Massey, the wife of Robert Massey, Guy's brother, Robert wrote "The Prisoner's Song" (see '25). She said she was with the brothers when her husband sang it and Guy wrote it down. Guy took it to New York and copyrighted it in his own name. Guy then convinced his cousin, Vernon Dalhart, to record it, and it became a huge hit. In his will, Guy willed the song back to Robert, but he never admitted Robert wrote it.

Ilona Massey (real name: Ilona Hajmássy; 1912–1974)   Ilona Massey had an impoverished childhood in Budapest, Hungary. She managed to scrape together enough money for singing lessons. She began her career dancing in the chorus at the Staats Opera. She came to America to appear in *Rosalie* ('37) and *Balalaika*, where she and a Russian Art Choir introduced "At the Balalaika" (see '40). She made only eleven films. She also appeared on radio and TV mostly in spy or espionage series. She became an American citizen in '46.

Louise Massey (real name: Louise Massey Mabie; 1902–1983)   Massey was a country and western singer, labeled "the original rhinestone cowgirl." Her career ran from approximately '18 until the early '50s. She formed a band in New Mexico in '18 with her father, her husband and two brothers. First called the Massey Family Band, they soon became Louise Massey and the Westerners. In '38, she and the band began recording and singing for NBC programs in New York City. She retired in '50. Massey was inducted into the National Cowgirl Hall of Fame in '82. See "My Adobe Hacienda" ('47).

Frankie Masters (1904–1991)   Frankie Masters led a very successful sweet-style band in the '30s and '40s. He also collaborated to write "Scatter-Brain" (see '39). It turned out to be his only major hit recording.

Robert Maxwell (1921–)   Robert Maxwell was co-writer of "Ebb Tide" (see '53). Robert, or Bob, began studying the harp at age 10. While in high school, he got a scholarship to Juilliard. By age 17 he was a member of the National Symphony Orchestra. During World War II, Maxwell served in the Coast Guard, serving with Rudy Vallee. Vallee arranged for Maxwell to tour with a band that was performing for servicemen. During the '50s, he recorded some harp albums for MGM.

Billy Mayhew   Billy Mayhew was the writer of "It's a Sin to Tell a Lie" (see '36).

Stella Mayhew (circa 1875–1934)   Stella Mayhew introduced "Hallelujah!" in the Broadway musical *Hit the Deck* (see '27).

Charles McCarron (1891–1919)   Charles McCarron was a Tin Pan Alley composer and lyricist. McCarron is credited with co-writing the lyrics for "Oh! How She Could Yacki Hacki Wicki Wachi Woo" (see '16) and "Blues (My Naughty Sweetie Gives to Me)" (see '20). He collaborated with other composers including Albert Von Tilzer and Chris Smith.

Joseph McCarthy (1885–1943)   Lyricist Joseph McCarthy wrote several hit songs from about '10 through the '30s. McCarthy began his career as a singer in Boston cafes. He moved to New York City and worked on the staff at Feist & Co., a music publishing company. In '14, he was a charter member of ASCAP and served as its director for most of the '20s. He collaborated on the Broadway musicals *Irene, Kid Boots,* and *Rio Rita*, plus several *Ziegfeld Follies*. McCarthy collaborated with such composers as Harry Tierney, Harry Carroll, Fred Fisher and Jimmy Monaco. Some of McCarthy's best-remembered songs include "You Made Me Love You" (see '13), "Where Did You Get That Girl?" (see '13), "They Go Wild, Simply Wild, Over Me" (see '17), "Ireland Must Be Heaven, for My Mother Came from There" (see '16), "I'm Always Chasing Rainbows" (see '18), "Alice Blue Gown" (see '20), "Irene" (see '20), "The Rangers' Song" (see '27) and "Rio Rita (see '27). McCarthy has been a member of the Songwriters' Hall of Fame since '70

Neal McCay   Neal McCay and Aline Crater introduced "Because You're You" (see '06) in *The Red Mill* and McCay, as the rather baudy governor of Zeeland, introduced "Every Day Is Ladies' Day with Me" (see '06) in the same production. McCay continued performing on Broadway through the mid–1910s, but *The Red Mill* was his biggest success.

John McCormack (1884–1945)   John McCormack became one of the greatest, most versatile singers of the 20th century. Not only did the Irish tenor sing famous Irish songs like "When Irish Eyes Are Smiling," he also was a much-admired opera singer, performing in music halls the world over. McCormack's most famous recordings were "I'm Falling in Love with Someone" (see '10), "Mother Machree" (see '11), World War I favorite "It's a Long, Long Way to Tipperary" (see '15), "The Sunshine of Your Smile" (see '16), "Somewhere a Voice Is Calling" (see '16), "The Star Spangled Banner" (see '16), "Send Me Away with a Smile" (see '18) and "All Alone" (see '25). McCormack was the No. 7 top recording artist of the 1910s and No. 35 of the '20s, qualifying him as the No. 18 top recording artist of the first half of the 20th Century. For more on McCormack, see http://www.mccormacksociety.co.uk/.

Bessie McCoy (real name: Elizabeth McAvoy; 1888–1931)   Bessie McCoy introduced "The Yama Yama Man" in the musical *The Three Twins* (see '09). Because she introduced this song and often sang it in vaudeville, she was known as "The Yama Yama Girl."

Junie McCree (1865–1918)   Junie McCree wrote the lyrics for "Carrie (Carrie Marry Harry)" (see '10), "Put Your Arms Around Me, Honey" (see '11) with composer Albert Von Tilzer. McCree also contributed the lyrics for "Take Me Up with You, Dearie" ('09).

James McGavisk   James McGavisk is primarily remembered today as the composer of "Gee, but It's Great to Meet a Friend from Your Home Town" (see '11).

McGuire Sisters   Phyllis (1931–), Dorothy (1930–), Christine (1929–). Three sisters from Middletown, Ohio, began singing together in '35 when Phyllis, Dorothy and Christine were four, five and six respectively. Their mother was pastor of First Church of God in Miamisburg, Ohio; where they often sang together at church functions, weddings and funerals. They quickly learned they had an uncanny ability to harmonize, that "family harmony" that is difficult to come by except in a filial way. Their voices blended naturally; even their own mother had difficulty telling them apart over a telephone. In '49 and '50, they toured military bases and veterans' hospitals around the country for the U.S.O. Also in '50, an agent and bandleader happened to hear them sing on a radio broadcast of a church service. He immediately went to the church to encourage them to sing pop music. Very soon the girls were singing with that agent's band in Dayton, Ohio. They began to receive national attention when they did eight weeks on Kate Smith's radio show in '52 and won *Arthur Godfrey's Talent Scouts.* Godfrey asked them to replace the Chordettes on his morning show for a week; they stayed six years. By the end of '52 they had signed with Coral Records and had their first single release, "One, Two, Three, Four." It wasn't until '54 that they made the top 10 with their cover version of the rhythm and blues song "Goodnight Sweetheart, Goodnight." Their eleventh single was a cover of another R&B song, the Moonglows' "Sincerely" (see '55), which became their first No. 1. By the early '60s, Phyllis left the group to become a soloist. She appeared in the film *Come Blow Your Horn* with Frank Sinatra. The sisters were inducted into the Vocal Group Hall of Fame in 2001.

Jimmy McHugh (real name: James Francis McHugh; 1894–1969) Songwriters' Hall of Fame member Jimmy McHugh had a very prolific career as a composer of popular songs. His first job in music was as a rehearsal pianist at the Boston Opera House, but he soon concentrated on popular music. He began working as a song plugger for the Boston office of Irving Berlin's publishing company and in '21, he moved to New York, where he began writing songs, especially for the Cotton Club revues in Harlem. One of his first successes came in '24 with one of his Cotton Club songs, "When My Sugar Walks Down the Street," with lyrics by Gene Austin. Another success from his Cotton Club years was "I Can't Believe That You're in Love with Me," with lyrics by Clarence Gaskill. In the early part of his career he collaborated with lyricist Dorothy Fields. Later he worked with several other important lyricists, including Harold Adamson, Johnny Mercer, Ted Koehler, and Ned Washington, in addition to Irving Mills. In the '30s McHugh worked on several Hollywood films. In the '50s McHugh organized the Jimmy McHugh Polio Foundation and Jimmy McHugh Charities. He also organized his own publishing company. McHugh's best-known hit songs include "I Can't Give You Anything but Love, Baby" (see '28), "Diga Diga Doo" (see '28), "On the Sunny Side of the Street" (see '30), "Exactly Like You" (see '30), "Cuban Love Song" (see '31), "I'm in the Mood for Love" (see '35), "I Won't Dance" and "Lovely to Look At" (see '35), "You're a Sweetheart" (see '38), "Comin' in on a Wing and a Prayer" (see '43), "Let's Get Lost" (see '43) and "I Couldn't Sleep a Wink Last Night" (see '44). McHugh and Dorothy Fields also co-wrote a new lyric based on an existing Oscar Hammerstein II lyric for Jerome Kern's "I Won't Dance" (see '35). Jimmy McHugh has been a member of the Songwriter's Hall of Fame since '70. At http://www.song writershalloffame.org/exhibit_audio_video.asp? exhibitId=51 you can hear audio clips of McHugh's "I Must Have That Man" performed by Billie Holiday, "On the Sunny Side of the Street" performed by Louis Armstrong, and "Cuban Love Song" performed by Lawrence Tibbett.

Lani McIntire Lani McIntire, "King of the Hawaiian Guitar," was co-writer of "The One Rose (That's Left in My Heart)" (see '37). McIntire's band was called variously Lani McIntire and his Aloha Islanders and Lani McIntire and his Hawaiians.

William C. McKenna William C. McKenna was the co-writer of "Has Anybody Here Seen Kelly?" (see '10).

McKinney's Cotton Pickers Drummer William McKinney (1894–1969) started his band in southern Kentucky in the early '20s. Starting as a quartet, it eventually transformed into the ten piece Cotton Pickers. In the late '20s McKinney lured arranger Don Redman to become the bandleader. Redman's leadership transformed the group into a more disciplined, more polished band. Redman arranged the scores, played trumpet and often performed vocals. Two of the group's sidemen who became well known are Fats Waller and Coleman Hawkins. Redman left the band in '31 and it was never quite as successful thereafter. The band's only big hit was their RCA Victor recording of "If I Could Be with You One Hour Tonight" (see '30). Recordings by McKinney's Cotton Pickers are available for listening at http://www.redhot jazz.com/bands.html.

Ted McMichael (1908–2001) Ted McMichael was one of the co-writers of "The Hut-Sut Song (a Swedish Serenade)" (see '41). McMichael was one of the founding members of the Merry Macs vocal quartet.

Jack McVea (1914–2000) Saxophonist Jack McVea was co-composer of "Open the Door, Richard" (see '47). Jack McVea's recording of the song appeared on the soundtrack of the '98 film *Lolita.*

F.W. Meacham (circa 1850–circa 1895) Bandleader and composer, F. W. Meacham wrote "American Patrol" (see '01).

Fred Meadows Fred Meadows was a co-lyricist of "You Were Only Fooling (While I Was Falling in Love)" (see '48).

Martha Mears (1908–1986) Martha Mears was the singing voice for Rita Hayworth in introducing "Long Ago and Far Away" in the movie musical *Cover Girl.* Ms. Mears was the singing voice for numerous Hollywood stars, most often uncredited in the film. Some of the female stars she sang for include Veronica Lake, Ellen Drew, Anne Shirley, Dorothy Lovett, Marjorie Reynolds, Lucille Ball, Marion Martin, Julie Bishop, Michele Morgan, Martha O'Driscoll, Audrey Totter, Sonja Henie and Hedy Lamarr.

Fred Meinken Fred Meinken was the composer on "Wabash Blues" (see '21).

Robert Mellin Born in England, Robert Mellin's first songwriting success was "My One and Only Love" with lyricist Guy Wood in '52. Mellin sometimes was composer, sometimes lyricist on his songs. His next success was when he furnished the English lyrics for "You, You, You" (see '53). In the late '50s and early '60s Mellin organized his own music publishing company. His next major songwriting achievement was writing the lyrics for Acker Bilk's "Stranger on the Shore." In the mid-'60s, he wrote soundtrack music for some Westerns.

James Melton (1904–1961) James Melton was a popular singer, Metropolitan Opera lyric tenor, producer and actor. He was raised on a Florida farm. A high-school teacher encouraged him to further his vocal studies. He studied at and graduated from Nashville's Ward-Belmont Conservatory. In '27, he moved to New York, where he sang at the Roxy during musical prologues and soon joined the Revelers vocal quartet, singing on radio and in concert tours across America and Europe. By '34 he became a solo performer and began to appear on radio, accompanied George Gershwin on a national tour, and was signed to a three-picture Warner Bros. film contract. "September in the Rain" premiered in the '35 movie musical *Stars Over Broadway*, but it was only heard there as instrumental background music. James Melton, who had starred in *Stars Over Broadway*, re-introduced the song in the movie musical *Melody for Two* (see '37). Melton made his Metropolitan Opera debut in '42. During the mid–'40s, he was featured on a weekly radio series, had a recording contract with RCA Red Seal, and was very active in wartime bond rallies, military hospital tours and benefit concerts. He appeared in the '46 MGM film *Ziegfeld Follies*. He began appearing on television, hosting his own musical series for one season in the '50s. He also appeared in nightclubs and produced a revue that toured the East Coast. He later opened an antique automobile museum in Florida.

Murray Mencher (1898–?) Murray Mencher was the composer of "Let's Swing It" (see '35). The website http://imdb.com credits him with writing "Merrily We Roll Along."

Nilo Menendez (1902–1987) Nilo Menendez wrote the Spanish version of "Green Eyes" titled "Aquellos Ojos Verdes" (see '41).

Frances Mercer (1915–2000) Frances Mercer, Hollace Shaw, Hiram Sherman, and Ralph Stuart introduced "All the Things You Are" in the Broadway musical *Very Warm for May*(see '40).

Johnny Mercer (real name: John Herndon Mercer; 1909–1976) Johnny Mercer's father was a wealthy Southern attorney with a flourishing real estate business, so he could easily afford to send John to a fashionable prep school in Virginia. However, when Johnny was in his late teens, his father's business collapsed and he was left deeply in debt. Suddenly Johnny couldn't afford to go to college, so he headed for New York City to try his luck at becoming an actor. Acting didn't pan out. His first break came in '30 when one of his song lyrics was sung on Broadway in *The Garrick Gaieties of 1930*, but a bigger break came when he won a singing contest sponsored by Paul Whiteman. When the Rhythm Boys left the Whiteman orchestra, Mercer was hired as their replacement. In addition to his singing, he often wrote material for the group. Whiteman introduced him to Hoagy Carmichael, and soon Mercer and Carmichael had a hit with "Lazybones." His career as a lyricist had begun. After Whiteman came stints with Benny Goodman and Bob Crosby. By this time Mercer had created enough attention to garner a contract to write for films. At first he served as lyricist for other composers, but eventually he wrote both music and lyrics. As president and co-founder of Capitol Records, Mercer was instrumental in the early recording careers of such musicians as Peggy Lee, Stan Kenton, Nat "King" Cole, Jo Stafford, and Margaret Whiting. By the mid–'40s, Capitol was responsible for one sixth of all records sold in the U.S. Mercer was a leading lyricist from the '30s into the '60s and remained active until his death in the mid–'70s. He also appeared on radio frequently and recorded often. He wrote lyrics for several Broadway musicals including *St. Louis Woman* ('46), with Harold Arlen and with Gene DePaul for *Li'l Abner* ('56), which included "Jubilation T. Cornpone." In '54, he wrote the lyrics to Gene DePaul's music for the classic Hollywood musical *Seven Brides for Seven Brothers*. Mercer wrote hit songs in four different decades, from the '30s through the '60s. Mercer wrote more than 1,000 songs, making him, along with Irving Berlin and Oscar Hammerstein II, one of the most prolific songwriters of all time. His most famous hit songs include "Lazybones" (see '33), "Goody Goody" (see '36), "I'm an Old Cowhand" (see '36), "Lost" (see '36), "Bob White (Whatcha Gonna Swing Tonight?)" (see '37), "Too Marvelous for Words" (see '37), "You Must Have Been a Beautiful Baby" (see '38), "And the Angels Sing" (see '39), "Day in — Day Out" (see '39), "Jeepers Creepers" (see '39), "Fools Rush in" (see '40), "Blues in the Night" (see '42), "Strip Polka" (see '42), "Tangerine" (see '42), "One for My Baby (and One More for the Road)" (see '43), "That Old Black Magic" (see '43), "G.I. Jive" (see '44), "Ac-cent-tchu-ate the Positive" (see '45), "Dream" (see '45), "Laura" (see '45), the Academy Award winner in '46 "On the Atchison, Topeka and the Santa Fe" (see '45), "Come Rain or Come Shine" (see '46), and the Academy Award winner in '51 "In the Cool, Cool, Cool of the Evening" (see '51). Publisher Edward Marks signed Johnny Mercer to write new lyrics for "The Glow Worm," which the Mills Brothers recorded and popularized (see '52). Other hits include "Autumn Leaves" (English lyrics for the French song (see '55), "Something's Gotta Give" (see '55), the Academy Award winner in '61 "Moon River," "Charade," and the Academy Award winner in '62 "Days of Wine and Roses." Mercer became the first songwriter to win the Best Song Oscar four times. Mercer had a posthumous hit when his wife allowed Barry Manilow to set music to one of his lyrics in the early '90s. It wasn't a giant hit, but "When October Goes" was a beautiful song and lyric. Mercer was also a popular recording artist. He was particularly popular in the mid- to late '40s. He had big hit recordings of "On the Atchison, Topeka and the Santa Fe" (see '45), "Ac-cent-Tchu-Ate the Positive" (see '45), "Candy" (see '45) with Jo Stafford, "Personality" (see '46) and "Baby, It's Cold Outside" (see '49) with Margaret Whiting. Mercer became the No. 20 top recording artist of the '40s. He was the founding president of the Songwriters Hall of Fame and he, himself, was elected to the Songwriters' Hall of Fame in '71. At http://www.songwritershalloffame.org/exhibit_audio_video.asp?exhibitId=18 you can hear audio clips of Mercer's "Jeepers Creepers" performed by Louis Armstrong, "Skylark" sung by Ella Fitzgerald, "Day in — Day Out" performed by Sarah Vaughan, "Come Rain or Come Shine" sung by Anita O'Day, "On the Atchison, Topeka and the Santa Fe," "Ac-cent-Tchu-Ate the Positive" and "In the Cool, Cool, Cool of the Evening" as recorded by Bing Crosby, "Moon River" performed by Sarah Vaughan, "Blues in the Night" as recorded by Rosemary Clooney, plus "That Old Black Magic" and "One for My Baby (and One More for the Road) sung by Frank Sinatra. The Johnny Mercer

Educational Archives can be reached at http://www.johnnymercer.com/.

Una Merkel (1903–1986) Una Merkel began her Hollywood career as a stand-in for Lillian Gish. She later appeared in several Broadway productions and returned to films. She became particularly known for her comic roles. She was a wise-cracking chorus girl in *Forty Second Street*. She, Ruby Keeler, Ginger Rogers and Clarence Nordstrom introduced "Shuffle Off to Buffalo" in that movie musical (see '33). She was nominated for the Oscar for Best Supporting Actress in *Summer and Smoke* ('62).

Ethel Merman (real name: Ethel Zimmerman; 1909–1984) One of Broadway's most charismatic performers from the '30s into the '50s, Ethel Merman was famous for her loud, belting style of singing. Although she also performed on radio, in movies and on television, she gained her greatest fame on the Broadway stage. After she began her career in *Girl Crazy* ('30), over the next thirty years she starred in more than a dozen musicals and appeared in fifteen films, including a half dozen movie musicals. Some of her most famous starring roles came in *Anything Goes* (see '34), *Annie Get Your Gun* (see '46) and *Gypsy* ('50). Ms. Merman introduced "Life Is Just a Bowl of Cherries" in the '31 edition of *George White's Scandals* (see '31). Merman and Jack Haley introduced "You're an Old Smoothie" in the musical *Take a Chance* (see '33). Her Hollywood musicals include *We're Not Dressing* ('34), *Kid Millions* ('34), *The Big Broadcast of 1936*, the film version of *Anything Goes* ('36), *Alexander's Ragtime Band* ('38), the film version of Berlin's *Call Me Madam* ('53) and *There's No Business Like Show Business* ('54).

Benny Meroff (1901–1973) Benny Meroff started his music career in the early '20s as a vaudeville violin, saxophone, and clarinet comedian. He formed his first band in the mid-'20s. One of his sidemen in the '20s was the young Benny Goodman. Meroff orchestra's home base was Chicago, but they toured often in the '30s and '40s. In the late '40s the group disbanded and Meroff went into semi-retirement. By far his most famous recording was of "Happy Days Are Here Again" (see '30).

Robert "Bob" Merrill (1921–1998) Songwriter Bob Merrill wrote several hits from the late '40s through the late '60s. In his early career he specialized in novelty songs. Some of his best-known songs include "If I Knew You Were Comin' I'd 'ave Baked a Cake" (see '50), "Sparrow in the Tree Top" (see '51), "I'm Yours" (see '52), "That Doggie in the Window" (see '53), "Make Yourself Comfortable" (see '54) and "Mambo Italiano" (see '54). He composed the scores and wrote the lyrics for several Broadway musicals, notably *Funny Girl* ('64), which premiered the song "People," among others.

Merry Macs Ted McMichael (baritone; 1908–2001), Joe McMichael (tenor; 1916–1944), Judd McMichael (tenor; 1906–1989), Cheri McKay (melody). The Merry Macs consisted of three brothers and one female. They began performing in the early '30s but did not reach prominence until the late '30s and early '40s. The female member changed during the early '40s. Their most popular recording was "Mairzy Doats" (see '44). The Merry Macs ranked as the No. 39 top recording artists of the '40s. The Merry Macs were inducted into the Vocal Group Hall of Fame in 2003.

Billy Merson Billy Merson was a popular British performer and songwriter of the music hall era. He gained considerable fame on the variety, pantomime and musical comedy stage and in '15 started making two and three-reel comedies for Homeland Productions. *Billy Merson Singing Desdemona* has been described as Britain's first sound film. Merson is now credited with writing the Al Jolson hit "The Spaniard That Blighted My Life" (see '13). He had accused Jolson of plagiarising the song after he had introduced it in a London music hall in '11.

Jack Meskill (1897–1973) Jack Meskill was co-lyricist of "Smile, Darn Ya, Smile" (see '31). Meskill also wrote "There's Danger in Your Eyes, Cherie" (see '30).

Georges Metaxa (1899–1950) Romanian Georges Metaxa and Libby Holman introduced "You and the Night and the Music" in the musical *Revenge with Music* (see '35).

Mayo Methot (1904–1951) Mayo Methot introduced "More Than You Know" in the Broadway musical *Great Day* (see '29). Methot played the second lead or the other woman in several films of the '30s and '40s.

George Meyer (1884–1959) George Meyer composed several popular songs and a few hits from '09 through the '40s. After high school, Meyer worked as an accountant for some Boston department stores. In the mid-'20s, he moved to New York City and became a song plugger for music publishers. In '14, Meyer was a charter member of ASCAP, and served as a director on two separate occasions. Meyer collaborated with Sam Lewis, Joe Young, Grant Clarke, Roy Turk, Arthur Johnston, Al Bryan, Edgar Leslie, E. Ray Goetz, Pete Wendling, Abel Baer and Stanley Adams. A few of his best-known songs are "When You're a Long, Long Way from Home" (see '14), "Where Did Robinson Crusoe Go with Friday on Saturday Night?" (see '16), "For Me and My Gal" (see '17), "Tuck Me to Sleep in My Old 'Tucky Home" (see '22), and "There Are Such Things" (see '43). George Meyer has been a member of the Songwriters' Hall of Fame since '70. At http://www.songwritershalloffame.org/exhibit_audio_video.asp?exhibitId=302 you can hear an audio clip of Meyer's "Tuck Me to Sleep in My Old 'Tucky Home" performed by Vernon Dalhart.

Joseph Meyer (1894–1987) During his early teen years, Joseph Meyer was sent to Paris to study violin for a year. After graduating from high school in San Francisco, Meyer worked in a San Francisco café entertaining patrons with his violin. After serving in the army during World War I, Meyer worked in a mercantile business. His songwriting career started in the early '20s, when he abandoned the retail business and moved to New York City. Meyer's first songwriting success came in '22. In collaboration with lyricist Harry Ruby, they wrote "My Honey's Lovin' Arms." Meyer worked with lyricist Buddy DeSylva to produce "California, Here I Come" (see '24). Meyer contributed songs to several Broadway scores, including *Big Boy, Charlot's Revue of 1925, Ziegfeld Follies of 1934* and *New Faces of 1936*. He also contributed to several film scores including *George White's Scandals of 1935*. Meyer worked with such renowned lyricists as Buddy DeSylva, Billy Rose, Ira Gershwin, Irving Caesar, Jack Yellen, Harry Ruby, Yip Harburg, Frank Loesser, Eddie De Lange, Al

Dubin, Al Jacobs, Carl Sigman and Bob Russell. In addition to the songs mentioned above, Meyer's song catalog includes "If You Knew Susie" (see '25), and "A Cup of Coffee, a Sandwich and You" (see '26), among others. The Songwriters' Hall of Fame honored Meyer with membership in '72.

Billy Meyers Billy Meyers was co-composer with Elmer Schoebel for "Nobody's Sweetheart" (see '24) and was a co-writer of "Bugle Call Rag" in '23 (see '32 when it was most popular).

Sherman Meyers Sherman Meyers was the composer of "Moonlight on the Ganges" (see '26).

Ray Middleton (real name: Raymond Earl Middleton, Jr.; 1907–1984) Ray Middleton is most famous for his portrayal of Frank Butler in the Broadway musical *Annie Get Your Gun*. He introduced "The Girl That I Marry," "They Say It's Wonderful," "Anything You Can Do" with Ethel Merman and "There's No Business Like Show Business" with several others from the cast. He also introduced "Here I'll Stay" in the Broadway musical *Love Life*.

A.H. Miles The lyricist of "Anchors Aweigh" (see '06), A. H. Miles, graduated from the Naval Academy in '07 and later served as the chapel choir director.

Bob Miller (1892–1955) Bob Miller was the record producer of "There's a Star-Spangled Banner Waving Somewhere" (see '43). He was a co-writer of the song under the name Shelby Darnell.

Glenn Miller (1904–1944) Glenn Miller became one of the most famous bandleaders of the big band era. His forte was arranging, and his unique clarinet-lead sound became what the public wanted to hear in the last years of the '30s and into the '40s. He also exerted a great influence on the popular music of the late war years by directing an air force band and broadcasting on radio in the United States and Great Britain. The band was headquartered in England. In '44, on a trip from England to Paris, the plane disappeared over the English Channel. His band continued to perform under the leadership of some of the other members of the band. Miller's most productive period of hit recordings was the years '39 through '43. Miller's biggest hit recordings were "Over the Rainbow" (see '39), "Moon Love" (see '39), "Wishing" (see '39), "Stairway to the Stars" (see '39), "The Man with the Mandolin" (see '39), "Blue Orchids" (see '39), his biggest hit "In the Mood" (see '40), "Careless" (see '40), "When You Wish Upon a Star" (see '40), "Tuxedo Junction" (see '40), "The Woodpecker Song" (see '40), "Imagination" (see '40), "Fools Rush in" (see '40), "Blueberry Hill" (see '40), "Chattanooga Choo Choo" (see '41), "Elmer's Tune" (see '41), "Song of the Volga Boatmen" (see '41), "You and I" (see '41), "Moonlight Cocktail" (see '42), "Don't Sit Under the Apple Tree" (see '42), "(I've Got a Gal in) Kalamazoo" (see '42), "A String of Pearls" (see '42) and "That Old Black Magic" (see '43). Miller was the composer of his theme song, "Moonlight Serenade" (see '39). Miller and his orchestra appeared in several films, most notably *Sun Valley Serenade* ('41) and *Orchestra Wives* ('42). Miller was one of the first inductees into the Big Band/Jazz Hall of Fame in '78. Glenn was inducted into the Popular Music Hall of Fame in 2001. Miller and his orchestra were the No. 11 top recording artists of the '30s and No. 2 for the 40s,

qualifying them as the No. 11 top recording artists of the first half of the 20th Century.

Marilyn Miller (real name: Mary Ellen Reynolds; 1898–1936) Marilyn Miller became probably the most popular singer and actress of the Broadway stage of the '20s. She began touring in vaudeville with her parents and toured the country for several years. She then performed in New York revues and graduated to musical comedy stardom in *Sally* (see "Look for the Silver Lining" in '21). She also had success in *Sunny* (see "Who?" in '26), *Rosalie* ('28) and *As Thousands Cheer* (see "Easter Parade" in '33). Ms. Miller and Paul Gregory introduced "Time on My Hands" in the Broadway musical *Smiles* (see '31).

Mitch Miller (real name: Mitchell William Miller; 1911–) Mitch Miller is probably best known for his *Sing Along with Mitch* albums and TV series in the late '50s and early '60s. Some of Miller's "sing-along" albums include *Sing Along with Mitch, Christmas Sing Along with Mitch, More Sing Along with Mitch, Still More Sing Along with Mitch, Party Sing Along with Mitch, Sentimental Sing Along with Mitch* and *Memories Sing Along with Mitch.* That "sing along" craze ran from the late couple of years of the '50s through the beginning of '60s. He became director of Mercury and later Columbia Records pop division. In that capacity he gave many new singers their starts, often conducting or producing their recording sessions. Miller and his orchestra accompanied Guy Mitchell on three hit recordings in '51 and '52. Miller's first success as a recording artist himself was "Tzena, Tzena, Tzena" (see '50), but his biggest success was the revival of the Civil War song "The Yellow Rose of Texas" (see '55).

Ray Miller Ray Miller was the leader of a popular '20s band. His band's most popular recording was of "I'll See You in My Dreams" (see '25).

The Mills Brothers Herbert (1912–1989), Harry (1913–1982), Donald (1915–1999). Three brothers from Piqua, Ohio, the Mills Brothers, were a very successful singing group from the early '30s through the '70s. At times an older brother, John, joined the group to play guitar or sing bass. The Mills Brothers' most productive time in the recording field was the early '30s through the early '50s. "Tiger Rag" (see '31) was their first big hit recording, but certainly not their last. Other big hits were "Dinah" with Bing Crosby (see '32), the hugely popular "Paper Doll" (see '43), "You Always Hurt the One You Love" (see '44) and the revival of '07's "The Glow-Worm" (see '52). The Mills Brothers became the No. 11 top recording artists of the '30s and No. 25 of the '40s, making them the No. 39 top-recording artists of the first half of the 20th Century. The Mills Brothers were inducted into the Popular Music Hall of Fame in 2002.

Irving Mills (real name: Frederick Allen Mills; 1894–1985) Lyricist Irving Mills was a very active songwriter in the '20s and '30s. In addition, he was a publisher (partner in Mills Music and at least four other companies), producer of movie musical shorts and radio shows, bandleader (Mills Blue Rhythm Band), manager for Duke Ellington for a time, and booster of many singers' recording careers, including those of Gene Austin and Rudy Vallee. Mills' songwriting credits include such lyrics as

"Mood Indigo" (see '31), "Minnie, the Moocher" (see '31) "It Don't Mean a Thing" (see '32), "Sophisticated Lady" (see '33), "Moonglow" (see '34), "I Let a Song Go Out of My Heart" (see '38), among others. Some '28–'30 recordings by Irving Mills' Hotsy-Totsy Gang and Irving Mills' Modernists are available for listening at http://www.red hotjazz.com/bands.html.

Kerry Mills (1869–1948) Kerry Mills was an important composer of popular music the late 1890s to the late 1910s. His music ranges from rag to cakewalk to marches. Mills was trained as a violinist and became head of the Violin Department at the University of Michigan's School of Music. It was there that he began composing popular songs. Mills moved to New York City in 1895 where he started a music publishing company. Some of Mills most memorable songs include "Meet Me in St. Louis, Louis" (see '04), "Red Wing" (see '07), and "Any Old Port in a Storm" (see '08).

Meade Minnigerode (1887–1967) Meade Minnigerode was a member of the '10 Yale class. He co-wrote the lyrics of "The Whiffenpoof Song" (see '09).

Issachar Miron (real name: Stefan Michrovsky; 1920–) Issachar Miron was a co-writer of "Tzena, Tzena, Tzena" (see '50). Yehiel Haggiz, a friend of Issachar Miron, was 30 years old and Miron was 19 years old when they wrote the tune to this song. American folksinger Pete Seeger helped Haggiz and Miron develop the song into what became the '50 hit song. For more on Miron, see http://issacharmiron.com/bio.html.

Mistinguett (real name: Jeanne Florentine Bourgeois; 1875–1956) Jeanne aspired to be an entertainer at an early age. A songwriter made up the name Miss Tinguette, which Jeanne made it her own by joining the two words together and eventually dropping the second "s" and the final "e" (Mistinguett). She made her debut as Mistinguett at the Casino de Paris in 1895. Her risqué routines captivated her Parisian audiences. She became the most popular French entertainer of her era and one of the highest paid female entertainers in the world. Like Betty Grable during World War II, Mistinguett's legs were insured for the then astounding amount of 500,000 francs. She was famous, or infamous, for her torrid love affairs with a much younger Maurice Chevalier, an Indian Prince, King Alfonso XIII of Spain and the future King Edward VII of England. Mistinguett had made "Mon Homme" (My Man) a hit in France and had planned to use it in her American debut in the *Ziegfeld Follies of 1921*. Ziegfeld lost interest in her and dropped her from the show before it opened. Read more in '21.

Abbie Mitchell (1884–1960) Abbie Mitchell began her musical comedy career in 1898 in Will Marion Cook's *Clorindy*. She performed with the famous George Walker and Bert Williams company and in the Cole and Johnson musical *The Red Moon*. In '19, she toured Europe with Cook's Southern Syncopated Orchestra. When she returned to the U.S., she performed on the concert stage and in opera. She also taught. Her final stage appearance was in George Gershwin's folk opera *Porgy and Bess*, where she introduced "Summertime" (see '35).

Charles Mitchell Charles Mitchell collaborated with Jimmie Davis on "You Are My Sunshine" (see '41).

Guy Mitchell (real name: Al Cernik; 1927–1999) Guy Mitchell was born in Detroit, Michigan of Yugoslavian immigrant parents. At age eleven, he signed with Warner Bros. to be groomed as a child star, but his film career never amounted to much. He performed with Carmen Cavallaro and his orchestra in the late '40s, appeared on *Arthur Godfrey's Talent Scouts*, and signed a recording contract with Columbia Records in '50. Mitchell became one of the top hit makers of the early '50s. Mitchell's first recording success came with "My Heart Cries for You" (see '51) and "My Truly, Truly Fair." After a couple of not-quite-so-popular releases, he had the biggest success of his career with "Singing the Blues" in '56, followed in '59 by another No. 1 hit with "Heartaches by the Number." Guy Mitchell became the No. 10 top recording artist of the '50s.

Sidney Mitchell (1888–1942) Lyricist Sidney Mitchell wrote several popular song and a few big hits during the '20s and '30s. Mitchell and Louis Alter wrote "A Melody from the Sky" (see '36) and "You Turned the Tables on Me" (see '36). Mitchell and Sam Stept wrote "All My Life" (see '36).

Vic Mizzy (1916 or '22–) Vic Mizzy was the composer of "My Dreams Are Getting Better All the Time" (see '45). Mizzy also wrote the theme songs for *Green Acres* and *The Addams Family* television shows. And he wrote the film scores of *The Ghost and Mr. Chicken, The Reluctant Astronaut, The Shakiest Gun in the West, The Love God,* and *How to Frame a Figg,* all starring Don Knotts. For more, see http://www.vicmizzy.com/biography.html.

Modernaires Hal Dickinson (1911–1970), Chuck Goldstein, Bill Conway, Ralph Brewster. Hal Dickinson, the founder and leader of the Modernaires, sang with Fred Waring in the mid-'30s and first began to gain national attention when they performed and recorded with Charlie Barnet and his orchestra in '36. The Modernaires worked with Paul Whiteman, but became most famous as a prominent feature of Glenn Miller's band in the '40s. During their time with Miller, they were prominently heard on "Chattanooga Choo Choo" (see '41), "Elmer's Tune" (see '41), "Moonlight Cocktail" (see '42), "Don't Sit Under the Apple Tree" (see '42), "(I've Got a Gal in) Kalamazoo" (see '42), and "That Old Black Magic" (see '43). The group's only hit recording after their band years was "To Each His Own" (see '46). The group began as a trio, then a quartet and later became a quintet in the mid-'40s when Dickinson's wife, Paula Kelly, joined. Although the personnel changed several times, the group performed often in the '40s and '50s and occasionally in later years. The Modernaires were inducted into the Vocal Group Hall of Fame in '99.

Halsey K. Mohr Halsey K. Mohr wrote the music for "They're Wearing 'Em Higher in Hawaii" (see '17).

Edith Moller Edith Moller is listed as co-lyricist for the German words to "The Happy Wanderer" ("Der Frohliche Wanderer") (see '54). The song's composer, Friedrich Wilhelm Moller's sister, Edith, was the conductor of an amateur children's choir. Her choir won a choral festival in North Wales. The festival was broadcast and the group's singing of this song as an encore turned the song into an instant hit in the United Kingdom. Ms. Moller's amateur choir was turned into a group that toured internationally as Obernbirchen Children's Choir. They appeared twice on *The Ed Sullivan Show*.

Friedrich-Wilhelm Moller Friedrich-Wilhelm Moller is the composer of "The Happy Wanderer" ("Der Frohliche Wanderer") (see '54). Also see Edith Moller's biographical sketch above.

James V. Monaco (1885–1945) Composer James V. Monaco came to the U.S. from his native Italy. He wrote numerous popular songs over a period from '11 through the mid-'40s. At the age of 17, Jimmy began his music career as a pianist in cabaret clubs and eventually was hired as a nightclub entertainer on Coney Island. In '14, he became a charter member of ASCAP. With a contract with Paramount Studios, he moved to Hollywood in the mid-'30s. He wrote the scores for such films as *The Road to Singapore*, *Rhythm on the River*, *Stage Door Canteen*, *Pin-Up Girl* and *The Dolly Sisters*, among others. Monaco collaborated with several lyricists including Johnny Burke, Joe McCarthy, Mack Gordon, Edgar Leslie, Grant Clarke and Sidney Clare. Some of his most famous songs include "Row, Row, Row" (see '13), "You Made Me Love You" (see '13), "I've Got a Pocketful of Dreams" (see '38), "Only Forever" (see '40), "I'm Making Believe" (see '44), and "I Can't Begin to Tell You" (see '45). He wrote several songs for Bing Crosby movies in the '30s and '40s. Jimmy Monaco has been a member of the Songwriters' Hall of Fame since '70.

Vaughn Monroe (1911–1973) Singer/bandleader Vaughn Monroe began his musical career as a trumpeter with Austin Wylie's orchestra. Monroe organized his own band in '40 and was leader and vocalist. After '53 he was strictly a soloist. His greatest period of popularity was from the mid-'40s into the early years of rock 'n' roll. By the late '50s he had dropped out of the music business. He returned again in the '60s and was semi-active until his death. Monroe's most popular recordings were "There I Go" (see '41), "When the Lights Go on Again" (see '42), "My Devotion" (see '42), "Let's Get Lost" (see '43), "There! I've Said It Again" (see '45), "Let It Snow! Let It Snow! Let It Snow!" (see '46), "Ballerina" (see '47), "Riders in the Sky" (see '49), and "Someday" (see '49). Vaughn Monroe became the No. 11 top recording artist of the '40s, No. 40 for the first half of the 20th Century. Vaughn Monroe sang "Mule Train" in the movie *Singing Guns* in '50. Even though it was not specifically written for the film, the song was nominated for the Academy Award for best song from film, but lost to "Mona Lisa."

Ricardo Montalban (real name: Ricardo Gonzalo Pedro Matalban y Merino; 1920–) Mexican native Ricardo Montalban is most famous as a movie and television star, but he did sing "Baby, It's Cold Outside" (see '49) in *Neptune's Daughter* with Esther Williams. He also starred in the Broadway musicals *Seventh Heaven* ('55) and *Jamaica* ('57), plus the movie musicals *Fiesta* ('47), *On an Island with You* ('48) and *Two Weeks with Love* ('50). In more recent years, he starred in the television series *Fantasy Island*.

Dave Montgomery (1870–1917) Comedian Dave Montgomery teamed with Fred Stone in 1894. This comedy team scored their biggest successes in *The Wizard of Oz* (see '03) and *The Red Mill* (see '06). Montgomery and Stone also starred in the musical *Chin-Chin* (see '15).

Art Mooney (1911–1993) Bandleader Art Mooney sprang to popularity with his recording of "I'm Looking Over a Four Leaf Clover" (see '48). With that success, he continued to revive oldies: '26's "Baby Face" and '34's "Bluebird of Happiness." By the late '50s Mooney's popularity had declined. Mooney's band also accompanied Barry Gordon in "Nuttin' for Christmas" ('55), which has remained a holiday staple.

Moonglows Bobby Lester (real name: Robert L. Dallas; 1930–1980), Harvey Fuqua (1929–), Alexander "Pete Graves" Walton (1936–), Prentiss Barnes (1925–). The Moonglows were a very influential rhythm and blues group from Cleveland, Ohio. They were originally called the Crazy Sounds, then the Moonlighters, before they were renamed by rock 'n' roll legendary DJ Alan Freed. They began recording on Chance Records, before moving to Chess Records, where they had their first hit, "Sincerely" (see '55). Later Fuqua fired all of the original group and hired a group known as The Marquees, made up of Marvin Gaye, Reese Palmer, Chester Simmons, and James Knowland to be the new Moonglows. Eventually, Fuqua became Marvin Gaye's manager for his solo career. The group was inducted into the Vocal Group Hall of Fame in '99.

Grace Moore (1901–1947) Singer Grace Moore starred in Broadway musicals during the '20s, in movie musicals and on radio in the '30s. She also sang with New York City's Metropolitan Opera from '28 to '31. On Broadway, she introduced Irving Berlin's "What'll I Do?" in *Music Box Revue of 1923* and Berlin's "All Alone" in the *Music Box Revue of 1924*. By the '40s her popularity peak had passed, but she remained active until her death in an airplane crash. Ms. Moore portrayed the life of the "Swedish Nightingale," Jenny Lind, in the '30 movie musical *A Lady's Morals*; she also starred in the '30 movie version of Sigmund Romberg's *New Moon*. She was nominated for the Best Actress Oscar for *One Night of Love* (see '34). She followed the success of '34 with *Love Me Forever* ('35). In '36, she starred in *The King Steps Out*, followed in '37 by *When You're in Love* and *I'll Take Romance*. The '53 movie *So This Is Love* was based on Moore's life. Grace Moore's only hit recording was "One Night of Love" (see '34) from the film of the same name.

John Charles Moore John Charles Moore was one of the co-writers of "Has Anybody Here Seen Kelly?" (see '10).

Phil Moore (1918–1987) Phil Moore played piano with several West Coast bands in the early part of his music career. In the early '40s he went to work for MGM studios, then transferred to New York City to be the music director for Mildred Bailey's radio show. He formed a small combo and appeared in a few films. Back in Hollywood, he backed many famous singers. He also founded the Singers Workshop to help aspiring young singers. His most famous contribution to the popular song market was "Shoo-Shoo Baby" (see '44).

Victor Moore (1876–1962) Victor Moore was a star of stage and screen. He appeared in over 58 films and 21 Broadway shows. Stanley Green in *Encyclopedia of the Musical Theatre* described Moore as "this potato dumpling of a man with the bleating voice and befuddled manner was the most endearing clown on the Broadway musical stage."

He first appeared on Broadway in *Rosemary* (1896). He also appeared in George M. Cohan's *Forty-five Minutes from Broadway*, and its sequel, *The Talk of New York*. He went on to star in such great Broadway musicals as Gershwin's *Oh, Kay!*, *Of Thee I Sing*, *Let 'Em Eat Cake*, Cole Porter's *Anything Goes!* and Irving Berlin's *Louisiana Purchase*. In his first Broadway musical, Moore introduced the title song from *Forty-five Minutes from Broadway* (see '06). Moore and his first wife, Emma Littlefield, toured the vaudeville circuit for many years. He also appeared in Hollywood films such as *Swing Time* with Fred Astaire and Ginger Rogers, *Make Way for Tomorrow*, the film version of *Louisiana Purchase* and *Ziegfeld Follies*. Moore did not announce his second marriage to Shirley Paige until they had been married for a year and a half. At the time of the announcement, he was 67 and she was 22.

Ed Moran Ed Moran was co-lyricist with Andrew B. Sterling for "I Sent My Wife to the Thousand Isles" (see '16). In such cases, it makes one wonder if the unknown, Moran, took his idea to the established songwriter, Andrew B. Sterling, who polished the lyric before it was published. There is no evidence that suggests such, but it makes one ponder.

Lois Moran (real name: Lois Darlington Dowling; 1909–1990) Lois Dowling trained as a dancer and at age 10 moved to Paris with her mother to study dance. She danced and sang at the Paris National Opera. She also appeared in a couple of French silent films. In '25, she made her Hollywood debut in *Stella Dallas*. She appeared in several early talkies, including *Words and Music* ('29) and *Mammy* ('30) with Al Jolson. In the early '30s, she took on Broadway. She and William Gaxton introduced the title song of the Broadway musical *Of Thee I Sing* (see '32). When she married Clarence Young, Assistant Secretary of Commerce, in '35, she retired. She appeared in the TV series *Waterfront* in the mid-'50s.

Jim Morehead Jim Morehead was the composer of "Sentimental Me" (see '50). "Sentimental Me" was first popularized by Ben Selvin and his orchestra and by the Arden-Ohman Orchestra in '25 and '26 respectively, but it was revived into popularity by the Ames Brothers

Neil Moret (real name: Charles N. Daniels; 1878–1943) In '04, composer Neil Moret co-founded Daniels & Russell Publishing Company in St. Louis and in the 1910s became an executive at Remick Music Company. He formed his own firm in '13 and from the mid-'20s until the early '30s, served as the president of Villa Moret, Inc. in San Francisco. Back in the 1890s, when Charles Daniels started his songwriting career by writing a march for John Philip Sousa, it was fashionable for composers to adopt European names, preferably French ones. So Daniels dubbed himself Moret. As a songwriter, Moret worked with the legendary lyricists as Gus Kahn, Richard Whiting, Harry Tobias, Gus Arnheim, Edwin Lemare and Ben Black. Moret's songs include "Hiawatha" (see '03), "Moonlight and Roses" (see '25), and "Chloe" (see '28). Other well known Moret songs include "You Tell Me Your Dreams, I'll Tell You Mine," "On Mobile Bay," "She's Funny That Way," "Sweet and Lovely" and "Peggy." Neil Moret has been a member of the Songwriters' Hall of Fame since '70.

Larry Morey Larry Morey was the lyricist of the songs from Disney's Snow White and the Seven Dwarfs, particularly including "Whistle While You Work," "One Song," and "Some Day My Prince Will Come" (see '38). Morey also wrote songs for *Bambi* and *The Reluctant Dragon*.

Carey Morgan Carey Morgan composed the music for "My Own Iona" (see '17). He also co-wrote the words and music for "Blues (My Naughty Sweetie Gives to Me)" (see '20).

Corrine Morgan (real name: Corrine Morgan Welsh; circa 1875–1945) Corrine Morgan is most remembered for her duet recordings with the Haydn Quartet and Frank Stanley. Her best known recordings include "Toyland" from *Babes in Toyland* with the Haydn Quartet (see '04), "Dearie" with Frank Stanley (see '05), "How'd You Like to Spoon with Me?" with the Haydn Quartet (see '06) and "So Long, Mary" from *Forty-five Minutes from Broadway* (see '06).

Dennis Morgan (real name: Earl Stanley Morner; 1908–1994) Dennis Morgan, Jack Carson and Martha Vickers introduced "A Gal in Calico" in the movie musical *The Time, the Place and the Girl* (see '46). Morgan began his Hollywood career as a bit player, but he eventually starred in several films, including *Kitty Foyle*, *My Wild Irish Rose*, *God Is My Co-Pilot*, *The Very Thought of You*, *Two Guys from Milwaukee*, *Two Guys from Texas* and *It's a Great Feeling*. He appeared with Jack Carson in several films. After retiring in the late '50s, Morgan appeared in a few cameo roles.

Helen Morgan (1900–1941) Torch singer Helen Morgan was immortalized in the '57 movie *The Helen Morgan Story*, which starred Ann Blyth (Gogi Grant did the singing for Blyth). Morgan was particularly popular as a singer in the '20s and '30s. Her Broadway debut was in the '25 edition of *George White's Scandals*, but by far her most important role was as Julie La Verne in the '27 and '32 productions of *Show Boat*. Ms. Morgan introduced "I've Got a Feeling I'm Falling" in the movie musical *Applause* (see '29). She introduced "Why Was I Born?" in the musical *Sweet Adeline* (see '29). In the late '20s she opened a nightclub, the House of Morgan. She continued to perform through the mid-'30s, appearing in several movies and on radio. By far her most famous recording was of "Bill" from *Show Boat*.

Russ Morgan (1904–1969) Bandleader Russ Morgan led a very popular band in the '30s and '40s and also composed several songs that it helped popularize. Morgan's first jobs in music were as a pianist in local clubs around his hometown (Scranton, Pennsylvania). Then he became well known as an arranger from some of the best-known big bands. With the aid of Rudy Vallee, Morgan formed his own band in the mid-'30s, using the slogan "Music in the Morgan Manner." His group appeared often on radio in the late '30s. Morgan's best known songs are "Somebody Else Is Taking My Place" (see '42) and "You're Nobody 'Till Somebody Loves You," popularized by Dean Martin in the '50s. Morgan's most popular recordings were "The Merry-Go-Round Broke Down" (see '37), "I've Got a Pocketful of Dreams" (see '38), "Cruising Down the River" (see '49) and "Forever and Ever" (see '49). Russ Morgan became the No. 17 top recording artist of the '30s and No. 19 of the '40s. Morgan continued to lead the band on a part-time basis in the '50s and '60s.

Victor Morley (circa 1871–1953) Victor Morley and Georgia Caine introduced Jerome Kern's "How'd You Like to Spoon with Me?" in *The Earl and the Girl* (see '05). Morley later became a director.

Joe Morrison (1908–?) Joe Morrison introduced "The Last Round-up" at the Paramount Theater in New York City (see '33).

Doretta Morrow (1927–1968) Doretta Morrow and Byron Palmer introduced "My Darling, My Darling" in the musical *Where's Charley?* (see '49). Ms. Morrow was the original Tuptim in *The King and I*, where she introduced "We Kiss in a Shadow" (see '51) and Marsinah in *Kismet*, where she and Richard Kiley introduced "Stranger in Paradise" (see '54). Ms. Morrow made only one film, *Because You're Mine* ('52), starring opposite Mario Lanza.

Dolly Morse (see Dorothy Terriss)

Theodore F. Morse (1873–1924) As a boy, Theodore Morse studied both the piano and violin. During his mid-teens, he left the military academy he attended for New York City. There he worked in a Harlem music shop and later as a salesman for the Oliver Ditson Music Company. He also began writing songs. His first published song, "Good-Bye Dolly Gray," came in 1897. It was written with Will D. Cobb and Paul Barnes and was published by his own company, Morse Music. When his company folded, Morse took a job with Howley, Haviland and Dresser, working as a pianist, composer and arranger. He became its principal composer and a full partner in the firm. In '14, he became a charter member of the performing rights society, ASCAP. Morse collaborated with several lyricists on the Alley, chiefly Edward Madden, Richard Buck, Howard Johnson, Al Bryan, Jack Mahoney and his wife, Theodora Morse. Morse co-wrote such well-known songs as "Dear Old Girl" (see '04), "Hurrah for Baffin's Bay" (see '03), "Blue Bell" (see '04), "Good Old U.S.A." (see '06), "Nobody's Little Girl" (see '07), and "M-O-T-H-E-R (a Word That Means the World to Me)" (see '16). Theodore Morse was an original member of the Songwriters' Hall of Fame in '70.

Ted Mossman Ted Mossman adapted Frederick Chopin's melody from "Polonaise in A Flat Major" into "Till the End of Time" (see '45).

Moya (real name: Harold Vicars; ?–1922) Moya was the composer of the music for "Song of Songs" (see '15). W. Maurice Vaucaire wrote the French words, while Clarence Lucas furnished the English version. Vicars was a pianist and conductor.

Gus Mueller (real name: Gustave Mueller; 1890–1965) Gus Mueller was co-lyricist with Buster Johnson on "Wang Wang Blues" (see '21). Mueller was a jazz clarinetist in Papa Jack Laine's band in New Orleans and later in Chicago. After serving in the Army in World War I, he moved to California, then joined Paul Whiteman's band. Some of Mueller's New Orleans contemporaries said "Wang Wang Blues" was all Mueller's. Mueller returned to California to play in the Abe Lyman Orchestra and stayed in the state where he worked in various bands and on film soundtracks. He retired after World War II.

Lewis F. Muir (1884–1950) Composer Lewis F. Muir began his career as a popular ragtime pianist in St. Louis saloons. After moving to New York City in '10, he began collaborating with lyricists. His first published song was "Play That Barbershop Chord." Collaborating with William Tracey, Edgar Leslie, Maurice Abrams and especially L. Wolfe Gilbert, Muir wrote such famous songs as "Ragging the Baby to Sleep," "Waiting for the Robert E. Lee," "Here Comes My Daddy Now (Oh Pop — Oh Pop — Oh Pop)," "Ragtime Cowboy Joe" and "Hitchy-Koo" (see '13). Lewis Muir was an original member of the Songwriters' Hall of Fame in '70. At http://www.songwritershalloffame.org/exhibit_audio_video.asp?exhibitId=248 you can hear an audio clip of Muir's "Waiting for the Robert E. Lee" performed by the Heidelberg Quintet.

Bill Munro Bill Munro's chief claim to fame in the popular music arena is as composer of "When My Baby Smiles at Me" (see '20).

C.W. Murphy (1875–1913) London-born songwriter, C.W. Murphy had several London hit songs, but his most famous song in the U.S. is probably "Kelly from the Isle of Man," which is most commonly known as "Has Anyone Here Seen Kelly?" (see '10).

George Murphy (1902–1992) George Murphy left college to become a dancer. He and his dance partner, Julie Johnson, who became his wife, performed on Broadway for several years. After his wife retired from show business, he became a Hollywood actor. He made 45 films. Murphy, June O'Dea and the chorus introduced "Love Is Sweeping the Country" in *Of Thee I Sing* (see '32). Murphy and Alice Faye introduced "You're a Sweetheart" in the movie musical of the same name (see '38). Murphy retired from films in '52, became a TV producer and in '64 was elected a Senator from California. He served for six terms.

Lambert Murphy (1885–1954) Lambert Murphy was a member of the Orpheus Quartet and was a tenor with the Metropolitan Opera Company. As a soloist, some of his most well known recordings include "Goodbye, Girls, I'm Through" (see '15) and "Roses of Picardy" (see '18). Lambert recorded for Victor.

Stanley Murphy (1875–1919) Stanley Murphy was a popular song lyricist who collaborated chiefly with Percy Wenrich, also with Albert Von Tilzer. He wrote or co-wrote the words for "Put on Your Old Grey Bonnet" (see '09), "Be My Little Baby Bumble Bee" (see '12), "Oh! How She Could Yacki Hacki Wicki Wachi Woo" (see '16) and "Daddy Has a Sweetheart (and Mother Is Her Name)," which was popularized in '20. He also contributed lyrics for some songs in the *Ziegfeld Follies of 1911*.

Billy Murray (real name: William Thomas Murray; 1877–1954) Billy Murray became one of the most popular singers in the U.S. during the early decades of the 20th century. Early in his career he worked in minstrel shows as a singer and eccentric dancer. From '03 until the early '30s he was primarily a recording artist. He made over 5000 recordings during his recording career. In addition to his solo efforts, he often recorded duets with Ada Jones, plus occasionally with Aileen Stanley. He also recorded with the Haydn Quartet, the Premier Quartet, and the American Quartet. Murray recorded his last side in '43 before retiring in '44. Murray was the top recording artist of the first decade of the 20th century, and number six of the second decade. He was still popular enough during the '20s to be one of the top thirty. He is the number two artist, behind Bing Crosby, of the first half of the 20th century. Murray's most well-known recordings were "Bedelia" (see '04), "Navajo" (see '04), "Meet Me in St. Louis, Louis" (see '04), "Alexander" (see '04), "Come Take a Trip in My Airship" (see '05), "Yankee Doodle Boy" (see '05), "Give My Regards to Broadway" (see '05), "In My Merry Oldsmobile" (see '05), Everybody Works but Father" (see '05), "The Grand Old Flag" (see '06), "Harrigan" (see '07), "Let's Take an Old-Fashioned Walk" (see '07) with Ada Jones, "Under Any Old Flag at All" (see '08), "Take Me Out to the Ball Game" (see '08), "Would You Like to Have Me for a Sweetheart" (see '08) with Ada Jones, "When We Are M-A-DOUBLE-R-I-E-D" (see '08) with Ada Jones, "Cuddle Up a Little Closer, Lovey Mine" (see '08) with Ada Jones, "Shine on, Harvest Moon" (see '09) with Ada Jones, "Carrie (Carrie Marry Harry)" (see '10), "By the Light of the Silvery Moon" with the Haydn Quartet see '10, "Be My Little Baby Bumble Bee" (see '12) with Ada Jones, "I Love a Piano" (see '16), "Pretty Baby" (see '16) and "That Old Gang of Mine" with Victor Roberts (see '23).

J. Harold Murray (1891–1940) During the late '20s and early '30s, J. Harold Murray was very active in vaudeville, operetta and Broadway musicals. His Broadway debut was in *The Passing Show of 1921*. One of his major successes came when he introduced the title song and "The Rangers' Song" in the musical *Rio Rita* (see '27). In '29 and '30, he appeared in five movie musicals. He returned to Broadway in '31 and starred in Irving Berlin's *Face the Music* in '32. He retired from the stage in '35, but appeared in a few musical film shorts during the late '30s.

Clarence Muse (1889–1979) Clarence Muse was co-writer with Leon and Otis Rene of "Sleepy Time Down South" (see '31). Muse sang in opera, was a minstrel performer and a vaudeville actor. He became the first African American film star, according to http://www.imdb.com. Muse held a law degree from Dickerson University in Pennsylvania. He fought demeaning stereotypes of African Americans in entertainment for most his career. Ironically, however, he was a supporter of the controversial radio and television series *Amos 'n' Andy*. He felt the series allowed black actors to portray roles such as doctors, bankers, judges and professors, which was not generally done in other series.

James E. Myers (1919–2001) James E. Myers co-wrote "Rock Around the Clock" using the pen name Jimmy DeKnight (see '55). There's debate over whether Myers really helped write the song. Myers was a composer, producer, musician and actor. In later years, Myers operated a Rock Around the Clock Museum out of his home.

J.W. Myers (circa 1869–1919) Welshman John W. Myers became one of the foremost baritone ballad singers of the first decade of the 20th Century, as well as a successful theatrical manager. Myers became the No. 9 recording artist of the first decade of the 20th Century and No. 35 for the entire first half of that century. Some of Myers' most popular recordings include "In the Shade of the Palm" (see '01), "On a Sunday Afternoon" (see '02), "Way Down in Old Indiana" (see '02) and "In the Good Old Summer Time" (see '02).

Josef Myrow (1910–1987) Josef (or Joseph) Myrow

wrote a few well-known songs. He also wrote for a few Hollywood films. Myrow's most famous songs include "You Do" (see '47) and "You Make Me Feel So Young." His son, Fredric, was also a composer and wrote for some Hollywood projects.

Johnny Napton Johnny Napton was co-writer of "My Devotion" (see '42). Napton played trumpet for Jimmy Dorsey's orchestra.

C. Naset C. Naset was co-lyricist with Frank Magine for "Dreamy Melody" (see '23).

Ogden Nash (real name: Frederick Ogden Nash; 1902–1971) Ogden Nash was one of America's famous poets. His first book, a children's book, *The Cricket of Caradon*, was published in '25. His first published poem appeared in the *New Yorker* magazine in '30; he joined the staff of that magazine in '32. Nineteen books of his poetry were published. His only important incursion into the music field came when he wrote the lyrics for and was co-librettist for the musical comedy *One Touch of Venus*, which included the hit song "Speak Low" (see '44). It was not his only venture on Broadway, however. He teamed with Vernon Duke on *Two's Company* ('52) and *The Littlest Revue* ('56).

May Naudain May Naudain introduced "The Glow Worm" to U.S. audiences in the musical *The Girl Behind the Counter* (see '08). The song had been written by Paul Lincke for the operetta *Lysistrata* in '02.

Al J. Neiburg (1902–?) Al J. Neiburg was co-lyricist of "It's the Talk of the Town" (see '33). He also wrote "I'm Confessin' (That I Love You)" and "Under a Blanket of Blue." Neiburg later ran his own publishing company.

Ed. G. Nelson Ed. G. Nelson was co-writer on "Peggy O'Neil" (see '21) and co-composer on "Ten Little Fingers and Ten Little Toes — Down in Tennessee" (see '22).

Ozzie Nelson (real name: Oswald George Nelson; 1906–1975) Ozzie Nelson recorded his first sides for Brunswick in '30 and his band was active until the early '40s. Ozzie was vocalist on many of the band's recordings, but so was Harriet Hilliard, his future wife, who joined the band in '32. Harriet Hilliard (see Ms. Hilliard's biographical sketch) married Ozzie in '35. Ozzie's most popular recording was "And Then Some" (see '35). Ozzie and Harriet became very famous on radio and television with their long-running sitcom-type show. Their show began on radio in '44 and switched to TV in '52, where it ran until '66. Their sons, David and Ricky Nelson, grew up on the show.

Henry Nemo (1907–1999) Henry Nemo was a songwriter and a Hollywood actor. Nemo was so "hip," he is often referred to as the "creator of jive talk." During the '30s, he was a Cotton Club fixture. It was there, with Duke Ellington, and others, he wrote "I Let a Song Go Out of My Heart" (see '38).

Ethelbert Nevin (real name: Ethelbert Woodbridge Nevin; 1862–1901) Composer Ethelbert Nevin began his professional career as a pianist and teacher in Pittsburgh and had his concert debut in 1886. At first, Nevin wrote mainly serious works for orchestra or piano solo, but he also experienced popular success with the "The Rosary" and "Mighty Lak' a Rose" (see both songs in '03). Ethelbert Nevin was an original member of the Songwriters' Hall of Fame in '70. At http://www.song writershalloffame.org/exhibit_audio_video.asp? exhibitId=304 you can hear audio clips of Nevin's "The Rosary" performed by Dame Clara Butt and "Mighty Lak' a Rose" performed by Paul Robeson.

New Orleans Rhythm Kings Leon Roppolo (clarinetist; 1902–1943), Paul Mares (leader/cornetist; 1900–1949), George Brunies (trombonist; 1902–1974), Benny Pollack (drummer and future bandleader; 1903–1971), Mel Stitzel (pianist). The New Orleans Rhythm Kings were one of the most influential jazz bands of the early to mid-'20s. The band had a New Orleans and a Chicago contingent. This white band has served as proof that African Americans were not the only ones who could play jazz with individuality and integrity. Mares, Brunies and Roppolo had been childhood friends from New Orleans. Future bandleader Ben Pollack joined the group as drummer early in the band's development. The New Orleans Rhythm Kings are credited as composers of "Make Love to Me" (see '54). The song began in '23 as "Tin Roof Blues," written by five players in the New Orleans Rhythm Kings plus Walter Melrose, a composer, author, and publisher during the '20s. Melrose wrote the original, more risqué, lyrics, but Bill Norvas and Allan Copeland contributed the present version in '53. The band broke up in '24.

Charles Newman (1901–1978) Charles Newman was a songwriter/composer, short story author, and musical director for films. He contributed the lyrics for "Sweethearts on Parade" (see '29) and "Let's Swing It" (see '35).

Lionel Newman (1916–1981) Composer Lionel Newman was a noted arranger and musical director for Hollywood films from the late '30s through the '50s. His brothers, Alfred and Charles, were also involved in the film industry. One of his best-known contributions to popular music was the song "Again" (see '49), which was introduced by Ida Lupino in the '48 film *Road House*.

Eddie Newton (real name: Eddie Walter Newton; 1869–1915) Eddie Newton was a ragtime pianist in Venice Beach, California when he met T. Lawrence Seibert a vaudeville entertainer who had written a sketch based on the tragic tale of Casey Jones, the brave engineer. Together they supposedly wrote the song "Casey Jones" (see '10), with Eddie composing the music and Tallifero supplying the lyrics. However, Wallace Saunders, an African American engine wiper, reportedly wrote the first poetic verses about Casey Jones. Then Wallace made up a catchy little tune for the verses. The song was picked up by other railroad men and was spread from station to station. Legend has it that one of the railroad men shared it with his brothers who were vaudeville performers. They reworked the lyrics and added a chorus. They began performing the song on the vaudeville circuit. The popularity of the song on the vaudeville circuit helped Casey Jones become a folk hero. When the song was published, T. Lawarence Seibert was credited as the composer and Eddie Newton as the lyricist.

Eileen Newton Poet Eileen Newton's contribution to popular music was as lyricist for "Somewhere a Voice Is Calling" (see '16).

Harold Nicholas (1921–2000) Harold Nicholas and Ruby Hill introduced "Come Rain or Come Shine" in the musical *St. Louis Woman* (see '46). Harold was the younger half of the famous Nicholas Brothers dance team. They appeared in several extraordinary dance sequences in films, including *Down Argentine Way, Tin-Pan-Alley, The Great American Broadcast, Sun Valley Serenade*, in which they helped introduce "Chattanooga Choo Choo," *Orchestra Wives* and *The Pirate*. Harold and his brother, Fayard, taught dance to Debbie Allen, Janet Jackson and Michael Jackson, among others.

Horatio Nicholls (1888–1964) Horatio Nicholls collaborated with Edgar Leslie to write "Among My Souvenirs" (see '28).

Alberta Nichols Alberta Nichols was co-composer with Saul Chaplin of "Until the Real Thing Comes Along" (see '36).

Red Nichols (real name: Ernest Loring Nichols; 1905–1965) Cornetist Red Nichols and his Five Pennies were one of the most popular and one of the most recorded jazz bands of the '20s. They actually recorded under several different names: Miff Mole and His Little Molers, the Hottentots, the Charleston Chasers, the Red Heads, the Louisiana Rhythm Kings, and the Arkansas Travelers. Red had studied cornet with his father, who was a college music professor. His cornet playing was influenced by Bix Beidebecke, which fit his Dixieland style. Some of his sidemen at various times included Jimmy Dorsey, Joe Venuti, Eddie Lang, and Pee Wee Russell. Once the swing style became popular in the mid-'30s, Red formed a big band, but his first love remained Dixieland. On the pop charts, Red's only really popular recording was "Ida! Sweet as Apple Cider" (see '27). Red was elected to the Big Band/Jazz Hall of Fame in '86. Red and his band were the No. 40 top recording artists of the '20s. In '59, Hollywood made a fact and fantasy movie about the band, *The Five Pennies*, which starred Danny Kaye as Red Nichols. Recordings between '27 and '39 by Red Nichols (Red Nichols and his Five Pennies, Red Nichols and his orchestra and Red Nichols' Stompers) are available for listening at http://www.redhotjazz.com/bands.html.

Alice Nielsen (1877–1943) Alice Nielsen sang with the Metropolitan Opera from '09 to '13. Her Columbia recording of the 1823 song "Home, Sweet Home" was very popular (see '15).

Ray Noble (1903–1978) Ray Noble was the first British bandleader to become successful in the United States. He had come to this country in '34. He became the arranger and musical director of the Radio City Music Hall in New York City. He also hired Glenn Miller to organize his band and to arrange charts for it. The Noble band was particularly successful in the late '30s and early '40s. In the late '30s he began to concentrate on radio work, where he served as music director for several famous shows, notably the Edgar Bergen and Charlie McCarthy show from '41 into the '50s. Noble was inducted into the Big Band/Jazz Hall of Fame in '87. As a composer, Noble's most famous songs include "Good Night, Sweetheart" (see '31), "Love Is the Sweetest Thing" (see '33), "My Little Grass Shack in Kealakekua, Hawaii" (see '34) and "The Very Thought of You" (see '34). Noble was elected to the

Songwriters' Hall of Fame in '96. As a bandleader, Noble had hit recordings of "Love Is the Sweetest Thing" (see '33), "The Very Thought of You" (see '34), "The Old Spinning Wheel" (see '34), "Isle of Capri" (see '35), "Let's Swing It" (see '35), and "Paris in the Spring" (see '35). In the late '40s his band accompanied Buddy Clark on a couple of hits: "Linda" (see '47) and "I'll Dance at Your Wedding" (see '48). Ray Noble became the No. 14 top recording artist of the '30s. At http://www.songwritershall offame.org/exhibit_audio_video.asp?exhibitId=235 you can hear an audio clip of Noble's "Goodnight Sweetheart" performed by George Metaxa with Ray Noble and the New Mayfair Orchestra.

Bob Nolan (real name: Robert Clarence Nobles; 1908–1980) Canadian Bob Nolan wrote his first song in the late '20s. In '31 he joined the Rocky Mountaineers to sing and play fiddle. In '33 he joined the group Pioneer Trio and within a few months added some members and became the Sons of the Pioneers. 1935 was a good year for the group; they signed a recording contract with Decca Records and appeared in their first film. Nolan remained with the group until '49. Nolan's best-known songs are "Tumbling Tumbleweeds" (see '34) and "Cool Water" (see '48). Both songs, as recorded by the Sons of the Pioneers, were inducted into the Grammy Hall of Fame: "Cool Water" in '86 and "Tumbling Tumbleweeds" in 2002. Bob is a member of the Nashville Songwriters Hall of Fame.

Clarence Nordstrom (1893–1968) Clarence Nordstrom appeared in a dozen or so Broadway musicals between '18 and the mid-'60s, including the *Ziegfeld Follies of 1925*, *Knickerbocker Holiday*, *The Time, the Place and the Girl* and *Guys and Dolls*. Nordstrom also appeared in several films. He, Ruby Keeler, Ginger Rogers and Una Merkel introduced "Shuffle Off to Buffalo" in the movie musical *Forty Second Street* (see '33).

Pierre Norman (real name: Joseph P. Connor; 1895–1952) Pierre Norman was co-composer of "You Brought a New Kind of Love to Me" (see '30). Norman also wrote "When I Take My Sugar to Tea." Norman studied at the Wyoming Conservatory and St. Bonaventure College. He was the pastor of St. John's Church in Cliffside, New Jersey and a chaplain of the New Jersey State Police and New Jersey National Guard. Norman primarily collaborated with Sammy Fain and Irving Kahal.

William Norris (1870–1929) William Norris helped introduce "The Tale of a Bumble Bee" in *King Dodo*. (see '01)

Alex North (real name: Isadore Soifer; 1910–1991) Alex North was the composer of "Unchained Melody" (see '55). He had studied music at the Curtis Institute, Juilliard and the Moscow Conservatory. North has received fourteen Academy Award nominations between the early '50s and the '80s, including *Streetcar Named Desire, Death of a Salesman, Viva Zapata!, The Rose Tattoo, The Rainmaker, Spartacus, Cleopatra, The Agony and the Ecstasy, Who's Afraid of Virginia Woolf?, The Shoes of the Fisherman, Shanks, Bite the Bullet, Dragon-slayer* and *Under the Volcano*. In '86, North received a Lifetime Achievement award from the film academy for his film music.

George A. Norton (1880–1923) George Norton wrote the lyrics for W. C. Handy's "The Memphis Blues" (see '14). When Handy sold the rights to the song to a New York publishing company for $50, the publisher hired George Norton to write the lyrics. Norton is also famous for writing the lyrics for "My Melancholy Baby" (see '28).

Bill Norvas Bill Norvas was co-lyricist of "Make Love to Me" (see '54). The song began in '23 as "Tin Roof Blues," written by five players in the New Orleans Rhythm Kings plus Walter Melrose, a composer, author, and publisher during the '20s. Melrose wrote the original, more risqué, lyrics, but Bill Norvas and Allan Copeland contributed the present version in '53.

Red Norvo (real name: Kenneth Norville; 1908–1999) Red Norvo and his wife, Mildred (Bailey), served as co-directors of their band from '36–'39. Red and Mildred created quite a lot of gossip when they married since Red was white and Mildred was Native American. Mildred was one of the best jazz singers of the era. Her brother, Al Rinker, was, along with Bing Crosby and Harry Barris, one of the Rhythm Boys who performed with Paul Whiteman's orchestra in the late '20s. Red had also been a soloist with Whiteman's orchestra in the late '20s. By the mid-'30s, he had formed his 10-piece band. The group had two years of recording success, '38–'39, before they broke up. After several years of forming and disbanding groups, Red joined the Benny Goodman band. He was vibraphonist of the Benny Goodman quartet, along with Goodman on clarinet, pianist Teddy Wilson, and bassist Slam Stewart. In '42, Red left Goodman for Woody Herman's small group, the Woodchoppers. Red Norvo and his orchestra's most popular recordings were "Says My Heart" (see '38) and "Please Be Kind" (see '38). Red Norvo became the No. 33 top recording artist of the '30s.

Jack Norworth (1879–1959) Jack Norworth first appeared on stage in vaudeville acts as a blackface comedian and later appeared in Broadway productions including *Ziegfeld Follies of 1909* and *The Jolly Bachelors*. Norworth was known as an actor and singer, performing mainly with his wife Nora Bayes. However, he also wrote several songs for vaudeville shows. Jack Norworth's most famous songs include "Take Me Out to the Ball Game" (see '08), "Shine on Harvest Moon" (see '09), and "Good Evening, Caroline" (see '09). Jack Norworth was an original member of the Songwriters' Hall of Fame in '70. The only prominent recording of Norworth was with his wife, Nora Bayes, on "Come Along, My Mandy" in '10. At http://www.songwritershalloffame.org/exhibit_audio_video.asp?e xhibitId=267 you can hear an audio clip of "Shine on Harvest Moon" performed by Billy Murray.

Ramón Novarro (1899–1968) Ramón Novarro and Evelyn Laye introduced "When I Grow Too Old to Dream" in the movie musical *The Night Is Young* (see '35). Novarro became one of the great luminaries of the early cinema. His work is not as widely known today, but he was one of the biggest attractions on the movie screens of the U.S. and abroad. For more on Novarro, see http://www. novarro.com/.

Ivor Novello (real name: David Ivor Davies; 1893–1951) Ivor Novello became a popular entertainer during the late 1910s. He was born in Wales to the well-known singer and teacher and a tax collector. He first became well known in the U.S. for his composition "Keep the Home Fires Burning" (see '16), which became a popular World War I song. After the war, he appeared on stage in the West End musicals. He also appeared in several successful Hollywood films. During World War II, Novello was convicted of illegal use of rationed gasoline and was briefly imprisoned. After his release he resumed appearing on stage until his sudden death in '51. The Ivor Novello Award is a prize awarded for songwriting, named for Ivor Novello, and awarded each year by the record industry to song writers and arrangers rather than to performing artists. Novello was portrayed in the fictional film *Gosford Park* (2001) and several of his songs were used on the film's soundtrack. In 2005 the Strand Theatre in London was renamed the Ivor Novello.

Donald Novis (1906–1966)   Donald Novis and Gloria Grafton introduced "My Romance" in the Rodgers and Hart musical *Jumbo* (see '35).

Jack Oakie (real name: Lewis Delaney Offield; 1903–1978)   Jack Oakie is mostly famous for his work in films, but he also was active on stage, radio and television. Born in Missouri, Jack grew up in Oklahoma, which is the origin of the "Oakie" part of his stage name. Oakie made his Broadway debut in '23 in the chorus of Cohan's *Little Nellie Kelly*. In '27, he moved to Hollywood, where he appeared in five silent films. He signed with Paramount Pictures at the dawn of the talkie era. After his Paramount contract ended in '34, he freelanced with remarkable success. He appeared in 87 films, mostly during the '30s and '40s. He and Dorothy Dell introduced "With My Eyes Wide Open, I'm Dreaming" in the film *Shoot the Works* (see '34). By the end of the '30s, Oakie was also on radio. He won an Oscar nomination for Best Supporting Actor for his role of Benzino Napaloni in Charlie Chaplin's film *The Great Dictator* ('40). Later in his career, he appeared in individual episodes of a number of TV series.

Ben Oakland (1909–1979)   Ben Oakland was a child prodigy, performing at Carnegie Hall in a piano concert at age 9. He later became accompanist for Helen Morgan and Georgie Jessel in vaudeville. Oakland contributed songs to the *Ziegfeld Follies of 1931, Earl Carroll's Sketch Book, Americana*, nightclub revues *George White's Gay White Way, Cotton Club Parade, Casino de Paree* and *Paradise Parade*, and film scores for *I'll Take Romance, The Awful Truth, My Little Chickadee, The Big Store* and *Show Business*. During World War II, Ben performed in USO shows for the soldiers. Oakland's chief collaborators were Oscar Hammerstein II, Paul Francis Webster, Herb Magidson, Don Raye, Milton Drake, Bob Russell, L. Wolfe Gilbert and Artie Shaw. Some of his most famous songs include "I'll Take Romance," "Java Jive," and "I'll Dance at Your Wedding" (see '48).

Will Oakland (1880–1956)   Countertenor Will Oakland's singing career began in the early 1900s in vaudeville and ended with television appearances before his death in '56. He recorded as a soloist and as a member of the Heidelberg Quintet. His recordings of "Mother Machree" and "I Love the Name of Mary" from *Barry of Ballymore* were both very popular (see both songs in '11). His recording of "I'm on My Way to Mandalay" with Henry Burr and Albert Campbell as the Lyric Trio was also especially successful (see '14).

Helen O'Connell (1920–1993)   Helen O'Connell is particularly remembered as a singer with the Jimmy

Dorsey orchestra from '39 through '43. She recorded often with the band and was featured on the very popular Dorsey recordings of "Amapola" (see '41), "Green Eyes" (see '41) and "Tangerine" (see '42). She left Dorsey in '43 and sang on radio for a short period. During the rest of the '40s she remained relatively inactive. When she returned to show business in the '50s, she often appeared on television.

Donald O'Connor (real name: Donald David Dixon Ronald O'Connor; 1925–2003)   Donald O'Connor was born into an Irish family of vaudevillians. He made several movie musicals from the late '30s through the mid–'50s, beginning at age 12 with *Melody for Two* ('37), and including *Sing You Sinners*, where Bing Crosby sang "Small Fry" to the 13-year-old Donald ('38), *Private Buckaroo* ('42), *Bowery to Broadway* ('44), *Yes Sir That's My Baby* ('49), *Call Me Madam* ('53), *There's No Business Like Show Business* ('54), and *Anything Goes* ('56). The crowning achievement of his film career was most likely *Singin' in the Rain* ('52). O'Connor is particularly famous for singing, dancing, and clowning "Make 'Em Laugh" in the movie musical *Singin' in the Rain* (see '52). He is also famous for his comic lead roles like the "Francis the Talking Mule" series of films.

James O'Dea (1871–1914)   James O'Dea, the husband of songwriter Anne Caldwell, wrote the lyrics for "Hiawatha" (see '03).

June O'Dea   June O'Dea, George Murphy and the chorus introduced "Love Is Sweeping the Country" in the Broadway musical *Of Thee I Sing* (see '32).

Charles O'Donnell   Charles O'Donnell's only major contribution to popular music was as the composer of "My Pony Boy" (see '09).

Charles O'Flynn   Charles O'Flynn was co-lyricist of "Smile, Darn Ya, Smile" (see '31).

Geoffery O'Hara (1882–1967)   Geoffrey O'Hara was a Canadian-American composer, singer and music professor. O'Hara was born in Canada, but moved to the U.S. in '04 and began performing in vaudeville. He began recording for Edison Records in '05. He held teaching positions at Teachers' College of Columbia University, Huron College and the University of South Dakota. During World War I he was a singing instructor of patriotic songs for American troops. O'Hara composed over 500 popular and patriotic songs, and hymns. He had only moderate success in the popular music field; however, his "K-K-K-Katy" (see '18) became one of the most popular tunes of the World War I era.

Phil Ohman (1896–1954)   Phil Ohman's first job was as a piano salesman at Wannamaker's in New York City in '15. Ohman was not just a salesman, but was a talented pianist himself. He and Victor Arden recorded hundreds of songs on piano rolls. During the early '20s Ohman worked as an arranger and composed both classical and popular music. In '22, he was hired as the pianist for Paul Whiteman's Orchestra, but he only stayed with Whiteman one year. He and Arden played vaudeville and small clubs in the city. In '24, they were hired to conduct the pit orchestra for the Gershwin musical *Lady Be Good*. They also worked on *Funny Face, Oh, Kay, Tip Toes* and *Spring Is Here*. The Arden-Ohman Orchestra was very successful between '26 and '32. Ohman and Arden split in '34. After the break-up Ohman organized an orchestra for the Trocadero nightclub in Hollywood. While there, he began scoring for films, writing songs and helping actors who needed to simulate piano playing on screen. Ohman was the composer of "Lost" (see '36).

Walter O'Keefe (1900–1983)   Walter O'Keefe was an actor, songwriter and short story author. He introduced "When Yuba Plays the Rhumba on the Tuba" in *The Third Little Show* (see '31). O'Keefe also appeared in *George White's Scandals of 1935*.

Zelma O'Neal (1903–1989)   Zelma O'Neal was a singer, dancer and comedienne whose greatest successes came on Broadway. She appeared in both the New York and London companies of *Good News*. As the co-ed Flo, she introduced "The Varsity Drag" (see '27) in *Good News*. She also starred in the musical comedy *Follow Thru* on Broadway, where she introduced "Button Up Your Overcoat" (see '29). O'Neal also appeared in the film version of *Follow Thru* ('30). Ms. O'Neal retired by the late '30s

Chauncey Olcott (1858–1932)   Chauncey Olcott was born in Buffalo, New York, but moved to London to study voice. When he returned to this country, he performed as a singer in minstrel shows and acted in several Broadway shows. Olcott wrote "My Wild Irish Rose" (see '00) without a collaborator. He often collaborated with Ernest Ball and George Graff. Olcott's other most famous songs were "I Love the Name of Mary" (see '11), "Mother Machree" (see '11), "Isle o' Dreams" (see '13) and "When Irish Eyes Are Smiling" (see '13). Chauncey Olcott was an original member of the Songwriters' Hall of Fame in '70. Olcott also had very popular recordings of "When Irish Eyes Are Smiling" (see '13) and "Too-Ra-Loo-Ra-Loo-Ral" (see '14). Olcott was one of the top recording artists of the 1910s.

Lotar Olias (1913–1990)   German composer Lotar Olias wrote "Du, Du, Du." Robert Mellin's English lyrics made it "You, You, You" (see '53).

Abe Olman (1888–1984)   Abe Olman composed the music for "Down Among the Sheltering Palms" (see '15), for "Oh Johnny, Oh Johnny, Oh!"(see '17) and for "O-HI-O" (see '21).

George Olsen (1893–1971)   George Olsen was the leader of an important pre-swing band. His organization was featured in several Broadway shows and in vaudeville. Olsen led the orchestra for more than thirty years, but his most productive years were from '26 to '33. His theme song was "Beyond the Blue Horizon." Olsen and his orchestra's most famous recordings were "Who?" (see '26), "Always" (see '26), "At Sundown" (see '27), "A Precious Little Thing Called Love" (see '29), "Say It Isn't So" (see '32), "Lullaby of the Leaves" (see '32) and "The Last Round-Up" (see '33). Olsen (along with his orchestra, of course) was the No. 8 top recording artist of the '20s and No. 29 for the '30s, qualifying him as the No. 35 top recording artist of the first half of the 20th Century.

Ole Olsen (John Sigvard Olsen; 1892–1963)   With Chic Johnson, Ole Olsen was half of a comedy team in vaudeville. The pair made several films; the most successful was *Hellzapoppin'* ('41). Olsen and Johnson were lyricists for "Oh! Gee, Oh! Gosh, Oh! Golly, I'm in Love" (see '23). Olsen and Johnson performed the song in *Hellzapoppin'*.

Haru Onuki   Ms. Haru Onuki introduced "Poor Butterfly" in the Hippodrome extravaganza *The Big Show* (see '17).

John Openshaw   John Openshaw was the composer of "Love Sends a Little Gift of Roses" (see '23).

The Original Dixieland Jazz Band   Nick LaRocca (bandleader, trumpet & cornet; real name: Dominick James LaRocca; 1889–1961), Larry Shields (clarinet; 1893–1953), Eddie Edwards (trombone; 1891–1963), Henry Ragas (piano; 1891–1919), Tony Sbarbaro (drums; real name: Tony Spargo; 1897–1969). The Original Dixieland Jass Band was an all-white band formed in '14 ("Jass" was changed to "Jazz" in '17; "jass" may have been slang for sexual intercourse). The leader of the group Nick LaRocca had learned music in New Orleans playing with "Papa" Laine's band. The ODJB left New Orleans, traveled to Chicago and eventually to New York City, where they became the first to record jazz in '17. The band had great success when they toured England in '19. They disbanded in '25. The band's most famous recordings were "Tiger Rag" (see '31), released in '18 and "Original Dixieland One Step)" (see '18). Other popular recordings by the group include "Darktown Strutters' Ball," "Home Again Blues," "Palesteena" and "St. Louis Blues." The Original Dixieland Jazz Band was one of the top recording artists of the '20s. The Original Dixieland Jass (Jazz) Band recordings between '17 and '36 are available for listening at http://www.redhotjazz.com/bands.html.

The Orioles   Sonny Til (real name: Earlington Carl Tilghman; 1928–1981), George Nelson (1926–1959), Alexander Sharp (1919–1970), Johnny Reed (1929–), Tommy Gaither (guitar; 1919–1950). The Orioles, an early R&B group, worked around the Baltimore area until they got their break on *Arthur Godfrey's Talent Scouts* show, which gave them enough exposure to sign a recording contract and book nightclub appearances on the rhythm and blues circuit of clubs. The group's most popular recording was of "Crying in the Chapel" (see '53). Sonny Til and the Orioles were inducted into the Vocal Group Hall of Fame in '98.

Nicholas Orlando's Orchestra   Nicholas Orlando's Orchestra recorded "Till We Meet Again" (see '19) with vocalists Harry MacDonough and Charles Hart. Their Victor recording was very successful. The flip side of the recording was a very popular recording of "Beautiful Ohio" by the Waldorf-Astoria Dance Orchestra.

Harold Orlob (1885–?)   Harold Orlob is primarily remembered for his part in writing "I Wonder Who's Kissing Her Now" (see '09). Orlob apparently wrote the tune, which Joe E. Howard published as his own. Orlob was writing material for Howard at the time. In the mid-'40s, when Howard's film biography was released Orlob came forward claiming he had written the song. The case was settled out of court when Howard agreed to share composing credit with Orlob.

Orpheus Quartet   Harry MacDonough (tenor, see his biographical sketch), Lambert Murphy (tenor, see his biographical sketch), Reinald Werrenrath (baritone, see his biographical sketch), William F. Hooley (bass). The

Orpheus Quartet's recording of "Turn Back the Universe and Give Me Yesterday" (see '16) was very popular.

Vess Ossman (real name: Sylvester Louis Ossman; 1868–1923) Vess Ossman was known as "The King of the Banjo." He became one of the most recorded ragtime musicians. His most successful period was between 1894 and the turn of the new century; however, his recordings of "The Old Folks at Home" (see '00) and "A Coon Band Contest" were quite well received.

Johnny Otis (real name: Ioannis (Yannis) Veliotes; 1921–) Greek-American Johnny Otis is a rhythm and blues pianist, vibraphonist, drummer, singer and bandleader. After playing in some swing bands, he formed his own group in '45. That group became the California Rhythm and Blues Caravan during the early '50s. Otis produced Etta James' "Roll with Me, Henry," which became known as "Wallflower (Dance with Me, Henry)," which Otis co-wrote with Hank Ballard and Etta James (see '55). As A&R (artist and repertory) for King Records, Otis discovered Jackie Wilson, Hank Ballard and Little Willie John. His best known recording was "Willie and the Hand Jive" in the late '50s. Otis was elected to the Rock and Roll Hall of Fame in 1994.

Hans Otten In '35 Hans Otten wrote "Du Kannst Nicht Treu Sein" which became "You Can't Be True, Dear" (see '48).

W.B. Overstreet W.B. Overstreet was a co-writer of "There'll Be Some Changes Made" in '29. The song was more popular in '41.

Harry Owens (1902–1986) According to http://www.squareone.org/Hapa/owens.html, "Harry Owens credits Hawaii with his rebirth in '34 when he first sailed past Diamond Head on Matson's S. S. Mariposa." Born in O'Neill, Nebraska, Owens came to the islands to lead the orchestra at the Royal Hawaiian Hotel in '34. He met several knowledgeable native Hawaiians who taught him a great deal about Hawaiian culture. Owens embraced it as his own and transcribed many ancient and 20th century Hawaiian songs which had never been written down before. Owens became one of Hawaii's great ambassadors as his band toured the mainland. He wrote his biggest hit and signature song, "Sweet Leilani" (see '37), when his first child was born and, when used in the Paramount film *Waikiki Wedding*, the song won an Academy Award. His friend Bing Crosby made the song a worldwide hit. Owens also wrote the music for "Linger Awhile" (see '24). Owens composed some 300 songs and made over 150 records for Decca.

Jack Owens Jack Owens was one of the co-writers of "The Hut-Sut Song (a Swedish Serenade)" (see '41) and the composer of "How Soon (Will I Be Seeing You?)" (see '48).

Jose Padilla (1889–1960) Jose Padilla was a Spanish composer (not the more recent alleged terrorist). Padilla was the composer of "Valencia" (see '26).

Bob Page Bob Page introduced "I'll Sing You a Thousand Love Songs" in the film *Cain and Mabel* (see '36).

Patti Page (real name: Clara Ann Fowler; 1927–) Patti Page was a popular nightclub, television and record-ing singer, who was particularly popular during the '50s. She began her career as a country singer on radio, but she quickly broke away to become a top entertainer in clubs and on records. She hit the big time with her hugely popular recording of "Tennessee Waltz" (see '50), the No. 1 hit of the entire decade. Page's most productive recording period was '50 through '57. Other extremely popular Page recordings were "All My Love" (see '50), "I Went to Your Wedding" (see '52) and "The Doggie in the Window" (see '53). Ms. Page was the No. 3 top recording artist of the '50s. In addition to her singing, she appeared in the film *Elmer Gantry* ('60). Ms. Page was inducted into the Popular Music Hall of Fame in 2004. Go to http://www.miss pattipage.com/ for more information.

Herman Paley (1879–?) Herman Paley's chief contribution to pop music history was as composer for "Sweet Little Buttercup" (see '18).

Byron Palmer (1925–) Byron Palmer and Doretta Morrow introduced "My Darling, My Darling" in the musical *Where's Charley?* (see '49).

Jack Palmer (1901–1976) Jack Palmer wrote "Everybody Loves My Baby" (see '25) with Spencer Williams.

John E. Palmer John E. Palmer wrote "The Band Played on" in 1895. Palmer sold his rights to the song to a vaudevillian, Charles B. Ward. As was the custom, once a person had paid for the song, it was theirs; they could publish it and take full credit. When Ward published it, he claimed to have written the music, but he did give Palmer credit for the words.

Frank Panella (1878–1953) Frank Panella was primarily known as a march composer, but he also wrote "The Old Grey Mare" (see '17).

Mitchell Parish (real name: Michael Hyman Pashelinsky; 1900–1993) Lyricist Mitchell Parish has been one of the most distinguished writers in the business. He specialized in adding lyrics to pre-existing music. Parish's family immigrated from Lithuania in '01, then later moved from Louisiana to New York City when he was a young boy. Parish had intended to become a lawyer, but after graduation from Columbia and N.Y.U., he became a songwriter. In the late 1910s, he was hired as a staff writer at a music-publishing house. He eventually established himself as a writer of songs for stage, screen and numerous musical revues. Parish's main focus was on writing individual popular songs not entire stage scores. Many of his songs have a romantic quality about them. Among his many collaborators were Hoagy Carmichael, Duke Ellington, Peter De Rose, Leroy Anderson, Glenn Miller, Sammy Fain, Frank Perkins, Will Hudson, Benny Goodman, Edgar Sampson, Raymond Scott. Some of Parish's most famous songs include "Star Dust" (see '31), "Sophisticated Lady" (see '33), "Stars Fell on Alabama" (see '34), "Hands Across the Table" (see '34), "Don't Be That Way" (see '38), "Deep Purple" (see '39) "Stairway to the Stars" (see '39), "Moonlight Serenade" (see '39), "Tzena, Tzena, Tzena" (see '50), "All My Love" (see '50) and "Blue Tango" (see '52). Others include "The Lamp Is Low," "Sweet Lorraine," "Sleigh Ride," "Ruby," and the English version of "Volare." Mitchell Parish was elected to the Songwriters' Hall of Fame in '72. At http://www.songwritershalloffame. org/exhibit_audio_video.asp?exhibitId=226 you can hear audio clips of "Stardust" sung by Nat "King" Cole, "One Morning in May" performed by Mel Torme, "Deep Purple" performed by Nino Tempo and April Stevens, "Sophisticated Lady" sung by Rosemary Clooney, "Stars Fell on Alabama" sung by Frank Sinatra, "Don't Be That Way" performed by the Benny Goodman Orchestra, "Volare" sung by Dean Martin, "Stairway to the Stars" performed by the Glenn Miller Orchestra with vocalist Ray Eberle, "Moonlight Serenade" performed by Glenn Miller and his orchestra and "Sweet Lorraine" performed by Nat "King" Cole and the "King" Cole Trio.

Fess Parker (real name: Fess Elisha Parker, Jr.; 1924–) Fess Parker introduced "The Ballad of Davy Crockett" in the television series *Davy Crockett*. His recording of the song competed with those by Bill Hayes and Tennessee Ernie Ford (see '55). Parker had been an athlete at the University of Texas, where he studied Drama, in the early '50s. He made a few films, but is mostly associated with portraying Davy Crockett in the TV series. He did appear in some other Disney films, including *Old Yeller* ('57). He also played Daniel Boone in a '60s TV series. After six years of that series, he retired and went into the real estate business.

Frank Parker (1906–) Frank Parker introduced "Life Is a Song (Let's Sing It Together)" (see '35) and "Tell Me That You Love Me" (see '35).

Ross Parker (circa 1914–1974) Ross Parker was one of the co-writers of "I Won't Tell a Soul (I Love You)" (see '38), "There'll Always Be England," referring to England's World War II problems, and "We'll Meet Again," which became a popular Vera Lynn recording.

Sol Parker Sol Parker was co-composer of "This Love of Mine" (see '41).

Cliff Parman Cliff Parman was one of the co-writers of "Pretend" (see '53). Parman was an orchestra arranger for stars like Connie Francis.

Geoffrey Parsons (1910–1987) Geoffrey Parsons was a co-lyricist of "Auf Wiederseh'n, Sweetheart" (see '52) and "Oh! My Pa-Pa" (see '54). British lyricist Geoffrey Parsons and John Turner (pen name for Jimmy Phillips) translated the original German into English. Parsons worked for the Peter Maurice Music Company, which was run by Jimmy Phillips. The company specialized in adapting foreign songs into English. Phillips, as the boss, would assign Parsons a project. When they were finished, Turner and Parsons shared credit.

Tony Pastor (real name: Antonio Pestritto; 1907–1969) Tony Pastor played tenor saxophone and sometimes sang with Irving Aaronson and his Commanders, Vincent Lopez and his orchestra and Artie Shaw and his orchestra beginning in the late '20s and extending in the late '30s. His most productive period with his own band was basically the '40s. Sisters Rosemary and Betty Clooney were his featured vocalists during the later '40s. His most popular recording was the Victor disk of "Bell-Bottom Trousers" (see '45) with Ruth McCullough as vocalist.

Les Paul (real name: Leslie Williams Polfuss; 1915–) Les Paul and his wife, Mary Ford, recorded several popular hits in the early '50s. Paul has also been widely known as a jazz guitarist and for the musical sound

effects and overdubbing (multiple recordings) experiments he developed. Les Paul and his Trio accompanied Bing Crosby on the '45 hit "It's Been a Long, Long Time," and Les, alone, had a minor hit with "Meet Mr. Callaghan" in '52. Les Paul and Mary Ford had No. 1 hits with "How High the Moon" (see '51) and the phenomenally popular "Vaya Con Dios" (see '53), which became the No. 4 hit of the decade. Other popular disks by the duo include "Mockin' Bird Hill," "The World Is Waiting for the Sunrise," "Just One More Chance," "Tiger Rag" and "I'm a Fool to Care." Most of their hits were revivals of old songs, except for "Vaya Con Dios." Les Paul was inducted into the Popular Music Hall of Fame and the Rock and Roll Hall of Fame in 2005. Les Paul and Mary Ford became the No. 6 top recording artists of the '50s.

John Howard Payne (1791–1852) John Howard Payne was an American actor and playwright. He is most remembered today as the author of "Home Sweet Home," which he wrote in 1822 (see 1915 when it was popularized again).

Bertram Peacock Bertram Peacock, who played Schubert, and Olga Cook, who played Mitzi, introduced "Song of Love" in the Broadway musical *Blossom Time* (see '22).

Harry Pease Harry Pease was co-writer of "Peggy O'Neil" (see '21) and "Ten Little Fingers and Ten Little Toes — Down in Tennessee" (see '22).

Jan Peerce (real name: Jacob Pincus Perelmuth; 1904–1984) Operatic tenor Jan Peerce introduced "A Beautiful Lady in Blue" over the radio on the Chevrolet Hour (see '36).

Peerless Quartet Henry Burr (tenor; see his biographical sketch), Albert Campbell (tenor; see his biographical sketch), Steve Porter (baritone; see his biographical sketch), Tom Daniels (bass). The Peerless Quartet was originally formed in the 1890s as the Columbia Male Quartet. They experienced a great deal of success beginning in '02. By '06, Frank Stanley had replaced Tom Daniels. Stanley then became both the lead singer and manager, as the group became the Peerless Quartet. Arthur Collins took Steve Porter's place in '09. After Stanley died in '10, John Meyer became the new bass and Henry Burr took over as leader. Arthur Collins left the group in late '18 and was succeeded by Frank Croxton. That lineup remained intact through '25 when Burr formed a new Peerless Quartet with three new partners until the group finally dissolved for good in '28. From '04 through '26, the quartet was responsible for numerous hit recordings including "Sweet Adeline" (see '04), "Let Me Call You Sweetheart" (as the Columbia Male Quartet, see '11), "I Didn't Raise My Boy to Be a Soldier" (see '15), "My Bird of Paradise" (see '15), "The Lights of My Home Town" (see '16), "Over There" (see '17) and "I Don't Know Where I'm Going but I'm on My Way" (see '18). The Peerless Quartet was the No. 24 recording artist of the first decade of the 20th Century, No. 5 of the second decade, making them the No. 14 top recording artist of the first half of the 20th Century. The Peerless Quartet was inducted into the Vocal Group Hall of Fame in 2003.

The Penguins Cleveland Duncan (lead vocalist), Curtis Williams (tenor), Dexter Tisby (baritone), Bruce Tate (tenor). The Penguins are primarily known for their version of "Earth Angel" (see '55), which was made more popular in a cover version by the Crew Cuts. This doo-wop quartet was never able to replicate the success of their only Top 40 hit, but the song has become an early rock 'n' roll classic. The Penguins, formed in '54, were all students at Fremont High School in Los Angeles. Not long after they organized, the group signed with the Los Angeles independent label Dootone Records. Their first single was going to be the up-tempo "Hey Sinorita," with the ballad "Earth Angel" as the B-side. When the record was released, Los Angeles radio stations got more requests for "Earth Angel."

Lee Penny Lee Penny was one of the writers of "My Adobe Hacienda" (see '47). This song had the distinction of being listed on both the hillbilly and the pop charts simultaneously, causing some to classify it as the first-ever "crossover" hit.

Buddy Pepper (real name: Jack R. Starkey; 1922–1993) Buddy Pepper was one of the co-writers of "Vaya Con Dios" (see '53). Pepper also collaborated on the title song from the Doris Day film *Pillow Talk*.

Frank Perkins (1908–1988) Frank Perkins was the composer of "Stars Fell on Alabama" (see '34). Perkins was also the composer of the score for *The Incredible Mr. Limpet* and conducted orchestras for films, including the '62 adaptation of *Gypsy*.

Betty Peterson Betty Peterson was the lyricist of "My Happiness " (see '48).

Bernice Petkere (1901–2000) Bernice Petkere was the composer of "Lullaby of the Leaves" (see '32). Ms. Petkere was born in Chicago to Canadian parents. She began performing in vaudeville at age 5 in an act with her aunt called "Baby Dolls." As a teenager, she sang with a dance band and was a pianist for the important publishing company of Waterson, Berlin and Snyder. She began her writing career in the '20s with "Starlight (Help Me Find the One I Love)," which was recorded by Bing Crosby. She also wrote many radio theme songs because her second husband, Fred Berrens, was the musical director at CBS. She moved to Southern California in the late '30s and wrote for the film industry.

Jack Pettis (1902–?) Jack Pettis was one of the co-writers of "Bugle Call Rag" (see '32). He and his collaborators had written the song in '23. Pettis was an early jazz pioneer. He played saxophone for the New Orleans Rhythm Kings in the early '20s. Then joined Ben Bernie's Orchestra, where he played a solo on "Sweet Georgia Brown" in a early short sound film. In '26, he began making recordings as the leader of his own band, with the Whoopee Makers and with Irving Mills' Hotsy Totsy Gang. He left the music business in '40 and disappeared.

Dave Peyton Dave Peyton was co-composer with Spencer Williams for "I Ain't Got Nobody" (see '16).

Edith Piaf (1915–1963) Edith Piaf was one of France's most admired singers and became a national icon. Her most famous song in the U.S. was "La vie en rose" (see '50). For more on Piaf, see http://en.wikipedia.org/wiki/Edith_Piaf.

Al Piantadosi (1884–1955) Composer and pianist Al Piantadosi was born in New York City. After graduat-

ing from high school, he began his entertainment career as a pianist in nightclubs and resorts. He eventually secured a position as a staff musician for music publishers. He toured through the U.S. as the accompanist for vaudeville star Anna Chandler. Piantadosi was a charter member of ASCAP in '14. Among his chief collaborators were Al Bryan, Grant Clarke, Joe McCarthy, Joe Goodwin and Edgar Leslie. Piantadosi wrote the music to such great hits as "Baby Shoes" (see '11), "The Curse of an Aching Heart" (see '13), "I Didn't Raise My Boy to Be a Soldier" (see '15), and "Send Me Away with a Smile" (see '18).

Pied Pipers John Huddleston, Chuck Lowry, Clark Yokum, Jo Stafford (Mrs. John Huddleston at this point; see her biographical sketch). The Pied Pipers started in '37 with seven men and a woman, but bandleader Tommy Dorsey couldn't afford eight singers, so they left in '38. Tommy soon hired back the four who became the famous quartet. After Stafford left in '45 to pursue a solo career, June Hutton replaced her. The group began to achieve national recognition on Tommy Dorsey's radio program in the late '30s. Johnny Mercer signed them to Capitol Records and they often backed him in recordings. The Pied Pipers became the biggest selling vocal group of the time and were named the Top Vocal Group for six consecutive years by *Downbeat Magazine*. The Pied Pipers' most popular recording was "Dream" (see '45), however they recorded often with Tommy Dorsey and backed many solo artists. A few of their popular recordings with Tommy Dorsey include "I'll Never Smile Again," "This Love of Mine," "There Are Such Things," "Oh, Look at Me Now," "Star Dust," "The One I Love Belongs to Somebody Else" and "Let's Get Away from It All." The Pied Pipers were one of the top thirty recording artists of the '40s. The group appeared in four films: *Las Vegas Nights, Ship Ahoy, DuBarry Was a Lady* and *Reveille with Beverly*. The Pied Pipers were inducted into the Vocal Group Hall of Fame in 2001.

Maceo Pinkard (1897–1962) Maceo Pinkard was educated at the Bluefield Colored Institute. Pinkard formed his own orchestra and toured throughout the country. In '14, he founded a theatrical agency in Omaha, Nebraska and eventually founded his own music-publishing firm in New York City. Pinkard wrote primarily without a collaborator. Some of his most well-known songs are "Sweet Georgia Brown" (see '25), "'Gimme' a Little Kiss, Will 'Ya' Huh?" (see '26) and "Here Comes the Show Boat" (see '28). Another well known Pinkard song is "Them There Eyes." Maceo Pinkard was inducted into the Songwriters' Hall of Fame in '84. At http://www.songwritershalloffame.org/exhibit_audio_video.asp?exhibitId=269 you can hear an audio clip of Pinkard's "Them There Eyes."

Ezio Pinza (real name: Fortunato Pinza; 1892–1957) Italian bass-baritone Ezio Pinza was best known as a Metropolitan Opera star until his appearance as Emile de Becque in *South Pacific*, where he introduced "Some Enchanted Evening" (see '49) and "This Nearly Was Mine." He appeared in a few unimpressive movie musicals: *Carnegie Hall* ('47), *Mr. Imperium* ('51) and *Tonight We Sing* ('53).

Tom Pitts Tom Pitts was co-writer of "I Never Knew I Could Love Anybody Like I'm Loving You" (see '21).

Frank Pixley   Frank Pixley's most significantly important contribution to popular music was as lyricist for "The Tale of a Bumble Bee" for the musical *King Dodo* (see '01). He also wrote "The Heidelberg Stein Song" and "The Message of the Violet" from *The Prince of Pilsen.*

Bobby Plater   Bobby Plater was a co-writer of "Jersey Bounce" (see '42).

The Platters   Tony Williams (lead vocalist; 1928–1992), David Lynch (tenor; 1930–1981), Paul Robi (baritone; 1931–1989), Herbert Reed (bass; 1931–), Zola Taylor (1938–). Buck Ram, who claims to have formed the group in '53, discovered the Platters. Ram, who was then managing the Penguins, refused to allow the Penguins to sign with Mercury Records unless the Platters were also given a contract. The Penguins had one hit, "Earth Angel," while the Platters became one of the most successful rhythm and blues groups throughout the '50s (the No. 14 top recording artists of the decade). Tony Williams left the group in '61 to go solo. He was replaced by Sonny Turner. By the mid-'60s only Herb Reed was left from the original group. The Platters' string of hits began with "Only You" (see '55). They had even more success in the late '50s with "My Prayer," "The Great Pretender," "The Magic Touch," "Twilight Time" and "Smoke Gets in Your Eyes." Several of their hits were revivals of old songs: "Smoke Gets in Your Eyes" (see '34), "My Prayer" (see '40), and "Twilight Time" ('44). The Platters were inducted into the Rock and Roll Hall of Fame in '90 and the Vocal Group Hall of Fame in '98.

Coy Poe   Coy Poe was a co-writer of "The Object of My Affection" (see '34) and "What's the Reason (I'm Not Pleasin' You)" (see '35).

Lew Pollack (1895–1946)   In his early years, Lew Pollack performed as a boy soprano in the famous Walter Damrosch choral group. Pollack later was a singer and pianist in vaudeville acts. He was one of the early writers of theme music for silent films including *What Price Glory* and *Seventh Heaven.* When sound entered the industry, he also wrote full scores for sound films including *Pigskin Parade* and *Rebecca of Sunnybrook Farm.* Pollack collaborated with songwriters such as Sidney Mitchell, Erno Rapee, Paul Francis Webster, Sidney Clare, Ned Washington, Ray Gilbert and Jack Yellen. He wrote or co-wrote "Charmaine" (see '27), "Miss Annabelle Lee" (see '27), "Diane" (see '28), "Angela Mia" (see '28), "Two Cigarettes in the Dark" (see '34), and "In the Middle of a Kiss" (see '35). Other Pollack songs include "At the Codfish Ball" and "Sing, Baby, Sing." Lew Pollack was an original member of the Songwriters' Hall of Fame in '70. At http://www.songwritershalloffame.org/exhibit_audio_video.asp?exhibitId=270 you can hear audio clips of "Angela Mia (My Angel)" performed by Paul Whiteman and his orchestra with vocals by Jack Fulton, Charles Gaylord, and Al Rinker and "Two Cigarettes in the Dark" sung by Bing Crosby.

Channing Pollock (1880–1946)   Channing Pollock was a playwright, critic, dramatic editor, lecturer, illusionist and broadcaster. His chief contribution to popular music was penning the English lyrics for "My Man" (see '21).

George S. Pomeroy   George Pomeroy was a member of the 1910 senior class at Yale. He co-wrote the lyrics of "The Whiffenpoof Song" (see '09).

Cole Porter (1891–1964)   When Cole Porter was born in Peru, Indiana in 1891 he was named for his Grandfather J.O. Cole, the richest man in Indiana due to his success during the California Gold Rush and multiplying his wealth in timber, coal and other enterprises. From the age of six, Cole began to exhibit his musical talent and his mother greatly encouraged that talent. The boy began to compose music by age ten, and his mother paid for them to be published. At age 14 he was sent to study at Worcester Academy where he learned a great deal about language and meter. Next he attended college at Yale, where Cole was a huge social success, and became famous for the songs he was constantly writing and singing. His "Bingo Eli Yale" and the "Yale Bulldog Song" were especially popular at the school. After Yale, he entered Harvard Law School, but had little interest in the law. After a couple of years, he transferred to Harvard's School of Arts and Sciences, where he planned to get a graduate degree in music. However, he left school in '16 and moved to New York City. He wrote his first show, *See America First*, in '16. Even though it wasn't very successful (it only ran 16 performances), he had begun his musical career. With the First World War raging, Cole moved to Paris in '17. He adored the fabulous social life of Paris. It was during those years that he met divorcee Linda Lee Thomas from Louisville, Kentucky. Even though she was older than Cole and was aware of his homosexual preferences, they were married in '19. They both loved the social life in Paris, Venice and the Riviera. E. Ray Goetz persuaded Porter to write the music for the Broadway musical *Paris*, which was to star Goetz's wife, Irene Bordoni. Cole wrote five songs for the show and experienced his first big success (see "Let's Do It" and "Let's Misbehave" in '28). For the remainder of the '20s and '30s, Porter was busy writing show after show and hit after hit. He wrote the music and lyrics for *Fifty Million Frenchmen* (see "You Do Something to Me" in '29), *Wake Up and Dream* (see "What Is This Thing Called Love?" '30), *The New Yorkers* (see "Love for Sale" in '31), *Gay Divorce* (see "Night and Day" in '32), *Anything Goes* (see "Anything Goes," "I Get a Kick Out of You" and "You're the Top" in '34), *Jubilee* (see "Just One of Those Things" in '35 and "Begin the Beguine" in '38), *Red, Hot and Blue* (see 'It's De-Lovely" in '37). As if he were not busy enough on Broadway, he found time to write film scores for *Born to Dance* (see "I've Got You Under My Skin" in '36) and *Rosalie* (see "Rosalie" in '38). Tragedy struck in the summer of '37 when Cole was thrown from a horse and the animal fell on top of him, crushing both legs and damaging his nervous system. He never recovered the full use of his legs and suffered a great deal of physical agony for the rest of his life. Over the next twenty years, he underwent thirty operations. His suffering didn't slow down his musical production, however. As soon as he could physically work he wrote *Leave It to Me* and *DuBarry Was a Lady* for Broadway. In the '40s Porter's work was divided between movie and stage musicals. Although the big hit songs became more rare, he continued producing at an astonishing pace. Hollywood productions of the decade were *The Broadway Melody of 1940, You'll Never Get Rich, Something to Shout About* (see "You'd Be So Nice to Come Home to" in '43), *Hollywood Canteen* (see "Don't Fence Me in" in '44), and *Night and Day*, his first film biography. Broadway productions of the decade included *Panama Hattie, Let's Face*

It, Something for the Boys, Mexican Hayride (see "I Love You" in '44), *Seven Lively Arts* and *Kiss Me Kate* (see Another Op'nin', Another Show" in '48). By the fifties Porter's production finally began to deteriorate, in volume and sometimes in quality. He provided the musical scores for Broadway's *Out of This World, Can-Can,* and *Silk Stockings*. He also wrote songs for the films *High Society* and *Les Girls*. After his mother and wife died in the '50s, he became rather reclusive. He very seldom wrote music and avoided the public. He died in '64 in Santa Monica, California after kidney surgery. Porter was noted for his sophisticated, clever lyrics and brilliant melodies supported by complicated beautiful harmonies. He was, of course, elected to the Songwriters' Hall of Fame when it was organized in '70. He was inducted into the Popular Music Hall of Fame in 2001. A 2004 movie biography of Cole Porter was titled *De-Lovely*. It starred Kevin Kline as Porter and Ashley Judd as Linda Lee Porter. More than 20 songs Porter wrote during his decades as one of Broadway and Hollywood's most prolific contributors are woven into *De-Lovely*. The film also features performances by latter-day pop and jazz performers covering Porter classics. Sheryl Crow, Elvis Costello, Alanis Morissette, Robbie Williams, Diana Krall and Natalie Cole are among the artists who appear in the guise of '30s and '40s crooners. Porter was an original member of the Songwriters' Hall of Fame in '70. At http://www.songwritershalloffame.org/exhibit_audio_video.asp?exhibitId=19 you can hear audio clips of Porter's "You're the Top," "Anything Goes," "Be Like a Bluebird," "The Cocotte," and "I'm a Gigolo" performed by Cole Porter, "I Get a Kick Out of You" and "I've Got You Under My Skin" sung by Frank Sinatra, "Night and Day" performed by Ella Fitzgerald, "Let's Do It (Let's Fall in Love)" performed by Louis Armstrong, "Easy to Love" sung by Billie Holiday, "Just One of Those Things" performed by Sarah Vaughan, "From This Moment on" sung by Rosemary Clooney, "Ev'ry Time We Say Goodbye" performed by Ella Fitzgerald, "Miss Otis Regrets" performed by Marlene Dietrich, and "I Am in Love" sung by Peggy Lee.

Jake Porter Jake Porter was a co-writer on "Ko Ko Mo" (see '55). The song was originally recorded by Gene and Eunice. They recorded it in Porter's basement studio. He got writing credit and owned the copyright. For more, see http://www.electricearl.com/dws/gene&eunice.html.

Steve Porter (1865–1946) Steve Porter began his entertainment career as a comedian in vaudeville during the 1890s. He sang baritone in the Columbia Male Quartet and the American Quartet from '09 to '19. In the period covered by this book, he had a particularly popular recorded version of "A Bird in a Gilded Cage" (see 1900).

George Posford (1906–1976) English composer George Posford wrote "At the Balalaika" (see '40). He had written it in '36 for the British musical *The Gay Hussar*.

Dick Powell (1904–1963) Dick Powell, the former trumpet player and band singer, became one of the most popular stars of the movie musicals of the '30s. He signed a Warner Bros. movie contract in '32. He became a star in the '33 film *42nd Street*, introducing the title song and several others in that production. He costarred in several movie musicals with Ruby Keeler: *Forty Second Street, Footlight Parade, Gold Diggers of 1933* (all in '33), *Dames,*

Flirtation Walk (both '34), *Shipmates Forever* ('35), and *Colleen* ('36). He made musicals without Keeler, including *Twenty Million Sweethearts* ('34), *Gold Diggers of 1935* and *1937,* and *Hollywood Hotel* ('37) to name only a few. Powell and Ruby Keeler introduced "Shadow Waltz" in *Gold Diggers of 1933* (see '33). Powell introduced "I Only Have Eyes for You" in *Dames* (see '34). Powell and Ginger Rogers "I'll String Along with You" in the movie musical *Twenty Million Sweethearts* (see '34). Powell and Alice Faye introduced "I've Got My Love to Keep Me Warm" in the movie musical *On the Avenue* (see '37). Powell also introduced "With Plenty of Money and You" in *Gold Diggers of 1937* (see '37) and "You Must Have Been a Beautiful Baby" in the movie musical *Hard to Get* (see '38). In the late '30s he was also very active on radio. In the mid-'40s he had a very popular radio mystery show: "Richard Diamond — Private Detective." After the '30s Powell's music career took a back seat to his acting and his dramatic work on radio. Powell turned his attentions behind the camera during the '50s, directing several films. He remained active as head of Four Star Television until his death of cancer. He was married twice, to actresses Joan Blondell and June Allyson.

Eleanor Powell (1910–1982) Dancer Eleanor Powell was a famous actress and superb dancer in several Broadway musicals and movie musicals, who was known for her exceptional tap routines. By age thirteen she was in Gus Edwards' kiddie troupe during summer vacations. Her Broadway career started in the late '20s, when she appeared in half-a-dozen Broadway musicals, but she didn't achieve stardom until she went to Hollywood in the mid-'30s. Her screen debut was in *George White's Scandals of 1935,* in which she showed critics and the movie audiences her considerable dancing talent. Her dancing featured a heel-and-toe style that was more sophisticated than most ordinary tap dancing. Her next starring role was in *Broadway Melody of 1936* opposite Robert Taylor, where she introduced "You Are My Lucky Star" and "Broadway Rhythm" (see '35). In the next several years she was very busy. Other movie musicals included *Born to Dance, Broadway Melody of 1938, Rosalie* (one of the top box-office attractions of 1937–38, see '38), *Honolulu, Broadway Melody of 1940* with Fred Astaire, *Lady Be Good, Ship Ahoy, Thousands Cheer, I Dood It, Sensations of 1945,* and *The Duchess of Idaho*. Ms. Powell and Nelson Eddy introduced the title song from the movie musical *Rosalie* (see '38). In the mid-'40s she married actor Glenn Ford and retired. She came back in the '50s for a television series. After a divorce from Ford in '59, she staged an elaborate nightclub act that was well received.

Felix Powell Felix Powell's most important contribution to popular music was as composer for the World War I classic "Pack Up Your Troubles in Your Old Kit Bag and Smile, Smile, Smile!" (see '17).

George Henry Powell (1880–1951) English lyricist George Henry Powell, using the pen name George Asaff, is primarily remembered today for writing one of the World War I era's most famous songs: "Pack Up Your Troubles in Your Old Kit Bag and Smile, Smile, Smile!" (see '17). Powell wrote the song with his brother, Felix.

Perez Prado (real name: Damaso Perez Prado; 1918–1989) Cuban Perez Prado formed his band in

Mexico in '48 and began to popularize the mambo beat. The mambo began to get more attention in the U.S. in '54 ("Mambo Italiano" and "Papa Loves Mambo"). Prado and his orchestra had a big hit with "Cherry Pink and Apple Blossom White" (see '55). They followed that success with "Patricia" in '58.

Jacques Prevert (1900–1977)   French poet and screenwriter Jacques Prevert wrote the French lyrics for "Autumn Leaves" (see '55).

Chilton Price (real name: Chilton Searcy) Chilton Price was a broadcast-station record librarian from Louisville, Kentucky, who became friends with country-western bandleader Pee Wee King. Price started bringing song ideas to King, and two of the ideas produced hit songs: "Slow Poke" and "You Belong to Me" (see '52). After attending the University of Louisville, Price played violin for the Louisville orchestra during the '30s and '40s. Despite having to share writing credit with King and Redd Stewart, she was simply grateful to them for helping her get the songs published, recorded and helping to make them hits. As of the early 2000s, she was still living in the Louisville area and was still writing songs.

Georgie Price (George Edwards Price; 1901–1964)   According to http://www.imdb.com, "when Georgie was born, his mother missed work as janitor of the building, and the landlord evicted the entire family of 11, carrying Mrs. Price and Georgie into the street in her bed. A famous lady social worker saved them, letting the family return home. Georgie started singing and dancing on the streets and subways of New York at a very early age, and in 1907, accompanied an older brother on his dry-cleaning delivery rounds. He sang for the wife of Gus Edwards, a Vaudeville entrepreneur, and was adopted by the Edwards, thereafter taking Edwards as a middle name. He and Lila Lee starred as "Little Georgie and Cuddles" in Gus Edwards' song review, *School Days*. Surrounded and adored by old-timers of vaudeville, he mastered many arts, including tap dancing, soft shoe, gag-writing, double-talk, and especially imitation, at which he was regarded as one of the best, not only for his accents and voices, but also for his ability to imitate dancers, singers (including Enrico Caruso, who offered to adopt him), and entertainers of the past — as taught to him by those who remembered them best." Georgie, as an audience stooge, introduced "By the Light of the Silvery Moon" in vaudeville (see '10). He went through some hard times during his adolescence, when he could no longer play children's parts. However, he soon became a headliner replacing Al Jolson in a Schubert production. He later became the first non-classical singer to get a long-term recording contract with RCA Victor. In the '30s, he bought a seat on the New York Stock Exchange, beginning a second career, but continued on in show business. He had a CBS radio show in the early '50s. Price was co-lyricist on "Angel Child" (see '22), which Georgie introduced in *Spice of 1922*.

Louis Prima (1911–1977)   Louis Prima was born in the French Quarter of New Orleans, where, as a child he studied the violin. He soon switched to the trumpet. Prima began his music career in his hometown of New Orleans during his late teens. His first group, Louis Prima and his New Orleans Jazzmen, naturally played New Orleans jazz style. At the beginning of swing in the mid–'30s,

Prima turned more toward popular music. Prima's first vocalist was Lily Ann Carol, but in '54, it became Keely Smith, who also became his wife. They became a major casino and supper club act. Prima wrote the well known "Sing, Sing, Sing" (see '38), which was popularized by Benny Goodman and his orchestra, but he may be most remembered as the voice of King Louie of the apes in Disney's *The Jungle Book*. Prima was inducted into the Big Band/Jazz Hall of Fame in '93.

George Primrose (1852–?)   George Primrose and his minstrels introduced "Carry Me Back to Old Virginny" in the 1870s (see '15) and it became a staple in the repertoire of most of the minstrel groups of the era.

Hughie Prince (real name: Hugh Prince) Hughie Prince was the lyricist of "Boogie Woogie Bugle Boy" (see '41). He wrote several of the songs from the Abbott and Costello film *Buck Privates*.

Prince's Orchestra   Charles A. Prince (1869–1937) was the pianist and leader of Prince's Orchestra. He was the musical director for Columbia Records and the director of their orchestra. He and his orchestra were most popular during the '10s and '20s. He recorded under such names as Prince's Band, Prince's Orchestra, Prince's Dance Orchestra, Prince's Military Band and Prince's Symphony Orchestra. Prince's most popular recordings were "Ballin' the Jack" (see '14), "Hello, Hawaii, How Are You? (see '16), and "The Star Spangled Banner" (see '16). Prince's Orchestra became the No. 11 top recording artist of the '10s, No. 37 for the first half of the 20th Century.

Yvonne Printemps (real name: Yvonne Wignolle; 1895–1977)   Yvonne Printemps was dancing at the *Folies Bergere* in Paris by age 13. She obtained her stage name as a nickname by her fellow chorus members because of her sunny disposition (Printemps means spring). She appeared as a teenager with some of the most famous stars of the era like Maurice Chevalier and Mistinguett. In '19, she married actor-playwright Sacha Guitry. They performed his plays in several North American cities. She received considerable international fame for her performance in Noel Coward's *Conversation Piece* ('34), where she introduced "I'll Follow My Secret Heart" (see '34). She divorced Guitry for the French film star Pierre Fresnay. They did not marry, but remained together for life. Ms. Printemps continued to perform on stage until she was in her sixties.

Sidney Prosen   Sidney Prosen was the writer of "Till I Waltz Again with You" (see '53).

Heinz Provost (real name: Fredinand Heinrich Proboscht; 1891–1959)   Austrian composer Heinz Provost wrote "Intermezzo (a Love Story)" (see '41).

William Pruette   William Pruette, as Henri de Bomvray, introduced "I Want What I Want When I Want It" in *Mlle. Modiste* (see '05).

Arthur Pryor (1870–1942)   Arthur Pryor was trombonist, band leader and soloist with the Sousa Band. Pryor was born on September 22, 1870, on the second floor of the Lyceum Theater in Saint Joseph, Missouri. Pryor directed the Stanley Opera Company in Denver until he joined the John Philip Sousa Band in 1892. During his dozen years with the Sousa Band, Pryor estimated that he played 10,000 solos. From 1895 to 1903 Pryor was assistant conductor of the Sousa Band. After he left the Sousa Band, he formed his own band that made its debut at the Majestic Theater in New York City in '03. His band toured until '09, when he retired to Asbury Park, New Jersey. Pryor and his band's most popular recording was "The Whistler and His Dog" (see '05), which Pryor wrote.

Cactus Pryor (real name: Richard Pryor) Cactus Pryor was one of the co-writers of "Don't Let the Stars Get in Your Eyes" (see '53). Pryor got his nickname while working in his father's movie theater in Austin, which was called "The Cactus Theater." He is a former talk show host and former news anchor on radio stations in Austin and Houston, Texas. He is currently Vice President of Broadcasting for an Austin station.

Eva Puck Eva Puck and her brother, Harry (see below) were a vaudeville act from 1898 until '11. They were known as the Two Pucks. Eva and Sammy White introduced "The Blue Room" in *The Girl Friend* (see '26). Puck and White married, but later divorced. Eva appeared as Ellie May Chipley in both the original '27 Broadway production of *Show Boat* and the '32 Broadway revival.

Harry Puck (1891–1964) Harry Puck was part of a brother-sister vaudeville act with his sister Eva from 1898 until '11. They were known as the Two Pucks. After his sister's marriage, Harry turned his attention to composing and the music publishing business. His most famous popular song credit is "Where Did You Get That Girl?" (see '13). He also wrote "California and You" and "Little House Upon the Hill." His sister returned to the act briefly, but they soon parted and both went on to perform in Broadway musicals. As a performer, he appeared in a number of Broadway musicals, including *Tangerine* ('21), *Lollipop* ('24), *Twinkle, Twinkle* ('26) and *Three Little Girls* ('30). Harry eventually worked for Paramount Pictures in Hollywood.

Charles Purcell Charles Purcell and Beatrice Lillie introduced "I Know That You Know" in Vincent Youmans' *Oh, Please!* (see '27).

W.T. Purdy W.T. Purdy, a corporation clerk who had never been to the state of Wisconsin, composed the melody for "On Wisconsin" (see '09).

Lew Qualding Lew Qualding was one of the co-writers of "Careless " (see '40) and the composer of "Sam's Song" (see '50).

Gertrude Quinland Gertrude Quinland helped introduce "The Tale of a Bumble Bee" in *King Dodo*. (see '01)

Dan Quinn (1859–1938) Dan Quinn became one of the top vocalists in the 1890s recording field. He recorded some 2,500 songs during his twenty year recording career. Most of his huge successes were in the pre–1900s era, but he did have considerable success with "Bill Bailey, Won't You Please Come Home" (see '02).

Dave Radford Dave Radford wrote the lyrics for "It's Tulip Time in Holland " (see '15).

Ralph Rainger (real name: Ralph Reichenthal; 1900–1942) Songwriters' Hall of Fame member Ralph Rainger became one of Hollywood's most prolific composers in the '30s and '40s. Rainger exhibited an early talent for composition. He won a scholarship to a prestigious New York music school, but dropped out after a year and began working his way towards a law degree. He graduated from Brown University Law School in the late '20s. After graduation, he decided against a career in law and devoted his life to music. He began taking jobs as a professional pianist, arranger and accompanist for vaudeville entertainers. It wasn't until '29 in the revue *The Little Show* that Rainger had his first commercial success with the song "Moanin' Low." In '30, Rainger met lyricist Leo Robin and they became a songwriting team. Robin and Rainger moved to Hollywood and produced some memorable film scores for Paramount. Some of the films on which they worked include *She Done Him Wrong, She Loves Me Not, The Big Broadcast of 1937, The Big Broadcast of 1938* and *Waikiki Wedding*. By the end of the '30s, the team left Paramount and signed with 20th Century Fox. In addition to Leo Robin, Rainger collaborated with Howard Dietz, Sam Coslow and Dorothy Parker. Rainger's most popular songs were "Moanin' Low" (see '29), "Please" (see '32), "Love in Bloom" (see '34), "June in January" (see '34), "Thanks for the Memory" (see '38), and "Ebb Tide" (see '53). Ralph Rainger was an original member of the Songwriters' Hall of Fame in '70. At http://www.song writershalloffame.org/exhibit_audio_video.asp? exhibitId=236 you can hear an audio clip of "Thanks for the Memory" sung by Bob Hope.

John Raitt (1917–2005) John Raitt got his first starring role on Broadway in *Carousel*. As Billy Bigelow, he introduced the very difficult "Soliloquy" and the romantic duet "If I Loved You" (see '45), among others. After several artistic successes over the next few years, Raitt achieved another major Broadway success in *The Pajama Game* ('54). As Sid Sorokin, the new superintendent of the Sleep Tite Pajama Factory, he introduced the song "Hey There" (see '54), which became a huge hit. Raitt's daughter, Bonnie, followed her father into the popular music field and has had considerable success as a recording artist.

Ben Raleigh (1913–1997) Ben Raleigh was lyricist of "You Walk by" (see '40) and "Laughing on the Outside (Crying on the Inside)" (see '46).

Buck Ram (1907–1991) Samuel "Buck" Ram was devoted to classical music as a child, but at age 15, switched from the violin to the saxophone. In college he studied law and in '33 passed the California Bar exam. Instead of practicing law, Ram went to New York City where he worked in a major publishing company supplying arrangements for several well-known bands. He wrote some songs for the Cotton Club and other NYC nightclubs, but his first significant writing success came when he collaborated with Walter Kent and Kim Gannon on "I'll Be Home for Christmas" (see '43). He moved to Hollywood and began to write for the silver screen. In '45, he co-wrote "Twilight Time," which was popularized by the Three Suns (it was revived by the Platters in '58). After some ill health in the late '40s, he returned to the music business in the early '50s and formed his own management company. His fortunes changed drastically when he became the manager of the Platters. Ram's many years of experience in the business helped turn the group into a huge international success. In the mid-'50s, the Platters scored a big hit with "Only You" (another Ram song, see '55). Other hit recordings include "My Prayer," "The Great Pretender," a revival of Ram's "Twilight Time" and the revival of the '33 song "Smoke Gets in Your Eyes."

Ande Rand   Ande Rand was listed as co-writer with Buck Ram of "Only You" (see '55).

Erno Rapee (1891–1945)   Composer Erno Rapee, born in Budapest, Hungary, is primarily remembered for a few songs he wrote in the late '20s as motion picture theme songs. He collaborated with Lew Pollack to write "Charmaine" (see '27), "Diane" (see '28) and "Angela Mia" (see '28).

David Raskin (1912–2004)   David Raskin learned to play the piano and clarinet from his father, who was a music shop owner and woodwind player with the Philadelphia Orchestra. By age twelve, David was leading his own dance band. After graduating with a music degree from the University of Pennsylvania, he became a sideman in local bands and worked occasionally for the Philadelphia radio station WCAU. When he relocated to New York City, he found work as a singer and radio conductor. Through famed pianist Oscar Levant, Raskin met George Gershwin who recommended him for a job at the publishing firm of Harms/Chappell. In '25, Raskin traveled to Hollywood where Charlie Chaplin hired him to write the score for *Modern Times*. In '36, he joined Universal Studios as a staff composer, then transferred to Columbia Pictures. Raskin wrote the scores for more than 400 films and television productions. His most famous popular song was the title song from *Laura* (see '45).

Willie Raskin   Willie Raskin collaborated with several well-known songwriters including Billy Rose, Billy Hill, Edward Eliscu, Sammy Fain, Irving Mills and Clarence Williams. His most famous collaboration was "Wedding Bells (Are Breaking Up That Old Gang of Mine)" (see '29), on which he shared lyricist credit with Irving Kahal.

Fred Rath   Fred Rath was co-lyricist with Al Dubin for "Just a Girl That Men Forget" (see '23).

Maurice Ravel (1875–1937)   Paul Durand adapted French classical composer Maurice Ravel's "Bolero" into "All My Love" (see '50). For more on Ravel, see http://en.wikipedia.org/wiki/Maurice_Ravel.

Eddy Ray   Eddy Ray wrote the words for "Hearts of Stone" (see '55).

Johnnie Ray (1927–1990)   Johnnie Ray was partially deaf since age twelve and began wearing a hearing aid at age fourteen. In '51 he signed a recording contract with Okeh. His first effort was a song he had written himself titled "Whiskey and Gin," which became a minor hit. Later that year he recorded two songs that were produced by Mitch Miller: "Cry" (see '51) and "The Little White Cloud That Cried" (see '52). The background singers were the Four Lads. "Cry" became a smash hit, reaching No. 1 on *Billboard's* chart and staying there for eleven weeks. "The Little White Cloud That Cried," written by Ray, peaked at No. 2 on *Billboard*. Johnnie's passionate, soulful vocal style made him a sensation, but he also became fodder for comedians and mimics. He was moved to Okeh's parent label, Columbia, where he recorded several disks, but he never achieved another monster success like the back-to-back hits "Cry" and "Little White Cloud..." When Ray signed a movie contract his first film was the Irving Berlin musical, *There's No Business Like Show Business*, in '54. A

few years later he made somewhat of a comeback in England. Johnnie developed liver problems and died of liver failure in '90.

Lilian Ray   Composer Lilian Ray furnished the music for "The Sunshine of Your Smile" (see '16).

Don Raye (1909–1985)   After graduating from New York University, Don Raye began his show business career appearing in vaudeville shows. In '35, he organized a nightclub act in New York and began writing his own material for the show. Raye moved to Hollywood in '40, but soon joined the U.S. Army to serve during World War II. After the war, Raye returned to songwriting. Raye worked with several collaborators, most notably, Gene De Paul. Other collaborators included Hughie Prince, Pat Johnston, Harry James, Freddie Slack, Artie Shaw, Charles Shavers and Benny Carter. Raye's best known songs include "Boogie Woogie Bugle Boy" (see '41) and "Mister Five by Five" (see '42). Other Raye songs include "Cow Cow Boogie," "They Were Doing the Mambo" and "Beat Me Daddy Eight to the Bar." Don Raye was inducted into the Songwriters' Hall of Fame in '85.

Gene Raymond (real name: Raymond Guion; 1908–1998)   Gene Raymond was a child performer and had performed on Broadway by the age of 12. His most productive period in films was in the '30s and early '40s. Raymond introduced "All I Do Is Dream of You" in the Hollywood film *Sadie McKee* (see '34). He married operatic singer/actress Jeanette MacDonald in '37. They were cast together in *Smilin' Through* ('41). By the end of the '40s his wife left the business and Raymond was very selective about the films he did.

Andy Razaf (real name: Andrea Paul Razafkeriofo; 1895–1973)   Lyricist Andy Razaf was the son of a Madagascar nobleman and a nephew of the Queen of Madagascar. Razaf studied music privately in Washington, D.C. where his father was stationed. He began writing songs for nightclub revues in the 1910s. Razaf also collaborated on a few Broadway scores. In the '20s Razaf collaborated with several composers, including Eubie Blake, James P. Johnson, JC Johnson, Paul Denniker, Thomas "Fats" Waller and Joe Garland. Razaf's most remembered songs include "Ain't Misbehavin'" and "Honeysuckle Rose" (see '29), "In the Mood" (see '40), and "Twelfth Street Rag" (see '48). Other Razaf songs include "Stompin' at the Savoy," "Memories of You," "S'posin'," "Christopher Columbus," "That's What I Like 'Bout the South," "Keepin' Out of Mischief Now," and "The Joint is Jumpin'." In the '50s Razaf began working as a newspaper columnist and continued that profession until his death. He was elected to membership in the Songwriters' Hall of Fame in '72. At http://www.songwritershalloffame.org/exhibit_audio_video.asp?exhibitId=305 you can hear audio clips of "Honeysuckle Rose" and "Big Chief DeSota" performed by Fats Waller.

Erell Reaves   Erell Reaves was lyricist of "Lady of Spain" (see '52). British writers Erell Reaves and Tolchard Evans wrote the song in '31, but it was put back into circulation in '52 when Eddie Fisher's recording of the song became a hit. Ian Whitcomb, a highly respected performer, composer, and music historian, claims on his website (http://www.picklehead.com/ian/uncle.html) that his uncle wrote "Lady of Spain." He also claims that the name

Erell Reaves was an amalgam of the last five letters of Damerell (he claims his uncle also wrote using the name Stanley J. Damerell) and the last six letters of Robert Hargreaves. He claims Tolchard Evans and Erell Reaves are the same person, his uncle.

John Redmond   John Redmond was co-lyricist of "I Let a Song Go Out of My Heart" (see '38) and "The Man with the Mandolin" (see '39).

Dave Reed, Jr.   Dave Reed, Jr. was lyricist for "Love Me, and the World Is Mine" (see '06) and "My Dear" (see '08).

Phil Regan (real name: Philip Joseph Christopher Aloysius Regan; 1906–1996)   Tenor Phil Regan introduced "All My Life" in the movie musical *Laughing Irish Eyes* (see '36).

Billy Reid (1902–1974)   British songwriter and bandleader Billy Reid wrote "The Gypsy" (see '46), "A Tree in the Meadow" (see '48), and "I'm Walking Behind You" (see '53).

Don Reid   Don Reid was the lyricist and co-composer with Sammy Kaye of the patriotic World War II song "Remember Pearl Harbor" (see '42).

Leo Reisman (1897–1961)   Leo Reisman was a talented violinist and pianist. After graduating from the New England Conservatory of Music, he became First Violinist with the Baltimore Symphony. He left the classical field to form his own dance orchestra that often played for high society dances. In '19, he brought his orchestra to New York City for an engagement at the Hotel Brunswick. When they left the Brunswick in '29, they transferred to Central Park Casino, and later to the prestigious Waldorf-Astoria Hotel. He broadcast from the Waldorf for the Philip Morris Cigarette radio program. Reisman's orchestra remained successful until his band went out of style during the Big Band era of the late '30s and early '40s. Reisman and his orchestra's most popular recordings were released between the late '20s and the mid–'30s. Some of his most famous recordings include "The Wedding of the Painted Doll" (see '29), "Night and Day" with Fred Astaire (see '32), "Paradise" (see '32), "Stormy Weather" (see '33), and "The Continental" (see '34). Reisman was the No. 27 top recording artist of the '20s and No. 10 of the '30s.

C. Francis Reisner   C. Francis Reisner co-wrote the lyrics for "Good-bye Broadway, Hello France" with Benny Davis (see '17) for the *Passing Show of 1917*.

Leon and Otis Rene   Leon (1902–), Otis. Leon and Otis Rene were co-writers with Clarence Muse of "Sleepy Time Down South" (see '31). The brothers also wrote "When the Swallows Come Back to Capistrano" and Leon later wrote the rock 'n' roll classic "Rockin' Robin." During the '40s, Leon and Otis ran the pioneering independent R&B labels Exclusive and Excelsior. They had their own record pressing plant, but their equipment could not press the 45 RPM speed so the labels went out of business in 1950. Leon formed Class Records in Los Angeles in '51. Their recordings were primarily R&B, jazz and some popular.

Harry Revel (1905–1958)   Harry Revel composed several hit songs for the movie musicals of the '30s. He collaborated with lyricist Mack Gordon on several hits. Revel was born in London, England. After graduating from the Guild Hall of Music in London, he toured with the Paris Hawaiian Band. Before immigrating to the U.S. in '29, Revel wrote for musical productions in Paris, Copenhagen, Vienna and London. After arriving in the U.S., he wrote the scores for *Ziegfeld Follies of 1931* and a couple of other shows. Revel moved to Hollywood to write for Paramount Pictures and later for 20th Century Fox. He wrote scores for such films as *We're Not Dressing, She Loves Me Not, Paris in the Spring, Two for Tonight, Poor Little Rich Girl, Four Jacks and a Jill* and *Love Finds Andy Hardy*. Revel collaborated with lyricists Mack Gordon, Mort Greene, Paul Francis Webster and Arnold Horwitt. Harry Revel's most famous songs include "Did You Ever See a Dream Walking?" (see '33), "Love Thy Neighbor" (see '34), "With My Eyes Wide Open, I'm Dreaming" (see '34), "Stay as Sweet as You Are" (see '34), "Paris in the Spring" (see '35), "When I'm with You" (see '36), "Goodnight, My Love" (see '37) and "Thanks for Everything" (see '39). Revel was an original member of the Songwriters' Hall of Fame in '70. At http://www.songwritershall offame.org/exhibit_audio_video.asp?exhibitId=306 you can hear an audio clip of "Stay as Sweet as You Are" performed by Sam Browne with Ambrose and his orchestra.

Eben E. Rexford (1848–1916)   Eben E. Rexford was born in Johnsburgh, New York. His gift with words was evidenced at a very early age. He was 14 years old when his first piece was published in the *New York Ledger* in 1862. Rexford wrote lyrics for sacred and secular works. His most well known secular poem was "Silver Threads Among the Gold," which was made into a song by Hart Danks (see '04). The song reportedly sold over three million copies.

Alvino Rey (real name: Alvin McBurney; 1908–2004)   Early in his career, Alvino Rey was attracted to the sound of the Hawaiian guitar, and later played the electric guitar. In the Big Band era, guitar was an unusual instrument in the bands, but Rey became famous for his guitar playing and for amplifying it so it could be heard among the other instruments. Rey joined Hoarce Heidt in '37 and recorded often with Heidt's band. In '38, he married one of the King Sisters, Louise, who also did vocals for Heidt. Soon after he left Heidt's band, he formed his own group and took the King Sisters with him. Beginning in '40, Rey's band recorded often for the Bluebird label. After '42, Rey primarily remained active in the music business by touring college campuses. Rey's most popular recording was "Deep in the Heart of Texas" (see '42).

Herbert Reynolds (real name: Michael Elder Rourke; 1867–1933)   Herbert Reynolds wrote the lyrics for the Sigmund Romberg operetta *Blue Paradise*. The popular song "Auf Wiedersehn" (see '15) came from that musical. He also wrote the lyrics for Jerome Kern's "They Didn't Believe Me" (see '15) and contributed some lyrics for the *Ziegfeld Follies of 1922*.

Betty Jane Rhodes (1921–)   Johnny Johnston introduced "I Don't Want to Walk Without You" in the movie musical *Sweater Girl*. Betty Jane Rhodes reprised the song later in the same film (see '42).

Helen Rhodes (real name: Helen Guy; circa 1858–1936)   Helen Rhodes was the composer of the famous wedding song "Because" (see '02) using the name Guy d'Hardelot. Rhodes was a French composer, pianist and teacher. She was born to an English father and a French mother near Bologne in the Chateau d'Hardelot (she took her pen name from her birth last name and the name of the castle). The old castle had been occupied by Henry VIII and Anne Boleyn. She studied at the Paris Conservatory and privately in London. At this point in history, it was not very acceptable for a woman to write songs, especially popular songs of love. Therefore, she assumed a pen name that was masculine.

Joe Ricardel (1911–2002)   Joe Ricardel wrote "The Wise Old Owl" (see '41). Ricardel and Redd Evans also wrote the jazz favorite "Frim Fram Sauce." Ricardel played violin, piano, saxophone, trumpet and clarinet

Gitz Rice (real name: Gitz Ingraham Rice; 1891–1947)   The name Lieutenant Gitz Rice became closely associated with one patriotic song he wrote with Harold Robe during the First World War: "Dear Old Pal of Mine" (see '19), in which a soldier laments his absence from his girlfriend. Rice was born in New Glasgow, Nova Scotia. He moved to Montréal to study at the McGill Conservatory and subsequently joined the Canadian Army. During the First World War, he saw active service in Europe, where he fought in several battles. Rice often performed in stage shows to entertain his fellow soldiers on the front lines between battles. The soldier-entertainers wrote and rehearsed new material during lulls in active duty. It was in this way that, in addition to singing and playing the piano for the concert parties, Rice polished his songwriting skills. Some sources also attribute the wartime ditty "Mademoiselle from Armentières, parlez-vous?" to Rice, but his authorship is unconfirmed. After the war, Rice continued to write and publish songs, traveled with vaudeville troupes.

Max Rich (?–1970)   Max Rich was the composer of "Smile, Darn Ya, Smile" (see '31).

Johnny Richards (1911–1968)   Johnny Richards was the composer of "Young at Heart" (see '54). Richards' tune had originated in '39 as "Moonbeam."

Harry Richman (real name: Harry Reichman; 1895–1972)   Harry Richman was one of the top vocalists in the '20s and '30s. He had a debonair image and a robust theatrical singing style. Richman achieved stardom in *George White's Scandals of 1926*. In the rest of the '20s he appeared in several Broadway shows and in top nightclubs. He introduced, wrote and/or popularized "Birth of the Blues" (see '26), "Miss Annabelle Lee" (see '27), "On the Sunny Side of the Street" and "Exactly Like You" (see '30), "Puttin' on the Ritz" and "There's Danger in Your Eyes, Cherie" (see '30), "I Love a Parade" (see '31), "Moonlight Saving Time" (see '31), "Let's Put Out the Lights" (see '32) and "Walking My Baby Back Home" (see '52, when it was most popular). During the '30s he continued to appear on Broadway and also acted in a few films. In the late '30s he was often heard on radio. By the mid- to late '40s he was only semi-active. He performed occasionally into the early '60s. "Puttin' on the Ritz" was Richman's only big hit recording (see '30).

Antonia Ridge   Antonia Ridge wrote the English lyrics for "The Happy Wanderer" (see '54).

Mike Riley (circa 1904–?)   Mike Riley played both trumpet and trombone. He is best remembered as the co-writer of "The Music Goes 'Round and Around" (see '36). In '27 Riley was playing trumpet in a band led by Jimmy Durante at the Parody Club. He next had stints playing trombone in several big bands. He joined Eddie Farley to form the Riley-Farley Orchestra. They split in '36 to lead separate bands.

Nikolai Rimsky-Korsakoff (real name: Nikolay Andreevich Rimsky-Korsakov; 1844–1908)   Rimsky-Korsakov was a Russian naval officer but soon discovered his love for music. In the mid–1800s he belonged to the group of progressive composers but later returned to the more traditional way of composing. He often combined uniquely Russian folksongs with the music of the Russian Orthodox Church. Rimsky-Korsakov wrote the first Russian symphony and Igor Stravinsky was one of his students. From the popular song perspective, Rimsky-Korsakoff's "Song of India" from the first movement of his *Le Coq D'Or Suite* and from his opera *Sadko* was very popular in '21. Several of his compositions have become very well known and have remained popular classics for years. His "Flight of the Bumble Bee" was turned into "Bumble Boogie" during the Big Band Era.

Blanche Ring (1877–1961)   Blanche Ring spent many years in vaudeville where she was famous for encouraging audiences to sing along with her. She made her Broadway debut in '02 in *The Defender*, where she introduced "In the Good Old Summer Time." She quickly became one of Broadway's top musical comediennes. Ring appeared in more than twenty musical productions, introducing some of the most popular hit songs of the early 20th century, including "Bedelia" (see '04), "Yip-I-Addy-I-Ay" (see '09) and "Come, Josephine in My Flying Machine" (see '11). Ring caused a sensation singing "I've Got Rings on My Fingers" in *The Midnight Sons* (see '09). She and the song became so popular that she reprised the song in her next show, *The Yankee Girl* in '10. Miss Ring had a featured role in *Strike Up the Band* ('30), and made her final Broadway appearance in *Right This Way* ('38). She also made several appearances in silent films and appeared in a few sound films, including *If I Had My Way* ('40), but didn't make much impact in the movies. The most successful of her four marriages was to actor Charles Winninger.

Dave Ringle   Dave Ringle was the lyricist on "Wabash Blues" (see '21).

Tex Ritter (real name: Woodward Maurice Ritter; 1905–1974)   Tex Ritter introduced the theme song from the classic western film *High Noon* (see '52) on the film's soundtrack. Ritter is primarily remembered as a singing-cowboy star of "B" westerns during the '30s and '40s, but he was also a country-music recording star. He is the father of actor John Ritter, who starred for several years on the TV sitcoms *Three's Company* and *Eight Simple Rules*.

E. Rivera   E. Rivera was co-lyricist of the English version of "Green Eyes" (see '41).

C.A. Robbins   C.A. Robbins was lyricist for Washington and Lee University's fight song, "Washington and Lee Swing" (see '10).

Harold Robe   Lyricist Harold Robe penned several

popular songs, but the only one that became particularly popular was "Dear Old Pal of Mine" (see '19).

Julian Robeldo   Julian Robeldo was the composer of "Three O'Clock in the Morning" (see '22).

Allan Roberts (1905–1966)   Allan Roberts was a co-writer of "You Always Hurt the One You Love" (see '44), "Into Each Life Some Rain Must Fall" (see '44) and "Put the Blame on Mame" (see '46).

Bob Roberts (1879–1930)   Bob Roberts' most popular recording was "Ragtime Cowboy Joe" (see '12), his last successful recording endeavor. According to *Pop Memories*, "among artists with more than one charted record, this was the biggest final hit by any recording artist."

Joan Roberts (1918–)   Joan Roberts as Laurey and Alfred Drake as Curly introduced "People Will Say We're in Love" in the musical *Oklahoma!* (see '43). Ms. Roberts performed on stage, screen and television. She played the role of Heidi Schiller in the 2001 Broadway revival of Stephen Sondheim's *Follies*.

Lee G. Roberts   Lee Roberts' chief contribution to pop music history was as the composer for "Smiles" (see '18).

Luckey Roberts (real name: Charles Luckeyth; 1887–1968)   Luckey Roberts was the composer of "Moonlight Cocktail" (see '42). Roberts was a jazz pianist, as well as a composer.

Paul Roberts (real name: Paul Metivier; 1915–)   Paul Roberts was a co-writer of "There's a Star-Spangled Banner Waving Somewhere" (see '43). Roberts was born in Dorchester, Massachusetts in '15. During the late '30s through the mid-'40s, Paul and his wife, Ann, were very popular entertainers throughout central and northern Maine, as well as the Maritime Provinces. It was during the early '40s while living in Skowhegan, Maine, that Paul wrote "There's a Star-Spangled Banner Waving Somewhere." Roberts had over 100 songs published.

Dick Robertson (1903–)   Dick Robertson was a co-writer of "A Little on the Lonely Side" (see '45). Robertson was a band singer who was also the band's leader. His most productive period in the recording field was between '37 and the early '40s. None of his recordings were particularly popular, the most successful ones only rising to No. 5 on the charts.

Leo Robin (1900–1984)   Lyricist Leo Robin was a prolific writer of popular songs from the mid-'20s into the '50s. He most often collaborated with composer Ralph Rainger. Robin studied at the University of Pittsburgh Law School and Carnegie Tech's drama school. After graduation, he worked as a publicity agent, a newspaper reporter and as a social worker. His biggest ambition was to be a playwright and in the early '20s he moved to New York City to try to achieve his goal. In New York, Robin began writing lyrics for songs for several different composers. Robin soon turned his attention to the Broadway stage. With Vincent Youmans and Clifford Grey, he produced *Hit the Deck*, which premiered "Hallelujah!" and "Sometimes I'm Happy" (see '27). Robin team with composer Richard A. Whiting to write "Louise" (see '29), which Maurice Chevalier introduced in film *Innocents of Paris*. In '30, Robin teamed with Ralph Rainger and they

soon moved to Hollywood to write for Paramount Pictures. They produced some of the most memorable film scores including *She Done Him Wrong, She Loves Me Not, The Big Broadcast of 1937, The Big Broadcast of 1938 and Waikiki Wedding*. By the end of the '30s, the team left Paramount and signed with 20th Century Fox. Robin and Rainger wrote several well-known songs; including "Beyond the Blue Horizon" (see '30), "Please" (see '32), "Love in Bloom" (see '34) and "June in January" (see '34). The pair received the Academy Award for Best Song for "Thanks for the Memory" (see '38). Robin's and Fred Hollander's "Whispers in the Dark" appeared in the movie musical *Artists and Models* (see '37). After Rainger's death in '42, Robin worked with many other composers including Jerome Kern, Arthur Schwartz, Harry Warren and Harold Arlen. Songs from those collaborations include "A Gal in Calico" (see '46), "The Lady in the Tutti Frutti Hat," "Zing a Little Zong," and "Hooray for Love." Robin also wrote the lyrics for "Prisoner of Love" back in the '30s, but it was most popular in '46. Robin collaborated with Jule Styne writing the score for the Broadway musical *Gentlemen Prefer Blondes*. The production starred Carol Channing and included the song "Diamonds are a Girl's Best Friend" (see '50). In the '50s, Robin was collaborating with Sigmund Romberg on the Broadway musical *The Girl in Pink Tights* when Romberg died. The musical was not completed until '54. Robin was inducted into the Songwriters' Hall of Fame in '72. At http://www.songwritershalloffame.org/exhibit_audio_video.asp?exhibitId=237 you can hear audio clips of "Beyond the Blue Horizon" performed by Bob Borger with George Olsen and his orchestra, "Thanks for the Memory" performed by Bob Hope, and "Zing a Little Zong" sung by Bing Crosby.

J. Russel Robinson (real name: Joseph Russel Robinson; 1892–1963)   J. Russel Robinson was a pianist and songwriter from Indianapolis. Robinson began his career in vaudeville around '08 as part of an act called the Robinson Brothers. His first published composition, "Dynamite Rag," appeared in '10. Although Robinson was white, he often collaborated with African American musicians and performers throughout his career, including Noble Sissle, Jo Trent, James P. Johnson, Fats Waller, and Cab Calloway, and was an accompanist to blues singers Lucille Hegamin and Lizzie Miles. As a pianist, Robinson cut a number of piano rolls for ORS Company. In early '19, the Original Dixieland Jazz Band's pianist, Henry Ragas, died suddenly. Robinson agreed to fill in on an eminent European tour and wound up staying in the band until it dissolved in '23. Although Robinson contributed songs to London stage productions, he didn't have much success as a Broadway-style songwriter. One of his songs, "Aggravatin' Papa (Don't You Try to Two-Time Me)," was introduced in *Plantation Revue*, an all-black cast musical in '22. It was with lyricist Roy Turk that Robinson enjoyed his biggest successes, but he also worked with Bernard, Sissle, Con Conrad, and others. His biggest hit songs were "Palesteena" (see '20) and "Margie" (see '21). In the '30s Robinson worked in radio and in '32 wrote the notorious song "Reefer Man" for Cab Calloway.

Jessie Mae Robinson (1919–1966)   Jessie Mae Robinson wrote "I Went to Your Wedding" (see '52) and "Keep It a Secret" (see '53).

Lilla Cayley Robinson   Lilla Cayley Robinson is

primarily remembered for writing the English lyrics for "Glow Worm" (see '08).

Alfred Robyn (1860–1935) Alfred Robyn is primarily remembered as the composer for several Broadway productions between '04 and '14. His most famous works include *A Yankee Tourist* and *The Yankee Consul*. His "Wouldn't You Like to Have Me for a Sweetheart?" from *A Yankee Tourist* was popularized in a duet recording by Ada Jones and Billy Murray (see '08).

Stanley Rochinski Stanley Rochinski brought Carmen Lombardo the lyric for "Powder Your Face with Sunshine" (see '49). Lombardo found it fascinating, so he set it to music.

Roy Rodde Roy Rodde was one of the co-writers of "Why Don't You Believe Me?" (see '52).

Richard Rodgers (1902–1979) Richard Rodgers became one of the most famous and most prolific composers of popular songs. He collaborated with lyricist Lorenz "Larry" Hart from '19 until '43, when he began his association with Oscar Hammerstein II. Rodgers and Hammerstein wrote together until Hammerstein's death in '60. Rodgers continued to write, producing both music and lyrics for some songs and collaborating with Stephen Sondheim and Martin Charnin in the '60s and '70s. He wrote more than 900 published songs, and forty Broadway musicals. Most of Rodgers' songs were written in a dramatic context, for movies and especially for the Broadway stage. In the first decade of their collaboration, Rodgers and Hart averaged two new shows every season. The golden period for Rodgers and Hart, and golden for the American musical, was '36 to '42. Rodgers and Hart produced one gem after another including *On Your Toes* ('36), *Babes in Arms* ('37), *I'd Rather Be Right* ('37), *I Married an Angel* ('38), *The Boys from Syracuse* ('38), *Too Many Girls* ('39), *Higher and Higher* ('40), *Pal Joey* ('40) and *By Jupiter* ('42). The Rodgers and Hart partnership came to an end in '43 just prior to Hart's death. Rodgers then joined forces with lyricist and author Oscar Hammerstein II. The first Rodgers and Hammerstein collaboration was *Oklahoma!*, a new genre of Broadway musical, the musical play. Rodgers joining forces with Hammerstein marked the beginning of the most successful partnership in Broadway musical history. After *Oklahoma!*, came *Carousel* ('45), *Allegro* ('47), *South Pacific* ('49), *The King and I* ('51), *Me and Juliet* ('53), *Pipe Dream* ('55), *Flower Drum Song* ('58) and *The Sound of Music* ('59). The team wrote one movie musical, *State Fair* ('45), and one for television, *Cinderella* ('57). Collectively, the Rodgers and Hammerstein musicals earned 35 Tony Awards, 15 Academy Awards, two Pulitzer Prizes, two Grammy Awards and 2 Emmy Awards. Despite Hammerstein's death in '60, Rodgers continued to write for the Broadway stage. *No Strings* in '62 earned him two Tony Awards. *No Strings* was Rodgers' only project where he worked solo, as composer and lyricist. He continued to write until the end of the '70s. The list of his successful songs is lengthy. A very limited list of some of his most famous songs includes "Manhattan" (see '25), "The Blue Room" (see '26), "The Girl Friend" (see '26), "My Heart Stood Still" (see '28), "Thou Swell" (see '28), "With a Song in My Heart" (see '29), "Lover" (see '32), "Isn't It Romantic?" (see '32), "Blue Moon" (see '35), "My Romance" (see '35), "There's a Small Hotel" (see '36),

"Where or When" and "My Funny Valentine" (see '37), "Bewitched" (see '50), "People Will Say We're in Love," "Oh, What a Beautiful Mornin'," and "The Surrey with the Fringe on Top" (see '43), "If I Loved You," "You'll Never Walk Alone" and "June Is Bustin' Out All Over" (see '45), "Some Enchanted Evening" and "A Wonderful Guy" (see '49), "Hello, Young Lovers" (see '51), "We Kiss in a Shadow" (see '51), and "Climb Ev'ry Mountain," which came in a period not covered by this book. The '48 film *Words and Music* was based on Rodgers and Hart's partnership. Rodgers was inducted into the Songwriters' Hall of Fame when it was organized in '70. At http://www.songwritershalloffame.org/exhibit_audio_video.asp?exhibitId=33 you can hear audio clips of "Oklahoma!" performed by the original cast from the musical, "Ten Cents a Dance" performed by Ruth Etting, "If I Loved You" and "Some Enchanted Evening" sung by Frank Sinatra, "Do-Re-Mi" and "Edelweiss" sung by Harry Connick, Jr., "Oh, What a Beautiful Morning" and "You'll Never Walk Alone" sung by Frank Sinatra, "Getting to Know You" performed by Gertrude Lawrence and "June Is Bustin' Out All Over" performed by Celeste Holm.

Alex Rogers (1876–1930) Alex Rogers was born in Nashville, Tennessee. He was the lyricist for many popular songs including "Let It Alone" and "Nobody" (see both songs in '06). He worked primarily with Bert Williams, who wrote the music for Rogers's lyrics. Rogers lived most of his life in New York City. He is said to have written 2,000 songs during his show business career (http://www.lib.utk.edu/refs/tnauthors/authors/rogers-a.html).

Ginger Rogers (real name: Virginia Katherine McMath; 1911–1995) Dancer and film star Ginger Rogers was one of the most popular performers in the movie musicals of the '30s and '40s, particularly when she costarred with Fred Astaire. When she left her Fort Worth, Texas home for New York City, she had a minor role in a '29 Broadway show before she drew considerable attention in *Girl Crazy*. She followed that success with some small roles in movies in the early '30s. Ginger, Ruby Keeler, Clarence Nordstrom and Una Merkel introduced "Shuffle Off to Buffalo" in the movie musical *Forty Second Street* (see '33). Ms. Rogers introduced "The Gold Diggers' Song," sometimes called "We're in the Money," in *Gold Diggers of 1933* (see '33). She first teamed up with Astaire in *Flying Down to Rio* ('34). The duo were not the stars of the film but were instantly popular with the film's audiences. Next came eight costarring roles in movie musicals that have become classics of the genre. Over her career Rogers appeared in more than seventy films, both musical and dramatic. She won an Oscar for her role in the '40 film *Kitty Foyle*. She seems to be primarily noted as Fred Astaire's dancing partner, but she also sang and introduced or helped introduce several popular classics: "Carioca" (see '34), "The Continental" (see '34), "I'll String Along with You" (see '34), "I Won't Dance" (see '35), "The Way You Look Tonight" (see '36), "A Fine Romance" (see '36) and "They Can't Take That Away from Me" (see '37).

Robert Cameron Rogers (1862–1912) Robert Cameron Rogers wrote the lyrics for "The Rosary" (see 1903).

Gonzalo Roig (1890–1970) Cuban composer Gonzalo Roig wrote "Quiereme Mucho" that became, in the English version, "Yours" (see '41).

Caro Roma (real name: Carrie Northey; 1866–1937)   Carrie Northey, using the pen name Caro Roma, wrote the music for "Can't Yo' Heah Me Callin' Caroline?" (see '14).

Sigmund Romberg (1887–1951)   Songwriters' Hall of Fame composer Sigmund Romberg, born in Nagykanizsa, Hungary, wrote several operettas that were very successful on Broadway and then as movies. Romberg showed musical ability at an early age, but his parents wanted him to go into something more sensible than music. They sent him to Vienna to study engineering, but instead, Romberg immersed himself in Viennese music. In '09, he moved to the United States and settled in New York City. He first found work in a pencil factory, but soon became a pianist in cafes. In '12, he formed his European salon and light music orchestra. Some of his early compositions attracted the attention of Broadway producers J.J. and Lee Shubert, who employed him as their house composer. By '17, Romberg had composed 275 numbers for seventeen musicals and revues. His first great success came in '17 with *Maytime*. The operetta was an adaptation of a Viennese operetta, *Wie einst im Mai*. Another Viennese operetta, *Das Dreimaederlhaus* became *Blossom Time* in '21. It was a fictionalized version of Franz Schubert's youth for which Romberg re-arranged several pieces of Schubert's music. Next came one of his greatest successes, *The Student Prince*, in '24. It was an adaptation of the German play *Old Heidelberg*. In '26, Romberg teamed up with Oscar Hammerstein II and Otto Harbach for *The Desert Song*, and with Hammerstein again for *New Moon* in '28. Also in '28, he wrote *Rosalie* with George Gershwin, with lyrics by Ira Gershwin and P.G. Wodehouse. Romberg continued to compose music for operettas, but none found favor, for the operetta vogue had passed. Throughout the '30s, he wrote the scores for several movies, including two with Hammerstein. In the '40s he toured America with his own orchestra, and regularly appeared on radio. At the time of his death, he was working with lyricist Leo Robin on a musical *The Girl in Pink Tights*, which was produced posthumously on Broadway in '54. Some of Romberg's most famous songs include "Auf Wiedersehn" (see '15), "Song of Love" (see '22), "Serenade" (see '24), " Desert Song" (see '27), "One Alone" (see '27), "Riff Song" (see '27), "Lover, Come Back to Me" (see '29), "Softly, as in a Morning Sunrise" (see '29), and "When I Grow Too Old to Dream" (see '35). Romberg was an original member of the Songwriters' Hall of Fame in '70. The '54 movie *Deep in My Heart* was based on the life of Romberg and featured many of his most famous songs. At http://www.song writershalloffame.org/exhibit_audio_video.asp? exhibitId=69 you can hear audio clips of "Song of Love" performed by Lucy Marsh and "Lover, Come Back to Me" performed by Billie Holiday.

Harold Rome (1908–1993)   Harold Rome was a noted composer and lyricist best remembered for his songs for several Broadway musicals. Rome learned to play the piano in his childhood and performed with several dance bands during high school. Rome attended Trinity College and Yale University where he studied architecture. An excellent swing pianist, he joined the Yale University Orchestra and supported himself by playing in nightclubs

and dance halls. After graduating from Yale in '29, the stock market crash made it difficult to find work as an architect, so he decided to try his luck as a musician. His first musical was *Pins and Needles* ('37), which was presented by members of the International Ladies' Garment Workers Union. World War II had broken out in Europe and Rome joined the U.S. Army special services, writing music and lyrics to entertain the troops. His other important musicals were *Call Me Mister* ('46), *Wish You Were Here* ('52), *Fanny* ('54), *Destry Rides Again* ('59) and *I Can Get It for You Wholesale* ('62). Rome's most famous songs were "My Heart Sings" (see '45), "South America, Take It Away" (see '46) and "Wish You Were Here" (see '52). Harold Rome was elected to the Songwriters' Hall of Fame in '82.

Ann Ronell (1906–1993)   Ann Ronell was a Jewish-American composer and lyricist best known for "Who's Afraid of the Big Bad Wolf?" (see '33) and "Linda" (see '47). She was nominated for the Best Song Oscar for "Linda," and with co-composer Louis Applebaum for the Best Score Oscar, for her work on the film *The Story of G.I. Joe*. She, Dorothy Fields, Dana Suesse, and Kay Swift were some of the first successful Hollywood and Tin Pan Alley female composers or librettists. Most of her music career was spent writing background music and conducting sound tracks for films. According to www.wikipedia.com, she was romantically involved with George Gershwin.

Mickey Rooney (real name: Joe Yule, Jr.; 1920–)   Mickey Rooney and Judy Garland introduced "Good Morning" in the film version of the Broadway musical *Babes in Arms* (see '39). Mickey made his stage debut at age 15 months as part of his family's vaudeville act. He made approximately 50 silent film comedies between '27 and '33, playing Mickey McGuire, a comic-strip character. In '34 he signed a film contract with MGM. He made 15 Andy Hardy films, many of them co-starring Judy Garland. Rooney gave some very memorable performances in films especially including *A Midsummer Night's Dream* ('35), *The Adventures of Huckleberry Finn* ('39), and *National Velvet* ('44). After serving in World War II, he returned to Hollywood, but his fame and box-office draw were never quite the same. In the mid–'50s, he starred in the TV series *The Mickey Rooney Show*. In the '60s, he toured nightclubs and theaters. He received the "Lifetime Achievement" Oscar in '83.

Malia Rosa (real name: May Singhi Breen; 1895–?)   May Singhi Breen as Malia Rosa was lyricist of "Forever and Ever" (see '49). May Singhi Breen was a very popular ukulele player and recording artist. She was called the "Ukulele Lady." She married Peter DeRose (see his biographical sketch).

Juventino Rosas (real name: Juventino Rosas Cadenas; 1868–1894)   Mexican composer, violinist and bandleader Juventino Rosas was the composer of "The Loveliest Night of the Year" (see '51). Irving Aaronson adapted Rosas' "Sobre las Olas," a waltz composed in the late 19th century, for this hit song.

Billy Rose (real name: William Samuel Rosenberg; 1899–1966)   Billy Rose was a successful lyricist, producer, nightclub and theater owner. One of his marriages was to superstar comedienne Fanny Brice. His most productive period as a songwriter came during the

'20s. After that he concentrated on his many other business ventures. After graduating from high school in New York City, Billy was trained in Gregg shorthand and as a teenager won a high-speed dictation contest. During World War I, Rose worked as the shorthand reporter for the War Industries Board. After the War, Rose returned to New York City and began working on Broadway. He collaborated with composers such as Ray Henderson, Mort Dixon, Dave Dreyer, Al Jolson, Vincent Youmans, Harold Arlen, Dana Suesse, Mabel Wayne and Harry Warren on scores for Broadway productions. Some of Rose's most famous lyrics include "Barney Google" (see '23), "You've Got to See Mamma Every Night" (see '23), "That Old Gang of Mine" (see '23), "A Cup of Coffee, a Sandwich and You" (see '26), "In a Little Spanish Town" (see '27), "Me and My Shadow" (see '27), "Tonight You Belong to Me" (see '27), "Here Comes the Show Boat" (see '28), "There's a Rainbow 'Round My Shoulder" (see '28), "Great Day" (see '29), "More Than You Know" (see '29), "Without a Song" (see '29), "I've Got a Feeling I'm Falling" (see '29), "I Found a Million Dollar Baby (in a Five and Ten Cent Store)" (see '31) and "I Wanna Be Loved" (see '50). Other well known Rose songs include "You Tell Her, I Stutter," "Does the Spearmint Lose Its Flavor on the Bedpost Overnight?," "Clap Hands, Here Comes Charley," "Don't Bring Lulu," "Fifty Million Frenchmen Can't Be Wrong," "Golden Gate," "It Happened in Monterey," "Back in Your Own Back Yard," "Cheerful Little Earful," "Would You Like to Take a Walk?," "It's Only a Paper Moon," and "The Night is Young and You're So Beautiful." Billy Rose was an original member of the Songwriters' Hall of Fame in '70. At http://www.songwritershalloffame.org/exhibit_audio_video.asp?exhibitId=307 you can hear audio clips of "You've Gotta See Your Mamma Every Night" and "That Old Gang of Mine" performed by Billy Murray, "It Happened in Monterey" performed by Jack Fulton with Paul Whiteman's Orchestra, "Would You Like to Take a Walk?," performed by Annette Hanshaw with Benny Goodman and his orchestra, and "I Found a Million Dollar Baby" sung by Nat "King" Cole.

David Rose (1910–1990)   Composer David Rose is most famous for the hits he composed for the orchestra he conducted. His two biggest hit recordings are of "Holiday for Strings" (see '44) and another of his own compositions "The Stripper" ('62). In the early part of his career he was primarily an arranger for several of the big bands, notably for Benny Goodman's band. In the late '30s he was musical director for the Mutual Broadcasting Network. By the late '40s he had begun a long relationship with comedian Red Skelton as orchestra leader on his radio and then television series ("Holiday for Strings" was the show's theme). Rose also wrote or arranged several musical scores for Hollywood films, including *Operation Petticoat* ('59) and *Please Don't Eat the Daisies* ('60).

Ed Rose   Ed Rose was co-lyricist on "Baby Shoes" (see '16) and lyricist for "Oh Johnny, Oh Johnny, Oh!" (see '17).

Vincent Rose (1880–1944)   Composer Vincent Rose was born in Palermo, Italy. He was particularly active as songwriter in the '20s. At the age of 17, he moved to the United States but returned to Palermo to study violin and piano at the Palermo School of Music. Back in

the U.S., Rose played violin and piano in dance bands in Chicago and Los Angeles. He finally formed his own group in '06. He led the orchestra until the early '40s; however, they did not receive much success in the recording field. Rose collaborated with lyricists such as Larry Stock, Jack Meskill, Al Lewis, Ray Klages, James Cavanaugh and Buddy DeSylva. Rose's most well-known songs include "Avalon" (see '21), "Linger Awhile" (see '24), "The Umbrella Man" (see '39), and "Blueberry Hill" (see '40). Vincent Rose was an original member of the Songwriters' Hall of Fame in '70.

Adrian Ross (real name: Arthur Reed Ropes; 1859–1933)   Adrian Ross was a lyricist of British musical comedies in the late 19th and early 20th century. He was also an esteemed Cambridge University don, historian, and a translator of French and German literature. He was the winner of the Chancellor's Medal for verse. He changed his name to Adrian Ross due to a concern that writing musicals would compromise his professional career. Under the name Adrian Ross he produced more than 60 libretti for the London stage. He is most famous in America for the lyrics and libretto he wrote for *The Merry Widow* (see '07).

Jerry Ross (1926–1955)   With Richard Adler, Jerry Ross wrote two Broadway scores that were extremely successful: *The Pajama Game* and *Damn Yankees*. "Hey There" and "Hernando's Hideaway" from *The Pajama Game* were big hits (see '54). "Heart" was the biggest hit song from *Damn Yankees* (see '55). Prior to their Broadway success, Adler and Ross wrote "Rags to Riches" (see '53). After their two Broadway successes, Ross died in '55. For more on Ross, see http://jerryross.net/.

Lanny Ross (real name: Lancelot Patrick Ross; 1906–1988)   Lanny Ross became a stage, screen, radio and television personality. At age six, he appeared on stage in New York City in *Disraeli*. During his teen years, he further developed his musical abilities. After he graduated from Yale with a law degree, he became a radio singer. Throughout the '30s, his signature song was "Moonlight and Roses." Ross appeared on many of radio's biggest shows, including *Maxwell House Show Boat* and *Camel Cigarette Camel Caravan*. In the mid-'30s, he was voted the Most Popular Male Vocalist. He had several lead roles in films, including *College Rhythm*, where he introduced "Stay as Sweet as You Are" (see '34). During World War II, he served in the Army and achieved the rank of major. After the war, he reestablished his entertainment career. In television's infancy, Ross performed on *Swift's TV Variety* and had his own show, *The Lanny Ross Show*.

Shirley Ross (real name: Bernice Gaunt; 1913–1975)   Shirley Ross is most famous for the duet she performed with Bob Hope of "Thanks for the Memory" (see '38). She and Hope followed that success with the duet "Two Sleepy People" in *Thanks for the Memory* (see '38). Otherwise, Ross acted and sang in several other movies, notably *The Merry Widow* ('34), *San Francisco* ('36) and *The Big Broadcast of 1937*, was vocalist with some of the big bands, made guest appearances on radio shows and starred in the '40 Broadway musical *Higher and Higher*.

Fritz Rotter (1900–1984)   Fritz Rotter was an Austrian author and composer. By age 17 Rotter was writing music for cabarets. Around '20, he moved to Berlin, where he wrote lyrics and composed music for films. Rotter's most well known song was "I Kiss Your Hand, Madame," for which he wrote the German lyrics (see '29). Fritz, using the pseudonym M. Rotha, wrote the words and music for "That's All I Want from You" (see '55). During World War II, Rotter fled Germany, eventually ending up in Switzerland.

Nick Roubanis   In '41, Nick Roubanis, a Greco-American music instructor, released a jazz instrumental arrangement "Misirlou," crediting himself as composer (see '47). However, the song most likely originated in Athens, Greece among the refugees from Smyrna (now Ismir, Turkey) during the '20s. The first known recording was in Greece around 1930.

Josephine V. Rowe   Josephine V. Rowe is only known for being the lyricist of "Macushla" (see '10).

Ruth Roye   Ruth Roye introduced "The Aba Daba Honeymoon" at the Palace Theater in New York City (see '14).

Harry Ruby (1895–1974)   Harry Ruby was a successful composer of popular songs, primarily with lyricist Bert Kalmar. Ruby grew up in New York City. In his early career, he worked as a pianist and song plugger for the Gus Edwards and Harry von Tilzer music publishing firms. Ruby also played in vaudeville acts, nickelodeons and cafes throughout the city. From '17–'20, Ruby collaborated with songwriters Edgar Leslie, Sam Lewis, Joe Young and George Jessel on the songs "Come on Papa" and "And He'd Say Oo-La-La Wee Wee." It wasn't until Ruby met Bert Kalmar in '20 that he had his greatest success. Songs from the Kalmar and Ruby collaboration include "I Wanna Be Loved by You" (see '28) and "Three Little Words" (see '30). Other Kalmar and Ruby songs include "So Long Oo Long," "My Sunny Tennessee" and "Who's Sorry Now?" Ruby wrote "Cecilia" (see '25) with Dave Dreyer. Moving to Hollywood in '30, Ruby contributed songs for several films including *Check and Double Check* and *The Kid from Spain*. Ruby also wrote screenplays including *Look for the Silver Lining* and *The Kid from Spain*. After Kalmar's death in '47, Ruby continued to write but wasn't as successful. In '50, Hollywood released *Three Little Words* based on the Kalmar and Ruby partnership. Ruby was an original member of the Songwriters' Hall of Fame in '70. At http://www.songwritershalloffame.org/exhibit_audio_video.asp?exhibitId=308 you can hear audio clips of "My Sunny Tennessee" performed by the Peerless Quartet and "A Kiss to Build a Dream on" performed by Louis Armstrong.

Gabriel Ruiz (real name: Gabriel Ruiz Galindo; 1909–1999)   Mexican songwriter Gabriel Ruiz became well known in his native country over radio and touring. By the early '40s, every famous vocalist in Mexico wanted to record a Ruiz song. In '38 Ruiz started writing music for Mexican films. His biggest U.S. hit song, "Amor," was introduced in *Broadway Rhythm* (see '44).

Bob Russell (real name: Sidney Keith Russell; 1914–1970)   Lyricist Bob Russell was particularly active in songwriting in the '40s and '50s. He also wrote music for several films. After graduating from Washington University, Russell worked for an advertising company as a copywriter. His early music career was spent writing special material for vaudeville acts and later for film studios.

Russell collaborated with several lyricists and composers including Duke Ellington, Harry Warren, Lester Lee, Carl Sigman, Lou Alter, Harold Spina, Peter DeRose and Bronislau Kaper. His best-known songs include "Frenesi" (see '40), "Maria Elena" (see '41), "Brazil" (see '43), "Don't Get Around Much Anymore" (see '43), "Babalu" (see '44), "Ballerina" (see '47) and "Misirlou" (see '47). Other well-known Russell songs are "Do Nothin' Till You Hear from Me," "You Came a Long Way from St. Louis," "I Didn't Know About You," and "Would I Love You? (Love You, Love You)." More recently, Russell wrote "He Ain't Heavy, He's My Brother" ('69). Russell, who wrote sometimes under the name S.K. and sometimes as Bob, is an original member of the Songwriters' Hall of Fame in '70. At http://www.songwritershalloffame.org/exhibit_audio_video.asp?exhibitId=280 you can hear an audio clip of "Do Nothing Till You Hear from Me" sung by Billie Holiday.

James J. Russell   James Russell is primarily remembered today as the writer of "Where the River Shannon Flows" (see '10). He wrote it in '05, but it was popularized in '06 and again, even more popular, in '10.

Jane Russell (real name: Ernestine Jane Geraldine Russell; 1921–)   Jane Russell and Bob Hope introduced "Buttons and Bows" in the movie *The Paleface* (see '48). Ms. Russell was probably as well known for her physical assets as for her film career. She first appeared in the Howard Hughes film *The Outlaw*, then starred opposite Hope in *The Paleface* and *Son of Paleface* ('52), plus opposite Marilyn Monroe in *Gentlemen Prefer Blondes* ('53).

Larry Russell   Larry Russell was one of the co-writers of "Vaya Con Dios" (see '53).

Lillian Russell (real name: Helen Louise Leonard; 1860–1922)   Born in Clinton, Iowa, Lillian Russell would become one of the most famous and beautiful actresses of the late 19th century and early 20th century. Little is known of her early life, except she had some musical training in Chicago. At the age of 18, she and her mother moved to New York City where she was offered a role in the chorus of Gilbert and Sullivan's operetta *H.M.S. Pinafore*. She first became Lillian Russell in 1879, when she made her first appearance at Tony Pastor's Theater. Her appearance was so successful that she stayed on with Pastor and starred in some of his comic operas. She was celebrated for her voice and her beauty. She soon became the companion of "Diamond" Jim Brady who showered her with extravagant gifts of diamonds and gemstones. Ms. Russell introduced "When Chloe Sings a Song" at Weber and Fields' Music Hall in an extravaganza titled *Whirl-I-Gig* in 1899 (see 1900) and she introduced "Come Down, Ma Evenin' Star" in the Weber and Fields extravaganza *Twirly-Whirly* (see '02). She was thereafter closely associated with the song.

Russell Wooding's Jubilee Singers   Russell Wooding's Jubilee Singers introduced "Great Day!" in the musical of the same name (see '29). The Singers also helped Lois Deppe introduce "Without a Song" in the same production (see '29).

S.K. Russell (see Bob Russell)

Dan Russo   Dan Russo collaborated with Ted FioRito and Ernie Erdman to pen "Toot Toot Tootsie" (see '23).

Benny Ryan   Benny Ryan's chief contribution to popular music was as co-lyricist with Bert Hanlon for "M-I-S-S-I-S-S-I-P-P-I" (see '17).

Frank Ryerson   Frank Ryerson was co-writer of "Blue Champagne" (see '41). Like Grady Watts, his collaborator on this song, Ryerson was a trumpeter in Glen Gray's orchestra.

Edgar Sampson (1907–1973)   Edgar Sampson was Chick Webb's alto saxophonist and arranger. He co-wrote "Don't Be That Way" with Benny Goodman (see '38). Mitchell Parish furnished the lyrics. Sampson was a composer, arranger, saxophonist and violinist. He was playing violin by age 6 and picked up the sax during his high school years. He started his professional career with a violin/piano duo with Joe Colman in '24. It wasn't long before he was playing with Duke Ellington's and Fletcher Henderson's bands. He joined Chick Webb's band in '33. It was during this period he wrote "Stomping at the Savoy" and "Don't Be that Way" (see above). He left that band in '36, and freelanced as a composer and arranger for Benny Goodman, Artie Shaw, Red Norvo, Teddy Wilson and Chick Webb.

Julio C. Sanders   Julio C. Sanders wrote the Argentine tango "Adios Muchachos" that was transformed into the popular song "I Get Ideas" (see '51).

Julia Sanderson (real name: Julia Sackett; 1884–1975)   Soprano Julia Sanderson co-starred with Donald Brian in *The Siren* ('11). Their chemistry clicked so well they were re-teamed for *The Girl from Utah*, where they introduced Jerome Kern's "They Didn't Believe Me" (see '15). Sanderson and Brian's last appearance together was in *Sybil* ('16). After "Love Is the Sweetest Thing" was introduced in the British film *Say It with Music*, it was premiered in the U.S. by Ms. Sanderson (see '33).

Ann Sands   Ann Sands and Jay Velie introduced "I Love You" in *Little Jessie James* (see '24).

Henry Sanicola   Henry Sanicola was the composer of some popular songs, but also served as associate producer or producer of several television shows during the '50s, most notably *The Frank Sinatra Show* in '57. Sanicola and Sinatra also teamed up to write the Christmas song "Mistletoe and Holly." Sanicola co-wrote "This Love of Mine" (see '41), which was popularized by Tommy Dorsey and his orchestra.

Joseph Santley (real name: Joseph Mansfield; 1890–1971)   Joseph Santley started his show business career as a child with his parents, where he was billed as "The World's Greatest Boy Actor." He began appearing on the New York stage beginning in '10. Joseph Santley introduced Irving Berlin's "The Girl on the Magazine" in the musical *Stop! Look! Listen!* (see '16). During the '20s he turned to film work at Paramount's Long Island City studio. His first feature film was the Marx Brothers film *The Cocoanuts*. He moved between Pathe, Monogram, Mascot, Republic Pictures, MGM and RKO throughout the '30s and into the '40s. He left feature films in the early '50s and moved to television, where he directed variety shows for such figures as Ethel Merman and Jimmy Durante.

William Saroyan (1908–1981)   Playwright and author William Saroyan and his cousin, Ross Bagdasarian, took an automobile trip through the western states in '49.

During the trip they adapted an Armenian folk song into "Come on-a My House" (see '51).

The Satisfiers   The Satisfiers introduced "All I Want for Christmas (Is My Two Front Teeth)" on Perry Como's radio show (see '48).

Robert Sauer   Robert Sauer was the composer of "When It's Springtime in the Rockies" (see '30).

David Saxon (1919–)   David Saxon was one of the co-writers of "There Must Be a Way" (see '45).

Fritzi Scheff (real name: Fredericka Scheff Yarger; 1879–1954)   Fritzi Scheff was the daughter of a prima donna with the Imperial Opera in Vienna. She made her debut at eight years old singing in a Gounod opera with the Frankfurt Opera company. After appearing with several other opera companies in Germany, she came to the U.S. and spent three years with the Metropolitan Opera in New York City. From opera she moved into operetta. Her signature song, "Kiss Me Again" from *Mlle. Modiste,* was written specifically for her by Victor Herbert (see '05). After operetta came vaudeville and appearances for Billy Rose in his show at the '39 New York World's Fair and at Rose's Diamond Horseshoe.

Victor Schertzinger (1890–1941)   Victor Schertzinger was a child prodigy on the violin. At age eight, he appeared as a prodigy violinist with several orchestras including Victor Herbert's and John Phillip Sousa's. His first published songs came in '13, but they are not particularly well known today. He also wrote background music for some of the early silent films. Once sound arrived in the late '20s, he contributed several songs to the "talkies." His most remembered songs are "Marquita" (see '28), "One Night of Love" (see '34), and "Tangerine" (see '42).

Elmer Schoebel (1896–1970)   Elmer Schoebel was a very respected pianist, bandleader and composer in the '20s. His band was called Elmer Schoebel and his Friars Society Orchestra. Schoebel began his music career playing piano for silent films. He was soon accompanying acts in vaudeville. For a couple of years in the early '20s, he recorded with the New Orleans Rhythm Kings. After that, he led his own group and toured with Isham Jones and his orchestra in the mid-'20s. By the '30s Schoebel was primarily a writer. Schoebel co-wrote the music for "Nobody's Sweetheart" (see '24) and "Bugle Call Rag" in '23 (see '32 when it was most popular).

John and Malvin Schonberger   The Schonberger brothers wrote the incredibly popular "Whispering" (see '20). Malvin wrote the lyrics, while John furnished the music.

Carl Schraubstader   Carl Schraubstader's chief claim to fame in the popular music field is as composer of "Last Night on the Back Porch" (see '24).

Walter Schumann (1913–1958)   Walter Schumann's music for the TV series *Dragnet* was a very integral part of Stan Freberg's "St. George and the Dragonet" (see '53). Schumann wrote music for many Hollywood films beginning in the late '40s.

Ira Schuster (1889–1945)   Ira Schuster was born in New York City. After graduating from high school he began working as a staff pianist at various publishing companies on Tin Pan Alley. Collaborating with songwriters Ed. G. Nelson, Joe Young, Jack Little, Larry Stock, Paul Cunningham and the Gershwin brothers, Schuster had a string of hits from the early '10s into the '30s. His best known songs were "Ten Little Fingers and Ten Little Toes" (see '22), and "In a Shanty in Old Shanty Town" (see '32). Schuster was also one of the first songwriters to form his own publishing company.

Wilber Schwandt Wilber Schwandt was co-composer of "Dream a Little Dream of Me" (see '31).

Arthur Schwartz (1900–1984) Composer Arthur Schwartz wrote several popular songs with lyricist Howard Dietz that became popular classics. Arthur Schwartz taught himself the harmonica and piano and by his mid-teens, was accompanying silent films at a Brooklyn theater. During his years of studying law, Schwartz also wrote songs and in '23 "Baltimore, MD, You're the Only Doctor for Me," became his first published song. In '28, he was introduced to Howard Dietz' lyrics while attending one of his Broadway shows. He was so impressed, Schwartz convinced Dietz to form a songwriting partnership with him. Schwartz was never totally dedicated to practicing law, so in the late '20s gave up law and devoted himself full-time to songwriting. Schwartz and Dietz' first Broadway score was *The Little Show* ('29), which included "I Guess I'll Have to Change My Plan." Some of their other Broadway productions include *Three's a Crowd, The Band Wagon, Flying Colors, Revenge with Music* and *At Home Abroad*. Schwartz wrote songs for several successful Hollywood films including *Thank Your Lucky Stars, The Time, the Place and the Girl, Excuse My Dust, Dangerous When Wet, You're Never Too Young* and *The Band Wagon*. Schwartz received two Academy Award nominations for Best Song: the first in '44 for the song "They're Either Too Young or Too Old" in the film *Thank Your Lucky Stars*; the second in '46 for the song "A Gal in Calico" from the film *The Time, the Place and the Girl*. In addition to Howard Dietz, Schwartz collaborated with some of the best lyricists of his day including Dorothy Fields, Frank Loesser, Johnny Mercer, Oscar Hammerstein II, Edward Heyman, Ira Gershwin, Leo Robin and Al Stillman. Among Schwartz's most famous songs are "I Guess I'll Have to Change My Plan" (see '29), "Something to Remember You By" (see '30), "Dancing in the Dark" (see '31), "Louisiana Hayride" (see '32), "You and the Night and the Music" (see '35), "They're Either Too Young or Too Old" (see '44), "A Gal in Calico" (see '46) and "That's Entertainment" (see '53). Schwartz was elected to membership in the Songwriters' Hall of Fame in '72. At http://www.songwritershalloffame.org/exhibit_audio_video.asp?exhibitId=224 you can hear an audio clip of "Dancing in the Dark" performed by the Revelers with Frank Black.

Jean Schwartz (1878–1956) Composer Jean Schwartz was born in Budapest, Hungary. In 1888, the Schwartz family immigrated to the U.S. and settled in New York City. His sister was responsible for Schwartz' early piano training. He soon became a pianist in a Coney Island band. Schwartz began his professional career working in the sheet music departments at various stores demonstrating the popular songs of the day. Later he was hired as a pianist and song plugger for an important music-publishing firm. He also performed in vaudeville with William Jerome and accompanied the Dolly Sisters.

Schwartz became one of the most prolific composers for the early Broadway stage. His scores include *A Yankee Circus on Mars, The Honeymoon Express, The Passing Show (1921 and 1923), The Midnight Rounders (1920 and 1921), Make It Snappy* and *A Night in Spain*. Schwartz also wrote individual songs for the musical productions, notably *Sinbad*. Schwartz collaborated with lyricists such as William Jerome, Harold Atteridge, Al Bryan, Clifford Grey, Grant Clarke, Sam Lewis, Joe Young, Milton Ager and Jack Meskill. Schwartz co-wrote such songs as "Any Old Place I Can Hang My Hat Is Home Sweet Home to Me" (see '01), "Bedelia" (see '04), "I Love the Ladies" (see '14), "Chinatown, My Chinatown" (see '15), "Hello, Hawaii, How Are You?" (see '16), "Hello, Central, Give Me No Man's Land" (see '18), "Rock-a-bye Your Baby with a Dixie Melody" (see '18), and "I'm All Bound 'Round with the Mason-Dixon Line" (see '18). Jean Schwartz was an original member of the Songwriters' Hall of Fame in '70. At http://www.songwritershalloffame.org/exhibit_audio_video.asp?exhibitId=278 you can hear an audio clip of "Ring a Ting Ling" performed by Ada Jones ('12).

Clinton Scollard (1860–1932) Oley Speaks took Clinton Scollard's poem "Sylvia" and turned it into a song. It is often used as an art song, but it was also popular in '14.

Clement Scott (1841–1904) Clement William Scott was a very influential London-based theatre critic for the *Daily Telegraph* in the final decades of the 1800s. From a popular music perspective, Scott was lyricist for "Oh, Promise Me" (see '07). Maewa Kaihau used a Scott tune for her song that became "Now Is the Hour" (see '48).

Maurice Scott (1878–1933) Maurice Scott was the composer of "I've Got Rings on My Fingers (Mumbo Jumbo Jijiboo J. O'Shea)" (see '09).

Winfield Scott (real name: Robie Kirk; 1939–) Winfield Scott wrote the words and music for "Tweedle Dee" (see '55). Scott teamed with Otis Blackwell to pen the Elvis Presley hit "Return to Sender" ('62). Robie Kirk was an R&B singer.

William Scotti William Scotti adapted the melody for "My Moonlight Madonna" (see '33) from Zdenko Fibich's "Poeme." Paul Francis Webster added lyrics.

Vincent Scotto (1876–1952) Vincent Scotto was born in Marseilles. Scotto wrote 60 operettas and some 4,000 songs. His most famous song in the U.S., "It's Delightful to Be Married" (see '07), was co-written with Anna Held. Scotto also composed the tune of "Vieni, Vieni" (see '37). John Royal, then vice-president of NBC, recommended this tune to Rudy Vallee. Vallee liked it, wrote the English lyrics and introduced it on the "Fleischmann Hour," his popular weekly radio program in '36.

Guy Scull Although for years the composer credited for writing Yale's famous "The Whiffenpoof Song" (see '09) was Tod B. Galloway, an Amherst graduate, but in more recent years, it appears to have been Guy Scull, a Harvard student.

Sholom Secunda (1894–1974) Sholom Secunda was born in Ukraine and was educated in America. He worked at a Jewish theater from '37 to the beginning of the '40s. He was the composer of "Bei Mir Bist du Schoen" (see '38).

Blossom Seeley (1892–1974)   Blossom Seeley was a well-known vaudeville and Broadway singer-dancer in the '20s. Her first marriage was to Hall of Fame baseball pitcher Rube Marquard, then later to entertainer Benny Fields. She appeared in the '33 movie musical *Broadway Thru a Keyhole*. The '52 movie *Somebody Loves Me* was based on Seeley and Fields. It starred Betty Hutton as Seeley and Ralph Meeker as Fields. Ms. Seeley's most popular recordings came with "Alabamy Bound" (see '25) and "Yes Sir, That's My Baby" (see '25).

Vivienne Segal (real name: Sonia Segal; 1897–1992)   Singer/actress Vivienne Segal was the romantic lead in the operettas *The Desert Song* and *The Three Musketeers*, but she turned more to comedy in *Pal Joey*, where she introduced "Bewitched (Bothered and Bewildered)" (see '50). In her Broadway debut, Ms. Segal introduced "Auf Wiedersehn" (see '15) in the operetta *Blue Paradise*. She also helped introduce the title song in *The Desert Song* (see '27). She appeared in almost twenty Broadway productions between '15 and the early '50s.

T. Lawrence Seibert (real name: Tallifero Lawrence Seibert; 1877–1917)   Eddie Newton was a ragtime pianist in Venice Beach, California when he met T. Lawrence Seibert, a vaudeville entertainer who had written a sketch based on the tragic tale of Casey Jones. Together they wrote the song "Casey Jones" (see '10), with Eddie composing the music and Tallifero supplying the lyrics. However, Wallace Saunders, an African American engine wiper, wrote the first poetic verses about Casey Jones. Then Wallace made up a catchy little tune for the verses. The song was picked up by other railroad men and soon spread from station to station. Legend has it that one of the railroad men shared it with his brothers who were vaudeville performers. They reworked the lyrics and added a chorus. They began performing the song on the vaudeville circuit. The popularity of the song on the vaudeville circuit helped Casey Jones become a folk hero. When the song was published in '02, T. Lawrence Seibert was credited as the composer and Eddie Newton as the lyricist.

Eddie Seiler   Eddie Seiler was one of the co-writers of "I Don't Want to Set the World on Fire" (see '41) and "When the Lights Go on Again" (see '42).

Ernest Seitz (1892–1978)   Canadian composer Ernest Seitz wrote the music for "The World Is Waiting for the Sunrise" (see '20).

Ben Selvin (1898–1980)   Violinist/bandleader/record company executive Ben Selvin started his music career in about '05. Beginning in '19, he made more recordings than anybody else in the world — 9,000 under approximately 40 different names for nine different companies. When he retired at age 65, RCA presented him with a gold disk. Selvin's biggest hit records were "I'm Forever Blowing Bubbles" (see '19), "Dardanella" (see '20), "Yes! We Have No Bananas" (see '23), "Manhattan" (see '25), "Oh, How I Miss You Tonight" (see '25), "Blue Skies" (see '27), "When It's Springtime in the Rockies" (see '30) and "Happy Days Are Here Again" (see '30). Selvin became the No. 5 top recording artist of the '20s and No. 37 of the '30s, making him the No. 21 top recording artist of the first half of the 20th Century. Ben Selvin and his orchestra recordings between '19 and '34 are available for listening at http://www.redhotjazz.com/bands.html.

Tot Seymour (1889–1966)   Tot Seymour was the lyricist of "And Then Some" (see '35). Tot Seymour became one of the first female lyricists on Tin Pan Alley. She worked on the staff for various publishing companies. She also wrote special material for singers including Fanny Brice, Mae West, Belle Baker and Sophie Tucker. Later, she moved to Hollywood, where she wrote for Paramount. Her chief collaborators were Vee Lawnhurst, Pete Wendling and Jean Schwartz. Seymour and Vee Lawnhurst were advertised as "the first successful team of girl songwriters in popular music history."

Terry Shand (1904–1977)   Terry Shand was a pianist, composer and band member. In '33 Shand began playing piano with Freddy Martin's band. After five years he organized his own band. Shand's best-known songs were "Cry, Baby, Cry" (see '38), "I Double Dare You" (see '38) and "Dance with a Dolly" (see '44), although the tune for this one was hardly original with Shand.

James R. Shannon (real name: James Royce)   James R. Shannon wrote the words and music for the famous Irish song "Too-Ra-Loo-Ra-Loo-Ral (That's an Irish Lullaby)" (see '14). A couple of years after "Missouri Waltz" was published as an instrumental, another edition of the song was published with lyrics written by James Royce, using the pseudonym J.R. Shannon (see '17).

Jack Sharpe   Jack Sharpe was the lyricist of "So Rare" (see '37).

Artie Shaw (real name: Arthur Arshawsky; 1910–2004)   Clarinetist/bandleader Artie Shaw and his orchestra were very popular in the late '30s. Along with Benny Goodman, Shaw is considered one of the best clarinet players of the swing era. He was also very temperamental and often seemed to be feuding with his own fans. In '39 he left the country reportedly in a protest against the jitterbug-dancing craze. Shaw started his career at age 15, playing saxophone in the pit band at New Haven's Olympic Theater. He then held a succession of jobs, including one with Red Norvo's band. In the early '30s he was a radio musician in New York City, and in '35 he took part in N.Y.C.'s first swing concert at the Imperial Theater, where he performed an original jazz piece. He formed his band soon after, but it did not rise to great popularity until his recording of "Begin the Beguine" brought him national fame in '38. Sales of all of Shaw's recordings reportedly total more than 43 million. Shaw's biggest hit recordings were "Begin the Beguine" (see '38), "They Say" (see '39), "Thanks for Everything" (see '39), and "Frenesi" (see '40). Shaw was elected to the Big Band/Jazz Hall of Fame in '90. Shaw was one of the top recording artists of the '30s.

Hollace Shaw (1910–1976)   Hollace Shaw, Frances Mercer, Hiram Sherman, and Ralph Stuart introduced "All the Things You Are" in the Broadway musical *Very Warm for May* (see '40).

Oscar Shaw (real name: Oscar Schwartz; 1889–1967)   Singer Oscar Shaw was an important leading man in the Broadway musicals of the '10s and '20s. He introduced "Ka-lu-a" in *Good Morning Dearie* ('20), "All Alone" in the *Music Box Revue of 1924* (see '25) and "Do-Do-Do" in *Oh, Kay!* ('26). He appeared in almost 25 Broadway productions between '08 and '32, when he played John P. Wintergreen, the Presidential candidate, in Gershwin's *Of Thee I Sing*.

Wini Shaw (real name: Winifred Lei Momi; 1910–1982) Winifred Shaw started her entertainment career as a child in her parents' vaudeville act. In '34, she signed a Warner Bros. contract, but her starring roles were mostly in small, minor films. However, Ms. Shaw introduced "Lullaby of Broadway" in the movie musical *Gold Diggers of 1935* (see '35). By the end of the '30s, her show business career had faded.

Larry Shay (1898–1988) Larry Shay was a composer and music coach for such greats as Al Jolson, Jimmy Durante and Sophie Tucker. Shay's career started during World War I, when he put together a band and show group for soldiers. In the '20s he worked in New York as a music coach. During the '30s, Shay went to Hollywood to serve as movie musical director for MGM. In addition to his work in the movies, Mr. Shay served as program director for NBC radio. His most remembered song is "When You're Smiling" (see '28), which he wrote with Mark Fisher and Joe Goodwin.

Mark Sheafe Mark Sheafe is credited as the composer of Washington and Lee University's fight song, "Washington and Lee Swing" (see '10).

Frances Shelley Frances Shelley introduced "What Is This Thing Called Love?" in Cole Porter's Broadway musical *Wake Up and Dream* (see '30).

Hiram Sherman (1908–1989) Hiram Sherman, Hollace Shaw, Frances Mercer and Ralph Stuart introduced "All the Things You Are" in the Broadway musical *Very Warm for May* (see '40). Sherman was primarily known as a Broadway actor, but he also appeared in a few films and some TV. A Navy veteran, Sherman won two Tony awards, one in '53 and another in '67.

Jack Sherr Jack Sherr wrote the English lyrics for "Yours" (see '41).

Ren Shields (1868–1913) Ren Shields was sometimes a popular-song composer and sometimes the lyricist. Some of his most popular songs include "Come Take a Trip in My Airship" (see '05), "In the Good Old Summer Time" (see '02), and "Waltz Me Around Again, Willie" (see '06). Other well known songs include "In the Shadow of the Pyramids" and "Steamboat Bill."

Jack Shilkret (real name: Jacob Schuldkraut; 1896–1964) Jack Shilkret was one year older than his brother Nat Shilkret (see below). Pianist and composer Jack directed successful bands during the '20s and '30s. Jack's most famous popular song composition is "Make Believe" (see '21). Jack also wrote for several Hollywood films.

Nat Shilkret (real name: Naftule Schuldkraut; 1895–1964) Nat Shilkret came to RCA Victor in '24 where he directed and arranged nearly all the '20s popular recordings. He also founded the Victor Orchestra, which recorded numerous songs and backed some of the era's greatest singers. After he left RCA Victor, he worked many radio shows as conductor of generic radio bands. In the mid-'30s he moved to Hollywood and became a music director for films. In the late '20s, Shilkret and the Victor Orchestra recorded several successful disks, but his most successful recording came with "Dancing with Tears in My Eyes" (see '30). Shilkret became the No. 14 top recording artist of the '20s. Nat was also the composer of "Jeannine (I Dream of Lilac Time)" (see '28). Also see the biographical sketch for the Hilo Hawaiian Orchestra, which Shilkret directed.

Jimmy Shirl Jimmy Shirl was one of the co-writers of "I Believe" (see '53).

Charles Shisler (1886–1952) Charles Shisler is mostly remembered in the popular music genre for writing the words and music for "Bring Me a Rose" (see '16). He continued to write and publish songs into the late '40s.

Dinah Shore (real name: Frances Rose Shore; 1917–1994) Dinah Shore became one of the top female singers from the early '40s through the late '50s. While attending Vanderbilt University, she sang on Nashville radio, using the song "Dinah" as her theme song. She adopted the song's title as her stage name and later legally made it her name. She left Tennessee for New York City in '37, sang on radio for a while, and then went back to college to get a degree in sociology. She signed a contract to sing with Ben Bernie's orchestra in '39, just as the band began a fill-in engagement on network radio. Within a short time she was nationally famous. By '44 she had her own radio program, and she grew even more popular in recordings, movies, and television. Shore won innumerable awards, including top vocalist on radio and records of '41. She had a top-rated television series from the mid-'50s into the early '60s. After a period of relative inactivity, she had a nationally syndicated talk show. Ms. Shore's most productive solo recording period ran from '42 into the early '50s. Her biggest hit recordings include "I'll Walk Alone" (see '44), "The Gypsy" (see '46), "Anniversary Song" (see '47) and "Buttons and Bows" (see '48). Ms. Shore became the No. 10 top recording artist of the '40s, No. 38 for the first half of the 20th Century. Her musical movies include *Thank Your Lucky Stars* ('43), *Follow the Boys* and *Up in Arms* ('44), *Belle of the Yukon* ('45) and *Aaron Slick from Punkin Crick* ('52). Her voice also appeared in the Disney cartoons *Make Mine Music* ('46) and *Fun and Fancy Free* ('47), She also appeared in the Jerome Kern screen biography *Till the Clouds Roll By* ('46).

Chester R. Shull Chester R. Shull was lyricist of "(It's No) Sin" (see '51). The song's composer George Hoven had met Chester R. "Chick" Shull when they both worked for the Old South Chester Tube Co. (Chester, PA). Shull was 34 years old when they wrote "(It's No) Sin." Shull retired from the Sun Oil Co. in '60.

Rudolf Sieczynski (1879–1952) Rudolf Sieczynski was an Austrian composer of Polish ancestry. His fame today rests almost exclusively on the nostalgic song "Wien, du Stadt meiner Träume (Vienna, City of My Dreams)," whose melody and lyrics he wrote in '14.

Florenz Siegesmund Florenz Siegesmund is listed as co-lyricist for the German words for "The Happy Wanderer" ("Der Frohliche Wanderer") (see '54).

Maurice Sigler (1901–1961) Maurice Sigler was one of the co-writers of "I Saw Stars" (see '34) and "Little Man, You've Had a Busy Day" (see '34).

Carl Sigman (1909–2000) Carl Sigman's childhood combined two rather unusual things: a love for baseball and classical piano. Since his mother expected him to become a doctor or lawyer, he studied law and was admitted to the New York State Bar. But his love of music far exceeded his desire to practice law. One of Carl's friends, Johnny Mercer, had already begun his songwriting career, so Carl collaborated with Mercer on "Just Remember," which became his first published song in '36. Carl was drafted in '42 and was attached to the glider division of the 82nd Airborne. He was awarded a Bronze star for his service in Africa. After the war, Carl quickly wrote "Ballerina" (see '47), "Civilization" (see '47), "Careless Hands" (see '49), "Enjoy Yourself" (see '50), "My Heart Cries for You" (see '51), "Many Times," using the name Jessie Barnes (see '53), and "Ebb Tide" (see '53) that charted highly. Carl wrote both lyrics and melodies with collaborators including Peter DeRose, Bob Hilliard, Bob Russell, Duke Ellington and Tadd Dameron. Others of his most popular songs were "Pennsylvania 6–5000," "It's All in the Game," "Answer Me, My Love," "Till," "Arrivederci Roma" and "What Now My Love." In '70 Carl wrote what would become his most popular song, "Where Do I Begin," the theme from the Ryan O'Neal/Ali McGraw blockbuster film *Love Story*. Carl Sigman's catalogue numbers some 800 songs. He was inducted into the Songwriters' Hall of Fame in '72. At http://www.songwritershalloffame.org/exhibit_audio_video.asp?exhibitId=233 you can hear an audio clip of Vic Damone singing Sigman's "Ebb Tide."

Frank Signorelli (1901–1975) Pianist Frank Signorelli started the Original Memphis Five in '17. He also played briefly with the Original Dixieland Jazz Band in the early '20s. Paul Whiteman said of Signorelli, he "tried to make a lady out of jazz." In '38, he joined the Paul Whiteman Orchestra. Signorelli was co-composer of "Stairway to the Stars" (see '39).

Abner Silver (1899–1966) Abner Silver wrote the music for "Angel Child" (see '22) and "Chasing Shadows" (see '35).

Frank Silver Frank Silver co-wrote one of the biggest novelty hits of the '20s, "Yes! We Have No Bananas," with Irving Cohn (see '23).

Al Silverman (see Al Stillman)

Dolores Vicki Silvers Dolores Vicki Silvers was the writer of "Learnin' the Blues" (see '55).

Louis Silvers (1889–1954) Born in New York City, Louis Silvers scored the first talking picture, *The Jazz Singer* ('27). He remained at Warner Bros. until '31, and then worked at several other studios as musical director, conductor and composer until his retirement in '46. He was music director for *Lux Radio Theater* for most of its long run ('34–'54). Silvers received four Oscar nominations: Best Score in '34 for *One Night of Love*, Best Score in '37 for *In Old Chicago*, for Original Score in '38 for *Suez*, and for Original Score in '39 for *Swanee River*. Silvers was the composer of "April Showers" (see '22), which Al Jolson introduced in *Bombo* on Broadway.

Ginny Simms (1915–1994) Ginny Simms was a very popular singer with Kay Kyser's orchestra from '34 to '41. She was voted the No. 1 female band vocalist in '41 in *Billboard's* college survey. She had ranked second in '40. Ginny sang on the Kyser hit recordings of "Three Little Fishies" (see '39) and "The Umbrella Man" (see '39), plus "With the Wind and the Rain in Your Hair," and "Alexander the Swoose." Ms. Simms appeared in the following

movie musicals: *That's Right, You're Wrong* ('39), *You'll Find Out* ('40), *Playmates* ('41), *Seven Days Leave* ('42), *Hit the Ice* ('43), *Broadway Rhythm* ('44) *Shady Lady* ('45), *Night and Day* ('46), and *Disk Jockey* ('51). Ginny introduced "Amor" in the movie musical *Broadway Rhythm* (see '44).

Margaret Simms Margaret Simms and Paul Bass introduced "Ain't Misbehavin'" in *Connie's Hot Chocolates* (see '29).

Nat Simon Nat Simon was the composer of "The Old Lamp-Lighter" (see '46). Simon also wrote "Poinciana" and "The Gaucho Serenade."

Moises Simons (1889–1945) Cuban composer Moises Simons wrote "Marta" (see '31). Simons also composed the song "El Mansiero," which became famous in the U.S. as "The Peanut Vendor" (see '31). Simons was a pianist, bandleader and composer from Havana.

Seymour Simons (1896–1949) Seymour Simons co-wrote "Breezin' Along with the Breeze" (see '26) and "Honey" (see '29) with Richard A. Whiting and Haven Gillespie. While most of America was reeling from the great Depression, songwriters Gerald Marks and Seymour Simons had reason to celebrate. Their one important songwriting collaboration, "All of Me" (see '32) became a big hit. Seymour Simons was born in Detroit. He received a bachelor of science degree from the University of Michigan and served as second lieutenant in the Army Air Force in World War I. Following discharge from the armed forces, he became well known in the Detroit area as a pianist, composer and orchestra leader. During the '20s, he wrote special material for a number of performers, including Nora Bayes and Elsie Janis. He worked in the radio production and booking business from '28 to '32 and operated his own orchestra playing for radio stations during the early '30s.

Frank Sinatra (real name: Francis Albert Sinestro; 1915–1998) Frank Sinatra was to the mid-'40s what Elvis Presley and the Beatles were to later generations: a superstar, charismatic entertainer. Sinatra began his rise to fame when he was hired to sing with Harry James' band in '39. He stayed with James for only a short time before he joined Tommy Dorsey's band. He left Dorsey in '42 and began to cause volcanic sensations among bobby-soxers in '43. In the late '40s he appeared often on radio, including stints on *Your Hit Parade*, and he starred in several movies. *Anchors Aweigh* in '45 established his credentials as a motion-picture actor (and he danced much better than one would have imagined in some fancy footwork with Gene Kelly). He also starred in *On the Town* ('49), one of the first films to be shot on location instead of in a studio. Frank was the lyricist of "This Love of Mine," which he sang with Tommy Dorsey and his orchestra (see '41). Sinatra introduced "Dolores" in his film debut in *Las Vegas Nights* (see '41) and "I Couldn't Sleep a Wink Last Night" and "A Lovely Way to Spend an Evening" in the film version of the musical *Higher and Higher* (see '44). In the early '50s Sinatra confined his appearances to nightclubs and television. Then, in '53, he won an Oscar for his acting as Maggio in *From Here to Eternity*. His other film credits are numerous; some of his most famous motion-picture appearances include *Young at Heart* (see '54), *The Tender Trap* and *Guys and Dolls* ('55),

High Society ('56), *Pal Joey* and *The Joker Is Wild* ('57), and *Can-Can* ('60). Sinatra sang the theme song on the soundtrack of the non-musical film *Three Coins in the Fountain* (see '54). He has recorded often, primarily for Columbia and for Capitol, until he formed his own company, Reprise. Sinatra's biggest solo hit singles include "Oh! What It Seemed to Be" (see '46), "Five Minutes More" (see '46), and "Mam'selle" (see '47). After the period covered by this book, his "Learnin' the Blues" and "Strangers in the Night" were very popular. He and his daughter, Nancy, had a No. 1 hit with "Somethin' Stupid" in '67. Of course, during his big band days, some recordings with Harry James, like "All or Nothing at All" (see '43) and with Tommy Dorsey, like "There Are Such Things," featured Sinatra's velvety voice (see '43). Other well-known Sinatra recordings include "I Couldn't Sleep a Wink Last Night," "Saturday Night (Is the Loneliest Night of the Week)," "Young at Heart," "Love and Marriage," and "All the Way." Sinatra was elected to the Big Band/Jazz Hall of Fame in '80. Frank was inducted into the Popular Music Hall of Fame in 2000. Surprisingly, especially to Sinatra's legion of fans, he was only the No. 14 top recording artist of the '40s and No. 21 of the '50s. He managed to rank No. 34 for the second half of the 20th Century. But all those figures seem incredibly low for the amount of adulation that Sinatra still generates.

John Siras   John Siras was one of the co-writers of the Depression Era gem "In a Shanty in Old Shanty Town" (see '32).

Noble Sissle (1889–1975)   Noble Sissle was born in Indianapolis, Indiana. His early interest in music came from his father, a minister and organist. After the family moved to Cleveland and before graduating from high school, Sissle joined a male quartet for a four-week run of the Midwest vaudeville circuit. After graduating, he joined a gospel quartet for a tour on the same circuit. Riding the wave of new interest in black entertainers, Sissle organized his own orchestra. In '15, he moved to Baltimore where he became songwriting partner with Eubie Blake. They had met as members of Joe Porter's Serenaders. When World War I broke out, Sissle enlisted and helped recruit members for the military band. Blake was too old for military service so he stayed stateside, putting music to the lyrics Sissle sent back. When the war ended, Sissle returned with hopes to bring African American theatrical shows back to Broadway. Sissle and Blake entered the white vaudeville circuit. They became one of the few black acts on the Keith circuit. There never was more than one African American act at the same venue. Sissle and Blake were billed as "The Dixie Duo." In '20, Sissle and Blake met Flournoy E. Miller and Aubrey Lyles who were veterans in black show business. The four men set out to write, direct, manage and star in their own musical comedy. The result, *Shuffle Along*, opened in New York City in '21. The most popular song to come out of the show was originally written as a waltz, but Lottie Gee, the young singer who was to perform it, complained that she couldn't sing it in waltz time, and the up-tempo "I'm Just Wild About Harry" became a hit (see '22). *Shuffle Along* was the first all-black musical to become a box office hit, and it started a resurgence of African American shows. Following the show's successful run and subsequent successful road tours, however, the team that created it broke up.

In the mid-'20s, Sissle and Blake toured Europe. While abroad, they began to have disagreements. They returned to the States, but Sissle decided to go back to Europe soon afterwards, and the team broke up. In the thirties, Sissle put together a successful orchestra.

Will E. Skidmore   Will Skidmore co-wrote the Bert Williams song "It's Nobody's Business but My Own" with Marshall Walker (see '19).

Sunny Skylar (real name: Selig Shaftel; 1913–)   Composer Sunny Skylar wrote literally thousands of songs, but only a few achieved hit status. He wrote the English lyrics for Consuelo Velazquez's "Besame Mucho" (see '44), the English words for Gabriel Ruiz's "Amor" (see '44), the words and music for "Hair of Gold, Eyes of Blue" (see '48), and was co-writer for "You're Breaking My Heart" (see '49), which was adapted from Ruggiero Leoncavallo's "Mattinata."

Walter Slezak (1902–1983)   Walter Slezak was the son of Leo Slezak, a Metropolitan Opera star. He was a medical student and a bank teller before he got his start in show business in the German silent film *Sodom and Gomorrah* ('22). He began his Broadway stage career in the '30s. He introduced "I've Told Ev'ry Little Star" in the musical *Music in the Air* (see '33). He went to Hollywood in the early '40s and appeared in over 100 films, mostly in character actor roles. He won a Tony award in '55 for his role in the Broadway musical *Fanny*.

A.B. Sloane   A.B. Sloane's lone lasting contribution to popular music was as composer for "Ma Tiger Lily" (see '00).

Ed Smalle (1887–1968)   Ed Smalle often sang duets with Billy Murray. He was also the pianist for the Revelers. His chief claim to fame was his recording of "That Old Gang of Mine" (see '23).

Beasley Smith (1901–1968)   Beasley Smith was active in the music business from the '30s. He was based in Nashville and his career included leading a band, composing, music publishing, and arranger for Dot Records. Smith collaborated with Haven Gillespie, Francis Craig, Marvin Hughes and Owen Bradley. His best known songs were "That Lucky Old Sun" (see '49) and "Old Master Painter" (see '50).

Bessie Smith (circa 1894–1937)   The "Empress of the Blues." That's what they called Bessie Smith, one of the chief pioneers in vocal blues music. Bessie was born into poverty in the segregated south. She began singing at the age of nine on the street corners of her hometown, Chattanooga, Tennessee. In '12 Bessie joined the Rabbit Foot Minstrels traveling show led by the legendary blues singer Gertrude "Ma" Rainey, who became Bessie's mentor. After performing in all sorts of sordid venues throughout the south, Bessie was signed to a recording contract by Columbia Records. She scored a major hit with "Down Hearted Blues," backed with "Gulf Coast Blues," (see '23). That disk eventually sold over a million copies. During the rest of the '20s, she toured regularly, particularly in vaudeville, often with such jazz greats as Louis Armstrong, Fletcher Henderson, James P. Johnson and later, Benny Goodman. Although she primarily performed to black audiences, Bessie did find popularity among whites as well. Most of her songs, like most blues, had themes of poverty, oppression, and unrequited love. Ms. Smith also appeared in the '29 motion picture short *St. Louis Blues*. By the opening of the '30s her career fell into a sharp decline. Some of that decline can be attributed to her long-standing alcoholism, which often made her very difficult to work with. Bessie had begun a comeback as a swing musician when her life was tragically cut short by an automobile accident in '37. While driving to a singing engagement in Mississippi with her current lover, Lionel Hampton's uncle, Richard Morgan, their car rear-ended a slow moving truck. Smith's left arm and ribs were crushed in the accident. A *Downbeat* magazine article suggested that Smith bled to death because she was not admitted at a "For Whites Only" hospital and reached a hospital that would treat African Americans too late. This accusation was never proved, but the rumor persists. The playwright Edward Albee dramatized her death in his '60 play *The Death of Bessie Smith*. In the decades that followed, her fame and record sales multiplied. She eventually found much more popularity among white listeners than during her lifetime. Future blues singers such as Janis Joplin were greatly influenced by Bessie Smith. Several of her recordings can be heard at http://www.redhotjazz.com/bessie.html.

Chris Smith (1879–1949)   Chris Smith wrote the music for several popular songs, including "Good Morning, Carrie!" (see '02), "He's a Cousin of Mine" (see '07), "You're in the Right Church but the Wrong Pew" (see '09), and "Ballin' the Jack" (see '14).

Clarence "Pine-top" Smith   (1904–1929) Clarence "Pine-top" Smith was famous for his boogie-woogie piano styling. In '28 he wrote "Pine Top's Boogie Woogie," which was popularized in '38 as "Boogie Woogie" (see '38). Smith toured the minstrel and vaudeville circuits throughout the '20s. He also played at rent parties, taverns and brothels. In '29, Smith was accidentally shot to death at a dance in Chicago.

Edgar Smith (1857–1938)   Edgar Smith's primary contribution to popular music was as lyricist or co-lyricist for "When Chloe Sings a Song" (see '00), "My Blushin' Rosie (My Posie Sweet)" (see '01) and "Come Down, Ma Evenin' Star" (see '03).

Harry B. Smith (1860–1936)   Lyricist Harry B. Smith began his professional life as a music critic for the Chicago *Daily News* and later a drama critic for the Chicago *Tribune*. Smith moved to New York City and began collaborating on Broadway scores with such composers as Reginald DeKoven, Victor Herbert, Jerome Kern, Sigmund Romberg and Ted Snyder. He wrote songs for numerous musical productions including *Whirl-I-Gig, Robin Hood, The Fortune Teller, Ziegfeld Follies* ('07, '08, '09, '10 and '12), *Miss Innocence, The Girl from Utah, Watch Your Step* and *Stop! Look! Listen!,* among others. Smith's most famous popular songs were "A Good Cigar Is a Smoke" (see '05), "You Belong to Me" (see '16) and "The Sheik of Araby" (see '22). Harry B. Smith was an original member of the Songwriters' Hall of Fame in '70. Smith was a charter member of ASCAP in '14 and served as a director from '14–'17.

"Whispering" Jack Smith (1899–1951)   Jack Smith used a half-whispering singing style because of an injury from gas in World War I. Most of his recording success came between '26 and '28. Smith's quiet baritone

voice helped popularize "'Gimme' a Little Kiss, Will 'Ya' Huh?" (see '26, for which he also co-wrote the lyrics with Roy Turk) and "Me and My Shadow" (see '27), plus a few other songs, but his audience had declined by the early thirties. Smith was the No. 30 top recording artist of the '20s. Listen to some of Smith's most popular recordings at http://great-song-stylists-uk.com/Jack%20Smith/whisperingjacksmith2.htm.

Joseph C. Smith's Orchestra   This group was an early dance band that achieved its major success between '17 and the very early '20s. The leader, Joseph C. Smith was a violinist. Their recording of "Smiles" (see '18) with vocalist Harry MacDonough was particularly popular. According to Tim Gracyk in his *Popular American Recording Pioneers: 1895–1925*, "This may be the first dance record to feature a vocal refrain, and several Smith records that followed would feature vocal refrains, a novelty at the time."

Kate Smith (real name: Kathryn Elizabeth Smith; 1907–1986)   Kate Smith is an extremely famous singer and occasional actress from just before and during World War II. She started her career on Broadway in *Honeymoon Lane* ('26) and followed that with *Flying High* ('30). After that she performed in vaudeville and in theaters across the country until she started her own radio show. She was particularly popular as a radio personality (the Kate Smith Hour, which aired weekly from '37–'45, plus a daytime radio show, Kate Smith Speaks), and the exposure got her a movie contract. She sang her theme song, "When the Moon Comes Over the Mountain," in *The Big Broadcast* ('32). She became a national personality when she starred in the '33 film *Hello Everybody*. Smith was always rather large, which hindered her screen career, but she continued to appear in films, although seldom as part of the main plot. She appeared in *The Hit Parade* ('37), which was a variety show with a large roster of stars. Next came a cameo appearance in *The Great American Broadcast* ('41), and she sang "God Bless America" in the movie version of *This Is the Army* in '43. She introduced Irving Berlin's "God Bless America" on her radio program in November of '39. Her performance of the number became so famous that she is almost exclusively associated with the song. In '50 Smith entered television with a Monday–Friday afternoon variety show, plus a mid-week primetime show, the *Kate Smith Evening Hour*. Her biggest hit recordings were her theme song, "When the Moon Comes Over the Mountain" (see '31), which she also helped write, and "River, Stay 'Way from My Door" with Guy Lombardo and his Royal Canadians (see '32). Ms. Smith was inducted into the Popular Music Hall of Fame in 2002. It is difficult to believe that over the years her "God Bless America" has not passed the million mark or more (see '40).

Muriel Smith (1923–1985)   Muriel Smith, singing for Zsa Zsa Gabor, introduced the title song from *Moulin Rouge*, sometimes called "Where Is Your Heart?" and most often titled "The Song from *Moulin Rouge*" (see '53). In addition to providing the singing voice for Ms. Gabor, she played the part of Aicha in the film.

Robert B. Smith (1875–1951)   Robert B. Smith is the brother of lyricist Harry B. Smith. Robert B. Smith's most successful lyrics were written for the Broadway stage. His first successful Broadway musical was *Twirly Whirly*, which featured "Come Down, Ma Evenin' Star" (see '03). Perhaps his most famous musical was *Sweethearts* written with composer Victor Herbert in '13. From that musical came "Sweethearts" and "The Angelus" (see '13). However, he also wrote the musical *The Debutante* with Herbert, which produced the song "The Springtime of Life" (see '14).

Samuel Francis Smith (1808–1895) Samuel Francis Smith, the lyricist for "America," was born in Boston, Massachusetts. He attended Eliot School and then a college preparatory school and the first public school in America. In 1825, he went to Harvard College (now University). Smith graduated from Harvard in 1829, with many honors. After working in journalism for a short time, he decided to become a minister. In 1830, he entered Andover Theological Seminary. In 1832 Smith translated a German poem for a friend. That new song became "America (My Country 'Tis of Thee)" (see '16). Smith became pastor of the Waterville Baptist Church, and later accepted the editor position at *The Christian Review* and became pastor at Newton Centre Baptist Church near Boston. After several years, he became secretary of the Baptist Missionary Union, a position that enabled him to travel all over the country. When Smith died in 1895, "America" was sung at his funeral.

Ted Snyder (1881–1965) Composer Ted Snyder moved to Chicago around the turn of the century where he worked as a café pianist. Later he became a staff pianist and song plugger for some music publishing companies. His first success as a songwriter came in '07 with "There's a Girl in This World for Every Boy," which he wrote with lyricist Will D. Cobb. In '08, Snyder moved to New York City where he formed his publishing company. Snyder hired a young songwriter named Irving Berlin as a staff writer in '09. Snyder and Berlin became publishing partners with Henry Waterson and a successful songwriting team. By '13, the publishing firm was reorganized as Waterson, Berlin and Snyder. Snyder teamed with lyricists such as Bert Kalmar, Edgar Leslie, Sam M. Lewis, Joe Young, Harry B. Smith and Francis Wheeler. The most popular song from Snyder's song catalog was "The Sheik of Araby" (see '22), however his most famous song was most likely his collaboration with Bert Kalmar and Harry Ruby on "Who's Sorry Now?" Snyder also included songs in many Broadway revues and productions including *Sinbad* and *Make It Snappy*. In '30, Snyder retired from the songwriting business and moved to Hollywood, California where he opened a nightclub. He was an original member of the Songwriters' Hall of Fame in '70. In '14, Snyder was a charter member of the new performing rights society, ASCAP. At http://www.songwritershalloffame.org/exhibit_audio_video.asp?exhibitId=244 you can hear an audio clip of "I'm Going Back to Dixieland" performed by Arthur Collins and Byron Harlan.

Alfred Solman (1868–1937) Alfred Solman's chief contribution to popular music was as composer for "There's a Quaker Down in Quaker Town" (see '16).

Song Spinners The Song Spinners enjoyed great success during the musicians' strike of the early '40s with an cappella recording of "Comin' in on a Wing and a Prayer" (see '43). They also accompanied Dick Haymes on "You'll Never Know" (see '43).

Sons of the Pioneers Leonard Franklin Slye (Roy Rogers; 1911–1998), Robert Clarence Nobles (Bob Nolan; 1908–1980), Lloyd Wilson Perryman (1917–1977), Vernon Tim Spencer (1908–1974), Thomas Hubert "Hugh" Farr (1903–1980), Karl Marx Farr (1909–1961). Elected to the Country Music Hall of Fame in '80, the Sons of the Pioneers, America's premier western singing group, was formed in '33 as the Pioneer Trio by Leonard Slye, Bob Nolan and Tim Spencer. In late '33 or early '34 they added Hugh Farr, a fine country fiddler, and in mid-'35 Hugh's guitarist brother, Karl. That quintet became the Sons of the Pioneers. In '36, tenor Lloyd Perryman joined the group. Comedian-bass player Pat Brady replaced Leonard Slye when he signed with Republic Pictures in '37 to become one of America's favorite singing cowboys, Roy Rogers. The songs composed by Bob Nolan and Tim Spencer were often inspired by their participation in western films, first in '35 with Charles Starrett, then in '41 with their old buddy Roy Rogers. Some of their most famous recordings include "Tumbling Tumbleweeds" (see '34), "Cool Water" (see '41) and "Room Full of Roses" (see '49).

Ann Sothern (real name: Harriet Lake; 1909–2001) Ann Sothern began her film career as an extra in '27. After working at MGM and on Broadway, she signed with Columbia Pictures. Her first film for that studio was *Let's Fall in Love*, where she introduced the title song (see '34). Next came *Kid Millions* with Eddie Cantor. After a couple of years, Columbia dropped her contract. She then signed with RKO, but her career still wasn't flourishing. In '38, she left RKO to return to MGM. Over the next several years, she appeared in a number of MGM feature films. In the early '50s, she turned to television. She starred in *Private Secretary* from '53 to '57, then in '58 in *The Ann Sothern Show,* which ran until '61. In '65, she became the voice of a car in *My Mother the Car*. She was nominated for an Academy Award for her role as the neighbor of Lillian Gish and Bette Davis in *The Whales of August* in '87.

Robert Sour Robert Sour was co-lyricist of "Body and Soul" (see '30).

John Philip Sousa (1854–1932) Composer John Philip Sousa was born in Washington D.C. His education was in private schools and then at a music conservatory. From 1880 to 1892, Sousa was the leader of the United States Marine Corp Band. In 1892, he formed his own band and traveled throughout the world. Some of Sousa's most memorable marches are "The Stars and Stripes Forever" (see '01), "Semper Fidelis" (see '02), "El Capitan" (see '09), plus "The Thunderer," "Washington Post March," "King Cotton," and "Hands Across the Sea." Sousa also wrote scores for Broadway productions including most memorably *El Capitan*. Sousa's Band's most popular recordings during the period covered by this book include "The Stars and Stripes Forever" (see '01), and "In the Good Old Summer Time" (see '03). Sousa was also a charter member of the American Society of Composers, Authors and Publishers (ASCAP) in '14. John Philip Sousa was an original member of the Songwriters' Hall of Fame in '70. Sousa's Band was the No. 13 top recording artist of the first decade of the 20th Century. The John Philip Sousa Library and Museum is in Champaign, Ill. At http://www.song

writershalloffame.org/exhibit_audio_video.asp?exhibitId=309 you can hear audio clips of Sousa's "Stars and Stripes Forever" performed by the Columbia Orchestra, "Semper Fidelis" performed by Sousa's Band, and "The Liberty Bell March" performed by the Edison Grand Concert Band.

Oley Speaks (1874–1948)   Oley Speaks was a railway clerk in Columbus, Ohio as a young man. He then decided to follow a career in music and took music lessons. He became a baritone soloist in a Columbus church, but in the late 1890s moved to New York City. He became soloist at the Church of the Divine Paternity and later at St. Thomas' Church. During the early years of the 20th century, he also pursued a successful career as a singer, touring the U.S., giving recitals and also appearing in oratorios. He also wrote many art (as opposed to popular) songs. His greatest popular successes, each reportedly selling over a million copies of sheet music, were "On the Road to Mandalay" (see '13), and "Sylvia" (see '14). He composed over 250 songs during his career.

Grace Spencer   Grace Spencer's recording of "Tell Me, Pretty Maiden" from *Florodora* (see '01) with Harry MacDonough was very popular.

Len Spencer (real name: Leonard Garfield Spencer; 1867–1914)   Len Spencer was one of the chief pioneers of the recording field. He became one of the most successful recording artists of the 1890s. In the era covered by this book, his recordings of "Hello, Ma Baby" (see '00), "Ma Tiger Lily" (see '00) and "Arkansaw (sic) Traveler" (see '02) were particularly successful. He also recorded several comedy records with Ada Jones.

Otis Spencer   Otis Spencer's chief claim to fame in the popular music arena is as co-composer with Martin Fried of "Broadway Rose" (see '21).

Tim Spencer (real name: Vernon Tim Spencer; 1908–1974)   Tim Spencer, one of the Sons of the Pioneers, wrote "Room Full of Roses" (see '49).

Larry Spier   Larry Spier was the composer of "Memory Lane" (see '24). He also named his music publishing company Memory Lane Music Co.

A.W. Sprague   A.W. Sprague was working in Bar Harbor when he heard a march called "Opie" by E.A. Fenstad. When Sprague was a student at the University of Maine, he rewrote the march and convinced his roommate, Lincoln Colcord to write the lyrics for what became "Stein Song" (see '30). Sprague and Fenstad are listed as co-composers. Sprague later joined the University of Maine faculty and became chairman of the Music Department.

Sylvester Sprigato   Sylvester Sprigato was a co-writer of "It Isn't Fair" (see '50).

Jo Stafford (real name: Jo Elizabeth Stafford; 1917–)   Jo Stafford was one of the most popular female vocalists of the mid–'40s and '50s. She formed a trio with her sisters and began singing on radio in the mid–'30s. She joined the Pied Pipers in '37 and remained with them for seven years, at which time she left to try it as a soloist. While with the Pied Pipers, she recorded the terrifically popular "Dream" (see '45). After she left the group, she performed often on radio and recorded regularly. She recorded a hick version of "Temptation" with

Red Ingle and the Natural Seven called "Tim-tayshun" (see '47). The disk label billed her as "Cinderella G. Stump." The hillbilly parody was her first solo million seller. Other very popular recordings include "Candy" (billed as Johnny Mercer, Jo Stafford and the Pied Pipers) in '45, her biggest-selling hit "You Belong to Me" (see '52) and "Make Love to Me" (see '54). She also had a *Billboard* No. 1 hit with "My Darling, My Darling" from *Where's Charley* in a duet with Gordon MacRae (see '49). With her husband, Paul Weston, she recorded several albums under the names of Jonathan and Darlene Edwards. The Edwards were a parody of a bad lounge act and won a Grammy for Best Comedy Album. She began retiring in the mid–'60s and left the music business completely in the mid–'70s. Her husband died in '96. She currently lives in California. She was inducted into the Big Band/Jazz Hall of Fame in 2003.

Felix Stahl   Felix Stahl was the composer of "Many Times" (see '53).

Johnny Standley   Comedian Johnny Standley had a very popular recording that topped the charts. His "It's in the Book" (see '52) was a parody of a fundamentalist preacher's rendition of "Little Bo Peep." Horace Heidt and his Musical Knights accompanied him on the recording.

Stanford Four   The Stanford Four introduced "By the Beautiful Sea" in vaudeville (see '14). The publisher hired a group of boys in sailor suits to perform the song in the Coney Island amusement park area to help familiarize the public with the song.

Aileen Stanley (real name: Maude Elsie Aileen Muggeridge; 1897–1982)   While still in her childhood, Aileen, her widowed mother, and her older brother sang and danced in vaudeville as Stanley and Aileen. She became a solo performer when her brother left the act. She took her stage name by reversing the name of the old family billing. In '20, she made a hit in New York City in the revue *Silks and Satins*. She also began her recording career in '20. The majority of her records were for the Victor Talking Machine Company, but she also recorded with Edison, Pathe, Okeh, Brunswick, Vocalion, Gennett and others. She even recorded for Black Swan Records, a basically African American label, under the name Mamie Jones. During the mid–'20s she was paired with Billy Murray on several Victor recordings. After she lost heavily in the Stock Market Crash of '29, she moved to London in the early '30s. Stanley's most popular solo recordings include "Sweet Indiana Home" ('22) and "Everybody Loves My Baby" ('25). She and Gene Austin recorded a popular duet of "When My Sugar Walks Down the Street" in '25. The most popular duet with Billy Murray was "It Had to Be You" in '24.

Frank Stanley (real name: William Stanley Grinsted; 1869–1910)   Frank Stanley began his entertainment career as a banjo player. He accompanied Arthur Collins on some of Collin's late 1890s recordings. He became famous as the leader and manager of the Peerless Quartet and for his many duet recordings with Henry Burr, Corrine Morgan and others. Stanley's most successful recordings in the era covered by this book include "Blue Bell" (see '04), "Good Evening, Caroline" (see '09) with Elise Stevenson and "Tramp! Tramp! Tramp!" from

Naughty Marietta (see '10). He also recorded often with Henry Burr as a duo and was a member of the Peerless Quartet.

Frank L. Stanton (1857–1927) Frank Stanton was the lyricist for "Mighty Lak' a Rose" (see '03).

Jack Stapp (1912–1980) Jack Stapp and Harry Stone, employees at WSM radio in Nashville, wrote "Chattanoogie Shoe Shine Boy" (see '50).

Kay Starr (real name: Katherine LaVerne Starks; 1922–) Kay Starr was born on an Indian reservation in Oklahoma. Kay's father was a full-blooded Iroquois Indian and her mother was of Native American and Irish descent. When her family moved to Memphis, she sang with jazz violinist Joe Venuti's band at age fifteen. She left Venuti to join Bob Crosby's band, which carried her to New York City. There she recorded with Glenn Miller, but she rejoined Venuti and spent two years with Charlie Barnet's band before embarking on a solo career. Her first recording contract was with Capitol, but she also recorded with Victor in the mid–'50s. Starr's biggest hit recordings were "Wheel of Fortune" which topped the *Billboard* chart for ten weeks (see '52) and "Rock and Roll Waltz" which topped the chart for six weeks in '56. See http://kaystarr.net/bio.html.

John Steel (1900–1971) John Steel is primarily remembered for introducing "A Pretty Girl Is Like a Melody" in the *Ziegfeld Follies of 1919*, "Lady of the Evening" in the second edition of *The Music Box Revue* and "What'll I Do?" in *The Music Box Revue of 1923*. He also sang in the *Follies* of '20, and '21. His biggest hit recordings were "A Pretty Girl Is Like a Melody" (see '19) and "The Love Nest" (see '20).

Lois Steele Lois Steele is a co-writer of Perry Como's hit "Wanted" (see '54). Her chief collaborator was Jack Fulton with whom she wrote "Ivory Tower" which Cathy Carr popularized in '56.

William Steffe (c. 1830–c.1890) In the mid–1850s William Steffe wrote a camp-meeting-style song with a traditional "Glory Hallelujah" refrain. It started with the words "Say, brothers, will you meet us on Canaan's happy shore?" The tune was catchy and was soon widely known. Early in the Civil War, a soldier named John Brown was a member of a regiment stationed in Boston. The regiment used Steffe's tune to sing a song about John Brown of Kansas who had recently made a stand against slavery. Their song was directed in jest towards their own John Brown. This version, using the words "John Brown's body lies a-mouldering in the grave, but his soul goes marching on," soon became popular among the Union troops. In December, 1861, at the suggestion of a friend, Julia Ward Howe wrote new words for Steffe's tune, which, of course, became "Battle Hymn of the Republic" (see '18).

Max Steiner (real name: Maximilian Raoul Walter Steiner; 1888–1971) Famous film composer Max Steiner emigrated to the U.S. from his native Austria in '14 to become conductor for Florenz Ziegfeld's musical productions. After several years of leading theater orchestras and working as chief orchestrator for one of New York City's leading music houses, he moved to Hollywood where he scored hundreds of films. Steiner was awarded the first Oscar ever given by the Academy of Motion Picture Arts and Sciences for his score for *The Informer* in '35. He won two other Academy Awards for his scores for *Now, Voyager* in '43, and for *Since You Went Away* in '45. Over the period of his Hollywood career, he received 18 Academy Award nominations. Surprisingly, his most famous work, the background score for *Gone with the Wind*, which included his most famous song, "Tara's Theme," never won an Oscar nor any other award. Some others of Steiner's most famous film scores include *Casablanca, Key Largo*, and *Life with Father*. A few of his film themes have become well known, especially "Tara's Theme" from *Gone with the Wind* ('39) and "Theme from *A Summer Place*" ('59). His biggest popular song success of the pre-rock era was "It Can't Be Wrong" from *Now, Voyager* (see '43). Max Steiner was inducted into the Songwriters' Hall of Fame in '95.

Sam Stept (1897–1964) Composer Sam Stept, born in Odessa, Russia, came to the United States from Russia in '00 and grew up in Pittsburgh. He led a dance band in the early '20s and did not begin composing until the late '20s. He wrote a few hit songs including "That's My Weakness Now" (see '28), "All My Life" (see '37) and "Don't Sit Under the Apple Tree" (see '42).

Andrew B. Sterling (1874–1955) After graduating from high school, Andrew Sterling began writing songs and special material for vaudeville acts. In 1898, he met composer Harry Von Tilzer and the two began a songwriting partnership that would last three decades. Other than von Tilzer, Sterling collaborated with Frederick Allen Mills, James Hanley, Raymond Sterling, M.K. Jerome, Ray Henderson, Bernie Grossman, Edward Moran and Bartley Costello. Some of Sterling's most famous songs include "Hello, Ma Baby" (see '00), "On a Sunday Afternoon" (see '02), "Goodbye, Eliza Jane" (see '03), "Alexander (Don't You Love Your Baby No More?)" (see '04), "Meet Me in St. Louis, Louis" (see '04), "All Aboard for Dreamland" (see '04), "What You Goin' Do When de Rent Comes 'Round" (see '05), "Where the Morning Glories Twine Around the Door" (see '05), "Wait 'Till the Sun Shines, Nellie" (see '06), "Under the Yum Yum Tree" (see '11), "Last Night Was the End of the World" (see '13), "The Song That Stole My Heart" (see '14), "Close to My Heart" (see '15), "I Sent My Wife to the Thousand Isles" (see '16), and "When My Baby Smiles at Me" (see '20). Andrew Sterling is one of the original members of the Songwriters' Hall of Fame in '70. At http://www.songwritershalloffame.org/exhibit_audio_video.asp?exhibitId=245 you can hear an audio clip of Sterling's "My Old New Hampshire Home" performed by Jere Mahoney.

Larry Stevens (1926–2000) Larry Stevens, Cornel Wilde, and Louanne Hogan, who dubbed the singing for film star Jeanne Crain, introduced "All Through the Day" in the movie musical *Centennial Summer* (see '46).

Elise Stevenson Soprano Elise Stevenson was born in Liverpool, England. She became a member of the Lyric Quartet and the Victor Light Opera Company. She was also a frequent duet partner of Frank Stanley, who also became her manager. Her most successful recordings include "Because You're You" from *The Red Mill* (see '07), "Are You Sincere?" (see '08), "Good Evening, Caroline" (see '09) with Frank Stanley, and "Shine on, Harvest Moon" (see '09) with Harry MacDonough (Ms. Stevenson was billed as Miss Walton).

Dorothy Stewart Dorothy Stewart wrote the English lyrics for "Now Is the Hour" (see '48).

Melville Stewart (1869–1915) Melville Stewart introduced "A Good Cigar Is a Smoke" in *Miss Dolly Dollars* (see '05). He and Audrey Maple introduced "Sympathy" in *The Firefly* (see '13).

Redd Stewart (real name: Henry Ellis Stewart; 1923–2003) Redd Stewart was one of the co-writers of "Tennessee Waltz" (see '50), "Slow Poke" and "You Belong to Me" (see '52). For more on Stewart, see http://www.rockabillyhall.com/ReddStewart1.html.

Slam Stewart (real name: Leroy Stewart; 1914–1987) Slam Stewart was an African American bass player. He specialized in jazz. He originally played violin but switched to bass. While he was attending Boston Conservatory of Music, he heard a guy singing while he played his violin. That inspired Stewart to do the same with his bass. He and Slim Gaillard formed the novelty act Slim and Slam in '37. Their biggest hit was "Flat Foot Floogee" (see '38, which they collaborated on with Bud Green. Throughout the '40s, Stewart worked with Art Tatum, the Benny Goodman Sextet and other jazz ensembles.

Al Stillman (1906–1979) Lyricist Al Stillman wrote several hits in the '40s and '50s. After graduating from New York University, Stillman worked as a newspaper writer, but in '33 he became a staff writer for Radio City Music Hall, a position he held for nearly 40 years. Stillman collaborated with several composers, including Arthur Schwartz, George Gershwin, Ernesto Lecuona, Robert Allen, Fred Ahlert, Percy Faith and Paul McGrane. His best-known lyrics were "Say 'Si, Si'" (see '36), "The Breeze and I" (see '40), and "I Believe" (see '53). Other Stillman well known songs include "Chances Are," "It's Not for Me to Say," "Moments to Remember," "Home for the Holidays," "You Alone (Solo Tu)," "Bless 'em All," "No, Not Much," "Mama Yo Quiero" and "Jukebox Saturday Night." As Al Silverman, Stillman was the English lyricist of "Tell Me That You Love Me" (see '35). Stillman was elected to the Songwriters' Hall of Fame in '82.

Larry Stock (1896–1998) By his eighth birthday, Larry Stock was playing the piano, and at twelve, was accepted by the school that later became the Julliard School. Graduating at sixteen, he continued his studies at the City College of New York. After college he intended to become a concert pianist, but with the Depression in full force, he had to settle for playing in clubs. Of course, that allowed Stock to spend his days writing songs. After almost a decade of songwriting, he experienced his first real success with "The Umbrella Man" (see '39), followed by "Blueberry Hill" (see '40). Another Stock song is "You're Nobody 'Til Somebody Loves You." Stock collaborated with Vince Rose, Al Lewis, Russ Morgan and James Cavanaugh. Larry Stock was posthumously inducted in the Songwriters Hall of Fame in '98.

Byron D. Stokes Byron D. Stokes is famous for writing the lyrics for "The Sweetheart of Sigma Chi" (see '12). Stokes wrote the words one June day while in class at Albion College. He took the words to Dudleigh Vernor, who completed the music that same day.

Robert Stolz (1880–1975) Austrian composer Robert Stolz wrote the waltz "Zwei Herzen im Dreivierteltakt" for the first German sound film. Joe Young's English lyrics turned it into "Two Hearts in Three-Quarter Time" (see '30). Stolz also composed operettas and was a well known conductor.

Fred Stone (1873–1959) Comedian Dave Montgomery teamed with dancer and actor Fred Stone in 1894. This comedy team scored their biggest successes in *The Wizard of Oz* (see '03) and *The Red Mill* (see '06). Montgomery and Stone also starred in the musical *Chin-Chin* (see '15).

Gregory Stone Gregory Stone was a co-composer of Benny Goodman's famous "Let's Dance" (see '35).

Harry Stone Harry Stone and Jack Stapp, employees at WSM radio in Nashville, wrote "Chattanoogie Shoe Shine Boy" (see '50).

Helen Stone Helen Stone was the lyricist of "Mexicali Rose" (see '38). She and Jack Tenny had written the song in '23. The Clicquot Club Eskimos popularized it on radio in '26. However, it was most popular in '38.

Eberhard Storch German composer Eberhard Storch wrote the music for "Auf Wiederseh'n, Sweetheart" (see '52). Total sales of this '49 German publication reportedly went over the 2 million mark.

Herbert Stothart (1885–1949) Herbert Stothart wrote songs for the stage and movies. He began in '20 and wrote most of his hits before the mid–'30s. Stothart is famous for co-writing "Bambalina" (see '23), "I Wanna Be Loved by You" (see '28) and "Cuban Love Song" (see '31).

Clarence A. Stout Clarence A. Stout was the writer of "O Death, Where Is Thy Sting?" (see '19).

G.H. Stover G.H. Stover wrote the lyrics for "On the Beach at Waikiki" (see '15). Henry Kailima contributed the music.

Jack Strachey (real name: Jack Strachey Parsons; 1894–1972) Jack Strachey was co-composer of "These Foolish Things Remind Me of You" (see '36).

Elaine Stritch (1925–) Elaine Stritch interpolated "Civilization" into the Broadway revue *Angel in the Wings* (see '47). Elaine Stritch studied at the Dramatic Workshop of the New School before making her Broadway debut in '46. Over the years, she starred in *Bus Stop*, a revival of *Show Boat* and Stephen Sondheim's *Company*. She has appeared in films and on TV, but Broadway seems to be her favorite medium.

John Stromberg John Stromberg's most lasting contributions to popular music were as composer for "When Chloe Sings a Song" (see '00), "My Blushin' Rosie (My Posie Sweet)" (see '01) and "Come Down Ma Evenin' Star" (see '03).

Leslie Stuart (real name: Thomas Augustine Barrett; 1863–1928) Leslie Stuart was an English composer of early musical theatre, best known for the hit show *Florodora*. Born in Southport, Stuart was working as organist at Salford Cathedral while he composed minstrel-style songs under the pseudonyms Lester Barrett and Leslie Stuart. "Tell Me, Pretty Maiden" and "The Shade of the Palm," both from *Florodora*, are his most popular songs in the United States (see '01). For more on Stuart, see http://math.boisestate.edu/GaS/british/composers/stuart.html.

Ralph Stuart Ralph Stuart, Hollace Shaw, Frances Mercer, and Hiram Sherman introduced "All the Things You Are" in the Broadway musical *Very Warm for May* (see '40).

Carl Stutz Carl Stutz and Edith Lindeman wrote "Little Things Mean a Lot" (see '54). Stutz was a Richmond, Virginia disk jockey, while Lindeman was the amusement editor for the Richmond Times-Dispatch.

Jule Styne (real name: Julius Kerwin Stein; 1905–1994) Jule Styne became a leading composer of music for movies and Broadway from the '40s through the '60s. Styne came to the U.S. from his native London as a small boy and studied music in Chicago. He wrote for the Broadway stage and for Hollywood musicals. His movie musical credits are numerous, but some of the most well known films he wrote for in Hollywood include *Sweater Girl, Youth on Parade, Follow the Boys, The Sweetheart of Sigma Chi* and *Romance on the High Seas*. With Betty Comden and Adolph Green, Styne wrote *Bells Are Ringing*, with "Just in Time" and "The Party's Over" plus *Do Re Mi*, which introduced "Make Someone Happy." Styne collaborated with Bob Merrill on the songs for *Funny Girl*, including "Don't Rain on My Parade," "I'm the Greatest Star," "The Music That Makes Me Dance" and "People." He collaborated with Leo Robin for the songs for *Gentleman Prefer Blondes*, which introduced "Diamonds Are a Girl's Best Friend" (see '50). Stephen Sondheim furnished the lyrics for Styne's music for *Gypsy*, which included "Let Me Entertain You," "Everything's Coming Up Roses" and "Together, Wherever We Go." With Bob Hilliard, Styne wrote "How Do You Speak to an Angel?" Styne teamed with Sammy Cahn to write the following famous songs: "I've Heard That Song Before" from *Youth on Parade* (see '43), "I'll Walk Alone" from *Follow the Boys* (see '44), "It's Been a Long, Long Time" (see '45), "Saturday Night Is the Loneliest Night of the Week" (see '45), "Five Minutes More" (see '46), "It's Magic" from *Romance on the High Seas* (see '48), "Three Coins in a Fountain" from *Three Coins in a Fountain*, which won the Academy Award for Best Song (see '54), plus "It's Been a Long, Long Time" (see '45), and "Let It Snow, Let It Snow, Let It Snow" (see '46). Other famous Styne songs include "Time After Time," "I Fall in Love Too Easily," "The Things We Did Last Summer" and "The Second Time Around" from *High Time*. Styne wrote "I Don't Want to Walk Without You" with Frank Loesser (see '42). Styne has been a member of the Songwriters' Hall of Fame since '72. At http://www.songwritershalloffame.org/exhibit_audio_video.asp?exhibitId=73 you can hear audio clips of "People" and "Don't Rain on My Parade" sung by Barbra Streisand, "Time After Time" performed by Frank Sinatra, "It's Been a Long, Long Time" performed by Al Jolson, "The Things We Did Last Summer" sung by Dean Martin, "It's Magic" performed by Keely Martin, "Let It Snow..." performed by Lena Horne, "I Still Get Jealous" performed by Louis Armstrong, and "I Fall in Love Too Easily" sung by Frank Sinatra. Styne's official website: http://www.julestyne.com/.

Dana Suesse (1909–1987) Dana Suesse was the composer of "You Oughta Be in Pictures" (see '34). Ms. Suesse was a composer and lyricist. As a child, she toured the Midwest vaudeville circuits as a dancer and pianist. In the mid-'20s, she and her family moved to New York City. She collaborated with Eddie Heyman, Irving Kahal, E.Y. Harburg and Billy Rose. She became known as "the girl Gershwin."

Arthur Sullivan (1842–1900) Composer Sir Arthur Sullivan is most often linked with lyricist W.S. Gilbert, with whom he wrote a succession of operettas that have remained a popular part of English repertoire. Gilbert and Sullivan's most famous operettas include *Trial by Jury, The Gondoliers, HMS Pinafore, The Pirates of Penzance, The Mikado*, and *The Yeomen of the Guard*. Dorothy Terriss, Mrs. Theodore Morse, using the pen name D.A. Esrom, wrote the lyrics for "Hail! Hail! The Gang's All Here" to Arthur Sullivan's music of "The Pirate's Chorus" from *The Pirates of Penzance* (see '18).

Marion Sunshine (real name: Mary Tunstal Ijames; 1894–1963) Marion Sunshine was co-lyricist of the English version of "The Peanut Vendor" (see '31). She and her sister were part of a vaudeville act called "Tempest and Sunshine." They also performed in the *Ziegfeld Follies of 1907*. Her husband was Eusebio Santiago Azpiazu, bandleader Don Azpiazu's brother and manager.

Harry O. Sutton Harry Sutton's only major contribution to popular music was as composer for "I Don't Care" (see '05).

Don Swander (1905–1996) Don Swander was the composer of "Deep in the Heart of Texas" (see '42).

Arthur Swanstrom Arthur Swanstrom co-wrote "Blues (My Naughty Sweetie Gives to Me)" (see '20) with Carey Morgan and Charles McCarron.

Kay Swift (1897–1993) Kay Swift was the first woman to write the score for a hit Broadway musical, *Fine and Dandy* ('30). Her most enduring songs are "Can't We Be Friends" (see '29), and "Can This Be Love?" Swift was also known in musical theater circles for her long-term romance with George Gershwin.

Marty Symes (1904–1953) Marty Symes was co-lyricist of "It's the Talk of the Town" (see '33). Symes also wrote "Under a Blanket of Blue" and "There Is No Greater Love."

Milton Taggart Milton Taggart was co-lyricist of "When It's Springtime in the Rockies" (see '30).

Harry Tally (1866–1939) Harry Tally sang tenor with the Empire City Quartet from approximately '00 until '15. Tally recorded a very popular version of "Wait Till the Sun Shines, Nellie" (see '06). He recorded for Columbia, Victor and Zon-o-Phone recording companies.

Tamara (real name: Tamara Drasin; 1907–1943) Singer Tamara came to the U.S. from her native Russia. Tamara introduced "Smoke Gets in Your Eyes" and "The Touch of Your Hand" in *Roberta* (see '34) and "I'll Be Seeing You" (see '44) and "I Can Dream, Can't I?" (see '50) in *Right This Way*. She died in an airplane crash on a trip to entertain servicemen during World War II.

Eva Tanguay (1879–1947) Canadian Eva Tanguay was a singer and vaudeville entertainer in the early years of the 20th century. Her family moved from Quebec to Massachusetts before she was six years old. She made her first appearance on stage at the age of eight. Next she entered a variety of amateur contests and eventually landed a spot with a comedy troupe before making her vaudeville debut in New York City in '04. With a mediocre voice, Eva became an audience favorite performing risque songs in scanty costumes. She had a very successful vaudeville career and eventually commanded the highest salary of any performer of her era. She lost most of her fortune in the stock market crash of '29. She became known as the "I Don't Care Girl," after her most famous song, "I Don't Care" (see '05). Ms. Tanguay sang on a few gramophone records and starred in two silent film comedies. She retired from show business in the '30s. Mitzi Gaynor portrayed Eva Tanguay in a fictionalized version of her life in the Hollywood motion picture, *The I-Don't-Care Girl* ('53).

Arthur F. Tate (1870–1950) Composer Arthur F. Tate's contribution to popular music was "Somewhere a Voice Is Calling" (see '16).

Tell Taylor (1876–1937) Tell Taylor was born in Ohio. He performed in vaudeville and established a music publishing house in Chicago. By far his biggest hit was "Down by the Old Mill Stream" (see '1), one of the most commercially successful Tin Pan Alley publications of the era.

Macy O. Teetor Macy O. Teetor was co-lyricist with Johnny Mercer of "Lost" (see '36).

Florenze Tempest Florenze Tempest introduced "I Love the Ladies" in the musical *Our American Boy* in '14.

Shirley Temple (1928–) Shirley Temple was the most popular child star the motion-picture industry has ever known. She had enrolled in dancing school when she was three. She began her film career in bit parts in *Baby Burlesks* shorts that spoofed hit films. Once she graduated to full-length films, she made more than 20 in the '30s. She and her films were top box-office attractions during the mid-'30s and '40s. In '34, she became a star in *Stand Up and Cheer*. Also in '34, came *Bright Eyes*, where she introduced "On the Good Ship Lollipop," *Baby, Take a Bow, Now and Forever*, and one of her most famous roles in *Little Miss Marker*. She received a miniature Oscar "in grateful recognition of her outstanding contribution to screen entertainment during the year 1934." Some of her other most famous films of the '30s include *Curley Top* ('35), *Poor Little Rich Girl* (where she introduced "When I'm with You," see '36), *Dimples* and *Stowaway* (also in '36), *Rebecca of Sunnybrook Farm* and *Little Miss Marker* ('38). Other popular films include *Miss Annie Rooney* ('42), *I'll Be Seeing You* ('44), *The Bachelor and the Bobby-Soxer* ('47) and *Mr. Belvedere Goes to College* ('49). As she grew up, she could not sustain her former popularity, so she left the business in the late '40s. She married actor John Agar in the mid-'40s but later divorced him. She married television executive Charles Black in '50. In more recent years she has been active in politics and served in the United Nations and as a U.S. ambassador. She is famous for introducing "On the Good Ship Lollipop" (see '35), "When I'm with You" (see '36), and "Goodnight, My Love" (see '37), plus "Animal Crackers in My Soup" and "Baby Take a Bow."

Fay Templeton (1865–1939) Fay Templeton was the daughter of theatrical parents. She began her show business career at age three singing between acts of her father's opera company. By the early 1880s Templeton was touring the country with her own light opera company. Her first brush with fame came with her appearance in *Evangeline* in New York City in 1885. In a succession of extravaganzas over the next several years, she became celebrated for her singing, her acting, and her dark, seductive beauty. She appeared with Weber and Fields in their burlesque productions beginning in 1898, where her comic talent was discovered. She starred in several Weber and Fields' productions including *Fiddle-dee-dee, Hoity Toity*, and *Twirly Whirly*, all of which also featured Lillian Russell. Ms. Templeton introduced "My Blushin' Rosie" in the Weber and Fields production *Fiddle-Dee-Dee* (see '01) and starred in George M. Cohan's *Forty-Five Minutes from Broadway*, where she introduced "Mary's a Grand Old Name" and "So Long, Mary" (see '06). After several years of semi-retirement, she returned to Broadway to appear in Weber and Fields' *Hokey Pokey* in '12 and several versions of *H.M.S. Pinafore*. She appeared in the film *Broadway to Hollywood* ('33) and in late '33 returned to Broadway in Jerome Kern's *Roberta,* where she introduced "Yesterdays."

Jack Tenny Jack Tenny and Helen Stone wrote "Mexicali Rose" in '23. The Clicquot Club Eskimos popularized it on radio in '26. However, it was most popular in '38, when Bing Crosby popularized it.

Sid Tepper Sid Tepper was a co-writer with Roy Brodsky for "Red Roses for a Blue Lady" (see '49). Tepper most often collaborated with Roy C. Bennett. They met in Brooklyn and published over 300 songs together. Tepper and Bennett wrote several songs for Elvis Presley films.

Dorothy Terriss (real name: Alfreda Theodora Strandberg; 1883–1953) Dorothy Terriss was born in Brooklyn, New York. There are conflicting reports in several sources regarding her name. Virginia Grattan, in *American Women Songwriters*, says she was born Terriss. Other sources say Terriss was a pseudonym. Terriss later married Theodore Morse and wrote under the name of Theodora Morse, Dolly Morse and D. A. Esrom (Morse spelled backwards). She was one of American popular music's finest lyricists and contributed to many of her husband's songs. Terriss and Morse were one of Tin Pan Alley's earliest husband-wife songwriting teams. Dorothy, or is it Theodora, not only wrote with her husband, but also collaborated with other composers. Though her work helped with her husband's success, her most successful songs were not with her husband. Some of those successes were: "Blue Bell" (see '04, using the name Dolly Morse), "Hail! Hail! The Gang's All Here!" (see '18, using the D. A. Esrom pseudonym), "Siboney" (see '29), "Wonderful One" using the name Dorothy Terriss, and one of her most famous works even though it never made it to No. 1 or any of the other lists to warrant inclusion in this book, and "Three O'Clock in the Morning" (see '22).

Edward Teschemacher (real name: Edward Frederick Lockton; 1876–1940) Edward Teschemacher is probably most famous for penning the lyrics for the wedding classic "Because" (see '02). He also wrote the words for "Love Is Mine" (see '12).

Dick Thomas (1915–2003) Dick Thomas was the composer of "Sioux City Sue" (see '46).

Harlan Thompson (1890–1966) Harlan Thompson was librettist and lyricist for the Broadway musical

Little Jessie James which spawned the hit song "I Love You" (see '24). Thompson wrote three other Broadway musicals between the mid-'20s and the early '30s.

Bonnie Thornton Bonnie Thornton, James Thornton's wife, introduced his "When You Were Sweet Sixteen" (see '00).

James Thornton (1861–1938) James Thornton's major contribution to popular music was a composer and lyricist for "When You Were Sweet Sixteen" (see '00).

Art Thorsen Art Thorsen wrote the music for Johnny Standley's comic masterpiece "It's in the Book" (see '52). Thorsen had been a bassist with Horace Heidt's band.

Three Flames Tiger Haynes (guitar; 1914–1994), Roy Testmark (piano), Bill Pollard (bass). The Three Flames were a popular black vocal/instrumental trio. They became among the first black performers to have their own TV show — *The Three Flames Show*— in '49 on NBC. The group's only major hit recording was of "Open the Door, Richard" (see '47).

Three Suns Al Nevins (guitar; 1915–1965), Morty Nevins (accordion; 1917–1990), Artie Dunn (organ; 1922–1996). The Three Suns trio was most popular in the late '40s and early '50s. Their only No. 1 hit was a revival of "Peg o' My Heart" (see '47), but their version of "Twilight Time" in '51 was also popular.

Lawrence Tibbett (1896–1960) Lawrence Tibbet was only six when his father, who was a Kern County deputy sheriff, was killed by bandits. After training with a Metropolitan Opera bass, Tibbet became a singer at the Metropolitan Opera in New York City in '23 and added another "t" to his name. Blessed with boyish good looks and a powerful voice, he was one of the first great opera stars to enjoy success in Hollywood films. He was nominated for the Academy Award for Best Actor for this role in his first film, *The Rogue Song* ('30). He introduced "Cuban Love Song" in the movie of the same name (see'31). By the early '40s Tibbett began to have vocal problems. He left the Met by the end of the decade. In the '50s, he succeeded Ezio Pinza in the Broadway musical *Fanny*.

George Tibbles (1913–1987) George Tibbles was one of the co-writers of "Woody Woodpecker" (see '48). His song was nominated for an Oscar. Tibbles was a screenwriter who contributed to such TV series as *My Three Sons, The Munsters, Alice* and *Who's the Boss?*

Harry Tierney (real name: Harry Austin Tierney; 1890–1965) Composer Harry Tierney studied music with his mother as well as at a New York conservatory. Early in his career, Tierney toured as a concert pianist. In '15 he worked for a music publisher in London and then in '18 became the staff composer at Remick, the Tin Pan Alley music publisher. Tierney wrote scores for several Broadway productions including *Irene, Kid Boots, Ziegfeld Follies* ('19, '20 & '24) and *Rio Rita*. Tierney moved to Hollywood in the early '30s to contribute songs to RKO studio films. While his chief collaborator was Joe McCarthy, Tierney also worked with lyricists Bert Hanlon, Benny Ryan, Al Bryan, Ray Egan and Anne Caldwell. Some of Tierney's most famous songs include "M-I-S-S-I-S-S-I-P-P-I" (see '17), "Alice Blue Gown" (see '20), "Irene" (see '20), "The Rangers' Song" (see '27) and "Rio

Rita" (see '27). Harry Tierney was an original member of the Songwriters' Hall of Fame in '70.

Floyd Tillman (1914–2002) Floyd Tillman was elected to the Country Music Hall of Fame in '84. During the '30s and '40s, Tillman wrote and recorded some of country music's most well known standards, some which became pop crossover hits. Tillman's "Slippin' Around" was a crossover hit for Jimmy Wakely and Margaret Whiting (see '49).

Martha Tilton (1915–) Martha Tilton is most remembered for her recordings of "I Let a Song Go Out of My Heart" (see '38), and "And the Angels Sing" (see '39) with Benny Goodman and his orchestra. She also experienced some success from '42 to '49 as one of the first artists to record for Capitol Records, although her biggest solo hit, "I'll Walk Alone," peaked at No. 4 on the charts in '44. After she left Capitol, she recorded for several other labels. Ms. Tilton also appeared in films. Her singing voice was also used in many films dubbed over other actresses including Barbara Stanwyck.

Dimitri Tiomkin (1894–1979) Ukrainne composer Dimitri Tiomkin became one of the most prolific film composers in Hollywood history. He has been nominated for the Academy Award twenty-three times. His Oscar winning scores include *High Noon* (see '52, he also won the Best Song Oscar for the title song, which is sometimes called "Do Not Forsake Me"), *The High and the Mighty* (see '54), and *The Old Man and the Sea* ('58). His success with songs like "High Noon" and "The High and the Mighty" caused producers to hire him to write other film scores hoping for the same success. Other Oscar nominated scores between '37 and '71 were for *Lost Horizon, Mr. Smith Goes to Washington, The Corsican Brothers, The Moon and Sixpence, The Bridge of San Luis Rey, Champion, Giant, Friendly Persuasion, Wild Is the Wind, The Young Land, The Alamo, The Guns of Navarone, Town Without Pity, 55 Days at Peking, The Fall of the Roman Empire* and *Tchaikovsky*. Tiomkin was educated at St. Petersburg Conservatory. His principal instrument was the piano, but he was also a conductor. He came to the U.S. in '25 and became a citizen in '37.

Charles Tobias (1898–1970) Charles Tobias began his long music career as a professional singer for music publishers and toured as a vaudevillian. He founded his own publishing firm in New York City in '23 and was later joined there by his brothers Henry and Harry Tobias. Tobias wrote with his brothers and other composers and lyricists such as Neil Moret, Nat Simon, Gus Arnheim, Jules Lemare, Anson Weeks, Jack Scholl, Cliff Friend, Don Reid, Sammy Stept, Lew Brown, Roy Turk and Al Sherman. Tobias contributed songs to Broadway shows like a couple of Earl Carroll productions, plus *Yokel Boy* and *Banjo Eyes*. He also collaborated with Sammy Fain on the Broadway score for *Hellzapoppin*. Beginning in the late '20s through the early '50s, Tobias also co-wrote songs for movie musicals such as *The Daughter of Rosie O'Grady* and *On Moonlight Bay*. Tobias co-wrote "When Your Hair Has Turned to Silver" (see '31), "Let's Swing It" (see '35), "Trade Winds" (see '40), "Rose O'Day" (see '42), "Don't Sit Under the Apple Tree" (see '42), and "The Old Lamplighter" (see '46). Later hits came with "All Over the World," "Those Lazy, Hazy, Crazy Days of Summer," and

"What Are You Doing the Rest of Your Life?" Charles Tobias was one of the original members of the Songwriters' Hall of Fame in '70.

Harry Tobias (1895–1994) The Tobias brothers, Charles, Henry and Harry, were all songwriters. Harry began writing songs in '11, the beginning of seven decades of songwriting. Harry's first published songs came in '16 with "Take Me to My Alabam'" and "That Girl of Mine." Tobias enlisted in the U.S. Air Force in '17, and spent World War I shouting song lyrics into megaphones to entertain our troops. After the war, Harry joined his brother Charles' music publishing company and the two brothers began collaborating. In the late '30s, Tobias moved to Hollywood to write for movie studios. Harry collaborated chiefly with his brother Charles, later with his brother Henry and even later with his son, Elliot. Tobais also wrote with Will Dillon, Gus Arnheim, Neil Moret, Jules Lemare, Phil Boutelje, Percy Wenrich, Al Sherman, Harry Barris, Jean Schwartz and Jack Stern. Harry Tobias' most famous songs include "Sweet and Lovely" (see '31) and "At Your Command" (see '31). His "Sail Along, Silv'ry Moon" was popularized later. Harry Tobias was inducted into the Songwriters' Hall of Fame in '83.

Genevieve Tobin (1899–1995) Genevieve Tobin was the daughter of an entertainer, so she began her stage career as a child. Her older brother, George, and younger sister, Vivian, were also stage and film actors. One of her biggest successes was she and William Gaxton introducing "You Do Something to Me" in Cole Porter's *Fifty Million Frenchmen* (see '29). After that production, she began to focus on films, including *A Lady Surrenders* ('30) and *Free Love* ('30). She then began to play more second lead or other woman roles. Once she married William Keighley, she retired from show business.

Nell Tollerton Two middle-aged British women, Eily Beadell and Nell Tollerton, wrote "Cruising Down the River" in '45. It won a nationwide song contest in Great Britain. The song became a big hit in the U.S. in '49.

Pinky Tomlin (real name: Truman Tomlin; 1907–1987) Pinky Tomlin got the nickname "Pinky" because of his pale hair and he sunburned easily because of his fair complexion. Pinky became a very good banjoist and at age 16 was hired by Louis Armstrong to work on a riverboat. Tomlin later gravitated to the guitar. Tomlin came to national attention when he introduced "The Object of My Affection" (see '34), a song he helped write. He earned a few featured roles in movies, as well as starring roles in four pleasant, low-budget features for Melody Pictures. Tomlin introduced "What's the Reason (I'm Not Pleasing You)?" in the film *Times Square Lady* (see '35). After too much touring soured him on the music business, he became an oilman. Pinky Tomlin's '81 biography was appropriately titled *The Object of My Affection*.

Mel Torme (1925–1999) Mel Torme is a very versatile entertainer: he sings jazz, plays drums and piano, and is an actor, a composer, and an arranger. His most famous song creation is "The Christmas Song (Chestnuts Roasting on an Open Fire)" (see '46). Some people called Torme "The Velvet Fog" because of his soft "misty" singing style. His only No. 1 hit recording was of "Careless Hands" (see '49), but his recording of "Again" was also very popular in '49. Mel is probably better known and

appreciated in jazz circles and was inducted into the Big Band/Jazz Hall of Fame in '90.

Al Trace (circa 1901–1993) Composer, bandleader, drummer Al Trace and his band used Chicago as their home base. As a youngster in Chicago, he played drums and sang occasionally with various bands. He formed his own group for an engagement at the '33 Chicago World's Fair. After the fair closed, the band performed at some of Chicago's best dining and dancing spots. Trace worked primarily in the Chicago area, but gained national fame for his composing and recording. He was most active in the '40s and '50s. He achieved national recognition for his songs "You Call Everybody Darling" (see '48) and "If I Knew You Were Comin' I'd 'ave Baked a Cake" (see '50), which he wrote under the name Clem Watts.

Ben Trace Ben Trace was one of the co-writers of "You Call Everybody Darling" (see '48). Ben was the brother of Al Trace. Al was one of the co-writers, writing under the name Clem Watts.

William Tracey William Tracey is primarily remembered as the lyricist for "Play That Barbershop Chord" (see '10) and for "Gee, but It's Great to Meet a Friend from Your Home Town" (see '11).

Arthur Tracy (real name: Abba Avrom Tracovutsky; 1899–1997) Arthur Tracy was born in Kamenetz-Podolsk, Moldavia. He came to the U.S. in '06, where he began his entertainment career in vaudeville. Known as "The Street Singer," Tracy made "Marta" his theme (see '31). He was a sentimental singer who achieved recognition over radio beginning in the early '30s. He signed on and off of his three-time-weekly radio show with "Marta." He appeared in the film *The Big Broadcast* in '32 and was in the cast of the British film *Limelight* ('36). His recordings sold well during the early '30s. His version of "Pennies from Heaven" was featured on the soundtrack of the Steve Martin film *Pennies from Heaven* ('81).

Barbara Trammel Barbara Trammel is one of the co-writers of "Don't Let the Stars Get in Your Eyes" (see '53).

Merle Travis (1917–1983) Merle Travis is famous in the country genre as both a performer and songwriter. In popular music circles, he is most known for co-writing "Smoke, Smoke, Smoke That Cigarette" (see '47) and for writing "Sixteen Tons" (see '55). Travis was particularly active in country music in the '40s and '50s. He was elected to the Country Music Hall of Fame in '77. Merle Travis appeared in approximately fifteen Hollywood films, mostly in the late '40s and early '50s.

Maria Tree Maria Tree introduced "Home, Sweet Home" in the operetta *Clari* or *The Maid of Milan* in 1823 (see '15).

Emma Trentini (1885–1959) Italian songstress Emma Trentini and Orville Harrold introduced "Ah! Sweet Mystery of Life" in the operetta *Naughty Marietta* (see '10). Ms. Trentini also introduced the soprano showpiece "Italian Street Song" in the same production (see '10) and "Giannina Mia" in *The Firefly* (see '13).

Bobby Troup (1918–1999) Bobby Troup was a senior at the University of Pennsylvania when he wrote the song "Daddy" (see '41) for a play — *The Mask and Whig*.

Just prior to World War II, Tommy Dorsey's orchestra recorded Troup's song and Troup arranged some songs for the band. After Marine Corps duty during the war, he decided to try his luck at songwriting. A cross-country drive to L.A. inspired another of his tunes, "Route 66" (see '46). Nat "King" Cole was one of the first big stars to record Troup's songs. Eventually he performed himself as a singer-pianist and helped his wife, Julie London, launch her career as a singer-actress. He began his own acting career in the '50s.

Orrin Tucker (1911–) Orrin Tucker conducted his orchestra in ballrooms and concerts in theaters all over the U.S. during the '30s. They also appeared on the radio version of *Your Hit Parade* for a year. He and his band's only really famous recording was of "Oh Johnny, Oh Johnny, Oh!" in '39 (see '17 when it was most popular) with vocalist Bonnie Baker but their version of "At the Balalaika" (see '40), with Gil Mershon doing the vocal, was also reasonably popular.

Sophie Tucker (real name: Sonia Kalish; 1884–1966) Show business legend Sophie Tucker was born in Russia. She first began singing in her father's café in Hartford, Connecticut in '05. She married Louis Tuck (later changed to Tucker for her stage name) in '06. Her first appearance in the *Ziegfeld Follies* came in '09. By '14 she was earning top money. Over her long career Tucker appeared on the stage, in movies, on radio and television and on recordings. Ms. Tucker's most famous recording was "Some of These Days" (see '27), which she popularized in both '11 and '27.

Roy Turk (1892–1934) Lyricist Roy Turk was born in New York City and attended City College. During World War I he served in the Navy. After the war, be began writing song lyrics, became a staff writer for a Tin Pan Alley music publisher, and later went to Hollywood where he wrote song lyrics for films. Among his collaborators were Fred Ahlert, Harry Akst, George Meyer, Charles Tobias, Arthur Johnston, Maceo Pinkard, and J. Russel Robinson. Turk's successful songs include "My Sweetie Went Away" (see '23), "Gimme a Little Kiss (Will Ya', Huh?)" (see '26), "I'll Get By" (see '44), and "Walkin' My Baby Back Home" (see '52). Turk also co-wrote Bing Crosby's theme song "Where the Blue of the Night Meets the Gold of the Day" (see '31). Other well known Turk songs include "Mean to Me," "I Don't Know Why (I Just Do)." Even though Turk died in '34, he was still reaping hits in the '60s. Elvis Presley recorded his '27 song "Are You Lonesome Tonight" and it became a No. 1 hit for him in '60. Roy Turk was one of the original members of the Songwriters' Hall of Fame in '70. At http://www.songwritershalloffame.org/exhibit_audio_video.asp?exhibitId=44 you can hear audio clips of "Walkin' My Baby Back Home" performed by Maurice Chevalier, and "I Don't Know Why, (I Just Do)" performed by Layton and Johnstone.

Alan Turner Alan Turner was a British operatic baritone who had a couple of successful recordings in the U.S. in the pre-'20s. His recording of "As Long as the World Rolls On" (see '08) and his rendition of "Till the Sands of the Desert Grow Cold" (see '13) were both very popular.

John Turner (real name: Jimmy Phillips) John Turner was a co-lyricist of "Auf Wiederseh'n, Sweetheart" (see '52) and "Oh! My Pa-Pa" (see '54). Britain's John Turner (pen name for Jimmy Phillips) and Geoffrey Parsons translated the original German into English. Parsons worked for the Peter Maurice Music Company, which was run by Jimmy Phillips. The company specialized in adapting foreign song lyrics into English. Phillips, as the boss, would assign Parsons a project. When they were finished, Phillips (or Turner) and Parsons shared credit.

Kay Twomey Kay Twomey was the lyricist of the World War II song "Johnny Doughboy Found a Rose in Ireland" (see '42). Twomey seems to have sometimes been the lyricist, sometimes composer of songs. She also wrote "Hey! Jealous Lover," which was popularized by Frank Sinatra in '57, and "Wooden Heart," which Elvis Presley sang in *G.I. Blues* in '60.

Rudy Vallee (real name: Hubert Prior Vallee; 1901–1993) Rudy Vallee taught himself the saxophone by listening to recordings of Rudy Wiedoelft. He attended college at the University of Maine and Yale. After college, he took the first name of his saxophone idol and dubbed himself Rudy Vallee. Since his principal instrument was the saxophone, he had no intention of singing. His first professional band was called Rudy Vallee and the Yale Collegians, but the university objected to a nightclub band using the institution's name, so he was forced to change it to Rudy Vallee and the Connecticut Yankees in '29. In '29, he starred in the early sound film *The Vagabond Lover* and began his weekly network radio show, which was to become the most popular variety program during the next decade. His radio theme song was "My Time Is Your Time." Sound systems and microphones were not yet very sophisticated, so when Vallee's voice needed amplification, he used a megaphone to help his singing be heard over his band. The megaphone became his trademark. Vallee was particularly important and heard from often in the '30s and to a degree in the '40s, after which his fame waned. He made a comeback in the '50s, more as a comic actor than as a singer. He had an important role in the '61 Broadway musical and the '67 movie version of *How to Succeed in Business Without Really Trying*. Vallee became the No. 18 top recording artist of the '20s and No. 7 of the '30s, making him the No. 28 top recording artist of the first half of the 20th Century. His most popular recordings include "Honey" (see '29), "Stein Song" (see '30), "Brother, Can You Spare a Dime?" (see '32), "Vieni, Vieni" (see '37) and "As Time Goes by" ('43). Other popular recordings include "Weary River," "Deep Night," "Marie," "Lonely Troubador," "When Yuba Plays the Rhumba on the Tuba," "I Guess I'll Have to Change My Plan," and "Let's Put Out the Lights." In addition, he was the composer of or lyricist for a few popular songs including "Deep Night" (see '29), "I'm Just a Vagabond Lover" (see '29) and "Betty Co-ed."

Egbert Van Alstyne (real name: Egbert Anson Van Alstyne; 1882–1951) Composer Egbert Van Alstyne was born in Chicago. After attending the Chicago Musical College and Cornell, Van Alstyne joined the circus and later toured the country on the vaudeville circuit. He moved to New York City around the turn of the century and worked as staff pianist for music publishers. His chief collaborators were Harry H. Williams and Gus Kahn. With Williams, he wrote "Navajo" (see '04), "In the Shade of the Old Apple Tree" (see '05), "Campmeetin' Time" (see '07), "Won't You Come Over to My House?" (see '07), "There Never Was a Girl Like You" (see '08), "Good Night, Ladies" (see '11) and "When I Was Twenty-One and You Were Sweet Sixteen" (see '12). With Kahn, he wrote "Memories" (see '16) and "Pretty Baby" (see '16). Egbert Van Alstyne was an original member of the Songwriters' Hall of Fame in '70. At http://www.songwritershalloffame.org/exhibit_audio_video.asp?exhibitId=283 you can hear an audio clip of "When I Was Twenty-One and You Were Sweet Sixteen" performed by Albert Campbell and Henry Burr.

Van and Schenck   Gus Van (real name: August Von Glahn; 1886–1968), Joe Schenck (real name: Joseph Thuma Schenck; 1891–1930). Van and Schenck sang and performed mainly comedy material. They were vaudeville stars and made several appearances in *The Ziegfeld Follies* in the late 1910s and early '20s. They made quite a few recordings for Emerson, Victor, and Columbia record companies. Some of their most popular recordings include "For Me and My Gal" (see '17), "Ain't We Got Fun?" (see '21), and "Carolina in the Morning" (see '23). This duo became the No. 32 top recording artists of the 1910s and No. 24 of the '20s. They also performed on radio and appeared in a few films.

Walter Van Brunt   Walter Van Brunt is said to have been Thomas Edison's favorite tenor. He began recording at age seventeen. In '17, at Edison's urging, he changed his last name to Scanlan and starred on Broadway in *Eileen*. He also appeared on radio with Billy Murray in the late '20s and early '30s. His recording of "I Want a Girl (Just Like the Girl That Married Dear Old Dad)" with the American Quartet (see '11) and his recording with Helen Clark of "Sympathy" from *The Firefly* (see '13) were well received.

Jimmy Van Heusen (real name: Edward Chester Babcock; 1913–1990)   Composer Jimmy Van Heusen grew up in Syracuse, where he began composing songs while he was still in high school. During his teens, he had a radio program on a Syracuse station and for that program, changed his last name to Van Heusen (inspired by the men's collar, and later shirt, manufacturer of the same name). After high school, Van Heusen attended Cazenovia College and Syracuse University where he studied music. In '33 Van Heusen moved to New York City and took a job as a staff pianist with Remick, the famous music publishing company. In '38, Van Heusen was put under contract with Remick as a songwriter and began collaborating with lyricist Eddie DeLange. Even though they worked together for only a short period of time, the team produced quite a number of songs. By '39, Van Heusen started working with another lyricist, Johnny Burke. Collaborating on Broadway shows, as well as over 30 films, the Van Heusen-Burke team became one of the most successful songwriting partnerships. Under contract with Paramount Studios, Van Heusen and Burke moved to Hollywood at the beginning of the '40s. Throughout his forty-year career, Van Heusen received ten Oscar nominations for Best Song in a Motion Picture and four Academy Awards for Best Song in a Motion Picture. In '56, Burke semi-retired from songwriting and Van Heusen started another successful partnership with legendary lyricist Sammy Cahn. Van Heusen and Eddie DeLange's most

famous songs were "Heaven Can Wait" (see '39) and "Darn That Dream" (see '40). Van Heusen and Johnny Burke's most popular songs include "Imagination" (see '40), "Moonlight Becomes You" and "Road to Morocco" (see '43), "Sunday, Monday or Always" (see '43), "Swinging on a Star" (see '44) the '45 Academy Award for Best Song, and "Personality" (see '46). Other well known Van Heusen and Burke songs include "Polka Dots and Moonbeams," "It's Always You," "Sleighride in July," an Academy Award nominee from *Belle of the Yukon*, "Day After Forever," "Would You?," "Aren't You Glad You're You?," "But Beautiful," "It Could Happen to You" and "Like Someone in Love." Van Heusen and Sammy Cahn collaborated on "The Tender Trap" from the film of the same name, "Love and Marriage" from TV adaptation of *Our Town*, which received the '55 Emmy Award for Best Song, "All the Way" from *The Joker Is Wild*, the '57 Academy Award for Best Song, "High Hopes" from *A Hole in the Head*, the '59 Academy Award for Best Song, "The Second Time Around" from *High Time*, "Call Me Irresponsible" from *Papa's Delicate Condition*, the '64 Academy Award for Best Song and "Come Fly with Me" from the film of the same name. His string of hits continued with the Academy Award nominee "My Kind of Town" from *Robin and the 7 Hoods*, Academy Award nominee "Thoroughly Modern Millie" from the film of the same name and Academy Award nominee "Star" from the film of the same title. Van Heusen composed the songs for all the Bing Crosby and Bob Hope "Road" films, and several other Crosby and/or Hope motion pictures. Jimmy Van Heusen was inducted into the Songwriters' Hall of Fame in '71. At http://www.songwritershalloffame.org/exhibit_audio_video.asp?exhibitId=100 you can hear audio clips of "Darn That Dream" performed by Mildred Bailey, "My Kind of Town" sung by Frank Sinatra, "Second Time Around" sung by Bing Crosby, "All the Way" performed by Lena Horne, "Ain't Love a Kick in the Head" performed by Dean Martin, "The Last Dance" and "Love and Marriage" sung by Frank Sinatra. For more see http://www.jimmyvanheusen.com/.

Jaramir Vejvoda   Jaramir Vejvoda wrote the tune for the Czech song "Skoda Lasky" in '27; lyrics were added in '34. It became "Beer Barrel Polka" after Lew Brown added English lyrics (see '39).

Consuelo Velazquez (c. 1917–2005)   Consuelo Velázquez was a Mexican songwriter. According to her obituary she was 88 years old, making her birth 1917, but most music resources list her birth date as August 29, 1924 in Ciudad Guzmán, Jalisco State, Mexico. Velázquez was the songwriter and lyricist of many Latin standard songs, most notably, of the enduring 1940s-era hit "Bésame Mucho" (see '44). Velázquez started her professional career as a classical music concert pianist, but later became a singer and recording artist. She composed the romantic ballad "Bésame Mucho" in '41, which was soon recorded by artists around the globe, making it an international hit. It became a big hit for Jimmy Dorsey in '44. English lyrics were added by Sunny Skylar and the song has been recorded by hundreds of great performers. Velázquez also was elected to the Mexican Congress.

Jay Velie (1893–1982)   Jay Velie was an actor and singer on Broadway for more than 50 years. He began his career in vaudeville with his sister, Janet, in '12. His first Broadway lead was in *Little Jessie James*, where he and Ann Sands introduced "I Love You" (see '24). Later, Mr. Velie appeared in *Our Town, Carousel, Call Me Madam* and *Sound of Music*.

F. Dudleigh Vernor According to the Albion College website, Mrs. Darleen Wellington Miller, a local piano and vocal teacher, assisted one of her pupils, F. Dudleigh Vernor, in composing the song "The Sweetheart of Sigma Chi," which today is considered to be the world's most famous fraternity song (see '12).

Virginia Verrill (1916–1999) Virginia Verrill's voice, dubbed into the soundtrack for Jean Harlow's, introduced "Did I Remember?" in *Suzy* (see '36). Ms. Verrill also introduced "That Old Feeling" in the movie *Walter Wanger's Vogues of 1938* (see '37).

Martha Vickers (real name: Martha MacVicar; 1925–1971) Martha Vickers, Jack Carson, and Dennis Morgan introduced "A Gal in Calico" in the movie musical *The Time, the Place and the Girl* (see '46). Ms. Vickers broke into the entertainment field as a model. David O. Selznick signed her as a starlet, but after nothing came of it, so she signed with Universal, with RKO and eventually Warner Bros. During World War II, she was a pin-up girl for U.S. soldiers.

Victor Light Opera Company Almost all of the singing stars at Victor recorded with this group between '09 and '26. Some of the most famous members include Harry MacDonough, Lucy Isabelle Marsh, Olive Kline, Reinald Werrenrath, Billy Murray, Ada Jones, Elsie Baker, John Bieling, Elsie Stevenson, Lewis James, Elliott Shaw, Wilfred Glenn, and Franklyn Baur. A recording billed as Ada Jones and the Victor Light Opera Co. of "The Yama Yama Man" was very popular (see '09). Otherwise, Lucy Isabelle Marsh's recording with the company of "Italian Street Song" (see '10) and the company's recording of excerpts from *Naughty Marietta* were their most well received recordings.

Victor Military Band The Victor Military Band's most popular recording was of "Poor Butterfly" (see '17). A medley from the musical *Katinka* was also quite popular in '17. Walter B. Rogers was the director of the Victor Military Band.

Victor Orchestra The Victor Orchestra, conducted by Walter B. Rogers, recorded a particularly successful rendition of "The Glow Worm" (see '08).

A.G. Villoldo Angel G. Villoldo's Argentine tango, "El Choclo," was written in '13. It was adapted into "Kiss of Fire" (see '52).

Nat Vincent (1889–1929) Jean Kenbrovin was the pseudonym for James Kendis, James Brockman, and Nat Vincent when they co-wrote the lyrics for "I'm Forever Blowing Bubbles" (see '19). Kendis, Brockman, and Vincent had separate contracts with publishers that led them to merge their names into Jean Kenbrovin for credit on "I'm Forever Blowing Bubbles."

Albert Von Tilzer (real name: Albert Gumm; 1878–1956) Albert Von Tilzer became an important songwriter from the early 1900s into the '20s. He was the younger brother of composer Harry Von Tilzer. Early in his life, Albert was a shoe buyer for a Brooklyn depart-

ment store and the music director for a vaudeville company. His brother Harry hired him as a staff writer for his music publishing company and in '03, Albert and his other brother, Jack, formed their own music-publishing firm. Von Tilzer worked on Broadway and also contributed songs to films in the '20s and '30s. Albert Von Tilzer's chief collaborators include Jack Norworth, Junie McCree, Lew Brown, Neville Fleeson and Cecil Mack. Highlights from Albert Von Tilzer's songwriting career include "Take Me Out to the Ball Game" (see '08), "Good Evening, Caroline" (see '09), "Carrie (Carrie Marry Harry)" (see '10), "Put Your Arms Around Me, Honey" (see '11), "I'm the Lonesomest Gal in Town" (see '12), "Oh, How She Could Yacki Hacki Wicki Wacki Woo" (see '16), "Forever Is a Long, Long Time" (see '17), "Give Me the Moonlight, Give Me the Girl" (see '18), and "I'll Be with You in Apple Blossom Time" (see '20). Other Von Tilzer songs include "Teasing," "Honey Boy," "I Used to Love You but It's All Over Now," "Dapper Dan" and "Roll Along, Prairie Moon." Albert Von Tilzer was an original member of the Songwriters' Hall of Fame in '70. The Von Tilzer brothers, see Harry Von Tilzer below, had changed their names from Gumm to sound more European. Their niece, Frances Gumm, would change her name to Judy Garland. At http://www.songwritershalloffame.org/exhibit_audio_video.asp?exhibitId=284 you can hear an audio clip of "Carrie" performed by Billy Murray.

Harry Von Tilzer (real name: Harry Gumm; 1872–1946) Composer Harry Von Tilzer was born in Detroit, but when he was a child, his family moved to Indianapolis where a theatrical company performed above his father's shoe store. That was Harry's introduction to show business. In his early teens, Harry ran away from home to join the circus. By 1887, he was playing the piano, composing and acting in a traveling repertory company. In 1892, he moved to New York City where he got a job as a saloon pianist. In 1899, he was made a partner in a publishing firm, renamed Shapiro, Bernstein and Von Tilzer. In '02, Von Tilzer left that firm to form Harry Von Tilzer Music Company. Von Tilzer primarily collaborated with Andrew B. Sterling, Arthur J. Lamb, Will Dillon and William Jerome. Von Tilzer collaborated with Arthur J. Lamb on "A Bird in a Gilded Cage" (see '00), and "The Mansion of Aching Hearts" (see '02). With Jerome, he wrote "The Green Grass Grew All Around" (see '13). With Andrew B. Sterling, he wrote "On a Sunday Afternoon" (see '02), "Goodbye, Eliza Jane" (see '03), "Alexander (Don't You Love Your Baby No More?)" (see '04), "All Aboard for Dreamland" (see '04), "What You Goin' to Do When the Rent Comes 'Round?" (see '05), "Where the Morning Glories Twine Around the Door" (see '05), "Wait Till the Sun Shines, Nellie" (see '06), "Under the Yum Yum Tree" (see '11), "Last Night Was the End of the World" (see '13) and "The Song That Stole My Heart" (see '14). Harry Von Tilzer's other famous songs include "Down Where the Wurzburger Flows" (see '03), "I'm the Sweet Bye and Bye" (see '03), "I Love, I Love, I Love My Wife, but Oh! You Kid!" (see '09), "I Want a Girl (Just Like the Girl That Married Dear Old Dad)" (see '11) and "I Sent My Wife to the Thousand Isles" (see '16). Other well known Von Tilzer songs include "The Cubanola Glide," "I'd Leave My Happy Home for You" and "When the Harvest Days are Over, Jessie Dear." In '14, Von Tilzer was a charter member of the performing rights society, American Society of Composers, Authors and Publishers or ASCAP. Harry Von Tilzer was one of the original members of the Songwriters' Hall of Fame in '70. The Von Tilzer brothers, see Albert Von Tilzer above, had changed their names from Gumm to appear more European. Here was a white man attempting to compose African American songs and an American posing as a German. Their niece, Frances Gumm, would change her name to Judy Garland. At http://www.songwritershall offame.org/exhibit_audio_video.asp?exhibitId=246 you can hear audio clips of "I'd Leave My Happy Home for You" performed by Arthur Collins and "My Old New Hampshire Home" performed by Jere Mahoney.

Bea Wain (1917–) Singer Bea Wain is best known as the vocalist with the Larry Clinton band during the late '30s. She sang with Fred Waring before she joined Clinton's group. She gained fame with Clinton's orchestra when they popularized several songs in '38 and '39. She left the band in '39 to work as a single. Although she continued singing for many years, she never regained her former popularity. She married radio announcer Andre Baruch. With Larry Clinton's band, she was the vocalist on "My Reverie" (see '38), "Cry, Baby, Cry" (see '38), "Heart and Soul" (see '38), among others.

Jimmy Wakely (real name: James Clarence Wakely; 1914–1982) Jimmy Wakely is best known as a singing cowboy in several films. His biggest record hits were mostly "honky-tonk, cheatin'" songs. He broke the mainstream pop barrier when he teamed with Margaret Whiting for several recordings, most notably "Slipping Around" (see '49). Wakely's singing might be called a combination of a country Bing Crosby and a highbrow Gene Autry.

Waldorf-Astoria Dance Orchestra The Waldorf-Astoria Dance Orchestra, directed by Joseph Knecht, recorded a particularly popular rendition of "Beautiful Ohio" for Victor (see '19). The flip side of the record was the very popular "Till We Meet Again" by Nicholas Orlando and his orchestra.

George Walker (1873–1911) George Walker was a vaudeville performer and partner of Bert Williams. The most successful duet recording Walker recorded with Bert Williams was "Good Morning, Carrie" (see '02).

James J. Walker (1881–1946) James J. Walker, often known as Jimmy Walker and colloquially as Beau James, became the mayor of New York City during the late '20s. Walker was the son of Irish immigrants. Before entering politics, Walker worked as a songwriter. His most popular song was "Will You Love Me in December (as You Do in May)?" (see '06). He studied law and was elected to the New York State Assembly in '09, he won election to the New York State Senate in '14 and was later majority leader of that body. He became Mayor of New York City in '26. The first few years of his tenure in office were a prosperous time for the city, at least partially due to the proliferation of speakeasies during the Prohibition Era. His affairs with chorus girls were widely known, and he left his wife, Janet, for showgirl Betty Compton without impairing his popularity. He won re-election by an overwhelming margin in '29. During the re-election campaign, he was denounced for immorality, both personal

and political. Increasing social unrest led to the investigations into corruption within his administration, and he was eventually forced to testify before the Seabury Commission. Facing pressure from Governor Franklin Delano Roosevelt, Walker resigned from office in '32 and fled to Europe until the danger of criminal prosecution appeared remote. He married Betty Compton while in Europe. When he returned to the United States, Walker became head of Majestic Records. A romanticized version of Walker's tenure as mayor was presented in the '57 film *Beau James,* which starred Bob Hope.

Marshall Walker Marshall Walker co-wrote the Bert Williams song "It's Nobody's Business but My Own" with Will E. Skidmore (see '19).

Chester Wallace Chester Wallace wrote the lyrics for "Moonlight on the Ganges" (see '26).

Oliver Wallace (1887–1963) Oliver Wallace composed music for several of Disney's classic cartoons. In '42, he was awarded an Oscar for his music and scoring for Disney's *Dumbo.* He also worked on *Cinderella, Alice in Wonderland, Peter Pan* and *Lady and the Tramp* for Disney. His "Der Fuehrer's Face" was a World War II comedy hit. Wallace's other best-known song is probably "Hindustan," which he co-wrote during World War I with Gitz Rice (see '19).

Fats Waller (real name: Thomas Waller; 1904–1943) Afro-American pianist, singer, composer Fats Waller was particularly popular and wrote most of his songs in the late '20s and '30s. Composer Thomas "Fats" Waller was born in New York City. The legendary pianist and singer learned the organ at Abyssinian Baptist Church in New York City where his father was pastor. Waller began his career as a singer and pianist in nightclubs and accompanied in various theatres as an organist. He also accompanied singer Bessie Smith. Leading and recording with his own band, Waller toured extensively throughout the United States and Europe. While his chief collaborator was lyricist Andy Razaf, Waller also worked with Stanley Adams, George Marion, Jr. and Clarence Williams. Waller's biggest hits were "I've Got a Feeling I'm Falling" (see '29) and "Ain't Misbehavin'" (see '29). Other Waller songs include "Honeysuckle Rose" (see '29), "Keepin' Out of Mischief Now" and "The Joint Is Jumpin'." Fats had a great deal of recording success during the last half of the '30s. His most popular recordings include "Truckin'" (see '35), "A Little Bit Independent" (see '35), "It's a Sin to Tell a Lie" (see '36), "All My Life" (see '36), "(You Know It All) Smarty" (see '37) and "Two Sleepy People" (see '38). Waller became the No. 18 top recording artist of the '30s. In '79 Broadway honored Waller with a revue, *Ain't Misbehavin',* which featured many of his best works and other songs that were identified with him. Waller was honored with membership in the Songwriters' Hall of Fame when it was organized in '70. He was elected to the Big Band/Jazz Hall of Fame in '89. Several Fats Waller recordings are available at http://www.redhotjazz.com/bands. html. At http://www.songwritershalloffame.org/exhibit_ audio_video.asp?exhibitId=285 you can hear an audio clip of Fats Waller singing his "Honeysuckle Rose."

Charles Walters (1911–1982) Charles Walters made his Broadway debut in '34's *New Faces,* but really gained attention in *Jubilee,* where he teamed with June Knight to introduce "Begin the Beguine" (see '38) and "Just One of Those Things" (see '35). After other featured roles in *I Married an Angel* and *DuBarry Was a Lady*, Walters choreographed *Let's Face It, Banjo Eyes* and *St. Louis Woman*. Walters also staged the dance scenes for several Hollywood films including *Girl Crazy, Meet Me in St. Louis* and *The Harvey Girls*. He then graduated to director of several MGM movie musicals including *Good News, Easter Parade, Lili, High Society, Jumbo* and *The Unsinkable Molly Brown*.

James Paul Warburg James Paul Warburg, writing under the name Paul James, was the lyricist of "Can't We Be Friends" (see '29). Warburg most often wrote with his wife Kay Swift.

Aida Ward Aida Ward, in her Broadway debut, interpolated "I Can't Give You Anything but Love" into *Lew Leslie's Blackbirds of 1928* (see '28). Ms. Ward introduced "I've Got the World on a String" at the Cotton Club in Harlem (see '32).

Charles B. Ward (1865–1917) John E. Palmer wrote "The Band Played On" in 1895. Palmer sold his rights to the song to a vaudevillian, Charles B. Ward. As was the custom, once a person had paid for the song, it was theirs; they could publish it and take full credit. When Ward published it, he claimed to have written the music, but he did give Palmer credit for the words.

Fred Waring (1900–1984) Fred Waring and his brother formed their first musical group in '16, a quartet called Waring's Banjazzatra. His Collegians were particularly popular during the '20s. He expanded his band to include a glee club, which became well known on radio in the mid–'30s and on television in the late '40s. They were billed as Fred Waring and His Pennsylvanians. Waring's recording successes ran from the mid–'20s into the early '30s. Some of his biggest hit recordings included "Memory Lane" (see '24) with a vocal by Tom Waring, "Sleep" (see '24) with vocals by Fred and Tom Waring, "Collegiate" (see '25), "Laugh, Clown, Laugh!" (see '28) with a Fred Waring vocal, "Little White Lies" (see '30) with vocalist Clare Hanlon, and "I Found a Million Dollar Baby (in a Five and Ten Cent Store)" (see '31) with vocals by Clare Hanlon and the Three Waring Girls. Waring is ranked as the No. 9 top recording artist of the '20s and No. 22 of the '30s, making him the No. 34 top recording artist of the first half of the 20th Century. In addition to his musical endeavors, he was an inventor (the Waring Blender) and manufacturer. He also founded the Shawnee Press to publish the arrangements the Pennsylvanians performed and was very active for many years in sponsoring workshops for choral directors. Waring's Pennsylvanians recordings between '23 and '84 are available for listening at http://www.redhotjazz.com/bands.html.

Jeanette Warner Jeanette Warner and Billy Kent introduced "Ballin' the Jack" in vaudeville (see '14). Warner and Kent are credited with being the creators of the fox trot dance.

Harry Warren (real name: Salvatore Guaragna; 1893–1981) Composer Harry Warren was one of the most successful writers of popular songs from the early '20s through the '50s. Harry Warren was born to Italian immigrant parents in Brooklyn, New York, the eleventh of twelve children. Warren taught himself to play several musical instruments, including the accordion and piano. At age 15 he left school and took his first job as a drummer with John Victor's brass band. He then got jobs with various touring carnival shows, as stagehand for a vaudeville theater, and as a property man and offstage piano player at the Vitagraph film studios. After serving in the U.S. Navy in World War I, Warren began writing songs. His first effort was never published, but it got him a job as staff pianist and song plugger for a music-publishing house. Warren's first published song was "Rose of the Rio Grande," written in '22 with Edgar Leslie and Ross Gorman. Warren wrote songs for several Broadway shows in the early '30s, including *Crazy Quilt* and *The Laugh Parade*. Between the late '20s and '33 he wrote songs for a few minor movies. He decided to make Hollywood his permanent home in '33 when he was hired to work with Al Dubin on Warner Bros. *Forty Second Street*. During the rest of the decade, Warren wrote some twenty movie musicals with Dubin. He also wrote some movie songs with Johnny Mercer during the '30s. Warren moved to 20th Century Fox in the early '40s, where he teamed with Mack Gordon. From the mid–'40s into the early '50s, he worked at MGM. Warren moved to Paramount at that point and it was there he wrote his last big pop hit, "That's Amore." Through the later–'50s, he mainly wrote scores for dramatic movies such as *An Affair to Remember* and *Separate Tables*. Warren collaborated with Johnny Mercer on "You Must Have Been a Beautiful Baby" (see '38), "Jeepers Creepers" (see '39), and "On the Atchison, Topeka and the Santa Fe" (see '45) from *The Harvey Girls*, which won the Academy Award for Best Song. With Edgar Leslie, Warren wrote "By the River Sainte Marie" (see '31). Warren and Mack Gordon collaborated on "At Last," "Chattanooga Choo Choo" (see '41), "(I've Got a Gal in) Kalamazoo" (see '42), "I Had the Craziest Dream" (see '43), "You'll Never Know" (see '43) from *Hello, Frisco, Hello*, which won the Oscar for Best Song, "My Heart Tells Me" (see '44), and "The More I See You" (see '45). Warren's most popular song co-written with Mort Dixon and Billy Rose was "I Found a Million-Dollar Baby (in a Five-and-Ten-Cent Store)" (see '31). Warren collaborated with Al Dubin on numerous songs. Some of the most popular ones include "Too Many Tears" (see '32), "Forty Second Street" (see '33), "Shuffle Off to Buffalo" (see '33), "You're Getting to Be a Habit with Me" (see '33), "Shadow Waltz" (see '33), "The Gold Diggers' Song (We're in the Money)" (see '33), "I'll String Along with You" (see '34), "I Only Have Eyes for You" (see '34), "Lullaby of Broadway" (see '35), "She's a Latin from Manhattan" (see '35), "I'll Sing You a Thousand Love Songs" (see '36), "Remember Me?" (see '37), "September in the Rain" (see '37) and "With Plenty of Money and You" (see '37). Other well known Warren and Dubin collaborations include "About a Quarter to Nine," "Boulevard of Broken Dreams," "I Love My Baby, My Baby Loves Me," and "Young and Healthy," among others. Warren composed the music for "That's Amore" (see '53). See Harry Warren's original manuscript of this song at http://www.harrywarrenmusic.com/frame set.html. In '80, Warren and Dubin's *Forty Second Street* was brought to Broadway. Nine additional Harry Warren songs from his various movie musicals were added to the original film score. On his 80th birthday in '71, he was elected into the Songwriters Hall of Fame. Go to http://www.harrywarren.org for a look at almost all of his songs, lyrics, some midi musical versions, etc. At http://www.songwritershall offame.org/exhibit_audio_video.asp?exhibitId=22 you can hear audio clips of "Would You Like to Take a Walk" performed by Annette Hanshaw with Benny Goodman and his orchestra, "Cryin' for the Carolines" performed by Waring's Pennsylvanians, "At Last" performed by Eva Cassidy, "Zing a Little Zong" sung by Bing Crosby, "She's a Latin from Manhattan" performed by Al Jolson, "Lulu's Back in Town" performed by Fats Waller, "We're in the Money" sung by Rosemary Clooney, "Jeepers Creepers" performed by Louis Armstrong, "I Found a Million Dollar Baby" sung by Nat "King" Cole, "Chattanooga Choo Choo" performed by Ray Anthony and his orchestra, "September Song" performed by Dakota Stanton, "Serenade in Blue" performed by Ethel Ennis, "There Will Never Be Another You" performed by Chet Baker, "The More I See You" sung by Nancy Wilson, "I Only Have Eyes for You" sung by Dinah Shore, "Lullaby of Broadway" performed by Ann Richards, "You're Getting to Be a Habit with Me" performed by Peggy Lee, "An Affair to Remember" sung by Nat "King" Cole, "That's Amore" sung by Dean Martin, "Keep Young and Beautiful" performed by Denny Dennis with Roy Fox and his Band, and "You'll Never Know" performed by Dick Haymes and the Song Spinners.

Frank Warshauer Frank Warshauer was a co-writer of "It Isn't Fair" (see '50).

Joe "Country" Washburne Country Washburne was co-lyricist of "One Dozen Roses" (see '42). Washburne was a first-rate jazz musician who had performed with Ted Weems and his orchestra. He eventually took over most of the arranging duties for Spike Jones and his City Slickers. Joe "Country" Washburne and his orchestra were regulars on Roy Rogers' radio program.

Ned Washington (1901–1976) Lyricist Ned Washington wrote several hits, primarily for Broadway shows and for films. Washington was nominated for the Oscar a dozen times. He began his career as a vaudeville Master of Ceremonies. His first songwriting success came in '28 with the song "Singing in the Bathtub," which was included in the musical revue *Earl Carroll Vanities of 1929*. Washington collaborated on several scores for Broadway including several editions of *Earl Carroll Vanities, Murder at the Vanities* and *Blackbirds of 1934*. In '34, he moved to Hollywood where he wrote complete scores for the Walt Disney films *Pinocchio*, which won the '40 Academy Award and Box Office Blue Ribbon Award and *Dumbo*. Subsequently, he also contributed songs to *No, No, Nanette, Little Johnny Jones, Brazil, The Greatest Show on Earth, Miss Sadie Thompson* and *Gulliver's Travels*. Washington collaborated with many composers including Victor Young, Dimitri Tiomkin, Lester Lee, Michael Cleary, Allie Wrubel, George Duning, Max Steiner, Jimmy McHugh, Bronislau Kaper, Walter Jurmann, Leigh Harline and Sam Stept. Some of Washington's most famous songs include "I'm Getting Sentimental Over You" (see '32), the Academy award winner for Best Song "When You Wish Upon a Star" (see '40), "The Nearness of You" (see '40), "My Foolish Heart" (see '50), the Academy Award winning "High Noon" (see '52) and "The High and the Mighty" (see '54). Another well known Washington song is "(I Don't Stand) A Ghost of a Chance with You." The Song-

writers' Hall of Fame elected Washington to membership in '72. At http://www.songwritershalloffame.org/exhibit_ audio_video.asp?exhibitId=311 you can hear an audio clip of Barbra Streisand singing "When You Wish Upon a Star."

Ethel Waters (1896–1977) Ethel Waters began her musical career in vaudeville in '17. Her blues recordings were particularly popular among jazz connoisseurs, but she became better known to a wider public when she introduced "Dinah" at the Plantation Club in New York City in the mid-'20s (see '32), then introduced "Am I Blue?" in the movie musical *On With the Show* (see '29), then back to Broadway to introduce "Until the Real Thing Comes Along" in *Rhapsody in Black* (see '36), "Heat Wave" in *As Thousands Cheer*, "Stormy Weather" in a Cotton Club revue (see '33) and "Taking a Chance on Love" (see '43) in *Cabin in the Sky*. She became one of the first African Americans to star on Broadway in a racially mixed cast in *At Home Abroad* in '35. Ethel Waters' most famous recordings were released between the mid-'20s and the mid-'30s and included "Am I Blue?" (see '29) and "Stormy Weather" (see '33). Several Ethel Waters recordings are available for listening at http://www.redhotjazz. com/bands.html.

Billy Watkins (1888–1945) Billy Watkins' duet recording of "By the Beautiful Sea" for Columbia with Ada Jones was very popular (see '14).

Deek Watson (1909–1969) Deek Watson, an original member of the Ink Spots, is credited as co-writer of "For Sentimental Reasons," but later research indicates that William Best most likely wrote both words and music. For more, see http://inkspots.ca/DEEK-BIO.html.

Paula Watson Paula Watson introduced "A Little Bird Told Me" (see '49), but Evelyn Knight then popularized it with a very successful recording.

Clem Watts (see Al Trace)

Grady Watts Grady Watts was co-writer of "Blue Champagne" (see '41). Watts was a trumpet player for Glen Gray's orchestra from the early '30s.

Bernie Wayne (1919–1993) Bernie Wayne was the composer of "You Walk by" (see '40) and "Laughing on the Outside (Crying on the Inside)" (see '46). Wayne also composed the melody for "There She Is," the Miss America theme song for many years.

John Wayne (real name: Marion Morrison; 1907–1979) John Wayne whistled the theme song from the film *The High and the Mighty* off and on throughout the movie (see '54). Wayne is not particularly well known for his musical skills. He is, of course, an extremely famous Hollywood film actor, known mostly for his western films. For more on Wayne, see http://en.wikipedia. org/wiki/John_Wayne.

Mabel Wayne (1898–1978) Composer Mabel Wayne studied voice and piano in Switzerland and attended the New York School of Music. Early in her career, she performed as a pianist and concert singer as well as a dancer in vaudeville acts. Wayne collaborated with several lyricists including L. Wolfe Gilbert, Kim Gannon, Billy Rose, Mitchell Parish, Sam Lewis, Joe Young and Al Lewis. Among Wayne's most famous songs are "In a Little

Spanish Town" (see '27), "Ramona" (see '28), and "Little Man You've Had a Busy Day" (see '34). Other well known Wayne songs include "It Happened in Monterey" and "A Dreamer's Holiday." Mabel Wayne was inducted into the Songwriters' Hall of Fame in '72. At http://www.song writershalloffame.org/exhibit_audio_video.asp? exhibitId=312 you can hear audio clips of "It Happened in Monterey" performed by Jack Fulton with Paul Whiteman and his orchestra and "Little Man You've Had a Busy Day" performed by Paul Robeson with Ray Noble and the New Mayfair Orchestra.

Fred E. Weatherly (real name: Frederic Edward Weatherly; 1848–1929)   Fred E. Weatherly is remembered as the lyricist of "Danny Boy" (see '13) and "The Roses of Picardy" (see '18). He was an English lawyer, who was also a songwriter and radio entertainer. As far as can be ascertained, Weatherly never visited Ireland.

Weavers   Pete Seeger (1919–), Lee Hays (?–1981), Fred Hellerman (1927–), Ronnie Gilbert (1926–). The Weavers evolved from the Almanac Singers, which consisted of Pete Seeger, Lee Hays and Woody Guthrie. Seeger and Hays founded the Weavers with Fred Hellerman and female lead singer Ronnie Gilbert. They made folk music a popular phenomenon in the early '50s. The Weavers' recording of "Goodnight, Irene" (see '50) with Gordon Jenkins and his orchestra spent thirteen weeks at the top of the *Billboard* chart an sold over two million copies. The same year, their version of the Israeli song "Tzena, Tzena, Tzena" (see '50) was also quite popular. Their version of the old Southern Highlands folk song "On Top of Old Smoky" (see '51) with the Terry Gilkyson chorus and Vic Schoen's Orchestra was also quite successful. The Weavers were inducted into the Vocal Group Hall of Fame in 2001.

Clifton Webb (real name: Webb Parmelee Hollenbeck; 1891–1966)   Actor, singer, and dancer Clifton Webb is best remembered for the twenty films he made, particularly the Mr. Belvedere roles he played. From the mid–1910s, Webb was a leading man and dancer in several Broadway musicals. He introduced or helped introduce "I've Got a Crush on You" in *Treasure Girl*, "I Guess I'll Have to Change My Plan" (see '29) in *The Little Show*, "Louisiana Hayride" (see '32) in *Flying Colors* and "Easter Parade" (see '33) in *As Thousands Cheer*. His last musical on Broadway was in '38, after which he turned to Hollywood.

Weber and Fields   Joe Weber (real name: Joseph Maurice Weber; 1867–1942), Lew Fields (real name: Lewis Maurice Schanfield; 1867–1941). Weber and Fields were an American comedy team. Both of these comics were born in New York City. By the age of eight they were already performing together in the Bowery, and turned professional shortly afterward. Appearing in beards, loud checked clothes, and derbies, they were adored by their fans. Fields was taller than Weber and more aggressive, while Weber became the brunt of all the jokes. They were noted for their slapstick antics and dialect jokes. They opened and managed Weber and Fields Music Hall on Broadway from 1896 until '04, where they presented many popular productions. They separated after a quarrel in '04, but they resumed their partnership in '12. They both retired in the early '30s.

Rex Weber   Rex Weber introduced "Brother, Can You Spare a Dime?" in *New Americana* (see '32).

Paul Francis Webster (1907–1984)   Paul Francis Webster was born in New York City, attended Cornell University and New York University. By '31 his career as a lyricist had begun and he would become one of Hollywood's most successful lyricists. In '35, he went to Hollywood intending to write for Shirley Temple films. Soon after he arrived on the West Coast, he became a freelance writer and in '41 he had his first real success with "I Got It Bad (and That Ain't Good)." After '50, Webster worked primarily with composer Sammy Fain. Together they won two Academy Awards, for the song "Secret Love" (see '54) from the film *Calamity Jane*, and for "Love Is a Many-Splendored Thing" (see '55) from the film of the same name. Working with composer Johnny Mandel, he won a third Academy Award for the song "The Shadow of Your Smile" from the '65 film *The Sandpiper*. Webster's long list of collaborators includes Sammy Fain, Johnny Mandel, Duke Ellington, Hoagy Carmichael, Harry Revel, Rudolf Friml, Lew Pollack, Jerry Livingston, John Jacob Loeb, Max Steiner, Alfred Newman, Bronislau Kaper, Frank Churchill, Franz Waxman, and Dmitri Tiomkin. Others of his best-known songs were "Masquerade" (see '32), "My Moonlight Madonna" (see '33), "Two Cigarettes in the Dark" (see '34), "Doctor, Lawyer, Indian Chief" (see '46), "The Loveliest Night of the Year" (see '51), plus "Friendly Persuasion," "April Love," "A Certain Smile," "The Green Leaves of Summer," "Somewhere My Love (Lara's Theme from *Doctor Zhivago*)," "The Twelfth of Never," "The Lamplighter's Serenade," "Song of Raintree County," and "Tender Is the Night," most of those popular after the period covered by this book. Paul Francis Webster was inducted into the Songwriters' Hall of Fame in '72. At http://www.songwritershalloffame.org/exhibit_audio_video .asp?exhibitId=74 you can hear an audio clip of "Two Cigarettes in the Dark" sung by Bing Crosby.

Harold Weeks   Harold Weeks had success with two songs that were quite popular in the late teens. Weeks wrote the words and music for "Chong" (see '19) and co-wrote the words and music for "Hindustan" (see '19) with Oliver G. Wallace.

Ted Weems (1901–1963)   Bandleader Ted Weems' group of musicians was particularly popular from the mid–'20s through the '30s. They experienced a revival in '47 and continued to be active through the early '60s. Some of Weems' most popular recordings include "Somebody Stole My Gal" (see '24), "The Man from the South" (see '30), and "Heartaches" (see '47). Most of his recording successes came between the mid–'20s and the early '30s, except for the revival in '47. Weems is ranked the No. 23 top recording artist of the '20s and No. 33 of the '40s (not among the top 40 recording artists of the '30s). Weems was inducted into the Big Band/Jazz Hall of Fame in 2003. Ted Weems and his orchestra recordings between '23 and '42 are available for listening at http://www.red hotjazz.com/bands.html.

Melle Weersma (circa 1908–1988)   Melle Weersma was the composer of "Penny Serenade" (see '39). Weersma was a pianist and accordion player.

Kurt Weill (1900–1950)   Composer Kurt Weill was a very successful writer for the German stage before he came to America. He composed *The Rise and Fall of the City of Mahagonny* in '27 and the very famous *The Threepenny Opera* (the origin of the song "Mack the Knife") in '28. When Weill's works, which were often attacks on the social and political life in Nazi Germany, were not allowed to be performed, Weill escaped to Paris, then to London, and on to New York City by '35. He became an American citizen in '43. *Knickerbocker Holiday*, which introduced "September Song" (see '39) was his first successfully produced musical in the United States. His other successful Broadway shows include *Lady in the Dark*, *One Touch of Venus* (see "Speak Low" in '44), *Street Scene* and *Lost in the Stars*. His *The Threepenny Opera* was revived on Broadway in updated English versions '52 and '54. Weill has been a member of the Songwriters' Hall of Fame since its inception in '70.

Irving Weiser Irving Weiser was the composer of "There I Go" (see '41).

George Weiss (1921–) George David Weiss had planned on a career as a lawyer or accountant, but his love for music led him to the Julliard School of Music where he perfected his writing skills. His Julliard experiences led to writing arrangements for bandleaders like Stan Kenton and Vincent Lopez. Weiss wrote some of the most popular pop songs of the '40s, '50s, and '60s. He worked with many collaborators, but a large number of his well-known songs were written with Bennie Benjamin. Some of their songs include "Oh! What It Seemed to Be" (see '46), "Rumors Are Flying" (see '46), "Surrender" (see '46), "Wheel of Fortune" (see '52), "Cross Over the Bridge" (see '54) and "How Important Can It Be?" (see '55). Weiss also had successful song hits with other composers, some later than this book covers. That list includes "Lullaby of Birdland," "What a Wonderful World," "The Lion Sleeps Tonight" and "That Sunday, That Summer." Weiss' movie scores include *Murder, Inc.* ('60), *Gidget Goes to Rome* ('63), *Mediterranean Holiday* ('64) and *Mademoiselle* ('66). Weiss collaborated on three Broadway musicals. The most successful one was *Mr. Wonderful* in '56, which featured the title song as well as "Too Close for Comfort." Weiss was inducted into the Songwriters' Hall of Fame in '84. At http://www.songwritershalloffame.org/exhibit_audio_video.asp?exhibitId=24 you can hear audio clips of "Rumors Are Flying" performed by Marjorie Hughes with Frankie Carle and his orchestra, "What a Wonderful World" performed by Louis Armstrong, "Mr. Wonderful" sung by Peggy Lee, "Lullaby of Birdland" performed by Sarah Vaughan, "Too Close for Comfort" performed by Ella Fitzgerald, "Oh, What It Seemed to Be" sung by Frank Sinatra.

Stephen Weiss Stephen Weiss was a co-writer of "They Say" (see '39) and "Music! Music! Music!" (see '50).

Frank Weldon Frank Weldon was the composer of "The Man with the Mandolin" (see '39) and a co-writer of "A Little on the Lonely Side" (see '45).

Georgia B. Welles Georgia B. Welles was the composer of "The Rosary" (see '03).

Robert Wells (1922–1998) Robert Wells was the lyricist of "The Christmas Song" (see '46).

Pete Wendling (1888–1974) Composer and pianist Pete Wendling was born in New York City to German immigrants. He started his working life as a carpenter, but gained fame during the mid-'10s as a popular music composer, producing such hits as "Oh! What a Pal Was Mary" (see '19) and "There's Danger in Your Eyes, Cherie" (see '30). Wendling was also one of the top pianists of his era.

Percy Wenrich (1887–1952) Percy Wenrich's mother taught him the organ and piano as a young boy and at the rather late age of 21, Wenrich enrolled in the Chicago Music College. His first published songs, "Ashy Africa" and "Just Because I'm from Missouri," were while he was still in college. After graduation, Wenrich worked as a music demonstrator in a Milwaukee store and staff writer for music publishing companies. Like most successful songwriters, he moved to New York City to ply his craft. Wenrich and his wife, Dolly Connolly, worked in vaudeville for over 15 years. He often collaborated with Harry Tobias as well as Alfred Bryan, Joe McCarthy, Stanley Murphy, Edward Madden, Jack Mahoney, Howard Johnson and Ray Peck. Wenrich's most famous songs include "Put on Your Old Grey Bonnet" (see '09), "Moonlight Bay" (see '12), "Way Out Yonder in the Golden West" (see '14), and "When You Wore a Tulip and I Wore a Big Red Rose" (see '15). Percy Wenrich was an original member of the Songwriters' Hall of Fame in '70. He was also a charter member of the performing rights society ASCAP in '14. At http://www.songwritershalloffame.org/exhibit_audio_video.asp?exhibitId=247 you can hear an audio clip of "Moonlight Bay" performed by the American Quartet.

Reinald Werrenrath (1883–1953) Baritone Reinald Werrenrath sang with the New York Metropolitan Opera Co. from '19 until '21. He also was the featured baritone of the Victor Light Opera Co. and he was a member of the Orpheus Quartet. Werrenrath's most successful recordings include "Hello, Frisco!" (see '15), plus to a slightly less extent "As Long as the World Rolls On" (see '08).

Louis Weslyn (1875–1936) Louis Weslyn's chief contribution to popular music was as co-writer, with Al Piantadosi, of the World War I song "Send Me Away with a Smile" (see '18).

Eugene West Eugene West was lyricist for "Broadway Rose" (see '21).

Paul Weston (real name: Paul Wetstein; 1912–1996) Paul Weston was a pianist, arranger, composer and conductor. After he graduated from Dartmouth College in '33, he became an arranger for Rudy Vallee's *Fleischman Hour* on radio. In '36 he became Tommy Dorsey's chief arranger; he stayed with Dorsey until '40. Next he became Dinah Shore's arranger and conductor, but also did some freelance work for Bob Crosby and his band. He went to Hollywood in the early '40s and worked on several films, including *Holiday Inn, Belle of the Yukon* and *Road to Utopia*. When Capitol Records began in '42, they hired Weston as musical director for the label. He also began radio work with Johnny Mercer and Jo Stafford. When Stafford signed with Columbia Records in '50, Weston followed. He and Ms. Stafford were married in '52. Weston was co-writer of "Shrimp Boats" (see '51). He was also the musical director of Danny Kaye's television show. He and his wife teamed up for a series of comedy albums based on her ability to deliberately sing off-key while Paul played the piano accompaniment like some hack pianist. They were called Jonathan and Darlene Edwards.

R.P. Weston (1878–1936) R.P. Weston was responsible for such song hits as "I've Got Rings on My Fingers (Mumbo Jumbo Jijiboo J. O'Shea) (see '09), the immortal "I'm Henry The Eighth, I Am" in '11 (popularized by Herman's Hermits in '65), plus World War I's tongue-twister "Sister Susie's Sewing Shirts for Soldiers."

Lawrence Wheat Lawrence Wheat, Marie Flynn and the chorus introduced "You're in Love" of the musical *You're in Love* (see '17).

Anna Wheaton Anna Wheaton's Columbia duet recording of "Till the Clouds Roll By" (see '17) with James Harrod was very popular. Her recording of "M-I-S-S-I-S-S-I-P-P-I" (see '17) was also quite popular.

C.E. Wheeler C.E. Wheeler co-wrote "Montmartre Rose" (see '25) with cabaret singer Tommy Lyman.

Francis Wheeler Francis Wheeler was co-lyricist with Harry B. Smith on "The Sheik of Araby" (see '22).

Frances White Frances White introduced "M-I-S-S-I-S-S-I-P-P-I" in the Ziegfeld revue *Midnight Frolics* (see '17).

Johnny White Johnny White was co-lyricist with Harry Pease on "Ten Little Fingers and Ten Little Toes — Down in Tennessee" (see '22).

Sammy White (1894–1960) Sammy White and Eva Puck introduced "The Blue Room" in *The Girl Friend* (see '26), while White also introduced the musical's title song (see '26). White and Puck married, but later divorced.

Paul Whiteman (1890–1967) Paul Whiteman had the most popular orchestra during the '20s, featuring sweet, lush arrangements with a danceable beat. Called the "King of Jazz," Whiteman began his career in symphonic work but left that field to play popular music in '19. His symphonic orchestra soon began to attract major attention with engagements at the best hotels and with several early recordings. The title "King of Jazz" is a little bit misleading, since Whiteman's orchestra was not particularly jazzy. However, all popular music in the '20s was called "jazz," so to say that Whiteman was the "King of Popular Music of the '20s" would be completely accurate. Among Whiteman's varied accomplishments, he organized the concert at Aeolian Hall in New York City that premiered George Gershwin's "Rhapsody in Blue" in '24. Whiteman and his orchestra starred in the '30 film *The King of Jazz*, which was dedicated to him. They also were popular radio personalities. Whiteman's biggest hit recordings include "Whispering" (see '20), "The Japanese Sandman" (see '20), "Wang Wang Blues" (see '21), "Cherie" (see '21), "Song of India" (see '21), "Say It with Music" (see '21), "My Mammy" (see '21), "Three O'Clock in the Morning" (see '22), "Hot Lips" (see '22), "Stumbling" (see '22), "Do It Again!" (see '22), "Parade of the Wooden Soldiers" (see '23), "I'll Build a Stairway to Paradise" (see '23), "Bambalina" (see '23), "What'll I Do?" (see '24), "Somebody Loves Me" (see '24), "Linger Awhile" (see '24), "All Alone" (see '25), "Valencia" (see '26), "The Birth of the Blues" (see '26), "In a Little Spanish Town" (see '27),

"My Blue Heaven" (see '27), "Angela Mia (My Angel)" (see '28), "Among My Souvenirs" (see '28), "Ramona" (see '28), "Together" (see '28), "Ol' Man River" (see '28), "Great Day!" (see '29), "Body and Soul" (see '30), "All of Me" (see '32), "Smoke Gets in Your Eyes" (see '34) and "Wagon Wheels" (see '34). Whiteman is the No. 1 top recording artist of the '20s, No. 6 of the '30s, qualifying him as the No. 3 recording artist of the first half of the 20th Century, behind only Bing Crosby and Billy Murray. Whiteman was elected to the Big Band/Jazz Hall of Fame in '93. Numerous Paul Whiteman and his orchestra recordings between '20 and '42 and Paul Whiteman's Rhythm Boys between '27–'28 and '32 are available for listening at http://www.redhotjazz.com/bands.html.

George Whiting George Whiting was the lyricist for "My Blue Heaven," the biggest hit song of the '20s (see '27).

Jack Whiting (1901–1961) Singer/dancer/actor Jack Whiting appeared in many Broadway musicals from '22 through the mid-'50s. He had the pleasure of introducing a number of songs, but only "You're the Cream in My Coffee" (see '29) became a major hit.

Margaret Whiting (1924–) Margaret Whiting, daughter of composer Richard Whiting, was a popular singer during the late '40s and early '50s. Her first professional success came as vocalist with Freddie Slack's orchestra. More success followed with Billy Butterfield's band. She next turned solo and reaped a No. 1 hit with "A Tree in the Meadow" (see '48). Her only other No. 1 hit came in '49 with "Slipping Around" (see '49), a duet with Jimmy Wakely. She became the No. 22 top recording artist of the '40s.

Richard A. Whiting (1891–1938) After graduating from Los Angeles' Harvard Military School, Richard Whiting began his career as a staff writer for various music publishers in New York City and in '12 became a personal manager. He moved to Hollywood in '19 and wrote the film scores for a dozen or more movies, including *Innocents of Paris, Monte Carlo, Transatlantic Merry-Go-Round, One Hour with You, Big Broadcast of 1936, Ready, Willing and Able* and *Hollywood Hotel*. Whiting collaborated with lyricists like B.G. DeSylva, Ray Egan, Johnny Mercer, Neil Moret, Leo Robin, Gus Kahn and Sidney Clare. Whiting produced hits like "It's Tulip Time in Holland (Two Lips Are Calling Me)" (see '15), "Till We Meet Again" (see '19), "Japanese Sandman" (see '20), "Ain't We Got Fun" (see '21), "Ukulele Lady" (see '25), "Breezin' Along with the Breeze" (see '26), "Sleepy Time Gal" (see '26), "Honey" (see '29), "Louise" (see '29), "Beyond the Blue Horizon" (see '30), "You're an Old Smoothie" (see '33), "On the Good Ship Lollipop" (see '35), "When Did You Leave Heaven?" (see '36) and "Too Marvelous for Words" (see '37). Whiting also wrote scores for Broadway including *George White's Scandals of 1919* and *Take a Chance*. Richard Whiting was an original member of the Songwriters' Hall of Fame in '70. At http://www.songwritershalloffame.org/exhibit_audio_video.asp?exhibitId=314 you can hear audio clips of "Beyond the Blue Horizon" performed by Bob Borger with George Olsen and his orchestra and "Ain't We Got Fun?" performed by Van and Schenck.

Ray Whitley (1901–1979) Ray Whitley collaborated with Gene Autry to write "Back in the Saddle Again" (see '40). One morning Whitley got a call from his RKO bosses, who wanted him to write a song for a new western film they were starting to shoot that day. As he explained the call to his wife, he said to her, "Well, I'm back in the saddle again." She thought that would make a good title for the song and he agreed. He dashed off the song in almost no time. He performed it for his bosses the next day. When Autry heard it, he thought it would fit his character perfectly. He and Whitley rewrote it slightly before Autry sang it in his next film. It became Autry's signature song.

Joan Whitney (1914–1990)   Joan Whitney wrote with Alex Kramer. Kramer coached some young vocalists in singing techniques. Joan Whitney was one of his pupils. They married and began a songwriting partnership. Their first success was "High on a Windy Hill" (see '41). Others among their best-known songs include "My Sister and I" (see '41), "It's Love, Love, Love" (see '44), "Candy" (see '45), "Love Somebody" (see '48) and "Far Away Places" (see '49).

Beth Slater Whitson (1878–1930)   Beth Slater Whitson wrote lyrics for an estimated 400 songs. She also wrote short stories, poems and a silent movie screenplay. Beth Slater was born in Hickman County, Tennessee, but moved to Nashville in '13. She married George M. Whitson in '16. Mrs. Whitson was one of the first early women songwriters. Her best-known lyrics today include "Meet Me Tonight in Dreamland" (see '10) and "Let Me Call You Sweetheart" (see '11). New Yorker Leo Friedman furnished the music for both lyrics. Mrs. Whitson also wrote "Don't Wake Me Up, I Am Dreaming" (see '10) with Herbert Ingraham.

Cornel Wilde (real name: Cornelius Louis Wilde; 1915–1989)   Film actor Cornel Wilde's chief contribution to music was when he, Larry Stevens and Louanne Hogan, who dubbed the singing for film star Jeanne Crain, introduced "All Through the Day" in the movie musical *Centennial Summer* (see '46).

Dudley Wilkinson   Dudley Wilkinson was the composer of "Because of You" (see '51).

Slim Willet (real name: Winston Lee Moore; 1919–1966)   Slim Willet was one of the co-writers of "Don't Let the Stars Get in Your Eyes" (see '53). Willet graduated with a journalism degree from Hardin-Simmons University in Abilene, Texas in '49. After working for a short time in the aircraft industry, he became a DJ on an Abilene country station. His radio popularity enabled him to form his first band, the Hired Hands. They soon were performing on The Big D Jamboree in Dallas and the Louisiana Hayride in Shreveport, LA. In the early '50s, he released a few singles that became hits on the country charts, "Red Rose," "No Love Song to You" and his biggest hit, "Don't Let the Stars Get in Your Eyes." In '94, Willet was named to the Country Music DJ Hall of Fame.

Bert Williams (real name: Egbert Austin Williams; 1875–1922)   Bert Williams was born on the island of Antigua. In 1888 his family moved to California and he began his entertainment career in 1892. He became a famous vaudeville artist, both with his partner George Walker and as a soloist. Williams and Walker were particularly important in popularizing the "cakewalk." As strange as it seems for a black person to appear in black-

face, Williams was famous for his performances in blackface. Williams became the first black to perform with whites on Broadway. His performances helped erase some of the racial barriers that existed during the early years of the 20th century. Williams most often wrote his own material, including his songs. Some of his most famous ones include "Nobody" (see '06), "Let It Alone" (see '06) and "That's A-Plenty" (see '09). Williams had a very successful recording career from the early years of the 20th century into the early '20s. Some of his most popular recording were "Good Morning, Carrie" (see '02) with George Walker, "Nobody" (see '06), "Let It Alone" (see '06), "He's a Cousin of Mine" (see '07), "Play That Barbershop Chord" (see '10), "It's Nobody's Business but My Own" (see '19) and "O Death, Where Is Thy Sting?" (see '19). Williams became the No. 14 top recording artist of the first decade of the 20th Century and No. 16 of the second decade, making him the No. 25 recording artist of the first half of the 20th Century.

Curley Williams (1914–1970)   Country singer and songwriter Curley Williams was the writer of "Half as Much" (see '52). Hank Williams popularized the song on the country-western charts, while Rosemary Clooney had the most popular version on the pop charts. For more on Williams, see http://www.hillbilly-music.com/artists/story/index.php?id=11576.

Curtis Williams   Curtis Williams was a co-writer of "Earth Angel" (see '55). Curtis Williams was the lead singer of the quartet that popularized the song, the Penguins. At first Williams was solely credited with writing the song, but a lawsuit proved that Jesse Belvin and Gaynel Hodge also had a hand in writing it.

Esther Williams (1922–)   Esther Williams was a teenage swimming champion. An MGM talent scout noticed her while she was working at a Los Angeles department store and offered her a film contract. Her film debut was in *Andy Hardy's Double Life* ('42). Soon MGM starred her in several "aqua-musicals," including *Bathing Beauty* ('44), *Neptune's Daughter*, where she and Ricardo Montalban introduced "Baby, It's Cold Outside" (see '49), and *Million Dollar Mermaid* ('52). She tried a few non-musical roles, but they weren't quite as successful. She retired from films in the '60s.

Hank Williams (1923–1953)   Hank Williams became the uncontested star of country music. He joined the *Grand Ole Opry* in '49. He enjoyed unparalleled commercial success for a country music star, but tragedy in the form of drugs, alcohol, and marital problems also hounded him. Hank Williams' most famous songs on the pop charts include "Cold, Cold Heart" (see '51), "Jambalaya" (see '52), and "Your Cheatin' Heart" (see '53). Other well known Williams songs that were more popular on the country charts include "Move It On Over," "I'm So Lonesome I Could Cry," "Kaw-Liga," "Lovesick Blues," "Hey, Good Lookin'," "Settin' the Woods on Fire," "I Can't Help It (If I'm Still in Love with You)," "Half as Much," "You Win Again" and "Take These Chains from My Heart." Just as country music was reaching a peak with songs crossing over into the pop market, Hank Williams died. In '61, Hank was elected a member of the Country Music Hall of Fame, has been inducted into the Rock 'n' Roll Hall of Fame and the Songwriters' Hall of

Fame. At http://www.songwritershalloffame.org/exhibit_audio_video.asp?exhibitId=315 you can hear an audio clip of "Your Cheatin' Heart" sung by Hank Williams.

Harry H. Williams (1879–1922) Harry H. Williams was lyricist for "Navajo" (see '04), "In the Shade of the Old Apple Tree" (see '05), "Campmeetin' Time" (see '07), "Won't You Come Over to My House?" (see '07), "There Never Was a Girl Like You" (see '08), "Good Night, Ladies" (see '11), and "When I Was Twenty-One and You Were Sweet Sixteen" (see '12). A Harry Williams was credited as co-writer of "It's a Long, Long Way to Tipperary," however, Jack Judge supposedly added this man to the writing credits because the man had lent him money. It seems unlikely this is the same person.

Hugh Williams (see Will Grosz)

Spencer Williams (1889–1965) Spencer Williams was one of the earliest recognized African American composers in popular music. Many of his songs, such as "I Ain't Got Nobody" (see '16), "Everybody Loves My Baby" (see '25), "Royal Garden Blues" and "Basin St. Blues" have become pop standards. Spencer Williams was born in New Orleans. He worked in Chicago in the early 1900s as a vocalist and pianist. There he often worked with another pianist, composer, and bandleader: Clarence Williams (they were not related). About the time of World War I, he began writing songs, such as "Squeeze Me," which he cowrote with Fats Waller. In '25, he traveled to Paris to write songs for Josephine Baker, who was then working at the famed *Folies Bergere*. In '30, he made several recordings, singing and playing the piano, with Teddy Bunn, and with Lonnie Johnson. In '32, he and his friend Fats Waller vacationed in France. But while Waller returned to the U.S., Williams moved to England, where he remained in residence until '51. He later made Sweden his home. He returned to the U.S. again in '57.

Tex Williams (real name: Sol Williams; 1917–1985) Country singer Tex Williams suddenly became a national personality when his recording of "Smoke! Smoke! Smoke! (That Cigarette)" became a big hit (see '47). He had begun to perform in his childhood in Illinois. In '47 he formed the Western Caravan band, which became very successful, particularly in Southern California. Williams appeared in several cowboy films between '35 and '55.

Johnnie Lee Wills (1912–1984) Country singer Johnnie Lee Wills was a co-writer of "Rag Mop" (see '50). For more on Wills, see http://www.texasplayboys.net/Biographies/johnnie_lee_wills.htm.

Meredith Willson (real name: Robert Meredith Reiniger; 1902–1984) Composer Meredith Willson was born in Mason City, Iowa, where he learned to play piccolo and flute in high school. In '19, at age 17, he enrolled in New York's Institute of Musical Art, where he studied the flute. For a couple of years in the early '20s, Willson toured the U.S., Cuba, and Mexico as the flutist with John Phillip Sousa's Band. In '24, he worked briefly in New York's Rialto theater orchestra and from the mid-'20s to the end of the decade he was flutist in the New York Philharmonic Orchestra and the New York Chamber Music Society. After serving as a Major in World War II, Willson continued songwriting while also working as music director of ABC radio and television net-

works. Throughout his diverse career, Wilson contributed scores and librettos to several Broadway scores including *The Music Man*, which earned him the New York Drama Critics, Tony and Grammy awards in '58, *The Unsinkable Molly Brown* and *Here's Love*. Acting as lyricist and composer for most of his career, Willson wrote "You and I" (see '41), plus "It's Beginning to Look a Lot Like Christmas," "May the Good Lord Bless and Keep You," "76 Trombones," "Till There Was You," and "Belly Up to the Bar, Boys." Willson was inducted into the Songwriters' Hall of Fame in '82.

Al Wilson Al Wilson was co-lyricist with Jim Brennan on "Song of India" (see '21). They wrote the lyrics to Rimsky-Korsakoff's famous melody.

Dooley Wilson (real name: Arthur Wilson; 1886–1953) Wilson received the nickname "Dooley" from a song he performed in whiteface ("Mr. Dooley") in Chicago around '08. He is most famous as the piano player/singer of "As Time Goes by" in *Casablanca* (see '43). Ironically, Wilson was a singer and drummer, not a pianist. The piano playing in the film was by Elliott Carpenter, while Wilson faked the hand movements.

Forest Wilson Forest Wilson was a co-writer on "Ko Ko Mo" (see '55). The original rhythm and blues version of "Ko Ko Mo" was by Gene and Eunice (Gene being Forest Gene Wilson and Eunice being Eunice Levy, also a co-writer of the song). For more on Gene and Eunice, see http://www.electricearl.com/dws/gene&eunice.html.

Teddy Wilson (real name: Theodore Shaw Wilson; 1912–1986) Teddy Wilson became one of the greatest jazz pianists. During the '30s, Wilson made a number of small band recordings that rank as jazz classics. Wilson began his professional career in Chicago, then moved to New York City in '33 to join Benny Carter's band called the Chocolate Dandies as pianist and arranger. In '35, Wilson joined Benny Goodman's band, becoming one of the first African Americans to perform with a white band. Wilson also played in the Goodman trio consisting of himself on piano, Goodman on clarinet, and Gene Krupa on drums. Vibraphonist Lionel Hampton joined Goodman in '36 and the trio was enlarged to a quartet. Wilson remained with Goodman until '39, participating in trio and quartet recordings that are considered masterpieces of chamber jazz. Wilson's most successful recordings with his own orchestra include "Carelessly" (see '37) and "You Can't Stop Me from Dreaming" (see '37).

Muriel Window (1891–1965) Muriel Window helped popularized "By the Beautiful Sea" when she interpolated the song into the revue *The Passing Show of 1914*.

Dick Winfree Dick Winfree was co-writer with Phil Boutelje for "China Boy" (see '22).

Franz Winkler Franz Winkler was the composer of "Forever and Ever" (see '49). The song had originated in Switzerland in '48 as "Fliege mit Mir in die Heimat."

J.E. Winner (real name: Joseph Eastburn Winner; 1854–1907) J.E. Winner wrote "The Little Brown Jug" using the pseudonym R.A. Eastburn in 1868 (see '00).

Septimus Winner (1827–1902) Septimus Winner was born in Philadelphia. His parents were Joseph Eastburn Winner and Mary Ann Hawthorne. He published lyrics and music, besides using his own name, under the pseudonyms of Alice Hawthorne, Percy Guyer, Mark Mason, Apsley Street, and Paul Stenton. His most popular songs were "Listen to the Mocking Bird" (1855, see '04), "Oh Where, Oh Where Has My Little Dog Gone?" (1864) and "Whispering Hope" (1868). Winner was a skilled serious composer as well, creating over 1,500 arrangements for various instruments and 2,000 arrangements specifically for the violin and piano. In addition to a catalog of over 200 popular songs, Winner is the author of just as many musical instruction books for 23 different instruments. He was a frequent contributor to *Graham's Magazine*, then edited by Edgar Allan Poe, and was the founder of Philadelphia's Musical Fund Society. He was especially popular for his ballads published under the pseudonym of Alice Hawthorne. Winner was inducted into the Songwriters' Hall of Fame in '70.

Charles Winninger (1884–1969) Charles Winninger was primarily a comic actor, but he sang enough to introduce "I Want to Be Happy" (see '25) in *No, No Nanette*. Winninger was Cap'n Andy Hawks in the original '27 Broadway production and the '36 film version of *Show Boat*. He also appeared in numerous films. Some of his most prominent movie musical appearances include *Three Smart Girls* ('36), *Three Smart Girls Grow Up* ('38), *Babes in Arms* ('39), *Ziegfeld Girl* ('41), *Coney Island* ('43) and the '45 version of *State Fair*, where he played the head of the Frake family from Iowa who were going to the fair.

Fred Wise (1915–1966) Fred Wise was one of the co-writers of "Misirlou" (see '47) and "'A'— You're Adorable" (see '49). Wise later wrote some songs for Elvis Presley films.

P.G. Wodehouse (real name: Pelham Grenville Wodehouse; 1881–1975) British native P.G. Wodehouse was an active lyricist for Broadway musicals from '16 through the '20s. His most memorable lyrics are "Leave It to Jane" from the musical of the same name (see '17), "Till the Clouds Roll By" from *Oh, Boy!* (see '17) and "Bill" from *Show Boat*.

Guy Wood (1911–2001) Guy Wood was the composer of "Shoo-fly Pie and Apple Pan Dowdy" (see '46). Wood came to the U.S. from his native England in the early '30s. He played saxophone for several different bands. From '39 to '42, he led his own group at New York's Arcadia Ballroom.

Haydn Wood (1882–1959) Haydn Wood is primarily remembered for his "Roses of Picardy " (see '18). Wood, an Englishman, wrote some two hundred songs. His other works include a body of light instrumental music and music of a more serious style.

Leo Wood Leo Wood was lyricist for "Cherie" (see '21), wrote the words and music for "Somebody Stole My Gal" ('18, see '24 when it was most popular) and was co-lyricist for "Runnin' Wild" ('22).

Eddie Woods Eddie Woods was co-lyricist of the English version of "Green Eyes" (see '41).

Harry Woods (1896–1970) Composer and lyricist Harry MacGregor Woods was born in North Chelmsford, Massachusetts. Woods had been born with a deformed left hand, but his mother, a concert singer, encouraged

him to learn to play the piano. When he attended Harvard University, he supported himself by singing in church choirs and giving piano recitals. After graduation, Woods settled on Cape Cod and intended to become a farmer. Woods didn't begin to cultivate his talent for songwriting until he was serving in the Army during World War II. After his discharge, Woods settled in New York City and began his career as a songwriter. His first songwriting successes came in '23 with the songs "I'm Goin' South" and "Paddlin' Madeleine Home." In '29, Woods began contributing songs to Hollywood musicals such as *The Vagabond Lover, Road House, Limelight,* and *She's for Me.* In '34, he moved to England for three years and worked for a British film studio. While Woods primarily created both the words and music for his songs, he also collaborated with Mort Dixon, Howard Johnson, Arthur Freed, Rube Bloom and Gus Kahn. Alone, and with his collaborators, he wrote "I'm Looking Over a Four Leaf Clover" ('27, see '48 when it was most popular), "The Man from the South" (see '30), "When the Moon Comes Over the Mountain" (see '31), "Just a Little Street Where Old Friends Meet" (see '32), "River, Stay 'Way from My Door" (see '32), "Just an Echo in the Valley" (see '32), "We Just Couldn't Say Goodbye" (see '32), "I'll Never Say 'Never Again' Again" (see '35) and probably his biggest hit song "When the Red, Red Robin Comes Bob, Bob, Bobbin' Along" (see '26). Other Woods songs that are well known include "Side by Side," "Heigh-Ho, Everybody, Heigh-Ho," "What a Little Moonlight Can Do,"and "Try a Little Tenderness." Woods was an original member of the Songwriters' Hall of Fame in '70. At http://www.song writershalloffame.org/exhibit_audio_video.asp? exhibitId=98 you can hear an audio clip of "Try a Little Tenderness" performed by Otis Redding.

Mary Hale Woolsey Mary Hale Woolsey was co-lyricist of "When It's Springtime in the Rockies" (see '30).

Bobby Worth (1912–2002) Bobby Worth was co-writer of "Do I Worry?," and lyricist of "'Til Reveille" and "Tonight We Love" (see '41). Composer/lyricist Bobby Worth was a child prodigy. He began playing the piano at age 2. He began performing classical concerts by age 10 and joined Gus Edwards' vaudeville act as a teenager. He also wrote the songs for Disney's *Fun and Fancy Free* ('47) and *Melody Time* ('48).

Horace Wright Horace Wright's Victor duet recording of "My Own Iona" with Rene Dietrich (see '17) was very popular. His recording of "O'Brien Is Tryin' to Learn to Talk Hawaiian," also in '17, was also quite successful. Helen Louise and Frank Ferera accompanied both of those recordings on Hawaiian guitars.

Robert Wright (1915–2005) Robert Wright teamed with George "Chet" Forrest on the music and lyrics for several popular songs, but they are best known for adapting classical material to popular songs. Their most famous adaptation was Alexander Borodin's music for the '53 Broadway musical *Kismet*. They also adapted Norwegian composer Edvard Grieg's music for *Song of Norway* ('44). One of their first transformations was Rudolf Friml's "Chansonette" into "Donkey Serenade" in '37. Other well-known songs that were Forrest-Wright collaborations are "At the Balalaika" (see '40) and "It's a Blue World." Songs from *Kismet* include "Stranger in Paradise" (see '54),

"Baubles, Bangles and Beads" and "And This Is My Beloved." Songs from *Song of Norway* include "Strange Music" and "I Love You."

Robert B. Wright (see Buddy Feyne)

Allie Wrubel (1905–1973)
After attending Wesleyan University and Columbia University, Allie Wrubel began his music career as a saxophonist in dance orchestras, most notably with the Paul Whiteman Orchestra. Wrubel started his own band and began writing his own material while touring throughout England and Europe. He moved from New York to Hollywood in '34 to write for the Warner Bros. film studio. Wrubel wrote songs for film musicals like *Dames, Flirtation Walk, We're in the Money, The Lady in Red, The Toast of New York* and *Private Buckaroo*. Wrubel signed with Walt Disney studios in the late '40s where he contributed to the films *Make Mine Music, Song of the South,* which included the Academy Award winning song "Zip a Dee Doo Dah" (see '47) and *Melody Time.* Wrubel collaborated with several lyricists including Abner Silver, Herb Magidson, Charles Newman, Mort Dixon, Ray Gilbert and Ned Washington. Wrubel co-wrote such famous songs as "Gone with the Wind" (see '37), "Music, Maestro, Please" (see '38), and "I'll Buy That Dream" (see '45). Some other well known Wrubel songs include "Mr. and Mrs. Is the Name," "The Lady in Red," "The Masquerade Is Over," "Everybody's Got a Laughing Place," and "The Lady from 29 Palms," among others. Allie Wrubel was an original member of the Songwriters' Hall of Fame in '70.

Jane Wyman (real name: Sarah Jane Mayfield Fulks; 1914–)
Jane Wyman began her professional career as a radio singer, which led to her first name change to Jane Durrell. In '36, at age twenty-two, she signed a contract with Warner Bros., and changed her name to Jane Wyman. She starred opposite her boyfriend and future husband, Ronald Reagan, in *Brother Rat,* and its sequel, *Brother Rat and a Baby.* She went on to star in many films and won a Best Actress Oscar nomination for her role as Ma Baxter in *The Yearling* and won the award in '49 for her role as a deaf-mute rape victim in *Johnny Belinda.* She appeared in the following movie musicals: *The Singing Marine, My Favorite Spy, Footlight Serenade, Hollywood Canteen, Night and Day, It's a Great Feeling,* and *Starlift,* but her biggest musical credits were introducing the Academy Award winning song "In the Cool, Cool, Cool of the Evening" (see '51) with Bing Crosby in the film *Here Comes the Groom* and introducing "Zing a Little Zong" with Crosby in *Just for You* in '52. The '50s she was nominated for the Oscar for her performances in *The Blue Veil* and *Magnificent Obsession.* She won the Golden Globe for Best Performance by an Actress in a TV Series Drama for *Falcon Crest.* She also guest-starred as Jane Seymour's mother on *Dr. Quinn: Medicine Woman.*

Bessie Wynn
Bessie Wynn, as Tom Tom, introduced "Toyland" in the original production of *Babes in Toyland* (see '04).

Jack Yellen (1892–1991)
Lyricist Jack Yellen was born in Poland. In 1897, his family immigrated to the U.S. After graduating from the University of Michigan, he found work as a reporter for a Buffalo newspaper. Later, he moved to New York City to become a songwriter. Yellen wrote the scores for several Broadway productions including *George White's Scandals* ('35 & '39) and *Ziegfeld Follies of 1943.* Yellen moved to Hollywood and became a screenwriter and lyricist for 20th Century Fox. Some of the films he worked on include *The King of Jazz, George White's Scandals* ('34 & '35), *Happy Landing, King of Burlesque, Sing, Baby, Sing* and *Rebecca of Sunnybrook Farm.* Yellen collaborated with many composers including Milton Ager, Abe Olman, Harold Arlen, Sammy Fain, Ray Henderson, Joe Meyer and Lew Pollack. Among Jack Yellen's most famous songs are "O-HI-O" (see '21), "Lovin' Sam (the Sheik of Alabam')" (see '23), "I Wonder What's Become of Sally" (see '24), "Ain't She Sweet?" (see '27), "Forgive Me" (see '27) and "Happy Days Are Here Again" (see '30). Other well known Yellen songs include "Are You from Dixie?," "Alabama Jubilee," "Big Bad Bill," "Are You Havin' Any Fun?" and "Happy in Love." Jack Yellen was elected to the Songwriters' Hall of Fame in '72. At http://www.songwritershalloffame.org/exhibit_audio_video.asp?exhibitId=317 you can hear an audio clip of Miss Patricola performing Yellen's "Lovin' Sam."

Alice Yorke (circa 1886–1938)
Alice Yorke introduced "Cuddle Up a Little Closer, Lovey Mine" in the Broadway musical *The Three Twins* (see '08).

Vincent Youmans (real name: Vincent Millie Youmans; 1898–1946)
Vincent Youmans became one of the most famous composers of popular songs in the '20s and early '30s. Many of his most famous hits were premiered in Broadway musicals. Youmans' career was shortened when he contracted tuberculosis and entered a Denver sanitarium in '34. Although he was able to leave the sanitarium periodically, his later musical endeavors were minimal. Music had not been Youmans' original ambition; he had hoped to become an engineer. In '14, he joined the U.S. Navy and served during World War I. After the war, Youmans began working as a song plugger and then as a rehearsal pianist for Victor Herbert's operettas. Eventually, Youmans achieved his own songwriting success with several Broadway productions including *Wildflower, No, No, Nanette, Oh, Please!, Hit the Deck, Great Day!, Smiles, Through the Years* and *Take a Chance.* He also wrote the film score to *Flying Down to Rio,* which included the Academy Award nominated song "Carioca." Youmans collaborated with Herbert Stothart, Otto Harbach, Oscar Hammerstein II, Irving Caesar, Anne Caldwell, Leo Robin, Clifford Grey, Billy Rose, Edward Eliscu, Edward Heyman, Harold Adamson, Mack Gordon, B.G. DeSylva and Gus Kahn. Youmans' most popular songs include "Bambalina" (see '23), "Tea for Two" (see '25), "I Want to Be Happy" (see '25), "Hallelujah!" (see '27), "Sometimes I'm Happy" (see '27), "I Know That You Know" (see '27), "Great Day" (see '29), "More Than You Know!" (see '29), "Without a Song" (see '29), "Time on My Hands" (see '31), "Flying Down to Rio" (see '34), "The Carioca" (see '34) and "Orchids in the Moonlight" (see '34). Vincent Youmans was an original member of the Songwriters' Hall of Fame in '70.

Joe Young (1898–1946)
Lyricist Joe Young began his career as a singer for music publishing firms in New York City. During World War I he entertained our troops in Europe. His first major songwriting success came in '14 with the songs "Don't Blame It All on Broadway" and "When the Angelus Is Ringing." In '16, he began a partnership with co-lyricist Sam M. Lewis that would last

until the '30s. The team wrote "If I Knock the 'L' Out of Kelly" (see '16) and for the Broadway show *Robinson Crusoe, Jr.,* an Al Jolson vehicle, which spawned the hit "Where Did Robinson Crusoe Go with Friday on Saturday Night?" (see '16). For the next decade and a half, Young and Lewis collaborated with such composers Walter Donaldson, Jean Schwartz, Ray Henderson, Harry Akst and Harry Warren. The hits produced during this time include "Hello, Central, Give Me No Man's Land" (see '18), "I'm All Bound 'Round the Mason Dixon Line" (see '18), "Just a Baby's Prayer at Twilight (for Her Daddy Over There)" (see '18), "Rock-a-bye Your Baby with a Dixie Melody" (see '18), "My Mammy" (see '21), "Tuck Me to Sleep in My Old 'Tucky Home" (see '22), "Five Foot Two, Eyes of Blue" (see '26), "I'm Sitting on Top of the World" (see '26), "In a Little Spanish Town" (see '27), "Laugh, Clown, Laugh" (see '28), "I Kiss Your Hand, Madame" (see '29), "Two Hearts in Three-Quarter Time" (see '30), "Lullaby of the Leaves" (see '32), "Snuggled on Your Shoulders" (see '32) and "Dinah" (see '32). A few other well known Young songs include "How Ya Gonna Keep 'Em Down on the Farm?," and "Cryin' for the Carolines." After '30, Young continued writing hit songs, but never collaborated with another lyricist. He worked with composers like Fred Ahlert, Carmen Lombardo, Harry Warren, Mort Dixon, John Shiras and Bernice Petkere. Young also wrote "In a Shanty in Old Shanty Town" (see '32), "Lullaby of the Leaves" (see '32), and "Snuggled on Your Shoulder, Cuddled in Your Arms" (see '32), "Life Is a Song (Let's Sing It Together)" (see '25), "Take My Heart" (see '36) plus "You're My Everything," and "I'm Gonna Sit Right Down and Write Myself a Letter." Joe Young was a charter member of ASCAP in '14. He was an original member of the Songwriters' Hall of Fame in '70. At http://www.songwritershalloffame.org/exhibit_audio_video.asp?exhibitId=96 you can hear audio clips of "Tuck Me to Sleep in My Old 'Tucky Home" performed by Vernon Dalhart, "Dinah" sung by Bing Crosby, and "Cryin' for the Carolines" performed by Waring's Pennsylvanians.

Rida Johnson Young (1869–1926) Lyricist Rida Young was born in Baltimore. After graduating from Wilson College, Young chose a career as an actress. However, she found her greatest talent was as a librettist and lyricist. She collaborated with some famous composers including Sigmund Romberg, Victor Herbert and Rudolf Friml. Her most famous Broadway credits are *Naughty Marietta* and *Maytime,* which included "Will You Remember?" Rida Young's most famous songs include "Ah! Sweet Mystery of Life" (see '10), "Tramp! Tramp! Tramp!" (see '10), "I'm Falling in Love with Someone" (see '10), "Italian Street Song" (see '10) (all from *Naughty Marietta*) and "Mother Machree" (see '11). Rida Johnson Young was one of the original members of the Songwriters' Hall of Fame in '70.

Victor Young (1900–1956) Composer and bandleader Victor Young was an important force in popular music from the early '30s until his death. He turned to popular music and composing from concert music in the late '20s. In the '30s he recorded often with his band; in the '40s his band usually backed singers. Victor Young was born in Chicago. At the age of ten, Victor went to study violin at the Warsaw Conservatory. After his concert debut and tour of Europe, he returned to the states. He

performed as concertmaster with a couple of theater orchestras before joining the Ted FioRito orchestra as violinist and arranger. In the '20s and the first half of the '30s, Young worked as music director for radio programs in Chicago and New York City. In the mid–'30s, he moved to Los Angeles where he formed his own orchestra. Victor Young and his Singing Strings' most popular recording was "She's a Latin from Manhattan" ('35). Other popular recordings were "Who's Afraid of the Big Bad Wolf," "The Last Round-Up" and "The High and the Mighty." Young was the No. 40 top recording artist of the '30s. As a popular songwriter, Young collaborated with lyricists like Will Harris, Jack Osterman, Ned Washington, Edward Heyman, Joe Young, Ray Evans and Jay Livingston. He wrote scores for more than 350 films including *For Whom the Bell Tolls, Samson and Delilah, The Greatest Show on Earth* and *Around the World in 80 Days,* which won the '56 Academy Award for Best Score in a Motion Picture. Young's most popular songs are "Sweet Sue (Just You)" (see '28), "Golden Earrings" (see '48) and "My Foolish Heart" (see '50). Other well known Young songs include "Street of Dreams," "(I Don't Stand) A Ghost of a Chance with You," "Stella by Starlight" and "When I Fall in Love," among others. Young was a charter member of the Songwriters' Hall of Fame in '70. At http://www.songwritershalloffame.org/exhibit_audio_video.asp?exhibitId=318 you can hear audio clips of "(I Don't Stand) A Ghost of a Chance with You" performed by Billie Holiday, "Love Letters" performed by Diana Krall, and "Street of Dreams" performed by Sarah Vaughan.

Maurice Yvain (1891–1965) Maurice Yvain is primarily known in the U.S. as the composer of Fanny Brice's immortal song "My Man" (see '21). The song was originally the French song "Mon Homme."

Hy Zaret (real name: William Stirrat; 1919–) Lyricist Hy Zaret was most active in the popular song field in the '40s and early '50s. His best known lyric was "Unchained Melody" (see '55) from the movie *Unchained,* which was nominated for the Best Song Oscar. No less than three versions of the song — by Les Baxter, Al Hibbler, and Roy Hamilton — hit the Top Ten that year, with Hibbler's version ranking highest. The song was successfully covered by countless others over the years, but the Righteous Brothers' '65 version has become the definitive version for later generations. Their recording was revived in '90 thanks to its inclusion in the film *Ghost.* Zaret's first major success as a songwriter came in '35, when he teamed up with Saul Chaplin and Sammy Cahn to co-write the pop standard "Dedicated to You." In the early '40s, he wrote "There I Go" (see '41). In the late '50s, Zaret turned his attention to educational children's music, collaborating with Lou Singer on a six-album series dubbed Singing Science.

Charles A. Zimmerman (1861–1916) Charles A. Zimmerman composed "Anchors Away" (see '06). Zimmerman was at the time a Lieutenant; he had also been bandmaster of the United States Naval Academy Band since 1887.

Leon Zimmerman Leon Zimmerman shared writing credit with Rudy Vallee on "I'm Just a Vagabond Lover" (see '29). The song was the object of several plagiarism suits, all of which were discredited.

Bibliography

Bergreen, Laurance. *As Thousands Cheer: The Life of Irving Berlin*. Cambridge, MA: Da Capo, 1996.

Billboard Publications. *Top Pop Singles of the Year*. New York: Billboard, 1982.

Camelli, Allen. *Our Century in Music*. New Rochelle, NY: Stonehouse, 1974.

Castronova, Frank V., editor. *Almanac of Famous People*. Detroit, MI: Gale, 1998.

Cowden, Robert H. *Popular Singers of the Twentieth Century*. New York: Greenwood, 1999.

DeRemer, Leigh Ann, project editor. *Contemporary Musicians*. Detroit, MI: Thomson, 2003.

Ewen, David. *All the Years of American Popular Music*. Englewood Cliffs, NJ: Prentice-Hall, 1977.

_____. *American Popular Songs*. New York: Random House, 1966.

_____. *American Songwriters*. New York: H.W. Wilson, 1987.

_____. *The Complete Book of Classical Music*. Englewood Cliffs, NJ: Prentice-Hall, 1965.

Gammond, Peter. *The Oxford Companion to Popular Music*. New York: Oxford University Press, 1991.

Green, Stanley. *Broadway Musicals: Show by Show*. Milwaukee, WI: Hal Leonard, 1994.

_____. *Encyclopedia of the Musical Theatre*. Cambridge, MA: Da Capo, 1976.

_____. *Hollywood Musicals: Year by Year*. Milwaukee, WI: Hal Leonard, 1990.

Hirschhorn, Clive. *The Hollywood Musical*. New York: Crown, 1981.

Hitchcock, H. Wiley, and Sadie, Stanley, editors. *The New Grove Dictionary of American Music*. New York: Grove, 1986.

Kingsbury, Paul, editor. *The Encyclopedia of Country Music*. New York: Oxford University Press, 1998.

Kinkle, Roger D. *The Complete Encyclopedia of Popular Music and Jazz 1900–1950*. New Rochelle, NY: Arlington House, 1974.

Larkin, Colin, editor. *Encyclopedia of Popular Music*. New York: Muze, 1998.

Mattfeld, Julius. *Variety Music Cavalcade*. Englewood Cliffs, NJ: Prentice-Hall, 1962.

Paymer, Marvin E., editor. *Facts Behind the Songs*. New York: Garland, 1993.

Payne, Phillip W., editor. The Swing Era—1936–1937. New York: Time-Life Books, 1970.

_____. The Swing Era—1937–1938. New York: Time-Life, 1971.

_____. The Swing Era—1938–1939. New York: Time-Life, 1971.

_____. The Swing Era—1940–1941. New York: Time-Life, 1971.

_____. The Swing Era—1941–1942. New York: Time-Life, 1971.

_____. The Swing Era—1944–1945. New York: Time-Life, 1971.

_____. The Swing Era—Into the '50s. New York: Time-Life, 1971.

_____. The Swing Era—Postwar Years. New York: Time-Life, 1972.

Raph, Theodore. *The Songs We Sang*. Theodore Raph, 1964.

Whitburn, Joel. *A Century of Pop Music*. Menomonee Falls, WI: Record Research, 1999.

_____. *Pop Memories*. Menomonee Falls, WI: Record Research, 1986.

Williams, John R. *This Was Your Hit Parade*. John R. Williams, 1973.

Internet Websites

http://digital.library.ucla.edu/apam/librarian?SEARCHPAGE&Browse

http://digital.nypl.org/lpa/nypl/lpa_home4.html

http://en.wikipedia.org/wiki/

http://hometown.aol.com/mgmfanatic/index.html

http://lcweb2.loc.gov/cocoon/ihas/

http://levysheetmusic.mse.jhu.edu/browse.html

http://libraries.mit.edu/music/sheetmusic/fileindex.html

http://library.indstate.edu/level1.dir/cml/rbsc/kirk/

http://library.msstate.edu/

http://lirama.net/

http://lyrical.nl/

http://nfo.net/index.html

http://parlorsongs.com/index.asp

http://scriptorium.lib.duke.edu/dynaweb/sheetmusic/

http://songfacts.com/

http://ucblibraries.colorado.edu/cgi-bin/sheetmusic

http://voxlibris.claremont.edu/sc/exhibits/cacroonin/cacroonin.html

www.authentichistory.com/audio/

www.barbershopharmony.bizland.com/

www.classicmoviemusicals.com/musicy.htm

www.dorothyfields.co.uk/

www.edisonnj.org/menlopark/vintage/columbia.asp.

www.edisonnj.org/menlopark/vintage/diamonddisc.asp

www.garlic.com/~tgracyk/century.htm

www.halcyondaysmusic.com/about.htm
www.harrywarren.org/songs.htm
www.imdb.com/
www.jazzhall.org/
www.johnnymercer.com/
www.kcmetro.cc.mo.us/
www.lib.unc.edu/mss/sfc1/hillbilly/HTML
www.libraries.psu.edu/speccolls/waring/
www.lorenzhart.org/main.htm
www.musicalheaven.com/

www.musicals101.com/index.html
www.musicweb.uk.net/encyclopaedia/
www.oldielyrics.com/
www.parabrisas.com/welcome.html
www.pdmusic.org/1900s.html
www.perfessorbill.com/index2.htm
www.redhotjazz.com/
www.songwritershalloffame.org/
www.umkc.edu/lib/spec-col/guidelin.htm
www.collectionscanada.ca/gramophone/

Index

499